SOUTH-WESTERN
LAW FOR BUSINESS AND PERSONAL USE

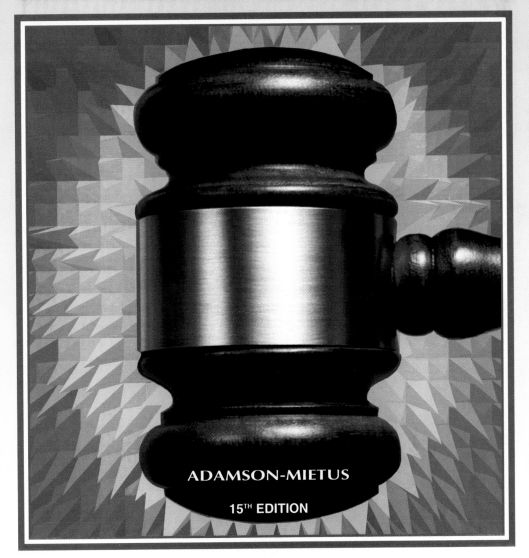

ADAMSON-MIETUS

15TH EDITION

VISIT US ON THE INTERNET
www.swep.com

South-Western Educational Publishing
an International Thomson Publishing company I(T)P®

www.thomson.com

Cincinnati • Albany, NY • Belmont, CA • Bonn • Boston • Detroit • Johannesburg • London • Madrid
Melbourne • Mexico City • New York • Paris • Singapore • Tokyo • Toronto • Washington

Team Leader Eve Lewis
Managing Editor Enid Nagel
Production Coordinator Carol Sturzenberger
Marketing Manager Nancy A. Long
Editors Darrell Frye, Nicole Christopher Toms
Consulting Editor Jeanne Busemeyer
Art and Design Coordinator Bill Spencer
Marketing Coordinator Christian L. McNamee
Manufacturing Coordinator Kathy Shaut
Team Assistant Tracey Roell
Editorial Assistant Laureen Palmisano
Marketing Assistant Yvonne Patton
Internal Design Anthony J. Libardi
Cover Photography Al Freni
Composition/Prepress Better Graphics, Inc.

About the Authors

John E. Adamson is Assistant Professor of Business and Law in the Department of Finance and General Business at Southwest Missouri State University. Adamson received a B.S. from the U.S. Military Academy at West Point, NY; an M.A. from Georgetown University; and an M.B.A and J.D. from the University of Virginia at Charlottesville. A decorated, disabled veteran and current mayor and school board member of Miller, MO, Adamson is author of numerous business law publications, with a concentration on environmental law.

Norbert J. Mietus is Professor of Law Emeritus in the School of Business Administration at California State University, Sacramento. Mietus received a B.S. from Marquette, an M.B.A. from Harvard, and a J.D. from UCLA and is a member of the California Bar. He has taught at Loyola Marymount, The University of California at Berkeley and California State University at Sacramento, and has written numerous books on the law and business.

ISBN: 0-538-68353-8

4 5 6 7 8 9 0   D   05 04 03 02 01
Printed in the United States of America

International Thomson Publishing

REVIEWERS

Contents

Contents

UNIT 2 Fundamentals of Contracts 96

IN PRACTICE 97   **THE PROJECT 210**

Contents

UNIT 3 Sales and Other Contractual Situations 212

IN PRACTICE 213   THE PROJECT 278

Contents

Unit 4 Property 280

Contents

Unit 5 The Law of Jobs 376

IN PRACTICE 377   THE PROJECT 464

FEATURES IN UNIT 5
Hot Debate 378, 390, 402, 418, 432, 448
A Question of Ethics 384, 392, 404, 412, 421, 439, 454, 456
Cultural Diversity in Law 384, 396, 409, 426, 435, 457
FYI 392, 409, 451, 456
Prevent Legal Difficulties 385, 397, 413, 427, 443, 459
Law in the Media 442

Contents

Unit 6 Forms of Business Organizations 466

FEATURES IN UNIT 6
Hot Debate **468, 488, 508, 522**
A Question of Ethics **471, 502, 511, 526**
Cultural Diversity in Law **475, 491, 514, 525**
FYI **475, 516**
Prevent Legal Difficulties **483, 503, 517, 529**
Law in the Media **512**
Law and the Internet **497, 524**

Contents

Unit 7 Borrowing Money and Paying Bills 536

FEATURES IN UNIT 7
Hot Debate 538, 550, 564, 578, 592
A Question of Ethics 543, 558, 566, 579, 601
Cultural Diversity in Law 544, 553, 571, 580, 602
FYI 557, 579
Prevent Legal Difficulties 545, 559, 573, 587, 605
Law in the Media 600
Law and the Internet 580, 598

Contents

Introduction to Students

You will soon find business law is one of your most valuable subjects. You will study true situations that show how business and personal law impacts not only business, but the lives of young people and adults as well. The learning package will help you achieve an understanding of legal principles you will use throughout your life. Use the plan outlined below to help you effectively study *Law for Business and Personal Use.*

HOW TO STUDY THE TEXTBOOK

➡ Each chapter opens with a Hot Debate. Read the Hot Debate scenario and then discuss with your class the questions that go along with it.

➡ Each chapter is divided into several lessons. Each lesson has a list of Goals at the beginning. Read the Goals and then scan the lesson to see where each Goal is addressed.

➡ Read each lesson slowly and carefully. Make notes of important points. In the Student Activities and Study Guide supplement, there is an outline of every lesson to help you take notes.

➡ Each main topic heading is followed by a What's Your Verdict? scenario. Try to answer the question. Then read the following paragraphs to learn the law that applies to What's Your Verdict? before you go on to the next topic.

➡ As you read, apply what you learn to your own experience or those of your family and friends. Think about situations within your own experience to which the law applies.

➡ After you have carefully studied the lesson, complete the exercises in Think About Legal Concepts and Think Critically About Evidence.

➡ After you complete all the lessons in a chapter, read the Concepts in Brief to refresh your memory. Then complete Your Legal Vocabulary, Review Legal Concepts, Write About Legal Concepts, and Analyze Real Cases.

➡ The exercises in Think Critically About Evidence help you apply what you learned in the chapter. Analyze Real Cases allows you to work with the facts from real lawsuits related to the topics in each chapter.

SPECIAL FEATURES

■ **Hot Debate** promotes thoughtful discussion of important legal issues.

■ **What's Your Verdict?** motivates you to learn new legal concepts.

■ **In This Case** demonstrates legal principles and concepts in action.

■ **Law in the Media** analyzes the effects of the media, including television and the press, on legal issues.

■ **Law and the Internet** discusses the emerging area of the legal aspects of the Internet.

■ **A Question of Ethics** presents ethical issues that arise within the legal framework.

■ **Cultural Diversity in Law** illustrates legal procedures and issues in other cultures. Also introduces concepts of international law.

■ **FYI** provides unusual or interesting facts or ideas related to the law.

■ **Prevent Legal Difficulties** provides helpful guidelines for dealing with the legal system as an individual, an employee, an entrepreneur and more.

REAL-WORLD CASE

■ **Case for Legal Thinking** presents important real-world cases for analysis and discussion.

PROJECT

■ **Entrepreneurs and the Law** allows you to apply the law to a real-life business situation.

HOW TO ANALYZE LEGAL SITUATIONS

Following each lesson and each chapter, you will find a number of real-life legal situations in Think Critically About Evidence. You also will find actual cases that have been decided by courts in Analyze Real Cases and Case for Legal Thinking. You may use the same method to analyze both types of exercises. To answer the question raised in an exercise or case, first read it carefully. Be sure you understand the question and the facts involved. Then determine the rule of law involved and reach a decision. You will find it helpful to answer these questions.

❏ What are the facts?

❏ What is the disputed point?

❏ What rule of law is involved?

❏ How does this rule apply to the facts?

❏ What is the answer or decision?

HOW TO ANALYZE ETHICAL SITUATIONS

An ethical dilemma is posed in A Question of Ethics. You can use the frameworks described in Lesson 2-2.

To analyze the dilemmas using ethical reasoning based on consequences

◆ Describe alternative actions that would improve the situation.

◆ Forecast consequences that would flow from each alternative described.

◆ Evaluate the consequences for each alternative by selecting a standard for judging right or wrong consequences.

To analyze the dilemmas using fundamental ethical rules

◆ "Universalize" the action in question.

◆ Determine whether the action is irrational, illogical, or self-defeating.

HOW TO READ CASE CITATIONS

Law cases are referenced in a way that makes them easy to find. There are three parts to a citation. For example, 28 A2d 309 identifies (1) a series of law books, (2) one volume in that series, and (3) the page where the case begins. In the example, A2d identifies the series of books that report the decisions of certain courts. The A stands for Atlantic Reporter, a series that reports the cases of appellate courts in the North Atlantic Region. The 2d indicates that the case appears in the second series of the Atlantic Reporter. The 28 in this example citation refers to Volume 28 in the series. The case begins on page 309.

LEGAL ADVICE

Consult a lawyer if you have any doubts about your rights or duties when your property, life, or liberty is endangered or if significant changes occur in your circumstances.

▲ Familiarize yourself with local, state, and federal laws to help avoid violations. Ignorance of the law is normally no excuse.

▲ Remember that as a minor, you are generally liable for crimes and torts and bound by contracts.

▲ If you are involved in a legal dispute, try to learn the other person's version and honestly seek a friendly solution out of court. In every court action at least one person loses and often both find the costs burdensome.

▲ If someone injures you or your property, do not rush to sign a statement releasing the person from liability in exchange for some payment of money. The damages may be greater than they appear at first. Consult your attorney immediately.

▲ Although oral agreements can be legally binding, you should write out all contracts that involve significant time, money, or detail and have both parties sign and receive copies.

LAW, JUSTICE, AND YOU

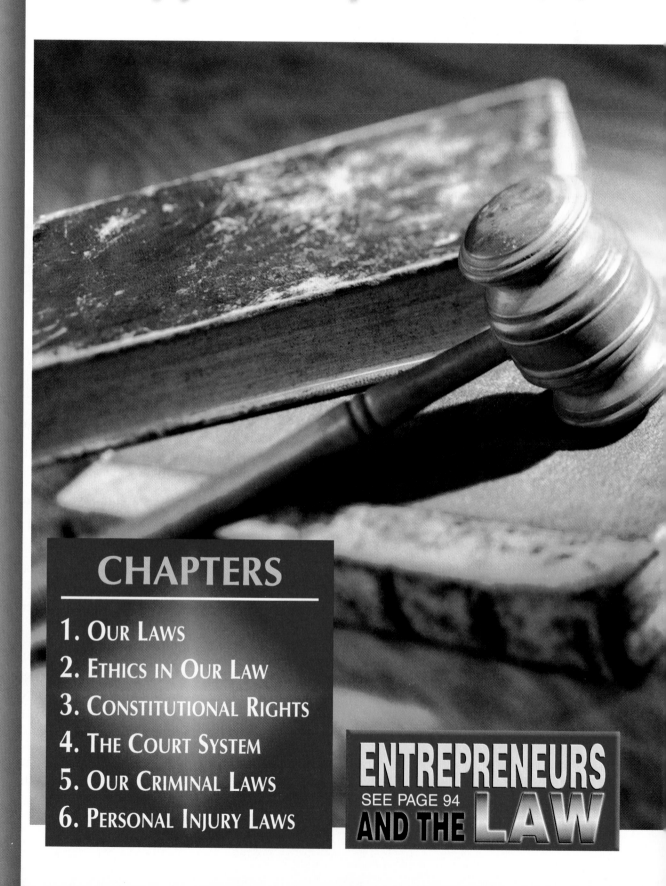

ENTREPRENEURS
SEE PAGE 94
AND THE LAW

Like many licensed practical nurses, Barbara Cicognani prepares herself every day for the medical emergencies her profession demands. However, the world in which Barbara chooses to practice her profession forces her to prepare for many other different forms of crises. Instead of treating patients in doctors' offices or hospitals, Barbara combines her nursing expertise and keen legal sensitivity by treating inmates within the walls of a county prison.

Barbara began her education at Waterloo Central School in central New York, where she graduated with a Regent's Diploma in 1964. After attending Albany Medical Center School of Nursing for three years on a nursing scholarship, she passed the LPN Nursing Boards, and became a Licensed Practical Nurse in 1997.

Barbara has had a variety of nursing positions in pediatrics, operating rooms, hospital and home nursing, and doctors' offices. She has worked in her present position as a corrections nurse in a county prison for three years. "Not being endowed with a strong gift of mercy, I find corrections nursing the perfect venue for my personal strengths and a very rewarding way to earn a living."

Barbara's responsibilities at the jail include conducting health screenings, answering inmate health concerns, and offering medical assistance for injuries and illnesses. A successful corrections nurse needs strong observation skills coupled with a keen awareness of inmate behaviors. A prison nurse must be able to react calmly and quickly to a variety of situations in a potentially volatile environment.

A nurse in corrections must also exhibit sharp psychological insights so that he or she is able to answer the needs of the inmates. Prisoners are often not aware that the stress of imprisonment itself can bring on physical and/or emotional symptoms. The nurse needs to recognize stress-induced problems and make suggestions for stress-reduction.

Many of the people that nurses in corrections encounter on a daily basis have not taken care of themselves physically for long periods of time, which is often due to drug and/or alcohol abuse. The nurse may need to address sensitive issues, such as, AIDS and STDs. These situations fill the corrections nurse's day with challenges that require fast, accurate judgments and even-handed responses.

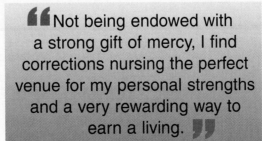

Legal issues are a particular concern for those who work in corrections. Nurses are affected by legal dilemmas because they must separate genuine medical ailments from fabricated inmate complaints. "Some inmates always seem to be finagling to establish a basis for a lawsuit, and medical personnel seem to be favorite targets of frivolous lawsuits. They may become extremely demanding, submitting frequent detailed complaints to elicit attention. These legal concerns revolve around . . . inmates trying to dictate what diagnostic tests they require or, alternately, refusing prescribed care. The corrections nurse often walks a fine line between dispensing needed medical care and refusing to be brow-beaten into reacting to demands without foundation."

Corrections can certainly be a very rewarding field for the strong-willed nurse who thrives on unpredictable challenges on a daily basis. Though sometimes frustrating, there are few dull moments for nurses who work in corrections!

> **❝** Not being endowed with a strong gift of mercy, I find corrections nursing the perfect venue for my personal strengths and a very rewarding way to earn a living. **❞**

LESSONS

HOT DEBATE

Donna Estes was driving south on National Avenue. She was doing 60 mph in a 50 mph zone. Wilma Sexton was driving north on the same street at the same time. She had been drinking and was weaving back and forth in her lane. Suddenly, Wilma noticed she was about to miss her turn. Signaling for a brief second, she made an abrupt left in front of Donna's vehicle. The cars collided. Both women received lacerations and broken bones. Both cars were totaled.

Where Do You Stand?

1. Who was at "fault"?

2. What arguments would Donna's attorney present at the civil trial to determine who was negligent?

3. What arguments would Wilma's attorney present?

GOALS

● **Explain the stages in the evolution of law**

● **Describe the differences between common law and positive law**

● **Describe the difference between law courts and equity courts**

WHAT IS LAW?

WHAT'S YOUR VERDICT?

Lorenzo and Bixby were discussing how much civilization had advanced since the beginning of recorded history. Bixby said he believes that the basic nature of man has not changed, but the number of facts we know has been multiplied many times over. Lorenzo nodded in agreement, "Just compare the laws they had way back then with the ones we have now. We're still making the same mistakes and still need the same protections from the conduct of others."

Do you think they are correct?

The **laws**, or enforceable rules of conduct in a society, reflect the culture and circumstances that create them. Laws may be grouped into an organized form called a **code**. When we compare one civilization's code with the codes of other civilizations, we see many similarities.

For example, the law code set down about four thousand years ago by Hammurabi, King of Babylon, had sections on criminal law, property law, business law, family law, personal injury law, labor law, and others. Such coverage is similar to that found in our country's law codes today.

Lorenzo and Bixby in *What's Your Verdict?* were right. The need for law has not changed significantly over our recorded history. We still make the same mistakes and still need the same protections from the conduct of others.

Stages in the Growth of Law

Most societies go through four distinct stages in forming their legal systems:

1. Individuals take revenge for wrongs done to them.
2. Awards of money or goods are substituted for revenge.
3. Court systems are formed.
4. A central authority figure intervenes to prevent and punish wrongs.

In the first stage, injuries inflicted on one human being by another are matters for personal revenge. Those who are wronged feel that justice can be done only through punishing the wrongdoers. Gang-related shootings in our inner cities often are a result of this type of attitude. Whether they occur in our cities or in a developing society, such incidents usually disrupt the normal routine of the people and result in harm to innocent bystanders.

The situation often leads to one individual seizing power and exerting control to bring peace to the society.

This individual (who we will call the *sovereign*) then brings about the second stage in the evolution of law. The sovereign awards money or goods as a substitute for revenge.

The sovereign then enters into the third stage by forming courts. Elders or priests generally preside over the courts. (For the most important matters the sovereign presides.) The sovereign's subjects can go to the courts to be heard when they are injured by another in some way.

Finally, the sovereign uses the courts to prevent problems from arising. The sovereign also issues laws to punish behaviors that injure others in certain ways. This is the fourth, and generally last, stage in the evolution of law.

Common Law v. Positive Law

Laws reflect the wisdom—or lack thereof—of their creators. In any society laws should be both predictable and flexible. A system of laws that is not predictable will not produce a stable society. Chaos, unrest, and the replacement of the system by one that can exercise control will follow.

A legal system that is too controlling and too rigid to change with the wants and needs of the people also will be overthrown. The best system of laws always gradually evolves towards a form that is most appropriate to the current standards of the people.

Law based on the current standards or customs of the people is called **common law**. Common law usually is pronounced by judges who use it to settle people's disputes. However, as noted earlier, some laws are set down by a sovereign or other central authority to prevent disputes and wrongs from occurring in the first place. Law dictated from above in this fashion is called **positive law**.

WHAT'S YOUR VERDICT?

The labor strike is in its fifth bitter week. The strikers are tense and angry. The workers who remain on the job are both angry and fearful about the situation. For several days nearly a thousand picketers gather at the company's main gate. They are chanting slogans and jeering those who enter the plant. The crowd begins to throw rocks at the workers who cross the picket line. Then a company truck is set on fire and destroyed.

What powers do the courts have that would be useful in this situation?

The world's two great systems of law are the English common law and the Roman civil law. Countries with systems patterned after the civil law have adopted written, well-organized, comprehensive sets of statutes in code form. Only one state in the United States—Louisiana—has law based on a civil law system.

The legal system used in the other 49 states is based on the English common law. English colonists transported this system of law to this continent. To understand how the common law works, we must look at how it developed.

English Common Law

Before the English common law system developed in England, feudal barons acted as judges within their territories. Disputes were settled on the basis of local customs and enforced by the barons' power. Because of this, the laws of England differed from region to region. Such variances worked a hardship on the people and made it difficult for a central government to maintain control.

THE KING'S COURTS Around 1150, King Henry II decided to improve the situation. He appointed a number of judges from a group of trusted nobles. King Henry gave these judges the power to order that wrongdoers pay with money or goods the parties they injured.

In good-weather months the judges would "ride circuit" into the countryside, holding court in the villages. During bad-weather months, the judges came together in London to hear cases that might have been decided unwisely on circuit. This court came to be called King's Bench (or Queen's Bench if the regent was female).

The baron's courts, which heard local cases before the King's courts were created, kept the power to decide some of the minor cases. However, the King's courts always took **jurisdiction** (the power to decide a case) over the most important cases.

JURY King Henry recognized that it was important to decide the court cases in harmony with the customs of the people. To do otherwise would cause unrest, if not revolution. The judges were instructed to empanel citizens from each region to help interpret the customs. This panel of citizens evolved into what we know today as the *jury*. The jury is an institution unique to the English common law system.

AN EXAMPLE The early system of English common law worked something like this: Let's say a farmer named William is on his way to market one morning in his ox cart. He is traveling through an unfamiliar region. As he approaches an intersection, he sees another person in a similar ox cart coming into the intersection from his right.

In William's region the right of way at an intersection goes to the person on the left, so he continues on, expecting the other person to rein in. The other party, a local resident named Gwen, does not yield and a collision results. Both William and Gwen are injured. Their oxen are gored. Their carts and other property

CULTURAL DIVERSITY IN LAW

Louisiana

The French Code Napoléon

The territory that is now Louisiana was claimed for France by the explorer Lasalle in 1682. French settlers brought many French influences to the state of Louisiana—customs, food, language, and law. Louisiana's legal system was developed using the French Code Napoléon (or Napoleonic Code) as a foundation. Over the years Louisiana has modified its legal system to correspond with those of the other 49 states.

The Napoleonic Code was derived from Germanic customs and Roman law. The Napoleonic code also was the model for the civil law codes of Italy, the Netherlands, Spain, and the Canadian Province of Quebec.

are destroyed. As a consequence, the next time the King's circuit-riding judge comes into Gwen's region, both people appear in court and request damages for their losses.

The judge needs to know who is at fault in the case in order to decide who must pay. To find out, the judge empanels a jury of 12 residents from the area and asks them which person, according to their customs, acted improperly. The jury determines that, because the right of way customarily goes to the person on the right in their region, William is at fault and must pay Gwen damages. The judge accepts the decision and orders William to pay.

William, however, is upset. He knows that throughout most of his travels the right of way is given to the person on the left. Therefore, he decides to take his case to the higher court—King's Bench in London—for appeal. That court will not be in session for several months yet, so William uses the time to collect information on other courts in England that have ruled on the issue of right of way.

Finally, the time comes to appear before King's Bench. The judges listen to William's appeal and Gwen's defense of the lower court's decision. The appellate court judges decide that it would be wisest to reverse the holding in the lower court (that the right of way should go to the person on the right). Instead, says King's Bench, the right of way will be given to the person on the left. They send the case back down to the lower court with instructions to enter a judgment for damages in William's favor.

From that point on, anyone in the kingdom will need to give the right of way to the person on the left. If any lower court, including the one in Gwen's region, decides a case using a different rule, the result can be appealed to King's Bench and reversed.

Advantages of English Common Law

The judicial process described in the example was repeated over and over in England throughout the centuries. As a result, a web of custom-based common law developed. The process used to achieve this end is called the English common law system.

The English common law system differs from a traditional system of common law in its uniformity. Because of this uniformity and because of its ability to adapt to changes in society, the English common law system has been a model for legal systems worldwide. As noted earlier, the system of law in the United States is based on the English common law.

Equity: An Alternative to Common Law

The English common law courts carefully followed *precedent.* This means the courts used prior cases as a guide for deciding similar new cases. Following precedent helped to provide stability in the law.

However, following precedent also had its disadvantages. First of all, it resulted in a rigid adherence to proper form. A misplaced period or misspelled word would nullify the effect of a document. Another disadvantage was that the courts of law were limited to granting the remedy of money damages. This meant that the common law courts had to wait until the harm actually occurred before they could take action.

For example, if a farmer decided to dam up the stream that watered his neighbors crops and animals, the courts of law had to wait until the harm had occurred and then award the neighbor damages for what the farmer did. The courts of law could not order the farmer to stop building the dam. This would be a waste of resources from the perspective of the country as a whole.

However, if the neighbor were a

noble, he might be able to get around the courts and directly petition the king for help. The king would refer the matter to his chancellor, who was usually a high clergyman respected for his equity, or fairness.

The chancellor would conduct a hearing under rules different from those of a common law court. There would be no jury, for example, and the remedies the chancellor could impose in the king's name were different from those available to the law courts.

The chancellor might order a decree to compel that something be done. Or, he might issue an *injunction* which ordinarily prohibits something from being done. For example, the chancellor could issue an injunction to stop the dam from being built. If the neighbor were not a noble, he would have no recourse to the king. The harm would be allowed to occur.

Eventually the king sensed a need for access to equitable remedies for all citizens. He created a system of equity courts and placed them under the chancellor's control. These courts were given the power to issue injunctions or to compel specific actions.

In the United States today, law courts and equity courts generally are merged. Most American courts can provide the help common law courts gave.

In *What's Your Verdict?* at the beginning of this lesson, the judge might grant the company a money award for the loss of the truck. The court also could issue an injunction to limit the number of picketers at the plant's entrance. Strikers who violate the injunction risk a jail sentence for contempt of court.

FYI

Four states in the United States administer law and equity separately. In Arkansas, Delaware, and Mississippi equity is administered in *chancery* courts; in Tennessee equity is administered in *law-equity courts.*

THINK ABOUT LEGAL CONCEPTS

Answer the following questions about legal concepts.

1. Substitution of damages for revenge is the first stage in the evolution of law. **True or False?**

2. The two systems of law in use today are the English common law and the **(a) American Constitution (b) French legal code (c) Roman common law (d) none of the above.**

3. A remedy of the English courts of law was the **(a) injunction (b) court order (c) disputation (d) none of the above.**

4. Louisiana is the only one of our 50 states whose law was not originally based on the English common law system. **True or False?**

5. Most American law courts can use either damages or an injunction or both as remedies in civil cases. **True or False?**

THINK CRITICALLY ABOUT EVIDENCE

Study the following situations, answer the questions, then prepare arguments to support your answers.

6. You are on your daily jog when a car negligently pulls out in front of you. Unable to stop, you run into it and injure yourself. Should you be able to recover damages for the harm done to you?

7. The driver of the car in exercise 6 becomes abusive towards you after your recovery. The driver follows you on your jogs and yells threats at you. He has recently taken to driving very close to you as you jog. What can you do legally to make him stay away from you?

8. Cracked Mirror, a locally well-known rock group, contracts to play for your high school prom. A week before the dance, the group cancels its appearance. A teacher finds out that the band took the opportunity to perform in a concert that will pay them $800 more. The class president's mother is an attorney and offers her services to the school. If you sue the band for damages, what would be an appropriate amount and why?

9. In exercise 8, could you fashion an equitable remedy that might prompt Cracked Mirror to decide to keep its commitment to play at your prom? (Certain remedies that may come to mind could violate portions of the U.S. Constitution and therefore could not be pursued.)

WHAT ARE THE SOURCES OF OUR LAWS?

WHAT'S YOUR VERDICT?

Congress requires cigarette makers to print these words on every cigarette package: "Warning: the Surgeon General has determined that cigarette smoking is dangerous to your health."

What type of law requires this?

Laws in this country are created at all three levels of government—federal, state, and local. The laws at each level consist mainly of constitutions, statutes, administrative regulations, and case law.

Constitutions

A *constitution* is a document that sets forth the framework of a government and its relationship to the people it governs. When constitutions are adopted or amended, or when courts interpret constitutions, **constitutional law** is made. You are governed by both the Constitution of the United States and the constitution of your state. The Supreme Court of the United States is the final interpreter of the federal Constitution. Each state supreme court is the final authority on the meaning of its state constitution.

Federal and state constitutions are concerned primarily with defining and allocating certain powers in our society. Constitutions allocate powers (1) between the people and their governments, (2) between state governments and the federal government, and (3) among the branches of the government.

ALLOCATION OF POWER BETWEEN PEOPLE AND GOVERNMENT The federal Constitution is the main instrument for allocating powers between people and their governments. It does this with its first ten amendments, called the *Bill of Rights*. The Bill of Rights protects people from actions of their governments. Among the personal rights granted in the Bill of Rights are freedom of religion, freedom of speech, and the right to remain silent if accused of a crime. The personal rights granted in the Bill of Rights will be discussed in detail in Chapter 3.

ALLOCATION OF POWER BETWEEN FEDERAL AND STATE GOVERNMENTS The federal Constitution also allocates powers between the federal and state governments. For example, many governmental powers over business are divided between state governments and the federal government on the basis of commerce. In general, the Constitution gives the federal government the power to regulate both foreign and interstate commerce. (*Interstate* commerce occurs between two or more states.) The power to regulate *intrastate* commerce (which occurs within one state) is left with that state.

ALLOCATION OF POWER AMONG THE BRANCHES OF GOVERNMENT State and federal constitutions also allocate governmental powers among the three branches of government: executive, legislative, and judicial. Constitutions allocate power to create a system of checks and balances among the branches of government. This ensures that no branch of government becomes too powerful. For example, the Constitution gives the courts, not Congress, the authority to conduct trials.

Statutes

The federal Constitution created the Congress of the United States. State constitutions created the state legislatures. These state and federal legislatures are composed of elected representatives of the people. Acting for their citizens, these legislatures enact laws called **statutes**. The law requiring cigarette warnings as discussed in *What's Your Verdict?* is a statute enacted by the U.S. Congress.

All states delegate some legislative authority to local governments. Thus, towns, cities, and counties can legislate on matters over which the state has given them authority. These laws are effective only within the boundary of the local governments that enacted them. Such legislation is created by a town or city council or by a county board or commission. Legislation at the local level usually is called an **ordinance.**

Administrative Regulations

Federal, state, and local legislatures all create administrative agencies. **Administrative agencies** are governmental bodies formed to carry out particular laws. The federal Social Security Administration, your state's division of motor vehicles, and your county's zoning commission are examples of administrative agencies. Although created by legislatures, administrative agencies usually are controlled by the executive branch of government. Thus, the President, governor, or mayor will supervise the agency's activities.

Legislatures sometimes give administrative agencies legislative powers and limited judicial powers. Legislative power means the agency is authorized to create administrative laws, also called *rules* and *regulations.* For example, the federal Social Security Administration might establish rules for determining *when* a student is a dependent of a widow or widower and qualified to receive social security payments.

If an agency has judicial power, it can hold hearings, make determinations of fact, and apply the law to particular cases. The Social Security Administration might, for example, hold a hearing that decides whether a *particular* student is in fact a dependent.

Cases

The judicial branch of governments creates **case law**. Case law usually is made after a trial has ended and one of the parties has appealed the result to a higher court. This appeal will be based on legal rulings made by the lower court in deciding the case. When the appellate court publishes its opinion on a case, that opinion may state new rules to be used in deciding the case and others like it. This process creates case law. Federal courts establish federal case law. Similarly, each state creates case law through its state courts.

The effectiveness of case law arises out of the doctrine of **stare decisis**. This is Latin for "to adhere to decided cases." This doctrine requires that lower courts must follow established case law in deciding similar cases.

The doctrine of *stare decisis* generally does not bind supreme courts. Generally, however, case law doctrines are carefully established and seldom revoked.

IN THIS CASE

Carol borrowed her stepfather's car without his express permission. The police stopped her, discovered the car was not registered in her name, then phoned her stepfather. When he said he did not know where his car was, Carol was arrested.

At her trial, Carol and her stepfather testified that she had his permission to use the car without asking each time. The trial judge nevertheless found Carol guilty of auto theft, which, the judge stated, occurs when one person takes the car of another without express permission. Carol appealed to the state supreme court. That appellate court issued an opinion stating implied permission is enough, and therefore, Carol was innocent. This rule then became state case law. The same supreme court could rule in a later but similar case that implied permission is not enough.

WHAT HAPPENS WHEN LAWS CONFLICT?

WHAT'S YOUR VERDICT?

When adopted, the U.S. Constitution provided that there could be no income tax. So when Congress levied a 2 percent income tax in 1894, the U.S. Supreme Court declared it unconstitutional. Many people wanted the federal government to raise money by taxing incomes because the burden imposed would be based on one's ability to pay.

Could the people do anything to change the effect of the Supreme Court decision?

Sometimes laws created by different levels of government conflict. For example, a city ordinance may conflict with a state statute on speed limits. Different types of laws created by the same level of government also may conflict. A federal administrative regulation may conflict with a federal court decision. In these situations, the legal rules for determining supremacy establish which law is valid and should therefore be enforced.

CONSTITUTIONS AND VALIDITY

Constitutions are the highest sources of law, and the federal Constitution is "the supreme law of the land" (U.S. Constitution, Article VI). This means that any federal, state, or local law is not valid if it conflicts with the federal Constitution.

Similarly, within each state the state constitution is supreme to all other state laws. When a law is invalid because it conflicts with a constitution, it is said to be **unconstitutional**. The appropriate supreme court determines whether a law is unconstitutional.

STATUTES AND VALIDITY Statutes or ordinances must be constitutional to be valid. Ordinances must not exceed the powers delegated to local governments by the states. Courts determine the constitutionality of statutes and ordinances. Courts also determine whether particular ordinances exceed the scope of powers delegated.

For example, a city enacted a law making it illegal to sell gasoline for more than $1 per gallon. It enacted another law making the death penalty mandatory for persons who commit murder within the city limits. Both ordinances were challenged in court. The first was invalidated because it conflicted with the federal Constitution, which gives the power to regulate commerce to the federal government. The second was invalidated because only the state has the power to set penalties for murder.

ADMINISTRATIVE REGULATIONS AND VALIDITY Administrative regulations also can be reviewed by courts to determine whether they are constitutional. The courts may invalidate a rule or regulation if it is outside the scope of powers delegated to the agency by the legislature that created it.

CASE LAW AND VALIDITY Courts are not the final authority on the effect of statutes. A legislative body has the power to nullify a court's interpretation of a statute or ordinance by abolishing or rewriting it. Administrative agencies also can revise their regulations when challenged.

Even when interpreting constitutions, courts are not the ultimate authority. The people, through votes for their representatives, have the power to amend constitutions if they disagree with the courts' interpretations. In answer to *What's Your Verdict?* the Sixteenth Amendment to the U.S. Constitution, adopted in 1913, gave Congress the power to lay and collect an income tax. This in effect nullified the U.S. Supreme Court decision.

WHAT ARE THE MAIN TYPES OF LAWS?

WHAT'S YOUR VERDICT?

Worthington was driving down the road well within the speed limit. At a stop sign he slowed to about 15 miles per hour, but he did not stop. As a result, he smashed into the side of Bates' Mercedes, causing $12,000 in damage.

Did Worthington violate civil or criminal law?

Laws may be classified in various ways. Common types of laws are civil laws, criminal laws, procedural laws, substantive laws, and business law.

Criminal v. Civil Laws

When the private legal rights of an individual are violated, the matter is governed by civil law. The use of the term **civil law** within the common law system refers to the group of laws that redress wrongs against individual persons. (Civil law in this sense does not refer to the comprehensive system of law mentioned in Lesson 1-1.) Civil law applies whenever one person has a right to sue another person.

For example when a tenant fails to pay the rent, the landlord has the right to sue the tenant. The police do not take action in civil conflicts. If a defendant loses a civil case, that defendant is liable. This means that she or he must pay money to the plaintiff. This is the primary help that courts grant in civil matters.

A **crime** is an offense against society. It disrupts the stable environment that we all depend upon to make civilization work. So, when the citizens' right to live in peace is violated by such activity, the offense is governed by **criminal law**. Acting in the name of all the people, the government investigates an alleged wrongdoing. If a crime is committed and the person responsible can be found, the government will prosecute. Conviction of a crime can result in a fine, imprisonment, and in some states, execution.

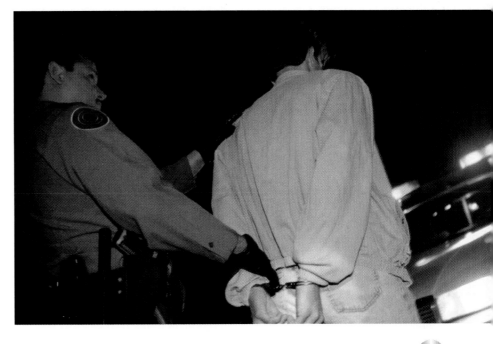

The Karla Faye Tucker Case

WAS JUSTICE SERVED?

Karla Faye Tucker and Daniel Ryan Garret were convicted in the brutal axe killing of a Texas couple. Brought to trial, both were sentenced to death. Garret died in prison of liver cancer, but Tucker lived on to face her sentence.

While in prison, Tucker claims to have experienced a religious conversion. Anti-death penalty advocates lobbied through the media to spare her life. Tucker was portrayed as an attractive, peaceful women, sorry for what she had done. Appeals for a verdict reversal failed. Tucker was executed by lethal injection.

Questions to Consider

1 **Do you think Tucker's portrayal in the media swayed public opinion about her execution?**

2 **Discuss the anti-death penalty lobbyists' use of the media to attempt to overturn the court verdict. What do you think motivated their actions?**

Usually when a crime occurs, private rights of the victim are violated also. A violation may be both a crime and a civil offense. Thus, the civil law may also apply. The victim of the crime may sue the wrongdoer.

In *What's Your Verdict?* Worthington committed both a crime and a civil offense. Driving through the stop sign was a crime. Worthington could be arrested, convicted in a criminal trial, and fined. In addition, Worthington committed a civil offense when he carelessly smashed into the side of Bates' Mercedes. Bates could probably win a separate civil trial and recover the $12,000.

Procedural v. Substantive Laws

Procedural law deals with methods of *enforcing* legal rights and duties. Laws that specify how and when police can make arrests and what methods can be used in a trial are procedural laws. Procedural laws

determine whether equitable remedies, such as an injunction, are available. The doctrine of *stare decisis* is a procedural law. Rules for determining the supremacy of conflicting laws are procedural laws.

In contrast, **substantive law** defines rights and duties. It is concerned with all rules of conduct except those involved in enforcement. Substantive laws define offenses, such as murder, theft, vehicular homicide, breach of contract, and negligence.

There are two types of procedural law: civil procedure and criminal procedure. *Criminal procedure* defines the process for enforcing the law when someone is charged with a crime.

Civil procedure is used when a civil law has been violated. Civil law is concerned only with private offenses. When a civil law is violated the injured party is entitled to protect his or her rights. Police and public prosecutors generally do not involve themselves in the dispute.

Business Law

Business law covers rules that apply to business situations and transactions. This book's table of contents shows that the scope of business law is broad. Business law is important for all students—not just those planning careers in business or law. Most business transactions involve a merchant and a consumer. As you study business law, you will gain legal knowledge that will make you a more competent consumer.

Business law is largely concerned with civil law, especially contracts. The area of the law pertaining to torts is another category of business law. **Torts** are private wrongs (civil offenses) against people or organizations. Torts are distinct from breaches of contracts. For example, torts may occur when manufacturers make defective products that injure users.

Business activities are also governed by criminal law at times. For example, criminal law would punish a firm that conspires with competitors to fix prices or an employee who steals company tools.

Laws of our various states do not have to be alike as long as they are constitutionally valid. However, with the growth of interstate commerce and large business firms, more uniformity among states of laws governing business and commercial transactions is important.

Committees of legal experts have written model laws covering such areas as sales, certain credit transactions, and business forms. Sets of these model laws were then offered to the states for adoption in place of their current statutes covering the areas. The result has been more uniformity in state commercial laws. The *Uniform Commercial Code (UCC)* is a widely adopted uniform business law. It governs such areas as sales of goods, certain aspects of banking, and leases of goods. You will learn more about the Uniform Commercial Code throughout this book.

THINK CRITICALLY ABOUT EVIDENCE

Answer the following questions about legal concepts.

1. The first ten amendments to the U.S. Constitution are known as the __?__ .

2. An offense that violates the right of citizens to live in peace is governed by **(a) administrative law (b) constitutional law (c) criminal law (d) common law**.

3. Legislative enactments at the local level are called __?__ .

4. *Stare decisis* is the doctrine that requires lower courts to adhere to existing case law in their decisions. **True or False?**

5. Torts are private wrongs committed against individuals or organizations. **True or False?**

6. As long as they are constitutionally valid, the laws of the various states **(a) do (b) do not have to be alike**.

7. Business activities are at times governed by the criminal law. **True or False?**

8. Businesses cannot commit torts. **True or False?**

9. The doctrine of *stare decisis* is a **(a) substantive law (b) procedural law (c) prohibitive law (d) none of the above.**

Study the following situations, answer the questions, then prepare arguments to support your answers.

10. Suppose the principal of your public school required all students to recite a prayer at the start of each school day. What level of government (federal, state, or local) is most likely to rule against such action?

11. In exercise 10, what type of law (constitutional, statutory, administrative, or case) requires such a ruling?

12. Sonoma County passed a law making it legal to drive 65 mph on freeways inside the county. A state law limited all vehicles anywhere in the state to 55 mph. What is the valid speed limit on freeways inside this county?

13. In 1896, the U.S. Supreme Court held in *Plessy v. Ferguson,* 163 U.S. 537, that equal treatment of different races is provided when public and semipublic facilities, even though separate, are substantially equal in quality. For years, railroad cars, buses, schools, and other facilities had separate and supposedly equal facilities for blacks. In 1954 black plaintiffs in Delaware, Kansas, South Carolina, and Virginia sought admission for their children to public schools on the basis of nonsegregation. Does the doctrine of *stare decisis* bar the U.S. Supreme Court from changing the law declared in *Plessy v. Ferguson*? (*Brown v. Board of Education*, 347 U.S. 483)

14. On a two-week vacation in a neighboring state, you buy several large firecrackers and take them home. A police officer notices them in your car on a routine traffic stop. She cites you for possession of an illegal explosive device, which is a felony in your state. Will the fact that possession of fireworks in the neighboring state is not even a crime be a defense for you?

As a citizen . . .

1. When moving to a new location, find out which county or city makes laws that may affect you.

2. Before beginning a new business, consult an attorney to learn about city, county, state, and federal laws and how they may affect you.

3. Study business law diligently so you can become an informed consumer who is knowledgeable about legal matters.

PREVENT LEGAL DIFFICULTIES

CHAPTER IN REVIEW

CONCEPTS IN BRIEF

1. Laws are the enforceable rules of conduct in a society.

2. The two great systems of law in the world are the English common law and the Roman civil law. The federal government and all states except Louisiana are based on the common law.

3. When no adequate remedy was available through the common law, a person could often obtain relief through a supplementary system of justice known as equity.

4. Sources of law include constitutions, statutes, cases decided by appellate courts, and regulations and rulings of administrative agencies.

5. A constitution is a document that sets forth the framework of a government and its relationship to the people it governs. In the United States both the federal government and state government have constitutions.

6. The common law operates through the doctrine of stare decisis. This doctrine requires lower courts to follow established case law in deciding similar cases.

7. Civil law is concerned with the private legal rights of individuals and governs relations between individuals. Criminal law deals with crimes (offenses against society) and governs violations of duties owed to society as a whole.

8. Procedural law deals with methods of enforcing legal rights and duties. Substantive law defines those rights and duties.

9. Business law is concerned with the rules that apply to business situations and transactions.

YOUR LEGAL VOCABULARY

Match each statement with the term that it best defines. Some terms may not be used.

1. Doctrine requiring lower courts to adhere to existing case law in making decisions

2. Group of laws defining the methods for enforcing legal rights and decisions

3. Enforced rules of conduct in a society

4. Law based on the customs of a group

5. Legislative enactments by a city

6. Government body formed to carry out particular laws

7. Group of laws defining and setting punishments for offenses against society

8. Basic fairness *criminal*

9. Power of a court to decide a case

10. Status of a law that conflicts with a constitution and which is therefore invalid

11. Laws enacted by state legislatures or federal legislatures

12. Law made when an appellate court endorses a rule to be used in deciding court cases

13. Group of laws that defines rights and duties

14. Laws grouped into an organized form

administrative agency
business law
case law
civil law
code
common law
constitutional law
crime
criminal law
equity
jurisdiction
laws
ordinance
positive law
procedural law
stare decisis
statutes
substantive law
torts
unconstitutional

15. Louisiana is the only one of our 50 states whose law was not originally based on the English common law system. What system was its law based on? How did this system come to be used?

16. Why should a constitution be considered the highest law of a nation or a state?

17. What does the phrase "interstate commerce" mean to you? Would you consider growing vegetables in your garden for your own consumption interstate commerce? Why or why not?

18. Why does the doctrine of *stare decisis* not bind supreme courts?

19. Why are city ordinances that are unconstitutional still on the books and being enforced?

20. Why are the fines the courts assess for criminal behavior generally paid to the government and not to the victim of the crime?

WRITE ABOUT LEGAL CONCEPTS

21. Would you rather be under the control of a system of common law or positive law? Write a paragraph to explain your answer.

22. Why is it important to have uniform state laws governing business? List and discuss at least four reasons in a paragraph.

23. HOT DEBATE The responding officer to the collision ordered a blood-alcohol concentration (BAC) test on both drivers. If Wilma is cited for DWI, what effect will this have on determining negligence? If Donna is cited for speeding, what effect should that have on the trial?

THINK CRITICALLY ABOUT EVIDENCE

Study the following situations, answer the questions, then prepare arguments to support your answers.

24. It is the year 1770. You are in the Colony of Virginia. You have a boundary dispute with your neighbor over where your land ends and hers begins. The highest court in the Colony rules in your favor. Is there any higher authority?

25. You are in France and are accused of a crime. You ask for a trial by jury. Why is one not available?

26. In a fit of anger a wealthy acquaintance of yours throws a bat at your car. The bat bounces off the side of the car and hits you in the face. Your friend Bill tells you that it won't do you any good to report it to the police. "Even if they do prosecute her, you can't get anything as a result." Is your friend correct?

27. Your friend Bill (from exercise 26) has shared with you his dream of getting rid of the income tax. He says that, if the people wanted to, they could pass a Constitutional Amendment that would eliminate the tax. Is he correct?

28. You are a citizen of the United States in 1791. In your mind, which is the most important government to you—the federal government or your state's government? Which one is making the laws that have the greatest effect on you?

ANALYZE
REAL CASES

29. Alaska enacted a statute known as "Alaska Hire." It required employers in the state to hire qualified Alaskan residents in preference to nonresidents. Hicklin, a nonresident, sued Orbeck, the state official charged with enforcing the statute. After the Supreme Court of Alaska found the statute constitutional, Hicklin appealed to the U.S. Supreme Court, which found the statute to be in conflict with the U.S. Constitution. Which supreme court is the final authority in this case? (*Hicklin v. Orbeck*, 437 U.S. 518)

30. The statute enacted by the U.S. Congress that created the Selective Service authorized it to register and classify draft-age men. It also authorized the Service to reclassify persons who fail to appear before the Service or who fail to provide it with certain information. Peter Wolff was registered with the Selective Service. During the Vietnam War, he received a deferment for being a student at the University of Michigan. When Wolff participated in a demonstration protesting U.S. involvement in the war, the Service eliminated his deferment. Is it legal for the Selective Service to do this? (*Wolff v. Selective Service*, 372 F.2d 817)

31. On March 30, 1981, as then President Ronald Reagan left the Washington Hilton Hotel after giving a speech, he was wounded by one of a series of bullets allegedly fired by John Hinckley. Three other men also were wounded, including James Brady, the President's press secretary, who received a severe wound to the head. President Reagan underwent surgery shortly thereafter at the hospital. Hinckley was arrested at the scene literally with the smoking gun. Soon after the criminal process was begun against him, he underwent two psychiatric examinations by order of the magistrate and then the chief judge involved in the case. Both examinations found him to be competent. On August 28, after being indicted by a federal grand jury, Hinckley pled not guilty to a battery of charges, including the attempted assassination of the President of the United States. Hinckley's lawyers then began their work. In two very important rulings they were able to suppress the use of evidence that would have been very damning to the defendant. They first had thrown out all answers he had given to questions prior to having his attorney present. This was done even though he had been read his Miranda rights three times before agreeing to answer those ques-

tions. Then Hinckley's attorneys were able to suppress allegedly incriminating material in the form of a diary gathered by the jailers when they checked Hinckley's cell for contraband and instruments useful in a potential suicide attempt. These rulings by the court were based on the Constitutional rights to counsel and to protection against improper searches and seizures. Do you consider their use in this case a proper application of such rights? Is the exclusion of the evidence the only possible remedy or could you come up with another one? If so, what is it and why would it be an improvement over the current policy? (*United States v. John W. Hinckley, Jr.,* 525 F. Supp. 1342)

32. In the Hinckley trial referred to above, the defense introduced evidence of Hinckley's psychiatric care immediately before the shooting. The defense also was able to introduce evidence showing that Hinckley had a fixation on actress Jodie Foster and believed that she would have to notice him if he carried out an act such as the assassination. His lawyers, who were hired by Hinckley's wealthy parents, pled him "not guilty by reason of insanity." After almost 24 hours of deliberation, the jury agreed and termed Hinckley not guilty by reason of insanity. He was then ordered confined at St. Elizabeth's Hospital, a mental institution in Wash-ington, D.C. Did Hinckley commit a crime? Why or why not? Regardless of the results in the criminal trial, could Hinckley be tried and found liable for a tort for the injury to the President? (*United States v. John W. Hinckley, Jr.,* 525 F. Supp. 1342)

33. Andrews was stopped by a police officer on a street where a murder had just been committed. The officer had no search warrant but arrested Andrews for carrying a concealed weapon. The officer relied on a clause in the Michigan Constitution. The clause stated a search warrant was not necessary if a police officer seized a firearm in the yard of any house in the state. The U.S. Supreme Court earlier held that the Fourth Amendment to the Constitution prohibiting unreasonable searches and seizures applied to the states. A U.S. court of appeals had held that the clause in the Michigan Constitution was in conflict with the U.S. Constitution. Must the Michigan courts recognize the superior authority of the U.S. Supreme Court and the U.S. Constitution? (*People v. Andrews,* 21 Mich. App. 731, 176 N.W.2d 460)

Silkwood v. Kerr-McGee Corporation
USSC 464 U. S. 238

FACTS Bill Silkwood, the father of Karen Silkwood, brought a lawsuit against her former employer, Kerr-McGee Corporation, to recover for injures she sustained in her employment. The lawsuit alleged that Karen died of plutonium poisoning while working at the Kerr-McGee plutonium fuel production facility near Crescent, Oklahoma. A jury trial resulted in a $10 million award to Karen's Estate. Kerr-McGee appealed.

APPEAL The appeal noted that the plant at which Karen worked was regulated by a federal agency known as the Nuclear Regulatory Commission (NRC). Kerr-McGee's attorneys pointed out that neither the rules and regulations of the NRC nor the act of Congress that created and empowered the NRC contained a provision that allowed recovery for a private person injured as a result of violations of NRC standards. As a consequence, the Oklahoma laws under which the $10 million was obtained were preempted by the superior federal laws.

Bill Silkwood's attorneys argued that Congress and the NRC had omitted any provision on private recovery because they had presumed such recovery would be pursued under state law as it had been.

DECISION The appeal was ultimately decided by the U.S. Supreme Court. In its opinion the Court noted that Congress probably omitted any mention of judicial recourse for persons injured in situation such as Karen's because it considered those parties free to bring lawsuits under state law. In so concluding, the Court stated:

Preemption should not be judged on the basis that the Federal Government has so completely occupied the field of safety that state remedies are foreclosed, but on whether there is an irreconcilable conflict between the federal and state standards or whether the imposition of a State standard in a damages action would frustrate the objectives of the federal law. We perceive no such conflict or frustration in the circumstances of this case.

PRACTICE JUDGING

1. **Who should win in this case?**

2. **What is the legal reasoning that led you to this conclusion?**

3. **If possible, look up the case in the law section of a library and see how the U.S. Supreme Court decided it and why.**

LESSONS

HOT DEBATE

Achmed emigrated to the United States from Iraq. He claimed Iraq's government would persecute him if he stayed there. The U.S. Immigration and Naturalization Service (INS) granted Achmed a temporary visa and began investigating his claim. The INS then denied his claim and revoked his visa. Achmed obtained a false ID to stay in the country. He told his employer, Julian, the whole story. Julian's lawyer told Julian he was legally obligated to inform the INS about Achmed. Julian believed that Achmed would be tortured if he returned to Iraq.

Where Do You Stand?

1. Should Julian inform the INS of Achmed's whereabouts? If so, why?

2. What are the reasons in favor of Julian not informing the INS?

ETHICS DEFINED

WHAT'S YOUR VERDICT?

While working in the school office, Jane discovered a copy of the exam to be given in one of her classes. She thought she could take it home with little chance of being caught. In thinking about whether to take the test home, she considered how helpful an "A" on the test would be and how important grades are to her. After she stole the test she told a friend, "It just felt so good to know that I wouldn't need to spend all that time studying to get an 'A'."

Has Jane made an ethical decision?

E thics is deciding what is right or wrong in a reasoned, impartial manner. Consider the three important elements in this definition:

1. decision about a right or wrong action
2. decision is reasoned
3. decision is impartial

The following sections discuss each of these important elements. The lesson concludes with how we can apply the study of ethics to making ethical business decisions.

Decision About a Right or Wrong Action

Many of your decisions have little effect on other persons or yourself. For example, your decision to buy blue jeans with wide instead of narrow pant legs has no ethical component. On the other hand, your decision to discontinue medical support for an unconscious, terminally ill relative is an intensely ethical decision. To involve ethics, a decision must affect you or others in some significant way.

Reasoned Decisions

We often act in response to our emotions. For example, after watching a movie, we recommend it to friends with such words as, "It really made me feel good." Or when someone asks us why we made a particular comment, we respond, "I don't really know, I just felt like it." What we mean is that our emotions guided these decisions. Our feelings directed our actions. But to make ethical decisions, we must usually base our decisions on reason, not on emotion. In *What's Your Verdict?* Jane made a decision based on emotion when she thought, "it just felt so good. . . ."

Often people reason about right and wrong by referring to a written authority that provides consistency. The law is such an authority. So are religious texts such as the Torah, the Bible, the Koran, and the Bhagavad Gita. For example, a person might reason, "I believe that God is the source of the Bible and the Bible tells me not to lie. Therefore, it would be wrong, or unethical, for me to lie."

Impartial Decisions

Impartiality is the idea that the same ethical standards are applied to everyone. If it is wrong for you to

engage in a certain action, then in the same circumstance it is also wrong for me. So, by definition, ethics does not value one person or group of persons more than any other does. Men are not more valuable than women. Caucasians are not entitled to more respect than people of other races. Each person is an individual and should receive equal respect and consideration from others.

Impartiality requires that in making ethical decisions, we balance our self-interest with the interest of others. To do this, we must learn to recognize the interests of others. Sometimes this is difficult. Our self-interest can cloud our perceptions and thus our ability to reason impartially.

Suppose you lose control of your car while backing out of your driveway. The next thing you know, you have struck and damaged your neighbor's station wagon, which is parked on the street. No one has seen you do this. You can't decide if you should tell your neighbor what you did. You might think, "I know my religion teaches me to tell the truth. But it would cost me more than $100 if I admit that I ran into Mrs. Anderson's vehicle. I can't afford that, but she can! So it must be okay to

deny my beliefs in this situation. I'm not going to tell her." If you come to this conclusion, you are not being impartial.

Impartiality is particularly important when organizations and institutions rather than individuals are involved. When we think about Mrs. Anderson, our emotions help us understand that she is a person who is entitled to the same treatment as we are. But when an ethical decision involves an organization, self-interest can make people conclude that their actions will not injure other people. "It was only the school's property," or "It doesn't matter, it was just the insurance company that was cheated." In reality, behind all organizations there are many people, such as taxpayers, employees, and customers. They are injured when the organization is injured. Property taxes may go up or insurance rates may be raised. When dealing with institutions, then, being impartial means considering how the people behind the institution are affected by our actions.

The law is an institution. It represents all the people in our country. When we injure the law, perhaps by violating it, by laughing at it, or by encouraging others to violate it, we

injure many other people who depend upon the law for protection and fairness.

IN THIS CASE

Gabe decided to walk to school instead of riding the bus because it was a nice day. On the way, he found a wallet containing $300 in cash and a driver's license. When he saw how much money there was, he felt elated. He could almost feel the fun he could have with it. Gabe also asked himself how much injury the loss of $300 might cause someone such as the owner of the wallet. At first he thought he would get much more pleasure from the money than anyone else could. In the end, he decided that he would want his wallet and money returned if he lost them, so he called the owner. When he returned the wallet the owner gave Gabe a $40 reward. Gabe's decision to walk to school did not have an ethical dimension to it because it didn't really affect anyone seriously. His decision about whether to return the wallet did have an ethical component. This decision would affect both Gabe and the owner of the wallet significantly.

Business Ethics

The reason you are learning about ethics in general is to prepare you to apply ethical concepts to business decision making. **Business ethics** are the ethical principles used in making business decisions. All too often, however, ethics are not considered when business decisions are made. The reason can be summarized in two words: profit maximization.

The idea of profit maximization is supported by those who would move factories offshore and cut jobs and pay in order to reduce costs and produce greater short-term profits. However, such activities tend to do little more than line the pockets of the business owners. This enriching the few at the expense of the many occurs because our free-market economy is far from perfect. To move toward a more ethically motivated economy, the profit maximization ethic will need to be replaced by the more humane ethical standards presented in this chapter.

THINK ABOUT LEGAL CONCEPTS

Answer the following questions about legal concepts.

1. Which of the following is not an element of our definition of ethics? **(a) making a decision that significantly affects you or others (b) making a decision based on reason rather than emotion (c) making a decision impartially (d) making a decision that places people above organizations**

2. A decision has an ethical component when it will affect you or others significantly. **True or False?**

3. When you treat everyone affected by a decision equally, you are being __?__ .

4. When our self-interest is at stake, it becomes very difficult to be impartial. **True or False?**

5. Ethical decisions are usually based on emotions rather than reason. **True or False?**

THINK CRITICALLY ABOUT EVIDENCE

Study the following situations, answer the questions, then prepare arguments to support your answers.

6. Gil received a scholarship offer to go to a top-ranked private college. Because the scholarship would cover only half his expenses, his parents would need to contribute more money for him to go there than they would if he went to the state university. That would probably leave less money to support his sister who was a year younger. The private college is farther away and most of Gil's friends are going to the state university. Does Gil's decision about which college to attend affect other people? Does it affect any of them significantly? Can you rank the people affected based on how significant the decision may be for them? Is this an ethical decision?

7. Conner walked past the candy section in the grocery store and quickly stuffed a handful of "Almond Joy" candy bars into her purse. A store security guard saw her do it and she was arrested. Her parents came to the police station after her arrest to take her home. Did Conner's shoplifting significantly affect anyone? If so, who? Was Conner basing her conduct on emotion or reason? Was she treating herself and the other customers and stockholders of the store equally?

8. Bill was madly in love with Jennifer. He couldn't think about anything else. He daydreamed in his classes and was close to flunking out of school. Does Bill's daydreaming in class have an ethical component? Who is most affected by this? Is Bill letting reason or emotion determine his conduct?

9. Voters faced two proposals on the ballot. One would build a new football stadium. Another would build new prisons. There is only enough money available to do one. Are voters being asked to make an ethical decision? Who is affected?

10. As Juanita was trying to decide how to allocate her monthly paycheck, she though of the many ways she could spend it. (1) She could treat herself to a makeover at the beauty salon because it would make her feel good. (2) She could repay money owed her sister because she would want to be repaid if anyone ever borrowed money from her. (3) She could get ahead on her monthly bills so she wouldn't worry so much. (4) She could enjoy the thrill of spending it all on lotto tickets. Which of these thoughts are reason-based and which are emotional reactions?

11. Mario was awarding end-of-year bonuses. As he looked over the list of employees, he rated each one based on how he felt about them. The political views of some of the employees affected his feelings. So did their physical attractiveness. Ultimately, Mario paid the bonuses in proportion to the employee's job performance. Which evidence suggests that Mario was not impartial? Which evidence suggests that he was impartial?

BASIC FORMS OF ETHICAL REASONING

WHAT'S YOUR VERDICT?

Tab inherited his grandparents' home. He built a garage for his car in the yard between his house and his neighbors' property line. Later, when he decided to build a fence on the border, he discovered that the garage was too close to the property line. So, he built the fence one foot onto the neighbors' property. Tab lived alone and three people lived on the neighboring property.

How can Tab evaluate the ethical character of his action?

Ethical reasoning about right and wrong takes two basic forms. One form is based on consequences. In this style of ethical reasoning, rightness or wrongness is based only on the results of the action. Particular acts have no ethical, or moral, character. An act that produces good consequences is good. An act that produces bad consequences is bad.

The other form of moral reasoning is based on ethical rules. In this style of reasoning, acts are either right or wrong. For example, telling the truth is always right, and lying is always wrong. In rule-based ethics, good consequences do not justify wrong or bad acts. For example, in rule-based ethics, you cannot justify lying by showing that it produces good consequences.

For almost all ethical decisions, these two forms of reasoning reach the same conclusion. In the decision of whether to lie or to tell the truth, for example, both forms usually conclude that one should not lie.

Consequence-based reasoning recognizes that lying usually produces bad consequences. Rule-based ethics says that lying is always wrong.

Ethical Reasoning Based on Consequences

Consequence-based reasoning first looks for alternative ways to alter the current situation. Then it attempts to forecast the consequences that will arise from each alternative. Finally, it evaluates those possible consequences to select the alternative that will generate the greatest good. These steps in consequential reasoning are described in the following paragraphs.

DESCRIBE ALTERNATIVE ACTIONS First, alternative actions that would improve things should be described. Two of the many alternatives Tab might consider are (1) building the fence on the neighbors' property without telling them, or (2) offering to buy a one-foot strip of the neighbors' property. In order to decide what is the best action to take, he must describe his alternatives in order to then evaluate them.

FORECAST CONSEQUENCES Second, the consequences flowing from each alternative must be described. This requires skill in predicting the future. It requires an ability to see things such as, "If I build the fence one foot inside my neighbors' property, they probably won't notice." Or "If they discover that the fence was built on their property, they will probably make me pay for the one-foot strip of property instead of making me tear it down."

EVALUATE CONSEQUENCES Third, the consequences for each alternative must be evaluated. There are two elements to the evaluation process.

1. selecting the standard for judging consequences as right or wrong
2. counting the persons affected

Philosophers usually call the standard for judging right or wrong **The Good.** The Good is the primary goal toward which human life should be directed. The Good involves alternative basic goals such as love, justice, truth, and pleasure. These goals

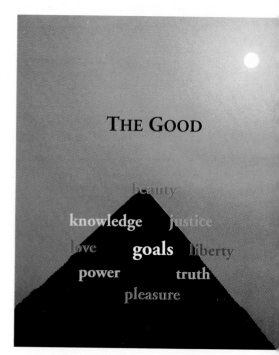

THE GOOD

beauty

knowledge   justice

love   **goals**   liberty

power   truth

pleasure

all motivate a reasoning person's actions and important decisions.

In *What's Your Verdict?* Tab must choose a goal with which to evaluate the alternative actions. Let's assume Tab chooses pleasure (from use of the land). In consequence-based reasoning, the standard is judged by "the greatest good for the greatest number" of people. Thus, for each alternative we must determine how many people will be positively and negatively affected. If Tab builds the fence on the neighbors' land without their consent, only his pleasure is increased. The pleasure of his three neighbors is decreased. Tab receives the benefit while his three neighbors bear the cost. So this alternative is ethically wrong in reasoning based on consequences where the good is pleasure.

To evaluate the consequences of buying the strip of land, we compare both the costs and the benefits for each person. For Tab, essentially the cost is the price paid for the land and the benefit is the ability to use the strip of land for his fence. For his neighbors, the cost is the loss of the land and the benefit is the money they receive for it. For the parties to agree voluntarily, Tab must prefer the land to the money and the neighbors must prefer the money to the land. If the sale can be voluntarily completed, four parties are positively benefited. Thus, in reasoning based on consequences where the good is pleasure, this alternative would be ethically good.

Fundamental Ethical Rules

With **fundamental ethical rules**, the acts themselves are judged as right or wrong. The standard for judging usually comes from one of two sources— a recognized authority or human reasoning.

DECISIONS BASED ON AUTHORITY An authority, such as the law or a religious text, can say that stealing is wrong. When an accepted authority has a rule on an issue, the rule tells the follower of that law or religion what is right and wrong. All religious authorities and all legal systems would condemn the act of building a fence on a neighbor's property without permission as a form of stealing. The act itself is basically wrong. In rule-based reasoning, the act is wrong even if it benefits more people than it injures. So building the fence on the neighbor's property without permission could not be justified by benefiting 10 people living on your property or by the neighbor being very rich.

DECISIONS BASED ON REASONING In addition to an authority, human reasoning also can show that some things are basically wrong. A test has been

IN THIS CASE

Gerry was late for a job interview. The rural road she was driving down was not heavily traveled. The posted speed limit was 55 miles per hour. She reasoned that by speeding she could benefit both herself and the interviewer. Gerry would make a better impression by arriving on time and the interviewer would not have to waste time waiting for Gerry to arrive. So she sped up to 70 miles per hour.

Gerry made an error in her ethical reasoning. She ignored some of the ways her actions affected other people. By speeding, she imposed a substantially greater risk of accident and injury on the other roadway users. Because she did not see this effect, she also failed to count some of the people affected by her decision. Also, she ignored the way her actions undermine respect for law. When these effects and people are counted, the action seems ethically wrong.

devised to determine whether an action is right or wrong. It involves picturing in your mind's eye everyone in the world doing the action. This is called **universalizing** the action. As you picture everyone doing the action, then ask, "Is this irrational, illogical, or self-defeating?" If it is any of the three, the action is inconsistent with reason and therefore ethically wrong.

We can apply the test to lying by imagining a world where everyone lies. Such a world would be illogical. There would be no point in lying, because no one would believe anyone. Similarly, if we imagine a world where everyone takes her or his neighbor's land, there would be no point in taking the land because another neighbor would promptly take it away from you. These pictures help us see that the actions of lying and stealing are inconsistent with human reason. Accordingly, in rule-based ethical reasoning, they are basically wrong.

Both authority and reasoning conclude that all human beings have dignity and worth. Religions usually say that humans are "made in the image of God" or "of Allah" and therefore must be treated with respect. Humans are unique because of their potential for reasoning about right and wrong. Both of these lines of argument lead to the conclusion that humans have moral rights. Moral rights are rightful claims on other people that flow from each person's status as a human being.

THINK ABOUT LEGAL CONCEPTS

Answer the following questions about legal concepts.

1. Reasoning based on consequences- and rule-based reasoning usually reach the same conclusion about what is right or wrong. **True or False?**

2. The idea that acts have a basic moral character is a feature of which form of moral reasoning? **(a) rule based reasoning (b) reasoning based on consequences**

3. In reasoning based on consequences, we are required to count everyone affected and to consider all the major ways they are affected. **True or False?**

4. In reasoning based on consequences, we are required to consider multiple alternatives and select the best one. **True or False?**

5. In reasoning based on consequences, the standard used to evaluate alternatives is called ___?___.

6. In rule-based reasoning, acts or rules are wrong if they are inconsistent with human reason. **True or False?**

THINK CRITICALLY ABOUT EVIDENCE

Study the following situations, answer the questions, then prepare arguments to support your answers.

7. Susan was driving friends to a concert. It was 8 P.M. and the concert began at 8:30 P.M. Because her friends still needed to pick their tickets up at the will call window, they started pressuring her to drive faster than the speed limit. She refused and said, "I just don't want to take a chance on getting a ticket." Is Susan using consequential reasoning or reasoning based on ethical rules here? Why?

8. In a trash basket she was emptying after school, Carol found a copy of the answer key for an exam she was scheduled to take the next day. Instead of using it, she returned it to the teacher, explaining how she found it. When the teacher asked why she did not use it to cheat. Carol said, "I just think it is wrong to cheat. When I take tests I am telling the teacher how much I really know. If I cheated it would be a form of lying. I believe lying is wrong. I won't lie even if it might help me." Is Carol using reasoning based on consequences or ethical rules here? Why?

9. Rosanna was trying to decide whether to share part of her lunch with Sheila and Fran, who had forgotten theirs. She decided not to, saying, "I just don't like Sheila, so I won't share with anyone." Has Rosanna made any errors in reasoning? If so, which errors?

10. Sharon knows about tax laws and how the Internal Revenue Service (IRS) audits tax returns. She knows a way to cheat on her tax return that would save her almost $2,000. She thinks her chance of being caught is about one in 100. Can this cheating be justified by reasoning based on ethical rules? Can it be justified by ethics based on consequences?

11. An ordinance of Walker County provided that all automobiles must pass a smog emissions test once a year. Ross was ticketed because his car had not been inspected and approved at an emissions testing center. Ross claimed to be a skilled mechanic who kept his car well tuned and cleaner than the law required. According to Ross, the law violated his natural rights. Explain why you agree or disagree with Ross.

12. Heather was trying to decide for herself about whether stealing could ever be justified. She thought about what the world would be like if the act of stealing were made universal. She saw that as soon as one person stole something, it would be immediately stolen from the thief. Is this universalized state more illogical because stealing has no purpose? Or is it self-defeating because eventually you would run out of things to steal?

G O A L S

● **Explain how our laws reflect ethics based on consequences and ethics based on reasoning**

● **Discuss why we are obligated to obey laws**

OUR LAWS REFLECT ETHICS BASED ON CONSEQUENCES

WHAT'S YOUR VERDICT?

In a coastal city of California, residents often could not sleep because people would drive late at night with their car windows down and their stereos playing full blast. On weekends and holidays, people put large home stereos in the back of their pickup trucks and played them as loud as possible. In response, the city council enacted a law making it illegal to generate noise in public above a certain decibel level.

Is there an ethical justification for this law?

In our country, the people—directly or indirectly—determine the laws that bind them. They do this by electing representatives to lawmaking bodies, such as city councils, state legislatures, and the Congress of the United States. In these elections and in the legislative bodies, **majority rule** prevails. The elected representatives must vote for laws acceptable to the majority of people they represent if they expect to be reelected.

Because this system is grounded on majority rule, it uses many of the features of consequences-based ethics. In this system, laws are judged to be right or good when they affect the majority of the people positively. Laws are judged to be wrong when they affect the majority negatively.

The Constitution of the United States seeks to ensure that our federal lawmaking system reflects the desires of our citizens. It does this by creating a national legislature composed of two bodies—the House of Representatives and the Senate. Together, these bodies are called Congress. The Constitution provides for the election of the members of Congress by the citizenry. States have similar legislative structures. This legislative structure promotes ethical reasoning based on consequences. (You will learn more about the U.S. Constitution and legislature in Chapter 3 of this book.)

In *What's Your Verdict?* the members of the city council tried to determine what the majority of citizens wanted. Some wanted the pleasure of playing their music loudly in public. But many more wanted the pleasure of a quiet community. So the law was passed in response to the majority will. It is justified by ethics based on consequences. It produces the greatest good for the greatest number. Clearly, this law restricts the conduct of those who want to play loud music. But does it violate their moral rights? No. Freedom to play loud music in public is not essential for the maintenance of human dignity. Therefore, it is not a right.

OUR LAWS REFLECT RULE-BASED ETHICS

WHAT'S YOUR VERDICT?

Almost everyone in a small community belonged to the same church. When members of a different denomination were considering buying land to erect a church, the city conducted a referendum (a direct vote by all the citizens on a proposed law). The referendum was on a zoning law that made it illegal to use any land in the city for any purpose other than residential housing. The law was enacted by majority vote. The effect of the law was to prohibit the construction of the proposed church in that city.

Is such a law ethically justified? Is such a law legal?

While most laws reflect the desires of the people governed, the laws desired by the majority sometimes conflict with moral rights. Stated another way, the majority may sometimes benefit from unjust laws. For example, the wealth of the majority of persons in a country might increase if it were to enslave a small percentage of the population. These people could be forced to work for free. Then the benefits of their free labor could be dis-

The United States of America is a country that recognizes and supports human rights. Other countries vary dramatically in the extent to which they do so. **Civil rights** (or civil liberties) generally are personal, human rights recognized and guaranteed by our Constitution. Among the civil rights recognized are freedom of religion, speech, and the press; freedom from unreasonable searches and seizures; the right to a speedy and impartial trial; the right to vote; and a host of others. You will learn more about our civil rights in Chapter 3.

The courts usually protect human rights. When the people or legislatures pass laws that undermine human rights, they are usually declared *unconstitutional*. This means that a court finds the law invalid because it conflicts with a constitutional provision. In *What's Your Verdict?* the zoning law adopted by majority vote is invalid. It is unconstitutional because it undermines freedom of religion.

Because courts perform the important duty of protecting natural rights,

we sometimes try to insulate judges from the will of the majority. Many judges are appointed, rather than elected. Federal judges are appointed for life, so they are free from the influence of the populace and elected officials. This permits judges to protect human rights without risking their jobs.

Our legal system primarily advances the will of the majority. It does this through the legislative process. But in this country we recognize that there are limits to majority rule. When the will of the majority conflicts with basic human rights, our legal system, particularly the judiciary, protects individual rights.

Our Declaration of Independence recognized these fundamental rights when it stated: "We hold these truths to be self-evident, that all men are created equal, that they are endowed by their Creator with certain unalienable Rights, that among these are Life, Liberty, and the pursuit of Happiness."

tributed to the majority. Historically, many countries adopted such laws. While these laws might benefit the majority, they violate the moral rights of the minority that is enslaved. The majority would be treating the minority in a manner inconsistent with their status as human beings.

Under the U.S. Constitution, the courts would declare such laws invalid because they deny "equal protection of the law" to the minority. We use other concepts of natural rights to protect political minorities from exploitation by those who make up the political majority. For example, the Fifth Amendment to the U.S. Constitution declares: "No person shall be . . . deprived of life, liberty, or property, without due process of law."

Ah, the joys of e-mail—instant communication of thoughts. You feel it, you say it, you send it. But, if your message is perceived as a threat, you could be prosecuted and convicted for it. In the first conviction of an online hate crime, a 21-year-old Los Angeles man was found guilty in federal court. He sent death threats by e-mail to more than 50 Asian students. The case set a precedent, as it put Internet communications on equal legal ground with telephone calls and postal mail. It also addressed civil rights violations committed online (hate crimes in this case).

The defense team argued this was a "stupid prank" and that so-called flames or abusive messages are commonplace with Internet culture and discussion groups. The jury thought otherwise and took the threats seriously. At first the Net was considered to be a fantasy land where users could be anonymous. This case shows that the legal system will not treat the Net differently from other forms of communication.

OTHER ETHICAL GOALS REFLECTED IN OUR LAWS

WHAT'S YOUR VERDICT?

Smyth was stopped for suspicion of drunk driving. The breathalyzer tests showed a blood alcohol level of 0.079 percent. State law defines drunkenness at 0.080 percent, so Smyth was not charged. Brown was stopped ten minutes later at the same location. Her test showed 0.081 percent blood level and she was arrested, tried, and found guilty. Her driver's license was revoked for one year.

Is there any ethical justification for treating Smyth and Brown so differently?

Often, matters simply need a consistent rule to assure order and predict ability. The rule need not be based on majority rule or on moral rights. Sometimes this means that the rule or law is arbitrary. For example, teachers are required to award grades on exams and for courses. Assume that the cutoff point between an "A" and a "B" is a 90-percent average. A student who has an 89-percent average and therefore receives a B may argue that the grade is unfair because it is arbitrary. After all, the student who receives an "A" for a 90-percent average has not done substantially better work. Yet the letter grades indicate a substantial difference. If the grade for the student with an 89-percent average is changed to an "A," then the argument for the student with the 88-percent average must be addressed and resolved the same way. In the end, everyone would receive the same grade.

A clear rule is needed, and it is perhaps more important that the rule exist than it is that the rule be completely fair. To be just, such rules of law must be communicated in advance and they must be applied consistently.

In *What's Your Verdict?* the law is clear and has been communicated to all drivers. Therefore it is just to treat Smyth and Brown differently.

WHY ARE WE OBLIGATED TO OBEY LAWS?

WHAT'S YOUR VERDICT?

During December vacation, Clementine worked part-time as a sales clerk in the jewelry department of a large department store. There was a watch that she wanted very much but could not afford. It was a busy time of the year and there were many opportunities for her to put a watch in her purse without being detected. She was convinced that the store management had not treated her fairly in the past.

Should Clementine take the watch if she thinks there is no chance of being caught?

We are obligated to obey the law because ethical reasoning demands it, because we have agreed to obey it, and because by obeying it we avoid punishment.

Ethics Demands That We Obey

Both ethics based on consequences and ethical rules conclude that we are obligated to obey the law.

According to consequences-based reasoning, when the law is violated, many more people are injured than are benefited. With rule-based reasoning, if we say that we have agreed to obey the law but violate it, we are breaking our promise. If we universalize promise breaking—imagining that everyone always breaks promises—there would be no point to promising. In this universalized state, promise breaking is illogical or pointless and thus wrong.

People who embrace formal religious principles (for example, Buddhists, Christians, Hindus, Jews, and Muslims) are taught to live in a manner that helps others. Hence, many religious people feel particularly obligated to obey the law in order to help others.

We Consent to Be Governed by Laws

Socrates was a philosopher who lived in Athens, Greece, from 470–399 B.C. He believed that he had promised to be governed by the laws of Athens. He expressed this promise by living in Athens and accepting the benefits of that society. Socrates believed that he should leave Athens, or not accept the benefits that it conferred on citizens, if he was not willing to obey all of its laws. Through this type of reasoning, Socrates concluded that it would be ethically wrong for him to violate the law of Athens. Socrates was charged with a crime and unjustly sentenced to death. When given the opportunity to escape, he declined, saying that to do so would be inconsistent with his moral beliefs. As a result, he was executed.

Socrates is widely regarded as a person of great integrity. **Integrity** is the capacity to do what is right even in the face of temptation or pressure to do otherwise. By giving up his life for his ethical beliefs, Socrates displayed the highest degree of integrity.

In *What's Your Verdict?* Clementine should not take the watch. She is required to obey the law because she has accepted the benefits of the society that made the law. Free schooling is one benefit this society has provided Clementine. Other benefits include police protection, safe roads, social security, and protection from foreign enemies in times of war. By accepting the benefits Clementine has demonstrated her consent to be governed by the law.

We Want to Avoid Punishment

Some people comply with the law primarily to avoid punishment. A person convicted of a crime may be fined, jailed, or, in some instances, put to death. While these penalties are widely known, there are many less well known penalties imposed on criminals. For instance, those convicted of serious crimes may be barred from jobs that require a security clearance. In many companies and governmental agencies, a security clearance is required for every employee. Also, some industries automatically exclude persons with criminal records from employment consideration. Banks, savings and loan associations, credit unions, and finance companies are but a few examples.

Employers often purchase fidelity bonds for persons who handle large sums of money, such as cashiers, managers of movie theaters, or supervisors of restaurants. A **fidelity bond**

is an insurance policy that pays the employer money in the case of theft by employees. Generally, those convicted of a serious crime cannot qualify for a fidelity bond.

Also, many professions are closed to those who are convicted of serious crimes. For example, before being licensed, prospective lawyers, public accountants, and medical doctors are

subject to a background check, which includes a check for criminal convictions. In *What's Your Verdict?* if Clementine is caught and convicted, her biggest penalty could be the one she would pay outside the judicial system. This penalty is the probable loss of many future job opportunities and her lasting embarrassment.

ARE WE EVER JUSTIFIED IN VIOLATING THE LAW?

WHAT'S YOUR VERDICT?

In the early 1960s, Dr. Martin Luther King, Jr., wanted to lead a march into Birmingham, Alabama, to protest racial segregation in that city. When he applied for a parade permit, his request was denied. Dr. King, knowing that his conduct was illegal, led the nonviolent march anyway. He was at the front of the line and allowed himself to be arrested, although he could have easily escaped. He went to jail. Community leaders were highly critical of Dr. King because he had violated the law. In response and while in jail, he wrote a famous letter attacking segregation laws as inconsistent with consequential and rule based ethical reasoning.

Is there an ethical justification for Dr. King's violation of the law?

Some persons care passionately about human rights and justice. Their concern for justice sometimes compels them to violate what they consider to be an unjust law—a law they believe to be in conflict with ethical reasoning. They violate the law by engaging in acts of civil disobedience. **Civil disobedience** is an open, peaceful, violation of a law to protest its alleged injustice. The goal of those who engage in civil disobedience is not to advance their self-interest but rather to make the legal system more just. The participants may be willing, or even eager, to be arrested in order to test the validity of the law in court.

In *What's Your Verdict?* Dr. Martin Luther King, Jr., engaged in civil disobedience. Dr. King believed that civil disobedience is justified only in

extremely limited circumstances. He and others conclude that civil disobedience is ethical only when

- a written law is in conflict with ethical reasoning
- no effective political methods are available to change the law
- the civil disobedience is nonviolent
- the civil disobedience does not advance one's immediate self-interest
- the civil disobedience is public and one willingly accepts the punishment for violating the law

As a result of Dr. King's efforts, many human rights were extended for the first time to several minority groups in this country.

In contrast to Dr. King, some persons are mere **scofflaws**. These are persons who do not respect the law. They simply assess the risk of being caught against the benefits they obtain by breaking the law. They think they are smart because they frequently violate valid laws without being caught. A scofflaw is never ethically justified in violating the law.

THINK ABOUT LEGAL CONCEPTS

Answer the following questions about legal concepts.

1. Many laws are based on ethics. **True or False?**

2. Majority rule usually advances this type of ethical reasoning. **(a) reasoning based on consequences (b) rule-based reasoning**

3. Legal rights are most often associated with which type of ethical reasoning? **(a) reasoning based on consequences (b) rule-based reasoning**

4. Where are the laws with the greatest ethical rules content most often found? **(a) in laws created by legislatures (b) in constitutions**

5. Arbitrary rules or laws are necessary to make social systems work. **True or False?**

6. Civil disobedience involves which of the following? **(a) violating the law (b) violating the law openly (c) violating the law openly and peacefully (d) violating the law openly, peacefully and accepting punishment for the violation (e) all of the above**

THINK CRITICALLY ABOUT EVIDENCE

Study the following situations, answer the questions, then prepare arguments to support your answers.

7. If a legislature enacted a law that made it illegal to shout "fire" in a movie theater, what would be the dominant ethical character of the law, consequences-based or rule-based reasoning?

8. When Congress passed the Civil Rights Amendment of 1964 making it illegal for employers to discriminate on the basis of race, religion, sex, or national origin, it exempted itself from the law. Can this action be justified by consequence-based reasoning? Can it be justified by rule-based reasoning?

9. Assume a state legislature enacted legislation which budgeted more money to educating rich children than to educating poor children. Also assume that the majority of children are rich. Would the dominant ethical character of this law be consequences-based or rule-based reasoning?

10. Your neighbor thought the tax system was corrupt. He thought it was far too complicated to be fair in the treatment of most people. So he refused to pay his taxes. He wrote the IRS expressing his views. When tax liens were filed against his property, he used the occasion to publicize the unfairness in the tax system. Is this civil disobedience? Why or why not?

11. Your uncle thought the tax system was unethical. As a result he failed to disclose some of his income to reduce the amount of tax he owed. In doing this he took great care to avoid being detected. Is this civil disobedience? Why or why not?

With your rights as a citizen go individual responsibilities. Every American shares them. Only by fulfilling our duties are we able to maintain our rights. Your duties as a citizen include the following. . .

1. The duty to obey the law.
2. The duty to respect the rights of others.
3. The duty to inform yourself on political issues.
4. The duty to vote in elections.
5. The duty to serve on juries if called.
6. The duty to serve and defend your country.
7. The duty to assist agencies of law enforcement.

PREVENT LEGAL DIFFICULTIES

(Adapted from *Law Day USA*, American Bar Association)

CHAPTER IN REVIEW

CONCEPTS IN BRIEF

1. Ethics applies when decisions affect people.

2. Ethical decisions must be grounded on reason and impartiality.

3. There are two basic forms of ethics: those based on consequences and those based on fundamental ethical rules.

4. Ethics based on consequences evaluates only the results or effects of acts.

5. The law tries to advance the goals of
   - reflecting the will of those governed
   - preserving natural rights
   - maintaining order

6. Both consequential and rule-based ethics compel us to obey the law.

7. Integrity is doing what is right even in the face of temptation or pressure to do what is wrong.

8. We are obligated to obey the law because, by accepting society's benefits, we have consented to be bound by its laws.

9. We are obligated to obey the law if we believe in helping others. Civil disobedience is only justified in rare and extraordinary circumstances.

10. We should obey the law if we desire to avoid punishment.

11. Civil disobedience is the open, peaceful violation of a law to protest its alleged injustice or unfairness.

YOUR LEGAL VOCABULARY

Match each statement with the term that it best defines. Some terms may not be used.

1. Open, peaceful conduct in violation of an alleged unjust law
   civ. dis.

2. Ethics that evaluates the results of an action
   con-base reason.

3. Making decisions that treat everyone the same
   impart.

4. A mental test to identify illogical actions
   univer.

5. Ethical decisions that evaluate only the act and not its consequences
   fund. eth.

6. Doing what is right even under pressure to act otherwise
   integrity

7. A person who does not respect the law
   scofflaw

8. Determining what is right or wrong action in a reasoned, impartial manner
   ethics

9. Insurance policy that pays the employer money in the case of theft by employees
   fidelity bond

10. Legitimate claims on other people, which flow from each person's status as a human being
    moral rt

11. Standard for judging right and wrong
    The good.

12. Personal, human rights recognized and guaranteed by our Constitution
    civ. Rt.

business ethics
civil disobedience
civil rights
consequence-based
   reasoning
ethics
fidelity bond
fundamental ethical
   rules
impartiality
integrity
majority rule
moral rights
scofflaw
The Good
universalizing

REVIEW LEGAL CONCEPTS

13. Identify a situation in your life where someone used consequence-based ethical reasoning.

14. Identify a situation in your life where someone used rule-based ethical reasoning.

15. Describe the three steps involved in making a decision using consequence-based ethics.

16. Explain the role of The Good in ethics based on consequences.

WRITE ABOUT LEGAL CONCEPTS

17. Use one to three words to identify a current event that others will quickly recognize. Next, write a paragraph evaluating someone's conduct in the current event using the ethics of reasoning based on consequences.

18. Use one to three words to identify a current event that others will quickly recognize. Next, write a paragraph evaluating someone's conduct in the current event using the ethics of rule-based reasoning.

19. Invent and write a scenario which raises an ethical issue. However, try to create a scenario where something is wrong in rule-based reasoning but right in reasoning based on consequences.

20. Invent and write a scenario which raises an ethical issue. However, try to create a scenario where the outcomes are judged good or bad depending upon which good is used in ethics based on consequences.

21. **HOT DEBATE** Write a paragraph giving reasons why Julian should inform the INS about Achmed's whereabouts. Write another paragraph giving reasons why Julian should not inform the INS.

THINK CRITICALLY ABOUT EVIDENCE

22. Jan was trying to decide whom to vote for in an upcoming election. After reviewing the candidates, she said, "I've decided to vote for Gary because I just feel better about him." Is Jan's decision based on ethics? If not, why?

23. Crawford was caught shoplifting by a store detective. The police were called, and he was arrested. When his parents came to bail him out of jail, they asked him why he did it. Crawford responded that he had applied for a summer job at the store, but he was not hired. He thought he was treated unfairly, and this justified the shoplifting. What do you think of Crawford's justification?

24. Staub, Conly, and Winfield were employees of the Prime Time Restaurant. They were aware that the owner never checked the totals on the sales checks against the cash in the register. Therefore, it would be very easy to steal from the cash register. However, they did not steal. When asked why, they gave the following reasons. Staub said he did not take the money because he was afraid of being caught. Conly said she did not take the money because she felt obligated to obey the law. Winfield said he did not take the money because of his religious beliefs. To which person do you best relate? Why?

25. The Seymours wanted their fifteen-year-old daughter, Anna, to help out in the family business, a convenience grocery store that was open twenty-four hours every day. The Seymours thought Anna could learn the business best this way. Since they would be paying Anna, they would not be benefiting financially. They insisted that state school attendance rules interfered both with parental rights to educate their children and with the children's right to get ahead faster. If the Seymours did not send Anna to school, would they be engaging in civil disobedience or acting as scofflaws? What action could the Seymours ethically take in response to the situation?

ANALYZE
REAL CASES

26. Poppy Construction Company was engaged in the business of developing, building, and selling a tract of houses in San Francisco. Mr. and Mrs. Burks, who were black, offered to purchase one of the houses. Poppy had a policy and practice of refusing to sell housing in the tract to blacks on the same conditions that the company applied to others. When their offer was rejected, Mr. and Mrs. Burks sued on the ground of racial discrimination. Racial discrimination was contrary to the law of California as well as to the U.S. Constitution. Poppy was required to accept the Burkses' offer to purchase the house. Is this law best justified by consequential or ethical rule based reasoning? (*Burks v. Poppy Construction Company,* 307 P.2d 313, Cal.)

27. The city of Chicago sued to stop the operation of the Commonwealth Edison Company's coal-burning, electricity-generating plant in nearby Hammond, Indiana. Chicago claimed that the plant emitted too much smoke, sulfur dioxide, and other harmful substances. The city also claimed that the plant was a common-law public nuisance because it caused "an unreasonable interference with a right common to the general public" to clean, unpolluted air. Edison argued that it had spent much money to reduce harmful emissions and that the emissions were now well below the levels prescribed by federal clean air regulations and by the city of Hammond. Edison also pointed out that "unpleasant odors, smoke, and film" already characterized the area in which the plant was located. The trial court refused to issue an injunction. Therefore, the city of Chicago appealed to a higher court, which affirmed (upheld) the trial court. How can this legal action be ethically justified? (*City of Chicago v. Commonwealth Edison Company,* 321 N.E.2d 412, Ill.)

28. Briney owned an old farmhouse in Iowa, which had been unoccupied for years. Although he had posted "No Trespassing" signs outside, there were intruders. To protect his property, Briney set a loaded shotgun inside the building and rigged it to fire if the bedroom door were opened. Soon after, Katko and a companion burglar broke into the house to steal old bottles they considered antiques. As Katko started to open the bedroom door, the shotgun went off, shooting off much of one leg. Although he was committing a crime by breaking into Briney's house, Katko sued Briney for damages and won. Is there a

form of ethical reasoning that justifies this legal result? (*Katko v. Briney,* 183 N.W.2d 657, Iowa)

29. Reader's Digest Association, Inc., promoted magazine subscriptions in 1970 by sending materials that included "simulated checks" to potential subscribers. The government concluded that use of simulated checks was, for some consumers, unfair and deceptive and thus illegal. Therefore, the government ordered the Digest to stop using "simulated checks or any confusingly simulated item of value." The Digest agreed to be bound to this governmental order. Later, the Digest mailed promotional material that used misleading "travel checks." After the government notified the Digest that these travel checks were illegal, the Digest mailed millions of additional checks to consumers. Was the conduct of the Digest that of a scofflaw or was the Digest engaged in civil disobedience? Explain. (*United States v. Reader's Digest Association, Inc.,* 662 F.2d 955).

30. Stu was a bartender at the Circle Inn, an establishment owned by O'Daniels. The bar had a rule that customers could not use its phones. Darrell Soldano came in and said he had been at Happy Jack's Saloon, a bar across the street. He told Stu that he had overheard a conversation where a patron of Happy Jack's threatened the life of another patron. Darrell asked for permission to use the bar's phone to call the police. Are the rules of an employer similar to rules of law? In this case, is there an ethical justification for violating this rule? Is the justification consequential, based on ethical rules or both? If Stu violates his employer's rule is he ethically obligated to tell the employer? (*Soldano v. O'Daniels,* 190 Cal. Rptr. 310)

31. Roy was a Native American. He was refused federal financial assistance for his two-year-old daughter through a food-stamp program and Aid to Families with Dependent Children. The reason Roy was refused benefits was because federal law required recipients of these programs to furnish a social security number, and Roy would not comply. His religious beliefs held that the use of social security numbers was dehumanizing. Thus, Roy believed that freedom of religion protected him from having to furnish one. Do you agree with Roy's belief about social security numbers? How do you think the judge decided this case, and why? (*Bowen v. Roy,* 476 U.S. 693)

CASE FOR LEGAL THINKING

Grimshaw v. Ford Motor Company
174 Cal. Rptr. 348

EVIDENCE Mrs. Gray, accompanied by 13-year-old Richard Grimshaw, set out in the family's new Pinto from Anaheim for Barstow to meet Mr. Gray in Barstow. As Mrs. Gray approached the Route 30 off-ramp where traffic was congested, she moved from the outer fast lane to the middle lane of the freeway. Shortly after this lane change, the Pinto suddenly stalled and coasted to a halt in the middle lane. A Ford Galaxie traveling immediately behind the Pinto was unable to avoid colliding with it. The Galaxie had been traveling from 50 to 55 miles per hour but before the impact had slowed to a speed of from 20 to 37 miles per hour. At the moment of impact, the Pinto caught fire and its interior was engulfed in flames. According to plaintiff's expert, the impact of the Galaxie had driven the Pinto gas tank forward and caused it to be punctured by the flange or one of the bolts on the differential housing so that fuel sprayed from the punctured tank and entered the passenger compartment. . . . When the occupants emerged from the vehicle, their clothing was almost completely burned off. Mrs. Gray died a few days later of congestive heart failure as a result of the burns. Richard Grimshaw managed to survive but only through heroic medical measures. He underwent numerous and extensive surgeries and skin grafts and faced additional surgeries over the next ten years. He lost portions of several fingers on his left hand, portions of his left ear, and his face required many skin grafts from various portions of his body.

OPINION Ford's objective was to build a car at or below 2,000 pounds to sell for no more than $2,000. Ordinarily marketing surveys and pre-liminary engineering studies precede the styling of a new automobile line. The Pinto, however, was a rush project, so that styling preceded engineering and dictated engineering design to a greater degree than usual. Among the engineering decisions dictated by styling was the placement of the fuel tank. The Pinto's styling . . . required the tank to be placed behind the rear axle, leaving only nine or ten inches of "crush space"—far less than in any other American automobile or Ford overseas subcompact. In addition, the Pinto was designed so that its bumper was little more than a chrome strip, less substantial than the bumper of any other American car produced then or later.

Prototypes as well as two production Pintos were crash-tested by Ford to determine, among other things, the integrity of the fuel system in rear end accidents. Prototypes struck from the rear with a moving barrier at 21 miles per hour caused the fuel tank to be driven forward and punctured, causing fuel leakage. Where rubber bladders had been installed in the tank, crash tests into fixed barriers at 21 miles per hour withstood leakage from punctures in the gas tank. The cost of the flaksuit or bladder would be $4 to $8 per car. A reasonable inference may be drawn from the evidence that despite management's knowledge that the Pinto's fuel system could be made safe at a cost of but $4 to $8 per car, it decided to defer corrective measures to save money and enhance profits. Ford's institutional mentality was shown to be one of callous indifference to public safety. . .

DECISION The judgment against the Ford Motor Company is affirmed.

PRACTICE JUDGING

1. **Which ethical system, consequence-based or reasoning based on ethical rules, most reflects the thinking used by the defendant, Ford Motor Company, in this case?**

2. **Which ethical system, or systems, most reflect the thinking used by the court in this case?**

LESSONS

3-1 FOUNDATIONS OF OUR CONSTITUTION

3-2 AMENDMENTS TO THE CONSTITUTION

3-3 DIVISION AND BALANCE OF POWER

HOT DEBATE

At the time of the American Revolution, no American Colonist was serving in the British Parliament. Yet taxes had been imposed on the colonists. Some people rallied for revolution. Their slogan: "Taxation without representation is tyranny!" Jake recalled this historical fact when he received his paycheck. "Look at that," he grumbled. "Deductions for federal income taxes, state income taxes, and social security taxes. And I pay sales taxes and property taxes, too. What we need is another revolution!"

Where Do You Stand?

1. **What would you say to calm Jake down?**

2. **What may he do to bring about effective change without attempting a revolution?**

GOALS

● **Name the documents written in the course of our nation's founding**

● **Explain the relationship between the Declaration of Independence and the Constitution**

OUR NATION'S FRAMING DOCUMENTS

WHAT'S YOUR VERDICT?

The Constitution was drafted in 1787. It was ratified by the ninth state, New Hampshire, in 1788. Four other states took longer to ratify. The vote of approval finally became unanimous in 1790, when Rhode Island became the thirteenth state to ratify.

Why did four states take longer to ratify?

Declaration of Independence

On July 4, 1776, delegates from the 13 original American colonies met in Philadelphia and formally adopted the **Declaration of Independence.** The Declaration charged King George III of England with "a history of repeated injuries and usurpation" for the purpose of establishing an "absolute tyranny. . . ." It declared that "all men are created equal, that they are endowed by their Creator with certain unalienable rights, that among these are life, liberty, and the pursuit of happiness." (See the full text of the Declaration of Independence in Appendix B on page 624.)

The authors of the Declaration of Independence believed that to secure these rights, they would need to institute their own government. This new government would derive its power from the people.

At the time the Declaration was adopted, the American War of Independence had already begun. In April 1775 British troops marched from Boston through Lexington and on to Concord. Their original mission was to destroy rebel military stores at Concord. The resulting war lasted more than eight years, with the colonies claiming ultimate victory.

Articles of Confederation

The 13 sovereign states united loosely in 1781 under a charter called the **Articles of Confederation.** The Articles of Confederation promised

● a one-house legislature (the Continental Congress) with two to seven representatives from each state; each state had one vote

● strict term limits placed on members of Congress, who were subject to recall by their states

● power to declare war, make peace, enter into treaties and alliances, manage relations with Indian nations, coin money, settle differences between states, establish a postal system, and appoint a Commander in Chief

● a national defense that would be paid for by the national government

Engrav'd Printed & Sold by PAUL REVERE BOSTON

- states would be asked, rather than required, to make payments to the national treasury
- major legislation, including bills relating to finance, would require a two-thirds vote for passage
- amendments to the Articles would require a unanimous vote of the states

Many people felt a need for a stronger central government than the one the Articles provided. Disagreement among the states regarding the Articles led to the calling of a special convention of delegates from the original 13 states.

Ratification of the U.S. Constitution

1	Delaware	December 7, 1787
2	Pennsylvania	December 12, 1787
3	New Jersey	December 18, 1787
4	Georgia	January 2, 1788
5	Connecticut	January 9, 1788
6	Massachusetts	February 6, 1788
7	Maryland	April 28, 1788
8	South Carolina	May 23, 1788
9	New Hampshire*	June 21, 1788
10	Virginia	June 26, 1788
11	New York	July 26, 1788
12	North Carolina	November 21, 1789
13	Rhode Island	May 29, 1790

*This provided the necessary two-thirds majority.

CULTURAL DIVERSITY IN LAW

England

The Magna Carta, Petition of Right, and Bill of Rights

The U.S. Bill of Rights is based on three English Documents: The Magna Carta, the Petition of Right, and the Bill of Rights. The Magna Carta is considered the basis for English constitutional liberties. This charter was granted by King John to English barons in 1215. The Magna Carta abolished many abuses and guaranteed certain liberties. The Petition of Right (1628) and the Bill of Rights (1689) reinforced the Magna Carta.

THE ORIGINAL 13

DE
NJ
PA
GA
CT
MA
MD
SC
NH
VA
NY
NC
RI

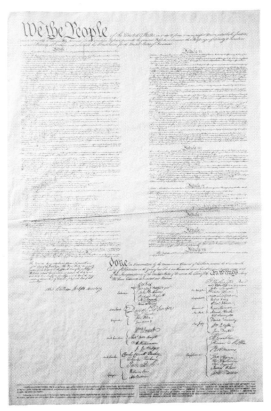

U.S. Constitution

The special convention, held in Philadelphia in the summer of 1787, drafted the initial **U. S. Constitution**. The seven articles of the Constitution provided a workable framework for a federal government "of the people, by the people, and for the people."

By June 1788, the Constitution had been ratified by delegates to special conventions in nine of the states. Our existence as a truly united country began on March 4, 1789, when Congress declared the Constitution effective and binding because nine states had already ratified.

Critics in the other four states claimed the wording of the Constitution failed to provide adequate protection of the human rights proclaimed in the Declaration of Independence. In *"What's Your Verdict?* Virginia, New York, North Carolina, and Rhode Island took longer to ratify because they felt this fundamental deficiency in the Constitution—the failure to protect human rights—had to be corrected. The situation was resolved by the adoption of the Bill of Rights.

The Bill of Rights

The **Bill of Rights**—the first ten amendments to the Constitution— was enacted as a shield against the possible violation of specified human rights by the federal government. Among the personal rights granted in the Bill of Rights are

- freedom of religion (First Amendment)
- freedom of speech (First Amendment)
- freedom to assemble peaceably (First Amendment)
- security in person and property against unreasonable searches and seizures (Fourth Amendment)
- right to remain silent if accused of a crime (Fifth Amendment)
- right to enjoy a speedy and public trial by an impartial jury (Fifth and Sixth Amendments)

- right to not be tried for the same crime twice (Fifth Amendment)
- right to a defense counsel in a trial and to confront witnesses against oneself (Sixth Amendment)
- protection from cruel or unusual punishment if convicted of a crime (Eighth Amendment)
- right to fair compensation for private property taken by the government for a public purpose (Fifth Amendment)
- protection from the taking of life, liberty, or property without due process of law (Fifth Amendment)
- a well regulated militia (Second Amendment)
- right to keep and bear arms (Second Amendment)

You will learn more about the Bill of Rights and additional amendments to the Constitution in Lesson 3-2.

Answer the following questions about legal concepts.

1. The Declaration of Independence was adopted on **(a) July 4, 1776 (b) July 4, 1789 (c) July 4, 1861**

2. The "inalienable rights" mentioned in the Declaration of Independence are "life, liberty, and the pursuit of __?__ ."

3. The American War of Independence lasted about **(a) two years (b) four years (c) eight years (d) ten years**

4. The 13 colonies originally created a common government under the "Articles of Incorporation." **True or False?**

5. Critics of the original Constitution claimed the wording failed to protect human __?__ .

6. __?__ was the thirteenth state to ratify the U.S. Constitution.

7. Which of the first 10 amendments guarantees freedom of the press? **(a) First (b) Second (c) Third (d) freedom of the press is not guaranteed in the Bill of Rights**

8. The original Bill of Rights contains the right of peaceful assembly. **True or False?**

9. Term limits on representatives were imposed by the Articles of Confederation. **True or False?**

Study the following situations, answer the questions, then prepare arguments to support your answers.

10. It is now 1793 and you are a citizen of one of the original states. You still hold a grudge against your fellow citizens of the now United States of America for fighting and winning the Revolutionary War. Every once in a while you stand up in the public square and voice these sentiments. Finally, the state prosecuting attorney brings criminal charges against you for treason. You maintain that your freedom of speech under the U.S. Constitution has been violated. The prosecutor replies that the Bill of Rights does not protect you from state actions. Is the prosecutor correct?

11. You are a citizen of one of the 13 colonies. The time is mid-July 1776. You have just heard of the issuance of the Declaration of Independence. What reasons might cause you to withhold your support of the Declaration?

12. It started as a fraternity stunt at a local college. But the stunt gained momentum over the next few days as other students took it seriously. The key idea was to tie up the evening rush-hour traffic at the busiest intersection in the city's business district as a protest against overseas military action by the government. "We'll stage a surprise rally," Tessa McEwen proposed, "then march back to the campus." About 600 students gathered as planned. They took over the intersection and all traffic stopped. Within minutes, the police moved in and forced the crowd to disperse. Several individuals who dropped their signs and "went limp" on the pavement were arrested. Did the police action violate the protesters' First Amendment constitutional right "peaceably to assemble?"

13. An English citizen and an American are comparing political freedoms in their two countries. The English citizen points out that American guarantees of freedom stem from rights won in England many centuries ago. Is this correct? If so, why was it necessary for us to fight a revolution to free ourselves from English control?

14. Referring to the debate in exercise 13, what does the Magna Carta have in common with the Bill of Rights? What other English political documents influenced our Bill of Rights?

15. Bill and Tom are upset about how the government intrudes into personal areas where each individual should have control. Harriet mentions that the right of privacy was intended to assure the common citizen that such intrusions would not occur. Tom takes out his copy of the Constitution and reads it carefully. He can find no mention of the right of privacy. "Who are you kidding, Harriet, there is no such right. It's not spelled out in our Constitution anyway." If he is correct, yet there is such a right, what might be its origin?

GOALS

● **Discuss how the Constitution has been a shield against violations of basic human rights**

● **Identify the basic human rights protected by the Bill of Rights and subsequent amendments**

AMENDMENTS AND RIGHTS: THE BILL OF RIGHTS

WHAT'S YOUR VERDICT?

Bill Murray and Arlene Childress were in love and talking about getting married. To find out if he was hiding any secrets from her, Arlene hired a private detective to investigate Bill's past. While visiting Bill's home one day, she wired a tape recorder into his phone system and began taping his calls. When Arlene told her friend Edna what she had done, Edna told Arlene that she had violated Bill's right to privacy. Arlene responded by saying that she did not believe the U.S. Constitution mentions a right to privacy.

Is the right to privacy mentioned in our Constitution or Bill of Rights?

U.S. Bill of Rights

The first ten amendments to the Constitution, known as the Bill of Rights, were adopted to ensure that U.S. citizens would enjoy the human rights proclaimed in the Declaration of Independence. The amendments in the Bill of Rights shown below are in the words of our founding fathers.

AMENDMENT I Congress shall make no law respecting an establishment of religion, or prohibiting the free exercise thereof; or abridging the freedom of speech, or of the press, or the right of the people peaceably to assemble, and to petition the Government for a redress of grievances.

AMENDMENT II A well regulated Militia, being necessary to the security of a free State, the right of the people to keep and bear Arms, shall not be infringed.

AMENDMENT III No Soldier shall, in time of peace be quartered in any house, without the consent of the Owner, nor in time of war, but in a manner to be prescribed by law.

AMENDMENT IV The right of the people to be secure in their persons, houses, papers, and effects, against unreasonable searches and seizures, shall not be violated, and no warrants shall issue, but upon probable cause, supported by oath or affirmation, and particularly describing the place to be searched, and the persons or things to be seized.

AMENDMENT V No person shall be held to answer for a capital, or otherwise infamous crime, unless on a presentment or indictment of a Grand Jury, except in cases arising in the land or naval forces, or in the Militia, when

in actual service in time of War or public danger; nor shall any person be subject for the same offense to be twice put in jeopardy of life or limb, nor shall be compelled in any criminal case to be a witness against himself, nor be deprived of life, liberty, or property, without due process of law; nor shall private property be taken for public use without just compensation.

AMENDMENT VI In all criminal prosecutions, the accused shall enjoy the right to a speedy and public trial, by an impartial jury of the State and district wherein the crime shall have been committed, which district shall have been previously ascertained by law, and to be informed of the nature and cause of the accusation; to be confronted with the witnesses against him; to have compulsory process for obtaining witnesses in his favor, and to have the assistance of counsel for his defense.

AMENDMENT VII In Suits at common law, where the value in controversy shall exceed twenty dollars, the right of trial by jury shall be preserved, and no fact tried by a jury shall be otherwise re-examined in any Court of the United States, than according to the rules of the common law.

AMENDMENT VIII Excessive bail shall not be required, nor excessive fines imposed, nor cruel and unusual punishments inflicted.

AMENDMENT IX The enumeration in the Constitution of certain rights shall not be construed to deny or disparage others retained by the people.

AMENDMENT X The powers not delegated to the United States by the Constitution, nor prohibited by it to the States, are reserved to the States respectively, or to the people.

Civil Rights

The Constitution serves as a shield for the civil rights of the people. **Civil rights** are personal, natural rights guaranteed by the Constitution. Preeminent is the shield of the First Amendment. It protects our rights to freedom of speech, freedom of the press, and freedom to assemble.

The First Amendment also protects the people's rights to practice the religion of their choice. Mankind's universal religious impulse has led to the construction of some of the most beautiful and enduring churches and temples throughout the world. Religion has inspired men, women, and children to their most noble and compassionate conduct toward their fellow beings.

However, misguided religious zeal has caused great violence and destruction. Over the centuries countless wars have been waged to win converts or eliminate heathens. The founders of our republic recognized this deep-seated religious impulse but wisely imposed a role of neutrality for the government. They created a wall of separation between church and state. The government tolerates all religions but supports none in any strictly religious efforts.

Due Process of Law

One of the most significant amendments in the Bill of Rights is the Fifth Amendment. It states, "No person shall be . . . deprived of life, liberty, or property, without due process of law. . ." Note that unlike the Declaration of Independence, the Constitution, does not mention "the pursuit of happiness." However, respect by others for one's life, liberty, and property surely helps one to be secure and content, if not consciously happy.

Legal rights are the benefits to which a person is justly entitled by law. **Legal duties** are obligations or standards of conduct toward other persons that are enforceable by law.

The legal right of one person generally imposes a legal duty on others. Frequently, legal rights and duties are also moral rights and duties, but this is not necessarily so.

My right to life, for example, imposes a duty on you not to injure or kill me. But no right is absolute. Thus, if I attack you without justification and threaten your life, you may reasonably defend yourself—even if it appears necessary to take my life. However, a person who unjustly kills another may be prosecuted for murder. Then the arrest, trial, and punishment of the alleged wrongdoer must be in accordance with due process of law.

Due process of law requires fundamental fairness in compliance with reasonable and just laws. If convicted, the criminal may be deprived of property by fine, of liberty by imprisonment, and even of life by lawful execution.

Due process of law is a concept embodied throughout the Constitution. It is assured by guaranteeing

* the right to assemble peaceably (First Amendment)

* the right to be secure against unreasonable searches and seizures (Fourth Amendment)

* the right not to be a witness against oneself in any criminal case (Fifth Amendment)

Think about the significance of what former U.S. Supreme Court Justice Louis D. Brandeis once wrote: "Those who won our independence . . . believed liberty to be the secret of happiness and courage to be the secret of liberty." Brandeis also wrote that the makers of the Constitution "conferred, as against the government, the right to be let alone—the most comprehensive of rights and the right most valued by civilized men."

* in criminal prosecutions, the right for the accused to a speedy and public trial by an impartial jury of the state and district where the crime was committed, and to be informed of the nature and cause of the accusation; the right

The expansive reach of the Internet has spurred a new debate over the individual's right to privacy. The debate surrounds our right to choose whether personal information about us can be disclosed. It also concerns our right to know how, when, and how much of our personal information is being used.

An Electronic Bill of Rights for this electronic age is a key government initiative. The Electronic Privacy Information Center has called for legislation to enact privacy policies for the Internet. Several pending bills (E-Privacy Act, Data Privacy Act, and Consumer Internet Privacy Act) would regulate Internet activity in the name of privacy.

to be confronted with the witnesses against him; to have a set process for obtaining witnesses in his favor, and to have the benefit of a defense counsel (Sixth Amendment)

- trial by jury in civil suits where the value in controversy exceeds $20 (Seventh Amendment)
- excessive bail will not be required nor excessive fines imposed, nor

cruel and unusual punishment inflicted (Eighth Amendment)

Peripheral Rights

Some rights are not explicitly mentioned in the U.S. Constitution or Bill of Rights, but courts have recognized them as necessary to protecting the rights that are mentioned. In *What's Your Verdict?* the right of privacy is such a peripheral right—it is not

specifically mentioned in the Constitution or Bill of Rights. In the 1960s the U.S. Supreme Court acknowledged the right of privacy as a separate right. The right of privacy has since been reinforced by several federal acts. Under these acts, it would not be just an invasion of privacy, but a crime, for Arlene to tap Bill's phone calls, both before and after marriage.

MORE CONSTITUTIONAL AMENDMENTS

WHAT'S YOUR VERDICT?

Ida presented a controversial talk to her high school class. "You speak of the shield of the Constitution. Maybe that's true today, but it was not always true. Originally, none of the women in our country—more than half of the adult population—could vote. The situation was even worse for women and men who happened to be black. They were slaves, and the Constitution validated that terrible practice." Several students protested. "That can't be true!" one said.

Was Ida telling the truth?

Among the nations of the world, there is no monopoly on virtue or vice. Human beings of all colors and of all races have been enslaved and maltreated—in ancient, medieval, and modern times. As recently as World War II, millions of innocent men, women, and children were slaughtered by the Nazis. Included were some six million persons who were murdered simply because they were Jewish. Today in India, despite formal legal bans on the custom, millions of people are considered "untouchables." They are relegated to menial work and are the victims of other discrimination.

Abolishing Slavery

Despite the solemn affirmation in the Declaration of Independence that "all men are created equal," the practice of slavery in our country for black men, women, and children originally

was tolerated under the Constitution. It continued until the issue was resolved through the bloodshed of the Civil War, which preserved the Union and abolished slavery.

In *What's Your Verdict?* Ida was telling the truth. Delegates from states that used slaves for menial labor lobbied successfully to keep this practice legal. The Constitution provided that Congress could not prohibit, prior to 1808, the "migration or importation of such persons . . . ." Slaves were further dehumanized by a provision in Article I that counted them as only three-fifths of a person for the purpose of apportioning representatives to Congress. Under Article IV, a slave who escaped to another state had to be returned to "the party to whom such service or labor may be due."

These provisions were negated by the Thirteenth Amendment, which states in part, "Neither slavery nor

involuntary servitude, except as a punishment for a crime whereof the party shall have been duly convicted, shall exist within the United States, or any place subject to their jurisdiction."

The Right to Vote

The Fifteenth Amendment provided the newly freed slaves the legal right to vote. It decreed, "The right of citizens of the United States to vote shall not be denied or abridged by the United States or by any State on account of race, color or previous condition of servitude."

Although the Thirteenth Amendment abolished slavery, and the Fifteenth guaranteed the former slaves the right to vote, racial discrimination continued in both the North and the South. Some southern states enacted a poll tax. This was a fixed payment per person required before the person could vote. Many former slaves could not afford to pay a tax in order to vote. Ultimately—more than 100 years after the Civil War began with the attack on Fort Sumter—the Twenty-Fourth Amendment provided that the right to vote in federal elections "shall not be denied or abridged . . . by reason of failure to pay any poll tax or other tax."

The Supreme Court subsequently applied the same rule to all state elections, declaring such taxes

Wyoming

Women's Right to Vote

The Wyoming territorial legislature granted women the right to vote fifty years before Congress passed the Nineteenth Amendment. The Wyoming law was enacted on December 10, 1869 in an attempt to attract female settlers.

unconstitutional under the Fourteenth Amendment. In the course of their struggle for genuine equality in civil rights, blacks also have advanced the cause of women and other victims of discrimination.

The exclusion of "gender" in the Fifteenth Amendment was a deliberate denial of voting rights to women of all races. This injustice was removed 50 years later when the Nineteenth Amendment provided "The right of citizens of the United States to vote shall not be denied or abridged by the United States or by any State on account of sex."

Students protested during the Vietnam War, in part, because they objected to being eligible to fight in a war at the age of 18—but not vote until age 21. One result of these student protests was the hasty enactment of an amendment that gave all citizens age 18 or older the right to vote. The Twenty-Sixth Amendment was approved overwhelmingly by the Senate and House in March 1971, and was ratified by 38 states within three months.

Limiting States' Powers

The Fourteenth Amendment opens with these sweeping provisions: "All persons born or naturalized in the United States and subject to the jurisdiction thereof, are citizens of the United States and of the state wherein they reside. No state shall make or enforce any law which shall abridge the privileges or immunities of citizens of the United States; nor shall any State deprive any person of life, liberty, or property, without due process of law; nor deny to any person within its jurisdiction the equal protection of the laws."

The Fourteenth Amendment was a gigantic step forward because, by its terms, state governments are barred from depriving any person of life, liberty, or property without due process of law. Recall that the Fifth Amendment had previously applied only to the powers of the federal government. The Fourteenth Amendment subjects the states to the same restraint.

Due process, as outlined in the Fifth Amendment, is not the only constitutional protection that state governments are required to respect. Other relevant amendments in the Bill of Rights have also been applied to the states. As a result, today the shield of the Constitution is effective

During the Vietnam conflict, young men and women in this country came close to open revolt. They embraced many forms of civil disobedience to make the point that they were being asked to bleed and die for their country, but had no input into making the decisions that caused the war or that might end it. Judged from the standpoint of the political "establishment" of the 1960s, their actions were illegal and improper. However, how would the American Revolutionaries have viewed them? Which viewpoint is the more ethical?

against abuse of power by *both* the federal and state governments. At both levels, statutes have been enacted to provide comparable protection against abuse of power by private individuals and corporations.

Answer the following questions about legal concepts.

1. Which of the first 10 amendments guarantees freedom of speech? **(a) First (b) Second (c) Third (d) freedom of speech is not guaranteed in the Bill of Rights**

2. The right of privacy is guaranteed in the Bill of Rights. **True or False?**

3. The __?__ Amendment extends due process protection to state acts.

4. The Sixth Amendment preserves the right to trial by jury in criminal trials. **True or False?**

5. The Fifth Amendment states no one shall be deprived of life, liberty, or property without __?__ .

6. Legal rights and duties are always the same as moral rights and duties. **True or False?**

7. Which of the following rights is included in the Sixth Amendment? **(a) the right to a speedy criminal trial (b) the right to a public criminal trial (c) the right to have defense counsel in a criminal trial (d) all of the above**

8. Which of the following issues does the Fourteenth Amendment address? **(a) voting (b) citizenship (c) privacy (d) slavery**

Study the following situations, answer the questions, then prepare arguments to support your answers.

9. Although you are innocent of the charge, while on vacation in another state, you are arrested and accused of burglary. You hire an attorney and at trial are found not guilty. A week later a witness comes forward and identifies you as being at the scene of the crime the evening it was committed. The prosecutor wants to try you again. What will prevent the prosecutor from doing so?

10. You own three acres of property to the west of the new State University's football stadium. The University seeks to take your property so as to turn it into a parking lot for the crowds that attend the games. Can they do so? Must they pay you anything for it? Why or why not?

11. As a part of your fight against the University's attempt to take your property, you print up a flyer stating your position on the matter. You try to distribute it on campus to interested students. University security personnel take you into custody, confiscate your flyers, and throw you off campus. You bring suit against the University alleging violations of your rights of __?__ (pick as many rights from the Bill of Rights as you think have been violated).

12. In your lawsuit to stop the University's attempt to take your land, the jury concludes that the University does not need the property as it has enough parking already. When the case is heard on appeal, the University tries to put in new evidence showing that in the current football season the stadium has been sold out. As a consequence, they will have to expand it and their need for parking will go up accordingly. What amendment will prevent this new evidence from being used by the appellate court to change the jury's determination?

13. Glen Turner is 28 years old. He lives with his wife and son in a small town in the Appalachian Mountains. Glen and his family are very poor. He is a coal miner but has no job because the mine shut down when the last veins of coal were cleaned out. Glen's wife also lost her job in the company office. Glen mournfully says, "Our threesome sort of enjoys life and liberty. But as to property, we haven't got any to speak of. The government's not going to deprive us of something we haven't got. So when you say owning property's a right under the Constitution, maybe that's true. But it's nothing for us. Nothing." Is Glen wrong? What could you say to him?

14. Bill Boyd was caught stealing a neighbor's tractor. Nonetheless, he has pled not guilty and asked that the court appoint an attorney for him. What provision of the Constitution requires the government to pay for Bill's defense attorney?

OUR SYSTEM OF CHECKS AND BALANCES

WHAT'S YOUR VERDICT?

June and Max were born during the same week almost 18 years ago. Both will soon legally become adults. "That means we can vote," said June. "I plan to register as a Democrat because we live in a democracy. How will you register?" Max replied, "We don't live in a democracy. We live in a republic. We should both register as Republicans."

Who is correct about our system of government?

Warren E. Burger, former Chief Justice of the U.S. Supreme Court, has pointed out that at the time the Constitution was drafted and adopted, "There was not a country in the world that governed with separated and divided powers providing checks and balances on the exercise of authority by those who governed."

The 55 delegates who drafted the U.S. Constitution displayed great foresight in devising a unique **system of checks and balances.** This system gives specific authority to each of the three basic branches of government.

Branches of Government

The three branches of government include the legislative, the executive, and the judicial.

LEGISLATIVE BRANCH The legislative branch at the federal level is the Congress. When the Constitution was drafted, the convention delegates were concerned with equal representation in Congress. States with small

populations worried they might lose some of the sovereignty and independence they enjoyed under the Articles of Confederation. States with large populations feared they would be dominated by the less populous states (of which there were many more), if each state had an equal number of votes.

The solution? The national legislature would consist of two bodies: (1) a Senate, with two members from every state—regardless of population, and (2) a House of Representatives, with seats allocated to the states in proportion to their population. The Senate could block any action of the House, and the House could block any action of the Senate. The existence of two bodies allows for various checks and balances. For instance, all bills for taxing or appropriating funds must originate in the House. But a majority vote of both bodies is required for passage of any bill.

A further check is available to the House of Representatives. The House

has the power to initiate the impeachment of any civil officer of the United States—including the President and Vice President—for treason, bribery, or other high crimes and misdemeanors. However, the Senate has the sole power to try all impeachment cases. **Impeachment cases** involve trying a government official for misconduct in office. Conviction in such cases requires a two-thirds vote of the members present. Finally, the people may vote their representatives out in elections to the House (for a two-year term), the Senate (for a six-year term), and the executive office (for a four-year term).

EXECUTIVE BRANCH The executive branch is headed by the President and Vice President. These officers are elected by a vote of the people. In the electoral process, citizens vote for the electors who are pledged to support candidates selected by political parties. (Because the President and Vice President are not elected directly by the people, the candidate who receives the most votes for president may not be elected. This situation occurred three times, in 1824, 1876, and 1888.)

A **political party** is a private organization of citizens who select and promote candidates for election to public office. Party members agree with these candidates on important governmental policies and legislation. Political parties are not mentioned in the Constitution.

JUDICIAL BRANCH The third branch of government is the judiciary. It is headed by the Supreme Court of the United States. Ultimately, the Supreme Court decides on the constitutionality of a statute passed by the legislative branch and signed by the President as head of the executive branch. The Supreme Court may also decide if a particular action or decision of the President exceeds the powers granted to the executive branch under the Constitution. If so, the action or decision is void.

Changing the Constitution

A major check is provided by the power of constitutional **amendment**, meaning change or alteration. The Constitution may be amended in two ways. The first way has been used for all amendments adopted to date: The amendment is proposed by a two-thirds majority vote in both the Senate and the House. The second way requires the legislatures of two-thirds of all the states to call a convention of all the states. The convention may propose one or more amendments. Thereafter, under either method of proposal, the amendment becomes a valid part of the U.S. Constitution only if it is ratified by the legislatures of three-fourths of the states, or if it is ratified by conventions in three-fourths of the states.

Our Form of Government

In a pure **democracy**, every adult citizen may vote on all issues. This is virtually impossible to make happen in our nation of more than 250 million people. Instead, we have a **republic** or a representative democracy. Voters select their representatives to the legislative, executive, and judicial branches of government.

Although representatives make the day-to-day decisions, the sovereign power ultimately resides in the people. This means that the highest final authority to decide what the law shall be rests with those citizens who exercise their right and duty to vote. In many elections only a minority of the total number of voters who are eligible actually exercise this right.

In *What's Your Verdict?* neither June nor Max is correct about what the political parties represent. Whether we live in a republic or a democracy does not determine whether we should all register and vote as Republicans or Democrats. Each citizen should study the issues and where the political parties and their candidates stand on the issues. Then we can register to vote for the party and/or candidates that most closely reflect our views.

DOES THE FEDERAL GOVERNMENT HAVE TOTAL GOVERNING POWER?

WHAT'S YOUR VERDICT?

It was July 4th. Several thousand people had assembled in the park for the annual celebration, complete with speeches and a band concert. The state's senior federal senator opened the ceremonies. "On this day, on all days," he said, "I am proud and pleased to be a citizen of the United States of America. I feel no less proud and fortunate to be a citizen of this great sovereign state that is ours. But I tell you: before I am a citizen of either the state or the country, I am a human being. So, too, are you who hear my voice. By divine providence we share with mankind the gifts of reason and freedom of will that dignify and unite us. Our humanity precedes our citizenship. Government exists only by the will and consent of the people. It is the people who control the government. Any control by the government of the people is by virtue of permission granted and maintained."

Does the senator's analysis conform to the governmental structure created by the U.S. Constitution?

The Constitution and the Bill of Rights were written by representatives of the people elected by voters in the 13 original states. These documents place a priority on the basic rights of human beings. This priority exists whether people act as individuals or in concert with each other. The Ninth Amendment recognizes this priority by stating, "The enumeration in the Constitution of certain rights, shall not be construed to deny or disparage others retained by the people."

Sovereignty of the States

The Tenth Amendment acknowledges the continued sovereignty of all of the states to govern their own citizens within their own borders. **Sovereignty** in this sense means freedom from external control. The Tenth Amendment declares, "The powers not delegated to the United States by the Constitution, nor prohibited by it to the States, are reserved to the States respectively, or to the people." Here it is evident that the Constitution is a shield against unlimited power of the federal government.

Article VI recognizes the Constitution to be "the supreme law of the land." It prevails over any possible contrary state constitution or law. At the same time, every state constitution and the respective statutes are supreme on matters that have not been given to the federal government. Powers kept by the states include control over most business law and contract law, most criminal and tort law, real property and probate law, and domestic relations law.

Powers of the Federal Government

The federal government has the duty to protect every state against invasion. It may raise and support armies, a navy, and an air force for national defense. The federal government has exclusive power to regulate interstate commerce (between states) and foreign commerce. However, each state retains authority to regulate intrastate commerce (trade within its own borders). The federal government alone may establish post offices, coin money, and tax imports and exports. Both federal and state legislatures may impose other taxes (on sales and on incomes).

Congress has the power to make detailed laws it considers appropriate for executing the powers given to it in the Constitution. The people, through their votes, ultimately control the entire governmental structure. Each adult retains power over choice of a place to live and to work, a career, friends, travel, holiday activities, and many other factors that determine personal lifestyle.

In *What's Your Verdict?* the senator's comments do accurately reflect the reality of the relationship between citizens and our government today. However, even after the Bill of Rights was added to the Constitution, certain deficiencies existed in the Constitution and in the resulting life of our nation. Additional amendments have been ratified through the years to correct these problems.

CULTURAL DIVERSITY IN LAW

Hungary

Democratic Representation

The history of democratic representation in Hungary is long and complicated. For nearly a thousand years, the only form of representation was a collection of nobles who met infrequently at different places around the country. The parliament was relatively weak, and Hungary was dominated by outside powers for much of the period. In 1867, the parliament gained considerable powers when the Austrian emperor Franz Joseph agreed that Hungary should be administered as a separate nation within the empire. The parliament continued throughout the rest of the nineteenth century and into the twentieth century as a semi-representative body. For most of this time, either an elite group or a dictator dominated the parliament. After the collapse of Communism in 1989, Hungary gained its first parliament that truly represented all Hungarians.

Answer the following questions about legal concepts.

1. Under our Constitution, all spending bills must originate in the __?__ .

2. Which of the following powers was not retained by the states? **(a) power to define and apply tort (personal injury) law (b) power to define and apply criminal laws (c) power to define and apply probate laws (d) the states retained all of the above powers**

3. Individual states in the United States can coin money. **True or False?**

4. The legislative branch of the federal government is the __?__ .

5. The U.S. Senate is made up of __?__ members from every state.

6. The U.S. House of Representatives is made up of the same number of members from each state. **True or False?**

7. The U.S. Senate has the power to initiate impeachment proceedings against a U.S. President. **True or False?**

8. The __?__ branch of government is headed by the President.

Study the following situations, answer the questions, then prepare arguments to support your answers.

9. You are a member of the House of Representatives of a large Midwestern state. Your state is running short of money to carry out some much needed programs. As a possible solution you suggest that the state government issue its own currency to people who work for it. The currency can be exchanged for dollar bills at a rate that is to be fixed by the state the first of every month. Is your idea constitutional?

10. Later in the House session mentioned in exercise 9, you become disenchanted with your fellow citizens when you learn that only 28 percent of those eligible to vote actually did so in the last election. Consequently, you pass a law requiring that everyone vote in every election. What arguments can you make in support of such a measure? Against?

11. The Equal Rights Amendment (ERA) was formally proposed in 1972. It provided: "Equality of rights under the law shall not be denied or abridged by the United States or by any state on account of sex." For more than ten years, proponents and opponents conducted vigorous campaigns in all states. When the time limit for approval elapsed in 1982, only 35 of the required state legislatures had voted in favor. Women in a sorority at a nearby college now wonder if another campaign should be launched to pass the ERA. How would you advise them?

As a citizen . . .

1. Carefully read and reread the Constitution as it has been amended. (See Appendix A on page 612.) This will enable you to become a properly informed citizen of the United States of America.

2. Pay special attention to the Bill of Rights and the Fourteenth Amendment to better appreciate their value in assuring our liberty and to be alert to possible threats that could erode vital freedoms for you and others.

3. When eligible, participate in government as a conscien-

PREVENT LEGAL DIFFICULTIES

tious voter. If you are able and willing, participate in the work of the political party of your choice. If you are one of the dedicated few, become a candidate for public office.

CHAPTER IN REVIEW

CONCEPTS IN BRIEF

1. The U.S. Constitution, as amended, is the shield of U.S. liberty.

2. The Bill of Rights is the popular name of the first ten amendments to the U.S. Constitution.

3. Under the First Amendment, Congress is barred from making any law to establish a public religion or to prohibit the free exercise of any private religion.

4. The First Amendment also protects free speech, free press, and freedom to assemble peaceably and the right to petition the government for redress if one is wronged.

5. The Fifth Amendment provides that no person shall be deprived of life, liberty, or property without due process of law.

6. Due process of law is assured by the First, Fourth, Fifth, Sixth, Seventh, and Eighth Amendments.

7. Slavery was finally banned by the Thirteenth Amendment, which was reinforced by the Fourteenth, Fifteenth, and Twenty-Fourth Amendments.

8. In 1920, the fundamental right of women to vote was recognized by ratification of the Nineteenth Amendment. In 1971, the voting age for all citizens was lowered to eighteen by the Twenty-Sixth Amendment.

9. The Fourteenth Amendment applied to the states the rule that no person shall be deprived of life, liberty, or property without due process of law.

10. A vigorous and useful balance of power exists among the three basic branches of government: legislative, executive, and judicial.

YOUR LEGAL VOCABULARY

Match each statement with the term that it best defines. Some terms may not be used.

1. Personal, natural rights guaranteed by the Constitution

2. Change or alteration

3. Governmental system wherein each citizen may vote directly to decide issues

4. Division and allocation of the powers of government between its various branches

5. Governmental systems wherein citizens elect representatives to decide issues

6. Freedom from external control

7. Obligations or standards of conduct toward other persons that are enforceable by law

8. Loose form of charter for common government for the 13 colonies prior to the adoption of the Constitution

9. Framing document that currently consists of 7 articles and 27 amendments

10. Concept of fundamental fairness in compliance with reasonable and just laws

11. The first ten amendments to the U.S. Constitution

amendment
Articles of Confederation
Bill of Rights
civil rights
Declaration of Independence
democracy
due process of law
impeachment cases
legal duties
legal rights
political party
republic
sovereignty
system of checks and balances
U.S. Constitution

12. The Constitutional Convention of 1787 was meant to make changes in the Articles of Confederation instead of create a wholly new document. Why do you think the Articles were discarded in favor of our current Constitution?

13. Can you foresee a time in our country when we might become a true democracy? If so, how could this occur?

14. While the system of checks and balances works to prevent the accumulation of too much power by any one branch of the government, it also causes problems in the functioning of government. What do you think some of these problems might be?

15. Could you get your friends and neighbors to sign the Declaration of Independence today? During the Vietnam era, young people around the country tried to do just that. Most citizens who read the document but were not told that it was the Declaration, refused to sign and, in some cases, reacted violently to its content. Why is that?

WRITE ABOUT LEGAL CONCEPTS

16. Write an essay on how the framers of the Constitution and the Bill of Rights could justify the maintenance of slavery and the denial of voting rights to women.

17. Write a paragraph stating your opinion about which is the most important right preserved by the Bill of Rights.

18. The Bill of Rights (shown on page 37) is in the language our founding fathers used. Rewrite the Bill of Rights in your own words.

19. HOT DEBATE Write an essay about the various ways a citizen may participate in making political decisions. Does Jake have all these options? Why do you think he is still disgruntled?

THINK CRITICALLY ABOUT EVIDENCE

20. After a worried discussion about the school funding problem in their area, a group of high school students decided to act. They agreed to contact the other five secondary schools in their area to obtain cooperation in a letter-writing campaign. Every student would be committed to sign and mail one copy of a standard form letter to each of their U.S. senators and to at least two of their ten representatives in the U.S. Congress. The letters would urge their representatives to get an amendment enacted to the Constitution that would recognize the human right of every person to formal education from kindergarten through the senior year at college. This education would be financed from the general funds of the federal government. Is there any flaw in the students' plan?

21. In 1919 the Eighteenth Amendment outlawed "the manufacture, sale, or transportation of intoxicating liquors. . . ." This law led to widespread illegal traffic in liquor by criminals. The controversial law also led to tacit approval of the illicit trade by many citizens who continued to buy and consume liquor. The Eighteenth Amendment was repealed by the Twenty-First Amendment, but individual states were permitted to continue to enforce Prohibition within their borders. By 1966, all individual states had abandoned Prohibition. According to experts, abuse of alcoholic beverages is the most serious drug problem in overall harmful effect on our society. Should Prohibition be reinstated? If not, what if anything should be done?

ANALYZE
REAL CASES

22. In 1951, during the Korean War, a dispute arose between our nation's leading steel mills and their employees, represented by the United Steelworkers of America, CIO. It concerned the terms of a new collective bargaining agreement. Lengthy negotiations failed to resolve the dispute. Governmental mediation efforts and recommendations did not help. When the union gave notice of a nationwide strike to begin in five days, President Harry Truman issued an executive order directing the Secretary of Commerce to seize and operate most of the steel mills. The President believed a work stoppage would endanger our national defense. The steel companies went along with the executive order, but they claimed that (a) the seizure was unlawful because it violated the U.S. Constitution and (b) Congress alone has power to make laws. Therefore, they requested and obtained a preliminary court injunction to end the seizure. However, the injunction was stayed (stopped) while the U.S. Supreme Court reviewed the matter. Did the President act beyond his powers under the Constitution? What sanction(s) can be imposed on the President if his actions are illegal? Does his action approach the institution of martial law? (*Youngstown Sheet & Tube Company v. Sawyer,* 343 U.S. 579)

23. A board of education in Champaign County, Illinois, granted permission to religious teachers to give religious instruction in public school buildings in grades four to nine. The instruction would last 30 minutes for lower grades, 45 minutes for higher grades, once each week. Subject to approval of and supervision by the superintendent of schools, the teachers were employed by a private religious group and included representatives of the Catholic, Jewish, and Protestant faiths. Only pupils whose parents requested religious instruction were required to attend the religious classes. Other pupils continued with their regular public school duties. McCollum, a resident with a pupil who was enrolled in one of the public schools, sued for a writ (i.e., court order) to end the religious instruction as a violation of the First Amendment to the Constitution. The writ was denied, and the Illinois Supreme Court upheld the denial. The parent appealed to the U.S. Supreme Court. Should the writ have been granted to end the practice as a violation of the First Amendment? (*McCollum v. Board of Education,* 333 U.S. 203)

24. In 1964, the owner of a motel in Atlanta restricted its clientele to white persons, three-fourths of whom were interstate travelers. Officers of the U.S. government charged that this policy violated the Civil Rights Act of 1964, which forbids such discrimination against blacks. The trial court ordered the motel to stop refusing blacks as guests because of their race or color. The motel owner appealed to the U.S. Supreme Court, claiming the Civil Rights Act was unconstitutional. Was it? Why or why not? Does the federal government have the power to regulate any matter that might in any way affect interstate commerce? (*Heart of Atlanta Motel, Inc. v. United States,* 379 U.S. 241)

25. Cleveland police had received information that a person wanted for questioning about a recent bombing was hiding in a particular two-family dwelling. There was said to be a large quantity of illegal lottery materials hidden in the home. Upon arrival, three officers knocked on the door and demanded entrance. Mapp, who lived on the top floor with her daughter, telephoned her attorney and then refused to admit the officers without a search warrant. Three hours later, reinforced by additional officers, the police returned. When Mapp did not answer immediately, they tried to kick in the door, then broke its glass pane, reached in, unlocked it, and entered. Meanwhile Mapp's attorney had arrived, but the officers would not let him see his client or enter the house. Mapp demanded to see a search warrant. When an officer held up a paper claiming it to be a warrant, Mapp grabbed the paper and placed it in her bosom. A struggle ensued during which the officer recovered the paper. Mapp was handcuffed for resisting the officer. The entire house was searched, but all that was found were certain allegedly "lewd and lascivious books and pictures." Mapp was convicted of knowingly having them in her possession. At the trial, no search warrant was produced nor was the failure to produce one explained. Mapp appealed to the U.S. Supreme Court for a reversal of her conviction because it was based on a search that was illegal under the U.S. Constitution. Was the evidence for conviction obtained in violation of the U.S. Constitution? If so, was it admissible in the trial against the defendant Mapp? (*Mapp v. Ohio,* 367 U.S. 643)

Gideon v. Wainwright
372 U. S. 335

BACKGROUND Gideon was charged in a Florida court with breaking and entering with the intent to commit a misdemeanor, which is a serious crime but not one punishable by death. Gideon appeared in court without legal counsel and requested the court to appoint a lawyer to defend him. The following exchange then occurred:

> **The Court:** Mr. Gideon, I am sorry, but I cannot appoint Counsel to represent you in this case. Under the laws of the State of Florida, the only time the Court can appoint Counsel to represent a Defendant is when that person is charged with a capital offense. I am sorry, but I will have to deny your request to appoint Counsel to defend you in this case.

> **Defendant:** The United States Supreme Court says I am entitled to be represented by Counsel.

FACTS After his request was disallowed, Gideon conducted his own defense as well as he could being a layman. He made an opening statement, cross-examined witnesses, presented his own defense witnesses, and made a short argument maintaining his innocence.

The jury then returned a guilty verdict. Gideon was sentenced to five years in state prison from which he filed the habeas corpus petition on which this case is based.

APPEAL The state supreme court of Florida considered the habeas corpus petition and denied all relief to Gideon. After Gideon wrote a

letter to the U.S. Supreme Court from his jail cell, the U.S. Supreme Court granted certioriari.

ISSUE Should a defendant in a state court have the right to counsel as mandated by the federal constitution?

DECISION The United States Supreme Court, in an opinion written by Justice Black, held that the Sixth Amendment required that in all criminal prosecutions the accused shall enjoy right to assistance of counsel. The decision of the Florida Supreme Court was reversed and the cause remanded so that counsel can be enjoyed by Gideon and other like defendants.

PRACTICE JUDGING

1. How should the Florida Supreme Court respond and why?

2. How are the counsels to be paid? Who is to determine if they do an adequate job?

3. What should be the sanction(s) imposed upon governments that fail to provide such legal services for their accused?

THE COURT SYSTEM

LESSONS

HOT DEBATE

Anthony Destin works as a systems analyst and computer programmer at a large fashion house called Berentinos. After two years on the job, Anthony learns that his co-worker Sarah Blake earns 35 percent more than he does. Anthony and Sarah were hired at the same time and have exactly the same job. Anthony has five years more experience in the field than Sarah does. Anthony discussed his concern with Tom Sortee, one of the designers. Tom commented that such discrimination against males has long been the rule at Berentinos. Anthony loves his work but can't help feeling he is being treated unfairly.

Where Do You Stand?

1. **What would likely happen to Anthony if he turns to the courts for help in ending the discrimination?**

2. **Does Anthony have a duty to anyone, legally or morally, to bring such a lawsuit?**

GOALS

- Explain how disputes can be settled without resort to the courts
- Name the different levels of courts and describe their powers

CAN DISPUTES BE RESOLVED PRIVATELY?

WHAT'S YOUR VERDICT?

7-Eleven sells franchises for stores bearing its name. The franchise agreement specifies that disputes between 7-Eleven and those who buy a franchise should be settled by arbitration rather than by a trial in court.

Can 7-Eleven compel its franchisees to use arbitration instead of litigation?

Many people decide too quickly to litigate—or take their disputes to court. When one person injures another or fails to keep a binding agreement, the parties may first try to negotiate a settlement themselves. The injured person should try to discuss the problem calmly with the wrongdoer. Together, they often reach a mutually acceptable solution.

In some cases, the parties invite an independent third party to act as **mediator.** The mediator tries to develop a solution acceptable to both sides of the dispute. The actions of a mediator are advisory. They do not bind the parties.

In other cases, the parties may retain an **arbitrator.** An arbitrator usually holds an informal hearing to determine what happened. The arbitrator's decision, unlike that of a mediator, is binding on both parties. The decision can be enforced by court order if necessary. Sometimes a provision for arbitration is included in the original agreement between the parties.

In answer to *What's Your Verdict?* 7-Eleven can require buyers of its franchises to use arbitration. By using negotiation, mediation, or arbitration, the disputing parties may avoid the costs, delays, and difficulties of a court trial.

DIFFERENT LEVELS OF COURTS

WHAT'S YOUR VERDICT?

Doyle made an illegal U-turn. A police officer saw it and gave him a citation (an order to appear in court). Doyle claimed that the sign forbidding a U-turn at that intersection was obstructed by a tree branch. The officer replied, "Sorry, sir. Tell it to the judge in court."

Why is a court necessary in this situation?

A **court** can be defined as a governmental forum that administers justice under the law. Courts decide civil disputes and criminal cases. A court may award damages in civil cases, impose punishment in criminal cases, or grant other appropriate relief. In *What's Your Verdict?* a court was necessary to decide whether Doyle was telling the truth and whether the blocked sign would be a valid defense.

Courts follow impartial and thorough procedures to make decisions. Witnesses are in some cases compelled to give testimony. The accused party is allowed equal opportunity to argue her or his side of the case. The two levels of courts are trial courts and appellate courts.

Trial Courts

A **trial court** is the first court to hear a dispute. As such, it has **original jurisdiction** over a case. Witnesses testify and other information is presented to prove the alleged facts.

A trial court consists not only of a judge but also of lawyers (who are officers of the court). Other jobs necessary for the court's operation include clerks, sheriffs or marshals, bailiffs, and jury members.

Clerks enter cases on the court calendar, keep records of proceedings, and sometimes compute court costs. Sheriffs or their deputies (who serve as bailiffs) summon witnesses, keep order in court, and take steps to carry out judgments in the *state court systems*. Marshals have these duties in the *federal court system*. Juries are citizens sworn by a court to decide issues of fact in court cases.

Appellate Courts

An **appellate court** reviews decisions of lower courts when a party claims an error was made during the previous proceeding. Appellate courts do not hear witnesses and generally do not accept new evidence. Appellate courts are concerned with errors of law rather than questions of fact.

Appellate courts examine the **transcript** (a verbatim record of what went on at trial). They also read **appellate briefs** (written arguments on the issues of law) submitted by the opposing attorneys. Appellate courts listen to attorneys' oral arguments. They also may question attorneys about the case. Finally, appellate courts decide whether the decision of the lower court should be *affirmed* (upheld), *reversed* (overturned), *amended* (changed), or *remanded* (sent back to the trial court for corrective action or possibly a new trial).

THINK ABOUT LEGAL CONCEPTS

Answer the following questions about legal concepts.

1. Courts **(a) award damages in criminal cases (b) hear witnesses at the appellate level (c) decide questions of fact at the trial level (d) enforce mediators' decisions (e) all of the above**

2. Appellate court review of trial court decisions is normally confined to matters of __?__ .

3. When an appellate court sends a case back down to a trial court for a new trial or other corrective action it is said to have __?__ the case. **(a) affirmed (b) reversed (c) remanded (d) none of the above**

4. There is no difference between mediation and arbitration. **True or False?**

5. To __?__ means to resolve a dispute in court.

6. Parties to a dispute may choose to use negotiation, arbitration, or mediation to avoid **(a)** , **(b)** , and difficulties of a court trial.

THINK CRITICALLY ABOUT EVIDENCE

Study the following situations, answer the questions, then prepare arguments to support your answers.

7. Your boss at Swift Electronics is getting ready to enter into a series of contracts with a new group of suppliers. She is concerned with avoiding the delays and high costs of any litigation that might result from the new agreements. She asks you for your recommendations. Do you have any ideas?

8. Your boss at Swift Electronics decides against the recommendations you made (see exercise 7). Six months later, a supplier sends the wrong projection device in response to your order. The supplier then refuses to correct the mistake. Your boss hires an attorney at $250 per hour and takes you to lunch to admit she made a mistake in not following your ideas. Ultimately, the case is set for trial. What type of jurisdiction will this court have? What will be done during the trial?

9. In exercise 8, who may be present during the trial? If there is an appeal, which of these parties will not have to appear again?

10. Don Long is convicted of second-degree murder for killing a woman he had been seeing over the last few months. The court sentenced him to 30 years in jail. One year after his trial, Don admits that he withheld evidence that would have cleared him. He states he did so to protect his twin brother, who actually committed the crime, but who was dying of cancer at the time. He further states that he did not want his brother to spend the last years of his life behind bars. His brother has since died. The evidence is conclusive as to his innocence. Should the court set aside his conviction due to the new evidence? What policies would support the court in not doing so?

ORIGINS OF OUR FEDERAL COURT SYSTEM

WHAT'S YOUR VERDICT?

Jim and Marla were discussing how U.S. Bankruptcy Courts were empowered to decide cases. Jim said that federal courts received their power from the U.S. Constitution. Marla thought Congress had created and empowered the bankruptcy courts.

Who is correct?

Through Article III of the Constitution, the people conferred the power to judge certain criminal and civil matters on a system of federal courts:

Section 1. The judicial Power of the United States shall be vested in one Supreme Court, and in such inferior Courts as the Congress may from time to time ordain and establish.

The Articles of Confederation did not allow for a Supreme Court, and some citizens did not think a Supreme Court would be needed under the Constitution. As a result, after George Washington's inauguration as our first president, it took nearly six months for Congress to utilize the power it was granted under Article III and pass the Federal Judiciary Act. This act "ordained and established" the U.S. Supreme Court (USSC) and the circuit courts of appeals.

Approximately a century after passing the Federal Judiciary Act, Congress established the federal district courts. Certain specialized courts, such as those concerned primarily with tax or bankruptcy matters, also were created as the need for them arose.

In *What's Your Verdict?* both Jim and Marla are correct. Ultimately, the federal courts received their power from the Constitution. However, the Constitution granted Congress the power to establish courts inferior to the U.S. Supreme Court. Congress used this power in creating and empowering U.S. Bankruptcy Courts.

JURISDICTION OF THE FEDERAL COURTS

WHAT'S YOUR VERDICT?

Susan Bean, a citizen of Illinois, sued Wallis Turk, a citizen of the state of Colorado, for the breach of a construction contract on Bean's new Chicago residence. More than $600,000 was at stake. Bean filed the suit in Illinois state court. Turk fought to remove the case to the federal courts.

Should the case be heard in federal or state court?

Currently there are three levels of federal courts with **general jurisdiction.** These are federal district courts, federal courts of appeals, and the U.S. Supreme Court. A court with general jurisdiction can hear almost any kind of case. A court with **special jurisdiction** hears only one specific type of case.

Federal District Courts

The federal (or U.S.) district court is the lowest level of federal court with general jurisdiction. This is the trial court of the federal system (the first court to hear the dispute). It has the power to determine the facts of the matter and to make initial determinations of the law to use in deciding the case.

In general, district courts have original jurisdiction over (a) federal questions, or cases that arise under the Constitution, U.S. law, and U.S. treaties; and (b) lawsuits between citizens of different states, between a U.S. citizen and a foreign nation, or between a U.S. citizen and a citizen of a foreign nation. These parties are said to have *diversity of citizenship.* More than $75,000 must be in dispute in federal diversity of citizenship lawsuits. If the amount is less than $75,000, the case should be litigated in a state court with proper jurisdiction.

The *Bean v. Turk* case in *What's Your Verdict?* should be tried in the federal courts. The case falls within the qualifications of the federal courts, which have priority in cases within their jurisdiction.

Federal Courts of Appeals

The federal courts of appeals have appellate jurisdiction over the district courts, certain specialized federal courts, and many federal administrative agencies. Such power is exercised when the result of a case in a lower court is appealed by one or more of the parties to the case. Appellate courts do not accept any new evidence or call witnesses. Instead, they review the trial transcripts and the written and oral arguments of the attorneys to reach a decision. No appellate court, not even the U.S. Supreme Court, can change the factual determinations of a jury.

There are 13 federal courts of appeal. Twelve of these are circuit courts, each of which is responsible for an assigned geographic area.

The First Amendment gives us freedom of speech. But just how freely can we speak? The courts have given books and newspapers the most leeway. However, television is strictly regulated. Now freedom of speech on the Internet is being examined by the courts.

The Communications Decency Act (CDA) brought the issue to the forefront. The CDA attempted to regulate speech on the Internet. A district court found the CDA unconstitutional. On appeal in *Reno v. ACLU*, the U.S. Supreme Court held that the CDA's "indecent transmission" and "patently offensive display" provisions abridged (or diminished) freedom of speech, as protected by the First Amendment. The Supreme Court felt government regulation of speech on the Internet would interfere more with the free exchange of ideas than encourage it.

The thirteenth is dedicated to the "federal circuit." As such, it handles patent cases appealed out of the district courts. It also handles appeals from federal courts with special jurisdictions and from such bodies as the International Trade Commission.

United States Supreme Court

The U.S. Supreme Court (USSC) has both original and appellate jurisdiction. Its original jurisdiction, according to the Constitution, is over "cases affecting ambassadors, other public ministers and consuls and those in which a state shall be party."

The most important function of the U.S. Supreme Court, however, is the exercise of its appellate jurisdiction. This jurisdiction is exercised over cases on appeal from the U.S. Courts of Appeals or from the highest courts of the various states. If the Supreme Court believes that a case contains a constitutional issue sufficiently important to be decided by it, the Supreme Court will issue to the last court that

FEDERAL COURT SYSTEM

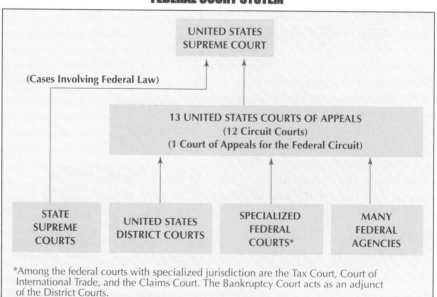

UNITED STATES SUPREME COURT

(Cases Involving Federal Law)

13 UNITED STATES COURTS OF APPEALS
(12 Circuit Courts)
(1 Court of Appeals for the Federal Circuit)

STATE SUPREME COURTS

UNITED STATES DISTRICT COURTS

SPECIALIZED FEDERAL COURTS*

MANY FEDERAL AGENCIES

*Among the federal courts with specialized jurisdiction are the Tax Court, Court of International Trade, and the Claims Court. The Bankruptcy Court acts as an adjunct of the District Courts.

heard the case a **writ of certiorari**. This "writ" or order compels the state court to turn over the record of the case to the Supreme Court for review.

Jurisdiction over state supreme court cases is limited to those in which a federal question has arisen. Such a question must be based on a federal law or on the U.S. Constitution. The decisions of the USSC that interpret or apply the Constitution are final and can only be overturned by the USSC itself or by a constitutional amendment.

THINK ABOUT LEGAL CONCEPTS

Answer the following questions about legal concepts.

1. A Supreme Court did not exist under the Articles of Confederation. **True or False?**

2. There are __?__ levels of courts with general jurisdiction in the federal system.

3. The federal trial courts are known as **(a) district courts (b) federal county courts (c) common law courts (d) criminal courts**

4. The USSC has original jurisdiction over cases involving citizens of different states in which more than $75,000 is at stake. **True or False?**

5. The USSC can change its mind about the interpretation of the Constitution once it has passed down a decision using that interpretation. **True or False?**

THINK CRITICALLY ABOUT EVIDENCE

Study the following situations, answer the questions, then prepare arguments to support your answers.

6. Ms. Tant of New York City recently sued Mr. Bloom, also of New York City. She claimed that he had run into and injured her while he was jogging. She asked for $50,000 in damages. When she filed her suit in federal district court, Mr. Bloom's attorney immediately objected on two grounds. What were they?

7. Ms. Tant's case (see exercise 6) was thrown out of federal court. She later filed it in the New York state court solely as a case involving Mr. Bloom's negligent jogging. When she lost, she appealed all the way to the highest New York state court but still lost. She then sought to appeal to the U.S. Supreme Court. Will the Supreme Court hear her case?

8. Samuel Train, a Missouri citizen, brought suit in federal court in Missouri against Val Dermit, a citizen of the state of Illinois. The suit alleged that, while vacationing near Branson, Missouri, Dermit had negligently run his small bass boat in front of Train's cabin cruiser. In trying to avoid what probably would have been a fatal collision for Dermit, Train ran his watercraft into a rock and it sank. Train alleges that the value of the craft is $84,000 based on its purchase price some three years earlier. In trying to get the suit dismissed, Dermit alleges that if the court considers the depreciation of the craft over the time it had been owned by Train, the craft was worth far less than the $75,000 jurisdictional limit for the federal district courts and probably has a market value of not more than $62,000. In a counterargument, Train states that the replacement cost of the craft is currently at least $94,000. If the suit is dismissed and must then be filed in a state court, Train may not be able to get jurisdiction over Dermit and will therefore go uncompensated. What value of the cabin cruiser do you think the court will use in making its determination?

9. Paul Stone sued his employer for assault and battery due to the actions of several of his female co-workers. While gathered around the coffee machine each morning, they would whistle at him, make sexual innuendoes, and touch and pinch him. When the case was dismissed from the state circuit court, Stone appealed. The intermediate court of appeals sustained the result in the lower court and Stone appealed to the state supreme court. When the state supreme court also sustained, Stone sought to appeal to the U.S. Supreme Court. Are there any federal issues in this case that would allow the U.S. Supreme Court to take jurisdiction? What might prevent the nation's highest court from so doing?

STRUCTURE OF STATE COURT SYSTEMS

WHAT'S YOUR VERDICT?

When Simon withheld the security deposit after Annie moved out of her apartment, Annie sued him in small claims court to get it refunded. When she lost, she told her friend that she would appeal it directly to the U.S. Supreme Court.

Can she do so?

The typical state legal system resembles the federal system. The state legislature makes the laws. The state executive branch enforces those laws in the courts of the state judicial branch.

The courts of general jurisdiction of the judicial branch are organized into three tiers. In the bottom tier is a geographically based trial-court system. An appellate layer of courts is next. Trial and appellate courts are controlled and supervised by a state supreme court as the ultimate level of appeal. In *What's Your Verdict?* Annie could not take her appeal directly to the U.S. Supreme Court, much less the state supreme court.

State Trial Courts

In most states trial courts (with general original jurisdiction over both criminal and civil matters), are known as circuit courts. In some states, however, they may be called superior courts, district courts, or

courts of common pleas. These are the courts of record in the state system.

A **court of record** keeps an exact account of what goes on at trial. The accuracy of this account is vital, as any appeal taken depends on it. The "record" may include a transcript of what was said, the evidence that was submitted, statements and determinations of the court officials, and the judgment of the court.

State trial courts also review the decisions of—or handle appeals from—courts of more specialized jurisdiction under them. In most cases, however, state trial courts actually retry the cases to make a proper record for the purpose of potential appeals.

A state trial court (or court of record) has original jurisdiction over cases before it. It therefore makes determinations of the facts in the case by using a jury. If a jury is not requested for the case, the presiding judge will determine the facts. Then the court of record will select and apply the law to the facts to reach a verdict in the case.

A TYPICAL STATE COURT SYSTEM

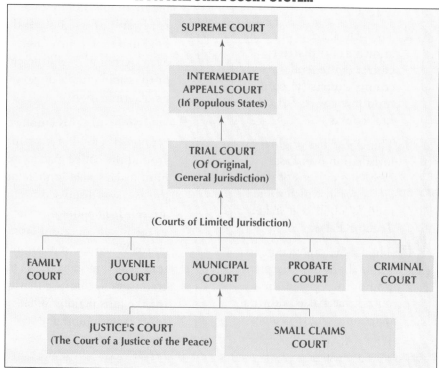

State Courts of Appeals

Typically, an appeal in a court of record is reviewed by a panel of judges in a state court of appeals. The panel of judges from the state court of appeals usually consists of no more than three judges. The panel evaluates the record of the case and then considers the attorneys' oral and written arguments. No new evidence can be introduced at this level. Evidence can only be introduced at the lower trial-court level, so that the facts remain unchanged. The judges at the appellate level instead check to be sure that the correct law was used to resolve the case.

If the court of appeals judges conclude that the trial court used the incorrect law, they may enter a judgment using what they consider to be the correct law. Sometimes the use of the wrong law interferes with the trial court's determination of facts or conduct of the trial. If this happens, the appellate court may send the case back down for a new trial. Or, the judges may conclude that the lower court used the correct law in the proper way. In this case, the lower court's judgment would stand.

State Supreme Courts

Generally, in whatever legal issue we confront, we are all entitled to a trial and to one appeal, if filed in a timely manner and in the proper form. In states with the intermediate level of courts of appeals, only cases that involve the most complex legal issues are taken to the justices of the state supreme court. (**Justice** is the title given to judges who sit on state supreme courts and the federal Supreme Court.) At the state supreme court level a panel of three or more justices reviews the legal issues and listens to the attorneys' oral arguments.

State supreme courts issue the final decision on matters of law appealed to them unless the U.S. Constitution or other federal issues are involved. If there is a U.S. Constitutional or other

federal issue, a further appeal can go to the U.S. Supreme Court. In several states, in addition to its appellate jurisdiction, the state supreme court has original jurisdiction over most state impeachment cases.

STATE COURTS WITH SPECIALIZED JURISDICTION

WHAT'S YOUR VERDICT?

Reid, age 15, was detained by the police for shoplifting and was referred to juvenile court.

Will Reid be treated differently in juvenile court than in an adult criminal court?

Below the circuit court level in most states are the courts that take care of specialized or relatively minor jurisdiction. These courts include the associate circuit, municipal, small claims, juvenile, and probate courts.

Associate Circuit Courts

Many states have a layer of courts below their main courts of general original jurisdiction. These lower courts are referred to as **associate circuit courts** or **county courts**. Such courts hear minor criminal cases, state traffic offenses, and lawsuits in which relatively small amounts are involved (usually no more than $25,000). Generally, these courts are not courts of record. However, they take a significant burden off the higher courts, even though appeals from their decisions can be taken to the circuit courts for a trial on the record.

City or Municipal Courts

Cities typically have courts that administer their ordinances. These **municipal courts** are usually divided into traffic and criminal divisions. As city ordinances often overlap with or duplicate state laws, less serious violations occurring within city limits are brought before such municipal courts

for their first trial. The result can then be appealed to the circuit court level if necessary. (Although the penalties for violating ordinances can be as severe, ordinances are not considered criminal laws. Only state and federal governments can make an act criminal.)

Small Claims Courts

Minor individual suits would not often be heard if not for the **small claims courts**. These courts handle disputes in which small amounts, generally $2,500 or less, are involved. Attorneys generally are not allowed in small claims courts. The judge hears the case without a jury or formal rules of evidence. Decisions of small claims court can be appealed to the circuit court.

Juvenile Courts

Younger members of society (those over 13 and under 18 years of age in most states) are referred to as **juveniles**. Our society typically believes that juveniles should not be held as responsible as adults for their criminal acts. To carry out this policy, special courts have been set up. In these courts the juvenile is entitled to his or her full constitutional rights, including the right to be represented by an attorney. If the juvenile is found

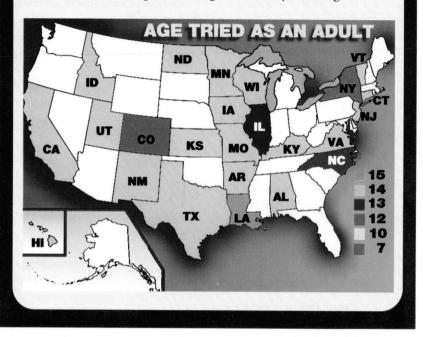

Washington D.C. and 26 states do not have a set minimum age for a child to be tried as an adult. The 24 states listed below do have a set minimum age—the range is 7 to 15 years of age.

AGE TRIED AS AN ADULT

15	
14	
13	
12	
10	
7	

A Question of ETHICS

At age 17, Horace Samuels was brought before the juvenile court charged with child molestation. He was convicted and, as a juvenile, was sentenced to probation in a foster home. While in the home, he was again caught and tried for the same offense. Again, he was tried as a juvenile. Now he is 18 and about to live on his own in an area in which many children of the same age that he has been charged with molesting also live. Horace's probation officer realizes that Horace has not been rehabilitated and is a potential danger to the neighborhood's young. The law requires that the juvenile's record remain closed so that he may begin a new life free and clear of his past mistakes. What should the probation officer do?

guilty of the charges brought, the court has wide powers in determining what should be done.

However, the emphasis for juveniles generally is on rehabilitation, not punishment. Possibilities open to the court include release into the supervision of parents, guardians, or governmental officials; placement in foster homes; and detention in correctional facilities.

These courts ensure that most of the criminal cases involving juveniles do not become public knowledge. The courtroom is closed while an informal hearing into the charges is conducted. Any records made on juvenile cases are not open to the public.

If rehabilitation fails or is shown to to be impossible, the young offender can be tried and punished as an adult. This occurs only in cases in

which a very serious offense was allegedly committed by the juvenile. For example, murder and certain other crimes may bring about trial and punishment through the criminal law system. Appeals from actions of the juvenile courts are directed to the circuit courts.

In *What's Your Verdict?* Reid would not be treated as an adult. He would be entitled to a juvenile court hearing where his age and level of maturity would be considered.

Probate Courts

Courts that administer wills and estates are called **probate courts**. When individuals die, their property and other interests must be divided according to their wishes and the appropriate laws. The procedure to accomplish this is formal and complex.

THINK ABOUT LEGAL CONCEPTS

Answer the following questions about legal concepts.

1. Which of the following is generally not included in the "record" of a case?
   (a) verbatim transcript
   (b) physical and documentary evidence
   (c) media coverage (d) all of the above are generally included

2. Attorneys generally are not required or not even allowed in a small claims court. **True or False?**

3. A state supreme court has the power to issue the final decision on all matters of law appealed to it. **True or False?**

4. A dispute between neighbors involving property damage of $8,500 would probably be heard in
   (a) federal district court
   (b) probate court
   (c) small claims court
   (d) associate circuit court

5. A state trial court has the power to hear some appeals. **True or False?**

THINK CRITICALLY ABOUT EVIDENCE

Study the following situations, answer the questions, then prepare arguments to support your answers.

6. Gwendolyn Hunt was driving while intoxicated when she hit and killed Felicia Meyers, a seven-year-old, in a school crosswalk. Gwendolyn was 16 years old at the time. However, she was on probation from a reduced sentence for driving 62 in a 35 mph residential speed zone. Should Gwendolyn be tried as an adult for vehicular manslaughter?

7. You are driving along a residential city street when you are stopped by a city police cruiser for speeding. You are given a citation and a summons to appear before a particular court. What court would that most likely be and why?

8. You are driving along the interstate highway headed for a ballgame in a nearby city. A state highway patrol car suddenly appears in your rearview mirror, lights flashing. You pull over and are cited for doing 80 in a 65 mph zone. Your receive a summons to a particular court. What court would that most likely be and why?

9. After a long illness, your uncle dies. He leaves a sizeable estate but no will is found for several weeks. Finally, one of his ex-wives appears with a document she claims to be a valid will. It shows her and her children by him receiving most of his property. Your parents and the deceased's other children contest the will. Should the federal or state courts handle this case? Why? Which court in which system is most likely to hear it?

10. George Matthews lives in the South. He ordered a $2,950 garden cultivator from a company in the Midwest. George paid for the cultivator C.O.D. (cash on delivery). After trying to use the cultivator, George found that the tines were made of a cheap, thin metal that was not adequate for use even on fairly loose soil. The company refused to refund George's money. Should George sue? What court would be available to him? Does the way jurisdictions are allocated make it unlikely certain cases will be litigated? What does this say about society's desire to afford justice to all?

As a citizen . . .

PREVENT LEGAL

DIFFICULTIES

1. To avoid expensive litigation should a dispute develop, when you enter a contract include a provision requiring the use of a mediator or an arbitrator.

2. To be sure of the rules and costs of any litigation that might develop under a contract or other legal document you sign, specify the jurisdiction in which such disputes must be resolved.

3. Have your parents see an attorney to make out a will and utilize other methods to avoid the expenses of probate.

CHAPTER IN REVIEW

CONCEPTS IN BRIEF

1. The levels of courts are trial courts, which have original jurisdiction, and appellate courts, which review decisions of lower courts.

2. Mediation and arbitration offer dispute resolution alternatives to litigation. Using these alternative methods of dispute resolution helps to avoid the costs, delays, and difficulties of a court trial.

3. The federal government and each state have separate court systems.

4. The federal courts receive their power from the Constitution. Federal courts can have either general or specialized jurisdiction.

5. The typical state court system is simular to the federal court system. Both the federal and state court systems have trial courts, appellate courts, and a supreme court.

6. In every state, there are juvenile courts with special jurisdiction over persons under the age of majority. These courts emphasize rehabilitation.

7. Juvenile courts treat minors as delinquents if they commit offenses that would be crimes for adults.

8. Probate courts settle the estates of decedents who die with or without a will.

9. Small claims courts feature relaxed rules of evidence and do not require representation by an attorney. The dollar amount that can be adjudicated usually is limited to around $2,500.

10. Municipal or city courts usually feature two divisions, one to handle traffic and another to handle violations of all other ordinances. Penalties for ordinance violations (which are not considered crimes) are less severe than federal and state criminal law penalties.

YOUR LEGAL VOCABULARY

Match each statement with the term that it best defines. Some terms may not be used.

1. Verbatim record of what went on at trial

2. Court that reviews trial court decisions to determine if a significant error of law was made during trial

3. Court in which an accurate, detailed report of what went on at trial is formed

4. Independent third party who develops a binding, court-enforceable dispute resolution

5. Order to a lower court to produce the record of a case for the Supreme Court to review

6. Power to hear a case in full for the first time

7. Individuals over 13 and under 18 years of age who are given special status under the criminal law

8. Title of a judge on the state or federal supreme courts

9. Tribunal that hears cases involving violations of ordinances

10. Power to hear only cases of a specific type

appellate brief
appellate court
arbitrator
associate circuit court
  (or county court)
court
court of record
general jurisdiction
justice
juveniles
litigate
mediator
municipal court
original jurisdiction
probate court
small claims court
special jurisdiction
transcript
trial court
writ of certiorari

11. What is the fundamental difference between arbitration and mediation?

12. Why are appeals taken on matters of law only?

13. Why should the federal courts handle cases involving private matters between citizens of different states (for example, cases involving diversity of citizenship with more than $75,000 at stake)?

14. Why shouldn't the USSC be able to substitute its own factual determinations for those of a jury in a lowly trial court?

WRITE ABOUT LEGAL CONCEPTS

15. Wherever we go we are charged with knowing all the laws, ordinances, rules and regulations that apply to us. "Ignorance of the law is no excuse." Because of the confusion this causes, there has been a movement in the last 50 years to make the state laws more uniform. From sales law to various parts of the criminal code, the effect has been positive. Should we now turn our attention to making the state court systems uniform? What are the advantages and disadvantages of such an idea?

16. Judges cost an extraordinary amount of money. To attract competent personnel to our judiciary, we must offer salaries of what a lawyer would earn in private practice. A way to provide the necessary salary levels is to save money elsewhere in the system. Many states use extensively trained non-lawyers to handle municipal courts and other more minor judiciary positions. Do you think this is a good idea? Why or why not?

17. **HOT DEBATE** Write a paragraph discussing the following question: if Anthony decides to file suit in state court against his employer, what federal court might ultimately claim jurisdiction? Under what circumstances?

THINK CRITICALLY ABOUT EVIDENCE

18. Gomez wanted to sue Shapiro for breach of contract but could not afford the expenses and time delays associated with litigation. What alternatives are available to resolve this matter?

19. If you were a witness to an incident involving a friend, would you be obligated to tell the complete truth even if it might cause your friend to lose the case? Would you have the moral strength to do that?

20. June lost her case in trial court. She thought that the plaintiff, Sid, had lied during the trial. On appeal, she requested that she be allowed to appear and explain why she thought Sid had lied. Will her request be granted?

21. Suppose someone has injured you. Do you have a duty to sue them for the injury even when the costs of the trial may be more than you can recover?

22. On May 7, Bart Masters turned 18. The evening of that day, he was caught stealing a woman's purse. "Don't worry," he told his friend Julia, "I just turned 18 today, they won't try me as an adult. I'm too close to being a juvenile." Is he correct?

23. Priscilla is being sued in small claims court by her landlord for past due rent. "Just wait," she exclaims. "Once I get in front of that jury, they won't award him the money. After all, he shut off the water several times and didn't even have heat in the building for over a month last winter." What is wrong with Priscilla's estimate of the situation?

24. Taylor and Fitz Coal Company had a dispute over the amount of money due under a mineral lease. They submitted the dispute to arbitration according to the provisions of the lease. The arbitrators awarded the lessor, Taylor, $37,214.67. Taylor did not like the amount awarded and filed suit in court. Will the court conduct a trial to determine whether the amount is fair? (*Taylor v. Fitz Coal Company,* 618 S.W.2d 432, Ky.)

25. Kent, a 16-year-old boy, was taken into custody by the police in Washington, D.C. He was held and questioned about breaking into an apartment, raping the occupant, and stealing a wallet. He admitted the offenses and volunteered information on several similar offenses. At the time, Kent was on probation for housebreaking and attempted purse snatching. Under the federal Juvenile Court Act, the case of any child 16 years of age or older who is charged with an offense that in the case of an adult would be a felony may, after an investigation by the juvenile court judge, be transferred by the juvenile court to the district court. The juvenile court waived its jurisdiction in Kent's case. Kent was tried and found guilty by a jury in the district court. Kent, admitting through his attorney that the juvenile court had the right to waive its jurisdiction, claimed nevertheless that the juvenile court had acted in an arbitrary manner by transferring him to the jurisdiction of the district court. Was the court within its rights in waiving jurisdiction? (*Kent v. United States,* 383 U.S. 541)

26. A government-owned P-51 fighter plane landed at a Los Angeles airport and waited on a runway for a tow truck, on instructions from the tower. Shortly thereafter, a plane owned by Douglas Aircraft Company began approaching the airfield to land. The Douglas aircraft struck the P-51, which was parked on the runway. The United States brought suit against Douglas, claiming that the Douglas pilot was negligent. During the trial, evidence was introduced indicating that the Douglas pilot was careless in not seeing the parked P-51, but that the airport was covered with a haze and the P-51 was painted in camouflage colors. Also, the Douglas pilot had "zigzagged" his plane while taxiing in order to

improve his forward vision. The trial was conducted before a jury. The government claimed that the issue of whether the Douglas pilot was negligent was an issue of law for the judge to decide. Douglas claimed that it was an issue of fact for the jury to decide. Which one is correct? (*United States v. Douglas Aircraft Company,* 169 F.2d 755, 9th Cir.)

27. A 17-year-old boy appeared in juvenile court to answer charges of vehicular homicide. The incident had occurred when he was 16. By the time the case actually went to trial the boy was 18. Should he be tried as an adult? Why or why not? (*Commission v. A Juvenile,* 545 N.E.2d 1164)

28. When a tip was received that marijuana was being grown in his greenhouse, Michael Riley's property was observed from a helicopter by an investigating officer. The helicopter flyover was deemed necessary because the items within the greenhouse could not be observed from a nearby road. Riley was subsequently arrested and tried for offenses stemming from his cultivation efforts. The defense challenged the use of the information acquired by the helicopter flyover saying that it was an illegal search under the Fourth Amendment to the U.S. Constitution. The Florida Supreme Court agreed with the defense. Could the State of Florida appeal the decision to the U.S. Supreme Court? Why or why not? (*Florida v. Riley,* 102 L.Ed. 2d 835)

29. Colleen Donnelly filed charges with the Equal Employment Opportunity Commission (EEOC) against her employer, Yellow Freight, for sex discrimination. After she filed the charges, Colleen received notice from the EEOC that she had 90 days to bring suit. This 90-day period was a procedure for claims under the federal Civil Rights Act of 1964. Within that period Donnelly did indeed file suit but in Illinois state court under an Illinois statute that also prohibits such discrimination. After the 90-day period had expired, however, she tried to take the suit to a federal court. Yellow Freight defended claiming that she could not make such a transfer as the 90-day period had expired for federal actions. Should she be allowed to go forward with her suit? Why or why not? (*Donnelly v. Yellow Freight System, Inc.,* 874 F.2d 402)

Texas v. Johnson
USSC, 109 Supreme Court Reporter 2533

BACKGROUND In 1984, during the Republican National Convention in Dallas, Texas, a political demonstration was held. The point of the demonstration was to protest the policies of the President of the United States, Ronald Reagan. Mr. Reagan was to be re-nominated by the convention for a second term. The demonstration also targeted several Dallas-based corporations for their government-related activities.

FACTS As the demonstration was being conducted, a protestor took an American flag from a pole outside one of the buildings. The protestor passed the flag to another protestor, Johnson, who subsequently doused it with kerosene and set it afire. As the flag of the United States of America burned, the protestors chanted, "America, the red, white, and blue, we spit on you." The protestor who set the flag afire was ultimately charged with a crime and tried in a Texas trial court.

LOWER COURT The trial court found Johnson guilty of violating a state statute which prohibited the desecration of state or national flags. The statute defined desecration as the physical mistreatment of such objects so as to seriously offend individuals likely to observe or discover the act.

APPEAL Johnson appealed his conviction on the basis of the First Amendment's guarantee of freedom of speech. A Texas Court of Appeals affirmed the conviction after stating that such a statute, which might have a potentially chilling effect on speech, deserved close scrutiny in its

application. However, said the court, the conviction could be upheld in this instance as being necessary to guarantee the peaceful nature of the assembly due to the highly inflammatory nature of a flag burning. The case was then appealed to the Texas Court of Criminal Appeals. The Court of Criminal Appeals reversed the decisions of the inferior courts and sent the case back to the trial court with instructions to dismiss the charges. The Court, in so doing, indicated that the statute was too broad in its reference to protecting against a breach of the peace. The U.S. Supreme Court then took jurisdiction by a writ of certiorari.

ISSUE Was the conviction of Johnson justifiable by the state of Texas as an attempt to protect against breaches of the peace or did the flag burning have overriding elements of communication that the state statute failed to protect?

DECISION The United States Supreme Court, in an opinion written by Justice Brennan, held that the First Amendment freedom of speech protection had indeed been violated by the application of the statute.

PRACTICE JUDGING

1. **Should the court affirm or reverse as a consequence?**

2. **The record did not contain any evidence indicating that a breach of the peace had indeed occurred. How do you think this affected the decision?**

3. **There is an exception for "fighting words" provided for governments who want to enforce statutes that might chill public speech. Could this exception have been applied to this situation in order to uphold the conviction?**

OUR CRIMINAL LAWS

CHAPTER 5

LESSONS

5-1 CRIMINAL LAW

5-2 CRIMINAL PROCEDURE

HOT DEBATE

Emily's father and mother both developed cancer due to hazardous and toxic materials illegally dumped in their water supply by the Northside Chemical Company. When Northside was able to avoid liability for its actions, Emily went to work for them under an assumed name. Five years later, she was discovered to have embezzled more than $1 million from the company and given it all to various charities aiding the victims of environmental pollution. Your friend Bill says Emily is a heroine and should not be punished for her crime.

Where Do You Stand?

1. **What arguments can you make for trying Emily?**

2. **What arguments can you make against trying her?**

WHAT ARE CRIMES?

WHAT'S YOUR VERDICT?

Davis, the chief accountant of the Del Norte Credit Union, cleverly juggled the company records over a period of years. During that time, she took at least $35,000 belonging to the credit union. When the theft was discovered by outside auditors, Davis repaid the money with interest.

Has she committed a crime despite the repayment?

The most fundamental characteristic of a **crime** is that it is a punishable offense against society. When a crime occurs, society—acting through police and prosecutors—attempts to identify, arrest, prosecute, and punish the criminal. These efforts are designed to protect society rather than to aid the victim of the crime.

Crimes contrast with *civil offenses,* which are offenses against just the victim, not society. For almost all crimes, the victim can sue identified criminals for civil damages. However, victims seldom do so because few criminals have the ability to pay judgments.

Crimes are defined by statute (laws enacted by state or federal legislatures). Statutes tell us what conduct is prohibited, so that we can conform our conduct to the law.

Elements of a Crime

Before anyone can be convicted of a crime, three elements usually must be proved at the trial. They are

1. a duty to do or not to do a certain thing
2. an act or omission in violation of that duty
3. criminal intent

DUTY State statutes prohibiting certain conduct usually describe duty. Less frequently, federal statutes or city ordinances identify criminal behavior. To establish duty in a trial, the prosecutor cites a statute to the judge.

VIOLATION OF THE DUTY The breach of duty—the specific conduct that violates the statute—is the **criminal act.** For example, all states have statutes that make battery a crime. These statutes often define criminal battery as "the intentional causing of bodily harm to another person." A breach of this duty could be proved in a trial by the testimony of a witness who saw the defendant punch the victim.

CRIMINAL INTENT The third element, criminal intent, must be proved in

most cases. Criminal intent generally means that the defendant (1) intended to commit the act and (2) intended to do evil. If in a basketball game you deliberately punch an opposing player, you display criminal intent. You have committed a crime. On the other hand, if you lose your balance, and while flailing your arms hit the nose of a bystander, there would be no crime. You did not intend the act nor did you intend to do evil.

In *What's Your Verdict?* Davis owed a duty, defined by state statute, to not take the credit union's money. Violation of this duty, the criminal conduct of taking another's property or money by a person to whom it has been entrusted, is **embezzlement.** This act could be proved with the testimony of the auditors. Davis' criminal intent can be established by her conduct. The acts were intentional and she intended to do the evil. So Davis did commit a crime. Her return of the money does not alter this fact.

Criminal intent creates two issues for corporations. First, can a corporation, which is an organization, form criminal intent the way humans can? The answer is yes. If the corporation's employees have criminal intent, their employer may be judged to have criminal intent. If the employees were doing their assigned duties and the criminal act benefits the organization, most courts will find criminal intent in the organization.

The second issue relates to corporate officers. When a corporate employee commits a crime, can officers be held criminally responsible? The answer is often yes. In many situations, the officer will be held criminally liable under the doctrine of **vicarious criminal liability.** Vicarious means substituted. The criminal intent of the employee is used as a substitute for the requirement of criminal intent for an officer.

Suppose the president of a company knows generally about very dangerous working conditions but does nothing to protect workers from the risks. If a worker is killed because a supervisor failed to take safety precautions, the president could be charged with the crime of homicide.

Criminal intent also is related to age. Under early common law, children under age 7 were considered to be below the age of reason. Therefore, they were considered incapable of having the criminal intent necessary for crimes. Those over age 14 were presumed to know the difference between right and wrong and so were as accountable as adults for their acts. For children ages 7 through 14, such knowledge had to be proved.

Today, statutes in most states fix the age of criminal liability at 18, but the figure ranges from 16 to 19. State statutes provide that minors as young as 7 may be tried and punished as adults if they are accused of serious crimes such as murder. Generally, however, what is a crime for an adult is juvenile delinquency for a minor.

To have criminal intent, one must have sufficient mental capacity to know the difference between right and wrong. Accordingly, insane persons are not held responsible for their criminal acts. Neither voluntary intoxication nor use of drugs relieves a person from criminal responsibility in most circumstances.

Some crimes do not require the element of criminal intent. For the less serious crimes where being sentenced to jail is very unlikely, criminal intent is not required. Traffic offenses are an example. A speeding driver who did not intend to speed or intend evil has still committed a traffic offense.

Another exception applies to actions involving extreme carelessness. Suppose you drive 80 mph through a residential neighborhood while drunk and kill a pedestrian. You may not have intended to speed or intended to do evil. However, your conduct was so careless that some courts treat it the same as criminal intent. You could be convicted of the crime of vehicular homicide.

Criminal Conduct

Criminal conduct may be classified in various ways. One type of classification is as follows:

1. crimes against a person (assault and battery, kidnapping, rape, murder)
2. crimes against property (theft, robbery, embezzlement)
3. crimes against the government and administration of justice (treason, tax evasion, perjury)
4. crimes against public peace and order (rioting, disorderly conduct, illegal speeding)
5. crimes against realty (burglary, arson, criminal trespass)
6. crimes against consumers (fraudulent sale of securities, violation of pure food and drug laws)
7. crimes against decency (bigamy, obscenity, prostitution)

CLASSIFICATION OF CRIMES

WHAT'S YOUR VERDICT?

Murdock was a witness at a civil trial for damages. Before testifying, he took an oath "to tell the truth, the whole truth, and nothing but the truth." Nevertheless, while being questioned by one of the attorneys, Murdock deliberately lied, hoping to help the defendant.

If this could be proved, could he be punished for a crime?

Crimes are classified as (1) felonies or (2) misdemeanors.

Felony

A **felony** is a crime punishable by confinement for more than a year in a state prison or by a fine of more than $1,000, or both—or even death. Murder, kidnapping, arson, rape, robbery, burglary, embezzlement, forgery, theft of large sums, and perjury are examples of felonies. People who lie under oath (as Murdock did in *What's Your Verdict?*) commit **perjury**. They may be imprisoned for two or three years.

Misdemeanor

A **misdemeanor** is a less serious crime. It is usually punishable by confinement in a county or city jail for less than one year, by fine, or both. Such crimes as disorderly conduct and speeding are usually misdemeanors. Some states classify lesser misdemeanors as **infractions**. Persons convicted of infractions can only be fined. Because there is no risk of being jailed, the defendant charged with an infraction is not entitled to a jury trial. Parking violations and littering are examples of infractions.

A Question of ETHICS

At one time in our history, there was a single sanction (punishment) for a felony. That sanction was death. Make two columns on a piece of paper and place ethical arguments for such a harsh penalty on one side and arguments against it on the other.

BUSINESS-RELATED CRIMES

WHAT'S YOUR VERDICT?

Officers of six competing cosmetics manufacturers met at a trade convention. All of the officers agreed to use the same wholesale prices. They also agreed to follow the lead of the biggest company in making future price changes. Each officer agreed to promote sales by advertising only within an assigned geographical region.

Were the officers and their companies guilty of any crime?

Like people, businesses are subject to general criminal law. Offenses committed in the business world typically are referred to as **white-collar crimes**. These crimes do not involve force or violence, do not cause injury to people, and do not cause physical damage to property.

Common examples of white-collar crimes are evading income taxes, defrauding consumers, cheating with false weighing machines, conspiring to fix prices, making false fire insurance and auto insurance claims, engaging in false advertising, committing bribery, engaging in political corruption, and embezzling.

Because physical violence is not involved, courts tend to be more lenient with white-collar criminals. Punishments usually include fines or short prison sentences.

In *What's Your Verdict?* the six officers were guilty of violating criminal portions of the antitrust laws. **Antitrust laws** state that competing companies may not cooperate in fixing prices or in dividing sales regions. Antitrust laws require that business firms compete with one another. Some of the more common business-related crimes follow.

LARCENY Larceny (commonly known as *theft*) is the wrongful taking of money or personal property belonging to someone else, with intent to deprive the owner of possession. **Robbery** is a variation of larceny. It is the taking of property from another's person or immediate presence, against the victim's will, by force or by causing fear. **Burglary** is another variation of larceny. It is entering a building without permission when intending to commit a crime. Other types of larceny include shoplifting, pickpocketing, and purse snatching.

Larceny may be either a felony or a misdemeanor. The classification is determined by the value of the property stolen and other circumstances. Robbery and burglary are always felonies. A thief who sells the stolen goods is guilty of the separate crime of selling stolen property.

RECEIVING STOLEN PROPERTY Knowingly receiving stolen property consists of either receiving or buying property known to be stolen, with intent to deprive the rightful owner of the property. One who receives stolen property is known as a *fence*.

FALSE PRETENSES One who obtains money or other property by lying about a past or existing fact is guilty of **false pretenses**. This crime differs from larceny because the victim parts with the property voluntarily. False pretenses is a type of fraud.

FORGERY Forgery is falsely making or materially altering a writing to defraud another. The most common forgeries are found on checks when one signs another's name without permission to do so. Forgery also includes altering a check, such as changing "$7" to "$70" and "Seven" to "Seventy." Forgery is usually a felony. Of course, if others authorize you to sign their names, there is no forgery.

BRIBERY Bribery is unlawfully offering or giving anything of value to influence performance of an official. Soliciting or accepting the bribe is also criminal. In many states, bribing nongovernmental parties is also a form of bribery called *commercial bribery*. Thus, paying a private company's purchasing agent to obtain a sale may be bribery. It is usually bribery when a professional gambler pays an athlete to lose a game intentionally. The federal Foreign Corrupt Practices Act of 1977 prohibits bribery in foreign countries by U.S. companies.

COMPUTER CRIME The computer revolution has created a range of problems for criminal law. For example, larceny is "the wrongful taking of the personal property of others." This traditional definition of the crime made it difficult to prosecute those who steal computer data. Many courts concluded that there was not a "taking" if an intruder merely copied the information in the computer. Even if an intruder copied and erased computer information, some courts concluded that there was no taking of "personal property" but only the loss of electrical impulses which no one really owns. In response, many states have created new criminal laws for computer-related crimes.

EXTORTION Extortion (commonly known as *blackmail*) is obtaining money or other property from a person by wrongful use of force, fear, or the power of office. The extortionist (blackmailer) may threaten to inflict bodily injury. Sometimes the extortionist threatens to expose a secret crime or embarrassing fact if payment is not made.

CONSPIRACY An agreement between two or more persons to commit a crime is called conspiracy. Usually the agreement is secret. The conspiracy is a crime separate from the crime the parties planned to commit. Depending on the circumstances, the crime may be either a felony or a misdemeanor. Business executives of competing corporations sometimes conspire to fix prices or to divide markets.

ARSON Arson is the willful and illegal burning of a building. Arson occurs when someone intentionally starts a fire and burns a structure without the owner's consent. In some states, arson also occurs if you burn your own building to defraud an insurer.

IN THIS CASE

Thompson and two others were convicted of conspiring to smuggle heroin into the United States and planning to distribute the drug. Thompson appealed the conviction. She claimed that no heroin was introduced as evidence to prove that the conspiracy was carried out. Therefore, the accused persons could not be found guilty. The court held that the crime of conspiracy is not dependent on the success of the planned scheme.

THINK ABOUT LEGAL CONCEPTS

Answer the following questions about legal concepts.

1. Legally, a crime is considered an offense against **(a) the victim (b) society (c) the court (d) none of the above.**

2. Which of the following is not an element of a crime? **(a) a duty not to do (or to do) a certain thing (b) an act or omission that fulfills that duty (c) criminal intent (d) all of the above**

3. In many situations, an officer of a corporation will be held criminally liable for the acts of an employee under the doctrine of __?__ .

4. Those charged with infractions are generally not entitled to a jury trial. **True or False?**

5. Which of the following crimes involves the taking of the property of another by force or violence? **(a) burglary (b) robbery (c) embezzlement (d) none of the above**

THINK CRITICALLY ABOUT EVIDENCE

Study the following situations, answer the questions, then prepare arguments to support your answers.

6. Mary received a citation for failing to remove the snow from the sidewalk in front of her dress shop. The fine was $60. Mary thought the citation was unfair because she did not have enough time to shovel the snow. She received the citation five hours after the snowstorm ended. In court she protested and asked for a jury trial. When she was told that the matter would be heard only by a judge, she said her constitutional rights to a trial by jury in criminal matters was being violated. Is she right?

7. Phillips developed a scheme to generate funds by sending bogus bills for a relatively small amount for District Sanitation Services to residents of certain affluent neighborhoods. Enough people paid these bills to make the practice quite profitable. Has Phillips committed a crime? If so, what crime?

8. A corporation was cited and charged with illegal pollution for dumping chemical wastes into a river. The dumping happened when an employee mistakenly opened the wrong valve. The company pleaded not guilty because the dumping was not intentional. Moreover, neither the company nor the employee knew of the ban on dumping this particular chemical. Is either argument a good defense?

GOALS

- Know the rights a person has when arrested
- Recognize a person's potential criminal liability for the actions of others
- Understand the justifiability of the common defenses to criminal charges

RIGHTS AND RESPONSIBILITIES

WHAT'S YOUR VERDICT?

A state law makes "hit-and-run" driving a crime. The law requires drivers of motor vehicles involved in an accident to stay at the scene, give their names and addresses, and show their driver's licenses. Barlow, who was arrested for violating this law, claimed that the law was unconstitutional. He said that the law violated his Fifth Amendment right against self-incrimination.

Is he correct?

One of the major objectives of the Constitution of the United States is to protect individuals from certain actions of the federal government. These constitutional limitations now also apply to state and local governments. The authors of the Constitution believed it was better for our society to give individuals too much liberty than to allow the government too much power. Thus, in this country, people suspected or accused of criminal conduct have rights that are not available in many other countries.

Rights When Arrested

The constitutional right to due process requires fundamental fairness in governmental actions. It requires fair procedures during an investigation and in court. For example, criminal defendants may not be compelled to testify against themselves. They have the right to cross-examine witnesses. Perhaps the most important right is the right of the accused criminal to be represented by a lawyer. For a person who cannot afford to hire a lawyer, a public defender or a private lawyer is provided by the state.

To convict a person of a crime, the evidence must establish guilt with proof beyond a reasonable doubt. This means the vast majority of the evidence (perhaps 90 percent) supports the guilty verdict. Defendants have a constitutional right to a trial by jury. There will be a jury if either the state prosecutor or the defendant requests one. In jury trials, the defendant is usually found guilty only if all the jurors vote to convict.

The rights of accused persons are subject to reasonable limitations. In *What's Your Verdict?* Barlow's right against self-incrimination was not violated by the law that requires one to remain at the scene of the accident and identify oneself. It is true that such actions would indicate involvement and could lead to criminal prosecution. However, the right against self-incrimination applies only to statements that would implicate the person in a crime. Merely identifying oneself as a party to an accident does not in itself indicate guilt.

Responsibility for the Criminal Conduct of Others

A person who aids another in the commission of a crime is also guilty of criminal wrongdoing. For example,

CULTURAL DIVERSITY IN LAW

France

Criminal Procedure

Criminal procedure in France —and most other European countries—is significantly different from criminal procedure in the United States and Great Britain. Many Americans became aware of these differences as a result of the investigation into the death of Diana, Princess of Wales. A few examples of the French system are

- persons accused of crimes are not presumed innocent until proven guilty
- victims and their families can become parties to investigations
- judges take an active role in trials, including examining and cross-examining witnesses
- persons accused of crimes have no protection from self-incrimination and can be compelled to testify
- testimony based on hearsay and opinion is allowed

one who acts as a lookout to warn a burglar of the approach of the police is an accomplice in the burglary. Similarly, one who plans the crime, or otherwise intentionally helps, is guilty of the same crime. In most jurisdictions, if someone is killed during a felony, all accomplices are guilty of the homicide.

As discussed previously in this chapter, corporations can be held vicariously liable for the conduct of their employees. Also, officers of corporations may be criminally liable for their actions as managers.

DEFENSES TO CRIMINAL CHARGES

WHAT'S YOUR VERDICT?

Will and Zack were arrested for possession of cocaine. Both signed confessions at the police station. At their trial, they claimed that their right to due process had been violated. They said they had not been advised of their right to remain silent and to have a lawyer present when questioned.

If true, are those good defenses?

The state must prove that the defendant is guilty beyond a reasonable doubt. But even when it appears this has been done, the defendant may escape criminal liability by subsequently establishing a defense. A **defense** often allows the defendant to escape liability. The defendant must produce the evidence to support any defense. There are two types of defenses: (1) procedural defenses and (2) substantive defenses.

Procedural Defenses

Procedural defenses are based on problems with the way evidence is obtained or the way the accused

person is arrested, questioned, tried, or punished. For example, a defendant who had confessed to a crime might assert the defense that she signed the confession only because she was threatened by the police. This would be a procedural defense.

Ignorance of the law is not a defense. The legal system assumes that everyone knows the law. Thus, if you park in a no-parking area because you did not see the sign, you have no defense.

In *What's Your Verdict?* Will and Zack should have been advised of their rights at the time of the arrest. If they were not so advised, their procedural rights under the Constitution were violated. Such a violation is a valid defense.

Substantive Defenses

Substantive defenses disprove, justify, or excuse the alleged crime. Most substantive defenses discredit the facts that the state sought to establish. For example, an eyewitness may have placed the defendant at the scene of the crime. The defendant may establish a substantive defense by showing that he was in the hospital at the time of the alleged crime. Self-defense, criminal insanity, and immunity are other examples of substantive defenses.

Self-defense is the use of the force that appears to be reasonably necessary to the victim to prevent death, serious bodily harm, rape, or kidnapping. This defense also extends to members of one's family and household and to others whom one has a legal duty to protect. You may not use deadly force if non-deadly force appears reasonably sufficient. Only non-deadly force may be used to protect or recover property. You may not set deadly traps to protect unoccupied buildings. In addition, a civilian may not shoot a thief who is escaping with stolen property.

Criminal insanity generally exists when the accused does not know the difference between right and wrong.

If the accused is criminally insane, there is no criminal intent and therefore no crime. At a trial, the defendant must prove the criminal insanity.

Immunity is freedom from prosecution even when one has committed the crime charged. Sometimes one criminal may be granted immunity in exchange for an agreement to testify about the criminal conduct of several other criminals. In other instances, there is no agreement. Instead, the government grants immunity to a reluctant witness to remove the privilege against self incrimination. A witness who refuses to testify after the grant of immunity is in **contempt of court.** Contempt of court is action that hinders the administration of justice. It is a crime punishable by imprisonment.

PUNISHMENTS FOR CRIMES

WHAT'S YOUR VERDICT?

To conserve water, a city ordinance prohibited the wasteful practice of allowing water to run into the streets and sewers. Gill turned the water sprinklers on in his garden and forgot to turn them off. The water ran into the street all night, making a considerable stream. Gill was cited for violating the ordinance.

What is an appropriate penalty for an offense of this nature?

"Let the punishment fit the crime" is more easily said than done. Any penalty provided by law and imposed by a court is called a **punishment.** The purpose is not to remedy the wrong but rather to discipline the wrongdoer. If reasonably swift and certain, punishment should also deter others from similar behavior.

In *What's Your Verdict?* Gill was guilty of an infraction, which did not require criminal intent. Nevertheless, his conduct was illegal so he would probably be fined. Criminal statutes ordinarily set maximum limits for punishment, but allow a judge discretion within those limits.

An accused person may agree to plead guilty to a less serious crime in exchange for having a more serious charge dropped. This is called **plea bargaining**. The accused voluntarily gives up the right to a public trial to avoid the risk of a greater penalty if convicted.

THINK ABOUT LEGAL CONCEPTS

Answer the following questions about legal concepts.

1. The authors of the Constitution believed it was better for our society to give individuals too much liberty than to allow the government too much power. **True or False?**

2. An individual who helped in a car jacking in which someone was killed by another car jacker can be charged with murder. **True or False?**

3. Which of the following is not a good defense to criminal accusations? **(a) immunity (b) insanity (c) indebtedness (d) all are good defenses**

4. Self-defense is a **(a) procedural defense (b) substantive defense.**

5. Immunity is never granted to someone who has committed the crime. **True or False?**

THINK CRITICALLY ABOUT EVIDENCE

Study the following situations, answer the questions, then prepare arguments to support your answers.

6. Sharon spent the weekend with her friend Amelia. Amelia proposed a plan for shoplifting compact disks (CDs) from a local music store. Sharon was to go to the store clerk, say she felt very ill, then pretend to faint. This distraction would allow Amelia, at the other end of the store, to place CDs in her shopping bag without risk of being seen. At first Sharon said she could not do something like that because it is against the law. Amelia argued that Sharon would not be breaking the law, only Amelia would. Is Amelia right? If a person can think of a way to profit by violating the law without risk, what reasons are there for not breaking the law?

7. Ben and Eric have been friends for years. One day Ben asks Eric to participate in an armed robbery that Ben has been planning. Eric agrees. Ben confides he has robbed several convenience stores recently and has never been caught. Police arrive during the robbery and both men are caught. The prosecutor wants to try Ben for his previous criminal acts but needs Eric's testimony. How would you advise the prosecutor to assure Eric's testifying to convict Ben?

8. Rosa shot a burglar in her home when he was about to enter her bedroom with a knife in his hand. What would be a good defense for her?

9. Art is charged with kidnapping. After listening to all the evidence, 11 of the 12 jurors found him guilty. The twelfth juror voted he was not guilty. Has Art been convicted of the crime?

10. Bob was driving 70 mph when he was pulled over by the state highway patrol. The last speed limit sign Bob had seen said 70 mph. The patrolman admitted that a nearer sign indicating a 55 mph speed limit had been blown down recently. Nonetheless, he wrote Bob a ticket. Why?

As a citizen . . .

1. Study business law carefully. Know which activities are identified as criminal in nature.
2. Never intentionally do something illegal.
3. Never misrepresent a fact to obtain the goods or services of others.
4. Never threaten others with an illegal act to compel them to do something.
5. If arrested, immediately contact a lawyer.
6. Know your rights and make use of them.

PREVENT LEGAL DIFFICULTIES

CHAPTER IN REVIEW

CONCEPTS IN BRIEF

1. A crime is a punishable offense against society. In order to convict, the prosecution must establish a duty, an act or omission in violation of the duty, and, in most cases, criminal intent.

2. Crimes are generally categorized as felonies or misdemeanors. Some states also recognize infractions.

3. Some crimes in which a business may be the victim are robbery, burglary, shoplifting, employee theft, passing bad checks, vandalism, receiving stolen property, and embezzlement.

4. Some crimes in which a business person or firm may be the perpetrator are income tax evasion, price fixing, false advertising, and bribery.

5. Generally, any adult capable of knowing the difference between right and wrong is responsible for his or her crimes.

6. Anyone accused of committing a crime has certain constitutional rights, including freedom from arrest without probable cause; the right to be represented by a lawyer; the right to cross-examine witnesses; the right to not testify against oneself; and the right to a speedy, public, fair trial.

7. Common substantive defenses are self-defense, criminal insanity, and immunity.

8. Crimes are punishable by fine, imprisonment, or both. Some states execute certain criminals.

YOUR LEGAL VOCABULARY

Match each statement with the term that it best defines. Some terms may not be used.

1. Legal position that disproves, justifies, or otherwise excuses an alleged crime
2. Falsely or materially altering a document to defraud another
3. Wrongful taking of another's property from their person or presence by threat of force or violence
4. Punishable offense against society
5. Agreement between two or more persons to commit a crime
6. Willful and illegal burning of a building
7. Crime punishable by either a fine of more than $1,000 or by confinement for more than one year in a state prison or by death
8. Substituted criminal liability
9. Freedom from prosecution even when one has committed the crime charged
10. Improperly obtaining money or other things of value by use of force, fear, or the power of office
11. Obtaining property by lying about a past or existing fact
12. A criminal defense based on how the evidence was obtained or how the accused was arrested, questioned, or tried

antitrust laws
arson
bribery
burglary
conspiracy
contempt of court
crime
defense
embezzlement
extortion
false pretenses
felony
forgery
immunity
infraction
misdemeanor
perjury
plea bargaining
procedural defense
punishment
robbery
self-defense
substantive defense
vicarious criminal liability
white-collar crime

13. Why must crimes be defined in statutory form?

14. Why are certain acts crimes in one state and not another? Why are there varying levels of punishment for the same crime in different states?

15. A prosecutor often does not have enough resources to try all the criminal cases that need to be pursued. What would you recommend be done in such a situation? What is being done?

WRITE ABOUT LEGAL CONCEPTS

16. An old adage of the law states, "As society becomes less secure, criminal punishments become more severe." Write a paragraph relating this to the United States' experience with the death penalty and other punishments in the last few years.

17. **HOT DEBATE** Write a persuasive essay stating why Emily should or should not be punished for her crime of embezzlement.

THINK CRITICALLY ABOUT EVIDENCE

Study the following situations, answer the questions, then prepare arguments to support your answers.

18. There was nothing Lucy wanted more than a stereo sound system. When Harper, an older student, offered to sell her a practically new deluxe system for just $100, Lucy agreed to buy. But then Lucy said, "Hey, how come so cheap?" Harper replied, "Had some happy hunting, and now I've got surplus stock." Later that day, the deal was completed. Has any crime been committed?

19. Buttler, a contractor, ordered $24,600 worth of plywood from K.C. Lumber Company without intending to pay for it. Buttler told the company it was to be used in building houses in a subdivision. When Buttler failed to pay for the plywood, the lumber company investigated. Its investigation revealed that after the plywood was delivered to the building site, Buttler had it transported across the state line, hidden, and resold for cash. A criminal complaint was then filed against Buttler. With what crimes could she be charged?

20. Bif was in Gail's office waiting to go to lunch with her. Gail owned a business in competition with Bif's business. When Gail excused herself to go to the restroom, Bif looked at her computer screen and saw part of a customer list. Bif had a blank diskette which he inserted into the computer. He quickly copied the file onto his diskette. Then he put his diskette in his pocket. The entire action took only 20 seconds. Bif finished long before Gail returned. Has Bif committed a crime? If so, what crime?

21. Paula's boyfriend moved to her home town, Oklahoma City, from Houston, Texas. Two weeks after he arrived, he asked her to phone his bank in Houston and inquire about his balance. She did so as a favor to him and found out the balance was over $40,000. As soon as she told him, he left and drove to Houston to remove it from his account. In Houston, he was arrested by the FBI for fraud and several related crimes. Paula was then charged with the federal crime of making a phone call across state lines for the furtherance of a fraudulent scheme. Her boyfriend only knew the scheme had been successful by the large balance in his old account. What would be a possible defense for Paula?

ANALYZE REAL CASES

22. The Royal Scotsman Inn built a motel that did not comply with the building code. Therefore, Scotsman was refused an occupancy permit. The chair of the county council approached a representative of the motel and offered to have "everything taken care of" in exchange for the payment of $12,000. Scotsman was faced with the possibility of a large loss of revenue. Therefore, Scotsman agreed to pay the money. The Federal Bureau of Investigation arrested the council chairperson after tape recording the discussion and seeing the exchange of the money. What crime did the council chairperson commit? (*United States v. Price,* 507 F.2d 1349)

23. Basic Construction Company was engaged in the road-paving business. Two of its lower-level managers rigged bids by giving competitors the prices that Basic would bid for work. That is a criminal violation of the Sherman Antitrust Act. Will Basic be criminally liable for the conduct of its manager? (*United States v. Basic Construction Company,* 711 F.2d 570)

24. Caesar's Palace is a gambling resort in Las Vegas. Boueri was a vice president there. His job was to act as the host for special, rich guests. As part of his job he would often arrange free airfare to Las Vegas as well as free food and free shows. Evidence was presented in a criminal trial which showed that Boueri also obtained free airline tickets for people who never received them. What crime has Boueri committed? (*State of Nevada v. Boueri,* 672 P.2d 33)

25. Pack was the president of Acme Markets, Inc., a large national retail food chain. Both Pack and Acme were charged with violating criminal provisions of the federal Food, Drug, and Cosmetics Act. They were charged with allowing interstate shipments of food contaminated by rodents in an Acme warehouse. Pack defended himself by stating that although he was aware of the problem, he had delegated responsibility for the sanitary conditions of food storage to responsible subordinates. Can Pack be criminally liable in these circumstances? (*United States v. Pack,* 95 S. Ct. 1903)

26. Feinberg owned a cigar store in a very poor neighborhood of Philadelphia. He sold cans of Sterno, which contains about 4 percent alcohol, to people in the neighborhood who mixed it with water and drank it to become intoxicated. After conducting this business for some time, Feinberg purchased a quantity of Institutional Sterno. It contained 54 percent alcohol. While the cans were marked "Danger," "Poison," and displayed a picture of a skull and crossbones, Feinberg did not warn his customers of the difference between the old Sterno and the Institutional Sterno. As a result, 33 people died from alcohol poisoning. Did Feinberg commit a crime? (*Commonwealth v. Feinberg,* 234 A.2d 913, Pa.)

27. To help attract convention business to the city, a group of hotels, restaurants, and various other businesses in Portland, Oregon, formed an association. The association was funded by contributions. Its members, to provide incentives for contributions to the association, agreed to stop doing or to curtail doing business with those who did not contribute. As a part of this effort, the Portland Hilton Hotel's purchasing agent threatened a Hilton supplier with the loss of the hotel's business unless such a contribution was forthcoming. Such activities and the agreement behind them are criminal violations of the federal antitrust laws. As a consequence, the federal government charged Hilton accordingly and a guilty verdict was returned at Hilton's trial. Hilton appealed, as it had been shown in court that the manager and assistant manager of the hotel had, on at least two occasions, told the purchasing agent not to participate in the boycott. He was instead to follow corporate policy and purchase supplies only on the basis of price, quality, and service. Should the decision be reversed on appeal given the employee's actions were clearly against corporate policy and firsthand directions by corporate executives? (*U.S. v. Hilton Hotels Corporation,* 467 F.2d 1000)

28. When a shopper appeared at her check-out counter with a large box marked chandelier, the clerk asked to see inside it before completing the transaction. In reaction, the shopper turned and pushed his shopping cart back into the store where he abandoned it. It was then discovered that the "chandelier" box contained around $900 worth of various tools that were for sale in the store. The shopper, Khoury, was apprehended and charged with grand larceny. In his defense, Khoury maintained that he could not be guilty of the offense because none of the goods had actually left the store. Is he guilty? Why or why not? (*People v. Khoury,* 166 Cal. Rptr. 705)

Miranda v. Arizona
USSC 86 S. Ct. 1602

BACKGROUND In 1963 a man named Ernesto Miranda, who had previously been described in court records as "seriously disturbed and having pronounced sexual fantasies," was arrested at his home on suspicion of rape and kidnapping. He was then taken to a Phoenix police station.

FACTS At the police station, the suspect was identified by the complaining witness, an eighteen-year-old woman. Thereafter, he was questioned by two officers. He was not advised of his right to have an attorney present at such a questioning. After a lengthy interrogation of approximately two hours, during which time his defense counsel was allegedly demanding to see him but not being allowed to do so, the officers convinced Miranda to sign a confession. The form of the confession as signed by Miranda included a statement that he was making the statement voluntarily and without being coerced by threats or promises of immunity. It also indicated, in a clear, typed paragraph at the top of the statement, to anyone who read it, that the statement was attested to with "full knowledge of my legal rights and the understanding that anything in the statement may be used against me."

LOWER COURT At the jury trial for his crimes, the written confession was placed into evidence over the defense counsel's objection.

Both interrogating officers testified also to the nature of the oral confession Miranda made during the interrogation. Ultimately, Miranda was convicted of the crimes and sentenced to 20 to 30 years imprisonment on each count.

APPEALS Miranda appealed his conviction to the Supreme Court of Arizona. That court upheld the lower court's conviction of Miranda on both counts. The Arizona Supreme Court, in reaching its decision, emphasized that Miranda did not ever even request counsel.

Miranda then took his appeal to the U.S. Supreme Court, alleging that he had not been informed of all his constitutional rights.

ISSUE The U.S. Supreme Court reviewed the matter in order to decide if Miranda could or should be convicted of any crime on the basis of his confession "obtained from defendant during incommunicado interrogation in police-dominated atmosphere, without full warning as to his or her constitutional rights."

DECISION In an opinion written for the U.S. Supreme Court by the then Chief Justice, Earl Warren, the Court decided that the confession was inadmissible as evidence in the trial and reversed the conviction. It also, thereafter, placed the burden on the government to demonstrate that, if the defendant waived his rights, such a waiver was made knowingly and intelligently.

PRACTICE JUDGING

1. If we are all charged with knowing the law, how could the court find that Miranda needed to be informed of his rights by the state?

2. Could Miranda be tried again for the same crime?

3. What justification would the Court have in imposing such a burden on the police? Would they not be practicing law by giving such legal advice?

4. Was excluding the evidence (the confession) the only sanction available to the U.S. Supreme Court? Can you think of some other sanctions that would still allow such evidence to be used but protect the innocent person who might be subjected to such a search?

LESSONS

6-1 OFFENSES AGAINST INDIVIDUALS

6-2 INTENTIONAL TORTS, NEGLIGENCE, AND STRICT LIABILITY

6-3 CIVIL PROCEDURE

HOT DEBATE

Your neighbor Shana is using a multipurpose woodcutting machine in her basement hobby shop. Suddenly, because of a defect in the two-year-old machine, a metal clamp from the machine breaks. The metal strikes Shana's left eye, badly injuring it. The manufacturer had provided a one-year warranty against defects on the machine.

Where Do You Stand?

1. Do you think the manufacturer should be responsible for paying Shana's medical expenses?

2. What defense(s) does the manufacturer have against a suit for damages for her injury?

GOALS

● **Distinguish a crime from a tort**

● **Discuss the elements of a tort**

● **Explain when a person is responsible for another's tort**

HOW DO CRIMES AND TORTS DIFFER?

WHAT'S YOUR VERDICT?

After an exhausting day of skiing, Josephina was driving home near sunset. She dozed off momentarily and crossed the highway dividing lane. She then crashed head-on into John's panel truck. Both drivers were seriously injured, and their vehicles were "totaled."

Although Josephina was asleep at the time, has she violated any rights of the other driver?

A crime is an offense against society. It is a public wrong. A **tort**, in contrast, is a private or civil wrong. It is an offense against an individual. If someone commits a tort, the person injured as a result can sue and obtain a judgment for money damages. The money is intended to compensate for the injury.

One act can be both a tort and a crime. In *What's Your Verdict?* Josephina committed an offense against society—the crime of reckless driving. Police will investigate the crime, then give her a ticket or possibly arrest her. A county or district attorney will prosecute her in a criminal trial. If convicted, she may be fined or jailed.

Josephina also committed a tort by injuring John and his property. John may bring a civil suit against her. If John wins, he can obtain a judgment against her as compensation for his injuries. Thus, Josephina's reckless driving caused her to be liable both criminally and civilly. She is criminally liable because her offense was committed against society. For this she may incur a fine and/or a jail term. She is civilly liable for money damages to John for the injury she caused him and his property.

ELEMENTS OF A TORT

WHAT'S YOUR VERDICT?

On a windy autumn day, Mason was burning dry leaves in his backyard. When he went inside to answer a telephone call, flames from the fire leaped to the next-door neighbor's fence and then to a tool shed where a small can of gasoline exploded. Soon the neighbor's house was ablaze, and it burned to the ground.

Did Mason commit a tort?

Like criminal law, tort law is a broad legal category. Just as there are many specific crimes, there also are many specific torts. Certain elements are common to most torts. In a trial, these elements must be proved to establish liability (legal responsibility). The elements of a tort are

1. duty (a legal obligation to do or not to do something)
2. breach (a violation of the duty)
3. injury (a harm that is recognized by the law)
4. causation (proof that the breach caused the injury)

DUTY By law, we all have certain rights. We also all have the duty to respect the rights of others. This principle has certain related duties. The following are the duties created by tort law:

1. the duty not to injure another (including bodily injury, injury to someone's reputation, or invasion of someone's privacy)

2. the duty not to interfere with the property rights of others, for example, by trespassing on their land

3. the duty not to interfere with the economic rights of others, such as the right to contract

Whether or not a duty exists in a certain situation is a question of law for the judge to decide. A judge will make this decision by consulting state case and statutory law and, on occasion, federal law.

VIOLATION OF THE DUTY A violation (or breach) of the duty must be proved before the injured party can collect damages. Whether a breach of a tort duty has occurred is almost always a question of fact for a jury to decide.

Many torts acknowledge a breach only when the defendant possesses a certain mental state at the time of the breach. Some torts require that the breach be intentional. These are classified as *intentional torts*. In other torts, intent is not required. It is enough if the breach occurred because someone was careless or negligent. These torts, based on carelessness, are classified as *negligence*. In still other torts, even carelessness is not required. Liability is imposed simply because a duty was violated and this caused injury. The last classification, where neither intent nor carelessness is required, is classified as *strict liability*.

INJURY Generally, injury resulting from the breach of duty must be proved. Thus, if you act recklessly, but no one is injured, there is usually no tort.

CAUSATION Causation means that breach of the duty caused the injury. There are degrees of causation. For

example, one can argue that the first people on earth are the ultimate cause of every injury that occurs in the world today. However, when the amount of causation is great enough for it to be recognized by the law, it is called *proximate cause*. Generally, proximate cause exists when it is reasonably foreseeable that a breach of duty will result in an injury.

Applying these elements to *What's Your Verdict?* Mason committed a tort because (1) he owed a duty to the neighbors not to injure their property; (2) he breached the duty when he left the fire unattended so it spread to the neighbor's property; (3) the injury occurred when the neighbor's house was burned; and (4) leaving the fire unattended was a proximate cause of the loss of the fence, the tool shed, and the house. Therefore, the neighbor can obtain a judgment against Mason for the value of the loss.

RESPONSIBILITY FOR THE TORTS OF ANOTHER

WHAT'S YOUR VERDICT?

Hunt was taking riding lessons from Saddleback Stables. Patterson, the Saddleback instructor, was a skilled rider although only 17 years old. Nevertheless, Patterson negligently lost control of the horse that Hunt was riding. As a result, Hunt was thrown to the ground and injured.

Who was liable for Hunt's injuries?

In general, all persons, including minors, are responsible for their conduct and are therefore liable for their torts. Thus, even children or insane persons may be held liable for injuring others. In *What's Your Verdict?* Patterson would be liable to Hunt even though Patterson was only 17 years old.

When one person is liable for the torts of another, the liability is called *vicarious liability*. With some exceptions, parents are not liable for the torts of their children. In some states

parents are liable, by statute, up to a specified amount of money for property damage by their minor children. This is usually designed to cover vandalism and malicious destruction of school property. Most states also provide that parents are liable, up to the limits of financial responsibility laws, for damages negligently caused by their children while operating motor vehicles.

Parents may also be liable if they give their children "dangerous instrumentalities," such as guns, without proper instruction. Similarly, parents may be liable for their children's continuing dangerous habits. For example, if a child continues to throw rocks at trains and vehicles, the parents may be liable if they fail to stop the child's behavior.

The most common example of vicarious liability is the liability of an employer for the acts of employees committed within the scope of the employment. In *What's Your Verdict?* Saddleback Stables was liable for the negligence of its employee Patterson. In such cases, the injured party may sue both employer and employee.

THINK ABOUT LEGAL CONCEPTS

Answer the following questions about legal concepts.

1. A tort is considered to be an offense against society. **True or False?**

2. A single act can be both a tort and a crime. **True or False?**

3. Degree of causation of a tort great enough to be recognized by law is called
   (a) **proximate cause**
   (b) **intimate cause**
   (c) **incidental cause**
   (d) **none of the above**

4. In order to establish liability for a tort, all of the following must be proved except (a) **duty** (b) **breach of duty** (c) **harm recognized by law** (d) **vicarious liability**

5. An insane person cannot be held liable for a tort. **True or False?**

6. When one party is held responsible for the tort of another, the liability is called __?__ liability.

7. Which of the following types of torts are based on carelessness? (a) **intentional torts** (b) **strict liability torts** (c) **negligence** (d) **none of the above**

8. If you act recklessly, but do not harm anyone, there usually is no tort. **True or False?**

9. Parents generally are held liable for the torts of their children. **True or False?**

Study the following situations, answer the questions, then prepare arguments to support your answers.

10. Philip drove a tractor-trailer rig onto a ferry boat. He left the rig in gear because of a problem with its brakes. Posted regulations prohibited the starting of engines before docking, but when the ferry was about 50 feet from the dock, Philip started his engine. That caused the tractor-trailer to jump forward and strike Herrick's car, which in turn hit Patton's car. Patton's car, at the head of the line, crashed through the ferry's barricades and plunged into the water. The car could not be recovered. What was the tort duty in this case? Where was the breach of the duty? What were the injuries? What was the proximate cause of the injury to Patton's car?

11. Felicia carelessly left a campfire before it was completely extinguished. The fire spread through the woods and caused the destruction of the lodge. Is Felicia liable to the owners of the lodge for the building and the surrounding trees? Is she liable to the lodge owners for the loss of income until the lodge can be restored? Is she liable to the persons who had reservations for the lodge but whose trips are now ruined?

12. Todd let his 10-year-old daughter, Julie, drive the family car. While she was driving, she turned her head to say something to her friend in the back seat, and swerved off the road. The car hit and destroyed a mailbox and damaged a fence. Who is liable for the damages to the property?

13. Monica kept a gun in her purse for self-defense because she had to travel through a dangerous section of the city on her way to work. One evening she carelessly left her purse where her son, age six, could reach it. While Monica was making dinner, she heard a shot and found that her son had fired the gun and hit a neighbor child in the leg. Who is liable? Why?

14. Patrick borrowed his friend John's car to impress a young lady he was dating. It was a new luxury car that John had saved four years to purchase. The paint on the car was designed to turn colors under various climatic and light conditions. While on the date, Patrick drove the car down a public road that had just been repaved with hot oil and gravel. The result was several nicks in the paint from flying rocks. Patrick then parked in front of his favorite restaurant, a sports pub on the far side of town. While in the restaurant, Patrick heard a special weather report that a thunderstorm with large hail was sweeping across the area and would arrive over the area of the restaurant in ten minutes. Unfortunately, for John's car, the date was going too well to break off and move the car under cover. Consequently, the hail left a multitude of pock marks on the top of the car. Is Patrick legally responsible for the damage done by the gravel, oil, and hail? Why or why not?

GOALS

● **Identify nine common intentional torts**
● **Define negligence and strict liability**

COMMON INTENTIONAL TORTS

WHAT'S YOUR VERDICT?

During deer-hunting season, Hart drove miles into the country in search of game. He parked his pickup truck along a dirt road, climbed a fence, and hiked into the woods. Hart thought the land was part of a national forest. However, it actually belonged to Quincy, who had posted "No Trespassing" signs. Confronted by Quincy, Hart apologized for his mistake and left.

Was Hart guilty of a tort?

Intentional torts are torts for which the defendant intended either the injury or the act. These torts contrast with negligence and strict liability, where intent to engage in the act or to produce the injury is not required. Specific intentional torts are presented below.

Assault

The tort of **assault** occurs when one person intentionally *threatens to physically or offensively injure another.* The threat can be made with words or gestures. The threat must be believable, so there must be an ability to carry it out. The threatened injury can be physical: a person may raise a fist threatening to punch you. Or the threatened injury can be offensive: a person might threaten unwanted sexual touching by threatening to kiss you.

Battery

A person has a duty to refrain from harmful or offensive touching of another. An intentional breach of the duty is a **battery**. Shooting, pushing in anger, spitting on, or throwing a pie in another's face are all batteries. An assault frequently precedes a battery. Thus, angrily raising a clenched fist and then striking someone in the face involves first an assault (the raised fist) and then a battery (the blow to the face). When the victim is hit without warning from behind, there is a battery without an assault.

Even though there is harmful or offensive touching, there may be no battery if the contact is not inten-

IN THIS CASE

Spencer, elderly and totally blind, thought Wills had swindled him. Spencer told Wills that he was going to "beat your face to a pulp." Because it was obvious that Spencer could not carry out his threat, there was no assault.

tional. Also, the contact may be justified. For example, when you act in self-defense, you have not committed a battery. Further, there may be consent to the contact. Thus, in a boxing match, there is no battery because the boxers consent to the offensive touching.

False Imprisonment

False imprisonment is depriving a person of freedom of movement without the person's consent and without privilege. People may be deprived of freedom of movement in many ways. For example, they may be handcuffed; locked in a room, car, or jail; told in a threatening way to stay in one place; or otherwise deprived of their liberty. Consent occurs when they agree to being confined. For example, when a burglary suspect sits voluntarily in a police car to describe his actions over the last hour, the suspect consents to being detained. If suspects are prevented from leaving when they want to, their consent evaporates.

When the police have probable cause to arrest people, they are privileged to imprison them. Privilege justifies the imprisonment. But if the police mistake the identity of one person for another, they may commit false imprisonment in the course of the arrest. Merchants in many states have a privilege to detain a person if they have a reasonable basis for believing the person was shoplifting. If they detain persons against their will without a reasonable basis, they falsely imprison them.

Defamation

Statements about people can injure them. If a false statement injures one's reputation, it may constitute the tort of **defamation**. If the defamation is spoken, it is slander. If the defamation is written or printed, it is libel. To be legally defamatory, the statement must (1) be false (truth is a complete defense), (2) be communicated to a third person (one's reputation is not harmed if no other person hears or reads the lie), and (3) bring the victim into disrepute, contempt, or ridicule by others.

IN THIS CASE

A news reporter on a radio program announced that an officer of a local corporation had a conflict of interest. The reporter said that a small company secretly owned by the officer was selling goods to the corporation at a high profit to the officer. This was true. Therefore, the news commentator was not guilty of defamation. Truth is a complete defense to a charge of defamation.

An exception to the definition of defamation exists for statements about public officials or prominent personalities. There is no liability in such cases unless the statement was made with *malice*. That means the statement was known to be false when made. This exception is intended to encourage free discussion of issues of public concern. For the same reason, legislators' statements, even those made with malice, are immune from liability if made during legislative meetings. Judges, lawyers, jurors, witnesses, and other parties in judicial proceedings are also immune from liability for statements made during the actual trial or hearing.

Invasion of Privacy

People are entitled to keep personal matters private. This is the right to privacy. Congress has stated that "the right of privacy is a personal and fundamental right protected by the Constitution of the United States." Invasion of this right is the tort of **invasion of privacy**. This tort is defined as the unwelcome and unlawful intrusion into one's private life so as to cause outrage, mental suffering, or humiliation.

This right includes freedom from unnecessary publicity regarding personal matters. So, unlike the law regarding the tort of defamation, publication of even a true statement about someone may be an invasion of privacy. This is because, as the U.S. Supreme Court put it, we should be protected when we have a reasonable "expectation of privacy." Thus, two-way mirrors in the women's restroom of a gas station would constitute an invasion of privacy. The right to privacy also includes freedom from commercial exploitation of one's name, picture, or endorsement without permission. The right to privacy bans illegal eavesdropping by any listening device, interference with telephone calls, and unauthorized opening of letters and telegrams.

However, the right of privacy is not unlimited. For example, the police are permitted to tap telephone lines secretly if they have a warrant to do so. Also, public figures, such as politicians, actors, and people in the news, give up much of their right to privacy when they step into the public domain.

Trespass to Land

The tort of **trespass to land** is entry onto the property of another without the owner's consent. However, trespass may consist of other forms of interference with the possession of property. Dumping rubbish on the land of another or breaking the windows of a neighbor's house are also trespasses.

Intent is required to commit the tort of trespass. However, the only requirement is that the intruder intended to be on the particular property. If a person were thrown onto another's land, there would be no intent and no trespass. If a person thought she was walking on her own property, but was mistaken, there would be a trespass because she intended to be there. Thus, in *What's Your Verdict?* Hart was guilty of trespass, even though he thought he was in a national forest.

Conversion

People who own personal property, such as diamond rings, have the right to control their possession and their use. This right is violated if the property is stolen, destroyed, or used in a manner inconsistent with the

A Question of ETHICS ❓

Angstrom went into a jewelry store and asked to see an expensive ring. The clerk handed it to him. While holding it, he asked the price on a matching necklace. As the clerk looked down to check the tag on the necklace, Angstrom laid the ring out of the clerk's sight behind a display on the counter. He then turned and started to walk out of the store. The clerk, thinking he was stealing the ring, yelled, "stop thief" and with other store personnel, grabbed him and threw him to the floor. When Angstrom was finally able to make the personnel listen, they found the ring and let him go with apologies. Now he is considering bringing suit because of their hasty action. Would it be ethical for him to do so as it appeared to be an honest mistake on the part of the store personnel?

owner's rights. If that happens, a **conversion** occurs. A thief is always a converter.

Conversion occurs even when the converter does not know that there is a conversion. So, the innocent buyer of stolen goods is a converter. The party injured by the conversion can receive damages. Or the converter can, in effect, be compelled to purchase the converted goods from their owner.

Interference With Contractual Relations

Parties to a contract may be able to breach the contract if they pay for the injury suffered by the other party; that is, if they pay damages. But if a third party entices or encourages the breach, that third party may be liable in tort to the nonbreaching party. This is called the tort of **interference with contractual relations**.

Fraud

Fraud occurs when there is an intentional misrepresentation of an existing important fact (that is, a lie). The misrepresentation must be relied on and cause financial injury.

Ordinarily a misstatement of opinion is not considered fraudulent. This is because the hearer should recognize that the statement is the speaker's personal view.

IN THIS CASE

Smith is trying to sell her home. While showing the property to Hernandez, Smith said, "This roof is in very good repair and has never leaked." Hernandez buys the house and later learns that the roof leaks and is in need of repairs costing $8,500. Hernandez also learns that Smith was given an estimate for similar repairs before the sale occurred. Smith committed fraud and is liable to Hernandez.

WHAT IS NEGLIGENCE?

WHAT'S YOUR VERDICT?

Britt was driving home late one rainy night after drinking alcohol all evening. With only one working headlight, she raced down residential streets at speeds up to 50 miles per hour. Meanwhile, Yee was slowly backing her station wagon out of her driveway, but she failed to look both ways when she should have. Britt rammed into the right rear end of Yee's car. Yee's station wagon was badly damaged, and she was injured.

Can Yee collect from Britt?

Negligence is the most common tort. Intent is not required for this tort, only carelessness. Like the other torts, negligence involves the elements of a duty, breach of the duty, causation, and injury.

Duty and Negligence

The general duty imposed by negligence law is the reasonable-person standard. This duty requires that we act with the care, prudence, and good judgment of a reasonable person so as not to cause injury to others.

For certain individuals, a different degree of care is applied. For example, children under age seven are presumed incapable of negligence. Older children are only required to act with the care that a reasonable child of like age, intelligence, and experience would act. If, however, a child undertakes an adult activity, such as driving a boat or a car, the child is held to the adult standard.

Professionals and skilled tradespersons are held to a higher degree of care in their work. These persons are required to work with the degree of care and skill that is normally possessed by members of the profession or trade. Thus, an attorney must act with the care and skill normally possessed by other attorneys in his or her community. Similarly, a plumber must perform work with the care and skill normally exercised by other plumbers in the community.

Breach of Duty in Negligence

The "reasonable-person" standard defines the duty. A defendant's conduct, such as Britt's in *What's Your Verdict?* is compared with the reasonable-person standard to determine whether a violation of the duty has occurred. We could conclude that a reasonable person would drive a car only at a safe speed, only when sober, and at night only when the car's lights work. Because Britt engaged in speeding, driving while intoxicated, and driving at night without proper lights, she clearly violated the reasonable-person standard.

Causation and Injury in Negligence

As with other torts, the violation of the duty must be the proximate cause of the injury. In *What's Your Verdict?* Britt's speeding was a breach of the duty and it is reasonably foreseeable that speeding will cause injury. In fact, speeding was the cause of the property damage to the station wagon and the personal injury to Yee.

Defenses to Negligence

At common law, a plaintiff cannot recover for loss caused by another's negligence if the plaintiff was *contrib-*

IN THIS CASE

Curtis tripped over an electric cord lying across a walkway in Emerson's Electric Shop. As a result of her fall, she suffered a broken hip. The cord was visible, and Curtis would have noticed it if she had not been wearing dark sunglasses indoors. In a legal action, the jury found her damages to be $50,000. But the jury concluded that because her dark glasses prevented her from seeing the cord, she contributed 40 percent of the total negligence. Therefore, the judge deducted $20,000 and awarded Curtis judgment for $30,000.

utorily negligent. This occurs when the plaintiff's own negligence was a partial cause of the injury. For example, in *What's Your Verdict?* Yee backed up without looking behind her. That and Britt's speeding were causes of the accident. So Yee was contributorily negligent. If she lived in a state that recognizes contributory negligence, she could not recover from Britt. Under this legal rule, it does not matter that one party, like Britt, was very negligent and primarily responsible for causing the collision while the other, like Yee, was only slightly negligent.

Most states have substituted *comparative negligence* for contributory negligence. Comparative negligence applies when a plaintiff in a negligence action is partially at fault. Then the plaintiff is awarded damages, but they are reduced in proportion to the plaintiff's negligence. Some states do not allow a plaintiff whose negligence was greater than the defendant's to recover.

Assumption of the risk is another defense to negligence. If plaintiffs are aware of a danger, but decide to subject themselves to the risk, that is a defense. Suppose you walk into a fast-food restaurant and see a sign stating "Danger! This floor is slippery due to mopping." Then, as you walk through the wet area, you slip, fall, and break your arm. The danger was created by the restaurant, but you assumed the risk after being informed of the danger. You could not recover in negligence because of the defense of assumption of the risk.

WHAT IS STRICT LIABILITY?

WHAT'S YOUR VERDICT?

Mrs. Lamm went to a grocery store and placed a carton of a carbonated soft drink in her shopping cart. One of the bottles exploded and the broken glass cut her leg.

Can she collect in tort from the grocery store or the bottler?

Sometimes the law holds one liable in tort on the basis of absolute or **strict liability**. This is liability that exists even though the defendant was not negligent. In essence, strict liability makes the defendant liable if he or she engaged in a particular activity that resulted in injury. In strict liability, proof of both the activity and the injury substitutes for proof of a violation of a duty.

Engaging in abnormally dangerous activities, such as target practice, blasting, crop dusting with dangerous chemicals, or storing flammable liquids in large quantities, gives rise to strict liability. If you engage in activities of this type and someone is injured as a result, you will be liable.

Ownership of dangerous animals also subjects one to strict liability. Domesticated animals (dogs, cats, cows, and horses) are not considered dangerous unless the owner knows that the particular animal has behaved in such a way. Bears, tigers, snakes, elephants, and monkeys are examples of wild or dangerous animals. If the dangerous animal causes injury, the owner is strictly liable.

A third strict liability activity is the sale of goods that are unreasonably dangerous. If the goods are defective,

the defect makes them dangerous. If the defect causes an injury, any merchant who sells those goods is strictly liable, as is the manufacturer.

Under strict liability, the manufacturer and any sellers in the chain of distribution are liable to any buyer of the defective product who is injured by it. The effect of strict liability is that the manufacturer held liable will increase the price and thus spread the cost to all consumers of the product. Without strict liability, the victim might receive no compensation because negligence may be difficult to prove. In *What's Your Verdict?* Mrs. Lamm could collect from either the store or the bottler under strict liability. The bottle was defective, and this defect made the product unreasonably dangerous.

FYI

Product liability laws vary from state to state. Because of this, manufacturers who distribute products across state lines are subject to many different laws.

THINK ABOUT LEGAL CONCEPTS

Answer the following questions about legal concepts.

1. An actual harmful or offensive touching is at the heart of the tort of assault. **True or False?**

2. A person who has consented to be detained by another cannot recover for the tort of false imprisonment. **True or False?**

3. Spoken defamation is **(a) libel (b) liable (c) slander (d) none of the above**

4. An unwelcome and unlawful intrusion into one's personal life so as to cause outrage, mental suffering, or humiliation is the tort of __?__.

5. An innocent buyer of stolen goods cannot be liable for conversion since the buyer had no intent to keep the goods from their rightful owner. **True or False?**

6. Which of the following is not a defense to negligence? **(a) contributory negligence (b) comparative negligence (c) violation of reasonable person standard (d) assumption of risk**

7. Strict liability may exist even when a defendant was not negligent. **True or False?**

THINK CRITICALLY ABOUT EVIDENCE

Study the following situations, answer the questions, then prepare arguments to support your answers.

8. Betty was at a baseball game seated one row behind a famous movie star. When Betty stood up to cheer, she was bumped by the person beside her. She lost her balance and fell into the lap of the movie star. He sued her for the tort of assault. Who prevails?

9. Every morning on the way to work, Sharon rides an elevator up 14 floors. Sometimes, when it is crowded, the elevator operator intentionally touches her in an offensive way. What can Sharon do legally?

10. Ham was a guest in Lane's home. While leaving the house, Ham was injured when she slipped on some ice that had formed on the steps leading from the door. Lane had cautioned Ham about the possibility of the steps being slippery, and Ham admitted seeing the ice. In a legal action claiming negligence, would Lane be liable?

11. Ashleigh has a pet boa constrictor named Pauline. She keeps it in the most expensive, escape-proof cage she can find. Regardless, the boa escapes and kills the neighbor's famed show cat which was valued at more than $5,000. Will Ashleigh be liable?

┌───┐
│   **G O A L S**   │
│   │
│ ● **Discuss what damages are available to victims of torts** │
│ ● **Explain the various stages of a civil suit**   │
└───┘

WHAT CAN A TORT VICTIM COLLECT?

WHAT'S YOUR VERDICT?

Horsley, the owner of a dry cleaning store, lived next door to Early, who was the editor of a small newspaper in their town. The two quarreled frequently and became enemies. As a consequence, when Early published a story on the drug problem in the town, he identified Horsley as "a drug dealer." This statement was untrue and defamatory.

What can Horsley collect from Early?

In some cases, an *injunction* (court order for a person to do or not do a particular act) may be issued to prevent a tort. However, the usual remedy for a tort is damages. **Damages** are a monetary award to the injured party to compensate for loss. The purpose of the award is to place the injured party in the same financial position as if the tort had not occurred. These damages are often referred to as *actual* or *compensatory damages*. However, in many cases, the loss may be difficult to measure. An example is where negligence causes bodily injury with ongoing pain and suffering or even death. Even so, a dollar value of the injury or loss must be set. This value is usually decided by a jury.

When a jury decides the amount of compensatory or actual damages, it is usually requested to consider reimbursing the plaintiff for lost wages, medical bills, and pain and suffering. Lawyers often will handle a civil lawsuit for a percentage of the recovery. This is referred to as taking the case on a *contingency fee* basis rather than being paid by the hour. Common percentages are 25 percent if the case is settled before a trial, 33 percent if the case must be won at trial, and 40 percent or more if the case is won on appeal.

In *What's Your Verdict?* if Horsley could prove that Early's defamation injured her business, she could probably get damages as compensation. If Horsley could prove that Early acted with malice (deliberate intention to cause injury), the jury might award her additional damages referred to as *punitive damages*. These damages would be awarded as punishment for Early's malicious defamation and as an example to deter others.

Punitive damages are always available where an intentional tort has been committed. The damage amount is meant to be set at a figure that would punish the defendant, not compensate the plaintiff. For example, if a large manufacturing company that makes a hundred million dollars in profits a year commits an intentional tort, the punitive damage award could run into the tens of millions. Because of its size, smaller amounts would not punish the company.

HOW IS A CIVIL CASE TRIED?

WHAT'S YOUR VERDICT?

Claxon's car collided with Da Lucia's in an intersection that had four-way stop signs. Claxon's car was badly damaged by Da Lucia's car, so she sued for damages. Claxon claimed Da Lucia was going at least 20 miles per hour and had not stopped, but had merely slowed down, for the sign. Da Lucia claimed he had stopped and had not yet reached five miles per hour. He said he entered the intersection first and Claxon tried to swing around his front end but had failed. Two witnesses saw the accident and could testify.

How can the court determine what really happened?

Judges and juries play different roles in trials. Judges always decide any issues of *law*. The issues of *fact* are left to the jury to decide, if one is sitting. In civil cases, there is not always a right to a trial by jury. Even when there is a right to a civil trial by jury, both the plaintiff and the jury may decide to forgo this right. When there is no jury, the judge decides the issues of both law and fact.

In *What's Your Verdict?* if the parties agreed to waive a jury trial, the judge would listen to the witnesses, including Claxon and Da Lucia, and then decide the issues of fact and law.

Civil juries are composed of 6 to 12 citizens who listen to the witnesses, review physical evidence, and reach their decisions. In most states, decisions in civil trials do not have to be unanimous.

After the jury for a specific case has been selected, the attorneys make opening statements. These opening statements briefly outline what the plaintiff and the defendant will try to prove. The evidence is then presented to the jury, first by the plaintiff and then by the defendant. **Evidence** includes anything that the judge allows to be presented to the jury that helps to prove or disprove the alleged facts. Evidence may consist of written documents, records, charts, weapons, photographs, and other objects.

Testimony is the most common form of evidence. **Testimony** consists of statements made by witnesses under oath. A **witness** is someone who has personal knowledge of the facts. Sometimes an *expert witness* (a witness who possesses superior knowledge about important facts) will give an opinion. For example, an engineer may be an expert witness testifying that skid marks indicate a car was going 70 miles per hour before a collision.

A **subpoena** is a written order by the judge commanding a witness to appear in court to give testimony. Willful, unexpected failure to appear is *contempt of court*. The judge can punish persons guilty of contempt of court by jailing them without a trial.

Following the presentation of the evidence, the attorney for each side gives a closing statement. During closing statements, each attorney summarizes the case, trying to persuade the judge (and the jury if there is one) to favor his or her side. After consultation with the attorneys, the judge then gives instructions to the jury. These instructions tell the jury what rules of law apply to the case.

IN THIS CASE

While waiting for a bus, Charles observed a collision. If there is a suit because of this accident, Charles could be subpoenaed as a witness by either side. Charles would be required to tell, under oath, the truth as to what he observed. If he fails to respond to the subpoena, he could be held in contempt of court, arrested, and jailed.

They also tell the jury what issues of fact they must decide.

For example, in a civil case involving an auto accident, the judge might instruct the jury that exceeding the speed limit in bad weather is negligence (a rule of law). The judge also may tell the jury to decide if the weather was bad at the time of the accident (a question of fact) and whether the defendant was exceeding the speed limit at the time of the accident (a question of fact). The jury then retires to the jury room for secret deliberation. In deciding, each juror must determine whether a preponderance (a majority of at least 51 percent) of the evidence supports the plaintiff's case. In a civil action, a majority vote of the jurors is usually required to find for the plaintiff. The jury's decision is called the **verdict**.

After the verdict has been returned, the judge renders a judgment. The **judgment** is the final result of the trial. It will normally be for a sum of money if the plaintiff wins. If the defendant wins, the judgment will merely be "judgment for the defendant." If either party believes the judge made a mistake, an appeal may be made to a higher court.

Examples of judicial error include incorrect instructions to the jury, admission of evidence that should have been rejected, or exclusion of evidence that should have been admitted. When there has been an error, the appellate court may modify or reverse the judgment of the lower court. Or it may order a new trial. If there is no error in the record, the reviewing court will affirm the judgment of the lower court.

HOW IS A JUDGMENT SATISFIED?

WHAT'S YOUR VERDICT?

Stevens brought a civil suit against Alvarez for breach of contract in building a warehouse. Stevens won a judgment for $35,000. Alvarez objected to the decision. However, she did not appeal because her lawyer told her that there was no basis for appeal. Nevertheless, Alvarez stubbornly refused to pay Stevens.

What steps could Stevens take to collect the judgment?

Ordinarily, when a civil judgment for the plaintiff becomes final, the defendant will pay the judgment. If the defendant does not pay, the plaintiff may obtain a writ of execution. *Execution* here means the process by which a judgment for money is enforced. The court directs that the defendant's property (for example, a savings account or car) be seized or sold. The proceeds, after deducting the costs of seizure and sale, are used to pay the judgment. In *What's Your Verdict?* Stevens could get a writ of execution, because Alvarez refused to pay voluntarily.

Answer the following questions about legal concepts.

1. Damages meant to punish the person who has committed a tort are called compensatory damages. **True or False?**

2. Compensatory damages are also referred to as __?__ damages.

3. A judge never determines a matter of fact. **True or False?**

4. In a civil case, the judge renders a judgment after hearing the jury's **(a) determination (b) resolution (c) verdict (d) none of the above**

5. Seizing a defendant's car to sell it to pay a damage award against him is known as **(a) recovery (b) liquidation (c) execution (d) all of the above**

Study the following situations, answer the questions, then prepare arguments to support your answers.

6. Stone had secretly criticized the large chemical company she worked for over a span of several years. Her inside information had led to many accurate stories in the local papers about toxic releases into the environment. Finally, the company discovered what she was doing and hired two thugs to rough her up. They did a very thorough job, and she had to be hospitalized for several weeks. Because she immediately reported her beating to the police, the thugs were captured. In a plea bargain with the prosecutor, they confessed who had hired them. Stone brought suit against the chemical company. For what types of damages could she sue? Why?

7. Stone lost $7,000 in wages and owed $22,000 in medical bills as a result of the beating in exercise 6. She had sustained a concussion and had a broken leg with numerous lacerations and abrasions. Thereafter, she consistently walked with a limp. The chemical company averaged $72 million in profits over the last five years. What damage award for each type of damages you selected in exercise 6 would be appropriate. Why?

8. Because the evidence against it was overwhelming, the chemical company decides to settle the case out of court for $16 million. What would be a typical attorney's contingency fee percentage share of this amount? If the case had to be won at trial and $20 million was awarded by the jury, how much would Stone's attorneys receive under a typical fee arrangement? If the chemical company appealed but lost, what would be Stone's typical attorney's share of the $20 million?

As a citizen . . .

PREVENT LEGAL DIFFICULTIES

1. Avoid legal liability for torts by consistently respecting other persons and their property.

2. If you commit a tort or are the victim of a tort that may lead to a lawsuit, promptly consult a lawyer. Critical evidence may be lost if you delay.

3. In some states, your own negligence, however slight, may bar any recovery under the doctrine of contributory negligence. However, in many states, the doctrine of comparative negligence may permit recovery.

Check with your lawyer.

4. If you injure a third party while on the job, both you and your employer may be liable. The employer, or an insurer, would probably pay, but the incident could cost you your job.

5. The automobile is the principal source of tort liability for most persons, young and old. Drive carefully.

6. If you are injured as the result of a tort, do not be rushed by insurance adjusters or others into signing a statement releasing the other party from liability. Let your lawyer decide if the settlement offer is fair.

CHAPTER IN REVIEW

CONCEPTS IN BRIEF

1. A tort is an unlawful act that causes private injury to the person or property of another. Most crimes are also torts, but not all torts are crimes.

2. Torts may be broadly classified as intentional torts, negligence, or strict liability. The most common tort is negligence, or the failure to act with reasonable care, thus causing a foreseeable injury to another.

3. In a tort caused by negligence, the negligent act (or failure to act) must be the proximate cause of the injury. That is, the injury must follow as a natural and reasonably foreseeable effect of the act (or failure to act).

4. Generally every individual is personally responsible for damage resulting from any torts committed by that individual. Employers are also liable for the torts of their employees if the torts are committed within the scope of the employees' employment.

5. In some states, if the injured person was also negligent and the negligence contributed to the injury, the injured person may be barred from recovering damages. In many states today, however, some recovery may be obtained under the doctrine of comparative negligence.

6. A person injured by a tort is entitled to damages—monetary compensation for the loss or injury suffered. The amount of damages is typically determined by the jury.

YOUR LEGAL VOCABULARY

Match each statement with the term that it best defines. Some terms may not be used.

1. Person who gives testimony

2. Deprivation of freedom of movement without consent or privilege

3. Intrusion into the private lives of others

4. Using property in a manner that is inconsistent with its owner's rights

5. The most common tort

6. False statement that injures a person's reputation

7. Intentionally made threat to physically or offensively injure another

8. Harmful or offensive touching

9. Written court order compelling a person to appear in court and to testify

10. Materials or statements presented in a trial to prove or disprove alleged facts

11. A monetary award to compensate for the loss caused by a tort

12. Intentional misrepresentation of an existing important fact, reliance upon which causes financial injury

13. Final result of a trial

14. Jury's decision in a case

assault
battery
conversion
damages
defamation
evidence
false imprisonment
fraud
intentional tort
interference with con-
    tractual relations
invasion of privacy
judgment
negligence
strict liability
subpoena
testimony
tort
trespass to land
verdict
witness

15. If certain acts are both crimes and torts, why couldn't we let the prosecutor both bring criminal charges against the defendant and bring suit for damages for the victim at the same time?

16. In most cases, in order to recover damages for emotional harm, a person must also show a physical harm. Why would society want to establish an additional barrier to someone who has been harmed by the commission of a tort?

17. Other countries with common law systems do not require a showing of malice in order for a public figure to recover against someone for defamation. Why do we have such a requirement in our laws?

18. Should the U.S. Supreme Court acknowledge that there is an "expectation of privacy" when a citizen is using a public restroom? Why or why not?

WRITE ABOUT LEGAL CONCEPTS

19. Some of the biggest damage awards have come from adding punitive damage amounts to actual damage figures. What purpose do such large awards serve?

20. **HOT DEBATE** Assume you are the manufacturer of the woodcutting machine. Write a letter to Shana stating the reasons why it will or will not pay her medical expenses.

THINK CRITICALLY ABOUT EVIDENCE

Study the following situations, answer the questions, then prepare arguments to support your answers.

21. Suppose you were involved in an accident where you scratched the fender of a parked car and no one saw what you had done. The law requires that you leave a note on the damaged car identifying yourself. If you were certain you could just drive away without anyone knowing what had happened, would you do it? What reasons can you state for the action you would take?

22. McDonald and Beck were sitting in a bar watching a professional football game. When they discovered they were rooting for opposing teams, Beck hit McDonald in the face, breaking McDonald's glasses and nose. McDonald called the police, who arrested Beck. Does McDonald have any legal claims against Beck?

23. Jackson was a lawyer, respected by his peers. He successfully represented several persons who were charged with income tax evasion. All three defendants were reputed to be leaders of an organized crime syndicate. The local newspaper then printed an editorial calling for the tightening of tax laws "to protect society against mobsters and shyster lawyers like Jackson who would sell their souls to the devil for 30 pieces of silver." Was this statement a tort?

24. Yardly and Whiple, ages 12 and 13, intentionally threw stones which smashed 57 windows in an old warehouse. The warehouse had been standing vacant for nine months. Yardly and Whiple were caught and disciplined by the juvenile court. Then the owner of the warehouse sued them and their parents for damages. The girls said they were "just having fun and not hurting anyone because the place was empty." Who, if anyone, is liable and why?

ANALYZE
REAL CASES

25. Town Finance Corporation (TFC) foreclosed on a mortgage following a dispute with Hughes as to whether a loan had been repaid. TFC had a locksmith remove the locks of Hughes' dwelling. When no one was home, TFC personnel then entered the house, seized household goods, and left the inside of the house in disarray. Hughes filed suit over the debt. The court held that the finance company had been paid and thus had no further right of action against Hughes. Hughes thereupon filed this action, which claimed malicious and willful trespass and asked both actual (compensatory) and punitive damages. Was Hughes entitled to judgment? (*Town Finance Corporation v. Hughes*, 214 S.E.2d 387)

26. Lewis, an undercover police officer carrying a concealed pistol, went shopping in a Dayton Hudson department store. There, a security officer became suspicious that he was a shoplifter. Lewis took some clothing into a fitting room, where there were signs stating, "This area is under surveillance by Hudson's personnel." In fact, the security guard observed Lewis from a grille in the ceiling. After he saw Lewis place the gun on a chair, he called the police. Eventually, Lewis was identified as an undercover officer. But he sued Dayton Hudson claiming that the spying in the fitting room was an invasion of his privacy. Will he recover? (*Lewis v. Dayton Hudson Corporation*, 128 Mich. App. 165)

27. A train stopped at the defendant's railroad platform. As it started up again, a man carrying a small package jumped aboard. He appeared unsteady and about to fall. Therefore a guard on the train, holding the door open, reached out to help him. Another guard, standing on the platform, pushed the man from behind. The man made it onto the train, but he dropped the package, which was about fifteen inches long. The package was wrapped in newspaper and contained fireworks that exploded when the package hit the rails. The shock of the explosion caused several scales at the other end of the platform, many feet away, to fall down. As they fell, they struck the plaintiff, injuring her. She sued the railroad, claiming the guards were negligent. Is the railroad liable? (*Palsgraf v. Long Island Railroad Company*, 162 N.E. 99, N.Y.)

28. An operator of a piece of earth-moving equipment was severely injured when his left pants leg caught between the rotating drums of the clutch, pulling his leg through the drums. The operator and his wife sued the manufacturer, claiming there was a defect in the design of the vehicle. They also claimed that the manufacturer knew of this defect. The evidence showed that a perforated guard was installed on the right side but not on the left. The evidence also showed that if there had been a guard on the left side, the accident would not have occurred. Should the operator be awarded damages? (*Carpenter v. Koehring Company*, 391 F. Supp. 206)

29. David Allen, age two, was attacked and severely bitten in the face and ear by a dog owned by Joseph Whitehead. Whitehead admitted that the dog barked frequently, was large, looked mean, and chased cars. On the other hand, no one had ever complained about the dog, it had never bitten anyone before, and it frequently played with other children. Is Whitehead liable for the injuries to David? (*Allen v. Whitehead*, 423 So. 2d 835, Ala.)

30. To get to the driveway of a service station, Nga Li attempted to make a left-hand turn across three lanes of traffic. In so doing she pulled into the path of an oncoming Yellow Taxi cab driven by Robert Phillips. Li's car was struck broadside by the cab and she was injured. When she sued the Yellow Cab Company, the evidence in the case led the jury to find that the cab's driver was negligent for driving so fast as to be unsafe under the conditions of travel at the time. However, the jury found that Li, in making her lefthand turn, also was negligent because her turn was made "at a time when a vehicle was approaching from the opposite direction so close as to constitute an immediate hazard." In a state using the doctrine of contributory negligence, would Li be awarded damages for her injuries? In a state using the doctrine of contributory negligence, would she receive a damage award? Which doctrine do you favor applying in this instance? Which doctrine seems fairer overall? (*Li v. Yellow Cab Company of California*, 532 P.2d 1226)

Nader v. General Motors
New York State Court of Appeals 255 N.E.2d 765

FACTS In the mid 1960s, Ralph Nader became famous as a consumer crusader. His fame was initially based on the writing of his book that alleged serious problems with the Chevrolet Corvair. The Corvair was a General Motors car. The title of the book conveys its nature: *Unsafe at Any Speed.*

SUIT Several years later, much to the shock of the nation, Nader brought suit against General Motors for invasion of his privacy. The case was filed in New York State Court but subsequently appealed to the highest court of that state, the Court of Appeals.

The Court of Appeals was called upon to determine which of the claims in his complaint to the court with original jurisdiction might be actionable as invasions of privacy. In other words, the Court had to decide which, if any, of the claims Nader might be able to present evidence about and possibly recover for in a subsequent trial.

CLAIMS The *claims* that Nader made were as follows:

1. That General Motors had tried to entrap him into an illicit relationship with several women in their hire.

2. That people hired by GM had conducted numerous interviews with Nader's friends about his viewpoints and had indicated that his views, sexual orientation, and personal habits were improper.

3. That GM's sleuths had watched him closely in public places for extended and unreasonable periods of time.

4. That people hired by GM had made harassing phone calls to him.

5. That GM had tapped his phone and eavesdropped on his private conversations.

6. That GM had conducted an extended investigation of him.

PRACTICE JUDGING

1. Consider each of these claims. Which ones do you think the New York Court of Appeals found actionable? Why and why not?

2. Consider the ways in which the protection of the right of privacy might have to expand given the various additional communication patterns we use in today's world. What guideline(s) would you use to select among the types of communications (fax, e-mail, cellular phone, cordless home phone, etc.) that should be protected?

ENTREPRENEURS AND THE LAW

PROJECT 1 LAW, JUSTICE, AND YOU

THE IDEA

Ben Windows worked as a machinist for Rebuilt Inc. Rebuilt manufactured heavy machinery. The company recruited Ben based on his class standing and some strong recommendations from instructors at the local technical school. Rebuilt was aware that Ben had served more than six months in jail as an adult for a string of burglaries he committed at age 17. Ben had two years to go on his parole. At Rebuilt Ben's mind was put to a legitimate purpose.

The idea arose from an OSHA (Occupational Safety and Health Administration) requirement for protective shields on the machine presses. No one at Rebuilt liked the shields. They were cumbersome and added 30 to 40 percent more time to each project. In fact, Rebuilt managers never ordered anyone to put the shields in place, except when OSHA inspectors visited the plant. Ben designed a rotating shield positioner that extended upwards from the central post of a press and suspended the shield from above. It would allow the machinist complete freedom of movement and solve OSHA's safety concerns.

THE PROTOTYPE

Ben made the prototype device in the basement of his rented suburban home. Only Kristen Stacy, Ben's classmate at the technical school, knew about his idea. And no one but Kristen had seen the prototype. Kristen now worked as a paralegal for a local law firm that specialized in invention development and production. She was impressed with the invention. Kristen told Ben she would review some of the cases her firm had handled and prepare a list of legal issues he would need to deal with in order to market the device.

Ben created a one-man assembly line in his basement. In less than a week he turned out 26 more devices. Ben named his invention the "Reelshield," because the shield positioning arm reminded him of a fishing reel. He bought some boxes and packaged all but two of the Reelshields, stamping each box with the "Reelshield" name. Ben loaded ten of the boxes into his pickup and was preparing to drive to Rebuilt and a couple of other machine shops to sell them. Then Kristen called. She had a few questions for him based on what she had found in reviewing her law firm's cases.

Divide into teams and perform one or more of the following activities, as directed by your teacher.

ROLE-PLAY

One condition of Ben's parole was that he be employed. Role-play a meeting between Ben, Ben's parole officer, Ben's machine shop instructor, Rebuilt's human resources director, and various other Rebuilt managers. This meeting is a follow-up to the job interview Ben had with the human resources director, which had gone quite well. In the role-play meeting, Ben, his parole officer, and instructor present evidence to convince Rebuilt managers to hire him.

RESEARCH

Prepare the list of questions that Kristen has for Ben on the legal issues he will need to deal with and the actions he will need to take to market his invention. Use this textbook and its table of contents as your information resource. Each team member should choose a different unit of the book and prepare questions that relate to that unit.

PRESENT

After all questions are prepared, team members will present their questions to the team. The team should discuss each question and decide which questions should go on the team list. After all teams have their list of questions prepared, each team will present its list to the class.

UNIT TWO

FUNDAMENTALS OF CONTRACTS

ENTREPRENEURS AND THE LAW
SEE PAGE 210

Gail Hallock, currently executive secretary to the Legal Council for a large HMO, embraces the philosophy that "every person today, no matter what their age, faith, financial status, religious belief, or physical limitations, has the opportunity to achieve their dreams . . . their career choice."

When Gail graduated from high school in 1963, her parents could not afford to send her to college. Instead of allowing this to discourage her, she obtained a student loan and completed three semesters of Business Administration before leaving school to get married.

Gail first used her education and people skills during her job as a clerk typist at a local manufacturing company. Through her employer, she continued her education by attending local seminars and night classes at a local community college.

With her ongoing education, Gail has had the opportunity to work in manufacturing, engineering, finance, human resources, office administration, and most recently, as a Legal Executive Secretary. Her experience includes working with Fortune 500 companies and their presidents, departmental positions and work groups within those companies. She has even worked for the U.S. Army in Saudi Arabia.

"I believe you should never limit your opportunities or choices. I never thought I would leave the town I was born and raised in, let alone live abroad and work for presidents of major companies. But I had the drive to follow my dreams and not get discouraged along the way."

As a legal secretary, Gail coordinates and assists with analyzing contracts. Gail considers the following skills necessary for success in her field: ability to analyze complex docu-

ments and customer problems, strong interpersonal skills, excellent written and oral communication skills, attention to detail, ability to assess needs and develop strategies to meet those needs, ability to train new employees and develop procedures to simplify workflow, computer, organization, and meeting coordination skills. "As a secretary you are the right hand for your boss and need to step in to assist however and whenever needed. I once was even asked to assist in managing a billion dollar building project at this HMO. Goes to show you that as a secretary you have diverse, challenging assignments."

Gail suggests that anyone interested in a career as an executive legal secretary should register for an Introduction to Paralegal course at a local community college. "This course gives you an overview of all the opportunities available as a paralegal." Gail points out that a paralegal need not be limited to a legal office environment. Positions are available in local and state government, public service companies, and large businesses such as the HMO for whom Gail works.

Gail explains that you will need 30 credit hours in order to become a paralegal. In order to become certified in Gail's state you are required to have 60 credit hours or five years of law office experience in addition to 30 credit hours.

> **❝** I believe you should never limit your opportunities or choices. I never thought I would leave the town I was born and raised in, let alone live abroad and work for presidents of major companies. **❞**

Gail's best advice: do not limit your choices, test the waters, and complete a summer internship program. With ongoing education, hard work, and an excellent work record, you can fulfill your dreams.

OFFER AND ACCEPTANCE

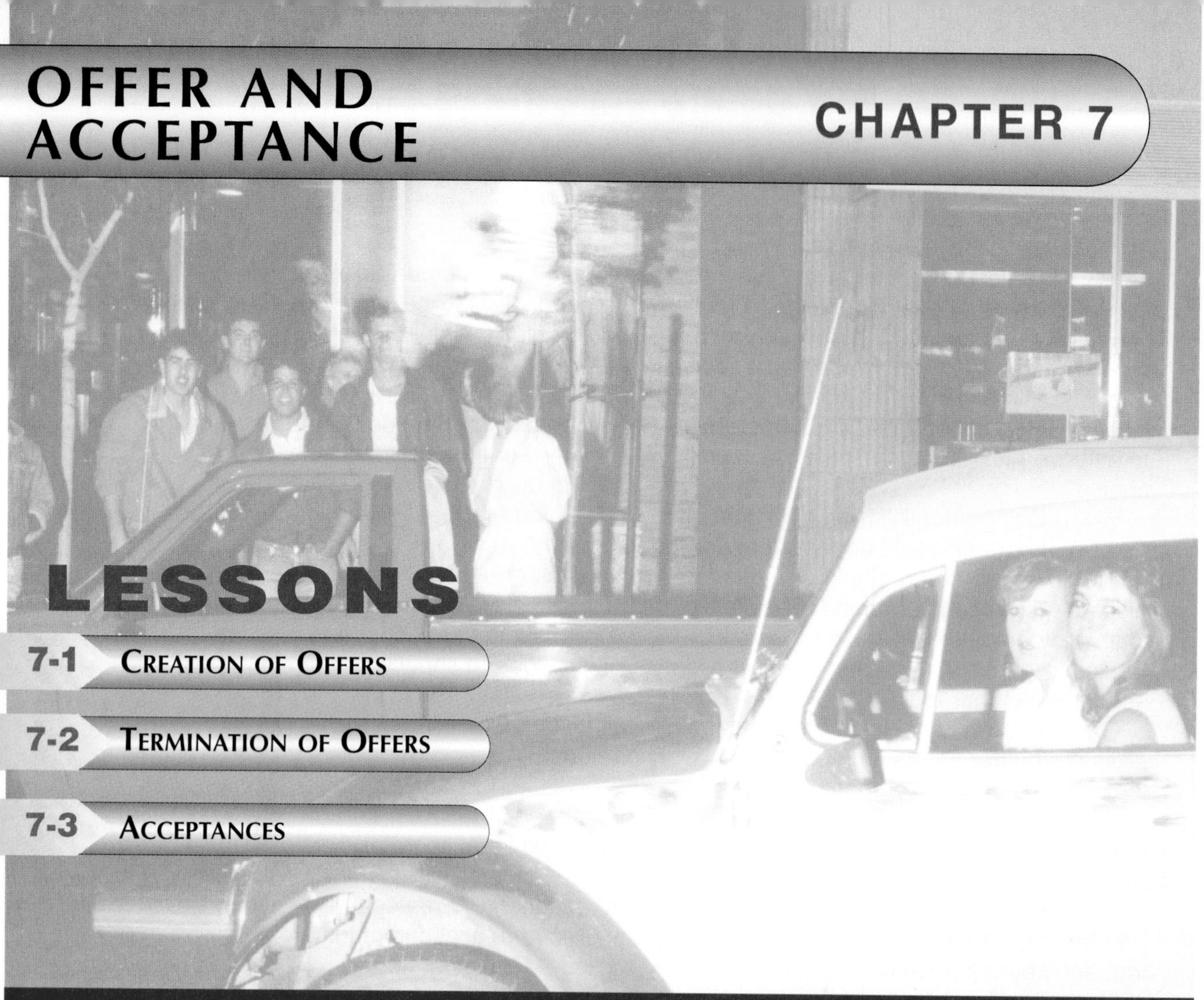

CHAPTER 7

LESSONS

7-1 CREATION OF OFFERS

7-2 TERMINATION OF OFFERS

7-3 ACCEPTANCES

HOT DEBATE

Celia had worked after school since she was 14 to save money for a car. When she turned 18, she bought a VW. Two weeks later she was driving a group of friends to school. The car stalled at a stop light and people behind her began honking. Celia became frustrated when the car wouldn't start and said, "I'll sell this thing for $300 right now!" Joan gathered three hundred dollars from her purse and handed it to Celia stating, "I accept, here's your money."

Where Do You Stand?

1. Should Celia be bound because the literal meaning of her words suggests she intended to sell the car?

2. Should Celia not be bound to sell the car because the circumstances (new car stalls and people are honking) suggest that she did not intend to sell?

● **List the elements required to form a contract**

● **Describe the requirements of an offer**

WHAT IS A CONTRACT?

WHAT'S YOUR VERDICT?

Pedro and Seamus were chatting during the break between classes. "Remember 'Great Moments in Sports', the video that I showed you last week?" asked Pedro. "You thought it was great and said you wished it was yours. I'll let you have it for fifteen bucks. Want it?" "Sure!" Seamus answered. "Bring it to school tomorrow, okay?"

Did the two friends create a contract?

A **contract** is an agreement that courts will enforce. Contracts between two parties are the basis for all economic activity. They are the legal links between the individuals and companies producing and consuming goods and services.

There are six major requirements that must be satisfied before courts will treat transactions as contracts. These requirements are

1. *Offer and Acceptance* There must be a serious, definite offer to contract. The terms of the offer must be accepted by the party to whom it was communicated.

2. *Genuine Assent* The agreement (offer and acceptance) must not be based on one party's deceiving another, on an important mistake, or on the use of unfair pressure exerted to obtain the offer or acceptance.

3. *Legality* What the parties agree to must be legal. So an agreement to pay someone to commit a crime or tort cannot be a contract.

4. *Consideration* The agreement must involve both sides receiving something of legal value as a result of the transaction.

5. *Capacity* To have a completely enforceable agreement, the parties must be able to contract for

themselves rather than being obligated to use parents or legal representatives.

6. *Writing* Some agreements must be placed in writing to be fully enforceable in court.

Contracts frequently result from the exchange of valuable promises. For example, a couple may want their home painted. Suppose a painter measures the exterior of their house and promises to paint the house within 30 days for $3,000. This is the offer. If the couple agrees to the time frame and the $3,000, this is the acceptance.

The painter is the **offeror**. He communicated a serious, definite proposal to the couple. The couple are **offerees** (persons to whom the offer is made). Without both offer and acceptance on mutually agreed terms, there is no contract. No particular language need be used.

In *What's Your Verdict?* Pedro and Seamus made a contract, even though delivery and payment will occur later.

REQUIREMENTS OF AN OFFER

An **offer** is a proposal by an offeror to do something, provided the offeree does something in return. If the offeree accepts the proposal, a contract arises. Generally, to create a valid offer

1. the offeror must appear to intend to create a legal obligation
2. the terms must be definite and complete
3. the offer must be communicated to the offeree

Expression of Intent to Create a Legal Obligation

The law will only recognize that an offer exists when the offeror *appears* serious about creating a legal obligation.

TEST OF THE REASONABLE PERSON The law is not concerned with what is actually in the mind of a person making a purported offer. Rather, it is concerned with the *appearance* of this person. So if you think you are joking, but a reasonable person would *interpret your conduct* as indicating that you intend to contract, you have made an offer. On the other hand if you are serious, but a reasonable person would interpret your conduct as a joke, then no offer is made. This is called the **test of the reasonable person**. It is an objective legal test used by jurors or judges rather than a subjective test based on what you say you were thinking. Businesses and

the law need a consistent way to determine when an offer is made. A subjective test would let people escape contractual responsibilities by lying about what they were thinking.

FACTS AND CIRCUMSTANCES The test of the reasonable person examines the offeror's words and conduct in light of all the relevant *facts and circumstances*. The words themselves may indicate an offer, but a reasonable person would disregard them because of the facts and circumstances under which they were spoken. When a teacher says to a business law class, "I offer to sell you my new car for $3,000," this probably isn't an offer but an example. Words spoken in obvious jest, frenzied terror, or anger would not be offers if a reasonable listener would realize that no offer was intended.

PRELIMINARY NEGOTIATIONS Information is often communicated without indicating an intent to contract. So, you might casually say, "Would you take $800 for that laptop computer?" You are probably trying to determine whether the other party is interested in selling and the ballpark price. This contrasts with an offer which might take the form, "Look Jeff, I'll give you $800 today for your laptop computer. Do you agree to my deal?" Sometimes one party states tentative terms, inviting others to make offers. If Jeff says, "I think I'm interested in selling

my laptop computer for around $1,000. Is anybody interested?"—this is not an offer to sell.

SOCIAL AGREEMENTS If two friends agree to go to the movies, no contract is intended. The friends don't think of this agreement as creating legal obligations. If either breaks the date, the other may be offended but cannot win a suit for breach of contract. Social arrangements do not create legal obligations.

Offer Must Be Complete and Clear

The terms of an offer must be sufficiently complete and clear to allow a court to determine what the parties intended and identify the parties' legal rights and duties.

COMPLETE If a purported offer is missing *essential* information, it is incomplete and legally ineffective. Nearly all offers must identify the price, subject matter, and quantity, either directly or indirectly.

The amount of information which is essential depends upon the complexity of the transaction. In most

IN THIS CASE

The Delgados agreed to buy and Oaknoll, Inc., agreed to sell one lot from among the 200 in a large suburban subdivision. Using their credit card, the Delgados paid $1,000 as a down payment and were given a receipt. The lots shown on the preliminary subdivision plan were of various sizes, shapes, and prices, but no particular lot was specified in the agreement. Because of this, an essential term was missing, and therefore no contract arose.

states the essential terms for the sale of real estate lots would include: (1) identity of the specific lot, (2) price, (3) full terms for payment, (4) date for delivery of possession, and (5) date for delivery of the deed. If one of those terms were missing there would not be a valid offer. In contrast, an offer for the sale of a candy bar by the local market typically identifies price, subject matter, and quantity (as many as are on the shelf). This is a valid offer.

CLEAR Each essential term must be identified clearly. The Delgados agreed on "one lot" but they didn't specify which lot. Therefore, although the offer touched on the essential term, it did not identify it clearly or definitely enough for courts to enforce an agreement.

IMPLIED TERMS In some contracts, a term might be implied by law or common business practice. For example, in contracts between merchants for the sale of goods, when the price is not specified, current market price is the basis for the contract.

ADVERTISEMENTS Advertisements in newspapers and magazines, on radio or television, or in direct mailings are generally not offers. Instead, courts treat them as *invitations* to customers to make offers. This is primarily because a person who advertises something for sale has a limited stock and cannot be expected to sell to the many thousands who theoretically might reply to the advertisement.

In *What's Your Verdict?* Anchors Aweigh advertised boats. When would-be buyers tendered (presented for acceptance) the purchase price of the cabin cruiser, the would-be buyers were the ones making an offer. Thus, Anchors Aweigh was not bound by contract to the seven would-be buyers who came to purchase the boats after they were out of stock. To promote good customer relations, businesses try to deliver advertised merchandise to all who

want to buy. Statutes prohibit false or misleading advertising.

Advertisements may occasionally be offers. This can occur in one of two ways. First, the ad must be clearly worded in ways that address the problem of numerous people receiving the ad for a limited amount of product. Someone selling a car could create an offer by writing a complete and clear ad, and in addition, writing that the car will be sold only to the first person to accept the terms contained in the offer. Or an ad may state "subject to stock on hand."

Second, an ad may become an offer if it asks the offeree to perform an act as a way of accepting. An ad which states that a clearly described new power lawnmower will be sold for $20 "to the first person to appear at the main door of a shopping mall on Saturday morning after 6:00 A.M." will be a valid offer.

Offer Must Be Communicated to the Offeree

A person who is not the intended offeree cannot accept the offer. Nor can a person accept an offer without knowing it has been made. That is because any action taken would not have been a response to the offer. Thus, an offer of a reward that is

made to certain persons or even to the general public cannot be accepted by someone who has never seen or heard of the offer. In such cases, the offeror may get what was sought, but most courts require that anyone who claims the reward must have known of the offer and acted in response to it when performing the requested act.

A Question of ETHICS

Sarah was talking with four friends at the entrance to their community college. When a bell called them to class, she absent-mindedly left her backpack behind. It contained a pocket calculator, her driver's license, and other items of value only to her. After class, she posted an ad on a student bulletin board, offering $25 to whoever returned her pack. Major, another student, had not seen the advertisement but he found the bag and returned it to Sarah. Is Major legally entitled to the reward? Is Sarah ethically obliged to give him the reward?

Answer the following questions about legal concepts.

1. If you don't satisfy the law's requirement for creating an offer, then you usually don't have a contract. **True or False?**

2. To be valid, an offer must indicate an intent to create a legal obligation. **True or False?**

3. Which of the following are reasons why an offer may not be valid? **(a) It is apparent that the speaker is joking. (b) It is clear that the speaker is trying to obtain additional information rather than commit to an agreement. (c) The subject of the agreement is only social. (d) all of the above**

4. The requirement that an offeror show an intent to contract is a(n) __?__ test rather than a test which focuses on the purported offeror's actual thoughts. *objective*

5. Which of the following is evidence showing an intent to contract? **(a) spoken or written words (b) conduct other than speaking or writing (c) other facts and circumstances (d) all of the above**

6. Advertisements can be offers when **(a) they are complete (b) they are clear (c) they address the problem of numerous recipients and a limited supply of the advertised product (d) all the above**

7. If an offer is made, it can be accepted by anyone who learns of it. **True or False?**

8. The test of the reasonable person is used by a jury or judge to evaluate all the relevant evidence to determine whether there has been a manifestation of an intent to contract. **True or False?**

9. To meet the contract requirement of genuine assent, the agreement must not be based on **(a) deception (b) an important mistake (c) using unfair pressure (d) all of the above.**

Study the following situations, answer the questions, then prepare arguments to support your answers.

10. The owner of a small color television set offers to sell it to a neighbor for $75. As the neighbor stands there thinking about the offer, a bystander says, "That's a bargain. I'll take it!" Is there a contract between the bystander and the owner?

11. Bill spent most of his month's allowance for expensive tickets to a rock concert after Lorene said she would go with him. On the morning of the event, Lorene phoned and said she was terribly sorry, but Tony, the high school's star fullback, had also asked her to go and she "just couldn't say no." Did she breach a contract? Could Tony be held legally liable if he knew Lorene had already promised to go with Bill? Was Lorene's conduct ethical? If Tony knew Lorene had already promised Bill she'd go with him, was Tony's conduct ethical?

12. The Nationwide Credit Union agreed to allow Heidi to borrow up to $10,000. Nothing was specified as to the length of the agreement, the rate of interest the credit union would charge, or the terms of repaying any loan. The credit union did not make a loan of $8,000 to Heidi when she requested it four years later. Is the credit union liable for breach of contract?

13. G. Whiz Sports Shop published this advertisement in the local newspaper: "Congratulations to the winners of the Tour de France! Now YOU TOO can be a champ! Get an 18-speed Blue Lightning bicycle for only $1,295—marked down from $1,795, the manufacturer's suggested retail price. What a bargain! Come and get it!" Baxter visited the discount store the following day and said, "I'll take one of the Blue Lightning bikes." The clerk replied, "Sorry, we had only ten bikes in stock and they've all been sold." Was the advertisement an offer?

GOALS

● Describe how an offeror can end an offer

● Tell how an offeree can end an offer

● Explain how the parties can create offers that cannot be ended by the offeror

HOW CAN OFFERS BE ENDED?

WHAT'S YOUR VERDICT?

Melissa offered her collection of baseball cards for sale for $3,000 to her friend and fellow collector, Raoul. Raoul asked if he could think it over and Melissa agreed. While Raoul was trying to raise the money, Melissa had second thoughts. So she called Raoul and said, "I've changed my mind, I'm not interested in selling the cards." Raoul responded, "It's too late, you promised to sell them to me, and I've got the money so I accept."

Was Melissa's offer terminated before Raoul tried to accept?

Once made, an offer does not last forever. There are several methods used to terminate offers.

Revocation by the Offeror

After an offer has been made, the offeror can generally revoke it anytime before it is accepted by the offeree. In *What's Your Verdict?* because Melissa revoked first, there was no offer alive when Raoul tried to accept. Therefore there was no contract. This is true even if the offeror promised that the offer would remain open for a particular period. The right to withdraw an offer before it is accepted is known as the right of **revocation**. A revocation is not effective until communicated to the offeree.

Time Stated in the Offer

In making an offer, the offeror may state how and when the offer must be accepted. For example, on October 10, the Mercantile Bank sent a letter to Boggs, who had applied for a loan.

In the letter, Mercantile offered to lend $50,000 on specified terms and stated that the acceptance had to be received no later than October 18. Boggs mailed an acceptance on October 17, but the letter did not arrive until October 20. Mercantile did not receive Bogg's reply by the time specified. Therefore the offer evaporated and there was no contract.

Reasonable Length of Time

When nothing is said in the offer about the length of its life, it is alive for a reasonable length of time. What is a reasonable length of time depends on all the surrounding circumstances. For example, a produce broker in New Jersey telephoned a customer in Florida offering to sell a truckload of tomatoes. If the offer to sell the tomatoes was not accepted within an hour, it probably would terminate automatically. That is because tomatoes are perishable produce which rot and therefore must be marketed and shipped quickly. The

seller may be in touch with many prospective buyers and they understand they must accept quickly.

In contrast, an offer to sell expensive durable equipment, such as a truck and trailer, would not terminate until a longer time had elapsed. At least several days would probably be reasonable. If the parties had bargained about the sale over a period of months, a week or longer might be appropriate. To avoid misunderstandings, it is prudent to specify at the outset the time available for acceptance.

Rejection by the Offeree

When an offeree clearly rejects the offer, the offer is terminated. For example, Kempsky offered to sell Del Rey a bicycle for $75, but Del Rey replied, "No, too much." The next day, Del Rey called Kempsky and said, "I've changed my mind. I'll take your bike for $75." However, Del Ray's earlier refusal was a rejection, which ended the offer. An offer is terminated by an offeree's rejection even if a time limit set by the offeror has not expired.

Counteroffer

Generally an offeree accepting an offer must accept it exactly as made. If the offeree changes the offeror's terms in important ways, a **counteroffer** results. In making a counteroffer, the

offeree says in legal effect, "I refuse your offer; here is my proposal." The counteroffer terminates the original offer. Then the counteroffer becomes a new offer. Unless renewed by the original offeror, the original offer can no longer be accepted by the offeree. (See In This Case, opposite.)

Death or Insanity of Either the Offeror or Offeree

Contracts are agreements voluntarily entered into by the parties and subject to their control. Death or insanity eliminates such control. Therefore the law acts for these parties when they can no longer act and terminates their offers.

HOW CAN AN OFFER BE KEPT OPEN?

WHAT'S YOUR VERDICT?

The Downings had placed their idle factory building on the market for $950,000. Robinson, a developer, was interested in buying it, but she needed time to persuade a group of investors to join her in a syndicate to purchase the building. Robinson offered $10,000 to the Downings to keep the offer open to her alone for 60 days. The Downings accepted the money.

Are they now legally bound to keep the offer open to Robinson?

Generally, an offeror is not obliged to keep an offer open for a specified time even if the offeror has promised to do so. Why? Because the offeree has given nothing in exchange for the promise.

Options

If the offeree gives the offeror something of value in return for a promise to keep the offer open, this agreement is itself a binding contract. It is called an **option**. The offer may not be withdrawn during the period of the option. In *What's Your Verdict?* Robinson held an option to buy the factory building. Thus, the Downings could not legally withdraw the offer. If they sold to a third party (who was unaware of the option) during the 60-day period, the Downings would be liable to Robinson for damages. Generally, the original offeror keeps the payment received for the option even if the offeree decides not to exercise the right to buy. Usually, if the original offer is accepted within the span of time allowed, money paid for the option is applied to the purchase price. However, this must be agreed to in advance.

Firm Offers

A special rule applies to merchants (those who regularly deal in the goods bought or sold). An offer by a merchant for the sale or purchase of goods stating in a *signed writing* how long it is to stay open is called a **firm offer**. The Uniform Commercial Code (UCC) makes firm offers binding for the time stated (but not more than three months). This is true even when nothing is paid by the offeree. Generally, neither death nor insanity of either party terminates an option contract or a firm offer.

Answer the following questions about legal concepts.

1. Offers expire at the time stated in the offer. **True or False?**

2. If an offeree clearly rejects the offer, the offer is said to be (a) counteroffered (b) revoked (c) expired (d) terminated.

3. When an offeree changes the offeror's terms in important ways, the offeror makes a(n) __?__ . counteroffer

4. Which of the following does not describe a method used to terminate offers? **(a) revocation by the offeror (b) offeror is admitted to the hospital for tests (c) counteroffer (d) death of the offeree**

5. An offeree who rejects an offer can later accept it if the acceptance occurs within a reasonable time after the rejection. **True or False?**

6. Which of the following will cause an offer to end? **(a) occurrence of an event, such as the passage of time, which the offer said would cause it to end (b) passage of a reasonable time if nothing is said in the offer about the length of its life (c) revocation by the offeror (d) counteroffer by the offeree (e) all of the above**

7. If an offeree gives the offeror something of value to keep an offer open, this is called a(n) __?__ . option

8. A barber, speaking to a longtime customer said, "I promise not to raise my prices for you this year." Is this offer binding? **Yes or No?**

9. A barber said, "I promise not to raise my prices for you this year if you pay me $10 today." Is this offer binding if you pay the ten dollars? **Yes or No?**

10. If a hardware store salesman said, "This price on the lawnmowers is good for 30 days," would this be a firm offer? **Yes or No?**

11. If a beauty salon hair designer said, "This price on the cut and dry is good for 30 days," then wrote it down on a piece of paper and signed it, would this be a firm offer? **Yes or No?**

Study the following situations, answer the questions, then prepare arguments to support your answers.

12. While at Prescott's garage sale, Wood noticed a large, metal tool chest in the corner, complete with about 400 standard and metric tools. Wood offered to buy it for $1,250 and said, "You can take a week to think about it before you decide whether to accept." Four days later, and before Prescott had responded, Wood told Prescott that he had found another set for less money and withdrew his offer. Can Wood withdraw his offer?

13. Frank saw a motorized wheelchair advertised in the paper. When he called, it was described to him and he drove out to see it. The seller was asking $900 for it, but it needed work. So Frank offered $700. The seller said she wasn't interested at that price. Later, Frank called and accepted the offer at the $900 price. However, the seller said it had been sold. Frank became upset and sued. Will the seller be liable? Why or why not?

14. Gus walked into his local hardware store to buy exterior paint for his house. It was on sale for $35 a gallon. Gus wanted to check around but didn't want to lose the chance to buy at the sale price. In response to Gus's request, the manager of the paint department wrote Gus a note stating, "Gus Almondson may buy up to 15 gallons of Old Dutch Exterior Grade paint for $35 per gallon anytime within the next two weeks." The manager signed and dated the note. Is this offer binding?

15. Phil was talking with Sharon about Opie, his Springer Spaniel dog. Phil explained that Opie has a strong personality, loves to snuggle up to people, likes to eat "people food," and is a good watchdog. Sharon liked Opie a lot and needed a dog. She asked Phil how much he paid for Opie. Phil said, "I paid $75, but I wouldn't sell Opie for ten times that amount. Sara said, "Well okay, it's a deal then. I'll give you $800, more than ten times the $75." Has Opie, been sold?

HOW ARE ACCEPTANCES CREATED?

WHAT'S YOUR VERDICT?

Darrow offered to trade his digital camera to Monette in exchange for her camcorder. Schorling, who had a camcorder of the same make and model, overheard the offer and said she would make the swap.

Did a contract result from Schorling's statement?

Acceptance occurs when a party *to whom an offer has been made* agrees to the proposal. To create an enforceable contract, the acceptance must

1. be made by the person or persons to whom the offer was made
2. match the terms in the offer
3. be communicated to the offeror

Who Can Accept an Offer?

An offer made to one person cannot be accepted by another. Accordingly, no contract resulted in *What's Your Verdict?* Only Monette, not Schorling, could have accepted Darrow's offer.

Sometimes, however, an offer is made to a particular group or to the public and not to an individual. For example, a reward offer may be made to the general public. Any member of the general public who knows of the offer may accept it by doing whatever the offer requires.

IN THIS CASE

RING LOST at Zuma Beach in front of beach house. Lady's yellow-gold band with 12 small diamonds. Inside inscribed: "Like diamonds. Forever. Yours, J.R.J." $1,000 reward. Call 555-8142.

Dowell saw this newspaper advertisement and rushed to the beach with a homemade sand sifter. About ten other people were also searching, using various devices. After four hours, Dowell shouted, "Eureka! I've found it!" She promptly returned the ring to its owner. She alone was legally entitled to the reward.

Acceptance Must Match the Offer

The offeror may specify the terms of the acceptance, such as when and how the acceptance must be made. To complete the agreement, the offeree must then comply with such

terms. Any change by the offeree in such required terms of the offer ends the original offer and results in a counteroffer. This is so even if the change is advantageous to the original offeror.

MIRROR IMAGE RULE The **mirror image rule** requires that the terms in the acceptance must exactly match the terms contained in the offer. If it varies any term, it is a counteroffer. This law applies to contracts for services (such as tax preparation) and realty (such as the sale of a home). Courts in some states apply this rule only when the term in the offer is material (important). By statute (the UCC), the mirror image rule has been changed in contracts for the sale of goods (such as books, computers, clothing, and food).

GOODS For the sale of goods, as with other types of contracts, if the offeror requires that acceptance must exactly match the terms contained in the offer, then any variation is a counteroffer. Absent this requirement in the offer, an unequivocal acceptance of an offer for a contract for a sale of goods *can* be valid even if it includes new or conflicting terms. In these cases, there is a contract on the terms where the offer and acceptance agree. The new terms or modified terms are treated as follows:

1. If a party is a consumer, not a merchant, then the new or changed terms are mere *proposals* and not a part of the contract unless agreed to by the original offeror.
2. If the parties are merchants, the new or changed terms are *not* a part of the contract if the original offeror objects, or in the absence of an objection, if the terms are material.
3. If the parties are merchants, the new or changed terms *are* part

of the contract if the original offeror is silent and the terms are minor (not material).

IN THIS CASE

On Thursday, the manager of Volume Value Vacuum, Inc. (VVV), offered by mail to sell model 234A vacuum cleaners to Susan's Shops, a retailer, at the bargain price of $129 each, with payment to be made on delivery. Susan accepted in writing but stated, "payment due 30 days after delivery." VVV said nothing in reply. A contract resulted on the area of agreement (model 234A at $129). Because both parties are merchants and VVV did not object to the modification, it will become a part of the contract if it is not material. Because an extension of credit is probably material, it does not become a part of the contract.

Acceptance Must Be Communicated to the Offeror

An acceptance must be more than a mental decision. It must be communicated to the offeror.

SILENCE AS ACCEPTANCE One is not obliged to reply to offers made by others. An offeror's attempt to word the offer so that silence would appear to be an acceptance will not work.

Sometimes, in a continuing relationship, the parties may agree in advance that silence is to be regarded as acceptance. For example, in a monthly book club, it may be agreed that failure to say "no" to a proposed shipment is to be regarded as "yes." Or a food market may have a standing order to have a wholesaler ship a certain amount of fresh produce every day unless the retailer breaks the silence with some notice. Only in situations such as these, where the parties have agreed in advance, can silence be acceptance.

UNILATERAL ACCEPTANCE In some offers, the offeror requires that the offeree indicate acceptance by performing his or her obligations under the contract. Contracts offered under these conditions are **unilateral contracts**. The offeror in a unilateral contract promises something in return for the offeree's performance and indicates that this performance is the way acceptance is to be made. For example, the offeror may publicly promise to pay a $100 reward to anyone who returns a lost dog. Many people learn of the offer. All may join the search. A promise to look for the dog does not create a contract. Only one person may find and return the dog, thus performing the act required to accept the offer and earn the reward.

When the offeree has begun performance of the act requested, the offer cannot be revoked until the offeree has had a reasonable amount of time to complete performance.

BILATERAL ACCEPTANCE Most offers are bilateral. This means the offer implies that it can be accepted by giving a promise instead of performing the

IN THIS CASE

Kulich, an art dealer, wrote Chiang, "I understand you are interested in selling your four-panel Chinese lacquer screen. I sold it to you in 1997 for $500 and said it would go up in value. Now I offer to buy it back for $3,000. Unless I hear from you to the contrary, I'll treat your silence as acceptance and send my truck to pick it up next Monday morning. The driver will bring my certified check for the full amount." Chiang did not reply. Chiang would not be bound to sell the screen.

contracted-for act. For example, a seller promises to deliver a load of topsoil in exchange for a homeowner's promise to pay $65. Offers for **bilateral contracts** require that the offeree accept by communicating the requested *promise* to the offeror. Until this is done, there is no contract. The promise can be implied from the offeree's conduct as well as from words. If the words used are ambiguous about unilateral and bilateral, courts will presume that the offer is for a bilateral contract.

WHEN ACCEPTANCE IS EFFECTIVE Contractual communications such as offers, acceptance, rejections, revocations, and counteroffers may be communicated orally, in person, or by telephone. They also may be communicated in writing and sent by mail, delivery service, e-mail, or facsimile (fax) machine. When the communication takes time, for example when sent through the surface mail, the question of when the communication is effective is very important. All forms of contractual communications but one take effect only when received. The exception to this is the acceptance, which is often effective when sent.

The offeror may require the offeree to use a certain communication method. If a different method is used, then it is treated as a modification of the offer. Business custom often implies a method to be used in an acceptance. On some stock and commodity exchanges, hand signals are used to communicate offers and acceptances. In many industries, next-day delivery service is the custom. When the required or the customary method is used, the acceptance is effective when sent unless the offeror specified the acceptance would be effective when received.

Often there is no specified or customary method for communicating acceptances. Most courts then say the acceptance is effective when sent by the same means used for the offer, or by faster means.

The UCC provides that an acceptance of an offer to buy or sell goods (tangible personal property) may be made "in any manner and by any medium reasonable in the circumstances" unless otherwise clearly "indicated by the language or circumstances." If the acceptance of an offer for the sale or purchase of goods is by a reasonable means, it is effective when sent. A "reasonable" method

incorporates all of the above rules but opens the door for a slower means to be reasonable in some situations.

It often becomes important to determine even more precisely when acceptance is effective. Oral acceptances are effective at the moment the words are spoken directly to the offeror. Acceptances effective when sent by mail generally take effect when properly posted (placed, with correct address and sufficient postage, under the control of the U.S. Postal Service). A telegram takes effect as an acceptance when it is handed to the clerk at the telegraph office or telephoned to the telegraph office. A fax transmission is instantaneous when the transmission lines are open and both sending and receiving equipment work properly. Therefore the effect is similar to instantaneous oral communication, but in a more durable form that is easier to prove in court.

The offeror may specify that an acceptance will not be binding until it is actually received. This avoids the confusion that arises when an acceptance is mailed yet never reaches the offeror because it is lost in the mail. It also avoids the requirement for using the rules above.

Study the following situations, answer the questions, then prepare arguments to support your answers.

6. Schneider offered to sell his motor home to Nunzio for $28,000. Schneider specified that in accepting, Nunzio must agree to pay the entire amount within 30 days. Nunzio accepted but changed the terms to $8,000 down and the balance in 20 equal payments with interest at 10 percent a year on the unpaid balance. Was there an acceptance?

7. Jonas wrote to Smith offering to sell 42 acres of farmland at $5,000 per acre with the purchase price to be paid at the closing. Smith replied, "I accept for the 42 acres, for the $5,000 per acre, but will pay the purchase price two days after closing." Is this an acceptance?

8. Office Suppliers, Inc., ordered 2,000 reams of 20 lb. paper from Dimension Paper for $1.75 per ream to be delivered at the Office Suppliers warehouse on April 24. Dimension responded that 2,000 reams would be delivered on April 25 at the price of $1.75 per ream. Office Suppliers made no further response. Has a valid contract been formed? If so, what are the terms? If not, why not?

9. On October 12, Gary sent by first-class mail an offer to sell his computer to Wanda. On October 14, Wanda received the offer. She thought about the offer and sent an acceptance by first-class mail on October 18. Gary received the acceptance on October 20. However, Gary had changed his mind about the price he wanted for the computer, and he had sent Wanda a revocation of his offer on October 16. Wanda received the revocation on October 19. Was a contract formed? If so, on what date? If not, why not?

10. Don wanted to buy an Audi Quatro. He sent by first-class mail a letter to three Audi dealers and a new car broker. The letter contained a description of the car, the price he would pay, and the delivery date. He indicated he would pay cash within five days after the acceptance. Don also specified that any acceptance would be effective only when received. A local Audi dealer and the new car broker accepted by letters arriving on the same day. Does Don have two contracts to purchase?

When you enter into a contract . . .

PREVENT LEGAL DIFFICULTIES

1. When negotiating contracts, assume the worst and include terms in the contract addressing potential problems.

2. For important contracts, put offers and acceptances in writing. If either an offer or an acceptance is made orally, promptly confirm it in writing.

3. Obtain and keep a copy of every important document you sign.

4. Express your intentions in offers and acceptances with clear, complete, and understandable language.

5. Remember that the offeror may specify how and when the offer must be accepted. Otherwise the offeree may use the same means used by the offeror, a faster means, or other reasonable means.

6. When appropriate, buy an option, if one is available, to keep the offer open for as long as you need.

7. For an offeror to withdraw or revoke an offer, the offeree must receive notice. For speed, use the telephone, e-mail, or fax machine to withdraw or revoke an offer.

8. Always examine the evidence in your possession which could be used in court to establish a particular contractual communication. If you don't have enough evidence, use a second communication to create the evidence. To facilitate proof of your acceptance by mail, use certified mail with *return receipt requested*. Also, keep a copy of your acceptance letter and other documents, including the offer.

CHAPTER IN REVIEW

CONCEPTS IN BRIEF

1. Contracts are agreements enforceable in court.

2. Freedom to contract is basic to life in a democracy. Our economy is built on contracts.

3. Contracts require a valid offer and acceptance, genuine agreement, legality, consideration, and capacity. Some contracts must be placed in writing.

4. The party making the offer is the offeror. The party accepting the offer is the offeree.

5. An offer must: (a) be made with the offeror's apparent intention to be bound by it, (b) be complete and clear, and (c) be communicated to the offeree.

6. If not accepted, an offer is ended (a) at the time stated in the offer, (b) or at the end of a reasonable time if no time is stated, (c) by rejection, (d) by counteroffer, (e) by the offeror's revocation, or (f) by death or insanity of either of the parties.

7. In general, an offeror is not obliged to keep an offer open for a specified time even if the offeror has promised to do so.

8. In contracts for the sale of services or realty, the offeree must accept the offer unconditionally and in the exact form and manner indicated by the offeror. In contracts for the sale of goods, acceptances can vary the terms of offer.

9. An acceptance must be communicated to the offeror. The acceptance is effective when sent if sent by the required means. If there is no required means, it is effective when sent by the customary means, the same means, or a faster means. A slower means will be effective under the UCC if it is reasonable under the circumstances.

YOUR LEGAL VOCABULARY

Match each statement with the term that it best defines. Some terms may not be used.

1. Binding agreement created by an offer that is accepted by a promise of performance *unilateral contract*

2. Offeror's act that invalidates an offer

3. Party to whom an offer is made *offeree*

4. Signed writing by a merchant promising to leave an offer open *firm offer*

5. Response by offeree, with new terms, which ends the original offer *counteroffer*

6. Requirement that the terms in an acceptance exactly match the terms in the offer *mirror image rule*

7. Affirmative response necessary to transform an offer into a contract

8. Contract to leave an offer open for a period of time in exchange for other consideration

9. Agreement that is legally effective and enforceable in court *contract*

10. Proposal that expresses willingness of the offeror to enter into a legally binding agreement

acceptance
bilateral contract
~~contract~~
counteroffer
~~firm offer~~
mirror image rule
offer
~~offeree~~
offeror
option
revocation
test of the reasonable
    person
~~unilateral contract~~

11. Tell how much detail must be contained in a valid offer for the sale of a used car.

12. Create an oral unilateral offer for the purchase of a book (select one that's in the classroom) for $15.

13. Invent and describe a situation where an oral offer for the sale of a used car for $399 is not valid because the facts and circumstances suggest that there is no manifestation of an intent to contract.

WRITE ABOUT LEGAL CONCEPTS

14. Write a script creating a valid offer and a valid acceptance for the sale of something unusual that might be found at a garage sale. Make the sale price less than $500. Be creative in selecting the item being sold.

15. Write an ad for the sale of a used car. Make sure the ad is not an offer.

16. HOT DEBATE Write a paragraph stating why Celia should or should not be legally bound to sell her VW to Joan.

THINK CRITICALLY ABOUT EVIDENCE

Study the following situations, answer the questions, then prepare arguments to support your answers.

17. Caryn offered to tutor Dottie in business law for six hours on the day before the final exam in return for $100. Dottie responded, "Let me think about it for a day, okay?" Two hours later Jim offered Caryn $150 to tutor him on the day before the final and she accepted. Dottie called Caryn an hour later and said, "I accept." Caryn said, "I'm sorry but I've already agreed to tutor Jim that day so I can't tutor you." Was there a contract between Caryn and Dottie?

18. Sam advertised his ski boat for sale, priced at $4,500, complete with outboard engine and trailer. Barbara paid Sam $100 for a ten-day option, the money to be applied to the purchase price if she exercised her right to buy. Two days later, Sam was killed. Is Barbara's option still valid?

19. On Monday, Abner offers to sell his trained golden retriever, Track, to Bob for $300 cash. "My offer is open until we go hunting next Saturday." On Tuesday, Carl offers Abner $400 for Track, in eight equal monthly payments of $50. Abner says "Sorry, my price is $300 cash." On Wednesday, Dan learns that Abner has offered to sell Track. Dan tells Abner, "I'll pay $300 cash when you deliver the dog at the end of this year's duck hunting season. But you can keep Track until then." Abner says, "Sounds like a good deal. Okay, you now own Track." He phones Bob and tells him of the sale. On Thursday, Carl phones Abner and says, "I accept your offer. I'll pay $300 cash. When can I pick up Track?" Abner replies, "Sorry, but Track's been sold." Has Abner breached a contract with Bob or Carl? Has he been ethical in his conduct?

ANALYZE
REAL CASES

20. Lee Calan Imports, Inc., advertised a 1964 Volvo station wagon for sale in a Chicago newspaper. Because of an error by the newspaper, the price was listed at $1,095 instead of $1,795. The advertisement made no mention of several material matters. Plaintiff O'Brien came in and said he wished to buy the station wagon. One of the defendant's sales representatives at first agreed but, upon discovering the erroneous price, refused to sell. Was there a binding contract? (*O'Keefe—Administrator of Estate of O'Brien v. Lee Calan Imports, Inc.*, 128 Ill. App. 2d 410, 262 N.E.2d 758)

21. Scheck wanted to sell a parcel of his real property. He made an offer to pay a commission to Marchiondo, a real estate broker, if Marchiondo caused the sale of the property to a particular buyer within six days. However, Scheck revoked his offer to Marchiondo on the morning of the sixth day. Later that day, Marchiondo obtained the prospect's acceptance of Scheck's offer, but Scheck refused to pay the commission. Marchiondo sued, claiming the offer could not be revoked because he had begun performance. The trial court dismissed the complaint, stating that Scheck could revoke his offer at any time before completion of the requested act. Marchiondo appealed. Who should win the case? (*Marchiondo v. Scheck*, 78 N.M. 440, 432 P.2d 405)

22. On December 23, the First National Bank had its sales agent Wyman mail a written offer to Zeller to sell a parcel of real property for $240,000. On January 10, Zeller had his purchasing agent mail a written offer to buy the property for $230,000. The same counteroffer was made in a telephone conversation on that day to Wyman, but Wyman told Zeller's agent that the offer to sell the land was no longer in effect. When Zeller's agent reported this news to Zeller, he promptly told his agent to wire an acceptance of the original offer at $240,000. Zeller's agent did as ordered and the telegram of acceptance arrived before the letter containing Zeller's counteroffer. The bank refused to sell, reminding Zeller that the offer to sell had been revoked and that its agent Wyman had so informed Zeller's agent in the telephone conversation on January 10. Nevertheless, Zeller sued the bank for specific performance and for damages. Who should win? (*Zeller v. First National Bank,* 79 Ill. App. 3d 170, 398 N.E.2d 148)

23. Epton orally bargained for an option to buy a 54 percent share of the ownership of the Chicago White Sox baseball club for $4.8 million from the defendant, CBC Corporation. The option, which was to have been reduced to writing, was to last one week in exchange for the payment of $1,000 by Epton. To exercise the option within the week, Epton was supposed to give CBC a certified or cashier's check for $99,000 as a down payment. Epton was also to notify the corporation in writing that he was exercising his option. Twice during the week, Epton orally assured CBC of his intent to exercise the option and he also offered to pay the $99,000 as soon as the option was signed by CBC. After the week had passed, CBC refused to sell, and Epton sued. He claimed that his oral notice of intent to exercise the option was sufficient. He said that failure of CBC to sign a written option agreement excused both the requirement of a written exercise of the option by him and the necessity of the $99,000 deposit. Who should win? (*Epson v. CBC Corporation*, 48 Ill. App. 2d 274, 197 N.E.2d 727)

24. This is an appeal of a trial-court verdict. The plaintiff is a stockbroker who sued customers to recover for the purchase price of certain uranium stock. The dispute arose with respect to the price per share at which the stock was ordered. The brokerage contends it was directed to buy the stock "as close to two cents as possible," while the customers contend the price was to be two cents per share. Pursuant to the order, the brokerage purchased the stock and several days thereafter sent a confirmation listing purchase of the stock at two and one-eighth cents per share. The customer declined to complete the purchase at that figure and refused payment. Later the brokerage sold the stock to other parties at a price undisclosed by the record. The trial court found the order to buy was given at two cents per share which plaintiff executed by purchasing the stock at two and one-eighth cents per share. Is there an enforceable contract? (*Baldwin v. Peters, Writer & Christensen,* 41 Colo. 529)

Lefkowitz v. Great Minneapolis Surplus Store
251 Minn. 188, 86 N.W.2d 689

FACTS On April 6, the defendant published the following advertisement in a Minneapolis newspaper:

Saturday 9 A.M. Sharp 3 Brand New Fur Coats Worth $100.00 First Come, First Served $1 Each

On April 13, the defendant again published an advertisement in the same newspaper as follows:

Saturday 9 A.M. 2 Brand New Pastel Mink 3-Skin Scarves Selling for $89.50 Out they go Saturday. Each . . . $1.00 1 Black Lapin Stole Beautiful, worth $139.50 . . . $1.00 First Come, First Served

The record supports the findings of the trial court that on each of the Saturdays following the publication of the above-described ads, the plaintiff [Lefkowitz] was the first to present himself at the appropriate counter in the defendant's store. On each occasion he demanded the coat and the scarf so advertised and indicated his readiness to pay the sale price of $1. Both times the defendant refused to sell the merchandise to the plaintiff, stating on the first occasion that by a "house rule" the offer was intended for women only and sales would not be made to men, and on the second visit that plaintiff knew defendant's house rules.

REASONING The defendant contends that a newspaper advertisement offering items of merchandise for sale at a named price is a "unilateral offer" which may be withdrawn without notice. He relies upon authorities which hold that, where an advertiser publishes in a newspaper that he has a certain quantity or quality of goods which he wants to dispose of at certain prices and on certain terms, such advertisements are not offers which become contracts as soon as any person to whose notice they may come signifies his accep-

tance by notifying the other that he will take a certain quantity of them. Such advertisements have been construed as an invitation for an offer of sale on the terms stated, which offer, when received, may be accepted or rejected and which therefore does not become a contract of sale until accepted by the seller; and until a contract has been so made, the seller may modify or revoke such prices or terms.

The test of whether a binding obligation may originate in advertisements addressed to the general public is "whether the facts show that some performance was promised in positive terms in return for something requested."

The authorities cited above emphasize that, where the offer is clear, definite, and explicit, and leaves nothing open for negotiation, it constitutes an offer, acceptance of which will complete the contract.

Whether in any individual instance a newspaper advertisement is an offer rather than an invitation to make an offer depends on the legal intention of the parties and the surrounding circumstances. We are of the view on the facts before us that the offer by the defendant of the sale of the Lapin fur was clear, definite, and explicit, and left nothing open for negotiation. The plaintiff, having successfully managed to be the first one to appear at the seller's place of business to be served, as requested by the advertisement, and having offered the stated purchase price of the article, was entitled to performance on the part of the defendant. We think the trial court was correct in holding that there was in the conduct of the parties a sufficient mutuality of obligation to constitute a contract of sale.

CONCLUSION Judgment affirmed.

PRACTICE JUDGING

1. If the store had not identified the quantity as "3 . . . fur coats," or "1 . . . stole," would this have affected the outcome of the decision?

2. If the store had advertised in the same way, but left out the statement, "First come, first served" would there have been a contract?

LESSONS

8-1   DURESS AND UNDUE INFLUENCE

8-2   MISTAKE, MISREPRESENTATION, AND FRAUD

HOT DEBATE

Your friend buys a digital camera for $519.97, including a carrying case and a special lens. In her excitement, she fails to note that the case and special lens are advertised as optional equipment supplied at an additional charge. The two items cost an extra $122.94, which is listed on the contract she signs. When the bill for $642.91 plus sales tax arrives, your friend objects.

Where Do You Stand?

1. **State three reasons why it would be fair to allow your friend to withdraw from the contract.**

2. **State three reasons why it would be fair for your friend to be bound to the contract.**

3. **Which reasons are more persuasive?**

GOALS

● **Define genuine agreement and rescission**

● **Identify when duress occurs**

● **Describe how someone may exercise undue influence**

GENUINE AGREEMENT AND RESCISSION

WHAT'S YOUR VERDICT?

Cameron owned a promising racehorse that Link had offered to buy for undisclosed parties. When Cameron refused to sell, Link lowered his voice and slowly said, "Listen, the people I represent don't take 'no' for an answer. If you don't sell, they'll hurt you. They'll hurt your family. Like a good friend, I'm telling you to sell. You're getting a fair price, just sign the contract." Cameron, who had secretly recorded the conversation, sold. Then he called the police.

Can he now rescind and get his horse back?

Papers or documents may indicate a valid offer and a valid acceptance. However, if one of the parties used physical threats to obtain the other's signature on a contract, there isn't really a genuine agreement. **Genuine agreement** (also called *genuine assent* or *mutual assent*) may be lacking due to fraud, misrepresentation, undue influence, duress, or mistake.

The absence of genuine agreement will make what appears to be a contract **voidable**. This means the injured party can rescind. **Rescission** is backing out of the transaction by asking for the return of what you gave in the transaction, and offering to give back what you have received.

To be effective, a rescission must be prompt. It must occur shortly after you discover that there is no genuine agreement. In addition, it must occur before you ratify the contract. **Ratification** is conduct suggesting you intend to be bound by the contract.

IN THIS CASE

Steven inspected a 5-year-old car with the intention of buying it. He asked the owner, Allan, how many miles were on the engine. Allan said, "As you can see from the odometer, it only has 30,000 miles on it, and I'm the only one who has ever owned it." A written contract was executed and Steven took the car to the local automobile dealer to be inspected. The dealer informed Steven that the car had often been serviced there, and that the odometer had been replaced at about 100,000 miles. This was fraud on Allan's part, making the contract voidable by Steven. But if Steven continued to make his monthly payments to Allan after discovering the fraud, this would ratify the contract and Steven would lose his ability to rescind.

Duress

Duress occurs when one party uses an *improper threat or act* to obtain an expression of agreement. The resulting contract is voidable. Much of the law of duress focuses on the nature of the threat.

THREATS OF ILLEGAL CONDUCT The threat to engage in illegal conduct, such as a crime or tort, to win agreement is always duress. Committing an act of violence (for example, stabbing), threatening a crime (threatening to stab), committing a tort (for example, unlawful detention), or threatening a tort to obtain a signature on a written contract is duress. The actual crime or tort, or the threat, may be to the physical life, liberty, or property of the victim, the victim's immediate family, or the victim's near relatives. In *What's Your Verdict?* Cameron acted under duress in making the contract and therefore could rescind it.

THREATS TO REPORT CRIMES If you observe a crime, you have a duty to report it to the proper authorities. If

A Question of ETHICS

Sherri learned that Laura intentionally failed to report half her income on her tax return. Then Sherri suggested that if Laura didn't buy Sherri's car at its blue-book price, Sherri would report the evasion to the Internal Revenue Service. Laura bought the car. Is Laura's tax evasion illegal, unethical, or both? Is Sherri's threat illegal, unethical or both?

The Lindbergh Kidnapping Case

WAS JUSTICE SERVED?

There is no better example of a crime that involves duress and the threat of illegal conduct than the kidnapping of a child. The most sensational kidnapping case of all time involved baby Charlie Lindbergh, son of the pioneer aviator and his wife, Anne Morrow Lindbergh. Charles Lindbergh had made aviation history by being the first person to fly nonstop across the Atlantic Ocean. On a cold weekend in March of 1932, while Charles and Anne were relaxing on the first floor of their home, baby Charlie was kidnapped from the second-floor nursery. The kidnappers left a chisel, a homemade ladder, and a ransom note demanding $50,000. Lindbergh and the police searched the immediate area, but to no avail.

The press went wild with speculation. They immediately descended upon the family home and trampled the entire area, erasing potential clues and possible evidence. Under great duress, and with the aid of police, Lindbergh met the demands of the kidnappers. Ransom money was delivered to a Bronx cemetery. The note received in return told them the baby was in a boat off the Massachusetts coast. Tragically, however, the child's dead body was found along a roadside two miles from the Lindbergh home.

Intensive police work over the next two years involved tracking down the marked ransom bills. It led them to their suspect, German-born carpenter Bruno Hauptmann, who was found to have more than $14,000 of the marked money in his garage. Police also found that a board cut from Hauptmann's attic floor was used in making the homemade ladder. Within hours, Hauptmann became the most hated man in the United States. The media and public itself clamored for an immediate death penalty. The media dug deeply into Hauptmann's life, revealing that he was an illegal German immigrant with a criminal record.

The media-dubbed "Trial of The Century," took place on January 2, 1935. More than 16,000 people, including reporters and other sensation seekers flooded the area. The media declared Hauptmann guilty before the actual trial began. During the trial, Hauptmann denied everything. It took the jury 11 hours to find him guilty of first-degree murder. He was electrocuted at Trenton State Prison on April 2, 1936. Shortly thereafter, Congress declared kidnapping a federal crime under the new "Lindbergh Law."

Questions to Consider

1. When the press descended upon the grounds of the Lindbergh mansion, they trampled over everything that could have been used as evidence. What could have been done to prevent this damage?

2. The media declared Hauptmann guilty before he went to trial. Can you think of examples where the modern media has passed judgment on a person accused of a crime?

you use a threat of reporting to coerce the criminal to contract with you, this is duress. It may also be the crime of *extortion*.

THREATS TO SUE The law encourages parties to settle conflicts without a suit. An important part of this process involves communicating a threat that you will sue if the other side doesn't settle. This happens frequently. But when the threat to sue is really made for a purpose *unrelated to the suit,* this may be duress.

For example, during divorce negotiations, a husband threatens to sue for custody of the children if the wife doesn't sign over valuable shares of stock. Because he doesn't really want custody of the children, this threat to sue makes the contract for the stock voidable. If the threatened suit is completely groundless, a resulting contract may be voidable for duress.

ECONOMIC THREATS Often when parties are bound by a valid contract, they will seek to modify it. Parties then are

tempted to use the economic power they have over one another to negotiate a favorable modification or settlement. If a manufacturer has a contract to pay a supplier $15 for a special computer part needed to maintain production, the supplier might threaten to withhold the parts unless the manufacturer agrees to a price of $20 each. If a disruption in the flow of parts would cause substantial injury to the manufacturer, then the courts would find the agreement on the new price an economic threat voidable for duress.

In economic duress cases, the courts look at both the *threat* and the *alternatives* available to the threatened party. If the threatened party had no choice but to enter into or modify a contract, then duress exists.

IN THIS CASE

Snap-On manufactures and sells hand tools such as wrenches to professional mechanics. It sold a distributorship to Eulich, but he was not successful and encountered significant financial difficulties. In Eulich's view his sales territory was too small. As a result Eulich terminated the dealership agreement. That agreement included a clause stating that on termination of the agreement, Snap-On might buy back any new tools owned by the distributor. Eulich attempted to turn in his tools but Snap-On delayed. Eulich's financial situation deteriorated to the point where he was unable to pay his personal bills and his wife needed to be hospitalized, though he had no medical insurance. Snap-On knew this. Finally, Snap-On accepted the tools. Before paying for the tools, Snap-On asked Eulich to sign an agreement promising not to sue Snap-On for claims arising out of the distributorship. He signed but later sued. The court looked at both the economic threat (not to buy back the tools) and Eulich's alternative (no money for wife's medical treatment) and found the agreement not to sue was based on duress. (*Eulich v. Snap-On Tool Corp.* 853 P.2d 1350)

WHAT IS UNDUE INFLUENCE?

WHAT'S YOUR VERDICT?

Smith was in the hospital near death. His nurse said she would not give him drugs for pain unless he signed a contract transferring certain stock to her for half its market value. Smith signed.

Is Smith bound?

Undue influence occurs when one party to the contract is in a position of trust and wrongfully dominates the other party. The dominated person then does not exercise free will in accepting unfavorable terms.

The two key elements in undue influence are the *relationship* and the *wrongful or unfair persuasion.* When a contract arises because of undue influence, the contract is voidable by the victim. In *What's Your Verdict?* the contract transferring Smith's stock is voidable by Smith.

The Relationship

A relationship of trust, confidence, or authority must exist between the parties to the contract. This relationship is presumed to exist between an attorney and client, wife and husband, parent and child, guardian and ward, physician and patient, or minister and congregation member. But a formal relationship is not necessary. So a relationship of trust could arise between a housekeeper and her elderly employer. It could also arise between a handicapped person and his neighbor.

Unfair Persuasion

Often the best evidence of unfair persuasion is found in unfair terms of the contract. For example, an elderly person, who is dependent on one child for daily care, may sell her home to that child for half its value. This is strong evidence of lack of free will.

A charge of undue influence can be overcome by proving that the contract is fair to both parties. To prevent a claim of undue influence, the

stronger party should act with scrupulous honesty, fully disclose all important facts, and insist that the weaker party obtain independent counsel before contracting.

Persuasion or nagging do not necessarily mean undue influence exists. Whether action rises to the level of undue influence is a difficult question of fact for a jury.

Answer the following questions about legal concepts.

1. Rescission for duress must be timely and occur before ratification. **True or False?**

2. Contracts created or modified by duress are voidable. **True or False?**

3. If duress is present, the victim can __?__ the contract. *resin*

4. If a person is subject to duress, he or she need not return what was received as a result of the contract. **True or False?**

5. Which of the following is a threat that can create duress? **(a) threat to shoot someone if she doesn't sign the contract (b) threat to sue (without grounds) if the victim doesn't modify the contract (c) threat to report the victim to the police if the victim doesn't sign an agreement (d) economic threat (e) all of the above can create duress**

6. When economic threats occur, courts look at **(a) the threat (b) the occupation of the party threatening (c) the victim's practical alternatives (d) both a & c (e) both a & b**

7. Undue influence requires a *formal* relationship, such as attorney and client, between parties to a contract. **True or False?**

8. Which are elements of undue influence? **(a) relationship of trust (b) persuasion (c) both a & b**

9. To prevent a claim of undue influence, the stronger party in a relationship of trust should **(a) act with scrupulous honesty (b) prevent disclosing important facts (c) insist the weaker party seek independent legal advice (d) all of the above**

10. If there is an offer and acceptance with no duress, undue influence, mistake, fraud, or misrepresentation, then there is __?__ . *genuine agreement*

11. When you perform an act which suggests you intend to be bound by the contract, you __?__ the contract. *RATIFY*

Study the following situations, answer the questions, then prepare arguments to support your answers.

12. Mary rented an apartment and later discovered that the roof leaked. She asked the landlord to make repairs, but he refused. Mary said that she would move out unless the landlord either made the repairs or lowered the rent. The landlord lowered the rent. Is Mary's conduct a form of duress?

13. Michelle rented an apartment and later discovered several housing code violations. She asked the landlord to make repairs, but he refused. Michelle said that she would inform the housing authorities unless the landlord either made the repairs or lowered the rent. The landlord lowered the rent. Is Michelle's conduct a form of duress?

14. Ted owned a thoroughbred racehorse that had been on a winning streak. Gifford wanted to buy Ted's horse. To induce Ted to sell, Gifford offered Ted twice the value of the horse. Ted accepted. Later Ted changed his mind and sought to rescind claiming economic duress. Will Ted prevail?

15. Evelyn was 86 years old and of sound mind. However, she relied upon her nephew Jerry, an accountant, to advise her in business matters. Jerry visited Evelyn often. During one of his visits, he persuaded her to sell him a valuable painting for about 80 percent of its true value. Evelyn agreed and signed a contract. Then she had the painting appraised and learned its true value. She continued with the transaction by accepting payment for the painting. About a year later she died. Her estate sued for rescission of the contract. Jerry defended by claiming that Evelyn had ratified by accepting payment after learning of the value of the painting. Who prevails, Evelyn's estate or Jerry?

GOALS

● Describe the kinds of mistakes that can make a contract void or voidable

● Determine when misrepresentation has occurred

● Identify when fraud has occurred

● Discuss the remedies for mistake, misrepresentation, and fraud

WHAT IS A UNILATERAL MISTAKE?

WHAT'S YOUR VERDICT?

Baglio wanted the gutters of his new house to be free of rust. The specifications in the contract he signed called for "rust-resistant steel gutters galvanized with zinc." After the house was built, he learned that galvanized steel gutters would eventually rust and require replacement. Aluminum or copper gutters are the kind he should have contracted for because they would not rust. Baglio now sues the contractor claiming a breach of contract because he did not get what he really wanted.

Will he win?

IN THIS CASE

Genetic Products, Inc., asked for construction bids (offers to build) for its new office building. Eight bids were received. Seven of them were within $100,000 of the architect's estimate of $3 million. However, the bid from New Horizon Builders was $800,000 below the architect's estimate. New Horizon's chief estimator had made a math error. This error reduced New Horizon's bid far below those of all other competitors. Genetics recognized this. Therefore, it may not seize upon New Horizon's unilateral mistake and demand performance at the bargain price created by the mistake.

A **unilateral mistake** occurs when one party holds an incorrect belief about the facts related to a contract. Generally, this does not affect the validity of the contract. In *What's Your Verdict?* Baglio alone was mistaken, so he will lose the lawsuit.

A mistake from failure to read a contract before signing is a unilateral mistake. So is a misunderstanding from a hurried or careless reading. Similarly, signing a contract written in language you don't understand will bind you even if you are mistaken about some of the contract's content.

Recognized Unilateral Mistake

If the unilateral mistake is a major one, and the other party to the contract is aware of the mistake, a court may grant rescission to the injured party.

Induced Unilateral Mistake

If one party has encouraged or induced the other to make the mistake, the contract is voidable. Assume you were looking at a tray of diamonds in a jewelry store. You chose the only stone on the tray that was a zirconium and offered a high price for it. The mistake would have been induced by the mixing of the zirconium with many real diamonds. Therefore, the contract would be voidable.

WHAT ARE MUTUAL MISTAKES?

WHAT'S YOUR VERDICT?

In a large Midwestern city, there were two streets named "Highland." Fisher owned the lot at 231 Highland Avenue. Neece, who lived in New York City, wanted to buy the lot at 231 Highland Boulevard. He wrote to Fisher, offering "to buy your lot on Highland" on specified terms. Fisher promptly mailed her acceptance of the offer.

Is the contract valid?

When there is a **mutual mistake** (also called a *bilateral mistake*) both parties have an incorrect belief about an important fact. Important facts that influence the parties' decisions about a contract are called **material facts**. If a mutual mistake occurs, the contract is void. If both a buyer and seller think that property is 41 acres and they contract for the sale based on this belief, then learn later that it is only 28 acres, this is a mutual mistake of fact. Their agreement is not binding.

Mistake About the Subject Matter

Mutual mistakes may occur as to the *existence* of the subject matter, as shown in the following example.

IN THIS CASE

Falkhausen, who lived in Indianapolis, owned a Formula One racing car that he kept in Miami. On March 18, he sold the car to Firenzi. The car had been destroyed in an accident on March 17 when the garage in which the car was stored burned to the ground. Neither Falkhausen nor Firenzi knew about the fire. Because of the mutual mistake as to the existence of the car, there was no contract.

The law treats a unilateral mistake about the identity of the subject matter of a transaction as a mutual mistake. Thus, in *What's Your Verdict?* the buyer's mistake as to the *identity* of the subject matter made the contract void. Neece, in his offer, was referring to the lot on Highland Boulevard. Fisher, in her acceptance, was referring to the lot on Highland Avenue. There was no genuine agreement between the parties.

Mistake of Law

In some states, when the mutual mistake is about the applicable *law,* the contract is still valid. For example, if both parties to a sale of raw land mistakenly believe that local zoning laws permit construction of duplexes on the lot, the contract would be valid though there was a mutual mistake. This is because all persons are presumed to know the law.

Other states treat mistakes of law in the same way as other mistakes. Unilateral mistakes generally have no effect upon the contract rights of the parties. Mutual mistakes create the right to rescind or void the contract.

WHAT IS MISREPRESENTATION?

WHAT'S YOUR VERDICT?

Nutri-Life offered a dietary supplement for sale. The package contained a statement that clinical studies at Harvard University had shown the drug reduced the risk of cancer by more than 30 percent if taken regularly. This statement was untrue.

Can customers get their money back if they learn of the deception?

In many contract negotiations, the parties make statements that turn out to be untrue. For example, in the sale of a car, the seller might say that it has 70,000 miles on it when in fact it has 150,000 miles on it. If the seller didn't know the true mileage because a prior owner replaced the odometer, this is an **innocent misrepresentation**. If the seller had known the statement were untrue, the seller would have engaged in **fraudulent misrepresenta-** **tion**. Both of these defenses make the contract voidable. Statements are treated as misrepresentation only if

1. the untrue statement is *one of fact* or there is active concealment, and
2. the statement is *material* to the transaction or is fraudulent, and
3. the victim *reasonably relied* on the statement.

Untrue Statement of Fact

In misrepresentation, the statement must be one of fact rather than opinion. Therefore the statement must be about a *past or existing* fact. If someone says, "This car will suit your needs well for at least the next year," this is a statement about the future and therefore must be an opinion. It cannot be the basis for misrepresentation. A seller's statement that, "I'm sure land values will increase at least 15 percent a year for the next three years," is a statement of opinion.

Opinions also can be distinguished from facts based on how concrete they are. Saying, "it really runs well," is a statement of opinion about the condition of the car. Statements like "This is the best tasting cola on the market" are mere sales talk. In contrast, if the seller said, "the engine was rebuilt 7,000 miles ago," this is the expression of a concrete fact. It is a misrepresentation if untrue.

When *experts* express an opinion, the law will treat the statement as a statement of fact. But this also can be the basis for misrepresentation. If an expert auto mechanic says, "The engine is in A-1 shape," and this is not true, it is a misrepresentation and the buyer could rescind. The packaging of the Nutri-Life dietary supplement in *What's Your Verdict?* involved an expert's opinion that constituted misrepresentation.

ACTIVE CONCEALMENT Active concealment is a substitute for a false statement of fact. If the seller of a house paints the ceiling to cover stains which indicate the roof leaks, this is *active concealment*. Similarly, if a seller places the price sticker on the TV screen to cover a wide scratch, this is active concealment.

SILENCE While in many situations the seller may remain silent about defects, there are three important situations where disclosure is required. The first is where a statement about a material fact omits important information. If a seller says, "I only drove this car once a week," then the seller must also disclose that this occurred while racing the car at the local drag strip. Half-truths cannot be used to conceal or mislead.

The second duty to break silence arises when a true statement is made false by subsequent events. A seller says, "No the roof doesn't leak." Later that night, it begins leaking and the seller ends up sleeping under an umbrella. This seller must break silence and disclose the defect to correct the buyer's misimpression.

The third situation arises when one party knows the other party has made a basic mistaken assumption. For example a buyer may assume that a foundation is solid, but the seller knows of a defect allowing water to flood the basement each spring. The seller knows repairs will cost 25 percent of the sale price. This mistaken assumption must be corrected.

Materiality

There are three ways an untrue statement can be determined to be material. First, a statement is material if the statement would cause a reasonable person to contract. Statements about total miles on a car and the number of miles since an engine was rebuilt would probably cause a reasonable person to complete the contract. A statement that a star's signature on a baseball card is his authentic autograph, when in fact it is a forgery, is a statement that would be material to a reasonable person.

Second, a statement can be material if the defendant knew this plaintiff would rely on the statement. Suppose a seller says the oil in the car was changed every 3,000 miles when it was only changed every 4,000 miles. This slight discrepancy would probably not be material to a reasonable person. If, however, a buyer says that the frequency of oil changes is very important to her, then statements about the frequency of oil changes would be material.

Third, if the defendant knew the statement was false, this makes the statement material. Therefore, if a seller lies about an otherwise non-material fact, this is material. So if a seller says, "I always had the car serviced at the local Chevrolet dealership," when in fact he had it serviced at the local gas station, this statement would be material.

Reasonable Reliance

Even though the statement is material, there is no misrepresentation unless the victim reasonably relied on it. A buyer may be told by a diamond expert that the stone is perfect, but then learns from an appraiser that it is not. If the buyer still completes the sale, the buyer isn't relying upon the statement. If a car dealer says the tires are new, but the buyer responds, "Two are as bald as you," there is no reliance.

Graffter sold a used car to Camacho for $16,000. Graffter told her that the car had been driven only 50,000 miles, had never been in an accident, and had the original paint. In fact, Graffter had stolen the car, set back the odometer from 90,000 miles, and repainted the exterior in the original color. Graffter stood between Camacho and the right rear end of the car to prevent her from seeing a crudely repaired fender that had been damaged in an accident. Later Camacho learned the truth.

Can Camacho rescind?

Fraud is based on misrepresentation. All the elements of misrepresentation must be proven or there is no fraud. In addition to misrepresentation, two additional elements must be proven to show fraud: *intent* and *injury*. If a victim can show fraud, courts will grant the victim assistance beyond rescission.

In *What's Your Verdict?* Graffter was a criminal who intentionally lied about the car and actively concealed the damaged rear fender. The deception injured Camacho because the car was not worth $16,000. Accordingly, Camacho could establish fraud.

Misrepresentation Must Be Intentional or Reckless

Fraud clearly exists when a person deliberately lies or conceals a material fact. Fraud also exists if a person recklessly makes a false statement of fact, without knowing whether it is true or false. To constitute fraud, in addition to intending to deceive, the misrepresentation must also be intended to induce the victim to contract.

The Misrepresentation or Concealment Must Injure

To establish fraud, there must be proof of injury. If there is an intentional misrepresentation, but no injury, there is no liability for fraud. Suppose you are looking at an antique motorcycle. The seller says,

"It is a 1938 Indian." The seller knows it is a 1937 Indian but intentionally lies thinking the newer bike is more valuable. If you buy it for $9,000 and it turns out to be worth $14,000, you haven't suffered an injury. While you could rescind based on misrepresentation, you could not establish fraud.

Remedies for Fraud

If a seller innocently misrepresents a material fact, the buyer may rescind. This remedy is also available for fraud. But if a victim can establish fraud, courts will also allow recovery of *damages* and *punitive damages*.

RESCISSION Contracts entered into as a result of misrepresentation or fraud are voidable by the injured party. Thus, the victim (such as Camacho in *What's Your Verdict?*) may rescind the

agreement. Normally when you rescind, anything you received must be returned. A deceived party who has performed *part* of the contract may recover what has been paid or given. A deceived party who has done nothing, may cancel the contract with no further obligation. If sued on the contract, the deceived party can plead fraud or misrepresentation as a defense.

DAMAGES Damages are available if fraud is proven. The party defrauded may choose to ratify the agreement rather than rescind. Then either party may enforce the contract. However the defrauded party who ratified may seek damages for loss created by the fraud. So, victim could recover the difference in value for a car with 70,000 miles on it (the fraudulent misrepresentation) and one with 150,000 miles on it (the truth).

Under the UCC, damages are available for innocent misrepresentation but the subject of the contract must be goods—tangible personal property.

PUNITIVE DAMAGES If fraud is proven, then punitive damages also become available. Punitive damages are a form of punishment. So a judge might award a victim $5,000 as a way to punish the party who committed fraud.

Grounds for Avoiding Contract	Elements	Remedies
Misrepresentation	1. Untrue statement of fact *or* active concealment *or* silence when disclosure is required 2. Materiality 3. Reasonable reliance	Rescission (And for sale of goods, damages)
Fraud	4. Intent to deceive *or* reckless statements intended to induce victim to contract 5. Injury	Rescission, Compensatory Damages, Punitive Damages

Answer the following questions about legal concepts.

1. Which type of mistake gives both parties the right to rescind? (a) unilateral mistake (b) bilateral mistake

2. Mutual mistakes can exist when only one party is mistaken about the identity of the subject of the transaction. **True or False?**

3. Rescission will be granted for unilateral mistake if (a) the mistake is induced (b) the mistake is material (c) the mistake is relied upon by the mistaken party (d) both a & c

4. Misrepresentation is an element in both innocent misrepresentation and fraud. **True or False?**

5. For misrepresentation, which of the following elements must be proven? (a) a false statement of fact (b) the fact must be material (c) the statement must be relied upon (d) all of the above

6. Courts will grant those injured by innocent misrepresentation (a) rescission (b) damages if the transaction is governed by the UCC (c) punitive damages (d) a & b

Study the following situations, answer the questions, then prepare arguments to support your answers.

7. Anne was shopping for a used washing machine. She found one she thought was in good condition. She asked the seller what shape it was in and the seller replied, "It is in great shape." In fact it needed major repairs. Is the seller's statement a misrepresentation?

8. Chip was shopping for a used computer. He found one and asked the seller if the processor was a Pentium II. The seller said, "Yes, it is a Pentium II processor." In fact it was a much slower chip. Is the seller's statement a misrepresentation?

9. Glenna found a computer she wanted. While describing all the components, the seller said it had a fast modem. Glenna said modem speed was very important to her and asked how fast it was. The seller said , "It's 56K," but she didn't really know how fast it was. In fact, it was a much slower modem. Has this seller committed misrepresentation? Has this seller committed fraud?

10. Audra's aunt was more than 80 years old. Audra took care of her in the mornings. One day Audra offered her aunt $100 for a family portrait and the aunt said, "Sure Audra, anything for you, my dear." The portrait was only worth the one hundred dollars. Has there been undue influence?

In making contracts . . .

1. Always carefully investigate before entering into an important transaction. When appropriate, consult trustworthy, independent experts. The other party in a transaction is seldom concerned with your best interest, and is generally not obligated to volunteer information or to disclose all the facts she or he knows.

2. Do not rush into a decision. Take time to review and understand the advantages and disadvantages of the proposed contract. Legitimate proposals will usually survive a delay.

3. Learn to distinguish between fact and opinion.

PREVENT LEGAL DIFFICULTIES

4. If you suspect or know of deception, do not enter into the contract.

5. If you believe you have been defrauded, act promptly to rescind the contract.

CHAPTER IN REVIEW

1. An offer and its acceptance must be made with genuine assent.

2. Duress consists of either an improper act or threat that induces the victim to make an unwanted contract. Such contracts are voidable by the victim.

3. Undue influence exists when one person, with trust, confidence, or authority, uses that power over the victim to obtain an unfavorable contract. The contract is voidable by the victim who acted without free will.

4. Generally a unilateral mistake of fact does not affect the validity of a contract.

5. Generally a mutual or bilateral mistake of material fact makes the agreement void. In some states, if the mutual mistake concerns the applicable law, the contract may be valid.

6. Misrepresentation occurs if a victim reasonably relied on a material or fraudulent misstatement of fact or a material fact was actively concealed.

7. Fraud exists when there is a deliberate false representation or a deliberate concealment of a material fact which influences the decision of the other party, causing injury. Contracts induced by fraud are voidable by the victim.

8. If a contract is voidable, the injured party must rescind shortly after the discovery that there is no genuine agreement. The injured party also must not engage in any activity that might ratify the contract.

9. Acts that can cause duress include threats of illegal conduct, threats to report crimes, threats to sue, and economic threats.

YOUR LEGAL VOCABULARY

Match each statement with the term that it best defines. Some terms may not be used.

1. Mistake about an important fact believed by both parties to a contract

2. Consent or agreement not clouded by fraud, duress, undue influence, or mistake

3. Contract in which the injured party can withdraw from the transaction

4. Statement of a material fact which is false but which the speaker thought was true

5. Deliberate false representation or concealment of a material fact, which is meant to and which does induce another to make an unfavorable contract

6. Approval of a voidable contract

7. Overpowering of another's free will by taking unfair advantage to induce the person to make an unfavorable contract

8. Use of an improper act or threat to obtain an expression of agreement

9. To offer to give back what you received via a contract while demanding return of what you gave

duress
fraud
fraudulent
    misrepresentation
genuine agreement
innocent
    misrepresentation
material fact
mutual mistake
ratification
rescission
undue influence
unilateral mistake
voidable

10. Describe the concept of mutual mistake.

11. Tell when a mistake by one party can be the basis for rescinding a contract.

12. Explain all the elements that must be proven to establish fraud.

13. What does reliance mean?

14. How is innocent misrepresentation different from fraud?

15. How is duress different from undue influence?

WRITE ABOUT LEGAL CONCEPTS

16. Write a short paragraph explaining the distinction between innocent and fraudulent misrepresentation.

17. Write two paragraphs describing those relationships in your family where undue influence could possibly occur.

18. Write a paragraph describing a television ad that could be the basis for misrepresentation if the statement made were untrue.

19. **HOT DEBATE** Write a letter, on behalf of your friend, to the camera shop. In the letter, explain what happened and ask the store to reduce the amount on the bill to $519.97.

THINK CRITICALLY ABOUT EVIDENCE

Study the following situations, answer the questions, then prepare arguments to support your answers.

20. In negotiations for the purchase of a ranch, Adler (the seller) discussed water rights with Folt, the buyer. Adler never mentioned an on-going dispute she had over such rights with a neighboring rancher. After the purchase, Folt realized that he had "bought a lawsuit" when his neighbor sued him over the water rights. In turn, he therefore sued Adler for rescission of their contract. Who will prevail, and why?

21. During negotiations for the sale of a well to be used to water animals, Hutton said the well was free of gypsum and brine (salty water). In fact, the well did contain gypsum, although there was no brine. The gypsum made the well unusable for watering animals. Curry, the purchaser, refused to pay, claiming the contract was voidable because of misrepresentation. Was it?

22. Ashbery, a salesperson, told Gelman that a new computer and its accounting software should do the work of at least five employees. Relying on this statement, Gelman bought the products. When Gelman found that he could eliminate only three employees but needed a new specialist, he claimed fraud. Was fraud committed?

23. Moser had no automobile liability insurance, although it was required by state law. She negligently collided with Chang's car. Chang threatened to sue if Moser failed to pay $1,000 for pain and suffering and $2,000 for car repairs. Moser gave Chang a check for $3,000. Then she stopped payment on it, claiming duress. Was it duress?

24. Olga Mestrovic, the widow of the successful artist Ivan Mestrovic, died. 1st Source Bank was the representative of her estate. It entered into a contract for the sale of Olga's home to the Wilkins. There was a lot of personal property in the home including a stove, dishwasher, and other items. The contract of sale provided that these items of personal property were also being sold to the Wilkins. When the Wilkins took possession of the realty, they found it in a cluttered condition which would require substantial cleaning. When they complained to the bank, it sent a bank officer to the scene. That person offered the Wilkins two options: Either the bank would pay to have the rubbish removed or the Wilkins could remove it and, "keep any items of personal property they wanted." No one thought there were any works of art on the property. The Wilkins accepted the latter option and later found eight very valuable drawings by Ivan Mestrovic. Was there a mutual mistake? Was there a mistake about the subject matter of the transaction? (*Wilkin v. 1st Source Bank,* 548 N.E. 2d 170, Ind. Ct. App.)

25. Devin and Joan Walker listed their property for sale with a real estate broker. In the listing the property was described as having 580 feet of highway frontage and 80,000 cubic yards of gravel. Cousineau, a contractor, bought the property with the intention of mining gravel on the property. Because there was snow on the ground, he did not perform a detailed inspection. When he began work, neighbors threatened to sue, and Cousineau learned that the road was only 410 feet wide and the property contained only 6,000 cubic yards of gravel. Can Cousineau rescind? What defense might the Walkers assert? (*Cousineau v. Walker,* 613 P.2d 608, Alaska)

26. Richard purchased a lot and model home from the defendant, a developer of residential real estate. The sales agreement provided that the sale was subject to zoning ordinances. At the time of the sale, the defendant delivered a plot plan to Richard. The plot plan showed a 20-foot side yard, which complied with minimum requirements of the zoning regulations. After taking possession of the house, however, Richard discovered that the building was, in fact, only 18 feet from the property line. Richard claimed that he relied on the representations of the developer, who should have known that the property did not meet the zoning requirements. Richard sought damages for the misrepresentation. Will he recover? (*Richard v. Waldman and Sons, Inc.,* 155 Conn. 343, 232 A.2d 307)

27. Defendant Darigold Farms was one of several dairies that submitted bids to supply 1.5 million half-pints of milk to the plaintiff, Clover Park School District. Its low bid was $.07013 per half-pint; the next lowest bid was $.072. A usually reliable Darigold secretary had seen penciled figures on a bid form and had erroneously typed them in the bid. The figures were actually the previous year's low price. Because the manager was away at the time, the bid was submitted without review. When the bids were opened on May 25, Darigold's manager immediately recognized the error and on the same day notified Clover Park, asking that the bid be rejected. Nevertheless, it was accepted by the school board on June 11. Darigold's lawyer told Clover Park that Darigold could not supply the milk at the bid price, but that Foremost Dairies would. Then Foremost backed out and Darigold persuaded Sanitary Cloverleaf Dairy to take over. It supplied milk until October, when it became insolvent and went out of business. Clover Park then sued Darigold for breach of contract. You decide. (*Clover Park School District v. Consolidated Dairy Products Company-Darigold Farms,* 550 P.2d 47, Wash.)

28. Treasure Salvors, Inc. located a Spanish ship on the ocean bottom in 55 feet of water about 46 miles off the Florida coast. The ship, the *Nuestra Señora de Atocha,* sank in a hurricane while heading from Havana to Spain in 1622. It was carrying "a treasure worthy of Midas: 160 gold bullion pieces, 900 silver ingots, over 250,000 silver coins, 600 copper planks, 350 chests of indigo and 25 tons of tobacco." On the mistaken assumption that the seabed where the *Atocha* lay was state land, Treasure Salvors made a series of contracts with Florida whereby the state was to receive 25 percent of all items recovered. After the U.S. Supreme Court, in another case, had decided that the continental shelf where the ship rested was federal land, Treasure Salvors sued to rescind its contract with Florida and to recover all items as the exclusive owner of the *Atocha.* You decide. (*Florida v. Treasure Salvors, Inc.,* 621 F.2d 1340)

Noble v. Smith
164 Cal. App. 3d 1001 (1985)

FACTS Noble contracted with the U.S. Navy to remodel the engine maintenance shop at El Toro Marine Corps Air Station. The contract price was some $647,500. The work included installation of heating, ventilating and air conditioning systems (HVAC) with a chilled water system.

In preparing his bid for the work, Noble solicited [informal] bids from subcontractors. He used $90,000 to cover the HVAC based on a bid for a subcontract by John Berry, president of American. Later the bid was reduced to $86,500.

Noble, sent Berry a contract for the HVAC work to be performed by American at its bid price of $86,500. Learning this, Coast (another bidder) warned Noble the $86,500 was not a reasonable bid as Coast's $94,000 bid had excluded the chilled water system from the HVAC.

Four weeks later, Berry told Noble he would not sign the contract. He testified he had a number of questions and "I knew going in it was a low bid." [Then Berry recommended Smith as a contractor who might do the work.]

Berry told Smith his $86,500 bid had a 20 percent profit margin. Smith signed that same day a contract identical to that turned down by Berry. Smith told Noble he had not done "much examination" of the plans or specifications and Ruff was going to look the job over. After checking the job site and the plans, Ruff told Smith the cost of the job "far exceeded" the contract price. The plans included the chilled water system in the HVAC which cost an additional $16,000 not contemplated by the [bid]. Smith promptly told Noble the $86,500 price would not cover the HVAC with the chilled water system. Noble responded with the comment he would get another contractor and "sue [Smith] for the difference."

Noble then awarded Coast two subcontracts, one for $94,000 and one for $16,000 for the chilled water system and sued Smith for the difference between his bid and the Coast bids.

REASONING Unilateral mistake is ground for relief where the mistake is due to the fault of the other party or the other party knows or has reason to know of the mistake.

Substantial evidence supports the conclusion Noble knew Smith's contract for the HVAC did not include the chilled water system.

To rely on a unilateral mistake of fact, Smith must demonstrate his mistake was not caused by his "neglect of a legal duty." This was Smith's first venture into contract waters deeper than $10,000. He told Noble the plans and specifications had not been reviewed by him; Ruff was to undertake that task after the contract was signed. Importantly, Smith related to Noble the profit assurance given him by Berry. In these circumstances, neither the trial court nor we could find Smith's conduct neglect of a legal duty.

While the [lower] court relied on mistake to void the contract, we find an alternative ground in fraud. Smith's consent was obtained by Noble's fraud in the suppression by Noble of the fact Berry's contract price for the HVAC did not include the cost of the chilled water system.

CONCLUSION Judgment affirmed that the contract should be voided.

PRACTICE JUDGING

1. Is the mistake material?

2. Is the mistake unilateral or bilateral?

3. What evidence supports the conclusion that fraud occurred?

MUTUAL CONSIDERATION

LESSONS

HOT DEBATE

For a college graduation present, a wealthy aunt promised to give Maureen two round-trip tickets for a cruise for her and a friend. The promised trip was to be along the "Mexican Riviera" from Long Beach, California, to Acapulco, Mexico. At the graduation exercises, however, her aunt gave her a kiss instead and said, "The stock market is down. Sorry, darling!"

Where Do You Stand?

1. State two reasons why you think Maureen should be able to recover the value of the trip from her aunt.

2. State two reasons why you think the aunt should not have to pay.

GOALS

- ● Define consideration
- ● Determine when there is no consideration

CONSIDERATION

WHAT'S YOUR VERDICT?

Your neighbors are going skiing in the Canadian Rockies near Calgary, Alberta. Their vacation will last 10 days. They unilaterally offer to pay you $30 on their return if you pick up their mail each day they are gone. You accept by picking up their mail every day.

Is there consideration for both parties? Is the contract enforceable?

The main purpose of consideration is to distinguish between social promises, such as offering a birthday gift, and more serious transactions where one thing is being exchanged for something else.

A **gift** is the transfer of ownership without receiving anything in return. A *promise* to make a gift is generally not enforceable. Only after a **donor** (the person giving the gift) transfers possession of the gift to the **donee** (the person receiving the gift) with the intent to transfer ownership, does the transaction irrevocably shift ownership to the donee.

There are three requirements of **consideration.**

1. Each party must give an *act, forbearance, or promise* to the other party.
2. Each party must *trade* what they contribute to the transaction (act, forbearance, or promise) for the other party's contribution.
3. What each party trades must have *legal value,* that is, it must be worth something in the eyes of the law.

Act, Forbearance, or Promise

In *What's Your Verdict?* what you contributed was picking up the mail each day. This is an *act.* It was traded for the neighbor's *promise* to pay the $30. Both this act and promise have value in the eyes of the law. When examining promises, we look for legal value in the underlying act that is promised. Similarly, if someone promises **forbearance** (to *not do something*), we look beneath the promise and ask if the forbearance has legal value.

Trading

In a typical contract, one party in effect says to another, "If you do this for me (pick up my mail), I shall do that for you (pay you $30)." A person promising an action or forbearance is the **promisor**. The person to whom the promise is made is the **promisee**. In most contracts, trading arises as one party exchanges a promise for the promise of the party on the other side. There has been a bargaining, or trading, of one promise for the other.

Consideration must be *mutual.* This means that each party must give

In today's world we all want instant results: Find the answer to a question by a quick search on the World Wide Web. Order a book by clicking a button at your favorite book vendor's Web page. Buy a share of stock or your favorite CD online. Even buy your next vehicle by searching, pointing, and clicking "I accept" on the purchase agreement.

But just how safe are the "cybercontracts" we make online? Can you legally consummate a contract by e-mail? Does a digital signature bind an electronic contract and make it enforceable? Electronic contracts raise complex legal issues. Although in most states the answer to whether the digital signature constitutes a legal contract would be yes, the answer to clicking the "I accept" is less clear-cut.

Internet law is evolving, and it will have many test cases over the course of several years. Many lawsuits have been brought before the courts, but the establishment of cybercontracting and Internet law is just beginning. Contrary to other actions in today's world, the law is just not established with a quick click of "I accept."

LAW and the INTERNET

consideration, and each must receive consideration. Consideration can be given by conferring (or promising to confer) a benefit or by incurring (or promising to incur) a detriment. If either of the parties does not give consideration, the other has no duty to perform as promised.

Legal Value

Legal value means there has been a change in a party's legal position as a result of the contract. In *What's Your Verdict?* you performed an act which involved a benefit to your neighbor (picking up mail). There is legal value because this changed (benefitted) your neighbor's legal position. Your neighbors, as promisors, benefitted your legal position by promising the $30. Because both the act (picking up the mail) and the promise (to pay $30) have legal value and were traded, consideration is present and there is a contract. Legal value (a change in legal position) is most commonly found in this form—in the *exchange of two benefits*.

Legal value can also be found in the exchange of *benefit for a detriment*. A detriment always arises when you promise forbearance—that is, promise to refrain from doing what you have a right to do. If your uncle said on your eighteenth birthday, "Look, if you refrain from smoking until your twenty-first birthday, I'll give you $25,000." You respond, "Yes, I accept." What you have promised is not a benefit to your uncle, but rather a detriment to yourself—you have given up a legal right. This is a change in your legal position and is thus valid consideration.

Legal value can also arise from the *exchange of two detriments*. If you say to your neighbor that you will forbear buying a dog if she will forbear building a fence, both parties have changed their legal positions. Therefore, there is consideration.

Adequacy of Consideration

Generally, what the parties give and get as consideration need *not* be of equal economic value. This idea is sometimes expressed as, "The courts do not inquire into the adequacy of consideration."

IN THIS CASE

While cleaning out his garage, Shreve found an old glass lampshade. He showed it to Laval, who thought it was an authentic Tiffany antique. Laval offered to buy it for $150, and Shreve accepted. When Shreve later learned that it was worth at least $450, he tried to cancel the contract and reclaim the lampshade. "Your miserable $150 was not a fair price!" he said. "That shade is worth at least three times as much!" Shreve sued, but lost because $150 is *sufficient* consideration for a $450 lamp.

The values that different people place on the same property may vary widely. For example, one person might gladly pay $60,000 for an original and exclusive high-fashion gown by a famous designer. Others would not be interested in owning such a gown for $60. A person also might place a higher value on a product at one time than at another. For example, when you have been baking for hours on the sunny side of a baseball stadium, you might willingly pay three times the grocery-store price for a cold soft drink.

Economic value is unimportant as long as there is genuine agreement. However, a big difference in economic value of what one gives and receives may be evidence of mutual mistake, duress, undue influence, or fraud. If the consideration received by one of the parties is so grossly inadequate as to shock the conscience of the court, the contract will be declared unconscionable. In such a case, the contract or the unconscionable clause may not be enforceable.

Nominal Consideration

In certain written contracts, such as publicly recorded deeds, consideration from one party may be identified as "one dollar ($1) and other good and valuable consideration." In such situations, the actual consideration may be substantially more. However, the parties either cannot state the amount precisely or do not want to publicize it. This token amount is known as **nominal consideration**. Courts will enforce contracts supported by nominal consideration if circumstances indicate that, in fact, consideration was given.

THINK ABOUT LEGAL CONCEPTS

Answer the following questions about legal concepts.

1. A promise of a gift is enforceable in court. **True or False?**

2. A valid gift arises when there has been a transfer of possession with the intent to transfer ownership. **True or False?**

3. The person who makes a gift is called the donee. **True or False?**

4. Consideration can be found in the exchange of benefits, or in the trading of a benefit for a detriment, or in bargaining to exchange two detriments. **True or False?**

5. To create an enforceable contract, the things exchanged must have approximately the same economic value. **True or False?**

6. Courts do not consider the __?__ of consideration.

7. If a contract required the payment of $10 for a property worth $100,000, the $10 would be **(a) nominal consideration (b) adequate consideration (c) sufficient consideration.**

THINK CRITICALLY ABOUT EVIDENCE

Study the following situations, answer the questions, then prepare arguments to support your answers.

8. After graduation from high school in June, you and three classmates plan to travel around the United States. The plan is to visit the capital cities of all 48 contiguous states, taking numerous pictures along the way. The Sunnyside Camera Shop offers to give you a dozen rolls of 36-exposure color film for the trip free if you agree to let it develop and print all the rolls you use, for a stated price per roll. You agree. Are both you and the Sunnyside Camera Shop legally bound? What is the consideration for each party?

9. A four-piece high school rock band practices for at least one hour most days of the week. Its studio is the garage of the drummer's home. The music was so loud that it violated a noise ordinance. Several neighbors offered to pay the rent at a local mini-warehouse as a practice room for a year if the group agreed to stop practicing at the drummer's home. The players agreed. Did the neighbors receive consideration? Did the rock band receive consideration? Did the rock band receive a benefit, endure a detriment, both, or neither? Was the contract enforceable? Would it make a difference if the band's music didn't violate the noise ordinance?

10. Gil found a nearly new engine in his neighbor's garage. He was experienced enough to see that it was in good shape. When he asked the neighbor how much she wanted for it, she said $65. Gil said, "Okay," even though he knew it was worth nearly $800. Is this a valid contract?

GOALS

● Identify when there is legal value

● Determine when there is a bargained-for exchange

LEGAL VALUE

WHAT'S YOUR VERDICT?

Lemsky employed Vork under a three-year contract. The contract called for Vork to manage a motel for Lemsky at $25,000 a year, as well as receive a free apartment. After six months, Flemming offered Vork $30,000 a year to manage a larger motel. Upon learning of the offer, Lemsky said to Vork, "You're competent. You're honest. I need you. I'll meet any offer you get from anyone else." Vork remains on the job.

Must Lemsky pay her the higher salary?

Legal value means there is a *change in the legal position* of the party as a result of the contract. When a benefit is promised, the promisee has his or her legal rights increased, so this has legal value. Thus if you promise to paint your neighbor's house for $3,000, you've increased your neighbor's legal benefits to include painting the house.

Illusory Promises

To be consideration, a promise must be binding. In other words, the promise must create a duty or impose an obligation. If a contract contains a clause which allows you to escape the legal obligation, the promise is said to be illusory. For example, you might have a clause stating that you will "paint the house—if you have time." This does not increase your legal obligation because you may never have time to paint the house.

TERMINATION CLAUSES Businesses often want the power to withdraw from a contract if business circumstances change. Therefore they include termination clauses in their contracts. If the clause gives one party the power to terminate the contract *for any reason,* the promise to perform would be illusory. On the other hand, if termination is allowed only after a change in defined circumstances, or after the passage of a certain length of time, or after 30-days' notice, the promise is not illusory. There is clearly a change in the party's legal obligations.

OUTPUT AND REQUIREMENTS CONTRACTS Buyers sometimes agree to purchase all of a particular producer's production. For instance, a steel company may buy all of the output of a nearby coal mining company. This is an **output contract**. On the other hand, a seller may agree to supply all of the needs of a particular buyer. For instance, a carburetor manufacturer may agree to supply all the carburetors needed for a certain make of vehicle. This is a **requirements contract**. While it may seem that one party could elect to stop production and thereby eliminate the obligation,

courts recognize these contracts as supported by consideration.

IMPLIED DUTY OF FAIR DEALINGS When termination clauses, output and requirements clauses, and other clauses create what would seem to be illusory promises, many states will find an implied duty of fair dealings. This means the clause cannot be exercised arbitrarily, but must be exercised in a way that constitutes fair dealings. By finding an implied duty of fair dealings, these courts have a basis for the presence of consideration.

Existing Duty

A person sometimes promises to do something that he or she is already obligated to do by law or by prior contract. Such a promise, or act, cannot serve as consideration.

EXISTING PUBLIC DUTY If on your sixteenth birthday, your aunt promised to pay you $10,000 if you promised to not purchase alcohol for two years and you said, "Okay," this would not be a contract. There is no consideration because it is illegal for you to purchase alcohol when you are 16 and 17 years old. While the agreement creates a benefit for you ($10,000), you don't incur a detriment because you are not giving up a legal right.

EXISTING PRIVATE DUTY If a contract creates a duty, this duty cannot be the basis of consideration in a different contract. In *What's Your Verdict?* Vork was still bound to work for Lemsky for an additional 30 months under the original contract. Therefore Lemsky's promise to pay more money is unenforceable. To hold Lemsky to the new promise, Vork would have to provide new, additional consideration. Otherwise Vork is obligated to carry out the contract as originally agreed upon.

The same rule holds true when a person demands further compensation for carrying out a contract already made.

SETTLEMENT OF LIQUIDATED DEBTS A **liquidated debt** is one where the parties agree that the debt exists and on the amount of the debt. When a *creditor* (a person to whom a debt is owed) agrees to accept less than the total amount due in full settlement from a *debtor* (a person who owes money to a creditor) there is no consideration if the debt is liquidated.

Assume that Shawver borrows $1,000 from Reno. The loan is to be paid in one year with interest at 10 percent per year, or a total amount of $1,100. On the due date, Shawver sends Reno a check for only $1,000, saying "Sorry, I'm strapped for cash. You will have to accept this in full payment." Reno *endorses* (signs) and cashes the check. Reno may later sue and recover the unpaid balance of

$100. She has received no consideration for the suggested agreement to reduce the amount due.

A debtor can settle a claim by paying less than the full amount if additional consideration is given. So payment of less than the full amount before the due date could be consideration. But there must be mutual agreement between the creditor and debtor to do so. Valid consideration exists because the creditor receives the benefit of early payment. Similarly, if something extra is given by the debtor, the new consideration supports a voluntary release by the creditor.

IN THIS CASE

Bailey owed Huff $500 but said he could pay only $300. Huff agreed to accept the lower sum together with a silver ballpoint pen in payment of the entire debt. The pen, although not worth $200, was sufficient new consideration for Huff's release from the remaining debt.

SETTLEMENT OF UNLIQUIDATED DEBTS In some cases, there is a genuine dispute between the parties about how much is owed. In such case, partial payment offered in full settlement by the debtor and accepted by a creditor settles the claim. For instance, a debtor may in good faith claim that a certain debt is $500. The creditor in good faith contends that it is $1,000. If the parties compromise on $750, their agreement is binding. Consideration is found in their mutual forbearance from litigating the amount owed. Such an agreement is called an **accord and satisfaction**.

The disputed claim for an unliquidated debt would be settled if the creditor cashed the debtor's check bearing a clear notation: "In full settlement of all claims outstanding."

RELEASE At the time most torts occur, the liability is unliquidated because the extent of damages is uncertain. If a party settles a claim at this point, this is called a **release**. The payment of money is sufficient consideration for the promise not to sue. Many people are hurt financially by signing releases too soon.

COMPOSITION OF CREDITORS Occasionally, a group of creditors will cooperatively agree to accept less than what they are entitled to, in full satisfaction of their claims against a debtor. In return, the debtor agrees not to file for bankruptcy. This is called a **composition of creditors**. Consideration for the promise of each creditor to release the debtor from full payment is found in the reciprocal promises of the other creditors to refrain from suing for the entire amounts due them. If the creditors did not agree to this arrangement, the debtor could file for bankruptcy, and the creditors might receive much less.

A Question of ETHICS

A motorist and her two young children are stranded in the parking lot of a shopping mall with a dead car battery. (Having just completed your driver's education course, you know how to jump-start a dead battery.) You connect the batteries of the two vehicles with your jumper cable. With your engine running, she turns her ignition key and her engine starts smoothly. Grateful, she asks for your address and promises to send you $25. Is she legally bound to keep her promise? Is she ethically bound to do so?

BARGAINED-FOR EXCHANGE

WHAT'S YOUR VERDICT?

Francis, a pedestrian, saw a car pulled over by the side of the road with a flat tire. He came to the driver's aid, replacing the flat with the spare tire. Then he accompanied the driver to the nearest gas station where her flat was repaired. She was thanked Francis and said she would give him $20 on her next payday. Later she changed her mind, and Francis sued.

Can Francis win the $20?

Mutual Gifts

The consideration on both sides must be *traded* one for the other. If they are not traded, then there are probably two gifts being made. In *What's Your Verdict?* Francis made a gift of changing the tires. Because the driver's promise was made *after* Francis changed the tire, the driver made a gift of promising $20. Neither party sought to exchange one thing for the other. Even where the gifts have legal value, they are not consideration unless they arise from a bargained-for exchange.

Past Performance

Recall that consideration is what one person asks of another in return for consideration. The bargaining takes place in the present, for immediate or future performance by both parties. Therefore, an act that has already been performed cannot serve as consideration. Such an act is called past consideration.

THINK ABOUT LEGAL CONCEPTS

Answer the following questions about legal concepts.

1. If a contract provides a way for one party to completely escape its obligations under the contract, then the promise is called __?__ .

2. Termination clauses make a contract invalid for lack of consideration. **True or False?**

3. Output clauses make contracts invalid. **True or False?**

4. If you already owe a duty, then that duty cannot be used as consideration. **True or False?**

5. If two acts have legal value and they are given independently of one another without being traded, they are not consideration. **True or False?**

6. Legal value means a change in one's legal position as a result of the contract. **True or False?**

7. If a court implies a duty of fair dealings, this can be the basis for consideration even when a promise seems illusory. **True or False?**

THINK CRITICALLY ABOUT EVIDENCE

Study the following situations, answer the questions, then prepare arguments to support your answers.

8. If a contract contains a clause stating that all the buyer's obligations could be extinguished by giving 30-days' notice, would this make the buyer's obligations under the contract illusory?

9. Georgia's neighbors approached her right after she received her driver's license and said they felt that she drove too fast on the roads where their kids often played. They struck a deal with her that if she stayed within the speed limit for the next three months they would pay her $200. Georgia agreed. Is there a benefit to the neighbors? Is there a benefit to Georgia? Is there a contract?

10. Kamiar owed Rubio $5,000, which was due in one year. There was no dispute as to the amount. However, Rubio needed money immediately, so Kamiar offered to pay $4,000 early in full settlement of the debt. If Kamiar pays the $4,000 early, may Rubio sue to collect the remaining $1,000 later?

11. Shea owed Barlow $1,200 that was due and payable. Shea had been temporarily laid off at work, so he asked Barlow to extend the due date for six months. Barlow agreed, but a month later sued Shea to collect the debt. Will she win?

GOALS

● Identify when promissory estoppel applies
● Discuss situations in which consideration is not needed

PROMISSORY ESTOPPEL

WHAT'S YOUR VERDICT?

Silvertone, a wealthy financier, strongly believes that world travel is essential for a balanced education. Accordingly, he told his twin niece and nephew that if they would "cap their college degrees with a trip around the world," he would pay all their expenses upon their return, up to $9,500 for each. Using savings and some borrowed money, the twins took off on a 90-day journey. Total reasonable expenses for each exceeded $9,500 by the time they returned home.

Is Silvertone liable to the twins?

There are important exceptions to the general rule that mutual consideration is necessary for a valid contract or binding promise. When someone intends a gift but consideration is not present, a promise may be enforced under the doctrine of **promissory estoppel**. The following conditions must be met:

- The promisor should reasonably foresee that the promisee will rely on the promise.

- The promisee does, in fact, act in reliance on the promise.

- The promisee would suffer a substantial economic loss if the promise is not enforced.

- Injustice can be avoided only by enforcement of the promise.

Silvertone is legally bound to reimburse each twin with $9,500. Although he received no consideration for his promise of a gift, he is *estopped* (or barred) from denying his liability under the doctrine of promissory estoppel. He could see that the twins would rely on his promise, they did in fact spend their money on the trip, and they would suffer an unfair economic loss unless he is required to pay. Injustice can be avoided only if Silvertone pays.

IN THIS CASE

Consolidated School District asked for bids to construct a new school building. Cardinal Construction, a general contractor, asked a variety of potential subcontractors to submit bids on parts of the job. Pleny Electrical submitted a bid for the electrical work. Cardinal told Pleny that its bid was the lowest and would be used by Cardinal in its bid on the new school building. Later, Pleny sought to withdraw its bid and substitute a higher price. Cardinal sued. However, the promise was one that Pleny knew Cardinal would rely on, Cardinal did rely on it in submitting its bid, Cardinal would be economically injured if the bid were not honored, and this would be unjust. Since all the elements of promissory estoppel were satisfied, the promise will be enforced.

EXCEPTIONS TO THE CONSIDERATION REQUIREMENT

WHAT'S YOUR VERDICT?

Branyan pledged $25,000 to the building fund of the community hospital. Relying on this and other pledges, the hospital's board of directors entered into a contract for construction of a new section.

Can the Branyans be held to their pledge?

Promises to Charitable Organizations

Individuals and business firms often contribute to charitable organizations, such as churches, schools, and hospitals not operated for profit. The contributions may be outright gifts or promises (pledges) to pay in the future. Because the party who makes the pledge receives nothing in return, one might assume that the pledge is unenforceable.

Courts generally enforce such promises provided the charity states a specific use for the money and actually acts in reliance on the pledge. For example, a hospital may have contracted for new facilities, as in *What's Your Verdict?* It would be unjust to deprive the hospital of promised support it reasonably relied on.

Statute of Limitations

The **statute of limitations** specifies a time limit for bringing a lawsuit. Once you become aware of a legal claim, you must sue before the statute of limitations passes or you lose the right to sue. In many states, the statute of limitations for breach of contract or torts is three years. If there is a breach of contract or a tort, you must bring suit within three years after the claim arises.

Some states will enforce a promise to pay a claim after the passage of the statute of limitations even though there is no consideration for the promise. These states do require that the promise be in writing.

Uniform Commercial Code

At common law a promise to leave an offer open is not enforceable.

Only when the offeree has provided consideration is this promise enforceable. Assume you received an offer from your neighbors to be paid $30 per week to mow their lawn, and they said you had a week to decide. This promise to leave the offer open for a week is not enforceable because it is not supported by consideration. To bind the neighbor you would need to pay them to leave the offer open. This would create an **option contract**.

FIRM OFFERS Under the UCC, a *merchant* who makes an offer in a signed writing to buy or sell goods and *promises to leave the offer open,* is bound for up to three months even when no payment or other consideration has been given for the promise. This is called a **firm offer**.

MODIFICATIONS At common law modification of a contract needs consideration. Under the UCC, however, a good-faith agreement that modifies an existing contract for the sale of goods needs no new consideration. For example, *after* a sale has been made, a seller could agree to give the buyers a valid warranty without further charge. This modification is enforceable though not supported by consideration.

Study the following situations, answer the questions, then prepare arguments to support your answers.

9. Laura wanted to go to graduate school after college and she knew it would be very expensive. Her dad told her that if she would major in math instead of history, he would pay tuition in graduate school for a master's degree. Laura majored in math but her dad refused to pay for her graduate school tuition. Can Laura compel her father to pay?

10. Welt entered into a contract with Carbonaro for the purchase of two dozen ultralight bike frames that he planned to resell from his retail bike shop. The price was $600 each. The parties wrote out all the terms of their contract and each signed. Later Welt learned that he could acquire similar frames for $525 each. Welt told Carbonaro that if it wanted to maintain Welt's goodwill it would reduce the price to $525. Carbonaro agreed. What is the consideration in the original contract? Is "maintaining goodwill" something which has legal value? Is the price of $525 enforceable? Why or why not?

11. When they were both freshmen in college, Steiner borrowed $200 from Faber so he could attend the big game in Chicago. Steiner never repaid the debt, and after five years it was barred by the statute of limitations. Then Steiner sent Faber a Christmas card on which he added this note: "I haven't forgotten those four 50's I borrowed from you for the big game. Now that I am working, I'll pay you. In addition, I'll take you to this year's big game at my expense." Is Steiner legally obligated to repay the $200?

12. Lemke's son bought a videocassette recorder from Dyer on an installment plan. When her son was unable to keep up the payments, Dyer came to repossess the recorder. Lemke promised in writing to make the payments if Dyer would allow her son to keep the recorder. If Dyer agreed, could Lemke hold him to his promise?

To prevent misunderstandings about contracts, remember that . . .

PREVENT LEGAL DIFFICULTIES

1. Generally both parties must give and receive consideration if their agreement is to be enforceable as a contract.

2. Adequacy or equality of consideration generally is unnecessary. It is sufficient when something of value is given and received.

3. Accepting money in exchange for giving up a legal right, such as the right to sue for damages after an accident, constitutes consideration and is binding. Consult a lawyer before making such an agreement in any major dispute.

4. A pledge to a charitable institution is generally binding and should not be made unless you intend to fulfill it.

5. Promises to make gifts cannot be enforced by the intended donee. An exception is made under the unusual conditions of promissory estoppel.

6. You should use care and good judgment in making contracts. Courts generally will not rescue you from "bad bargains" or unfavorable deals voluntarily made.

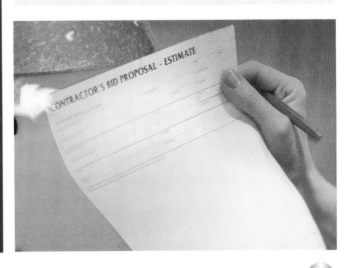

CHAPTER IN REVIEW

CONCEPTS IN BRIEF

1. Consideration is necessary to make a promise binding. Consideration may consist of a promise, an act, or a forbearance.

2. Each party to the contract gives consideration and each party receives consideration. Such trading is a test of the existence of a contract. It is the reason for the performance of the contract.

3. The adequacy, equality, or fairness of the consideration given and received is immaterial as long as the consideration has some value and is voluntarily agreed to by both parties.

4. Performing or promising to perform an existing obligation is not consideration.

5. Past performance is not consideration for a promise given now or in the future.

6. Pledges to pay money to charitable organizations are usually enforceable even though no consideration was given to the pledgers for their promises.

7. Agreements modifying contracts for the sale of goods need no consideration to be binding.

8. Under special circumstances, promises of gifts are enforceable under the doctrine of promissory estoppel.

YOUR LEGAL VOCABULARY

Match each statement with the term that it best defines. Some terms may not be used.

1. Agreement by all creditors to accept something less than the total amount of their claims in full satisfaction of a debtor's obligations

2. Token consideration, which bears no relation to the real value of the contract

3. Promise or action of one person in exchange for the promise or the action of another person

4. Refraining from doing what one has a right to do

5. Voluntary transfer of ownership of property without consideration

6. Change in the legal position of a party as a result of the contract

7. Act that has already been performed and thus cannot be consideration for a promise in the present

8. Enforcement of a promise to avoid injustice, even though no consideration is given for it

9. Person who makes a promise

10. Person to whom a promise is made

11. Merchant's binding written promise to keep open an offer to buy or sell goods

accord and satisfaction
composition of
    creditors
consideration
donee
donor
firm offer
forbearance
gift
legal value
liquidated debt
nominal consideration
option contract
output contract
past consideration
promisee
promisor
promissory estoppel
requirements contract
release
statute of limitations

12. Give an example for consideration as an act and consideration as a promise to forbear.

13. Give an example of an enforceable promise to make a gift and unenforceable promise to make a gift.

14. Identify three promises that you have made with your family or the people with whom you live.

15. Evaluate each promise you identified in exercise 14 and decide whether it is enforceable in court.

WRITE ABOUT LEGAL CONCEPTS

16. Write a short paragraph describing legal value.

17. Write a paragraph describing bargained-for exchange.

18. HOT DEBATE Write a half-page opinion, the way a judge would, resolving the Hot Debate which appeared at the beginning of this chapter.

THINK CRITICALLY ABOUT EVIDENCE

Study the following situations, answer the questions, then prepare arguments to support your answers.

19. Glenn contracted to provide the labor for an addition to Reid's home for $10,000. When Glenn was partially through, he realized that the job was more time-consuming than anticipated. Therefore he refused to continue until Reid promised to pay an additional $2,000. Is Glenn legally entitled to the extra $2,000?

20. Mackey, who had no children, told Lark that if she would attend his alma mater, Aloha College, and graduate, he would pay all expenses she incurred. Relying on loans and some of her own funds, she financed her way through college and earned the degree. Now Mackey says Lark suffered no detriment and he got no benefit. Since there was no consideration, he need not pay as promised. Is Lark right?

21. Kari promised to deed ten acres of land to the Ezlers. In reliance on the promise, they took possession of the land, cleared it, installed an irrigation system over a one-acre section, and planted fifty young fruit trees. Then Kari, seeing the

improved property, changed her mind. May the Ezlers compel the transfer even though they gave Kari no consideration?

22. Mary received a diamond brooch from the estate of her maternal grandmother. It was appraised at $7,500. Because it did not fit in with her sports-oriented lifestyle, Mary sold the brooch to a jeweler who told her, "The setting is old-fashioned, but the diamond is forever the same. I'll give you $3,500 cash." Later Mary wondered whether she received legally sufficient consideration. Did she? Can she rescind the transaction if she can prove that she received much less than the brooch was worth?

23. When Bob began college at age 21, his godmother promised to give him $1,000 at the end of each of the following four years if he remained in school and refrained from smoking tobacco and/or chewing. She also promised a bonus of $1,000 if and when he received his bachelor of science degree. Are the godmother's promises legally enforceable? What are the ethical implications of her promises?

24. Marine Contractors Company, Inc., did various kinds of marine repair work within a 100-mile radius of Boston, Massachusetts. The company maintained a trust fund for the benefit of retired employees. The trust agreement provided that employees who resigned could withdraw their share of the fund after waiting five years. Hurley, general manager of the company, had accumulated $12,000 in the trust fund. When Hurley resigned, the president of Marine offered to pay his $12,000 immediately if he would agree not to compete with Marine directly or indirectly within 100 miles of Boston for five years. The parties made a written contract which set forth a "consideration of One Dollar and other good and valuable consideration." The contract also stated that the parties have "set their hands and seals" to the contract. Within four months after leaving Marine's employ, Hurley began doing repair work similar to that of Marine. Soon after, he organized his own company, hiring two supervisors of Marine. Marine sued to stop Hurley from breaking his contract. Hurley defended with a plea of no consideration. Do you agree with Hurley or with Marine? (*Marine Contractors Company, Inc. v. Hurley*, 310 N.E.2d 915)

25. Under a written contract with the Robert Chuckrow Construction Company, Gough agreed to do the carpentry work on a commercial building. Gough was to supply all necessary labor, materials, and other requirements to complete the work "in accordance with the drawings and specifications." After Gough's employees had erected thirty-eight trusses, thirty-two trusses fell off the building. Gough did not claim that the plans or specifications were defective or that Chuckrow was to blame for the collapse. Gough was told by a Chuckrow representative to remove the fallen trusses and to rebuild and erect them. Gough was also told to submit an additional bill for this work. He completed the job and submitted the additional bill. However, Chuckrow paid only the amount promised under the original written contract. Therefore Gough sued Chuckrow for the extra costs of reconstruction. Is he entitled to the added money? (*Robert Chuckrow Construction Company v. Gough*, 159 S.E.2d 469, Ga.)

26. Hoffman and his wife owned a bakery in Wautoma, Wisconsin. Lukowitz, an agent for Red Owl Stores, Inc., represented to and agreed with Hoffman that Red Owl would erect a grocery store building for them in Chilton and stock it with merchandise. In return, the Hoffmans were to invest $18,000 and Hoffman was to operate the store as a Red Owl franchise. In reliance on Red Owl's assurances and advice, the Hoffmans sold their bakery, paid $1,000 down on a lot in Chilton, and rented a residence there. In negotiations over some seventeen months, Red Owl boosted the required investment to $24,100; then to $26,000; and finally to $34,000, which was to include $13,000 from Hoffman's father-in-law. Red Owl insisted the $13,000 must either be a gift or a loan that would be inferior in claim to all general creditors. Hoffman balked and sued for damages. Should the Hoffmans win? If so, on what grounds? (*Hoffman v. Red Owl Stores*, 133 N.W.2d 267, 26 Wis. 2d 683)

27. Petty, a general contractor, made a series of purchases from Field Lumber Company. Field's records showed a total price of $1,752.21. Petty admitted he owed $1,091.96, but denied liability for the difference of $660.25. He claimed the difference was a result of an unauthorized $292.60 purchase by an employee, plus related finance charges. Petty sent a check for $500 along with a letter stating that the check must be accepted in full settlement of the total claim or returned. Field phoned to say the lumber company required full payment, but nevertheless Field cashed the check and sued for the full balance it claimed was due. Can Field Lumber Company now recover the full amount? (*Field Lumber Company v. Petty*, 512 P.2d 764, Wash.)

28. Burt made two pledges of $50,000 each to the Mt. Sinai Hospital of Greater Miami. He made the pledges "in consideration of and to induce the subscriptions of others." Nothing was said as to how the funds were to be used. Mt. Sinai Hospital did not use his pledge to induce others to subscribe. Nor did the hospital undertake any work in reliance on Burt's pledge. Burt died in the following year. Up to the time of his death, he had paid $20,000 on his pledge. The executors of his estate now refuse to pay the balance. Must they do so? (*Mount Sinai Hospital of Greater Miami, Inc., v. Jordan*, 290 So. 2d 484, Fla.)

BACKGROUND Tom Waits agreed to be a recording artist and songwriter for Third Story Music (TSM). TSM transferred its rights in Waits' music to Elektra/Asylum Records (a division of Warner Communications). Under this agreement, Warner obtained from TSM the worldwide right to "manufacture, sell, distribute and advertise records or other reproductions and to permit others to do any or all of the foregoing. . ." This clause also specifically stated that Warner "may at our election refrain from any or all of the foregoing." TSM was to receive as a royalty a percentage of the amount earned by Warner.

Bizarre/Straight Records sought to compile and market an album of previously-released Waits' compositions. Bizarre presented a licensing proposal to Warner. Warner would not do the deal unless Waits agreed. Waits refused.

TSM brought suit against Warner for contract damages. Warner defended by asserting that the clause in the agreement permitting it to "at (its) election refrain" from doing anything to profitably exploit the music is controlling.

REASONING Both sides rely on different language in the California Supreme Court decision in *Carma v. Marathon*. In *Carma*, the court recognized that "in situations where one party is invested with a discretionary power affecting the rights of another," that "[s]uch power must be exercised in good faith."

The *Carma* court also stated: "The general rule [regarding the covenant of good faith] is plainly subject to the exception that the parties may, by express provisions of the contract, grant the right to engage in the very acts and conduct which would otherwise have been forbidden by an implied covenant of good faith . . . there can be no implied covenant where the subject is completely covered by the contract."

[An implied covenant of good faith can be the basis for consideration when there otherwise would be none because the promise is illusory.] "If what appears to be a promise is an illusion, there is no promise. . . ."

"The tendency of the law is to avoid the finding that no contract arose due to an illusory promise when it appears that the parties intended a contract. . . .

The TSM/Warner agreement states that Warner may market the Waits recordings, or "at [its] election" refrain from all marketing efforts. Read literally, this is a textbook example of an illusory promise. At the same time, there can be no question that the parties intended to enter into an enforceable contract with binding promises on both sides. Were this the only consideration given by Warner, a promise to use good faith would necessarily be implied under the authorities discussed.

The illusory promise was not, however, the only consideration given by the licensee. Warner promised to pay TSM a guaranteed minimum amount no matter what efforts were undertaken. It follows that consideration is present.

Warner bargained for and obtained all rights to Waits' musical output, and paid legally adequate consideration. That it chose not to grant a license in a particular instance cannot be the basis for complaint on the part of TSM as long as Warner made the agreed minimum payments and paid royalties when it did exploit the work.

CONCLUSION The judgment is for Warner.

PRACTICE JUDGING

1. **Where is the consideration on each side?**

2. **If Warner had not promised the royalty payments, would the court have found consideration present here?**

3. **If the promise of royalty payments had not been made, would the court have still found for Warner?**

LESSONS

10-1 CAPACITY RIGHTS

10-2 LIMITATIONS ON CAPACITY RIGHTS

HOT DEBATE

Angela was a 17-year-old high school student who, at her boyfriend's urging, signed a contract to work as a model for a modeling agency. Angela claimed she was 22 years old. She received her first assignment a week later. It involved flying to New York City for a magazine photo shoot. The day before the photo shoot, Angela's father Simon learned what his daughter had done. Simon called the agency and informed them that Angela would not be at the photo shoot the next day, and that he would not allow his daughter to be a model. As result, the magazine had to cancel the photo shoot and they lost over $5,000.

Where Do You Stand?

1. **Can Simon prevent Angela from carrying out the terms of the contract? Why or why not?**

2. **Can Angela be held liable for the magazine's losses? Why or why not?**

WHAT IS CAPACITY?

WHAT'S YOUR VERDICT?

Susan, age 16, walked into a fur shop out of curiosity and became enthralled with the idea of owning a fur jacket. A persuasive sales lady told her she would be able to use it for the rest of her life and that it was a good investment. Her aunt had recently died and willed her enough for the jacket. A week later, she realized that at this time in her life she didn't have a use for a fur jacket.

Can Susan get her money back?

The major requirements for the creation of a contract are satisfied if there is an offer, acceptance, mutual assent, and consideration. Still, certain parties to contracts are assumed by the law to lack the maturity and experience to protect their self-interests. The law grants these parties special contractual rights designed to protect them from being cheated.

Parties who have special contractual rights are minors, the intoxicated, and the mentally incapacitated. **Minors** are under the age of majority, which is 18 in most states. Minors, mentally incapacitated, and intoxicated persons "lack contractual capacity." Persons who are not minors, not intoxicated, or not mentally impaired possess the capacity to contract. **Contractual capacity** is the ability to understand that a contract is being made and its general meaning.

Capacity Rights

There are two basic protections granted to those who lack capacity. When protected parties purchase things classified as **necessaries**—things needed to maintain life and lifestyle—the protected, or special, parties need pay only the fair market value rather than the contracted price. When these parties purchase **non-necessaries**—things that for them are relative luxuries—they must pay the contracted price, but the protected parties have the option to *disaffirm* the contract.

Disaffirmance involves giving back the consideration by both parties. In *What's Your Verdict?* Susan purchased a non-necessary and could disaffirm by returning the jacket and requesting her money back.

If a protected party leased a luxury condominium for one year by paying two months' rent and a cleaning deposit, he or she could disaffirm a week later by giving possession back to the landlord, and recover the payments. Minors may disaffirm contracts for non-necessaries during their minority. They may also disaffirm for a reasonable length of time after achieving their majority.

After the age of majority, the power to disaffirm is immediately cut off if the person *ratifies* the contract. **Ratification** is acting toward the contract as though one intends to be bound by it. The chart below shows how special parties are treated in contracts for non-necessaries.

Minors

In most states, people under the age of 18 are legally minors. The law may refer to them as "infants" or persons living during the minor (shorter) part of their lives. They also may be referred to as being in their **minority** or under the **age of majority**. In a few

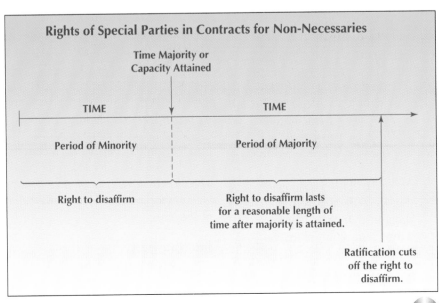

Rights of Special Parties in Contracts for Non-Necessaries

Time Majority or Capacity Attained

TIME — TIME

Period of Minority — Period of Majority

Right to disaffirm — Right to disaffirm lasts for a reasonable length of time after majority is attained.

Ratification cuts off the right to disaffirm.

states, the age of majority is 19 or 21. Minority ends the day before the birthday of the age of majority.

Emancipation

Emancipation is the severing of the child-parent relationship. It ends the duty of the parent to support a child and the duty of the child to obey the parent. A minor naturally becomes emancipated upon reaching the age of majority. But a minor may also be emancipated before that time.

Early emancipation can occur formally or informally. Formal emancipation occurs when a court decrees the minor emancipated. Informal emancipation arises from the conduct of the minor and the parent. The following are evidence of informal emancipation:

1. the parent and minor agree that the parent will cease support
2. the minor marries
3. the minor moves out of the family home
4. the minor becomes a member of the armed forces
5. the minor gives birth
6. the minor undertakes full-time employment

States differ greatly in their treatment of emancipated minors. Some give them full contractual capacity and others don't. If you become emancipated, you may lose your capacity protection.

Mental Incapacity

Mental incapacity is much less precisely defined than minority. The test is whether the party understands the consequences of his or her contractual acts. Thus people with severe mental illness, severe mental retardation, or severe senility lack capacity.

If a judge rules that a person is insane, then this person has a complete lack of capacity. All contracts executed by this person are void, whether for necessaries or non-necessaries.

Intoxication

Intoxication can arise from using alcohol such as beer or vodka, from using drugs such as marijuana or LSD, or inhaling products such as glue or aerosols. While the courts often articulate the same definition of incapacity as for the mentally impaired—does the person understand the consequence of their contractual acts—many courts are reluctant to allow disaffirmance for intoxication when it may injure another. These courts allow disaffirmance only for those who were so intoxicated that they did not know they were contracting. This stricter standard is used because intoxication is a voluntary act.

IN THIS CASE

Emily was 88 years old when she contracted to sell her family home to her daughter Gail for about 15 percent of its value. At the time, she was suffering from advanced Alzheimer's disease and didn't understand the consequences of the transaction. Two months later Emily died. Her will provided for all her property to be split equally among her four children. The other children sued to have the deed set aside because Emily lacked the mental capacity to contract. Emily did not understand the consequences of the transaction. Because this is the requirement for mental capacity, her estate can disaffirm the contract to sell the home.

IN THIS CASE

Joe drank a six-pack of beer on a Sunday afternoon while watching a pro football game. Joe often drank this much. After the game, Gordon, a real estate agent, came to Joe's house and presented an offer to buy from someone who had recently viewed his home. The price was $202,000. Joe signed the contract even though he felt a little tipsy. Later, someone offered $230,000. Although Joe had been drinking, he cannot disaffirm the contract based on intoxication. He did not satisfy either court standard for intoxication.

CULTURAL DIVERSITY IN LAW

Early America

Child Labor Laws

In early American culture, children began to work as soon as they were able. At first this meant working on the family's farm or business. But later, child labor took place in factories.

The social acceptance of child labor began to decline in the early 1800s. By the end of that century, state legislation was being drafted to keep children under 14 from working outside the home. In 1938 the Fair Labor Standards Act prohibited the employment of children under 16. This act signaled that the federal government thought that child labor was wrong and required federal regulation.

WHICH CONTRACTS CAN BE DISAFFIRMED?

The two rights given those who lack capacity are the right to disaffirm contracts for non-necessaries and the right to pay a fair price instead of the contract price for contracts for necessaries. Because these rights are mutually exclusive, it is important to understand the difference between necessaries and non-necessaries. Necessaries are goods and services that are reasonably required to maintain a person's lifestyle. These include basic food, clothing, shelter, and transportation. All other goods and services are for non-necessaries, or relative luxuries.

NECESSARIES The standard for necessaries can vary from one person to another. To be necessaries, the things contracted for must be suitable to that party's economic and social status. The person must not already possess those goods or services. For example, a minor must not have them supplied by parents or guardians. In *What's Your Verdict?* if the parents of both Garcia and Wesley provided adequate shelter, the apartment would not be a necessary.

Courts usually find such things as food, clothing, shelter, education, medical care, and tools used to earn a living to be necessaries. Some courts hold that an automobile is a necessary when it is essential for the minor to earn a living.

NON-NECESSARIES Those things not needed to maintain one's economic or social status, perhaps cosmetics, jewelry, liquor, tobacco, perfume, audio equipment, travel for pleasure, and expensive food for parties are likely to be *non-necessaries*.

CAPACITY IN ORGANIZATIONS

Some people who work for organizations have the capacity to bind the organizations to contracts. If someone has this capacity, it is said to be within his or her **scope of authority**, or within the range of acts the organization has authorized him or her to do. Capacity to contract can be created when the employer tells an employee that they are authorized to bind the organization.

Capacity also can be created when the organization leads others to believe that a person has certain authority, for example when the organization gives the title of purchasing agent to an employee. So a person selling shoes probably could not bind the shoe store to a contract for the lease of a new store in a shopping center. The salesperson has capacity to sell the shoes, but doesn't have the capacity to contract for the store in any other way. It would be within the shoe store owner's scope of authority to contract for the lease.

When doing business with organizations, it is important to ensure that the person signing the contract has the scope of authority to bind the organization. People acting outside the scope of their authority are generally personally liable when the organization isn't. In *What's Your Verdict?* Caryn may be liable to Alicia for the lost profit on the sale of the roses.

A Question of ETHICS

Perkins is a regional sales manager for an automobile manufacturer. She is responsible for visiting 15 car dealerships in one state. The dealerships are all independent business owners who buy cars from the manufacturer and then resell them to the public. Perkins's job is to "push" certain models to the dealers at different times to compensate for oversupply from the manufacturer. As part of her job, she often takes the owner and salespeople of a dealership to lunch. Over lunch, Perkins's guests often order several drinks. After these "three-martini lunches," Perkins then gets down to business with the owners and salespeople. She often does not know if her guests are drunk or not when she begins her pitch. Does Perkins have an ethical obligation to determine whether the dealers have had too much to drink? Do the owners have an ethical obligation to refrain from drinking at lunch, knowing that they will be asked to commit to deals with Perkins after lunch?

THINK ABOUT LEGAL CONCEPTS

Answer the following questions about legal concepts.

1. All contracts of those who lack capacity are void. **True or False?**

2. The law treats all the contracts of those lacking capacity in the same way. **True or False?**

3. Which contracts by those lacking capacity can be disaffirmed? **(a) those for necessaries (b) those for non-necessaries (c) those for either necessaries or non-necessaries**

4. What is the most common age of majority? **(a) 21 (b) 18 (c) 16 (d) 9**

5. The test for mental impairment is "Did the person understand the consequences of his or her contractual acts?" **True or False?**

6. The standard for distinguishing between necessaries and non-necessaries is the same for all persons. **True or False?**

7. Each person in an organization has a scope of authority that determines which contracts by that person can bind the organization. **True or False?**

THINK CRITICALLY ABOUT EVIDENCE

Study the following situations, answer the questions, then prepare arguments to support your answers.

8. Clare was age 17, a minor in her state, when she bought a week's worth of groceries at a local supermarket. Later she discovered she spent too much money and was going to be over her weekly budget. So she took the groceries back and asked for her money back. If she sues, will she get her money back?

9. Tanya, a minor, was the daughter of a construction worker. When she was 17, she bought an evening gown for $400 to wear to a school dance. After the dance, Tanya decided she didn't like the dress and returned it asking for the money back. Is she legally entitled to the money?

10. Janice had been drinking all afternoon before she went into a used car lot. There she signed a contract to purchase a two-year-old car for as much as it would cost for the same model new. She sought to disaffirm the contract based on intoxication. At the trial, she testified that she understood she was buying a car, that she understood the price identified in the contract for the car, but that she didn't realize that she could get a newer car for the same price. Is Janice likely to succeed in disaffirming this contract on the basis of intoxication?

GOALS

- **Identify the time when a contract cannot be disaffirmed**
- **Identify contracts that cannot be disaffirmed**
- **Explain the consequences of misrepresenting age**

TIME OF DISAFFIRMANCE AND RATIFICATION

WHAT'S YOUR VERDICT?

While still a minor, Beach bought a stereo sound system on credit from McReam's Electronic Cloud for $500. Beach paid $100 down and promised to pay $50 a month on the unpaid balance until the debt was paid. After making four payments, two of which were made after he reached the age of majority, Beach decided to disaffirm the contract and return the equipment.

Can Beach do this?

Generally, a person lacking contractual capacity can disaffirm a contract for non-necessaries

1. any time while still under the incapacity, or
2. within a reasonable time after attaining capacity.

After attaining capacity, a person may ratify the contract made while under an incapacity. Ratification is action by the party indicating intent to be bound by the contract. For a minor, ratification must occur *after* achieving majority. Ratification may consist of either of the following:

1. giving a new promise to perform as agreed, or
2. any act (such as making payments to the seller) that clearly indicates the party's intention to be bound.

In *What's Your Verdict?* Beach ratified the contract by making payments after reaching majority. This act cut off his power to disaffirm. Once ratification occurs, it may not be withdrawn.

RETURN OF GOODS OR SERVICES

WHAT'S YOUR VERDICT?

Lamon, a minor, bought a diamond engagement ring and a necklace for his fiancée, Morgan. He paid for the items in weekly installments of $10. On the day Lamon achieved majority, he and Morgan quarreled. Morgan returned the ring to Lamon but refused to part with the necklace.

Can Lamon return the ring to the jeweler and receive a refund for the ring and necklace?

In *all states,* when a minor disaffirms, anything of value the minor received and still has must be returned. The minor is then entitled to get back everything that was given to the other party.

LOSS OF VALUE In most states, if minors are unable to return exactly what was received under the contract they can still get back everything they gave. This is true even if a minor returns used or damaged goods. It is also true even if a minor returns nothing because the goods have been lost, consumed, or destroyed.

In *What's Your Verdict?* Morgan was legally entitled to keep the necklace because it was an ordinary gift not connected with the proposed marriage. Lamon could return the ring to the jeweler and demand a refund of the money he had paid for both pieces of jewelry. Lamon is entitled to the money he had paid on the ring. In most states, he is even entitled to what he had paid on the necklace. That is because he returned everything that was still in his possession.

In *some states,* however, a minor must return everything received in a condition as good as it was when it was received. If this cannot be done, the minor must pay the difference in value, or deduct the difference from the amount to be refunded. In these states, Lamon could be unable to recover the price of the necklace.

OBLIGATIONS OF PARTY WITH CAPACITY The party lacking capacity can generally disaffirm contracts for non-necessaries, yet the party lacking capacity can enforce them against the party with capacity. On the other hand, generally the party with capacity can neither enforce nor avoid all or any part of a contract for non-necessaries with a party lacking capacity.

WHAT CONTRACTS CANNOT BE DISAFFIRMED?

WHAT'S YOUR VERDICT?

Upon graduation from high school, Robinson, age 17, began a business doing electrical work. He bought $375 in tools from Muller. The venture was a disappointing failure. Discouraged after a month, Robinson asked Muller to take back the tools and to return his $375 payment.

Must Muller do so?

Some contracts of minors for non-necessaries cannot be disaffirmed. These exceptions vary considerably from state to state. The statutes and cases of your state are the only definitive source on this topic. The most common exceptions follow.

COURT-APPROVED CONTRACTS In all states, minors cannot void any contracts approved for them by a court. For example, minors who are employed as actors or actresses or as professionals in sports usually have their contracts approved by a court. Once approved, these contracts may not be disaffirmed.

MAJOR COMMITMENTS In all states, contracts to enlist in the armed services and contracts for educational loans cannot be disaffirmed. Similarly, marriage contracts cannot be disaffirmed.

BANKING CONTRACTS In most states, minors are permitted to make deposits in banks and in savings and loan associations. Most states also permit minors to make withdrawals as if they were adults, without any right to disaffirm these transactions.

INSURANCE CONTRACTS More than one-half of the states provide that minors who are over a certain age may not disaffirm certain contracts of life insurance.

WORK-RELATED CONTRACTS In most states, minors who engage in a business or trade cannot disaffirm agreements involving their businesses. Accordingly, in *What's Your Verdict?*, Robinson would not be able to avoid his contract if he lived in a state with such a law.

SALE OF REALTY In some states, a minor who owns real property and sells it or borrows money against it cannot disaffirm until after achieving majority.

APARTMENT RENTAL In a few states, the lease of an apartment cannot be disaffirmed even if the apartment is not a necessary.

MISREPRESENTING YOUR AGE

WHAT'S YOUR VERDICT?

Ron, a mature-looking minor, lied about his age when he bought an extensive wardrobe of clothing from the Casuals Shop. Ron showed his older brother's driver's license as identification. He also used his brother's name on the installment contract. By October, Ron had paid $325 on the $785 contract. He then became bored with the wardrobe and returned it to the store and demanded the return of all payments.

Must the store return the money?

Minors have been known to misrepresent their ages. In most states, minors who lie about their age may nevertheless disaffirm their contracts. However, in these states, a minor who gives a false age may be held liable for the *tort of false representation.*

Minors are liable for their torts and delinquent or criminal conduct, although they still have capacity rights. Thus, the other party to the contract may collect from a minor any damages suffered because of the minor's fraud even though the minor may be able to disaffirm the contract.

In *What's Your Verdict?* Ron is within his rights as a minor in disaffirming the contract. But his act was also a tort (fraud). Therefore in most states, the Casuals Shop could probably hold back from the refund an amount of money sufficient to cover the decrease in value of the wardrobe as returned. Or the store could hold back the full amount if nothing was returned. Ron could be held liable in damages for deceiving the seller, and these damages could exceed the price of the goods he lied to get.

THINK ABOUT LEGAL CONCEPTS

Answer the following questions about legal concepts.

1. Any contract entered into while a minor can be disaffirmed. **True or False?**

2. A contract for non-necessaries entered into while a minor can be disaffirmed **(a) anytime (b) anytime after achieving majority (c) anytime during minority (d) within a reasonable time after achieving majority (e) both c & d**

3. Acting toward the contract as though you intend to be bound by it—after achieving majority—is the definition of __?__ .

4. If a minor lies, saying she is an adult, this eliminates her capacity rights. **True or False?**

5. State statutes sometimes eliminate the minor's ability to disaffirm contracts for non-necessaries such as life insurance. **True or False?**

6. In most states, to disaffirm, a minor must pay for any loss or damage to the goods or service received in order to be entitled to get back what the minor gave. **True or False?**

THINK CRITICALLY ABOUT EVIDENCE

Study the following situations, answer the questions, then prepare arguments to support your answers.

7. Richard bought car insurance while he was 16. He had a perfect driving record until he reached the age of majority, 21 in his state. The day after his birthday, Richard disaffirmed the insurance contracts and asked for the return of his payments. Is he legally entitled to the money?

8. Linda subscribed to a "Book of the Month" program on her sixteenth birthday. She received monthly books from the publisher until her twenty-first birthday. She continued receiving books for another six months, then attempted to disaffirm. Will she succeed?

9. In Juan's state, the age of majority is 21. Three weeks after his eighteenth birthday, Juan joined the Marine Corps. After two weeks of boot camp, he decided he didn't like the lifestyle. So he told the Marines he was disaffirming his contract to join. Will he succeed?

10. Beverly was 14 when she bought a used motorcycle that wouldn't run. Beverly made repairs and got it going. She rode it illegally for more than six months. Then a leak developed in a gas line and the bike caught fire. It was a total loss. Beverly returned the burned-out motorcycle to the seller and asked for all her money back. Will she succeed?

In making contracts . . .

PREVENT LEGAL DIFFICULTIES

1. When contracting, always ask yourself if the person on the other side has full contractual capacity.

2. When judging age, be conservative. Ask for identification for anyone who looks like they are younger than 30 years old.

3. If the people you want to contract with have alcohol on their breath, consider waiting until another time.

4. The other party in a transaction is seldom primarily concerned with your best interests and is generally not obligated to volunteer information about their capacity.

5. When contracting with the elderly, generate evidence that they possess mental capacity. Consider having an impartial party observe the negotiations.

6. Don't rely on intoxication or drugs as a basis for disaffirming a contract.

CHAPTER IN REVIEW

CONCEPTS IN BRIEF

1. Necessaries are those things needed to maintain life and lifestyle. Contracts for necessaries by those lacking contractual capacity cannot be disaffirmed.

2. Non-necessaries are not needed to maintain life and lifestyle. Those lacking contractual capacity are not bound by contracts for non-necessaries.

3. Disaffirmance is giving back what you got and getting back what you gave.

4. Those lacking contractual capacity can disaffirm contracts for non-necessaries all during the time of their incapacity and for a reasonable time thereafter.

5. Minors are those under the age of majority.

6. Many states eliminate the ability of minors to disaffirm some contracts for necessaries.

7. After reaching majority, a person may ratify a contract made during minority. This can be done either by an express promise or by an act such as payment. In most states, silence or the failure to disaffirm within a reasonable time is considered ratification.

8. The test for mental capacity or intoxication is less precise than for minority. The test for mental incapacity is whether the party understands the consequences of the contractual acts.

9. The contractual party having capacity has no right to disaffirm the contract just because the party lacking capacity has the right to do so.

10. Employees bind their employers to contracts they execute on their behalf if they are acting within their scope of authority.

YOUR LEGAL VOCABULARY

Match each statement with the term that it best defines. Some terms may not be used.

1. Severing of the parent-child relationship

2. Within the range of authorized acts

3. Goods and services reasonably needed to maintain one's lifestyle

4. Inability to understand the consequences of a contract because of alcohol

5. Act after regaining capacity indicating an intent to be bound by the contract

6. Ability to understand that a contract is being made and its general meaning

7. Giving back what you have received under a contract and requesting the return of what you gave

8. Things not needed to maintain life or lifestyle

9. Period of time when a young person lacks full contractual capacity

10. A severe mental illness, retardation, or senility

11. Either 18, 19, or 21 in most states

12. One who has not yet reached the age of majority

age of majority
contractual capacity
disaffirmance
emancipation
intoxication
mental incapacity
minor
minority
necessaries
non-necessaries
ratification
scope of authority

13. Identify three things you've bought recently and classify them as necessaries or non-necessaries.

14. For the three things you've bought recently (from exercise 13), tell whether it would be possible for you to ratify the contract after reaching majority.

15. If any of the three things you've bought recently can be the basis for ratification, describe the exact conduct you might engage in after achieving majority to constitute ratification.

16. Assume you were going to buy a two-year-old car at a bargain price from a woman who was 86 years old. Explain the steps you would take to create evidence that she has mental capacity.

17. Assume you were going to buy a two-year-old car at a bargain price from a man with a lot of alcohol on his breath. Explain the steps you would take to create evidence that he has capacity.

WRITE ABOUT LEGAL CONCEPTS

18. Write a one-paragraph summary of the law of capacity as it applies to minors.

19. Write a one-paragraph summary of the law of capacity as it applies to the intoxicated.

20. Write a one-paragraph description of what you would do to protect your legal interests if dealing with a 90-year-old man who wanted to rent an apartment to you.

21. **HOT DEBATE** Write a letter to Angela as if you were the magazine's attorney explaining why Angela should be held responsible for the $5,000 lost due to the cancelled photo shoot.

THINK CRITICALLY ABOUT EVIDENCE

22. On her sixteenth birthday Jaymie bought a used car from Allen for $6,000 cash. Jaymie comes from a middle-class family and uses the car to drive to and from school. She could take a bus to school, but it is more fun to drive. She also drives her friends on errands and takes occasional short trips out of town for fun. Six months after buying the car, the crankshaft in the engine broke. The cost of a new engine would have been about $3,200 so Jaymie decided to disaffirm the contract to purchase the car. Legally, can she?

23. On her sixteenth birthday, Laurisa bought a used computer from Stuart for $100 cash. Laurisa is from a wealthy family and receives an allowance of $200 a week. Six months after buying the computer, the hard drive crashed so Laurisa decided to disaffirm. Legally, can she?

24. June stopped by a bar on the way home from work and drank three gin and tonics. Then she bought a six-pack of beer at the local grocery store and drank three cans before her husband came home. June and her husband then began drinking whiskey and water and each finished two drinks. A salesperson from Metropolitan Life Insurance came over and sold June a life insurance policy that cost $900 per year. Is there evidence indicating that June may be able to disaffirm?

25. Larson was 69 years old and trying to sell his home. He had it appraised, and the estimated value was $300,000. He listed the home with a local real estate broker for $330,000. When Perry offered him $305,000 he counteroffered at $320,000. When Perry balked at the price, he lowered his offer to $315,000 and she accepted. Is there evidence that Larson possesses the mental capacity to contract?

26. Sixteen-year-old Johnny Hays went to Quality Motors, Inc., in Tennessee, to buy a car. When a salesperson asked about his age, Johnny sidestepped the question. The salesperson refused to sell except to an adult. Hays left and returned shortly with a companion of 23, whom he had just met. The salesperson then sold Hays the car. The bill of sale was made out to the companion who, with the help of the salesperson, later transferred the title to Hays. When Hays' father, Dr. D. J. Hays, discovered the sale, he called Quality Motors and asked them to take the car back. The company refused. Dr. Hays tried to return the car on three more occasions. Finally, the car was put into storage. Johnny Hays found the keys to the car and took it on a trip, damaging it in two accidents. As a result, the car was not in running condition at the time of the trial. Can Johnny disaffirm? Who will bear the loss due to the damage? (*Masterson v. Sine,* 216 Ark. 264)

27. W. O. Lucy and J. C. Lucy, the plaintiffs, sued A. H. Zehmer and Ida Zehmer, the defendants, to obtain title to the Ferguson Farm for $50,000, as allegedly the Zehmers had agreed. Lucy had known the Zehmers for about 20 years. One night Lucy stopped in to visit the Zehmers in the combination restaurant, filling station, and motor court they operated. While there, Lucy tried to buy the Ferguson Farm just as he had tried many times before. This time he tried a new approach. Lucy said to Zehmer, "I bet you wouldn't take $50,000 for that place. " Zehmer replied, "Yes, I would too; you wouldn't give fifty." Throughout the evening, the conversation returned to the sale of the Ferguson Farm for $50,000. At the same time, the parties continued to drink whiskey and engage in light conversation. Eventually Lucy got Zehmer to write up an agreement to the effect that Zehmer would sell to Lucy the Ferguson Farm for $50,000 complete. Later, Lucy sued Zehmer to go through with the sale. Zehmer argued that he had been drunk and that the offer had been made in jest and hence was unenforceable. What evidence supports the conclusion that Zehmer was intoxicated? What evidence supports the conclusion that Zehmer was not intoxi-

cated? Is Zehmer bound? (*Lucy v. Zehmer,* 196 Va. 493)

28. Webster Street Partnership owned real estate in Omaha, Nebraska. It leased an apartment to Matthew Sheridan and Pat Wilwerding for one year at a rental of $250 per month. Although Webster Street did not know this, both Sheridan and Wilwerding were younger than the age of majority when the lease was signed. Both minors had moved out of their homes voluntarily and were free to return there at any time. Sheridan and Wilwerding paid $150 as a security deposit. They paid for two months, for a total of $500, then failed to pay for the next month on time. Webster Street notified them that they would be required to move out unless they paid immediately. Unable to pay rent, Sheridan and Wilwerding moved out of the apartment. Webster Street later demanded that they pay the expenses it incurred in attempting to re-rent the property and assorted damages and fees, amounting to $630.94. Sheridan and Wilwerding refused on the ground of minority to pay any of the amount demanded. Further, they demanded the return of their security deposit. Webster Street then sued. Is the apartment a necessary? Can Sheridan and Wilwerding disaffirm? (*Webster Street Partnership v. Sheridan,* 368 N.W. 2d 439, Neb.)

29. Kevin Green was 16 years old when he purchased a 1979 Camaro for $4,642.50 from Star Chevrolet. Shortly after the purchase, the car blew a head gasket and couldn't be driven. Thereafter Kevin informed Star that he was disaffirming the contract. He offered to return the car, but Star would not accept it unless it was repaired. In January 1982 Kevin brought suit for the purchase price. The car was not used for four or five months until Kevin repaired the blown head gasket himself. In June 1982 the car was in an accident which substantially reduced its value. In an insurance settlement arising out of the accident, Kevin received $1,500 as a salvage payment for the Camaro. He used the salvage money to buy another car. Star then sued Green. What resulted? (*Star Chevrolet v. Green,* 473 So. 2d 157, Miss.)

CASE FOR LEGAL THINKING

Hauer v. Union State Bank of Wautoma
192 Wis. 2d 576

EVIDENCE Kathy Hauer suffered a brain injury in a motorcycle accident. She was subsequently judged to be incompetent, and the court appointed a guardian for her. Hauer's guardianship was later terminated based upon a letter from her treating physician.

Ben Eilbes met Hauer and convinced her to take out a $7,600 loan to help him in his business, using her mutual fund as collateral. Eilbes then contacted Shroeder, assistant vice president of the bank, to arrange for the loan. Shroeder called Hauer's stockbroker and financial consultant to verify Hauer's mutual fund. He was told that Hauer needed the interest from the mutual fund to live on.

TRIAL The jury found that Hauer lacked the mental capacity to enter into the loan and that the Bank failed to act in good faith toward Hauer in the loan transaction. The Bank appeals.

REASONING A review of the record reveals that there is credible evidence the jury could have relied on in reaching its verdict. First, Hauer was under court-appointed guardianship approximately one year before the loan transaction. Second, Hauer's testimony indicates a complete lack of understanding of the nature and consequences of the transaction. Third, Hauer's psychological expert testified that Hauer was "very deficient in her cognitive abilities, her abilities to remember and to read, write and spell . . . Barnes further testified she was "incompetent and . . . unable to make reasoned decisions" on the date she made the loan.

The trial court offered two explanations for voiding the contract and not holding Hauer liable for repayment of the loan: (1) the law and policy of the "infancy doctrine," and (2) the jury's finding that the Bank failed to act in good faith.

Our Supreme Court held that a minor who disaffirms a contract might recover the purchase price without liability for use, depreciation, or other diminution in value. Generally, a minor who disaffirms a contract is expected to return as much of the consideration as remains in the minor's possession. However, the minor's right to disaffirm is permitted even where the minor cannot return the property.

However, a "contract made by a person who is mentally incompetent requires the reconciliation of two conflicting policies: the protection of justifiable expectations and of the security of transactions, and the protection of persons unable to protect themselves against imposition."

Absent fraud or knowledge of the incapacity by the other contracting party, the contractual act of an incompetent is voidable by the incompetent only if avoidance accords with equitable principles.

The Bank argues that it does not have an affirmative duty to inquire into the mental capacity of a loan applicant to evaluate his or her capacity to understand a proposed transaction. We agree. However, a contracting party exposes itself to a voidable contract where it is put on notice or given a reason to suspect the other party's incompetence such as would indicate to a reasonably prudent person that inquiry should be made of the party's mental condition.

Judgment affirmed.

PRACTICE JUDGING

1. What evidence indicates that Hauer had mental capacity?

2. What evidence indicates Hauer did not have mental capacity?

3. Which evidence do you think is weightier, that indicating capacity or that indicating lack of capacity?

LESSONS

11-1 WHICH AGREEMENTS ARE ILLEGAL?

11-2 ENFORCEABILITY OF ILLEGAL AGREEMENTS

HOT DEBATE

A friend offered Stacey $100 if he would "get rid of" a neighbor's barking dog. "You'll be the hero of this whole block," the friend said. "Just take it far out of town and give it to some farmer," said the friend. The dog had bitten a young boy who was teasing it. When neighbors reported the barking to the animal control office, the owners were always able to make the dog stop barking just before the officers arrived on the scene. Stacey agreed. He "got rid of" the dog and asked for the money. His friend refused to pay. Stacey sued his friend.

Where Do You Stand?

1. **Why should Stacey be able to collect the money?**

2. **Why shouldn't Stacey be able to collect the money?**

ILLEGAL AGREEMENTS

WHAT'S YOUR VERDICT?

Razer agreed with several published articles that criticized laws prohibiting the production, possession, and use of marijuana. The authors of the articles claimed such legislation was unrealistic and often violated civil rights. Razer agreed so heartily that he bought several dozen marijuana plants from a friend, Sara. Then he rented a patch of isolated land and persuaded the owner to accept a share of the anticipated crop as rent. After harvesting the first crop, Razer sold his share to Sara.

Were any of his agreements illegal?

Agreements can be void and unenforceable because they involve contracting for an illegal act. For example, if Sam contracted with Murder Incorporated to shoot his ex-girlfriend and refused to pay after the homicide had been committed, Murder Incorporated could not win a suit against him for breach of contract. The contract between Sam and Murder Incorporated is unenforceable because it is an illegal agreement.

On the other hand, other contracts can require a violation of the law and yet be enforceable. If you ordered stationery from a shop in a nearby mall but the business license of the shop had expired, the shop would be in technical violation of the law for engaging in business without the proper license. If the shop breaches the contract, could you sue and recover? Yes, you could. While there is a minor illegal act by the shop, you have not knowingly violated the law.

How can we distinguish these kinds of cases? There are basically four ways:

First, statutes sometimes explicitly state that certain contracts are unenforceable. For example, most states have statutes which make private betting contracts unenforceable.

Second, courts look at the impact of violation of a statute on the *public welfare*. So even though the homicide statute says nothing about the enforceability of contracts to murder, courts would rule them void because they have a big impact (possible loss of a life) on the public welfare.

Third, courts look at how directly the contract and the violation of the statute are connected. In the homicide example, the contract was for a homicide. In the business license example, the contract was for stationery.

Fourth, the courts look at how involved the parties are in the violation of a statute. In the murder contract, one party did the murder and the other paid for the murder. This is deep involvement in violation of a homicide statute. On the other hand, when you ordered stationery, you

were completely unaware that the shop's business license had expired. There is no direct involvement on your part in violation of the law.

Almost any agreement to commit a felony (a serious crime) will be an illegal agreement. In *What's Your Verdict?* all of Razer's agreements were criminal and therefore void.

Contracts Made Illegal by Specific Statute

State legislatures enact laws making certain contracts illegal.

ILLEGAL GAMBLING Most states either forbid or regulate gambling. Typically, they have statutes which make gambling agreements void. **Gambling** involves an agreement with three elements: payment to participate, a chance to win based on luck rather than on skill, and a prize for one or more winners. A **wager**, one of the most common forms of gambling, is a bet on the uncertain outcome of an event, such as a football game.

Most states have legalized some form of gambling under regulated conditions. *Pari-mutuel betting* (a form of betting in which those who bet on the winner share the total prize pool) at racetracks is sometimes permitted. State-run lotteries are common as a means of raising money. Bingo also is permitted in many states, often on a modest scale for financing charitable, religious, or educational projects.

AGREEMENTS TO PAY USURIOUS INTEREST Almost all states provide that, with certain exceptions, lenders of money may not charge more than a specified **maximum rate of interest**. Generally, the penalties specified by these statutes vary. In some states, the lender cannot collect some or all of the interest. However, the borrower must usually repay the principal. The maximum interest rate varies among the states and 18 percent is a

Native Americans

Tribal Gaming

In many states that permit gambling or "gaming," casinos are being operated by Native American tribes. The tribes, recognized as "sovereign nations," depend on the revenue from the casinos as an important part of their tribal economy. Tribal gaming has stimulated community growth and economic development within many once-impoverished Native American nations.

The large-scale tribal gaming operations began in the early 1980s, about the same time as the emergence of lotteries in many states. Since then, several court cases have shaped the relationship between the sovereign nations' gaming operations and the states. In 1987 in *California v. Cabazon* the Supreme Court upheld the tribes' rights as sovereign nations to conduct gaming on Indian lands. They may conduct the gaming free of state control if similar gaming is permitted outside the reservation. The Indian Gaming Regulatory Act, passed by Congress in 1988, affirms the tribes' right to conduct gaming on their lands. This Act requires states to negotiate with the tribes as equal sovereigns. However, it also gives states the power to regulate gaming.

common maximum. Lending money at a rate higher than the state's maximum allowable rate is **usury**.

Sometimes a person borrows money for which interest will be charged but no exact rate is stated. In such a case, the rate to be paid is the **legal rate of interest**, which is specified by state statute. In about one-half of the states, this rate is 7 percent or less per year. In most of the other states, the legal rate ranges between 8 and 12 percent.

Many states permit licensed loan companies and pawnbrokers to charge a **small loan rate of interest**. This rate is typically 36 percent a year, usually on loans of up to $2,000. Because the dollar amount loaned is relatively small, the overhead cost per dollar loaned is high. Presumably the risk of loss from defaults is also high on such loans. Therefore the states allow a higher interest rate to loan companies and pawnbrokers to protect people against criminal loan sharks, who illegally charge extremely high rates (often 50 percent monthly).

AGREEMENTS INVOLVING ILLEGAL DISCRIMINATION
Some agreements are unenforceable because they violate anti-discrimination statutes. For example, an agreement between a motel chain and a local manager to not accept guests of a particular race or national origin would be unenforceable because it violates the federal Civil Rights Act of 1964. Agreements may also be illegal as violations of the Constitution. For example, a contract between a residential subdivision developer and a home buyer providing that the buyer would not sell to a member of a particular race would be unenforceable because it violates the Fourteenth Amendment to the Constitution.

Agreements That Obstruct Legal Procedures
Agreements that delay or prevent justice are void. Examples include promises to

- pay non-expert witnesses in a trial to testify, or pay for false testimony
- bribe jurors
- refrain from informing on or prosecuting an alleged crime in exchange for money or other valuable consideration (called **compounding a crime**)

A *court* or *prosecutor* may make a penalty dependent upon a criminal's making restitution (for example, returning a stolen car). However, the victim may not make reporting a crime dependent upon restitution.

IN THIS CASE
After school, a new student named Judy robbed Melinda of $400. Instead of reporting the crime to the police, Melinda confronted Judy three days later, told her to return the money, and threatened to call the police if she didn't. Judy said she would pay $40 a week for 10 weeks. This agreement is void.

Agreements Made Without a Required Competency License
All states require that persons in certain occupations and businesses pass exams and receive a license to ensure that they are competent. Persons engaged in trades, such as barbers, plumbers, and electrical wiring installers typically require a **competency license**. Professionals such as physicians, teachers, lawyers, and pharmacists must have competency licenses. Real estate brokers, insurance agents, and building contractors are subject to such regulation. Persons who lack the required competency license may not enforce the contracts they make in doing the regulated work.

In contrast, if the license is a **revenue license**, whose purpose is only to raise revenue rather than to protect the public, contracts made by the unlicensed person are valid. Generally, the only penalty for failure to get such a license is a higher fee when the license is later obtained.

IN THIS CASE

Shaun learned two computer programming languages in his spare time and started a business helping people create web pages. He operated out of his home after school and was earning about $3,000 a month. The city where Shaun lived required a business license to operate any business there. Shaun didn't have the license. When a client encountered financial difficulty, it refused to pay, saying Shaun was unlicensed. The client must pay because the business license only raises revenue, it doesn't regulate competency.

Agreements That Affect Marriage Negatively

The law encourages marriage and family life by making agreements that harm or interfere with marriage unenforceable. For example, Mimi is an illegal immigrant and Bill is a U.S. citizen. It would be an illegal contract if Mimi agreed to pay Bill $5,000 in exchange for his promise to marry her so she could obtain citizenship. Similarly, a father's promise to pay his daughter for not marrying would be unenforceable. Also it would be illegal for a boss to agree to pay her assistant money in exchange for his promise to divorce his spouse.

Agreements That Restrain Trade Unreasonably

Our economic system is based on the concept of free and open competition. This creates profits for producers who benefit consumers the most.

Hence, both state and federal laws seek to prevent monopolies and combinations that restrict competition unreasonably.

PRICE FIXING When competing firms agree on the same price to be charged for a product or service, this injures consumers. It deprives them of the lower prices which competition would produce. **Price fixing** is a crime under federal law. Agreements to fix prices are therefore unenforceable.

IN THIS CASE

All ten pharmacy owners in the city of Weston meet to discuss common problems. During the discussion, they agree that all the stores would match the prices charged for certain items by a discount outlet that had recently opened in the town. They also agree that they will charge no less than specified minimum prices for some 50 other high-volume items. Because these agreements restrained free trade and controlled prices, they were illegal and void.

One form of price fixing is **bid rigging**. This occurs when competitors who bid on jobs agree that one bidder will have the lowest bid for a particular job. It is illegal because typically the bid riggers take turns being the lowest bidder and set the bid price higher than if there were real competition.

IN THIS CASE

Colgate manufactured and sold soap to retailers. It identified suggested retail prices and refused to sell to retailers who did not adhere to the prices. The government prosecuted Colgate for a form of price fixing called *resale price maintenance*. The Supreme Court ruled that this activity is legal as long as there is no *agreement* between retailers and Colgate and as long as Colgate does nothing else to enforce resale price maintenance. (*U.S. v. Colgate*, 250 U.S. 300)

RESALE PRICE MAINTENANCE Manufacturers engage in **resale price maintenance** when they want retailers to sell their product at particular prices. They may identify a "suggested retail price." This is legal. However, manufacturers may not *agree or contract* with retailers to sell the product at a particular price because that would involve two parties fixing the price. On the other hand, manufacturers can identify a suggested price and refuse to sell to retailers who do not adhere to the price.

ALLOCATION OF MARKETS The same injury to competition produced by price fixing can be achieved if competitors *divide* markets between themselves. This practice is known as **allocation of markets**. If the Ford dealers in a state agree that they will not sell to residents outside the county where their dealership is located, this eliminates price competition for Fords and injures consumers. Therefore agreements to allocate markets are illegal and unenforceable.

COVENANTS NOT TO COMPETE Price fixing and market allocations are agreements not to compete. One type of agreement not to compete is sometimes enforceable. When persons are hired they may agree that they will not compete with their employer after the employment terminates. But these covenants become illegal if they are unreasonable in:

- time period for the limitation
- geographic area to which the limitation applies
- employer's interest protected by the limitation

An agreement not to compete for 20 years would likely be illegal. Often an agreement not to compete anywhere in the United States is ruled to be illegal. In contrast, an agreement not to engage in the printing business for five years in the city or county where the former employer is located probably would be enforceable. The employer's interests protected by the covenant not to compete must be significant. Trade secrets are the most commonly recognized employer interests.

THINK ABOUT LEGAL CONCEPTS

Answer the following questions about legal concepts.

1. All contracts that involve an illegal act are unenforceable. **True or False?**

2. Contracts in which one person pays another to commit a felony are unenforceable. **True or False?**

3. Gambling arises when luck is the determinant of whether you can collect on the agreement. **True or False?**

4. Which of the following would be unenforceable agreements? **(a) wager between two private persons (b) gambling agreement between two private persons (c) both a & b**

5. Charging interest at a rate higher than allowed by law is called **(a) compounding a crime (b) wagering (c) excessive interest (d) usury**

6. If you agreed to pay a witness to be sure that she testified for you at a trial, this agreement would be unenforceable. **True or False?**

THINK CRITICALLY ABOUT EVIDENCE

Study the following situations, answer the questions, then prepare arguments to support your answers.

7. Crump owned a restaurant. She applied to the state liquor control board for a $500 license to sell alcohol. When the application was denied, Lynch, a customer, told Crump that he knew someone on the board and could get her a license for $7,500. Crump paid Lynch the money but never received the license. Can she recover the money?

8. Dixon, a wholesaler, was on the brink of bankruptcy. He bought fire insurance policies for more than twice the value of the building and contents from two companies. Then he arranged to pay a character known only as "Sparky" $10,000 to "torch" his business building. Was the agreement with Sparky valid? Could Dixon legally collect on his insurance policies if Sparky torched the building?

9. A remote community and the surrounding countryside had no doctor. The city council advertised for help, offering free office space, a six-bed infirmary, and a three-year contract. Glamorgan applied and was accepted. Three months later, the council learned that although Glamorgan had a medical degree, she had failed to pass the state examination required to practice medicine. No patients complained, but the council summarily discharged her. Glamorgan sued for breach of contract. Will she win the lawsuit?

- Describe how courts help parties to illegal contracts under the common law
- Describe how courts help parties to illegal contracts under the UCC

HOW DO COURTS TREAT PARTIES TO ILLEGAL CONTRACTS?

WHAT'S YOUR VERDICT?

A young couple, the Guptas, wanted to provide for the college education of their infant daughter. They received this offer in the mail from the True Bonanza Mining Corporation, which seemed perfect for their need: "Join us now for only 10 cents a share of stock. Become part owner of a gold and silver mine with already proven mineral deposits. In ten years, you will be rich enough to retire!" The Guptas used all their savings to buy 10,000 shares of Bonanza stock. Months later they learned that Bonanza had violated the law. Its "proven mineral deposits" were commercially worthless aluminum oxides. The sales agreement was illegal.

Can the Guptas recover their $1,000?

Generally, courts treat illegal agreements in two different ways depending upon whether they are governed by the common law (sale of services or realty) or the UCC (sale of goods).

Common Law

In contracts for the sale of services or realty, courts generally will help neither party to the illegal agreement. Courts will not enforce the agreement. Further, courts will leave the parties where they are. This is so even if one party has performed and the other has not. If you've already paid Murder Incorporated and they haven't done the job, you can't get **restitution** —recovery of your payment. However, there are four major exceptions to these rules.

PROTECTED VICTIMS In some cases the law that was violated was designed to protect a party to the agreement. For example, *blue-sky laws* prohibit sales of worthless stocks and bonds. Such securities have no more value than a section of the blue sky. The victim may obtain restitution to recover money paid. Thus, in *What's Your Verdict?* restitution would be available to the Guptas.

Parties to an illegal agreement are often not equally blameworthy. For example, by lying one party might persuade a gullible person to enter an illegal agreement. Where the illegal agreement was created by fraud, duress, misrepresentation or undue influence, the victim may obtain restitution.

THE EXCUSABLY IGNORANT The excusably ignorant can either enforce the legal part of the contract *or* obtain restitution. A person is excusably ignorant who

- does not know the contract is illegal, but
- the *other party knows* the transaction is illegal, and
- the illegality is *minor*

IN THIS CASE

Cindy agreed to star in a series of plays in summer stock at Shoreside Theater. The theater, however, had not been inspected for building code compliance after recent minor renovations. The theater knew this. Cindy did not. Cindy's ignorance of this fact is excusable because it would be very difficult for her to determine this. While failure to obtain the inspections is usually serious, this may not be the case if the renovations are minor. Therefore Cindy can enforce the legal part of the contract. If the theater owner had not been aware of the failure to inspect, then Cindy could not enforce the agreement.

RESCISSION BEFORE THE ILLEGAL ACT If a party rescinds before the illegal act occurs, then restitution will be available. For example, if you paid $50 to another student to steal an advance copy of a final exam, then changed your mind and called off the deal before the theft, you could recover the $50 payment. In this way, the law creates an incentive to stop illegal acts.

DIVISIBLE CONTRACTS Illegal contracts often contain a combination of legal and illegal provisions. Courts may enforce the legal part of a contract if it is **divisible**. Divisible generally means that separate consideration is given for the legal and illegal parts of the contract. Suppose a retailer contracts to sell camping and hunting supplies, including a pistol. If the seller fails to comply with a state law that requires a 30-day waiting period and a police clearance of sale of a handgun, this part of the contract is illegal. However, a court would probably enforce the legal provisions of the contract because the amount paid for the pistol (the illegal part) can be distinguished from the amount paid for everything else (the legal part).

On the other hand, suppose a single bid for all electrical contracting work on an office building specifies wiring and terminals in conflict with the building code. This contract would probably not be divisible because labor, wiring, terminals, and other costs were not broken out as separate items. This contract is **indivisible**.

The UCC

A major provision in the UCC governing the sale of goods makes agreements or contract clauses that are unconscionable unenforceable. Also, the UCC establishes an additional remedy for courts when dealing with such agreements. **Unconscionability** occurs when there is a grossly unfair contract that parties under ordinary circumstances would not accept.

UNCONSCIONABILITY The UCC makes **unconscionable contracts** for the sale of goods subject to the rules for illegality. Unconscionability has two elements.

- **Procedural unconscionability** is shown by *how* the contract is created.
- **Substantive unconscionability** is established by *terms* of the agreement.

Most (but not all) courts require *both* procedural and substantive unconscionability before the contract is deemed unconscionable and illegal.

Procedural unconscionability arises when contracts contain very fine print, light typesetting or elements of fraud, duress, undue influence, or misrepresentation. It can also be established by showing that a party had no real alternatives, was time pressured, or possessed unequal bargaining power.

Substantive unconscionability arises from unfair terms in the agreement. It can take the form of a price so high that it shocks the conscience of the court or very one-sided terms such as the elimination of important

IN THIS CASE

Barb was shopping for a car. She found a nearly new Bronco at a used car lot. The odometer said the car had 22,000 miles on it. The dealer presented Barb with a contract to review that showed the 22,000 miles. He asked her to read the contract and discuss any concerns before signing it. After she finished reading the contract, the salesperson took it to be signed by the sales manager. The salesperson returned with the signed contract and the manager's initials on each page. Barb then signed the contract and initialed each page. She didn't notice that the page with the odometer disclosure had been switched. The new page stated that the original odometer had been replaced at 66,000 miles and the car had been driven 88,000 miles. Barb paid almost twice the Blue Book value of the Bronco. Procedural unconscionability existed in the switching of the documents. Substantive unconscionability existed in the very high price paid by Barb. The court might exercise its power under the UCC and simply reduce the price.

remedies (for example, restitution) for one party.

ADDITIONAL REMEDY When the court finds a contract illegal for unconscionability, it can refuse to enforce the contract, or it can enforce the legal part and refuse to enforce the illegal part. This remedy is similar to the common law. In addition, courts can also modify the terms of an agreement to make it fair. This is the new remedy.

Answer the following questions about legal concepts.

1. Restitution is **(a) the enforcement of an agreement (b) getting back something you have given**

2. In general, illegal agreements cannot be enforced, but restitution is available. **True or False?**

3. Illegal agreements are not enforceable unless one party has performed all of the obligations. **True or False?**

4. A party to an illegal contract can *either* enforce the agreement *or* obtain restitution if they **(a) are excusably ignorant (b) are a protected victim (c) rescind before the illegal act occurs (d) none of the above**

Study the following situations, answer the questions, then prepare arguments to support your answers.

5. A new boss was scheduled to take over Patty's department in three weeks. Patty agreed to pay Nancy $600 to remove unflattering information from her personnel file so she would look good to the new boss. The day before Nancy was going to do it, Patty called and told her not to. She also asked for her money back. Nancy never took the information. Could Patty sue and recover her money?

6. Randy entered into a contract to provide a computer program to a New Jersey school district. He used without permission parts of a computer program copyrighted by another programmer. The portion of the program that violated the copyright law cost $12,000 and the part that didn't violate the copyright law cost $44,000. He delivered both parts to the school district. Can he recover anything for his work?

7. Cliff worked as a site manager for an oil-drilling company. When a drill bit broke, he called Texas Bit Company, a bit manufacturer. Cliff asked for a bit able to cut quickly through granite. The salesperson recommended their model 2123 which was described as a high carbon steel bit with diamonds embedded on the cutting edges. The salesperson quoted a fair price but she said there were no warranties and that the product was being sold, "as is." This is an unusual practice in this industry. Cliff didn't think he could get that type of bit from anyone else without a big delay, so he ordered it. It turned out that the bit was made only of low-carbon steel and it cut very slowly. Is there procedural unconscionability here? Is there substantive unconscionability here? Did the bit company create an unconscionable contract?

In making contracts . . .

PREVENT LEGAL DIFFICULTIES

1. Wagering is illegal in most states. Even where legal, most persons who wager lose in the long run. Therefore do not bet unless you can afford to lose.

2. Most states permit a wide range of interest rates, so shop for loans as carefully as you shop for goods and services.

3. Report any crimes or information you have that may help authorities prosecute crimes. Never accept money or something of value to refrain from reporting such information.

4. Deal only with persons who are reputable and properly licensed when contracting for professional or skilled services.

5. Do not rush into a decision. Take time to review and understand the advantages and disadvantages of the proposed contract. Legitimate proposals will usually survive a delay.

6. If you are in business, be careful not to agree with competitors to charge a certain price or to sell only in certain geographic areas.

CHAPTER IN REVIEW

CONCEPTS IN BRIEF

1. To be valid, a contract must not violate the law (constitutional, statutory, or case), nor be contrary to public policy in its formation, purpose, or performance.

2. Among agreements that violate law or public policy and are therefore void and unenforceable are those that
   - require committing a crime or tort
   - obstruct legal procedures
   - injure public service
   - are made by persons without a required competency license
   - involve payment of usurious interest
   - involve illegal gambling, wagers, or lotteries
   - threaten the freedom or security of marriage
   - involve price fixing or market allocation
   - include an unreasonable promise not to compete
   - are unconscionable

3. Illegal agreements are usually unenforceable and restitution is not available. Exceptions are sometimes made to this rule when
   - the violated law was meant to protect one of the parties
   - one party is excusably ignorant
   - a party rescinds before the illegal act occurs
   - the contract is divisible into legal and illegal parts

YOUR LEGAL VOCABULARY

Match each statement with the term that it best defines. Some terms may not be used.

1. A bet on the uncertain outcome of an event *wager*
2. Competitors' agreement to split market areas between themselves *allocation of markets*
3. Grossly unfair contract for the sale of goods *unconscionable contract*
4. Mechanism used by governments only to raise money *revenue license*
5. Accepting something of value for a promise not to inform on or prosecute a suspected criminal *compounding a crime*
6. Rate specified by statute when interest is called for but no percentage is stated in the contract *legal rate of interest*
7. Charging interest on a loan beyond the legally permitted maximum rate *usury*
8. Gross unfairness in how a contract is created *procedural unconscionability*
9. Competitors agree to charge the same amount for a product or service, thus injuring consumers *price fixing*
10. Manufacturer attempts to influence the retail price of its product or service
11. Competitors who bid on jobs agree that one bidder will have the lowest bid for a particular job *bid rigging*
12. Involves agreement with the following three parts: payment to participate, chance to win based on luck rather than skill, and a prize for one or more winners *gambling*
13. Higher interest rates that loan companies and pawnbrokers may charge on loans up to $2,000 *small loan rate of interest*
14. Element of unconscionability shown in the terms of a contract *substantive unconscionability*

allocation of markets
bid rigging
competency license
compounding a crime
covenants not to compete
divisible contracts
gambling
legal rate of interest
maximum rate of interest
price fixing
procedural unconscionability
resale price maintenance
restitution
revenue license
small loan rate of interest
substantive unconscionability
unconscionable contract
usury
wager

15. Describe the way courts classify contracts for unlicensed work.

16. Explain what usury is.

17. Tell how courts treat parties to a contract that is illegal because of usury.

18. Describe the two elements of unconscionability.

19. Write one sentence identifying a local merchant. Next write three sentences that describe three different illegal agreements that merchant might enter into related to the business.

20. For each of the three agreements in exercise 19, determine whether the illegal agreement is one which results in a court: (a) leaving the parties where they are, (b) allowing one party to obtain restitution, or (c) allowing one party to enforce the legal part of a broader contract.

21. Create a valid, written, four-sentence contract for the sale for $50 of the following items found at a garage sale:
  • a lamp
  • a bookcase
  • 26 books

22. List four licenses that are held by people you know. For each license, indicate whether it is a revenue or competency license.

23. **HOT DEBATE** Write one sentence giving a reason why Stacey should be able to collect the money. Write another sentence giving a reason why Stacey should not be able to collect the money.

24. A door-to-door salesperson appeared at Jamaya's front door selling encyclopedias. The set cost more than $600 for the hardbound deluxe edition. She signed the contract and paid $200 with the balance due when the books were delivered in 30 days. When the books arrived, she refused to pay. Jamaya claimed the contract was illegal because the salesperson didn't have a business license to operate in her city. If the allegation can be proven, can Jamaya recover the $200 she paid?

25. The Franklins, Ali and Lomalinda, had no medical insurance and urgently needed money for emergency surgery for their infant child. They could not qualify for a bank loan and they did not belong to a credit union. An acquaintance referred them to someone named "Slye, who'll lend you money on sight. No collateral. No credit report. Just show him you've got a steady job." The Franklins borrowed $2,500 from Slye and agreed to pay $325 on the first of each month "in 12 easy installments." Later a lawyer told them that the loan contract was illegal. Was it? How much money must the Franklins repay?

26. Trent, a minor, bought a copyrighted compact disc recording of a current hit from Shawn. After making a copy of the disc, Trent found a defect in the CD. He tried to return it to Shawn for a full refund. Shawn suspected the illegal copying and refused the refund. Can Shawn assert illegality as a defense here? Did Trent act legally and ethically in making a copy?

27. Moser had no automobile liability insurance, although state law required it. She negligently collided with Chang's car. Chang threatened to call the police if Moser failed to pay $1,000 for pain and suffering and $2,000 for car repairs. Moser gave Chang a check for $3,000. Then she stopped payment on it. If Chang sues, will she recover?

ANALYZE REAL CASES

28. Roger Morris, Ph.D., signed an employment contract with Baxter International that contained a covenant not to compete. It read: "I [Morris] will not render services for one year after the termination of my employment . . . to any Competing Organization within such geographic area where the organizations compete." Morris possessed no information that would be useful to a competing organization. When he left Baxter he went to work for its major competitor. Baxter sued to enjoin the new employment. Will Baxter prevail? (*Baxter International, Inc. v. Morris,* 976 F.2d 1189)

29. Blubaugh, a farmer, leased a combine from John Deere Leasing (JDL). The lease document was printed on two sides of the paper but one side was printed in very small, light type. Blubaugh read and signed the front side but did not notice or read the other side of the document. It contained unusual provisions making Blubaugh liable in the event of breach for much more money than the unpaid lease payments. When Blubaugh breached, JDL sued. The trial judge required a magnifying glass to read the fine print. Is there evidence of procedural unconscionability here? Is there evidence of substantive unconscionability? Was the contract illegal? Must Blubaugh pay more than the balance of the lease payments? (*John Deere Leasing Company v. Blubaugh,* 636 F. Supp. 1569, Kan.)

30. Dixon, a motor vehicle purchaser, sued the Wisconsin Finance Company with which he had entered into an installment contract. He also sued its Illinois sister corporation, alleging that the contract was void under Sales Finance Agency Act because the finance company was not licensed to do business in the state of Illinois. The license was not a competency license. Will Dixon prevail? (*Dixon v. Mercury Finance Company of Wisconsin,* 694 N.E.2d 693, Ill.)

31. Richard purchased a lot and home from Waldman and Sons, Inc., a real estate developer. The sale was subject to zoning ordinances. At the time of the sale, the Waldmans delivered a plot plan to Richard showing a 22-foot side yard, which complied with minimum requirements of the zoning regulations. After taking possession of the house, however, Richard learned the side yard was too narrow to comply with the zoning ordinances. He claimed he relied on the representations of the developer. Richard sought damages for the misrepresentation. Will he recover? (*Richard v. Waldman and Sons, Inc.,* 232 A.2d 307 Conn.)

32. 1st American Systems, Inc., an insurance company, sought an injunction against Rezatto, a former employee. Rezatto had agreed when hired not to compete with his employer for a 10-year period after termination. 1st American Systems alleged that Rezatto breached the employment contract by engaging in the insurance business in the same area as the employer within ten years after the termination of employment. Should the injunction be issued? (*1st American Systems, Inc. v. Rezatto,* 311 N.W.2d 51, S. D.)

33. Franklin Life Insurance Co. issued a policy that named Burne as a beneficiary. The policy provided for double indemnity accidental death benefits because of the death of the insured. The insured had been struck by an automobile and was kept alive in a vegetative state for four and a half years before he died. The policy provided that the accidental death benefits would be paid only if death occurred within 90 days of the accident, and that such benefits would not be paid if death occurred during a time when premiums were being waived due to the insured's disability. Will the beneficiary be allowed to recover the insurance? (*Burne v. Franklin Life Ins. Co.,* 301 A.2d 799, Pa.)

34. At a public auction by the Arizona Department of Transportation, notice was given that the successful bidder would be required to close the transaction within 30 days from notice of approval. A bank managed the auction for the Department of Transportation. At the auction, Renaissance Homes, Ltd., was the high bidder. Subsequently Renaissance asked the bank for and received 120 days' extension to close the transaction in return for a $15,000 earnest money deposit. The bank returned this deposit to Renaissance Homes because of a dispute by Renaissance Homes with the Department. When Renaissance Homes did not close the transaction, the bank paid $125,000 to the Arizona Department of Transportation as earnest money forfeited for breach of contract. The bank sued to recover the $15,000 from Renaissance Homes. The bank's agreement with Renaissance Homes for the 120-day extension was in violation of Arizona's competitive bidding statutes. Should the bank be allowed to recover the $15,000? (*Chicago Title Insurance Co. v. Renaissance Homes, Ltd.,* 679 P.2d 517, Ariz.)

Ransburg v. Haase
586 N.E. 2d 1295 (Ill. Ct. App.)

FACTS The Ransburgs resided in Peoria, Illinois. They orally hired David William Haase Associates, a local business, to act as the architect, construction manager, designer, and decorator of a house that the Ransburgs wanted to have built in Vail, Colorado. The parties discussed this project both in Peoria and in Colorado. The parties agreed that Haase would provide budgetary control. They also agreed to a construction budget of $949,500 and a completion date. Haase was to receive $80,000 as compensation for services. The cost of the project exceeded $1.2 million. The Ransburgs alleged that Haase had failed to meet contract terms and that he held himself out as an architect but is not a registered architect in Illinois or any other state. They sought recovery of the fees paid to Haase. The trial court dismissed this count. The Ransburgs appealed.

REASONING The initial question is whether Haase acted in violation of the Illinois Architecture Act when he represented to the Ransburgs that he is an architect and undertook to provide architectural services in connection with the construction of a residence in Colorado. The allegations in the complaint plainly charge Haase with offering professional services as an architect in Peoria where he operated a design and decorating business. Regardless of where the services were furnished, holding himself out to the Ransburgs as an architect in Illinois was a violation of the Illinois Architecture Act.

As a general rule, courts will not enforce a contract involving a party who does not have a license called for by legislation that expressly prohibits the carrying on of the particular activity without a license where the legislation was enacted for the protection of the public, not as a revenue measure. The purposes of the Illinois statute prohibiting the practice of architecture without the required registration have long been held to be for the protection of the public.

Applying the general rule to the case before us, it does not appear that the contract would be enforceable. Do Illinois courts recognize a cause of action to recover money previously paid to a defendant for architectural services which have been rendered but for which defendant was not licensed? Although it is a general rule that parties to a void contract will be left where they have placed themselves with no recovery of money paid for illegal services, exceptions to the rule have been recognized under two different rationales:

(1) that the person who paid for the Service is not *in pari delicto* [equally at fault] with the unlicensed person, and

(2) that the law in question was passed for the protection of the person who paid and it appears that the purposes of the law would be better effectuated by granting relief than by denying it.

To allow the unlicensed architect to retain the fee paid is to allow him to practice architecture in the state of Illinois without a license and to reap the rewards thereof. The purpose of the Illinois licensing act can best be effectuated by recognizing the Ransburgs' right to recovery.

Case remanded for further proceedings.

PRACTICE JUDGING

1. **Would the outcome be different if the Ransburgs' had known Haase was not an architect?**

2. **Are Haase's failures to meet the terms of the contract relevant to this case?**

LESSONS

HOT DEBATE

Anne promised her best friend, Sally, that she would pay for all Sally's wedding expenses if Sally would pay Anne's college tuition for a semester. Sally paid the tuition of $3,200. Time passed and the friends fell out of touch. After 12 years, Sally became engaged. When she contacted Anne about paying for the wedding, Anne said she didn't remember the promise.

Where Do You Stand?

1. **Why should Anne be required to pay for the wedding?**

2. **Why should Anne not have to pay for the wedding?**

GOALS

● **Describe the statute of frauds**

● **Discuss the consequences of failure to comply with the statute**

● **Describe what writing satisfies the statute under the common law and the UCC**

● **Explain how the signature influences enforcement of contracts**

is made. A person may enter many other business agreements without the formality of a written contract. Sometimes a contract may be implied from conduct. For example, a person may hail a bus, board it, deposit the proper coins, and later get off. No words are spoken or written by either passenger or driver, yet there is a valid contract.

MUST ALL CONTRACTS BE IN WRITING?

WHAT'S YOUR VERDICT?

While they were playing golf, Haka orally agreed to buy an apartment building from Simon. In a later telephone conversation, Haka promised Simon $100,000 as a down payment on the purchase price with the balance to be paid within five years. Simon promised to deliver the deed to the property at the time the down payment was made. Both parties were satisfied that all the terms had been completely negotiated. Later Haka found a better deal and told Simon he was backing out.

Is Haka's contract with Simon enforceable?

IN THIS CASE

Simon owned a 14-foot sailboat. Carl admired it and asked Simon if he would sell. Simon said. "Yes, for $480." Carl said, "That's a fair offer, but I just don't have that much money." He counteroffered at $380. Simon said, "Okay, I'll sell her to you for the $380." This was an acceptance of Carl's counteroffer and created a contract. This contract is enforceable, though nothing was placed in writing and no one even shook hands. Most oral contracts are enforceable.

Certain contracts are not enforceable in court unless a signed writing proves their existence. For example, contracts to transfer an interest in real property (land, buildings, and things permanently attached to them) must be evidenced by a writing and signed by the party against whom enforcement is sought. In *What's Your Verdict?* the oral agreement between Haka and Simon would not be enforceable.

Most contracts are enforceable even if there is no writing, or written proof. But just because a contract is unenforceable, it is not necessarily illegal. The parties may choose to carry out their agreement even if it does not meet the legal requirements for a writing.

Enforceable contracts can be created in face-to-face conversation. For example, in the sale of goods, payment by buyer and delivery by seller often occur at the time the agreement

WHAT IS THE STATUTE OF FRAUDS?

In early England, plaintiffs and defendants would often commit **perjury**. That is, they would lie under oath to prove a contract, though none really existed. To address this problem, England adopted a statute in 1677 that required certain contracts to be in writing and be signed by the party against whom the contract was to be enforced in court. Because the statute was designed to prevent fraud and perjury, it was called the Statute for the Prevention of Frauds and Perjuries.

The name **statute of frauds** is now commonly used to designate statutes that require certain contracts to be evidenced by a signed writing in order to be enforceable in court. The writing need not be a formal contract itself. The writing may consist of a letter or a sales slip if such writing identifies the necessary information.

Contracts Within the Statute of Frauds

A contract is said to be **within the statute of frauds** if it is required to be in writing. It is **without the statute of frauds** if it is not required to be in writing. Contracts within the statute of frauds include

- contracts to buy and sell goods for a price of $500 or more

- contracts to buy and sell real property or any interest in real property
- contracts that require more than one year to complete
- promises to pay the debt or answer for a legal obligation of another person
- promises to give something of value in return for a promise of marriage

If a contract is within the statute of frauds, but there is either no writing or no signature, how courts will treat the parties turns on the extent of contractual performance.

Executed Contracts

An **executed contract** is one that has been fully performed. Both parties have done all they promised to do.

If an executed contract is within the statute of frauds, but there is either no writing or no signature, the courts leave the parties where they are. Neither party can reverse the contract.

Executory Contracts

An **executory contract** is one that has not been fully performed. Something agreed upon remains to be done by one or both of the parties.

An executory contract within the statute of frauds, but not signed or not in writing, is unenforceable. This means neither party can compel performance from the other. In *What's Your Verdict?* the employment contract cannot be enforced since it was unwritten and it required more than one year to complete.

The executory contract in violation of the statute of frauds is different from an illegal contract. One way is that restitution is available. Further, if a benefit was conferred in reliance on the oral agreement, its value can be recovered. It is recovered by suing based on quasi-contract. A **quasi-contract** exists when some element of an enforceable contract is missing (such as a signed writing), yet courts award money to prevent the unjust enrichment of one party.

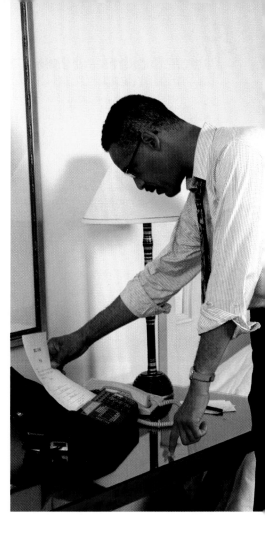

IN THIS CASE

Peg and Paul Dowell ordered "Steak of the Month" from a mail-order company in Texas. They paid $220 by check, which the seller cashed. Just before Christmas, two large Porterhouse steaks were delivered. During each of the following 11 months a different steak was to be delivered. The contract will be executory until all promised steaks are delivered. Then it will be an executed contract.

WHAT WRITING DOES THE STATUTE REQUIRE?

WHAT'S YOUR VERDICT?

Sue orally agreed to provide interior decorating services for a law firm for two years at a rate she found attractive. She wrote a signed letter to the law firm expressing her appreciation for the business, which she described as "interior decorating services, not to exceed 10 hours per week." The law firm replied with its own signed letter which described the transaction as, "services for 24 months at $3,500 per month."

Do these writings satisfy the statute of frauds?

A writing need not be in any special form to satisfy the statute of frauds.

Multiple Writings

A series of writings—such as an exchange of letters, telegrams, or faxed messages—is sufficient. In *What's Your Verdict?* the two letters satisfy the statute. The writing may be printed, typed, or handwritten with pen or pencil.

Content Requirements Under the Common Law

What must the writing contain? Under the common law, there is great variability. States have adopted statutes that differ significantly for

transactions governed by the common law. Because of the Uniform Commercial Code, states are uniform in their treatment of transactions for the sale of goods.

ALL ESSENTIAL TERMS The most demanding and common content standard used by states is that the writing must contain all the essential terms that would be required to create a valid offer. In general, this would include

1. names of the parties
2. description of the subject matter
3. price
4. quantity

5. other essential terms
6. signature

"Other essential terms" can include time or method of delivery, terms of payment, methods of financing, date for transfer of possession and so forth, depending upon the nature of the transaction. Most states require that contracts for the sale of real estate provide a legal description (as opposed to a street address) of the realty.

EVIDENCE OF A CONTRACT The least demanding common content standard merely requires that the writing indicate the existence of a contract. States that use this standard do not require that the writing contain all the essential terms.

Because the standards vary so much from state to state, it is a good practice to ensure that, in important transactions, all the essential terms are included in the writing.

Content Requirement Under the Uniform Commercial Code

Since the UCC is essentially the same in each state, it establishes a uniform content standard. Under the UCC, the writing must indicate only

- the quantity of goods
- that a contract has been created between the parties

Signature Requirement

Under the original statute, only a signing party could be successfully sued on the contract. That remains the law for transactions governed by state common law (service and realty transactions). So if there is only one signature, only one of the parties may be able to enforce the contract. This legal reality has led to the practice of asking the party on the other side to sign and then treating the transaction as concluded without signing yourself. This produces the unfair result that the party who doesn't sign can back out while the signing party cannot.

UCC AND SINGLE SIGNATURE The UCC changes the single signature issue in important ways. It provides that between merchants (those who regularly deal in the goods being sold), a writing signed and sent by one party is treated as the writing of the other party if not objected to within 10 days after receipt.

FORM OF THE SIGNATURE The signature may be written, stamped, engraved, or printed. It may consist of any mark that is intended as a signature or authentication of the writing. The purpose of the statute is to prevent frauds by requiring proof of the contract's existence that is hard to fake. Signatures are somewhat hard to forge.

THINK ABOUT LEGAL CONCEPTS

Answer the following questions about legal concepts.

1. Enforceable contracts can often be created without a writing. **True or False?**

2. The name of the law that identifies contracts that must be evidenced by a writing is the ___?___ .

3. A contract "within" the statute of frauds means that a contract need not be placed in writing. **True or False?**

4. If a transaction is within the statute of frauds but not in writing then, as with illegal contracts, restitution is not available. **True or False?**

5. Where there are contractual obligations unperformed, the contract is called ___?___ .

6. The statute of frauds does not influence an unwritten, executed contract. **True or False?**

7. The amount of writing required by the statute of frauds depends on whether the transaction is governed by the UCC or the common law of contracts. **True or False?**

8. All of the following are essential terms required to create a valid offer except **(a) the names of the parties to the contract (b) a description of the subject matter (c) the name of the person preparing the contract (d) all of these are required.**

THINK CRITICALLY ABOUT EVIDENCE

Study the following situations, answer the questions, then prepare arguments to support your answers.

9. Sheila walked into the local Wal-Mart, chose a $20 dress, walked to the checkout counter, paid for the dress and left the store. Is this agreement executory or executed? Is this a completely valid contract though nothing was placed in writing?

10. Jeanne went to SOHO, a local dress shop. She found a dress she liked for $180 and asked if she could put it on layaway. The owner said, "Yes, but you've got to put $20 down and pay at least $20 a week until it is paid." Jeanne said, "Okay," and paid the $20. Is the store bound by this agreement even if nothing was placed in writing?

11. Julian agreed with a national auto parts chain to pay $900 for a remanufactured engine for his older car. He took delivery of the engine and paid the money, though nothing was placed in writing. Two days later he saw an ad by another chain offering the same engine for $600. Is this contract within or without the statute of frauds? Is it executory or executed? Can Julian withdraw from the agreement because nothing was placed in writing?

GOALS

- Identify those contracts which are within the statute of frauds
- Describe exceptions where contracts within the statute need not be in writing to be enforced

WHAT CONTRACTS ARE WITHIN THE STATUTE OF FRAUDS?

WHAT'S YOUR VERDICT?

Cervante and Joan were good friends. When they graduated from high school, both were 18. They planned to marry, but first they wanted to become financially secure. So they shook hands and agreed to become partners in operating a small restaurant serving Indian cuisine. "This is just the beginning," Joan said. "'Til death do us part!" both said.

Are they legally bound to remain partners in business until one dies?

To be enforceable under the statute of frauds, five important types of executory contracts must be evidenced by a writing and signed by the party against whom the contract is to be enforced. As an alternative, the contract may be provable by some other writing, such as a letter signed by the party who is being sued. A plaintiff seeking to enforce the contract can readily sign if his or her signature is missing. Since either party might later want to sue for breach, both parties should sign when the contract is made.

Contract for the Sale of Goods for $500 or more

Goods (such as a book, car, or TV) are tangible personal property. If parties agree to buy and sell goods for a price of $500 or more, their contract must be evidenced by a writing.

If a contract for the sale of goods is for less than $500, then it need not

be in writing. However, a modification of that contract which brings the total price above $500 must be in writing and signed.

IN THIS CASE

Khan bought a new car and wanted to sell her old car. She advertised in the local paper and Khazari agreed to buy the car for $1,885. He promised to pay and to take delivery when he received his paycheck in two weeks. If Khan refused to sell as promised, Khazari could enforce their agreement only if Khan had signed their agreement. On the other hand, if Khazari refused to buy as promised, Khan could collect damages only if Khazari had signed.

IN THIS CASE

Don orally agreed with a gun shop to buy a used rifle (a good) for $480. This agreement is without the statute of frauds. However, Don called the shop the next day and asked them to add a used seven-power scope for the gun which cost an additional $100. Because this modification moves the total price above the $500 mark, the agreement must be placed in writing to be enforceable.

The Uniform Commercial Code provides exceptions to the statute of frauds. In these cases, a writing and signature are not required

- when goods are ordered to be specially manufactured and they are not suitable to be sold to others in the ordinary course of the seller's business
- when goods have been ordered and paid for and the seller has accepted payment
- when goods have been received and accepted by the buyer
- when the party against whom enforcement is sought admits during legal proceedings that the oral contract was made

These exceptions are discussed further in Chapter 15.

Contract to Sell an Interest in Real Property

Real property includes land and buildings permanently attached to land. Transfers of real property or of lesser interests—such as a lease, the right to pump oil or to cut timber—must be in a properly signed writing

to be enforceable. In most states, oral leases for one year or less are enforceable. Some states require that contracts employing real estate brokers satisfy the statute of frauds.

IN THIS CASE The Schmidts orally agreed to sell their mountain cabin, and the Cardonas orally agreed to buy it. The price agreed upon was $28,950. Before the oral contract was executed, the Schmidts got a better offer in writing from Murata. Could the Cardonas still hold the Schmidts to their original oral promise to sell for the agreed-upon price? No, the Cardonas cannot hold the Schmidts to their oral promise to sell. However, since Murata made his offer (to buy) in writing, the Schmidts could hold him to this promise.

As an exception to the general rule, courts will enforce the oral contract if the seller has delivered the deed or if the buyer has also done all of the following:

- made partial or full payment,
- occupied the land, and
- made substantial improvements to the land

Contracts That Require More Than One Year to Complete

Courts will not enforce a contract that cannot be performed within one year unless there is a signed writing to prove the agreement. The year begins at the time the contract is made, not at the time contractual performance is to begin.

This time provision does not apply to agreements that might be executed within one year. This is true even if such agreements are not actually carried out within that time. The test is not whether the agreement is actually performed within one year, but whether there is a possibility of performance within one year. To illustrate, two persons, such as Cervante and Joan in *What's Your Verdict?* shake hands and orally agree to be business partners. But they do not specify a definite time period. Because either partner may quit or die within one year, their agreement does not require more than one year to complete, and it need not be in writing. Either party could withdraw at anytime without liability to the other.

Contract to Pay a Debt or to Answer for the Legal Obligation of Another Person

Another provision of the statute of frauds requires a writing for a promise to answer for the debt or default of another. So if Dad tells his daughter's landlord that he will pay

IN THIS CASE Late in March, Bulger, the human resources manager of Data Dot Data Inc., orally promised to employ Gramling in the company's information processing department. The job was to be for eleven months at $2,000 a month plus a customary package of fringe benefits. Gramling was to report for work one month after receiving her high school diploma the following June. Gramling discussed the offer with her parents. The next day she telephoned Bulger and accepted it. However, this agreement was not an enforceable contract by either Gramling or Data Dot Data Inc. When Gramling reported for work as promised, Bulger said, "Sorry, business is too slow. We've changed our minds." The oral agreement was not enforceable because the contract required more than one year to complete, even though the employment period was for less than one year.

the rent if she defaults on a three-month lease, this promise is called a **collateral promise**. It must be in writing to be enforceable. This contrasts with a **primary promise** to pay. A primary promise exists if Dad says, "I'll rent the apartment and you bill me. Then I'll let my daughter stay there." This agreement is enforceable without a writing.

Often a person dies without enough assets to pay all the debts. In these cases, the person in charge of settling the deceased person's unpaid debts (often a relative) may agree to pay the debt personally instead of trying to pay it from the deceased person's assets. This is a promise to answer for the debts of another. Such

Puccini predicted a revival of "one-man bands" featuring accordion music. Mike's Music Box shop had the accordion Puccini needed but it cost $1,495. Puccini had neither the necessary cash nor credit. His friend, Muniz, told the music shop owner, "Sell Puccini the accordion on a 15-month installment contract. If he fails to make any payment, I will pay the balance due." After three months, Puccini defaulted. However, the oral promise Muniz made is not enforceable. If Muniz had said, "Sell the accordion to Puccini, but bill me. I will pay you," it would have been a direct, primary promise to the seller. As such, the oral promise would have been enforceable in court.

a promise is not enforceable unless placed in writing.

EXCEPTION—MAIN PURPOSE RULE A third party is liable for an oral promise to pay another's debt if the main purpose of the promise serves the promisor's own interest. This is called the **main purpose rule**. Suppose an owner of a house under construction is anxious to see it completed. After the building contractor fails to pay on time, the driver of the delivery truck refuses to unload a shipment of lumber. If the homeowner orally promises to pay the lumberyard if the contractor doesn't pay for needed supplies, the homeowner cannot defend using the statute of frauds. The main purpose rule applies.

Contract for Which the Consideration Is Marriage

A signed writing is required for agreements in which one party promises to marry in return for something other than the other's promise to marry. If Sue and Bill agree to marry each other, this is outside the statute of frauds. If Alice agrees to marry Buck because he promised to deed his house to her, this is within the statute of frauds. In some U.S. subcultures, a parent of the woman may promise to pay a dowry to the man in return for his promise to marry. This agreement must be placed in writing to be enforceable.

In some states, if one party breaches either an oral or written contract to marry, the victim of the breach may successfully sue for damages. The trend, however, is to ban such "heart balm" suits.

THINK ABOUT LEGAL CONCEPTS

Answer the following questions about legal concepts.

1. A good is tangible personal property. **True or False?**

2. Contracts for the sale of goods for __?__ or more must be evidenced by a writing to satisfy the statute of frauds.

3. Which transaction would be without the statute of frauds? **(a) contract for the sale of a car for $299 with all obligations to be completed within 20 days (b) contract for the sale of a car for $299 with payment due in 18 monthly installments of $50 each (c) both a & b**

4. Which transaction would be within the statute of frauds? **(a) promise to answer for the debt of another (b) promise given in exchange for marriage (c) promise to pay $30 for groceries within 10 days (d) both a & b**

THINK CRITICALLY ABOUT EVIDENCE

Study the following situations, answer the questions, then prepare arguments to support your answers.

5. Suzy entered into an oral contract with Hugh for the purchase of 16 used CDs by country and western singers. Suzy handed over the $300 price and Hugh gave her the 16 CDs. Is this transaction within the statute of frauds?

6. Jack and Ted were in a sporting goods store looking at exercise equipment. Jack wanted to buy a set of weights but he didn't have the cash or the credit. Ted orally told the owner of the store that he would pay if Jack didn't make his payments on time. Jack got the weights and took them home. Is Ted's promise primary or collateral? Does it fall under the main purpose rule? Is the transaction with Ted enforceable in court?

7. Jason's father, Phil, died. He left credit card bills totaling $17,000 and some additional small bills. His only asset at the time of death was a savings account with $6,000 in it. One of the credit card companies called Jason. In his grief, Jason orally promised to pay them the balance on his dad's account, $2,000. Is this promise enforceable in court?

WHAT IS THE PAROL EVIDENCE RULE?

WHAT'S YOUR VERDICT?

Highman bought a new personal computer from Advance Electronics. She signed the store's usual contract, which contained a clause stating that it was the complete agreement between the parties. Later, Highman alleged that as part of the bargain, the salesperson orally promised that if the list price were reduced within two months, Highman would be refunded the amount of the reduction. The list price was reduced, but Advanced Electronics refused to pay the refund to Highman.

Can Highman recover the refund?

Parties sometimes make enforceable oral agreements. Other times, part of the agreement is oral and part is in writing. Frequently the parties place the whole agreement in writing. Some writings are intended to be the final and complete agreement between the parties. Such final and complete writings invoke the parol evidence rule.

To determine whether a writing is intended by the parties to be the complete agreement, the courts look at the length and detail of the writing. Often, writings will be clear on this issue by including an **integration clause**. An example of an integration clause is: "It is agreed that the terms written here constitute the entire and final contract between the parties."

Consequences of Applying the Parol Evidence Rule

With certain exceptions, the **parol evidence rule** will bar testimony about what was said prior to the execution of the final writing or at the time of signing. This makes the final writing the source of evidence about the terms of the contract. Thus, if a complete final written agreement for the sale of a house is signed, then a court will not admit oral testimony that, prior to the parties' signing the written agreement the seller had said he would paint the exterior before vacating.

The rule keeps out preliminary inquiries, initial proposals, negotiations, and other discussions that are not the final agreement. These inadmissible spoken words are called **parol statements** or **parol evidence**.

In *What's Your Verdict?* Highman could not recover the refund. Evidence of the salesperson's oral promise would be parol evidence. In complete and final writings, both parties should carefully include all terms that they deem essential.

Exception to the Parol Evidence Rule

Even when there is a written agreement or an integration clause, parol evidence may be admissible. Parol evidence is admissible

1. to clarify ambiguities in the written agreement
2. if the written contract was not intended to be a complete agreement
3. if a condition necessary to the existence of the contract never occurred
4. if fraud, forgery, illegality, mistake, or misrepresentation occurred
5. to show the parties reached another agreement or terminated the contract under consideration after executing the written contract
6. to show that the contract is voidable because a party lacked contractual capacity

WHAT'S YOUR VERDICT?

Milo contracted with Corrigan for the installation of a complete burglar alarm system for $2,900. The printed standard form contract provided that Milo was to pay $900 down and the balance at $100 a month for 20 months. Failure to pay any installment when due would accelerate the debt and make the entire balance due. The payments were to be made on the first day of each month. Milo explained that he did not receive his paycheck until the tenth. Therefore, he said he would prefer to make the payments on that date. Corrigan agreed and in the margin wrote in "tenth," and initialed it on Milo's copy only. During the first month, Corrigan demanded the full balance when Milo failed to make the payment on the first day.

Is Corrigan entitled to the full balance immediately?

Even when parties put their agreement into a signed contract, the written words may be unclear or require interpretation. This sometimes happens when filling in blanks on standard forms. Also, modifying terms on a standard form may cause contradictions among terms. Further, one party may use a word that seems perfectly clear, yet it has a totally different meaning for the other party.

Specific Rules of Construction

If there is a conflict between the typeset print and something typewritten or handwritten, the later writings—not the conflicting typeset print—determines the contract's meaning. This is because the writing is likely to have occurred after the typesetting. Similarly a typewritten agreement which includes a conflicting handwritten statement or clause will be interpreted based on the handwritten portion. In *What's Your Verdict?* the handwritten modification prevails over the typeset, so Corrigan is not entitled to the full balance immediately.

When contracts refer to amounts of money, they often describe the amount with numerals, such as "10," and also with words such as "ten." If there is a conflict between the numeral and the word, and one of them is ambiguous, then the unambiguous expression will prevail. For example, "Two twenty-five dollars ($2.25)" will be interpreted by reliance on the numerals. When both the writing and the numerals are unambiguous, then the writing prevails. For example, "Two hundred twenty five and 00/100 ($235.00)" will be interpreted in reliance on the words. This is because more mistakes are made when writing numerals.

Analysis

The first thing a court will do is interpret the contract in terms of the **parties' principal objective**. By looking at the main objective, courts can see which clauses should prevail over others. Further, if an agreement can be interpreted in two ways, the courts will choose the way that renders the agreement a contract. Interpreting each clause in the light of all other provisions of the contract is another way to follow the parties' principal objective. Every word is given effect if this is reasonable.

REAL ESTATE MORTGAGE

THIS MORTGAGE made this ____**20th**____ day of ____**October**____, 20--, between **Bernard and Mariah Easton (husband and wife), 6720 Observatory Lane, Cuyahoga Falls, Ohio**, Mortgagors, and the LAST NATIONAL BANK of Akron, Summit County, Ohio, a corporation doing business under the laws of the United States with its principal office in Akron, Ohio, Mortgagee.

    WITNESSETH: That whereas, Mortgagors are jointly indebted to Mortgagee for money borrowed in the sum of $___**One hundred and thirty-four thousand, five hundred**___ Dollars ($___**134,900**___) to secure the payment of which Mortgagors have executed their promissory note of even date herewith in the said amount together with interest as stated in said note, payable within ten (1) years.

Find the mistakes in this contract. Which numbers prevail?

Words

The plain and normal meaning of ordinary words will be used to determine the meaning of the contract. Where the words are ambiguous, they will be given the meaning that the parties intended. Prior relationships of the parties may indicate how the words should be interpreted.

Legal and other technical terms are given their technical meaning unless the contract as a whole shows that a different meaning is intended. Where both parties are members of a trade or profession, both parties are presumed to know the trade custom or practice, and the contract is interpreted in light of that trade custom or practice.

Authors of Ambiguity

Courts will interpret ambiguities against the party who drafted the contract. Often consumers are asked to accept and sign **contracts of adhesion**. These are contracts such as credit purchases or life insurance policies, that are prepared by the stronger parties (usually the sellers), with the help of skilled lawyers, who naturally favor the interests of their clients. Generally, the terms of such contracts are not negotiable. The weaker parties (usually the consumers) must "take it or leave it." In such contracts, courts interpret ambiguity against the author. Statutes in some states now require that the language of consumer contracts be clear, simple, and understandable to the average person.

Implied Reasonableness

Contracts often include implied terms as a matter of reasonableness. Thus, a clause requiring "payment in cash" usually may be satisfied by check. Promised services must be performed with reasonable care and skill even when this is not stated. When no time for performance is mentioned, a reasonable time is allowed.

THINK ABOUT LEGAL CONCEPTS

Answer the following questions about legal concepts.

1. An integration clause is helpful in determining whether the writing is intended to be the __?__ and __?__ contract.

2. Unless there is an integration clause, the parol evidence rule does not apply. **True or False?**

3. The parol evidence rule will bar testimony about what parties said after the execution of the complete final contract. **True or False?**

4. Parol statements can be admitted to prove which of the following? **(a) fraud (b) illegality (c) a conflicting agreement existed before the signing (d) a & b**

5. When there is a conflict among terms, handwriting prevails over typewriting, and typewriting prevails over typesetting. **True or False?**

6. Ambiguity will be construed against the author. **True or False?**

7. Contracts offered by stronger parties on a "take it or leave it" basis are called __?__ .

8. The last thing a court will do is interpret a contract in terms of the parties' principal objective. **True or False?**

Study the following situations, answer the questions, then prepare arguments to support your answers.

9. A salesperson tries to persuade you to buy an electronic musical instrument. The price is $499, plus carrying charges of $72. The salesperson says, "You'll soon be the life of the party. If not, just return it and get your money back." You sign an installment payment contract, which includes an integration clause but which says nothing about a return privilege. Can you hold the seller to the promise to accept a return?

10. Silvio Development Company bought an insurance policy to cover the risk of damage to its corporate helicopter. For coverage, the standard printed insurance policy required that every pilot of the plane be licensed by the Federal Aviation Agency (FAA) and have a minimum of 500 logged (recorded by the pilot) flying hours. A typewritten addition specified that every pilot had to have a minimum of 200 logged helicopter flying hours. When the plane crashed, the pilot had logged only 75 helicopter flying hours. However, she was FAA licensed and had logged more than 2,000 flying hours in conventional planes. Must the insurance company pay?

11. When Torres leased an apartment from Leon, they used a printed form provided by Leon, the landlord. One sentence stated: "No advance deposits shall be required other than for one month's rent." However, Leon had typed in: "Tenant shall pay a $400 refundable cleaning and repair deposit upon taking possession. No charge shall be made for ordinary wear and tear." Torres drew a line through the $400 and wrote in $200. Both parties signed and each received a copy of the lease. Which provision governs the refundable deposit—the printed ($0), the typewritten ($400), or the handwritten ($200)?

12. Under a written contract, Cabrera bought a used sedan from Sharpe's Previously Owned Cars Inc. The salesperson had knowingly falsely assured her that the car was in "tip-top condition . . . with just 45,000 miles driven by only one previous owner." Later, in checking official registration records, Cabrera discovered that the sedan had three previous owners and that the odometer had been set back from 70,000 miles. In court, Sharpe's attorney claims that under the parol evidence rule, introduction of the salesperson's oral statements is barred because there was an integration clause in the written contract. Is this parol evidence admissible?

When you enter a contract . . .

1. If the contract is complex or involves much time or money, put it in writing even when the statute of frauds does not require this. Try to anticipate and provide for all important contingencies and possible problems. If needed, obtain the assistance of a qualified lawyer.

2. If a prepared contract is presented to you for your signature read it carefully, especially if it is a contract of adhesion. If the contract involves a large sum of money, or if it is complex in details, have your lawyer review it before you sign.

PREVENT LEGAL DIFFICULTIES

3. Insist that all terms of the contract that you do not understand be defined and explained. Make necessary changes, or reject the entire contract.

4. Make sure that all changes are written into the contract on all copies as well as on the original, and that all changes are initialed by both parties.

5. Be sure all desired terms are expressed in writing or included by specific reference to any other relevant document(s).

6. When any payments have been made in cash, be sure to get a receipt if payment is not acknowledged in the contract.

7. For contracts within the statute of frauds, be sure the party on the other side signs.

CHAPTER IN REVIEW

CONCEPTS IN BRIEF

1. Unless so required by the statute of frauds, contracts need not be in writing to be enforceable.

2. An express contract is stated in words—written or spoken. An implied contract is shown by conduct of the parties and by surrounding circumstances.

3. An executory contract has not been fully performed. An executed contract has been completed by both parties.

4. A quasi-contract exists when some element of a valid contract is missing, yet it is enforced as if it were a contract. This is done to prevent unjust enrichment of one party.

5. To be enforceable, the following contracts must be in writing (or evidenced by some other written proof) and signed by the party against whom enforcement is sought:

   • contracts to buy and sell goods for a price of $500 or more

   • contracts to buy and sell real property or any interest in real property
   • contracts that cannot be performed within one year after being made
   • contracts to pay a debt or answer for a legal obligation of another person
   • contracts having marriage as the consideration

6. A memorandum of an agreement need not be in any special form. The requirements for the content of a writing under the common law vary greatly from state to state.

7. The terms of a written contract may not be changed by parol evidence unless the original writing is clearly ambiguous. Parol evidence may also be used to show that a written agreement is not binding because of mistake, fraud, illegality, or because a party was a minor.

YOUR LEGAL VOCABULARY

Match each statement with the term that it best defines. Some terms may not be used.

1. Rule under which oral testimony cannot be used to contradict terms in a complete, final, written contract

2. Contracts not required to be in writing

3. Promise to pay a debt that is not conditioned upon failure of another to pay

4. Contract that has been fully performed

5. Promise to pay a debt but only if someone else fails to pay

6. Method of contract interpretation focused on the main goals of the parties to the contract

7. Obligation that is enforced as if it were a contract in order to prevent unjust enrichment of one party

8. Law stating that certain agreements are not enforceable unless they are in writing and are signed by the party against whom the contract is to be enforced

9. Contract that has not been fully performed

10. Contract in which the more powerful party dictates all the important terms

collateral promise
contract of adhesion
executed contract
executory contract
integration clause
main purpose rule
parties' principal objective
parol evidence
parol evidence rule
parol statements
perjury
primary promise
quasi-contract
statute of frauds
within the statute of frauds
without the statute of frauds

11. Name the categories of contracts that are within the statute of frauds.

12. Describe the range of content requirements for contracts for services within the statute of frauds.

13. Describe the content requirements for contracts for goods that are within the statute of frauds.

14. Identify situations where parol evidence is admissible.

WRITE ABOUT LEGAL CONCEPTS

15. Invent a situation involving the sale of after-school tutoring. Write a related contract that includes enough content to satisfy the most demanding state requirements.

16. Invent a situation involving the sale of a used car. Write a related contract which includes the minimum content required to satisfy the UCC.

17. Write a dialogue between two people that creates some oral statements which would be admissible and some which would not be admissible for a contract of employment for three years.

18. **HOT DEBATE** Write a paragraph arguing that Anne should be required to pay for the wedding or that she should not be required to pay.

THINK CRITICALLY ABOUT EVIDENCE

19. During the final week of Al's junior year at East High, an officer from Granite Inc. offered him a job. "After you get that diploma," the officer said, "show up ready for work." "I'll be there," Al replied. Was this a contract enforceable in court?

20. Van and Trip are competent adults. Under a written contract, Van bought Trip's motor scooter for $800. Van gave Trip a check for $300 as a down payment and took delivery of the scooter. On the way home, she bought some gas at a self-service station and got a granola bar from a vending machine. How would you classify these contracts as to extent of performance?

21. Bruno bought Hummel's condominium using a written contract. The title was to be transferred in 30 days. Bruno then orally agreed to buy specified items of Hummel's furniture for the lump sum of $2,800. When she took possession of the condominium, however, she decided not to buy any of the furniture. Is Bruno legally permitted to change her mind this way without any legal liability to Hummel? Is such conduct ethical?

22. Central-Cal Lands Corp. orally agreed to sell a 640-acre ranch to Ceres Inc. for $3,280,000. Ceres paid $125,000 and immediately took possession. Can Central-Cal legally withdraw from the agreement?

23. Kelley was admitted to University Hospital as an emergency heart transplant patient. The next day, the hospital's business manager discussed the cost of the surgery with Kelley's two sons. Both sons told the manager, "Do whatever is necessary to save his life, and we will pay you." When the hospital presented the staggering bill to the junior Kelleys, they said the contract was oral and, therefore, they were not liable. Is that true?

24. Cornelius, an elderly bachelor, was at the town cafe. In front of several witnesses who will vouch for the story, Cornelius made the following statement to Barbara, a young waitress: "I can't give you a castle in Spain. But if you marry me, I will deed to you a half interest in Meadowland Acres, the best farm in the county. And I'll give you 75 cows, 200 hogs, and 5,000 chickens." Barbara said, "I will," and they were married. Is Cornelius legally bound to keep his promise?

ANALYZE
REAL CASES

25. For a nine-year period, Kiyosi served as a teaching associate and lecturer at Indiana University, Bloomington. Meanwhile, he continued to study and write to qualify for a Ph.D. degree. He relied on an oral promise by the defendant university that upon obtaining the degree, he would be appointed to a permanent position with perpetual renewals, starting at the rank of assistant professor. It was customary for the university to make such appointments for terms of three years. When Kiyosi received his Ph.D., he was appointed assistant professor, but was told that he would not be reappointed for the following year. He then sued for damages for breach of contract. The university officials claimed that the statute of frauds barred his action because a lifetime contract cannot be performed within one year. You decide. (*Kiyosi v. Trustees of Indiana University,* 166 Ind. App. 34, 333 N.E.2d 886)

26. Unit, Inc., was the general contractor for a real estate development owned by Sciota Park, Ltd. Unit subcontracted to plaintiff Wilson Floors Company the job of furnishing and installing flooring materials. When Unit fell behind in making promised payments for completed work, Wilson stopped work. The Pittsburgh National Bank had already loaned $7 million to Sciota for the project, which was now two-thirds completed. The bank representatives orally assured Wilson that if it returned to work, it would be paid. Wilson did so and finished the job. When Wilson was not paid, it sued Unit, Sciota Park, and the Pittsburgh Bank for the $15,443.06, plus interest. Wilson received judgment. When Sciota and Unit failed to pay, Wilson sought recovery from the bank. The bank claimed it was not liable because a promise to pay another's debt had to be in writing. You decide. (*Wilson Floors Co. v. Sciota Park, Ltd.,* 54 Ohio St. 2d 451, 377 N.E.2d 514)

27. For safekeeping, Kula deposited $18,300 with the cashier of a Nevada hotel casino and was given a receipt for the money. Kula and a friend, Goldfinger, gambled in the hotel's casino. (Casino gambling is legal in Nevada.) Kula made withdrawals and deposits from time to time with the casino cashier and at the time had a balance of $18,000. One evening Goldfinger lost $500 in gambling and was unable to pay it. He asked the shift boss, Ponto, to telephone Kula for a guarantee of the loss. Ponto did so and received Kula's authorization to give Goldfinger credit up to $1,000 but no more. Ponto confirmed this but stated that Kula had also said Goldfinger could gamble the entire deposit of $18,000. Goldfinger was permitted to gamble until he lost $18,000. The casino tried to collect the amount from Kula on his alleged oral promise to cover Goldfinger's debt to $18,000. The casino did this by refusing to return to Kula the amount he had on deposit. Kula was willing to honor his oral guarantee of Goldfinger's debt up to $1,000 but no more. Kula sued the hotel for return of his deposit. Should he get it? (*Kula v. Karat, Inc.,* 531 P.2d 1353)

28. Nicolella, a building contractor, was asked by Palmer to submit a bid for the construction of an addition to a food market. After reviewing the plans and specifications for the addition, Nicolella bid $57,027 for the job. Palmer subsequently made two revisions of the written plans. Thereafter, the parties entered into a written contract. At the time of its execution, Nicolella orally asked Palmer if changes in the plans would materially affect the bid and Palmer said no. Palmer added that if there were any substantial changes, the price paid would be adjusted. After the start of construction, Nicolella discovered that 1,340 square feet had been added to the building. Palmer orally urged Nicolella to continue and said that any additional amount claimed would be paid. Upon completion of the job, Nicolella asked for an additional $10,653, based on the original price per square foot. Palmer refused to pay, so Nicolella sued, alleging that Palmer's statements had been made fraudulently. Could the terms of the original written agreement be varied by any prior or contemporaneous promises made by Palmer? Was Palmer bound by his later oral promise to pay any additional amount claimed by Nicolella? (*Nicolella v. Palmer,* 432 Pa. 502, 248 A.2d 20)

CASE FOR LEGAL THINKING

McCoy v. Spelman Memorial Hospital
845 S.W.2d 727

EVIDENCE McCoy was looking for a better job when he saw Spelman's advertisement for an assistant hospital administrator. After a telephone interview with Alan Abramovitz, Spelman's personnel director, McCoy was invited to interview with Spelman's board of directors and with Meyer. At the end of these interviews, McCoy understood that Spelman would offer him the position and that he would later receive written confirmation of the offer's terms.

Meyer sent McCoy a letter that stated:

> To reconfirm the offer, it is as follows: We will pay for the moving expenses. . . . I would like you to pursue your Master's Degree at an area program. We will pay 100% tuition reimbursement. Effective September 26 you will be eligible for all benefits. A starting salary of $48,000 annually with reviews and eligibility for increases at 6 months, 12 months and annually thereafter. We will pay for the expenses of 3 trips, if necessary, in order for you to find housing. As you have agreed, it is necessary for you to live in the Smithville School District but not until you have found and arranged for permanent housing. Vacation will be for 3 weeks a year after one year, however, we do allow for this to be taken earlier.

According to McCoy, the board asked him for a three to five year commitment, but the September 14 letter did not indicate a specific duration for employment.

McCoy accepted the offer and began work. Less than a year later he was terminated for allegedly inadequate management skills. The trial court determined that no employment contract existed between McCoy and Spelman, and it entered summary judgment in favor of Spelman and Meyer on the breach of contract claim.

McCoy asserts that the contract was oral—that the board's asking him for a three to five year commitment constituted an employment contract, and the agreement was memorialized by the September 14, 1988, offer letter. Spelman and Meyer argued to the trial court that an employment contract must be in writing to be enforceable—as required by the statute of frauds. McCoy argues that the letter satisfied the statute because it constituted a "memorandum or note" of the oral agreement.

OPINION We disagree. The statute of frauds, §432.010, RSMo, provides, "No action shall be brought . . . upon any agreement that is not to be performed within one year from the making thereof, unless the agreement upon which the action shall be brought, or some memorandum or note thereof, shall be in writing and signed by the party to be charged therewith, or some other person by him thereto lawfully authorized [.]"

To satisfy the statute of frauds, an employment contract—and its memorandum or note—must contain all essential terms, including duration of the employment relationship. Without a statement of duration, an employment at will is created which is terminable at any time by either party with no liability for breach of contract.

McCoy's argument that the letter constituted a memorandum of an oral contract fails because the letter does not state an essential element, duration. The letter did not state that Spelman was granting McCoy employment for any term. Moreover, the letter did not memorialize an agreement. It confirmed "the offer" which McCoy still had to accept.

PRACTICE JUDGING

1. Is the law of Missouri the same as the law in the vast majority of other states?

2. What would the outcome be if the letter identified a term of employment but omitted the language related to reviews for pay raises?

LESSONS

HOT DEBATE

June was an accomplished opera singer. She contracted to sing for the San Francisco Opera over Labor Day weekend for $5,000. About a month before her performance, she was offered another role that paid twice as much. June offered to pay the $5,000 to her friend Sara, an equally accomplished opera singer, to fill in for her on Labor Day weekend. Sara agreed. When June told the San Francisco Opera, they said they wouldn't pay the money.

Where Do You Stand?

1. **Why should the San Francisco Opera have to pay June?**

2. **Why should the San Francisco Opera not have to pay June?**

G O A L S

- Describe which rights can be assigned
- Identify what duties can be delegated

ASSIGNING CONTRACTUAL RIGHTS

WHAT'S YOUR VERDICT?

Whippet bought a high-powered sports coupe from Oriental Motors for $32,000. After a down payment of $2,000, the balance, plus a finance charge, was to be paid in installments over the following 48 months. Oriental Motors needed cash to restore its inventory of new cars. Therefore, it immediately sold Whippet's contract to the finance company and told Whippet to make all installment payments to the finance company.

Is such a transfer of contract rights legal?

Persons frequently have **contractual rights** (something they will receive under a contract) that they transfer to others. Such transfer is called an *assignment*. The party who transfers the contractual right to another is the **assignor**. The party who receives this contractual right is the **assignee**.

Assignable Rights

Generally, a party may assign contractual rights to another, provided performance will not be materially changed. **Performance** is the fulfillment of contractual promises as agreed. A right to collect a debt is assignable because performance remains the same after assignment. In *What's Your Verdict?* when Whippet was notified of the assignment, he became obligated to pay the finance company instead of Oriental Motors. Retailers and restaurants assign to issuers of credit cards the right to collect the amounts due from customers who have used the cards. In exchange, the credit card companies immediately pay the retailers and restaurants the face amount of the credit slips, less an agreed percentage.

Non-assignable Rights

Contractual rights may not be assigned if performance would be materially changed (changed in an important way). Additionally, contractual rights may not be assigned if performance becomes substantially more difficult. For example, Chris has a claim against Ted for $1,000. Chris may not assign that claim in 1,000 parts to the 1,000 students at Central High because such an assignment would make Ted's paying off the debt substantially more difficult.

Rights that may not be transferred include

1. a right created under a contract that prohibits transfer of the contractual rights
2. claims for damages for personal injuries
3. claims against the United States
4. rights to personal services, especially those of a skilled nature, or when personal trust and confidence are involved
5. assignments of future wages, as limited by state statutes

IN THIS CASE

Ford, a dentist, owed Bentin $5,000 for office furniture. Bentin agreed to accept $1,000 in cash and $4,000 in orthodontic services for his children as payment for the debt. Soon after, Bentin needed the money, so he assigned his right to receive the dental services to Lakely. Unless Ford consented, this assignment would not be valid because it included rights to personal services of a skilled, professional nature.

Form

Assignment of contractual rights is usually made voluntarily by the assignor. While an assignment is usually valid whether oral or written, a written assignment is always wiser. State statutes sometimes require that certain assignments be in writing. No consideration is necessary to make a valid assignment.

DELEGATING CONTRACTUAL DUTIES

WHAT'S YOUR VERDICT?

Ramirez hired Norton to come to her home and care for her two young children while she was at work.

Could Norton legally delegate the child-care duties to a well-qualified third party?

Contractual duties are legal obligations created by a contract. If you order a shirt and promise to pay $60, you have the duty to pay and the seller has the right to collect. Routine duties can often be transferred to another party. This is known as **delegation of duties.**

A person cannot delegate to another any duty where performance requires unique personal skill or special qualifications. In *What's Your Verdict?* Norton cannot delegate the duty of caring for the children. The task involves special qualifications of trust and skill. Similarly, a contract creating a duty can prohibit delegation.

A person who delegates contractual duties remains legally obligated and responsible for proper performance even though someone else may actually do the required work. Thus, a general contractor who agrees to build a house is responsible for providing the finished structure as promised. However, general contractors typically delegate most of the work to independent subcontractors.

Subcontractors lay foundations and do masonry, carpentry, plumbing, electrical, painting, and other work. The general contractor makes individual contracts with them and pays them. The subcontractors are responsible to the general contractor for proper performance. But the general contractor remains responsible to the buyer for the finished job. Sometimes contracting parties will both assign rights and delegate duties.

IN THIS CASE The Pyramid Builders, a ready-mix concrete company, received more orders than it could fill on schedule. Therefore it arranged to have a competitor, Gibraltar Inc., supply certain customers. Pyramid would bill the customers and turn over the proceeds to Gibraltar. If the concrete delivered was faulty, Pyramid remained liable to the customer for damages. In turn, Gibraltar would be liable to Pyramid if Gibraltar were at fault.

WHAT ARE THE OBLIGATIONS OF OBLIGORS?

WHAT'S YOUR VERDICT?

Ginsburg, a concert violinist, purchased "a genuine Stradivarius" violin from Krone for $250,000. Ginsburg paid $50,000 down and agreed to pay the balance in 24 equal monthly installments. Krone knew the violin was not a Stradivarius. He immediately assigned his right to collect the balance of $200,000 to Continental Finance for $90,000 in cash. Continental notified Ginsburg of the assignment. Krone then disappeared. Shortly after, Ginsburg discovered the fraud.

Can Ginsburg refuse to pay Continental if it tries to collect?

An **obligor** is the one who owes a duty under a contract. In *What's Your Verdict?* Ginsburg is the obligor who owes the duty to pay the balance of the money.

Notice to Obligor

Until notified that an assignment has occurred, the obligor may continue to pay the assignor. After notification, however, the obligor is liable to the assignee for performance. To protect newly acquired rights, the assignee should promptly notify the obligor of the assignment.

Obligor's Liability

Courts sometimes say that the assignee "stands in the shoes of the assignor." This means that the assignee receives exactly the same contractual rights and duties as the assignor had—no more and no less. If a contractual right is transferred, this does not change the legal rights of the other party to the contract. Assume Sally promises to give you 10 ballet lessons and you promise to pay her $200. Even if she assigns the right to your payment to a finance company, you don't need to pay if she fails to provide the lessons. In *What's Your Verdict?* Continental stands in the place of Krone, so Ginsburg can refuse to pay Continental because of Krone's fraud. This is true even though Continental is unaware of the fraud.

Obligor's Breach

In all assignments, the assignor guarantees to the assignee that the assignor has a right to assign and that the assigned right is legally enforceable. However, the assignor typically does not promise that the obligor will perform as promised in the original contract. If the obligor breaches, the assignee, not the assignor, must sue for the breach. Of course the assignment may include specific language making the assignor liable for breach by the obligor.

THINK ABOUT LEGAL CONCEPTS

Answer the following questions about legal concepts.

1. If a person is to receive something under a contract, this is called a(n) ___?___ .

2. If a person is obligated to do something under a contract, this is called a(n) ___?___ .

3. The party transferring a right in an assignment is called the **(a) assignee (b) assignor (c) obligor**

4. If the contract creating the rights and duties prohibits delegation or assignment, the parties may still delegate or assign. **True or False?**

5. Which of the following duties cannot be delegated? **(a) those which the contract says cannot be delegated (b) those which involve special qualifications (c) no duty can be delegated (d) both a & b**

THINK CRITICALLY ABOUT EVIDENCE

Study the following situations, answer the questions, then prepare arguments to support your answers.

6. Your parents contract to have a new house built. Shortly thereafter, your father's employer promotes him. The new position requires a move to corporate headquarters in Atlanta, Georgia, which is 2,000 miles away. Can your parents transfer their rights and duties under the building contract to someone else for the construction of the same house in a different location?

7. Tori operated a graphic design and printing shop. Gerov contracted to have Tori design and print 25,000 brochures in full color promoting a variety of international tours. Under their contract, Tori also agreed to address and mail envelopes containing the brochures to a select list of prospects. Tori delegated the addressing, stuffing, and mailing of the envelopes. Is this a valid delegation? Does Tori remain liable to Gerov for proper completion of the entire job?

8. Zack bought an automobile insurance policy. The policy contained a clause prohibiting assignment of the policy without written consent of the insurer. Later, when his car was stolen, Zack notified the insurer. After six months, during which the car had not been recovered, Zack assigned to Pragg his claim for payment under the policy. The insurance company refused to pay because it had not given its written consent to the assignment. Must the insurance company pay? Was the insurance company ethical in refusing payment of Zack's claim?

9. Your school orders 50 new uniforms for its marching band. The contract is with Quality Uniforms Inc., a firm with whom the school has done business for 12 years. A week before the first public performance by the band, Quality states that it has overbooked its business and has delegated the sewing to New Era Uniforms. Can the school cancel the contract or must it accept the uniforms from the new company?

GOALS

● Describe how contracts are usually satisfied

● Explain the ways contracts can be discharged other than by performance of their terms

---

HOW ARE CONTRACTS USUALLY DISCHARGED?

WHAT'S YOUR VERDICT?

Wesley promised to loan Hudson $900 within three months in return for Hudson's promise to paint Wesley's home. Hudson did not paint the house as promised. She did offer to give Wesley an aquamarine ring that had a retail value of about $1,000, and a wholesale value of $500 instead of painting the house.

Must Wesley accept the ring instead of the painting of his home?

When a contract is made, the parties take on certain duties. **Discharge** of a contract is a termination of duties that ordinarily occurs when the parties perform as promised. Most contracts are discharged by complete performance of the terms of the contract.

Failure to provide complete performance is a **breach of contract**. When one party commits a major breach, the other party may regard her or his obligation as discharged. In *What's Your Verdict?* Wesley need not accept the ring. Hudson is in major breach of the contract. Because of Hudson's major breach, Wesley need not loan the money. In sales contracts under the Uniform Commercial Code (UCC) this is termed a **cancellation**.

Occasionally, **substantial performance** occurs. This happens when substantially all the duties are performed but a minor duty under the contract remains. Then there has been only a minor breach. A minor breach does not discharge the duties

of the non-breaching party the way a major breach does. The party who has substantially performed can sue and recover what is due, less the cost of completing the remaining work. If

---

A Question of ETHICS ?

Kitchen Construction Company Inc. remodeled the Hamill's kitchen. The new cabinets were made of top-grade plywood instead of solid wood as specified in the contract. (The mistake was caused by a purchasing department error.) The contract was substantially performed because the breach was unintentional and minor. The Hamill's were responsible for the full price less a deduction for the lower cost of the plywood. Does this seem ethical to you?

IN THIS CASE

On January 5, Graham Roofers contracted to remove the old shingles and to install a new fireproof roof on the home of the Sterlings. The job was to be completed "by March 30, at the latest," to be ready for anticipated heavy spring rains. Late in February, Graham notified the Sterlings that because of a rush of orders, his crews were "swamped" and he could not get to the job until late April or early May. This was an anticipatory breach. The Sterlings have the choice of waiting for performance or immediately proceeding as though Graham had breached the contract.

the failure to perform is deliberate, the victim may treat it as a major breach.

Sometimes a party who **defaults** (fails to perform) notifies the other party to a contract before the time of performance has arrived that he or she will not perform. This is called an **anticipatory breach**. The victim may wait until the promised time of performance, or the victim may treat the notice as evidence of a breach of contract and immediately sue for damages.

Contracts often identify a duty but don't say when it must be performed. In these cases, the duty must be performed within a reasonable time. If it is not performed within a reasonable time, this is a breach. A judge or jury determines a reasonable time after examining the circumstances in each case. Thus a contract to ship tomatoes (which rot quickly) might have a reasonable time for performance of several hours while a contract to ship used cars (which don't change in value quickly) might have a reasonable time of seven days.

In other instances, the contract identifies a date for performance. Most courts will rule that performance shortly after the date is only a minor breach. Again, the circumstance in each case will influence how much time after the specified date will be allowed before the delay is treated as a major breach.

When a contract states that performance is to occur by a specified date, and that "time is of the essence," failure to perform by that date is generally regarded as a major

breach. If so, the duties of the non-breaching party are discharged. Time is "of the essence" when a contract deals with property that rapidly fluctuates in value or property that is perishable. Courts look to the subject matter of the contract and the individual circumstances of the case to determine whether time is "of the essence." These words placed into a contract are not necessarily controlling.

HOW ELSE CAN CONTRACTS BE DISCHARGED?

WHAT'S YOUR VERDICT?

Diaz was the owner of a landscape service. He contracted to maintain the yard of Reingold while she sailed around the world in a 45-foot yacht. Reingold planned to write and take photographs for a national magazine and had no fixed itinerary or schedule for the journey.

When would the contract with Diaz terminate?

In addition to discharge by complete performance, a contract may be discharged by

1. agreement
2. impossibility of performance
3. operation of law

By Agreement

When the parties prepare their contract, they may agree that it will terminate

- on a specified date or upon the expiration of a specified period of time (for example, a fresh food supply contract with a school district to terminate on the last day of school)

- upon the happening of a specified event (in *What's Your Verdict?* the contract to maintain the yard would terminate when Reingold returned from her voyage around the world)

- upon the failure of a certain event to happen (for example, a construction loan contract upon failure to get a required building permit)

- at the free will of either party upon giving notice (for example, when one partner decides to retire from business and gives the required notice as specified in the partnership agreement with her associates)

The parties who have made a contract may later mutually agree to change either the terms of the contract or the nature of their relationship. They may do so without any liability for breach.

RESCISSION By rescission the parties may agree to unmake or to undo their entire contract from its very beginning. Each party returns any consideration already received, and both are placed in their original positions in so far as possible.

ACCORD AND SATISFACTION Parties may decide that the present contract is not what they want, and so replace it with a new contract. This discharges their original contract by **substitution**. The parties may also agree to change the obligation required by the original contract. An agreement to make such a change is an **accord**. Performance of the new obligation is called a **satisfaction**.

A compromise of a disputed claim or a composition of creditors is an accord. Carrying out the new agreement is the satisfaction. Thus, an accord and satisfaction discharge the previous obligation.

Vanvoor borrowed $650 from Banta. Vanvoor could not repay the loan on schedule. The parties then agreed that Vanvoor would work off the debt by doing 30 hours of painting, electrical, and plumbing work in Banta's home during the next three months. The agreement to change the required performance was an accord. Vanvoor's completion of the agreed-upon work was the satisfaction. Together, this accord and satisfaction discharged Vanvoor's original obligation to pay $650.

NOVATION A party entitled to receive performance under a contract may release the other party from the duty of performance and accept a substitute party. This is a **novation**. In effect, a new contract is formed by agreement of the three parties who are involved.

Revell had contracted to install a skylight in the roof of Sinclair's workshop. Because of pressures to complete other jobs before the rainy season began, Revell asked Sinclair if she would accept a qualified substitute carpenter named Lowry, who was willing to do the job for the same price. All three parties were agreeable. By novation, Lowry took Revell's place in the original contract, thus releasing him from all duties to perform and depriving him of all rights to be paid.

By Impossibility of Performance

Impossibility of performance refers to external conditions rather than an obligor's personal inability to perform. For example, the fact that a borrower does not have the money to repay a debt does not make the contract impossible to perform. A contract is considered discharged by impossibility of performance in such cases as destruction of the subject matter of the contract through no fault of the parties or a change of law that makes a contract illegal to perform.

As a general rule, a contract is not discharged when unforeseen events make performance more costly or difficult. For example, increased prices of needed supplies, a strike of needed workers, difficulty in obtaining materials or equipment, or a natural disaster (such as a flood or earthquake) may delay performance. Generally, these events do not discharge the contractual obligations. These events should be anticipated as possibilities and be provided for in the contract when it is made. Otherwise a party who fails to perform because of such events could be held liable for major breach of contract.

Sundstrum, a wholesaler, contracted to supply various airplane parts to Arcadia Airport at a price of $17,686. However, Sundstrum later defaulted. He claimed that it was impossible to deliver at the contract price because the manufacturers had increased their prices to him by more than $8,600. The court held him to the contract. The fact that the contract was no longer economically profitable did not mean that it was legally and physically impossible to perform.

Parties may, and commonly do, include "escape hatch" language in their contracts. Such language permits modification, or even termination, of performance without liability for damages in the event of inability to perform on schedule because of specified conditions, such as foul weather and labor strikes.

Also, under unusual circumstances recognized by the UCC, a sales contract may be discharged by conditions that make performance impracticable. Increased cost alone is not enough. But a possibility not thought of by the parties, such as a surprise war or an unexpected *embargo* (legal stoppage of commerce), may suffice. Even a shutdown of major supply sources could discharge the contract for the sale of goods if it prevented the seller from getting supplies or if it caused an extreme increase in cost beyond what could reasonably be anticipated.

DESTRUCTION OF THE SUBJECT MATTER

Sometimes performance depends on the continued existence of some specific thing. Destruction of that thing terminates the contract if the destruction was not the fault of the parties to the contract.

IN THIS CASE

Blitz was a famous jockey. He contracted to ride the thoroughbred White Flash in the Kentucky Derby. A week before the race, the horse stumbled during a workout, broke a leg, and had to be destroyed. Blitz's employment contract was discharged. He was free to contract to ride another horse in the Derby.

The result of destruction of the subject matter is different if the seller has other sources of supply and the parties did not specify one and only one source as acceptable. For example, suppose that because of a fire, a wholesale lumber broker loses her main supply source. If the broker has access to other sources of lumber, and if her contract does not limit her to one particular source, she is legally bound to deliver the lumber. This is true even if the broker's resulting cost is much higher than she had anticipated.

PERFORMANCE DECLARED ILLEGAL A contract that is legal when made is discharged if and when it later becomes illegal. A new statute, a court ruling, or an administrative decision might cause illegality.

IN THIS CASE

Tippner contracted with Barnell to build a warehouse on land owned by Barnell. Before construction began, the city council passed a zoning ordinance restricting the site to residential dwellings. The construction contract was thereby discharged.

DEATH OR DISABILITY If the contract requires personal services, death or disability of the party who was to provide such services terminates the agreement. This rule does not apply when others are available to perform, as in partnerships or corporations that

continue to do business. Likewise, it does not apply where the contract simply calls for payment of money, delivery of goods, or transfer of title to land by the decedent. In each of

IN THIS CASE

The Daily Tribune contracted for the consulting services of Chi Liang, an expert in computer networks, at a rate of $600 a day. Liang agreed to supervise the installation of a computer system with integrated software programs. The Tribune's newsroom, pressroom, circulation and advertising departments, and business office were all included. After Liang had completed his work linking the newsroom and pressroom, he suffered a stroke and was unable to continue. Liang's contractual obligation was discharged by impossibility.

these cases, the decedent's personal representative can and is required to perform.

By Operation of Law

A contract may be discharged or the right to enforce it may be barred by operation of law. This happens when the promisor's debts are discharged in bankruptcy. It also happens when the time allowed for enforcement of the contract has elapsed because of the statute of limitations.

Alteration of a written agreement also usually discharges the agreement by operation of law. **Alteration** is a material change in the terms of a written contract without consent of the other party. To discharge the contract, the alteration must be

IN THIS CASE

Carey's Complete Cleaners contracted to clean all rooms and public spaces of Dahl's office building. A contractual clause in small print allowed a 10 percent discount if the charges were paid in advance in one lump sum instead of in 12 monthly installments. After the contract had been signed by both parties, and before giving Dahl her copy, Carey secretly crossed out the clause referring to the discount. This material alteration discharged Dahl from any obligation under the contract. Dahl could thereupon insist on inclusion of the clause or seek damages through court action.

- material, thus changing the obligation in an important way
- made intentionally, and not by accident or mistake

- made by a party to the agreement, or by an authorized agent
- made without consent of the other party

WHAT IS THE EFFECT OF TENDER OF PERFORMANCE?

WHAT'S YOUR VERDICT?

Zamorsky, a professional artist, agreed to paint Quincy's portrait for $5,000. Five sittings of two hours each were scheduled at times selected by Quincy, but he failed to appear for any of them. To accommodate her client, Zamorsky then offered to come to Quincy's home or office for rescheduled sittings at his convenience. Quincy rejected this proposal. Is Zamorsky's legal obligation discharged?

Is Quincy liable for damages?

future interest charges that might otherwise become due. To be valid, the tender of money must consist of the exact amount due in legal tender. **Legal tender** is currency or coins.

A tender of only part of the debt is not a valid tender. If the debtor offers less than the amount due, the creditor may refuse it without losing the right to later collect the entire amount due.

An offer to perform an obligation is a **tender**. If the duty requires the doing of an act, a tender that is made in good faith but is rejected will discharge the obligation of the one offering to perform. In *What's Your Verdict?* Quincy refused Zamorsky's offer to perform as agreed. Thus, Zamorsky's obligation was discharged, and Quincy is liable for damages.

If the obligation requires the payment of money, rejection of an offer to pay the money does not discharge the debt nor does it prevent the creditor from collecting later. It merely relieves the debtor of court costs or

Answer the following questions about legal concepts.

1. Which of the following creates a discharge of all contractual duties?
   (a) complete performance
   (b) major breach
   (c) promissory estoppel

2. Where the parties agree to substitute one party for another, this is called a(n)
   (a) novation (b) substitution (c) accord

3. Which of the following will discharge contractual duties? (a) destruction of the subject matter
   (b) death of a party contracting to render personal services (c) change in law which makes a contractual duty illegal
   (d) all of the above

Study the following situations, answer the questions, then prepare arguments to support your answers.

4. Your school orders 50 new uniforms for its marching band. The contract states that "time is of the essence," and if the goods are not received in time for the first performance by the band on September 1, the old uniforms will be used for another year. The manufacturer does not deliver the uniforms until September 3. Can the school cancel the contract? Would it be ethical for the supplier to delay the delivery until October 10 because of a rush order from another school that provided a higher profit?

5. In January, Doolan Construction Company promised to remodel Kemper's kitchen during July when Kemper would be visiting relatives in Canada. Their written contract called for work to start on July 1, and to be completed before August 2. In April, Doolan phoned and said he could not start the job before July 20, if then. What can Kemper do?

6. Tina, age seven, was playing accountant at her father's desk in his absence. When she found a stack of interesting papers, she "corrected" all of them, adding zeros to numbers ("500" thus became "5000") and drawing lines through words. The "interesting papers" were promissory notes, owned by her father, representing claims against debtors totaling about $17,000. Have these contractual claims been discharged by Tina's changes?

To protect yourself . . .

1. As a prospective assignee, determine whether the assignor is subject to any defense that may affect your claim. Do this by promptly checking with the obligor (debtor). Remember that you, as the assignee, acquire only such rights as the assignor possessed.

2. Do not forget that the assignor does not agree to pay the debt if the debtor fails to do so. If you wish the assignor to remain liable, include a provision to that effect in the written assignment agreement.

3. If you are an assignee, be sure to notify the obligor (debtor)

PREVENT LEGAL DIFFICULTIES

of the assignment as soon as practicable.

4. Be aware that "time is of the essence" in many contracts. If a contract calls for performance by a certain time, failure to perform may be a breach of contract. When appropriate, include this requirement in your contract, and clearly state that failure to perform at the time agreed upon may be treated as a breach.

5. Remember that hardship and higher costs do not make performance impossible. Bad weather, fires, strikes, inability to obtain materials, or similar difficulties could cause hardship. To be protected against damages for failure to fulfill a contract because of such events, include in the contract a clause to that effect.

CHAPTER IN REVIEW

CONCEPTS IN BRIEF

1. A party may generally assign rights under a contract as long as the performance will not be materially changed. One is not released from contractual duties by making an assignment.

2. Duties may not be delegated when they involve personal judgment or skill, as with artists and professional experts.

3. An assignee acquires only such rights as the assignor has under the contract.

4. Until notification of assignment is received, performance may still be properly made to the original contracting party.

5. A material breach of contract generally permits the other party to regard his or her obligation to perform as discharged.

6. The obligation of one party is discharged when a written contract is materially and intentionally altered by the other party without the consent of the former.

7. An obligation calling for an act is discharged by a tender of performance that corresponds exactly to the agreement. A tender of payment does not discharge an obligation to pay money.

YOUR LEGAL VOCABULARY

Match each statement with the term that it best defines. Some terms may not be used.

1. Breach that extinguishes the other party's duty to perform

2. Transaction by which a party transfers contractual rights to another

3. Notification, before the scheduled time of performance, of refusal to perform contractual terms as agreed upon

4. Termination of contractual obligations

5. A breach that does not extinguish the other party's duty to perform

6. Material change in the terms of a contract, made intentionally by one party without consent of the other

7. Doing all the things you promised in a contract

8. One who transfers contractual rights

9. Turning over to another party one's duties under a contract

10. Agreement between the parties to a contract to change the obligation required

11. Person who owes a duty under a contract

12. Offer to perform an obligation

13. Failure to perform a legal duty or agreement

accord
accord and satisfaction
alteration
anticipatory breach
assignee
assignment
assignor
breach of contract
complete performance
contractual duties
contractual rights
default
delegation of duties
discharge of contract
major breach
minor breach
novation
obligor
satisfaction
substantial performance
substitution
tender

14. Tell how to determine whether a right can be assigned.

15. Explain how to determine if a duty can be delegated.

16. Tell how courts determine whether a breach is major or minor.

17. Describe the different consequences for major and minor breach.

WRITE ABOUT LEGAL CONCEPTS

18. Write a short contract for the fictitious sale of a car between two of your classmates. Make the money to be paid in two weeks and the title is to be delivered in one week. Now for each of the two classmates, write a sentence describing the rights and duties created by this contract.

19. Think through all the contracts you've entered into over the last week. Now make a list of all the rights and duties created by these contracts. Choose two rights or duties and write a sentence saying why that right or duty can or cannot be assigned or delegated.

20. Write an invented fact pattern involving a contract. Now write a short description of how accord and satisfaction could alter the parties legal rights.

21. **HOT DEBATE** Write a short paragraph giving reasons why the San Francisco Opera should pay June. Write another paragraph giving reasons why the Opera should not have to pay June.

THINK CRITICALLY ABOUT EVIDENCE

22. Cullen purchased a Holee Donuts franchise. The contract contained a clause that forbade transfer of the business without consent of the franchisor. After six years of successful operation, Cullen wanted to sell the business to his manager. Was he legally permitted to do this?

23. Mercado contracted with Hidden Valley School District to provide a bus and to serve as the driver for a five-year period. After two years, Mercado died and his adult son became owner of the bus. He proposed to become the driver and complete the remaining three years of the contract. Must Hidden Valley accept his services?

24. Bradmaker operated a profitable lunch bar in a downtown business district. He sold the business to Olefson for $60,000. Olefson later assigned the contract to Ogden with Bradmaker's knowledge and consent. By then only $30,000 of the debt remained to be paid. Within six months, however, Ogden closed the lunch bar. He also stopped making payments. Bradmaker sued Olefson for the unpaid balance. Is Olefson liable?

25. Ferrazzi, a distinguished Italian sculptor, contracted to create a large bronze abstract design for the lobby of the Martindale Mart. He was to receive $75,000 upon completion and installation of the sculpture. Shortly thereafter, Ferrazzi was injured in an accident. Unable to fulfill his agreement, he asked his friend Drinano to do the work for him. Drinano was an equally competent sculptor. Must Martindale Mart accept Drinano's services?

26. Ohler Oil Company contracted to sell and to deliver 500 barrels of fuel oil on the first of each month for one year to the Monson Mushroom Factory (an indoor farm). Ohler delivered the oil for the first two months, but none during the third month. Ohler said there was unprecedented demand and it was allocating available supplies to all customers. Monson notified Ohler that it was canceling the contract because of Ohler's breach. Was Monson justified in its action?

27. Eugene Plante was a general contractor who built a house for Frank and Carol Jacobs for a contract price of $26,765. The buyers paid $20,000 but refused to pay the balance, claiming that the contract had not been substantially performed. Plante sued, and the court ruled in his favor but first deducted the cost of repairing plaster cracks in the ceilings and a number of other defects. The buyers were dissatisfied with the judgment and appealed, notably because the trial court had allowed nothing for the misplacement of a wall between the kitchen and the living room. This enlarged the kitchen and narrowed the living room by one foot. Real estate experts testified during the trial that this did not affect the market price of the house, yet to move the wall would cost about $4,000. How should the appellate court decide? (*Plante v. Jacobs*, 103 N.W.2d 296, Wis.)

28. In August, Tanner contracted to pay $300 to the Swanola Club to have his minor daughter participate as one of eight maids in the following year's carnival ball. Tanner paid $50 down, but one month later, he notified Swanola that his daughter would not participate because it might interfere with her college studies. He failed to pay the balance of $250 due before December 15. The contract gave Swanola "the option either to cancel the agreement and retain the cash portion paid as damages, or, in the alternative, to enforce payment of the entire consideration." Tanner claimed that Swanola was not entitled to the full contract price because it had never tendered performance by delivering the ball gown and other items as agreed. (Tanner's daughter had been measured for her gown by the Swanola dressmaker. Also, the daughter had found time to participate as a maid in a ball sponsored by another organization that same carnival season.) Only seven maids appeared in the Swanola ball. Six months after the ball, Swanola sued for the $250 balance. The trial court allowed Swanola to retain only the $50 deposit. Swanola appealed. You decide. (*Swanola Club v. Tanner*, 209 So. 2d 173, La.)

29. The defendant, Sunset Packing Company, contracted to buy Schafer's strawberry crop. It also contracted to furnish 150–200 laborers to harvest the crop beginning June 1. A recruiting fee of $15 per laborer was to be paid by Schafer, who gave Sunset a check for $2,000 as advance payment. Sunset recruited the laborers in Texas, but they went to Idaho to work in the sugar beet harvest. Two days before June 1, Sunset notified Schafer that it would be impossible to supply the laborers as agreed upon. Sunset said, however, that it would make available 100 laborers from its own labor force if Schafer would pay Sunset an extra $20 per ton of harvested strawberries. Schafer then recruited his own labor force, but at a greater cost. Later he sued Sunset for $17,880 in lost profits. Sunset claimed that it was discharged from its contractual obligation because of impossibility of performance. Do you agree with Sunset? (*Schafer v. Sunset Packing Company of Oregon*, 474 P.2d 529, Or.)

30. The Washington Trader was a giant oil tanker owned by the plaintiff, American Trading and Production Corporation. In March 1967, the defendant, Shell International Marine, Ltd., contracted for the ship to carry a load of oil from Texas to India. The total fee agreed upon was $417,327.36. No reference was made in the contract for the route to be taken; this was to be a decision of the shipping company. The route around Africa's Cape of Good Hope was an acceptable route. However, the price was based on passage through the Suez Canal (the invoice contained a Suez Canal toll charge). The Washington Trader headed for the Mediterranean Sea and the Suez. When the ship reached Gibraltar, it was warned of possible violence in the Middle East. Nevertheless, it continued. Upon reaching the Suez Canal, the ship found the canal closed by the Arab-Israeli War. The ship turned back and took the long route around Africa, at an added cost of $131,978.44. It arrived in Bombay some 30 days later than originally expected. American Trading then billed Shell for the full amount. When Shell refused to pay, American Trading sued. American claimed that the war made it impossible to perform as originally agreed. Shell, it said, should pay the extra cost because otherwise Shell would be unjustly enriched. You decide. (*American Trading and Production Corporation v. Shell International Marine, Ltd.*, 453 F.2d 939, 2d Cir.)

FACTS Byron Dragway, a dragstrip located in Byron, Illinois, needed work. Byron's insurance company insisted that the dragstrip be equipped with concrete retaining walls. Ronald Leek, Byron's president, decided to use the occasion to make other repairs, including resurfacing the 25-year-old surface. The dragstrip's starting area (the "starting pads") had a concrete surface, while the remainder of the track was asphalt. Leek hired Randy Folk to do all of the work. When Folk finished, Leek refused to pay, claiming that the work was shabby and would need to be entirely redone. Folk sued. The trial court gave judgment for Folk in the amount of $140,000, finding that, although there were problems, he had substantially performed. Byron Dragway appealed.

OPINION A contractor is not required to perform perfectly, but rather is held only to the duty of substantial performance in a workmanlike manner. Whether substantial performance has been given will depend upon the relevant facts of each case. However, the burden is on the contractor to prove the elements of substantial performance.

Duane Nichols, president of the UDRA, testified that the association is the largest owners and drivers association in the nation. It sponsors racing events throughout the country, featuring pro stock cars, super-charged funny cars, dragsters, and exhibition cars, which travel between 180 and 260 miles per hour. Inspecting the new track in fall 1987, Nichols observed that the new concrete [starting] pads were extremely smooth, plus there were significant dips in the concrete surface. Nichols particularly noted a dip where the concrete met the asphalt, an imperfection that would cause cars' tires to spin sideways. He observed several puddles in both asphalt lanes, where the surface dipped. Also, in fall 1987, Nichols attended a local meet held at Byron. Cars were having problems getting down the track, and several of them lost control, with one crashing. Nichols stated that no future UDRA events should be held at the track until the surface was repaired.

As to plaintiff's workmanship, the evidence points convincingly to its poor quality. [One expert] stated the defects of both the concrete starting pads and the asphalt surface were so severe that the total replacement of both was necessary. John Berg of Rockford Blacktop thought that the new asphalt surface would have to be ground off prior to the installation of a new surface. Ronald Colson and Duane Nichols, of the UDRA, found that both the concrete pads and asphalt track were unsafe, and the UDRA board refused to sponsor any future events until the new surface was thoroughly repaired. Folk did not substantially perform. Judgment reversed, in favor of Byron Dragway.

PRACTICE JUDGING

1. **Describe the resurfacing in a way that would constitute substantial performance.**

2. **Argue that there is evidence supporting the trial judge's decisions that substantial performance existed.**

LESSONS

14-1 REMEDIES FOR BREACH OF CONTRACT

14-2 DENIAL OF REMEDIES FOR BREACH OF CONTRACT

HOT DEBATE

Victoria needed her van repaired. The dealership estimated that the repairs to her transmission would take three days to complete. Because Victoria had a relative flying into town in four days, she asked the service manager if he was sure the work would be done within the three days. He replied, "Yes, for sure." Victoria left the van and went home. On the third day the dealership said it would take an additional two days. Victoria took two hours to arrange for a rental car to drive her relative around. She was angry and felt she'd been cheated out of the two hours and the cost of the rental car.

Where Do You Stand?

1. Why should Victoria be able to recover the cost of the rental car from the dealership?

2. What are the reasons in the dealership's favor for not reimbursing Victoria the cost of the rental car?

GOALS

- Distinguish between minor and major breach
- Describe when the remedies of rescission and specific performance are available
- Define four types of damages and tell when they will be awarded by courts

TYPES OF BREACH AND REMEDIES

WHAT'S YOUR VERDICT?

Eve planned to open a sportswear shop in a small store space in a mall scheduled to open November 30. In a contract, Designs Inc. assured her that all work would be completed by November 10 and acknowledged that timely completion was essential. On October 15 the manager of Designs Inc. told Eve that her crews were working double shifts on the "anchor" stores in the mall. "Sorry, but we can't get you in before December 30. Eve immediately hired another firm to do the job. It finished on November 12, but charged 25 percent more.

Does Eve have an enforceable claim against Designs Inc.?

The law divides breaches of contract into two categories: the major (or material) breach and the minor breach. Different remedies are granted for injuries caused by minor and major breaches. A **remedy** means the action or procedure followed to enforce a right or to get damages for an injury to a right.

The significance of any breach, and therefore its classification as major or minor, is an issue of fact to be decided by a judge or a jury. They will try to determine whether a reasonable person would, in light of the particular facts and circumstances, view the breach as major or minor.

Two guidelines help in classifying major versus minor breaches. The primary guideline is the significance of the breach in relation to the entire contract. For example, if a contractor builds a 12-room home for you but fails to paint four of the rooms, this

would probably be a minor breach. The cost of painting the rooms is quite minor in comparison to the cost of building a house. On the other hand, if a painting contractor agrees to paint the inside of your 12-room house but fails to paint four of the rooms, this would probably be a major breach. In *What's Your Verdict?* the breach is material because the contract terms make time of completion essential and because the value of Christmas sales is so large in relation to the typical cost of interior work.

The basic remedies for major breach of contract include the following:

1. rescission and restitution—canceling the contract and returning whatever has been received under it
2. money damages—the payment

of money to compensate for injury

3. specific performance—a court order commanding the breaching party to perform what was promised in the contract

How Does Minor Breach Affect the Victim's Duties?

The party injured by a minor breach must generally continue to perform the duties defined by the contract. The only remedy generally available for a minor breach is money damages, to recover the cost of completing the minor duty. Thus, if a buyer paid cash to have a new home built and upon moving in discovered that four rooms were not painted, the buyer could sue and recover the cost of painting the rooms. If the purchase price had not been paid, the buyer could recover damages through **offset**. That is, the buyer could deduct the cost of the painting from money to be paid for the house.

How Does Major Breach Affect the Victim's Duties?

If the breach is classified as a major breach, then the injured party need not continue performing the duties defined by the contract. In addition, the victim can choose among the remedies of restitution, compensatory money damages, consequential money damages, liquidated money damages, and specific performance.

What are Rescission and Restitution?

Rescission and restitution are intended to place the parties in the same legal position they were in before contracting. Rescission allows the parties to treat the contract as canceled. **Restitution** permits the injured party to recover money or property (or the value thereof) given to the defaulting party. Thus, if a seller of realty committed a major breach by failing to deliver the deed, the buyer could sue for restitution and recover any money paid for the property. When rescission is granted, all the contractual obligations of the parties are extinguished. Restitution also is usually available when the parties have attempted to contract, but failed, and in the process one party has delivered something of value to the other.

Types of Money Damages

Money damages may be compensatory, consequential, liquidated, punitive or nominal.

COMPENSATORY An award of **compensatory money damages** seeks to place injured parties in the same financial position they would have been in if there had been no breach. Specifically, the remedy grants the "benefit of the bargain." For example, if a homeowner contracted to sell at $65,000, when the fair market value of the property was $75,000, the buyer would be receiving a $10,000 "bargain." If the seller then committed a material breach, the buyer could recover the amount of her "bargain," $10,000, as compensatory money damages.

If the breach arises from failure to perform satisfactorily, the value of the reduced performance will become compensatory money damages. If John promises to rebuild your carburetor and replace your spark plugs, and you paid $200 in advance for the work, but John only finished the carburetor, you could sue for value of the spark plug work.

CONSEQUENTIAL In awarding **consequential money damages**, the court again tries to place injured parties in the same financial position they would have been in if the contract had been performed. This remedy grants money for the foreseeable injuries caused by the breach. Consequential damages are generally foreseeable when a reasonable person would know that a breach would

cause the injury. For example, suppose you contracted for the purchase of a new set of *Encyclopedia Britannica* at the unusually low price of $300. If you breached by not paying the money, there would probably be no compensatory damages available to the seller, because there was no bargain for the seller. However, because the lost profits are generally foreseeable, you would probably be liable for that amount.

IN THIS CASE

Rivera had the concession rights to sell food, drinks, and souvenirs at a big football post-season bowl game. Some 60,000 reserved seat tickets had been sold for the event. As part of her preparations, Rivera contracted with Ace High Novelty Company for 10,000 pennants, noisemakers, and other items imprinted with the emblems and in the colors of the two competing teams. Although Rivera had emphasized the absolute necessity of delivery at least eight hours before game time, the goods arrived two days after the game had been played. Rivera can recover lost profits from Ace because these consequential damages are generally foreseeable.

Consequential damages are specifically foreseeable if the defaulting party has been told that breach will cause the injury. For example, suppose a buyer tells the seller that she needs to take possession of her commercial property on or before January 1. She says that eight boxcars of ski boots will be arriving then and must be stored on the property. The buyer may also say she'll need to rent other property to store the boots if delivery of possession is delayed. This makes the injury specifically foreseeable, and the seller will be liable if

her breach causes the buyer to be forced to rent storage space. Consequential damages may be granted for both major and minor breaches.

LIQUIDATED Parties to a contract sometimes agree that a certain amount of money will be paid if a certain breach occurs. This is called **liquidated money damages**. A liquidated damages clause might state

> In the event the purchaser fails to pay the balance of the purchase price for said computer, the seller shall retain the amounts already paid hereon as liquidated damages.

Not all liquidated damages clauses are enforceable. When the amount of the liquidated damages is punitive, the clause will not be enforced. Punitive means punishing. A liquidated damages clause will be enforced only when it stipulates an amount reflecting a reasonable attempt to forecast the damages that would result from the breach. If it does reflect a reasonable forecast, it will be enforced even when no damages are actually suffered.

When the liquidated damages clause is not enforceable, the injured party can collect damages only by proving other money damages. For example, suppose a contract clause provided that the seller must pay a daily rental rate of $1,000 for every day of delay on delivering a $30,000 used truck to the buyer. This clause clearly would not be enforced because it attempts to punish the seller.

PUNITIVE Under certain circumstances, such as fraud or when an intentional tort is involved in a breach of contract, the courts will award **punitive damages**. Such damages are added to other money damages. Their purpose is to punish and to make an example of the defendant. This could happen, for example, when a dishonest seller cheats a buyer by falsely saying a necklace is made of of solid, 18-carat gold when in fact it is gold-plated copper or highly polished brass.

NOMINAL Failure to perform a duty under a contract is a legal wrong. Therefore courts will award **nominal damages**, or a small amount, even when there is no actual injury. This could happen when, after a breach, the plaintiff finds a replacement product at a lower price. Nominal damages are granted in recognition of the rights that have been violated.

SPECIFIC PERFORMANCE

WHAT'S YOUR VERDICT?

Kelly contracted to buy 160 acres of land from McCall. She planned to build an amusement park on the land. When McCall learned of her plan, he refused to transfer the title.

Did Kelly have any recourse?

Sometimes money damages are not an adequate remedy for breach of contract. Therefore a court may give the injured party the special relief of specific performance. In a **decree for specific performance**, the court orders the defendant to do exactly what was promised in the contract.

Money Damages Inadequate

Generally, money damages suffice as a remedy for breach of contract. The victim may use the money to buy similar goods from someone else. A decree of specific performance would not be available to a buyer of 16 place settings of Corning Ware dishes. This is because Corning Ware dishes

Fraud is one of the fastest growing threats facing consumers today. Because many consumer transactions now take place over the Internet, consumers also face the prospect of online fraud. In 1996, the National Consumers League started the Internet Fraud Watch project and the National Fraud Information Center website. Consumers can access the website to get tips on how to avoid scams and fraud 7 days a week, 24 hours a day. Of the more than 60,000 visits and 1,300 e-mails received per week, many involve travel fraud. Travel fraud is growing quickly and involves bargain vacation packages, travel vouchers, and prize trips "for a small fee." In Operation Trip-Up, the Federal Trade Commission and 12 other law enforcement agencies brought 36 separate actions against travel-related scams. Attorneys general in many states have established special task forces to handle Internet fraud. To curb Internet fraud, education is the key to protection. Before you purchase, check it out!

can be purchased from another source. Actual money damages will protect plaintiff's financial position.

Subject Matter Unique

Specific performance is generally available when the subject of the contract is unique. A contract to purchase a 1932 Rolls Royce is specifically enforceable because it is

a unique antique auto. In contrast, a contract to purchase a particular new car located on a dealer's lot probably is not specifically enforceable because that car is not really unique.

When the contract is for the sale of real property, specific performance will be granted because every parcel of land is distinctively different from all others, if only as to location. Accordingly, in *What's Your Verdict?* Kelly could win a suit for specific performance. The court would order McCall to transfer title to the property with a properly signed deed delivered to Kelly.

Ability to Supervise

The court must be capable of supervising the specific performance. A court would have great difficulty in supervising the construction of a home or other structure. Similarly, it is too difficult for courts to supervise personal service or employment contracts, and therefore these contracts are usually not specifically enforceable. However, a court may grant an injunction prohibiting the defaulting party, such as an athletic coach or a key laboratory scientist, from working for anyone else during the period of employment agreed to under the contract. The person who breached the contract would still be liable for any money damages suffered by the employer.

In addition to personal service and employment contracts, courts will not specifically enforce contracts in which terms are vague or ambiguous.

Clean Hands

Specific performance is an equitable remedy. A court will not award the remedy unless the party seeking it is blameless and has acted reasonably and fairly throughout the transaction. This is often called "clean hands."

THINK ABOUT LEGAL CONCEPTS

Answer the following questions about legal concepts.

1. Which remedy seeks to place the parties in exactly the same position they would have been in if the contract had been performed? **(a) liquidated damages (b) restitution (c) specific performance**

2. If a liquidated damages clause is ___?___, the clause will not be enforced and the injured party can only collect by proving other money damages. *punitive*

3. Specific performance will be granted if **(a) money damages are an adequate remedy (b) the subject matter of the contract is unique (c) the duty to be performed is difficult for the court to supervise (d) any of the above**

THINK CRITICALLY ABOUT EVIDENCE

Study the following situations, answer the questions, then prepare arguments to support your answers.

4. A college football coach has directed his team to division championships five times. With two years remaining in his current three-year employment contract, he notifies the college president that he is resigning in order to coach a professional team at a higher salary. Is the coach legally free to change employers? Is the professional team legally free to hire him? What can the college legally do?

5. You were hired to work as an aide at a youth camp in Alaska for three months, beginning on June 10. Because of an increase in camp fees and airfares, enrollment drops sharply. After the first two-week session, the director no longer needs your help, and so she fires you. Is the director acting legally? Is she acting ethically? Do you have any legal remedy?

6. The Bethlehem Steel Company contracted with the city of Chicago to supply and erect the steelwork for a certain section of an interstate highway. The price agreed upon was $1,734,200. The contract also provided that the steel company would pay as liquidated damages $1,000 for each day the work was extended and uncompleted beyond a specified date. The work was completed 52 days after the date agreed upon. Is the company liable for $52,000?

7. Stu bid $122 million for a Picasso painting, and the seller accepted the bid. Then the seller received a higher bid, $160 million. The seller told Stu the painting would not be delivered. What are Stu's remedies?

> ### GOALS
>
> ● **Describe the election of remedies**
> ● **Describe the requirement to mitigate damages**
> ● **Explain how the statute of limitations and bankruptcy affect remedies for breach of contract**

HOW CAN ELECTION OF ONE REMEDY BAR USE OF ANOTHER REMEDY?

WHAT'S YOUR VERDICT?

Jim "Fastball" Smoot, an unknown baseball pitcher, signed a five-year contract to play for a major league team in Denver for $120,000 a year. After two months, Smoot had won three and lost one in four starts, and had 37 strike outs and an earned-run average (ERA) of 1.75. He then contracted with a competing team in Seattle for $12 million a year, thereby breaching his contract with Denver.

What remedies are available to the Denver team?

An injured party must elect, or choose, a remedy when suing. Specific performance and damages cannot be recovered for the same breach because specific performance is not available when damages are an adequate remedy. Giving the victim the actual benefit of the contract (specific performance) while also giving the benefit of the bargain (compensatory damages) would be double counting. So specific performance and compensatory damages cannot be combined.

Similarly, rescission and restitution places the victim in the pre-contract position. Damages places the victim in the same post-contract financial position, so combining these remedies is not permitted. Under the UCC however, these remedies can be combined for a breach of contract for the sale of goods.

Restitution and specific performance are essentially opposites, so you could not combine these remedies. In *What's Your Verdict?* the Denver team could recover the two months' wages ($20,000) as restitution. But if the team elects this remedy, they would lose the ability to sue for damages and the ability to obtain an injunction prohibiting Smoot from playing for Seattle.

HOW CAN FAILURE TO MITIGATE DAMAGES ELIMINATE REMEDIES?

WHAT'S YOUR VERDICT?

In a valid written contract, Allente Associates, an advertising agency, employed DeChant to be its European representative based in Paris, France, for a three-year period. His salary was set at $12,000 a month, plus a housing allowance, travel expenses, and other fringe benefits. After two years, Allente fired DeChant because it had decided to use local native talent to perform DeChant's customary duties. DeChant had similar employment opportunities but decided to "make lemonade out of lemons" as he put it. He immediately drove to a resort in Monaco, on the Mediterranean, for 12 months of the three R's (rest, recreation, and recuperation).

Has DeChant's failure to seek comparable employment eliminated his ability to recover from Allente?

The injured party must usually take reasonable steps to **mitigate damages**. This means one must act to minimize one's injury. If you contracted for a daily supply of 10-cent bolts used to assemble a car and the supplier breached, you could not recover the consequential damages associated with the production line's being halted unless you made a reasonable attempt to find substitute bolts.

Similarly, in most states, a landlord must take reasonable steps to re-rent an apartment vacated in breach of a lease. In *What's Your Verdict?* DeChant's failure to mitigate by finding comparable employment will eliminate or dramatically reduce the available damages.

HOW CAN WAIVER ELIMINATE REMEDIES?

WHAT'S YOUR VERDICT?

When Lister bought her new automobile, she received a customary limited warranty from the manufacturer. It provided protection against defects in materials or workmanship on most components of the car for one year or 12,000 miles, whichever came first. One door did not fit properly and a whistling of wind could be heard when Lister drove faster than 50 miles per hour. Also, in heavy rains, water leaked into the trunk. Because Lister drove only in town, at low speeds, in good weather, she never bothered to complain about the defects.

Has her failure to act within one year been a waiver of her right to claim a breach of warranty?

Sometimes a party intentionally and explicitly gives up a contractual right. This is called a **waiver**. If a creditor says, "I will accept your late payment without a late charge," this is a waiver. Waivers also arise by implication from conduct. So if one party consistently sends late payments and is not charged the late fee specified in the contract, the rights to collect a late fee on future payments may be waived. In *What's Your Verdict?* Lister waived her rights under the warranty.

A Question of ETHICS ?

Assume that you are a landlord and that you live in a state that does not require lessors to mitigate damages. You have a tenant leave 3 months before the end of a lease. Then you rent the apartment to a new tenant at a higher rental rate. Would you use the law to recover the unpaid rent? Do you think of yourself as a person who would do anything legal if it is in your self-interest? Or would you decline to exercise a legal right if you thought exercising this right was unfair?

HOW CAN THE STATUTE OF LIMITATIONS ELIMINATE REMEDIES?

WHAT'S YOUR VERDICT?

Raley sold a used videocassette recorder to his friend and neighbor, Parr, for $495 on credit. Over a six-year period, Parr always had some excuse for not paying when Raley tried to collect. Exasperated, Raley finally filed suit in small claims court.

Will the court consider the claim even though it is six years old?

Statutes in all states deny any remedy if suit is not commenced within a certain time after a legal claim, such as breach of contract, arises. Such laws are called **statutes of limitations**. While the time period varies among the states, four years is a common time for contracts and three years is a common time for torts. About half of the states allow more time to sue on written contracts than on oral ones. In *What's Your Verdict?* Raley has probably waited too long to file his suit. The statute of limitations would bar Raley from suing Parr.

The UCC provides that an action for breach of a contract for the sale of goods must be begun within four years after the cause of action arises. In their original agreement, the parties may shorten the period to not less than one year, but may not lengthen it. The statute begins to run from the moment there is a right to sue for a breach or default.

In the case of minors and others who lack capacity to contract, allowance is made for their period of incapacity. Thus, a minor is given a reasonable time after reaching majority to file suit.

IN THIS CASE

Fredman borrowed $500 from McNulty for one year at 7 percent interest. Each year for 10 years, Fredman sent the interest but no payment on the principal. Finally, McNulty decided she must take steps to collect the debt. So she filed suit. Fredman pleaded that the statute of limitations outlawed the debt. This was not a good defense. His annual payments of interest acknowledged the existence of the debt and kept it alive.

HOW CAN BANKRUPTCY ELIMINATE REMEDIES?

WHAT'S YOUR VERDICT?

Greene had overextended himself financially by buying too many items on installment plans. Then he lost his job. His wife required major surgery and was hospitalized for almost two months. Soon after, Greene was found guilty of negligence in an automobile accident and was held liable for $155,000 more than his insurance policy coverage. Greene can see no way of paying his creditors, yet bill collectors are at his door almost daily.

Is there anything he can legally do to get rid of his debts?

Years ago, a person who could not or did not pay debts as they came due could be jailed. Such punishment is costly for society, impractical, and unreasonable. A debtor cannot earn money to pay a debt while in prison. Moreover, the debtor's dependents may be forced to rely on public relief for support.

Under the U.S. Constitution, Congress has established uniform laws on bankruptcies that permit the discharge of (excuse of) debts. Under these laws, debtors can get a fresh

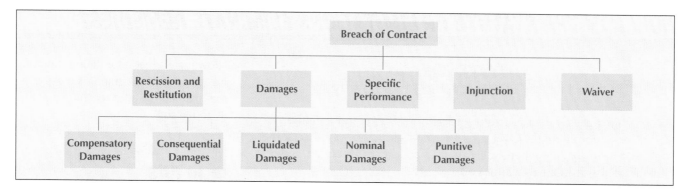

start, and creditors share fairly in whatever assets are available. **Bankruptcy** is a legal proceeding whereby a debtor's assets are distributed among his or her creditors to discharge the debts. In *What's Your Verdict?* Greene should file a proper voluntary petition with the bankruptcy court. If the petition were approved, he possibly would be permanently excused from paying all of the debts listed in *What's Your Verdict?* Note that if Greene had willfully and maliciously caused the automobile accident, or if the accident were caused by his intoxication, the judgment debt of $155,000 would not be discharged.

CULTURAL DIVERSITY IN LAW

International

Comity Principle

Countries engaging in international trade generally practice the principle of *comity*. Under this principle, each country agrees to respect the laws of the country with which it is doing business—if those laws are consistent with its own laws.

The principle of comity works something like this: Suppose a seller in Kenya has formed a contract with a buyer in America. The American buyer does not perform as promised in the contract. The seller sues the buyer in a Kenyan court, which awards damages. Because the buyer's assets are in the United States, the judgment can only be enforced by a U.S. court of law. If the laws and procedures of the Kenyan court are consistent with those in the United States, the U.S. court will enforce the Kenyan court's judgment.

Answer the following questions about legal concepts.

1. Which remedies are mutually exclusive? **(a) damages and restitution for services (b) specific performance and damages (c) specific performance and restitution (d) all of the above**

2. The UCC and the common law have different rules for determining when remedies are mutually exclusive. **True or False?**

3. In contracts for the sale of goods, rescission can be combined with damages. **True or False?**

4. The party injured by a breach has a duty to __?__ damages. *mitigate*

5. Waiver can be express or implied from conduct. **True or False?**

6. When do we begin counting the passage of time under the statute of limitations? **(a) when the contract is created (b) when the contract is ended (c) when a breach occurs (d) both a & b**

Study the following situations, answer the questions, then prepare arguments to support your answers.

7. While under contract with the county, Pyramid Paving improperly applied asphalt to the public gravel road in front of your family's home. Soon after application, large cracks appear and your family complained. It took the city six years to file suit. What defense can Pyramid assert?

8. Fulton sold traffic-signal equipment to the city of Philadelphia. The city installed the equipment, put it to use, and found that it did not work satisfactorily. The equipment did not meet the contract specifications for being weatherproof. But the city used the lights and did not complain to Fulton for more than a year. Does Fulton have any defense to a lawsuit for breach of contract?

9. Taipei Yang ordered 900 solid brass bowls for indoor plants from the East-Meets-West Company, which imports such goods from Singapore. Yang had included the bowls as a special in his holiday gift catalog and expected to generate a net profit of at least $9,000 from their sale. When the shipment arrived and was opened, Yang scratched the bottom of one bowl and determined that it was steel with a surface plating of brass. Yang complained to the supplier, who pleaded ignorance and apologized. Nothing further was said and Yang paid the full price. Three months later he thought he should get a reduction in price because of the defect. Will he succeed?

10. Bender was found guilty of manslaughter for causing the death of another driver in an automobile accident. Bender had been drinking and had been "showing off" his car to the passengers. At the trial, all of the passengers testified that they had tried to get him to stop, but he would not do so. In a separate civil action, judgment was rendered against Bender for a total of $650,000 for willful and malicious battery. Although he had no liability insurance, Bender just laughed. He said that when he got out of jail, he would "go through bankruptcy and shake the debt off." Would Bender's conduct be legal? Would it be ethical?

When seeking a remedy for breach of contract . . .

1. Negotiate, and if feasible, mediate or voluntarily arbitrate, before you litigate. A lawsuit should be the final resort because it is costly in time, money, and goodwill.

2. As a creditor seeking payment of an overdue debt, try to get at least a partial payment. In most states, such payment extends the time for filing suit before the claim is barred by the statute of limitations.

3. Do not delay too long. If the debtor is uncooperative or defiant, sue. To rest on legal rights is to risk losing them.

PREVENT LEGAL DIFFICULTIES

4. If you wish to rescind or to cancel your obligation, you must show that the other party breached the agreement in a material way. If you have paid anything, you may be able to recover what has been paid. If you have performed any service, you are entitled to be compensated.

5. Always keep accurate records and be prepared to show that you actually suffered a monetary loss if you seek more than nominal damages. You must also show that you made a reasonable effort to mitigate the damages.

6. If you seek specific performance, you must show that money damages will not adequately compensate you for your loss. You must also show that you are able, willing, and ready to fulfill your obligation.

CHAPTER IN REVIEW

CONCEPTS IN BRIEF

1. In case of a breach of contract, the injured party has various remedies. An injured party may (a) rescind or cancel the contract, (b) recover the amount of loss through damages, and (c) in certain cases, require specific performance or obtain an injunction.

2. After default, the injured party usually may recover the amount already spent in carrying out the obligations incurred as part of the contract. But the injured party should not increase the damages. Instead, the damages should be mitigated—that is, reduced if reasonably possible.

3. Generally, a party to a contract has the option of breaching it. The courts will not punish such action by awarding punitive damages unless an intentional tort or crime is involved. Rather, the court will award compensatory damages, possibly including special consequential damages. Sometimes the court will award either liquidated or nominal damages.

4. When the legal remedy of damages is not adequate, the court may grant the equitable remedy of specific performance, or of rescission, or it may grant an injunction prohibiting specified acts.

5. At the time of entering into a contract, the parties may agree to pay a specified, reasonable amount of damages if actual damages would be difficult to prove in case of default. Such damages are known as liquidated damages. The amount must not be so excessive that it would constitute a penalty.

6. A remedy for breach of contract may be barred (a) by the lapse of the time prescribed by a statute of limitations or (b) by the debtor's discharge in bankruptcy.

YOUR LEGAL VOCABULARY

Match each statement with the term that it best defines. Some terms may not be used.

1. Law setting time limit for bringing a lawsuit

2. Damages that are agreed upon before a possible breach of contract

3. Legal proceedings discharging debts and distributing assets

4. Means used to enforce a right or to compensate for an injury

5. Ending a contract by placing parties in the same position as if there had been no contract; neither party gets damages

6. To reduce damages if reasonably possible

7. Remedy permitting the injured party to recover money or property that had already been given to the defaulting party

8. Deducting the cost of completing or fixing a minor breach from payment of the contract price to the breaching party

9. Token amount awarded when rights have been violated, but there is no actual injury

10. Amount of money awarded to compensate for a plaintiff's loss

bankruptcy
compensatory damages
consequential damages
decree for specific performance
liquidated damages
mitigate
nominial damages
offset
punitive damages
remedy
rescission
restitution
statute of limitations
waiver

11. Explain how compensatory and consequential damages are calculated.

12. Describe those situations where specific performance will not be granted.

13. Tell which remedies can and cannot be combined.

14. Explain how a statute of limitations works.

15. Write a short contract for the sale of a desk. Include an enforceable liquidated damages clause.

16. Make a list of five things that might be the subject of a contract but where specific performance would not be available. After each item write one sentence which states why this remedy is not available.

17. **HOT DEBATE** Write a letter to the dealership on behalf of Victoria. In the letter, outline the reasons the company should reimburse her for the cost of the rental car.

18. Hoglund reneged on his promise to sell his car to Elsen. Elsen went to nearby Los Angeles and found the same model with lower mileage, in better condition, and priced $600 below Hoglund's. Nevertheless, Elsen was incensed by Hoglund's conduct and wanted to sue him. To what damages, if any, is Elsen entitled?

19. Madison Unified High School District had plans to build a new high school. Madison awarded the contract for construction to Empire Builders Inc., which bid $2.6 million. The contract contained a liquidated damage clause that provided for payment of $1,500 a day for every day that completion was delayed beyond the expected 24-month construction period. Could the liquidated damage clause be enforced?

20. Good contracted to build a house for Stern according to Stern's plans. After the house was completed, there were several defects that Good refused to fix. Stern then contracted with Madden to do the necessary corrective work for $8,000 and then sued Good for $8,000 in compensatory damages. Stern also demanded $10,000 in punitive damages "to punish Good and set an example for others." Is Stern entitled to compensatory damages? Is Stern legally or ethically entitled to punitive damages?

21. When Smythe bought a mattress and foundation at Big Bazaar, a recently hired and soon-to-be-fired clerk mishandled the records of the sale. As a result, the store never charged the price of $475 to Smythe's account. For four years (the statutory period of limitation for such accounts), Smythe received no bill and made no payment. Then she boasted to friends about how "sweet it is to snooze at the expense of Big Bazaar." Is Smythe still legally obligated to pay for the goods? Is she ethically obligated to pay?

22. Gordon, a wholesaler of women's clothing, contracted to buy 6,000 woolen wrap-around robes from Shine. Shine, who used nonunion labor in her factory in New York City, had purchased the required bolts of cloth in several colors and her employees had almost completed cutting the cloth into proper pieces. Gordon then surprised and shocked Shine with a letter in which he said, "Let's cancel the deal. I got an offer I couldn't refuse from an outfit in Shanghai. Their price is about half of yours. What could I do? But you'll get my next order, I guarantee you that!" Does Shine have a cause of action (right to sue) against Gordon? How should Shine mitigate the damages? Did Gordon behave in an ethical manner toward Shine?

23. Seismic & Digital Concepts, Inc., was a manufacturer of computer hardware. Digital Resources Corporation produced computer software. Digital Resources sold software to Seismic and sued when Seismic refused to pay for the software. Seismic countersued for damages because of late delivery of the goods—they were delivered 10 to 25 days after the date specified in the contract. There was no indication in the contract that "time was of the essence." Moreover, Seismic had accepted and used the software, and for about five months had even asked Digital Resources to do additional work. Is Digital entitled to judgment? (*Seismic & Digital Concepts, Inc. v. Digital Resources Corporation*, 590 S.W.2d 718, Tex.)

24. Union Oil Company was the owner of a truck stop. Union sued the general contractor and subcontractors who had constructed the large service station to recover the cost of repairing the cracked parking area pavement. Union claimed the defendant had not followed specifications for the base material used for fill. When the contractor, Kennon Construction, refused to make the needed repairs, Union had the work done by others at a cost of $58,659 and then sought to recover this sum. The contractor's superintendent admitted under oath that he had not followed the specifications, but he said that Union had approved the substitute material. Union denied this, and the notes of Union's representative supported Union's testimony. The defendant's witnesses could not remember times or dates or present any records on the matter. Should Union win? (*Union Oil Company of California v. Kennon Construction*, 502 F.2d 792, 6th Cir.)

25. Under a written contract, plaintiff Shirley MacLaine Parker agreed to play the female singing-dancing lead in defendant 20th Century-Fox Film Corporation's planned production of a musical entitled "Bloomer Girl," to be filmed in Los Angeles. Fox Films was to pay MacLaine a minimum of $53,571.42 a week for 14 weeks, starting May 23. Before then, Fox decided not to produce the picture. In a letter dated April 4, Fox offered to employ MacLaine in a dramatic, western-type movie to be produced in Australia instead. She was given one week in which to accept. She did not, and the offer lapsed. She then sued for the agreed-upon $750,000 guaranteed compensation. Fox defended by saying MacLaine had unreasonably refused to mitigate damages by rejecting the substitute role. Is MacLaine entitled to receive the damages? (*Parker v. 20th Century-Fox Film Corporation*, 474 P.2d 689, Cal.)

26. Knutton operated a music company. Cofield was the owner of a restaurant. Knutton and Cofield contracted for the installation of a jukebox in the restaurant, agreeing to share the receipts obtained. The contract provided that if Cofield discontinued use of the jukebox before the end of the agreed-upon period, he would pay Knutton a sum of money for the unexpired time. The sum would be based on the average of the amount paid to Knutton per day while the machine had been used. Before the contracted time expired, Cofield disconnected the jukebox and installed one from another supplier. Knutton sued for damages for breach of contract. Cofield claimed the damages sought were a penalty for the breach and not liquidated damages, as claimed by Knutton. Was Cofield correct? (*Knutton v. Cofield*, 160 S.E.2d 29, N.C.)

27. The plaintiffs filed a class action suit against the state of Colorado, certain officials, and the contractors on a tunnel construction project. The purpose of the suit was to seek recovery of funds alleged to have been expended unlawfully in the construction. The plaintiffs claimed that as citizens and taxpayers, they were beneficiaries of the contract for the tunnel construction. Therefore, they claimed, they were entitled to sue on the contract that was made on their behalf even though the contract was made with the state of Colorado and did not mention any individuals by name as beneficiaries. May these plaintiffs properly sue? (*Gallagher v. Continental Insurance Company*, 502 F.2d 827, 10th Cir.)

28. McIntosh entered into an agreement with Magna Systems, Inc., to the effect that McIntosh would provide assistance in the developing Magna's educational materials. Magna would pay an annual fee of $35,000 for three years to McIntosh or provide McIntosh the option of purchasing 25 percent of Magna's authorized stock in lieu of the annual fees. When he wasn't paid, McIntosh sued alleging that he had performed all contractual obligations but Magna refused to pay. Among the counts of McIntosh's complaint was one seeking punitive damages. There was no fraud or intentional tort committed by Magna. Will McIntosh recover punitive damages? (*McIntosh v. Magna Systems, Inc.*, 539 F. Supp. 1185, N.D. Ill.)

Campbell Soup Co. v. Wentz
172 F.2d 80

EVIDENCE Campbell Soup Company contracted with Wentz for the purchase of all the Chantenay red carrots he could grow on his 15-acre farm. The contract price was $30 per ton. One clause in the contract allowed Campbell to refuse the carrots and at the same time prohibit Wentz from selling them to others. After execution of the contract, the market price of Chantenay carrots rose to $90 per ton, and a shortage developed. When Wentz harvested the carrots he began selling them to others at the high price and refused to deliver his crop to Campbell at the contract price. Campbell sued for specific performance to obtain Wentz's carrots at the contract price. The trial court declined to grant the decree, holding that carrots were not unique, therefore the remedy at law (damages) was adequate.

OPINION The trial court denied equitable relief. We agree with the result reached, but on a different ground from that relied upon by the District Court. . . .

We think that on the question of adequacy of the legal remedy the case is one appropriate for specific performance. It was expressly found that at the time of the trial it was "virtually impossible to obtain Chantenay carrots in the open market." This Chantenay carrot is one that the plaintiff uses in large quantities furnishing the seed to the growers with whom it makes contracts. Its blunt shape makes it easier to handle in processing, and its color and texture differ from other varieties. The preservation of uniformity in appearance in a food article marketed throughout the country and sold under the manufacturer's name is a matter of considerable commercial significance and one which is properly considered in determining whether a substitute ingredient is just as good as the original. . . .

Judged by the general standards applicable in determining the adequacy of the legal remedy we think that on this point the case is a proper one for equitable relief. We see no reason why a court should be reluctant to grant specific . . . [performance] . . . when it can be given without supervision of the court or other time-consuming processes against one who has deliberately broken his agreement. Here the goods of the special type contracted for were unavailable on the open market, the plaintiff had contracted for them long ahead in anticipation of its needs. We think if this were all that was involved in the case that specific performance should have been granted. . . .

HOLDING We are not suggesting that the contract is illegal. Nor are we suggesting any excuse for the grower in this case who has deliberately broken an agreement entered into with Campbell. We do think, however, that a party who has offered and succeeded in getting an agreement as tough as this one shouldn't come to the chancellor and ask the court for help in the enforcement of its terms. That equity does not enforce unconscionable bargains is too well established to require elaborate citation.

PRACTICE JUDGING

1. **Exactly what part of this contract does the court find "unconscionable"? Is it the low price? Is it the ability of Campbell to prohibit Wentz from selling the carrots to others? Do you find anything objectionable?**

2. **Would the judge have reached a different conclusion if Chantenay carrots were available in the marketplace, but at the price of $600 per ton?**

3. **What do you think of the ethical character of Wentz's and Campbell's conduct in this situation?**

PROJECT 2 FUNDAMENTALS OF CONTRACTS

PROTECTING THE IDEA

Ben Windows' idea for a "Reelshield" seemed to be working out. His good friend Kristen had called his attention to the legal issues he needed to take care of before he could start marketing the devices. Most importantly, Ben's idea needed to be protected so that it could not be claimed or exploited by anyone else. He met with a lawyer from Kristen's law firm to discuss how to go about protecting the idea. The lawyer listened to Ben's description of the Reelshield and his assessment of the market for it. Then he made several recommendations:

First, Ben should not explain the workings of the Reelshield to anyone else without having them first sign a non-disclosure agreement. Next, Ben should meet with the owners of Rebuilt to see if they will give up all claims on Ben's invention. Rebuilt might argue that because Ben is employed there, the idea is the company's property to use and develop. The lawyer suggested that Ben be prepared to offer consideration to Rebuilt for giving up these claims. Ben also should have a preliminary patent search run to see if a similar device has already been patented. If the preliminary patent search finds no conflicts, Ben should contract for a professional engineer to draft blueprints of the Reelshield for a patent application. Then, he should contract with a lawyer specializing in patent law to draft the actual application.

ADDITIONAL ISSUES

The lawyer also advised Ben that making the devices in his rental home is against the zoning laws of the city. Therefore Ben should see about leasing a small manufacturing facility for his production line. The lawyer closed the meeting by telling Ben that as the business progresses, many other steps will need to be taken. He told him they should meet again soon to discuss the additional steps.

After the meeting, Ben tells Kristen he is concerned about how he will finance the project. He used all of his savings to pay for building the first few Reelshields. He does not know how he will find the money for the legal and engineering work that needs to be done. After listening carefully, Kristen looks Ben squarely in the eyes and says, "You know I've believed in you since we met in school. I have some savings, too. Let me lend you the money and you can pay me back when things get going." At first, Ben declined. Then, seeing that Kristen was serious, he said, "All right, but we'll get the lawyers to make it formal. Thank you so much."

ACTIVITIES

Divide into teams and perform one or more of the following activities, as directed by your teacher.

PREPARE LEGAL DOCUMENTS

As a team, prepare the following legal documents that Ben's lawyer has recommended: (1) non-disclosure agreement (how should this be worded to protect Ben?) (2) lease agreement for new assembly plant (3) promissory note to Kristen to ensure that Ben will pay back the money he borrows.

NEGOTIATE

Ben needs to settle the issue of Rebuilt's possible claims on his invention. The lawyer suggests that Ben be prepared to offer consideration to Rebuilt for agreeing to give up these claims. Divide the team into two. One side should represent Ben's interests and the other side, Rebuilt's. Prepare different contract alternatives, dependent upon Rebuilt's attitude towards giving up its claims on the Reelshield. (For example, Ben could supply Rebuilt with the devices at cost, or even for free. Also, Rebuilt could be used as the site for testing not only the Reelshield but any inventions Ben might come up with in the future. To protect Ben, a limit on time or number of units to be supplied could be placed on the deal.)

USE TECHNOLOGY

Have one or more group members conduct an Internet search to find out how to apply for a patent. The member(s) who conduct(s) the search should then present the findings to the group.

SALES AND OTHER CONTRACTUAL SITUATIONS

ENTREPRENEURS AND THE LAW

SEE PAGE 278

Kathryn Redwine chose to enter the legal field because of its diversity. "The legal profession has allowed me the opportunity to tap into many different aspects of the law, such as Criminal, Contract, Medicare/Medicaid, and Equal Employment Opportunity. With the legal profession you are not limited to one aspect."

Kathryn began her study at Colorado University at Boulder, Colorado, where she earned a degree in Sociology, with an emphasis in Criminology and Juvenile Delinquency. She volunteered for a youth gang alternative program and in Boulder's Probation Department.

Kathryn believes her undergraduate degree helped determine the type of law she wanted to practice. "Sociology allowed me to understand the mechanics of how society functions and enabled me to deal with people from all walks of life."

After graduating, Kathryn enrolled in Southern University Law Center, one of three predominately African-American law schools in the United States. She was appointed liaison to the Corrections and Sentencing Committee of the American Bar Association. She also clerked for Capital Area Legal Services, where she drafted briefs and interviewed indigent clients.

After law school graduation, Kathryn became an Employee Relations Research Assistant/Consultant for Kaiser Permanente Health Plan of Colorado, one of the nation's largest HMOs. Here Kathryn conducted internal investigations for all Equal Employment Opportunity Commission complaints. She also helped recruit other minorities.

Kathryn accepted her current position as an Appeals Analyst within Kaiser after she passed the bar exam. Her primary responsibility is to maintain the appeals process, which includes contract interpretation for all 330,000 Kansas City and Colorado members. Kathryn forms recommendations and decisions based on her analysis of applicable laws, statutes, and medical facts.

Kathryn explains that there are many paths to a legal career. "Some individuals may choose the route I chose, that is, entering into a law program directly after obtaining their undergraduate degree. Others may choose to enter a paralegal program, which will allow them the opportunity to do research, meet with prospective clients and draft pleadings. Still others may decide that they would rather do court reporting, work for a probation department or be a legal assistant."

Kathryn considers the following among her greatest strengths: excellent communication, organizational and administrative skills, ability to work well under pressure, and a strong sense of teamwork.

"A person who wants to be an attorney should have exceptional management skills; enjoy research; have strong interpersonal communication, problem resolution, and human relations skills; have the ability to assess situations, analyze options, and achieve desired results; be organized, self-motivated, and detail-oriented with a dedication to confidentiality and follow-through procedures; and be able to complete simultaneous tasks accurately in a rapid-paced environment. If someone has those skills and the motivation to become an attorney, I say welcome to the ranks of esquire!"

> **❝ The legal profession has allowed me the opportunity to tap into many different aspects of the law, such as Criminal, Contract, Medicare/Medicaid, and Equal Employment Opportunity. With the legal profession you are not limited to one aspect. ❞**

LESSONS

15-1	**SALES**
15-2	**OWNERSHIP**
15-3	**SPECIAL RULES FOR SALES CONTRACTS**

HOT DEBATE

A bride-to-be wants her wedding gown to be custom-made from a unique new fabric. A bridal shop quotes a price of $1,750. When the bride-to-be orally agrees, the shop places a special order for the fabric and cuts it to fit. Then the wedding is canceled. The bride-to-be seeks to avoid the contract because it was not in writing. The bridal shop brings a lawsuit to recover the agreed price.

Where Do You Stand?

1. **Discuss the legal and ethical reasons for the plaintiff's (bridal shop's) suit.**

2. **Discuss the legal and ethical reasons in the defendant's (bride-to-be's) favor.**

WHAT IS A SALE?

WHAT'S YOUR VERDICT?

At the Dan-Dee Discount Department Store, Jack and Jean Medina signed a contract to buy a clothes washer and dryer set. The Dan-Dee salesperson explained that although the set on display was not in stock, "We will deliver and install it within two weeks." While shopping at the store, the Medinas left their car in the store's automobile service department to have the engine's idling speed adjusted and to have squeaks in the door eliminated. The charge for labor was $45. There was no charge for parts or supplies. The service attendant recommended replacing the car's tires, and the Medinas agreed. The cost of the tires was $300, plus $25 for balancing and installation. The Medinas also bought a new battery for $59. It was installed free of charge.

Were all of these agreements sales?

A **sale** is a contract in which *ownership* of (*title* to) goods transfers immediately from the seller to the buyer for a price. If the transfer of ownership is to take place in the future, the transaction is a **contract to sell** rather than a sale. **Price** is the consideration for a sale or contract to sell goods. It may be expressed in money, in services, or in other goods. When parties exchange goods for goods, the sale is a **barter**.

Sales of Goods Under the UCC

The Uniform Commercial Code (UCC) governs sales of goods. It also governs contracts to sell goods in the future. **Goods** are tangible (touchable), movable personal property, such as airplanes, books, clothing, and dogs. By UCC definition, goods do not include the following:

1. money (except rare currency or rare coins, which are collectible items with value that may exceed their face amounts)

2. intangible (not touchable) personal property, such as legal rights to performance under a contract, transferred by assignment rather than by sale

3. patents and copyrights, which are exclusive rights given by the federal government to inventors and writers

4. land and other forms of real property, which are transferred by conveyance and are subject to special rules (as discussed in Unit 4 on Property)

Under the UCC, a sales contract may be made in any manner sufficient to show agreement. The resulting contract suffices if the parties by their actions recognize the existence of a contract. This is true even though a court might not be able to determine precisely when the contract was made, and even though one or more terms are left open in accordance with customs of the trade.

Payment occurs when the buyer delivers the agreed price and the seller accepts it. Receipt of goods means that the buyer takes physical possession or control of the goods. Receipt usually involves actual delivery. However, delivery may be constructive. This happens when there is no actual transfer of possession of the goods, but the recipient has the power to control them, as intended by the parties involved. Examples would be when the buyer gets the keys to a car or receives a warehouse receipt for stored goods.

Acceptance of goods means that the buyer has agreed, by words or by conduct, that the goods received are satisfactory. Acceptance is shown when the goods are used, resold, or otherwise treated as if they were owned by the buyer. Acceptance may also be indicated when a buyer fails to reject the goods within a reasonable time, if the buyer has had adequate opportunity to inspect them.

In general, the law of contracts has been simplified and made less strict in its application to sales of goods. For example, the price for goods usually is fixed in the contract. However, the parties may indicate that the price is to be set in a certain way at a later date. This method is especially used in long-term contracts when consid-erable instability of prices is expected. Ordinarily, when nothing is said about the price, a contract results if all other essentials are present, and provided the parties do not express a contrary intent. In such a case, the buyer is required to pay the price that is reasonable at the time of delivery.

Contracts for Personal Services

In many situations, the contract is primarily for personal services. Such contracts are not sales because any goods supplied are merely incidental. In *What's Your Verdict?* the work on the car engine and the doors was a contract for services. Any goods supplied, such as lubricants, were inci-dental. Even if a specific charge was made for them, the contract would remain one for the services that were the dominant part of that agreement.

On the other hand, the transfer to the Medinas of title to the tires was a sale of goods, even though a small charge was made for related labor. The battery also was acquired in a sale of goods, with no charge for labor. The Medinas' agreement to buy the washer and dryer at a later date was not a sale. Instead, it was a contract to sell—a contract in which ownership of goods is to transfer in a sale in the future. In both sales of goods and contracts to sell, the seller is known as a **vendor**. The buyer is known as the **vendee** or the *purchaser*.

MUST DELIVERY AND PAYMENT BE MADE AT THE SAME TIME?

WHAT'S YOUR VERDICT?

The Baumgartens bought Hannukah gifts for their three young children during the Sunrise Center's October lay-away sale. Delivery was scheduled for early December, and payment was due before January 15 of the following year.

When did the Baumgartens become owners of the gifts they had purchased?

In the basic sales transaction, payment, delivery (transfer of possession), and transfer of title take place simultaneously at the seller's place of business. Even if payment or delivery, or both, take place later, title still passes when the buyer selects (identifies to the contract) and agrees to buy existing goods in the seller's store.

At the appropriate time fixed in the sales contract, the buyer has a duty to pay, and the seller has a duty to trans-fer possession. Generally neither is obligated to perform until the other does. Thus, unless it is otherwise agreed (as when the sale is on credit), or if it is the custom of the trade, the seller may retain the goods until the buyer makes payment in full. Similarly, the buyer may refuse to pay the price until the seller delivers all the goods. The buyer is entitled to a receipt when payment is made.

A **bill of sale** is a receipt that serves as written evidence of the transfer of ownership of goods. Such a document is sometimes required by statute, as in the case of automobile sales. If a bill of sale is signed by the seller, buyer, or both, it can satisfy the requirements of the statute of frauds for a signed writing. However, neither a sales contract nor a bill of sale nec-essarily identifies the parties nor explains the terms of the transaction.

A bill of sale makes resale of the property easier because it provides the owner with written evidence of ownership. When goods are lost, stolen, or destroyed, as in a fire, the document can be used to help prove value. The bill of sale is not absolute proof of ownership because other persons may have acquired claims against the goods since the bill of sale was issued. Also, dishonest persons may forge such documents to help dispose of stolen property.

To encourage business, most sellers extend credit to qualified buyers, including other business firms. Some retailers do most of their business selling to customers who use credit cards or charge accounts, or who pay in installments. Thus, the buyer may get both title and possession before payment. In *What's Your Verdict?* assuming the goods were set aside for the Baumgartens at the time of the sale, they received title in October, possession in December, and paid for the goods in January.

OTHER METHODS OF SALES CONTRACTING UNDER THE UCC

WHAT'S YOUR VERDICT?

The Tastie Treat Shop mailed an order for 500 one-pound boxes of fruit and nut candies to the Chocolate Castle Company. Chocolate Castle could have accepted the order by mail, telephone, wire, or fax machine. Instead, it immediately shipped the candy and simply added the usual amount to the next invoice mailed to the Tastie Treat Shop.

Was the Chocolate Castle Company's acceptance of the order valid?

Sales contracts may be made through a traditional exchange of offer and acceptance. But the UCC also recognizes alternative methods. Instead of telephoning, sending a facsimile (fax), or mailing an acceptance, the seller may simply ship the goods and thereafter notify the buyer of this action. In *What's Your Verdict?* the Chocolate Castle Company's immediate shipment of the order to the Tastie Treat Shop did constitute a valid acceptance.

Under the UCC, an offeror may state that the offer to buy or to sell goods must be accepted exactly as made or not at all. Otherwise the offeree may accept and still change some terms of the contract or add new ones. Recall that in most contract negotiations such changes would end the original offer and would be considered a counteroffer. Under the law of sales of goods, however, the new term is treated as a *proposal for addition* to the contract.

The provision of the UCC for a new term to be treated as a proposal for addition to the contract helps to avoid what courts have called the "battle of the forms." This battle occurs when a merchant buyer makes an offer with a preprinted *purchase order form*. It contains detailed terms, often many that clearly favor the buyer. In response, a merchant seller accepts by using a *sales order form* with differing terms, which favor the seller.

When both parties are merchants, a new term inserted by the offeree automatically becomes part of the

IN THIS CASE

A pottery manufacturer offered to sell red clay flowerpots in three different sizes to a garden supply store. The store accepted the offer but specified that the pots had to be packaged in sets of three (with one of each size) rather than in bulk as described in the offer. This was a material change in the terms. The pottery maker did not object or revoke the original offer. Instead it packaged and shipped the goods as requested. Thus a contract resulted, with no other change in terms.

contract if the offeror fails to object within a reasonable time. However, the new term must not materially alter the offer. In addition, the original offer must not expressly bar such changes. If the new term is a *material* (important) alteration, it is included in the contract only if the original offeror expressly agrees to be bound by it.

UNCONSCIONABLE SALES CONTRACTS

WHAT'S YOUR VERDICT?

FrostiFresh Corporation sold a refrigerator to Nguyen. A recent immigrant, Nguyen spoke, read, and wrote Vietnamese and French, but he did not speak English. The refrigerator was sold on an installment payment contract. The negotiations and sale of the refrigerator were made in French. However, the written contract was entirely in English, although the seller knew that Nguyen could not read English. FrostiFresh paid the manufacturer $348 for the refrigerator. FrostiFresh then sold it to Nguyen on the installment plan for $3,146, plus a credit charge of $546.

Was this agreement unconscionable?

The UCC provides that a court may find that a contract or a clause of a contract is **unconscionable**, that is, grossly unfair and oppressive. An unconscionable contract or clause offends an honest person's conscience and sense of justice, as does the contract in *What's Your Verdict?* The terms need not be criminal nor violate a statute, but they are unethical.

Contracts of adhesion are more likely to be unconscionable. This is so because in such contracts one of the parties dictates all the important terms. The weaker party must generally accept the terms as offered or not contract at all.

A court that decides whether a clause of a contract is unconscionable may do any of the following:

- refuse to enforce the contract
- enforce the contract without the unconscionable clause
- limit the clause's application so that the contract is no longer unfair

The law is not designed to relieve a person of a bad bargain. A person may be legally bound by the purchase of overpriced, poor quality, or unneeded goods.

Answer the following questions about legal concepts.

1. Rare coins, even though currency, can be considered goods under the UCC. **True or False?**

2. Patents are goods. **True or False?**

3. Which of the following would not be considered goods under the UCC's law of sales? **(a) passenger plane (b) computer (c) six acres of land (d) all of the above are goods under the UCC**

4. Contracts to sell are not governed by the UCC's law of sales. **True or False?**

5. In a basic sale, ___?___ , transfer of possession, and transfer of ___?___ take place at the same time.

THINK CRITICALLY ABOUT EVIDENCE

Study the following situations, answer the questions, then prepare arguments to support your answers.

6. The Caribbean Mill sold a quantity of standard electrolytic copper bars to Pollard. The contract was complete in all respects except that it failed to state the price. Was the contract a valid one, thus enforceable in court?

7. At Ellen's request, her doctor prescribed and injected her with a drug. The drug had been tested and approved for sale by the federal Food and Drug Administration. It had been manufactured by maker *A*, sold to wholesaler *B*, then sold to retail pharmacy *C*, which sold it to the doctor. The doctor charged Ellen $15 for the drug and $50 for his services. Twenty years later, Ellen's daughter developed a cancer traceable to the drug that her mother had taken. Was the doctor a seller and therefore liable for breach of warranty?

8. As Brackston was examining a China place setting in the Nook and Cranny Shoppe, the place setting slipped from her hands. It smashed into countless pieces when it hit the floor. After the proprietress swept up the mess, she pointed to a sign on the wall that said, "Handle with Care! If You Break It, You Buy It." She then rang up a sales charge of $300 plus $18 sales tax. Was Brackston the vendee in a sales contract?

9. After their business law class, Alexa and Ronald were discussing contracts of adhesion. Ronald insisted that when a "big ticket item," such as a television, is sold on credit terms, the seller prepares the contract. "You agree to it as written or you're out of luck. No sale." Alexa argued, "That's the truth, but not the whole truth." Can you explain what Alexa meant by her comment? Is it ethical for a seller to use contracts of adhesion?

GOALS

- Discuss the benefits and burdens of ownership of property
- Compare the various methods of acquiring property
- Explain the unique role of merchants and why and how they are treated specially by the law

RESULTS OF OWNERSHIP

WHAT'S YOUR VERDICT?

Leister won $2 million in a state lottery. When he received the first of 20 promised annual payments, he went on a spending spree. He bought a new car which he carelessly wrecked, clothes which he never even wore, and a mink coat for a casual friend he met in a bar. He staged a wild New Year's Eve party for 50 new friends, during which the revelers smashed their crystal champagne glasses in a fireplace. Through court action, relatives now seek to stop Leister from using his money and goods so wastefully.

Will they succeed?

It is important to know the difference between a sale and a contract to sell because both benefits and burdens generally go with ownership. Therefore it is necessary to know when ownership transfers from one party to another. A person who *sells* (transfers to another party the ownership of goods for a price) says, in effect, "I hereby transfer to you the legal right to use, control, and dispose of these goods."

Ownership carries valuable rights. Any rise in value (as in prices of securities, output of land, or increase in animal weight or number) belongs to the owner. Moreover, goods generally may be enjoyed and used as the owner pleases. They may be squandered or even destroyed, as in *What's Your Verdict?* Leister's relatives will fail unless they can prove he has become mentally incompetent, which is unlikely.

Ownership also involves duties and burdens. The owner may be taxed in proportion to what is owned. The freedom to use one's property may be limited by governmental regulations for the common good, as by speeding and zoning laws. Property should be protected and maintained. If it is cared for improperly or used in a manner interfering with the rights of others, the owner may be liable for resulting torts.

In recent years, penalties also have been imposed for violations of environmental protection laws. In some cases, the owner's responsibility may extend to cover the use of the goods by other persons. For example, the owner of an automobile may be held responsible for injuries caused by another person operating the car with the owner's permission.

The owner suffers loss when goods deteriorate because of the passage of time and the action of natural forces such as sun, wind, rain, snow, oxygen, and other elements. When goods are destroyed or damaged without the legal fault of any person, the owner loses unless covered by insurance.

For example, if a storm destroys your camping tent, you suffer the loss unless it was properly insured. The result is the same when your possessions are lost, stolen, or destroyed by fire. In effect, your goods are also under a never-ending assault by the economic forces of obsolescence (becoming out of date) and depreciation (declining in value because of wear and tear, and other reasons).

A Question of ETHICS

Destiny Pharmaceuticals sponsored a great deal of research in the area of locating and developing new drugs from plants growing in isolated areas. A recent expedition to the central Amazon region of Brazil brought back several potentially beneficial discoveries. An exceptionally rare tree, known to be very beneficial to the life systems in the rain forest, could produce what the chemists at Destiny labeled "Revita." Revita had been shown to reverse the effects of Alzheimer's Disease in more than 60 percent of those tested. Regrettably, it was found in the bark of the rare tree and harvesting it usually exposed the tree to invasion of parasites and, ultimately, death. Revita, however, would help millions of people and would produce large profits for Destiny. Should Destiny market the drug?

SALES COMPARED WITH OTHER TRANSFERS OF OWNERSHIP AND POSSESSION

WHAT'S YOUR VERDICT?

Both Brian and Claire became electronic data processing specialists during their service in the U.S. Army. When they retired from the Army, they decided to open a retail electronics specialty store. Using savings, borrowed funds, and (a) money donated by their parents, they (b) purchased a parcel of land that had a suitable building. They (c) rented the empty lot next to the building to use as parking space, under a five-year contract. They (d) bought a supply of personal computers and related equipment and (e) agreed to purchase an equal quantity of a new PC model scheduled for production within six months. They (f) traded their two sports cars for a company truck, and (g) raised additional money by transferring, to a buyer, a note receivable (commercial paper) for $27,000 that Brian had received in partial payment when he sold his house trailer. To get more cash for working capital, (h) Brian and Claire transferred to a bank all rights to collect on a group of accounts receivable they had obtained from sales made on credit. They (i) obtained all their store display cases by renting them from the manufacturer. In every instance noted, Brian and Claire obtained possession of property needed for their business.

What types of transactions did they utilize?

In most cases, the UCC treats all buyers and sellers alike. In some cases, it treats merchants differently from casual sellers. A **merchant** is a seller who deals regularly in a particular kind of goods or otherwise claims to have special knowledge or skill in a certain type of sales transaction. In *What's Your Verdict?* Brian and Claire became merchants after retirement from the Army.

Contrast merchants with **casual sellers** who sell only occasionally or do not otherwise meet the definition of merchant. You would be a casual seller if you sold your private automobile. A used-car dealer selling the same car would be a merchant. In general, the UCC holds merchants to a higher standard of conduct than it does casual sellers. Merchants may be required to have licenses to sell. They are also usually subjected to special taxation and closer regulation by the government.

In *What's Your Verdict?* most of the business transactions Brian and Claire engage in as merchants will be sales, or the opposite of sales—purchases. This will be true when they acquire inventory and other equipment from suppliers, and when they sell their stock in trade to customers. However, they could acquire property in a variety of other transactions. The transactions lettered in *What's Your Verdict?* are: (a) gift; (b) conveyance; (c) lease; (d) sale; (e) contract to sell; (f) barter; (g) negotiation; (h) assignment; and (i) bailment.

Transaction	What Type of Property Is Involved?	Is a Contract Involved?	Is Ownership Transferred?	Is Possession Transferred?	What is the Evidence of a Transaction?
(a) Gift	Personal or Real Property	No	Yes	Usually yes	Usually none; Deed for Real Property
(b) Conveyance	Real Property	Usually (may be gratuitous)	Yes	Usually yes	Contract; Deed
(c) Lease	Real Property (Usually)	Usually (may be gratuitous)	No	Yes	Lease (a Contract)
(d) Sale	Goods (Tangible Personal Property)	Yes	Yes	Usually yes	Contract; Bill of Sale
(e) Contract to Sell	Goods	Yes	No	Usually yes, but not immediately	Contract
(f) Barter	Goods	Yes	Yes	Usually yes	Contract
(g) Negotiation	Negotiable Instruments	Usually	Yes	Yes	Commercial Paper (Contracts)
(h) Assignment	Contract Rights	Usually	Yes	Yes, when contract is performed	Contract
(i) Bailment	Personal Property	Usually	No	Yes	Contract (in Commercial Bailment)

This table summarizes and compares important effects of nine common transactions involving property, both personal and real. Note how the legal effects reflect the intent of the parties.

Answer the following questions about legal concepts.

1. There is no difference in the time ownership is transferred in a sale versus a contract to sell. **True or False?**

2. Ownership involves duties as well as rights. **True or False?**

3. Is risk of loss always placed on the owner of the goods? **Yes or No?**

4. A person selling items at a once-a-year garage sale would be considered a **(a) casual merchant (b) casual seller (c) merchant (d) none of the above.**

5. To a vendor, the transaction is a sale; to a vendee, the transaction is a (an) __?__ .

6. Which of the following is not a means of ownership transfer? **(a) barter (b) contract to sell (c) negotiation (d) all of the above transfer ownership**

7. A person with a large collection of movies on laser discs needs money. She contracts with a well-known seller of the discs to put them in his store and sell them for her at an appropriate price. Is she a merchant? **Yes or No?**

8. Is the right to destroy goods transferred in a sale? **Yes or No?**

9. Ownership rights are not absolute. **True or False?**

10. The owner of property that causes environmental pollution or otherwise violates the laws of the land may be punished. **True or False?**

11. Which of the following persons are held to the highest standards of conduct by the UCC? **(a) casual seller (b) casual buyer (c) merchant**

12. Goods may lose value due to wear and tear. This is referred to as depreciation. **True or False?**

13. Goods may lose value by becoming out of date. This is referred to as depreciation. **True or False?**

Study the following situations, answer the questions, then prepare arguments to support your answers.

14. Every two weeks, Ericson held a garage sale to resell items she had purchased at other such sales. When the city and state governments tried to tax her sales, Ericson claimed that she was merely a casual seller and therefore did not have to pay a sales tax. Was she correct?

15. Danny Destello received several million dollars as the star and co-owner of a motion picture that was a box-office sales success. Danny then spent $2 million on jewelry for friends and himself. His older brother told him, "I admire your success, and I guess I should envy you and your friends. But I don't. Even if the friendships are genuine, the burdens of such ownership will exceed the benefits." What are some of the possible burdens and benefits of such legal ownership?

16. Paul Broderick worked in a store that sold audio CDs. He also was an avid collector of old vinyl recordings. He particularly sought those "records" with the "big band" sound of the 1950s. To pursue his hobby, he advertised in several magazines for old vinyl records, attended swap meets, and bought and sold multiple copies of the records that he considered truly collectibles. He even published a newsletter for other collectors called "Blast from the Past." Would you consider him a merchant? Why or why not? Should he charge sales tax on the records he sells? Why or why not?

17. Which of the following property "rights" do you consider to be the most protected from government regulation? (a) transferring property that you own freely (b) holding property that you own to the exclusion of all others (c) destroying property that you own that may be of considerable worth to others or to society as a whole. Justify your selection.

GOALS

- Explain the need for the statute of frauds
- Discuss the instances in which the statute of frauds will be applied

STATUTE OF FRAUDS

WHAT'S YOUR VERDICT?

Chilton orally agreed to buy an imported camera from the Open Shutter Shop for $748.98. The camera she wanted was not in stock, but a shipment was expected any day. Therefore the salesclerk prepared a memorandum of the sale, signed it, and gave Chilton a copy. A week later the clerk phoned and said, "Your camera is ready." Chilton replied that she did not want it because she had learned that the identical model could be purchased for much less by mail from a New York City discount store.

Is Chilton liable to Open Shutter for breach of contract?

Sales contracts, like other contracts, are generally valid and enforceable in court whether they are oral, written, or implied from the conduct of the parties. However, as you may recall, under the statute of frauds, sales of goods for $500 or more must be evidenced by a writing to be enforceable in court.

In good business practice, both parties sign a written sales contract and each party gets a copy. This provides both parties with a useful legal record, and it reinforces mutual good faith. Normally both parties expect to perform, but either party could breach the contract. If that happens, the injured party can sue for damages. The written contract goes a long way towards proving the existence and terms of the agreement.

In *What's Your Verdict?* the price of the goods was more than $500. Therefore the sale was governed by the statute of frauds. Open Shutter is bound because its clerk signed the contract. Chilton is not bound because she did not sign, but she could enforce the agreement against Open Shutter if she so desired.

Not all the terms of a sales contract have to be in writing to satisfy the statute of frauds. Essentially, all that is required is a writing, signed by the party being sued, which satisfies the court that a contract to sell, or a sale, has been made. The number or quantity of goods involved in the transaction must be contained in the writing. The contract is not enforceable beyond the stated quantity.

However, the time and manner of performance; credit and warranty terms; packaging, labeling, and shipping instructions; and even the price need not be included for the writing to satisfy the statute. If necessary, this information can be provided later in oral testimony in court.

A variation of the statute of frauds applies only to contracts between merchants. The law generally requires a signature of the person being sued. Between merchants, however, the signature of the party who is suing may suffice to prove an otherwise unenforceable sales contract. If a merchant sends a written confirmation of an oral contract to another merchant within a reasonable time after this oral agreement was made, the confirmation binds both parties. If the second merchant sends a written objection to the confirmation within ten days, the confirmation is not binding.

CULTURAL DIVERSITY IN LAW

International

CISG

The Convention on Contracts for the International Sale of Goods (CISG) is a United Nations agreement that regulates international sales contracts. The CISG has been adopted in nearly 40 countries. Once a country adopts the CISG, it becomes part of that country's domestic law.

The CISG applies to international transactions under the following conditions: (1) the contract involves the commercial sale of goods (2) the contract is between parties whose "places of business" are located in different countries (3) the places of business are located in countries that have adopted the convention.

The CISG governs contract formation and the rights and obligations of the buyer and seller.

WHAT'S YOUR
VERDICT?

La Fargo telephoned an order to Hoban's Brick and Tile Works for ceramic tiles imported from Mexico priced at $663. In accordance with the oral contract order, the proper tiles were delivered. Later that day, La Fargo notified Hoban's that she refused to accept the goods. Hoban's insisted that the oral contract was binding and sued for damages.

Who should win?

IN THIS CASE

Ramirez visited Petrosiki's Paint Pot and orally ordered 40 gallons of shingle stain. The stain was priced at $13 a gallon. It was to be charged to her account and delivered the following Monday. Nothing was signed. Ramirez took one five-gallon can home with her. However, her husband was displeased with the color, and she disliked the way it went on. Therefore she refused to accept the balance of the order. Ramirez was within her rights in doing so. She was bound by the contract only for the five gallons that she had received and accepted.

Under certain circumstances, oral contracts for the sale of goods priced at $500 or more may be valid and enforceable. These exceptions to the requirements of the statute of frauds include the following:

Goods Received and Accepted by the Buyer

Receiving the goods does not in itself make an oral contract binding under the statute of frauds. Both receipt and acceptance are necessary. A buyer may receive goods without accepting them.

Under the UCC a buyer can accept goods in three ways.

1. After a reasonable opportunity to inspect the goods, the buyer signifies to the seller that the goods conform to the contract, or will be retained in spite of their nonconformity.

2. The buyer acts inconsistently with the seller's ownership (for example, uses, consumes, or resells the goods).

3. The buyer fails to make an effective rejection after having a reasonable opportunity to inspect the goods.

In *What's Your Verdict?* La Fargo effectively rejected the goods even though they conformed to the contract. She could legally do this because the statute of frauds required that the contract (for goods priced at $500 or more) be in writing and signed by her as buyer. Alternatively, to make the oral contract binding, La Fargo had to receive and accept the goods. Here, she received the goods but did not accept them. Therefore Hoban's loses the suit. Hoban's could have prevented this costly problem by requiring La Fargo's signature on a suitable writing before shipping the tiles.

Note that if the buyer has received and accepted only some of the goods, the oral contract is enforceable only for those goods received and accepted.

Buyer Pays for Goods and Seller Accepts Payment

When payment in full has been accepted by the seller, the oral contract is enforceable in full. When *partial* payment has been accepted by the seller, the oral contract is enforceable only for the goods paid

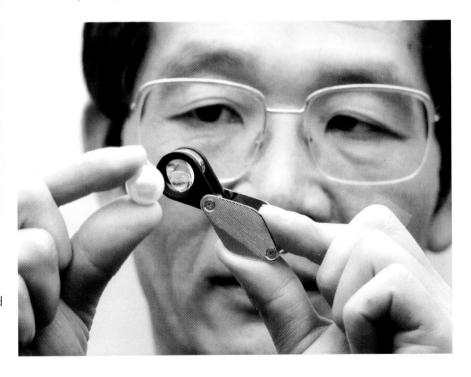

for if the goods can be divided and the price can be apportioned fairly. If the goods are indivisible and there can be no dispute as to quantity, the contract is enforceable in full.

IN THIS CASE

At an auction, Zutto bought a handmade, oak rolltop desk from Winslow for $1,250. Zutto paid $250 and left to get a truck with the balance still due. When Zutto returned, Winslow told her the desk had been sold to another person for $1,500. He explained that the contract with her was oral and therefore not enforceable. Winslow was wrong; Zutto's partial payment for the indivisible goods (the oak desk) made the oral contract enforceable. If the goods had been divisible (for example, 50 reams of paper), the contract would be enforceable only for the quantity paid for. Winslow is liable to Zutto for damages measured by the extra amount she must now pay someone else for an equivalent desk.

GOODS SPECIALLY MADE NOT SUITABLE FOR SALE TO OTHERS A seller can enforce an oral contract for nonsalable goods if

1. the seller has substantially begun to manufacture them
2. the seller has made contracts to obtain the goods from third parties.

PARTY AGAINST WHOM ENFORCEMENT SOUGHT ADMITS ORAL CONTRACT MADE A party against whom enforcement of an oral contract is sought may admit in legal pleadings or testimony that he or she agreed to part or all of a contract. In such a case, a signed writing is not necessary for the enforcement of the part of the contract that was admitted.

THINK ABOUT LEGAL CONCEPTS

Answer the following questions about legal concepts.

1. Generally, orally made sales or contracts to sell are valid and enforceable in court. **True or False?**

2. Under the statute of frauds, sales of goods valued at __?__ or more need to be evidenced by a writing to be enforceable in court.

3. Do both parties have to sign the writing to satisfy the statute of frauds? **Yes or No?**

4. If a buyer resells the goods, the UCC treats the buyer's action as an acceptance. **True or False?**

5. If a party admits in court the existence of a contract, it becomes enforceable against that party even if the admission is only oral. **True or False?**

THINK CRITICALLY ABOUT EVIDENCE

Study the following situations, answer the questions, then prepare arguments to support your answers.

6. When Soule bought a sweater for his wife, the clerk deliberately lied to him. She said that the garment was a pure silk and mohair, hand-knitted import from Italy. In fact, it was a machine-made, domestic, polyester-and-wool mix. Did the clerk violate the statute of frauds by her conduct? Did the clerk act ethically?

7. Grant had long admired Kahn's collection of records featuring the big bands of the 1930s. One day Kahn orally agreed to sell the collection to Grant for $275. When Grant appeared with the money, however, Kahn said she had changed her mind and refused to deliver. Moreover, she insisted she was acting within her legal rights. Kahn said she had learned that her collection was worth at least $1,000. Therefore, she said, a signed writing was required to make the contract enforceable. Did Kahn state the law correctly?

8. Harrison orally agreed to buy two electric guitars and a matched set of drums from Rudolph. The price was $1,250, payable with $800 in cash and a bass saxophone. Harrison paid the price in full. However, Rudolph refused to deliver the guitars and drums, and he sent the saxophone back and mailed a certified check for $800 to Harrison. He explained that he had decided to start another rock group. Rudolph claimed that their oral agreement was not enforceable. Is he right?

In sales, be aware that . . .

1. During your lifetime, you will probably enter into more sales contracts than any other type of contract—as both buyer and seller. Knowledge of the law of sales will help you to make successful transactions.

2. Your best protection against poor-quality merchandise is knowledge of goods and their value, followed by careful comparison shopping.

3. Your best protection against sales fraud is the integrity of the seller (as reflected in the seller's established reputation) coupled with your caution.

4. When you make a major purchase, make sure your insurance is adequate. It should provide for coverage against possible loss of valuable purchased property. If appropriate (as in automobile purchases), it should also provide protection against possible liability for injury to others.

5. It is a good idea to put a sales agreement in writing even if it is for goods worth less than $500. Although this is not required by the statute of frauds, doing so can avoid misunderstandings and prevent costly litigation. If the goods are worth $500 or more, insist on compliance with the statute of frauds.

6. The other party should sign the contract or memorandum and give you a copy. The other party may properly require that you sign, too.

7. You are bound by oral contracts for goods priced at $500 or more if you have received them and accepted delivery. You may be bound in full or in part if you have made some payment. You usually are bound when you order custom-made goods.

8. For expensive "big ticket" items, you should get a bill of sale marked "paid" when you pay the full price.

CHAPTER IN REVIEW

1. Both sales of goods and contracts to sell goods are governed by a combination of basic contract law and special UCC provisions on sales. Transfers of ownership of other types of property, such as intangible personal property and real estate, are governed by different laws.

2. Both benefits and burdens go with ownership of goods.

3. Merchants generally are held to a higher standard of conduct by the UCC than are casual sellers.

4. Neither payment nor delivery is essential for transfer of title.

5. Unless otherwise required by statute, sales or contracts to sell may be oral, written, or implied from the conduct of the parties.

6. To be enforceable, a sale or contract to sell goods for $500 or more must be evidenced by a writing. The writing must specify at least a quantity of goods involved and must be signed by the party who is sued or by that party's agent. The writing is not essential when

   - buyer has received and accepted the goods
   - buyer has paid for the goods in full and the seller has accepted payment
   - goods custom-made for the buyer are not suitable for sale to others in the ordinary course of business, and the seller has begun manufacturing or has contracted to obtain the goods
   - party seeking to avoid the contract admits during legal proceedings that the oral agreement was made.

7. Price may consist of anything such as money, services, or goods—whatever was agreed upon by the parties as consideration.

8. Payment occurs when the buyer delivers the price and the seller accepts it.

9. Receipt of goods occurs when the buyer takes physical possession or control of the goods.

10. Acceptance of the goods occurs when the buyer indicates that the goods received are satisfactory.

11. A bill of sale may provide useful evidence of the transfer of title to goods.

YOUR LEGAL VOCABULARY

Match each statement with the term that it best defines. Some terms may not be used.

1. Transfer of ownership of goods from a seller to a buyer for a price

2. Consideration for a sale or a contract to sell

3. An exchange of goods for goods

4. Tangible, movable personal property

5. Label for a seller who claims special knowledge in a certain type of sales transaction

6. Receipt showing evidence of a transfer of ownership of goods

7. Seller who does not meet the definition of a merchant

8. Delivery of the agreed-upon price and the concurrent acceptance of it by the seller

barter
bill of sale
casual seller
contract of adhesion
contract to sell
goods
merchant
payment
price
sale
unconscionable
vendee
vendor

9. Why should the law of sales be different from the law of contracts?

10. Does barter hold certain advantages over a sale for money?

11. Arguably, the law of sales helps facilitate the smooth transfer of goods in commerce. It also

provides clear standards that are in general uniform from state to state. Why should the governments of the states devote their time and resources to accomplish such ends?

12. Should the same time and resources be devoted to helping other subgroups such as teachers, clergy, actors, lawyers, etc.?

13. Consider the various special rules and laws that the UCC imposes on merchants that it does not impose on casual sellers. Why should merchants under the UCC's law of sales be held to higher standards of knowledge than others?

14. Why is a bill of sale not considered a contract?

WRITE ABOUT LEGAL CONCEPTS

15. **HOT DEBATE** Write a persuasive opening statement for a trial that emphasizes the legal and ethical points in the plaintiff's favor. Write a persuasive opening statement that emphasizes the legal and ethical points in the defendant's favor.

THINK CRITICALLY ABOUT EVIDENCE

16. Paul, a graduate student at the university, repeatedly sold his blood to a blood bank to pay for his tuition and books. Should the law of sales apply to all these transactions?

17. One day, on his way back from selling his blood, Paul became light headed and crashed his car into a light pole. The car was repairable but the charges for parts and labor totalled more than $2,000. Should he have to pay sales tax on this whole amount? Why or why not?

18. When the economy turned sour and a large number of people sought to sell their blood, the blood bank wrote a term in its contracts that, in order to sell blood to the blood bank, each "donor" had to sell at least three pints a month to it or would have to refund any payments made to them in a month where the quota was not met. This meant that the donors would be very low on their own blood supply. What might a court do when confronted by such a term in a contract? What would be the result?

19. One visit Paul could only bleed out three quarters of a pint of blood. The blood bank refused to pay anything for what had been donated until Paul could complete the donation of a full pint of blood that the sales contract called for. Paul maintained that he should be paid pro rata for the amount he had given. Who is correct under the law of sales?

20. When Paul returned to complete the delivery of blood, the blood bank refused to pay, yet kept the full pint and resold it to a hospital. Paul then maintained that the blood bank had accepted the goods he had for sale and should pay. Is he correct?

21. Paul had type B-negative blood. It was extremely rare. As a consequence, when the blood bank received a request for that type, it called Paul and orally promised to pay him $645 per pint. Paul gave two pints in less than three weeks, but the blood bank only paid him the standard $35 per pint. Was the oral contract enforceable? Why or why not?

ANALYZE REAL CASES

22. Gillispie, a minor, was injured when two bottles of a soft drink exploded. The accident occurred as Gillispie was carrying the bottles to the checkout counter in the defendant's self-service store. Had a sale taken place even though Gillispie had not yet paid for the goods? If so, the store could be liable for the injury. You decide. (*Gillispie v. Great Atlantic and Pacific Tea Company*, 187 S.E.2d 441, N.C.)

23. Shriber, an officer of Nelly Don, Inc., orally agreed with a representative of the defendant DHJ Industries, Inc., to buy 75,000 yards of colorfast fabric from DHJ. A few days later, Shriber confirmed this agreement by telephone, and then sent a Nelly Don purchase order form. The form included these words, "This purchase order shall become a binding contract when acknowledged by Seller, or upon whole or partial shipment by Seller." In response, Shriber received a DHJ sales order form. At the bottom, just above the lines for signatures, this statement appeared, "This contract is subject to all the terms and conditions printed on the reverse side." On the reverse side was a clause requiring settlement of any controversy by arbitration. Shriber signed. Later, a dispute arose as to whether the fabric delivered was colorfast and machine washable. The plaintiff buyers claimed fraud and sued. The defendant sellers said the dispute had to be settled by arbitration and not in court. Was the arbitration clause binding? (*N & D Fashions, Inc. and Nelly Don, Inc. v. DHJ Industries, Inc.*, 548 F.2d 722)

24. Cargill, Inc., the plaintiff, is a large grain company. Warren, an agent of Cargill, managed its grain elevator in Hingham, Montana. On August 24, Warren orally contracted to buy from Wilson, the defendant farmer, 28,000 bushels of wheat at $1.48 per bushel and 6,000 bushels of higher protein wheat at $1.63 per bushel. Warren prepared two standard grain purchase written contracts. He signed them for Cargill, as its agent, and he also signed Wilson's name. A few days later, he delivered copies to Wilson, who made no objection. On August 30, Wilson received a $10,000 loan from Cargill. The check was attached to a detachable part of the standard grain contract, and it incorporated the two contracts by specific references to their numbers. Wilson endorsed and cashed the check. The loan was interest-free because it was an advance payment for the wheat. During September and October, Wilson delivered 11,000 bushels of ordinary wheat at the agreed-upon price of $1.48, and 6,000 bushels at the then-current, higher market price. Then Wilson refused to deliver any more wheat. Cargill sued for damages. Wilson claimed he was not bound because of the statute of frauds. Who should win? (*Cargill, Inc. v. Wilson*, 532 P.2d 988, Mont.)

25. Jordan Paper Products, Inc., sued to recover $22,089.48 owed to it under an oral contract by Burger Man, Inc., an Indiana fast-food chain. The contract was for various paper products that Jordan had prepared at Burger Man's order, to specially identify the fast-food chain to its customers. Burger Man maintained that the oral contract was unenforceable because of the statute of frauds. You decide. (*Burger Man, Inc. v. Jordan Paper Products, Inc.*, 352 N.E.2d 821, Ind.)

26. Albert Reifschneider knew farming. Born and raised on a farm, he had been marketing his crops for more than 20 years. He had extensive experience in farm futures (these are contracts made between farmers and buyers for the purchase of crops to be harvested at some future time) and the farm marketplace. One year he orally contracted to sell more than 12,000 bushels of corn from the fall harvest to the Colorado Kansas Grain Company. Treating Reifschneider as a merchant, the company sent him a written confirmation of the oral deal which he did not respond to in any manner. When Reifschneider refused to deliver the corn, the Grain Company sued him for breach of contract. Who won and why? (*Colorado-Kansas Grain Co. v. Reifschneider*, 817 P. 2d 637)

27. The Palermos needed carpeting for their home. Colorado Carpet Installation, Inc., agreed to do the job for a price that, including carpet and labor, totalled more than $500. When Mrs. Palermo did not like how the job was being done, the Palermos sought the services of another contractor. At that point, Colorado Carpet sued for enforcement of the oral contract. The Palermos replied that, as the contract was for more than $500, it was unenforceable under the statute of frauds which required contracts for more than $500 to be in writing to be enforceable. The issue at trial became whether or not the contract was for the sale of goods or services. What do you think? (*Colorado Carpet Installation, Inc. v. Palermo*, 668 P.2d 1384)

Advent Systems, Ltd., v. Unisys Corporation
U.S. Court of Appeals, Third Circuit, 925 F. 2d 670

BACKGROUND In the pre-1990 developing world of computers, Unisys Corporation was a major competitor of IBM. When Unisys was approached in the mid-1980s by Advent Systems, Ltd., a software developer, Unisys saw a chance to make a major improvement in its market position. Advent had developed a computer-based data management system that allowed engineering drawings and specialized documents to be transformed into a database. The database could then be improved, tailored, and reused again and again for different projects.

FACTS In June of 1987, Unisys agreed with Advent to sell the system throughout the United States for an initial two-year period. Advent was required to provide the technical personnel that might be necessary to produce a successful installation of each individual system.

In the summer of 1987, however, Unisys failed in an attempt to sell the Advent developed system to Arco, a large oil company. This cast a negative light on the properties and marketability of the Advent system. Regardless, progress continued on the joint sales and training programs in the United States.

Finally, however, the relationship split apart. Unisys, in a period of downsizing, determined that it would be better off if it developed its own system. Therefore, in December, 1987, Unisys informed Advent that their relationship was at an end. Similarly, negotiations between Unisys'

United Kingdom subsidiary and Advent came to an end.

LOWER COURT Advent promptly filed a complaint against Unisys alleging a breach of contract. Unisys defended by contending the sale of the software was, in essence, a sale of goods and, therefore, there was no breach of contract suit. Advent countered that software was not a good and that Advent was basically contracting to sell Unisys the services of its technical personnel.

DECISION The trial court found in favor of Advent. A jury awarded Advent $4,550,000 as a result of Unisys' "breach of contract." The case was appealed to the U. S. Court of Appeals.

APPEALS The case was appealed to the U.S. Court of Appeals, 3rd Circuit. On appeal, Advent continued to base its arguments on a breach of contract claim for the providing of services. Unisys also followed its previous line of reasoning in the lower court. Before the appellate court, it basically said that the transaction was a sale of goods and, therefore, subject to the statute of frauds in the Uniform Commercial Code. As the agreement lacked an explicit term on quantity, the statute of frauds would, therefore, preclude any suit and recovery.

ISSUE Was the transaction a sale of goods or a providing of services?

PRACTICE JUDGING

1. Should the trial court's decision be reversed because the transaction was a sales contract, or should the decision be affirmed as the transaction was for services?

2. What is the legal reasoning that led you to this conclusion?

3. Can you envision any time when computer software would not be as you decided it should be? What are the circumstances of the transaction, if so?

LESSONS

16-1 THE POWER TO TRANSFER OWNERSHIP

16-2 RISK OF LOSS AND INSURABLE INTEREST

HOT DEBATE

While you are having dinner one evening, your laptop computer is stolen from the front seat of your car. You do not report the theft for a week and a half. The police discover that the computer was sold to an innocent purchaser by a pawn shop that has since gone out of business. The new "owner" of the laptop is a pastor of a church that ministers to the homeless. She bought the laptop from a pawn shop before you reported the theft to the police. When you approach the pastor to get the computer back, she refuses. She says that the church needs it desperately to keep track of its "flock." It is especially important during the current winter season, when knowing where the homeless can seek shelter means life or death. You file suit for the return of the computer.

Where Do You Stand?

1. **What are the legal reasons for your suit?**

2. **What sort of legal arguments could you anticipate the attorney for the church making? Why?**

 G O A L S

- Describe various types of goods
- Discuss who may transfer ownership of goods
- Explain what is required for transfer of ownership of goods
- Identify when the ownership of goods has transferred

WHO MAY TRANSFER THE OWNERSHIP OF GOODS?

WHAT'S YOUR VERDICT?

Brad stole a cassette player from Fuller's car. He then sold it to Standon, who knew it was stolen.

Did either Brad or Standon receive good title to the cassette player?

Generally, only the true owner of goods may legally transfer ownership of those goods. As a general rule, the buyer of goods receives only the property rights that the seller has in the goods and nothing more. Therefore, the person who buys stolen goods from a thief receives possession, but not title, because the thief did not have good title to give. This is true whether the buyer is innocent or knows that the goods were stolen. In *What's Your Verdict?* neither Brad nor Standon received title to the cassette player. Because Standon knew it was stolen, he is guilty of the crime of receiving stolen property.

Unfortunately, stolen goods are seldom recovered. If they are recovered, they have often been damaged or stripped of parts. Even when recovered in good condition by the police, stolen goods often cannot be clearly identified as property of the victim and therefore are not returned. The police are compelled to sell such goods at public auction.

As with most general rules, there are exceptions to these rules about transfer of ownership. Such exceptions include the following.

1. Persons authorized to do so may transfer another's title.
2. Buyers in a sale induced by fraud may transfer better title than they have.
3. Holders of negotiable documents of title may transfer better title than they have.
4. Merchants who keep possession of goods they have sold may transfer better title than they have.

Authorized Persons

Persons may validly sell what they do not own if the owner has authorized them to do so. Salespeople in retail stores are so authorized. Auctioneers and sheriffs are also authorized when they sell, under court order, stolen or repossessed goods or foreclosed property.

Buyers in a Sale Induced by Fraud

If an owner of goods is induced by fraud to sell the goods, the buyer obtains a voidable title. Upon discovering the fraud, the victimized seller may cancel the contract and recover the goods unless an innocent third party has already given value and acquired rights in them. Such a third party is known as a **good faith purchaser**. Thus, a fraudulent buyer with voidable title may transfer valid title to a good faith purchaser. To act in good faith, the purchaser must not have reason to suspect the person who has the voidable title. The defrauded seller must seek damages from the original fraudulent buyer.

IN THIS CASE

Downy lied about his income and assets when he bought a dinette from Furniture World on credit. After making the first of 12 payments, Downy defaulted. Furniture World then checked Downy's credit record and discovered the fraud. Downy had already sold the dinette to Tilly, who honestly thought that Downy was the owner. As a good faith purchaser, Tilly received good title to the dinette. Furniture World must suffer the loss unless it can locate Downy and recover from him.

Holders of Negotiable Documents of Title

In business, certain documents are often used as a substitute for possession of goods. Examples are warehouse receipts issued by public warehouses and bills of lading and airbills issued by common carriers. These documents may be nonnegotiable or negotiable. If the documents are negotiable, the goods are to be delivered to the bearer, who is the person in possession of the document, or to the order of a named party. Such persons, also known as *holders,* are deemed to have title to the goods. They may transfer ownership of the goods by transferring the documents alone. A holder who is named in the negotiable document must sign as well as deliver the document to transfer it to a third party.

Merchants With Possession of Sold Goods

Occasionally a buyer will allow the merchant seller to temporarily retain possession of the goods after the sale. If, during this period, the merchant resells and delivers these goods to a good faith purchaser, the latter receives good title. But the merchant must replace the resold goods or be liable in damages to the original buyer for the tort of *conversion.*

IN THIS CASE

When their new home was almost finished, the Howlands bought a set of new living room furniture from Eaton's Fine Furniture Shop. Eaton was to retain possession of the furniture under a layaway plan until the house was completed. Eaton assumed that she would have no trouble replacing the furniture before this completion date. Therefore she sold the Howlands' furniture to Hopkins, a good faith purchaser who took immediate delivery. Hopkins thus obtained a valid title. If Eaton is unable to replace the set when the Howlands demand delivery, she will be liable to them for damages for the tort of conversion.

REQUIREMENTS FOR TRANSFER OF OWNERSHIP

WHAT'S YOUR VERDICT?

O'Dell was preparing for a gala New Year's Eve charity ball. He could not decide which of three tuxedos to buy from Signet Styles. At O'Dell's request, the manager set all three aside until the next day so O'Dell's friend could come in to help him decide. That night a fire destroyed the store and its contents.

Must O'Dell pay for the tuxedos that were set aside?

For ownership of goods to be transferred in a sale, the goods must be both existing and identified. **Existing goods** are physically in existence even though they may not be in a fully assembled and immediately deliverable condition. Existing goods also are owned by the seller. **Identified goods** have been specifically designated as the subject matter of a particular sales contract. The identification of such goods may be

CULTURAL DIVERSITY IN LAW

International

Negotiable Bills of Lading

In international transactions, ownership often is transferred using negotiable bills of lading. These documents are bought and sold while cargo is literally floating on the open seas. When the document is sold, so is the cargo. It is not uncommon for oil to change hands 20 times between the time it leaves the Persian Gulf and arrives in the United States.

Negotiable bills of lading have been a part of commerce for centuries. Many European countries used them as early as the sixteenth century.

done by the buyer, the seller, both, or by a mutually agreed-upon third party. Typically, when identified, the goods are marked, separated, or in some way made distinct from similar goods that the seller might have on hand.

In *What's Your Verdict?* there was no intent to buy all three tuxedos, and no selection had been made of the one to be bought. Therefore, even though the goods were existing, they had not been identified. Thus, there never was a contract to buy any one tuxedo. Consequently, ownership and risk of loss for all three items remained in the seller.

Unless goods are both existing and identified, they are **future goods**. Any contract for the sale of future goods is a contract to sell rather than a sale. Neither ownership nor risk of loss passes at the time of the agreement.

An important exception to the process of identification is made for *fungible goods*. These are goods of a homogeneous or essentially identical nature. With fungible goods, by nature or trade usage, each unit is regarded as equal to every other unit. Examples are a quantity of corn or oil of a given variety and grade, or thousands of cases of identical canned fruit in a warehouse. In many states, ownership and risk of loss in fungible goods pass without selection or identification of specific goods. The buyer therefore becomes the owner at the time of the agreement.

WHEN DOES OWNERSHIP TRANSFER?

WHAT'S YOUR VERDICT?

Chien Huang ordered electronic equipment worth more than $3 million from Inter-Continental Traders, a Seattle exporter. The equipment was to be shipped to a company in the People's Republic of China. The sales agreement, signed by both parties, stated that title and risk of loss would pass "when all necessary governmental permits are obtained." The Chinese government granted an import permit and necessary clearance to allow the exchange of Chinese currency into dollars to pay for the order. However, the U.S. State Department refused to grant an export permit because of the classified nature of some of the equipment.

Did a sale take place?

Recall that ownership of goods brings with it a bundle of rights and benefits. These rights and benefits are offset by a related bundle of duties and burdens. When ownership transfers from one party to another, the nature of the duties and burdens are important to know.

Once goods are existing and identified, disputes may arise over who has title to the goods at particular times. Sometimes creditors of the seller, or creditors of the buyer, may claim possession in order to collect money due. Other disputes may concern who bears the risk of loss if the goods are damaged, stolen, or destroyed before the transaction is completed. A risk-bearer may want or need the protection of casualty insurance. Generally, the person who has title to the goods will bear the loss, but this is not always the case.

In deciding when title transfers from seller to buyer, courts first examine the sales agreement to see if the parties have clearly specified when they intended for title to pass. If they have expressed such intent, courts will generally uphold their agreement. In *What's Your Verdict?* no sale took place. The agreement said that title and risk of loss would pass "when all necessary governmental permits" were obtained. Therefore Inter-Continental Traders would retain title to the goods because this condition had not been met.

If the parties do not specify when title is to pass, courts first determine if there is any applicable custom or usage in the particular trade that can settle the question. If there is no agreement on the matter and no available trade custom or usage, courts look to the Uniform Commercial Code (UCC) for a solution.

Common situations involving transfer of title are discussed below. Note that neither the method of payment nor the time of payment governs the outcome.

Seller Delivers Goods To Their Destination

If the contract requires the seller to deliver the goods to their destination, title passes when the goods are tendered at that specified destination. **Tender of delivery** means that the seller places (or authorizes a carrier to place) the proper goods at the buyer's disposal and notifies the buyer so that delivery can be received. The manner, time, and place for tender are determined by the agreement and the UCC. When the seller is required to do additional work, title does not pass until such work is completed.

Seller Ships, But Does Not Deliver, Goods to Their Destination

If the contract requires or authorizes the seller to ship the goods but does not obligate the seller to deliver them to the destination, title passes to the buyer at the time and place of shipment, when possession is transferred to the carrier.

A Question of ETHICS

In the Hot Debate at the beginning of the chapter, you sought to recover your stolen laptop from an innocent purchaser, a pastor of a church that ministered to the homeless. The laptop was being used by the church to track and monitor the welfare of the homeless. Nonetheless, you have filed suit to force the computer's return, a move that will result in a considerable loss of resources for the church. How can you ethically justify doing this? Does the church itself have an ethical interest in returning it to you? What is that interest? Have you acted in a manner that would indicate the relative importance of the laptop to you? If so, how did you act and how do your actions bear on the moral justifiability of your claim?

Answer the following questions about legal concepts.

1. The buyer of stolen goods does not get "legal" possession. **True or False?**

2. An innocent buyer of stolen goods gets title to the goods. **True or False?**

3. A fraudulent buyer of goods may transfer __?__ title to a good faith purchaser. **(a) valid (b) voidable (c) void (d) all of the above**

4. In determining when title is to pass, the courts will first look at the sales agreement. If nothing pertinent is found, the courts will look at trade customs or usage. Only as a last resort will the courts look at the __?__ .

5. If the seller is to tender the goods at the place of sale, title passes at the time and place where the sales contract is made. **True or False?**

THINK CRITICALLY ABOUT EVIDENCE

Study the following situations, answer the questions, then prepare arguments to support your answers.

6. After Carr refurbished her home, she held a yard sale for things she did not need. Included was a large crosscut saw, which she sold to Sutro. She did not know that her husband had borrowed the saw from a neighbor. Did Sutro become the owner?

7. Smith's Bookstore handled rare books. Needing money, Smith's sold an old edition of the Bible to Aubley. Smith's received $20,000 as a deposit of one-half the purchase price. The rest was to be paid upon delivery of the book. Smith's then sold the same book to James on the same terms. Finally, Smith's sold and delivered the book to Salmon for the full $40,000. All three buyers acted in good faith and without notice of the other transactions. Who gets title to the book?

8. Corcoran was suddenly transferred from Portland, Oregon, to company headquarters in Schenectady, New York. Before moving, he hastily rented his house to Mr. and Mrs. Shwin, who had shown him convincing credentials of their credit worthiness. The Shwins also bought all the household furniture and equipment for $10,000. They put 5 percent ($500) down, with the balance to be paid in 19 equal installments of $500 each. The Shwins were prompt in paying the rent and the $500 installment for two months. Then they disappeared. Their credit records had been forgeries, and before vanishing they had sold almost all the furniture and kitchen equipment to good faith purchasers. Did the purchasers get good title?

Seller Delivers Document of Title

When customary, or when the parties have agreed that the seller is to deliver a document of title (for example, an airbill), title passes when and where the document is delivered. For example, Degory bought 600 tons of oats from Delta. The oats were stored in a public grain elevator. Title passed when an authorized agent of Delta delivered a negotiable warehouse receipt for the oats to Degory.

Buyer Takes Possession at Place of Sale

If the seller is to tender the goods at the place of sale, title passes at the time and the place where the sales contract is made.

GOALS

● **Explain when the risk of loss from seller to buyer transfers in different situations**

● **Explain when insurable property interests transfer in different situations**

WHEN DOES RISK OF LOSS TRANSFER?

WHAT'S YOUR VERDICT?

Alda had stored 200,000 pounds of Idaho potatoes in Berle's Cold Storage house. On December 17, Alda sold 25,000 pounds to Clark. On December 20, Alda notified Berle, who issued a negotiable warehouse receipt to Clark for 25,000 pounds. On February 15, Clark paid the storage charges and ordered shipment of the potatoes to New Orleans. On February 16, Berle shipped the goods.

When did the risk of loss transfer to the buyer, Clark?

The transfer of the risk of loss from seller to buyer does not always occur when title transfers. Possible alternatives regarding when the transfer of risk of loss takes place are discussed below.

Seller Ships Goods by Carrier

If the seller is required to deliver the goods to a particular destination but is allowed to use a carrier, such as a railroad, to make the delivery, the risk of loss passes to the buyer at the destination, upon tender of delivery. This is true even if goods that are shipped by carrier are still in the possession of the carrier.

Suppose the seller is not required to deliver the goods to the buyer at a particular destination. If the seller then uses a carrier to transport the goods, the risk of loss passes to the buyer when the goods are delivered to the carrier.

Commercial buyers often use the shipment term **FOB**, which means "free on board." Assume that the seller is in Atlanta and the buyer is in New York City. In this case, "FOB Atlanta" means the seller agrees to deliver the goods no further than the carrier's freight station in Atlanta. Title and risk of loss transfer to the buyer at that point. On the other hand, if the terms are "FOB, buyer's warehouse, New York City," the seller must deliver the goods to the buyer's warehouse in New York City. The title and the risk of loss remain with the seller until delivery takes place. In the absence of contrary arrangements, the buyer pays the transportation charges in the first situation described and the seller pays the charges in the second.

IN THIS CASE

Cook's Christmas Tree Corner ordered 50 cases of fragile ornaments from a wholesaler. The contract did not require delivery to Cook's or to any other designated destination. The wholesaler routinely shipped the ornaments using an independent trucker selected by Cook's. The shipment was lost when the trailer that contained the ornaments was stolen at an overnight truck stop. Unless covered by insurance, Cook's must bear the loss because it owned the goods.

In shipments from foreign countries, it is not uncommon for the seller to quote a CIF *(cost, insurance, freight)* price. This means that the seller contracts for adequate insurance and for proper shipment to the named destination and then adds these items to the price or cost of the goods. The risk of loss passes to the buyer when the seller delivers the goods to the carrier, such as a seagoing ship. However, the insurance provides protection against loss from any identified risks.

Goods Held by Bailee

Sometimes goods are held for a seller by a bailee. A *bailee* has temporary possession of another person's goods, holding them in trust for a specified purpose. A public warehouse is an example of a bailee. The goods may be sold by the owner, yet the contract may call for delivery to the buyer without the goods being moved. The risk of loss transfers to the buyer under such circumstances in any of the following situations:

* when the buyer receives a negotiable document of title covering the goods (for example, a negotiable warehouse receipt)
* when the bailee acknowledges the buyer's right to possession of the goods
* after the buyer receives a non-negotiable document of title (for example, a non-negotiable warehouse receipt) or other written direction to a bailee to deliver the goods. (The buyer must have had a reasonable time to present the document to the bailee, who must have honored it.)

In *What's Your Verdict?* the risk of loss passed from Alda to Clark on December 20, when Berle issued the negotiable warehouse receipt. (Bailments are discussed more fully in Chapter 20.)

Either Party Breaches After Goods Identified

The seller sometimes breaches by providing goods so faulty that the buyer rightly rejects them. The risk of loss then remains with the seller until the defects are corrected.

IN THIS CASE

Galaxy Furniture Company shipped a truckload of chairs and sofas to Brenda's Bargain Basement. Without unloading the tractor-trailer, inspection disclosed that Galaxy had mistakenly shipped sofas and chairs upholstered in costly Italian leather. Brenda had ordered the durable but much cheaper vinyl upholstery models. Brenda promptly notified Galaxy of the error and asked for instructions on what to do with them. After a week, the unloaded trailer was still parked in back of Brenda's warehouse. Then a fire of undisclosed origin destroyed the trailer (along with some other vehicles). Galaxy suffers the loss unless properly insured.

Goods Neither Shipped by Carrier Nor Held by Bailee

In any case not covered previously, the risk of loss falls on the buyer upon receipt of the goods if the seller is a merchant. If the seller is not a merchant, the risk of loss transfers to the buyer as soon as the seller makes a tender of delivery.

IN THIS CASE

Abigail bought a camper trailer at a garage sale. The seller said that Abigail could take the trailer home at any time. Abigail went home to get a pickup with a trailer hitch. Upon returning, Abigail was told that during her absence, an unidentified person had backed into the trailer, causing extensive damage to it. If the person cannot be found, Abigail will have to bear the loss. That is because the seller was not a merchant and the seller had made an effective tender before Abigail left to get the pickup.

WHEN DO INSURABLE PROPERTY INTERESTS TRANSFER?

WHAT'S YOUR VERDICT?

Frosty-Frolic Company was a fresh-food packer and processor. In a sales contract with Goodman, Frosty-Frolic agreed to pack a quantity of head lettuce grown near Salinas, California, and to place the "Soaring Eagle" brand label on the cartons. The lettuce was routinely dehydrated, cooled, packaged, placed in the special cartons, and stacked on pallets in Frosty-Frolic sheds for daily shipment as ordered by Goodman.

At what point did Goodman obtain the right to insure the goods against possible loss?

The buyer obtains a special property interest in goods at the time of their identification to the contract. This special interest gives the buyer the right to buy insurance on the goods. The physical act of identifying goods usually takes the form of setting aside, marking, tagging, labeling, boxing, branding, shipping, or in some other way indicating that the specific goods are to be delivered or sent to the buyer in fulfillment of the contract.

Thus, in *What's Your Verdict?* Goodman obtained an insurable interest when the lettuce was identified as hers (when placed in "Soaring Eagle" cartons). If the goods already exist and have been identified to the contract, the property interest of the buyer arises when the contract is made.

In addition to the insurable interest, the buyer has the following rights:

1. to inspect the identified goods at a reasonable hour
2. to compel delivery if the seller wrongfully withholds delivery
3. to collect damages from third persons who take or injure the goods

TRANSFER OF OWNERSHIP AND RISK OF LOSS IN SPECIFIC TRANSACTIONS

WHAT'S YOUR VERDICT?

Cutting Edge Inc., a manufacturer, sold 250 gasoline-powered chain saws to Valu-Line, a large retailer. The full price was due in six months, and Cutting Edge agreed to accept the return of any saws not sold by then. Two months later, after only 25 saws had been sold, Valu-Line filed a bankruptcy petition. Cutting Edge demands return of the unsold saws. Valu-Line's other creditors claim that title to the saws had passed to the retailer. Therefore, under the bankruptcy law, all creditors should share in the claim to the saws.

Who is right?

The following transactions merit special attention because of the frequency with which they occur or because of the uniqueness of the rules that apply to them.

Cash-and-Carry Sales

When the buyer in a sales contract is a consumer who pays cash and takes immediate delivery, title passes to the buyer at the time of the transaction. This is the most common type of transaction for groceries and other low-priced items. Risk of loss passes upon the buyer's receipt of the goods from a merchant and on tender of goods by a casual seller.

The seller may insist on payment in legal tender. Checks are commonly used but are not legal tender. Acceptance of a check by the seller is not considered payment until the check is paid at the bank. But use of a check by the consumer in a cash-and-carry sale does not affect the timing of the transfer of title or risk of loss.

Sales on Credit

The fact that a sale is made on credit does not affect the passing of title or risk of loss. A **credit sale** is simply a sale that, by agreement of the parties, calls for payment for the goods at a later date. Ownership and risk of loss may pass even though the time of payment or delivery is delayed.

COD Sales

Goods are often shipped **COD**, which means collect on delivery. The carrier collects the price and transportation charges upon delivery and transmits this amount to the seller. If the buyer does not pay, the goods are not delivered. Thus, in effect, the seller retains control over the possession of the goods until the price is paid. In a COD arrangement, the buyer loses the right otherwise available to inspect the goods before payment. Nevertheless, ownership and risk of loss transfer just as though there were no such provisions.

Sale or Return

A **sale or return** is a completed sale in which the buyer has an option of returning the goods. When goods are delivered to a merchant buyer in a sale or return, the ownership and risk of loss pass to the buyer upon delivery. Such a transaction is a true sale. But in a sale or return transaction, if the buyer returns the goods within the fixed or a reasonable amount of time, ownership and risk of loss pass back to the seller. This is true whether the sale is made for cash or on credit. The returned goods must essentially be in their original condition.

Normally goods held on sale or return are subject to the claims of the buyer's creditors, who can seize the goods under court order. In *What's Your Verdict?* all of Valu-Line's creditors share in the claim to the saws. Cutting Edge was but one of many claimants.

The sale or return provision should not be confused with the return privilege granted to customers of some retail stores. These stores allow customers to return most purchases that have not been used, even if they are not defective. This return privilege is not required by law, but stores offer it to promote goodwill and increase sales in the long run.

Sale on Approval

Sometimes goods are delivered to the buyer in a **sale on approval**, "on trial," or "on satisfaction." In such a case, prospective ownership and risk of loss do not pass until the prospective buyer approves the goods. This may be done by words, payment, any conduct indicating approval, or retention of the goods beyond a specified or reasonable time. While in possession of the goods, the prospective buyer is liable for any damage to them caused by his or her negligence. Normally, the prospective buyer may reject the goods for any cause, whether or not it is reasonable.

Sale of an Undivided Interest

A person who sells a fractional interest in a single good or in a number of

goods that are to remain together makes a **sale of an undivided interest**. Ownership and risk of loss pass to each buyer at the time of the sale of each undivided interest.

Auction

An **auction** is a public sale to the highest bidder. When an auctioneer decides that no one will bid any higher for the goods on sale, the bidding is closed, usually by the pounding of the auctioneer's gavel. In doing so, the auctioneer accepts the bid on behalf of the owner of the goods. Ownership passes to the buyer at that time. Risk of loss passes whenever the auctioneer acknowledges the buyer's right to possess the goods, typically upon tender of the goods in exchange for payment.

Auction sales are "with reserve" unless specifically announced in advance to be "without reserve." "With reserve" means that if nothing to the contrary is stated, an auctioneer may withdraw the goods anytime before announcing completion of the sale. If "without reserve" the goods must be sold to the person who makes the highest bid even if it is the first and only and ridiculously low.

Bulk Transfer

A **bulk tansfer** is the transfer, generally by sale, of all or a major part of the goods of a business in one unit at one time. Such goods include materials, supplies, merchandise, and equipment if sold with the inventory.

The law protects creditors of the occasional dishonest merchant who would otherwise sell out secretly, keep the proceeds, and disappear. The UCC requires notice to the seller's creditors before the bulk transfer is made. The seller is required to list all creditors. The buyer is required to notify those creditors of the forthcoming transfer of ownership and to pay their claims or to make other arrangements with them. If the buyer does not do this, creditors of the seller may make claims against the inventory and

equipment after the buyer takes possession.

An innocent third party who in good faith buys some or all of the goods from a bulk transferee gets good title. But if such third party pays no value or knows the buyer failed to comply with requirements of the bulk transfer law, the creditors can retake the goods.

THINK ABOUT LEGAL CONCEPTS

Answer the following questions about legal concepts.

1. The transfer of the risk of loss from seller to buyer always occurs when title transfers. **True or False?**

2. CIF means **(a) cost in freight (b) customer insures freight (c) cost including freight (d) none of the above**

3. If a buyer properly rejects faulty goods, the risk of loss stays with the seller until the defects are corrected. **True or False?**

4. An insurable interest is acquired by the seller when the goods are identified to the contract? **True or False?**

5. A buyer can always inspect the goods before paying, even in a COD sale. **True or False?**

6. The carrier collects the price and transportation charges upon delivery, then transmits this amount to the seller in **(a) COD sales (b) cash-and-carry sales (c) a sale or return (d) sales on credit.**

IN THIS CASE

Clarke bought a one-half interest in a traveling carnival. On the day after the purchase, the truck and trailer carrying the big tent to the next city were totally destroyed in a crash and fire. Clarke claimed that he should not have to bear any part of the loss because the owners had not yet determined which part of the carnival belonged to whom. However, the contract showed an intent to continue the carnival's operation under joint ownership. There was no intent to divide the various properties into separately owned parts. Therefore Clarke was wrong. From the time of the purchase, he was part owner of all the carnival properties. As such, he had to suffer one-half of the loss.

Study the following situations, answer the questions, then prepare arguments to support your answers.

7. Donatti, of California, ordered 400 pounds of fresh blueberries from Margeson, a produce broker in New Zealand. The terms called for shipment by airfreight, FOB Donatti's cold-storage plant in Los Angeles. The blueberries were properly packed and shipped by airline common carrier, but they were mishandled upon arrival at the Los Angeles International Airport. Delivery was delayed, and when the fruit was finally delivered it was not edible. Who must suffer the loss?

8. Burby was a dealer in fuel and related supplies. Burby sold a quantity of oak firewood to Buckminster. Nothing was said about delivery to a carrier or transfer to a bailee. After the goods were set aside and were ready for delivery, they were stolen by burglars. Who suffers the loss?

9. To finance a trip for the high school band, the director bought "safe and sane fireworks" priced at $4,000 wholesale. The director paid cash in a sale-or-return contract. Band members took turns as salesclerks in the Fourth of July booth provided by the distributor. Several items did not sell at all. The wholesale price of those fireworks sold by midnight on July 4 was only $1,286.50. What should the director do?

10. Ever since grade school, Annette and Barb had talked about going into business together after college. Late one evening, Annette and Barb were discussing plans for a mail-order business. They agreed that they would not want to face the headaches and risks of selling goods on credit. Annette said they should avoid all losses by selling only for cash or certified check. Barb said they should avoid all losses by selling only on a COD basis. Will these strategies avoid all losses?

To protect yourself in the actual sales transaction. . . .

1. Remember that ownership of goods will not necessarily prevent transfer of title to them contrary to your wishes when

- You have authorized others to sell the goods for you. They may violate your instructions.

- You have been defrauded in a sales transaction and have given a voidable title to the wrongdoer. Before you cancel the contract and try to get your goods back, the wrongdoer can transfer good title to a good faith buyer.

- Someone has wrongfully obtained possession of a negotiable warehouse receipt, a negotiable bill of lading, or a negotiable airbill for your goods. The wrongdoer can give good title by negotiating, that is, transferring, the paper.

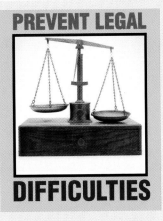

PREVENT LEGAL DIFFICULTIES

- You have allowed the person who sold to you to keep possession of your goods. The person who sold them to you might sell them again.

Be alert to the following possibilities. . . .

2. It is wise to act promptly in identifying goods to the sales contract and in completing performance. Delay may lead to complications.

3. Important written sales contracts ideally specify precisely when title to goods and risk of loss of goods are to transfer.

4. As a buyer or a seller, carry adequate insurance when appropriate to cover any insurable interest you may have in goods that are the subject matter of the sales contract.

5. Assure yourself of the integrity and financial responsibility of buyers before selling goods to them on credit, on sale or return, or on approval.

6. When the buyer's credit is questionable, sell for cash or on a COD basis.

7. If you buy an entire business inventory or a major part of one, be sure to comply with UCC rules governing bulk transfers, if applicable in your state.

CHAPTER IN REVIEW

CONCEPTS IN BRIEF

1. Generally the owner of goods is the only one who can legally transfer title to them. Exceptions are made for a party who
   - is authorized by the owner to sell the goods
   - has obtained good title to the goods by fraud and sells them to a good faith purchaser
   - is the holder of a negotiable document of title
   - is a merchant seller who has retained possession of previously sold goods.

2. Before ownership in goods can pass, goods must be both existing and identified.

3. In determining when title and risk of loss pass in a sales transaction, the terms of the sales contract are given top priority. If those terms do not provide an answer, then trade customs and usage may provide the determining customary rule. If not, UCC rules are used to make the determination.

4. The buyer obtains an insurable property interest when goods are identified to the contract.

5. In cash-and-carry sales, title passes at the time of the transaction. If a check is used, the payment is conditional until the check is paid by the bank on which it is drawn.

6. COD terms by a seller do not affect the time of transfer of ownership or of risk of loss. But the terms do reserve control of the goods to the seller until payment is received.

7. In a sale or return sale, ownership and risk of loss generally pass to the merchant buyer upon delivery.

8. At an auction, title passes when the auctioneer signifies acceptance of the bidder's offer. Unless otherwise announced, the auctioneer may refuse all bids and withdraw the goods.

9. Notice of a bulk transfer of the inventory and equipment of a business must be given to creditors of the seller before the sale takes place.

YOUR LEGAL VOCABULARY

Match each statement with the term that it best defines. Some terms may not be used.

1. Physically existing goods owned by the seller

2. Goods that are not both existing and identified

3. Goods of an essentially identical nature to one another

4. To place the goods at the buyer's disposal

5. Sale that, by agreement, calls for payment for the goods at a later date

6. Public sale to the highest bidder

7. Collect on delivery

8. Innocent third party to a fraudulent transfer of goods who gives value to and acquires rights in the goods

9. The transfer, generally by sale, of all or a major part of the goods of a business in one unit at one time

auction
bulk transfer
CIF
COD
credit sale
existing goods
FOB
fungible goods
future goods
good faith purchaser
identified goods
sale on approval
sale or return
sale of an undivided
   interest
tender of delivery

10. Why should an innocent purchaser from a thief receive only possession whereas an innocent purchaser of another's goods from a repairman of those goods get good title?

11. Why should the risk of loss to fungible goods pass at the time of the agreement instead of when the goods are existing and identified to the contract?

12. Why should the courts give priority to the actual sales contract when determining when the ownership of goods passes from seller to buyer?

13. What are the advantages and disadvantages to allowing ownership to be transferred by the passage of documents of title?

WRITE ABOUT LEGAL CONCEPTS

14. Should checks be considered "legal tender?" Write a paragraph stating arguments for both sides of the issue.

15. Are COD sales still useful? Make a list of instances in which they fill a need.

16. **HOT DEBATE** Write an argument in favor of your recovering the computer. Write an argument that emphasizes the legal and ethical points in the church's favor.

THINK CRITICALLY ABOUT EVIDENCE

17. Trina, a computer programmer, had her laptop computer stolen. She reported it stolen and gave the police its serial number. Three months later, the police recovered a laptop that was the same make and model as Trina's. However, the serial number had been removed. Trina tried to obtain the computer from the police but they declined her request and put the computer up for sale at the next police auction. Trina sued to recover what she considered to be her computer. Who won and why?

18. Shortly after her lawsuit against the police department was resolved, Trina decided to buy a new laptop from a 1-800 phone order seller. As Trina and the seller agreed, the seller shipped Trina's new computer to a warehouse near Trina's home. The warehouse then notified Trina to come and pick up the computer. Through no fault of the warehouse, the computer was drenched with water and rendered inoperable during a minor

fire. Trina tried to return the computer to the seller for a new one, saying that the seller had to bear the loss. The company refused to accept the return. Trina sued the computer company for her money back or another computer. Who won and why?

19. Shortly after her lawsuit against the computer company was resolved, Trina took her new laptop into a computer store for needed repairs. When Trina returned to pick it up, she found it had been sold by one of the store's salespeople to an innocent purchaser. Evidently, due to a bookkeeping error and its mint condition, Trina's laptop had been shelved with the store's regular stock and was snapped up by the first customer that saw it. Before Trina's attorney could bring suit against the shop, it went out of business. She then sued to recover the laptop from the customer who purchased it from the store. Who won and why?

20. During World War II, Lieber was in the U.S. Army and was one of the first soldiers to occupy Munich, Germany. Lieber entered Adolf Hitler's apartment with some companions and removed some of his clothing, decorations, and jewelry. In 1968, Lieber was living in Louisiana when his chauffeur stole the collection and sold it to a dealer. The dealer then sold the collection to Mohawk who bought the collection in good faith. Through collectors' circles, Lieber learned that Mohawk had his collection. He demanded its return. Who gets the collection? (*Lieber v. Mohawk Arms, Inc.*, 314 N.Y.S.2d 510, N.Y.)

21. Lane had a boat dealership in North Carolina. In February, he sold a new boat, a 120-HP motor, and a trailer to a man who represented himself to be "John Willis." Willis gave Lane a check for $6,285 and left with the goods. The check proved to be worthless. Less than six months later, Honeycutt bought the three items in South Carolina from a man whom he had known for several years as "John R. Garrett." In fact, this was Willis, using an alias. Later, while searching for Willis under the alias of "John Patterson," the Federal Bureau of Investigation contacted Honeycutt. Honeycutt said that (a) he had paid a full price of only $2,500; (b) Garrett had nothing to show he was the owner; (c) he did not know from whom Garrett got the boat; (d) Garrett said he was selling the boat for someone else; (e) Garrett signed what he called a "title" (the document was nothing more than a "Certificate of Number" issued by the state Wildlife Resources Commission, not the "certificate of title" required by statutes); (f) Garrett forged the signature of the purported owner, John F. Patterson, on the so-called title. Plaintiff Lane now claims that defendant Honeycutt was not a good-faith purchaser and therefore should return the boat to him, with damages for a wrongful detention. Who has title to the boat? You decide. (*Lane v. Honeycutt*, 188 S.E.2d 604, N.C)

22. Consolidated Chemical Industries purchased three heat exchangers from Falls Industries, in Cleveland. The contract specified that after identification the machines were to be crated securely. They were then to be delivered, without breakage, to the destination, the Consolidated plant in East Baton Rouge. Because the machines were not crated securely, the exchangers were badly damaged in transit. Consolidated refused to accept them, and Falls sued. Falls claimed that risk of loss had passed when the goods were delivered to the carrier. Do you agree? (*Falls Industries, Inc. v. Consolidated Chemical Industries, Inc.*, 258 F.2d 277)

23. The plaintiff, a Los Angeles manufacturer of men's clothing, sold a variety of clothing to the defendant, a retailer in Westport, Connecticut. The plaintiff prepared four invoices covering the clothing and stamped them "FOB Los Angeles," and added the words "goods shipped at purchaser's risk." The plaintiff delivered the goods to the Denver-Chicago Trucking Company. When the truck arrived in Connecticut with the goods, the defendant's wife was in charge of the store. She ordered the driver to unload the cartons and place them inside the store. The driver refused and left with the goods. The defendant complained to the plaintiff, who filed a claim against the trucking company. No reimbursement was obtained by the plaintiff, and the defendant never received the goods. Now the plaintiff seller sues the defendant buyer for the purchase price. Who is right? You decide. (*Ninth Street East, Ltd. v. Harrison*, 259 A.2d 772, Conn.)

24. In June, plaintiff Multiplastics, Inc., contracted with defendant Arch Industries, Inc., to make and to ship 40,000 pounds of plastic pellets, which were to be delivered at the rate of 1,000 pounds a day after Arch gave "release instructions." Multiplastics produced the pellets within two weeks. Arch refused to give the release orders, citing labor difficulties and its vacation schedule. On August 18, Multiplastics wrote, "We have warehoused these products for more than 40 days . . . however we cannot warehouse . . . indefinitely, and request that you send us shipping instructions." Multiplastics followed this with numerous telephone calls seeking payment and delivery instructions. In response, on August 20, Arch agreed to issue the release orders but never did. On September 22, the Multiplastics factory, including the 40,000 pounds of this order, was destroyed by fire. The pellets were not covered by Multiplastics' fire insurance policy. Therefore Multiplastics sued Arch for breach of contract and also claimed that the risk of loss had passed to the buyer. You decide. (*Multiplastics, Inc. v. Arch Industries, Inc.*, 348 A.2d 618, Conn.)

BACKGROUND Numismatic Funding Corporation sold rare collectible coins by mail throughout the United States. In general, buyers would request specific coins and Numismatic would ship them on the terms discussed below.

FACTS Numismatic Funding Corporation sold by mail rare collectible coins throughout the United States. Early one year, Numismatic mailed a sizeable shipment of such coins to Frederick Prewitt. Prewitt was a commodities broker in St. Louis, Missouri, with whom the Corporation had done business on at least two other occasions. The shipment of rare gold and silver coins was valued at over $60,000. The would-be sales transaction was governed by the terms set down in the documents that were enclosed with the coins. These terms stated that Prewitt could buy part or all of the shipment which was available to him on a "14 day approval basis."

The accompanying invoice stated that the title did not transfer until the seller was paid in full. Also the buyer was given 14 days from the receipt of the goods to settle the account in full. No directions were provided as to how to return the unwanted coins. After examining the coins, Prewitt told his wife to send them back to Numismatic by certified mail. She did so within the 14-day period. She also insured each of the two packages the coins were returned in for $400.

Numismatic Funding Corporation never received the coins. Prewitt then sued to be declared free of responsibility for the loss.

TRIAL COURT At the trial it was noticed by the court that Numismatic's sales technique was to not only mail out coins requested by a prospective retailer, but also to send out unsolicited merchandise at the same time. The trial court then found for Prewitt, in effect, deciding that Prewitt had acted properly under the laws and, in doing so, avoided legal responsibility for the loss.

APPEAL Numismatic then appealed to the Eight Circuit Court of Appeals.

ISSUE Who bore the risk of loss for the solicited and the unsolicited merchandise that Numismatic sent to Prewitt?

PRACTICE JUDGING

1. **Who must bear the loss for the rare coins?**

2. **What legal theory prompted you to answer question 1 as you did?**

3. **What is the status of the unsolicited merchandise? What is the source of the law that decides the issue of the unsolicited merchandise?**

CONSUMER PROTECTION

LESSONS

HOT DEBATE

Edison buys a lawnmower from a department store. Because of a defect in design, a protective plastic flap binds the lawnmower whenever the lawnmower is pulled backwards. For efficiency's sake Edison removes the flap. Later, as he is pulling the mower backwards, he trips and falls backwards. Due to the lack of the protective flap, his foot shoots upwards into the mower blade. Edison, who was only wearing tennis shoes, loses half his foot. Later, he brings suit against the manufacturer.

Where Do You Stand?

1. List and discuss the legal reasons supporting Edison's suit.

2. List and discuss the legal reasons supporting the manufacturer.

WHY DOES THE LAW PROTECT CONSUMERS?

WHAT'S YOUR VERDICT?

Simmons wanted his car painted. He saw a newspaper advertisement for "car painting, $99.99 complete." He went to the place of business, contracted for the service, and selected a dark blue metallic finish. However, when the paint job was completed and Simmons examined the car, the color was obviously light blue. Simmons complained, but the manager claimed the color was close enough to the color Simmons had selected and refused to make any correction.

What should Simmons do?

A **consumer** is an individual who acquires goods that are primarily intended for personal, family, or household use. It was once thought that consumers, forewarned by the legal phrase *caveat emptor* (meaning "let the buyer beware") would be adequately protected by their own ability to judge a product's safety and utility. The forces of supply and demand in a competitive marketplace were to keep product makers and sellers committed to producing the best product for the money.

Unfortunately, these measures proved to be inadequate. In our affluent, technology-oriented society, the complexity and sheer abundance of products make it difficult for the consumer to properly judge the quality or advantages and disadvantages of a product. Products often are so complex that most people cannot repair them if they break down.

In addition, the products often are offered by huge corporations capable of manipulating, rather than being controlled by, the marketplace. As a consequence, large corporations are not always responsive to consumer complaints. Their sales volumes are not dependent on their reputations with consumers. Many sellers rely heavily on intensive advertising campaigns that cost millions of dollars. Such advertising can be more effective in creating consumer attitudes toward the product than actual first-hand experience or word-of-mouth recommendations.

In response, local, state, and federal governments have passed legislation to help restore a balance of power between sellers and buyers in the marketplace. These laws fund agencies that add to the traditional contract, tort, and criminal protection against such abuses. For example, anyone who has been deceived while contracting may still sue the wrongdoer rather than waiting for a governmental agency to act.

However, an individual court action to correct a consumer's problem is generally costly and time-consuming. When the product in question costs little or the potential damage claims are low, court action is often not worth the required effort and expense. To help overcome this problem, **class actions** have been authorized by court rules. A class action allows one or several persons to sue not only on behalf of themselves, but also on behalf of many others similarly wronged.

When the government acts on behalf of the injured consumer through the proceedings of an administrative agency, it may investigate and issue a **cease-and-desist order** to a company. This is an order requiring the company to stop the specified conduct. If the defendant violates the order, heavy civil penalties may be imposed. Often a defendant will sign a consent order rather than resist the charge in a long legal battle. A **consent order** is a voluntary, court-enforceable agreement to stop an illegal or questionable practice. An agency may also order **restitution**, the return to customers of money wrongfully obtained.

In settling a dispute with a business, a consumer may seek help or advice from the state attorney general's office (many maintain toll-free consumer hot lines), the local Better Business Bureau, and, if appropriate, even the customer service department of the corporation involved. In *What's Your Verdict?* Simmons might take any of these actions, and as a last resort, he might take his problem to small claims court.

Overall, consumer laws

1. help protect against the production and sale of substandard or dangerous consumer goods

2. prohibit improper trade practices

3. require licenses and inspections to help ensure compliance with the law

4. provide remedies for persons injured.

PROTECTION AGAINST SUBSTANDARD GOODS

WHAT'S YOUR VERDICT?

The Annihilator Pest Company developed and sold thousands of robot cockroach traps called the Terminator. The human user of the trap simply placed it on the floor of the room and the device would pursue, kill, and consume any roaches on the surface it occupied. Recent consumer reports have shown that the computer chip that controls the trap is too sensitive to vibration and causes the Terminator to go out of control and attack mice, house pets, and even furry house slippers.

What is the Annihilator required to do?

Although the ultimate responsibility for protection against substandard goods rests with the consumer, the law provides help in the following areas.

Safety Standards

Each year millions of people are injured and thousands are killed by products in use around the home. As a response, in 1972 the Consumer Product Safety Act was enacted. This law created the Consumer Product Safety Commission (CPSC) and gave it authority to issue and enforce safety standards for most consumer products.

The CPSC requires any manufacturer, distributor, or retailer discovering the failure of its products to comply with safety regulations to report that fact to the commission. The CPSC also receives reports from the nation's hospitals on product-caused injuries. If the CPSC determines that a product is substantially hazardous, the manufacturer, distributors, and retailers of the product must notify purchasers about the hazard and then either recall and repair the product, replace it, or refund the purchase price.

Often the mere threat of CPSC action causes responsible parties to recall their product "voluntarily." In *What's Your Verdict?* Annihilator must notify those concerned and implement an appropriate remedy. Failure to comply could lead to a fine and imprisonment. If necessary, the CPSC has the power to seize the hazardous product and ban it from the marketplace.

Consumers who think the CPSC is not taking action where needed may sue in federal district court to have a protective rule established. If victorious, consumers may be awarded an amount to cover reasonable attorney's fees, as well as their court costs.

The CPSC maintains a toll-free telephone service. Consumers can call the CPSC and, among other things, report claims concerning unsafe products, find out about product recalls occurring in the last few months, and get information about unsafe children's products.

Drugs, Food, and Cosmetics

The federal Food and Drug Administration (FDA) requires that the production facilities for cosmetics, food, and drugs be clean and that the products be prepared from ingredients fit for human use or consumption. A product that does not meet the minimum standards for purity and quality set by the FDA is considered *adulterated*. Such a product may be confiscated by the government. The U.S. Department of Agriculture also inspects canners, packers, and processors of poultry and meat entering interstate commerce to help ensure that the products are free of disease and were processed under sanitary conditions.

In addition, the FDA requires that labels on regulated products give the name and address of the manufacturer, packager, or distributor, and reveal the quantity, such as the weight or the fluid ounces. Nutritional labeling also is required. Labels include information such as the fat, sodium, carbohydrate, and protein amounts provided by a serving.

Drugs are regulated by the FDA to ensure their safety for users and to be certain of their effectiveness for the purpose sold. Without FDA approval, new drugs cannot be marketed in this country. In addition, the FDA determines which drugs are prescription and which may be sold "over-the-counter." The FDA has been criticized for its extremely cautious approach to granting new drug approval. Its procedures have led some Americans to go beyond our borders for certain drugs alleged to be life-saving and pain-easing.

Standards for Weights and Measures

The U.S. Constitution gives Congress the power to set standards for weights and measures. To do so, Congress created the National Bureau of Standards. This government body provides standardized sets of actual weights and measures to the state and local governments. With proper inspection, testing, and enforcement at state and local levels, the measurement of a gallon of gasoline, pound of bananas, or foot of rope is uniform throughout the country. Most states inspect and test weighing and measuring devices at least once a year. Seals certify the accuracy of such devices as gasoline pumps, supermarket scales, and taxicab meters. Violations of the weights and measures laws are punishable by fine, imprisonment, or both. The goods involved may be confiscated.

PROTECTION AGAINST UNFAIR TRADE PRACTICES

WHAT'S YOUR VERDICT?

A national magazine planned to increase subscriptions by giving away prizes of up to $1 million in a drawing. People contacted in a huge mail campaign could enter the drawing by return mail, whether or not they actually subscribed to the magazine. Instructions on how to enter would be placed in the text of the promotional material so a person contacted would have to read about the magazine in order to find out how to enter the drawing. A senior officer of the magazine canceled the plans because she thought it was an illegal lottery.

Was she correct?

Generally, an **unfair trade practice** is any method of business that is dishonest or fraudulent or that illegally limits free competition. To protect consumers, the federal and state governments have enacted numerous laws prohibiting such practices. Chief among these are federal antitrust laws and the Federal Trade Commission Act. They are designed to prevent unfair trade practices in *interstate commerce* (business conducted between persons in two or more states). States have similar laws for *intrastate commerce* (business conducted wholly within one state). Unfair trade practices take many forms.

Agreements to Control or Fix Prices

The part of the free market system that serves the consumer best is *competition.* Competition is the force that drives efficient businesses to create new and better products and services. Competition also drives inefficient firms out of business. Some individuals and companies enter into agreements to control or fix prices and thereby try to ensure their survival by eliminating competition. Such agreements are illegal and unenforceable. Violators are subject to criminal penalties.

False and Misleading Advertising

False and misleading advertising is advertising that intentionally deceives, makes untrue claims of quality or effectiveness, or fails to reveal critically important facts. Claiming that a mouthwash prevents and cures colds and sore throats when it does not is one example of such advertising.

A store practices another form of improper advertising when it uses an understocked, low-priced "come on" to lure prospective buyers into the store. Once there, the would-be buyers find that the advertised item has been sold out and the customers are then deftly redirected to a better, but more expensive product. This practice is referred to as **bait and switch**.

The advertisement is not considered deceptive if it states how many of the advertised item are available or states that the supply of the item is limited. Many stores that want to maintain customer goodwill give rain checks when even reasonably stocked items are exhausted. Rain checks permit customers to purchase the items later at the advertised price.

The *Federal Trade Commission (FTC)* has the main responsibility for preventing false and misleading advertising. If necessary, the FTC may order an advertisement terminated. Where the advertiser has created a false impression that will persist even without the advertisement's being run anymore, the FTC may order corrective advertising. *Corrective advertising* requires the advertiser to admit the wrongdoing and state the truth in a prescribed number of future advertisements.

Illegal Lotteries and Confidence Games

To be a **lottery**, a gambling scheme or game must have three elements:

1. a required payment of money or something else of value to participate
2. the winner or winners to be determined by chance rather than by skill
3. a prize to be won.

Holding or participating in such a gambling scheme is illegal and violators are subject to fine and imprisonment. However, many states have exempted by statute certain religious

Sending mass, unsolicited advertisements over the Internet is a practice known as *spamming*. Many receivers consider these unsolicited e-mails to be the electronic equivalent of junk mail. However, spammers say they have a First Amendment right to send their e-mails. Many states have bills before their legislatures to regulate spamming. These bills would either prohibit junk e-mail altogether or require spammers to provide toll-free phone numbers and return e-mail addresses so recipients can ask to be removed from the e-mailer's list. Regulatory and legal debates about First Amendment rights are not new. How they unfold for the Internet is one issue the courts will be considering for years to come.

and benevolent groups from the lottery prohibition. These groups are allowed to run bingo and other games to produce revenue for their activities. Also, some states hold their own lotteries to generate revenue for state projects, like education.

The use of lotteries by businesses to promote sales remains an unfair method of competition. In *What's Your Verdict?* the promotion was legal because no payment was required to participate. Even so, the FTC would monitor such a game to ensure that all promised prizes are awarded.

Other prohibited schemes are often disguised as legitimate business undertakings. These are sometimes referred to as *confidence games.* Such games typically involve a fraudulent device whereby the victim is persuaded to trust the swindler with the victim's money or other valuables in hopes of a quick gain. One example of the confidence game is the pyramid sales scheme. A chain letter is one such pyramid scheme.

In the chain letter scam, the sender swindles the recipient by convincing him or her to send money to the person whose name appears at the top of an enclosed list. After sending the money, the recipient is supposed to place his or her name at the bottom of the list and mail copies of the letter

and the list to friends. The swindler's name and aliases comprise the first two or more names on the initial list. Initiating or participating in such a scheme is a felony under the law in most states.

Unfair Pricing and Service

Some of the more common unfair pricing methods include intentionally misrepresenting that goods are being sold at a considerable discount and stating that the price charged for the goods is a wholesale price. Both of these unfair pricing schemes are illegal.

Representing goods or services as being free when purchased with another good that is sold at an inflated price to cover the cost of the first is also an unfair pricing method. Reputable merchants often give away truly free samples to introduce new products. Merchants may have legitimate "two-for-one" and "one-cent" sales as long as the cost of the main item is not artificially raised for the sale.

Consumers of repair services may have problems related to unfair pricing. These problems may occur when the estimated price of a repair is significantly less than the actual price. They may also occur when the repair service charges the consumer for repairs that were not authorized.

Most states require businesses to provide consumers with written estimates of repair costs before the work is performed.

Mislabeled Goods

Mislabeling a good to make it more marketable is an unfair method of competition prohibited by law. Even the shape or size of a container must not mislead the consumer into thinking the package contains more than it does. However, some empty space in a package may be necessary to prevent breakage of its contents or may legitimately result from the settling of the contents after filling.

The law also requires that certain products carry warning labels. Poisons and insecticides must have appropriate "Danger" labels. Cigarette packaging and advertisements must carry warnings indicating the danger smoking poses to the health of the user and to others.

Used Articles Sold as New

Many illegal misrepresentations involve selling used articles as if new or in a better condition than they actually are. The most common instance occurs when no indication is given that the goods are secondhand. For example, in used cars, odometers (which show total miles the car has traveled) are sometimes turned back, and the cars are then sold for a much higher price. This activity is illegal.

Other Unfair Trade Practices

There are many other forms of unfair trade practices and competition.

CONFUSING BRAND NAME OR TRADEMARK
One unfair trade practice is the use of a brand name or trademark so similar to a competitor's that it confuses or deceives the public.

UNORDERED MERCHANDISE Sending unordered merchandise and demanding payment for it or its return is also an unfair trade practice. According to federal law, when someone deliber-

ately sends unordered merchandise through the mail, the recipient is under no obligation to return it or to pay for it.

COMMERCIAL BRIBERY Another unfair practice is commercial bribery, which occurs in several different situations. A supplier giving a corporation's purchasing agent money "under the counter" in exchange for an order from the supplier is commercial bribery. A manufacturer paying a retail salesperson "push money" for extra effort in promoting the manufacturer's product also involves commercial bribery. A spy employed in "industrial espionage" to find out a competitor's secrets is also engaging in commercial bribery. In all these instances and others, such bribery is prohibited by law.

FRAUDULENT TELEMARKETING AND INTERNET SCHEMES Fraudulent telemarketing and Internet schemes are additional examples of unfair trade practices. Most companies who contact potential customers by telephone or conduct business on the Internet are honest and legitimate. However, consumers must be wary of those who are not. They should be especially cautious with offers of "get-rich-quick" schemes. Such offers often involve real estate or precious metals. Offers of free gifts and travel also are common in fraudulent schemes.

Whether contacted by a telemarketer or through the Internet, consumers should always check a company out first before sending money or pressing the "I accept" button.

FTC Guidelines

The FTC has adopted many guidelines and regulations that are intended to correct abusive trade practices by requiring businesses to act certain ways. These include the following.

1. Would-be creditors must explain to their intended borrowers the methods of figuring finance charges.

2. Under certain circumstances, sellers, manufacturers, or both must provide written warranties to their customers.

3. Businesses selling door-to-door (legally referred to as *home solicitation sales*) must give purchasers three days to cancel contracts for purchases of $25 or more.

THINK ABOUT LEGAL CONCEPTS

Answer the following questions about legal concepts.

1. Legally, a person buying goods for her or his business is not a "consumer." **True or False?**

2. Is restitution a remedy used by consumer protection agencies? **Yes or No?**

3. Local governments do not have any consumer protection laws. **True or False?**

4. The elements of a lottery are ___?___, chance, and consideration. **(a) price (b) money (c) luck (d) none of the above**

5. Which of the following is regulated by the CPSC? **(a) drugs (b) firearms (c) toys (d) cosmetics**

THINK CRITICALLY ABOUT EVIDENCE

Study the following situations, answer the questions, then prepare arguments to support your answers.

6. You properly terminated your membership in a record club four months ago, yet you receive a compact disc through the mail from the club. It is the new release of your favorite artist. You play it repeatedly for more than a month before you receive a letter from the club stating that it made a mistake in sending the disc to you and asking that you either return the disc unused or pay for it. Do you have an ethical obligation to do so? Do you have a legal obligation to do so?

7. A friend gives you a copy of a letter containing the "offer of a lifetime." The letter offers you the opportunity to make thousands of dollars simply by sending $1 to everyone on a 10-name list, typing in your name in the number 10 position, and deleting the name at the top of the list. You then are to give copies of the new list and the letter to 10 of your friends. Is complying with the terms of the letter ethical? Is it legal?

8. In a national television advertising campaign, FunTime fruit drink was said to contain "natural food energy." The FTC discovered that the "natural food" providing the energy was sugar and held that the advertisement therefore created a false impression. What remedy would you recommend that the FTC use to correct the situation?

STATE AND LOCAL GOVERNMENT PROTECTION

WHAT'S YOUR VERDICT?

As Wilson and Pequot were driving past the Downtown Electronics Warehouse, Pequot noticed their going-out-of-business sale. "They had a sale like this last year and I bought a C.D. player. I thought I was getting a great deal because they were getting rid of all their merchandise. They stayed in business though, and I paid more than the regular price for the same C.D. player at other stores."

Are such sales by the Downtown Electronics Warehouse legal?

Although the latest wave of consumer protection laws have been developed at the federal level, a variety of state and local laws also protect consumers. Taken with the federal effort, the coverage of these consumer protection laws is quite far reaching. In fact, the old adage of *caveat emptor* has been somewhat replaced by *caveat venditor* or "let the seller beware."

Licensing Laws

Consumer protection often begins with licensing suppliers of consumer goods and services. This is particularly true for those who provide health services, such as doctors, nurses, laboratory technicians, and pharmacists. Also, teachers, lawyers, accountants, construction professionals, realtors, insurance agents, and beauticians, among others, are licensed in most jurisdictions.

Certain businesses and institutions also must pass inspection before they receive operating licenses. Examples include hospitals, rest homes, private schools, check-cashing services, and insurance companies. Failure to maintain minimum standards may cause suspension or cancellation of the license.

Businesses offering repairs on cars, electronic equipment, watches, and the like are often required to give written estimates and detailed bills for all work performed. Similarly, states regulate special sales by retail businesses, such as bankruptcy sales and going-out-of-business sales. Often a special license is required and the businesses must shut down after the sale or be guilty of fraud, as would likely be the case in *What's Your Verdict?*

Remedies Available to Injured Consumers

Instead of compelling consumers to rely on various officials to take appropriate legal steps to prevent or remedy harm, many states have given consumers rights against those who take unfair advantage or cause injury. Using these rights in situations where an agency has not acted, the victim may sue for damages and get a court order preventing future violation of the statute the agency was supposed to enforce. These remedies are especially useful when consumers join together in a class action.

Sanitation and Food Adulteration Laws

States and localities usually provide for the inspection of businesses where food is handled. Meat markets, bakeries, restaurants, hotels, and other businesses are rated on their

FYI

Laws that protect consumers of automobiles and other vehicles are called "lemon laws." (Lemon laws are so-called because chronically defective vehicles are referred to as "lemons.") Lemon laws exist at both state and federal levels.

Lemon law protection works like this: A consumer returns a vehicle with a major defect to an authorized dealership for repair within the warranty period. If the dealership tries unsuccessfully to fix the vehicle several times (the number varies by statute), the consumer should then, in writing, request a refund or a replacement vehicle. If the request is not met, the consumer should seek the help of an attorney.

cleanliness and are required to display their ratings. Food handlers may be subject to periodic health examinations. Laws also regulate the purity and quality of such products as milk, meat, fruit, and vegetables sold in such businesses.

Safety Laws

To offer additional protection, especially in emergencies, laws govern the type of construction, location, accessibility, occupancy rate, and type of use of buildings where the public gathers. Detailed regulations apply to fire escapes, elevators, parking, sprinkler systems, exit location and marking, and sanitary facilities.

All of these safety laws are designed to protect consumers and to assist them in deciding which products and services best meet their needs.

WHAT IS PRODUCT LIABILITY?

WHAT'S YOUR
VERDICT?

Tackett removed a safety guard from his power radial saw. This was contrary to a warning prominently printed on the guard. Because of a manufacturing defect, a saw blade broke. The safety guard was not in place, so the blade hit and seriously injured Tackett.

Can Tackett recover for the injury caused by the defective product?

The rules for determining who is legally liable for injuries caused by a defective product have been expanded in recent years to protect injured plaintiffs.

Privity of Contract

At common law, warranty liability depended on the contract between the buyer and seller, who were said to be in privity of contract. **Privity of contract** is the relationship that exists between or among the contracting parties as a result of their legally binding agreement.

Only the immediate contracting buyer was permitted to sue, and suit could be brought only against the immediate contracting seller. Thus, an injured consumer could sue the retailer, but not the wholesaler or the manufacturer. This was true even if the wholesaler or manufacturer were primarily responsible for the defect and better able to pay.

Now, however, the UCC broadens the common law rule so that all injured persons who are the buyer's family, household, or guests may sue. Moreover, courts in most states now permit the injured party, even a nonuser, to sue retailers, intermediate sellers, and manufacturers.

Today, a manufacturer or producer that makes inaccurate or misleading statements in advertising or labels is liable for resulting injuries to consumers. If the goods are defective and therefore dangerous, the maker is similarly liable for resulting harm. In either case, not only the manufacturer or producer but also intermediate sellers and the immediate supplier may be liable.

Recovering Damages

A product liability suit may be based on a breach of warranty or on the torts of fraud, negligence, or *strict liability*. While these alternative legal theories can be used as a basis for recovery, the injured consumer may still have difficulty recovering damages.

A person injured by a defective product might find that there is no warranty, that the warranty is not applicable, or that the warranty has expired. The injured person, even if defrauded, might discover that the seller's misbehavior is difficult to prove. Fraud requires proof of intent, an elusive element. Finally, negligence, even if present, is difficult to

CULTURAL DIVERSITY IN LAW

Japan

Product Liability

When seeking damages for product-related injury in Japanese courts, consumers must demonstrate not only that the product caused an injury, but that the company was negligent in the way it designed or manufactured the product.

Unlike U.S. courts, the Japanese court system does not allow punitive damages. Consumers must pay their attorney a percentage of what they hope to gain in damages. There are no juries to persuade, because there are no jury trials.

prove because the defective product may have been designed and made many months or years before in some distant factory by workers who cannot be identified or located.

Today, a person injured by a defective product is most likely to recover damages by relying on strict liability. The trend in many states is to hold the manufacturer, wholesaler, and retailer strictly liable if someone is injured because of a defective condition in the product that caused it to be unreasonably dangerous to the user or consumer. The liability is imposed without reliance on warranties. Strict liability is imposed regardless of the presence or absence of fraudulent intent or negligence.

There is no liability if the injury was suffered while the product was used for a purpose for which it was not intended (using gasoline to clean clothes). Likewise, there is no strict liability if the product is used for a purpose which could not reasonably be foreseen (trying to climb a mountain using ropes made for tying packages). Likewise, liability may be barred if the product has been altered by the user (lengthening a ladder by nailing extensions to its legs).

Liability also may be barred if the injured person is personally found guilty of improper conduct that causes the accident. Examples of this include driving on a defective tire after discovering the defect, failing to service or to maintain an engine, or taking an overdose of medication. Finally, there generally is no liability if one is hurt when improperly using a product that may be dangerous when misused (knives and firearms).

In *What's Your Verdict?* Tackett's removal of the fully adequate safety guard bars his recovery. Legally, the injury was the result of Tackett's action, not the defect in the saw.

THINK ABOUT LEGAL CONCEPTS

Answer the following questions about legal concepts.

1. Local governments do not have any consumer protection laws. **True or False?**

2. Special state __?__ often are necessary for businesses to hold bankruptcy or going-out-of-business sales.

3. Detailed safety regulations apply to **(a) elevators (b) sprinkler systems (c) exit signs (d) fire escapes (e) all of the above**

4. Although several legal theories are available to form the basis for a product liability suit, injured consumers may find it difficult to recover damages. **True or False?**

THINK CRITICALLY ABOUT EVIDENCE

Study the following situations, answer the questions, then prepare arguments to support your answers.

5. When Winslow decided to install a brick walk in front of his home, he bought three sacks of standard Pyramid-brand mortar mix from the U-Can-Do store. Instructions on the bags warned against direct contact with skin. Although Winslow had sensitive skin, he repeatedly touched the wet mix with his bare hands because he was not skilled in using a trowel. This burned his hands and he developed an allergic rash. Is either U-Can-Do or Pyramid liable to him under any theory of product liability?

6. Kent was critically injured when he dropped a running lawnmower on his foot. At the time he dropped it, Kent was using the lawnmower to trim the top of a three-foot-high hedge. He sued the retailer, wholesaler, and manufacturer of the lawnmower on a product liability theory. Kent claimed an automatic shutoff should have been built into the lawnmower for times when it was not in contact with the ground. Will Kent win? Why or why not?

7. The students in Ms. Romboldt's law class were writing a script for a skit intended to dramatize points of law about product liability. One idea was to have someone play the role of Barbara Walters interviewing Ralph Nader, the consumer activist. Student Jack Parish suggested this question: "As a consumer of goods, what warranty would you choose to have if you could have only one?" How would you answer?

EXPRESS AND IMPLIED WARRANTIES

WHAT'S YOUR VERDICT?

Bligh, a sales agent employed by Total Environments, persuaded the Fletchers to install a central air conditioning system. Bligh assured them that "this unit will keep all rooms at 68 degrees even on the hottest summer days and the coldest winter mornings." The unit failed to perform as promised.

Do the Fletchers have any rights against Total Environments?

To induce prospects to buy, sellers often promise more than their products can provide or do. An example is Bligh's statement in *What's Your Verdict?* When such a precise factual claim is part of the bargain, the seller legally promises the buyer that the product will perform as stated. The price paid is consideration for the product and any included warranty. In sales, a **warranty** is a statement about the product's qualities or performance that the seller assures the buyer is true.

Warranties may be either express or implied. Because they involve sales of goods, warranties are governed by the Uniform Commercial Code (UCC). An assurance of quality or promise of performance explicitly made by the seller is an **express warranty**. An example is: "Use our brand of oil and you won't need to change your engine oil for 10,000 miles."

In *What's Your Verdict?* Bligh made an express warranty. As Bligh's employer, Total Environments is liable because the warranty was breached. A breach of warranty is a breach of contract. There is no intent to deceive, so it is not the tort of fraud for which punitive damages might be claimed and collected.

An express warranty may be oral or written. It may even be implied by conduct. If the contract is written, the warranty must be included in the writing, or it probably will be excluded from the agreement by the parol evidence rule. However, if the warranty is given after the sale, it may be oral even though the sales contract was written. A warranty or any other term may be added to a sales contract later by mutual agreement, and no new consideration is required.

Under the Magnuson-Moss Warranty Act, the Federal Trade Commission has established certain minimum standards that must be met by sellers who give written warranties on consumer products that cost more than $15 and that normally are used for personal, family, or household purposes. Sellers are not required to give warranties. If sellers do give warranties, prior to the sale, sellers must make available to consumers a single document, in simple and readily understandable language. The following information must be included:

1. to whom the warranty is extended (for example, if it is limited to the original buyer)

2. a description of the product and any excluded parts

3. what the *warrantor* (one who makes a warranty) will and will not do in the event of a breach of warranty

4. when the warranty begins (if different from purchase date) and when it ends

5. the step-by-step procedure to obtain performance of warranty obligations

6. the availability of any informal methods of settling disputes

7. any limitation on how long implied warranties last

8. any exclusion or limitation on incidental or consequential damages

9. the words "This warranty gives you specific legal rights, and you may also have other rights which vary from state to state."

An express warranty that obligates the seller to repair or to replace a defective product without cost to the buyer and within a reasonable time is a **full warranty**. Any warranty that provides less protection than a full warranty is a **limited warranty**, and the seller must identify it as such.

Sellers' Claims

A positive statement about the value of goods or a statement that is just the seller's opinion does not create a warranty. Sellers often enthusiastically overstate the merits of the goods they are trying to sell. Making statements such as "superb quality," or "best on the market," is exaggerated sales talk called **puffing**. Such words are not warranties or statements of fact. They are merely personal opinions. Buyers should not—and generally do not—accept such opinions at face value. *Caveat emptor* or "let the buyer beware" provides the only measure of protection when sellers make such statements.

Sometimes, however, the buyer has good reason to believe that the seller is an expert. If a buyer asks for the seller's opinion as an expert, the seller's word as to the quality of the article becomes part of the basis of the bargain. In such a case, it may be taken as a warranty. This is particularly true with merchants. For example, a statement by a jeweler that a diamond is flawless may be relied on as a warranty.

IMPLIED WARRANTIES

WHAT'S YOUR VERDICT?

While adding a large new family room to their home, the Tanakas asked the Alpha Electric Service Company what size circuit breaker they would need to carry the increased electrical current load. After reviewing the list of equipment planned for the entertainment center of the room, the Alpha expert recommended a 15-ampere breaker. Following installation, however, the breaker consistently cut off the power whenever two or more of the listed items of equipment were operating at the same time. The breaker was mechanically perfect, but it was not adequate for the current load.

Do the Tanakas have any legal rights against Alpha?

Sellers are free to decide whether to give any express warranties. However, the law compels all sellers to honor certain implicit, unstated warranties, in order to ensure minimal standards of contractual performance. This rule applies whether or not explicit warranties are given by the seller. An implicit warranty obligation imposed by law on all sellers is called an **implied warranty**.

The three warranties discussed in the following sections are made to all purchasers by all sellers, including casual sellers as well as professional merchants. These warranties are implied by law and need not be mentioned in the contract. Only if the parties specifically agree is any one or more of these warranties excluded.

WARRANTY OF TITLE Implicit in the act of selling, the seller warrants that he or she has title to the goods and the right to transfer them. This warranty is implied by law. Note, however, that it is excluded when it is obvious that the seller does not have title, such as when a sheriff, by court order, sells a debtor's goods to satisfy a judgment.

Warranty Against Encumbrances

Also implicit in the act of selling is the seller's warranty that the goods shall be delivered free of all encumbrances (claims of third parties, for example for an unpaid balance) of which the buyer is not aware at the time of contracting. This warranty does not ensure that the goods are free of encumbrances at the time of the sale, but rather that they will be free at the time of delivery. This distinction enables the seller to comply with the warranty by paying off any third-party claimants before transferring ownership.

WARRANTY OF FITNESS FOR A PARTICULAR PURPOSE A buyer who needs goods for a specific purpose often tells the seller about that purpose. Then

- the buyer relies on the seller's skill and judgment for a selection of appropriate goods
- the seller has ample reason to know of that reliance.

In such circumstances, the seller makes an implied warranty that the goods delivered to the buyer are reasonably fit for the stated purpose. If they prove to be unfit, the buyer has a right of action for breach of warranty. Therefore, in *What's Your Verdict?* the Tanakas have a right of action for breach of an implied warranty of fitness for a particular purpose.

This warranty does not arise when the buyer

- personally selects the goods
- orders the goods according to the buyer's own specifications
- does not rely on the skill and judgment of the seller, because of independent testing or for other reasons.

The warranty could arise even when the buyer asks for goods by patent or brand name. However, this variation applies only if the seller knows the purpose for which the goods are required and if the buyer relies on the seller's selection. For example, the buyer might ask for a "Buzzer" brand name chain saw to fell a stand of 30 trees with trunks two feet in diameter.

When the seller selects the proper model, the buyer is relying on the seller's judgment, expertise, and implied warranty of fitness for a stated purpose. Contrast this with the case of a buyer who insists on getting goods of a particular brand and specifies the model, size, or number, obviously not relying on the seller's knowledge. In this case no warranty of fitness for a particular purpose arises.

ADDITIONAL INFORMATION ABOUT WARRANTIES

WHAT'S YOUR VERDICT?

Marquez built and sold a machine for wrapping individual pieces of candy in foil to Frobisher, a candy manufacturer. The machine was built according to Frobisher's directions and specifications. Unknown to either party, Rodmann, a European candy manufacturer, held a Swiss patent on such a machine. She also had registered it with the U.S. Patent Office to protect the U.S. monopoly rights. Rodmann sued Marquez for an injunction against further production and for damages. Rodmann won the suit.

Must Frobisher indemnify Marquez, thus making good his loss?

In addition to express and implied warranties, there are also warranties implied by law for merchants and express warranties made by all sellers. Also, there are certain times when warranties may be excluded.

Warranties Implied by Law for Merchants

Merchants are typically held to higher standards in their dealings with consumers than are casual sellers. This is certainly true in the area of warranties. In addition to the warranties made by all sellers (as previously discussed), the following warranties are, by law, also made by merchants.

WARRANTY AGAINST INFRINGEMENT A merchant makes an implied warranty that the goods in which she or he normally deals shall be delivered to a buyer free of any third party's claims for patent, copyright, or trademark *infringement* (unauthorized use). This warranty may be excluded by agreement between the parties.

If the buyer furnishes specifications to the seller that lead to a claim of infringement against the seller, the buyer is obligated to indemnify the seller for any loss suffered because of the infringement. Accordingly, in

What's Your Verdict? Frobisher must indemnify Marquez and also pay damages to Rodmann.

WARRANTY OF MERCHANTABILITY Every merchant who customarily deals in goods of a particular kind makes an implied **warranty of merchantability** to all buyers of the goods. Basically, a warranty of merchantability requires that the goods be fit for the ordinary purposes for which such goods are used.

All goods sold must pass without objection in the trade under the sales contract description. Buyers must not balk at accepting them. If the goods are fungible, like grain, they must be at least of fair, average quality within the description. Within variations permitted by the contract, goods must be of even kind, quality, and quantity. If required by the contract, they must be adequately contained, packaged, and labeled. Finally, they must conform to any promises or affirmations of fact made on the label or on the container.

This implied warranty of merchantability greatly increases the merchant's duties of care and performance beyond those of the casual seller. It extends, for example, to food sold, which must be whole-

The warranty of merchantability may be expressly excluded by agreement of the parties. Also, when a buyer has examined the goods or a sample or model before contracting, there is no implied warranty of merchantability as to those defects that a reasonable examination would have revealed. This also applies if the buyer refused to examine the goods, sample, or model before contracting.

Express Warranties Made by All Sellers

In addition to warranties implied by law, sellers may make express warranties.

WARRANTY OF CONFORMITY TO SELLER'S STATEMENT OR PROMISE Every seller is bound by any express statement of fact or promise that is part of the bargain. It is desirable to have such statements in writing.

WARRANTY OF CONFORMITY TO DESCRIPTION, SAMPLE, OR MODEL When a description of the goods or a sample or model is made part of the contractual agreement, there is an express warranty that all the goods shall conform to the description, sample, or model used. This is true even if the words "warrant" or "guarantee" do not appear in the contract. It is also true even if the seller had no intention to give such a warranty.

Exclusion of Warranties

A seller may offer to sell goods without any warranties. This is most likely to occur if the goods are known to have defects or if they are a new design or model. To sell goods without a warranty, the seller must refrain from making any express warranties, and use appropriate language that will exclude implied warranties.

For example, to exclude or modify the broad warranty of merchantability or any part of it, the seller must men-

some and fit for human consumption. It includes foods and drinks that are sold and served to be consumed elsewhere or on the premises, as in restaurants and in fast-food shops. Drugs for human use must also be safe and wholesome. Buyers of perishable foods and drugs must also handle them properly.

Merchantability requires that any warranty protection that is customary in the trade be extended to all buyers. For example, the seller of a pedigreed animal, such as a dog or horse, is expected to provide documentation of the lineage of the animal because such proof is customary in the trade.

tion "merchantability" in a disclaimer. A **disclaimer** is a notice of exclusion. To exclude or modify any implied warranty of fitness, the exclusion must be in writing and must be conspicuous (easily seen or noticed). A statement such as the following would cover both merchantability and fitness: "There are no warranties of merchantability or fitness that extend beyond the description on the label."

Unless circumstances indicate otherwise, all implied warranties are excluded by such expressions as "with all faults," "as is," or other similar words.

> ### IN THIS CASE
> The Space Rockets, a professional football team, contracted for new uniforms from Arkwright Mills. At the time of the order, sample uniforms in particular colors and fabrics were referred to and included as part of the agreement. Arkwright is legally obligated to provide goods that match the samples.

> ### IN THIS CASE
> At a sale in a discount store, Doty bought 20 pounds of shelled walnuts. They were packed in one-pound sealed plastic bags and were sold at a bargain price "as is." When Doty opened one package, he discovered that the walnuts were edible but were stale and unpalatable. Doty claims a breach of warranty of merchantability. Doty is not entitled to a refund because the walnuts were bought "as is."

Answer the following questions about legal concepts.

1. An express warranty may be given orally and still be legally effective. **True or False?**

2. A warranty that obligates the seller to repair or replace the defective product with only a labor cost to the buyer is still a full warranty. **True or False?**

3. *Caveat emptor* is Latin for
   (a) **let the buyer beware**
   (b) **let the seller beware**
   (c) **let the ruler beware**

4. The warranty of __?__ is implied against merchants of food products to be sure those products are fit for human consumption.

Study the following situations, answer the questions, then prepare arguments to support your answers.

5. When the Grandiose Motor Car Company introduced its new model, sales lagged. After three months, only 7,500 cars had been sold. To stimulate sales, Grandiose added four years to its standard one-year warranty. It also extended the warranty on the cars already sold. Is Grandiose legally bound to the early buyers for the extra four years even though no new consideration was paid?

6. While in Florida, Van Loon decided to go fishing for tarpon. Visiting Stanton's Sports Shop, Van Loon explained his specific need to the salesperson. Van Loon then bought the fishing gear the salesperson recommended. During the first trip out, Van Loon had repeated strikes, but the line was too light for the weight of the fish. The line broke every time even though handled properly. What legal rights, if any, does Van Loon have against Stanton's?

7. Using a newspaper classified ad, Canby sold to Pegler stereo equipment that he bought less than a year earlier. A week later, Pegler tried to return the merchandise to Canby. Pegler claimed that there was a breach of the warranty of merchantability because the compact disc programmer did not work properly. Is Canby liable?

For protection as a consumer . . .

1. Be aware that not every assurance of quality or performance made by a seller is a warranty.

2. Know the implied warranties for goods you buy and watch for sellers' statements of limitation and warranty exclusion.

3. When appropriate, tell the seller how you intend to use the goods. If the seller has superior knowledge and advice upon which you can reasonably rely, you will be protected by an implied warranty of fitness for your purpose.

4. Make certain that any express warranty you receive is in writing to avoid later disputes as to its meaning or existence.

5. Use special care in buying goods "as is." Inspect the

PREVENT LEGAL DIFFICULTIES

goods to be sure that you are willing to take them without the benefit of warranties.

6. Practice comparison shopping for value and price and never purchase on impulse, in haste, or in frustration.

7. Be cautious of "bargains." Usually they are authentic, but occasionally they are a part of

a bait-and-switch scheme or they are loss leaders surrounded by overpriced goods.

8. Do not gamble. Remember that even in free and honest gambling contests, the vast majority of participants receive nothing.

9. When you have a valid complaint about a fraudulent or unfair business practice, take action, both for yourself and for others who may be similarly victimized in the future. Complain to the business involved, the Better Business Bureau, the local prosecutor, the state attorney general, the FTC, the CPSC, and any other governmental body with jurisdiction. If all else fails, consider taking legal action.

CHAPTER IN REVIEW

CONCEPTS IN BRIEF

1. Buyers have long been urged to beware by the Latin phrase *caveat emptor*. The complexity of today's products and the inaccessibility of their makers now require consumers not only to beware but to be aware of the various federal, state, and local laws designed to inform and protect them.

2. Federal agencies and state and local governments work together to ensure safe products, services, and sanitary facilities for consumers.

3. Unfair trade practices include price fixing, false advertising, illegal lotteries, improperly labeling goods, and selling used articles as new.

4. Many businesses are licensed. Reports of improper goods or services can be made to their licensing authorities at the state and local levels.

5. Generally, any person injured by a defective product may bring suit against any manufacturer or merchant in the chain of distribution of that product. Depending on the circumstances, the suit may be based on warranty, fraud, negligence, or strict liability.

6. Warranties may be express or implied. Express warranties are oral or written promises by the seller about product quality or performance. Implied warranties are imposed by law and are effective even when not mentioned by the seller. You should inspect goods sold by merchants. However, merchant sellers normally are bound by the important implied warranty of merchantability unless explicitly disclaimed.

YOUR LEGAL VOCABULARY

Match each statement with the term that it best defines. Some terms may not be used.

1. Notice of exclusion of warranty
2. Return of improperly obtained money or property
3. Individual who buys primarily for household use
4. Greatly exaggerated sales talk
5. Let the buyer beware
6. Let the seller beware
7. Obligation implicitly imposed on all sellers
8. Comprised of prize, chance, and consideration
9. Lawsuit made possible by the procedural joining of similarly situated plaintiffs
10. Explicit assurance of quality or performance by seller
11. Dishonest, fraudulent, or anti-competitive business method
12. Voluntary, court-enforceable agreement to stop an illegal practice
13. Warranty requiring that goods fit the ordinary purposes for which they are used
14. Claims of third parties against the goods
15. Relationship between parties to a legally binding agreement

bait and switch
caveat emptor
caveat venditor
cease-and-desist order
class action
consent order
consumer
disclaimer
encumbrances
express warranty
false and misleading advertising
full warranty
implied warranty
limited warranty
lottery
privity of contract
puffing
restitution
unfair trade practice
warranty
warranty of merchantability

16. Should a written contract include all express warranties?

17. Why are sellers not required to give warranties in every transaction?

18. How do the terms "puffing" and *"caveat emptor"* relate to one another?

19. Who can bring suit for product liability under the UCC?

20. What are the normal sanctions available to a consumer protection agency?

21. How would you prove a bait and switch had occurred?

WRITE ABOUT LEGAL CONCEPTS

22. Write a paragraph stating your opinion on what is the most important implied warranty.

23. Make a list of the reasons that *caveat emptor* does not work as well now as it once did in protecting consumers?

24. HOT DEBATE Write a persuasive opening statement that emphasizes the legal and ethical points in Edison's favor. Or, write a persuasive opening statement that emphasizes the legal and ethical points in the manufacturer's favor.

THINK CRITICALLY ABOUT EVIDENCE

25. The Motleys entered Penn's Nursery and asked for a 50-pound sack of ZAP, a brand-name weed killer, to kill the narrow-leafed devil grass in their lawn. ZAP was advertised as "effective, when properly used, against crabgrass and other broad-leafed weeds and grasses." The Motleys applied the chemical according to directions, but the devil grass survived. They sued the manufacturer, claiming a breach of warranty. They also sued Penn's for failure to give them proper advice as to what kind of weed killer to buy. Will the Motleys win their suit against the manufacturer? Will they win their suit against Penn's?

26. Gallo, an experienced glider pilot, rented a glider at a commercial glider port. While in flight, she lost control because of a defect in the tail assembly. The glider crashed while landing, and Gallo was permanently disabled. Although several years old, the glider had been properly maintained. There was no warranty in effect on the glider. Does Gallo have any legal recourse?

27. The Baby-Bright Crib was banned as a hazardous product by the CPSC. The Sabatinas bought one of the cribs and then learned of the ban. What should they do now?

28. A computer store chain buys "factory rebuilt" computers and sells them to customers without disclosing their origin or used condition. Is this practice illegal?

29. A coffee manufacturer incorrectly states the volume of coffee in one of its packages. Thousands of these packages are on the market. If necessary, can the packages be confiscated by the government to remedy the situation?

30. After an hour of persistent persuasion by a door-to-door salesperson, the Arnos signed a contract to buy magazine subscriptions. The next morning, the Arnos did some quick calculating and were appalled to discover that they had agreed to spend $257.40—a sum they could not afford—for magazines. Can the Arnos cancel the contract without being liable for damages?

ANALYZE
REAL CASES

31. Every week for a year and a half, Newmark was given a shampoo and set by employees of Gimbel's. Then a new product ("Candle Wave," made by the Helene Curtis company) was applied to Newmark's hair. As a result, Newmark suffered contact dermatitis of the scalp, with substantial hair loss. Newmark sued Gimbel's for breach of the implied warranty of fitness for a particular purpose. Gimbel's argued that it was providing a service and not selling goods in this transaction. Therefore it could not be held liable for breach of warranty with reference to the product of Helene Curtis. It could only be held liable, it claimed, if its own employees were proved negligent. Could a jury find Gimbel's liable if the wave solution was defective and caused the injury? (*Newmark v. Gimbel's Inc.,* 258 A.2d 679, N.J.)

32. Mahaney purchased a used car from Perry Auto Exchange. Mahaney was told that the car was in "perfect, A-1, and first-class condition." A written statement given to Mahaney at the time of the sale described the car as being in "good operating condition." Mahaney had no opportunity to investigate the truth of these statements. Later, it was determined that the car had a problem in the differential and had no brakes at the time of the sale. Mahaney sued for rescission. Were Perry's statements merely puffing or were they warranties upon which the rescission could be based? (*Mahaney v. Perry Auto Exchange,* 85 N.E.2d 558, Ohio)

33. On January 1, plaintiff Werner bought the *White Eagle,* a wooden sloop, from defendant Montana, and the parties signed a bill of sale. The previous October they had signed an intent to purchase and sell. During their negotiations, the seller had assured the buyer orally that the hull would "make up" from swelling when placed in the water and would be watertight. At the end of June, Werner put the boat in the water. He allowed more than six weeks—a sufficient time—for the planking to swell to form a watertight hull. But the hull still leaked. The boat could not be sailed. Werner then checked the hull and for the first time discovered extensive dry rot which required substantial repairs. In a letter in September, he demanded that Montana take the boat back and refund the purchase price of $13,250. The defendant refused, and so Werner sued for rescission. Montana argued that the oral assurances he had given that the boat was watertight could not be admitted at the trial because of the parol evidence rule. Who should win? (*Werner v. Montana,* 378 A.2d 1130, N.H.)

34. Through radio and television, the defendant's stores advertised a "top quality . . . Queen Anne Console Magic Stitcher" sewing machine, along with a sewing chair, for the "close-out price of just $29.50." Under the sales plan, a "lead person" would accept the customer's order, taking a deposit as small as 25 cents. After that, a demonstrator would visit the customer and "kill the sale" by having the machine jam in use. The demonstrator would also say that the customer could lose an eye if the machine jammed. Then the demonstrator would attempt to "step-up" the sale and persuade the customer to buy a higher priced machine. In about 19 months, only 26 of the advertised machines were sold, although 10,951 customers entered into conditional sales contracts for such machines. The 26 advertised machines were sold at a time when the defendants had received complaints from the television station and the Better Business Bureau. The defendants were prosecuted for conspiring to sell merchandise by means of deceptive and misleading advertising. The prosecutor gave evidence that the defendants never intended to sell the advertised machines, which actually cost them $45 each. Are the defendants guilty as charged? (*People v. Glubo, Exelbert, Epstein, and Atlantic Sewing Stores, Inc.,* 158 N.E.2d 699)

35. Registration of a "MONOPOLY" trademark for use on clothing was sought by a New York-based corporation named Tuxedo Monopoly, Inc. The makers of the "MONOPOLY" board game, General Mills Fun Group, opposed the application. The Patent and Trademark Office Trademark Trial and Appeal Board sustained the opposition and would not allow the registration. On appeal to the U.S. Court of Customs and Patent Appeals, Tuxedo's attorneys argued that monopoly was a common term and that, regardless, there was very little likelihood of confusion between a trademark used on a game and one used on clothing. They also pointed out that the court had previously allowed the registration of the famous "DIXIE" cup mark by a company using it as its mark on waxed paper. If the court finds a likelihood of confusion exists, it will affirm the Board's decision. How should the court rule? (*Tuxedo Monopoly, Inc. v. General Mills Fun Group, Inc.,* 648 F.2d 1335)

CASE FOR LEGAL THINKING

Blevins v. Cushman Motors
Supreme Court of Missouri, 551 S.W. 2d 602

FACTS Maxwell and Blevins teed off on 13, then hopped into their golf cart and motored out to Maxwell's ball. Maxwell fired his second shot, then drove the cart toward Blevins' ball. As the car approached the ball at approximately 5 mph, it entered a shady area of the course on which a light dew lay. At that point the cart went into a 10- to 15-foot skid. It was like "being on ice." The cart then tipped over. Maxwell was thrown free. However, Blevins, who failed in his attempt to jump from the cart, was pinned under it when it came to rest. Blevins brought suit on product liability grounds based on strict liability in tort, not negligence. He sued for his personal injuries. In addition, his wife brought suit for loss of consortium (the fellowship of husband and wife in companionship and sexual relations).

TRIAL COURT'S DECISION The court found for Mr. and Mrs. Blevins. Both received very substantial awards.

APPELLATE COURT DECISION The Missouri Court of Appeals upheld the decision of the trial court and maintained the amount of the awards.

MISSOURI SUPREME COURT'S DECISION Cushman Motors, manufacturer of the cart, approached the Missouri Supreme Court arguing that although Missouri courts had used strict liability in tort to decide cases involving a defect in manufacturing, the courts of the state should not use such a standard to decide a case involving a defect in design. Instead, the negligence theory should be used to determine whether the maker of the product was liable.

The Supreme Court decided, "There is no rational distinction between design and manufacture in this context, since a product may be equally defective and dangerous if its design subjects protected persons to unreasonable risks as if its manufacture does so."

PRACTICE JUDGING

1. What arguments can you make to justify Cushman's distinction between design and manufacture?

2. What arguments can you make against such a position?

3. According to the excerpted text of the Supreme Court's decision quoted above, was it correct to use strict liability in tort to determine the result in this case?

LESSONS

18-1 LEGAL ASPECTS OF MARRIAGE

18-2 LEGAL ASPECTS OF DIVORCE

HOT DEBATE

Ben, 16, had been dating Betsy for several months when he told his parents about the relationship. Ben's father had been in business with Betsy's dad and the partnership ended poorly. When his father heard the news, he told Ben to stop seeing Betsy. Ben refused, and his father grounded him. When Ben continued to see Betsy, his father took away the car Ben bought with his own money, stopped paying Ben's tuition, cut off his allowance, and spent the funds saved for Ben's college. He even threatened to spank Ben. Ultimately, with his mother's backing, Ben brought suit against his father for "improper parenting." Ben's father's attorney quickly filed a motion to dismiss the suit. The motion stated that "improper parenting" was not a legitimate cause of action and that the father had acted within his powers as a parent under the law. The lower court dismissed the suit, and Ben appealed to the state court of appeals.

Where Do You Stand?

1. **Make a persuasive argument that emphasizes the legal reasons supporting Ben's suit.**

2. **Make a persuasive argument that emphasizes the legal reasons supporting his father's actions.**

GOALS

- Discuss how the law affects premarital and marital relationships
- Explain the uses of prenuptial agreements
- Name the rights and duties of husbands and wives

PREMARITAL RELATIONSHIPS

WHAT'S YOUR VERDICT?

Jim and Mary are both 16 years old. While dating they have intimate relations, and Mary becomes pregnant.

Will the law compel them to marry?

Marriage is a legal union of a man and woman as husband and wife. No law specifies a minimum age for dating, although there are still state laws setting a minimum age for marriage without parental permission. Typically, this minimum age is 18. No law restricts the choice of marital partners, with one exception—close relatives may not marry.

If parents tell their minor child not to date or not to see a specific person, they can enforce that order only with the "reasonable force" that they may use to see that their other directions are carried out. If that fails, parents have no legal means to achieve their ends short of having their child labeled "incorrigible" in a juvenile delinquency proceeding. Parental use of excessive force may result in charges of child abuse.

Criminal laws against consensual premarital sexual intercourse have generally been eliminated over the past couple of decades. However, if pregnancy results and the male responsible is identified, he will be required to pay his share of the female's medical bills and to contribute to the child's support until the child reaches adulthood. This is true

even if the father is a minor. Beyond that requirement, no law exists to force the parents of an illegitimate child to marry. In *What's Your Verdict?* Mary and Jim may remain single.

A man and woman who live together outside of marriage are said to *cohabitate.* Such living arrangements were considered illegal in most states until the late 1970s. Cohabitation is still illegal in some states, although such laws are seldom enforced.

THE MARITAL CONTRACT

WHAT'S YOUR VERDICT?

Grady and Cheryl are engaged to be married. Grady's parents strongly disapprove of the upcoming marriage. They finally convince Grady to break the engagement.

Can Cheryl bring a successful lawsuit against Grady's parents for interfering with her contract to marry Grady?

If one party in a heterosexual relationship proposes marriage and the other accepts, a binding contract results. If both later mutually agree to end their engagement, the contract is *annulled.* This means that the law considers their agreement void and never to have existed. If only one party wants out of the contract and refuses to perform, a breach-of-promise suit may be brought by the other party.

Such suits at one time were notorious because juries set abnormally

CULTURAL DIVERSITY IN LAW

Muslim Culture

Marriage Rules

In Muslim countries, such as Saudi Arabia and Kuwait, the Muslim religious rules of marriage are part of the legal rules as well. In these countries, arranged marriages are common. There may be little or no contact between the bride and groom prior to the marriage. A dowry—or payment from the groom to the bride's father—is made. (In some other cultures dowry payments are made by the bride's family to the groom or the groom's family.) Polygamy, the taking of multiple wives, is legal in some Muslim countries. In these situations the husband may take up to four wives, provided each wife shares equally in the husband's companionship and worldly goods.

high figures to compensate the jilted party (usually the woman) for the actual damages, humiliation, and hurt feelings that accompanied the break-up. Today, some states allow such suits only where the woman is pregnant and her ex-fiancé is the father. Other states have placed a cap on the amount of damages that can be awarded. Many states have banned breach-of-promise suits altogether.

If third parties interfere with the engagement, a few states allow damage suits against the intruders. Such suits, however, cannot be brought against the parents who try to prevent their son or daughter from marrying. In *What's Your Verdict?* Grady's parents may try to keep him from marrying Cheryl. Cheryl could not successfully sue them for interfering with her contract to marry Grady.

When a relationship breaks down, gifts given by one party to the other may create legal problems. If the gift, such as a ring, is given in expectation of marriage, the courts generally order it to be returned. However, some states allow the woman to keep the ring if the man breaks off the engagement. Gifts other than those given in expectation of marriage can be kept by the recipient.

HOW DO YOU GET MARRIED?

WHAT'S YOUR VERDICT?

Zed lived with Tamra for about two years. Although they never applied for a marriage license, they told everyone that they were married. Recently, they split up, and now Tamra is about to marry another man. However, Zed claims that she cannot enter another marriage because she is his common-law wife.

Is he correct?

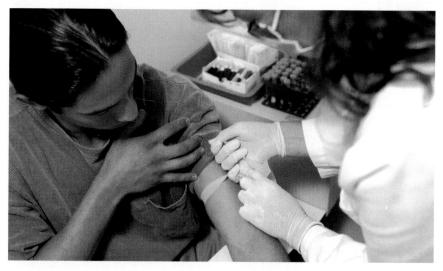

Couples may get married by following the laws of the state in which they wish to marry. An alternative way to marry is to enter into a common-law marriage.

State Marriage Requirements

Each state has its own requirements for marriage. Most couples begin the process by appearing before the city or town clerk. The couple must apply for and pay a fee for a marriage license. In the vast majority of states, if the parties are over 18 years of age, they do not need their parents' consent. With parental consent, most states allow minors as young as 16 years old to marry.

Some states require a blood test before the license is issued to show that the applicants are free from various communicable diseases. A

mandatory waiting period of three days from application to issuance is common. Once the license has been issued, any authorized religious or civil officials—court clerks, mayors, judges, rabbis, ministers, priests, and even ship captains at sea—can perform the ceremony.

An attempt has been made to standardize state laws for marriage and divorce. The Uniform Marriage and Divorce Act has been adopted by eight states. These states include Illinois, Kentucky, Missouri, Minnesota, Colorado, Montana, Arizona, and Washington. Marriage laws in the other states vary. The marriage laws in each state are described in the table on page 266.

Common-Law Marriage

Common-law marriages have their roots in the American frontier. Because of the absence of suitable

authorities, many pioneers could not follow the legal methods for becoming husband and wife. As a consequence, the law recognized **common-law marriages** that occurred when a single woman and a single man lived together, shared common property, and held themselves out as husband and wife over a prolonged period of time (usually 10 years or longer).

Today, about one-fourth of our states allow common-law marriages, although all states must recognize such a union if it is legal in the state in which it occurred. In *What's Your Verdict?* even if Tamra and Zed lived in a state that allowed common-law marriages, they did not remain together long enough to be considered as having a common-law marriage. Therefore, Tamra is free to marry another.

COMMON-LAW MARRIAGE

MT ID IA PA RI UT CO KS OK DC SC AL GA TX

STATES WHERE IT IS RECOGNIZED

DUTIES AND RIGHTS OF WIVES AND HUSBANDS

WHAT'S YOUR VERDICT?

Your friend Bill's mother died three years ago. Now his father plans to remarry. Bill is concerned that his father's fiancée will have a claim against the family home and other property.

Is there anything Bill can do to prevent such a claim?

Traditionally, the law sees husband and wife as parties to a marriage contract for life and for the benefit of each other. The practical and legally recognized purposes for marriage are procreation, raising children, and filling sexual, economic, and companionship needs.

Marital Consortium

The law recognizes these purposes as mutual duties of the wife and husband and calls them the **marital consortium**. In most states, if either spouse suffers an injury that prevents fulfillment of these marital duties, the other can sue the party who caused the harm for damages for "loss of consortium."

The most important duty of both spouses is to provide for the support, nurture, welfare, and education of their children. Other obligations

jointly entered into, such as contracts, notes, and income tax returns, also are the mutual responsibility of the marital partners.

Parenthood Rights and Duties

Parents are obligated by state laws to support their children until they reach adulthood. An exception applies if a minor child takes legal measures to become "emancipated". Financial support of a couple's children is a joint obligation. This duty may be divided according to each spouse's financial position. Both parents in a married couple have custody rights to their children. Likewise, both have an equal voice in decisions that arise while raising them.

Some couples may choose to adopt children. The legal process of **adoption** creates a parent-child relationship. Adoptive parents have the

CULTURAL DIVERSITY IN LAW

Massachusetts & Tennessee

Adoption Law

In 1851, Massachusetts passed a major adoption law—the first in the United States. Today adoption laws are the focus of attention in many states. Much of the attention is centered on access to adoption records. Laws vary from state to state but most states allow some access. As new adoption laws are enacted, they are also being challenged. In 1997 the U.S. Supreme Court let stand a decision by the U.S. Court of Appeals for the Sixth District that Tennessee's open records statute does not violate the federal Constitution.

State	Earliest legal age of marriage with parental consent	Earliest legal age of marriage without parental consent	Medical examination required for license	Required wait after license / expiration of license (in days)
Alabama	14	18		– / 30
Alaska	16	18		3 / –
Arizona	16	18		– / 365
Arkansas	17 M / 16 F	18		– / –
California	None	18	✓	– / 90
Colorado	16	18		– / 30
Connecticut	16	18	✓	4 / 65
Delaware	18 M / 16 F	18		1 / 30
District of Columbia	16	18	✓	3 / –
Florida	16	18		– / –
Georgia	None	16	✓	3 / 30
Hawaii	15	16	✓	– / –
Idaho	16	18	✓	– / –
Illinois	16	18		1 / 60
Indiana	17	18		3 / 60
Iowa	None	18		3 / 20
Kansas	None	18		3 / –
Kentucky	None	18		– / –
Louisiana	18	18		3 / –
Maine	16	18		3 / 90
Maryland	16	18		2 / 180
Massachusetts	14 M / 12 F	18		3 / –
Michigan	16	18		3 / –
Minnesota	16	18		5 / –
Mississippi	None	17 M / 15 F	✓	3 / –
Missouri	15	18		– / –
Montana	16	18	✓	– / 180
Nebraska	17	19	✓	– / 365
Nevada	16	18		– / 365
New Hampshire	14 M / 13 F	18	✓	3 / 90
New Jersey	16	18	✓	3 / 30
New Mexico	16	18	✓	– / –
New York	16	18	✓	1 / 60
North Carolina	16	18		– / –
North Dakota	16	18		– / 60
Ohio	None M / 16 F	18	✓	5 / 60
Oklahoma	16	18	✓	– / 30
Oregon	17	18		3 / –
Pennsylvania	16	18	✓	3 / 60
Puerto Rico	18 M / 16 F	21	✓	– / –
Rhode Island	16	18	✓	– / –
South Carolina	16 M / 14 F	18		1 / –
South Dakota	16	18		– / 20
Tennessee	16	18		3 / 30
Texas	14	18		3 / 30
Utah	14	18		– / 30
Vermont	14	18	✓	1 / –
Virginia	16	18	✓	– / 60
Washington	17	18	✓	3 / 60
West Virginia	18	18	✓	3 / –
Wisconsin	16	18	✓	5 / 30
Wyoming	16	18	✓	– / –

same rights and duties to the adoptive child as they would to a child born of their union. Adoptions are governed by state law and must be approved by the courts.

Property Rights and Duties

Property acquired during the marriage may be kept in the name of the husband, the wife, or both. Either marital partner can buy and sell property of all types in her or his own name and have sole control of the respective earnings and credit. Such was not always the case, especially for the woman in the relationship.

At times, spouses bring property into marriage that they want to keep in their own names. They don't want the other spouse to have claim over it, especially in the event of death or divorce. Keeping a spouse from getting property rights can be accomplished with a **prenuptial agreement**.

By entering into a prenuptial agreement, the marital partners-to-be typically give up any future claim they might have to part or all of the other's property. Such a contract is especially useful when one or both are entering into their second or subsequent marriage and want to reserve the property from a previous marriage for the children of that bond.

In What's Your Verdict? Bill could recommend that his father enter a prenuptial agreement with his fiancée by which she would give up any property claims she might acquire by the marriage.

The actions of one spouse may incur liability for the other. For example, the wife or husband may take care of the household while the other works outside the home. This often happens when there are young children in the family. In such a circumstance, the wage-earning spouse is legally responsible for the debts incurred by the other spouse in purchasing food, clothing, medical care, furniture, and any other items necessary to run the household.

Prenuptial Agreement

Whereas the bonds of matrimony are about to surround and forever join them to one another and whereas they are of the belief that their commitments to one another should be explicit and known, the following agreement, whose terms shall have precedence over all otherwise applicable statutory requirements, is hereby entered into on this 17th day of June, 20—, by Ms. Monica Sacks of 900 Blind Tree Lane, West Amherst, N. Y., and Mr. Bernard Wells, no current address, of that same city.

It is, therefore, agreed, as Ms. Sacks has considerable property left to her by her deceased husband, Mr. Toby Sacks, and can expect to acquire more as a function of the sound management of said estate, that:

1. Mr. Wells hereby relinquishes any and all claims, rights, or other interests and estates that the forthcoming marriage might bestow upon him in Ms. Sacks' property with the exceptions as to those granted by the following terms of this agreement.
2. That Mr. Wells shall enjoy during the term of the marriage a monthly stipend of $5,000, to be spent as he deems necessary.
3. That, should the marital union be broken and divorce ensue, Mr. Wells should receive a lump sum payment of $1,000,000 in full settlement of any claims he might have for maintenance or other support.
4. That said payment shall be forthcoming within three months of the entering of a decree of divorce in a court of this state with appropriate authority.
5. That the terms of this agreement expressed in paragraphs 2, 3, and 4 above, shall be null and void if Mr. Wells is shown to have been unfaithful to Ms. Sacks from this time forward.

IN WITNESS HEREOF, we, the undersigned, have set our hands and seals on the day and year first above written.

Monica Sacks
Monica Sacks

Bernard Wells
Bernard Wells

THINK ABOUT LEGAL CONCEPTS

Answer the following questions about legal concepts.

1. A marital contract is legally binding. **True or False?**

2. Even if both parties agree to end their contract to marry, the contract is still valid. **True or False?**

3. The voiding of a marital contract is referred to as an (a) **alleviation** (b) **allois** (c) **annulment** (d) **none of the above.**

4. If a party to a marital agreement wants out of the marital contract but the other party does not, a __?__ suit may result.

5. In most states, parental consent to marry is still required for any party under the age of 18. **True or False?**

6. Is common-law marriage still possible in some of the states of the United States? **Yes or No?**

7. Marital consortium includes the sharing of property. **True or False?**

8. By entering into a(n) __?__ agreement, the marital partners-to-be typically give up any future claim they might have to any or all of the other's property.

9. A parent-child relationship is artificially created by the legal process of (a) **adhesion** (b) **alignment** (c) **assignment** (d) **none of the above.**

THINK CRITICALLY ABOUT EVIDENCE

Study the following situations, answer the questions, then prepare arguments to support your answers.

10. Becky and Tom are engaged. Tom has told her he does not want children. Becky knows that she cannot conceive because of an illness she had a few years ago. Should she tell Tom that she cannot have children?

11. Maria is an only child. Her mother died when she was eight years old. Now, seven years later, her father is engaged to remarry, and Maria objects. She is afraid that her father's new wife will come between her and her father and that the new wife will end up with the family home after her father dies. Ethically, should Maria try to persuade her father not to marry? Is there a legal device that would help resolve part of her worries?

12. Marcel is 22 years old and Heather is 16. They are very much in love and planned to get married right away. After Heather's parents refused to consent to her marriage, Heather and Marcel eloped. Can Heather's parents have the marriage annulled even though Marcel is an adult?

13. Michael was driving home late one night when a tractor-semitrailer truck ran a red light and struck his vehicle. Even though Michael was wearing a seat belt and his air bag properly deployed, he was critically injured. Several months later it became obvious that he was permanently paralyzed from the waist down. Michael has grounds for a lawsuit against the trucking company and the driver of the tractor semi-trailer. What cause of action does his wife have? How do you think a judge will decide?

14. Ben and Tanya were married for several years before Tanya took her first job. Newly graduated from college, she was able to get a high-paying job in computer imaging. When she brought home her first paycheck, she announced to Ben that she was not going to put the check in their joint account, but instead keep it solely for her own use. Ben responded that, because they were married, the money belonged to them both. Who is correct and why?

15. Orlando and Mary lived together for 14 years in Oklahoma City. During the latter part of their cohabitation, they both claimed to be married to one another. In addition, they added Mr. and Mrs. to their address and held a joint bank account in those names. Now they are living apart from one another. Orlando currently lives in California. He has fallen in love with another woman and plans to marry her. As a consequence, he hires an attorney to determine whether he and Mary were legally married. What will the attorney check first? What other elements of common-law marriage might be significant in the determination? Is Orlando free to marry another?

G O A L S

- Discuss ways other than divorce by which marriages can end
- Identify grounds for a traditional and a no-fault divorce
- Name topics usually covered in a separation agreement

riage may be terminated within a reasonable time by an annulment proceeding. The marriage stays valid until the annulment. In *What's Your Verdict?* Rhonda could void her marriage by annulment on the grounds that Samuel refused to have children.

A **void marriage**, on the other hand, creates no rights or duties for either party and is considered invalid

ENDING MARRIAGES LEGALLY

WHAT'S YOUR VERDICT?

After they were married a short time, Samuel told Rhonda that he did not want to have children. Despite several months of discussion, he remained firm.

Can Rhonda end their marriage due to his firm decision?

A marriage may end several ways. The death of either spouse, annulment, divorce, or a variety of illegalities may bring about the end of a marriage. Legal consequences of a spouse's death are discussed in Chapter 24.

Annulment ends many marriages. An **annulment** is a court order that cancels a marriage because of a problem that existed from the beginning of the marriage. Annulments serve to end marriages considered to be either voidable or void.

Problems such as refusal to have children or fraudulent grounds for the marriage contract may produce a **voidable marriage**. Fraudulent grounds for marriage include either spouse lying to the other as to wealth, condition of pregnancy, freedom from disease, willingness to have a child, past marriage, or age. Such a mar-

LAW IN THE MEDIA

The Menendez Brothers

WAS JUSTICE SERVED?

Some marriages end with the death of one or both spouses. Such was the case with Jose and Kitty Menendez. Their marriage ended tragically with both their deaths—at the hands of their children, Lyle and Erik.

Defense attorney Leslie Abramson contended that both brothers had been lifelong victims of their father's sexual abuse. The actions of Lyle and Erik following the murders, however, suggest that their motive for the murders had to do with inheriting the family fortune. No less than 24 hours after the murders, the brothers took their father's safe to a probate attorney and tried to get it open.

Whatever the brothers' motive, the trial attracted sensational media attention. The public was provided with blow-by-blow reporting of the trial in the tabloids, general press, radio, and television. A made-for-television movie was quickly produced to tell the tragic story.

The brothers' first trials ended in deadlock, with separate juries split between the charges of manslaughter and murder.

Questions to Consider

1. **Think about the psychological effect on the public mind of the intensive press coverage. Did it serve to create either sympathy or animosity for the brothers? Did it make television viewers feel that they had an important stake in the outcome? If so, why?**

2. **Do you think the first trials would have gone on as long and with the same results if they had been conducted without television? If not, how do you think the results would have been different?**

from the beginning. Such a marriage typically occurs whenever laws are violated by the matrimonial union. For example, if one partner is already married when the second marriage occurs, the second is a void marriage. A person who knowingly marries a second spouse while still married to the first is a **bigamist**. Bigamy is a crime. Another example of a void marriage is one based on an incestuous relationship (a marriage between close relatives).

MARRIAGE ENDED BY DIVORCE

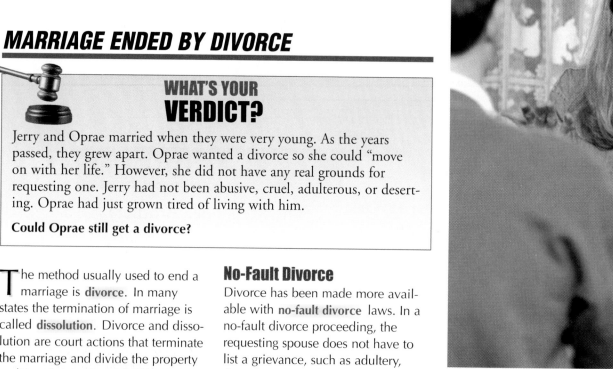

WHAT'S YOUR VERDICT?

Jerry and Oprae married when they were very young. As the years passed, they grew apart. Oprae wanted a divorce so she could "move on with her life." However, she did not have any real grounds for requesting one. Jerry had not been abusive, cruel, adulterous, or deserting. Oprae had just grown tired of living with him.

Could Oprae still get a divorce?

The method usually used to end a marriage is **divorce**. In many states the termination of marriage is called **dissolution**. Divorce and dissolution are court actions that terminate the marriage and divide the property and remaining responsibilities between the parties. Divorce rates increased greatly during the twentieth century. The chart labeled "Divorces and Annulments" on page 271 shows the number of divorces granted per 1,000 people since 1910 in the United States.

No-Fault Divorce

Divorce has been made more available with **no-fault divorce** laws. In a no-fault divorce proceeding, the requesting spouse does not have to list a grievance, such as adultery, desertion, or cruelty, against the other. Instead the court recognizes the right of either the wife or the husband to terminate a marriage unilaterally or of both spouses to end the marriage by mutual agreement. In *What's Your Verdict?* Oprae could get a divorce even though there were no possible grounds for it other than being bored with Jerry.

A no-fault marriage dissolution may be initiated by either spouse. The dissolution is granted after testimony that there is no chance of repairing the marriage relationship. In most no-fault states *irreconcilable differences* are stated as the legal reason for dissolution. After the dissolution request is filed, the couple must usually wait about six months before it is final. In some states couples must meet with a marriage counselor to try to save their marriage.

State Divorce Laws

In some states, the first step toward divorce is **separation.** In such an event the spouses maintain separate living quarters, but their marital rights and obligations remain intact. To alter these rights and obligations, the parties or their lawyers must negotiate a

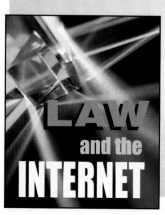

Individuals who are considering or seeking a divorce can find a wealth of information via the Internet. One needs only to type the words "divorce law" into an Internet search engine, such as Infoseek or AltaVista. Resulting information will be in the form of articles or FAQs (frequently asked questions) on topics ranging from individual state laws to child custody and support issues. Referrals to numerous divorce-related websites will be found as well. Those wishing to communicate with other people who are going through similar situations may even participate in live chat groups.

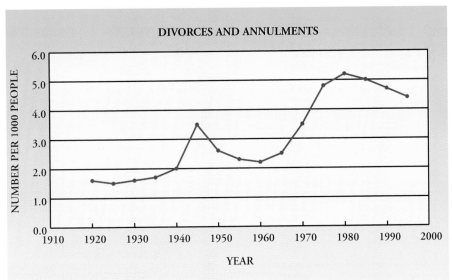

DIVORCES AND ANNULMENTS

legal separation agreement. This separation agreement contains terms covering such items as child custody, child support, alimony, and property division. If the parties fail to reconcile their differences during the period of separation and instead go through a divorce proceeding, the separation agreement often becomes the basis for the final divorce decree.

Issues to be Resolved

Many issues need to be resolved when a couple divorces. These include the issues of division of marital property, child custody and support, and alimony payments.

DIVISION OF PROPERTY In most states marital property laws are based on the English common law. The property brought into a marriage by a spouse will remain that spouse's property should the marriage end. During the marriage, whatever is earned, inherited, or received as a gift also remains the property of the spouse who earned or received it. States that do not follow this common-law rule are called *community property* states. You will learn more about community property laws in Chapter 19.

Regardless of the law followed, most states provide some type of equitable distribution of marital prop-

erty upon the dissolution of a marriage. Judges distribute property fairly between the spouses. They consider issues such as the age and earning power of each spouse, length of the marriage, and contributions of each spouse to the marriage. If one of the spouses has stayed home to raise children and or take care of the household, the value of those services are considered as well.

CHILD CUSTODY AND SUPPORT The issue of child custody is concerned with the division of the physical and other care and control responsibilities for a child. The welfare of the child is the most important consideration in determining who will have custody of the child. Under the Marriage and Divorce Act, the factors a court must consider in awarding custody include

- parents' wishes as to custody
- child's wishes as to custody
- child's relationship with parents, siblings, and others who may affect the child's best interest
- child's adjustment to home, school, and community
- physical and mental health of all persons concerned.

Many divorcing couples are awarded *joint custody* of their children. In these situations the responsi-

bility of raising the children is shared. With joint custody, both parents usually remain more interested and involved with their children.

Even if joint custody is not awarded, both parents have a duty to support minor children. The court typically orders the noncustodial parent to pay child support to the custodial parent. **Child support** is the monetary payment by a parent to provide a dependent child with appropriate economic maintenance. These payments help pay for the needs and wants of the child, including housing, food, clothing, and other expenses.

ALIMONY **Alimony** is the support paid by the wage earner of the family to the other spouse. Alimony is usually paid at regular intervals. It may, in some cases, be a lump-sum payment. Alimony is not intended to penalize the person ordered to pay it. The amount to be paid is set by the court. Factors considered by the court are the paying spouse's income, financial resources, earnings outlook, current debts, number of dependents, and number of spouses (former and subsequent).

A Question of ETHICS ?

Debra Cater had lived her whole life at the direction of others. As the oldest child, she had been controlled by her mother while growing up. Upon marriage, she had been ordered around by her husband who told her how to behave and dress.

Finally, she became aware that her husband was having an affair with a woman at the business he owned. The affair had been long-running, but Debra felt that she had been blinded to it by the trust she placed in others' directions for her life.

Ready to finally live life on her own terms, Debra filed for divorce at the age of 40. Her husband vowed that she would get no further support from him, even though the couple had a young son, Tony.

To prepare for living on her own, Debra decided to finish college and then go to law school. Unfortunately, she realized that Tony would have to be without her a great deal, especially in the evenings. Debra would have to be in the library studying, when she should be focusing on him. In addition, the law school she would attend was hours in driving time from his father. So Tony would be basically alone.

Nonetheless, Debra felt she could not wait any longer to prepare herself for independence. What would you advise Debra to do? On what ethical grounds is your advice based?

THINK ABOUT LEGAL CONCEPTS

Answer the following questions about legal concepts.

1. A void marriage is considered to have never been valid. **True or False?**

2. A voidable marriage is considered to have never been valid. **True or False?**

3. Could a person avoid a marriage if the person's spouse had lied significantly about his or her age? **Yes or No?**

4. The ___?___ agreement often becomes the basis for the divorce decree.

5. Child support is a part of alimony. **True or False?**

6. An annulment can end a marriage. **True or False?**

7. Before the advent of no-fault divorces, which of the following was not a typical ground for divorce? **(a) desertion (b) cruelty (c) adoption (d) all of the above were such grounds**

8. Bigamy always produces a void marriage. **True or False?**

9. An incestuous marriage is a void marriage. **True or False?**

10. Which of the following is usually given as the legal reason in a no-fault marriage dissolution? **(a) bigamy (b) irreconcilable differences (c) cruelty (d) desertion**

Study the following situations, answer the questions, then prepare arguments to support your answers.

11. The night after Zeke and Shanda were married, Shanda admitted that she was pregnant by another man. Can Zeke end their marriage? How?

12. Ben Thomas was a writer. He was married to Agnes, a stockbroker. Ben stayed home to write and to take care of their two children. But because Ben's writing had not sold, Agnes provided the sole financial support to the family. If Ben and Agnes ever divorce, would Agnes have to pay for Ben's support?

13. After they had been married several months, Alfie admitted to his wife that he was not a secret agent of British Intelligence with a double zero "license to kill." She immediately sued to have their union annulled on the grounds he had lied to her about his profession. Will she be successful?

14. If Alfie's wife in exercise 13 is not successful annulling their marriage, what would be another approach to ending the marriage?

15. Bernice and Bernie were married. He was a Certified Public Accountant making $75,000 per year. She was an antitrust lawyer making almost exactly the same amount. In the event of divorce, who will pay whom alimony?

16. Bernice and Bernie, the married couple in exercise 15, argued all the time. Bernice, who had been promoted to partner in the law firm, felt that the main reason for the arguments was the fact that she was now making almost twice Bernie's salary. However, she felt that if there were some way the two of them could live apart for several months, the effect on Bernie might be such that he would see that relative earning power didn't matter when it came to the potential loss of the woman he loved. Is it legally possible for a married couple to live apart but keep their marital rights and obligations intact? Explain.

17. Several months later, instead of realizing how much he needed Bernice, Bernie has drifted further away. The arguments have been replaced by silence. Bernice is considering filing for divorce. The couple has no children. However, she hesitates because she still loves Bernie. Bernice also thinks that she must have grounds such as adultery, desertion, or cruelty upon which to base her filing. A friend tells her that she needs to move on with her life and that no substantial grounds for divorce are necessary. Is the friend correct? What sort of divorce is the friend referring to?

PREVENT LEGAL DIFFICULTIES

1. Understand that your actions have consequences and that your premarital relationships may have long-term effects.

2. Realize that hasty, ill-considered decisions in selecting a marital partner may become lifelong mistakes. Make your decisions with the long-term good of both you and your partner in mind.

3. Consider marriage a serious contract between husband and wife that requires each to fulfill their duties with mutual concern and respect for each other.

4. Use prenuptial agreements to avoid subsequent conflicts over property ownership and division.

5. In the event of divorce, seek legal counsel and carefully consider and fulfill the obligations, such as child support and alimony, being assumed.

6. If your marriage ends in divorce, make all decisions relative to your children with their best interest in mind. Joint custody with cooperating and involved parents helps the children grow up in a balanced and healthy environment.

CHAPTER IN REVIEW

CONCEPTS IN BRIEF

1. In most jurisdictions, a gift given by one party in a relationship to the other in anticipation of marriage must be returned to the giver if the parties do not marry.

2. Parental consent to marry is generally required for individuals under age 18.

3. Annulments are available based upon fraud where either spouse lied about such things as freedom from diseases, past marriages, age, preference towards having children, and wealth.

4. Suits involving loss of consortium may succeed against individuals who cause harm that prevents a spouse from fulfilling marital duties.

5. In a prenuptial contract, marital partners-to-be may renounce any claim to their future spouse's property that they might otherwise acquire through marriage.

6. Even though a married couple may separate or divorce, such obligations as alimony and child support, where appropriate, remain legally enforceable.

YOUR LEGAL VOCABULARY

Match each statement with the term that it best defines. Some terms may not be used.

1. Voiding of a marital contract

2. Marital union treated as valid by the law until terminated at the option of one or both parties due to improper grounds

3. Marital union with no legal effect whatsoever

4. Person who is married to two or more people at the same time

5. Court action terminating a marriage

6. Divorce procedure in which no cause need be shown for termination of the union

7. Generally the first step towards divorce

8. Care and control of a minor

9. Legal process that creates a parent-child relationship

10. Legal union of a man and woman as husband and wife

11. Marital relationship legalized by a couple holding themselves out as husband and wife, sharing home and property for an extended period

12. Money paid by parent to provide child with economic maintenance

13. Mutual obligations of wife and husband undertaken to fulfill the purposes of their union

14. Legal contract resolving property and other claims that might result from a marriage

15. Term in some states for the ending of a marriage

adoption
alimony
annulment
bigamist
child custody
child support
common-law marriage
dissolution
divorce
marital consortium
marriage
no-fault divorce
prenuptial agreement
separation
void marriage
voidable marriage

16. What are the advantages of parental control over when and to whom a child marries?

17. What sort of "reasonable force" do parents have at their disposal for enforcing their decisions against their children? Can they refuse to feed them ("go to bed without your supper"), beat them, or imprison them ("you're grounded")?

18. Why does the government require parental consent for marriages of persons under 18 years old?

19. What is the purpose of breach-of-promise lawsuits?

20. Imagine that you are engaged to be married. Write a letter to your fiancée stating reasons for or against having a prenuptial agreement.

21. Write an essay explaining what you would most like to see changed about our divorce laws.

22. HOT DEBATE Write a persuasive opening argument that emphasizes the legal and ethical points in Ben's favor. Or, write a persuasive opening argument that emphasizes the legal and ethical points in his father's favor.

Study the following situations, answer the questions, then prepare arguments to support your answers.

23. Billy and his first cousin, Sally, were raised together as children. They both have the same values, go to the same school, have the same friends and are extremely happy together. One day, Billy asks Sally for her hand in marriage. Sally says yes. They are both 17. What problems might they encounter in fulfilling their desires to marry?

24. Tom and Juanita are lovers. Several years into their relationship, Juanita has a child by Tom. They do not marry, however. Now, Juanita has broken off their relationship but expects Tom to help pay for the child's support. Must he do so by law? What rights does Tom have with the child? What interest does the government have in making sure that someone has responsibility for the child?

25. Alexandra and Thomas are engaged. Before they marry, Thomas meets Marcia and falls in love with her. He then breaks off his engagement. Alexandra is humiliated by the rejection. Further, she and her parents have already invested thousands of dollars in wedding preparations. What legal cause of action might she have against Thomas? Could she also sue Marcia in some states? Why?

26. Stephanie and Alfred moved to Missouri after 15 years of living in Oklahoma. All during the time they were together in Oklahoma, they held themselves out as husband and wife, lived together, and shared common property. Now Alfred wants to leave Stephanie. He has been the sole wage earner the whole time they have been together. Therefore, he wants to take all the property except a bed and an old car. Stephanie believes that Alfred owes her far more than that. She feels they have been married at common law and, therefore, she has the same rights as any other divorcing spouse. Alfred points out that Missouri does not have common-law marriage, so she has no such rights. Who is correct?

27. Antonio and Doris have been married a year when Antonio is injured in a freak chemical accident that leaves him unable to conceive a child. Antonio has sued the negligent parties for his loss. What cause of action does Doris have stemming from the same incident?

28. More than four years after they were married, George Woy sought an annulment of his marriage to Linda Woy on the basis of fraud. In his petition he alleged that at the time of the marriage ceremony he was unaware that she had a dependence on illegal drugs, and that, had she not concealed the fact from him, he would have refused to marry her. Should the court grant an annulment on this basis? (*Woy v. Woy*, 737 S.W.2d 769)

29. When they remarried each other, Robert Root owed Nila Root several thousand dollars of unpaid child support from their first marriage. A month and a half after their second marriage ceremony, Nila filed to dissolve their second marriage and demanded payment of the back child support. Should the court allow her to collect the money, as she is still married to Robert? (*In re Marriage of Root*, 774 S.W.2d 521)

30. James and Anna Nesbit were contemplating divorce. They entered into a property settlement agreement, but James died before the divorce became final. His will provided a greater amount of property for Anna than did the settlement agreement. Which document should be enforced? (*Crist v. Nesbit*, 352 S.W.2d 53)

31. Three days before their marriage, Donna Rinvelt and Arnold Rinvelt signed a prenuptial agreement drafted by the latter's attorney. The document stated that each party would keep all rights in their separate property and could dispose of it without any claims upon it by the other spouse. The document also contained the following clause:
Divorce: In the event that the marriage of the parties shall end in divorce, annulment, or separate maintenance, it is hereby agreed that their respective rights in and to the property of the other spouse shall be limited as follows:

(a) The Prospective Husband shall be entitled to ten percent (10%) of the net estate of the Prospective Wife, net estate meaning gross estate less all expenses.

(b) The Prospective Wife shall be entitled to ten percent (10%) of the net estate of the Prospective Husband, net estate meaning gross estate less all expenses.

As a consequence of this latter provision, Donna Rinvelt was awarded almost a quarter of a million dollars of Arnold's property by the divorce court.

Arnold brought an appeal asking that the award be thrown out. What arguments could be made in this regard? What arguments could Donna make to the contrary? What do you think the court decided? (*Rinvelt v. Rinvelt*, 475 N.W.2d 478)

32. Thea Ella Curless brought an action for divorce against Timothy Dean Curless. The judgment and decree granted the divorce, awarded custody of the two children, a boy, Trist, age 13, and a girl, Tobi, age 10, to their father with rights of visitation to the mother. The court divided the personal property and debts according to the agreement between the parties and awarded the house to Timothy Curless with Thea Curless' equity secured by a second mortgage in the amount of $36,000, to be paid in installments of $600 per month with 10 percent interest. After entering judgment, the trial judge denied Mrs. Curless' motion for a new trial and denied the children's motion to intervene, as well as their motion to have a guardian appointed for them. Mrs. Curless is a junior high school teacher with a master's degree in education. Timothy Curless is employed by the Union Pacific Railroad. The court heard conflicting testimony as to how much time Mr. Curless' job keeps him away from home and how much time Mrs. Curless' employment and extracurricular activities kept her from attending to the children. The court also heard conflicting facts about which spouse did more or less than his or her share of household duties and attending of children. The court heard testimony to the effect that Mr. Curless is an alcoholic but that he has "quit drinking." Mr. Curless testified that he had not had a drink since he made a commitment to give up alcohol four years ago. There was evidence that Mr. Curless had been a user of marijuana and had a marijuana plant in his home. Mr. Curless testified that he had had "no involvement with any drugs for 45 days," and had not had a marijuana plant in his home for the last "eight or nine years." Finally, the court held, and the parties do not seriously contend otherwise, that both parties are "fit" and proper persons to have care and custody of the children. Because of the divorce court's rulings in the case, Thea Curless has brought an appeal before the Supreme Court of Wyoming. Should the court uphold the divorce court's determinations or reverse them? Why or why not? (*Curless v. Curless*, 708 P.2d 426)

CASE FOR LEGAL THINKING

Ivana Trump v. Donald J. Trump
Supreme Court of New York, Appellate Division, 582 N.Y.S.2d 1008

FACTS The Trumps were married in 1977. On December 24, 1987, they entered into a postnuptial agreement. Both spouses did so under the advice of separate counsel. The agreement of December 1987 superceded three previous agreements of 1977, 1979, and 1984, respectively.

Two paragraphs of the 1987 agreement are under primary scrutiny in this case. The first is Paragraph 9(b) which set out the parties' rights and obligations in the event of divorce. These rights and obligations included the husband's obligation to pay $350,000 per year to the wife as maintenance and $10,000,000 in a lump sum within 90 days after the entry of the final divorce decree.

The second paragraph (Paragraph 10) provides that without obtaining Mr. Trump's advance written consent, Mrs. Trump can not publish, or cause to be published, any diary, memoir, letter, story, photograph, interview, article, essay, account, or description or depiction of any kind, whether fictionalized or not, concerning their marriage or any other aspect of Mr. Trump's personal, business, or financial affairs. She also could not assist or provide information to others in connection with the publication or dissemination of any such material or excerpts.

The agreement goes on to terminate any of Mr. Trump's obligations under paragraph 9(b) if a breach of the agreement occurs. It also provides that, in the event of divorce, the terms and conditions of this agreement shall supercede any divorce decree.

In 1990, Mrs. Trump initiated a divorce action against Donald J. on the grounds of cruel and inhuman treatment. Concurrently, she brought suit to have the agreement voided as she maintained it violated her rights to a property division available under state law.

TRIAL COURT DECISION The court granted Mrs. Trump her divorce. Later, after extensive negotiations between the parties, the court issued a judgment that reflected the result of these negotiations, i.e., that Mrs. Trump would accept the lump sum payment of the $10 million in return for allowing the agreement to be enforceable. Regrettably, the court, although including all the other terms of the agreement by reference, did not include paragraph 10 of the agreement in its judgment. Mr. Trump appealed the court's unilateral action which was taken without explanation or notice to the parties.

APPELLATE COURT DECISION "Since it is clear that the trial court exceeded its limited authority to disturb the terms of a separation agreement and paragraph 10 does not, on its face, offend public policy as a prior restraint on protected speech, we modify to incorporate the terms of said agreement into the . . . judgment as agreed to by the parties."

PRACTICE JUDGING

1. **What is the significance of the omitted term? Could you infer that Mrs. Trump gave up anything of value in the negotiations in return for its being omitted?**

2. **Do you think the courts should have the discretion to pick and choose what sections of a contract they are going to enforce, even though all sections are valid under the law?**

3. **Mrs. Trump argued against the reinclusion of the term by saying that it involved a "prior restraint" on what she might publish. This, she maintained, would be a violation of her Constitutional rights. Do you agree? Why or why not?**

ENTREPRENEURS AND THE LAW

PROJECT 3 SALES AND OTHER CONTRACTUAL SITUATIONS

SELLING THE DEVICES

After receiving the go-ahead from his attorney, Ben finally placed several of the Reelshields in the hands of Rebuilt. Now word was spreading. The machinist's union meeting featured a presentation about the Reelshield. The next day many union members asked their employers to try it out. Soon Ben received several phone inquiries, and now he had two orders for the devices. One machine shop wanted 15 units and another, 10 units. Both orders had been placed over the phone. The 15-unit order had been confirmed by a letter restating the terms of the deal. The second order required a modification or two of Ben's standard design due to the low ceiling of the buyer's shop. This shop had an excellent reputation and generally did business on just a handshake. Ben was amazed that both buyers had not blinked an eye when he had named the selling price of $1,331 for each Reelshield. He had intended to sell them for around $500 each, which was double his cost. Kristen had suggested that he start asking more than $1,000, as they were such useful items and he had a patent-based monopoly.

LOCATION AND SHIPPING

Ben leased a small factory in an industrial park just outside town. A city representative visited him and advised him to obtain a business license as soon as possible. Ben had moved his equipment and supplies into the structure and was set to begin his first production run. Ben's immediate goal was to be able to fill the many orders he had, and those that soon would be on his way. He also needed to devise a way to get the finished product to the buyers. Ben knew he would have to be careful in packaging as well as in choosing a transport company.

PROFITABLE VENTURES

(One month later.) The size of his profit still staggered Ben. Even with the lease payments and paying for supplies for the backlog, he would be able to pay Kristen back in full plus interest. Also amazing was the answer Kristen gave when he asked her to marry him. She said yes! However, she also said her parents were not convinced he was the man for her.

Divide into teams and perform one or more of the following activities, as directed by your teacher.

DISCUSS AND PRESENT

As a team, discuss the legal status of the orders for 10 and 15 Reelshields. Use the following questions as a guide: Is each order valid in the form received? What happens if legal disputes arise about the details of the transactions? What advice, both legal and financial, would you give Ben about accepting future orders? One team member should record the team's answers to the questions. Another member should present the team's advice for Ben to the class.

PREPARE LEGAL DOCUMENTS

Draft a sales contract for the orders for the 10 and 15 Reelshields. (Keep in mind the advice your group had for Ben in the activity above.) Next, draft a sample shipping contract Ben can use in shipping out these and subsequent orders. Be sure to include terms (such as COD, FOB, etc.) that would protect him from loss or damage to the goods.

BRAINSTORM

As a team, brainstorm the terms of a prenuptial agreement that would satisfy Kristen's parents. They are concerned about protecting Kristen's sizable inheritance. They are also concerned about her well-being should she and Ben divorce, with or without children. Have a group member record each idea. Draft a prenuptial agreement based on the team's ideas.

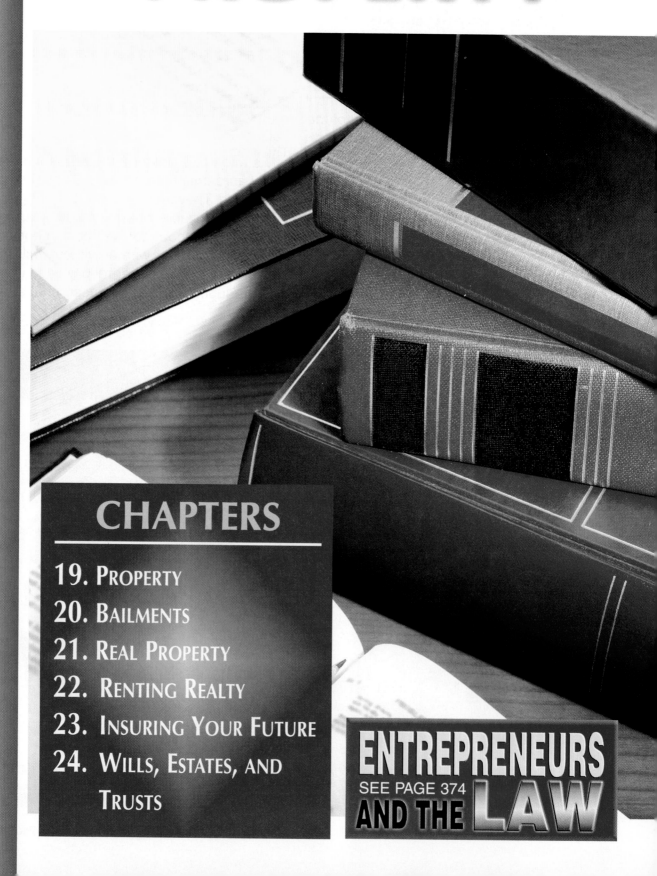

UNIT FOUR

PROPERTY

ENTREPRENEURS
SEE PAGE 374
AND THE LAW

Warren Zaretsky is a marketing strategist and media producer. He specializes in producing communication programs to support the launch of new companies, new products, and new concepts. Over 15 years, he has produced, written, and directed a wide range of award-winning corporate and marketing communications in film, video, and live programs. His clients include many of America's top corporations, including Apple Computer, AT&T, Coca Cola, Chrysler, IBM, Kodak, and Motorola.

Before forming his own production company, Zaretsky was a Product Manager for GAF Corporation, a Director of Marketing for Berkey Photo, Inc., and General Manager of Gordon/Glynn Productions. He is a graduate of Wayne State College, with graduate studies at Los Angeles State College, and the University of California, Riverside.

Over the years Zaretsky has provided creative production services for his clients in virtually every medium. He has staged large-scale presentations for trade shows, global conferences, and national sales meetings. He's created TV commercials, corporate image films, new-product videos, CD-ROMs, and sales-training programs. He also has developed and produced feature film projects, documentaries, and television "pilot" shows.

"Running my own company, I've had to be aware of the standard range of business law issues," Zaretsky said. "But as an independent producer I've also had to learn about entertainment law, and issues like 'work-for-hire,' intellectual property, copyrights, and royalties. The creative business can get very complicated. Frequently I've needed to consult with two or three different and specialized attorneys on the same project. To me, the law is

as much a creative tool as a camera or my editor. The success of my business and each individual production depends on how well I employ those tools to achieve my vision."

As an example, Zaretsky produced and directed a global sales conference for the giant French and American owned Rhone-Poulenc Rorer pharmaceutical company. The theme of "Teamwork: Working In Concert" was illustrated using a chamber symphony orchestra. Three videos, numerous computer graphic presentations, and overall conference design were developed in the United States. The actual production was staged in Madrid, Spain. "I needed my company's general council to review contracts with the client and 'independent contractor' agreements with my main production team. I went to an entertainment lawyer to help me obtain music rights, performance rights, and to negotiate future royalties with the orchestra. And then, because of all the agreements and insurances for crew and equipment in Spain, I required a bilingual specialist in international law."

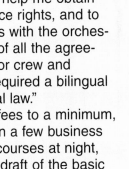

To keep hourly legal fees to a minimum, Zaretsky says he's taken a few business and entertainment law courses at night, and writes his own first-draft of the basic contracts. He then presents the drafts to the attorneys for review and finalizing. "It's like producing a TV commercial. You could spend weeks or even months creating and developing the ideas, writing the script, and designing the story-board—that's where the hours, and the costs really build up. Once you've got it on paper, you could shoot it in a day."

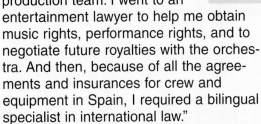

> **"**To me, the law is as much a creative tool as a camera or my editor. The success of my business and each individual production depends on how well I employ those tools to achieve my vision.**"**

United States Patent Application

Sheet 1 of 2

LESSONS

HOT DEBATE

Sue and Bill were married for 12 years when Bill died. They owned their own home. In his will, Bill left everything to his elderly mother who was very poor and in need of money for a place to live. Sue had worked part time to help make the payments on the mortgage. She was the one who did all the cleaning and maintenance. Sue felt she should be able to keep the home but she also knew she could support herself if she didn't get the home.

Where Do You Stand?

1. Why should the mother receive the home?

2. Why should Sue receive the home?

GOALS

- Distinguish between real, tangible personal, and intangible personal property
- Determine what body of law governs various transactions for the purchase of goods and/or services
- Discuss the types of intellectual property

WHAT IS PROPERTY?

WHAT'S YOUR VERDICT?

Winkler rented her cabin in Ocean City to Hanson for the summer season.

Did Hanson acquire property under the lease?

When someone speaks of property, you probably think of tangible things you can see or touch. Tangible things include this book, clothing, diamond rings, buildings, land, cars, and boats. But thinking about property should also bring to mind intangible things, or things you cannot see or touch.

For example, both the goodwill of a brand name and the secret formula by which a product is made are intangible. Other examples of intangible property include patents for inventions, the copyright of this book, the franchise to open a particular business in your town, and the right to collect money under an automobile insurance policy.

According to the law, **property** is (1) a thing, tangible or intangible, that is subject to ownership and (2) a group of related legal rights. For example, suppose you own some land with a house that you correctly call property. Ownership of the land and house gives you a number of legal rights. These include rights to (1) possess, use, and enjoy it; (2) dispose of (by gift or sale), consume, or even destroy it; and (3) give it away by will after death.

You also have the right to lease your property to a tenant. If you lease your property, the tenant "acquires" an interest in the property. The tenant acquires the right to use your land and building, while you continue to own them. In *What's Your Verdict?* Hanson acquired a property interest in the cabin.

CLASSIFICATIONS OF PROPERTY

WHAT'S YOUR VERDICT?

Sonia wrote a poem. She wondered if the law would protect it from being used by other people without her permission.

What class of property is Sonia's poem? What body of law protects it?

Property can be classified as real or personal. Personal property can be either tangible or intangible.

Real Property

Real property (sometimes called *realty*) is land. It includes not only the surface of the earth, but also the water and minerals on and below the surface. Real property extends down to the center of the earth and, with certain limits, includes the airspace above the land. Real property also includes anything permanently attached to the land, such as buildings.

Tangible Personal Property

Personal property (sometimes called *personalty*) is something that is either movable or intangible. The rights to use such things also are considered personal property. Items of tangible personal property are often called **goods**. Goods are *mobile*—they are easily moved. Therefore, your watch, car, and clothing are tangible personal property. The law that generally governs transactions in goods is the Uniform Commercial Code (UCC). While this is state law, it is basically the same in every state.

In business law, property or goods contrast with *services*. Services are always intangible. When you hire a lawyer, accountant, physician, or auto mechanic, you are purchasing services. Transactions for the purchase of services are governed by the common law of contracts. This is a body of primarily state case law.

Some transactions are mixed transactions, involving a purchase of both tangible personal property and

LAW and the INTERNET

You spend countless hours creating a website. Then, when surfing the net, you find entire portions of your website running in an online magazine—without any attribution to you.

As reported in *PC World Online,* that is what happened to Bob Minnick who created "Beginner's Central," a series of how-to Web pages for cyberspace newcomers. Minnick asked Mark Voorhees of "Information Law Alert" whether his home page was protected under copyright law. The answer: Yes. According to Voorhees, copyright law protects all original work whether or not it bears the copyright symbol or some other explicit statement of ownership. You cannot use somebody's work as your own or distribute it without permission. Certain limited uses are allowed under the "fair use" provision of U.S. copyright law. The bottom line is, always site your source. And remember, copyright laws apply online as well as offline.

services. In a mixed transaction, the dominant component will determine which law (UCC or common law of contracts) applies.

If you want the local automobile dealership to repair your front disk brakes, you would purchase the services of the mechanic to replace the brake pads. You also would purchase the brake pads, which are tangible personal property. The mechanic's labor is a service, and if you supplied the brake pads, the repair would be governed by the common law of contracts. On the other hand if you bought the pads from the automobile dealership and installed them yourself, this purchase would be governed by the UCC. If you purchased both the brake pads and the mechanic's labor from the auto dealership, the common law of contracts would apply because the labor or service aspect is the dominant component of the transaction.

Intangible Personal Property

Personal property includes not only tangible, but also intangible property. **Intellectual property** is purely intangible—that is, one cannot touch it. Intellectual property includes copyrights, patents, trade secrets, servicemarks, and trademarks. The creation,

use, and transfer of interests in intellectual property are generally governed by federal statutes. In *What's Your Verdict?* Sonia's poem is intellectual property governed by federal law.

COPYRIGHT A **copyright** protects the *expression* of a creative work, such as the work of an author, artist, or composer. Owners of the copyright have the exclusive right to reproduce, sell, perform, or display the work. Copyrights owned by the creator of the work last for the life of the creator plus 70 years. After a copyright period expires, the work can be used by anyone without cost or obtaining permission. An author can transfer ownership of the copyright to others.

Copyrighted works can include songs, books, computer programs, and architectural plans. The expression must be *fixed* and *original.* Fixed means it is expressed in a permanent way others can understand, for example in writing, painting, computer language, or a blueprint. It is the fixed expression, not the idea, that is protected. If you wrote a book about the Civil War, it is only the way you used the words that would be protected.

Copyright arises upon creation of the original work. The creator's rights

are increased if the work is registered with the U.S. Copyright Office. Registration allows the creator to collect damages for **infringement.** Infringement is the unauthorized copying, sale, display, or performance of the work.

Not all unauthorized uses of copyrighted works infringe on the copyright. **Fair use** is the very limited use of copyrighted works by critics, researchers, news reporters, and educators. The most important factor in determining whether the defense of fair use is available is the economic impact of the use.

Another factor is the quantity of the copied material in relation to the size of the whole copyrighted work. One novelist might quote a paragraph from another novelist's 300-page book. That would be fair use because it does not injure the first novelist by causing reduced sales of the quoted novel. Also, the paragraph is a small portion of the original, copyrighted novel. Teachers may use very limited portions of copyrighted materials in their classes.

TRADEMARKS AND SERVICEMARKS Business firms may acquire property rights known as trademarks. A **trademark** is

Trademark Protection

Then and Now

Trademarks have been used for centuries. Ancient Chinese potters and medieval sword makers used pictures and symbols as their trademarks. The American patriot and silversmith Paul Revere marked his work with his initials.

The rights of trademark owners were not clearly established until the nineteenth century. The Paris Convention of 1883, along with subsequent amendments, is an international treaty organization that requires members to recognize the trademark rights of foreign producers. Registration of trademarks in the United States officially began in 1870. The Lanham Act, enacted in 1946, is the current federal trademark law.

a word, mark, symbol, or device that identifies a product of a particular manufacturer or merchant. The mark must be unique and identify and distinguish the product. For example, the word "Kodak" is a trademark. It is included in the name of the owner, the Eastman Kodak Company, and it identifies products made by that company. However, descriptive words, such as "35mm camera," are not trademarks, and they may be used by any company. A **servicemark** is a unique word, mark, or symbol that identifies a service as opposed to a product.

All states and the federal government have trademark registration laws. Registration is not essential. However, if a trademark is registered it is easier to prove ownership of the mark. Common law protection lasts forever if a unique trademark establishes the product in the minds of the public and the trademark is used continuously. The originating company loses its exclusive property right to the trademark if either of the following occurs:

1. the company permits competitors to refer to similar products by the unique trademark, or
2. the trademark is used generally as a descriptive generic term.

Examples of terms that have become generic are "shredded wheat" and "cellophane." In contrast,

the terms "Xerox," "Levi's," and "Scotch Tape" remain the property of the original owners.

PATENTS A **patent** is the grant of the exclusive right to make, use, and sell a novel or new, nonobvious, useful product or process. *Novel* and *nonobvious* mean no one has ever thought of the product or process before. *Useful* means the product or process can help people do things. Like copyrights, patents can be transferred to others. A patent is good for 20 years and is not renewable.

An inventor will sometimes patent improvements to the original product and thereby extend the practical life of the initial patent. Patents are also given for original designs, such as a unique chair, or original processes, such as one for refining oil into rubber. Patents also are given for certain new and distinct varieties of plants and other biological creations.

TRADE SECRETS Sometimes a business firm will have important ideas or knowledge that cannot be copyrighted or patented. These ideas can still be protected as trade secrets. A **trade secret** is commercially valuable information that the owner attempts to keep secret. If an employee leaves a company and sells a secret formula, process, or customer list, the former employee and the buyer of the trade secret will be liable to the employer.

	What is protected?	Registration required?	Duration?	Examples
	Features of Intellectual Property			
Patent	Ideas, designs, or processes that are novel, non-obvious, and useful	Yes	20 years	Industrial chemical manufacturing processes, prescription drugs
Copyright	Fixed expressions of creativity	No, but recommended	70 years past the death of the creator	Novels, poems, songs, photographs
Trademark	Distinctive mark, word, or symbol associated with a particular product	No, but recommended	Indefinite	Logos, emblems, catch phrases

Answer the following questions about legal concepts.

1. Property is either a tangible or intangible thing and legal rights related to it. **True or False?**

2. Transactions for both goods and services are always governed by the UCC. **True or False?**

3. Copyrights held by authors are protected by federal law for the life of the author plus 50 years. **True or False?**

4. Patents are only available for new, useful, non-obvious products or processes. **True or False?**

5. To be protected by law, a trade secret **(a) must be copyrightable (b) must be patentable (c) must be commercially valuable (d) must have had efforts to keep it secret (e) both c and d**

6. A unique word, protected by federal law, that identifies a business's product is called a __?__ .

7. Which of the following would be governed by the common law of contracts? **(a) contract for the sale of a case of soft drink (b) contract for the purchase of a new computer for $1,500 which includes a service agreement worth about $150 (c) purchase of an SAT prep course for $600 that includes about $150 worth of books**

8. Which of the following would be governed by the common law of contracts? **(a) contract for the sale of an automobile (b) contract for the purchase of brake pads for the automobile (c) contract for the purchase of a laptop computer (d) contract to have your family's lawn mowed weekly for the next year**

9. The common law of contracts governs **(a) a contract for the sale of a 1999 automobile (b) a contract for the purchase of brake pads for the car (c) a contract for the purchase of a laptop computer (d) a contract to purchase vacant land.**

Study the following situations, answer the questions, then prepare arguments to support your answers.

10. Roberts had an above-ground swimming pool installed on his land. It was not permanently attached to the realty and could be easily disassembled and moved to another location. Then Roberts received a real estate tax assessment bill with an increased assessed value because of the pool. Roberts sued for a deduction, claiming that the pool was personal property. Will he prevail? *(Roberts v. Assessment Board of Review of the Town of New Windsor, 84 Misc. 2d 1017, N.Y.)*

11. AlphaTech developed a computer program that linked together several otherwise incompatible programs. AlphaTech then entered into an agreement with Omega. The agreement stated Omega was to use its equipment to place AlphaTech's program and one of Omega's programs on a CD, and ship orders to customers. The contract terms specified that for each CD sold, Omega was to receive 50 cents for the CD, 2 cents for its program, and 12 cents for placing AlphaTech's program on the CD. What body of law governs this contract?

12. Steven was president of a successful chemical company. He developed a non-patentable process for making soap better. At first, he treated his process as a secret. But later his pride caused him to disclose the technique to a number of people. When one of these people started a competing business using his process, he sued claiming theft of a trade secret. Will Steven prevail?

13. Mary developed a hair dye, from natural ingredients, that could be washed with hot water without changing the color. She took the dye to a chemist who said that most chemists were aware of the dye's properties. Which approach is most likely to help Mary protect her formula—a patent, copyright, or trade secret?

G O A L S

● Discuss seven ways of acquiring property
● Distinguish between mislaid and lost property
● Identify some of the legal limitations on the use of property

HOW IS PROPERTY ACQUIRED?

WHAT'S YOUR VERDICT?

Five friends were discussing how they each had acquired their watches. Appleton bought his with earnings from his job at the local fast-food restaurant. Baird received hers as a graduation gift. Cameron inherited hers from an aunt who had died. Dawson, a skilled watchmaker, made his own. Engler found hers on the street. She had not been able to find the owner.

Did each friend have equal ownership rights in his or her wristwatch?

R eal or personal property is most commonly acquired by contract, gift, or inheritance. In addition, personal property may be legitimately acquired by accession, intellectual labor, finding, or occupancy. Real property may be acquired by adverse possession, dedication, and eminent domain. In *What's Your Verdict?* even though each friend acquired a watch through a different means, each friend had equal ownership rights in his or her own wristwatch.

Acquiring Ownership by Contract

Any kind of property may be acquired and transferred, or bought and sold, by contract. People acquire most of their property by earning money and using it to purchase property.

Acquiring Ownership by Gift

To create a valid gift, the person making the gift, the **donor**, must do two

things: (1) manifest an intent to transfer ownership and (2) deliver the property. **Delivery** is a shift of physical possession of the property to the new owner, the **donee**. Thus, you could transfer ownership of a watch by giving it with a birthday card to your nephew. This would display the intent to transfer ownership as well as shift the physical possession. A donee has a right to disclaim or reject a gift within a reasonable time after learning of the gift.

Often the law allows a symbol of the subject matter of the gift to be substituted in delivery. Thus, the keys to a car or a deed to real property could be used in place of the car or realty itself. A mere promise to make a gift creates no legal obligations.

Sometimes a gift is conditional, as when a man gives his fiancée an engagement ring. If the two mutually agree not to get married after all, or if the woman breaks the engagement,

IN THIS CASE

Schuster dangled a certificate for 100 shares of stock in front of his niece, a senior in high school. "Melinda," he said, "you've been doing so well in all your classes that I'm giving you this stock." Melinda had no ownership rights in the stock because, as yet, there was no delivery. If Schuster had given her the indorsed stock certificate, however, there would have been delivery and ownership would have shifted.

the man may generally reclaim the gift. In most states, if the man breaks the engagement the woman is entitled to keep the ring.

Another type of conditional gift is made when a donor expects to die

IN THIS CASE

Three friends were flying across the Rocky Mountains in a small airplane. An unexpected storm caused ice to form on the wings so the plane crashed in an isolated area. Only the pilot, Gary, was hurt and his injuries appeared critical. "I'll never make it," he said. "Here, Jim, take my diamond ring. Lisa, you take my watch." Gary insisted, and so Jim and Lisa accepted the gifts before Gary lapsed into unconsciousness. Within hours, however, a helicopter rescued them, and Gary survived. He is entitled to the return of his ring and watch.

You probably view the e-mail you send as your own personal property. But what about the e-mail you send at work? Many companies now have e-mail policies about who owns the e-mail correspondence and whether the company considers the messages to be confidential. The courts have ruled that e-mails are the property of the company. In *Shoars v. Epson*, the judge found in favor of the company and stated that it had the right to tap into, read, and print employees' e-mails. The court reasoned that the company's property right in the computers prevailed. The company's ethics was not of consequence, according to the current law.

In most cases involving e-mail, the judges have marked their opinions as "Not For Publication," which indicates they feel the statutes need updating. The bottom line: Be careful before you press the Send button. E-mail messages are neither confidential nor your private, exclusive property.

justice by letting the improver keep the property after paying fair value for the original item.

Acquiring Ownership by Intellectual Labor

You can acquire personal property rights by original production. Authors or inventors have exclusive property rights in their own productions prior to the time their creations are published or marketed. Authors or inventors can request and obtain recognition of their creations from the federal government. The government may then issue a patent or register a copyright.

soon. The gift may be conditional upon the death's actually occurring. Donors who survive may take back their gifts.

Acquiring Ownership by Accession

Personal property may also be acquired by accession. **Accession** is the right of an owner of property to an *increase* in that property. The

increase may be natural or man-made. Thus, farm crops and the offspring of animals belong to the owner of the land or the animals. When new parts are put into an item of property, they generally become part of the property. For example, if a modem is installed in your computer, it becomes part of the computer.

If, by mistake, someone improves another's property, courts seek to do

Acquiring Ownership by Finding

Anyone who loses property has the right to recover it from any finder. One must simply prove true ownership. When a finder of property knows who the owner is, the finder must return the property. Under some laws, a finder must try (for example, by newspaper advertising) to locate the property owner. If the owner is unknown, either the *finder* or the *owner of the place the property was found* may keep the property until the true owner appears. Which one has this right depends on whether the property is lost or mislaid.

Finders keep *lost* property and owners of the place where the property was found keep *mislaid* property. **Lost property** is created when the owner unknowingly leaves the property somewhere or accidentally drops it. If, while attending a football game, your coat falls from the bleachers, and someone finds it on the ground, the finder, not the school, is entitled to possession. Statutes permit the finder to become the owner if the true owner does not reclaim the property within a stated time, often 60 days.

Mislaid property is intentionally placed somewhere but then forgotten. If you hung your coat on a coat rack in a restaurant while you ate, and then walked out without your coat, it would be mislaid. The finder of the coat would be required to turn it over to the restaurant. Because you may come back looking for the coat, this law helps owners find mislaid property.

Acquiring Ownership by Occupancy

Occupancy means acquiring title by taking possession of personal prop-erty that belongs to no one else. A common example is personal property that has been discarded by the owner. In such a case, the finder who takes possession becomes the owner.

Like discarded or abandoned property, wildlife is considered unowned. A properly licensed person who takes possession of a wild animal on public lands by killing it becomes the legal owner. Similarly, one may become the owner of shells by picking them up on a public beach. However, property on private lands belongs to the owner of the real property and may not be acquired by occupation.

Acquiring Ownership by Inheritance

A person may acquire both real and personal property by inheritance from others after they die. If a person leaves a valid will, it will specify who gets each item of property. If a person dies without a will, he or she is said to die *intestate*. In that situation, the courts will follow the instructions of a state statute that declares how a deceased's property is to be divided among surviving relatives.

LIMITATIONS ON OWNERSHIP

WHAT'S YOUR VERDICT?

Jordan, who lived alone, was very fond of animals. After his retirement, he began to care for stray dogs in his home and yard. Within one year, he had 27 dogs. Neighbors were reluctant to interfere until the noise became intolerable.

Could the neighbors compel Jordan to dispose of his dogs?

An owner of property is not permitted to use that property in an unreasonable or unlawful manner that injures another. In *What's Your Verdict?* Jordan could be compelled to correct a nuisance. The government may adopt laws to protect the public health, safety, morals, and general welfare. All such laws limit the owner's ownership and freedom of use.

Thus, a city may require that buildings be maintained at a certain level of livability. Cities or counties may also enact laws that prohibit the keeping of livestock or other animals in certain sections. Governments may regulate the purity of food and drugs sold to the public. Governments may even destroy private property, such as shipments of canned fish that are infected with deadly botulism.

Answer the following questions about legal concepts.

1. Ownership of property shifts when you make a promise of a gift. **True or False?**

2. The right of an owner of property to an increase in that property is __?__.

3. Gifts conditional upon a marriage or an impending death are not valid if the marriage or death does not occur. **True or False?**

4. Who has the right to possession of *lost* property when the true owner cannot be found?
(a) the owner of the place where the property is found (b) the finder

5. If you were sailing off the coast of California and left a fishing line streaming behind the boat for three hours, then you hooked a tuna and reeled it in, under which legal process would you become the owner of the fish?
(a) accession (b) gift
(c) occupancy (d) intestacy

6. Property that is intentionally placed somewhere but then forgotten is __?__.

7. If, while you were biking on a mountain trail, your watch fell off your wrist, the watch would be
(a) lost (b) mislaid

8. If a person dies without a will, they are said to die __?__.

Study the following situations, answer the questions, then prepare arguments to support your answers.

9. Sheri found a portable computer in the trash bin behind the girls' gym after school. She thought to herself that someone must have intended to throw it away. She took the computer home and tested it to see if it worked. It worked fine and Sheri used it for more than two weeks. One day Skip saw her using the computer and claimed it was his. He said that he had lost it about two weeks ago and that he has a receipt to show he bought it. Who is entitled to the computer and why?

10. While on a ski trip in Vermont, you (a) find a pair of skis in a parking lot, (b) pick up some firewood along a public road, and (c) shoot two rabbits you plan to eat for dinner. By what legal processes can you become the owner of these things?

11. Yvette gave her nephew, Jake, 100 shares of stock in Gold Stake Oil Co. for his sixteenth birthday. She handed the shares, worth about $2,000, to Jake right after Jake successfully blew out all his candles. Two days later, Gold Stake discovered a large oil field. The value of the stock increased 100 times to $200,000. As a result, Yvette demanded the return of the shares. Must Jake return the stock?

12. Dani worked as a server at Shift's Place, a restaurant and bar. Patrons frequently left things in the bar or cloakroom. Dani was responsible for closing Shift's. Closing required her to clean all the rooms and tables and lock the windows and doors before leaving. In closing, she discovered a full length fur coat in the cloakroom and one diamond earring under a bar stool. The fur coat had a label sewn into it with the name, address, and phone number of Tonya. Who is entitled to possession of the fur coat and the earring, Dani, Shift's, or Tonya?

13. Martin owned a 20-unit apartment building. Upon inspection, the city determined that Martin's building did not meet the building code because it did not have fire doors in the hallways. The city informed Martin that he could not rent the units until he installed the fire doors. Does the city have the right to infringe upon Martin's ownership right in the building?

14. A national aluminum company offered to buy used aluminum cans for recycling. One Saturday, the members of the Junior Optimist Club picked up three truckloads of cans from along the sides of a heavily traveled county road. Under what legal doctrine did the club members acquired ownership? What process did they use to transfer ownership of the cans to the aluminum company?

PROPERTY OWNERSHIP

WHAT'S YOUR VERDICT?

Beth and Maureen inherited a 12-acre tract of land from their parents. Beth moved onto the property, and Maureen stayed in her former home. Beth decided Maureen could have the back six acres and she would keep the front six acres.

Can Beth exclude Maureen from part of the tract of land they co-own?

There are two basic ways to own property—in severalty or by co-ownership. These are examined in detail in the following sections.

Ownership in Severalty

Ownership in severalty exists when someone owns property by themselves. This is the most common form of ownership for personal property. If you owned a stamp collection, you would probably own it in severalty.

Co-Ownership

Co-ownership exists when two or more persons have ownership rights in the same property. Co-ownership may take one of several forms: joint tenancy, tenancy in common, tenancy by the entireties, or community property.

All forms of co-ownership have two attributes in common. The first is that all co-owners have equal rights of possession. **Equal rights of possession** means that no co-owner can exclude any other co-owner from any physical portion of the property. This is the most basic attribute of co-ownership.

The second attribute common to co-ownership is the right of partition. The **right of partition** allows any co-owner to require the division of the property among the co-owners. Sometimes the partition is physical, as when a co-owned farm is divided into two parcels. Usually partition is financial. For example, a co-owned airplane could be sold and the proceeds of sale divided among the three co-owners.

In *What's Your Verdict?* Beth had no right to exclude Maureen from the front six acres of their tract. They could, however, agree on a division, or ask a court to divide the property.

JOINT TENANCY **Joint tenancy** is the equal co-ownership of the same property with the *right of survivorship*. Each joint tenant must always have an equal ownership interest, for example 50/50 with two owners or 25 percent for each of four owners. The **right of survivorship** means that if one of the joint owners dies, the deceased co-owner's interest is divided equally among the remaining joint tenants. If the right of survivor-

ship conflicts with provisions of a will, the property passes via the right of survivorship, not the will.

Because the interest in a joint tenancy passes automatically on death, joint tenants often use this form of co-ownership to leave property to the other joint tenant(s). In this way, they do not have to incur the costs and delays of probate.

A joint tenant's interest may be transferred while the joint tenant is alive. But a transfer would end the joint tenancy with regard to the transferred interest. Rather than a joint tenant, the new co-owner would be a tenant in comon, which is discussed in the next section.

A Question of ETHICS

Fran learned that owning property together with someone in joint tenancy allows one co-owner to receive another's interest when that person dies. So Fran asked her 78-year-old uncle to pay half and become a co-owner of resort property with her. When he asked what form of co-ownership they should use, Fran said, "Because we will own it together, we should be joint tenants." Is Fran's conduct ethical?

TENANCY IN COMMON In **tenancy in common** the shares may be *unequal* and there is *no* right of survivorship. Upon the death of any tenant in common, that person's interest passes to the heirs (relatives entitled to inherit) or to the beneficiaries designated in the will, if there is one. The heirs or beneficiaries then become tenants in common with the other owners. Any

IN THIS CASE

Smith, Locke, and Pitt were friends and co-workers at a local factory. The three friends could not afford to purchase vacation trailers individually. Together, however, they were able to buy one. Smith contributed 50 percent, Locke contributed 10 percent, and Pitt contributed 40 percent. They agreed to allocate the time when each owner could use the trailer in proportion to his contribution. Tenancy in common would be the appropriate form of ownership in this case. Although all owners have the right of possession, they can agree to give exclusive use to one or the other at certain times. This is true of all forms of co-ownership.

number of co-owners may be tenants in common of a particular piece of property. Tenants in common may sell their interest without the others' consent.

TENANCY BY THE ENTIRETIES In some states, **tenancy by the entireties** is a form of co-ownership between husband and wife. Tenancy by the entireties is limited to married couples, carries the right of survivorship, and may not be sold or mortgaged without the spouse's consent. As in a joint tenancy, the interests must be equal.

A divorce or separation usually transforms a tenancy by the entirety into a tenancy in common. Both joint tenancy and tenancy by the entirety must be created with special language so the nature of the right of survivorship is communicated adequately.

COMMUNITY PROPERTY In some states, all property acquired by husband and wife during their marriage is presumed to be community property.

With **community property**, each spouse owns a one-half interest in such property. Generally, while the spouses are alive, both must consent to disposal of community property. In some states, there is a right of survivorship. In other community property states, the spouse who dies may dispose of his or her half through a will.

Property owned by either spouse at the time of marriage or received as

IN THIS CASE

All of the property belonging to John and Sally Yaun was community property. Domestic difficulties developed between them. Although there was no divorce, John made a will in which he left all the community property to his nephews and nieces. If John dies, it is clear that he may not legally deprive his widow of at least her half of the community property. In some states, he could will *his half* of the community property to relatives or strangers.

a gift or inheritance is **separate property**. Such property becomes community property only if the owner formally or informally treats it as community property and mixes it with other community assets.

Features Type of Co-ownership	May any number co-own?	Must interests be equal?	Is consent of co-owners required for sale?	Is there a right of survivorship?	Must co-owners be married?	Can a will replace survivorship?
Tenancy in common	Yes	No	No	No	No	N/A
Joint tenancy	Yes	Yes	No	Yes	No	No
Tenancy by the entireties	No, just 2	Yes	Yes	Yes	Yes	No
Community property	No, just 2	Yes	Yes	Yes*	Yes	In some states

*In some states a deceased spouse's one half interest in community property passes automatically to the surviving spouse. In other states it can pass via a will to someone other than the surviving spouse, but if there is no will, it then passes to the surviving spouse.

Answer the following questions about legal concepts.

1. When there is only one owner of property, she or he is said to own in __?__.

2. All co-owners have the right to occupy all the property and the power to cause a partition of the property. **True or False?**

3. Which form(s) of co-ownership have the right of survivorship? **(a) tenancy in common (b) joint tenancy (c) tenancy by the entireties (d) b and c**

4. The right of survivorship allows property to pass on an owner's death to co-owners without a will. **True or False?**

5. Which form(s) of co-ownership allow different ownership interests? **(a) tenancy in common (b) joint tenancy (c) tenancy by the entireties (d) community property**

6. Which form(s) of co-ownership allow a co-owner to sell without the consent of the other co-owners? **(a) tenancy in common (b) joint tenancy (c) tenancy by the entireties (d) a and b**

7. Which form(s) of co-ownership require that the co-owners be married? **(a) tenancy in common (b) joint tenancy (c) tenancy by the entireties (d) b and c**

Study the following situations, answer the questions, then prepare arguments to support your answers.

8. You combine your savings with five friends to buy a large sailboat. What form of ownership makes the most sense for your group?

9. For ten years, Trudy and her brother Bert invested their savings in a 12-unit apartment house. They held the title as joint tenants. Then Bert got married. Shortly after the wedding, he was killed in an automobile accident. In his will, Bert left all his property to his wife. His sister and his widow are now in a dispute over who should get his share of the apartment house. Who will get Bert's share?

10. Michael and Julia are married. They co-own a chain of record stores as tenants by the entireties. Michael decides he wants to sell the record stores and go into the plumbing business. Can he sell his half interest without Julia's consent?

11. Foxx, Flynn, and Hammond were auto mechanics. The three also had equal shares as tenants in common in a drag racer nicknamed "The Green Monster." After a disagreement, Foxx wanted to get out of the arrangement. She demanded the engine as her share of the commonly owned racer. Is she entitled to it? What are the other methods available to Foxx to get out of the arrangement?

Manage and use property wisely . . .

1. Do not misuse your property in any way that injures others.

2. Use public property with care. Vandalism, destruction, and theft deprive innocent persons of the benefits of use and also cause higher taxes, which burden all taxpayers.

3. Do not infringe upon the copyright, trademark, or patent of another.

4. If you become a co-owner, be sure to take title in an appropriate form. Use tenancy in common with strangers, associates, and friends. Use joint tenancy with a spouse or other person whom you want to have the full owner-

ship by right of survivorship when you die.

5. In community property states, be sure to keep separate property separate, with clear independent records, if you do not want it to become community property.

CHAPTER IN REVIEW

CONCEPTS IN BRIEF

1. Property is a group of rights or interests that are recognized by society and protected by law. The term may refer to the things themselves—both real and personal, tangible and intangible—in which one may have legal rights and interests.

2. Real property is land, including the surface of the earth, surface and subsurface water and minerals, the airspace above, and anything permanently attached to the land.

3. Personal property is any intangible or movable tangible property. Intangible personal property includes copyrights, patents, servicemarks, trademarks, and trade secrets.

4. Rights in property may be acquired by contract, gift, accession, intellectual labor, finding, occupancy, or inheritance.

5. The true owner of property is entitled to it over anyone who finds it. However, if the owner is not known, a finder is entitled to possession of lost property. The owner of the property on which mislaid property is found is entitled to temporary possession.

6. Ownership by one person is ownership in severalty. Co-ownership may take the form of joint tenancy or tenancy in common. In some states, husband and wife hold property by tenancy by the entireties. In other states, property acquired during marriage is community property.

YOUR LEGAL VOCABULARY

Match each statement with the term that it best defines. Some terms may not be used.

1. An item that is intentionally placed somewhere but then forgotten
2. Co-ownership of property without the right of survivorship
3. Ownership of property by one person alone
4. Right of an owner of property to an increase in the property
5. Exclusive, monopolistic right to make, use, and sell a novel, nonobvious, useful product or process
6. Means of acquiring title by taking possession of personal property that belongs to no one else
7. Exclusive right to produce, sell, copy or publish a creative work
8. Land and things permanently attached to the land
9. Form of co-ownership, other than community property, where neither co-owner may sell without the consent of the other
10. Co-ownership of property with the right of survivorship available to persons who are not husband and wife
11. Very limited use of copyrighted material allowed in certain circumstances
12. Unique word, mark, or symbol that identifies a service of a particular company or person
13. A thing subject to ownership and the related legal rights
14. Unique word, mark, or symbol that identifies a product
15. Unauthorized copying, sale, display, or performance of the work
16. Allowance of a co-owner to require the physical or financial division of the property among the co-owners

accession
community property
co-ownership
copyright
fair use
infringement
intellectual property
joint tenancy
lost property
mislaid property
occupancy
ownership in severalty
patent
personal property
property
real property
right of partition
right of survivorship
servicemark
tenancy by the
   entireties
tenancy in common
trademark
trade secret

17. Identify items of property you can see in your classroom and classify them as real or personal.

18. Explain how copyright law works.

19. Explain how patent law operates.

20. Describe the right of survivorship in joint tenancy.

21. Write a paragraph describing tenancy in common.

22. Write a paragraph describing joint tenancy.

23. Write a paragraph describing tenancy by the entireties.

24. **HOT DEBATE** Write a paragraph explaining why you think Bill's mother should receive the home. Write another paragraph explaining why Sue should be able to keep the home.

Study the following situations, answer the questions, then prepare arguments to support your answers.

25. Your mother operates a small lumber business. She owns a tract of land with a stand of trees on it. She cuts down the trees, saws them into construction lumber, and sells the wood to builders. She also is building a house as a business venture. The house is about one-third finished, and one-half of the framing for the walls is completed. Your mother is concerned about her insurance coverage because it covers only personal property. Which parts of her property are realty and which are personalty?

26. Jeff's school has a computer laboratory. Jeff also has a computer at home and decides to copy the school's word processing program for his personal use. The program is copyrighted by its developer. Is it legal for Jeff to make a copy for himself? Would it be ethical for Jeff to make a copy if he first obtains permission from the school's principal?

27. Voila!, a French firm, manufactures expensive leather goods. It marks all of its products with a crest or seal that depicts its registered trademark. Imperial sold six counterfeit handbags bearing the Voila! mark. The purchaser was a private investigator that Voila! had employed. Voila! sued Imperial for trademark infringement. Imperial did not manufacture the handbags, but only sold them. Will Voila! prevail?

28. Kurt and his best friend bought a motorcycle when they were 17 years old. Because they were such good friends they decided to co-own the bike as joint tenants. Five years later, Kurt married. He wrote a will which stated that upon his death all of his personal property should go to his wife. While driving to work one day he crossed some railroad tracks at the same time as a train. Kurt's car was crushed, and he was killed. Who owns Kurt's interest in the bike?

ANALYZE REAL CASES

29. Gem Electronic Distribution installed Make-a-Tape systems in their retail stores. Make-a-Tape is a coin-operated magnetic tape duplicating system. In two minutes, it can reproduce on a blank tape the complete musical selections already recorded on another tape that takes 35 to 45 minutes to play. Elektra Records sued Gem to restrain it from using Make-a-Tape to produce unauthorized copies of Elektra sound recordings, which are copyrighted. Who should win? Would it be ethical for Gem to make the machine available for use by its customers if it knew that 95 percent of its users violated the copyright laws? (*Elektra Records Company v. Gem Electronic Distributors, Inc.,* 360 F. Supp. 821, E.D.N.Y.)

30. Joseph's aunt sent him $5,000 as a gift. Later, she sent a letter stating that upon her death the money was to be distributed among Joseph and his brothers and sisters. After the aunt died, Joseph kept the money and was sued. Joseph defended himself by claiming that a valid gift of the money occurred before the letter was sent, so the letter is of no legal significance. Is Joseph correct? (*In re Gordon's Will,* 27 N.W.2d 900, Iowa)

31. Betty Dolitsky was in a booth of the safety deposit room of the Dollar Savings Bank when she discovered a $100 bill in an advertising folder that the bank had placed in the booth. She turned the money over to the bank. A year later after the money had not been claimed by its true owner, Betty asked for it. The bank refused. Betty sued. Who prevails? (*Dolitsky v. Dollar Savings Bank,* 119 N.Y.S.2d 65)

32. Hamilton and Johnson were tenants in common of a parcel of land. Hamilton wanted to end the relationship and brought a suit for partition of the property. A forced sale of the property would be inconvenient for Johnson and would cause him some loss. Must the court, nevertheless, divide the property? (*Hamilton v. Johnson,* 137 Wash. 92, 241 P. 672)

33. Alejo Lopez was a married man. Without divorcing, he married a second time. He and his second wife, Helen, purchased property and tried to take title as tenants by the entireties. Later Alejo divorced his first wife and then remarried Helen. When he died, a question arose as to whether the property was owned in tenancy by the entireties. Is it? (*Lopez v. Lopez,* 243 A.2d 588, Md.)

34. On his wife's birthday, Leopold Cohn wrote in the presence of his entire family the following:

    West End, N.J., Sept. 20, 1911

    I give this day to my wife, Sara K. Cohn, as a present for her (46) forty-sixth birthday (500) five hundred shares of American Sumatra Tobacco Company common stock.

    Leopold Cohn

    That writing was immediately delivered to his wife. Six days later, Leopold died. At that time, Leopold owned 7,213 shares but the stock was in the name of and in the possession of his firm, A Cohn & Co., in which he was a partner. Is this a valid gift? (*Matter of Cohn,* 176 N.Y.S. 225)

35. Bernice Paset went into the Old Orchard Bank to gain access to her safety deposit box. Once inside the vault, she went into an examining booth, which contained a small table and a chair. The chair was partially under the table. When Bernice pulled the chair out she discovered $6,325 in cash on the seat of the chair. Is this property abandoned, lost, or mislaid? Who, between Bernice and the bank, is entitled to possession of the property? (*Paset v. Old Orchard Bank,* 378 N.E.2d 1264)

36. E. I. DuPont de Nemours & Co. (DuPont) developed a new process for production of methanol. Although it had not patented the process, it had taken steps to keep the process secret. In order to implement the discovery, DuPont began construction of a refinery. During the construction process an aircraft was observed circling low above the construction site. When DuPont traced the aircraft by its numbers, they discovered that the occupants were photographers who had taken aerial pictures of the plant for an undisclosed client. DuPont believed the photographs might communicate the nature of their trade secret. Accordingly, they sued the photographers to obtain the identity of their client. DuPont then planned to sue the client for misappropriation of a trade secret. Would DuPont prevail in such a suit against the client? (*DuPont v. Christopher,* 621 F.2d 1012)

Marcus v. Rowley
Pfaelzer, District Judge

BACKGROUND This is an appeal from a suit for copyright infringement. The plaintiff is a public school teacher who owns a registered copyright to a booklet on cake decorating. The defendant, also a public school teacher, incorporated a substantial portion of the copyrighted work into a booklet which she prepared for use in her classes.

EVIDENCE Plaintiff, Eloise Toby Marcus was employed by San Diego Unified School District ("District") as a teacher of home economics. Plaintiff wrote a booklet entitled "Cake Decorating Made Easy." Plaintiff's booklet consisted of 35 pages of which 29 were her original creation. Plaintiff properly registered the copyright for "Cake Decorating Made Easy," and 125 copies of the booklet were published.

Defendant, Shirley Rowley ("Rowley"), teaches food service classes in the District. She enrolled in one of plaintiff's cake decorating classes and purchased a copy of plaintiff's book. During the following summer, Rowley prepared a booklet entitled "Cake Decorating Learning Activity Package (LAP)" for use in her food service classes.

Rowley admits copying 11 of the 24 pages in her LAP from plaintiff's booklet. Rowley did not give plaintiff credit for the 11 pages she copied, nor did she acknowledge plaintiff as the copyright owner with respect to the pages.

REASONING In determining whether the use made of a work in any particular case is a fair use, the factors to be considered shall include:
1. the purpose and character of the use, including whether such use is of a commercial nature or is for non-profit educational purposes
2. the nature of the copyrighted work
3. the amount and substantiality of the portion used in relation to the copyrighted work as a whole
4. the effect of the use upon the potential market for or value of the copyrighted work.

The facts that Rowley used the LAP for a nonprofit educational purpose and the LAP was distributed to students at no charge were not disputed. These facts necessarily weigh in Rowley's favor. Nevertheless, a finding of a nonprofit educational purpose does not automatically compel a finding of fair use.

[Another] factor to be considered is the amount and substantiality of the portion used in relation to the copyrighted work as a whole. In this case, almost 50 percent of defendant's LAP was a verbatim copy of plaintiff's booklet and that 50 percent contained virtually all of the substance of defendant's book. This case presents a clear example of both substantial quantitative and qualitative copying.

[Also] to be considered with respect to the fair use defense is the effect which the allegedly infringing use had on the potential market for or value of the copyrighted work. Under these circumstances . . . the fact that plaintiff suffered no pecuniary damage as a result of Rowley's copying supports a finding of fair use.

CONCLUSION The order of the district court is reversed. Summary judgment is entered for the plaintiff.

PRACTICE JUDGING

1. If only a page had been copied, would this be fair use?

2. If Rowley had given Marcus credit, would this be fair use?

3. If the 11 pages had been copied and credit given, but the plaintiff suffered financial injury, would this judge have concluded that the usage was fair?

LESSONS

HOT DEBATE

Janice walked into a well-known restaurant. She hung her cashmere coat on a rack near her booth. After eating, she left without the coat. Another patron, Sally, noticed the coat when Janice hung it up. Sally also noticed that Janice forgot it. So when Sally left, she took Janice's coat home with her. As soon as Janice got home, she called the restaurant and asked them to hold her coat so she could pick it up. The restaurant said that the coat was not there.

Where Do You Stand?

1. **Does Janice have grounds to sue the restaurant for the loss of her coat? Why or why not?**

2. **Is the restaurant responsible for reimbursing Janice for the cost of the coat? Why or why not?**

HOW IS A BAILMENT CREATED?

WHAT'S YOUR VERDICT?

Roberta's parents own a television set with a built-in videocassette recorder. One evening they rent a video Roberta wants to see.

What is the legal relationship between the parents and the video store?

If you lend your pen to a friend, you are involved in the legal relation of bailment. The transaction is neither a sale nor a gift, because your friend must return the pen to you. A **bailment** is the transfer of possession without the transfer of ownership.

Temporary possession and control of goods is the focus of the bailment relationship. The **bailor** is the party who gives up possession of the property. The **bailee** is the party who accepts possession and control. In *What's Your Verdict?* a bailment was

created between Roberta's parents and the video store. The video store was the bailor, and Roberta's parents were the bailees.

Bailments have four characteristics: (1) the subject is personal property; (2) a transfer of temporary possession; (3) a transfer of temporary control; and (4) both parties intend return of the goods.

Personal Property
The subject of the bailment must be personal property. Real property, such as land or buildings, cannot be bailed. Real property is leased under different rules of law.

Transfer of Temporary Possession
Usually property is bailed by the person who has title to the goods, but property may be bailed by any person in possession. This includes the owner's agent or employee, a finder, or even a thief.

There are two ways to transfer possession and control of goods. In **actual bailments**, bailees receive and accept the goods themselves. When you rent a car, get behind the steering wheel, and drive off, you receive and accept the car in bailment.

Constructive bailment occurs when the bailee receives and accepts a symbol of the personal property. If you asked to borrow your neighbor's truck, and received and accepted the keys, you would be entering into a constructive bailment for the truck.

Transfer of Temporary Control
In order for a bailment to arise, both possession and control of the goods must shift from the bailor to the bailee. Disputes often arise over cars left in parking lots. Suppose a car owner drives onto a lot, parks the car, but keeps the key. The owner can later drive the car away without permission of an attendant. The owner gave up possession but not control. In this case there is no bailment. There *is* a bailment, however, if an attendant takes possession of the car and gives the owner a claim check that must be turned in to get the car back. In this situation both possession and control are given to the bailee.

It is possible for a person to have temporary control of another's personal property yet not have a bailment. This occurs with **custody**. A person hired to guard the paintings in an art museum has custody of the art but is not a bailee. The owners of the art do not give complete control of the art to the guard. They authorize the guard to watch over the goods, but the owners retain control.

Goods To Be Returned
Both bailor and bailee must intend that the goods be returned to the bailor. In some bailments, the bailor identifies another party to whom the goods must be delivered.

Usually the bailee must return the identical goods. The goods may be modified somewhat, as a result of agreed-upon use, repairs, processing, or aging. Also, some goods are fungible. **Fungible** means there is no difference between one unit of the goods and another. A gallon of 90-

A Question of ETHICS

Ed borrowed a power drill from his father, and ruined it by trying to drill into concrete. Ed then borrowed his neighbor's drill. But this time he didn't try to drill into concrete. He felt it would be irresponsible to ruin his neighbor's drill. Should Ed's relationship determine his duty or should the transaction of borrowing determine it?

octane gasoline is the same as, or fungible with, another gallon of 90-octane gasoline. When the subject of the bailment is fungible, the bailee need only return the same quantity as received, not the exact same unit of the goods.

HOW DOES A BAILMENT END?

WHAT'S YOUR VERDICT?

Ruden leased a heavy-duty pile driver from Max Power Controls for six months with the right to renew upon 30-days' notice. Three months later, Ruden was killed in an industrial accident.

Was the bailment ended?

The bailment ends when the time agreed upon by the parties has elapsed, when the agreed purpose has been achieved, or when the parties mutually agree to end it. If no termination time is stated, either party may end the bailment. Thus, the bailor might ask for return of the property. Or the bailee may no longer need the property and return it. If the bailed property is destroyed or damaged so badly that it is not fit for the intended purpose, the bailment ends.

Death, insanity, or bankruptcy of one party can end the relation when the bailee's duties cannot be performed by another, or the bailment is one that may be ended at will. Normally, however, if there is a contractual bailment for a fixed period, death or incapacity does not end the relation. The rights and duties of the deceased are transferred to the personal representative of the estate. This applies to Ruden's case in *What's Your Verdict?*

GOALS

- Identify types of bailments
- Identify the duties of bailees and bailors
- Describe how to modify a bailee's duty of care

BAILEE'S DUTY OF CARE

WHAT'S YOUR VERDICT?

Patricia borrowed her neighbor's small sailboat for the afternoon. While she was sailing, a strong wind ripped the sail.

What type of bailment was created? How does that affect Patricia's liability for the damage to the boat?

Most legal problems with bailments arise when something happens to the goods while they are in the possession of the bailee. The type of bailment determines the degree of care the bailee must exercise over the goods. As bailments benefit the bailees more, the bailees' duty of care increases so they must take better care of the bailed goods.

Levels of Care

In general, there are three levels of care: extraordinary, ordinary, and minimal. In a trial, the burden of showing that the required level of care has been met rests with the bailee.

Extraordinary care generally means the bailee will be strictly liable for any damage, loss, or injury to the goods. When goods are bailed with common carriers and hotels an **extraordinary bailment** arises. The duty of care is extraordinary. Thus a common carrier is strictly liable for injury to the bailed goods. The only time such a bailee is not liable is when the loss is caused by an act of war, unforeseeable acts of God, or acts of police.

When only one of the parties benefits from the bailment, a **gratuitous bailment** arises. When the party benefited is the bailee, there is a gratuitous bailment for the sole benefit of the bailee. This applies if you lend your calculator to a classmate without charge. The bailee's duty of care for this type of bailment is extraordinary care.

In *What's Your Verdict?* Patricia is a gratuitous bailee. The bailment is for her sole benefit, so she must exercise extraordinary care. She is liable for the damage to the boat. High winds are not unforeseeable acts of God. Damage caused by a tornado would have been considered an act of God. In that case, Patricia would not have been liable.

Ordinary care means that the bailee will be liable if *negligent* in some way. A **mutual-benefit bailment**, in which consideration is given and received by both bailor and bailee, invokes the duty of ordinary care. Assume that you left your car at a repair shop and paid $27.99 for an oil change. You would receive the benefit of the oil change, and the repair shop would receive the benefit of the $27.99. Mutual-benefit bailments result from contracts, whereas gratuitous bailments do not because there is no exchange of consideration.

Minimal care generally means that the bailee must not ignore, waste, or destroy the bailed property. Minimal care is called for with **involuntary bailments**, which arise without the

During a severe storm on a lake, a rowboat was torn loose from Compton's pier. The next morning, Sprague found the boat on his beach on the other side of the lake. As an involuntary bailee, Sprague is required to act with minimal care for the boat and in seeking the owner. Thus, he should probably tie the boat up so it will not float farther away. This duty would be violated if he simply pushed the boat back into the water.

consent of the bailee. This can happen, for example, when your neighbor's trash cans blow onto your property. For valuable property, the bailee must make a minimal effort to identify the owner. Involuntary bailments also arise when mail is delivered to the wrong addressee.

A bailment for the sole benefit of a bailor also calls for minimal care. This type of bailment would arise if your parents agree to care for a neighbor's house plants without

charge while the neighbor is on vacation. Your parents' duty of care in this case would be minimal.

Modification of Duty of Care

There are three common ways to modify the nature of the bailee's duty of care: (1) by legislation, (2) by contract, and (3) by disclaimer.

MODIFICATION BY LEGISLATION An industry may seek to avoid the duty of care established by the common law by lobbying for legislation with a state legislature or regulatory body. For example, under the common law, hotels are held to the standard of extraordinary care. In many states hotels have obtained laws eliminating this liability.

As common carriers, airlines would owe the duty of extraordinary care for passengers' luggage. However, the industry has persuaded the Federal Aviation Administration to adopt a regulation limiting liability to $750 per item of luggage. Laundries and dry cleaning establishments often have special legislation limiting their duty of care. On the other hand, legislatures may increase the duty or limit the ability of the industry to modify the duty of care.

MODIFICATION BY CONTRACT When the bailor and bailee negotiate a contract, they can usually modify the duty of care. Suppose General Motors negotiated with a transportation company to deliver cars to local auto dealers. The parties could agree in the contract that this bailment for mutual benefit would create an extraordinary duty of care for the transportation company. Or, they could agree that the duty would be minimal. The bailee cannot, however, be relieved of liability for willful or deliberate injury to the bailed property.

MODIFICATION BY DISCLAIMER Often merchants attempt to modify the duty of care with a disclaimer. A **disclaimer** is a sign, label, or warning reducing

the bailee's duty of care. Thus, a garage may have a sign on the wall stating that it is not liable for loss of items left in a car. A restaurant may have a sign indicating that it is not responsible for loss of coats left on coat racks. A parking lot might have a ticket with small print on it stating that it is not liable for any loss or damage to the car.

Usually disclaimers only become a part of the contract when the bailor is aware of the limitation before the purchase. So a limitation in small print on a claim check or parking ticket is insufficient notice, unless the bailor has read it or was specifically told about the limitation in advance. Courts often find disclaimers not enforceable.

Van Dyke Productions engages in commercial photography. It bought Kodak motion picture film for a project in Alaska. The film boxes contained a disclaimer saying that Kodak was not liable, except for replacing the film, for any "warranty or other liability of any kind." After shooting the film, Van Dyke sent it to the Eastman Kodak Company for processing. While processing the film, an employee of Kodak made a mistake and much of the film was damaged. Van Dyke sued Kodak. Because this was a bailment for mutual benefit, Kodak owed a duty of ordinary care. The negligence of the employee violated this duty. But the disclaimer attempted to modify Kodak's duty by eliminating the duty of care. The court interpreted the language of the disclaimer as not applying to negligence because that word was not used in the disclaimer.

goods for possible defects. Failure to inform the bailee of known or reasonably discoverable defects makes the bailor liable for any possible resulting injury.

Bailments for the Sole Benefit of Bailee

Friends or relatives often borrow equipment and other personal property from one another without charge. These transactions are gratuitous bailments, but they are for the sole benefit of the bailee.

For example, a friend might borrow a ladder or jewelry. The bailee-borrower may use the goods, but only as agreed. The bailor-lender is obligated to inform the bailee of known defects. The bailor who knows of a loose rung in a ladder, yet says nothing, may be liable for any resulting injuries suffered by the bailee.

BAILOR'S DUTY OF CARE CONCERNING PROPERTY CONDITION

WHAT'S YOUR VERDICT?

For a family outing, Hua rented a rubber raft from the River's Edge Rental Company. River's Edge was having a busy day and did not take time to check the raft for damaged spots and slow leaks before letting Hua take it. After rafting down a smooth section of river and seeing rapids ahead, Hua's family noticed their raft was losing air.

Will the River's Edge Rental Company be liable if Hua's family is injured because of the raft's condition?

The bailor's duty concerning the condition of the property depends upon the type of bailment.

Mutual-Benefit Bailments

In a mutual-benefit bailment, there is a bailor's duty to provide goods fit for the intended purpose. A bailor in a mutual-benefit bailment who fails to inform the bailee of defects which reasonably could be discovered is liable for any resulting injuries. Thus, River's Edge in *What's Your Verdict?* would be liable to Hua's family for any injuries resulting from the company's failure to find the damaged spots on the raft.

A bailee who has been told about or discovers a defect cannot collect damages if injured because of the

defect. The bailee is held to have assumed the risk. This could happen, for example, if a bailee drives a rented truck with defective brakes after being told of the dangerous condition.

Bailments for the Sole Benefit of Bailor

Suppose your friend goes on vacation and leaves her dog, house plants, and car with you. These are gratuitous bailments for the sole benefit of the bailor. Unless otherwise agreed, you may not use these things unless the use is necessary to preserve or maintain them.

In a bailment for the sole benefit of the bailor, before transferring possession the bailor should examine the

WHAT IS THE BAILEE'S DUTY TO RETURN THE GOODS?

WHAT'S YOUR VERDICT?

During dinner at the Vail Ski Lodge, Adam carelessly left his parabolic skis near a blazing fireplace in the main lounge. By the time he returned to the lounge, the heat had caused the edges to separate from the skis at several points. Adam took the skis to the Vail Ski Hut and had them repaired. Now he wants the skis for the coming weekend but doesn't have the cash to pay for the repair.

Must Vail Ski Hut give him the skis and simply bill him?

The bailee's duty to return the property compels the bailee to return the bailed property according to the terms of the bailment agreement. A bailee entitled to payment may exercise the **bailee's lien** and retain possession until paid. If payment is delayed unreasonably, the bailee may sell the property to recover the fee and related costs.

In *What's Your Verdict?* Vail Ski Hut has the right to keep the skis until paid and to sell them if not paid within a reasonable time.

THINK ABOUT LEGAL CONCEPTS

Answer the following questions about legal concepts.

1. The level of care a bailee must exercise over the goods is determined by __?__ .

2. When both parties benefit from a bailment, it is called a mutual-benefit bailment and the bailee's duty of care is ordinary. **True or False?**

3. When the bailment is only for the benefit of the bailor, the duty of care is minimal. **True or False?**

4. The bailee will be liable if negligent in some way with (a) **extraordinary care** (b) **minimal care** (c) **ordinary care** (d) **none of the above.**

5. Only one party benefits from a/an (a) **mutual-benefit bailment** (b) **gratuitous bailment** (c) **extraordinary bailment.**

6. In a (a) **gratuitous bailment** (b) **mutual-benefit bailment** there is no exchange of consideration.

THINK CRITICALLY ABOUT EVIDENCE

Study the following situations, answer the questions, then prepare arguments to support your answers.

7. During the fall harvest, most of the Roman Beauty apples picked at Scott's Orchard were immediately placed in the Kool-Tech Storage Co. warehouse. Scott paid a monthly fee for the storage, and the contract specified that the apples would be stored at temperatures between 40 and 55 degrees. When Scott removed some of the apples three months later, many had begun to rot because Kool-Tech had failed to keep the building at the proper temperature. Who is liable for this loss?

8. Cararro rented a car and, because it wasn't his, treated it harshly. He gunned the engine before engaging it in gear, drag raced, and intentionally burned a cigarette hole in the upholstery. When a friend asked why he did it, he said, "Since the car isn't mine, who cares? Besides, it's kind of fun. It makes me feel good, kind of powerful." Is Cararro acting ethically? Why or why not? Is Cararro liable for the damage? Why or why not?

9. Boyd borrowed a lawn edger from her neighbor Enbanks. The edger's circular blade was defective, but Enbanks did not know this. While Boyd was using the edger, the blade snapped. A piece of metal lodged in Boyd's eye, blinding it. Was Enbanks liable for the injury?

10. Widdington inherited an old 90-foot navy-patrol boat. She delivered it to Ol' Jon Silver's Shipyard, located near the oceanfront. Widdington contracted with Jon Silver for a conversion of the patrol boat into a houseboat for $130,000. After the work was completed, but before Widdington came to get her boat, a tidal wave destroyed the shop and all the boats in the immediate vicinity. Is Jon Silver liable for the loss of Widdington's boat? Or must Widdington pay the $130,000?

11. Buz asked his neighbor Hazel if he could borrow her chain saw. Hazel had a feeling that something was wrong with it, but she knew nothing concrete she could point to. She thought, "It doesn't matter. Buz will have to look out for himself." Hazel didn't say anything to Buz about her concern. The chain saw malfunctioned while Buz was cutting a log. The saw bucked back and hit Buz in the shoulder, making a large gash in his skin and sawing partway into his collar bone. Was Hazel legally liable for the injury?

12. Charles borrowed his roommate's laptop computer to complete an assignment for his business law class. After he finished the assignment, he tried to remove his floppy disk from the disk drive, but it was stuck. He then damaged the disk drive in trying to remove the disk. Who is the bailor in this situation? What type of bailment is this? Who is liable for repairing the computer?

G O A L S

● **List the most common types of bailments**
● **Describe the legal features of the most common types of bailments**

BAILMENT FOR TRANSPORT

WHAT'S YOUR VERDICT?

Starr Shippers, an interstate trucking company, just transported Morgan's large box of valuable tools to New York. Starr, the carrier, refuses to release the box until paid for its services. Morgan says he needs the tools in order to earn money to pay the charges. He demands credit.

Must Starr release the tools?

A **common carrier** agrees, for a fee, to transport goods for anyone who applies, provided the goods are lawful and fit for shipment. Although passengers may be transported by common carriers, only their baggage is governed by bailment law. In *What's Your Verdict?* the trucking company was a common carrier.

A common carrier has the right to

1. enforce reasonable rules and regulations for the conduct of its business (for example, it may enforce rules stating how goods must be packed)

2. charge an amount negotiated with the bailor or, if the carrier is regulated, charge the scheduled rate

3. charge **demurrage**, that is, a fee for use of the transportation vehicle when it is not loaded or unloaded at the agreed time

4. enforce a **carrier's lien**, that is, retain the goods until charges for transportation and incidental services are paid.

In *What's Your Verdict?* Starr would not be required to release the box of tools until Morgan has paid for not only the transportation but also any demurrage.

BAILMENT FOR HIRE

WHAT'S YOUR VERDICT?

Rosetta rented a sports utility vehicle from Avis for a week's trip with her children. Because they were having so much fun, she wired Avis and said she would take the vehicle for another week. This extended use was not authorized. On the way to return the vehicle, a drunk driver smashed into it. Rosetta was not at fault for the accident.

Is Rosetta liable to Avis?

A bailment for hire arises when the bailor, for a fee, provides personal property (such as a car, truck, tool, machine, or other equipment)

for use by the bailee. Under the common law the bailee is required to act with ordinary care. However, most rental contracts modify the duty of care making the bailee strictly liable for property damage.

Typically the rental companies ask the bailee to initial those parts of the contract which modify the duty of care. The bailee must abide by the contract, using the property only for the stated purposes and returning it at the agreed time. In *What's Your Verdict?* Rosetta's unauthorized use of the vehicle for the second week made her liable for the damages.

BAILMENT FOR SERVICES

WHAT'S YOUR VERDICT?

Systematics Electronics prepared computer files for its annual catalog and price list. It sent the files to the Bocca Press and Bindery for printing and binding into booklets. After the job had been done, a fire broke out in an adjacent building and spread to the Bocca plant. All the booklets were ruined by fire, smoke, and water.

Must Systematics pay for the job?

When a person delivers goods to be serviced, repaired, or made into a finished article, a bailment for services results. For example, the bailor may deliver wool cloth to a tailor to have a suit made. Or a bailor may deliver clothes to a dry cleaner to be laundered or a watch to a jeweler to be repaired.

As in *What's Your Verdict?* a bailor may send computer files to a printer to have booklets made. If the goods are damaged or destroyed, but the bailee has exercised ordinary care in their protection, the loss falls on the bailor who owns them. Moreover, the bailor must pay for any work done by the bailee before the accident. In *What's Your Verdict?* Systematics must pay for the job. Only if the fire was caused by Bocca's negligence or intentional wrongful act, like arson, would Bocca be liable.

BAILMENT FOR SALE

WHAT'S YOUR
VERDICT?

Werner owned a retail sporting goods store. A supplier, Irresistible Lures, offered Werner a counter card that displayed a new type of fishing lure. Werner agreed to display the card when the sales agent said, "You pay nothing and return any lures not sold. Just deduct 50 percent of each sale for yourself and send the balance to us."

Was Werner a bailee?

Goods may be sent on consignment by a manufacturer to a retailer. With **consignment**, ownership remains with the manufacturer or wholesaler (the bailor) until the goods are sold. Retailers who display and sell consigned goods (like Werner in *What's Your Verdict?*) are bailees.

Bailment also is created when a merchant sends goods "on approval" to a prospective buyer. In a **sale on approval** the prospective buyer may use the goods to decide whether to buy them. During this time the prospective buyer is a bailee of the goods.

Ownership shifts if the bailee agrees to buy the goods. At that point the bailment ends. If the bailee rejects the goods, they must be returned. This arrangement is common in merchandising books, cassettes, and compact disks.

THINK ABOUT LEGAL CONCEPTS

Answer the following questions about legal concepts.

1. In a consignment, the retailer is a bailee. **True or False?**

2. A common carrier does not have the right to retain possession of the goods until the charges for transportation and accompanying services are paid. **True or False?**

3. If goods involved in a bailment for services are damaged or destroyed, the loss always falls on the bailee. **True or False?**

4. The fees a common carrier receives for use of its vehicle in the event that it is not loaded or unloaded at the agreed time is called (a) **incidental charges** (b) **a carrier's lien** (c) **demurrage.**

5. If the prospective buyer may use the goods before deciding whether to purchase, the seller is making a ___?___.

Study the following situations, answer the questions, then prepare arguments to support your answers.

6. Hanson bought and contracted to have delivered a large industrial stamping machine weighing 11,000 pounds. When a common carrier truck arrived with the machine, it took Hanson a week to locate a crane that could lift the stamping machine off the truck. Is he liable for the rental value of the truck while it waited to be unloaded?

7. Shanhon wanted to ship a box containing an unstable chemical compound. He contacted Interstate Trucking, which ordinarily transported anyone's goods for a fee. Interstate refused to transport the box because the shipper thought the package was unsafe. Shanhon also had contacted the local railway office about traveling to the adjoining state. What type of carrier is Interstate Trucking? Was it acting lawfully in refusing to transport Shanhon's package? If Shanhon travels by rail, what type of carrier is the train? Would bailment law cover Shanhon and/or his baggage?

8. Mertz was responsible for a short-term project that involved sending a large mailing to potential customers. In order to prepare the mailing, Mertz rented a photocopier for a three-month period. What type of legal relationship was created between Mertz and the company that rented Mertz the machine? If the machine was damaged while Mertz was renting it, who would be responsible for the damages?

9. Wingate took her chair to a local shop, Just Like New, to be reupholstered. Just Like New finished the work on May 22. It notified Wingate that the chair was ready and placed the reupholstered chair in a locked storage room at the rear of its building. Wingate planned to pick up the chair May 23, but on the night of May 22, someone broke into the storage room and stole some items, including Wingate's chair. What relationship existed between Wingate and Just Like New? Who bears responsibility for the loss? Must Wingate pay for the work already performed by Just Like New?

10. NewMark Co. sent Breggler a postal meter with the understanding that Breggler could try it out for 60 days. If at the end of the 60 days Breggler wanted to keep the postal meter, she was to pay for it. If she was dissatisfied or just decided she did not want it, she was to return it to NewMark before the end of the 60-day period. What relationship was created between NewMark and Breggler during the 60-day period? Who owned the postal meter during the 60-day period?

For Bailees

1. Before you take possession of or use bailed goods, be sure you have adequate liability and property insurance coverage. You are usually required to pay if you damage or destroy the bailed property or injure someone with it.

2. If you have performed services on bailed goods, do not return them until you have been paid for your services or are satisfied that the bailor's credit is good.

3. When you find and take possession of something of value belonging to another person, you become a constructive bailee. Act reasonably in caring

PREVENT LEGAL DIFFICULTIES

for the property and seeking the true owner.

For Bailors

1. Although a bailee may be liable for willful or negligent conduct which damages your goods or injures third parties, it is still wise to carry appropriate property and liability insurance to cover possible losses.

2. Spell out the terms of the bailment contract in writing whenever practicable. Always get a receipt for goods transferred to a bailee.

3. If the bailee is to repair or service the goods, be as precise as practicable about prices and work to be done.

4. If you rent a car or other equipment that could be dangerous if in faulty condition, inspect it carefully and correct defects before delivering it to the bailee.

CHAPTER IN REVIEW

CONCEPTS IN BRIEF

1. In a bailment, the bailee has possession and control of personal property belonging to the bailor.

2. Every bailment has four characteristics: the subject is tangible personal property; the bailor transfers temporary possession to the bailee; the bailor transfers temporary control to the bailee; the goods must be returned to the bailor or to someone the bailor specifies.

3. A bailment may be terminated by agreement, an act of either party, destruction of the subject matter, or operation of law (such as by death of a party).

4. Bailments created for the benefit of both parties are mutual-benefit bailments. Bailments created for the benefit of only one party are gratuitous bailments. Mutual-benefit bailments arise from contracts because there is an exchange of consideration.

5. In a mutual-benefit bailment, the bailee must exercise ordinary care. In a gratuitous bailment for the sole benefit of the bailee, the bailee must exercise extraordinary care. In a gratuitous bailment for the sole benefit of the bailor, the bailee need exercise only minimal care.

6. In a mutual-benefit bailment, the bailor is liable for damages caused by known or reasonably discoverable defects in the property unless the bailee has specifically been informed of such defects.

7. Common types of mutual-benefit bailments are those for transport, for hire, for services, and for sale.

YOUR LEGAL VOCABULARY

Match each statement with the term that it best defines. Some terms may not be used.

1. Bailment in which the bailee can try out the goods before buying them

2. Duty of care when the bailment is involuntary

3. Bailment in which the bailee receives and accepts a symbol of the personal property rather than the property itself

4. Right of a bailee to hold goods until paid

5. One who undertakes, for hire, to transport goods or passengers for anyone who applies

6. Fee for delay by party shipping goods in loading or by party receiving goods in unloading

7. Control of another's personal property, under the owner's direction

8. Bailment in which one party receives no benefit

9. Bailee's duty of care when the bailment is for the sole benefit of the bailee

10. Party who gives up temporary possession and control of personal property

11. Bailment in which the bailee is liable for all damage, loss, or injury, such as a bailment with a hotel or a common carrier

12. Sign, label, or warning reducing the bailee's duty of care

actual bailment
bailee
bailee's lien
bailment
bailor
carrier's lien
common carrier
consignment
constructive bailment
custody
demurrage
disclaimer
extraordinary bailment
extraordinary care
fungible goods
gratuitous bailment
involuntary bailment
minimal care
mutual-benefit
   bailment
ordinary care
sale on approval

13. Create a factual scenario where property is mislaid.

14. Create a factual scenario where property is lost.

15. Create a factual scenario where the bailee's duty of care is ordinary care.

16. Create a factual scenario where the bailee's duty of care is extraordinary care.

WRITE ABOUT LEGAL CONCEPTS

17. Identify an object in your classroom. Next write a five-line dialogue where you ask the teacher for permission to take the item home. In the dialogue describe the duty of care that applies to this bailment.

18. **HOT DEBATE** Write a letter from Janice to the restaurant demanding to be reimbursed for the coat. Write a letter from the restaurant to Janice telling her why they will not reimburse her.

THINK CRITICALLY ABOUT EVIDENCE

Study the following situations, answer the questions, then prepare arguments to support your answers.

19. Babbitt rented a paint-spraying outfit from Baron. The equipment was in good working condition, and Babbitt knew how to use it properly. However, when Babbitt was shifting position between two buildings, she carelessly sprayed the neighbor's building and the top of the neighbor's car parked below. The neighbor sued Baron. Is Baron liable?

20. Bortez, a sales representative, had a breakfast appointment with a prospective buyer. They were to meet in the restaurant of the Grand Prix Hotel. Bortez left his attaché case, which contained almost $30,000 worth of sample watches, with the clerk in the hotel checkroom. The clerk gave him a receipt that stated in fine print: "Not liable for loss or damage from any cause beyond a maximum of $100." Bortez, in a hurry, stuffed the stub into his pocket without reading it. The clerk left his post briefly to go to the restroom. When he returned, the case was gone. Is the Grand Prix liable? If so, for how much?

21. Burg customized and sold new vans and serviced old ones. Jake and Jayne Slinker were trusted employees who had been carefully hired and trained and had worked for Burg for ten years. Jake did metalworking and woodworking; Jayne did upholstering. One holiday weekend, the Slinkers and an accomplice stole three vans and disappeared. The first van belonged to Adams, who had brought it in to have the engine tuned. The second van belonged to Yates, a friend who had asked Burg if he could leave the van on the lot with a "For Sale" sign. Burg had agreed and did not charge Yates. The third van was a very valuable vehicle, built by Burg, and sold to Mox. Mox had loaned the van to Burg, free, for display in the latter's exhibit at a Civic Auditorium show scheduled for the following week. What is Burg's liability, if any, to Adams? to Yates? to Mox?

22. Nettles has 500 skeins of navy blue yarn stored at South Side Warehouse, which also stores yarn for other customers. When Nettles returns to pick up the yarn, must South Side give him exactly the same skeins that he left, or can it give Nettles any 500 skeins of navy blue yarn?

23. Plaintiff Wall drove his car into a self-parking lot at O'Hare Airport in Chicago. He entered through an automatic gate and received a ticket bearing the date and time of arrival. He parked, locked the car, and left with the keys. Normally, when ready to depart, he would walk to his car and, using his keys, would enter the car and drive it to the exit. There an attendant would take the ticket and compute and collect the parking fee. This time his car had been stolen. He sued the defendant, Airport Parking Company of Chicago, for damages. Is the defendant liable? (*Wall v. Airport Parking Company of Chicago*, 244 N.E.2d 190, 41 Ill. 2d 506)

24. Mrs. Carter took her fur coat to Reichlin Furriers to be cleaned and stored. She was given a receipt for the coat. On the front of the receipt an employee had written the number "100." On the back of the receipt, the words, "the . . . amount recoverable for loss or damage to this article shall not exceed . . . the depositor's valuation appearing in this receipt. . ." Also on the front of the receipt was a place for the customer's signature, but Mrs. Carter had not signed it. The coat was lost. Is Reichlin liable for its market value of $450 or only for the $100? (*Carter v. Reichlin Furriers*, 386 A.2d 648)

25. A student enrolled in flight school. While 900 feet above the ground on a practice flight in the school's aircraft, the student discovered that the rudder was stuck. As a result of the stuck rudder, the plane crashed into the ground, and the student was seriously injured. Is the school liable to the student for the injury? (*Aircraft Sales and Service v. Gannt*, 52 A.2d 388)

26. Loden shipped a quantity of perishable cucumbers from Yuma, Arizona, to Los Angeles via the Southern Pacific Company Railroad. However, the carrier failed to deliver the goods within the ordinary and usual time. On January 25, a railroad inspector was sent out to check the track structures. The inspector discovered that heavy rainfall had damaged two bridges. Repairs were started on January 26, and the tracks were joined on January 28. The making of these repairs further delayed the shipment of Loden's cucumbers. When the cucumbers finally arrived in Los Angeles on January 29, they were spoiled. Loden sued the railroad for $10,000 in damages. Which party is liable for the damages? (*Southern Pacific Company v. Loden*, 19 Ariz. App. 460, 508 P.2d 347)

27. Armored Car Service, Inc. had its employees pick up at the Miami Springs Junior High School a locked money bag containing $1,511.25. The money was supposed to be deposited in the proper cafeteria fund account at a certain bank. However, the bag was mistakenly delivered to the First National Bank of Miami. First National provided a receipt for the bag but made no record of the bag's handling or disposition. Presumably, the bag was stolen. Armored Car Service indemnified the high school and now seeks to recover its loss from First National. (a) What kind of bailment was created by the mistake? (b) Is the First National Bank of Miami liable as bailee? (*Armored Car Service, Inc. v. First National Bank of Miami*, 114 So. 2d 431)

28. A woman parked in a parking lot. An attendant asked her to leave her keys in the car. The car was stolen and was later recovered but it had been damaged. Must the parking lot company be held liable? (*Agricultural Insurance Co. v. Constantine*, 58 N.E.2d 658, Ohio)

29. Allen left his car with the defendant parking lot. Allen's golf clubs were in the trunk of the car but Allen did not tell defendant of their presence. The car was stolen and later recovered but the golf clubs were missing. Is the defendant liable for the golf clubs? (*Allen v. Houserman*, 250 A.2d 389, Del.)

30. Singer owned air conditioning units. He stored them in Stoda's warehouses. A fire destroyed the air conditioners. Singer sued and showed that Stoda knew the sprinkler system in the warehouse did not operate, the fire alarm would not automatically activate, and no security guards were present. Is Stoda liable? (*Singer Company v. Stoda Corporation*, 436 N.Y.S.2d 508, N.Y.)

31. The plaintiff delivered his show horse (a registered Tennessee Walking mare) to the defendant's stables for breeding. Plaintiff said the mare was skittish and would kick. The defendant placed the mare in a stall next to a stall which held defendant's stallion. After she was left unattended for 18 minutes, the mare was found with a broken leg and had to be destroyed. No one knew how the injury occurred. Is the defendant liable? (*David v. Lose*, 218 N.E.2d 442, Ohio)

Numismatic Enterprises v. Hyatt Corp.
797 F. Supp. 687

FACTS Mark Teller was a partner with Norman Applebaum in Numismatic Enterprises. The business bought and sold rare coins. The partners traveled to Indianapolis, Indiana, for a convention of coin dealers. They brought a large black briefcase with a double lock on it containing rare coins worth more than $300,000.

When they arrived at the Hyatt Regency Hotel, an employee named Ms. Atkinson took them to the safe-deposit room and assigned them a box. Atkinson gave them one of the two keys required to open the box. When this occurred, Teller told Atkinson that he was with the coin show. Then Teller signed a Safe Deposit Record form and Atkinson signed as a witness.

Later, when Teller opened the safe deposit box to retrieve the coins, the box was empty. The partners sued, claiming that Hyatt had breached its duty as a bailee.

OPINION The Indiana statute provides: "A hotel, apartment hotel, or inn, or the proprietor or manager thereof, shall not be liable for the loss of or damage to any merchandise samples or merchandise for sale, whether such loss or damage is occasioned by the negligence of such proprietor or manager or his agents or otherwise, unless the guest or other owner shall have given prior written notice of having brought such merchandise into the hotel and of the value thereof, the receipt of such notice shall have been acknowledged in writing by the proprietor, manager or other agent and in no event shall liability exceed the sum of four hundred dollars ($400.00) unless the manager or proprietor of such hotel, apartment hotel or inn shall have contracted in writing to assume a greater liability."

In the present case, there does not appear to be any dispute that the plaintiffs failed to comply with the statute's requirements. Although it might be argued that the hotel had sufficient notice under the statute as a result of its employee's observation of the coins and her conversation with the plaintiff.

The court found persuasive the defendant's argument that the Safe Deposit Record cannot be construed as sufficient notice under the Indiana Innkeeper's statute. It did not inform the Hyatt Regency of the fact that the plaintiffs were bringing their merchandise into the hotel or the estimated value thereof. Although the Hyatt Regency's agent (Atkinson) signed the Safe Deposit Record, thereby witnessing the Plaintiff's execution of the form (and at least implicitly, the fact that Teller had read the "Rules and Regulations Governing Safe Deposit Boxes"), her signature hardly constitutes a written acknowledgment that the Hotel had received sufficient notice under the statute. Even if Ms. Atkinson's signature could somehow be interpreted as the equivalent of a written acknowledgment that plaintiff Teller was bringing merchandise into the Hotel (on the theory that Teller provided Atkinson and her employer with "notice" of that fact when he (1) told her he was with the Coin Show, and (2) proceeded to place the partnership inventory in the safe deposit box while in her presence), it would nevertheless fail to constitute a valid acknowledgement. Under the statute, an innkeeper's agent must acknowledge notice which includes a declaration of the value of the guest's merchandise. The defendant shall accordingly take nothing.

PRACTICE JUDGING

1. If there were not a special statute in Indiana, what duty of care would Hyatt owe?

2. How would this case have been decided if there were not a special statute for innkeepers in Indiana?

3. Which do you think is more fair, this innkeeper's statute or the bailee's usual duty?

LESSONS

HOT DEBATE

The Bryants owned a condominium and were required to pay property tax on both the real and personal property. The tax rate on the real property was 1 percent of its value. The rate for personal property was 4 percent. The Bryants owned a digital TV system with surround sound which was wired into each room, with speakers concealed in the walls. The receiver, tuner, and amplifier were permanently built into a closet which had been remodeled to accommodate the equipment.

Where Do You Stand?

1. Why should the stereo be taxed at 1 percent as real property?

2. Why should the stereo be treated as personal property and taxed at 4 percent?

REAL PROPERTY RIGHTS

WHAT'S YOUR VERDICT?

The limb of an apple tree growing on Gilbert's land extended over the boundary onto Oster's lot. One day Gilbert discovered that Oster had cut the limb off at the point where it crossed the boundary.

Did Oster act legally?

Realty or **real property** includes land, things permanently attached to land, and certain rights to use the land of others.

Surface Rights

The basic physical element of realty is **land**. The buyer of real property usually purchases the surface rights or the right to occupy the surface of a piece of land.

Right to Air Space

The air space above the surface of the land is also part of the realty. Ownership of that space is called the *right to air space*. The ownership power, except for the right to exclude aircraft from flying over, extends to the upper atmosphere.

If the branch of a neighbor's tree grows into your air space (as Gilbert's tree did in *What's Your Verdict?*), you have the right to force its removal. This is seldom done because both property owners generally benefit from the vegetation. However, in *What's Your Verdict?* Oster did act legally. While surface rights and the right to air space are usually owned

by the same party, occasionally one party owns the surface rights and another owns the right to the air space.

IN THIS CASE

New York City sold the air space over certain highways to developers. They then built structures, such as office buildings, over the highways. The city then owned the surface rights and the developers owned the air space.

Mineral Rights

Realty also includes the earth beneath the surface. The right to dig or mine that earth is called a **mineral right**. In theory, ownership of mineral rights extends down from the land surface to the center of the earth.

SOLID MINERALS Ownership of solid minerals such as coal, iron ore, cop-

per ore, nickel, and uranium usually extends downward from the perimeter of a surface parcel. The owner of the mineral right has the power to remove any mineral located within that area.

FLUIDS Ownership of fluids such as oil (a liquid) and natural gas (a vapor) also usually extends downward from a surface area. However, the *doctrine of capture* grants ownership of these fluid minerals to the party who extracts (or captures) them. Thus, if a person drilled an oil well on a quarter-acre lot and began pumping from a pool of oil that extended beneath a 25-acre area, all the oil could be removed under the doctrine of capture. This is so even though the oil was originally another's property and, because of the pumping, it flowed from one location to another. Note that the well shaft itself may not extend into realty owned by others.

Water Rights

Water on the surface or under the ground is a part of the realty. Control of that water is called a **water right**. Control of water rights is governed by individual states. States use two systems for regulating the use of water. The major system is the *riparian rights system*. Riparian rights allow those who own land *abutting* a body of water to make use of it. Thus, ownership of the adjoining land (or the land beneath the water) carries with it the right to use the water.

The other system, used by a minority of states, is called the *prior appropriation system*. Prior appropriation does not connect the right to use the water with the adjoining land. Rather, it grants the first party to use the water priority in subsequent years over other potential users. The amount of the initial use determines the amount of water that may be used in later years.

REAL VS. PERSONAL PROPERTY

WHAT'S YOUR VERDICT?

Vada owns a mobile home. She claims that she can change the home into real property by removing its tires, placing it on a concrete foundation, and connecting it to the city water and sewer system.

Is Vada correct?

The ability to distinguish between real and personal property is critical to understanding many transactions. Different bodies of law govern transfers of real and personal property. The Uniform Commercial Code generally governs the sale of personal property. The sale of realty is governed by the common law of contracts.

Tax treatment of real and personal property varies greatly. Property tax rates established by local counties are different for real and personal property. Income tax treatment of real and personal property varies in important ways, too.

The usual test for distinguishing real and personal property is that real property is land and immovable things attached to the land. In contrast, personal property is a movable thing. Sometimes real and personal property are very closely connected—for example, a stove (perhaps personal) and a house (real). In these situations the law uses finer tests than the general test of mobility. These are the tests of attachment, adaptation, and intention.

Attachment

In most cases the *permanency of the attachment* to realty will determine whether property is real or personal.

STRUCTURES Structures or buildings are part of the real property if they are permanently attached to the land. Classrooms in a high school are part of the realty. However, a house trailer sitting on wheels used as a temporary classroom is usually considered personal property. If the wheels of the house trailer were removed and it were connected to a permanent foundation, it would be realty.

Vada's mobile home in *What's Your Verdict?* will be legally classified as real property after she removes the tires, places it on a concrete foundation, and installs permanent plumbing. A small garden shed resting on top of the ground would be personalty. If the garden shed were bolted to a cement pad, it would probably be realty.

FIXTURES When personal property is permanently attached to realty it is called a **fixture** and treated as real property. Thus, personal property like stoves and dishwashers become a part of the realty if they are permanently attached. In most cases a free-standing stove is personalty, but a built-in stove is realty.

CROPS Permanency of attachment is also the test for classifying crops. When a crop is harvested annually, as is corn, then it is treated as personal property even while in the ground. It is personal because the law views it as not *permanently* attached to the land. On the other hand, if the crops are *infrequently harvested*—less often than once a year—as are Christmas trees, they are a part of the realty until severed from the ground. Grapevines and rose bushes would be real property. Grapes and roses raised would be personal property if harvested at least once a year.

A contract to sell growing crops separately from the land is a contract for the sale of goods. The sale is governed by the UCC. It doesn't matter if the crops sold are harvested by the buyer or the seller.

Adaptation

This test will cause certain items to be classified as realty because they are *truly essential to the functioning of realty.* Thus a toilet in a residence is usually attached with about the same degree of permanency as a free-standing stove (personalty). But since the toilet is more essential to the functioning of the residence, it is considered adapted to it and is treated as realty. Similarly, the key to the front door is treated as real property in some states under the doctrine of adaptation.

Intention

Sometimes parties reach agreements about how property is to be classified. For example, a landlord and a tenant might agree that the dishwasher installed by the tenant could be removed at the end of the lease period. This would be an indication of an intention to treat the property as personal. Without this display of intention, the dishwasher would, if permanently attached, become realty and, therefore, the property of the landlord at the end of the lease.

Items of personal property attached to realty by business tenants are called **trade fixtures**. Unlike other fixtures, trade fixtures are treated as personalty because they are usually not intended to be permanent. Thus if a baker permanently attaches ovens to a rented bakery shop, they would still be treated as personalty because the landlord and tenant probably intended that they should be removed at the end of the lease period.

THINK ABOUT LEGAL CONCEPTS

Answer the following questions about legal concepts.

1. Land is the only component of real estate. **True or False?**

2. The owner of realty generally owns **(a) the land (b) minerals under the surface (c) space above the land (d) all of the above.**

3. The water in a river is treated by the law as real property. **True or False?**

4. A contract to sell crops growing in the ground is a contract for the sale of **(a) goods (b) realty (c) goods, if severed by seller (d) realty, if severed by buyer.**

5. Adaptation requires that things be permanently attached to realty before they can be treated as real property. **True or False?**

6. Parties may agree to treat something as personal property even though the law classifies it as real property. **True or False?**

THINK CRITICALLY ABOUT EVIDENCE

Study the following situations, answer the questions, then prepare arguments to support your answers.

7. Clarence sold Delbert a parcel of land on which there was a house, a barn, unharvested crops, and a house trailer. The house trailer was on a cement foundation, connected to the city electricity line and plumbed into the water and sewer systems. Delbert protested when Clarence removed the trailer, and Delbert sues to recover it. Who should prevail, Clarence or Delbert?

8. Jerry's mother and father entered into a contract for the purchase of a house. The house contained many desirable features, such as a built-in dishwasher, wall paintings, throw rugs, and a built-in workbench in the garage. The contract Jerry's parents signed stated that they had purchased only the "real property." Which items stay with the house and which can the sellers take with them?

9. Sam inherited a farm from his mother. Forty years later a neighbor discovered oil. Sam wonders who would be the owner of the oil under his neighbor's property. He also wonders if there is any oil under his property and if there is, who most likely owns it. Who owns the oil under the neighbor's land, and who would own the oil under Sam's land?

10. Consiglio owned a building in West Yarmouth, Massachusetts. He rented it to Carey for summer seasons. Carey operated a restaurant in the building and paid rent of $4,500 to $8,500 per month. After Consiglio and Carey discussed the possibility of Carey's purchasing the building, Consiglio raised the rent to $35,000 per month in an attempt to encourage Carey to conclude the purchase. Instead of purchasing, Carey prepared to move to another nearby building. Consiglio then brought suit to prevent Carey from removing certain items of restaurant equipment Carey installed. Consiglio claimed the items were real property. The equipment in question includes a walk-in freezer, a compressor supplying the cold air to the freezer, two air conditioners, and a bar. The air conditioners were installed in two of the three window casings. They were large units, and their installation necessitated removal of the sash from each casing. The freezer, 12-feet high, and too high to be brought into the building, was installed at the back wall of the building on an insulated concrete slab. A hole was cut in the rear wall of the building to provide access to the freezer door. The freezer is portable. The compressor is located outside the building and is attached only to the freezer. Will the injunction be granted to stop Carey from removing these items? If Carey owned the building, would these items be treated as real or personal? (*Consiglio v. Carey*, 421 N.E.2d 1257)

G O A L S

● Describe the major estates in land
● Identify the legal names of parties involved in deeding realty
● Describe the processes for transferring ownership of land

MAJOR ESTATES IN LAND

WHAT'S YOUR VERDICT?

Susan gave her daughter Emily a deed to a five-acre lot next to her home with the hope that Emily would live there. In the deed, Susan wrote that the property was being deeded on the condition that Emily not keep any livestock on the property. Emily did build a home on the property, but she also built a stable and kept horses there.

Will Emily lose ownership of the realty because of the horses?

Ownership of realty is usually acquired by purchase, gift, or inheritance. But everyone does not receive the same *powers of ownership*. The powers of ownership are defined by the estate in land that the new owner receives. Each **estate** is comprised of a certain bundle of ownership rights. The words used in the deed, will, or lease determine which estate is transferred. The party who gives up ownership powers is called the *grantor*. The party who receives ownership powers is called the *grantee*. When an estate is transferred from a grantor to a grantee by deed, the transaction is called a **conveyance**.

One parcel of land usually supports only a single estate. For example, most owner-occupied homes involve just one estate. Occasionally, however, two or more estates exist in the same parcel. Thus both the landlord and the tenant own estates in a rented apartment. The tenant's ownership rights include the right to

occupy (called the *right of possession*) the property. The landlord's ownership rights include the powers to collect the rent and regain possession at the end of the lease.

When more than one estate exists in a single parcel, the respective owners each owns a *separate* estate with *separate* powers of ownership. This contrasts with *co-ownership* where two people own *together* the same single estate. The following paragraphs discuss the powers of ownership of the major estates in land.

Fee Simple Absolute

A **fee simple absolute** is the estate with *all* the ownership rights. The owner of this estate exercises all the power allowed by law. If this estate is present, there can be no other estate in the same land. Almost all buyers of homes and farms and commercial property purchase the fee simple absolute estate.

Conditional Estates

Conditional estates make the ownership conditional on some act or event. For example, ownership may exist only "so long as no alcoholic beverages are served on the premises." The owner of this conditional estate has the right of possession. But if beer were served, ownership would shift from the owner of the conditional estate to the one who conditionally conveyed the property. Similarly, if a deed made ownership conditioned on not having horses on the property, ownership of the realty would be lost by violating that condition. Thus, in *What's Your Verdict?* Emily would lose ownership of the five-acre lot.

Whenever there is an estate other than fee simple absolute, there must be a second corresponding estate. In the conditional estates, the second estate is made up of the ownership

---

CULTURAL DIVERSITY IN LAW

Honduras

Foreign Land Ownership

Honduras, a country in Central America, restricts foreigners from owning land there. The National Security provisions of the Honduran constitution prohibit non-Hondurans from owning land within 40 kilometers of Honduran borders. The Honduran Agrarian Reform law limits the amount of farmland a foreign company or individual can own.

power retained by the grantor of the conditional estate. This nonpossessory estate is called a *future interest*.

Life Estates

A life estate is ownership only for the length of a life. The owner of a life estate has the right of possession and exercises all the ownership powers except the right to permanently dispose of the property. The length of the ownership period is generally measured by the life of the holder of the life estate. For example, a husband might convey his home "to my wife Julia, for life." Julia would own the home only for her lifetime. She could not transfer the property by will upon her death. Upon Julia's death, the property would go back to her husband, or to whomever he specified.

Nonfreehold Estates

Nonfreehold estates, sometimes called *tenancies*, involve ownership for a limited period of time. Tenants who are renting real property own nonfreehold estates. The length of ownership is specified in a lease, indicated by the payment period, or lasts only as long as the landlord desires.

TRANSFER OF OWNERSHIP

WHAT'S YOUR VERDICT?

Eaton, a land developer, wanted to buy a full square block along Michigan Avenue in downtown Chicago as the site for a new hotel-office-store complex. The property was owned by twelve different individuals and corporations, some of whom refused to sell. Eaton asked the city government to use its power of eminent domain to acquire the entire block and then to transfer the block to her. Eaton claimed this was justified because the public desperately needed the new complex. She also said construction would provide many jobs, and the neighborhood would be improved. Eaton said she would pay fair market value for the property.

Could the city comply with Eaton's request?

The principal ways of transferring ownership of real property are by deed as evidence of a sale, by gift, or by inheritance. Ownership can also be transferred by adverse possession, by dedication, and by eminent domain.

Deed

A deed is the legal document used to transfer ownership of real property. The two major types of deeds used to convey realty are the quitclaim deed and the warranty deed. The *quitclaim deed* transfers any interest the grantor may have in the real property, but doesn't guarantee that the grantor owns anything or that the grantee receives anything. A grantee has no legal claim against the grantor based on the quitclaim deed. The *warranty deed*, however, protects the grantee by providing several enforceable grantor's warranties. The principal warranties include the following:

- The grantor has the legal ability to transfer the realty described by the deed.

- There are no undisclosed claims or encumbrances (for example, liens, mortgages, or overdue taxes) against the property.

- The grantee shall have quiet enjoyment of the property (no one with superior title will disturb the grantee's possession).

Inheritance

Ownership of real property may be transferred through a will. If owners die without a will (that is, die *intestate*), then all their property, including their realty, will be distributed as required by state statutes.

Adverse Possession

In some situations, a person who publicly occupies another's land for a number of years may be treated by the law as the new owner of the realty. Suppose you bought a

600-acre farm and the legal description of the boundary included 10 adjoining acres that belonged to an absentee neighbor. If you fenced your farm and included the 10 acres, or otherwise occupied this land for the statutory period, you could become its owner. This is because of the doctrine of adverse possession.

Adverse possession occurs when you adversely and exclusively possess in an open and notorious way the land of another private person. Possession must be continuous for the statutory period of 5 to 21 years, depending on state law.

Adverse means that the occupation is without the consent of the owner. If an owner said you could occupy the land, either for rent or without charge, you could not become an adverse possessor. *Open and notorious* means that the occupation must be visible to the public, including the owners, upon inspection. Erecting fences, planting crops, building barns, and grazing cattle constitute open and notorious occupation. *Continuously* means that the occupation is uninterrupted. If a couple occupied your land for two years, then moved away, then returned two years later and occupied it for another six years, they would *not* satisfy a statutory requirement that the adverse possession occur for seven years.

Many states require the payment of property taxes on the occupied land before adverse possession can be asserted. Some states also require that adverse possessors have a legal basis for concluding that they own the property.

Dedication or Eminent Domain

Dedication typically involves giving real property to the government, such as a city, for use as a park or roadway. As with any other gift, the dedication is effective only if the government accepts the property.

In contrast with dedication, **eminent domain** is the power of the government to take private property for public use in exchange for the fair market price. If the owner is unwilling to sell at a price that the government thinks is fair, the government initiates a condemnation proceeding.

A *condemnation proceeding* is a hearing to determine fair compensation for the owner and acquire ownership for the government. If not satisfied with the price offered, the owner may demand a trial by jury to set a just price.

Property taken under eminent domain must be for a public use, such as for highways, airports, parks, or schools. Privately owned railroads and utilities may also exercise this power for such essentials as land for tracks and switching yards and for telephone and electric lines. Eminent domain may not be used for other private purposes even though the public may benefit and a fair price is offered. Thus, in the *What's Your Verdict?* the city would not comply with Eaton's request.

A Question of ETHICS ?

Governments have the constitutional power to condemn and rezone property. Both of these activities bring the needs of society into conflict with the interests of individual landowners. Do you think a reasonable balance should exist between private interests and the public good? Can you think of situations where this process would produce an unjust result?

Answer the following questions about legal concepts.

1. An estate is a particular bundle of legal rights in real property. **True or False?**

2. Which of the following statements is true? **(a) A landlord and tenant own separate estates in the same parcel of property. (b) The landlord and tenant are co-owners.**

3. The length of a life estate is usually measured by the life of the grantor. **True or False?**

4. Which of the following is the most common and greatest estate? **(a) conditional estate (b) life estate (c) nonfreehold estate (d) fee simple absolute**

5. The ___?___ deed provides the most protection to grantees.

6. Adverse possession can occur in secret. **True or False?**

7. Which of the following does not have the right of possession? **(a) fee simple absolute (b) conditional estates (c) future interests**

8. A quitclaim deed guarantees that the grantor receives what is described in the deed. **True or False?**

9. Taking by eminent domain can only occur when there is a legitimate public purpose for the taking. **True or False?**

Study the following situations, answer the questions, then prepare arguments to support your answers.

10. Atushi conveyed a life estate for his lifetime to his niece, Tomomi, with a quitclaim deed. Three years later Atushi died. What estate is owned by Tomomi after Atushi's death?

11. With a warranty deed, Anistasio conveyed a life estate to his niece, Terresa, for her lifetime. Six months later Terresa died. What estate did Anistasio own during Terresa's lifetime? After Terresa's death?

12. Sally bought a 236-acre farm for more than $1 million. She received a warranty deed. The deed contained language that made ownership conditional on the owner's not being Jewish. At the time she bought the property, Sally was a Methodist. Later, she fell in love with a Jewish man and converted to Judaism. What estate does Sally own?

13. Juan bought a farm and took title with a warranty deed. He then built a fence around the farm. He misjudged the boundary so that his fence ran 25 feet inside the property of his neighbor Swensen. The fence remained in place for 22 years and Juan paid taxes on all the enclosed realty. Then Swensen died without a will. The statutes of his state specified his brother, Phil, would receive his real property in the event Swenson died without a will. Phil had a surveyor check the boundary of the farm and this identified the misplaced fence. Phil then hired a bulldozer operator to level the fence. Juan obtained an injunction to halt the leveling and filed suit asking a court to determine who owns the disputed land. Who will prevail, Juan or Phil?

14. Smith owned a home in a suburban development and had been trying to sell it for over a year. Alex expressed interest in purchasing the property and the parties reached an agreement on the purchase price. They executed a contract that contained a legal description of all the terms of the sale. This agreement only referred to a sale of the realty, and nothing was ever communicated between the parties about any of the personal property. Smith executed a warranty deed conveying fee simple absolute to Alex. At that point the parties realized that they had transferred title only to the realty, and they were uncertain about the legal status of many of the items in the home. These items included valuable throw rugs; drapes; a workbench bolted to the studs in the garage; a built-in dishwasher; a washer-dryer combination in the laundry room; a fireplace screen bolted to the stone fireplace; a matching fireplace set consisting of a shovel, tongs, and broom; garden hoses; and a garden shed resting on 2 × 4s in the back yard. Which of these items belong to Smith and which belong to Alex?

GOALS

● Describe and distinguish licenses and easements
● Describe when a restrictive covenant binds buyers
● Distinguish between valid and invalid zoning
● Describe the duties owners owe to persons injured on their realty

LICENSES AND EASEMENTS

WHAT'S YOUR VERDICT?

A friend bought Isabel a ticket to her favorite movie. Isabel had seen it nine times before and was bored during parts. To entertain herself, Isabel started reciting the lines as they were spoken by the actors. Those sitting near her complained to the manager of the theater.

Can the theater eject Isabel?

Two important rights that others have in your land are licenses and easements.

Licenses

Someone who owns a fee simple estate in land controls all the ownership rights associated with that land. Frequently an owner will give some right in the land to another. For example, a theater owner may grant someone the right to sit through one showing of a film. This kind of temporary, oral right to come upon the land of another is called a license.

A *license* is a temporary, revocable right to some limited use of another's land. It is personal, nontransferable, not inheritable, and not an estate in land. Stores grant implied licenses to their customers to enter the store to shop for goods. Because oral licenses are revocable, the theater patron (like Isabel in *What's Your Verdict?*) would become a trespasser upon failure to leave immediately when asked.

Easements

Irrevocable rights to some limited use of another's land are usually called **easements**. In contrast with licenses, easements are generally given for substantial periods of time—for example, for five years, fifty years, or forever. To comply with the statute of frauds, easements should be in writing. Easements may be granted to allow a neighbor to drive across your land, for a utility company to bury a sewer pipe or hang power lines, or to make any other use that does not constitute exclusive possession. Easements may be appurtenant, in gross, by necessity, or by prescription.

EASEMENT APPURTENANT When easements are given to neighboring landowners and the easement benefits the neighbor's land, then it is called an *easement appurtenant*. Appurtenant means attached to the land. Thus an easement to drive farm equipment across a neighbor's land in order to farm an otherwise inaccessible parcel would be an easement appurtenant.

Easements for access roads or water ditches are easements appurtenant. These easements are generally transferred when the land benefitted by the easement is sold.

EASEMENTS IN GROSS Easements that do not benefit neighboring land, but benefit a person or business, such as easements for access given to a nonneighbor, or for telephone lines and poles, are called *easements in gross*. The person benefitted generally cannot transfer his or her rights.

EASEMENT BY NECESSITY An owner may sell part of her property, and the buyer can only gain access by crossing the seller's property. If nothing has been stated about an easement, the law will assume the parties intended the buyer could cross the property of the seller. An *easement by necessity* is created in such a case.

EASEMENT BY PRESCRIPTION If someone makes systematic use of your property for a long period of time, typically 15 to 21 years, then the law will acknowledge an *easement by prescription* arising from the use.

RESTRICTIVE COVENANTS AND ZONING ORDINANCES

WHAT'S YOUR VERDICT?

Lindsay purchased two acres from Glenn. In writing Lindsay promised he would not buy a pickup truck during the time he owned the land.

Will this restrictive covenant bind Lindsay and future purchasers of the land?

Many times when you buy property, there are restrictions on how you can use the property. These restrictions can come in the form of restrictive covenants or zoning ordinances.

Restrictive Covenants

A **restrictive covenant** is a promise usually made in writing by the buyer to the seller. Usually the promise limits the use of the land in some way. For example, the buyer may contract with the seller, promising not to graze sheep on the land. If the buyer who gave the covenant resells, the new owner is bound only if the covenant is the kind that runs with the land.

Restrictive covenants *run with the land* when they meet all four of the following legal tests.

1. The original parties must have intended the covenant to run with the land.
2. It must touch and concern the land. This means that the covenant must affect the use of the property or affect the title to the property.

3. The buyer must have had notice of the covenant at the time of purchase. Notice exists when the buyer is told about the restrictive covenant or when a copy of the restrictive covenant is recorded.
4. There must be a chain of ownership connections between the original promisee and the current owner. This is called *privity of estate.*

If one of the tests is not passed, then the restrictive covenant does not bind subsequent purchasers. In *What's Your Verdict?* the restrictive covenant binds the buyer (restricting Lindsay from buying a pickup truck), but not subsequent purchasers. This would be so because this particular promise does not touch and concern the land.

Note that sellers can extract the same promise from buyers by a restrictive covenant, by transferring a conditional estate, or by separate contract. If the restrictive covenant is broken, the owner may be required to pay damages or may be enjoined from future breaches. In contrast, if the condition of conveyance is violated, the violator loses ownership.

Zoning Ordinances

The owner's use of his or her realty can also be restricted by zoning ordinances. **Zoning ordinances** are adopted by cities or counties to regulate the location of residential, business, and industrial districts. Generally states can only enact zoning ordinances when they promote the health, safety, morals, and general welfare of the community.

Courts generally support the government's right to enforce community goals at the expense of individual landowners. For example, a commercial area could be rezoned residential. If the zoning reduces the value of the owner's land, the owner would bear the loss and could not recover from the local government for the financial injury.

Invalid Zoning

Zoning is not enforceable if it exceeds the constitutional powers of the state. This occurs when the ordinance is clearly arbitrary, unreasonable, or without substantial relation to the public health, safety, morals, and general welfare.

Zoning cannot be used unreasonably to eliminate an existing use. Thus a zoning ordinance restricting use of an area to residential could not be used to eliminate an already existing cemetery. (The cemetery in a residential zone is called a *nonconforming use.*) Recently, however, some courts have begun to allow reasonable zoning ordinances that eliminate existing uses.

Spot Zoning

Spot zoning is the treatment of a single property in a manner inconsistent with the treatment of similar properties in the area. It is usually prohibited. However, a **variance** may be granted by a city or county to allow a landowner to make some use of his or her land that is inconsistent with the general zoning ordinance. Usually the owner must appear before the variance board and establish hardship and lack of injury to others.

LIENS FILED AGAINST REAL PROPERTY

WHAT'S YOUR VERDICT?

Jerry, a high school student, installed a lawn sprinkler system for the Wyatts while he was on summer break. Although the system worked well, the Wyatts failed to pay Jerry for his work or the system itself.

What can Jerry do to get the money the Wyatts owe him?

A lien is a legal right in another's property given as security for the performance of a financial obligation. A "mortgage" is a lien; so is a "trust deed." These are called *voluntary liens.* The owners of the realty consent to (or volunteer) the lien, usually because they receive money in return for granting the lien.

Involuntary liens arise without the consent of the owner. For example, if an owner does not pay property taxes when due, the taxes often automatically become a lien against the property. This is called a *tax lien.* If the tax lien is not paid, the taxing authority can *foreclose* (cause the property to be sold) to pay the debt.

Mechanic's liens are another example of involuntary liens. A mechanic is someone who supplies labor or material that is used to improve real property. A carpenter can be a mechanic; so can a plumber, a lumber yard, or a high school student who installs lawn sprinklers during summer breaks. Jerry in *What's Your Verdict?* can record a mechanic's lien against the Wyatts' property. Then he can file suit, prove the claim, and foreclose on the property in order to get the money for the system and his work on it.

DUTIES OWED TO THOSE ENTERING YOUR LAND

WHAT'S YOUR VERDICT?

Luke has guests at his house for a swimming party. He knows the sliding glass door leading to the pool cannot be seen when the patio lights are on and the house lights are off.

Does Luke have a duty to warn his guests of the glass in the door?

A possessor (a person who owns a possessory interest in land) may owe certain tort duties to others who come on the land. Under the common law, the extent of the duties depends on whether the people are trespassers, licensees, or invitees. Some courts ignore these distinctions and hold possessors liable if they fail to take reasonable steps to prevent harm to those entering their land.

Trespassers

A **trespass** occurs when a person is on the land without a right to be there. Thus, when a neighbor walks upon your land without your consent, the neighbor is a trespasser. Generally, a trespasser takes the property as the trespasser finds it. The possessor does not have any duty to the trespasser to keep the land in a reasonably safe condition. However, the possessor cannot intentionally cause harm to the trespasser.

If the possessor knows that the trespasser is on the land, or that persons constantly trespass on the land, then various tort duties are imposed upon the possessor with respect to the condition of the land. An **attractive nuisance** is something that attracts children to trespass. It broadens the possessor's responsibility.

Licensee

A *licensee* is a person whom the possessor of land has permitted to be on that land. A social guest is an example. The possessor of land has the duty to disclose to the licensee any known nonobvious dangers on the land. In *What's Your Verdict?* Luke has a duty to warn his guests of the glass in the door. If he fails to warn them, and someone is injured by shattering the glass, Luke would be liable for damages for their injuries.

Invitee

An invitee is either a public invitee or a business visitor. A public invitee is a member of the public invited by the land's possessor to enter or remain on the land for a public purpose. A business visitor is invited on the land to do business with the possessor. When a retail store invites prospective customers to enter the store and consider making purchases, the customers become business visitors. The possessor of land has the duty to invitees to keep the premises in a reasonably safe condition. The possessor also has a duty to warn invitees of dangers on the land of which the possessor should be aware and which are not reasonably discoverable by the invitee.

Answer the following questions about legal concepts.

1. Which of the following are features of a license? **(a) short-term (b) revocable (c) usually unwritten (d) right to a limited use of another's land (e) all of the above**

2. Easements appurtenant benefit nearby land. **True or False?**

3. Only those restrictive covenants which __?__ bind subsequent purchasers of the realty.

4. The greatest tort duties are owed to invitees, lesser duties are owed to licensees, and the least duties are owed to trespassers. **True or False?**

Study the following situations, answer the questions, then prepare arguments to support your answers.

5. In 1942 a deed properly created a perpetual easement of right to receive light, air, and unobstructed view over certain property now owned by Friedman. Friedman erected a television antenna, and Petersen—as owner of the property benefited by the easement—sought an injunction to compel removal of the obstruction. Friedman argues that the parties who created the easement back in 1942 could not have intended to bar such television installations, since they were not even known of at the time. Is the easement valid? (*Petersen v. Friedman,* 162 Cal. 2d 245)

6. Bentley had been in business at a particular location in Cleveland, Ohio, for many years. When the government's Redevelopment Agency sought to buy her land for redevelopment purposes, Bentley refused to sell. Can she be compelled to sell?

7. Pete owned a large garage from which he operated his tire repair business. He installed several automatic tire changers (machines that remove the rubber tires from the steel wheels on which they are mounted). The property was zoned commercial and Pete's garage conformed to the zoning. Other property owners complained to the city council about the noise at Pete's business. The council responded by rezoning the property R-1, limited to single family residences. Is this zoning valid?

When dealing with real property . . .

PREVENT LEGAL DIFFICULTIES

1. If your personal property is to be attached to real property in any transaction, agree in writing who will get it. Put the agreement in writing, whether the contract involved is a sale, lease, or mortgage.

2. When purchasing real property, protect your interest by
   - having the property properly surveyed, particularly if it is an irregularly shaped parcel or has borders that are uncertain
   - requiring a deed containing all possible warranties
   - securing title insurance if it is available
   - being represented in the transaction by a professional. If there is anything distinctive about the transaction, use a real estate lawyer.

3. Be sure that any deed to land you have purchased is promptly recorded.

4. To prevent adverse possession, owners of realty, especially raw land, should check it periodically to see if someone is occupying it without your consent.

5. If you are asked to convey property and want to be free of possible future obligations, use a quitclaim deed.

6. If the government seeks to take your land by condemnation under its right of eminent domain, consult a lawyer. You have a constitutional right to a trial by jury to determine the fair price that must be paid.

CHAPTER IN REVIEW

CONCEPTS IN BRIEF

1. The rights that exist in real property include surface rights, rights to air space, mineral rights, and water rights.

2. Personal property becomes realty when that is what is intended, when it is permanently attached to the realty, or when it is adapted to the realty.

3. The rights and powers of ownership are determined by the estate in land received by the purchaser. Fee simple absolute is the most common and greatest estate. Other major estates are conditional estates, life estates, nonfreehold estates, and future interests. Ownership is usually transferred with a warranty deed which provides great protection to grantees.

4. Real property is usually transferred by deed evidencing a sale. Ownership can also be transferred by gift, inheritance, adverse possession, dedication, or eminent domain.

5. A license is a temporary, revocable right (privilege) to some limited use of another's land. Easements are irrevocable rights to some use of another's land.

6. Zoning regulates land use to promote community goals, health, safety, or general welfare.

7. Only restrictive covenants that run with the land bind later purchasers.

8. Possessors of land owe tort duties to trespassers and greater duties to licensees and invitees.

YOUR LEGAL VOCABULARY

Match each statement with the term that it best defines. Some terms may not be used.

1. Greatest possible bundle of ownership rights in, and powers over, realty

2. Personal property attached to realty in such a way that it is regarded as real property

3. Method of acquiring title by occupying land belonging to another, without the other's consent, for a certain uninterrupted period of time, under prescribed conditions

4. Document used to evidence transfer of ownership of real property

5. Estate or tenancy that involves ownership for a limited period of time

6. Agreement limiting your use of your property

7. Personal property attached to realty by a business tenant

8. Property right allowing one person to extract things, such as minerals and oil

9. Property right one has in the land of another, such as a right to cross the other's land

10. Power of the government to take private property for public use upon payment of the fair market price

11. Control of water that is part of the realty

adverse possession
attractive nuisance
conditional estate
conveyance
dedication
deed
easement
eminent domain
fee simple absolute
fixture
land
lien
life estate
mineral right
nonfreehold estate
real property
restrictive covenant
trade fixture
trespass
variance
water right
zoning ordinances

12. Describe the legal features of a life estate.

13. Describe the legal feature of a conditional estate.

14. Describe the legal features of fee simple absolute.

15. Explain what a future interest is.

WRITE ABOUT LEGAL CONCEPTS

16. Assume you are a buyer of the place where you live. Write a paragraph that could be included in a contract of sale describing which items of personal property would go to you as part of the sale.

17. Write a paragraph describing a situation in which a person is a licensee.

18. Write a paragraph describing a situation in which a person is an invitee.

19. HOT DEBATE Write a paragraph explaining why the stereo should be taxed at 1 percent as real property. Write another paragraph explaining why the stereo should be taxed at 4 percent as personal property.

THINK CRITICALLY ABOUT EVIDENCE

Study the following situations, answer the questions, then prepare arguments to support your answers.

20. Stu bought a parcel of land in a New York City neighborhood that included both an office building and residences. He began building a three-story home on the parcel. The owner of an adjoining office building sued Stu claiming that she owned the airspace above the second story and asking the court to halt Stu's construction. If the neighbor's claim is true, can she stop the construction?

21. A butcher installed a very heavy refrigerated display case in a rented space in a shopping mall, wired it into the electrical system, plumbed it into water and sewage systems, and bolted it to the floor. Is the display case realty or personal property?

22. Brand sold property to Alioto and conveyed it with a quitclaim deed. There was a mortgage on the property that neither Brand nor Alioto knew about at the time of the conveyance. Who will lose money because of this mortgage, Brand or Alioto?

23. Purcey gave a written easement to her neighbor Pitzer allowing Pitzer to run a water ditch across Purcey's property to irrigate Pitzer's land. Purcey sells her property to Riddell, who fills in the ditch because, "it's dangerous for my kids." Pitzer sues. Who prevails?

24. Swit bought a single-family residence and converted it into a halfway house for delinquent teenagers. Neighbors objected to the increased risk of crime in the neighborhood. Then the neighbors filed suit claiming that the residents of the home were not, "a single family," as required by the applicable zoning ordinance. Who prevails, Swit or his neighbors?

25. The city of Westerly maintained an old-fashioned Merry-Go-Round near a beach. All summer both kids and adults would ride it. It was shut down during the winter. Occasionally, kids would climb the fence around the Merry-Go-Round, start the electrical motor, and ride it for free. Shelly, age 12, climbed the fence, started the motor, but had her hand crushed when it was caught between a v-belt and a pulley on the motor. Is the city of Westerly liable to Shelly?

ANALYZE
REAL CASES

26. The Pentecostal Tabernacle Church had just built a new church building when dissension broke out among the members, and they split into two factions. As a consequence, payments on the building loan were not made, and foreclosure resulted. Williams bought the church building at the foreclosure sale. Trustees of the church then brought suit to recover the pews from the building. Williams defended by claiming that the pews were fixtures and were therefore to remain in the building. Evidence disclosed that removal of the pews would leave holes and broken bolts in the tiled floor. However, the pastor and a trustee of the church testified that when the pews were installed it was intended that they were to be removed later and placed in another wing of the building. Two ex-trustees of the church disputed that intention during their testimony. Are the pews real property? (*Sims v. Williams,* 441 S.W.2d 385)

27. W. E. and Jennie Hutton executed a warranty deed conveying their interest in a parcel of land to the local school district. The words of conveyance stated: "This land to be used for school purposes only; otherwise to revert to grantors herein." The property was used for a school for 32 years. Then the property was used by the school district for storage purposes. When this occurred, the heirs of the Huttons filed suit to recover the property from the school district. Who owns the land? (*Mahrenholz v. County Board of School Trustees of Lawrence County,* 417 N.E.2d 138, Illinois)

28. Holmes was engaged in the business of raising and processing chickens. He bought property in Clackamas County, Oregon, on which he planned to erect a chicken-processing plant. To prepare for construction, he spent $33,000 to install a well system, plant special grass, and run soil tests to determine where drain fields for the plant's sewage should be located. Later Clackamas County enacted an ordinance zoning the property Rural Agricultural-Single Family Residential. The zoning prohibited further construction of the chicken-processing plant. Holmes continued work and the county sued. The trial court enjoined defendant from further construction. He appealed. What resulted? (*Clackamas County v. Holmes,* 508 P.2d 190, Oregon)

29. The Davis family rented an apartment in a complex controlled by McDougall. The laundry room in the complex contained a washing machine with tub, agitator, and roller-type wringer. The roller wringer was designed to release automatically when misused. However, the release mechanism was defective. Jodi Davis, age 3, climbed up on a stool, started the washer and inserted her hand in the roller wringer, causing permanent injuries to her fingers, hand, and wrist. Her parents sued on her behalf, alleging that the landlord maintained an attractive nuisance. The trial court granted McDougall's motion for summary judgment and ruled that the washing machine was not an attractive nuisance. Jodi's parents appealed. What resulted? (*Davis v. McDougall,* 480 P.2d 907, Idaho)

30. The Wakes operated a cattle ranch in Cassia County, Idaho. During the spring and fall, they drove their cattle over land owned by the Johnsons. Eventually the Wakes sold their cattle ranch to the Nelsons. The new owners continued to use the Johnsons' land as a cattle trail twice a year. This went on for about sixteen years before the Johnsons objected and locked the gates to the cattle trail. The Nelsons sued, claiming an easement by prescription. Is there an easement by prescription here? (*Nelson v. Johnson,* 679 P.2d 662)

31. Smith bought two lots along the shore of Lake Pepin and built a cottage, which he mistakenly extended over the boundary line into a third lot, Parcel X8. Smith cleaned all three lots, seeded X8 with grass, and used it in the sporadic and seasonal manner associated with lakeshore property. Burkhardt had a warranty deed to X8 but did not challenge Smith's possession for more than twenty years. Now Smith claims title to X8 by adverse possession. Burkhardt argues that the entire parcel was not actually occupied nor was it usually cultivated. Burkhardt also argues that Smith's possession was not hostile because it was based on a mistaken boundary line and because Smith paid no taxes on X8. Does Smith get title to Parcel X8 by adverse possession? (*Burkhardt v. Smith,* 17 Wis. 2d 132)

Parrish v. Richards
336 P.2d 122

BACKGROUND This is an action to enjoin maintenance of a tennis court and fence allegedly built in violation of a real property restrictive covenant.

EVIDENCE The parties are contiguous owners of real property. . . . [The Richards'] residence is located between those of plaintiffs, Parrish and Peterson. Prior to the acquisition by any of the parties of any of the tracts of land here involved, there had been placed upon and against such lands certain restrictive covenants recorded in the office of the County Recorder of Salt Lake County, Utah. The covenant here involved reads as follows:

> Use of Land: Each lot is hereby designated as a residential lot, and none of said lots shall be improved, used or occupied for other than private residence purposes, and no flat or apartment house . . . shall be erected thereon, and no structure shall be erected . . . other than a one-, two-, or three-car garage, and one single family residence, not to exceed one story in height. . . .

Prior to August 1, [the Richards'] leveled their land on the south side and laid down a concrete apron in the southwest corner measuring 78 feet by 36 feet for a tennis court. Around and upon such concrete [the Richards'] placed a six-foot wire fence. [The Richards'] testified that they do not intend to put up any overhead lights or floodlights whatsoever over the tennis court. Parrish brought suit, alleging that the described construction of the tennis court is a "structure" erected and placed upon the property in violation of the above-mentioned restrictive covenant. Parrish also alleged that the construction inter-fered with their view; that there had been no waiver of the covenant on their part; that the value of their property had diminished as a result of the construction; and they prayed for an injunction permanently enjoining the defendants from proceeding with the construction.

REASONING OF APPEALS COURT The trial court followed the correct doctrine that in the construction of uncertain or ambiguous restrictions, the courts will resolve all doubts in favor of the free and unrestricted use of property and that it will "have recourse to every aid, rule, or canon of construction to ascertain the intention of the parties." In applying that doctrine to the situation, the court concluded that the fence surrounding said tennis court does not violate the covenant. Garages and other similar buildings which are of solid construction are of a different character entirely. Structures of that kind, which are solid, obstruct the view for the neighborhood and crowd the area with buildings, which would reduce the beauty of it. It seems quite plain that the covenant was intended to prevent the blocking of the view and the crowding of the buildings which would reduce the beauty and utility and therefore depreciate the value of the property within the subdivision. But the objections which validly may be made against solid constructions do not exist in regard to a flat concrete slab for a tennis court. Nor does the wire fence around it obstruct the view.

CONCLUSION Based upon the foregoing, it is our opinion that the trial court was correct in its conclusion that the tennis court and fence are not the type of structure prohibited by the covenant. Affirmed, for [the Richards'].

PRACTICE JUDGING

1. **Is this restrictive covenant the type that would run with the land?**

2. **How would this judge rule if the structure were (a) a basketball court (b) a patio with a brick barbecue about four-feet high (c) a small garden shed 10-feet square (d) a workshop about 10-feet square?**

LESSONS

HOT DEBATE

Sally rented an apartment that had been constructed only a month before she moved in. After she had lived in the apartment for a week, she discovered the fan in her bathroom didn't work. Because she was knowledgeable about electrical work, Sally made the repair to the fan herself. Then she told her landlord about the problem and her solution. She asked to be compensated for her work at $35 per hour, the going rate for electricians in her community.

Where Do You Stand?

1. **What, if any, are the legal reasons why Sally should be compensated for fixing the fan?**

2. **What, if any, are the legal reasons why the landlord should not have to compensate Sally for fixing the fan?**

WHAT IS A LEASE?

WHAT'S YOUR VERDICT?

Curtis entered into an oral agreement with Kearne to lease Kearne's cabin for three months during the winter ski season. However, skiing was poor that year because there was little snowfall. Therefore Curtis tried to avoid the contract. Curtis claimed that the lease was not enforceable because it was not in writing and because of the poor skiing conditions.

Must this lease be in writing to be enforced?

A **lease** is an agreement in which one party receives temporary possession of another's real property in exchange for rent. **Rent** is the consideration given in return for temporary possession. The lease creates a relationship between the person conveying possession of realty (called the **landlord** or *lessor*) and the person receiving possession (called the **tenant** or *lessee*). The ownership interest of the tenant is called a **leasehold estate**. In contrast to rental of real property, rental of personal property creates the relationship of bailment between a bailor and bailee.

When a written document describes the rental transaction, the document is called the *lease* or rental agreement. Most leases constitute a blending of the law of conveyance (that is, transferring ownership of realty) and the law of contracts. The conveyance aspect of the transaction is concerned with transferring a leasehold estate to the tenant. The contract aspects relate to the agreements be-

tween the parties on such issues as the amount of the rent, who shall repair the realty, and the amount of security or cleaning deposits.

A lease may be oral. However, under the statute of frauds, leases that extend for more than one year must be in writing or courts may refuse to enforce them. In *What's Your Verdict?* the lease was for only three months, so the oral agreement was binding. As the tenant, Curtis was entitled to possession during the three months of the lease. In addition, the landlord did not agree to deliver a good snowfall. Even if a writing is not required, it is a good idea to put the important terms of a lease in written form to avoid disputes.

IN THIS CASE

Several months ago, your brother entered into a nine-month lease for an apartment. All the terms were agreed upon orally. Now, upon discovering that the apartment can be leased for more money, the landlord has told your brother to vacate. The landlord claims that their oral agreement is unenforceable. However, this oral lease is enforceable.

TYPES OF LEASEHOLD ESTATES

WHAT'S YOUR VERDICT?

The two Adams sisters leased an apartment from Pena. They were to pay rent on the first day of each month. No time limit for the lease was specified.

What type of leasehold estate was created?

There are four basic types of leasehold estates (that is, tenants' ownership interests) that can be created by a lease. These estates are a periodic tenancy, a tenancy for years, tenancy at sufferance, and a tenancy at will.

Periodic Tenancy

A **periodic tenancy** arises when the leasehold is for a renewable period of time with rent due at stated intervals.

For example, the parties may agree that the rent is "three hundred dollars per month payable in advance." This language suggests that the lease is intended to run for longer than one month, yet the lease specifies no ending date.

Leases that create a periodic tenancy sometimes identify a rental period, such as from "week to week," "month to month," or "year to year." If the lease does not state the period,

then the frequency with which rent is paid will be assumed to be the period. When rent is paid by the month (as in *What's Your Verdict?*) the tenancy is referred to as a **tenancy from month to month**.

In general, this tenancy continues for the length of the payment period and is automatically renewed unless one party gives adequate notice of termination. Often the notice of termination must equal the length of the payment period. Thus, where rent is paid every two months, most states would require a two-month notice to terminate. The period may vary depending on state law. Sometimes there is a requirement in the lease that this notice be in writing and be given a certain number of days before the end of the lease period.

Tenancy for Years

When a leasehold is for a definite period of time—such as six months, one year, or ninety-nine years—it creates a **tenancy for years**. It has this name even when the period of the lease is less than one year. The fea-

ture that distinguishes a tenancy for years from a periodic tenancy is the identification of a date for the ending of the lease. Thus, if a lease states that the rental period is from May 1 to August 15, this is a tenancy for years because August 15 is specified as the ending date. At the end of the lease period, a tenancy for years terminates automatically without a requirement of notice.

Tenancy at Sufferance

Tenants often have a hard time leaving the rented property before the day when the lease ends. If a tenant remains in possession after a lease has expired, a **tenancy at sufferance** arises. The tenant is then called a *holdover tenant.*

When there is a tenancy at sufferance, the landlord generally has a choice of remedies. The holdover tenant can be *evicted*—that is, be forcibly removed from the property by the sheriff. Further, the tenant is liable for reasonable rent for the holdover period. In some states the landlord can collect double or triple

rent for the holdover period. If the tenant holds over, the landlord may—as an alternative to eviction—compel the tenant to pay rent for another lease period.

If the holdover tenant pays and the landlord accepts additional rent, a periodic tenancy is generally created for the same period or term as the prior lease. Therefore, if the prior lease were for one year, the tenant would be liable for another full year's rent. If the old lease were for one month, the landlord would be obligated to provide the premises for another month.

IN THIS CASE

Anne rented an apartment to Clare, a college freshman. The lease was for a nine-month period from September 1 to May 30, and rent was due in advance every month. Clare paid the rent on May 1 for May. Then she decided she wanted to go to a summer school session which lasted two months. She paid a month's rent on June 1 without disclosing her plans. The payment was accepted by Anne. Clare and Anne initially created a tenancy for years because the termination date was identified. When Clare stayed in the apartment after the end of May, a tenancy at sufferance existed. When Anne accepted the rent in June, Clare ceased being a tenant at sufferance and both Anne and Clare were bound to a lease for another nine-month period.

Tenancy at Will

If a party possesses land with the owner's permission but without an agreement as to the term of the lease or the amount of the rent, a **tenancy at will** results. Such a leasehold may be terminated at any time by either party with minimal notice.

THINK ABOUT LEGAL CONCEPTS

Answer the following questions about legal concepts.

1. All leases must be in writing to be enforceable in court. **True or False?**

2. Which of the following must be in writing to be enforceable by a court? **(a) lease for a period of two months (b) lease for a period of six months (c) lease for a period of 12 months (d) lease for a period of 24 months (e) both c and d**

3. If the landlord and tenant do not identify an ending date for the lease but they do identify a payment period, then the lease is a **(a) periodic tenancy (b) tenancy for years (c) tenancy at sufferance (d) tenancy at will.**

4. If the landlord and tenant identify an ending date for the lease, then the lease is a **(a) periodic tenancy (b) tenancy for years (c) tenancy at sufferance (d) tenancy at will.**

5. A tenancy for years must last at least one year. **True or False?**

6. A tenant who occupies the property after the lease has expired has which tenancy? **(a) periodic tenancy (b) tenancy for years (c) tenancy at sufferance (d) tenancy at will.**

7. If a potential lessor and lessee agree that property will be leased and the tenant moves in before a lease is negotiated, the tenancy by which that person occupies is called a tenancy at __?__ .

THINK CRITICALLY ABOUT EVIDENCE

Study the following situations, answer the questions, then prepare arguments to support your answers.

8. Smith agreed to allow Winchell to come upon his property on the condition that he pay at least $660 per month. Smith agreed that if Winchell made the monthly payments for 10 years he would be the owner of the realty. Is this a lease?

9. You moved into an apartment some time ago under a lease which identified the ending date as December 31. You plan to move out as of December 31 but do not tell the landlord. Two days before the lease expires, while you are packing, your landlord appears and informs you that because you did not give notice of your intent to leave, you owe rent for an additional month. Is the landlord right?

10. Church and Jaspers planned to remain in their Vine Street offices only until their one-year lease expired on June 1. On May 15 they entered into a two-year lease for new office space on Seventeenth Avenue. This lease was to commence June 1. On May 25 Church and Jaspers discover that the occupant of the Seventeenth Avenue offices, whose lease expires on May 31, has not vacated and does not plan to do so until June 15. Can Church and Jaspers remain in their old offices until June 15?

TENANTS' RIGHTS

WHAT'S YOUR VERDICT?

Trip, the landlord of an apartment building, asked to show Louis's apartment to a prospective renter. The lease did not provide for such tours. Louis needed undisturbed use of his apartment on the day his landlord wanted to show it.

Could Louis legally deny the request?

Tenants have both rights and duties created by a lease. Tenants' rights will be discussed first.

Right of Possession

The tenant has a right to the possession of the real property starting at the time agreed upon in the lease. In addition, unless otherwise provided in the lease, the tenant's possession is to be exclusive of all other persons and is for the duration of the lease. Landlords generally do not have a right to enter leased premises for inspection unless this right is given in the lease.

Louis, in *What's Your Verdict?*, could legally deny Trip's request to show the apartment to a prospective renter. If a landlord is given the right to enter and inspect the leased premises, most states require that the landlord give reasonable advance notice and that the landlord inspect at a reasonable time of the day.

If the landlord blocks the tenant from possession of all the real property, an **eviction** has occurred. The tenant may recover damages from

the landlord if the eviction is improper.

Under some circumstances, the tenant may claim a constructive eviction and refuse to pay rent. A **constructive eviction** occurs if the landlord fails to perform certain duties as defined in the lease or imposed by statute *and if* the tenant abandons the premises because of such a breach.

CULTURAL DIVERSITY IN LAW

Mexico

Tenants' Rights

In Mexico, a tenant who has been leasing a house for more than five years has preferential rights to buy the property if the owner decides to sell.

For example, if the landlord fails to heat residential premises and this forces the tenant to move out, there has been a constructive eviction. If the lessor fails to keep residential premises in a condition fit for human habitation, perhaps because of infestation by insects or rodents, this could amount to a constructive eviction if the tenant leaves the premises because of such condition.

Right to Use the Property

The tenant is allowed to use the leased property in the manner specified in the lease. If a particular use is not mentioned in the lease, the tenant may use the property for any purpose for which it is designed or customarily used.

IN THIS CASE

The Bartleys leased a house from Atlas Properties. The lease limited the use of the property to occupancy by a single family. To help the family finances, the Bartleys installed bunk beds on the second floor and rented the area to eight college students. A tenant who agrees to lease a house as a single-family residence may not use the building as a boardinghouse. Therefore the Bartleys were in violation of their lease.

Right to Assign the Lease or to Sublet

Unless restricted by the terms of the lease, a tenant may assign the lease or may sublet the premises. An **assignment of a lease** takes place when the tenant transfers his or her entire interest in the lease to a third person. Although the new tenant becomes liable to the landlord for the rent and performance of other conditions of the lease, the original tenant also remains liable.

Subletting occurs when the tenant does either of the following:

- leases all of the property to a third person for a period of time that is *less than* that remaining on the lease, or
- leases *part* of the property to a third person for part or all of the term remaining.

When the property is sublet, the original tenant continues to be directly liable to the landlord for performance of the lease. Leases often require the landlord's prior approval of assignment or subletting. However, courts have held that the landlord must have a valid reason if consent is withheld.

TENANTS' DUTIES

WHAT'S YOUR VERDICT?

Susan rented an apartment for six years. New carpet had been installed, although it was rather cheap. Susan treated the apartment with reasonable care, but when she moved out the landlord wrote her saying the carpet was "threadworn" and gave her a bill for $900 for new carpet.

Is Susan liable for the cost of new carpet?

A lease creates certain duties for the tenant.

Duty to Pay Rent

A tenant's most important duty is to pay the agreed-upon rent when it is due. Although rent is usually expressed as a fixed sum of money, it may consist of a share of the crops of a farm or a percentage of the profits of a business. The tenant may be evicted for failure to pay rent.

Before leasing property in a tenancy for years or a tenancy from month to month, landlords sometimes require the payment of the first and last months' rent. Thus, if the tenant fails to make prompt payment for the next period's rent, the landlord can use the last month's rent for the month during which legal steps are taken to evict the tenant. In residential rentals, a "cleaning" or "security" deposit is almost always required. The amount of this deposit should be refunded at the end of the lease period if the property is left as clean and undamaged as it was when first occupied, less ordinary wear and tear. In *What's Your Verdict?* Susan would not be liable for the cost of new carpet if the old carpet was only damaged by ordinary wear and tear during her tenancy.

Duty to Take Care of the Property

A tenant owes a *duty of reasonable care* to return the property in substantially the same condition it was in when the lease began. This ordinarily includes responsibility for making all minor repairs. The tenant is not liable for wear and tear caused by ordinary use. However, the tenant is liable for deterioration caused by willful misuse or negligence. In some states by statute, and sometimes based on the lease, landlords make all repairs. This can include even such minor repairs as replacing faucet washers and electric fuses.

The tenant normally is under no obligation (in fact, has no right) to make major structural changes or to make improvements without the consent of the landlord. For example, if the roof leaks, the necessary repair is the responsibility of the landlord. However, the tenant is legally expected to act reasonably and to take appropriate steps to prevent avoidable damage until the landlord has been notified and can make needed repairs. The tenant is obligated to *notify* the landlord when major repairs are needed. In a few states, the tenant may apply up to a full month's rent toward essential repairs if the landlord does not make the repairs after reasonable notice.

Torts Duty

A business or residential tenant in possession of leased property has a duty of care to those who enter the property. An injury to a licensee or invitee caused by a tenant's negligence is the responsibility of the tenant in the areas under the tenant's control. The tenant may even be held liable if the landlord had the responsibility under the lease to make repairs, which, if they had been made, would have avoided the injury. A tenant can buy liability insurance to protect against loss from injury claims.

In the majority of states, lessees assume liability for injuries to themselves and to others (torts) that occur on the leased property. An exception to this rule exists when the landlord knows the defective condition but does not disclose it to the tenant, and the tenant would not be able to identify the problem after a reasonable inspection. The landlord is also liable for injuries occurring on portions of the property, such as hallways, which the landlord controls. In general, the landlord controls the common areas. These are areas used by all the tenants. Thus if a tenant's guest is injured because of a defective diving board in the pool area of an apartment complex, the landlord is likely to be liable.

Answer the following questions about legal concepts.

1. In a tenancy, the right of possession is owned by the __?__ .

2. The landlord does not have the right to enter the premises whether or not the lease states that right exists. **True or False?**

3. If the landlord is responsible for heating an apartment and fails to do so, this will be a(n) __?__ if it causes the tenant to move out.

4. A tenant may not use the property in ways prohibited by the lease. **True or False?**

5. If a tenant transfers her interest in the lease for all but the last month, which of the following has occurred? **(a) subletting of the premises or (b) assignment of the lease**

6. If a tenant fails to pay the rent on time, the landlord may confiscate the cleaning deposit. **True or False?**

7. Which of the following is not one of the tenant's duties if a major repair becomes necessary? **(a) to notify the landlord of the problem (b) to take reasonable steps to prevent avoidable damage (c) to make the necessary repairs**

Study the following situations, answer the questions, then prepare arguments to support your answers.

8. Three weeks before you are scheduled to move out of an apartment, the landlord tells you that he wants to begin showing the apartment to other prospective tenants. Must you allow him to do this even though your lease says nothing about showing the apartment? Ethically, should you allow the apartment to be shown even if you are not legally obligated to do so?

9. Fidel rented property from De Baca. The lease agreement contained a clause prohibiting assignments. Fidel sublet a portion of the property for a period shorter than the unexpired term of the lease. De Baca sues to evict Fidel. Who prevails?

10. Perry owned apartments in a college town. Apartments were easy to rent when school started in September, but they were often vacant during summer months. Pablo moved to town in the middle of the summer and rented one of Perry's apartments for only $250 per month. The written lease was a periodic tenancy from month to month. Pablo said, "This is such a good deal, you can count on me as a tenant for the next year." Perry said nothing in response. He planned to give Pablo 30 days' notice at the beginning of August so he could rerent the apartment for $400 per month for the academic year. Legally, can Perry do this? Is it ethical?

11. Smith rented an apartment from Jerry on a month-to-month basis for $700 per month. At the time Smith first saw the apartment, there was a large tear in the carpet right behind the entryway door. The carpet there often bunched up and it was easy to trip on if you didn't notice it. On Saturday, Smith was entertaining guests when her boss arrived. The boss rang the doorbell and let herself in when no one answered. She then tripped on the torn rug, fell and broke her arm. She sued both Smith and Jerry for her medical expenses, lost wages, and pain and suffering. Smith is nearly broke, but Jerry her landlord is a multi-millionaire. Is Jerry liable?

12. Betty Reiman, a 14-year-old girl, had been helping Mrs. Green prepare to return home from the hospital. As part of the preparations, Betty went to the roof of Mrs. Green's apartment building to collect some of Mrs. Green's laundry. Betty had hung the laundry to dry on a clothesline up there. While on the roof, Betty tripped and fell backward through a skylight on the roof. She then sued Moore, who owned the building, for her injuries. Is Moore responsible for Betty's injuries? (*Reiman v. Moore*, 108 P.2d 452, Cal.)

GOALS

- Describe the lessor's rights when rent is not paid and the lessor's duties to maintain the premises
- Tell when the lessor is liable for injuries on the property
- Describe the lessor's duties under the Fair Housing Act

LANDLORDS' RIGHTS AND DUTIES

WHAT'S YOUR VERDICT?

McElroy leased a store building from Steward for one year. After three months, McElroy moved all her possessions from the building and left town, defaulting on her rent. Steward did not relet the store.

Is McElroy liable for the rent for the remaining nine months?

Often, the rights and duties of a tenant find their complements in the rights and duties of a landlord.

Right to the Rent

The landlord's primary right is to the rent agreed upon in the lease. If the tenant fails to pay the rent, the landlord may take legal action to recover the rent and evict the tenant.

TENANT VACATES EARLY A tenant who vacates the property before the end of the lease remains liable for the unpaid rent. In some states, the tenant is liable for the rent even if the landlord allows the property to remain empty. Other states require that the landlord make a good-faith effort to rerent the property. This is called the *duty to mitigate* (to keep damages to a minimum). If the property is not rerented, the original tenant is liable for the rent remaining on the lease. If it is rerented, but at a lower rental amount, the original tenant is liable for the difference.

In *What's Your Verdict?* McElroy's liability depends on the law of the state where the property is located. In some states, Steward can allow the premises to remain empty and sue McElroy for the unpaid rent. Other states will require that Steward try to lease the premises to someone else before collecting from McElroy.

TENANT FAILS TO VACATE If the tenant fails to pay rent and remains in possession, the landlord may sue to *evict* the tenant. The landlord may include the claim for overdue rent in the same suit. However, the landlord may not take the law into his or her own hands, personally evicting the tenant and placing the tenant's belongings on the sidewalk. If the tenant refuses to leave the premises, a court order directing the sheriff or other official to evict the tenant must be obtained.

Right to Regain the Realty and Fixtures

At the end of the lease term, the lessor is entitled to regain possession of the real property. If a tenant has added fixtures to the realty, they belong to the landlord. This general rule does not apply to trade fixtures added by business tenants.

Duty to Maintain the Premises

While the responsibility for minor maintenance of the leased property generally falls on the tenant, there are important exceptions to this rule. For example, when a number of tenants rent portions of a building, the landlord is responsible for all the upkeep of the exterior and the public, or common, areas. Common areas are those not under the specific control

of any one tenant. Public areas include common hallways, stairs, elevators, yards, and swimming pools.

A landlord is required to provide residential property in a condition fit for human living. This is sometimes called the implied **warranty of habitability**. In some states and in many large cities, the law—in the form of a housing code—may prescribe in detail the required condition of such properties. A representative city housing code makes provisions such as these:

- There shall be no exposed electrical wiring.
- The roof shall not leak.
- Every ceiling and wall shall be smooth, free of loose plaster and wallpaper, and easily cleanable.
- Outside doors and windows shall have tight-fitting screens.
- Every unit shall have a private bathroom.
- Gas stoves shall be properly vented and connected..

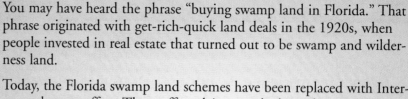

You may have heard the phrase "buying swamp land in Florida." That phrase originated with get-rich-quick land deals in the 1920s, when people invested in real estate that turned out to be swamp and wilderness land.

Today, the Florida swamp land schemes have been replaced with Internet real estate offers. These offers claim you don't need money to start (or even need a real estate brokers' license) to get rich selling real estate. You just need to say yes—then send money! These land deals typically don't even involve land. What you receive for your money is either a seminar or book on making money. And all you learn is that your investment money now belongs to someone else.

If such an e-mail offer comes to you, you may want to simply press the Delete key before trying to make quick money through real estate over the Internet.

Often, violation of housing codes is a violation of the warranty of habitability. If that warranty is violated, the tenant may recover damages, become entitled to a reduction in rent, or terminate the lease.

Torts Duty

One who is injured because of the faulty condition of common areas could bring suit for damages against the landlord. In addition, a landlord may be held liable for injuries that result from defective conditions in the property in the tenant's exclusive possession if the conditions are concealed or are not readily apparent.

Duty to Pay Property Taxes

In the absence of contrary agreement, the landlord pays all property taxes and assessments on the leased property. However, long-term leases of commercial property commonly provide that the tenant will pay such taxes and assessments, as well as premiums for fire insurance.

Fair Housing Act Duties

The Fair Housing Act makes it illegal for the lessor, or the lessor's agent, to

discriminate on the basis of race, religion, sex, national origin, handicap, or family status. A lessor must allow a handicapped person to pay for reasonable modification to the property on the condition that the property is returned to its original condition at the end of the lease. In addition, lessors may not discriminate against families with children unless the facility falls with the "housing for older persons" exception.

Duty on Voluntary Termination

A lease can be terminated by agreement before the expiration of the term. This extinguishes the obligations of the parties. For example, the tenant can surrender the lease to the landlord and the landlord can accept. Mere abandonment of the premises without assent by the landlord is not surrender; it is a breach of the lease. Any *material* breach generally gives the injured party (landlord or tenant) the right to terminate the lease.

Answer the following questions about legal concepts.

1. All states require the landlord to mitigate damages if a tenant abandons the lease before the end of the term. **True or False?**

2. If a landlord rerents property abandoned by the lessee, but for less rent, the tenant is liable for the difference. **True or False?**

3. The name of the process where a landlord seeks to have a sheriff or other official remove a tenant is __?__ .

4. The lessor is responsible for all repairs for **(a) common areas (b) the tenant's premises (c) both a and b**

5. It is illegal to discriminate on the basis of race, religion, sex, and national origin in the rental of housing. **True or False?**

Study the following situations, answer the questions, then prepare arguments to support your answers.

6. In the midst of a very cold winter, the central heating unit in Manlie's apartment complex failed. Several tenants notified the landlord, who happened to be out of town. Unless action were taken immediately, all the pipes in the building would burst. The cost of the repairs was less than $50, but no one wanted to spend the money. What were the tenants' duties in this situation?

7. Moya rented an apartment in a large complex owned by Johnson. Moya's guest, Perkins, was injured when he fell on the icy sidewalk leading up to the building where Moya's apartment was located. Perkins sued both Moya and Johnson. Who is liable, Moya or Johnson?

If you are a tenant . . .

PREVENT LEGAL DIFFICULTIES

1. Written residential leases are generally prepared by the landlord or the landlord's attorney. Thus, such leases often contain many clauses that protect the landlord's interests. Read with understanding before you sign. If the terms are unacceptable to you, request a change. If you are refused, go elsewhere.

2. You may not remodel or significantly change the premises without the consent of your landlord.

3. You may be held liable if someone is injured because of the faulty condition of the premises if such condition was caused by your negligence. Normally you, the tenant, have the obligation to make necessary *minor* repairs and to notify your landlord of the need for major repairs. Protect

yourself with careful maintenance and with adequate liability insurance.

4. When you move, give your landlord proper notice. Such notice is required in periodic tenancies. Failure to give adequate notice may obligate you to pay additional rent even after you vacate the premises.

5. If you are a tenant in a tenancy for years, be sure to vacate,

removing all belongings and trade fixtures, before expiration of the lease or arrange to renew the lease. If you stay beyond the lease period without permission, you could be treated as a trespasser or be held liable for as much as another full lease period's rent.

6. If a "cleaning" or "security" deposit is required, it is a good idea to conduct an inspection of the premises with the landlord and with witnesses both before occupying and immediately after vacating.

7. If your job requires frequent moves on short notice, you may try to include a clause in your lease providing that the lease will end if such a move becomes necessary.

CHAPTER IN REVIEW

CONCEPTS IN BRIEF

1. The relationship between landlord and tenant always involves real property.

2. A landlord-tenant relationship may be a tenancy for years, a periodic tenancy, a tenancy at will, or a tenancy at sufferance.

3. Generally the tenant is responsible for paying the rent, taking reasonable care of the premises, and using the premises only for the agreed purposes.

4. To claim constructive eviction, the tenant must vacate the real property.

5. A tenant may assign the lease or sublet the premises unless there is a restriction in the lease.

6. The landlord must make major repairs, see that the tenant is not deprived of the use of the leased property, and pay the taxes.

7. A lease may be terminated by expiration of the lease period, by agreement of the parties, or at the option of either party upon material breach by the other. In a periodic tenancy, either party seeking to terminate must give the other party proper notice.

YOUR LEGAL VOCABULARY

Match each statement with the term that it best defines. Some terms may not be used.

1. Consideration given by a tenant

2. Ownership interest of a tenant

3. Periodic tenancy in which the rent is paid by the month

4. One who, through a lease, transfers to another exclusive possession and control of real property

5. One who, through a lease, is given possession of real property

6. Lease that exists for a definite period of time

7. Tenancy created when the tenant remains in possession after the lease has expired

8. Tenant's transfer of partial interest in the lease to a third person

9. Agreement in which tenant obtains possession of real property of the landlord in exchange for rent

10. Legal action taken to remove a tenant from possession of all the landlord's real property

11. Transfer to a third person by the lessee of the entire interest in the lease

12. Results if a party possesses land with the owner's permission but without an agreement as to the term of the lease or the amount of the rent

assignment of a lease
constructive eviction
eviction
landlord
lease
leasehold estate
periodic tenancy
rent
subletting
tenancy at sufferance
tenancy at will
tenancy for years
tenancy from month to month
tenant
warranty of habitability

13. Describe a situation where an estate at will is created.

14. Describe a situation where a tenancy at sufferance is created.

15. Describe how the room where you sleep could be rented so that a periodic tenancy would arise.

16. Describe when a lease does not need to be placed in writing yet will still be enforceable in court.

WRITE ABOUT LEGAL CONCEPTS

17. Write a paragraph describing the condition of an apartment at the beginning of a lease. Write another paragraph describing the difference between apartments at the end of leases after "normal wear and tear" and after deterioration because of willful misuse.

18. Write a paragraph describing the parts of a typical apartment complex, where the landlord will be liable for injuries to guests.

19. Write a paragraph describing the parts of a typical apartment complex where the tenants will be liable for injuries to guests.

20. **HOT DEBATE** Write a letter from Sally to the landlord explaining the reasons why she should be paid for the repairs she made. Then write a response from the landlord to Sally explaining the reasons why she should not be paid.

THINK CRITICALLY ABOUT EVIDENCE

Study the following situations, answer the questions, then prepare arguments to support your answers.

21. Strovic orally leased a restaurant from Quinn for five years. Within a year, Strovic had built a large following, and business was booming. Quinn then demanded more rent. When Strovic refused, Quinn sought to evict him and to lease the now well-established property to someone else who would pay higher rent. Can Quinn do this?

22. Slovin entered into a month-to-month tenancy of an apartment for $450 per month. When he married, his wife moved in with him. The landlord did not discover this until three months later. The landlord told Slovin that he owed an extra $100 per month for the time during which the wife had also occupied the apartment. In addition, he told Slovin that the rent for the next month would be $600. What are Slovin's legal obligations to the landlord?

23. Hirschey moved away to college and leased an apartment for nine months, to end on the first of June. After her final examinations were over (on the first of June), she moved out of the room without saying anything to the landlord. The landlord now seeks to collect an additional month's rent because Hirschey did not give notice of termination. Can the landlord collect?

24. Romero rented a farmhouse under a three-year lease. At the end of the lease, Romero and the landlord walked through the farmhouse to inspect for damage. In an empty upstairs room the landlord found a window that was jammed open. It was obvious that rain and snow had come through the open window and damaged the curtains and carpeting. Who is liable for this damage, Romero or the landlord?

25. Houser opened a hamburger shop in a building that she leased for five years from Livingston. The long hours impaired Houser's health and after one year she sold the business to Todd, assigning the lease as part of the deal. When Todd later defaulted on rent payments, Livingston tried to collect from Houser. Is Houser liable?

26. Platt leased the Arctic Circle Drive Inn to Peterson under a tenancy for years. The term was 10 years. At one point Peterson fell two months behind with the rent. In response, Platt let himself into the property after everyone else was gone. He changed the locks and prohibited Peterson and his employees from entering the establishment. Because Peterson was unable to gain access, many of the goods perished. He then sued Platt, claiming that Platt's actions were illegal. He asked that Platt be required to pay for the spoiled goods. Will Peterson prevail? (*Peterson v. Platt,* 678 P.2d 41)

27. Wallenberg leased certain property from Boyar in a tenancy from month to month, beginning October 1. The rent was payable in advance on the first of each month. On November 27, Wallenberg left without notifying the landlord. Is Boyar entitled to rent for the month of December? (*Boyar v. Wallenberg,* 132 Misc. 116, 228 N.Y.S. 358)

28. Lemle rented an expensive home in the Diamond Head area of Honolulu. The home contained six bedrooms and the roof was made in the Tahitian style with corrugated metal covered by woven coconut leaves. After moving in, Lemle and his family discovered the roof was infested with rodents. For two days after moving in, they all slept in the downstairs living room because of their fear of the rodents. After the landlord tried without success to exterminate the rodents, Lemle and his family moved out and demanded return of their deposit and prepaid rent. Is Lemle entitled to the return of the rent? (*Lemle v. Breeden,* 462 P.2d 470, Hawaii)

29. James Kreidel was engaged to be married and planned to attend school. He entered into a lease of an apartment from May 1, 1972, to April 30, 1974. Before the lease period began, Kreidel's engagement was broken. As a student, Kreidel then had no means of support and therefore had no way to pay the rent. On May 19, 1972, he wrote the landlord explaining his situation and stating that he was abandoning the lease. Although the landlord had the opportunity, he did not rerent the apartment until September 1, 1973. Is James liable for the rent from May 1, 1972, to September 1, 1973? (*Sommer v. Kreidel,* 378 A.2d 767, N.J.)

30. Garcia leased an apartment in East Harlem in New York City. The lead-based paint on the walls was peeling and flaking off. Garcia's two children were eating the paint chips. Consuming lead-based paint can cause mental retardation and death. Garcia complained to the landlord without effect. Then he bought the necessary supplies and repainted. He then brought suit against the landlord for his expenses. Will he recover? (*Garcia v. Freeland Realty, Inc.,* 314 N.Y.S.2d 215, N.Y.)

31. Dr. Eldredge leased a 45-acre farm located in Gem County, Idaho, to Joseph W. Jensen and Rhea Bell Jensen for five years. After the first year, the Jensens defaulted in their rental payments but remained in possession. At the beginning of the fourth year, Dr. Eldredge sold the property to third parties. The Jensens elected to treat the sale as constructive eviction and abandoned the premises. Dr. Eldridge sued for unpaid rent of $1,200. The Jensens defended claiming damages of $5,000 for early termination of the lease. Who will prevail? (*Eldredge v. Jensen,* 404 P.2d 624, Idaho)

32. Sharon Fitzgerald leased, on a month-to-month basis, a house from Roger Parkin. At the time the lease was created, Roger promised to make certain repairs. After repeated demands by Sharon, and the passage of three and a half months, Roger had not made the repairs. Sharon obtained an inspection from city authorities, which resulted in a citation of Roger for eight violations. One month later, Roger served Sharon with a 30-day notice to quit the premises. Roger then initiated an action to evict Sharon. Sharon defended the action on the ground that Roger was engaged in retaliatory eviction. Roger claims that his reason for evicting Sharon is that one of Sharon's rent checks bounced, another check had been late, and that she had kept a dog on the premises in violation of the lease. Who will prevail? (*Parkin v. Fitzgerald,* 240 N.W.2d 828, Minn.)

33. Under a five-year lease, Dr. Joseph Davidow rented space for his medical office from Inwood North. Inwood was to provide hot water, air-conditioning, and electricity, as well as security, janitorial, and maintenance services. During the lease period, the roof leaked, the air-conditioning did not work properly, and cleaning and maintenance were not done as promised. There was often no hot water and for several days there was no electricity. Davidow moved about a year before the lease ended. Inwood sued for the unpaid rent. Will Inwood win? (*Davidow v. Inwood North Professional Group— Phase I,* 747 S.W.2d 373, Tex.)

Cherberg v. Peoples National Bank of Washington
564 P.2d 1137 (Washington)

BACKGROUND James Cherberg and his wife claim the tort of intentional interference with business expectations arising from the willful refusal of the Joshua Green Corporation, their landlord, to perform duties owed them under a commercial lease. A jury verdict for $42,000 was entered in favor of the Cherbergs.

EVIDENCE James and Arlene Cherberg leased a portion of the Lewis Building on Fifth Avenue in downtown Seattle and invested approximately $80,000 in the establishment of a restaurant business at that location. Joshua Green Corporation acquired the Lewis Building in February, subject to the Cherberg lease. In April Peoples National Bank of Washington, the owner of the property abutting the Lewis Building on the south, commenced demolition of the existing buildings on its property for the purpose of constructing a high-rise office tower. The demolition work resulted in the exposure of the south wall of the Lewis Building. It was found to be structurally unsafe and in need of substantial repairs to satisfy requirements of the City of Seattle Building Department. The premises here at issue were located within the Lewis Building but did not abut the south wall.

The lease between the parties required the lessee to make necessary repairs to maintain the premises, excepting the outside walls and other structural components of the building, and reserved to the lessor the use of the roof and outside walls of the building.

Upon learning of the problems with the south wall, the lessor contacted the Cherbergs, indicating that the Green Corporation would probably elect not to repair the wall and that the City might order the building closed. The Cherbergs responded that the lessor was obligated under the lease to make repairs and that they would suffer substantial damage should their tenancy be disrupted.

TRIAL COURT'S DECISION The trial court, at the conclusion of testimony, instructed the jury that Green Corporation was liable for damages caused by the failure to repair the outside wall. It further instructed the jury with regard to the elements of the tort of intentional interference with business expectations that, if the jury concluded that the defendant's actions were willful, damages for mental suffering, inconvenience, and discomfort would be compensable. The jury made a special finding of willful action and returned a verdict of $42,000.

REASONING The first issue is the rights and duties of the parties with regard to the unsafe condition of the south wall of the building.

A landlord has a duty to maintain, control, and preserve retained portions of the premises subject to a leasehold in a manner rendering the rented premises adequate to the tenant's use. Failure to fulfill this duty results in liability on the part of the lessor for injury caused thereby, and failure to fulfill this duty, by omission to repair, can in a proper case constitute an actionable constructive eviction.

The willful refusal to adequately maintain retained portions of a building so as to allow the tenant to enjoy the beneficial use of the rented portion of the building is a breach of an implied duty owed by the landlord to the tenant under Washington law. On these facts, this breach of duty was sufficient to constitute an actionable constructive eviction and provides a basis for the conclusion that the landlord was liable for any damages stemming from that breach.

CONCLUSION The judgment in favor of the Cherbergs is upheld. It is so ordered.

PRACTICE JUDGING

1. Can the lease create a duty to repair, which differs from the duty presumed by the law?

2. Who had the duty to maintain the interior of the restaurant, the lessor or lessee? If the lessor had not retained control over the exterior walls, would the court have ruled differently?

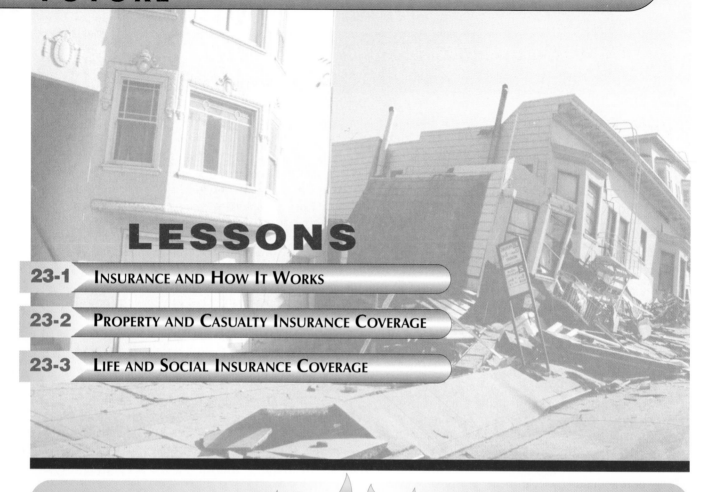

LESSONS

23-1 INSURANCE AND HOW IT WORKS

23-2 PROPERTY AND CASUALTY INSURANCE COVERAGE

23-3 LIFE AND SOCIAL INSURANCE COVERAGE

HOT DEBATE

You start a successful business. To insure against loss due to employee dishonesty, you must have fidelity insurance. You apply for it knowing that Joan, one of your managers, has served a prison term for theft. She has had many opportunities to take money from your business, but she has not done so. If you tell the insurance company about Joan's record, your rates would be so high that you would have to fire her to stay in business. Two years after you take out the policy, another employee steals $50,000. The insurance company performs a background check on all your employees. It finds out you knew but did not report Joan's record and refuses to pay the claim.

Where Do You Stand?

1. **If you sue to force the insurance company to adhere to the policy, what are the legal reasons supporting your suit?**

2. **What are the legal reasons in favor of the insurance company?**

GOALS

● **Discuss the common types of insurance**

● **Identify when an insurable interest is present**

WHAT IS INSURANCE?

WHAT'S YOUR VERDICT?

Bertellino is about to open a bicycle sales, exchange, and repair store. Because she is unsure how large the market is for such an enterprise, she asks an insurance agent to write a policy that would pay back any amount she might lose from business operations.

Will the agent be able to sell her a policy that insures her against the risk of doing business?

Insurance is a contractual arrangement that protects against loss. One party (usually an insurance company) agrees to pay money to help offset a specified type of loss that might occur to another party. The loss may be the death of a person, property damage from earthquake, or injury resulting from exposure to many other risks.

When one party pays to compensate for such harm, that party is said to indemnify, or make good, the loss to the suffering party. The party who agrees to indemnify is called the insurer. The party covered or protected is the insured, and the recipient of the amount to be paid is the beneficiary. In some cases, notably under life insurance contracts, the insured will not be the beneficiary.

Insurance makes an important contribution to society. By collecting relatively small premiums from many persons, an insurer builds a fund from which to pay insureds that suffer a covered loss. This process spreads losses among a greater number of people.

The written contract of insurance is called a policy. The face value of a policy is the stated maximum amount

that could be paid if the harm a person is insured against occurs. However, a person who suffers a loss covered by insurance recovers no more than the actual value of the loss, even if this amount is less than the face value of the policy.

IN THIS CASE

Carlson carried $10,000 of insurance coverage on his car to pay for repairs to it in the event he alone caused an accident that damaged the vehicle. Driving home from bowling one foggy night, he hit a telephone pole. The repairs cost $4,200. The insurance company would have to pay only this actual loss amount, not the $10,000 face value of the policy.

The consideration for a contract of insurance is called the premium. The possible loss arising from injury to or death of a person or from damage to property from a specified peril is called the risk.

The risk of most financial losses can be covered by insurance. Certain risks, however, cannot be covered. In *What's Your Verdict?* Bertellino cannot be insured against a business loss. This illustrates one of the most important risks for which a policy of insurance cannot be written. The risk of doing business is too unpredictable and too subject to the control of the would-be insured. If she were insured, Bertellino could simply neglect the business and yet collect on the insurance when the store failed. The best protection against the risk of doing business is found in hard work, good products, and excellent service.

COMMON TYPES OF INSURANCE

WHAT'S YOUR VERDICT?

To raise funds for a trip to the New Year's Day Parade in New Orleans, the Band Boosters planned a fall festival complete with contests and games. Some of the planned events involved a risk of injury to participants and spectators alike.

What kind of insurance would protect the Band Boosters against liability for negligence or other torts that might result in injury to individuals at the fundraiser?

There are seven major types of insurance. These are (1) life insurance, (2) fire insurance, (3) casualty insurance, (4) social insurance, (5) marine insurance, (6) inland marine insurance, and (7) fidelity and surety bonding insurance.

Life Insurance

Insurance that pays the beneficiary a set amount upon the death of a specified person is life insurance.

There are three common types of life insurance—term, whole or ordinary, and endowment. In addition, insurance companies have developed combination policies to meet the changing needs of their customers.

TERM INSURANCE Term insurance is written for a certain number of years—generally one, five, or ten years. If the insured dies within the policy term, the beneficiary receives the face value of the policy. If the term ends before the insured dies, the contract ends with no further obligation on the insured or the insurer. Term insurance is a relatively inexpensive type of life insurance.

WHOLE LIFE INSURANCE Whole life insurance (sometimes called ordinary or straight life insurance) provides for the payment of premiums for as long as the insured lives or until age 100. The premiums remain constant and a portion of the premium goes into a savings program against which the insured can borrow at a relatively low interest rate. If the insured dies, the face value (less any outstanding loans against it) is paid to the beneficiary.

A variation of whole life insurance is limited pay life. The policyholder pays premiums over a shorter period of time (usually 10, 20 or 30 years) and at a higher amount. Coverage extends beyond the period of making payments. The beneficiary receives the face value of the policy when the insured dies, whether the death occurs during the period when premiums are being paid or after all payments have been made. Limited pay life has the advantage of enabling the insureds to pay premiums while in their high-earning-power years.

ENDOWMENT LIFE INSURANCE Endowment life insurance requires the insurer to pay the beneficiary the policy's face amount if the insured dies within the period of coverage (usually 20 years or until the insured reaches retirement age). If the insured lives to the end of the coverage period, the owner of the policy (usually the insured) is paid the face value. Premiums for endowment policies are high, but this type of policy has been attractive to people who need a large lump sum available at a set point in time. For example, this money could be used to buy a retirement home.

Fire Insurance

Insurance that indemnifies for loss or damage due to fire (and usually smoke as well) is fire insurance. The typical fire insurance policy coverage may be increased to cover losses due to perils such as rain, hail, earthquake, and windstorm.

Casualty Insurance

Casualty insurance provides coverage for a variety of specific situations in which the intentional, negligent, or accidental acts of others or mere chance may result in loss. Some of the most important types of casualty insurance include the following.

BURGLARY, ROBBERY, THEFT, AND LARCENY INSURANCE Such insurance protects against losses resulting from identifiable criminal behavior. In addition, this form of insurance may also protect against the mysterious disappearance of property, that is, when the cause of the property's vanishing cannot be ascertained.

AUTOMOBILE INSURANCE This type of insurance indemnifies for losses arising from or connected to the owner-

ship and operation of motor vehicles. This important insurance coverage will be discussed later in this chapter.

LIABILITY INSURANCE Such insurance provides protection against claims of parties who suffer injury or other loss as a result of negligence or other torts committed by the insured. In *What's Your Verdict?* if the Band Boosters were insured under a suitable liability policy, the organization would be protected against claims arising from the fundraiser.

DISABILITY, ACCIDENT, OR HEALTH INSURANCE These policies protect the insured from the financial consequences of hospital bills and loss of income stemming from accident or illness.

Social Insurance

Under the provisions of the Social Security Act and related acts, millions of Americans insure themselves against unemployment, disability, poverty, and medical expense problems.

Marine Insurance

Marine insurance indemnifies for loss of or damage to vessels, cargo, and other property exposed to the perils of the sea. It is perhaps the oldest type of insurance, dating back to ancient times.

Inland Marine Insurance

Inland marine insurance covers personal property against loss or damage caused by various perils where the property is located. The property is also covered while it is being transported by any means other than on the oceans.

Fidelity and Surety Bonding Insurance

Fidelity insurance provides coverage against financial loss caused by dishonesty. Such dishonest acts include embezzlement or failure of one person to perform a legal obligation to another, such as constructing a building as promised. Contracts of fidelity insurance are often known as surety bonds.

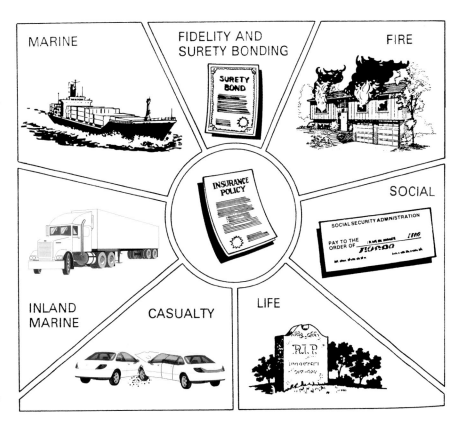

MARINE

FIDELITY AND SURETY BONDING

FIRE

SOCIAL

INLAND MARINE

CASUALTY

LIFE

INSURABLE INTEREST

WHAT'S YOUR VERDICT?

When Sanders bought Dante's only car, she offered to pay him an extra $100 for the two months of protection still remaining on his automobile insurance policy. Dante refused, saying he alone did not have the power to transfer its protection to her.

Was he correct?

Insurance is intended to be a personal contract between the insurer and the insured. In *What's Your Verdict?* Dante was correct. Merely buying goods that have been insured does not transfer the benefits of the insurance policy to the new property owner. Even if paid, the insured cannot transfer or assign the benefits of the policy to a third person without the permission of the insurer.

A person with contractual capacity can acquire insurance if he or she would suffer loss if the insured property is damaged or destroyed or if the insured person is injured or dies. This potential to sustain loss is referred to as an **insurable interest**.

Insurable Interests in Property

Any person who would suffer a direct and measurable monetary loss if property were damaged or destroyed has an insurable interest in that property. Note, however, for the insurer to be legally obligated to pay, an insurable interest in property must exist at the time of the loss. A person may not insure property, then sell it, and expect to be paid if the property is later damaged or destroyed.

A person need not hold all the property rights (title, possession, use, a security interest, or some future interest) in the insured property in order to have an insurable interest. Just one of these rights would be sufficient. Many individuals may all have an insurable interest in the same property at the same time.

IN THIS CASE

Severson planted a large cucumber crop on her farm. To help her at harvest time, she bought a cucumber picker from a farm supply store for $7,300. She paid $2,300 in cash and financed the balance. The seller, Equipment Unlimited, retained a security interest in the device. Both Severson and Equipment Unlimited have an insurable interest in the cucumber picker.

Insurable Interests in Life

A person has an insurable interest in her or his life. Everyone who meets the insurance company's requirements and is legally competent may acquire a life insurance policy on herself or himself. Would-be beneficiaries seeking to take out a policy on another person's life must demonstrate that they would suffer direct financial loss if the insured died.

Creditors may insure their debtors, business people may insure their partners or key employees, and husbands and wives may insure one another. Courts frequently rule against adult children having insurable interests in their aging parents. Brothers and sisters ordinarily do not have insurable interests in each other.

Unlike property insurance, the insured has to demonstrate only an insurable interest at the time the policy is taken out, not at the time of the death of the person whose life is insured.

THINK ABOUT LEGAL CONCEPTS

Answer the following questions about legal concepts.

1. The party who agrees to indemnify another is termed the **(a) insurer (b) insured (c) beneficiary.**

2. The face amount of a policy is always paid whenever the covered loss is sustained. **True or False?**

3. The risk of any and all financial losses can be covered by insurance. **True or False?**

4. Which type of insurance covers loss of or damage to property while it is being transported? **(a) marine (b) surety (c) fidelity (d) none of the above**

5. The beneficiary's insurable interest must exist at the time of loss for a life insurance policy to pay. **True or False?**

6. An insurable interest in property must exist at the time of loss for a fire insurance policy to pay. **True or False?**

THINK CRITICALLY ABOUT EVIDENCE

Study the following situations, answer the questions, then prepare arguments to support your answers.

7. Copeland contracted for fire insurance coverage for the full value of her $225,000 home at an annual cost of $1,187. Harvest States Insurance Company issued the policy. Identify the **(a) insurer (b) insured (c) subject matter (d) risk (e) face value (f) premium.**

8. Your parents are concerned about the advancing age of their parents. They apply for life insurance on the lives of each of your grandparents, to be used to pay for funeral expenses. Will the applications be accepted?

9. Lampson sold Stark a large recreational vehicle for $52,500. However, Lampson forgot to cancel the insurance he held on the vehicle. One month after Stark bought the recreational vehicle, it was totally destroyed by fire. Shocked by the occurrence, Lampson then remembered the policy and immediately filed a claim for the loss of the recreational vehicle with his insurance company. Will he be able to collect?

10. Buck and Shannon formed a partnership to market a new type of computer memory device that Buck had developed. Shannon, who was in poor health, had all the business contacts that would make the venture a success. Buck worried that she would lose her $250,000 investment if Shannon died. Therefore, Buck insured Shannon's life for $250,000. A year later, Shannon quit the partnership and retired. Buck decided to keep the insurance in force, however, and when Shannon died eight months after she retired, Buck sought to collect the $250,000 from the insurance company. Will she be successful?

> ## GOALS
>
> ● **Know the types of coverage provided by property and casualty insurance**
>
> ● **Understand the coverages provided in an automobile insurance policy**

PROPERTY AND CASUALTY INSURANCE

WHAT'S YOUR VERDICT?

Waste Not, Want Not, an environmentally oriented rock group, insured its $28,000 worth of equipment with two different companies. When the group's tour bus overturned and the equipment was destroyed, the group tried to collect in full from both companies.

Will it be allowed to do so?

The general type of insurance intended to indemnify for harm to the insured's personal or real property brought about by perils such as fire, theft, and windstorm is **property insurance**. The type of insurance that indemnifies for losses resulting from accident, chance, or negligence is **casualty insurance**. There is some overlap between these two. Certain types of casualty insurance (for example, automotive policies) are written to indemnify for both casualty and property losses. Examples of casualty insurance include workers' compensation, disability insurance, and health insurance. Liability insurance, which protects the insured against other parties' claims of negligence or other tortious conduct, is also a type of casualty insurance.

The purpose of all property and casualty insurance is indemnification for loss. This means that a person who experiences a loss recovers no more than the actual value of the loss. In *What's Your Verdict?* Waste Not, Want Not's total recovery from both insurance companies could not exceed $28,000.

Although property and casualty insurance can be obtained to indemnify for almost any peril that might cause a loss, certain exceptions to coverage relieve the insurance company from paying. These exceptions, known as **exclusions**, are expressly stated in the policy.

Many states make certain that all exclusions are easily noticeable within a policy. States may require that exclusions be set in a different style and larger size of type, in a different color of print, or both. Examples of common exclusions include losses due to war, invasion, rebellion, nuclear disaster, depreciation, and pollution.

Fire Insurance

The type of property insurance that covers the direct loss to property resulting from fire, lightning strike, or removal from premises endangered by fire is known as **fire insurance**. Any fire insurance contract written to cover these risks is composed of a basic or *standard fire policy* and one or more forms that modify the standard policy to make it apply to the

specific type of property being insured.

The standard fire policy itself is composed of basic policy provisions required by the law of the state in which the policy is written. All the states have such provisions. Some forms include a Dwellings and Contents Form for homes and a Mercantile Building and Stock Form for businesses. For those who have no need for policies to cover the building itself, such as renters and tenants, there are special forms covering only the contents and other personal property.

The standard policy and forms may also be modified by **endorsements** (also known as *riders*). Endorsements are attached to the policy and forms to provide for special and individual needs. Endorsements help, for example, in determining whether a loss was caused by fire, lightning, wind, explosion, or some other peril.

Suppose that a truck crashes into a building and explodes, causing a fire. In such a case, it would be hard to tell how much of the loss was caused by the impact of the truck, how much by the explosion, and how much by the resulting fire. To avoid this difficulty, a fire insurance policy may be issued with an *extended coverage endorsement.* This endorsement adds coverage for damage by windstorm, hail, explosion, riot, smoke, aircraft, and vehicles. Therefore, it would not be necessary to determine the exact cause of the damage, because all possible causes would be covered. Because of the frequency of the losses covered by an extended coverage endorsement, such an endorsement usually is added routinely to the Dwellings and Contents Form.

Regardless of the particular forms or endorsements added to the standard fire policy, three steps must be taken to prove that a particular loss should be indemnified.

First, the insured must show that there was an actual fire. A glow or a flame is required. Damage to an item resulting from scorching, blistering, or smoke due to being too near to a heat source is not enough.

Second, the actual fire has to be hostile. A *hostile fire* is either (1) a fire started by accident, negligence, or a deliberate act uncontrolled by the insured or (2) a *friendly fire* (a fire in its intended place) that becomes uncontrollable.

Third, the hostile fire has to be the natural and foreseeable cause of the loss. This cause is referred to as being the proximate cause of the harm. Generally, a hostile fire is considered the proximate cause of damage produced not only by the burning, but also produced by scorching, smoke, techniques used in extinguishing the fire, and actions in removing goods endangered by the fire.

As the capability of fire departments to respond to alarms and quickly suppress fires has increased over the years, the number of structures totally lost to fire has decreased markedly. In recognition of this fact and the needs of their insureds to keep premiums low, insurance companies developed coinsurance.

Coinsurance is a clause in a fire insurance policy that requires the insured to maintain coverage equal to a certain percentage of the total current value of the insured property. The coverage amount, therefore, must be increased as the property value increases. In the event of loss, the insurance company will fully indemnify up to the face amount of the policy unless the insured has failed to keep that face amount at the proper level.

Inland Marine Insurance

Modeled after insurance covering goods being transported on the high seas, **inland marine insurance** was developed by fire insurance companies to indemnify for loss to most personal property while it is being transported across land or inland waterways. However, the carrier, such as the automobile, airplane, or railroad car, is not covered by this insurance. In response to the changing needs of insureds over time, the basic inland marine policy was altered to produce a second type, called a *personal property floater.* This was issued to cover any and all of an insured's personal property against practically any peril regardless of the location of the property. The term *floater* means that the protection floats with, or follows, the property.

Rather than have the policy written to cover all the insured's personal property, it is also possible to contract for coverage of scheduled (specifically identified) property, such as jewelry, furs, stamp collections, musical instruments, livestock, athletic equipment, wedding presents, and photographic equipment. One can also arrange to insure a single piece of personal property, such as an organ or a neon sign. Mail-order dealers frequently take out a blanket policy to cover all losses, including breakage and mysterious disappearances of shipped goods. Laundries and dry cleaners may take out policies covering possible losses to customers' property in their possession. Such a policy is known as *lessee insurance.*

Although the application of the personal property floater is quite broad, some losses are excluded from coverage. Examples include losses caused by wear and tear, repair efforts, dampness, temperature, war, confiscation, and dishonesty of a party to whom the goods have been entrusted.

Liability Insurance

Liability insurance is a type of casualty insurance that indemnifies against personal injury or property damage claims for which the insured is legally responsible. Generally, liability coverage is limited to harm

CULTURAL DIVERSITY IN LAW

International

History of Property Insurance

As far back as the fourteenth century in Europe, ships' cargos were protected against risk by marine insurance. The oldest known marine insurance policy written in English covered the voyage of a ship called the Santa Crux around 1555. By the late seventeenth century, private homes were being insured in London. The sale of insurance to private individuals and businesses became widespread in the late nineteenth century.

accidentally caused by the insured. Intentional infliction of harm by the insured is not covered.

Liability coverage is a major part of most automobile insurance policies. Coverage for liability claims not arising out of the operation of a motor vehicle is often offered as part of a homeowner's or an apartment dweller's insurance policy.

Many persons engaged in providing personal services, such as beauty salon operators, and most businesses usually carry liability insurance. Persons rendering professional services, such as hospital operators and physicians, usually purchase coverage for malpractice through liability insurance. Television and radio broadcasting companies also carry liability insurance to protect against liability for defamation.

AUTOMOBILE INSURANCE

WHAT'S YOUR
VERDICT?

While driving, Williams was momentarily blinded by the sun reflecting off a passing car. Consequently, he missed an upcoming curve, and his car overturned. Although his vehicle was totally destroyed, Williams was not injured because he was wearing his seatbelt.

What type of insurance would cover Williams for the loss of his vehicle in this situation?

A variety of coverages may be provided by **automobile insurance**. Primary among these is coverage for liability. An automobile insurance policy's liability coverage obligates the insurer to represent and provide for the insured's defense if the insured is accused of or sued for negligent ownership, maintenance, or use of the motor vehicle. In addition, if necessary, the coverage indemnifies for the payment of damages resulting from such negligence.

Automobile liability insurance coverage may be augmented by an *omnibus clause.* An omnibus clause extends similar coverage to all members of the named insured's household and to any person not in the household who is given permission to drive the insured's car.

Automobile liability insurance also commonly provides coverage for the insured and members of the insured's family when such persons are operating non-owned vehicles with the owner's permission. This coverage applies to all borrowed or substitute automobiles. Examples include automobiles used when the car described in the policy has broken down or is being repaired or serviced. Also, if one purchases another automobile to replace the insured car, generally all the coverage under the policy applies to the replacement car for a limited time as specified in the policy.

When one becomes liable for damage or injury while driving a vehicle he or she does not own, the car owner's policy provides the primary coverage. The driver's policy then provides coverage up to its face amount for any excess liability.

Because insurers are contractually liable for legitimate claims against their insureds, the insurers have the right either to settle such claims out of court or to defend their insureds in court. Since the insurer has potential liability under the policy, only the insurer can make a settlement with claimants against the insured. If the insurer requires the presence of the insured as a witness at any legal hearings, most automobile insurance policies provide for payment of lost wages to the insured.

Liability claims against the insured that the insurer may have to pay include bodily injury or death of third parties and damage to the property of

third parties. Third parties are persons other than the insured or insurer.

Other types of coverage available under the typical automobile insurance policy are medical payments coverage, collision and comprehensive coverage, and uninsured and underinsured coverage.

Medical Payments Coverage

Medical payments coverage pays for the reasonable medical claims of occupants of the insured's vehicle who are injured in an automobile accident. An occupant is one who is in, upon, entering, or leaving a vehicle. The coverage also applies to the insured and the insured's family members while such persons are driving or riding in another's vehicle. This kind of coverage is mainly for vehicle occupants. However, it also covers the named insured and the family members if a vehicle strikes those persons while walking, riding bikes, roller skating, or sledding.

Collision and Comprehensive Coverage

Two types of automobile insurance coverage indemnify insureds for damage to their own vehicles. The first, **collision insurance**, protects against direct and accidental damage due to (a) colliding with another object, such as a tree or bridge abutment, and (b) upset, such as the overturn suffered by Williams in *What's Your Verdict?* Collision coverage would provide Williams compensation for the loss of his vehicle in the accident.

Collision coverage pays only the actual cash value (the cost new minus an allowance for age and use) of the vehicle or its damaged parts less any deductible. Thus, for each loss the insured pays up to the amount of the deductible. The insurer pays the rest up to the policy limit.

The second type of automobile insurance coverage indemnifying insureds for damage to their own vehicles is comprehensive coverage. (Sometimes it is called *other than col-*

lision insurance.) **Comprehensive insurance** indemnifies against all damage to the insured's car *except* that caused by collision or upset. The causes covered by comprehensive insurance, which could occur for any reason, include fire, theft, water, vandalism, hail, and glass breakage. Theft includes loss of the car and any part of the car, such as hubcaps. However, loss of clothing and other personal property left in the car generally is not covered unless the loss is by fire. Similarly, most policies require extra premiums to cover compact disc players, radios, and stereos. Any damage done to a car, such as broken locks, is covered.

Uninsured and Underinsured Coverage

When an accident is caused by the negligence of a driver who is uninsured and potentially insolvent or who leaves the scene and cannot be found, innocent parties involved in the accident may have to bear their own losses. Certainly their collision and medical payments coverage may help, but significant amounts of loss, for example, lost wages and the medical payments that exceed the limit of their policy, may not be indemnified.

Consequently, many vehicle owners carry a supplemental coverage to a regular policy. This additional coverage, called *uninsured motorists coverage*, allows the insured to collect damages from his or her own insurance company when they are not collectible from the person who caused the harm. In most states, the coverage is limited to compensation for bodily injury, death, lost wages or support, and pain and suffering. Indemnification for property damage is generally excluded from this coverage. In this same vein is *underinsured motorists coverage* which compensates the insured when the negligent driver does not have *sufficient* insurance to cover damages. Like uninsured motorists coverage, underinsured motorists coverage excludes payment for property damage.

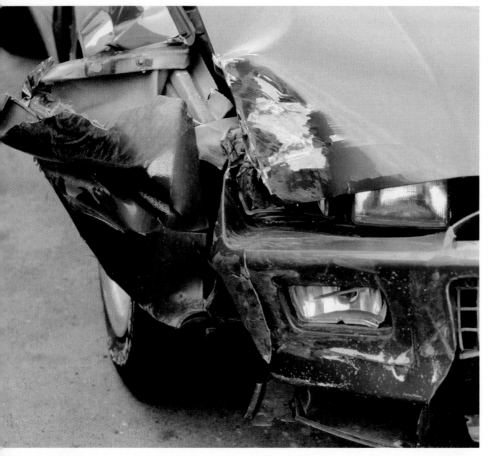

No-Fault Insurance

Finally, it should be noted in a discussion of automobile insurance, that, to curtail the growing case loads of our court systems, some states have instituted no-fault insurance systems. No-fault insurance requires that parties to an automobile accident be indemnified by their own insurance company regardless of who is at fault. Therefore, a court trial to determine who is at fault in an accident may be avoided. The indemnification of the losses by the insurance company takes the place of the damages that might have been awarded. However, if the medical claims of an injured person are larger than a set amount or the injuries are permanent, a suit can be brought for all alleged damages, including pain and suffering.

Generally, property damage is not covered at all by a no-fault system. This is because it is not likely that people will sue for the amounts involved. Insurance companies tend to resolve such claims fairly and efficiently without court involvement.

THINK ABOUT LEGAL CONCEPTS

Answer the following questions about legal concepts.

1. Automobile insurance may be written to indemnify for both casualty and property losses. **True or False?**

2. Depreciation is a common exclusion to property insurance coverage. **True or False?**

3. Which of the following is not covered in the standard fire policy? **(a) losses due to fire (b) losses due to lightning strikes (c) losses due to inept attorneys (d) none of the above are covered**

4. A friendly fire that becomes uncontrollable is considered a hostile fire for fire insurance purposes. **True or False?**

5. A(n) ___?___ clause extends auto insurance coverage to members of the insured's household.

THINK CRITICALLY ABOUT EVIDENCE

Study the following situations, answer the questions, then prepare arguments to support your answers.

6. Scandinavian Fire Insurance Company insured Carnes against fire. One day while ironing, he left the room to answer the telephone and negligently forgot to turn off the iron. The iron fell from the ironing board, and the carpet caught fire. The fire then spread to the drapes. As flames engulfed the room, smoke damaged the remainder of the house. Will the loss be covered by the policy?

7. To protect her inventory, Olivet, owner of an appliance store, carried a coinsurance fire policy. The policy required that Olivet carry insurance in the amount of 80 percent of the current inventory value. Late one night, fire totally destroyed the inventory, which was valued at $100,000 when the loss occurred. The face value of Olivet's policy was $80,000. For how much of the $100,000 loss will the insurance company pay?

8. Some of the wiring in Thomas' car shorted out and started a fire. Before the blaze could be extinguished, the car was destroyed. What type of automobile insurance coverage would indemnify Thomas?

9. Olsen negligently backed into Sabatino's car. Olsen was very apologetic and, after a few minutes of negotiating, paid Sabatino for the damage. Olsen then asked his automobile insurance company to reimburse him under its liability coverage for the amount he had paid Sabatino. Must the insurance company do so?

GOALS

- Identify common provisions in life insurance contracts
- Explain the types of social insurance

LIFE AND SOCIAL INSURANCE

WHAT'S YOUR VERDICT?

Borrego worries about what would happen to her and her family if she would lose her job.

What kind of insurance would help her if that happened?

Life insurance is a contractual arrangement under which an insurer promises to pay an agreed-upon amount of money to a named party upon the death of a particular person. Given the uncertainties of today's world and its fast-paced mode of living, such insurance is crucial to families, businesses, and responsible individuals throughout our society.

Social insurance indemnifies persons, at least partially, from the harsh financial consequences of unemployment, disability, death, or forced retirement. Since the late 1930s, programs under the federal government's Social Security Act have been instrumental in providing such protection. In *What's Your Verdict?* Borrego would likely be assisted during a time of unemployment by compensation provided under the Social Security Act.

Without the protection of life and social insurance, the potentially adverse impact of death, disability, unemployment, or advancing age would have to be borne solely by the individuals directly affected. Society finds it important to do as much as possible to protect against the adverse consequences of such occurrences.

LIFE INSURANCE

WHAT'S YOUR VERDICT?

Edmonton was the beneficiary of her uncle's term life insurance policy. When her uncle, a Navy pilot on active duty, was killed in a terrorist bomb explosion overseas, the insurance company refused to pay the policy's face value of $100,000.

Can the insurance company legally be forced to pay the policy?

The insurer of life agrees to pay to a named beneficiary or to the insured's estate the amount stated in the policy, in accordance with the policy provisions. However, life insurance policies sometimes contain provisions that exempt the insurer from liability when death is due to certain causes, such as the crash of a private airplane.

Policies may also provide for exemption from liability in case of the policyholder's death during military service abroad or at home. In cases where death occurs under an exemption, the insurer is liable for return of the premiums paid or cash value (less loans against the policy), instead of the proceeds. In *What's Your Verdict?* if such an exemption were in Edmonton's uncle's policy, the insurance company could not legally be forced to pay the $100,000.

In addition to exemptions, a life insurance policy usually contains an *incontestability clause.* Such a clause prohibits the insurer from refusing to perform due to misrepresentation or fraud after the policy has been in effect for a specified period of time—usually one or two years. However, if the misrepresentation or fraud involves the age of the insured, the policy is not voided regardless of the length of time it has been in effect. Instead the insurer provides the face amount of insurance that the premium would have bought if the insured's correct age had been known.

A similar clause requires the insurer to pay even if the insured commits suicide after one or two years from the date the policy was issued. If the suicide occurs before the one- or two-year limit, the insurer is required to return only the premiums paid.

By statute, most life insurance contracts must also provide for a period of time, called the *grace period,* during which an overdue premium can be paid to keep the policy in force. Typically, this period is one month. If an insured fails to pay the premium before the grace period expires, the policy terminates, or *lapses.* A policyholder in good health who pays the back premiums can revive or *reinstate* a lapsed policy.

In addition to these common provisions, it is possible to write additional coverage into a life insurance policy. One way is through *double indemnity coverage,* which requires the insurer to pay twice the face amount of the policy if the death of the insured is accidental. Triple or quadruple coverage may also be purchased, if desired. Such coverage usually excludes certain causes of death, such as suicide, illness or dis-

ease, wartime military service, and certain airplane accidents. It also is inapplicable after a certain age, such as 65 or 70.

The second additional coverage, *disability coverage,* provides for protection against the effects of total permanent disability. At a minimum, it cancels the requirement for payment of policy premiums while the insured is totally disabled. It often provides money to replace lost wages.

SOCIAL INSURANCE

WHAT'S YOUR VERDICT?

Farley had just started college when his mother died unexpectedly. Her paycheck had been the Farley family's sole source of support for more than a decade.

Is there a social insurance program that might help Farley and the rest of his family?

The primary source for *social insurance* coverage in this country is the federal government's Social Security Act. Coverage provided under the act is frequently labeled RSDHI (for Retirement, Survivors', Disability, and Health Insurance). Unemployment compensation, which is designed to lessen the financial hardship of losing one's job, is also provided indirectly through programs under the act. Unemployment compensation programs, however, are controlled by the individual states.

RETIREMENT INSURANCE An eligible person may elect to begin receiving social security retirement insurance checks as early as age 62 or may wait until age 66 or 70. However, the amount of the monthly income differs considerably between the three options, in favor of the person who retires later. Whatever option is chosen, the checks from the social security retirement insurance program are meant to provide supplemental

income only. Too often, individuals rely solely on these checks for their retirement income. This is not the purpose of the program.

During the working years, each individual is responsible for accumulating savings. This savings should provide enough income that, when added to the social security retirement amount, will allow an adequate standard of living during the retirement years. All too often, people retire only to find that they have to return to some form of employment to make ends meet.

SURVIVOR'S INSURANCE Survivors of a person eligible for benefits under the system may also receive benefits if they are a widow or widower age 60 or older (or, if disabled, age 50 or older); a widow or widower of any age if caring for a child under age 16 or a child that is disabled; or a dependent child. In *What's Your Verdict?* assistance may likely be provided to Farley and his family by survivors' insurance benefits.

A Question of ETHICS ?

Under the current Social Security Act, all working people have a portion of their paychecks withheld as a FICA tax. (FICA stands for Federal Insurance Contributions Act). These funds are used to pay social security retirement insurance benefits to current retirees. There is some debate about whether funds will be available to pay benefits to current contributors when they retire. Is it ethical of the federal government to deduct this tax from workers' paychecks when they can't guarantee the benefits?

DISABILITY INSURANCE A severe, long-lasting disability is one that prevents the eligible person from being able to do "any substantial work." Before any payments can be made, it must be established that the condition is physical or mental, and is expected to continue indefinitely or result in death. The disabled person must have earned a certain number of work credits within a specific time period. The eligible person must not refuse reasonable medical treatment.

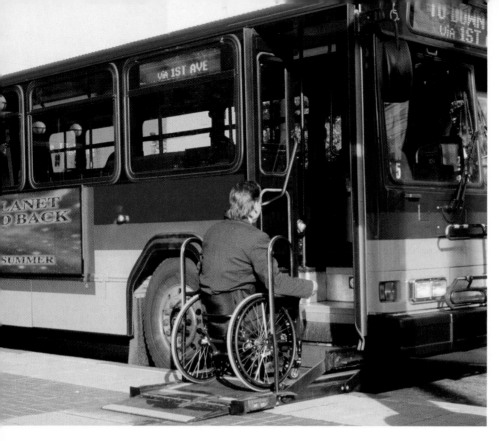

hospital for necessary treatment. Persons with enough work credits and who are age 65, those with permanent kidney failure, or those covered for extensive periods by the disability program if under age 65 are eligible.

Medical insurance, the second basic Medicare program, helps pay for items not covered by hospital insurance. These include services of physicians and surgeons. Also included are services such as ambulance charges, X-rays, radium treatments, laboratory tests, surgical dressings, casts, and home visits by nurses or therapists. The patient pays relatively small yearly deductibles, and then medical insurance generally pays either a large percentage or all of the costs of the covered services.

Unlike hospital insurance coverage, financed primarily from the social security tax, contracting and paying premiums for medical insurance coverage are voluntary. Each person enrolled in the medical insurance plan pays a monthly premium. The federal government pays an equal amount out of general revenues.

The following ordinarily are considered severe enough to meet the test of disability:

- loss of both arms, both legs, or a leg and an arm
- heart and lung diseases that cause pain or fatigue on slight exertion
- progressive cancer
- brain damage that results in loss of judgment or memory
- loss of vision, inability to speak, deafness

HEALTH INSURANCE In the last two decades, the costs of medical care have risen so dramatically that a major illness involving extended hospitalization and treatment threatens not only the physical well-being but also the financial livelihood of the patient and the patient's family. As a consequence, *health insurance,* which indemnifies against the cost of medical care necessary to regain physical well-being after an illness, has become very important. *Medicare* provides such coverage primarily for those age 65 and over. Private insurance companies provide similar coverage for those not protected by the Social Security Act.

Medicare consists of two basic programs. The first, *hospital insurance,* helps pay for hospital expenses and the costs of follow-up treatment. To receive payments under this program, an eligible person must enter a

The Social Security Administration (SSA) is the government agency that runs the Social Security program in the United States. The SSA has one of the most extensive websites of any government agency. When you visit http://www.ssa.gov you can perform a number of functions. You can learn about the history of the SSA and its plans for the future. You can inquire about all of the benefits that the SSA offers, such as retirement income and Medicare medical insurance. You can also request many of the services the SSA offers directly from the website. The SSA accepts requests from the website for personal earnings and benefits summaries. Companies also can download forms used to report employees' earnings and wages to the SSA. Before the growth of the Internet, you had to visit an SSA field office in person to receive many of these services. Now you can receive these services and even contact your field office directly from your home or office computer.

Answer the following questions about legal concepts.

1. Which of the following indemnifies against the cost of medical care necessary to regain physical well-being after an illness? **(a) survivor's insurance (b) disability insurance (c) health insurance (d) life insurance**

2. Unemployment insurance is provided directly by the Social Security Act. **True or False?**

3. A(n) __?__ clause prohibits an insurer from refusing to perform due to fraud or misrepresentation after a policy has been in effect for one or two years.

4. Double-indemnity coverage requires the insurer to pay half the face amount of the policy if the death of the insured is accidental. **True or False?**

5. Which of the following types of social insurance provides health insurance and hospital insurance for people age 65 and older? **(a) retirement insurance (b) survivor's insurance (c) disability insurance (d) Medicare**

Study the following situations, answer the questions, then prepare arguments to support your answers.

6. A month after his release from jail, Bill Bravo insured his own life in a double indemnity policy. Two months later, he was killed while attempting to hold up a bank. The insurance company refused to pay the benefits to Bill's wife and son, even though the policy contained no provision excluding liability if the insured died as a result of violating the law. Under what legal grounds can the insurance company refuse to pay this claim?

7. When Henecker took out his life insurance policy, he misrepresented his age as 27. In reality, he was 34. Will the insurance company be required to pay on the policy when Henecker dies?

8. Shuster had a $100,000 triple indemnity life insurance policy. Three years after contracting for it, she committed suicide. Will the insurance company have to pay $300,000?

PREVENT LEGAL DIFFICULTIES

1. Be honest in answering all questions on insurance applications. A false representation or warranty or concealing a material fact may allow the insurance company to avoid the policy rather than pay for the loss.

2. Carefully read the insurance contract to be familiar with all its terms. Pay special attention to stated exclusions and conditions.

3. Select your potential insurers with caution as to their financial reserves and their reputation for good service in case of loss.

4. Be aware of the expiration dates, cancellation terms, and renewal provisions of your policies. Move quickly to acquire other coverage if a policy lapses or is terminated.

5. One of the most frequently incurred and potentially disastrous liabilities results from a lawsuit based on bodily injury and property damage in an automobile accident. To protect yourself, carry adequate automobile liability coverage.

6. If you are sued as a result of an accident and you have complied with the policy requirements, your insurer is required to defend you. Thus, if you are involved in an accident, no matter how trivial it may seem to you, report it to your insurer immediately.

CHAPTER IN REVIEW

CONCEPTS IN BRIEF

1. Although insurance is an excellent way to protect against possible loss, certain risks such as that of doing business cannot be covered.

2. Losses covered by a fire insurance policy will be indemnified only upon a showing that they were most likely caused by a hostile fire.

3. A property or casualty insurance policy can be assigned only with the consent of the insurer. The right to recover from an insurer a loss that has already been sustained may be assigned by the insured without consent of the insurer.

4. Coinsurance requires the insured to keep the face value of the policy equal to a certain percentage (usually 80 percent) of the current value of the insured property.

5. The basic purpose of automobile insurance is to provide coverage against liability. It can also provide medical payments coverage, collision and comprehensive coverage, and uninsured and underinsured coverage.

6. No-fault insurance, which indemnifies the insured for various losses sustained in an automobile accident regardless of who had legal responsibility for the accident, is now required by some states.

7. Federal disability insurance provides monthly benefits for a worker and dependents if a severe, long-lasting disability is suffered.

8. Social Security retirement insurance provides monthly benefits for a worker and dependents when the worker retires at age 62 or later.

YOUR LEGAL VOCABULARY

Match each statement with the term that it best defines. Some terms may not be used.

1. To make good a loss

2. Party who will indemnify if loss occurs

3. Stated maximum amount that can be paid under a policy

4. Consideration for a contract of insurance

5. The potential loss that has been insured against

6. Potential to sustain loss due to the covered risk

7. Indemnifies for loss from personal negligence, chance, and accident

8. Exceptions to insurance coverage

9. Modification to the standard fire policy made to satisfy individual needs

10. Requires that, in the event of loss, insureds be indemnified by their own insurance companies

11. Clause in a fire policy that requires the insured to maintain coverage equal to a certain percentage of the total current value of the insured property

12. Insurance to cover personal injury or property damage claims for which the insured is legally responsible

automobile insurance
beneficiary
casualty insurance
coinsurance
collision insurance
comprehensive insurance
endorsements
exclusions
face value
fire insurance
indemnify
insurable interest
insurance
insured
insurer
liability insurance
life insurance
no-fault insurance
policy
premium
property insurance
risk

13. Do you think you could find insurance to cover your potential losses from a trip to Las Vegas for gambling? Why or why not?

14. Why does the insurable interest in property have to be present at the time of loss?

15. What is the purpose of fidelity insurance?

16. The insurable interest in life only has to be present when the policy is taken out. Can you think of situations where this might lead to problems?

17. Why should renters and tenants have fire and liability insurance?

18. Write an imaginary letter to an automobile insurance company. In your letter, state the reasons why they should not charge you the maximum premium amount for your age group on automobile insurance coverage.

19. **HOT DEBATE** Write a persuasive opening statement that emphasizes the legal and ethical points in your favor. Write a persuasive opening statement that emphasizes the legal and ethical points in the insurer's favor.

Study the following situations, answer the questions, then prepare arguments to support your answers.

20. An abandoned store surrounded by high, dry weeds stood adjacent to a frequently traveled road near Ashleigh's home. She realized that the store would be destroyed if just one cigarette butt were thrown from a passing vehicle. Therefore, even though she did not own it, she decided to insure the building against loss by fire. After she obtained the insurance, there was a fire. Legally, will Ashleigh be allowed to collect?

21. Claudia James took out a $200,000 life insurance policy on her husband and named herself as beneficiary. Three months later they were divorced, and a month after that her ex-husband died in a car accident. Claudia sought to collect on the policy, but the insurance company refused to pay. The company said she lacked an insurable interest both at the time the policy was taken out and at the time of death. Is the company legally obligated to pay the $200,000?

22. McNeely owned a go-cart track on which the public was invited to race the small motorized carts that she provided. Collisions and upsets occurred relatively frequently. What type of insurance would it be advisable for McNeely to have?

23. Dr. Bray performed a tympanoplasty (eardrum replacement) on Azle. The operation appeared to be successful, but one year later the doctor found the ear canal to be completely closed due to the growth of scar tissue from areas where Dr. Bray had drilled improperly. What type of insurance would protect Dr. Bray from a malpractice suit by Azle?

24. Sarnof took a summer job to earn money for his college education. On his way home from work late one evening, a drunken driver ran a red light and smashed into Sarnof's car. Sarnof's medical bills were more than $45,000 and his injuries prevented him from working for the rest of the summer. Unfortunately, the drunken driver had only the minimum state-required liability coverage ($10,000). The driver also had little or no assets or income to pay for Sarnof's losses. Sarnof's automobile insurance policy had liability and uninsured motorist protections. Must Sarnof absorb the majority of his medical bills and losses himself?

ANALYZE REAL CASES

25. Antrell made an offer to purchase a building on the Leech Lake Indian Reservation for $300. He paid $100 in cash at the time he made the offer and received the keys to the structure. Without examining the property, his insurance company issued a policy with a face value of $16,000. Several months later, fire totally destroyed the structure. At the time of the loss, Antrell had not paid the balance of the purchase price nor had the title been transferred. The company claims that the plaintiff did not have the required insurable interest and that, therefore, the company was not liable on the policy. Do you think the company should pay? (*Antrell v. Pearl Assurance Company,* 89 N.W.2d 726)

26. Lakin sued the Postal Life and Casualty Insurance Company for its failure to pay him, as beneficiary, under an insurance policy on the life of his business partner, Hankinson. Evidence presented at the trial showed that Hankinson had contributed neither capital nor skills to the alleged partnership, that he could not issue partnership checks, and that he could not hire or fire employees. In addition, it was disclosed that Lakin paid the policy premiums and had made no settlement of "partnership" interests after Hankinson's death. Should the insurance company be ordered by the court to pay the $25,000 face amount to Lakin? (*Lakin v. Postal Life and Casualty Insurance Company,* 316 S.W.2d 542)

27. In the life insurance policy agreed to by James McElroy was a term that read, "if the insured is over the age of 54 years at the date hereof, this policy is void. . . ." McElroy was indeed over 54 at the time. When he died three years later, his beneficiary sued for the face amount of the policy claiming it should be paid because of a two-year incontestability clause in the same policy. Should the court order the insurance company to pay the policy's face amount? (*Hall v. Missouri Ins. Co.,* 208 S.W.2d 830)

28. Milburn carried automobile damage and theft insurance on his Cadillac sedan as required by the creditor on his car loan. Milburn could no longer make the payments. He turned the car over to an automobile salesperson to sell. The salesperson ultimately disappeared with the car. The insurer, Manchester Insurance Company, refused to pay, and World Investment Company, Milburn's creditor on the loan, sued Manchester. Manchester claimed the policy insured against theft which, as larceny, involved a taking against the owner's will. Because Milburn voluntarily delivered the car to the salesperson, no theft had occurred. World Investment Company claimed that the word "theft" should be given its common meaning of "steal" and so the insurance company should pay. What do you think? (*World Investment Co. v. Manchester Insurance and Indemnity Co.,* 380 S.W.2d 487)

29. When Wilson and his passenger Davison were injured in an automobile accident, the insurance company stated that the policy on Wilson excluded coverage of more than one person in a single accident. Davison sued, contending that because the exclusion of coverage in the policy was not in a different color or type than the rest of the policy as required by state statute, the term was void. The insurance company pointed out that although the exclusion did not appear in a different color or type of print, it was in a section of the policy clearly labeled "exclusions." Should Davison be allowed to collect? (*Davison v. Wilson,* 239 N.W.2d 38)

30. The Consolidated School District No. 1 of Dallas County, Missouri, contracted for fire insurance to cover its high school buildings. The policy has a 90-percent coinsurance clause. During the term of the policy, a fire caused a partial loss to the buildings, amounting to more than $45,000 in damages. At the time of the fire, the structures were valued at approximately $80,000 and the amount of the policy coverage stood at $50,000. How much of the $45,000 loss should the policy cover? (*Templeton v. Insurance Co. of North America,* 201 S.W.2d 784)

31. Gary Stallings was on active duty with the National Guard when the three-quarter-ton truck he was driving overturned and caused a fellow Guard member and passenger, Robert Ward, bodily injury. Stallings was the named insured in Michigan Mutual Liability Company's "Auto-Guard" Family Insurance Policy. When Ward sued Stallings for the injuries, Michigan Mutual refused to defend Stallings and denied responsibility to pay any judgment that might result. In addition to other coverages, the policy obligated the company to defend and pay judgments up to the policy limit if the insured was driving a "nonowned automobile." The company maintained that the three-quarter-ton army truck with canvas top and doors was not an automobile. What do you think? (*Michigan Mutual Liability Company v. Stallings,* 523 S.W.2d 539)

Hall v. Wilkerson
Federal Circuit Court of Appeals, 926 F.2d 311

BACKGROUND At the time of the automobile accident that is the origin of this suit, Wayne Wilkerson was residing in the home of Gwendolyn Hall. Before she left for France one spring, Hall gave permission to Wilkerson to continue to reside in her house and to drive her car under certain prescribed conditions. In particular, there were to be no drugs in her car, and she considered alcohol to be a drug just like any other.

FACTS Unfortunately, Wayne Wilkerson liked to drink—and he drank a lot. So after having consumed a large quantity of beer one day, he was involved in an accident. The accident involved only one vehicle. In the accident both of Wilkerson's passengers, Susan Kilmer and Richard Schock, were seriously injured. The car Wilkerson was driving in the accident regrettably was Gwendolyn Hall's.

LOWER COURT Gwendolyn Hall's insurance company and the injured parties brought this suit seeking a determination of whether or not Wayne Wilkerson was an insured at the time of the accident.

The lower court concluded that Wilkerson's use of alcohol was indeed a violation of the conditions imposed on his being able to use Hall's vehicle with permission. Therefore, he was not an "insured" under Hall's policy.

APPEALS The state law where the accident occurred requires that insurance coverage be maintained under such permissive use clauses in a policy if the driver's deviation is slight and inconsequential. It will not be permissive use if the deviation is substantial.

ISSUE Gwendolyn Hall's automobile insurance policy read:

"Who is an insured (under this policy)?"

The policy then answered its own question as follows:

"For YOUR car—YOU, any RELATIVE, and anyone else using YOUR CAR if the use is (or is reasonably believed to be) with YOUR PERMISSION, are INSUREDS."

PRACTICE JUDGING

1. Should the policyholder have the power to eliminate insurance coverage by imposing conditions on permission to drive, as Gwendolyn Hall did in this case? (For example, what if Hall had granted Wilkerson permission to drive on the condition that he neither damage the car nor involve it in an accident?)

2. If Wilkerson is not an insured, the injured parties lose a major source of funding to pay for the expenses of recovering from their injuries. This may prevent them from receiving treatment that would enable them to engage in gainful employment and/or may force them into conditions of financial hardship. On the other hand, holding that they are unable to recover from their injuries because Wilkerson is not an insured may send a warning to others to be careful about the persons from whom they accept rides under similar circumstances. From a societal standpoint, which alternative do you think should be chosen? Why?

3. How do you think the appellate court should hold? Why?

LESSONS

24-1 LEGAL CONSEQUENCES OF DEATH

24-2 TRUSTS

HOT DEBATE

Tom Blackwell was in a motorcycle accident and suffered extensive brain injuries. Life support monitors detected no brain function. Tom had $7,000 in assets and no health insurance. Soon his assets were, by court order, exhausted to pay for his care. The cost to keep him "alive" per year would be more than $200,000 in state funds. These funds could be put to use for patients who had more promise of recovery. Tom had no relatives and had never expressed an opinion about life support. When the state brought suit to have the court issue an order to remove the equipment, several religious groups intervened to argue against the request.

Where Do You Stand?

1. List the reasons in favor of keeping Tom alive.

2. List the legal reasons supporting the state's suit.

GOALS

- Explain why an orderly distribution of a decedent's estate is necessary
- Discuss the benefits of making a will
- Describe how a valid will is made

DEATH AND THE LAW

WHAT'S YOUR VERDICT?

Dennis, a bachelor living in Maine, often thought he should make a will but repeatedly put off doing so. In the meantime he amassed considerable property. One day without warning, Dennis died of a heart attack.

How will his property be distributed?

When a person dies, the law looks for his or her instructions to resolve some basic legal issues that arise. These issues include how the debts of the person who dies (called the **decedent**) are to be paid and what is to be done with the remaining property. The necessary instructions are found either in the wishes of the decedent as expressed in a will, in statutes (especially if the decedent did not leave a will), or in both.

Death Without a Will

Those who die without a valid will are said to have died **intestate**. When a person dies intestate, as in *What's Your Verdict?,* a special court (generally called a probate court or surrogate's court) has the power to settle the affairs of the decedent. This court appoints a personal representative known as an **administrator** (if male) or **administratrix** (if female) to take charge of the intestate's property. This representative uses the property of the deceased, called the **estate**, to pay all debts, including the costs of administering the estate. The remainder of the property will then be distributed

in accordance with the state's intestacy statute. Dying without a professionally drafted will can cause the beneficiaries to pay considerable administrative expenses and needlessly large estate taxes.

Intestacy statutes vary from state to state. Generally, intestacy statutes call for a surviving spouse to receive one-third to one-half of the estate with the remainder divided equally among the children. If there are no surviving children or grandchildren, then that share goes to the decedent's parents or, if they are dead as well, to the decedent's sisters and brothers and their children.

Death With a Will

It is usually much to the advantage of all concerned if the decedent dies **testate** (leaving a valid will). A **will** is a legal expression, usually in writing, by which a person directs how her or his property is to be distributed after death (see illustration on next page). The maker of the will is called the **testator** (if male) or the **testatrix** (if female). In contrast to the intestacy statutes (which distribute a decedent's

estate without regard for need), a will allows a person to direct his or her estate's resources to where they can do the most good.

A will also allows its maker to name a personal representative (**executor** if male or **executrix** if female) to carry out the directions in the will. The testator can specify that the executor or executrix be exempted from posting bond (paying the court a sum of money to insure the duties are properly performed). A will also may be used to name a guardian for minor children of the testator or testatrix. Through the will, the named guardian can be exempted from posting a bond.

"Living will" is a term used for a document directed to attending physicians regarding a person's choices about the use of life-support systems in treatment for terminal illness or vegetative state. Be sure to distinguish "living wills" from the wills described in this chapter. The term is a poor label. A more descriptive term for "living will" would be "Directive to Physicians." An alternative to accomplish the same end would be using a durable power of attorney—which confers on a chosen or court-appointed individual the right to make health care decisions, such as removal of life support.

CREATION AND EXECUTION OF A VALID WILL To counteract the possibility of forgery, the law has strict requirements regarding the preparation and execution of valid wills. To be valid, a will must conform to the state laws regarding creation and execution. The most basic requirements in almost every state are the following:

1. The testatrix or testator must have **testamentary intent**, or the clear intention to make a will. A person must not be pressured into signing the document

against his or her desires by the undue influence of others. Likewise, the signer must not be misled into thinking that the document is something other than a will.

2. The testator or testatrix, at the time the will is executed, must have testamentary capacity to make the will. **Testamentary capacity** means the maker must know, at least in a general way, the kind and extent of the property involved, the persons who stand to benefit, and that he or she is making arrangements to dispose of his or her property after death. Lapses into senility by the maker may bring the will of an elderly person into question due to the possible lack of capacity. In most states a person under age 18 does not have testamentary capacity.

3. Ordinarily the will must be in writing and, in most states, signed at the end of the document to prevent unauthorized additions. The signing must be witnessed by at least two adults. In some states, three witnesses must sign. These witnesses should not be individuals who will inherit under the will. The witnesses must be advised that they are watching the testator's or testatrix's will being signed as they do so.

AMENDMENT OF A VALID WILL A will takes effect only upon the death of the maker. Therefore, it can be changed or canceled at any time during the maker's life. However, this ability to change the document as often as desired, coupled with the fact that the contents of a will are proved only after the death of the maker, opens the way to potentially false claims under forged documents.

Regardless of the potential problems in making changes, it is, nonetheless, important that the maker

of a will keep it current. Marriage, divorce, the birth of children, and other significant changes in a person's life should be reflected in the document by periodic amendments or by a new will. In states requiring a formal will, changes must be made using a **codicil**, which is a formal, written, and witnessed amendment. A codicil must be executed with the same formalities as a will.

SPECIAL TYPES OF WILLS There are exceptions to the rules for the creation, execution, and altering of a valid will. For example, many states recognize a **holographic will** as valid

even without witnesses. A holographic will is one that was written entirely by the decedent's own hand and signed by him or her. Where a valid holographic will is used, changes require appropriate additions or deletions (before witnesses if necessary) in the handwriting of the maker.

A **nuncupative will** (or oral will) is recognized in some states if proclaimed during the maker's last illness or by service personnel on active duty. However, the will must be witnessed and is often limited to controlling the distribution of personal property.

LAST WILL AND TESTAMENT
REBECCA BIRK FAULSTICH

I, Rebecca Birk Faulstich, of 1875 El Rey Way, San Francisco, California, declare that this is my will. I revoke all wills and codicils that I have previously made.

FIRST: I am married to Kevin Alan Faulstich and we have one child, Jeffrey Michael, born March 12, 20—.

SECOND: After payment of all my debts, I give my estate as follows:

(A) To my twin sister, Rachel Ann Wilson, I give my personal clothing, jewelry, and sporting equipment, if she should survive me.

(B) To my beloved husband, Kevin, I give all the residue if he should survive me for thirty (30) days.

(C) To our son, Jeffrey Michael, I give all the residue if my husband should not survive me for thirty days and if my son should survive me for thirty days.

(D) To the Regents of the University of California (to provide student scholarships and awards without reference to financial need, in order to encourage excellence of effort and achievement), I give all the residue if neither my husband nor my son should survive me for thirty days.

THIRD: I nominate my husband as the executor of this will. If for any reason he should fail to qualify or cease to act as such, I nominate my sister, Rachel, as executrix. If for any reason she should fail to qualify or cease to act as such, I nominate the Central City Bank, a California corporation, to act as executor. I direct that neither my husband nor my sister be required to post bond as executor or executrix.

IN WITNESS WHEREOF, I have hereunto set my hand this _18th_ day of _January_, 20—, in San Francisco, California.

Rebecca Birk Faulstich
Rebecca Birk Faulstich

The foregoing instrument was subscribed on the date which it bears by the testatrix, Rebecca Birk Faulstich, and at the time of subscribing was declared by her to be her last will. The subscription and declaration were made in our presence, we being present at the same time; and we, at her request and in her presence and in the presence of each other, have affixed our signatures hereto as witnesses:

Diana P. Davis residing at _432 Third Street_
San Francisco, California
Adam T. Price residing at _1644 Prospector's Point_
San Francisco, California

Lee was fatally injured in an automobile accident late one evening. As she lay dying, she told three witnesses that she was making a will and that she wanted her valuable collection of paintings to go to her good friend Anne. In a state that allows nuncupative wills, if the witnesses' testimonies were properly and promptly reduced to writing, Lee's dying wish as to the disposition of her property would be carried out.

REVOCATION OF A WILL A will is subject to partial or total change at the desire of the testator. A will is only intended to take effect upon the testator's death. Anytime before that moment, as long as the testator has testamentary intent and testamentary capacity, the will can be amended. A will also can be completely revoked. A will may be completely revoked, rather than being amended, in several ways. Doing something to the will that clearly indicates intent to revoke it, such as destroying it or defacing it, will accomplish this end.

According to some state statutes, the marriage of the maker or the birth or adoption of a child by that individual works as an automatic termination. Divorce, on the other hand, does not produce such an automatic revocation. However, a divorce settlement does revoke the parts of a will with which the settlement conflicts once the divorce occurs.

Finally, a will may be revoked by a written revocation in a later will. Such a document must either explicitly state, "I hereby revoke all prior wills," or contain provisions that conflict with the prior will so that it impliedly revokes the preceding document.

WHAT'S YOUR VERDICT?

Benson owed Cane $1,750. Cane did not learn of Benson's death until eight months after it occurred. By that time, the period for presenting claims against the estate had elapsed.

Can Cane still legally collect the $1,750 from the estate?

Whether a person dies with or without a valid will, a probate court will supervise the handling of the decedent's estate.

Procedure for Estate Resolution

Regardless of whether a person dies testate or intestate, the first item of business on the executor's or administrator's list is to offer proof of death to the appropriate court. This proof may be in the form of a death certificate, official notification of death from an armed service, or even testimony of the deceased's presence in a disaster that resulted in unidentifiable or irretrievable bodies. In the last case, the court can take judicial notice of the situation and issue a declaration of death.

If a person simply vanishes without a trace, after several years he or she can be declared dead under the "Enoch Arden laws." (These laws were named for a poem by Tennyson about a seaman who returns home after a long absence to find his "widow" married to another.) Almost without exception, the time required under such laws is either five or seven years of absence.

After proof of death is established, the personal representative's duties are

1. assembling, preserving, inventorying, and appraising the assets of the estate and collecting the debts owed to it
2. giving public notice of the estate and the necessity for

filing claims against it within the statutory period
3. paying valid claims against the estate
4. distributing the remaining property according to the will or statute

The personal representative will be liable for failure to reasonably carry out her or his duties. Depending on the size and types of property in the estate, the task can be quite complex. As indicated above, the personal representative must properly give public notice that all creditors of the estate have a set time, typically six months, to file a claim or go unpaid. He or she must then determine which claims are valid and pay them where possible. In *What's Your Verdict?* because Cane did not file within the proper period, the estate will not pay the $1,750. Note, however, that although six months are given to file such claims, the full procedure of settling an estate can take several months beyond this. This is especially true if the validity of the will is challenged or contested or if the meaning of the will is unclear in some of its provisions.

Distributions Without a Will

Although the laws of intestate succession vary considerably from state to state, a good general idea of their content can be obtained by reviewing those of the state of Hawaii. (See the Cultural Diversity in Law feature on following page.)

Hawaii

Distributions Without a Will

If a person dies intestate in Hawaii:

- With no spouse but one or more children surviving, the children inherit equal shares in the real and personal property.
- With a spouse and one or more children or grandchildren surviving, the spouse gets one-half of the real and personal property and the children share equally in the remainder. If a child is deceased but has surviving children, those children share equally in the deceased child's share.
- With a spouse and no children or grandchildren surviving, the spouse gets one-half of the real and personal property and the deceased's parents receive the remainder. If the deceased's parents are not alive, the deceased's brothers and sisters receive equal shares in the remainder.
- With no spouse, no children, and no grandchildren surviving, the deceased's parents each receive one-half of the real and personal property or, if only one parent survives, he or she receives it all. If both of the deceased's parents are dead, the brothers and sisters of the deceased share equally.

Distributions With a Will

If there is a valid will, its terms are to be followed. However, there may be statutory provisions allowing certain relatives to override the will's terms and receive more of the estate than the will provided. For example, in some states the surviving spouse may elect to receive one-third to one-half of the decedent's property instead of the share provided under the will.

Because of the number of technicalities and potential problems, the settling of a decedent's estate with or without a will is best carried out with the professional help of a lawyer.

One of the most complex will-related issues has to do with how the testator has decided to split the property among the lineal descendants. The testator may specify that the living lineal descendents split the property equally, be they children, grandchildren or even further down the lineal tree. This is referred to as a *per capita* distribution. Or the testator may specify that the lineal descendants split equally what a deceased parent would have received but receive nothing if the parent still lives. This latter is referred to as a *per stirpes* distribution. See the chart on page 367 which illustrates these two methods of distribution.

If There are No Inheritors

If there are no inheritors, the property of the deceased **escheats** or reverts to the state.

LAW IN THE MEDIA

MICHIGAN VS. KEVORKIAN

On November 22, 1998, the CBS newsmagazine *60 Minutes* aired a videotape showing Dr. Jack Kevorkian in the act of carrying out a mercy killing. (Mercy killing, or euthanasia, involves ending the life of a hopelessly sick or injured individual in a painless and merciful way.) The subject of the videotaped mercy killing, 52-year-old Thomas Youk, suffered from Lou Gehrig's disease. Youk had asked Dr. Kevorkian for his assistance. He was terrified of otherwise choking to death.

After viewing the *60 Minutes* segment, Michigan prosecutors charged Dr. Kevorkian with first-degree murder. The doctor had been tried and acquitted three times in Michigan on "assisted suicide" charges. In those cases, Dr. Kevorkian had provided the suicide apparatus and drugs to terminally ill people, who then used the materials to end their own lives. In the *60 Minutes* videotape, Kevorkian himself injected Youk with a fatal dose of potassium chloride. Since Dr. Kevorkian's acquittals in Michigan, the state passed a new law forbidding assisted suicide. The law went into effect in September 1998.

Questions to Consider

1 Dr. Kevorkian sent the videotape to *60 Minutes* himself. What do you think motivated him to do so?

2 Do you think *60 Minutes* made the right choice in airing the mercy killing? What do you think motivated their decision?

Answer the following questions about legal concepts.

1. Those who die without a valid will are legally termed to have died inter-state. **True or False?**

2. A will written entirely by the decedent's own hand and signed by her or him is legally termed a(n)
   (a) nuncupative will
   (b) graphic will
   (c) express will (d) none of the above

3. The fact that a testator crossed out all the provisions of his current will may be sufficient evidence that it has been revoked. **True or False?**

4. If there are no inheritors of the decedent's estate, the property ___?___ to the state.

5. The legal term for an oral will is a(n) ___?___ will.

6. The insertion of a codicil on a will does not have to be witnessed. **True or False?**

7. The typical time for all creditors of the estate to file a claim against it is
   (a) four months (b) six months (c) ten months (d) twelve months

8. The personal representative of the estate can be held personally liable for failure to properly carry out his or her duties. **True or False?**

Study the following situations, answer the questions, then prepare arguments to support your answers.

9. Sid went to his attorney's office and described in detail how he wanted his estate distributed upon his death. The lawyer made extensive notes and prepared a 12-page will. He called Sid and read it to him over the phone. Sid made a few minor changes. The lawyer then prepared a final copy. On his way to the lawyer's office to sign the document, Sid died of a heart attack. Was the final copy a valid will? Why or why not?

10. Toa was ill. She did not think she could afford an attorney, so she sat down and wrote on notebook paper what she wanted done with all of her property upon her death. She signed at the end and dated the document in front of four neighbors, who also signed as witnesses. Will Toa's estate be distributed according to her wishes or in some other manner?

11. Hilda executed a will on the first day of January. On the first day of June in the same year she executed a second will, which contained many provisions in conflict with the first will. She died on the first day of December. Which will governs the distribution of her estate?

12. Eric executed a valid will dividing his property among his wife and three children. The will was not altered for 22 years. Then Eric separated from his wife but did not divorce her. He wrote a second will, which left all his property to their children. After Eric's death, his wife sued to receive a fair share of his estate. Will she succeed?

13. Evangel Smith was appointed the personal representative to settle the estate of Everett Smith. Evangel provided the appropriate public notice necessary to give creditors a fair chance to file their claims against the estate. Unfortunately, due to the negligence of the staff he hired, some of the claims were lost. Evangel settled the estate and distributed the proceeds without discovering the lost claims. Now the unpaid creditors want their money. Can Evangel be held personally liable for the debts of the estate? Why or why not?

14. Evander was the lineal descendant through his father, Eston, of his grandfather, Elias Fieldstone. When Elias died he left an estate worth $5,000,000. Elias' will called for the estate to be distributed per capita among his lineal descendants. These included four children and seven grandchildren, of which Evander was the youngest. Regrettably, Evander's father had died during the time between when the will was made and Elias' death. All the other lineal descendants were alive and well. How much will Evander receive from the distribution of Elias' estate (not considering taxes and administration charges)?

G O A L S

● **Explain the usefulness of trusts**

● **Name and describe the various types of trusts**

● **Distinguish between express and implied trusts**

CREATION OF TRUSTS

WHAT'S YOUR VERDICT?

Pedro wanted to keep his family in close contact. Consequently, he bought a large vacation home on the beach at the Jersey Shore and gave a standing invitation to each of his children and grandchildren to visit him as often as they could. As he grew older, Pedro worried that upon his death his children would merely sell the property and split the proceeds rather than using it as a rallying point.

What legal device can Pedro use to prevent this from happening?

At times, people may wish to transfer the immediate control of some or all of their property to another party with instructions on how it is to be managed for the benefit of the transferor or a third party.

When the transferee of the property is a separate entity under law, a **trust** has been created.

A trust can be created to accomplish any conceivable legal purpose. The legal entity that has the title to the subject property is known as the **trustee**. The trustee must utilize the property in the trust in such a way as to accomplish the trust's objectives.

The creator of a trust is known as the **settlor**. The party for whose benefit the trust is managed in accordance with the settlor's wishes is the **beneficiary**. The trustee has a fiduciary duty (requiring the highest care and loyalty) to the beneficiary. The trustee cannot cause the beneficiary to acquire liability to third parties through the trust management. In addition, the trust does not usually terminate at the death of the trustee. Another person is simply appointed to fulfill the trustee's role and the operation of the trust continues.

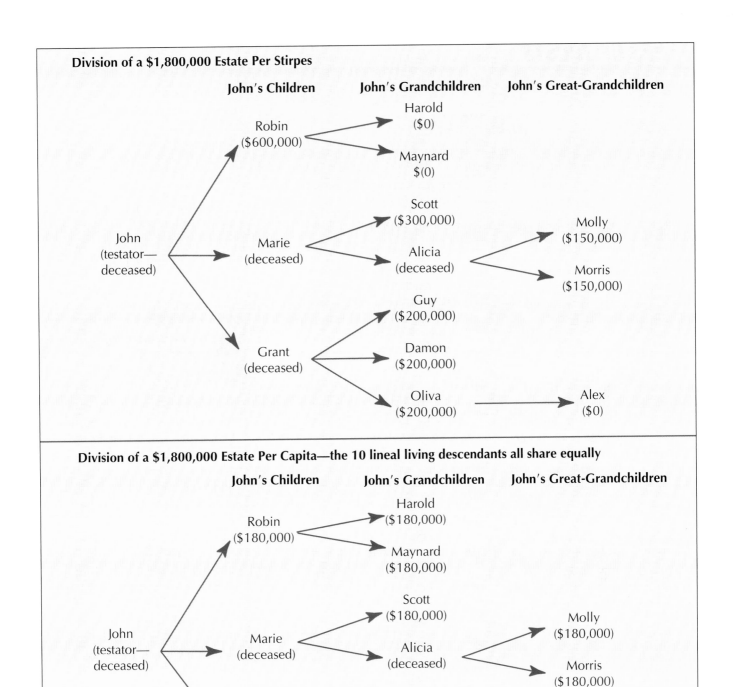

Division of a $1,800,000 Estate Per Stirpes

John's Children   John's Grandchildren   John's Great-Grandchildren

John (testator—deceased)

Robin ($600,000)
- Harold ($0)
- Maynard $(0)

Marie (deceased)
- Scott ($300,000)
- Alicia (deceased)
  - Molly ($150,000)
  - Morris ($150,000)

Grant (deceased)
- Guy ($200,000)
- Damon ($200,000)
- Oliva ($200,000)
  - Alex ($0)

Division of a $1,800,000 Estate Per Capita—the 10 lineal living descendants all share equally

John's Children   John's Grandchildren   John's Great-Grandchildren

John (testator—deceased)

Robin ($180,000)
- Harold ($180,000)
- Maynard ($180,000)

Marie (deceased)
- Scott ($180,000)
- Alicia (deceased)
  - Molly ($180,000)
  - Morris ($180,000)

Grant (deceased)
- Guy ($180,000)
- Damon ($180,000)
- Oliva ($180,000)
  - Alex ($180,000)

Per Stirpes and Per Capita Divisions of an Estate

Finally, if it is not mentioned in the trust document, trustees have the right to be paid for their services. The probate court or state law will determine just how much the trustee's fee might be in such a case. However, the settlor may also detail in the trust document how much the trustee will receive for her or his services. If the pay is inadequate, it is wise for the settlor to keep in mind that the person nominated for the trusteeship is free to decline it. In *What's Your Verdict?* Pedro should create a trust to manage the property with the objective of prolonging his family's contact with one another.

TYPES OF TRUSTS

WHAT'S YOUR VERDICT?

Oliver formed a charitable trust to raise money to install air conditioners at the local high school. He transferred to the trust several items of property that were to be sold for the cause. Unfortunately, the school building burned before that purpose could be fulfilled.

What is to be done with the property owned by the trust?

Trusts are basically known by the timing and purpose of their creation. A trust may be created during the lifetime of the settlor. This type of trust is known as an *inter vivos* **trust**. A trust created after the death of the settlor in accordance with directions in her or his will is labeled a **testamentary trust**.

A trust created for the fulfillment of an altruistic purpose (such as that mentioned in *What's Your Verdict?*) is known as a **charitable trust**. Alternatively, a trust created for a private purpose is known as a **private trust**. One type of private trust is called a **spendthrift trust**. This trust protects the beneficiary's interest in the subject property from the beneficiary's creditors. The beneficiary can have no control whatsoever in such a trust arrangement, so creditors cannot reach the property in the trust.

The trusts mentioned above are usually created by a written or oral statement in which the terms are explicitly stated by the settlor. As a consequence, they are all properly labeled **express trusts**.

The law, however, also makes provisions for at least two types of *implied trusts*. The first implied trust is known as a **resulting trust**. This trust is formed when the entity intended to receive the benefit of an express trust cannot do so. In such a case a resulting trust is formed to hold the property for its original owner. In *What's Your Verdict?* a resulting trust would be formed around the property in the charitable trust for the benefit of Oliver.

The other type of implied trust is known as a **constructive trust**. Such a trust is created to require a person holding property to transfer it to another because retention of the property would be a wrongful and unjust enrichment of the holder. Property obtained through fraud, duress, or like means is deemed to be held by the wrongdoer in constructive trust for the person wronged.

A Question of ETHICS

Brenda Mathews sat beside her mother, Anne, on her hospital bed. Anne was suffering from cancer and had been drifting in and out of consciousness. Suddenly, Anne opened her eyes and said, "Brenda, I must tell you something. You have a sister I put up for adoption years ago. Her name is Belinda Smith, and she lives in Palmetto, California. I have never contacted her but I want you to. Tell her that I'm thinking of her even now." Brenda nodded. "Brenda, you know how much I love you for taking care of me these last few years. My $500,000 life insurance policy will help you and your sister, and reward you for your care." Suddenly, Anne gasped and then died. When Brenda returned home that evening, she found the policy. It was made out to her mother's estate. Now Brenda is faced with a dilemma. Should she tell anyone about her sister and share the money? Or should she receive her reward as a faithful daughter by taking the life insurance proceeds in full?

LAW and the INTERNET

People who wish to transfer control of property before their deaths may execute an *inter vivos* trust. Through the Internet, "Living Trust Makers" are offered in an easy-to-use interview format. This product comes with available online Legal and Program Help. It assists users in making appropriate decisions for themselves and their family, such as deciding what property to put in a trust, how to transfer property, how to distribute property after death, and how to manage property left to young beneficiaries. In question still are the legal framework, binding contractual considerations, and the legal enforceability of the trust should it be contested. These issues should be resolved with the help of an attorney.

Answer the following questions about legal concepts.

1. A trust terminates at the death of the settlor. **True or False?**

2. A trust terminates with the death of the trustee. **True or False?**

3. A resulting trust may be created due to the death of a trust's beneficiary. **True or False?**

4. A trust created by the will of a deceased settlor is known as a(n) **(a) inter vivos trust (b) end of vivos trust (c) testamentary trust (d) none of the above**

5. A charitable trust is created for a(n) __?__ purpose.

6. In a spendthrift trust the beneficiary's creditors can utilize the trust's property to satisfy the debts owed them by the beneficiary. **True or False?**

7. Is a resulting trust an express trust? **Yes or No?**

8. The two types of implied trusts are the private trust and the spendthrift trust. **True or False?**

9. The trustee has a responsibility requiring the highest degree of care and loyalty to the beneficiary. This is referred to as a **(a) fiduciary duty (b) legal caretaker's duty (c) lawful caretaker's duty (d) none of the above**

Study the following situations, answer the questions, then prepare arguments to support your answers.

10. Terry was named in his parents' will as the trustee of the family farm. He does not want the position as he has little or no interest in farming. His brother, Harold, has worked the farm for the last five years and would be a far better trustee. His parents chose Terry, however, because he was older. What can Terry do in this situation?

11. If Terry does take the position described in exercise 10, he will lose time that he could spend working on his new insulation business. Worse, the will does not mention the possibility of any pay for Terry. What can he do to help the situation?

12. Terry decides to repair the farmhouse. He solicits bids from different contractors and chooses the low bidder. However, when it comes to the contract to insulate the farmhouse, he has his firm do it and sends the estate a bill that is $1,000 more than the cost if other firms had bid the job. When his brother discovers what Terry has done, Terry merely states that the extra charge was to help pay for his time as trustee. Has Terry acted legally? Why or why not?

13. Dr. Anders teaches law in a Midwestern university. At the end of one of his classes, a student brought up a brand new laptop that had been left behind by an unknown departing student. Dr. Anders accepted the computer for "safekeeping." What sort of responsibilities does he have as a consequence? What kind of trust might be imposed on him if he sells the laptop?

1. Be sure to make a legally proper will. Failing to do so may cause clashes between your potential beneficiaries. This may leave lifelong animosities and cost a great deal in legal fees.

2. Dying without a professionally drafted will can cause the beneficiaries to pay considerable administrative expenses and needlessly large estate taxes.

3. A will takes effect only upon the death of the maker. Therefore, it can be changed or canceled at any time during the maker's life. Use an attorney to be sure the will and any

PREVENT LEGAL DIFFICULTIES

subsequent changes are placed in the proper form.

4. You can create trusts to formally direct the use of your resources to achieve the ends you desire.

CHAPTER IN REVIEW

CONCEPTS IN BRIEF

1. The basic requirements for a valid, formal will are testamentary intent and capacity, a general knowledge of what is being done, and a signed writing with witnesses.

2. A will can be revoked or changed at any time prior to the testator's death.

3. Creditors' rights against the estate and the rights of a surviving spouse to a share of the estate may not be defeated by a will that attempts to give the property to others.

4. In essence, a trust can be created to accomplish any conceivable legal purpose.

5. The beneficiary can have no control whatsoever in a spendthrift trust arrangement.

6. A resulting trust is formed when the entity intended to receive the benefit of an express trust cannot do so. The resulting trust is intended to hold the property for its original owner. Note that it differs from a constructive trust, which is imposed on someone wrongfully holding the property of another but which is also imposed to benefit the true owner.

YOUR LEGAL VOCABULARY

Match each statement with the term that it best defines. Some terms may not be used.

1. A deceased person

2. To die without a will

3. Intestate's personal representative (female) appointed to settle the estate

4. Property of the deceased

5. To die with a valid will

6. Male maker of a will

7. Orally made will

8. Creator of a trust

9. Trust created for private reasons

10. Court appointed representative for a decedent

11. Trust created for the fulfillment of an altruistic purpose

12. Trust in which the terms are explicitly stated by the settler

13. Will written and signed entirely by the hand of the maker

14. Legal vehicle used to transfer the immediate control of property to another party

15. Trust created during the lifetime of the settlor

administrator/
   administratrix
beneficiary
charitable trust
constructive trust
decedent
escheat
estate
executor/executrix
express trust
holographic will
inter vivos trust
intestate
nuncupative will
private trust
resulting trust
settlor
spendthrift trust
testamentary capacity
testamentary intent
testamentary trust
testate
testator/testatrix
trust
trustee
will

16. Is it fair for individuals under age 18 not to have testamentary capacity? Why or why not?

17. What changes in the settlor's life should cause the updating of a will.

18. Why would a holographic will be disallowed?

19. Why do some states require a formal will?

20. Is a spendthrift trust fair to the creditors of the settlor? Why or why not?

21. Does a resulting trust carry out the wishes of the original owner? Why or why not?

22. Could a constructive trust be used in situations in which the property is not wrongfully obtained from the true owner? Why or why not?

WRITE ABOUT LEGAL CONCEPTS

23. Draft a will for yourself.

24. How could you use a trust in your life? Draft a document to set it up.

25. What qualities would you want in the trustee of your estate? List them in order of importance.

26. **HOT DEBATE** Write a persuasive argument that emphasizes the legal and ethical points in favor of the state's petition. Or, write a persuasive argument that emphasizes the legal and ethical points in favor of continuing life support for Tom.

THINK CRITICALLY ABOUT EVIDENCE

27. Tim had a considerable estate. He also had three children whom he loved dearly. He did not want to show any favoritism between them in the distribution of his estate after his death. Therefore, he decided not to make out a will and let the state handle the matter according to its rules. Is this a good idea? Why or why not?

28. On his deathbed Tim finally is persuaded to make a will by his youngest child, Paula. The other two children are rushing to be at Tim's bedside but have not arrived yet. A nurse overhears Paula telling Tim that the other two children died several years ago and that they should, therefore, receive nothing. Tim, nodding his head in agreement, then signed the will leaving everything to Paula. Two friends of Paula then signed as witnesses. Will the will stand up in probate court?

29. Not only was Tim's will attacked by the other two children as soon as it was filed in probate court but Tim's wife suddenly reappeared. She had been thought to have drowned two years before when a golf cart she was driving veered into a canal near their Florida home. She is extremely upset that Tim has willed away all the property. Does she have any rights in the matter?

30. Suspicious of the validity of the will, the probate court appointed a neutral party rather than Paula as executor. The executor discovered that, about two months before his death, Tim had set up a spendthrift trust for Paula. Tim had set it up with more than $500,000 in principal. Should the amount in the trust be included in the estate for distribution? Why or why not?

31. Paula has a number of creditors mainly because of her frequent visits to the horse track and her uncanny ability to steadily bet on losers. Will these creditors want to have the $500,000 included in the estate if Tim's will is held to be valid? Will they want the amount to be included in the estate if the will is invalidated?

ANALYZE REAL CASES

32. Ralph Mangan was wounded by a gunshot in 1971. He was hospitalized and later moved to a nursing home. There, he executed a will dated February 23, 1972. After his release from the nursing home, he was cared for by his brother for a short time. Because of Ralph's advanced age and medical problems, he was again hospitalized. In May 1972, he returned to the nursing home and in June was adjudicated incompetent. He died in August 1972. His will was filed for probate and was contested on the grounds that Ralph was disoriented because of his advanced age, heart disease, and the gunshot wound. The will left property to someone described as a nephew when there was no such nephew. Witnesses testified that during Ralph's first stay in the nursing home he was self-reliant and was able to handle his own business affairs. Ralph's attorney testified that Ralph appeared to be of sound mind at the time he executed the will. Ralph had discussed the details of the will with the attorney and had mentioned a number of nephews, cousins, and other distant relatives. Ralph's physicians testified that Ralph had periods of disorientation and periods of lucidity. Is Ralph's will valid? (*Edward L. Mangan v. Joseph J. Mangan, Jr.,* 554 S.W.2d 418)

33. Joyner wrote out her will and took it to the neighbors to type and sign as witnesses. She only told them that it was a "piece of paper" that she wanted "fixed up so as I can sign it so that [her son] could have a place to live." The neighbors knew that she was asking them to sign the paper so her property would be properly disposed upon her death. Did Joyner's failure to announce that it was her "last will and testament" render the will invalid? (*Faith v. Singleton,* 692 S.W.2d 239)

34. When Adams died, it was discovered that his will created a charitable trust in favor of several educational institutions as long as they admitted only "members of the White Race." The will also declared that, should these institutions have admitted other than members of the white race, the funds should go to Hermitage Methodist Homes of Virginia, Inc. No racial limitation was placed on Hermitage's ability to receive the benefits of the trust. What should be done with the trust? (*Hermitage Methodist Homes of Virginia, Inc. v. Dominion Trust Co.,* 387 S.E.2d 740)

35. When the administrator of Courziel's estate opened the safe deposit box that contained a copy Courziel's will, he found the will was missing the last page. Unfortunately this page contained Courziel's signature and those of the witnesses to the document. Courziel had sole control over the box. Should the "will" be enforced? (*Board of Trustees of the University of Alabama v. Calhoun,* 514 So. 2d 895)

36. Gillespie, during a visit to his bank, dictated a codicil to his will. It was typed and signed by Gillespie before he left the bank. However, it was not until later that two bank employees signed the document as witnesses. They were not present to see Gillespie actually sign the document. Would the probate court treat the codicil as valid? (*Brammer v. Taylor,* 338 S.E.2d 207)

37. Mr. Suarez purchased a $50,000 insurance policy on himself from Liberty National Insurance Company. As beneficiary, he designated his mother, Guarina Cardona. Months later Suarez met with his insurance agent to change the beneficiary on his policy from Cardona to Zeigler. At the meeting Suarez indicated that he wanted the policy payoff to be used for the benefit of his two children, Ebony and Antonio. After Ziegler agreed to carry out Suarez's wishes, Suarez changed the beneficiary to Zeigler. However, when the insurance agent submitted the change of beneficiary form to Liberty National, the company never actually changed the beneficiary. Not knowing this, Ziegler faithfully paid the premiums on the policy until Suarez's death. Afterwards this suit was brought to correct the matter. What sort of trust device could be used by the court to see that Suarez's wishes would be carried out? Why? (*Ziegler v. Cardona,* 830 F. Supp. 1395)

38. When Edwin Fickes died his will provided that a trust should be established and that it should be split "in equal portions between the grandchildren then living" upon the death of his last surviving child. When that occurred, there were eight surviving grandchildren. Four of these were adopted. Two of the adopted grandchildren had been adopted before Fickes died. The other two were adopted afterwards. Which grandchildren should receive a portion of the estate? (*Connecticut National Bank v. Chadwick,* 217 Conn. 260)

BACKGROUND The plaintiff, John Morse, son of the decedent, Marvin, brought this action to contest his father's will. He alleged that his father lacked testamentary capacity and was under the undue influence of his second wife when he made out the contested document. The Lower Court decided in favor of the son and ruled that it was not the father's legitimate last will and testament. Barbara Volz, the personal representative of the estate of John Morse's second wife-now deceased, brought this appeal.

FACTS When the father's first wife lay dying, he began to exhibit behavior that seemed questionable. He drank more and refused to visit her in the hospital. He would isolate himself in his study with a bottle of scotch and take long solitary walks. He was so irritable that he struck his granddaughter, yelled and screamed at family, friends, and neighbors, and stormed from the house to return only to grab more scotch and find his room.

This behavior struck his son, John, as exceptional as he had never seen his father act in such a way. After the death of his first wife, the father refused to make the funeral arrangements or attend the visitations. To John, he had always been a kind and understanding man. John and his wife, Claire, decided to live permanently near the father and had a caring relationship with him for several years after the first wife's death. Then the father's eyesight began to fail and he became depressed and reclusive. He began to drink heavily.

Obsessed with money, the father moved into the basement of his house and slept on a cot to save on utilities. He also experienced memory lapses and could not recall the events of past days or even hours. After his house was burglarized, the father began to prowl it at night carrying a .20 gauge shotgun.

Then he began seeing Inga, the woman who would become his second wife. Inga was at the time seeing another man named Eldon Zion. Following a luncheon with her friend Zelma and Marvin, Inga telephoned Zelma and said that, although she loved Eldon, she was going to date Marvin because Eldon "had no money and was not a Mason."

When Marvin announced his impending marriage to Inga, his son noted that the date for the wedding was during the time the son and his wife would be in Italy. At the same time, the father also said that he had been to an attorney and "everything has been taken care of to protect all of our children."

After the wedding, the father made out the new, contested will. "At the time there was nothing at all unusual about him," testified the attorney chosen to craft the will and who took the decedent through it "rather carefully" afterward. The attorney also said "He was quite capable of making a will."

The will in question left everything to Inga, if she survived him, and to her children, if she predeceased him. The will expressly stated that the decedent left nothing to his son as "he does not have the need for what I may leave in my estate."

Various experts testified to the possibility that the decedent may have been subject to early senile degeneration or Alzheimer's Disease at the time of the making out of the will.

PRACTICE JUDGING

1. **Did the decedent have testamentary capacity?**

2. **Did the decedent act of his own free will in cutting out his son and the son's family or was Inga's influence too great?**

3. **How should the court rule in this case?**

ENTREPRENEURS AND THE LAW

PROJECT 4 PROPERTY

PATENT PROTECTION

Ben hired an engineer and a patent lawyer with the funds Kristen provided him. They immediately set about the tasks necessary for filing the patent application. The drawings were done and the lawyer began identifying the claims (the characteristics that set Ben's invention apart from all others) that would be made on the Reelshield to obtain the patent.

POTENTIAL LIABILITY

Ben just heard that Rebuilt, without consulting him, had sold one of its Reelshields for $5,000. The purchaser, Metalworx, had improperly installed the device, and the machinist using it had been injured. Ben was concerned as to his potential liability stemming from the situation. Soon he was served with a complaint and summons: *Grayson v. Windows, Metalworx Inc., and Rebuilt Inc.,* the process read. The injured machinist was bringing suit and had named all parties potentially responsible.

Ben was worried and immediately called Kristen. She assured him that her firm would defend him and that the cost would not be prohibitive. "It's not your fault, and we'll be able to show that with just a deposition or two," she commented. "So don't worry about it. Just get busy on those new orders." Then she thanked him for repaying so quickly the money he had borrowed from her.

INSURANCE NEEDS

Before she hung up, Kristen reminded Ben to set up a meeting with a local business insurer. "You need some insurance protection—for you and the business. There's too much riding on it now to take any further risks. We'll also get someone from the law firm to advise us on wills and trusts."

Ben felt snowed under for a moment, then rebounded when Kristen said, "I know this is a lot to think of, but once it's done a lot of worries will be off your shoulders. Besides, I'll be there to help, if you want me." Ben smiled, "You can count on that. Thanks. Love you." Kristen paused, "I'm proud of the way you are handling things, Ben, and I love you too."

ACTIVITIES

Divide into teams and perform one or more of the following activities, as directed by your teacher.

PREPARE LEGAL DOCUMENTS

Your team is the patent attorney Ben hired. Draft a patent application that includes the following sections: (1) Background of the Invention; (2) Detailed Description of the Invention; (3) and Claims. Divide the team into three groups, and have each group work on a different section. Assemble the sections and submit the completed application to your teacher.

ARGUE

Divide the team into four groups, each representing a party named in the lawsuit (*Grayson v. Windows, Metalworx Inc., and Rebuilt Inc.*) Each group should prepare an opening argument to use in the event of a trial. After each side presents its argument, the team should vote on which party is liable for the injury.

DEMONSTRATE

Divide the team into five groups. Each group should choose one of the following types of insurance Ben will need: liability insurance, property insurance, fidelity insurance, life insurance, disability insurance. Discuss Ben's needs for each type of insurance.

BRAINSTORM

Project into Ben and Kristen's future. What provisions will they need in their wills presuming the business keeps growing and they marry and have children? Make a list of the provisions. Share your list with the class.

ENTREPRENEURS
AND THE LAW

SEE PAGE 464

Sharon Lamm is President of Lamm Associates, Ltd.—an Adult Learning and Organization Development consulting firm. "While in school, if anyone had told me I would be President of my own firm at such a young age, I never would have believed them. I had a strong mentor who encouraged me to follow my heart and dreams. That was the best advice I had. It led me to explore careers in the world outside of school."

Sharon earned a BS in Business Administration and a BA in Psychology from the State University of New York at Geneseo, and a Masters of Industrial and Labor Relations from Cornell University. She is currently a doctoral candidate in Organization and Leadership at Columbia University.

Sharon completed two internships while in college. She first interned at Exxon Chemical in Louisiana. At Exxon, Sharon acted as a human resource generalist and conducted Equal Employment Opportunity research. Sharon's second internship was with Morgan, Lewis, and Bockius, a Washington, DC law firm. There she researched collective bargaining negotiations for the Major League Baseball Association. "The internships helped me cement my career path. I wanted to work with people and in training and organizational development. I also learned that while I enjoyed negotiations and the law behind human resources, I did not want to be an attorney."

Sharon feels her internships helped her land a job with ARCO Chemical Company. At ARCO, Sharon held positions ranging from human resource generalist to senior international training and organization development consultant. "Without my internships, I don't feel a company as prestigious as

ARCO would have been interested in giving me my start. Internships definitely prepared me for what the real world was like as opposed to the world of theory you learn about in school. You need to know both."

At Lamm Associates, Sharon currently develops programs tailored to meet individual clients' needs. "I start out with a client assessment through interviews and focus groups. Then I review the assessment with the client prior to prescribing a program or intervention. Then I develop the program and work with the client on implementation."

Sharon believes the following skills are necessary in her profession: self-confidence, intuition, courage, humility, flexibility, responsibility, strong public speaking and writing skills, the ability to think and respond quickly, and a willingness to model desired behaviors.

Programs such as Equal Employment Opportunities, Affirmative Action, and discrimination laws always have a strong impact on Sharon's field. She also needs to keep updated on the National Labor Relations Board and labor laws. "Professional liability is an up and coming area for lawsuits. For example, if a company feels that I made matters worse or harmed them in any way, they could sue me. Because of this, you need to keep up on all areas of law pertinent to this field."

Sharon's best advice: "I cannot speak highly enough about the value of internships, shadowing programs, personal growth, continuing education, and personal development. My advice is learn about yourself and what makes you happy. Then *Go For It* and success will follow!"

> **"** While in school, if anyone had told me I would be President of my own firm at such a young age, I never would have believed them. I had a strong mentor who encouraged me to follow my heart and dreams. **"**

LESSONS

Bruce owned an apartment building. He hired a maintenance manager named Tom to "make minor repairs requested by tenants such as fixing plumbing leaks, replacing light switches, and replacing broken garbage disposals." Things worked well until Tom ordered a new refrigerator and stove for one of the apartments without consulting Bruce. Tom had given the business card Bruce had printed for him to the appliance store. The card described Tom as the "Manager of Maintenance" for the apartment complex. Based on that business card, the retailer delivered the appliances.

Where Do You Stand?

1. Why should Bruce be bound to pay for the appliances?

2. Why should Bruce not be bound to pay for the appliances?

GOALS

- Describe when an agency relationship exists
- Identify who is qualified to be a principal and who is qualified to be an agent
- Discuss how the law treats principals and agents who lack contractual capacity

WHAT IS AN AGENCY RELATIONSHIP?

WHAT'S YOUR VERDICT?

Jose worked at the Civic Center Service Station. His duties included selling gasoline, oil, and accessories, for which he either collected cash or made out credit tickets. Jose also changed oil and filters, provided lubrication services, and cleaned the premises.

Was Jose an agent, an employee, or both?

A person who does work for pay (for example, bagging groceries or reading water meters) under the supervision and control of another person is an *employee*. But some employees have a special legal status because they make contracts for their employer. When one person is authorized to alter another's legal relationships, the relationship of **agency** exists.

Agency exists, for example, when a salesperson makes sales contracts with customers for a business owner. The person who authorizes another to alter one of his or her legal relationships (the business owner) is a **principal**. The party authorized by the principal to act on his or her behalf (the salesperson) is the **agent**. The agent represents the principal in reaching agreements that bind the principal and a **third party** (customers).

In *What's Your Verdict?* Jose was an employee when he changed oil and filters, lubricated cars, and cleaned the premises. But when he

sold gas, oil, and accessories, the agency relationship existed. Agency existed because Jose was altering the legal relationships of the service station by making contracts on its behalf. The service station or its

IN THIS CASE

Sharon was a physician and a member of the Army reserve. She was called to active duty during Operation Desert Storm and was sent to Saudi Arabia. She and Dennis wanted to marry but they were separated by more than 6,000 miles. So Sharon asked her friend Gail "to stand in for her" during the wedding ceremony. Gail did, and on behalf of Sharon said, "I do." Gail was Sharon's agent because she altered Sharon's legal relationship with Dennis— Gail bound Sharon to the marriage relationship.

owner is the principal. Jose is both the owner's agent and an employee. Customers are the third parties. The diagram on the next page illustrates these parties and their relationships.

ALTERING LEGAL RELATIONS Contracting is the most common way of altering legal relationships. But there are other ways an agent can alter legal relationships as well. You can use agency to marry someone, divorce someone, sue someone, waive your legal rights, or alter your legal relationships in a variety of other ways.

SCOPE OF AUTHORITY The agent must act within the granted scope of authority in order to bind the principal. The **scope of authority** is the range of acts authorized by the principal.

IN THIS CASE

Smiley bought a motorscooter from The Wheels Shop. The salesperson gave her a signed card offering a free engine adjustment within three months of purchase. If the salesperson is not there when Smiley requests an adjustment, Smiley is still entitled to performance. The salesperson's signature was binding on the owner as principal, just as if the owner had personally signed the card.

ACTS BEYOND AUTHORITY If the agent has acted *outside* the scope of authority, the principal is not bound. Thus, in the example, if the salesperson had, without authority, executed a deed to Young's home, Young would not be bound. The salesperson would have been acting outside the scope of authority.

Generally, agents are not personally liable for the contracts that they

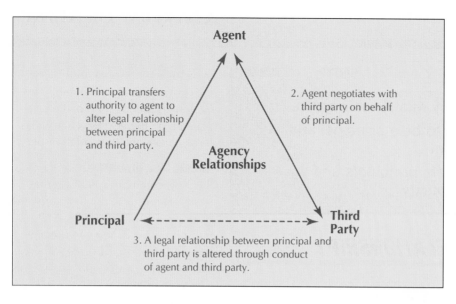

1. Principal transfers authority to agent to alter legal relationship between principal and third party.

2. Agent negotiates with third party on behalf of principal.

Agent

Agency Relationships

Principal

Third Party

3. A legal relationship between principal and third party is altered through conduct of agent and third party.

FIDUCIARY DUTIES All agents owe to their principals obligations called fiduciary duties. In essence, **fiduciary duties** require that the agent serve the best interests of the principal. The specific fiduciary duties are those of loyalty and obedience, reasonable care and skill, confidentiality, and accounting. If an agent violates a fiduciary duty, the principal may sue and recover damages from the agent.

CONSENSUAL NATURE Agency is consensual. Even if you contract to make someone your agent, both parties always have the power to terminate the agency relationship. While there may be contractual liability for ending the agency, no one can be compelled to continue in an agency relationship.

negotiate on behalf of their principals. However, when the agent acts outside the scope of authority and the third party suffers an injury as a result, the third party can recover from the agent. Of course a person who is not an agent has no authority and cannot bind another party.

WHO CAN BE A PRINCIPAL?

WHAT'S YOUR VERDICT?

Carey, a minor, wished to sell her rollerblades. She agreed to pay Fischer 10 percent of the sales price of $100 if Fischer would sell them for her. Fischer agreed, but after he had found a buyer, Carey decided not to sell. She claimed that, as a minor, she had the power to avoid the agency agreement and to avoid the contract made by Fischer, her agent.

Was Carey correct?

capacity (minors, the legally intoxicated, or the insane). Thus the law tries to protect third parties with a warranty of capacity. A **warranty of the principal's capacity** is imposed by law on the agent. The law assumes that the agent promised the third party that the principal had capacity. If the principal lacked capacity, avoided the contract, and thus injured the third party, the third party can recover from the agent.

Minors, and others who lack contractual capacity, can be principals and act through agents. However, they retain their rights flowing from a lack of contractual capacity. So they may disaffirm contracts *made with* their agents for non-necessaries. In *What's Your Verdict?* Carey may avoid her contract to pay Fischer 10 percent. In addition, minors may avoid contracts *made through* their agents. So Carey can avoid the contract with the buyer of her rollerblades.

Contracts made through agents can be avoided by those who lack

IN THIS CASE

Tanya was a minor. She moved out of her parents' home before graduating from high school. A salesperson appeared at her apartment one night when her sister was there but Tanya wasn't. He offered a year's supply of groceries and a large capacity refrigerator for only $225 per month. Tanya's sister phoned her and asked if she wanted the deal. Tanya said yes and her sister signed the contract on Tanya's behalf. When Tanya learned that the fair market value of the groceries and refrigerator was only about $80 per month, she refused to pay more for these necessaries. The company then sued the sister and recovered the difference from her because she did not tell the salesperson that Tanya was a minor.

WHO CAN BE AN AGENT?

WHAT'S YOUR VERDICT?

Tricia Cousins, a 17-year-old minor, was asked to buy a car on behalf of Mrs. Cousins, her elderly grandmother. Mrs. Cousins signed documents appointing Tricia as her agent for this purpose. Then Tricia found a car and executed a contract to buy it, signing as an agent. Later, her grandmother decided she did not like the color and said she was not bound by the contract because Tricia was underage.

Is Mrs. Cousins correct?

To protect the public, all states require that agents in certain occupations be licensed. This usually requires passing a professional examination. Licensing is often required of auctioneers, insurance agents, lawyers, stock brokers, and real estate brokers.

The general requirement is that an agent must be able to *understand* the transaction entered into on behalf of the principal. An agent who cannot understand the transaction lacks agency capacity for that transaction.

Minors, and others who lack contractual capacity, may themselves be agents. Thus, minors who lack legal capacity to act for themselves can generally act for and bind adults in contracts. Adult principals cannot later avoid the resulting contracts simply because of the minority of their agents. Only in the situation where the minor is unable to understand the transaction is the minor unable to act as an agent. In *What's Your Verdict?* Tricia's grandmother is wrong. Mrs. Cousins is bound by the contract even though her agent, Tricia, was a minor.

THINK ABOUT LEGAL CONCEPTS

Answer the following questions about legal concepts.

1. Every employee is an agent. **True or False?**

2. If an agent acts outside the agent's authority, then **(a) principal is not bound (b) agent is liable to the third party for any injury caused by acting outside the scope of authority (c) both a and b.**

3. Minors who act through agents have the same rights they would have if they acted directly. **True or False?**

THINK CRITICALLY ABOUT EVIDENCE

Study the following situations, answer the questions, then prepare arguments to support your answers.

4. Alonzo hired Lawrence to help him sell a valuable Persian rug. He authorized Lawrence to sell it for $400,000 cash. Lawrence did so. Later, Alonzo discovered that the rug was worth more than $600,000. Because Alonzo was a minor, he disaffirmed the contract, returned the $400,000 to the buyer, and got the rug back. The buyer sued Lawrence for $200,000—the difference between the $400,000 contract price and the $600,000 value. Will she collect?

5. Sweet Store, Inc., hired Li to work in the store. Mrs. Sweet, the owner, asked Li to be in charge of the vegetable displays. This involved spraying the vegetables with water periodically and sorting out vegetables that lost the fresh look. Another employee was in charge of ordering and taking deliveries of the vegetables. Cash register clerks were in charge of selling the vegetables. One day, Li was taking a break on the loading dock when a load of vegetables arrived. He signed the shipping receipt, although he was not authorized to do so. Unfortunately, the order was short and about $600 worth of vegetables were missing. Is the store liable for the loss because of Li's signature?

GOALS

- Identify the sources of an agent's authority
- Describe the acts of an agent which bind the principal
- Explain what happens when an agent acts outside the scope of express authority

CREATION OF AGENCY AUTHORITY

WHAT'S YOUR VERDICT?

Taylor was planning a birthday party for a friend. She asked another friend, Logan, to buy the cake. Logan agreed. Taylor told her to charge the cake to Taylor's account at the bakery. Taylor also gave Logan the keys to her car.

What forms of agency authority does Logan have?

Agency authority is created when a principal authorizes an agent to represent the principal. When the principal agrees to pay the agent, the agency relationship arises from a contract between the agent and the principal. In other instances, there is no contract.

One person, such as Logan in *What's Your Verdict?* may simply agree to help another in altering legal relationships with third parties. In cases where the agent receives no consideration, and there is no contract, the agency is called a **gratuitous agency**.

Agency authority may be created in a variety of ways. These include an express grant of authority, an implied grant of authority, creation by apparent authority, and ratification.

Express Grant of Authority

Express authority is directly communicated by the principal to the agent. It may be oral or written. In *What's Your Verdict?* Taylor gave Logan express authority to purchase the cake. If written, the grant may be in an informal letter or a carefully drafted document. Any writing that appoints someone as an agent is called a **power of attorney**.

Implied Grant of Authority

Implied authority is the power to do anything that is reasonably necessary or customary to carry out the duties expressly authorized. Thus, an agent's implied authority flows out of the express authority. In *What's Your Verdict?* there may be implied authority for Logan to buy some gas for the car if it is needed and charge it to Taylor.

Implied authority may be expanded in an emergency. In *What's Your Verdict?* if Taylor's car caught on fire while Logan was driving it on the errand, Logan would have implied authority to promise money to someone to assist in putting out the fire. Taylor would be liable to pay for this help.

Apparent Authority

Agency authority may sometimes result from the *appearance* created by the principal. This does not create a conventional authority because there has been no agreement between the principal and the agent. **Apparent authority** is created when a principal leads the *third party* to reasonably believe that a particular person has agency authority. The apparent authority must always come from the principal's words or conduct. It can never arise from the words or conduct of the agent alone.

POWER OF ATTORNEY
GENERAL

Know All Men by These Presents: That I, _____

_____

the undersigned (jointly and severally, if more than one) hereby make, constitute and appoint _____

_____

as a true and lawful Attorney for me and in my name, place and stead and for my use and benefit:

(a) To ask, demand, sue for, recover, collect and receive each and every sum of money, debt, account, legacy, bequest, interest, dividend, annuity and demand (which now is or hereafter shall become due, owing or payable) belonging to or claimed by me, and to use and take any lawful means for the recovery thereof by legal process or otherwise, and to execute and deliver a satisfaction or release therefor, together with the right and power to compromise or compound any claim or demand;

(b) To exercise any or all of the following powers as to real property, any interest therein and/or any building thereon: To contract for, purchase, receive and take possession thereof and of evidence of title thereto; to lease the same for any term or purpose, including leases for business, residence, and oil and/or mineral development; to sell, exchange, grant or convey the same with or without warranty; and to mortgage, transfer in trust, or otherwise encumber or hypothecate the same to secure payment of a negotiable or non-negotiable note or performance of any obligation or agreement;

(c) To exercise any or all of the following powers as to all kinds of personal property and goods, wares and merchandise, choses in action and other property in possession or in action: To contract for, buy, sell, exchange, transfer and in any legal manner deal in and with the same; and to mortgage, transfer in trust, or otherwise encumber or hypothecate the same to secure payment of a negotiable or non-negotiable note or performance of any obligation or agreement;

(d) To borrow money and to execute and deliver negotiable or non-negotiable notes therefor with or without security; and to loan money and receive negotiable or non-negotiable notes therefor with such security as he shall deem proper;

(e) To create, amend, supplement and terminate any trust and to instruct and advise the trustee of any trust wherein I am or may be trustor or beneficiary; to represent and vote stock, exercise stock rights, accept and deal with any dividend, distribution or bonus, join in any corporate financing, reorganization, merger, liquidation, consolidation or other action and the extension, compromise, conversion, adjustment, enforcement or foreclosure, singly or in conjunction with others of any corporate stock, bond, note, debenture or other security; to compound, compromise, adjust, settle and satisfy any obligation, secured or unsecured, owing by or to me and to give or accept any property and/or money whether or not equal to or less in value than the amount owing in payment, settlement or satisfaction thereof;

(f) To transact business of any kind or class and as my act and deed to sign, execute, acknowledge and deliver any deed, lease, assignment of lease, covenant, indenture, indemnity, agreement, mortgage, deed of trust, assignment of mortgage or of the beneficial interest under deed of trust, extension or renewal of any obligation, subordination or waiver of priority, hypothecation, bottomry, charter-party, bill of lading, bill of sale, bill, bond, note, whether negotiable or non-negotiable, receipt, evidence of debt, full or partial release or satisfaction of mortgage, judgment and other debt, request for partial or full reconveyance of deed of trust and such other instruments in writing of any kind or class as may be necessary or proper in the premises.

Giving and Granting unto my said Attorney full power and authority to do and perform all and every act and thing whatsoever requisite, necessary or appropriate to be done in and about the premises as fully to all intents and purposes as I might or could do if personally present, hereby ratifying all that my said Attorney shall lawfully do or cause to be done by virtue of these presents. The powers and authority hereby conferred upon my said Attorney shall be applicable to all real and personal property or interests therein now owned or hereafter acquired by me and wherever situate.

My said Attorney is empowered hereby to determine in his sole discretion the time when, purpose for and manner in which any power herein conferred upon him shall be exercised, and the conditions, provisions and covenants of any instrument or document which may be executed by him pursuant hereto; and in the acquisition or disposition of real or personal property, my said Attorney shall have exclusive power to fix the terms thereof for cash, credit and/or property, and if on credit with or without security.

The undersigned, if a married woman, hereby further authorizes and empowers my said Attorney, as my duly authorized agent, to join in my behalf, in the execution of any instrument by which any community real property or any interest therein, now owned or hereafter acquired by my spouse and myself, or either of us, is sold, leased, encumbered, or conveyed.

When the contest so requires, the masculine gender includes the feminine and/or neuter, and the singular number includes the plural.

WITNESS my hand this _____ day of _____ , 19 ___

_____   _____

_____   _____

State of _____ , ⎫
                                    ⎬ SS.
County of _____ ⎭

On _____ , before me, the undersigned, a Notary Public in and for said

State, personally appeared _____

_____

known to me to be the person _____ whose name _____ subscribed

to the within instrument and acknowledged that _____ executed the same.

(Seal) _____

Witness my hand and official seal.   Notary Public in and for said State

Stanton was unhappy with a power lawn mower he had purchased from Lacey's Department Store. It was hard to start. Carla, who was in charge of Lacey's Customer Relations Department, had express authority to handle exchanges and refunds. In this case, she allowed Stanton to return the mower, and she gave him a full cash refund. Carla assumed that Lacey's would return the mower to the manufacturer. Later, the store manager told Stanton he should have asked the manufacturer for the refund. Stanton need not do so because Carla had apparent authority to bind the store. Her apparent authority was created when Lacey's made her the head of its customer relations department.

Ratification

If a person acts outside the scope of his or her authority, the principal is not bound. However, a principal who later agrees to the transaction can be bound. This approval of a previously unauthorized act, or an act outside the agent's scope of authority, is called **ratification**. A principal impliedly ratifies an agency transaction by knowingly accepting its benefits. For a valid ratification, the following conditions must be met:

- the third person must have believed that by dealing with the principal's agent, he or she was making a contract with the principal

- before ratification, the principal must have full knowledge of all material facts

- the principal must show an intent to ratify

- the principal must ratify the entire act, not just one part of the transaction

- the principal must ratify before the third person withdraws from the unratified transaction.

CULTURAL DIVERSITY IN LAW

International

Exporting—Part 1

Companies engaged in direct exporting (selling directly to overseas companies) may hire full-time *employees*. These employees include full-time export managers and international sales specialists. Their duties include developing new products for overseas markets, pricing, and packaging and labeling products for export, among others.

Instead of hiring its own employees, companies also may conduct business with overseas companies through *foreign sales agents*. These are agents of the companies who work on commission, earning a percentage of the sales they make.

A Question of ETHICS

Mary Louise was Karen's executive assistant. On December 1, Karen told Mary Louise to draw up a list of their most important customers and send each one a nice present for Christmas. The next day Mary Louise took the list to Karen with her suggestion for a gift. Karen was in a hurry and didn't even look at the list of customers or the gift suggestions. Karen told Mary Louise "just go with whatever you have now." Mary Louise then ordered a $100 fruit basket to be sent to 150 customers. When the bill for $15,000 came on December 15, Karen was extremely upset. She threatened to fire Mary Louise as she yelled, "How am I going to explain this to accounting? I only wanted to spend about $50 on 10 customers." She also wanted to know if Mary Louise would be willing to call each of the customers and ask for the fruit basket back. Did Karen have an ethical obligation to point out her planned budget to Mary Louise? Did Mary Louise have an ethical obligation to explain that she was about to spend $15,000 on Karen's behalf? Can Karen justify her anger if the goodwill created by the gifts generates more than $1 million in new sales?

Answer the following questions about legal concepts.

1. Express authority comes from the principal to the third party. **True or False?**

2. Which of the following are types of authority?
   (a) **express authority**
   (b) **implied authority**
   (c) **apparent authority**
   (d) **all of the above**

3. The scope of implied authority can be based on either express authority or on an emergency. **True or False?**

4. Apparent authority arises out of the principal's conduct toward the agent. **True or False?**

5. When someone acts outside the scope of express authority, but the principal accepts the benefits of the transaction with knowledge of all its terms, this is called __?__ .

Study the following situations, answer the questions, then prepare arguments to support your answers.

6. Jane asked Kroger to represent her in selling her farm. She executed a formal power of attorney authorizing Kroger to negotiate a sale and to execute all necessary documents to transfer title to her real property. Then Jane left for vacation. When she returned, she learned that Kroger had sold the farm at an attractive price. He also sold two tractors and a truck. Is Jane bound by Kroger's conduct in selling the farm? In selling the tractors and the truck?

7. William Kirchberg was a food broker. He represented O'Day in 55 deals for the purchase of lettuce from Arakelian Farms (AF). For each transaction, AF sent bills to O'Day and he paid them. Then Kirchberg terminated the agency relationship with O'Day. AF was not notified of the termination. Then, Kirchberg placed 20 more orders, purportedly on behalf of O'Day. AF delivered the lettuce and billed O'Day but was not paid. AF sued O'Day. At the trial, O'Day's defense was that Kirchberg was not his agent. What is the result? (*O'Day v. Arakelian Farms,* 540 P.2d 197)

8. Cook executed a power of attorney authorizing Shornack to sell 22.5 acres of his farmland for $10,000 per acre. Cook provided a general description of the property. Before finding a serious candidate, Shornack showed the property to 12 prospects. Shornack and the buyer then walked around the boundary of the property based on Cook's description. When the legal description for the deed was prepared, it described a plot of 26.5 acres. The buyer paid for the extra four acres. When presented with the cash, Cook balked at selling that much of his property. Is Cook bound to sell the additional four acres? If Cook accepts the cash, is he then bound to the sale of the extra four acres?

If you are a third person dealing with an agent, remember that . . .

1. You should verify the extent of the agent's authority directly from the principal. If you are uncertain about the authority or honesty of the agent, make payment by a check payable to the principal.

If you are an agent, remember that . . .

2. When you sign anything for your principal, make it unmis-

PREVENT LEGAL DIFFICULTIES

takably clear that you are signing as an agent. Always write the name of the principal first, then add "by" and your signa-

ture followed by the word "agent." If you exceed the scope of your authority and that injures the third party, you may be liable for that injury.

If you are a principal, remember that . . .

3. Your agent's acts become your acts. Use care in selecting agents. If you discharge your agent, protect yourself against apparent authority by notifying those the agent dealt with in your name.

CHAPTER IN REVIEW

CONCEPTS IN BRIEF

1. The relationship of principal and agent is created when one person authorizes another to alter legal relations, for example by assisting in contracting with third persons.

2. Principals are bound by the contracts negotiated by their agents when the agents have acted within the scope of their agency authority.

3. Principals are not bound by agreements that are outside the scope of the agent's authority.

4. Apparent authority arises when the principal leads the third party to believe a person has agency authority.

5. The test for determining the capacity of agents is "Do they have the mental capacity to understand the transaction?"

6. Minors can have agency capacity for transactions they negotiate for principals.

7. Agency authority may be created by express grant or by implied grant, or it may result from appearance. Unauthorized action may also bind the principal if the action is later ratified by the principal.

8. The fiduciary duties compel the agent to act in the best interest of the principal.

9. Agents owe fiduciary duties to their principals.

10. Ratification arises when the principal accepts and retains the benefits of a transaction negotiated by an agent who acted outside the scope of the agent's authority.

11. The agent is liable to the third party if the agent acts outside the scope of authority and thereby injures the third party.

YOUR LEGAL VOCABULARY

Match each statement with the term that it best defines. Some terms may not be used.

1. Agent's implied promise that the principal has contractual capacity

2. Party who works through an agent to bind a principal

3. Authority of an agent to do anything necessary or customary to carry out expressly authorized duties

4. Authority created when a principal leads a third party to believe that someone has agency authority

5. Obligations of an agent to serve the principal's best interests

6. Authority directly granted by a principal to an agent orally or in writing

7. Agency that is not based on a contract

8. Principal's assent to unauthorized acts of an agent

9. Writing that creates agency authority

10. A person who authorizes another to alter one of his or her legal relationships

11. A party authorized to act on another's behalf

12. The range of acts authorized by the principal

agency
agent
apparent authority
express authority
fiduciary duties
gratuitous agency
implied authority
power of attorney
principal
ratification
scope of authority
third party
warranty of the
   principal's capacity

13. Describe a transaction where a person is an employee but not an agent.

14. Describe a transaction where a person is both an employee and an agent.

15. Describe a transaction where a principal creates apparent authority.

16. Describe a transaction where an agent acts outside the scope of authority.

WRITE ABOUT LEGAL CONCEPTS

17. Create a one-paragraph scenario where an agent is given express authority.

18. Create a one-paragraph scenario where an agent has implied authority.

19. Create a one-paragraph scenario where a principal ratifies conduct outside the scope of authority.

20. **HOT DEBATE** Write up a new job description for Tom. Redefine Tom's job in a way that explicitly forbids him from making expensive purchases.

THINK CRITICALLY ABOUT EVIDENCE

Study the following situations, answer the questions, then prepare arguments to support your answers.

21. Susan celebrated her sixteenth birthday. Two weeks later she went shopping for a car using money she inherited. She became frustrated with the process and asked her father to select and purchase an appropriate car on her behalf. She trusted her dad to know what she would like and also thought he was more knowledgeable. He found a car and purchased it, signing as her agent. Unfortunately dad bought a large gray four-door sedan and Susan wanted something sporty. Can Susan disaffirm?

22. Simington hired Alice to work in his shoe store fitting shoes. Her job description limited her duties to that task. One day Simington left Alice alone in the store without any instructions. When a customer came it, she sold him the store's most expensive shoes at a third of their retail value. Is Simington bound?

23. Newman executed a power of attorney authorizing Sanchez to sell his car at the highest price possible, but for not less than $2,800. Sanchez received an offer for $2,200 from Derry and accepted it. Is Newman bound?

24. When Kraus discharged his purchasing agent, Stacey, and terminated their agency relationship, Stacey became angry. To get even, Stacey made two contracts that included terms that were unfavorable to Kraus, yet were reasonable in the competitive market. The first contract was with an old customer, A, who thought Stacey was still the purchasing agent for Kraus. The second contract was with a new customer, B, who had never heard of Stacey or Kraus before. Is Kraus liable on either of these contracts?

ANALYZE REAL CASES

25. Nissan Motor Corporation appointed McKnight as its Denver area agent and dealer for the sale of its automobiles. McKnight purchased automobiles and parts from Nissan. He then sold them as he desired and at prices he set without any control from Nissan. The question arose as to whether an agency existed. What is your judgment? (*United Fire and Casualty Company v. Nissan Motor Corporation,* 164 Colo. 42, 433 P.2d 769)

26. Serges owned a retail butcher shop. One of his managers borrowed $3,500 from David for use in the butcher shop. Serges claimed that the manager had no authority to borrow money. Nevertheless, Serges made payments of $200. Serges also told David on several occasions that the full sum would eventually be paid. Was Serges liable? (*David v. Serges,* 373 Mich. 442, 129 N.W.2d 882)

27. Desfossess was a mobile-home-park developer. He hired Notis, a licensed real estate broker, at a weekly salary. Notis's job was to assist Desfossess with the special assignment of acquiring land for mobile home parks. Desfossess asked Notis to negotiate on his behalf for the purchase of a tract suitable for a mobile home park. Notis suggested a certain parcel and received authority to purchase it in his own name, with Desfossess as the undisclosed principal. Notis reported to Desfossess that the land would cost $32,400, although Notis knew it could be and was purchased for $15,474.62. It also appeared that Notis, before becoming Desfossess's agent, had obtained an option for $1,000 to purchase the land but did not reveal this to Desfossess. Desfossess sued for the difference between what he had paid Notis and the cost of the land. Notis claimed that if Desfossess, as his former principal, had any right at all, it would be only to rescind the contract and to return the land to Notis. Who was correct? (*Desfossess v. Notis,* 333 A.2d 89)

28. Smith and Edwards operated a sporting goods shop in Brigham City, Utah. Sponsors of the Golden Spike Little League made arrangements with the store to purchase, at a substantial discount, the players' baseball uniforms and equipment. The sponsors picked up $3,900 worth of merchandise without making any payments. After a demand for full payment, Smith and Edwards sued the sponsors. The sponsors defended by asserting that they were agents of Golden Spike Little League, acting within the scope of their authority, and thus were not personally liable. The trial judge found that Golden Spike Little League was a loosely formed voluntary association and thus not a legal entity upon which liability could be imposed. Are the sponsors liable? If the sponsors avoided liability, do you think this would be ethical? (*Smith and Edwards v. Golden Spike Little League,* 577 P.2d 132, Utah)

29. Mrs. Terry is dealing with Alice, a clerk in Peters Department Store. Mrs. Terry sees a cashmere sweater she likes, but she notices it is slightly soiled. Alice, pushing for a sale, agrees to mark it down from $25 to $15, which she has no authority to do. Mrs. Terry says, "fine," asks that the sweater be delivered, and promises to pay C.O.D. The manager of Peters sees the item being wrapped, corrects the bill, and sends it out to Mrs. Terry. On seeing her sweater accompanied by a bill for $25, Mrs. Terry calls the store. She is told by Peters that Alice had no authority to mark down the price. Mrs. Terry also is told that she should either pay the bill or return the sweater. Is Mrs. Terry entitled to her bargain? Why or why not? (From Mearns, "Vicarious Liability for Agency Contracts," 48 Virginia Law Review 76.)

30. ABC Transportation hired Agnes as its president. After a few years of hard work, Agnes was successful in making ABC profitable. Agnes asked for substantial salary increases and his relationship with the company deteriorated. He then copied customer lists and recruited an ABC vice-president to help him start a new company to engage in the same business. ABC filed suit against Agnes. Has Agnes violated his fiduciary duties? (*ABC Trans., etc. v. Aeronautics Forwarders, Inc.* 379 N.E.2d 1228.)

31. Rae Abramson and Ruth Pailet were sisters who together owned a parcel of real property. They desired to lease the property. Dr. Albert Abramson, Rae's husband, helped them rent it. Dr. Abramson assisted them in leasing the property to Cenla Equipment Company, Inc., for five years. After about three years, Cenla stopped paying rent. Thereafter, Cenla approached Dr. Abramson with a request that the lease be terminated. After checking with the sisters, he informed Cenla that the termination was acceptable and no further rent would be owed. When the rental income stopped, Ruth Pailet (plaintiff) filed suit against Cenla (defendant), stating that she did not agree to the termination of the lease. Who prevails? (*Pailet v. Guillory,* 315 S.2d 893, Ct. App., Louisiana)

FACTS The First Parish Unitarian Church of East Bridgewater hired Rich as its minister. At this time a Church Committee ran the church. As Rich's role in the Church expanded, he began to perform many of the duties of the Committee. The Church also expanded, from 12 families to more than 400. After about 10 years the Committee stopped meeting. Rich then ventured into real estate and other unrelated business ventures. To finance these, he gave mortgages on the church property which he, but not the Church Committee, executed. When the businesses he established failed, the creditor sought to foreclose on the mortgages. Church members claimed the mortgages were invalid because the Committee did not authorize them. The lower court found for the mortgage holders and the Church appealed.

The Committee claims that it did not know of the existence of the mortgages. Thus its failure to repudiate the mortgages resulted not from a ratification of the transactions but from ignorance of essential facts. Generally, in order to establish ratification of unauthorized acts of an agent, a principal must have "knowledge of all material facts . . ." However, a qualification to this rule is that one cannot "purposefully shut his eyes to means of information within his own possession and control." This is especially true of the Committee that functioned as the "business center" of the Church and had a duty to keep itself informed of Church business.

Further, the Committee was not totally ignorant of Rich's actions. From the many indications of the radical physical and structural changes to the Church and surroundings, it should have

been obvious to the Church that "something was afoot." The very nature of the construction and renovation indicated that large expenditures were being made. Although Rich was far from candid in his disclosures, he did inform Church members of various projects at Church events through annual reports and publications.

OPINION We conclude that the Committee's knowledge of substantial and costly physical changes at the Church should have provoked an investigation by the Committee which would have led to the discovery of the mortgages. In these circumstances, the Committee's failure to act "will be deemed to constitute actual knowledge." By failing to disavow the mortgages, the Church ratified the transactions, a ratification that may be inferred without a vote by the Committee.

Accordingly the mortgages are valid. Affirmed.

PRACTICE JUDGING

1. **Do you think the church or the mortgage holders should pay?**

2. **What specific conduct does the court point to as constituting the ratification?**

LESSONS

26-1 AGENT'S FIDUCIARY DUTIES

26-2 OTHER LIABILITIES IN AGENCY

HOT DEBATE

Susan is a real estate broker. She agreed to be Alicia's agent to assist in selling her home. Alicia told Susan she was in a financial bind and needed cash. Susan showed the property to more than 25 potential buyers but no one made an offer. Finally, in exasperation, Susan said to a prospect, "Look, I've shown this property to at least 25 other people and no one seems interested! I know the seller is in a financial bind and desperately needs cash. Why don't you offer 70 percent of the listing price and I'll try to get her to accept it?"

Where Do You Stand?

1. Has Susan acted fairly in this situation?

2. How might Susan not have acted fairly?

GOALS

● Describe each fiduciary duty of an agent

● Identify when each fiduciary duty has been violated

● Explain the principal's remedies for an agent's violation of a fiduciary duty

WHAT ARE AN AGENT'S FIDUCIARY DUTIES?

WHAT'S YOUR VERDICT?

Susan gave Wallace an antique Chinese bronze mirror to sell for her at the highest possible price. Without telling Susan, Wallace sold the mirror to his wife for half its value.

If Susan discovered what occurred, could she recover the rest of the mirror's value from Wallace?

In many respects, the agent's duties to the principal are the same as those of an ordinary employee. However, the agent has the additional ability to bind the principal in dealings with third parties. Therefore, agents must be honest and show good faith. The law encourages this by requiring four fiduciary duties.

Fiduciary duties owed by agents to principals are loyalty, care and skill, confidentiality, and accounting. If an agent violates a fiduciary duty and that injures the principal, the agent will be liable for the injury. In *What's Your Verdict?* Susan could recover the lost profits from Wallace.

Loyalty and Obedience

The agent's core duty is the **duty of loyalty and obedience**. It requires that agents place the interests of their principals above the interests of all others.

SECRET PROFITS The duty of loyalty means that the agent may not secretly benefit from the agency transaction. Thus, agents may neither buy from

IN THIS CASE

Buck was a real estate broker. He obtained a listing on Marlene's home, which made him her agent. Later Buck spent almost two weeks working with a prospective buyer, and they became friends. The buyer, who was interested in Marlene's home, asked Buck, "What is the minimum price Marlene would accept for this property?" Buck knew what that price was. However, Buck must place Marlene's interests above the interests of his friend the buyer. He may not tell the buyer what Marlene's lowest price is.

nor sell to themselves, their relatives, or their friends without prior approval from their principals. In addition, any profits the agent earns in performing the agency duties belong to

the principal, unless otherwise agreed.

OBEDIENCE This duty also means that the agent must obey the instructions of the principal. Of course an agent should not follow instructions to do an illegal or immoral act. For example, a sales agent may not lie about a product even if the principal has ordered such fraudulent conduct. If a principal orders an agent to do something illegal or immoral, the agent should resign from the agency relationship.

Reasonable Care and Skill

In representing one's principal, an agent must satisfy the **duty of reasonable care and skill**. This requires the agent to exercise the

degree of care and skill that a reasonably prudent person would use in a similar situation. Failing to satisfy the fiduciary duty of reasonable care and skill renders the agent liable to the principal for the resulting loss or injury.

IN THIS CASE
The Merritts owned the Pony Express Inn. Because the inn was located in a high crime area, security was a concern. Therefore, the Merritts told their employees to limit the cash on hand by dropping all cash over $200 into a floor safe controlled by an automatic timer. Kate, the weekend manager, thought this was too bothersome, so she simply left the receipts in the cash drawer and dropped the excess in the safe at the end of her shift. One Sunday, Kate was robbed. The robbers fled with the $3,000 that was in the cash drawer. Kate would be held liable for the loss of the $3,000. A prudent manager would not leave so much money in the cash drawer when a safe was available.

DUTY TO COMMUNICATE At a minimum, reasonable care and skill requires the agent to communicate to the principal any information that would affect the principal's decisions.

Confidentiality

Agents owe the fiduciary duty of confidentiality to their principals. The **duty of confidentiality** requires the agent to treat information about the principal with great caution. Information that is obviously confidential must be kept confidential.

Some information is not obviously confidential. But if a principal asks an agent to treat any information as confidential, the agent must do so. This

IN THIS CASE
Harold represented a seller, Martha, in a real estate transaction. While negotiating with the buyer, Janice, over the phone, Harold heard Janice talking to her husband about making an offer at a higher price if the first offer was not accepted by Martha. The duty to communicate requires that Harold tell Martha this information before she decides whether to accept Janice's offer.

duty of confidentiality survives the agency relationship. So the duty binds the agent even years after the agency relationship has ended.

IN THIS CASE
When acting as the agent of Harry, Sue learns that Harry is about to go into bankruptcy. This information is valuable and obviously confidential. If Sue tells people about it and this injures Harry, he could recover from her for the injury.

Accounting

Agents owe the **duty of accounting** to the principal. It requires an agent to account to the principal for all money and property of the principal that comes into the agent's possession. The agent must promptly notify the principal of the receipt of money from third parties and must make an accounting within a reasonable time. An accounting is a formal statement (usually in writing) that tells the principal what happened to all of the principal's money or property.

A Question of ETHICS

Rich, who often donated animals to the city zoo, sent his agent Alice to Africa to buy an elephant. Rich gave Alice $9,500 for travel and other expenses. While in Africa, Alice took a side trip to visit friends. When she returned, she did not deduct those expenses from the total. Is this ethical? Is it legal?

COMMINGLING The agent may not commingle. **Commingling** is mixing the funds or property of the principal and agent. If commingling occurs and there is a loss, the agent bears that loss.

TRUST ACCOUNTS Money of the principal held by the agent must usually be deposited in a bank, in an account separate from that of the agent. The separate accounts for the funds of principals are called **trust accounts**. Professional agents such as lawyers, accountants, real estate brokers and stockbrokers maintain trust accounts that are separate from their personal and office checking accounts. If a client's funds are placed in a personal or office account, that would be commingling. Such action would subject the agent to both professional sanctions (such as disbarring a lawyer) and liability to the principal for any loss.

FYI

The word fiduciary comes from the Latin word *fidere* which means "to trust." This word is also the source of the words fiancée, affidavit, confide, federal, and defy.

Answer the following questions about legal concepts.

1. Agency law tries to make it safe for the principal to trust the agent. **True or False?**

2. The obligations agents owe principals are called __?__ duties.

3. Which of the following is the most basic duty of an agent?
(a) **loyalty and obedience**
(b) **reasonable care and skill** (c) **confidentiality**
(d) **accounting**

4. If an agent makes a profit on an agency transaction without the principal's knowledge or consent, which of the fiduciary duties would be violated?
(a) **loyalty and obedience**
(b) **reasonable care and skill** (c) **confidentiality**
(d) **accounting**

5. If an agent fails to tell the principal about an important part of a transaction, which of the fiduciary duties would be violated?
(a) **loyalty and obedience**
(b) **reasonable care and skill** (c) **confidentiality**
(d) **accounting**

6. The duty of confidentiality lasts only as long as the agency relationship lasts. **True or False?**

7. Commingling occurs when an agent mixes together the funds of more than one principal. **True or False?**

Study the following situations, answer the questions, and then prepare arguments to support your answers.

8. Jeff hired Sally, a real estate broker, to help sell his home. While she was trying to sell the home, a buyer asked Sally what Jeff's bottom price was. She told the buyer (without Jeff's permission) and the house sold. Has Sally done anything legally wrong?

9. Newman authorized Sanchez to sell his car at the highest price possible, but for not less than $2,800. Sanchez received an offer of $3,000 from Hack. Nevertheless, Sanchez sold the car to his buddy Glenn for $2,800. When Newman learned of this, he attempted to collect $200 from Sanchez. Will he succeed?

10. Laura, an elderly woman, was physically disabled and confined to a wheelchair. Her nephew Richard kept her financial records for her for free. During the course of paying Laura's bills, Richard learned that she was interested in car racing magazines and subscribed to three of them. He thought that was interesting and told his mother about it. Does Richard owe any duties to Laura? Has he violated any legal duty?

11. Anita retained Lynn as her lawyer. Lynn settled a lawsuit for more than $200,000 and the check was mailed to Lynn at her law office. Lynn deposited the check in her personal account and she used the money to pay monthly bills. When Anita asked about the money, Lynn stalled her saying it might take another month to arrive. Anita eventually became suspicious and checked with the defendant only to learn the judgment had been paid. If Anita calls the bar association in her state, will they discipline Lynn?

12. Alto was hired as a purchasing agent for Stargate, a motion picture animation company. In his resume, he misrepresented his background and skill. His first assignment was to buy the film stock on which Stargate printed their animations. Because Alto wasn't familiar with the different grades of film, he purchased more than $27,000 worth of stock that couldn't be used. Stargate had to bare that loss. Is there any agency law that would allow Stargate to recover from Alto?

13. Weston was a real estate broker. He listed Smythe's home for sale. When Weston obtained an offer at the listing price, Smythe rejoiced, and broke out the champagne. The offer was conditioned upon the buyer obtaining financing at 7.5 percent interest within 30 days. Weston told both the buyer and Smythe that she would easily be able to find a lender at that rate. Business was booming for Weston and he didn't have a chance to follow up on the buyer's financing situation. When the 30 days expired, the seller refused to complete the sale. Has Weston violated a fiduciary duty? If so, which one?

GOALS

- Describe a principal's liabilities
- Describe an agent's liabilities

WHEN IS A PRINCIPAL LIABLE?

WHAT'S YOUR VERDICT?

Jim signed an agreement with Jesse, appointing Jesse to find a buyer who would pay $35,000 for Jim's antique car. If Jesse found a buyer who was ready, willing, and able to buy the car, Jesse was to receive a commission of 10 percent of the price. Jesse found a ready, willing, and able buyer for the car at the agreed price, but Jim refused to enter into a sales contract.

Is Jesse entitled to the commission?

When a principal enters into an agency relationship, a failure to fulfill obligations can create a liability to either the agent or to the third party.

Liability to the Agent

After a principal gives an agent certain tasks to perform, the principal has a duty to cooperate with the agent so that the tasks can be performed. Failure of the principal to fulfill her or his obligations gives the agent the right to quit and recover any damages. The principal's main obligation is the duty to pay what was promised for the agency services. In *What's Your Verdict?* Jim is legally obligated to pay, because Jesse completed the assigned task.

If an agent properly incurs expenses, the principal must reimburse the agent. If the agent suffers any loss because of the principal's instructions, the principal must indemnify, or repay, the agent the amount lost.

Contractual Liability to the Third Party

As long as agents act within the scope of their authority, principals are bound by the agreements with the third parties. Principals also are liable when the unauthorized acts of agents

are ratified. **Ratification** occurs when the principal accepts the benefits of the unauthorized transaction with the third party.

Agent's Torts, Fraud, and Crimes

If torts or fraud are committed by an agent, the agent is liable. The *principal* also will be liable if the principal directed the agent to engage in the illegal activity, or the agent was acting to advance the interests of the principal. For example, if a sales agent defrauds a customer in order to make a sale, the principal is liable for any damages that result.

IN THIS CASE

Bridges was the credit manager of White Appliances. Bridges wrongfully took possession of Diane's truck while attempting to collect a past-due account from Diane. White Appliances was liable to Diane for damages because Bridges, its agent, had committed the tort of conversion while acting within the scope of his authority. Bridges was also liable for the wrongdoing.

Usually, the principal is not liable for an agent's crime unless the crime itself has been authorized or ratified. As an exception to this rule, the principal is generally liable for the illegal sale, by the agent, of intoxicating liquor or adulterated foods. Thus, a bar owner, the principal, would be liable if the agent, a bartender, illegally served liquor to a minor.

WHEN IS AN AGENT LIABLE TO THIRD PERSONS?

WHAT'S YOUR VERDICT?

Sara was authorized to sell rugs and carpeting for the Magic Carpet Company, Inc. However, she was not authorized to make purchases. While on a sales trip to New York, Sara had a rare opportunity to buy seven small oriental rugs at low "distress sale" prices. She did not have enough time to contact her home office. Therefore, she simply signed the contract as a purchasing agent for Magic Carpet.

Is Sara liable for the purchase price?

An agent can be liable to third persons if the agent's acts are outside his or her scope of authority or if the principal lacks capacity.

Agent's Acts Outside the Scope of Authority

If an agent acts without authority from the principal, the agent becomes personally liable to the third party for resulting injury. That is because the agent implies the promise that he or she has appropriate authority. This usually arises when an agent exceeds the authority given by the principal.

In *What's Your Verdict?* Sara was personally liable because she exceeded her agency authority.

However, if Magic Carpet later ratifies the purchase, Sara would no longer be personally liable. In some cases, a person will act as agent for an alleged principal when absolutely no authority has been given for any action. Again, only the "agent" is liable to the third party unless the "principal" ratifies or has given apparent authority.

Principal's Lack of Capacity

The agent warrants the principal's capacity to the third party. If it turns out that the principal does not exist, or that the principal is able to avoid the contract for lack of contractual capacity, the agent will be liable. Normally, to bind the principal and

to avoid personal liability an agent will sign the name of the principal to a contract and add words to indicate that the signature is by an agent.

Sometimes the agent is not allowed to disclose the principal's existence or identity. The principal in such a case is known as an **undisclosed principal**. The agent is liable on such a contract. However, with most contracts, when the third party learns the identity of the principal, the third party may generally elect to hold either the principal or the agent to the agreement. But the third party may not enforce the agreement against both.

IN THIS CASE

Maria contracted for a supply of paper bags and cartons for her employer, Tasti-Town Tamales. She properly signed the contract as follows: Tasti-Town Tamales, by Maria Costa, Purchasing Agent.

HOW IS AN AGENCY TERMINATED?

WHAT'S YOUR VERDICT?

Daisy entered into a one-year written contract with the Sweet Magnolia Nursery as its sales agent in North and South Carolina. After six months, company sales dropped far below expectations. Daisy was the last to be hired, and so she was the first to be fired—even though her manager admitted that her performance had been satisfactory.

Did the nursery have a legal right to terminate the agency?

Generally, both the agent and the principal have the power but not the right, to terminate the agency at any time. The principal terminates

by revoking the agent's authority. The concept that the principal has the power but not the right means that the principal may end the agency

relationship but must pay damages for doing so.

In *What's Your Verdict?* the nursery could revoke Daisy's authority. As a result, Daisy could no longer bind the nursery. This illustrates that the nursery had the power to terminate the agency, but it did not have the *right*. It would be liable in damages for breach of the one-year agency contract.

In a similar way, the agent has the power to quit at any time. However, he or she may lack the right to do so unless the principal has breached the contract. If an agent wrongfully terminates the agency before the contract expires, the principal is entitled to damages.

Gratuitous Agency

A gratuitous agency exists when the agent receives no consideration. Usually, a gratuitous agent cannot recover any damages if the authority is revoked. Likewise, a principal normally cannot recover any damages from a gratuitous agent who abandons the agency.

Agreement

An ordinary agency expires at the time provided in the contract that created it. This may be a particular length of time, the occurrence of an event, or the completion of certain tasks. If no time is stated in the agency contract, the agency continues for a reasonable time. An agency can be ended at any time if both the principal and agent agree to terminate it.

Operation of Law

An agency is ordinarily terminated upon the death, insanity, or bankruptcy of either the principal or the agent. Also, if it becomes impossible to perform the agency, such as if the subject matter of the agency is destroyed or if a change of law makes the agent's required actions illegal, the agency is ended.

When the authority of an agent is terminated by the principal's voluntary act, the principal should promptly notify third persons who have previously dealt with the agent. If the principal does not give individualized notice, the agent is likely to have apparent authority to make binding contracts between the principal and third persons as long as the third persons do not know of the termination. Others who may have heard of the agency also are entitled to notice. This can be given by publishing the fact of the termination in a newspaper of general circulation in the area.

CULTURAL DIVERSITY IN LAW

International

Exporting—Part 2

Companies who export products may work through their own employees or through foreign sales agents. They also may conduct overseas business using independent contractors, such as foreign distributors or export management companies.

Foreign distributors are usually located in the country with which the company is doing business. They assume the risks of buying and warehousing the goods. They also typically service the products they sell, train end users to use the product, extend credit to customers, and advertise the products.

Export management companies are consultants that advise manufacturers and other exporters. They conduct research targeted to specific countries, exhibit goods at foreign trade shows, prepare export documentation, handle language translations, and make shipping arrangements.

Answer the following questions about legal concepts.

1. The principal is liable to the agent for failure to pay the agreed amount for the agency service. **True or False?**

2. If an agent acts outside the scope of authority, the principal will still be bound if the principal __?__ the agent's unauthorized acts.

3. Both principals and agents have the ability to terminate the agency but they may be liable for damages if they do so. This is called the __?__ .

Study the following situations, answer the questions, then prepare arguments to support your answers.

4. Stu agreed to pay a 6 percent commission to his friend if the friend found a buyer for his collection of CD's. After the friend found a willing buyer, Stu backed out. Could the friend recover the commission in small claims court?

5. Tanya had her mother negotiate the purchase of her wedding dress. She told her mother not to spend more than $1,000. The mom fell in love with another dress and signed a contract to buy it as, "Alice Burhman, agent for Tanya Burhman." Is Tanya liable?

6. Kathy was Jon's agent in selling cattle. In the course of a sale Jon lied about the health of a herd. He denied that the cows had hoof and mouth disease when he knew they suffered from it. Is Kathy liable for Jon's conduct?

7. Jayne worked as a sales agent for Brandon. While on the road, she became so fed up with her whole life that she shot a customer. Is Brandon liable?

8. Susan, a minor, hired an attorney to represent her in the sale of her car. The lawyer did not disclose to the buyer that Susan was a minor. Later Susan disaffirmed the sale. Will the lawyer be liable to the buyer?

If you are a principal, remember that . . .

1. Your agent, in effect, stands in your shoes. Your agent's acts become your acts. Therefore, use care in selecting an agent.

2. If you discharge your agent, protect yourself by notifying those with whom the agent has been dealing in your name. To inform all others who may have heard of the agency, publish a notice in a journal of general circulation in the area.

3. If the agent acts outside the scope of authority, be cautious about ratifying the transaction when its benefits are presented to you. First, examine the whole transaction, then decide whether you want to be bound to it.

If you are a third person dealing with an agent, remember that . . .

1. You should learn the extent of

PREVENT LEGAL DIFFICULTIES

the agent's authority from the principal.

2. If you pay an agent money, be sure that the agent has authority to accept it. You should also obtain a receipt with the name of the principal on it. The receipt should state the date, amount, and purpose of the payment and should be signed by the agent.

3. If you are uncertain about the authority or honesty of the agent, make payment by a check payable to the principal.

If you are an agent, remember that . . .

1. When you sign anything for your principal, make it unmistakably clear that you are signing as an agent. Always write the name of your principal first, then add "by" and your signature followed by the word "agent."

2. You must be loyal to your principal and exercise reasonable care and skill in obeying all proper instructions.

3. If you handle your principal's money or other assets, you should keep them separated from your own.

CHAPTER IN REVIEW

CONCEPTS IN BRIEF

1. The fiduciary duty of loyalty requires the agent to place the interests of the principal above the interests of anyone else.

2. The duty of reasonable care and skill requires the agent to act with the level of skill appropriate to the transaction.

3. The duty of confidentiality compels agents to keep secret obviously confidential information. In addition, the agent must honor a principal's request to treat other information confidentially.

4. The fiduciary duty of accounting compels the agent to tell the principal what happened to any of the principal's money that was controlled by the agent.

5. Commingling is mixing the money of the principal and agent. It is a violation of the fiduciary duty of accounting. Trust accounts are used to prevent commingling.

6. The principal is liable to the agent for the agreed compensation.

7. The principal is liable to the torts of agents if they advance the interests of the principal.

8. The agent is liable to the third party if the agent acts ouside the scope of authority and thereby injures the third party.

9. Both the principal and the agent have the power, but not the right, to terminate most agency relationships.

10. Agency usually is terminated upon the death, insanity, or bankruptcy of the principal or agent. When terminated voluntarily by the principal, third parties should be notified to prevent the agent from acting with apparent authority.

YOUR LEGAL VOCABULARY

Match each statement with the term that it best defines. Some terms may not be used.

1. Mixing together the money of the agent and the principal

2. Duty that requires all agents to place the interests of the principal above the interests of all others

3. Agent's obligation to act competently

4. Duty to treat information about the principal very carefully

5. Group of duties owed by the agent to the principal

6. Checking account that assists an agent in fulfilling the duty of loyalty

7. Principal's assent to unauthorized acts of an agent

8. The ability to end an agency relationship

9. Duty to account for all money and property of the principal that comes into an agent's possession

10. A principal whose identity or existence is not allowed to be disclosed

commingling
duty of accounting
duty of confidentiality
duty of loyalty and
    obedience
duty of reasonable
    care and skill
fiduciary duties
power to terminate
ratification
trust account
undisclosed principal

REVIEW LEGAL CONCEPTS

11. Describe the fiduciary duty of loyalty.

12. Explain the fiduciary duty of reasonable care and skill.

13. Describe the fiduciary duty of confidentiality.

14. Tell how the fiduciary duty of accounting is met by real estate brokers.

WRITE ABOUT LEGAL CONCEPTS

15. Create a one-paragraph scenario where the fiduciary duty of loyalty has been violated.

16. Create a one-paragraph scenario where the fiduciary duty of reasonable care and skill has been violated.

17. Create a one-paragraph scenario where the fiduciary duty of confidentiality has been violated.

18. **HOT DEBATE** Write a paragraph to describe legal reasons why Susan's conduct may be legal. In another paragraph, describe reasons why Susan's conduct may not be legal.

THINK CRITICALLY ABOUT EVIDENCE

19. Sharon helped a friend, Gil, who was moving to another state. She agreed to sell at a garage sale those things Gil didn't want to take with him. Sharon liked Gil's old records and though she was offered $100 for them at the sale, she kept them and paid Gil $25. Was this legal?

20. Bud was a real estate broker. He was acting as the agent in finding a buyer for Crib's home. A seller made an offer of $250,000 for the property but said, "If Mr. Crib doesn't accept this offer, I will raise it by $15,000." Bud knew that the duty of loyalty compelled him to tell Crib of the buyer's statement. Is this fair to the buyer? Why or why not? What could Bud do in future transactions to allow him to treat buyers more fairly?

21. Baroni asked her boyfriend, Sid, to help her sell her car. She promised to pay Sid 10 percent of the sales price. Sid agreed. Later, when trying to sell the car, Sid stated that a rebuilt engine had just been installed. This was not true. Kate bought the car. When she discovered the deception, she sued Baroni. Is Baroni legally responsible?

22. When Kraus discharged his purchasing agent, Stacey, and terminated their agency relationship, Stacey became angry. To get even, Stacey made three contracts that included terms that were unfavorable to Kraus, yet were reasonable in the competitive market. The first contract was with an old customer, A. The second contract was with a new customer, B, who had heard of the agency but had never been contacted by Stacey. The third contract was with a total stranger, C, who had never heard of the agency. Is Kraus liable on any of these three contracts?

23. Huy owned an auto repair shop. His favorite employee was Tom. Huy always sent Tom to buy supplies from a wholesaler in town. Once Huy told Tom, "Here's a check for $600. Use it to buy a new spray paint gun and a compressor to replace the ones that are broken." When Tom got to the wholesaler's place of business, he saw that they were running a sale on car paints. So he spent the money on paint. Has Tom acted outside the scope of his express authority? Has Tom acted outside the scope of his apparent authority? Will Tom be liable to Huy for the cost of the paint?

24. MBank hired El Paso Recover Services to repossess the Pontiac Trans-Am owned by Sanchez because she was late on her loan payments. The repossessor went to Sanchez's home with a tow truck and tried to hook the car to the tow truck. Sanchez, who was cutting her grass at the time asked what they were doing. The repossessors didn't respond. Sanchez then locked herself in the car to try to stall them until the police arrived. The repossessor finally towed the Trans Am on a high-speed trip, with Sanchez inside, to a repossession lot where they left the car in a fenced and locked yard. Police later rescued Sanchez. She sued MBank. Will she recover? (*MBank of El Paso v. Sanchez*, 836 S.W.2d 151, Tex.)

25. Jerry and JoAnn Cameron sought to purchase a home. They contacted a real estate salesperson, who showed them several homes. In the process of showing homes to the Camerons, this agent allowed them to look at the multiple listing book that contained a description of the property they ultimately bought. That description stated that the home contained 2400 square feet of space. After the purchase, the Camerons learned that in fact it contained only 2,245 square feet. The Camerons filed suit against Terrell & Garrett, the real estate agents of the seller, who had submitted the information for the multiple listing book. Terrell & Garrett had obtained the square footage information from the seller. (*Cameron v. Terrell Garrett, Inc.*, 599 S.W. 2d 680, Ct. Civ. Apls. Tex.)

26. Margaret Berry was admitted to the hospital in February. In March, she executed a power of attorney designating her niece, Irene Montanye, as her agent. In April, Margaret suffered a stroke. She remained in a comatose or semi-comatose condition until her death in June. On April 30, Mrs. Montanye, acting under the power of attorney, transferred some $109,000 of the decedent's funds into a trust account in the name of the decedent in trust for Ann R. Scully, administratrix of this estate. Heirs of the decedent objected that the transfer of the funds was void because at the time of the transfer and thereafter the decedent was mentally incompetent by reason of being in a comatose or semi-comatose state and, therefore, the agency was revoked. Is the transfer valid? (*In re Estate of Berry*, 329 N.Y.S.2d 915)

27. On August 28, Harry O'Neill was seriously injured in an assault by an off-duty employee of Cinema One, an Anchorage theater. On February 4 of the following year O'Neill filed suit against North Pole Enterprises (NP), Cinema One's owner. NP was served with the complaint and summons on February 29 and given until March 20 to respond. NP was insured by Ambassador Insurance Company (AIC). The policy designated Kenneth I. Tobey, Inc., as its agent and authorized representative. A few days after it was served, NP contacted its local insurance agent, Ralph Blanchard, who sent copies of the complaint and summons to Tobey, located in Seattle. Tobey mailed those materials to AIC's home office in New Jersey. The suit papers were received by AIC on March 16. The next day, AIC wrote to Crawford and Company, an Anchorage adjusting firm, asking Crawford to contact local counsel for advice on O'Neill's complaint. Apparently, Crawford did not receive the request until March 24. By that time, a default had been entered against NP. Crawford then obtained counsel for AIC, who, on March 25, moved to set aside the default. Before that motion could be heard, however, O'Neill offered to settle for policy limits, provided his settlement offer was accepted by April 30. AIC accepted O'Neill's offer and settled the case for $100,000 (O'Neill's injuries were severe and his suit asked for more than $2,000,000 in damages). Later, AIC discovered that the policy in effect at the time of the assault provided no coverage for NP's Cinema One operation. In addition, the policy excluded from its coverage claims based upon "assault and battery." On November 3, AIC filed suit against Tobey and others, seeking indemnification for the loss it incurred in settling with O'Neill. AIC alleged it had been estopped from raising these policy defenses in O'Neill's suit, because of negligence on the part of Tobey, its agent. Tobey's negligence, according to the complaint, consisted of (1) his failure to advise AIC in a timely manner of the lawsuit; (2) his failure to take further action to avoid entry of the default; and (3) his failure to advise NP of the lack of coverage under the policy. Should AIC recover its losses from Tobey? Why or why not? (*Ambassador Insurance Company v. Kenneth I. Tobey, Inc.*, Supreme Court of Alaska, 618 P.2d 572)

Burchett v. Marcum
1998 WL 157409 (Ohio)

EVIDENCE On February 1, 1994, Mr. Matt Marcum, owner and employee of Marcum Transport and Rigging Incorporated [MTRI], entered into an oral employment contract with Mr. Tim Burchett. Mr. Burchett was to be paid $75 per day plus expenses for work to be performed in Charles City, Iowa. The men traveled to Charles City and arrived on February 2. Mr. Burchett stayed in Charles City from February 2 until February 12th with room and board paid by Mr. Marcum. Work on the particular project in Charles City did not begin until after February 12th.

According to trial testimony, a problem arose between Mr. Marcum and Mr. Burchett. Mr. Marcum terminated Mr. Burchett's employment on February 11th. Tim Burchett's father wired him money so that he could return home. MTRI offered to reimburse Mr. Burchett for the cost of the bus trip home.

Burchett filed an action in the Small Claims Division, seeking damages for lost wages.

TRIAL COURT The lower court held Mr. Marcum personally and individually liable, finding that he personally hired Mr. Burchett and never held himself out as an officer acting on behalf of MTRI, his corporation.

Mr. Marcum argues that the judgment of the lower court is against the manifest weight of the evidence and is contrary to law as "Mr. Marcum should not be personally liable because he was acting within his authority as an agent for the Marcum Transport Inc."

REASONING It is established law that an agent who discloses neither the agency relationship nor the identity of the principal is personally liable in contractual dealings with third parties. However, where the existence of the agency and the identity of the principal are known to the third party and the agent acts within the scope of authority and in the name of the principal, the agent is not ordinarily liable on the contracts made.

APPEAL The testimony of Mr. Marcum, the corporation's employees, and Mr. Burchett's wife provided strong evidence that Mr. Burchett was aware of the existence of the corporation and Mr. Marcum's role as agent. Mr. Marcum testified that he hired Mr. Burchett as an employee of the corporation. Mr. Burchett admitted observing the corporate logo on equipment and vehicles to be used on that project. Mr. Burchett's wife testified that she saw the corporate logo on the equipment where Mr. Burchett was working.

Mr. Burchett testified that he had worked for the corporation one week prior to the Charles City job, sanding down a corporate truck for painting. Mr. Burchett even asked for a wage advancement on the Charles City job. Mr. Burchett further testified that he received the advancement on a bluish-green colored check with "somebody's" name on it, although he was unsure whose name it contained. Mr. Marcum maintains that the check was a corporate check and that he did not pay corporate employees with personal checks. No contrary evidence was presented to show that it was not a corporate check. The corporation's other employees testified that throughout the scope of their employment, they were always paid by corporate check. Further, expenses for the trip to Charles City were paid by the corporation.

CONCLUSION The trial court judgment is hereby reversed.

PRACTICE JUDGING

1. Why would Burchett sue Marcum instead of his corporation?
2. What evidence indicates that Marcum's status as an agent was disclosed?

EMPLOYMENT CONTRACTS

LESSONS

HOT DEBATE

Brenda was 14 years old. Her next door neighbor, Bob, owned a small logging company and offered Brenda a job as a "saw mechanic." This job involved cleaning, tuning, sharpening, and testing chain saws. Testing involved cutting a thick log while wearing gloves and safety goggles. The job paid $14.00 per hour, a rate very attractive to Brenda. When Brenda told her dad about the opportunity, he said he thought the job was too dangerous for someone her age. She said she thought he was just being sexist.

Where Do You Stand?

1. Do you agree with Brenda or her father about the job being too dangerous for someone Brenda's age?

2. Should Brenda, her father, Bob or someone else decide whether Brenda can take this job or not?

GOALS

- Define employment and contrast it with other relationships where one person works for another
- Describe how the *terms* in employment contracts are created
- Discuss the duties imposed by law on employees

WHAT IS EMPLOYMENT?

WHAT'S YOUR VERDICT?

Phil and his teenage daughter Elaine trimmed the branches from a large, dead tree in front of their house. They also dug around the base and cut through most of the roots. Then they tried to pull the main trunk out of the ground with a long, heavy rope. Seeing them struggle, their neighbor Steve came out and helped.

Is Elaine an employee of Phil? Is Steve an employee of Phil?

Employment is a legal relationship based on a contract. The parties to this contract are the employer and the employee. The party who pays is the **employer**. The party who does the work is the **employee**. In general, **employment** exists when an employer contracts to pay an employee to do work under the employer's supervision and control.

If there is no contract to pay for work, or if there is no supervision and control, the relationship between the parties is not one of employment. In *What's Your Verdict?* neither Elaine nor Steve is an employee. There was no contract for pay. Elaine was helping her father with a family chore. Steve was a good neighbor and friendly volunteer.

Sometimes people use the words "employment" or "hiring" to refer to relationships that are not actually employment relationships. This occurs most frequently when someone contracts to have a job done but does not supervise or control the worker. For example, suppose a homeowner promises to pay $3,500 to a roofing company to install a new roof. There is a contract for pay.

However, because the homeowner will not direct and control the workers, this is not a contract of employment. Rather, it is what the law calls hiring an **independent contractor**. In general, an independent contractor agrees to produce a finished job without being supervised, while an employee agrees to do a range of tasks under the direction and control of the employer.

TERMS OF THE EMPLOYMENT CONTRACT

WHAT'S YOUR VERDICT?

Sid applied for a part-time job as a cook in a Mexican restaurant. Sid and the manager, Leslie, discussed hours and agreed that Sid would work from 3 P.M. to 5:30 P.M. on Mondays, Wednesdays, and Fridays. Sid was given a company personnel manual that described the pay scale and fringe benefits. It showed that he would be paid $6 per hour. In addition, Leslie told Sid how she wanted the food cooked.

What are all the terms of this employment contract?

Employment contracts are unusual because their terms can come from a variety of sources. The terms can be derived from

- express agreements between the employer and employee
- implied agreements between the employee and employer
- state and federal laws.

Express Agreements

Express employment contracts are oral or written documents. Detailed written contracts are used most often with sports professionals, entertainers, top-level managers, and union members. These written contracts typically describe all of the elements of the employment relationship. For example, a contract of employment for a specific period contains an express term identifying the length of employment.

A party who violates an express term is liable for breach. Often the contract describes the liability for breach of any of the terms of the contract. However, only a small percentage of employment contracts are *completely* in writing.

Most employment contracts are partly written and partly oral. In *What's Your Verdict?* Sid's hours have been agreed upon orally, so this is an express term. The hourly rate and fringe benefits are in writing in the company personnel manual, so these also are express terms. Compensation is almost always an express term. So are fringe benefits. Often the employer and employee also expressly agree upon the time required for advance notice of termination.

Implied Agreements

Notice that Sid and Leslie said nothing about the length of time Sid will be employed. When hiring hourly workers, custom or trade practice determines whether length of employment is specified.

Sid, like most other employees, is employed in a job that is terminable

at will. This employer-employee relationship is known as **employment at will**. It means an employee can be discharged at any time because there has been no agreement about the length of his employment. It also means an employee may quit a job at any time without being liable for breach of contract. Employment contracts can always be identified as either "at will" or "for a specific period."

Frequently, other terms also are implied from the way individual employers supervise their employees. For example, in a particular restaurant there may be an implied term that requires waiters and waitresses to pool their tips and to share them with the people who clear tables. Factory workers may be required to provide their own safety shoes and gloves. Such implied terms come from the rules of a particular employer rather than from customs of the industry or trade group.

Terms Imposed by Law

State and federal laws provide many important terms for each employment contract. The law sometimes becomes a part of each employment

contract whether or not the employer and employee want it included. In *What's Your Verdict?* Sid is entitled to receive, and Leslie is required to pay, at least the minimum wage specified by federal law. Federal law would dictate this part of Sid's employment contract even if Sid and Leslie had expressly agreed upon a lower amount.

A Question of ETHICS ?

Suppose you were hired under a contract for three years as a research scientist. After six months on the job, a competing firm offers you twice the pay. You can breach your current contract, pay damages, and still come out ahead financially. Will you break your contract and your promise? What reasons support your decision?

EMPLOYEE DUTIES

WHAT'S YOUR VERDICT?

Vito hires Winston as a welder for a three-year period. Vito requires all welders to wear protective helmets and goggles while working. Winston, who has long hair that makes it difficult to wear the helmet, refuses to do so.

Can Vito discharge Winston without liability?

IN THIS CASE

Ash was the assistant to the president of Pinos Point Properties. She had confidential information that her company was going to make an offer on a certain piece of land for $250,000 but would be willing to pay as much as $350,000 for it. Ash told this to the owners of the land, who agreed to give her one half of any amount over $250,000 that they received. After the purchase was made for $350,000, Pinos Point learned of Ash's action. Pinos justifiably dismissed Ash and sued her for damages.

An employee has a duty to fulfill the agreements made with the employer. The employee also has duties created by state case law. These duties include the following:

Obedience

Each employee is bound by the **duty of obedience**. This means the employee has a duty to obey the reasonable orders and rules of the employer. This duty exists whether or not the employee has expressly agreed to it. In *What's Your Verdict?* the company would be within its rights in discharging Winston because the rule that Winston disobeyed was reasonable. However, an employee cannot be required to act illegally, immorally, or contrary to public policy.

Reasonable Skill

The **duty of reasonable skill** requires that those who accept work possess the skill, experience, or knowledge necessary to do it. The employer need not keep the employee, nor pay damages for discharging the employee, if the employee does not perform with reasonable skill. Thus, a welder whose welds keep breaking could be fired for the lack of reasonable skill.

Loyalty and Honesty

An employee owes the **duty of loyalty and honesty** to the employer. The employee is obligated to look out for the employer's best interest. By committing a fraud upon the employer, or by revealing confidential information about the business, an employee may be justifiably discharged. Such a worker may also be liable for damages.

Reasonable Performance

Employees owe the **duty of reasonable performance** to employers. An employer is justified in discharging an employee who fails to perform assigned duties at the prescribed time and in the prescribed manner. Occasional minor failure to perform as expected ordinarily is not sufficient grounds for dismissing an employee. On the other hand, any employee may be discharged if unable to do the work because of illness or injury.

Answer the following questions about legal concepts.

1. All people paid for their work are employees. **True or False?**

2. Which of the following is not a test to determine whether a person is an employee? **(a) payment for work (b) supervision and control (c) respondeat superior**

3. Which of the following is not a source of the terms in an employment contract? **(a) express terms spoken or written (b) implied terms (c) the law (d) none of the above**

4. Which of the following is not a duty owed by employees to employers? **(a) duty of obedience (b) duty of reasonable performance (c) duty of reasonable skill (d) duty of honesty (e) none of the above**

5. If someone contracts to have a job done, but does not control or supervise the worker, the worker is an independent contractor. **True or False?**

6. Federal law is likely to supply which of the following terms in employment contracts? **(a) job title (b) minimum wage (c) job location**

7. When no length of employment is specified, the employer-employee relationship is known as employment __?__ .

Study the following situations, answer the questions, then prepare arguments to support your answers.

8. At the beginning of the summer you were hired as a food server by a local restaurant. Unfortunately, neither you nor your employer discussed how long the job would last. You will be starting college soon in a different state. May you quit this job then without legal liability?

9. The High Country Lumber Company hired Mason to haul trees from a forest site to a lumber mill 25 miles away. Mason used his own truck, began and ended work when he pleased, paid for his own gasoline, and worked by himself. He was paid $8.50 per log. Was Mason an employee of High Country Lumber Company?

10. Sharp worked as a machinist building models of new products. His firm was working on a contract for a new doorknob for Costcorp, Inc. Sharp approached one of Costcorp's competitors and showed them a design that his firm had developed. Is this grounds for firing Sharp?

11. Francis was hired as a cook at a local restaurant. He said he was experienced in cooking breakfast items and could handle lunch, too. In fact, his only experience was as a dishwasher, although he had carefully watched cooks work. On the first day, he was fired because he was too slow. Was the employer acting legally?

12. Susan was hired to park customers' cars at a local restaurant. All her pay was in the form of tips and she worked during all the hours the restaurant was open. She had no direct supervisor and parked the cars in a lot nearby. When she was unable to work, the restaurant placed a sign at their entrance telling customers to self-park. Is Susan an employee?

13. Darrel, a high school student, was friends with an adult neighbor, Bill. Bill operated an auto tune-up business from his garage. Darrel often helped out. At first he would drop by for an hour in the evening and just watch. Then he started handing tools and parts to Darrel. Occasionally Bill would give Darrel a $5 bill or take him to dinner. Darrel showed up about twice a week, but there was never any advance notice. Is Darrel an employee?

14. Ignacio was hired as a computer programmer at a software company. The contract identified the pay as $5,000 per month. It said nothing about how long Ignacio would be employed. Three months after being hired, the company's business slowed. Though Ignacio had done a fine job, he was laid off. Is this legal?

GOALS

● Describe the employer's duties that arise out of the express terms of the employment contract

● Explain the employer's duties imposed by law

EMPLOYER'S DUTIES TO EMPLOYEES

WHAT'S YOUR VERDICT?

Dale hired Frye to run her office for one year for $1,800 a month. One month, Dale had financial problems and temporarily withheld $100 from Frye's paycheck. Dale promised to make it up the next payday, which she did. Three months later, Dale withheld $200, and so Frye quit.

Was Frye legally justified in quitting?

Employers owe a variety of duties to employees. Some of these duties arise out of the express terms agreed upon by the parties. In *What's Your Verdict?* Dale violated the express term related to pay, and Frye was justified in quitting. In other cases, the law imposes the duty by agreement instead. The following are the principal obligations, created by law, which the employer owes to the employee.

Reasonable Treatment

An employer is required to treat workers in a reasonable manner. If the employer commits an assault or battery upon an employee, the employee may quit the job without liability. The injured employee also may sue for damages.

Safe Working Conditions

An employee is entitled by law to reasonably safe working conditions (including safe tools, equipment, machinery, and the building itself).

IN THIS CASE

Gerhart had been hired as a vacation replacement for clerical employees of the Dairyland Creamery. He promised to work all summer. When Gerhart made a number of mistakes, his supervisor reprimanded him and called him "stupid." There was no assault or battery. There was only an insult and reprimand, which did not constitute unreasonable treatment. Normally under such circumstances, employees like Gerhart who have promised to work for a specific period would have no right to quit and could be held liable for breach of contract if they did.

The working conditions must not be harmful to the employee's health, safety, morals, or reputation. If the employer does not provide safe working conditions, the employee may quit without breaching the contract.

IN THIS CASE

Pittman contracted to work for six months as a forklift operator for Corder Moving and Storage Company. The brakes on her forklift were not working properly, and the lift was slipping. On three occasions, Pittman reported these defects to her supervisor. However, no repairs were made. After a near-accident caused by these unsafe conditions, Pittman walked off the job. There were four months left on her employment contract. Pittman had the right to leave her job. She also had the right to report the unsafe conditions to the Occupational Safety and Health Administration (OSHA) of the U.S. Department of Labor.

Fair Labor Standards

The federal government has enacted the Fair Labor Standards Act to establish the minimum wage and maximum hours for all employees under the jurisdiction of the act. Maximum hours that can be worked at regular rates of pay are 40 per week (with no daily maximum). If more than 40 hours are worked in one week, overtime must be paid at one and one-half times the regular rate.

Not all workers are covered by this act. The minimum wage and overtime requirements of the law do not apply to executives, administrators, and professional workers. In addition, the hourly provisions apply only partially to workers in seasonal industries. Special rules apply to trainees, apprentices, student workers, and handicapped workers. In certain circumstances they may be paid at 85 percent of the minimum wage.

Payroll Deductions

Certain governmental programs are financed by payments made by employees. Typically the employer deducts money from the employee's paycheck. These are sometimes called **payroll deductions**. Thus, the employer is legally obligated to withhold a percentage of the paycheck to cover the employee's federal and state income tax obligations. Similarly, the employer must withhold certain amounts for the employee's portion of social security payments (sometimes called FICA, which stands for Federal Insurance Contributions Act).

Other payments often are made from the funds of the employer. **Workers' compensation** is an example. This is a payment into an insurance fund that compensates employees for their injuries on the job. It eliminates the need for employers to compensate employees directly for on-the-job injuries.

Similarly, employers must make payments for unemployment insurance. Unemployment insurance provides short-term income for people who have recently lost their jobs. This is discussed later in this chapter.

Duties to Minors

Both the federal government and state governments have labor laws protecting minors.

STATE LAWS Every state government regulates the conditions and types of employment permitted for persons under age 18. These are often termed child-labor laws. When state child-labor laws have stricter standards than federal laws, the state laws rule. Although the federal and state laws vary, they are all based on the following principles:

- a person's early years are best used to obtain an education
- certain work is harmful or dangerous for young people
- child labor at low wages takes jobs from adults

The states usually specify a minimum age for employment during school. All states place a limit on the number of hours a young person may work. In calculating the maximum number of hours, the hours of school often are combined with the hours on the job while school is in session. For example, a common maximum is 48 hours (school and outside work combined) in one week. Most states maintain controls over those hours, and most require a **work permit** if the individual is under the age of 18.

In addition, many states have child labor laws that

- set the maximum number of working hours in one day
- prohibit night work
- prescribe the grade in school that must be completed before being able to work
- set the required age for certain hazardous occupations

In some states minors may work only between 5 A.M. and 10 P.M. Moreover, the job must not be classified as hazardous.

Hazardous Occupations Not Available to Minors

- Mining
- Manufacturing explosives, brick, or tile
- Operating power-driven hoists
- Logging and saw milling
- Driving motor vehicles or acting as an outside helper on such vehicles (except for incidental, occasional, and school bus driving)
- Slaughtering or meat packing
- Operating circular saws, band saws, or guillotine shears
- Wrecking or demolishing buildings or ships
- Roofing
- Excavating

FEDERAL LAW The Fair Labor Standards Act sets the minimum protection for young workers. This law makes it illegal for people under fourteen years old to work, except in entertainment and agriculture. Fourteen- and fifteen-year-olds are only permitted to work *limited hours* after school in non-hazardous jobs. Unless modified by state law, sixteen-and seventeen-year-olds can work unlimited hours in non-hazardous jobs.

Exceptions for some child labor laws exist for young people. These include working for their parents in non-manufacturing jobs, working in agricultural jobs after school, delivering newspapers, and working as actors.

Military Service and Voting

The Military Selective Service Extension Act of 1950 requires that certain military persons be re-employed by their former employer after honorable discharge from the service. Persons receive this protection who have been drafted, enlisted, or called to active duty. To qualify for reemployment veterans must still be able to perform the work.

More than one-half the states provide that workers must be given sufficient time off with pay, at a time convenient to the employer, to vote in regular primary and general elections.

CULTURAL DIVERSITY IN LAW

Mexico

Child Labor

Child labor in Mexico for children under the age of fourteen is illegal. Nevertheless, millions of children are employed, often in hazardous jobs. In the state of Guanajuato, for example, shoe manufacturing is an important industry. In the Mexican shoe industry, it is customary to employ young boys. These boys are called *zorritos*, meaning "little foxes." Conditions for the *zorritos* often are hazardous. They are exposed not only to dangerous machinery but also to toxic substances. One particularly toxic substance is the glue that holds the shoes together.

EMPLOYER'S DUTY TO THOSE INJURED BY EMPLOYEES

WHAT'S YOUR VERDICT?

Walker was an electrician for Centurion Electrical Service. One day Walker was sent to repair mixing machines at Molecular Chemical Company. Walker did the work in a negligent manner, causing several thousand dollars' worth of damage to the machines.

Was Centurion liable for the damage? Was Walker liable for the damage?

If an employee, acting *within the scope of employment,* commits a tort (injures persons or property), the employer is liable for the damages. It is immaterial that the employer did not authorize the act. If an employee commits a tort but is not acting within the scope of the employer's business, the employee alone is liable for any resulting injuries. Even if an employee intentionally causes damage, the employer may be held liable if the employee has acted with the intention of furthering the employer's interests. In *What's Your Verdict?* Walker was acting within the scope of her employment so both Walker and Centurion are liable for the damage.

Generally, if a person is an independent contractor rather than an employee, the person who hired the contractor is not liable for the contractor's torts. If the job is inherently dangerous, such as blasting with dynamite, the party who hired the independent contractor may be liable to those injured.

Answer the following questions about legal concepts.

1. Many of the employer's duties to employees are created by statutes. **True or False?**

2. Which of the following is not a duty owed by the employer to the employee? **(a) duty of reasonable treatment (b) duty to provide safe working conditions (c) duty to follow Fair Labor Standards (d) none of the above**

3. State laws designed to protect minors restrict the hours minors can work. **True or False?**

4. A __?__ is required before a minor can work.

5. An employer is liable for the torts of an employee if the employee was acting within the __?__ when the tort occurred.

6. Any party who hires an independent contractor may be liable for the independent contractor's torts if the work **(a) involves overtime (b) involves vehicles (c) requires professional skill (d) is inherently dangerous.**

7. If there is no pay agreed to, then the relationship of employment probably does not exist. **True or False?**

Study the following situations, answer the questions, then prepare arguments to support your answers.

8. Socow's father was an operator of a backhoe. For three summers, the father trained his son to operate backhoes. When Socow became 14 years old, he applied for a job with a local construction firm as a backhoe operator but was turned down because of his age. Was the construction company's conduct legal?

9. Your friend is hired as a ride operator with a traveling carnival. At a county fair, he carelessly fails to secure the safety bar over the seat on a small roller coaster. Two riders are thrown out and seriously injured. Who is liable for the injuries?

10. Walgreen Company planned to open a restaurant in Duluth, Minnesota. A.J. Gatzke, a district manager for Walgreen, was sent to Duluth to supervise the opening. Gatzke obtained a room—paid for by Walgreen—in a motel owned by Edgewater Motels, Inc. One day after work, Gatzke and another Walgreen employee went to a bar near the motel. There Gatzke drank four brandy Manhattans in about one hour. Then Gatzke went back to his motel room where, apparently, he smoked several cigarettes after completing an expense account report. The butt of one cigarette was apparently thrown into a wastebasket in the room. The room caught on fire and the fire spread to the entire motel. Gatzke escaped uninjured, but the damage to the motel was more than $330,000. Edgewater Motels sued both Gatzke and his employer, Walgreen Company. Who is liable? (*Edgewater Motels, Inc. v. Gatzke*, 277 N.W.2d 11)

11. Cerney operated a computer programming business and just signed an important new contract that required overtime for all personnel. Sharon began working for Cerney after school because she could program in a useful language. When she was hired, she was told she would be paid $14 dollar per hour. However her first paycheck had a third of the pay taken out for federal and state taxes, social security (FICA) taxes, and other deductions. Are the deductions legal?

12. Ace Highway Company hired Demolition Experts Inc. to do the blasting on a mountain road they were building. Demolition Experts Inc. was an independent contractor. At the first blast, a bystander was hit by a flying rock and paralyzed for life from the neck down. The victim sued Ace Highway. If negligence is proven, can the victim recover from Ace?

13. Ellie worked at the local grocery store as a bagger. She was paid $10 per hour. Usually she worked only 20 hours per week. The week before Christmas, several baggers called in sick and Ellie ended up working 55 hours. What will her gross pay be?

GOALS

● Tell when an employee is liable for quitting a job

● Describe when an employer is liable for firing an employee

● Explain the rights of a fired employee

TYPES OF EMPLOYMENT CONTRACTS

WHAT'S YOUR VERDICT?

After suffering a stroke, Ching hired Vennet as a nurse and companion for one year. Four months later, Ching died.

Was Vennet's contract terminated?

Contracts of employment for a specific period are terminated in the same ways as other contracts. The usual method of termination is by performance of the contractual obligations. As with other contracts, courts look to the terms of the employment contract to determine the obligations of the parties. The express and implied terms, and those imposed by law, define these obligations. If material obligations are not performed, breach of contract occurs. Material breach extinguishes the obligations of the other party to the contract.

Suppose an employer fails to pay the employee an agreed-upon monthly check. This would be a breach of the contract. Because it is material, the employee would be justified in quitting or in abandoning the job without liability for breach of contract. Similarly, if the employee fails to live up to the material obligations of the job, the employer may treat the contract as terminated and discharge the employee without liability. In *What's Your Verdict?* the contract was terminated by impossibility of performance. Death made it impossible for Vennet to be a nurse and companion to Ching.

Employment Contracts Terminable at Will

As discussed, many employment contracts are terminable at the will of either the employer or the employee. This occurs because the employer and employee generally do not specify a length of time for the employment relationship. The law then assumes that either party may terminate employment at any time without liability.

For example, if an automobile repair shop hired a mechanic for $17 per hour and a competitor later offered the mechanic $20 per hour, there would generally be no liability for quitting the $17 per-hour job. On the other hand, the repair shop manager could fire the mechanic without giving any reason for doing so.

WRONGFUL DISCHARGE There are limitations on this power to terminate without cause. Firing because of race, religion, gender, age, handicap, pregnancy, veteran status, or national origin is job discrimination and illegal. Federal law also prohibits an employer from dismissing an employee for engaging in union activities. Further, most states now deny the power to terminate at will when it is used to retaliate against those who

- refuse to commit perjury at the request of the company
- insist on filing a workers' compensation claim
- report violations of law by the company
- urge the company to comply with the law

When an employer fires an employee for one of the above reasons, it commits the tort of **wrongful discharge**.

VIOLATION OF CONTRACT TERMS Employers who make promises orally or in company documents such as employee handbooks to "treat employees fairly" may cause this promise to become a part of the employment contract. When such terms are part of the employment contract, the employer

cannot fire an employee without a fair reason.

The Tananna Valley Medical Group hired James Eales as a physician's assistant. At that time it made promises to James that as long as he did his job, he could stay until retirement. Six years later he was fired without cause. The Alaska Supreme Court held that the employer's promise was enforceable.

Employment Contracts for a Specific Length of Time

If the employment contract is for a certain length of time, it is breached if one party terminates early. For example, if a basketball player signs a three-year contract for $600,000 a year to play for a professional club, this would be a contract for a specific length of time. If the player breaches the contract by deliberately refusing to come to scheduled games (a breach of the employee's duty of obedience), the employer would probably be justified in terminating the contract. In addition, because the player caused the termination, the player may be liable for damages. Thus, if the club has to pay $1 million per year to obtain the services of an equally talented replacement, the player might be liable to the club for the difference in pay for the remainder of the contract term.

Employment Contracts With Governments

In general, public employees (those who work for a government) are entitled to *due process* before being discharged. This means that they are entitled to notice of the reasons for the discharge along with a hearing. In a hearing, they are given the opportunity to present their own evidence and to challenge the claims of the governmental employer. For this reason, it is more difficult to discharge public employees than private sector employees.

Right to Unemployment Compensation

Workers who have been terminated despite having complied with all the terms of their employment contract are said to have been **discharged without cause**. This means the cause of the discharge was not the employee's conduct. An employee who is discharged without cause is entitled to unemployment compensation benefits. **Unemployment compensation** is money paid by the government (or a private insurance fund) to workers who have lost their jobs through no fault of their own.

If an employee has been discharged because of violating an employment obligation, then the employee is said to be **discharged for cause**. The worker discharged for cause generally is not entitled to unemployment compensation. Unemployment compensation payments are made by the states in cooperation with the federal government under the Social Security Act of 1935. There is usually a period of one or two weeks after termination before payments begin. Then a percentage of the regular wage is paid to the unemployed person every week for a limited period of time. Unemployment compensation generally is not available to those who quit voluntarily, strike, or refuse to accept similar substitute work. It is often available to part-time workers.

A Question of ETHICS

You just interviewed Danny Mitchell for the job of receptionist for your own company. You had intended to pay the person hired $9.25 per hour because that is the competitive rate for receptionists in your community. You decide that Danny is perfect for the job. Before making the offer, you ask, "How much pay do you need to take this job?" Danny responds, "Anything above $7.00 per hour."

What pay rate will you use in your offer? What reasons support your decision?

THINK ABOUT LEGAL CONCEPTS

Answer the following questions about legal concepts.

1. Most private sector employment contracts are ___?___ .

2. Which of the following is the factor which determines whether an employment contract is terminable at will?
(a) rate of pay (b) age of the employee (c) whether a length of time for the employment is specified (d) all of the above

3. If an employer fired an employee who discovered that the employer was underreporting sales on tax returns, this firing would be a ___?___ .

4. Unemployment insurance will be denied if the employee was fired for cause. **True or False?**

THINK CRITICALLY ABOUT EVIDENCE

Study the following situations, answer the questions, then prepare arguments to support your answers.

5. Amit was the night clerk at the Indian Inn. He had several duties besides working at the main desk. Therefore, he was not allowed to sleep while on the job, even if business was slow. On several occasions, the manager of the inn found Amit sleeping and warned him not to do so. If Amit continued to fall asleep on the job, would the manager be justified in discharging him? If discharged, could Amit collect unemployment compensation?

6. A neighborhood meat market had employed Swenson as a butcher for 12 years. Her boss had always praised her job performance. After a large grocery store was built nearby, drawing away many of the market's customers and reducing its sales, Swenson was given a 30-day notice of termination. She protested, claiming she had always been a very good employee. Was Swenson discharged for cause? Can Swenson collect unemployment insurance?

7. Smith and Alonzo agreed that Smith would temporarily be paid less than minimum wage. They did this because Alonzo could not afford to pay more and Smith had no other employment opportunities. They executed an agreement that clearly indicated Smith's consent to the arrangement. Is Smith entitled to the minimum wage or has she waived this right?

8. Inez worked as a cashier in an all-night cafeteria. One night two men followed her home from the swing shift. They assaulted her at her home demanding "the money and the deposits." They thought she took money home from the cafeteria to deposit in the bank the next morning. Inez filed a claim for workers' compensation. Was she injured on the job?

When you become an employee . . .

1. Realize that you and your employer are parties to a contract in which you both have rights and duties.

2. Before you go to work, learn as much as you can about the job. Find out about hours, pay, duties, dress, fringe benefits, and any other related matters.

3. Avoid tardiness and absenteeism.

PREVENT LEGAL DIFFICULTIES

4. Remember that in addition to reasonable skill and performance, you owe your employer loyalty, honesty, and obedience. However, the duty of obedience does not require employees to engage in illegal, immoral, or unsafe activities.

5. Remember that you are personally responsible for your own negligent acts. This is true even though the injured party may also be able to recover from your employer.

CHAPTER IN REVIEW

CONCEPTS IN BRIEF

1. Employment is a form of contract.

2. An employee is distinguished from an independent contractor by the fact that an employer has the power to supervise and control the employee's work. An independent contractor is not subject to direction and control, but is only responsible for the finished job.

3. Contracts of employment may be express (oral or written) or implied (shown by conduct).

4. Among the duties imposed by law on the employee are the duties to obey reasonable rules and orders, perform the prescribed duties with reasonable skill, be loyal and honest, and perform the prescribed duties at the proper time and in the proper manner.

5. Among the duties imposed by law on the employer are the duties to ensure reasonable treatment of employees, provide safe working conditions, comply with fair labor standards, withhold payroll deductions, comply with child-labor laws, reemploy discharged military personnel, and give employees time off from work to vote.

6. An employer is liable for injuries to the person or property of third parties if employees acting within the scope of their employment cause the injuries. The employee is also liable for such acts.

7. Employment contracts are terminated in the same ways as other contracts. Material breach of contract by the employee is cause for discharge. The employee is justified in quitting if the employer does not fulfill an important part of the agreement.

YOUR LEGAL VOCABULARY

Match each statement with the term that it best defines. Some terms may not be used.

1. Governmental payments to those who recently lost their jobs

2. Payment for injuries that occur on the job

3. Party who engages another to work for pay

4. One who contracts to do something for another but is free of the latter's direction and control

5. Contractual relationship in which one party engages another to work for pay under the supervision of the party paying

6. Party who works under the supervision of another for pay

7. The obligation to look out for the best interests of the employer

8. The obligation to perform the job tasks with competence

9. Firing an employee in retaliation for reporting violations of law by the company

10. Document obtained from the state allowing a person under 18 years old to work

11. Employment relationship whereby employee may be discharged at any time because no agreement was made about length of employment

12. Money withheld from an employee's paycheck

discharged for cause
discharged wthout
   cause
duty of loyalty and
   honesty
duty of obedience
duty of reasonable
   performance
duty of reasonable skill
employee
employer
employment
employment at will
independent contractor
payroll deductions
unemployment
   compensation
workers' compensation
work permit
wrongful discharge

13. Describe the difference between an independent contractor and an employee.

14. Explain how courts will decide whether an employment contract is terminable at will.

15. Describe the sources of the terms in an employment contract.

16. Tell the class about the basic provisions of the Fair Labor Standards Act.

WRITE ABOUT LEGAL CONCEPTS

17. Write a short description of a job you know about. Next write two or three sentences describing an employment contract for that job that makes it terminable at will. Last, write another two or three sentences describing an employment contract for the job that makes it not terminable at will.

18. Write a short description of a job you know about. Next, write a job description (a statement of the job's duties and responsibilities) as if the job were for an independent contractor. Last, write a job description for the job as if it were for an employee.

19. Assume that the job in question is that of a personal secretary for the head of a large department of 40 people. Write two separate paragraphs describing the processes the law would require you to follow if you were going to fire the secretary. In the first paragraph, assume the secretary works in a private sector job that is terminable at will.

20. HOT DEBATE Write a paragraph giving reasons why Brenda should be able to take the job. Write a paragraph giving reasons why Brenda should not be able to take this job.

THINK CRITICALLY ABOUT EVIDENCE

21. Chin interviewed Caroline for a position as a cashier in her grocery store. She described the job responsibilities, the days and hours Caroline would work, the attitude she wanted Caroline to communicate to customers, and the hourly pay. After the interview, Chin said she would hire Caroline and they shook hands. Describe three terms of this employment contract that are express and three that are imposed by law.

22. Myron owned Crossroads Service Station. He directed Pat, an employee, to put re-refined oil into the unlabeled oil jars displayed for sale. Pat knew that the law required re-refined oil to be labeled "re-refined." Therefore, Pat refused to fill or display the jars. Was Pat's disobedience grounds for discharge? If discharged, could Pat collect unemployment compensation?

23. Jeff was a secretary at Elmhurst Elementary, a public school. Ms. O'Daley, the principal wanted to fire him because he was often late. Describe how Jeff's employment contract differs from that of a secretary in a private organization. Describe the steps Ms. O'Daley must take to fire Jeff.

24. Chia was hired as an electrical engineer but there was no agreement about the length of the employment period. At the time he was hired he was told that he would not be fired unless he failed to perform his job. The employee's handbook said the same thing. Later when the company changed product lines, it fired Chia. Can Chia recover for breach of the employment contract?

ANALYZE
REAL CASES

25. Thomas P. Finley worked for Aetna Life Insurance. Aetna had a company personnel manual that stated that employees would "not be terminated so long as their performance is satisfactory." Finley was fired. He sued and asserted that the language in the personnel manual meant that he was not terminable at will but rather entitled to employment as long as he performed satisfactorily. Can a personnel manual supply such terms of the employment contract? (*Finley v. Aetna Life and Casualty Company,* 202 Conn. 190)

26. Gale, an umpire, was a member of the Greater Washington Softball Umpires Association. During a game in which Gale was officiating, a player objected to his decision on a play. The player then struck Gale with a baseball bat, causing injuries to Gale's neck, hip, and leg. Gale claimed that he was an employee of the association and so sought workers' compensation for his injuries. The association asserted that its members were independent contractors. It based this assertion on the fact that the umpires had full charge and control of the games, and that the association did not direct the worker in the performance or manner in which the work was done. The evidence presented showed (a) that the umpires were paid by the association from fees collected from the teams; (b) that the umpires, while assigned to the games by the association, were not obligated to accept the assignments; (c) that the association conducted clinics, administered written examinations, and required members to wear designated uniforms while officiating; and (d) that the umpires had to meet with the approval of committees of the association who observed a member officiating during a probationary period. Under these circumstances, do you believe Gale was an employee of the association or an independent contractor? (*Gale v. Greater Washington Softball Umpires Association,* 311 A.2d 817)

27. Whirlpool operated a manufacturing facility that used overhead conveyors to transport parts around the plant. Because the parts sometimes fell from the overhead conveyor belt, Whirlpool installed a wire screen below the conveyor belts to catch them. Maintenance workers were required to retrieve fallen parts from the screen, which was about twenty feet above the floor of the plant. On two occasions, maintenance workers fell through the screen onto the floor. One of the workers was killed by the fall. Shortly thereafter, Vergil Deemer and Thomas Cornwell asked that the screen be repaired. When repairs were not made, these men complained to OSHA. The next day they were told by their supervisor to climb out onto the screen to retrieve fallen parts. When they refused, they were sent home without pay. Was their refusal a violation of their duty of obedience? (*Whirlpool v. Marshall,* 445 U.S. 1)

28. Lucky Stores, Inc., owned a building with a large sign spelling out "ARDENS" on it. Lucky hired Q.R.I. Corporation as an independent contractor to remove the sign. The removal work was inherently dangerous because each letter was about six feet high and two and one-half feet wide and weighed between fifty and sixty pounds. Q.R.I. workers safely removed the letter "A" and loaded it on their truck. They also safely removed the letter "R" and leaned it against the truck. Then, for a moment, one worker negligently released his hold on the letter. A gust of wind blew the letter into contact with seventy-nine-year-old Smith, injuring her seriously. Is Lucky liable to Smith for damages? (*Smith v. Lucky Stores, Inc.,* 61 Cal. App. 3d 826, 132 Cal. Rptr. 628)

29. McGraw-Hill hired Weiner. When he applied for the job, he signed a job application stating that he had read McGraw-Hill's handbook on personnel policies. The handbook stated that the company would discharge employees only when there was "just and sufficient cause." Later, Weiner was fired. Weiner claimed the firing was without just cause and therefore in violation of his employment contract. Does Weiner's employment contract include the statements in the personnel handbook? If Weiner were fired without just cause, will McGraw-Hill be liable for breach of contract? (*Weiner v. McGraw-Hill, Inc.* 443 N.E. 2d 441, New York)

30. Central Indiana Gas Co. hired Frampton. Later Frampton was required to serve on a jury. Because he missed work for jury duty, he was fired. He sued. Will he win? (*Frampton v. Central Indiana Gas Co.,* 297 N.E. 2d 425, Indiana)

Progress Printing Co. v. Nichols
421 S.E.2d 428 (Virginia Supreme Ct)

EVIDENCE At the time Nichols began work as a pressman for the Progress Printing Company he was given a copy of the Employees' Handbook. The handbook stated that Progress would not discharge or suspend an employee "without just cause" and that the company "shall give at least one warning notice in writing" before termination. Later, the company's personnel director gave Nichols a form that stated in part:

> I have received a copy of the Progress Printing Employee Handbook. . . . I agree to follow the procedures and guidelines it contains. . . . The employment relationship between Progress Printing and the employee is at will and may be terminated by either party at any time.

Nichols and the personnel director both signed the form. Nichols became upset over Progress's failure to correct a recurring defect in a print job, and he refused to complete that job. Nichols was fired on the following day without the prior written notice promised by the Employee Handbook. Nichols then sued for wrongful discharge in a Virginia trial court. After that court ruled in his favor and awarded him $9,000 in damages, Progress appealed.

OPINION In Virginia, as in a majority of jurisdictions, the employment relationship is presumed to be "at will," which means that the employment term extends for an indefinite period and may be terminated for any reason. This presumption may be rebutted if sufficient evidence is produced to show that the employment is for a definite, rather than an indefinite, term. Progress argues that Nichols failed to rebut the presumption because the handbook did not constitute an enforceable employment contract and, even if it did, the subsequent execution of the acknowledgment form created an at-will employment relationship.

A number of jurisdictions have held that termination-for-cause provisions contained in employee handbooks can bind the employer if those provisions are communicated to the employee in a sufficiently specific manner. We have held that an employment condition that allows termination only for cause sets a definite term for the duration of the employment. We nevertheless agree with Progress that the acknowledgment form specifically superseded and replaced the [just cause] provision with the agreement that the employment relationship was at will.

We base this holding on a number of grounds. The termination-for-cause language of the handbook and the employment-at-will relationship agreed to in the subsequent acknowledgment form are in direct conflict and cannot be reconciled in any reasonable way. If the documents are considered a single contract, this conflict fails to provide sufficient evidence to rebut the presumption of employment at will. In any event, the acknowledgment form was not a part of the handbook and was executed 13 days after Nichols began work. Under these circumstances, the form reflects an understanding between the parties separate from that contained in the handbook. Execution of the form memorialized reciprocal commitments that satisfy the requisites of a contract; that is, there was an offer of employment at will; the employee continued service, which constituted the consideration; and the employee accepted by performance.

Progress did not breach the employment at will contract when it terminated Nichols. The trial court decision is reversed.

PRACTICE JUDGING

1. **Would the decision have been different if the acknowledgment had been signed first and the handbook later provided to Nichols?**

2. **Which do you think is better evidence of the understandings of the parties, the signed agreement or the statement in the handbook?**

LESSONS

28-1 HOW ARE UNIONS ESTABLISHED?

28-2 RELATIONS IN A UNIONIZED WORKPLACE

HOT DEBATE

You are employed as a fruit picker at a large orchard. You and your co-workers are dissatisfied with your wages and working conditions. You think wages are too low and hours are too long. Much of the work requires you to stand on ladders that can be dangerous. Your employer says she cannot stay in business if wages are higher or hours shorter.

Where Do You Stand?

1. **Should this employer be required to spend the time and money to negotiate over these issues?**

2. **Should she be able to hire anybody who is willing to work under the conditions she specifies?**

GOALS

● Explain the roles of state and federal labor laws

● Describe the history of labor law

● Discuss the processes for establishing a new union, changing unions, and eliminating union representation

STATE AND FEDERAL REGULATION OF EMPLOYMENT

WHAT'S YOUR VERDICT?

Jerry is employed as an administrative assistant in an electronic component factory. The company ships its products throughout the United States and to many other countries.

Is Jerry's employment subject to state employment law, federal employment law, or both?

In labor-management relations, both federal and state laws exist. These laws are usually in harmony. If there is a conflict between state and federal laws, federal law prevails. Also, federal guidelines define which employers are not subject to federal jurisdiction. If a retail store sells less than $500,000 worth of goods annually, it is governed by the state. In *What's Your Verdict?* Jerry's employment is subject to both state and federal laws.

HISTORY OF LABOR LAWS

WHAT'S YOUR VERDICT?

Boston boot makers formed an association with the intent to negotiate higher wages. The state of Massachusetts prosecuted them, alleging that the boot makers were engaged in a criminal conspiracy to extort higher wages. Further, the state alleged that the wage increases would be passed on to consumers, thereby injuring them.

Is the conduct by the boot makers criminal?

An understanding of the history of labor law will help you see how the law evolved, and this will help you understand current labor law. Labor unions did not engage in strikes in the United States until the 1800s. The law then responded with hostility. One line of reasoning held that an employment contract existed between employers and union members. Strikes then were attempts to pressure, or extort, employers into accepting terms they would otherwise reject. Courts held that strikes, boycotts, and similar tactics were simply actions in breach of the employment contract. Many companies immediately fired any employee suspected of harboring sympathies toward unions.

Companies could do this because employment contracts are terminable at will. Other companies made new employees promise not to join a union. These employment contracts earned the name **yellow-dog contracts**.

A second line of legal reasoning held that union activities were criminal conspiracies. Unions were held to be organizing their members to extort higher wages at the expense of the consuming public. The courts supported this claim until about 1842. After that time, the courts ceased classifying unions as criminal conspiracies. In *What's Your Verdict?* the boot makers are not engaged in criminal conduct.

Another judicial response to unions was the **ex parte injunction**. This is an injunction issued by a judge after hearing only one side of an argument. If the employer could show potential injury flowing from a strike, many judges would issue an injunction prohibiting the strike. If employees struck in the face of the injunction, they could be arrested and imprisoned for contempt of court. Also, injunctions were used to prohibit attempts to organize employees into unions when they were working under yellow-dog contracts.

In 1890, Congress passed the Sherman Antitrust Act, which prohibited restraints of trade and made business monopolies illegal. Some judges thought this act also made unions illegal. For example, in the *Danbury Hatters* case, the U.S. Supreme Court held that the Sherman Antitrust Act did apply to unions. Congress responded by enacting the Clayton Act, which exempted unions from the Sherman Antitrust Act. The history of U.S. labor law reveals great hostility toward unions.

THE NATIONAL LABOR RELATIONS BOARD

WHAT'S YOUR VERDICT?

Joyce was a union member who frequently complained about working conditions. Even though she did more work than was required of her, she was fired. When she asked why, her boss stated that it was because of her pro-union and anti-management attitude.

Must Joyce and/or her union go to court to get this matter settled?

Today, most labor relations problems are resolved through a federal administrative agency instead of through the courts and Congress.

That agency, the National Labor Relations Board (NLRB) administers the rights and duties given to workers, employers, and unions. The NLRB was created by the National Labor Relations Act (also known as the Wagner Act). Representatives of the union, employers, and individual workers are entitled to file charges and to take part in hearings before the NLRB. A party that is dissatisfied with the board's order may seek review in the federal courts.

In *What's Your Verdict?* Joyce need not go to court. She or her union can file a complaint with the NLRB. The board would probably order the employer to reinstate her.

HOW ARE UNIONS ESTABLISHED?

WHAT'S YOUR VERDICT?

Joan felt that her employer did not treat its employees fairly. When she asked the employer to address issues of sexual harassment in the workplace and unsafe working conditions, she was ignored. When she talked with other employees in her machine shop, she discovered that her views were widely shared. Joan decided that the only way to get management to listen was to organize the other workers into a union.

If Joan organizes a union, how would bargaining units be formed?

Employees may organize into unions and bargain collectively with their employers. Or they may voluntarily decide not to organize into unions and bargain individually.

The Bargaining Unit

To establish union representation, a series of steps need to be taken. One step involves determining which employees should be represented together. Within a unionized company, any group of employees whose employment contract is negotiated together is called a **bargaining unit**. The NLRB may determine the appropriate unit, but there are statutory requirements.

Common employment interests such as training are important considerations in who should be included in the bargaining unit. Employees who have supervisory responsibilities or those who have a confidential role in creating management-labor policies cannot be in a bargaining unit.

Sometimes one union represents several bargaining units in negotiating with a single employer. Each unit is entitled to select its own union to bargain with the employer. However, in *What's Your Verdict?* all the nonsupervisory workers in Joan's machine shop could probably become a bargaining unit.

Voluntary Recognition

To establish a union, the organizers obtain employee signatures on authorization cards. An **authorization card** indicates the worker wants to be represented by a particular union. If a sizable percentage of workers sign authorization cards for a particular union, it may approach management and ask to be recognized as the exclusive bargaining representative.

NLRB Petition

If management denies voluntary recognition, the union can ask the NLRB to conduct a **representation election**. At least 30 percent of the employees in the bargaining unit must sign authorization cards or a petition. If the 30-percent requirement is met, the NLRB will conduct hearings to determine who is in the bargaining unit and who is eligible to vote. To select a bargaining representative (a union), workers in the bargaining unit vote secretly in an election conducted by the NLRB. Majority vote governs. If a union is selected, it becomes the exclusive negotiator for all the employees in the bargaining unit. The NLRB will then acknowledge that union as the exclusive bargaining agent. This is called **certification**.

Certification Campaigns

Often management is hostile to the possibility that a union will represent workers. So labor law makes certain conduct illegal during organizing campaigns. Thus, it is illegal for an employer to fire or to threaten to fire union sympathizers to discourage unionization. Similarly, employers may not threaten to close a plant, to automate the workplace to reduce the number of workers, or to move work out of the country just to avoid unionization. In addition, management may not support one union over another. Labor unions are similarly regulated. During certification campaigns they may not picket, make threats, or engage in violence.

Decertification

If a union has been certified and later 30 percent of the employees decide they want different or no representation, they can petition the NLRB to conduct a **decertification election**. At this election, employees can reject union representation or select a different union. If a majority rejects representation, workers will negotiate individually with the employers. An employer cannot file a decertification petition. Managerial employees are not permitted to vote in certification or decertification elections or to be represented by a union.

A Question of ETHICS

Cork did not think his employer treated women fairly. During a campaign to unionize the workplace, he considered spreading a false rumor about management's "sexist attitudes." He knew if he did this the union would win the campaign. Cork reasoned that spreading the false rumor was wrong but the result would be good because the union would ensure that women were treated fairly.

THINK ABOUT LEGAL CONCEPTS

Answer the following questions about legal concepts.

1. Today, all workers have the right to unionize. **True or False?**

2. The group of workers for whom a union negotiates a common contract is called the ___?___ .

3. Who conducts the certification election? **(a) the union (b) management (c) the petitioning workers (d) the NLRB**

4. Who determines the membership in the bargaining unit? **(a) the union (b) management (c) the petitioning workers (d) the NLRB**

5. What percentage of workers in a bargaining unit must vote in favor to create a union? **(a) 10% (b) a majority (c) 20% (d) 30%**

6. Members of a union who petition the NLRB to change unions or eliminate union representation are asking for ___?___ .

THINK CRITICALLY ABOUT EVIDENCE

Study the following situations, answer the questions, then prepare arguments to support your answers.

7. Friends of your family own a large bakery. They claim their workers are not allowed to join a union because all of the workers are paid union-scale wages or better. Are your friends correct?

8. Jacob was unhappy with his working conditions and wanted to start a union. He knew many other employees were also sympathetic to the idea of union representation. How many coworkers must support an election before the NLRB will conduct a certification election? How many must vote to support a union for it to become the exclusive bargaining agent?

9. At Alta Corporation, 5 of the 20 machinists and 20 of the 30 assembly workers favored unionizing. Describe how the petition for certification and the votes on certification would fare if the bargaining unit were defined as (1) the machinists, (2) the assembly workers, or (3) a combination of both.

10. At Hotel Delta, 25 percent of the maids and laundry workers and two-thirds of the clerical staff favor unionizing. The maids and laundry workers who favor a union want the Teamsters to represent them while the clerical staff who favor a union want their own union. Describe what you think the NLRB will do in creating bargaining units. How do you think the workers will be represented?

GOALS

- Explain how union certification affects employees
- Discuss unfair labor practices by unions and management

UNION CERTIFICATION

WHAT'S YOUR VERDICT?

Phil was an employee of Long Distance Trucking, Inc. Union organizers collected signatures from 30 percent of the employees in Phil's department and the NLRB conducted an election. Phil voted against having a union, but by a majority vote of the bargaining unit, the employees chose the union. Phil did not like the contract the union negotiated. The contract required that union dues be deducted from his pay even though Phil was not required to join the union. Further, he tried to make an individual contract with the company.

What rights does Phil have in this situation?

Exclusive Bargaining Representative

Once a union has been certified, it is the exclusive bargaining representative for everyone within the unit. Whether or not they are union members, all workers in each bargaining unit are bound by the collective agreement reached between the union and the employer. In *What's Your Verdict?* Phil could not negotiate an individual employment contract with his employer.

Union Shop

Workers are not required to join a union unless the employer has agreed to have a union shop. In a **union shop**, non-union employees may be hired, but they must join the union within a stated maximum period, usually 30 days. The agency shop is a variation of the union shop. In the **agency shop**, employees are not required to join the union, but if they do not, they must nevertheless pay union dues as a condition of employment. In *What's Your Verdict?* Phil is working in an agency shop. The union, in effect, acts as the employees' agent in dealing with the employer.

Open Shop

In the **open shop**, employees are not required to belong to a union or to pay dues. The union bargains collectively with the employer and agrees to an employment contract binding union and nonunion workers.

Closed Shop

In the closed shop, the employer agrees that workers must belong to the recognized union before they can be hired. The closed shop was outlawed by the Labor Management Relations Act (also known as the Taft-Hartley Act).

Right-to-work laws have been enacted by a number of states. Such laws prohibit compulsory union membership and ban the union shop, closed shop, and agency shop. In states with right-to-work laws, unions may function, but only with open shops.

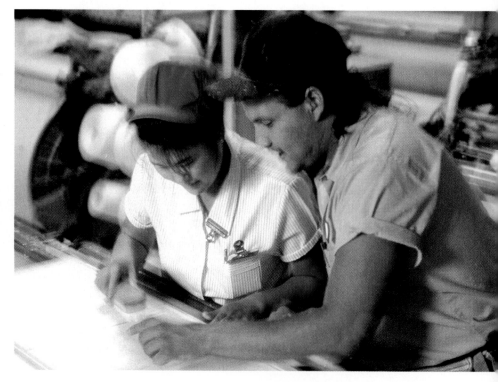

COLLECTIVE BARGAINING

WHAT'S YOUR
VERDICT?

Ace Inc. manufactures automobile parts for several U.S. car companies. The same union represents all of its manufacturing employees. Historically, labor and Ace management negotiated five-year contracts. The current round of negotiations was unsuccessful. During one session, union and management representatives got very angry at each other. At one point, someone threw a chair across the bargaining table. Because of these incidents and the unlikelihood of reaching an agreement, Ace refused to continue negotiating. It said it was prepared to continue paying workers under the old contract but that it was unwilling to negotiate with the current leaders of the union.

What alternatives are available to solve this problem?

Collective bargaining is the process whereby the union and the employer negotiate a contract of employment that binds both sides. Unions choose their own negotiators. Management or lawyers typically represent the company. Pay and fringe benefits are the most commonly negotiated issues. However, grievance procedures, hours, overtime, pensions, health care, working conditions, and safety issues are also frequently negotiated. An employer is not required to bargain over such issues as product prices or designs, plant location, or quality of products. These are strictly management matters even though they do affect the company's ability to pay wages.

Many factors influence the bargaining power of labor and management. These include the company's profitability, availability of substitute workers, prevailing labor rates, the competitiveness of the industry, and foreign competition. The union has legal power flowing from the ability to **strike**, that is to collectively stop working to force an employer to give in to union demands. The employer has legal power flowing from the ability to lock out. A **lockout** occurs when an employer temporarily closes down operations to induce the union to agree to the employer's position.

Great economic pressure results on both sides if either a strike or a lockout occurs. Employee wages usually cease and production often stops. This economic pressure is reinforced by the legal requirement that both management and labor bargain with each other. Failure to bargain is an unfair labor practice. In *What's Your Verdict?* Ace committed an unfair labor practice by refusing to continue negotiations. The union could file a complaint with the NLRB, which might issue an order compelling management to negotiate in good faith.

Collective bargaining sometimes breaks down or becomes deadlocked. Negotiations are **deadlocked** when the union and employer cannot agree on important issues. When this happens, a governmental representative may try to bring the parties together to settle their differences. In **mediation** (also known as conciliation), a mediator (conciliator) talks with both sides and attempts to achieve a compromise. However, such a person has no power to compel agreement.

UNFAIR PRACTICES BY MANAGEMENT

The Wagner Act and other federal and state statutes require that employers treat unions fairly by allowing them to organize. These statutes also require that management engage in good-faith negotiations (collective bargaining) with unions. These laws define certain actions of employers as **unfair labor practices** and prohibit such actions. The following are management unfair labor practices.

1. Interfering with employees' efforts to form, join, or assist unions. Such interference can take a variety of forms. For example, it would be an unfair labor practice to refuse to deduct union dues for union members, to disrupt organizing meetings, or to threaten to fire employees to keep them from organizing a union. Similarly, employers may not threaten to stop operations, replace workers with machines, or move the factory just to avoid unionization.

2. Dominating a union or giving it financial or other support. This preserves the ability of unions to represent the interests of employees. In the past, some companies tried to influence certification elections. Sometimes, they wanted the least aggressive union to win. Other times they tried to win favor with union leaders by contributing money to their election campaigns.

3. Encouraging or discouraging union membership. Employers may not threaten to blacklist employees. Employers blacklist employees by placing their names on a list of pro-union persons and sending it to other employers with the purpose of making it difficult for the employees to find work.

4. Refusing to bargain in good faith with the union. This means management must participate actively in attempting to reach an agreement. It must make honest and reasonable proposals and must listen to the arguments of the union. Management must attempt to find a common ground with the union. However, the law does not require that management agree to a union proposal; management need only engage in good faith bargaining.

Similarly, it is an unfair labor practice to discharge or otherwise discriminate against an employee for filing charges of labor law violations or for testifying about such charges. In *What's Your Verdict?* Mulroy's employer was guilty of an unfair labor practice. The employer could be required to rehire Mulroy and to

pay her the wages lost while barred from the job.

After Paul had voted against forming a union, he tried to negotiate directly with management. He also complained loudly to other employees about how much money was being deducted from his paycheck for union dues. In response, some union officials went to management and asked that Paul be fired. The union officials implied that labor negotiations would go more smoothly if management agreed to this request. As a result, Paul was fired.

Does Paul have a claim against the union?

The Taft-Hartley Act and other statutes require that unions treat employees and management fairly. The actions described below are unfair labor practices by unions.

1. Refusing to bargain collectively in good faith with the employer.

2. Attempting to force an employer to pay for featherbedding. Featherbedding is payment for services not performed. If the work is performed, there is no featherbedding even though the work may be unnecessary.

3. **Picketing** (patrol the employer's property with signs) by uncertified unions to try to force the employer to bargain with that union. Certifying elections are the appropriate method for compelling an employer to bargain with a particular union. It is also an unfair labor practice for a union to picket in an effort to force employees to select that union as their representative within 12 months after losing a valid representation election.

4. Engaging in strikes and boycotts prohibited by law. Most strikes are legal if they are conducted without violence. Those situations where strikes and boycotts are illegal are discussed in the following section.

5. Requiring payment of an excessive or discriminatory fee for initiation into the union.

6. Forcing or to attempt to force employees to support that union or to restrain employees from supporting competing unions. A union may, however, try to persuade employees to support it.

7. Causing or to attempt to cause an employer to discriminate against an employee because of union-related activities.

In *What's Your Verdict?* Paul could sue the union for engaging in an unfair labor practice.

After congressional testimony about corruption and violence in a few unions, Congress passed legislation designed to limit union corruption. The Labor-Management Reporting and Disclosure Act (also known as the Landrum-Griffin Act) requires that unions operate in a manner that gives members full voice in decision making. The law was intended to ensure that union members themselves could correct abuses of power by entrenched leadership through free and open elections.

See the Union Bill of Rights, at right. This document describes rights that union members have with regard to their unions.

UNION BILL OF RIGHTS

ELECTIONS	Union members have the right to equal opportunities for nominating candidates for union offices, and the right to vote by secret ballot in union elections.
MEETINGS	Union members have the right to meet with other members to express views about candidates or other business.
DUES	Union members have the right to vote by secret ballot on increases in dues, initiation fees, and assessment levies.
LAWSUITS	Union members have the right to sue, to testify in court or before any administrative agency or legislative body, and to communicate with any legislator.
DISCIPLINE	Union members are protected from union disciplinary action, unless the member is served with written charges; given time to prepare a defense; and afforded a fair hearing. (Members may be disciplined from nonpayment of dues without such elaborate due process.)
MANAGEMENT	Union members have the right to obtain information about union policies and financial matters, to recover misappropriated union funds for the union, to inspect union contracts, and to be informed of provisions of this act.

WHEN MAY UNIONS STRIKE?

An **economic strike** is one where the dispute is over wages, hours, or conditions of employment. An employer may respond to an economic strike by giving any striking employee's job to someone else. In *What's Your Verdict?* Zeus could give replacement workers the jobs of striking union members. However, when there is an economic strike, unions commonly refuse to settle unless striking members are rehired.

If the strike is over an unfair labor practice by management, the employer may not permanently give the striking worker's job to someone else. When such an **unfair labor practice strike** is over, the employer must reinstate the striking worker even if this requires transferring or discharging the replacement.

Strikes of public (governmental) employees are generally prohibited even though such workers may unionize and bargain collectively. Sometimes public workers (including police officers, teachers, and fire fighters) strike, or stay away from work claiming illness. In such cases, the workers and their leaders are subject to court orders directing them to return to work. If they ignore the court order, they may be fired or jailed.

The president of the United States has the power to obtain an injunction in federal court forcing a **cooling-off period** of 80 days when a national emergency strike is threatened. A **national emergency strike** is one that involves national defense or major industries, or would imperil national health or safety. Strikes and lockouts are illegal during the cooling off period.

WHEN MAY A UNION BOYCOTT?

A **boycott** is a refusal to buy or to use someone's products or services. A **primary boycott** involves the employees' refusals to buy their *employer's* products or services. Primary boycotts are legal. Typically, they are accompanied by a strike and by picketing at the employer's place of business. Usually the striking employees also encourage others, such as customers and suppliers, to boycott the employer.

Sometimes, however, striking employees try to get customers to stop buying the products or services of a third party. Such action against a third party is known as a **secondary boycott**. It is generally illegal. In *What's Your Verdict?* the action was an illegal secondary boycott by the union. The picketing would have been legal if the picketers had urged customers of the stores to stop buying only dresses made by the New York manufacturer, not all products.

Although generally illegal, secondary boycotts are legal when the National Labor Relations Act, or state statutes similar to the NLRA, do not apply. This would be the case with farm labor in most states. Thus, farm workers engaged in labor disputes with farmers have encouraged consumers to not buy anything at grocery stores carrying nonunion grapes and lettuce. This secondary boycott is legal because the farm workers are not covered by the National Labor Relations Act.

CULTURAL DIVERSITY IN LAW

Mexico

Labor Laws

In Mexico, labor relations are regulated by the Federal Labor Law of Mexico. Under this law, labor unions are favored and so are easy to form. If union members decide to strike, the plant will close. This forces the union and company to settle the strike quickly.

Mexican law also favors job security for workers. If an employee passes a 30-day trial period, the person may not be terminated for lack of job qualifications.

Answer the following questions about legal concepts.

1. Certification means that a union is the exclusive bargaining representative for a bargaining unit. **True or False?**

2. Which of the following is illegal according to the Taft-Hartley Act?
(a) **union shop**
(b) **agency shop** (c) **open shop** (d) **closed shop**

3. Management's First Amendment rights allow it to say anything in an attempt to defeat the union during a certification campaign. **True or False?**

Study the following situations, answer the questions, then prepare arguments to support your answers.

4. Sharpe was a union leader. In the midst of intense negotiations, a stranger approached her and engaged her in a discussion. The stranger offered her $20,000 if she would support a management proposal. Although Sharpe knew this was an unfair labor practice, she also recognized that it would be difficult to prove. Would she be acting legally in accepting the money and supporting the proposal?

5. The Electrical Workers Union represented most of the workers in the General TV Plant. In a dispute over wages, the union went on strike and began picketing the plant. They also picketed nearby stores that carried the General televisions, asking that shoppers not purchase them. Is any of this conduct illegal?

6. Alonzo owns his own machine shop and has several close friends among his employees. The NLRB is about to conduct a certification election. Alonzo knows he could persuade his employee friends to spread rumors that if the union is certified, he would move his shop out of the country. He is also certain that such rumors could never be traced back to him. Would this action be legal? Would it be ethical for Alonzo to spread such rumors if they would cause the union to lose the election?

If you are an employee, remember . . .

1. You and your coworkers generally have the legal right to organize into unions and bargain collectively with your employer.

2. An employer may not legally discharge you for engaging in union activities. An employer that does so is guilty of an unfair labor practice.

3. If you belong to a union, you have a right to vote for your officers in secret elections and to see accurate and timely information on union finances and activities.

PREVENT LEGAL DIFFICULTIES

If you are an employer, remember . . .

1. Unions are legal. If they represent your workers, you should cooperate with them in good faith for the common good of all parties involved.

2. You may not discharge or otherwise discriminate against your workers because they join a union or because they refuse to join a union (unless there is a legal union shop).

3. You must bargain collectively in good faith with representatives of any union chosen by a majority of the workers in each bargaining unit. You are not obligated to make any concessions, such as boosting wages, reducing hours, or changing conditions of employment. However, if you refuse to compromise and make some concessions, there may be a strike, and it may continue indefinitely.

CHAPTER IN REVIEW

CONCEPTS IN BRIEF

1. The NLRB will conduct a certification election if it receives a petition or signed authorization cards for 30 percent of the employees in a bargaining unit. If a majority of employees vote for the union, it becomes their exclusive bargaining representative.

2. In a union shop, employees must join the union, usually within 30 days after being employed. In an agency shop, they need not join the union but must pay union dues. In an open shop, employees are not required to join the union or to pay union dues.

3. Common unfair labor practices by management include interfering with employees trying to form a union, favoring one union over another, trying to dominate a union, discriminating against union members, and refusing to bargain in good faith.

4. Common unfair labor practices by unions include refusing to bargain in good faith, featherbedding, picketing an employer when the union is not the exclusive bargaining agent, forcing employees to support the union, and discriminating against employees who do not support the union.

5. If a strike is over economic issues, the employer may hire permanent replacements for the jobs held by strikers. If the strike is over an unfair labor practice, permanent replacements cannot be hired.

6. Primary boycotts are directed against the employer; secondary boycotts are directed against a third party.

7. Primary boycotts are legal. Secondary boycotts are often illegal.

YOUR LEGAL VOCABULARY

Match each statement with the term that it best defines. Some terms may not be used.

1. A process by which a union ceases to be the exclusive bargaining agent for employees

2. State laws that ban both the union shop and the closed shop

3. Establishment in which all employees must belong to the union, either when they are hired or within a specified time after they are hired

4. Boycott by striking employees that is directed mainly against their employer

5. Concerted stoppage of work to force an employer to yield to union demands

6. Patrolling by union members with signs alongside the premises of the employer during a labor dispute

7. Union or employer actions that violate the rights of employees with respect to union activity

8. Attempt by a neutral third party to achieve a compromise between disputing parties

9. Employer's shutdown of operations to bring pressure on employees

10. Establishment in which nonunion members do not pay union dues

agency shop
bargaining unit
boycott
certification
closed shop
collective bargaining
decertification election
economic strike
ex parte injunction
lockout
mediation
open shop
picket
primary boycott
right-to-work laws
secondary boycott
strike
unfair labor practices
unfair labor practice strike
union shop
yellow-dog contracts

11. Describe the roles of state and federal governments in labor relations.

12. Describe the history of labor law.

13. Explain the steps involved in establishing a new union.

14. Tell how workers could change to have a different union represent them.

15. Describe how the law regulates management and union conduct during certification elections.

16. Invent four examples of unfair labor practices by a union.

17. Invent four examples of unfair labor practices by management.

18. Explain when boycotts are legal and illegal.

WRITE ABOUT LEGAL CONCEPTS

19. **HOT DEBATE** Write a letter from the employees to the employer outlining the points you would like to negotiate with her.

20. Write a short paragraph describing the voting procedures used in establishing a union.

21. Write two paragraphs describing labor-management conflicts that you have learned about through the news or other sources.

22. Write two paragraphs about the balance of power that the law gives to management and to unions. Reach a conclusion about whether you think the balance favors one side or the other.

THINK CRITICALLY ABOUT EVIDENCE

23. When a national union sent organizers to try to persuade Baker's workers to join the union, Baker called three of her most trusted employees to her office. She urged them to organize a new union limited to company employees. She offered to provide the union with office space and time for officers to conduct union business. Baker then gave the three workers money to buy printed notices and refreshments for an organization meeting. Was Baker's action legal?

24. O'Donnell felt that management at the company where he worked was engaging in unfair labor practices. He complained in public and filed charges with the NLRB. Those charges were dismissed. Later he was called to testify about charges filed by the union. O'Donnell's bosses hinted that they would get even. About two months later, the company decided to eliminate O'Donnell's job. Does he have any recourse?

25. Joan and the other members of her union were striking for higher wages. Management made a public announcement that workers who failed to report on the following Monday would be perma-

nently replaced. Can an employer permanently replace striking union members? Can a union continue striking until the employer agrees to rehire the striking employees?

26. A strike at the Titan Stone Works was in its fifth week when Paxton, a federal mediator, was called in. After long discussions with both sides, she persuaded the union representatives to accept certain terms. The terms were a major concession on the part of the union but seemed to her to be fair to all parties involved, including the buying public. Titan rejected the terms even though it was financially able to meet every demand. Can Paxton compel Titan to sign the proposed contract?

27. Employees of the city of Manchester became dissatisfied with their working conditions. As a result, 35 percent petitioned the NLRB for a representation election. They established a local, unaffiliated union that won the election. When they were unsuccessful in their negotiations with the city council, they went on strike. Is any conduct by these employees illegal?

28. The United Steelworkers of America, a national union, had a provision in its constitution that imposed requirements to be satisfied before a member could run for leadership positions in local affiliates. The limitation was that to be eligible to be a local officer, the union member must have attended at least one-half of the regular local meetings for the three years prior to the election. Is this restriction legal? (*Local 3489 United Steelworkers of America v. Usery,* 97 S. Ct. 611)

29. Mary Weatherman was the personal secretary to the president of Hendricks County Rural Electric Membership Corporation. One of her friends at the firm was involved in an industrial accident that resulted in the loss of one of his arms. Shortly after the accident, he was dismissed. Mary, concerned about the plight of her friend, signed a petition seeking his reinstatement. Because of this conduct Mary also was discharged. Mary filed a charge with the NLRB, alleging an unfair labor practice. The company defended itself by claiming that because Mary was a confidential secretary, she was not covered by the National Labor Relations Act's definition of "employee." Who is right, Mary or the company? (*NLRB v. Hendricks County,* 102 S. Ct. 216)

30. During a union-organizing campaign at Portage Plastics Company, some members began wearing union buttons on the job. Because a button fell into a grinder and caused loss of material and because of the increasing division among the employees, the president of Portage prohibited the wearing of either union or nonunion badges at work. Other jewelry and hair attachments were still permitted even though such ornaments had also fallen into equipment and caused losses on prior occasions. Immediately after the president gave his order, a strike was started in protest. Was the company rule on union badges an unfair labor practice? Would it make any difference if the union agreed, after the order, that its members would not wear badges? (*Portage Plastics Company v. International Union, Allied Industrial Workers of America, AFL-CIO,* 163 NLRB No. 102)

31. Kuebler was a member in good standing of the lithographers union when it struck the Art Gravure Company. Several months after the strike began, Kuebler met in a nonsecret meeting with 12 or 13 other strikers. Their purpose was to discuss "the widening gap" between the labor and management bargaining committees and to "try to straighten this thing out to where we could get back to work." Later, a three-person committee from the group communicated its views to the Union Negotiating Committee. Kuebler returned to the picket line. When the strike finally ended, the trial board off the local union charged and found Kuebler guilty of attending "a meeting . . . held for the purpose of undermining the Union Negotiating Committee." Kuebler was suspended from the union for three months and was fined $2,000. He filed a notice of appeal to the membership and requested several items: copies of charges against him, with supporting facts; names of the persons on the executive board who had accused and tried him; a copy of the decision in writing showing how each member had voted; and a copy of the transcript of the evidence and proceedings at his trial by the union trial board. This information was refused, and so Kuebler sued for relief in the U.S. district court. Had the union violated Kuebler's rights? Had Kuebler been denied a fair hearing? (*Kuebler v. Cleveland Lithographers and Photoengravers Union Local,* 473 F.2d 359)

32. The Greenpark Nursing Home hired First National Maintenance to maintain its facilities. First National in turn hired employees to work for it on the premises of the nursing home. These employees of First National formed a union. Shortly after, First National decided, for financial reasons, to cancel its maintenance contract with the nursing home. Anticipating a complete layoff, the union sought to negotiate with management over the decision to terminate this contract. Management refused to negotiate on this issue. Was this refusal to negotiate legal? (*First National Maintenance v. NLRB,* 452 U.S. 666)

FACTS Mohawk Liqueur Corporation's collective bargaining agreement with Local 42 (the union) was about to expire, and the parties were negotiating a new contract. The parties disagreed on many issues but talks continued. Then Mohawk submitted its final offer, including a statement that it would not pay the final cost of living adjustment (COLA) due under the *old* contract, for work already performed. The union declared this an unfair labor practice, and struck. Mohawk unilaterally implemented its final offer and refused to pay the COLA. Negotiations resumed and about two months later Mohawk agreed to make the old COLA payment. It then warned the workers that they would be permanently replaced if they failed to return by August 4.

On August 3, the union met. The workers agreed that the COLA payment was no longer an issue but voted to continue the strike. The employees hoped to force Mohawk to divulge the names of certain workers the company planned to discharge, to offer a general amnesty to all strikers, and to grant certain financial benefits. Mohawk replaced all striking workers. On August 11 the union voted to return to work. Mohawk reinstated some but not all of the strikers, and five months later the parties reached a new contract.

The Board determined that what had begun as an unfair labor practice strike had changed into an economic one, and that Mohawk had lawfully replaced some workers permanently. The union appealed.

DECISION Employees who take part in an economic strike run the risk of permanent replacement by new hires. But unfair labor practice strikers are entitled to reinstatement if they wish to return to work and, if denied reemployment, are also entitled to back pay from the date of denial.

The causes of a strike can, of course, change over time. Sometimes a strike that starts for economic reasons is prolonged by the employer's subsequent unlawful conduct and is thereby "converted" from an economic to an unfair labor practice strike.

The members' meeting's avowed purpose was to decide whether to prolong the strike. The minutes of the meeting, the motion by which the strikers decided not to return to work, and the testimony before the Administrative Law Judge all demonstrate that the reasons for continuing the strike had nothing whatsoever to do with Mohawk's prior violations of the NRLA. The May 31 COLA came into the deliberations only when the Union negotiator and attorney explained why it was no longer a reason to strike. The evidence relating to both the August 11 negotiating session (such as testimony that the parties agreed the COLA issue had been "settled" and the Union's announcement that it was withdrawing its COLA grievance) and the August 12 Union meeting also supports the Board's conclusion that the strike was prolonged for reasons entirely unrelated to Mohawk's unfair labor practices.

The Board's order, declaring the permanent replacements lawful, is affirmed.

PRACTICE JUDGING

1. What is the unfair labor practice alleged by the union?

2. Would the outcome for fired workers have been different if the union had not made demands unrelated to the COLA?

3. If the COLA questions had not been settled and the additional demands had been made, would this be an unfair labor practice strike or an economic strike?

EMPLOYMENT DISCRIMINATION

CHAPTER 29

LESSONS

29-1 ILLEGAL EMPLOYMENT DISCRIMINATION

29-2 PROVING ILLEGAL DISCRIMINATION

29-3 SPECIFIC LAWS MAKING UNJUSTIFIED DISCRIMINATION ILLEGAL

HOT DEBATE

Phan's parents were born in Vietnam. They spoke Vietnamese in the home. Phan did not learn English until he began kindergarten. Upon graduating from high school, Phan's language skills were still below par. When Phan applied for a job, he was asked to take an English grammar test. He took the test but failed, and therefore was denied employment. Phan contended that his life circumstance caused him to fail the test. The prospective employer said it didn't care about Phan's life circumstance, only how well he could do the job.

Where Do You Stand?

1. Why should Phan have been given the job?

2. Why should Phan have not be given the job?

GOALS

- Define illegal discrimination
- Define legal discrimination
- Identify members of protected classes

UNJUSTIFIED DISCRIMINATION

WHAT'S YOUR VERDICT?

Clare has been working at Rich Manufacturing for three years. Lisa has been working there for two months. They both operate computerized machine-tooling equipment. The machines perform many operations, such as drilling, cutting threads, turning, deburring, and surfacing metal objects. Lisa is faster. When a promotion opportunity came along, it was given to Lisa. Clare protested, saying that she was being discriminated against because Lisa would be earning almost 30 percent more money than she would.

Is Clare correct? Is she a victim of unjustified discrimination?

Discrimination is treating individuals differently. **Employment discrimination** within the workplace is treating individuals differently on the basis of race, color, gender, national origin, or religion. Our law attempts to protect people from being judged on the basis of their membership in these groups. Being judged simply on the basis of group membership is a form of unjustified discrimination. Instead of judging people by the groups to which they belong, the law compels employers to judge each person as an individual.

It is a form of discrimination to pay more money to those who work harder. However, this is a form of justified discrimination. An important point for understanding this chapter is knowing the difference between justified discrimination and unjustified discrimination.

The law attacks unjustified discrimination in a practical way. It identifies group characteristics that may not be considered when making employment decisions. The courts have attached the label **protected classes** to people within these groups. Members of protected classes are often, but not always, minorities. Employment discrimination law is designed to ensure that membership in a protected class is not a significant factor in employment decisions.

Justified discrimination is permitted and even encouraged. Workers fairly judged as dependable, skilled, creative, smart, or hard working usually receive more favorable treatment. They earn more money and have more job opportunities. Thus, in *What's Your Verdict?* Clare is being justifiably discriminated against. She is only pointing out the fact that Lisa is being treated better. If the employer has a good reason for the treatment (for example, Lisa works faster), the discrimination is justified. Much of employment discrimination law concerns balancing justified and unjustified discrimination.

TYPES OF UNJUSTIFIED DISCRIMINATION

WHAT'S YOUR VERDICT?

Stephanos is Greek and has a strong accent. He is living in the United States. He has a Ph.D. in engineering from a Greek university. When Stephanos applies for engineering jobs, he often encounters resistance from those who do not feel that a person with a strong accent can do good engineering work. Stephanos knows that, unlike many countries, the United States has laws that forbid employment discrimination. He assumes these laws are aimed at helping minority groups in this country like blacks and Hispanics. He does not think these laws could protect him.

Is Stephanos correct?

A variety of federal statutes define the criteria that employers cannot consider when making employment decisions. These criteria and the associated protected classes of persons are presented below.

RACE AND COLOR The protected class based on race or color includes all persons who are not white. So, African Americans, Asians, Filipinos, Hispanics, Native Americans, and others are members of a protected class.

GENDER Employers may not discriminate against females or males based on their gender. In addition, sexual harassment is illegal.

PREGNANCY Employers may not discriminate because of a person's childbearing condition or plans.

AGE People over age 40 are protected against discrimination on the basis of their age.

RELIGION People who have religious beliefs of any kind are members of a protected class. This category could include everyone.

DISABILITY The physically and mentally disabled are afforded limited protection against discrimination.

NATIONAL ORIGIN People are protected against discrimination based on their country of origin. So those who do not speak English or who are not citizens of the United States are protected to a limited extent. In *What's Your Verdict?* Stephanos is being discriminated against because his accent is a signal of his national origin. That is illegal.

THE SCOPE OF PROTECTION

WHAT'S YOUR VERDICT?

Gifford is African-American. He works for a company that has a good reputation for hiring people of both sexes, from all racial groups, and without regard to age, religion, handicap, or national origin. About half of Gifford's colleagues and superiors are African-American. Pay rates are equal among the majority and all protected classes. Gifford's only complaint about the company is that white males seem to be assigned overtime more often than anyone else. Gifford concludes that because the company does such a good job in hiring protected classes, he does not have a legal basis for suing.

Is Gifford correct?

The most obvious forms of employment discrimination arise out of the hiring decision. In the past, this country's employment advertisements often included such language as "men only," "no black people need apply,"

and "persons between the ages of 16 and 30 years only, please."

Conditions of Employment

Today the law makes illegal not only unjustified discrimination in hiring,

but also unjustified discrimination in any "term, condition, or privilege of employment." This means it is illegal to discriminate against protected classes in any aspect of the job. If the unjustified discrimination is displayed in pay, promotions, training, overtime, educational opportunities, travel requirements, shift rotations, firings, layoffs, post-employment letters of recommendation, or any other aspect of employment, it is illegal. Thus, in *What's Your Verdict?* Gifford could win a suit even if the employer discriminated only in allocating overtime.

Organizations Subject to These Laws

Most employers with 15 or more employees and engaged in interstate commerce are subject to federal employment discrimination laws. This means that almost all employers except some small businesses are subject to the laws described in this chapter. Agencies of state governments, employment agencies, and labor unions also are generally subject to anti-discrimination laws.

CULTURAL DIVERSITY IN LAW

European Union

National Origin Discrimination

In the treaties forming the European Union, workplace discrimination on political and religious grounds are not addressed. However, the treaties do cover discrimination on the basis of national origin. According to the treaties, citizens from each country in the European Union are free to follow their economic interests anywhere within the Union—without the fear of being discriminated against on the basis of national origin.

European Union treaties also address sex discrimination. Pregnant workers cannot be fired and are entitled to take a minimum 14-week maternity leave.

THINK ABOUT LEGAL CONCEPTS

Answer the following questions about legal concepts.

1. An employer can never discriminate. **True or False?**

2. In general, employment law makes it illegal to consider a group characteristic when hiring individuals. **True or False?**

3. "Protected classes" refers to members of groups that are illegal to discriminate against. **True or False?**

4. Which of the following people working in the United States is not a member of a protected class? **(a) woman (b) Asian man (c) Hispanic father (d) Spanish uncle (e) none of the above**

5. Which of the following U.S. residents is not a member of a protected class? **(a) Asian woman (b) Panamanian man (c) Hispanic aunt (d) French artist (e) none of the above**

THINK CRITICALLY ABOUT EVIDENCE

Study the following situations, answer the questions, then prepare arguments to support your answers.

6. Sven immigrated to the United States at age 12 and obtained citizenship at age 18. He speaks with a thick accent. When he applied for a job as a bank clerk, someone else was selected because the other person was more accurate in counting money. Has Sven been the subject of discrimination? Was the discrimination justified or unjustified?

7. Atushi is Japanese. "We Wash Windows" is a company that washes windows in a commercial building where many windows are six or seven feet off the ground. Taller people can wash these windows more quickly. When Atushi applied for a window washer job he was told they don't hire Japanese because the typical Japanese person is shorter than other people. Atushi is six feet, four inches tall. Has Atushi been the subject of discrimination? Was the discrimination justified or unjustified?

8. Shaun was born in Ireland and immigrated to this country when he was 32 years old. He found work as a computer programmer and was the most efficient worker in his department. When overtime was available, it was always offered to someone else. When Shaun asked his boss why, the boss said, "We can't discriminate in hiring but the company can do whatever it wants in awarding overtime." Is the boss right?

9. Susie owned a florist shop employing three people in a state that had no laws against employment discrimination. She hired her nephew, Bill, without considering anyone else for the job. Is this a form of discrimination? Is it illegal in her state? Is it illegal under federal law?

GOALS

- Explain how unequal treatment can be proved
- Identify employers' major defenses in discrimination suits
- Explain what constitutes sexual harassment

HOW CAN UNEQUAL TREATMENT BE PROVED?

WHAT'S YOUR VERDICT?

Geraldo, an Hispanic, had 10 years of experience as a finish carpenter. He applied for a job with a local construction company but was turned down. The company continued advertising the position and eventually hired Jake. Jake was white. He did not have as much experience as Geraldo. At the trial, the company was not able to justify its decision to hire Jake instead of Geraldo.

Will the court find in favor of Geraldo or the company?

Unequal treatment (sometimes called **disparate treatment**) means that an employer treats members of a protected class less favorably than other employees. In order for the treatment to be considered unequal, it must be intentional.

Direct and Indirect Evidence

Cases based on unequal treatment have taken two forms, based on the nature of the evidence.

DIRECT EVIDENCE In the past, unequal treatment was often both intentional and open. Newspapers carried want ads that listed jobs as "men only." Some firms would publicly refuse to hire African-Americans, Asians, Cajuns, Mexicans, mulattos, Puerto Ricans, or women. Flyers would sometimes state, "no Irish" or "no Jews need apply." Sometimes women would receive letters stating, "I am sorry, but we have a policy against hiring women in these positions."

IN THIS CASE

Pan American World Airways (Pan Am) had a "female only" policy for flight attendants. A male, Diaz, applied for the job and was turned down because of his gender. He sued. At the trial, he offered direct proof of the policy. Pan Am admitted that it had the policy. This was proof of Pan Am's intent to discriminate. Pan Am lost the suit.

To win a case where the discrimination is admitted, the employee need only prove that she or he was denied employment because of membership in a protected class. Today, most direct-evidence litigation focuses not on the decision to hire,

but on decisions related to other aspects of the employment relationship. Thus, if an employer offered life insurance as a fringe benefit but the amount was less for women than for men (on the grounds that women outlive men), this would be intentional unequal treatment.

INDIRECT EVIDENCE Today most cases involve situations where the employer denies any intention to illegally discriminate. To establish a case against such an employer, an employee must show the following:

1. the person was a member of a protected class
2. the person applied for the job and was qualified
3. the person was rejected
4. the employer held the job open and sought other persons with similar qualifications

In *What's Your Verdict?* Geraldo, a member of a protected class, applied for a job for which he was qualified. He was rejected, and the company held the job open and later hired Jake. The court presumed that the discrimination was intentional and Geraldo won the suit.

Employer's General Defense: Business Necessity

Once the employee has shown, with either direct or indirect evidence, that unequal treatment occurred, the employer may defend by establishing one of several defenses. These defenses attempt to show that the unequal treatment was justified by a reason that is legal. Thus, in an indirect proof case, the employer's most common defense is that the employee's skills or work history was the reason for not hiring. This general defense is sometimes called business necessity or job relatedness.

Business necessity means that the

employer's actions were meant to advance the business rather than to create unjustified discrimination.

IN THIS CASE Star Plumbing advertised a position that stated that applicants would be considered only if they had five years of residential plumbing experience. Chu, an Asian, had the experience. He applied for the job but was turned down. Later, Star hired Sue, a white woman, for the job. She also had the experience. Chu sued and attempted to prove the discrimination with indirect proof. He established in court that he was a member of a protected class, that he had the experience, that he applied and was rejected, and that the job was held open for others. At that point in the trial, Star proved that when it checked Chu's references it discovered that he had been recently fired from other jobs for drinking at work. Star won the suit because it had a valid general defense. It discriminated against Chu because of business necessity.

Defense of Bona Fide Occupational Qualification

Another defense available to an employer is called the bona fide occupational qualification (BFOQ). A **bona fide occupational qualification** is a job requirement that compels discrimination against a protected class. Thus, if an employer hired actors to play parts in a stage show, some of the parts would be for men and the employer could decide to hire only men. Similarly, employers could request only male or female models for a fashion show.

To establish the BFOQ, the discrimination must truly be essential to the business. The fact that discrimination is helpful is not enough. When airlines were fighting to preserve female-only flight attendants, they presented surveys showing that a high proportion of their passengers preferred to be served by women. The courts rejected this argument and held that being female is not necessary to perform the job.

Defense of Seniority

Seniority can be another justification for unequal treatment. A **bona fide seniority system** is one that rewards employees based on the length of employment rather than merit and is not intended to discriminate. In the law, a bona fide seniority system can justify discrimination. If an employer pays union members on the basis of seniority, promotes on

the basis of seniority, or lays employees off on the basis of seniority, unequal treatment of protected classes will be tolerated. The Supreme Court will permit seniority to be used even when it perpetuates past discrimination.

Pretexts

Employers often assert business necessity or BFOQ as a pretext, or a cover, for discriminating. For example, a company hires a male instead of a female, Julie, for a job. The company says the reason is that the job involves a lot of travel. Because Julie is the mother of three children, the company says that would make travel harder for her to schedule. Julie could establish that this reason is a not business necessity but a pretext by showing that men with three or more children had been hired for the job.

Sharon's Machine Shop manufactures fire hydrants. When finished, each hydrant weighs approximately 175 pounds. Part of the job description for hydrant assemblers states that a person hired for this job be able to lift 175 pounds ten times in two minutes. This requirement is similar to the actions required to assemble the hydrants.

Is this job requirement a form of illegal employment discrimination?

Many companies have a policy (like the one at Sharon's in *What's Your Verdict?*) that is regarded as **neutral on its face**. This means that the policy makes no reference to a protected class. But note that in *What's Your Verdict?* more men will probably be able to satisfy this job requirement than women. So the policy has a disparate, or different, impact on a protected class. **Disparate impact** indicates that the policy eliminates more members of protected classes than members of the majority. If prison guards are required to be six feet tall, this would eliminate a higher proportion of Asians, Hispanics, and women than white and black males. Agility tests, height tests, weight tests, educational requirements, and tests of clerical abilities all have a disparate impact on a protected class.

The courts treat cases involving job requirements quite differently from cases involving unequal treatment. To win a suit claiming disparate impact, the employee need not prove an intention to discriminate. But the employee must identify a specific employment practice and show statistically that the practice excludes members of a protected class. Even then the employee will lose if the employer is able to show that there is a legitimate business necessity for the practice.

In *What's Your Verdict?* Sharon's weight-lifting test is neutral on its face. But it can be statistically shown that a smaller proportion of women will pass the test. Therefore, it has a disparate impact. However, the test is justified by business necessity because it is clearly job-related.

In the past, such practices as requiring high school graduation, written aptitude tests, height and weight tests, and subjective interviews have been attacked by employees on the basis of disparate impact.

Statistical Proof of Disparate Impact

The employee must establish that fewer members qualified for the job when the challenged employment practice is used than when it is not. This involves examining two groups:

1. the **applicant pool** (those qualified for the job without regard to the challenged practice)
2. the **workforce pool** pool (persons actually in the workforce)

The percentage of protected class individuals in each pool is then compared. If the percentage in the applicant pool is statistically higher than the percentage in the workforce group, this suggests disparate impact. But one other element, causation, must be proven. **Causation** is a linking of the challenged practice and the difference in percentages of protected class persons. After causation is established, the employee has proven disparate impact.

Employer Defenses

Employers can avoid liability even after the employee has shown disparate treatment. If the challenged practice is justified by business necessity, there is no liability. Thus, if weight lifting is required on the job, it does not legally matter that the requirement excludes a protected class from the job. In addition, an employer can utilize the defenses of bona fide occupational qualification and seniority.

IN THIS CASE

Lenny's Trash Collection Company in Denver, Colorado, paid $18 per hour to its trash collectors. It required job applicants to lift 130 pounds. Of 150 trash collectors, only 3 percent were women. In Denver the percentage of women in the unskilled workforce is about 40 percent. Lucy challenged the practice. Her lawyer's statistician found that the difference between 40 percent of women in the unskilled labor pool and the 3 percent of women in Lenny's workforce was statistically significant. Lenny's evidence showed that most women did not want to work in trash collecting. Lenny's statistician proved there was not a statistically significant difference between the 4 percent of women who would apply and the 3 percent in the workforce. Lenny's and Lucy's evidence pointed to different causes for the small percentage of women in the workforce. Lucy has not established disparate treatment

PROVING PATTERN AND PRACTICE OF DISCRIMINATION

WHAT'S YOUR VERDICT?

Beck wanted to be considered for advanced training at her company's headquarters. Their bosses nominated employees for the training. In Beck's job classification, there were about 80 men and 60 women. Beck's boss nominated her. Of the 20 people nominated for the home-office training, half were men and half were women. Of the 10 people selected for the training, all were men.

Is Beck's employer liable for employment discrimination?

In some cases, the government can initiate proceedings against a company for employment discrimination when there is evidence of a pattern and practice of discrimination. In this type of litigation, the government merely shows a statistically significant difference between the protected class composition of the pool of qualified applicants and the workforce. In *What's Your Verdict?* Beck's employer would probably be liable under pattern and practice.

SEXUAL HARASSMENT

WHAT'S YOUR VERDICT?

Fran and Shayla worked in payroll at a trucking company. Many of the drivers flirted with both Fran and Shayla by calling them "honey," asking for dates, and flattering their figures. Although Fran loved it, Shayla would become upset after some of the remarks. She complained to their boss, but he refused to do anything.

Is the company liable for sexual harassment?

employee's ability to work. In instances where a supervisor sexually harasses a subordinate, the employer is strictly liable.

Generally, the employer is liable for the conduct of non-supervisory employees only when the harassment is either known or should have been known to supervisors and they failed to act to prevent further occurrences. In *What's Your Verdict?* Shayla's boss knew about the harassment. Therefore, the trucking firm will be liable if Shayla brings a hostile environment case.

One form of sex discrimination is sexual harassment. Sexual harassment takes two forms: quid pro quo and hostile environment.

Quid Pro Quo

Quid pro quo means one thing is exchanged for another. The most vivid illustration of this form of sexual harassment is when a boss threatens to fire a subordinate unless sexual favors are provided. Continued employment is being exchanged for sexual favors. The employer may offer any term, condition, or privilege of employment, such as a raise, or a favorable evaluation.

Hostile Environment

A **hostile environment** arises when unwelcome sexual comments, gestures, or contact interfere with an

A Question of ETHICS ?

Suzie works in the accounting department of a manufacturing company. Seven other women work in the same room. Men from the plant often walk by and joke with the women. Most of the women enjoy the interaction but it makes Suzie uncomfortable. Should Suzie ask everyone to stop because she finds the flirtation offensive?

Answer the following questions about legal concepts.

1. Which of the following are grounds for illegal discrimination? **(a) disparate treatment (b) disparate impact (c) pattern and practice (d) all of the above**

2. Which type of illegal discrimination is most concerned with one person? **(a) disparate treatment (b) disparate impact (c) pattern and practice (d) none of the above**

3. Most disparate treatment cases today involve which type of proof? **(a) direct proof (b) indirect proof**

4. Employers may discriminate against protected classes if it is justified by business necessity. **True or False?**

5. If a member of a protected class proves disparate treatment, the employer will not be liable if it can show the defense of seniority or BFOQ. **True or False?**

6. A job requirement may be illegal although it appears on its face not to discriminate against a protected class. **True or False?**

7. To establish that a job requirement that is neutral on its face is illegal, the plaintiff must establish that it produces which of the following? **(a) disparate treatment (b) disparate impact (c) pattern and practice**

Study the following situations, answer the questions, then prepare arguments to support your answers.

8. Pablo interviewed people to serve as clerks at his dry cleaning business. Pablo thought that he would get more repeat business if he hired attractive male clerks. He advertised and told females that he was only interested in male clerks so they need not bother with an interview. Would this form of discrimination be proved directly or indirectly? Would the case be one based on disparate impact or disparate treatment?

9. Finance America reimbursed employees for their job-related educational expenses. Janice applied for reimbursement for a course, but was told, "This isn't job related." She learned that another employee, Gail, had been turned down, too. Later, Janice met four men with similar jobs who had taken the same course and had been reimbursed. What type of discrimination occurred? What defense is Finance America most likely to employ in this case?

10. As a condition of employment, Duke Moving required a high school education or a satisfactory score on a general intelligence test. Both requirements were designed to improve the quality of the workforce but neither requirement was shown to improve job performance. Griggs claimed that the test discriminated against him. He said that, as a minority member, he had not had the educational opportunity afforded others. Moreover, he said, the test did not relate to skills and qualifications that were necessary for employment at Duke. Was Griggs legally correct? If he sued, what type of discrimination would Griggs claim?

11. E-Com hired computer programmers even if they didn't know Java, the main programming language used by the company. But to be hired without knowing Java, applicants had to pass a "Test of Basic Programming Ability." Different racial groups performed very differently on the test. Asians passed at the rate of 38 percent while some other groups passed at the rate of only 12 percent. E-Com had done studies showing that applicants who passed the test produced twice as many lines of computer programming as those who didn't pass the test. Is the test neutral on its face? Does the test produce a disparate impact? Is the test illegal?

12. Ajax Trash Removal company had a policy that required employees to be able to lift 120 pounds. It also had a policy that trash cans weighing more than 65 pounds would not be picked up. In your opinion, is the employment policy (regarding 120 pounds) legal?

13. Joyce was at her first day on the job. When she started her computer, it automatically drew an explicit picture of a nude woman on the screen. Is this sexual harassment? What should Joyce do to ensure that nothing like this happens again?

GOALS

● Describe the Civil Rights Act of 1964

● Name the laws which make discrimination on the basis of age, pregnancy, and disability illegal

LEGISLATION PROHIBITING DISCRIMINATION

WHAT'S YOUR VERDICT?

Jannette was employed in a glass factory. Her job was to inspect and pack glass jars in cartons. Men also were employed in the same capacity, but they were occasionally required to lift the packed cartons. The women were paid 10 percent less than the men were.

Is the difference in pay illegal?

The federal government has enacted a number of statutes to prohibit discrimination in employment.

The Civil Rights Act of 1964

With some exceptions, the Civil Rights Act of 1964 forbids employers, employment agencies, and unions from discriminating in hiring, paying, training, promoting, or discharging employees on the basis of race, color, religion, national origin, or sex. An employer may discriminate in selecting one worker over another if the standard set is necessary for proper performance of the job. For example, a prospective pilot of an airplane may be required to understand radar and navigation equipment. That person may also be required to react quickly to emergencies and to be free of potentially fatal heart diseases.

The Civil Rights Act sets up the Equal Employment Opportunity Commission (EEOC). The EEOC has the authority to investigate and conciliate complaints of job discrimination and to prosecute suspected offenders.

If an employer has discriminated in the past, the courts may mandate an **affirmative action plan** to remedy the past discrimination. Most employers that contract with the federal government also must submit affirmative action plans. These are positive steps aimed at offsetting past discrimination by bringing the percentages of minorities and women in the workforce up to their corresponding percentages in the pool of qualified applicants. Because the federal government is the biggest buyer of goods and services in the country, most large employers are directly affected by affirmative action.

Equal Pay Act of 1963

The Equal Pay Act prohibits wage discrimination on account of sex. Women who do the same work or substantially equal work as that of men must be paid at the same rate. This means that when the same skill, effort, and responsibility are required and when the job is performed under similar working conditions, women must be paid the same as men. Thus, in *What's Your Verdict?* the court held

that Jannette and the other women were entitled to equal pay for equal work and that "equal work" did not mean identical duties. Differences in pay are allowed if based on any of the following:

1. merit system
2. seniority system
3. system basing pay on quantity or quality of production
4. system based on any factor other than gender

Age Discrimination in Employment Act of 1967

The Age Discrimination in Employment Act forbids discrimination against workers over the age of 40 in any employment practice (hiring, discharging, retiring, promoting, and compensating). Exceptions are made when age is a necessary consideration for job performance. Such occupations include bus drivers, fire fighters, and police officers.

Americans with Disabilities Act of 1990

The Americans with Disabilities Act (ADA) requires that employers not engage in unjustified discrimination against disabled persons on the basis of their disability. The act attempts to prevent employers from automatically assuming that disabled persons cannot perform work. A **disability** substantially limits a major life activity. It can be physical or mental. However, current use of illegal drugs is not a disability under ADA. Neither are sex-related traits or conditions such as homosexuality or transexuality. A person with a contagious disease may be protected under the ADA, although the courts determine this based on individual medical judgments.

The ADA defines a qualified individual with a disability as one who can perform the essential functions of

workers. Most states and many cities have enacted similar laws. In addition, the Supreme Court has interpreted the Fourteenth Amendment to apply to employment. The Supreme Court also has extended to employment the civil rights laws passed in 1866 and 1870.

These efforts have modified the old common-law concept that an employer has complete freedom in hiring and, subject to liability for breach of contract, freedom in discharging workers. Essentially, current laws, regulations, and court decisions require that job applicants be judged on their merits as individuals, not as members of any group or class.

the job or who could perform those functions with a reasonable accommodation. Thus employers must now make a reasonable accommodation for the qualified disabled worker. A reasonable accommodation is not required if it would produce an undue hardship for the employer. Factors considered in determining whether there would be undue hardships are the cost of the accommodation and the financial resources of the employer.

Pregnancy Discrimination Act

The Pregnancy Discrimination Act is a statute that makes it illegal to discriminate because of pregnancy, childbirth, or related medical conditions. Accordingly, an employer may not fire, refuse to hire, refuse to promote, or demote a woman because she is pregnant.

The act also makes it illegal for fringe benefits to discriminate on these bases. Thus, an employer cannot carry an insurance policy that insures all physical conditions except pregnancy.

Federal anti-discrimination laws such as those just discussed have been enacted because of past injustices in the hiring, paying, training, transferring, and discharging of

LAW IN THE MEDIA

WOMEN AND CRIME

According to psychologist Elizabeth Carll, Ph.D., female perpetrators of crimes are given much more media attention and coverage than male perpetrators of similar crimes. This discrimination can be explained, Carll says, by society's tolerance for violence against women and crimes of passion by men. When a woman commits a crime of this nature, the media can't seem to provide enough coverage.

Take, for example, the case of Amy Fisher, who was sentenced to eighteen months in prison for the attempted murder of Mary Jo Buttafuoco, the wife of her lover. The coverage of this story in the newspapers and on television lasted for more than a year.

Questions to Consider

1 **Can you think of more examples of women receiving excessive coverage in the media after committing a crime? Why do you think our society is so fascinated by women who commit crimes?**

2 **Ninety-five percent of domestic violence victims in the United States are women. How do you account for the disparity between this fact and the coverage of female crimes in the media?**

3 **Do you think punishments women receive for crimes of passion are equal to those men receive? Think of examples to justify your opinion.**

Answer the following questions about legal concepts.

1. Which law prohibits discrimination based on race, religion, sex, or national origin in any term, condition, or privilege of employment? **(a) ADA (b) Equal Pay Act (c) Civil Rights Act of 1964**

2. Which law prohibits discrimination based on gender in the payment of wages? **(a) ADA (b) Equal Pay Act (c) Age Discrimination in Employment Act (d) Pregnancy Discrimination Act**

3. The law that protects workers over age 40 is called the __?__ .

Study the following situations, answer the questions, then prepare arguments to support your answers.

4. When Servo-Technologies faced financial difficulties it began laying off employees. The majority were over the age of 40, although they constituted only 5 percent of the workforce. Is this legal? What statute, if any, was violated?

5. Har Foundry had a long history of employment discrimination against black people. When it began doing work for the federal government, it was required to submit a lot of additional paperwork. What plan should Har likely develop?

6. Boyce's mother, Martha, went to college after her husband died. She studied accounting and graduated when she was 52 years old. When she applied for positions with large accounting firms, she was never seriously considered because of her age. The firms seemed to hire only people in their 20s and 30s. Has Martha been the victim of illegal employment discrimination? What statute, if any, was violated?

7. Irene was a Jehovah's Witness. She believed that other members of her religion were more honest than the general population. When she was asked to hire a bank teller for her employer, she advertised the job as one available only for members of her religion. Is Irene's action legal? Would it be legal if Irene could prove in court that members of her religion were in fact more honest?

As an employee . . .

1. Approach every job in a professional manner. Do not seek to be judged on the basis of your race, sex, disability, national origin, or other group characteristic. Seek to be judged on the basis of your job performance.

2. Do not flirt with coworkers.

3. If you suspect that you are being discriminated against because of your membership in a protected class, contact the EEOC.

As an employer . . .

1. Do not ask questions on job applications that require the

PREVENT LEGAL DIFFICULTIES

disclosure of race, religion, sex, national origin, handicap, or pregnancy status.

2. Do not ask questions in job interviews about maternity plans, child care abilities, birth control practices, number of children, or other related factors.

3. Carefully train your supervisory employees both to avoid unwanted sexual comments and to respond intelligently to complaints about the unwelcome sexual conduct of coworkers.

4. Train your supervisory employees to focus on the job performance of their subordinates. Help them become sufficiently impartial so that their biases do not play a role in their employment decisions.

CHAPTER IN REVIEW

CONCEPTS IN BRIEF

1. The law attacks only unjustified discrimination.

2. Discrimination is illegal when it is based on race, color, sex, pregnancy, age, religion, disability, or national origin.

3. Employment discrimination laws generally apply only to firms with 15 or more employees.

4. There are two ways to prove unequal treatment: directly and indirectly.

5. The employer's principal defenses are business necessity, bona fide occupational qualification, and bona fide seniority system.

6. In a disparate impact case, the employee must show that the challenged practice caused a statis-tically significant difference in the percentage of protected class members in the pool of qualified applicants and the workforce.

7. Sexual harassment may consist of quid pro quo or hostile environment harassment. It can include any unwelcome sexual comment, gesture, or touch in the workplace.

8. Employers that have engaged in discrimination in the past and those with federal contracts may be required to implement affirmative action plans.

9. The employer should evaluate persons with dis-abilities only on their ability to do the essential functions of the job, possibly with reasonable accommodation.

YOUR LEGAL VOCABULARY

Match each statement with the term that it best defines. Some terms may not be used.

1. All the people who work for an employer that has been charged with employment discrimination

2. Interference with an employee's ability to work due to unwelcome com-ments, gestures, or touching of a sexual nature at work

3. Label for a workplace policy that does not seem on the surface to discrimi-nate against any protected class

4. When a business practice has the effect of reducing the number of workers from a protected class in the workforce

5. Job requirement that, of necessity, requires the hiring of a person of a particu-lar race, sex, or national origin

6. Linking a job requirement with underrepresentation of a protected class in the workforce

7. Groups that employment law protects

8. System that rewards employees for length of employment rather than merit

9. Those qualified for the job

10. Has the authority to investigate and conciliate complaints of job discrimina-tion and to prosecute suspected offenders

affirmative action plan
Americans with Disabilities Act (ADA)
applicant pool
bona fide occupational qualification (BGOQ)
bona fide seniority system
business necessity
causation
disability
disparate impact
employment discrimination
Equal Employment Opportunity Commission (EEOC)
hostile environment
neutral on its face
protected classes
quid pro quo
unequal treatment
workforce pool

11. Explain the difference between justified and unjustified discrimination.

12. Describe the element of disparate treatment and its main defenses.

13. Describe the elements of disparate impact and the way it is proven in court.

14. Explain what pattern and practice means.

WRITE ABOUT LEGAL CONCEPTS

15. Write an ad for a job as a server in a restaurant which creates direct evidence of disparate treatment.

16. Write a job description for a high school teacher which contains two types of job requirements. One type might create a disparate impact. Another type will not create a disparage impact.

Which requirements are likely to create a disparate impact?

17. **HOT DEBATE** Write a letter from the employer to Phan explaining the reasons he will not be hired for the job. Write a letter from Phan to the employer explaining why he should be hired.

THINK CRITICALLY ABOUT EVIDENCE

18. A fast-food restaurant surveyed its customers to determine their preference for food servers. The survey indicated that the customers clearly preferred girls to boys as servers. Therefore the restaurant advertised for and hired female servers only. This caused its business to increase substantially. Brett applied for a job but was denied an interview because of his sex. Is Brett entitled to an interview for this job?

19. Suppose you were in charge of hiring 15 workers to assemble very small electrical components to make a toy. If you believed that females of Asian ancestry were most likely to do this type of work well, would you limit your interviews to this group of persons only? Would your decision be different if you were certain there would be no legal risk?

20. Peter owned a small restaurant that specialized in Indian food. He had fewer than 15 employees and therefore knew that most employment dis-

crimination laws did not apply to him. Is Peter ethically obligated to follow these laws anyway?

21. Jerry owned a small printing shop. He had medical insurance coverage for all his employees. The policy was periodic, renewable once each year. One of Jerry's employees contracted acquired immune deficiency syndrome (AIDS). As the disease progressed, medical expenses for this employee skyrocketed, but they were covered by the insurance. A clause in the policy allowed the insurance company to raise the premium when the employer renewed the policy. On the annual renewal date, the insurance company presented Jerry with a 1,000 percent premium increase for continued coverage. If he paid the premiums, it would bankrupt his company. Is Jerry ethically obligated to pay the increase to protect his AIDS-infected employee? Has the insurance company acted ethically?

22. Ann Hopkins worked for Price Waterhouse, a large accounting firm. It was a practice to make professional employees partners in the firm after several years. Ann had been distinctively successful in the performance of her job. Of about 600 partners in the firm, only eight were women. When Ann was being considered for partnership, a committee of all male partners evaluated her. Several members of the committee made comments such as the following: "She should go to charm school;" "She needs to learn to dress, walk, and talk like a woman;" and "She should wear jewelry and makeup." Ultimately the committee turned her down for partnership. She was also told the comments of the members of the committee. Ann sued, claiming unequal treatment. Will she prevail? (*Price Waterhouse v. Hopkins,* 109 S. Ct. 1775)

23. Wards Cove Packing Company operated canneries in remote areas of Alaska. The workers in the canneries were primarily Filipinos and native Alaskans. These jobs were unskilled and the pay was low. The workers in non-cannery jobs were primarily white. These positions were highly skilled and highly paid. Antonio was a canner and he sued for employment discrimination. He claimed that the difference in the composition of the cannery and non-cannery workforces established that Wards Cove was illegally discriminating. Will he prevail? (*Wards Cove Packing Company v. Antonio,* 109 S. Ct. 2115)

24. Henderson worked as a radio dispatcher for the Dundee, Florida, police department. The police chief, she alleged, subjected her to repeated sexual comments and requests that she have sexual relations with him. She said that because she refused, the chief refused to allow her to attend the police academy. Further, he suspended her for two days for violating a minor office policy that had never been enforced before. She interpreted the suspension as a threat that she would be fired unless she gave in to her boss's advances. Eventually Henderson quit and then sued the city claiming sexual harassment. Will she prevail? (*Henderson v. City of Dundee,* 682 F.2d 897)

25. United Airlines had certain minimum requirements for the position of flight officer. The applicant had to have 500 hours of flight time, be 21 to 29 years of age, have a commercial pilot's license and instrument rating, and have a college degree. When Spurlock, a black, applied for the position, no one knew his race. At the time, he had only 204 hours of flight time and only two years of college, mostly in music education. His written application was rejected. Therefore Spurlock sued United, claiming racial discrimination in violation of Title VII of the Civil Rights Act. He pointed out that of approximately 5,900 flight officers in United's employ at the time, only nine were blacks. Was United guilty of illegal discrimination? (*Spurlock v. United Airlines, Inc.,* 475 F.2d 216)

26. Shiela Grove and David Klink were both tellers for Frostburg National Bank. Both were high school graduates. They had worked for the bank for the same length of time performing the same duties. Occasionally, Klink performed miscellaneous tasks that were not assigned to Grove. A male supervisor, David Willetts, set the salaries for both tellers. Klink's salary was significantly higher than Grove's. Has the bank violated the Equal Pay Act? (*Grove v. Frostburg National Bank,* 549 F. Supp. 922)

27. Johnson Controls, Inc., manufactures batteries made primarily of lead. Lead is a dangerous substance for pregnant women because exposure to lead can harm the fetus. For this reason, Johnson Controls excluded women who are pregnant or who are capable of bearing children from jobs that involve exposure to lead. Numerous plaintiffs, including a woman who had chosen to be sterilized to avoid losing her job, entered a federal district court class action suit alleging that Johnson Controls' policy constituted illegal sex discrimination under Title VII. Is this illegal discrimination? (499 U.S. 187, U.S. Sup. Ct., 1991)

CASE FOR LEGAL THINKING

EVIDENCE Theresa Harris worked as a manager for Forklift Systems, Inc. During Harris's two and one-half years with Forklift, she was subjected to gender-based insults and unwanted sexual innuendoes from Charles Hardy, the firm's president. Hardy told Harris, for example, "You're a woman, what do you know?" and "We need a man as the rental manager." Once he suggested that he and Harris negotiate her raise at the Holiday Inn. Hardy would also ask Harris and other female employees to get coins from his front pants pocket and to pick up objects that he threw on the ground. Most of these incidents occurred with other employees present.

After Harris complained to Hardy, he apologized and promised to stop. Later however, he inquired whether Harris had promised sex to a customer with whom she had concluded a deal on Forklift's behalf. Shortly thereafter Harris quit. She then sued Forklift for hostile environment sexual harassment in federal district court. Although it considered Harris's claim "a close case" the trial court found for Forklift. It did so in part because it concluded that Hardy's actions were not sufficiently severe to seriously affect Harris's psychological well being. Ultimately, Harris appealed to the U.S. Supreme Court.

REASONING Title VII makes it "an unlawful employment practice for an employer . . . to discriminate against any individual with respect to his compensation, terms, conditions, or privileges of employment, because of such individual's race color, religion, sex, or national origin." . . . The phrase "terms, conditions, or privileges of employment" evinces a Congressional intent to strike at the entire spectrum of disparate treatment of men and women in employment which includes requiring people to work in a discriminatorily hostile or abusive environment. When the workplace is permeated with discriminatory intimidation, ridicule and insult that is sufficiently severe or pervasive to alter the conditions of the victim's employment and create an abusive working environment, Title VII is violated.

This standard . . . takes a middle path between making actionable any conduct that is merely offensive and requiring the conduct to cause a tangible psychological injury. . . . Conduct that is not severe or pervasive enough to create an environment that a reasonable person would find hostile or abusive is beyond Title VII's purview. Likewise, if the victim does not subjectively perceive the environment to be abusive, there is no Title VII violation. But Title VII comes into play before the harassing conduct leads to a nervous breakdown. A discriminatorily abusive work environment, even one that does not seriously affect employees' psychological well-being, can and often will detract from employees' job performance, discourage employees from remaining on the job, or keep them from advancing in their careers. We therefore believe the district court erred in relying on whether the conduct seriously affected plaintiff's psychological well being or led her to suffer injury. Such an inquiry may needlessly focus the fact-finder's attention on concrete psychological harm, an element Title VII does not require.

DECISION Reversed and returned to the district court.

PRACTICE JUDGING

1. If Hardy had not made the statements regarding negotiating the raise, "at the Holiday Inn," would a different decision have been reached?

2. If Hardy had not made the statements regarding negotiating the raise, "at the Holiday Inn," and had not asked "female employees to get coins from his front pants pocket," would a different decision have been reached?

LESSONS

30-1 EMPLOYER'S TORT LIABILITY

30-2 WORKERS' COMPENSATION

30-3 OSHA

HOT DEBATE

Susan worked after school as a cashier at a local grocery store. In the parking lot outside, a robbery occurred. The robber, in an attempt to scare a bystander, fired a gun in the air twice. As he brought the weapon parallel to the ground, he fired again. This bullet struck Susan in the thigh causing paralysis in her right leg. The robber escaped. Susan sued the grocery store.

Where Do You Stand?

1. Why should the store not be required to pay Susan for her injury?

2. Why should the store be required to pay?

> ## G O A L S
>
> ● **Discuss the relationship among negligence suits, workers' compensation, and OSHA**
>
> ● **Explain when the employer is liable to the injured employee**

INTRODUCTION TO JOB SAFETY

WHAT'S YOUR VERDICT?

Crow was a steelworker working on the fifth story of a fifteen-story apartment project. His employer, Nu-Dimensions, Inc., provided all workers with protective helmets as required by law. One day, because of the intense heat, Crow removed his helmet and worked bareheaded while the supervisor was off-duty. A large bolt fell from the employer's construction crane and hit Crow on the head, fracturing his skull. It was common for objects to fall from the top floor of a construction project.

Could Crow recover any money for injuries due to this on-the-job injury?

Our legal system has three ways of dealing with injuries to employees. These are the negligence suit, workers' compensation, and job safety requirements. To understand these systems, you need to understand their history.

Negligence Suits

In the common-law approach, the employees sue the employer for damages by bringing a **negligence suit** against them. Employees win their negligence suits if they prove in court that the employer's negligence caused their injury. This system attempts to make the party at fault bear the financial loss associated with the injury. By making employers liable for the injuries caused by their negligence, the common law encouraged employers to protect employees.

REASONABLY SAFE WORKING CONDITIONS

The law imposes on employers the general duty to *provide reasonably safe working conditions* for employees. This duty may be violated in several ways. For example, an employer might fail to provide a safe workspace, safe tools, or safe machinery. Similarly, the employer would violate the duty if there were an insufficient number of co-workers to do a job safely or if employees were given inadequate safety instructions. When the employer violates the duty to provide safe working conditions and this causes injury to workers, the employer has probably committed the tort of negligence.

DIFFICULTIES FOR EMPLOYEES IN NEGLIGENCE SUITS

The common-law system had many problems. The injured worker had several reasons for not suing the employer. For example, the employee had to hire an attorney. The employee who sued also risked being fired. Even if an employee proved

that the employer's negligence caused the injury, the employee would not collect if the employer proved any one of the following **common-law defenses**:

- the employee had *assumed the risk* involved
- the employee was *negligent*
- the *negligence of a co-worker* caused the injury

Assumption of risk occurs when a person is aware of a danger that could cause injury, but voluntarily remains in the dangerous situation. In *What's Your Verdict?* Crow assumed the risk of being hurt by falling objects when he remained on the job after seeing other objects fall.

Contributory negligence means that the employee carelessly did something that contributed to her or his injury or death. This defense can be effective even when the employee's negligence is very slight in relation to the employer's. In *What's Your Verdict?* Crow was contributorily negligent because he removed his safety helmet.

Co-worker negligence means simply that a co-worker is the cause of the injury. It also prevents recovery from an employer. In *What's Your Verdict?* if the employer could show that a co-worker caused the bolt to fall, the employer would not be liable. These common-law defenses prevented employees from winning most negligence suits. However, until the early 1900s, the negligence suit was the only recourse for workers injured on the job.

Workers' Compensation

Because employees had great difficulty in winning negligence suits, around 1890–1910 state legislatures enacted laws to help injured employees. These **workers' compensation statutes** require most employers to obtain insurance to pay benefits to injured employees. The benefits are paid without regard to fault. So the insurance pays even when the employer is not a cause of the injury.

The workers' compensation system was created as a *substitute* for negligence suits. If the injured employee is covered by workers' compensation, no negligence suit is ordinarily allowed against the employer. On the other hand, if a worker is not covered by workers' compensation, then the negligence suit *is* allowed. Because the amount an employer must pay for workers' compensation insurance is somewhat related to the firm's safety record, employers still have an incentive to maintain a safe workplace.

Occupational Safety and Health Administration

The third approach relies on workplace safety standards enacted and enforced by federal and state administrative agencies. The **Occupational Safety and Health Administration (OSHA)** enacts safety regulations and inspects workplaces. It can impose fines and even shut down plants when it finds violations of its laws. OSHA does not allocate loss based on fault (as in negligence suits) or provide money for medical expenses without regard to fault (as in workers' compensation). Rather, it seeks to make the workplace safer by trying to *prevent* injury.

In *What's Your Verdict?* Crow probably could not recover from his employer in a suit for negligence because Crow's failure to wear his helmet was a cause of his injury. Crow was more at fault than the employer was. If the employer had workers' compensation coverage, Crow would not be allowed to sue the employer. Workers' compensation could probably pay some of Crow's lost wages and all of his medical expenses. The injury might lead to an OSHA investigation. If OSHA finds that any of its safety regulations have

been violated, it would require the unsafe condition to be eliminated.

Additionally, it might fine the employer.

RECOVERING FROM THE EMPLOYER FOR NEGLIGENCE

WHAT'S YOUR VERDICT?

Shue worked as a model for the Carlisle Modeling Agency. While modeling for a magazine layout at Carlisle's studio, she was raped by the photographer who had been hired by Carlisle.

Can Shue recover from Carlisle for her injuries?

The general rule is that an employee cannot sue the employer for on-the-job injuries if the employee is covered by workers' compensation. But there are several important exceptions. In these exceptional circumstances, an injured employee (or the family of an employee who is killed on the job) can still sue the employer for negligence. The cases differ in the extent to which they allow common-law defenses. In some situations, no common-law defense is available, in others all defenses are available.

Employer Fails to Provide Workers' Comp Insurance

If state law requires that an employee be covered but the employer has not purchased workers' compensation insurance, the injured employee can sue the employer for negligence. In these cases, the employer generally may not use the employers' common-law defenses of assumption of the risk, contributory negligence, or co-worker negligence. Thus, the employee has the possibility of recovering large sums of money while the employer is almost defenseless. This possibility creates a great incentive for the employer to purchase workers' compensation coverage.

Employee Coverage Not Required

If an employee is not required to be covered by workers' compensation and is injured because of the employer's negligence, the employee may sue the employer. In these cases, the employer may usually use all the common-law defenses.

Injury Not Covered by Workers' Compensation

In some cases, the employee is injured because of the negligence of the employer but workers' compensation does not cover the injury. In *What's Your Verdict?* Shue's injury did not arise from a risk of her work. There is nothing about being a model that significantly increases the risk of being raped. So the injury was not covered by workers' compensation. But Shue could sue Carlisle for not adequately screening its employees. While the law would allow Carlisle to assert the defenses of contributory negligence or assumption of the risk, neither is likely to be an effective defense. Therefore, Shue is likely to prevail.

Employer Commits an Intentional Tort

In some states, even when covered by workers' compensation, an employee may sue the employer for intentional actions that the employer knows will cause injury. This most often occurs when the conduct of the employer is criminal, is an intentional tort, or is an intentional violation of a safety regulation.

THINK ABOUT LEGAL CONCEPTS

Answer the following questions about legal concepts.

1. Which of the following is *not* a common-law defense to a negligence suit against an employer? **(a) contributory negligence (b) co-worker negligence (c) OSHA violations in the workplace (d) assumption of the risk**

2. If an employee is covered by workers compensation, then that worker generally cannot bring a suit against the employer for negligence. **True or False?**

THINK CRITICALLY ABOUT EVIDENCE

Study the following situations, answer the questions, then prepare arguments to support your answers.

3. If you were working at a car wash and were injured when you slipped on the wet floor because a friend who worked there distracted your attention by throwing a wet towel at your head, which common-law defense would be most useful to the car wash owner in a negligence suit?

4. Jameston, a school custodian, is injured when student lockers fall on him while he is cleaning the hallway. All of the schools' employees are covered by the school's workers' compensation insurance policy. Has the school violated its duty to provide a safe workplace? Can Jameston recover in a suit against the school for violation of this duty?

5. Mary Lou works as a bar tender in an upscale restaurant. She is not covered by workers' compensation. When opening a refrigerator, an electrical short was created, Mary Lou was shocked, fell backwards, and hit her head on the floor suffering a concussion. Has the restaurant violated its duty to provide a safe workplace? Can Mary Lou recover in a negligence suit against the restaurant?

GOALS

- Determine the injuries for which workers' compensation is liable
- Describe the defenses available to workers' compensation insurers
- Identify employees who need not be covered by workers' compensation

OPERATION OF WORKERS' COMPENSATION

WHAT'S YOUR VERDICT?

Turpin was a production-line worker in a steel desk factory. His job was to use a hydraulic shear to cut large pieces of sheet metal into smaller sizes for desk drawers. One morning while Turpin was setting up his shear, Gillis, his friend and co-worker, watched. Gillis believed that the main power supply for the machine was off. As a joke, he pressed the two "ON" buttons while Turpin's arm was under the shear's blade. Turpin's arm was cut off.

Can Turpin recover from his employer for the loss of his arm?

Negligence suits under the common law were risky for both employers and employees. Most injured employees collected nothing because of the common-law defenses. However, when employees did win, they sometimes were awarded amounts that would bankrupt the employer. Today's workers' compensation laws reflect a public policy objective of moving away from allocating risks based on fault and toward no fault. Thus, the common-law defenses are not available to the insurer. The cost of this insurance is passed along to consumers in the form of slightly higher prices for goods and services.

In *What's Your Verdict?* Turpin would recover workers' compensation benefits even though the injury was caused by a co-worker and the employer was not at fault. Note that before workers' compensation, no money would have been paid, because Turpin only would have been able to sue for negligence. He probably would have lost this suit against his employer because of the defense of co-worker negligence. Although the co-worker, Gillis, was legally responsible, he probably had no money to pay a judgment.

General Coverage

Employees are generally protected by workers' compensation insurance if they are injured

1. by accident or disease, including job-related stress
2. in the scope of employment
3. from risks of that employment

Generally, these terms are satisfied if a worker is injured on the job and the injury is caused by the work.

IN THIS CASE

Boal assembled fire hydrants for the Richmond Foundry. The job required him to lift finished fire hydrants weighing up to 140 pounds. One day, while lifting fire hydrants, Boal suffered a hernia. Boal can collect workers' compensation benefits.

Winning a Workers' Compensation Award

The decision about whether a person is entitled to benefits is made at a hearing conducted by a state administrative agency. This agency is often called the Workers' Compensation Board or the Industrial Accident Commission.

Hearing procedures for the Workers' Compensation Board and the Industrial Accident Commission are much less complicated than those of a trial. For small claims, the injured worker does not need a lawyer. However, when the claim or injury is significant, a lawyer who is a specialist in the field should represent the person.

What Does the Injured Employee Receive?

If a worker covered by workers' compensation is injured because of the job, the worker becomes entitled to benefits. Sometimes there is a lump-sum payment to cover such things as pain and suffering involved with injuries such as loss of a hand, or loss of life. All medical expenses usually are covered. Most states will also pay a percentage of lost wages. Compensation for lost wages is typically about 80 percent. In nearly every case, the payment is much less than if the injured party had won a negligence suit.

If an accident makes it impossible for a worker to continue in the former job, most states also pay for vocational rehabilitation. **Vocational rehabilitation** is training for another type of job. Often the amount of the benefit is increased if the employer is grossly negligent or reduced if the employee is grossly negligent. A 10 percent increase or reduction is typical.

Paying for the Insurance

Workers' compensation benefits are paid from one of three sources. Employers may purchase a workers' compensation insurance policy from a private insurance company, participate in a state-administered workers' compensation fund, or be self-insured. Insurance companies and state funds charge amounts that reflect the riskiness of the business and each employer's safety history. The amount paid out by those that are self-insured depends on the number and severity of workplace injuries. So employers have an incentive to make the workplace safe to reduce their costs of workers' compensation coverage.

INJURIES COVERED

WHAT'S YOUR VERDICT?

Johnson, a jailer for the Tarrant County Sheriff's Department, was cleaning his service revolver at his residence at approximately 9:15 p.m. when he accidentally discharged his revolver into his left leg and foot. Johnson had reloaded the revolver after cleaning it and left the room temporarily. When he returned, he saw oil dripping from the revolver. He then picked it up, spun the cylinder to disperse the oil, and having forgotten that he reloaded it, pulled the trigger.

Can Johnson recover workers' compensation for this injury?

Scope of Employment

To recover from workers' compensation, the injured employee must have been acting within the scope of employment at the time of the injury. Scope of employment generally means acting for the benefit of the employer. For example, an auto accident while driving to or from work would usually not be within the scope of employment because you do that primarily for yourself. On the other hand, an employee doing an errand for the employer on the way home from work is likely to be within the scope of employment.

The facts in *What's Your Verdict?* were adapted from a Texas case where the court wrote:

> The Texas Workers' Compensation Act provides a definition of scope of employment: "an activity performed by an employee while engaged in or about the furtherance of the affairs or business of the employer." All county jailers were required to own a weapon, and each officer had the responsibility for cleaning and maintaining his or her own weapon. Because the sheriff's department did not provide an area at the jail for officers to clean their weapons, officers were permitted to clean their weapons at home or "anywhere," as long as they showed up for work each day with a clean weapon. Johnson is entitled to workers' compensation. (*Esis, Inc., v. Johnson*, 908 S.W.2d 554)

Risks of Employment

There are risks associated with jobs and these are the risks that workers' compensation generally covers. Thus, while a person assembling heavy fire hydrants could recover for a hernia, a clerical worker who suffered a hernia while picking a piece of paper off the floor might not collect benefits. That is because the injury may not have been caused by the job, but rather by weak abdominal muscles.

Similarly, a person who suffers a stroke or heart attack on the job will not be entitled to death benefits

IN THIS CASE

Stacy Lee Bratcher worked for Cherokee Drilling & Development Corporation. On the day he died, he complained that he had not slept much the past few days and said he was going to the company's trailer to take a nap. A member of the crew later found that Mr. Bratcher had collapsed across the edge of the bathtub in the trailer. Mr. Bratcher's widow sued for death benefits for an injury alleged to have been sustained in the course of employment. Dr. Christopher L. Hall who performed the autopsy concluded that the "manner of death was natural, rather than work-related." Bratcher had an aneurysm that could have burst at any time. The injury arose from a personal defect which proved to be fatal from a strain totally unrelated to the deceased's employment. The risk was one Mr. Bratcher would have confronted irrespective of type of employment. Mr. Bratcher's widow may not recover workers' compensation. (*Employers' Casualty Company v. Bratch*, 823 S.W.2d 719)

unless there are features of the job that led to these events. In all states insurers are not liable to employees who intentionally injure themselves.

Workers' Compensation or Negligence

Injured employees sometimes desire to sue for employer negligence rather than accept the small payments offered by workers' compensation. This is particularly true where there are major injuries. So in some cases, a worker may argue that an injury was caused by the employer's negligence but that it was not a risk of the job or was outside the scope of employment.

IN THIS CASE

Sharon worked for Safeway Supermarkets. After finishing her shift as a butcher, she walked through the store toward the parking lot and stepped in a puddle of Pepsi that hadn't been properly mopped up. She fell and injured her back. Because the workers' compensation awards are small in her state, she wanted to sue for employer's negligence. She claimed she was acting outside the scope of her employment at the time of the accident. The argument was rejected on the grounds that workers' compensation covers workers who are at the job site for short periods before and after work.

WHO IS NOT COVERED?

WHAT'S YOUR VERDICT?

Boy Scout Troop 1416 was looking for a moneymaking project to help fund its July camping trip. It contacted Southern Manufacturing which hired the troop on a one-time basis to wash all the company cars.

Are the Scouts covered by workers' compensation?

Not all workers are required to be covered by a plan of workers' compensation.

FEW WORKERS OR CASUAL WORKERS

Frequently, companies with three or fewer employees are not required to provide workers' compensation insurance. Similarly, in most states, casual workers need not be covered. **Casual workers** are those who do not work regularly for one employer. In *What's Your Verdict?* the Scouts would be casual workers. In addition, servants, housekeepers, and agricul-

A Question of ETHICS

Smyth, who was just starting a new lumberyard, hired only two employees. He did not purchase workers' compensation insurance for them. When asked why, he said, "There are two reasons: state law doesn't require it and I don't have enough money invested in the business to worry. If someone sues the corporation, I'll just take it into bankruptcy." Is Smyth's conduct ethical?

tural workers often are not required to be covered.

INDEPENDENT CONTRACTORS Independent contractors need not be covered. An independent contractor is someone hired to accomplish a task, but who is *not supervised* while doing so. If you hired a neighbor to repair your car's broken transmission, he or she would probably be an independent contractor, not an employee.

OTHER SYSTEMS OF COVERAGE Rather than being covered by state workers' compensation laws, employees of railroads, airlines, trucking firms, and other common carriers engaged in interstate commerce are governed by a special federal law. Longshore and harbor workers also operate under a different federal law and are not subject to state workers' compensation laws. A special statute also governs the crew on seagoing vessels. Often state and federal employees are covered by a separate system.

THINK ABOUT LEGAL CONCEPTS

Answer the following questions about legal concepts.

1. When a worker is covered by workers' compensation, this is generally the employee's exclusive remedy for job-related injuries. **True or False?**

2. Which defenses are available to an insurer when sued by an injured employee? **(a) contributory negligence (b) assumption of the risk (c) co-worker negligence (d) none of the above**

3. Which defenses are available to an insurer when sued by an injured employee? **(a) contributory negligence (b) assumption of the risk (c) co-worker negligence (d) injury arose outside scope of employment**

4. Which defenses are available to an insurer when sued by an injured employee? **(a) assumption of the risk (b) injury arose outside scope of employment (c) injury was not a risk of the job (d) both b and c**

THINK CRITICALLY ABOUT EVIDENCE

Study the following situations, answer the questions, then prepare arguments to support your answers.

5. Wynett was a delivery driver for Federal Express. One Friday, he departed from his delivery route to see his girlfriend, Latasha. Latasha lived nearly 60 miles away from Wynett's delivery area. As he pulled up to Latasha's home, he was hit in the rear end by a large tractor-trailer. This caused whiplash. Was this injury a risk of the employment? Was Wynett acting within the scope of employment? Can Wynett recover workers' compensation for this injury?

6. Lambert hired Mayer, a casual worker, to apply anhydrous ammonia, a fertilizer, to the soil on her farm. Lambert was not required to provide workers' compensation insurance, so Mayer was not covered. Lambert said to Mayer, "Be careful when you handle this stuff; it might burn you." However, Mayer had never used this type of equipment before, and Lambert did not explain to him how to handle the tank or the hose or what to do if he was sprayed on his body. Mayer lost control of the hose and was sprayed in the face with the chemical, blinding him in one eye. He sued Lambert for negligence, claiming that he was not properly instructed in how to handle the equipment. Who wins?

7. Jerold hired a construction worker to install a shake shingle roof on his home. The work was to be completed within 30 days. All the decisions about materials, methods, and time when the work would be done were left to the contractor. Must Jerold purchase workers' compensation insurance for the contractor? Why or why not?

8. A 27-year-old retail store employee was raped twice by a store security guard. The security guard had been convicted of violent sex crimes before the store hired him. In her lawsuit the plaintiff sought $50 million, plus punitive damages. The store has asked a judge to dismiss the woman's lawsuit, contending that her only recourse is to pursue a workers' compensation claim. Is rape a risk of the job? What evidence of negligence by the employer is there here? If there is a negligence suit against the employer, what defenses could the employer assert?

GOALS

- **Name two ways OSHA protects employees**
- **Explain how OSHA obtains employer compliance with its requirements**

HOW DOES OSHA PROTECT EMPLOYEES?

WHAT'S YOUR VERDICT?

Browning Processing Company prepares fruits and vegetables for the market. An OSHA inspector ordered the company to install clutches on the prune-pitting machines and to provide electrical grounding of all electric typewriters and word processors.

Must Browning comply?

In 1970, the U.S. Congress enacted the **Occupational Safety and Health Act (OSHA)**. This law created the Occupational Safety and Health Administration and empowered it to enact rules and regulations designed to achieve safety in the workplace. The Department of Labor enforces those rules.

The basic policy behind this legislation was to *directly prevent* injuries by requiring that workplaces be safe. This law applies to firms with 11 or more employees engaged in interstate commerce. State administrative agencies often apply similar safety laws to smaller organizations or those not engaged in interstate commerce.

The General Duty Clause

In general, OSHA enforces two types of laws. The first type is the **general duty clause**. It requires that employers provide a place of employment free from hazards that are likely to cause death or serious physical harm. If this general duty requirement is violated, OSHA can fine the company and/or shut down the plant.

Specific Regulations

The second type of OSHA law includes specific workplace safety regulations. Many of these regulations were hastily established shortly after this federal administrative agency was formed. These regulations cover most aspects of work. They spell out safety training requirements; safety clothing and equipment to be worn by workers; and the construction, maintenance, and shielding of equipment.

Minimum standards are established for lighting, ventilation, and sanitation. For example, OSHA specifies that spray paint booths must be vented to the exterior of the building and that they must be constructed of metal rather than wood. Another example is the requirement that hair protection (hairnets) be worn when working near equipment such as drills.

Minor violations of OSHA regulations are usually resolved by bringing the workplace into compliance, although employers can be fined. In *What's Your Verdict?* Browning Processing would be required to comply with OSHA's demands because the lack of clutches and electrical grounding violates specific OSHA regulations. If the company did not comply, it could be fined.

Workplace Inspection

OSHA uses workplace inspections to ensure compliance with its general

FYI

Both the *Occupational Safety and Health Act* and the *Occupational Safety and Health Administration* are commonly referred to as OSHA.

A Question of ETHICS ?

Your friend complained about fumes at her workplace. She said the fumes were causing eye burn, headaches, and nausea. She asked the company to install exhaust fans, but it did not. So she reported the problem to OSHA. Shortly after, her employer told her that her services were no longer needed, so she left. You are aware that fumes where you work are causing health problems for many employees. Are you ethically obligated to complain to OSHA even if that means risking your job? Will the law protect you if you report safety violations to OSHA?

Canada

Canada Labour Code

Occupational Health and Safety in Canada is regulated by Part II of the Canada Labour Code. In addition to defining the duties of employers and employees, Part II of the Code also establishes three employee rights: (1) the right to know about workplace hazards, (2) the right to participate in correcting those hazards, and (3) the right to refuse dangerous work.

The last major amendments to Part II of the Code passed the Canadian Parliament in 1984. The federal government in Canada plans to change the code dealing with workplace safety issues. With these proposed changes, the framers of the legislation (representing labour, management and government) are aiming for a better balance between the roles and responsibilities of employers, employees, and government.

A mechanism for an "internal resolution process" that will guide workplace parties without government intervention will be included in the revised legislation.

duty clause and specific regulations. While an employer may deny OSHA inspectors access to the workplace, inspectors can easily obtain a search warrant giving them authority to inspect.

Employers are required to file periodic safety reports describing work-related injuries. If there is an injury requiring hospitalization of three or more employees or resulting in a death, the Department of Labor must be notified within eight hours. These reports often prompt OSHA inspections.

Employees also may anonymously call OSHA to report safety violations. OSHA will then send inspectors to the workplace. Employers may not discriminate against workers who

have informed OSHA of safety violations.

Dealing With OSHA Violations

In most simple cases, employers deal with OSHA officials without a lawyer. The problems usually involve technical engineering and safety issues rather than legal issues. Inspectors and company supervisors are best equipped to deal with these problems. However, some OSHA violations become serious because the cost of compliance can be prohibitive, pushing some companies into bankruptcy. In these situations, the employer needs immediate expert legal help. Unless one acts quickly, some rights to appeal the safety citation may be lost.

JOB SAFETY & HEALTH PROTECTION

The Occupational Safety and Health Act of 1970 provides job safety and health protection for workers by promoting safe and healthful working conditions throughout the Nation. Provisions of the Act include the following:

Employers

All employers must furnish to employees employment and a place of employment free from recognized hazards that are causing or are likely to cause death or serious harm to employees. Employers must comply with occupational safety and health standards issued under the Act.

Employees

Employees must comply with all occupational safety and health standards, rules, regulations and orders issued under the Act that apply to their own actions and conduct on the job.

The Occupational Safety and Health Administration (OSHA) of the U.S. Department of Labor has the primary responsibility for administering the Act. OSHA issues occupational safety and health standards, and its Compliance Safety and Health Officers conduct jobsite inspections to help ensure compliance with the Act.

Inspection

The Act requires that a representative of the employer and a representative authorized by the employees be given an opportunity to accompany the OSHA inspector for the purpose of aiding the inspection.

Where there is no authorized employee representative, the OSHA Compliance Officer must consult with a reasonable number of employees concerning safety and health conditions in the workplace.

Complaint

Employees or their representatives have the right to file a complaint with the nearest OSHA office requesting an inspection if they believe unsafe or unhealthful conditions exist in their workplace. OSHA will withhold, on request, names of employees complaining.

The Act provides that employees may not be discharged or discriminated against in any way for filing safety and health complaints or for otherwise exercising their rights under the Act.

Employees who believe they have been discriminated against may file a complaint with their nearest OSHA office within 30 days of the alleged discriminatory action.

Citation

If upon inspection OSHA believes an employer has violated the Act, a citation alleging such violations will be issued to the employer. Each citation will specify a time period within which the alleged violation must be corrected.

The OSHA citation must be prominently displayed at or near the place of alleged violation for three days, or until it is corrected, whichever is later, to warn employees of dangers that may exist there.

Proposed Penalty

The Act provides for mandatory civil penalties against employers of up to $7,000 for each serious violation and for optional penalties of up to $7,000 for each nonserious violation. Penalties of up to $7,000 per day may be proposed for failure to correct violations within the proposed time period and for each day the violation continues beyond the prescribed abatement date. Also, any employer who willfully or repeatedly violates the Act may be assessed penalties of up to $70,000 for each such violation. A minimum penalty of $5,000 may be imposed for each willful violation. A violation of posting requirements can bring a penalty of up to $7,000.

There are also provisions for criminal penalties. Any willful violation resulting in the death of any employee, upon conviction, is punishable by a fine of up to $250,000 (or $500,000 if the employer is a corporation), or by imprisonment for up to six months, or both. A second conviction of an employer doubles the possible term of imprisonment. Falsifying records, reports, or applications is punishable by a fine of $10,000 or up to six months in jail or both.

Voluntary Activity

While providing penalties for violations, the Act also encourages efforts by labor and management, before an OSHA inspection, to reduce workplace hazards voluntarily and to develop and improve safety and health programs in all workplaces and industries. OSHA's Voluntary Protection Programs recognize outstanding efforts of this nature.

OSHA has published Safety and Health Program Management Guidelines to assist employers in establishing or perfecting programs to prevent or control employee exposure to workplace hazards. There are many public and private organizations that can provide information and assistance in this effort, if requested. Also, your local OSHA office can provide considerable help and advice on solving safety and health problems or can refer you to other sources for help such as training.

Consultation

Free assistance in identifying and correcting hazards and in improving safety and health management is available to employers, without citation or penalty, through OSHA-supported programs in each State. These programs are usually administered by the State Labor or Health department or a State university.

Posting Instructions

Employers in States operating OSHA approved State Plans should obtain and post the State's equivalent poster.

Under provisions of Title 29, Code of Federal Regulations, Part 1903.2(a)(1) employers must post this notice (or facsimile) in a conspicuous place where notices to employees are customarily posted.

More Information

Additional information and copies of the Act, OSHA safety and health standards, and other applicable regulations may be obtained from your employer or from the nearest OSHA Regional Office in the following locations:

Atlanta, GA	(404) 562-2300
Boston, MA	(617) 565-9860
Chicago, IL	(312) 353-2220
Dallas, TX	(214) 767-4731
Denver, CO	(303) 844-1600
Kansas City, MO	(816) 426-5861
New York, NY	(212) 337-2378
Philadelphia, PA	(215) 596-1201
San Francisco, CA	(415) 975-4310
Seattle, WA	(206) 553-5930

Washington, DC
1997 (Reprinted)
OSHA 2203

Alexis M. Herman, Secretary of Labor

U.S. Department of Labor
Occupational Safety and Health Administration

This information will be made available to sensory impaired individuals upon request.
Voice phone: (202) 219-8615; TDD message referral phone: 1-800-326-2577

Answer the following questions about legal concepts.

1. Which of the following is not a way our legal system deals with employee injuries? **(a) negligence suit (b) arbitration (c) workers' compensation (d) job safety requirements**

2. OSHA's general duty clause requires employers to provide a "workplace free from hazards." **True or False?**

3. OSHA has power to shut down an unsafe plants that violate the general duty clause. **True or False?**

4. OSHA regulations control such specific issues as how paint booths must be ventilated. **True or False?**

Study the following situations, answer the questions, then prepare arguments to support your answers.

5. Bill operated a bakery with only 16 employees selling bread in two states. Is the bakery subject to regulation by OSHA?

6. ABCO stored trichlorethelene in 55 gallon drums at floor level. A forklift nicked a drum and the liquid spilled out without people immediately realizing it. Fumes spread throughout the plant. Five people fainted. The fire department was called and ambulances took the workers to the hospital. The chemical was cleaned up within 2 hours and production restored. What legal obligations remain for ABCO?

7. Circo-Pacific manufactured circuit boards—the base on which electrical components are mounted by soldering. Peery worked as a dip solderer, inserting the bare boards into a small tub of molten solder to coat the copper circuits. The building in which he worked leaked and, when it rained, water dripped into the tub and splashed molten solder onto Peery's arm, causing numerous slight burns—the largest about half the size of a pencil eraser. Peery complained to his boss about the problem several times but his boss dismissed the complaints saying, "Don't be such a sissy." Peery finally complained to OSHA. An inspector arrived at the plant and cited the company. The fine was $500. A month later, Peery was transferred to a job that paid much less than that of dip solderer. He complained to OSHA that he was being discriminated against because of his complaint. Is he correct? What is the result?

As an employee . . .

1. Determine whether you would be covered by workers' compensation insurance before accepting a job involving safety risks.

2. Follow all safety precautions, use all safety devices prescribed for your job, and follow the employer's safety regulations.

3. Think about the elements of your work that might cause injury to you or to a co-worker. If there are serious risks, discuss them in a friendly way with your boss. If your boss is not helpful, consider discussing the situation with the people at OSHA.

PREVENT LEGAL DIFFICULTIES

As an employer . . .

1. Inspect your workplace to identify and to eliminate risks to the safety and health of your workers.

2. Identify lawyers in your area who specialize in employment law.

3. Verify that all your workers are covered by workers' compensation. If some are not covered, ask your attorney to review their status.

4. If you hire servants, agricultural or casual workers, or independent contractors who are not covered by workers' compensation, ask your lawyer for advice on how to limit your liability for injuries to them.

5. Consider asking OSHA inspectors to conduct an informal inspection of your workplace.

CHAPTER IN REVIEW

CONCEPTS IN BRIEF

1. Negligence suits are based on determining who is at fault. These suits generally cannot be brought if the injured worker is covered by workers' compensation.

2. Negligence suits can be brought by an injured worker if (a) a worker should have been covered by workers' compensation but was not, (b) a worker was not required to be covered by workers' compensation, (c) the injury to the worker is not covered by workers' compensation, or (d) the employer does something that it knows will cause injury.

3. In a suit for negligence, the worker must establish that the employer was negligent and this caused the injury.

4. Even when the employer is negligent, the worker cannot win if the employer can establish any of the applicable common-law defenses.

5. Workers' compensation pays benefits to those injured in the course of their employment from the risks of the job. The benefits usually include all medical payments, some lost wages, and sometimes, vocational rehabilitation.

6. The employer pays the workers' compensation premiums. The amount is based in part on the safety record of the employer.

7. OSHA enforces both a general duty clause and specific workplace regulations.

8. OSHA inspectors can obtain search warrants to inspect the workplace. Most violations do not involve a fine if the violation is eliminated. Serious violations can lead to heavy fines and plant closing.

YOUR LEGAL VOCABULARY

Match each statement with the term that it best defines. Some terms may not be used.

1. When a worker knows there is danger on the job but agrees to do it anyway

2. Retraining of an injured worker

3. Laws that provide compensation for workers (or their dependents) when the workers are injured (or killed) in the course of employment

4. Federal agency that administers the Occupational Safety and Health Act

5. Persons who do not work regularly for a certain employer

6. When a worker does something to partially cause his or her own injury

7. Part of the Occupational Safety and Health Act requiring that employers provide a workplace free from hazards likely to cause serious harm or death

8. A suit, brought by an employee against an employer, that claims the employer's carelessness caused the employee's injury

9. Consists of assumption of risk, contributory negligence, and negligence of a co-worker

10. A fellow employee is responsible for one part of your injury

assumption of risk
casual workers
common-law defenses
contributory negligence
co-worker negligence
general duty clause
negligence suit
Occupational Safety and Health Act (OSHA)
Occupational Safety and Health Administration (OSHA)
vocational rehabilitation
workers' compensation statutes

11. Describe when an employee can maintain a negligence suit against an employer.

12. Describe the employer's safety duty under tort law.

13. Invent a situation where an employer would be able to escape liability in a negligence suit by an injured employee by asserting the defense of contributory negligence.

WRITE ABOUT LEGAL CONCEPTS

14. Write a scenario similar to *What's Your Verdict?* Make the evidence suggest that an employee who is injured could sue for employer negligence.

15. Write one paragraph describing how the employer's liability for negligence is determined. Write a second paragraph describing how an insurer's liability for workers' compensation is determined.

16. Write a scenario similar to *What's Your Verdict?* Make the evidence suggest that an employee who is injured was acting outside the scope of employment.

17. **HOT DEBATE** Write a letter from the store's lawyer to Susan's lawyer claiming why it is not responsible for her injury.

THINK CRITICALLY ABOUT EVIDENCE

18. Blake worked for West Oregon Lumber Company as a wood sorter. In violation of Oregon law, the company did not carry workers' compensation insurance. While sorting wood on a table, Blake knocked a piece off, and it fell and hit his foot. Blake sued the employer for negligence. The lumber company asserted contributory negligence as an employer's defense. Will Blake win?

19. Atlas Warehouse was equipped with an old-fashioned freight elevator that had a manually operated gate on each floor. When the elevator reached a floor, the employee had to raise the gate and then lower it after getting off. Lacey, a supervisor delivering a message to Ritter, stepped off the elevator after raising the gate. She did not lower the gate because she intended to get back on immediately. While she was talking with Ritter, the elevator was moved to another floor. After her conversation, Lacey returned to the elevator. Not noticing it had been moved, she stepped into the shaft and fell to her death. What would be the employer's liability in a negligence suit?

20. Fries and Brack were employed as truck drivers by different companies, and both were covered by workers' compensation. Late one afternoon, Fries was rushing to make a delivery. In haste, Fries negligently rammed into Brack's truck. Brack suffered fatal injuries. Brack's widow later received a lump-sum workers' compensation benefit of $55,000. Is this all she can collect?

21. Randle worked at the Hide Tanning Company, which employed only two people. The company did not carry workers' compensation insurance because the state law did not apply to very small firms. A large wooden vat of acid with an open top was mounted on a wooden stand six feet off the ground. Because the stand was old and rickety, the person working near it was afraid that it would collapse and spill the acid on them. An OSHA inspector cited the company for violation of the general duty clause. Two days after the citation, the vat broke, spilling acid on Randle. Randle sued the employer and introduced the citation as evidence of the company's negligence. The company objected, claiming that OSHA inspections have nothing to do with suits for employer's negligence. Is the company correct?

22. Abell and his brother had been hired as laborers to help prepare the grounds for the county fair. They were to be paid by the hour and were to furnish their own tools. No understanding was reached concerning the length of their employment, but it was understood that it would be "for one or two weeks." The work to be done consisted of "odd jobs," such as cleaning up and making minor repairs. Abell died when he was struck by a tractor while working. In light of these facts, were Abell's survivors entitled to workers' compensation benefits? (*Wood v. Abell*, 300 A.2d 665)

23. Thornton was employed as production foreman with the defendant corporation. On several occasions, Thornton had reprimanded an employee, Sozio, for failure to wear safety glasses and had reported this to the employer. On one occasion, Sozio threatened Thornton, saying, "I'll take care of your eyes later." Nine days after Sozio's employment had been terminated, Thornton saw him in a bar. At that time Sozio said, "Remember me, remember me?" and attacked Thornton, causing him to lose the sight of one eye. Thornton claims that he is entitled to workers' compensation benefits because his injuries arose out of and had their origin in his employment and because the injuries were in the course of the employment. His employer claims that the injuries did not occur on the job even though they did arise out of the employment. Sozio, no longer an employee, had deliberately inflicted the injuries. Therefore, the employer argues, Thornton is not entitled to workers' compensation benefits. Is Thornton entitled to benefits? (*Thornton v. Chamberlain Manufacturing Corporation*, 62 NJ. 235, 300 A.2d 146)

24. Bailey managed a gasoline station. He was required to use his station wagon to make emergency calls for the station. Tools were carried in the car, and the service station paid for the gas and oil it used. Bailey owned another car that was used as a "family car." One morning while driving to work, Bailey was struck and killed by a train. His wife filed a claim for workers' compensation benefits. The Industrial Commission denied the claim, stating that travel to and from work is not covered by workers' compensation insurance. Was Bailey's death caused by his work? Is his widow entitled to the death benefit? (*Bailey v. Utah State Industrial Commission*, 16 P.2d 208, Utah)

25. Eckis, age 22, was a full-time employee of Sea World, an amusement park. Eckis served as secretary for Burgess, the director of animal training. Eckis, who was an excellent swimmer, had worked as a model. When Burgess asked her to ride "Shamu, the Killer Whale" in a bikini for some publicity pictures, she eagerly agreed. Burgess knew Shamu was conditioned to being ridden only by persons wearing wet suits and had attacked riders in bathing suits. Eckis was warned in general terms of the danger, and she fell off during one practice session while wearing a wet suit. When a trainer told Eckis he would not watch her ride Shamu "because it was really dangerous," Burgess reassured Eckis and she rode Shamu three different times. Each time she wore a bikini instead of a wet suit. During the second ride, Shamu's tail was fluttering, indicating that the whale was upset. During the third ride, Eckis fell off and Shamu bit her on her legs and hips and held her in the tank until she was rescued. As an employee, Eckis qualified for modest workers' compensation payments but had no other insurance benefits. Therefore, she sued for more money in a civil action. She claimed that the employer was negligent, had defrauded her, and was liable for the acts of an animal with dangerous tendencies. The jury awarded Eckis damages of $75,000. Sea World appealed. Was workers' compensation Eckis's only remedy? (*Eckis v. Sea World Corporation*, 64 Cal. App. 3d 1)

26. Barlow's Inc. was an electrical and plumbing contractor. An OSHA inspector appeared at Barlow's place of business and asked to inspect the premises. There had been no injuries at Barlow's and the inspector did not possess a search warrant. Barlow's denied the inspector access to the business. OSHA sued to compel Barlow to admit the inspector without a warrant. Who prevails, Barlow or OSHA? (*Marshall v. Barlow's Inc.*, 436 U.S. 307)

EVIDENCE Deborah Tolbert, a secretary employed by the Martin Marietta Corporation, was raped by a Martin Marietta janitor while on her way to lunch within the secured defense facility where she worked. She sued Martin Marietta, alleging that it had negligently hired the janitor and had negligently failed to make its premises safe for employees. Martin Marietta moved for summary judgment, claiming that Tolbert could not sue in negligence because workers' compensation was her sole remedy.

REASONING The sole issue is whether the Colorado Workmen's Compensation Act covers Tolbert's injury. If it does, workers' compensation is her exclusive remedy and this tort action is barred. Tolbert asserts that her injury is not covered by workers' compensation, presumably because she expects that a tort action would yield a larger recovery. Martin Marietta, on the other hand, apparently is willing to pay the workers' compensation award to avoid risking a large tort verdict. Workers' compensation applies where the injury or death is proximately caused by an injury or disease arising in the course of the employee's employment and is not intentionally self-inflicted. Although her injury did arise in the course of her employment, Tolbert contends that it did not "arise out of" the employment.

Courts have interpreted the "arising out of" language in two different ways: "positional risk" or "increased risk."

The positional-risk doctrine has been defined thus:

Any injury arises out of the employment if it would not have occurred but for the fact that the conditions and obligations of the employment placed claimant in the position where he was injured. Invoking this rule, Martin Marietta asserts that Tolbert's injury is covered by workers' compensation because: (1) her employment placed her within the building where she was injured, and (2) the assault was a neutral force.

Under the increased-risk test, compensation is awarded only if the employment increases the worker's risk of injury above that to which the general public is exposed. If Colorado presently applies the increased-risk analysis, Tolbert would not be covered by workers' compensation. Certainly her employment as a secretary within a secured defense facility would not be expected to increase her risk of sexual assault above that to which women in the general public are exposed.

The rape was a nonemployment-motivated act directed at the plaintiff because she was a woman. Tolbert was not raped because of the nature of her duties or the nature of her workplace environment, or because of any incident or quarrel growing out of the work. [In Colorado,] An injury arises out of the employment if it would not have occurred but for the fact that the conditions and the employment placed claimant in the position where he was injured.

The workers' compensation statute has not abolished Tolbert's tort claim. Adopting this position has the additional advantage of providing employers an incentive to make reasonable efforts to screen prospective employees so as to avoid hiring rapists or those having the identifiable characteristics of potential rapists. Martin Marietta's motion for summary judgment denied.

PRACTICE JUDGING

1. If the janitor had no prior criminal record, what do you think the outcome of the negligence suit would be?

2. Which test, positional-risk or increased-risk, allows more recovery under workers' compensation?

ENTREPRENEURS AND THE LAW

PROJECT 5 LAW OF JOBS

EMPLOYMENT CONTRACTS

Ben was a physical wreck. There just weren't enough hours in the day for one person to get all the work done. It was time to hire some help. Kristen had mentioned that he could double his production, pay his workers almost half again the going rate, and still produce a remarkable profit. Ben liked the idea. He also liked the idea of hiring ex-cons like himself who wanted a new chance on life. He would train each one while filling the orders.

Ben also needed help in the office. If he could find an experienced secretary who knew how to set up an efficient front office, he could avoid many start-up mistakes. Suddenly, he had an idea. Patricia Johns ran the front office at Rebuilt so well that even the machinists spoke of her with respect. Perhaps he could lure her away from Rebuilt.

ADVERTISING

Ben knew he would have to generate some new business to ensure that his employees had enough to do. His first move would be to place an ad in Machinist's Monthly, the industry trade magazine. Some narrative and a decent picture of the Reelshield should generate quite a few inquiries. Also, he was con-

sidering raising the price of the Reelshield to $2,000 per unit. Many of his customers had mentioned that the device seemed to be priced too low. It had caused them to wonder about the quality of the materials used in building the Reelshield.

INDEPENDENT PRODUCT AGENTS

Ben also considered contracting with some independent sales agents. These agents traveled around the country selling various items like the Reelshield to factories. They typically worked on a commission basis. Ben realized that the creation of such an agency had to be done with care. He had to be sure each salesperson had adequate production information and would convey any unanswered questions back to him.

JOB DISCRIMINATION AND HARRASSMENT

Finally, Ben remembered how he had been treated when looking for a job as an ex-con. He wanted to be sure that his employees were hired without being subject to any form of illegal discrimination. He also wanted to be sure that the job environment was free from all types of harassment.

Divide into teams and perform one or more of the following activities, as directed by your teacher.

PREPARE LEGAL DOCUMENTS

Draft some standard contracts for Ben's prospective employees. Consider the following issues: What clauses might you put into the contracts of the ex-cons? What legal problem(s) might arise with trying to lure Johns away from Rebuilt? What solutions can you propose? Share your contracts with the class.

BE CREATIVE

Divide the team into two groups. Members of one group should contact trade journals and find out about advertising in the journal. (Ask each trade journal to send a copy of its

adverising contract. Be sure to find out how they screen advertisers for legitimacy, the lead time for the ad, and if there are any other constraints.) The other group should prepare various ads to submit to the trade journals. When each group has completed its assignment, the groups should present their results to the team and then to the class.

ROLE-PLAY

Divide the team up into student pairs. Each pair should role-play the interview between Ben and an independent sales agent candidate. Students should alternate playing Ben and the candidate.

UNIT SIX

FORMS OF BUSINESS ORGANIZATIONS

CHAPTERS

ENTREPRENEURS
SEE PAGE 534
AND THE LAW

Moletas. To hear it, one might think of an Italian dish being prepared as the feature of the day. Few would guess that "moletas" are knife grinders. To Richard Nella, owner of Nella Cutlery Inc., the term represents a trade that spans four generations. The knife grinder trade dates back prior to the year 1000 and is considered to be the core technology that makes all other technologies possible.

The strong tradition of moletas, or knife grinders, has always been a very powerful influence to Rich in choosing his career path. Like many moletas, Rich feels a personal responsibility and desire to advance his trade so that succeeding generations can proudly continue in a vibrant business.

Rich had completed all his coursework for a master's degree in ergonomic engneering at Alfred University in New York when he decided to join his family tradition of knife grinding. "I saw it as a way to bring my engineering knowledge into a proven trade and enhance and improve on tradition."

Rich started Nella Cutlery Inc. in 1985. The cutlery is a full service operation for professional food preparation equipment, machines, and tools. The business manufactures, repairs, rents, and sells equipment, knives and tools used by food service professionals.

With his wide customer base, Rich must rely on vendors from all over the world. To meet these needs, Rich developed an Excel worksheet with 3-D references and a Web query worksheet to check the current price of a product and its exchange to U.S. dollars. The vendors update their prices and product availability on a daily basis. "I saw a way to improve this process by introducing computers into my business. To simplify the bidding, quote, and pricing process, I now use software to integrate these processes."

Rich also improved his business by designing special grinding machinery. The new equipment increased efficiency while reducing costs. "I used my technological background and expertise and brought it into the knife grinding trade."

To be a successful entrepreneur, Rich believes the following skills are necessary: inner drive to constantly improve, self-motivation, ability to learn quickly, good listening skills, multi-task and detail-oriented, strong selling skills, and capacity to motivate and deal with diverse people. "I have to be able to sell to customers, motivate my work staff, know the product, know the systems and technology, and know all facets of the business in case one of my staff are on vacation or off for the day."

A business owner must also be aware of all legalities concerning hiring, subcontracting, the Equal Employment Opportunities Commission, employment, trade infringement, copyright, collections, bankruptcy, non-compete agreements, and theft. "When I developed the machine, I had to make sure it was patented or anyone could have built one and I would have had no legal recourse. Because of all the various legal ramifications directed at business owners today, it is imperative that you have good legal counsel at your fingertips."

Today, the moläs (pushcarts with mounted grindstones) that Rich Nella's ancestors used for years have been replaced by more modern equipment. However, the service and dedication brought to the trade by his ancestors four generations ago continues.

> **Because of all the various legal ramifications directed at business owners today, it is imperative that you have good legal counsel at your fingertips.**

FORMS OF BUSINESS ORGANIZATION

LESSONS

HOT DEBATE

Bill found a lump in his neck. The x-rays ordered by Dr. Compton at St. John's hospital emergency room turned up negative. Months passed, and the lump grew. Another doctor diagnosed it as being a malignant growth on Bill's carotid artery. After experimental surgery saved his life, Bill filed suit against St. John's. He then discovered that the emergency room was run by a subcontractor, Emergency Physicians, Inc. Bill also found that at the time he was treated there, Dr. Compton was a recovering drug addict and had lost his license to practice in Texas. The x-rays he ordered only showed Bill's neck from the top of the lump up. St. John's hospital has petitioned the court to be dismissed as a defendant. It contends that only Dr. Compton and Emergency Physicians, Inc., should be held liable.

Where Do You Stand?

1. What are the legal reasons that support retaining St. John's as a defendant?

2. What are the legal reasons in favor of dismissing St. John's as a defendant?

GOALS

● **Discuss the basic attributes of the sole proprietor-ship, partnership, and corporation**

● **Determine which one form of organization may be best in a particular situation**

● **Explain the risks of utilizing each form of business organization**

WHAT IS A SOLE PROPRIETORSHIP?

WHAT'S YOUR VERDICT?

Shirley wants to open a sporting goods store. She hesitates because she thinks the expenses would be prohibitive. She lists the costs of renting or buying required space; hiring help; buying a computer to keep records; buying a large inventory; obtaining a charter from the state; and paying for licenses, legal fees, and accounting fees.

Should these costs cause her to drop her plans?

There are three principal forms of business organization:

1. sole proprietorship
2. partnership
3. corporation

Of the three, the simplest, most flexible, and easiest to start is the **sole proprietorship**, which is owned by one person. The owner of a sole proprietorship has relatively unlimited control over the business and keeps all the profits. However, the sole proprietor also has unlimited personal responsibility for all debts and for other liabilities that the business may incur. In case of breach of the proprietor's contract, or a tort, his or her personal property as well as all of the business property may be seized to pay damages awarded by courts. But careful management, along with adequate public liability insurance, limits those risks and makes them tolerable.

Sole proprietorships are by far the most numerous legal form of business organization. Most independent contractors listed in the Yellow Pages of telephone directories are sole proprietors. Many expand their businesses with the help of employees and agents. Corporations are fewer in number, but they have a much larger sales dollar volume and employ many more workers.

There are no particular legal requirements for organizing or conducting a sole proprietorship. When started, many sole proprietorships are conducted out of the owner's home, garage, or van. No help need be hired, no computer is required for the simple records, and inventory may be limited and often purchased on credit. No charter is needed from the state, although a local business license and perhaps a permit to collect sales taxes for transmittal to the state, may be required. Some types of businesses, such as those selling food or securities, are subject to special governmental regulations regardless of the legal form of organization.

In *What's Your Verdict?* Shirley should not necessarily drop her plans. She should survey her potential market to confirm the need for such a business in that location at the present time. She should also be reasonably sure that she has the necessary knowledge and ability, as well as sufficient capital, for the venture. Usually, it is highly desirable to have prior experience as an employee in a similar business.

WHAT IS A PARTNERSHIP?

WHAT'S YOUR VERDICT?

Bard and Chung organized and operated the Dusk t' Dawn Club. They agreed to share profits and losses equally. They also agreed to pay rent of either $500 a month or 6 percent of their gross revenues, whichever amount was greater, for use of Allyn's warehouse. Kardine was hired as manager for $1,000 a month plus 3 percent of the net profits.

Are Bard, Chung, Allyn, and Kardine all partners in the business?

The law that controls partnerships in most states is the Uniform Partnership Act (UPA). According to the UPA a **partnership** is an association of two or more persons (who are called *general partners*) to carry on, as co-owners, a business for profit. This may be referred to as a general partnership. The general partners share all profits equally. They also equally share all losses if any are suffered. The partners may agree among themselves to a different distribution. However each remains fully liable without limit to outside creditors for debts owed by the firm. This unlimited liability limits the popularity and utility of the general partnership form of business organization.

In *What's Your Verdict?* Bard and Chung were partners, but the others were not. Neither Allyn nor Kardine owned part of the business. Their sharing of the gross revenue or net profits was merely a method of paying them rent and salary.

A partnership combines the capital, labor, skill, and knowledge of two or more persons. Often the resulting combination serves to multiply the strength of the parties: one plus one equals three or more in talent and productivity. Unique abilities can be better developed and utilized through specialization. Thus bigger projects become manageable.

Because of their close relationship and ability to bind each other legally in contracts and torts involving third parties, partners should be selected with painstaking care. If possible, one

should choose as partners only persons who are socially compatible, financially responsible, ethical and morally trustworthy, professionally competent, physically fit, and willing

to work hard. As with sole proprietors, competence and integrity, coupled with adequate public liability insurance, make the risks of unlimited liability tolerable.

WHAT IS A CORPORATION?

WHAT'S YOUR VERDICT?

Kate, a prosperous banker, and Eric, an engineer, agreed to invest in a promising fiberglass boat manufacturing business. Kate was too busy to devote a lot of time to the new business, but Eric wanted the benefit of her business judgment on major decisions. At the same time, Kate and Eric could not afford the risk of unlimited liability to third parties.

What form of business organization would be appropriate?

A **corporation** is a legal entity or artificial person in the eyes of the law. It has an existence distinct or separate from the real persons who organize, own, and run it. Therefore, it is the corporation that makes or loses money. The corporation also

may injure people and even commit crimes.

As a consequence of the corporation's being treated as an entity in its own right under the law, investors in a corporation only run the risk of losing what they have invested in it, not

all their personal wealth. The corporation, but not the investors, may be hit with a large lawsuit. The corporation—not the investors—may lose money and go bankrupt from the business. This limit on the owners' potential risk makes the corporate form very attractive. Unlike the partnership the corporate form also features free transferability of ownership. A corporation can have perpetual life as a result. A partnership, however, ends if a partner withdraws, dies, or goes bankrupt.

Corporations have the ability to attract large sums of capital because investors' liability is limited. Efficient corporations generally have greater financial strength than do other forms of business organization. This enables corporations to attract superior workers by offering generous salaries and fringe benefits. In *What's Your Verdict?* these corporate advantages would appeal to both Kate and Eric making the corporation their likely informed choice as a form of business organization.

MAJOR FORMS OF BUSINESS ORGANIZATION

	Sole Proprietorship	Partnership	Corporation
Requirements for Organizing	None	Agreement of the parties	State charter; organizational fees
Legal Status	Owner is the business; not a separate entity	Not a separate entity in many states	Separate entity from owners
Liability	Unlimited liability	Unlimited liability (except limited partnership)	Limited liability of shareholders
Management	Owner decides	Partners have equal say in management unless otherwise specified in agreement	Directors (elected by shareholders) set policy and appoint officers
Dissolution	Owner decides; terminates upon owner's death	Terminates by agreement of partners or upon a partner's death, withdrawal, bankruptcy	Does not necessarily end
Ease of formation	Just do it	Moderately hard	Difficult
Duration	Death or disinterest of proprietor	Death, bankruptcy, or withdrawal of any partner	Can be perpetual
Ability to attract professional managers	Poor	Moderate	Excellent

A Question of ETHICS ?

Dennis Rice formed and owned 51 percent of the stock in Silver Veins Inc., a Delaware Corporation intended to invest in silver futures. The other 49 percent was owned by various charities and pension plans Dennis had solicited as investors. Once the investors paid in their money, Dennis hired himself as the chief executive officer. He then arranged a salary package that paid him so much each year that no funds were left to pay dividends. Consequently, the other investors received no return on their money. Is this ethical? Is this legal?

Answer the following questions about legal concepts.

1. Which form of business organization does not involve unlimited personal liability for its owners? **(a) sole proprietorship (b) partnership (c) corporation**

2. Which form of business organization does not terminate upon the death of its owners? **(a) sole proprietorship (b) partnership (c) corporation**

3. Which form of business is the easiest to set up? **(a) sole proprietorship (b) partnership (c) corporation**

4. Which form of business has the greatest potential to bring together large sums of capital? **(a) sole proprietorship (b) partnership (c) corporation**

5. Which form of business has the greatest potential for attracting professional managers? **(a) sole proprietorship (b) partnership (c) corporation**

6. Which form of business organization needs a charter from the state? **(a) sole proprietorship (b) partnership (c) corporation**

7. The UPA governs **(a) proprietorships (b) partnerships (c) corporations.**

8. Which form of business organization is looked upon as being an artificial entity, separate from its owners? **(a) sole proprietorship (b) partnership (c) corporation**

Study the following situations, answer the questions, then prepare arguments to support your answers.

9. One day Sol had an idea to make money. He went out and bought large blocks of tickets for the main entertainment attractions in Branson, Missouri, and then called several tour directors to see if they would buy them. When they did, Sol charged them a dollar extra per ticket. What form of business organization does Sol most likely have?

10. Sol hired Nadine to deliver the tickets in his car to the theaters just as the tour busses arrived. If Nadine has an accident on such an errand, what are the potential consequences for Sol's business and his personal assets?

11. After several months of brokering tickets to tour directors, Sol thought it would be a good idea if he offered his ticket service to people on the World Wide Web. His friend Tom was a computer programmer and Sol made him an offer to join the business. Tom would control computer marketing of the tickets and, rather than a salary, would receive a percentage of the profits. What form of business organization exists between Sol and Tom?

12. If Sol and Tom's employee is delivering tickets and has an accident, what are the potential consequences for their business and personal assets?

13. As Sol and Tom's business continued to grow, they decided it would be a good idea to open a storefront on the main access road into Branson. Unfortunately, they did not have the capital they needed to build the building. Their business was still too new to get a loan from the bank and their personal credit standings would not support a loan the size they needed. Sol and Tom did have some friends who were interested in investing in their business, but the friends did not want to be exposed to unlimited personal liability that might come with certain types of business organizations. What type of business organization seems ideal in this situation (sole proprietorship, partnership, or corporation) and why?

14. If Sol and Tom go forward with the new storefront and the new form of business organization and now the employee is delivering tickets and has an accident, what are the potential consequences for the owners' business and personal assets?

15. Sol and Tom have been running their business for a decade now. It has grown to the point where it is difficult to keep up with all the work they have to do. One day Sol mentions they are making so much money that they could hire professional managers to run the business. They could live on the dividends from their stock ownership. Tom thought about this and nodded. "Of course," said Tom, "just because we want to hire a professional manager doesn't mean we could find one to work for us." What could Tom and Sol do to attract managers to their business?

G O A L S

● **Explain how a partnership is formed**

● **Identify different types of partnerships and partners**

● **Discuss the ways in which a partnership can be terminated and what happens when this occurs**

HOW IS A PARTNERSHIP CREATED?

WHAT'S YOUR
VERDICT?

Abbie Pinegar and her sister Ashlee wanted to form a partnership to run a hot dog stand at this year's county fair. After talking about what was required, they agreed that each would pay for one half of the supplies and rental of space for the stand. They also agreed that they would alternate days spent running the booth and that the profits would be split equally. Any decisions they could not agree on would be made by their mother.

Does their partnership agreement have to be in writing?

"Strong fences good neighbors make" is the old adage. The same is certainly true about "good partners." The strong fences of a partnership are the terms and conditions that the partners agree on to guide them in managing the partnership. These terms and conditions comprise the **partnership agreement**.

Although best in an explicit written form, the partnership agreement need not be in writing unless required by the statute of frauds. As discussed previously, the statute of frauds requires a writing signed by the party being sued to make the contract enforceable if it cannot be performed within one year from the date it is made. Therefore, if two persons agree at the time they form their partnership that it is to last longer than one year, their agreement must be in writing and signed by both persons to be enforceable by both. In *What's Your Verdict?* the agreement

to operate a booth in this year's fair does not have to be in writing.

If the parties do not agree on a specific length of time for their partnership to continue, their agreement need not be in writing. After all, the contract could be performed within one year, even though it could last for many years. Nonetheless, the time, resources, and detail involved make it highly desirable to put every partnership agreement in writing, preferably with the assistance of a lawyer. This encourages thoughtful review of the many potential problems of the new business. It also helps to avoid future costly controversies by spelling out rights and duties of the partners in advance. A sample partnership agreement is found on page 474.

Under the UPA, a partnership is legally treated, in some respects, as an entity. This means that it is a distinct, real being in the eyes of the law. A partnership:

1. may take title to, and transfer property in its own name

2. is regarded as a principal, for which each partner may act as agent, making contracts in the firm's name

3. must use its own assets to pay its creditors before any individual partner's assets may be seized.

For most purposes, a partnership is legally treated as an aggregation or group of individual partners, with the following results.

1. Each partner must pay income taxes on her or his share of the net profits even if they are not distributed but are retained in the business. The firm pays no income tax but files an information return. This enables the Internal Revenue Service (IRS) to cross-check the accuracy of the partners' individual tax returns.

2. The firm, in the absence of a permissive statute, must sue and be sued in the name of all the partners.

3. All debts of the firm not paid out of firm assets are chargeable to every partner. (This reflects the unlimited liability of general partners, which many persons understandably fear.)

4. When any partner drops out of the firm for any reason, the partnership is dissolved. However, prior arrangements can be made to continue the operation of the partnership business without interruption.

5. The partnership is handicapped when it comes to attracting large sums of new capital beyond the amount originally invested.

GENERAL PARTNERSHIP AGREEMENT FORMING
"DOWN THE DRAIN"

Date, identity of partners, and purpose of partnership

Name, location, and records availability

Duration and termination procedure

Capitalization

Funding of reserve

Division of profits and losses, payout schedule

Account location, withdrawal procedure

Duties and limitations

Nonroutine decision-making procedure

By agreement made this 11th day of September, 20--, we Amy Brock, Martin Espinoza, and Gerald Hunt, the undersigned, all of Castletown, Kansas, hereby join in general partnership to conduct a plumbing installation and repair business and mutually agree to the following terms:

1. That the partnership shall be called "Down the Drain" and have its principal place of business at 166 Oak Street, Castletown, Kansas, at which address books containing the full and accurate records of partnership transactions shall be kept and be accessible to any partner at any reasonable time.

2. That the partnership shall continue in operation for an indefinite time until terminated by 90 days' notice provided by one or more of the partners and indicating his, her, or their desire to withdraw. Upon such notice an accounting shall be conducted and a division of the partnership assets made unless a partner wishes to acquire the whole business by paying a price determined by an arbitrator whose selection shall be agreed to by all three partners. Said price shall include goodwill, and the paying of same shall entitle the payor to continue the partnership business under the same name.

3. That each partner shall contribute to the partnership: $10,000 for initial working capital and the inventory and equipment (including trucks—which shall be marked with the partnership name, address, and logo) of their current individual plumbing businesses.

4. That in return for the capital contribution in item 3, each partner shall receive an undivided one-third interest in the partnership and its properties.

5. That a fund of $50,000 be set up and retained from the profits of the partnership business as a reserve fund. It being agreed that this fund shall be constituted on not less than 15 percent of the monthly profits until said amount has been accumulated.

6. That the profits of the business shall be divided equally between the partners, that the losses shall be attributed according to the subsequent agreement, and that a determination of said profits and losses shall be made and profit shares paid to each partner on a monthly basis.

7. That the partnership account shall be kept in the First National Bank of Castletown and that all withdrawals from same shall be by check bearing the signature of at least one of the partners.

8. That each partner shall devote his or her full efforts to the partnership business and shall not engage in another business without the other partners' permission.

9. That no partner shall cause to issue any commercial paper or shall enter into any agreements representing the partnership outside the normal conduct of the plumbing business without notice to the remaining partners and the consent of at least one other partner and further that all managerial and personnel decisions not covered by another section of this agreement shall be made with the assent of at least two of the partners.

IN AGREEMENT HERETO, WE ARE

Amy Brock   Martin Espinoza   Gerald Hunt

Signatures

Amy Brock   *Martin Espinoza*   *Gerald Hunt*

KINDS OF PARTNERSHIPS AND PARTNERS

WHAT'S YOUR VERDICT?

Avery invested $100,000 as a limited partner in a partnership organized to operate an amusement park. On opening day, an accident on a roller coaster severely injured 17 people. The damages awarded to the accident victims totaled nearly $7 million. That amount far exceeded the value of the partnership's assets and insurance coverage.

Will Avery be held liable for unpaid liability claims against the partnership?

Partnerships may be classified according to their purpose and according to the extent of the liability of the partners.

Classification by Purpose

Classified by purpose, partnerships are either trading or non-trading and are either general or special. A **trading partnership** buys and sells goods and services commercially. A **non-trading partnership** provides professional and noncommercial assistance, such as legal, medical, or accounting advice. A general partnership conducts a general business, such as a retail store. A **special partnership** may be formed for a single transaction, such as the purchase and resale of a farm.

Sometimes a proposed project (for example, construction of the Hoover Dam at the Arizona-Nevada border) is too big for a single person or business firm to handle alone. (See photo of the Hoover Dam on page 476.) Two or more persons or firms then associate together, combining their resources and skills in a **joint venture** to do the one complex project. Because the joint venture is so similar to a general partnership (which may also be formed to do a single project), many courts as well as the IRS treat it as such. However, unlike the rule for general partnerships, death of a participant does not cause dissolution of the joint venture. The joint venture normally continues until the project is completed.

Classification by Extent of Liability

Classified by extent of liability of partners, partnerships are either general or limited. In a **general partnership**, all the partners assume full personal liability for debts of the firm. In a **limited partnership**, at least one partner must be a general partner, with unlimited liability. However, one or more partners may be **limited partners**, who are liable only to the extent of their investment.

The Uniform Limited Partnership Act (ULPA) has been adopted with few amendments in almost all the states. Unlike a general partnership, a limited partnership can be created only by proper execution, recording, and publication of a certificate that identifies the partners and states basic facts about their agreement. Limited partners contribute capital and share profits and losses with general partners.

In *What's Your Verdict?* if the limited partnership had been properly formed and Avery had not participated in the management of the business, she would be liable only to the extent of her $100,000 investment.

Classification of Partners

General partners may be further classified as silent, secret, or dormant. A **silent partner** may be known to the public as a partner but takes no active part in management. A **secret partner** is not known to the public as a partner yet participates in management. A **dormant partner** is neither known to the public as a partner nor active in management. All such partners, when identified, can be held liable without limit for partnership debts.

A **nominal partner** is not a partner. However, nominal partners hold themselves out as partners, or let others do so. Parents sometimes become nominal partners to assist children who have taken over the family business. Consequently, if a partnership liability arises, they are liable as partners. A third party, acting in good faith, may rely on the reputation of the nominal partner and therefore extend credit to the firm. If so, all partners who consented to the misrepresentation are fully liable. If all members consent, the firm is liable.

A minor who enters into a partnership agreement generally has special status. In most states, such a partner retains all of the rights and privileges of a minor. Thus, the minor normally can plead minority as a defense and not pay if sued by a creditor of the partnership. The minor may also withdraw and thus dissolve the partnership without being liable for breach of contract. Some states, however, do hold a minor liable on contracts made as either an individual proprietor or as a partner in connection with business.

Because limited partners do not share in the managerial control of the business, their liability for firm debts and losses is limited to the amount of capital they invest. Limited partners who participate in management lose their status and become liable without limit as general partners.

This rule has been relaxed and defined by the Revised Uniform Limited Partnership Act (RULPA), which has been adopted by a majority of the states. Under RULPA, a limited partner does not participate in the managerial control of the business solely by doing such things as:

1. being an independent contractor for, or an agent or employee of, the limited partnership
2. consulting with or advising a general partner
3. attending a meeting of the general partners
4. proposing, approving, or disapproving (by vote or otherwise) the dissolution, change in the nature of the business, admission or removal of a general or limited partner, or amendment to the partnership agreement.

ENDING A PARTNERSHIP

WHAT'S YOUR VERDICT?

Paradiso is a partner in a successful certified public accounting firm. While vacationing, she becomes personally liable for a large amount of damages that result from her negligence in an automobile accident. She therefore files for bankruptcy and has these and other debts discharged.

What effect will this have on the partnership?

When any partner ceases to be associated in the ordinary operation of the business, **dissolution** of the partnership occurs. Dissolution is normally followed by a **winding-up period**, which concludes with the actual **termination** or ending of the partnership. During the winding-up period, all partnership business in process at the time of dissolution is concluded, creditors of the business are satisfied if possible, and each partner's share is accounted for and distributed. When the winding-up process is completed, termination of the legal existence of the partnership actually occurs.

Dissolution of a partnership may be caused by action of one or more of the partners, operation of law, or court decree. These situations are discussed in the sections that follow.

Action of One or More of the Partners

A partnership may be dissolved by agreement of the parties. For example, if the original agreement is for one year, the partnership concludes at the end of that year. Sometimes a firm is organized for a specific purpose, such as the development of a large tract of farmland into a subdivision for houses. Sale of the last lot and house would end the partnership. Also, the parties may unanimously agree at any time to terminate their relationship.

Withdrawal of a partner for any reason dissolves the partnership. The partnership agreement may permit such withdrawal without penalty, preferably after a reasonable advance notice. In such case, the withdrawing partner would not be liable to the remaining partner(s) for any drop in profits that might result. If the withdrawal violates their agreement, the withdrawing partner would be liable in damages for any injury resulting from the breach of contract. If the organization is a **partnership at will**, a partner normally may withdraw at any time without liability to associates. The withdrawing partner could be liable for resulting losses if the sudden withdrawal was unreasonable.

Operation of Law

Death of any partner dissolves the partnership. This is a serious disadvantage of the partnership form of organization. Prudent partners simply anticipate this inevitable event and specify what action shall be taken when it happens. For example, they may agree that the surviving partner(s) will continue with a new firm and pay for the decedent's share over a period of years.

Bankruptcy, a kind of financial death, also automatically dissolves the partnership. This is true whether the bankruptcy is suffered by any of the partners (such as Paradiso in *What's Your Verdict?*) or by the firm itself. Although rare, subsequent illegality also dissolves the partnership. For example, a professional partner-

ship of doctors would be dissolved if any member lost the license to practice.

Court Decree

Partners, if living, usually arrange for dissolution privately. If necessary, however, one partner may petition a court to order dissolution if another partner has become insane, otherwise incapacitated, or guilty of serious misconduct affecting the business.

Also a court may act if continuation is impracticable, or if the firm is continuously losing money and there is little or no prospect for success. This could happen when there are irreconcilable differences between the partners. For example, irreconcilable differences could be the result of decisions to add or drop a major line of merchandise or to move a factory to another location to reduce labor costs.

Answer the following questions about legal concepts.

1. Which of the following is active in management of a partnership but unknown to the public? (a) **silent partner** (b) **dormant partner** (c) **limited partner** (d) **none of the above**

2. Which of the following is known to the public but does not participate in management? (a) **silent partner** (b) **dormant partner** (c) **limited partner** (d) **none of the above**

3. Which of the following does not participate in management and is only potentially liable for her/his investment in the partnership? (a) **silent partner** (b) **dormant partner** (c) **limited partner** (d) **none of the above**

4. If a partner dies the partnership is dissolved. **True or False?**

5. Can a partnership agreement be structured so as to continue the partnership business even if the partnership is dissolved? **Yes or No?**

6. If we form a partnership to prepare income taxes for businesses over the next five years, can we terminate the business after just a year if we both agree to do so? **Yes or No?**

Study the following situations, answer the questions, then prepare arguments to support your answers.

7. Zeno, Smith, and Cospit were partners in Fly by Night, a small, overnight, parcel delivery service. In forming their partnership, they provided for continuation of the business if any partner should die. Their written agreement specified that the business would continue uninterrupted, under the same name, with management and control by a new partnership composed of the surviving partners. The business is now showing a profit of more than $500,000 a year and has net assets valued at more than $5,000,000. How would a retiring partner receive a fair share without having to liquidate the business regardless of the partnership agreement provisions to the contrary?

8. Tole and Hunt orally agreed to sell Christmas trees and share any profits or losses equally. What type of organization have they formed? Must they pay income taxes individually on their profits or will the organization pay as a legal entity?

9. Peterson and Goebel orally agree to fix up a park for the local children. What type of organization have they formed? Could they raise money for the group without changing to a different type of organization?

10. Brooke was 17 years old when he entered into a partnership with Beale, age 22. Their agreement to operate a dog-training school was for three years. After six months, Brooke decided to withdraw. Was he liable for breach of contract? Why or why not?

11. Sanferd and Sontag were partners in a very successful real estate development firm. After all the lots in their latest subdivision were sold they decided to look around for another undeveloped part of town. Acting independently of one another one day, they both bought separate sections of land for the partnership to use for its next subdivision. Neither one had the other sign the contract for purchase. Is the partnership bound to buy both parcels of land? Why or why not?

12. Although Sandferd and Sontag's partnership agreement was not in writing, they had agreed that the partnership would terminate after five years. Shortly after the contracts were made to purchase the land referred to in exercise 12, it became obvious that a new round of capital contributions to the firm would be necessary. As Sandferd had originally provided more than two thirds of the capital for the firm and shared in the profits by the same proportion, Sontag maintained that Sandferd had to pay in that proportion of the new capital requirement. Sandferd refused, saying that they had agreed that after the original capital contribution, he would only have to pay one half. If the partnership agreement does not declare otherwise, the state partnership act requires a pro-rata contribution from each of the partners, in which both would contribute 50 percent. How much do the partners have to contribute and why?

PARTNERS' DUTIES

WHAT'S YOUR VERDICT?

Fineman was one of five partners in a firm of certified public accountants. Her duties included management of the office. As such, she bought all office equipment. Recently, she purchased an advanced photocopying system for $25,000, a competitive price. Several days later, she met the seller, Fisher, at a dinner party. Fineman convinced Fisher to give her a 5 percent discount on the price because clients of her accounting firm might be inclined to buy similar equipment when they learned of its use from her. Fineman now claims the $1,250 discount belongs to her alone because she obtained it on her own time after the original contract was signed.

Is she correct?

By law or by agreement each partner has a duty to do the following.

COMPLY WITH PARTNERSHIP AGREEMENT AND DECISIONS Each partner must comply with the partnership agreement, including later provisions properly added and related decisions properly made.

USE REASONABLE CARE In performing partnership duties, partners must use reasonable care. However, they are not personally liable for the full loss caused by their own errors in judgment, mistakes, and incompetence. Any resulting financial burden rests on the firm and is shared by all partners. This harsh reality affirms the importance of selecting competent persons as partners.

ACT WITH INTEGRITY AND GOOD FAITH A partnership is a fiduciary relationship of utmost trust and confidence. Each

partner is legally bound to act with the highest integrity and good faith in dealing with the other partner(s). No partner may personally retain any profit or benefit unless the other partners are informed and consent. In *What's Your Verdict?* Fineman was wrong in claiming the discount. All profits or benefits flowing from the firm's business belong to the firm, to be shared by all partners equally or as otherwise agreed.

NOT CONDUCT COMPETING BUSINESS Unless there is a contrary agreement, a partner may not do any business that competes with the partnership or prevents performance of duties to the firm. A partner may, however, attend to personal affairs for profit, as long as the firm's business is not sacrificed. A partner who withdraws from the firm may compete with it unless validly prohibited by the partnership agreement.

KEEP ACCURATE RECORDS A partner should keep accurate records of all business done for the firm and give the firm all money belonging to it. Moreover, every partner should disclose to the other partner(s) all important information that concerns the firm's business.

PARTNERS' RIGHTS AND AUTHORITY

WHAT'S YOUR VERDICT?

Palm, a partner in the Bobbin' Cork Bait Shops, normally purchased the inventory for the business. Unknown to her, the other three partners voted to no longer deal with Trout Attractions, Inc., one of their main suppliers. Before finding out about their decision, Palm contracted for $1,000 worth of lures from Trout.

Is the partnership bound by the contract?

In the absence of contrary agreement, legal rights of partners are shared equally. Partners may, however, agree as to who shall have particular rights and duties.

Partners' Rights

The principal rights a partner has include the following:

RIGHT TO PARTICIPATE IN MANAGEMENT Every partner, as a co-owner of the business, has an equal right to participate in its management. Acting alone, a partner may buy, sell, hire, fire, and make other routine decisions in carrying on the ordinary day-to-day activities of the firm. In effect, each partner acts as an agent for the firm and for the other partners. All partners are bound by the result, unless the partner lacked the necessary authority, and the person with whom the contract was made knew this. In *What's Your Verdict?* the $1,000 contract resulted from a routine decision by Palm, a partner with apparent authority. Consequently, the partnership is bound.

In addition to routine decisions, each partner has the right to do the things normally done by managers in similar firms. This includes the right to inspect the partnership books at all times, unless otherwise agreed.

When a difference of opinion arises as to ordinary matters connected with the business, a majority vote of the partners decides the issue. Unless otherwise agreed, each partner has one vote regardless of the amount of capital contributed. If there is an even number of partners and they split equally on a question, no action can be taken. A pattern of such deadlocks can eventually lead to dissolution. To forestall such an outcome, it is often helpful to provide in the partnership agreement that deadlocks over specified matters shall be settled by arbitration.

Unanimous agreement of all the partners is required to make any change in the written partnership agreement, however minor it may be. All partners must also agree to any fundamental change that affects the very nature of the business (for example, changing its principal activity or location). In addition, under the UPA, unanimous agreement is required for decisions to:

- assign partnership property to creditors
- *confess judgment* (allow a plaintiff to obtain a judgment against the firm without a trial)
- submit a partnership claim or liability to arbitration
- do any act that would make it impossible to carry on the business.

The preceding rules governing the use of managerial authority may be changed by agreement. Often, by agreement, work is divided according to talents and interests. Certain partners have exclusive control over specific activities, such as selling, purchasing, or accounting and finance. By specializing in this way, efficiency and productivity increases.

RIGHT TO PROFITS Partners are entitled to all profits earned. In the absence of contrary agreement, both profits and losses are shared equally regardless of different amounts of capital contributed or time spent. However, the partners may agree to divide the profits and/or the losses in any percentages desired. Often, profits will be shared equally, but a partner with a large amount of outside income may agree, for tax purposes, to take all the losses. Outsiders, however, are not bound by such internal agreements and may hold any or all general partners liable without limit for all partnership debts.

RIGHT IN PARTNERSHIP PROPERTY

Partnership property consists of all cash and other property originally contributed by the partners as well as all property later acquired by the firm. The property is held in a special form of co-ownership called **tenancy in partnership**. In tenancy in partnership, each partner is a co-owner of the entire partnership property and is not the sole owner of any part of it. For example, if a firm of two partners owns two identical trucks, neither partner may claim exclusive ownership of either vehicle. Therefore, a partner has no salable or assignable interest in any particular item of property belonging to the

IN THIS CASE For several years, Gohegan and Briddle had been partners in Dealing In Wheeling, a bicycle retail and repair business. Gohegan wanted to hire two well qualified mechanics in order to divide the shop work and to give the partners more time for sales promotion. Briddle objected, saying "If you hire, I'll fire. . . . We can't afford it now." With the partners deadlocked, no one was hired.

partnership. However, the interest of a partner in the firm may be sold or assigned to another party. The buyer or assignee is not a partner but is entitled to that partner's share of the profits, and of the assets upon dissolution.

Each partner has an equal right to use firm property for partnership purposes, but no partner may use firm property for personal purposes unless all other partners consent.

RIGHT TO EXTRA COMPENSATION A partner who invests more capital, brings in more business, or works longer and harder than his or her associates is not entitled to extra pay or a larger share of the profits unless all the partners so agree. Common sense and fairness often dictate that a partner who gives more should receive more, but all partners must agree to this.

IN THIS CASE

Hudson, DeSoto, and Auburn were partners in an advertising agency. Hudson brought in most of the firm's accounts. He spent most of his days playing golf, tennis, or racquetball with prospective clients and friends. De Soto, a brilliant artist and copywriter, did most of the production. He often worked 10-hour days, seven days a week. Auburn had no creative talent and little energy. He spent no more than four hours a day delivering and picking up copy and layouts. Unless the partners agree, however, none is entitled to receive extra pay or a larger share of the profits.

A Partner's Authority

Unless otherwise agreed, each partner has an equal right to participate in management and to act as an agent for the firm. Generally, the law implies to each member the authority

necessary to carry on the business. This includes the right to do the following.

MAKE BINDING CONTRACTS FOR THE FIRM Acting within the scope of the particular business, each partner can make binding contracts deemed by that partner to be necessary or desirable, regardless of the possible folly of the deals. Any internal agreement limiting powers of a partner is binding on the partners, but not on third parties that do not know about the limitation. However, a partner who violates such internal agreement is liable to the other partners for any resulting loss.

No partner can bind the firm in contracts that are beyond the scope of the firm's business as publicly disclosed. Partners engaged in an aerial photography business, for example, would not be bound by a contract by one of the partners to use the plane for air ambulance service. Even if a partner has acted beyond authority in making a contract, the other partners may choose to ratify the act. If they do, the partnership is bound, as a principal would be in an ordinary agency.

RECEIVE MONEY OWED TO AND SETTLE CLAIMS AGAINST THE FIRM In the eyes of the law, all partners are assumed to have received any payments to the firm even if the partner who actually received the money disappears. Also, each partner may adjust debts of the firm by agreement with creditors. Each may compromise firm claims against debtors, settling for less than is due. However, a partner may not discharge a personal debt by agreeing to offset it against a debt owed to the partnership.

BORROW MONEY IN THE FIRM'S NAME In a trading partnership, any partner can borrow for partnership purposes. In such borrowing, the partner can execute promissory notes binding the firm and can pledge or mortgage partnership property as security. Partners in a nontrading partner-

ship generally do not have such power.

SELL A partner can sell in the regular course of business any of the firm's goods and give customary warranties. Acting alone, however, a partner may not sell the entire inventory in a bulk transfer because this could end the business.

BUY Any partner can buy for cash or credit any property within the scope of the business.

DRAW AND CASH CHECKS AND DRAFTS A partner can draw checks and drafts for partnership purposes and can indorse and cash checks payable to the firm.

HIRE AND FIRE EMPLOYEES AND AGENTS Each partner has the authority to hire and fire employees, agents, and independent contractors to help carry on the business.

RECEIVE NOTICE OF MATTERS AFFECTING THE PARTNERSHIP When one partner is served with a summons and complaint against the firm, all are deemed to have received the notice, even if they are not informed. Likewise, one partner's declarations and admissions in carrying on the business bind all partners even when contrary to the best interests of the firm.

A PARTNER'S CREDITOR'S RIGHTS A creditor of a member of a partnership cannot reach specific partnership property to satisfy the debt owed to him or her. In other words the creditor cannot take the partnership's trucks or computers or other assets to satisfy the debt. However, a creditor can go to court and get a judgment against the partner. Then the creditor could ask the court to assess the judgment against the partner's interest. The creditor would then receive whatever distributions that would normally go to the partner out of profits or sales of assets. The creditor has no rights in the partnership as far as managing is concerned and the debtor remains as a partner.

Between or among themselves, partners may make any agreements they choose regarding authority to run the business. Outsiders, however, may not be aware of such secret internal agreements. When this is the case, the partnership firm and all of its members are liable without limit for all obligations of the firm that arise out of contracts made by any partner within the scope of the firm's business. In *What's Your Verdict?* the firm and both partners are bound. If a loss results, Cotter could seek full recovery from Pinell because Pinell had violated their agreement in buying the equipment.

The partnership and all partners are liable when any partner commits a tort (for example, negligence or fraud) while acting within the ordinary course of the business. The wrongdoer would be obligated to indemnify the partnership for any damages it had to pay to the injured party. If the other partners had authorized or participated in the tort, all would share the blame and no indemnity would be payable.

Liability for certain crimes committed in the course of business, such as selling alcoholic beverages to minors, is also imposed on the partnership and all the partners. Generally, however, if the business of the firm does not require the criminal activity, neither the partnership nor the partners who do not authorize or take part in

the crime are held criminally liable. Thus, a partner who kills a pedestrian while negligently driving a company car on firm business will alone be *criminally* liable. However, the wrongdoer as well as the firm and the other partners are *civilly* liable for damages.

When a judgment is obtained against a partnership, and the partnership assets are exhausted, the individually owned property of the general partners may be legally seized and sold to pay the debt. Creditors of the respective individual partners, however, have first claim to such property. Any partner who pays an obligation of the firm with personal assets is legally entitled to recover a proportionate share from each of the other partners.

A partner cannot escape responsibility for firm debts by withdrawing from the partnership. One who withdraws remains liable for all debts incurred while a member. A new partner who joins the firm is liable for both existing and new debts of the business. However, creditors with claims that arose before the new partner joined the firm are limited, with respect to the new partner, to action against only the new partner's share of partnership property.

Answer the following questions about legal concepts.

1. A partner has a duty to use __?__ care in performing partnership duties.

2. A partner may engage in other businesses, even if they compete with the partnership. **True or False?**

3. Every general partner has an equal right to participate in management of the firm. **True or False?**

4. A partner who invests more time or money in the partnership has a right to a larger percentage of the profits. **True or False?**

5. Partnership property is held by the partners in a __?__ in partnership.

Study the following situations, answer the questions, then prepare arguments to support your answers.

6. Laird and Ball were partners in an indoor tennis center. Laird, a wealthy surgeon, contributed all the capital. Ball, a former tennis champion with an international reputation, contributed her name and agreed to work full time at the center. They agreed to split the profits equally. The losses, however, were all to be charged to Laird. Can the partners legally receive different proportions of the losses and the profits?

7. Adams, Starnes, and Williams were partners in a burglar and fire alarm service. Adams would mount his own camper cabin on the back of one of the company's pickup trucks every weekend and drive it into the country on overnight fishing trips. Starnes would take the company's laptop computer home every weekend to work on her version of the "great American novel." On weekends, Williams used the company's photocopying machine to run off copies of the weekly bulletins for his church. No partner was aware of any other partner's action. Did each have a legal right to borrow the firm's equipment? Why or why not?

8. Aki, Degas, and Kline were partners in an air-conditioning business. They obtained a $275,000 contract to install units in a candy factory. Long before the job was finished, Kline accepted the final payment of $100,000 and disappeared with the money. Must Aki and Degas absorb the loss and complete the job for the $175,000 already paid to them, without being paid an additional $100,000 by the candy factory?

Before going into business as a sole proprietor or partner. . .

1. Be reasonably sure that your formal education and experience (preferably in a similar business) have prepared you to do a competent job.

2. Be sure to comply with applicable licensing, registration, and other legal requirements.

3. If you are a partner, put the partnership agreement in writing, with the aid of a qualified lawyer. Include appropriate language covering each partner's:

  • duties and authority

PREVENT LEGAL DIFFICULTIES

  • share of profits and losses, if not intended to be equal
  • salary or right to withdraw

earnings (drawing account)
  • vacation and sick-leave rights, and rights to withdraw from the partnership

4. In the partnership agreement, include provisions covering:
  • periodic valuation of each partner's interest
  • methods for raising additional capital if needed
  • possible addition or withdrawal of a partner
  • amicable resolution of disputes, as by arbitration
  • possible continuation of the business after dissolution.

CHAPTER IN REVIEW

CONCEPTS IN BRIEF

1. Sole proprietorships are the most simple and numerous form of business organization. The owner makes all decisions, keeps all the profits, and is liable without limit for all losses.

2. A partnership is an association of two or more persons to carry on, as co-owners, a business for profit. Profits and losses are shared equally unless otherwise agreed. Every general partner is liable without limit to creditors for debts of the business.

3. A corporation is a legal entity that exists separately from its owners. Investors in a corporation risk losing only what they have invested.

4. In a partnership, unless otherwise agreed, all partners have a right to participate in management with equal authority.

5. Any partner, acting alone, may normally make routine business decisions for the firm. A majority must resolve disputes about ordinary matters.

6. In dealings with one another, partners are bound to act with the highest integrity and good faith. They must keep one another informed about the business, maintain accurate records, and take no secret profits.

7. Partners own firm property as tenants in partnership. Each may use the property for company business but not for personal purposes without consent of the other partners.

8. Limited partnership is a special form in which one or more limited partners contribute capital but not managerial services. Financial liability of a limited partner for the firm's debts cannot exceed the amount of capital such a partner has invested.

9. Partnerships may be terminated by action of the partners, operation of law, or decree of court.

YOUR LEGAL VOCABULARY

Match each statement with the term that it best defines. Some terms may not be used.

1. Simplest form of business organization

2. Association of two or more to do business as co-owners for profit
   partnership

3. Partnership organized for a single transaction
   sole proprietorship.

4. Partner with limited liability

5. Partner who is publicly known but not actively managing
   silent partner

6. Partner who is not publicly known but is actively managing

7. Form of ownership by which partners hold partnership property
   silent partner secret partner.

8. Conclusion of a partnership's legal existence

9. Partner who is not publicly known and not actively managing
   dormant partner

10. Partnership that provides professional and noncommercial assistance or advice

11. Change in partners' relationship due to a partner's ceasing to be associated with the partnership's ongoing purpose

12. Artificial person created as a legal entity by the authority of federal or state law

corporation
dissolution
dormant partner
joint venture
limited partner
limited partnership
nominal partner
non-trading
    partnership
partnership
partnership agreement
partnership at will
secret partner
silent partner
sole proprietorship
special partnership
tenancy in partnership
termination
trading partnership
winding-up period

13. What are the major problems with the sole proprietorship form?

14. What is the primary advantage to the general partnership form?

15. What interest does the state have in allowing businesses to adopt the corporate form?

16. If you were a professional manager looking for a lifetime or even a long-term position, under what terms would you consider a partnership or a sole proprietorship as a potential employer?

WRITE ABOUT LEGAL CONCEPTS

17. Design a form of business organization that would be especially useful to a small business owner. What would be its attributes?

18. What protection can you design into your business form in exercise 17 for small investors that have no part in the management of the business?

19. HOT DEBATE Write a persuasive opening statement that emphasizes the legal and ethical points in favor of including St. John's as a responsible defendant in Bill's case. Or, write a persuasive opening statement that emphasizes the legal and ethical points in favor of dismissing St. John's as a defendant.

THINK CRITICALLY ABOUT EVIDENCE

20. At the end of the school year, you buy more than 100 books from other students. During the summer, you clean all the books and rebind some. In September, you sell them at a profit to incoming students. What legal form of business organization are you probably using?

21. Jonnas and Schmidt entered into a partnership for five years to conduct a catering business. It proved to be very successful. However, after two years, Schmidt's husband's employer offered him a promotion and transfer to corporate headquarters in Los Angeles, 2,000 miles away. Schmidt and her husband decided that he should accept the promotion and they would move. Could she sell out to Topper, a trustworthy, well-qualified assistant, transferring all duties and assigning all her rights, title, and interest in the firm? Could she simply assign her interest to Topper?

22. The written agreement of a professional partnership stated that, during the first year of operations, no partner could draw more than $300 earnings per week, and that no partner could take a vacation. All members would have to rely on personal savings and credit if they needed more funds. The business prospered beyond expectations. After six months, four of the five partners agreed to increase the permitted draw to $500 a week, and three of the five voted to permit up to one week of vacation without pay. Are these modifications legal and binding?

23. Stanton and Tokun agree to work together as partners for a year. Both are experienced in treating wooden shingle and shake roofs to make them fire resistant and waterproof, which prevents rotting and extends the life of the roof. Stanton puts up the $20,000 capital needed for equipment and supplies. Both agree to work full time, and each draws a salary of $2,500 a month. Stanton does all of the difficult sales work, as well as helping on site. Tokun is slow on the job and repeatedly fails to show up, falsely claiming to be sick. In fact, he goes fishing and hunting on long weekends. At the end of the year, the firm shows a net profit of $25,000 after all expenses and the return of Stanton's capital contribution. How should the net profit be divided? Why?

ANALYZE
REAL CASES

24. Lewis owned a vacant building. He persuaded Dinkelspeel to open and to conduct a business called The Buffet in the property. Together, they purchased furniture, fixtures, and merchandise. They agreed that Dinkelspeel was to run the business and that profits were to be divided equally. Lewis's interest was not to be disclosed to the public, although he was to raise necessary funds and provide the building space. When the International Association of Credit Men sued both parties for goods sold to The Buffet, Lewis denied liability as a partner. Is he a partner? If so, what kind? If he is a partner, what is his liability? (*International Association of Credit Men v. Lewis,* 50 Wyo. 380, 62 P.2d 294)

25. On January 1, 1969, Vernon and Engel became partners in a food brokerage business. Later, they disagreed about the way profits were being divided and expenses were being paid. On August 1, 1970, they dissolved the partnership by mutual agreement. Vernon ran the business during the winding-up period. He claimed that Engel had violated their agreement and therefore was not entitled to his share of the profits. Vernon also argued that because he had carried on the business during the winding-up period, Engel was not entitled to any commissions collected during that time. Is Vernon right? (*Engel v. Vernon,* 215 N.W.2d 506)

26. Gast brought suit for back wages against a partnership headed by general partner Petsinger. To improve his chances of recovering a court award, Gast maintained that the limited partners in the business were really general partners and were fully liable along with Petsinger. Gast based his claim on the partnership agreement that gave the limited partners the rights and powers to receive distributions of profits and dissolution funds; prevent the transfer of assets of the firm; examine the books and records; attend meetings; hear reports of the general partner; and transfer, sell, or assign their interests to third parties. Should the limited partners in the agreement be considered general partners? (*Gast v. Petsinger,* 228 Pa. Super. 394, 323 A.2d 371)

27. Cooper and Isaacs were partners in a business that sold and distributed janitorial supplies. Their written agreement provided that the partnership "shall continue until terminated by sale of interests, mutual consent, retirement, death or incompetency of a partner." After eight years, Cooper filed an action seeking dissolution because of irreconcilable differences between the partners regarding matters of policy. He also asked for appointment of a receiver to manage the partnership property until the business was wound up. Isaacs claimed such dissolution was in violation of the partnership agreement. Was Cooper's action a wrongful dissolution? (*Cooper v. Isaacs,* 448 F.2d 1202, D.C.)

28. L.W. Clement and his brother Charles formed a partnership in the 1920s to run a plumbing business. The partnership lasted some 40 years. However Charles ultimately became suspicious of the way L.W., who had total control over the partnership finances, was handling partnership funds. He filed an equity suit maintaining that L.W. had used partnership funds to invest in personal real estate and insurance policies. The chancellor of equity heard the case and awarded Charles one half interest in the real estate and insurance policies in question. The appellate court reversed the chancellor's decision saying that Charles had no claim as he could not trace the flow of partnership funds into L.W.'s investments. The Supreme Court of Pennsylvania then agreed to hear the case. The issue as perceived by the Pennsylvania Supreme Court was whether L.W. owed to Charles the duty of negating the inference that the source of the funds for the investment was the partnership coffers. Decide. (*Clement v. Clement,* 260 A.2d 728)

29. More than 40 medical doctors held partnership interests in a health club. One of the partners, Dr. Witlin, died, and as prescribed by the partnership agreement, the other doctors purchased his share in the partnership. In so doing, they paid his widow a little over $65,000. The amount offered for the share (and originally accepted by Mrs. Witlin) was determined by a committee of the remaining partners and based on the book value of the partnership's assets. The goodwill associated with the health club's name and the intrinsic value of an ongoing business were not included in the valuation because it only considered such book value. Also, the partnership was about to sell the club for an amount that would have doubled the widow's payout. This fact was not told to Mrs. Witlin, however. Mrs. Witlin sued to overturn the transaction. Should the court do so? Why or why not? (*Estate of Witlin v. Rio Hondo Associates,* 83 Cal. App. 3d 167)

Lenkin v. Beckman
575 A.2d 273

BACKGROUND The law firm of Beckman and Kirstein was comprised of Robert Beckman and David Kirstein and located in Washington D.C. Both partners were well schooled and had many years in education and government service between them, including teaching at Harvard Law, serving as counsel to the Civil Aeronautics Board, and working as a trial attorney for the Antitrust Division of the United States Department of Justice. Forming a law practice with another attorney, the resulting partnership signed a 10-year lease for office space in a Washington D.C. building owned by Melvin Lenkin.

FACTS The lease had a clause that stated that the individual partners as well as their successors in interest in the lease could not be held personally liable under its terms. One year after entering into the lease, the partnership was dissolved by the withdrawal of Beckman and Kirstein's other partner. Beckman and Kirstein then came into being. A little more than a year after the new partnership was formed and nearly eight years before the lease was to expire, Lenkin received a letter from Beckman informing Lenkin that the lease was going to be terminated in a month. Lenkin then filed suit against Beckman and Kirstein for the balance due on the lease.

LOWER COURT Beckman and Kirstein immediately filed a motion to dismiss based on the prohibition in the lease against holding partners individually liable. The lower court granted the motion and also held that, as a partnership cannot be sued in the District of Columbia, Lenkin could not even get a judgment against the part-

nership of Beckman and Kirstein. As a consequence, Lenkin was left without a remedy. He then appealed.

APPELLATE COURT The appellate court assessed the assumption that the partnership property automatically becomes the personal property of the individual partners upon dissolution. This would mean that the property of the partnership would be invulnerable to suit in this case due to the lease clause prohibiting individual partner liability. The second assumption assessed was that the partnership itself is immune from suit. This would mean that suit could not be brought even if the partnership entity did retain property.

ISSUES Should assets be retained in the partnership to complete the winding-up process for the partnership and before the assets become the personal property of the partners? Should such assets be open to suit by such a creditor as Lenkin even given the prohibition in Washington D.C. law against suing a partnership?

PRACTICE JUDGING

1. **How would you rule on the first issue and why?**

2. **If you rule that the property should remain in the partnership until the winding-up process is complete, how would you justify suing the partnership in conflict with D.C. law so that the assets could be properly used to satisfy partnership creditors?**

LESSONS

32-1 CREATING A CORPORATION

32-2 FINANCING, OPERATING, AND TERMINATING A CORPORATION

32-3 CORPORATE POWERS AND SHAREHOLDER RIGHTS

HOT DEBATE

A famous civil trial involved a car that exploded into flames upon a minor rear-end collision. Evidence at the trial suggested that executives of the car manufacturer knew this before the model was introduced to the market. In order to make greater profits, they marketed the car without making any changes. The executives' actions cost lives of innocent car buyers. A Detroit prosecuting attorney brought criminal charges against them. The manufacturer's safety engineer testified that when he would not sign off on the car for production, he was fired. The attorneys for the defendants moved to dismiss the charges due to the business judgment rule.

Where Do You Stand?

1. List the legal steps that would lead to the conclusion that the executives should be tried as an exception to the business judgment rule.

2. What are the legal points in favor of dismissing the charges?

ADVANTAGES OF CORPORATIONS

WHAT'S YOUR VERDICT?

Several high school teachers are the incorporators, directors, officers, employees, and shareholders of a small corporation. The company runs boats through the white-water rapids of a river every summer.

If a customer is injured due to employee negligence, who is liable for the damages?

The last chapter introduced the corporate form of business and a few of the reasons many businesses, large and small, utilize it. These businesses obtain the authority to exist in the corporate form by complying with the incorporation statutes of one of the 50 state governments. Congress, by special legislative acts, also creates some corporations (for example, the Federal Deposit Insurance Corporation, or FDIC) to serve specific national interests.

Although corporations are far outnumbered by sole proprietorships and partnerships, corporations do most of the business in this country. This is because the corporation has attributes (or advantages) that are essential for large-scale enterprises. Some of these attributes are attractive to small business ventures, too. The advantages of corporations are perpetual life, limited liability, transferability of ownership interests, ability to attract large sums of capital, and professional management.

Perpetual Life

Unlike the sole proprietorship, a corporation is a legal entity separate and distinct from its owners and managers. Therefore it can continue to function after they die. Under the law, a corporation may continue indefinitely with new owners, managers, and employees.

Limited Liability

Creditors normally cannot collect claims against the corporation from persons who own shares in the corporation. The corporation itself is liable without limit for its debts. All of a corporation's assets may be seized under court order to pay delinquent claims. But the individual stockholders stand to lose only the amount they have invested. It is this limited liability that makes the corporation an appropriate form of business organization for investors such as the high school teachers in *What's Your Verdict?* They are willing to assume risks entrepreneurs face. But they

want a ceiling or limit on the amount they might lose if someone successfully sues the business for heavy damages or if the business fails and cannot pay its debts.

Under unusual conditions, courts may hold the shareholders personally responsible for corporate debts. This practice is called "piercing the corporate veil." A court may take this extreme action, more likely with small corporations, if shareholders fail to keep corporate assets separate from their own or if they hide behind the corporate form for improper purposes, such as to avoid just debts.

Transferability of Ownership Interests

A major advantage of the corporate form over the partnership form is the ease of transferring ownership interests in the firm. Normally, individual owners can sell their interests in the corporation without disturbing the company's operations or getting the consent of other owners. The stock of most large corporations is traded (bought and sold) on the New York Stock Exchange or the American Stock Exchange. By contacting a stockbroker, any person may buy or sell a reasonable number of shares of any listed stock within minutes when the exchanges are open.

Ability to Attract Large Sums of Capital

Many investors feel comfortable and reasonably secure when buying stock in corporations. This is because their liability as owners of the corporation is limited to the amount they have invested. Moreover, as owners they may readily sell their individual shares, or buy more. Finally, the corporation may have perpetual life, outlasting present owners, directors, and employees, all of whom may be replaced without terminating the business. As a result, large sums of money may be raised. Small and large investments by thousands of persons and institutions are combined to fund giant corporations.

Professional Management

Because they can and do raise substantial amounts of capital, efficient corporations generally have greater financial strength than do other forms of business organization. This enables such corporations to attract superior

workers by offering generous salaries and fringe benefits. Moreover, because the corporation is not automatically dissolved by the death of any owner or manager, it usually provides better assurance of continued employment.

DISADVANTAGES OF CORPORATIONS

WHAT'S YOUR VERDICT?

Dorn and several other people plan to start a business. They reject the partnership form of organization because none of them is willing to become liable without limit for the firm's debts. They consider the corporate form of organization, but reject it because they know it could result in paying more income taxes.

Is there an alternative legal form of organization that they could use?

There are some important disadvantages to the corporate form. The federal government taxes net income when earned. This income is taxed again after distribution to the shareholders. Some states also tax the corporation income, and then the shareholders, on income received.

Small corporations that elect to be treated as "S corporations" can avoid the multiple federal taxation. S corporations are referred to as such because they are organized under subchapter S of the Internal Revenue Code. For tax purposes only, an S corporation is treated as a partner-

ship. The S corporation form would provide a good solution to *What's Your Verdict?* of Dorn and her associates.

In addition to the taxation disadvantage, it is costlier and more troublesome to organize a corporation than it is to organize a sole proprietorship or partnership. In addition, large corporations are subject to extensive regulation of the sale of their stocks and bonds to the public. Finally, juries sometimes tend to favor individuals in legal disputes with corporations. But, overall, the advantages of the corporation often outweigh its disadvantages, especially for big enterprises.

DIFFERENT TYPES OF CORPORATIONS

WHAT'S YOUR VERDICT?

Appleberry, Jackson, and Smythe urge members of their service club to create a separate organization for a special project. They plan to open a permanent, year-round farm and camp for underprivileged city children. The planners hope that the farm will be self-supporting. Practically, however, they anticipate that expenses will exceed revenues because so many people are expected to visit and use the farm facility. All edible fruits and vegetables produced there will be used to feed the campers or given to the poor. Field crops, such as corn and hay, are to feed the cattle and hogs. All excess costs are to be covered by anticipated donations obtained in an annual fund-raising auction.

What type of corporation would be suitable for the group?

Corporations are classified according to their place of incorporation and purpose. If a corporation is chartered in a particular state, it is a

domestic corporation in that state. A corporation doing business in that state but chartered in another state is termed a *foreign corporation*. Finally,

a corporation chartered in another nation doing business in the state is an *alien corporation*.

In terms of purpose, a corporation is either public or private. A *public corporation* is established for a

IN THIS CASE

Koba Ltd., a South Korean corporation, and Tarpon Chasers Inc., a U.S. corporation incorporated in New Jersey, do business in Florida. Koba Ltd. is an alien corporation and Tarpon Chasers Inc. is a foreign corporation in Florida.

governmental purpose. Incorporated cities, state hospitals, and state universities are public corporations. Private citizens establish a *private corporation* for business or charitable purposes. (Sometimes a private corporation is called a *public corporation* because the public broadly owns its stock. This differentiates it from a private corporation, where only one or a small number of shareholders own the stock. The latter type also is known as a *close* or *closely held corporation*.)

Private corporations are further classified as profit making, nonprofit, and public service corporations. A *profit making corporation* is a private corporation organized to produce a financial profit for its owners. Examples include banks, manufacturing and merchandising companies, and airlines.

A *nonprofit corporation* is organized for a social, charitable, or educational purpose. It may have revenues that exceed expenses, but it does not distribute to owners any earnings as profits. If a nonprofit corporation engages in business for profit, it must, like any other business, pay income taxes. Churches, colleges, fraternal societies, and organizations (such as the service club in *What's Your Verdict?*) are typically organized as nonprofit corporations.

Finally, a *public service corporation* (also called a *public utility*) is generally a private company that furnishes an essential public service. Electric, gas, and water companies are examples. However, they are closely regulated as to the quality of service they must provide, the prices they can charge, and the profit margin they may earn. Competition in providing such services needed by most persons would be needlessly wasteful. Therefore such public utilities usually receive monopolistic franchises and special powers of eminent domain to acquire needed real estate.

HOW IS A CORPORATION FORMED?

WHAT'S YOUR VERDICT?

Delatronics Inc., a Delaware corporation, wants to incorporate a subsidiary corporation in another state. The subsidiary will make electronic component parts for Delatronics' products.

Could Delatronics serve as an incorporator of another corporation?

Typically, a corporation is formed as a result of the efforts of one or more persons called **promoters**. These individuals bring together interested parties and take preliminary steps to form a corporation. Regardless of the promoters' efforts, however, the resulting corporation is not liable on any contract made on its behalf by them. The promoters cannot bind an organization that is still to be created. Usually, though, once it comes into being the corporation adopts such contracts and is thereby bound by them. The promoters, however, also remain liable on such contracts.

In most states to create a corporation, an application for incorporation must be filed with a state. The application is submitted to the proper state official, usually the Secretary of State, of the state in which incorporation is sought. This application is accompanied by or contains the articles of incorporation. **Articles of incorporation** filed by the incorporators serve as the basic plan of operation. (See the sample articles of incorporation on the next page).

The articles are signed and submitted by one or more persons called **incorporators**. At least one of the incorporators must have legal capacity to enter into a binding contract. Thus, the incorporators cannot all be minors. A corporation, such as Delatronics in *What's Your Verdict?* may be an incorporator.

Articles of incorporation generally contain the following elements:

1. name of the corporation
2. duration (indefinite or perpetual)
3. purpose, or purposes, for which the corporation is organized, which may be broadly stated (for example, "any purposes legal for a corporation in this state")
4. number and kinds of shares of capital stock to be authorized for issuance
5. location of the corporation's principal office and the name of its agent to whom legal notices may be given
6. number of directors or the names and addresses of the persons who are to serve as directors until the first annual meeting of shareholders or until their successors are elected (in some states, the incorporators serve as directors until the shareholders elect their replacements)
7. name and address of each incorporator
8. any other provision consistent with the law

To indicate approval, a state may issue a certificate of incorporation or a charter. Once the corporation receives the corporate charter or after the articles of incorporation are properly filed with the state, shares of stock are sold. The shareholders (owners) then meet and elect a board of individuals to administer the corporation. This group then hires the managers who will run the company on a day-to-day basis. These managers then use the capital collected in return for the sale of the shares of stock to begin doing business in the corporate form.

THE STATE OF MISSOURI
OFFICE OF THE SECRETARY OF STATE

ARTICLES OF INCORPORATION

(As Required by Revised Statutes of Missouri, Section 351.055)

1. **The Name of the Corporation shall be:** The Checkered Flag Company.

2. **The Address, including street and number, if any and its initial registered office in this state, and the name of its initial registered agent at such address:** Omar Bradley Johnson, Agent, at 213 First Street North West, Miller, MO 65707.

3. **The number, class, and right of the holders of authorized shares:** 100,000 common shares each with full ownership rights and voting authority.

4. **A current shareholder's right to purchase shares in a new stock issue:** Each current shareholder shall have the right to purchase a pro rata share equal to her or his ownership percentage of each subsequent issue at the public offering price of that issue.

5. **The name and place of residence of each incorporator:**
   Omar Bradley, Johnson Miller, MO 65707
   Charles Edgar, Johnson, Miller, MO 65707

6. **The number of corporate directors and the names and addresses of those chosen to fill those positions until the stockholders can elect their replacements:** Three (3) directors shall constitute the initial Board of Directors of The Checkered Flag Company. They are:
   Omar Bradley Johnson, 213 First Street North West, Miller MO 65707
   Charles Edgar Johnson, 1717 E. Delmar, Miller, MO 65707
   Jacqueline Alexis Johnson, 213 First Street North West, Miller, MO 65707

7. **The number of years the business is to continue:** The business is to enjoy perpetual existence.

8. **The purpose(s) for which the business is formed:** The Checkered Flag Company is to involve itself in racing competitions with the hope of profiting thereby.

THINK CRITICALLY ABOUT EVIDENCE

Answer the following questions about legal concepts.

1. Only a state can authorize the creation of a corporation. **True or False?**

2. Corporations are the most numerous form of business in the United States. **True or False?**

3. The __?__ sign the articles of incorporation.

4. All corporations are subject to double taxation. **True or False?**

5. A corporation that furnishes a utility such as water, sewer, etc., is known as a public service corporation. **True or False?**

6. Which of the following is not required to be in the articles of incorporation? **(a) name of the corporation (b) period of duration of the corporation (c) purpose, or purposes, for which the corporation is organized (d) all of the above are required**

7. In the event of problems, individual stockholders in a corporation generally stand to lose only what they have invested in the corporation. **True or False?**

8. When courts take the action of holding shareholders personally responsible for the debts of the corporation, it is referred to as "piercing the corporate veil." **True or False?**

Study the following situations, answer the questions, then prepare arguments to support your answers.

9. Several juniors at Metropolitan High School plan to organize a corporation named Teenage Noteworthy Talent, Inc., (TNT for short). Drawing on the talents of high school students, they hope to arrange part-time jobs and full-time summer jobs as tutors, models, playground helpers, keyboard operators, tour guides, and clerks. Can they incorporate their business?

10. The Lacklands bought 5,000 shares of stock in Space Age Motion Pictures Inc., a speculative company created to imitate the fabulous success of producers of such space dramas as Star Wars. Were the Lacklands correct when they said, "At $25 a share, we can't lose more than $125,000; one big hit and we're millionaires!"?

11. Alibi Corporation, named for the creative suggestion service it provides via a 1-800 number, earned more than $75,000 last year. It paid income taxes on that amount and was left with an after-tax gain of more than $50,000. $25,000 of that was distributed in the form of dividends to the five shareholders. Will the shareholders have to pay taxes on the dividends?

12. Billy and Brady Anderson have just graduated from the University of Virginia with Masters in Business Administration degrees (MBAs). They are about to begin their careers as professional managers. In their final months in the MBA program they interviewed with some of the largest companies in the country. As graduation approached, they each had narrowed their choices down to two firms. Billy had job offers from a corporation and a large partnership. Brady had offers from a corporation and a sole proprietorship. The two brothers discussed the relative merits of each job offer. Billy said, "Of course for professional managers like we will be, the form of the business does make a difference." What are the advantages and disadvantages of working for each of these business forms (sole proprietorship, partnership, corporation)?

13. Brady Anderson, see exercise 12, noted that he would like to have a share of the ownership in the business he worked for. It would motivate him as a manager. What he did to save or make money for the business would mean more money for him directly. Billy nodded in agreement. Which form of business organization would be the best in this regard? Why?

14. Billy noted that he wanted to put whatever organization he went to work for on the fast track for growth. Expansion into new areas with new stores and/or production facilities would be a necessity. Which form of business organization is best suited to attract the capital needed to fulfill Billy desires for the future? Why?

GOALS

● **Explain how a corporation is financed**

● **Discuss the duties of corporate directors and officers**

● **Discuss the procedure for terminating corporations**

WHAT ARE SHARES OF STOCK?

WHAT'S YOUR VERDICT?

Anderson is an incorporator of the newly formed Galaxy Space Research Corporation. Bailey is a director. Chou is the president. Davies, Espinosa, and Freidberg are shareholders who own most of the stock.

If the corporation buys an electronic microscope, who owns it?

Corporations issue units of ownership known as **shares of stock**. A person who owns one or more shares of stock is a **shareholder** (or *stockholder*).

The corporation uses the money received from the initial sale of stock to buy equipment, supplies, and inventory; to hire labor; and to pay other expenses. As goods and services are produced and sold, more income flows into the business. Often earnings are reinvested. Also more shares of stock may be sold and money may be borrowed to provide for further expansion.

A shareholder might receive a *stock certificate,* which is written evidence of ownership and rights in the business. Stock ownership does not transfer title to specific corporate property to the holder. The corporation, as a legal person, remains the owner of all corporate property. In *What's Your Verdict?* Galaxy Corporation owns the electronic microscope.

Par and No-Par Stock

Stock may have a *par value,* which is the face value printed on the certificate. If it does not have a par value, it is *no par stock* and is originally sold at a price set by the board of directors of the corporation. When either par or no-par stock changes hands in later transfers, the price may be higher or lower. This market price is determined by many factors, including past and anticipated future profits. Profits, in turn, are affected by general economic conditions of the country and of the particular field of endeavor.

Corporations may have one or more kinds of stock. **Common stock** is the basic type, with the right to vote in corporate elections. Shareholders of common stock typically have one vote per share owned, and they generally receive dividends. **Dividends** are distributions of profits earned by the corporation.

To attract additional funds from investors, who want greater assurance of payment of dividends, some corporations also issue **preferred stock**. Owners of preferred stock usually have no voting power, but they are legally entitled to a stated dividend, if it is earned, before the common

shareholders get anything. For example, the preferred shareholder may be entitled to receive $7 per share each year before any distribution of profits is made to the common shareholders. If profits are high, the common shareholders may get more money than the preferred shareholders. Preferred shareholders also generally have a priority right to be repaid the face value of their stock from the corporation's funds obtained in a liquidation. **Liquidation** occurs when all of the business assets are sold, all debts are paid, and the corporate existence is ended.

Preferred stock may be cumulative. With *cumulative preferred stock*, if the promised dividend is not paid in a given year, it remains due and payable in the future. Each year the unpaid dividends *cumulate* (add up) and must be paid in full before the common shareholders receive any dividends. (The corporation must earn profits before it can pay dividends.)

In some cases, the preferred stock also can be participating. For example, in a given year, if dividends are distributed, the *participating preferred stock's* shareholder receives the basic dividend as contractually agreed, and the common shareholder receives an equal amount per share. Then any remaining profit to be distributed that year is divided between the preferred and common shareholders. This remaining profit can be divided equally or in any ratio as previously agreed.

WHO CONTROLS THE BUSINESS OF THE CORPORATION?

WHAT'S YOUR VERDICT?

Max organized the Integral Cable TV Corporation and owned most of its stock. However, he was no longer actively employed in its management or operations. Nevertheless, during a trip to London he claimed he was "acting for his company" when he contracted for services of an English theater group to present five Shakespearean dramas for Integral.

Is Integral bound by Max's contract?

As noted earlier, a corporation is a legal person in the eyes of the law. It must act through human agents elected by the shareholders, appointed by the directors, or hired by the officers. No shareholder, even one that owns most or all the stock, can act for the corporation or bind it by contract merely because of such ownership. In *What's Your Verdict?* Max had no authority to represent the corporation and therefore Integral is not bound.

Shareholders

Shareholders indirectly control the affairs of a corporation by electing the directors. They also have the power to vote on major issues, such as changing the corporate articles, merging with another company, or selling out in a corporate takeover. Antitrust laws do not forbid acquisitions or mergers of dissimilar companies. Large size in itself is not illegal.

Directors as Fiduciaries

As their name indicates, **directors** are responsible for overall direction of the corporation. Elected by shareholders, they serve as the corporation's board of directors. They are fiduciaries and as such are duty-bound to act in good faith and with due care, oversee the corporation, and formulate general policies. They must not act fraudulently or illegally. Most states apply the standard of the Model Business Corporation Act. This requires that the director act "in a manner he reasonably believes to be in the best interests of the corporation, and with such care as an ordinary prudent person in a like position would use under similar circumstances." Failure to do so can make the director liable in damages to the shareholders.

Duties of Directors

The directors are the top officials of the corporation. They set major goals and determine basic policies (for example, whether to sell for cash, credit, or both, and whether to expand or reduce operations in a given area). They appoint and set the salaries of the top officers of the company: typically the president, vice president, secretary, and treasurer. Acting together, the directors have the power to make contracts for the corporation, but they delegate the day-to-day duties of running the business to the officers they have selected.

The directors are expected to exercise their own best judgment in appointing the officers and in overseeing their work. The directors alone may declare dividends and authorize major policy decisions. Therefore they may not have others serve as substitutes at board meetings to deliberate and vote for them.

Requirements for Directors

The number of directors varies among corporations. Most states allow the shareholders to determine the number. Some states require at least three. Other states require only one director, who also can be the sole officer and sole shareholder. This gives the corporation the attributes of a sole proprietorship plus the advantage of limited liability for its owner.

Statutes sometimes require that directors be shareholders. A few states require that directors be adults.

Some states require that the president of the company serve as a director, while in many corporations all the directors are officers. This is called an *inside board* and is not considered ideal because the directors naturally tend to approve their conduct as officers. Better results are sometimes obtained from an *outside board,*

which has no officers in its membership and which presumably scrutinizes corporate performance more objectively and critically. Probably the best form is a *mixed board,* with some officers to provide information and detailed understanding and some outsiders "to ask the embarrassing questions."

POWERS AND DUTIES OF CORPORATE OFFICERS

WHAT'S YOUR VERDICT?

After Karporev was selected as vice president of a large U.S. electrical products company, it was disclosed that he was a citizen of the Soviet Union. Several shareholders sought a court order to compel his dismissal.

Was Karporev legally qualified to serve in the position?

Directors generally employ managing officers and delegate to them necessary authority to conduct the firm's day-to-day business. Corporate managing officers commonly include a president, a vice president, a secretary, and a treasurer. However, the duties of two or more of these positions may be combined. Other positions may be created as required. Many states and the Model Business Corporation Act permit one

person to hold two or more offices, except that the president may not also serve as secretary. This helps to prevent falsification of records.

The board of directors usually appoints officers, although in some corporations they are elected by the shareholders. Generally there are no restrictions on the selection of officers. Thus, they do not necessarily have to be shareholders or directors,

have certain qualifications, or be a certain age. In *What's Your Verdict?* Karporev was legally qualified to serve as vice president.

Because the officers of a corporation are its agents, they are fiduciaries governed by applicable principles of agency law. The articles of incorporation, the governing rules of the corporation, and the board of directors may impose limitations.

Officers are legally accountable to the corporation for willful or negligent acts that cause loss to it. However, neither shareholders, directors, officers, nor other corporate employees can be held personally to be criminally or civilly liable to parties outside the corporation for honest errors of judgment made in the course of business. This is referred to as the **business judgment rule**.

HOW DO CORPORATIONS END?

WHAT'S YOUR VERDICT?

According to its articles of incorporation, Fun Foods Inc. was created to operate restaurants and food stands at the state fair for the duration of the event.

When the fair ended, how was the corporate existence terminated?

A variety of causes may bring about the dissolution or termination of a corporation. These include the following:

Specification by the Incorporators or by Agreement of the Shareholders

A corporation terminates upon expiration of the agreed-upon period of its existence. In *What's Your Verdict?* Fun Foods, Inc., was automatically terminated when the fair ended, as specified in the articles of incorporation. A corporation may also end before the agreed-upon time if the shareholders (usually those with a majority of the voting power) voluntarily vote to do so.

Forfeiture of the Charter

The state may bring judicial proceedings for the forfeiture of the charter of a corporation that has been guilty of certain acts. Examples of such acts are (1) fraudulent submission of articles of incorporation, (2) flagrant misuse of corporate powers, and (3) repeated violation of the law. Forfeiture is rare because the state does not monitor corporate affairs, and aggrieved persons can seek private relief in court.

Consolidation or Merger

A **consolidation** of corporations can occur with the approval of the boards of directors and a majority of the shareholders in each of the corporations involved. The two corporations cease to exist and a new corporation is formed.

In a **merger** one corporation absorbs the other. The surviving corporation retains its charter and identity; the other disappears. Again, approval must be given by the directors and by the shareholders of the merging corporations.

A combination through either consolidation or merger must not violate antitrust laws by interfering unreasonably with free competition. An illegal monopoly occurs when one company controls the supply of goods, excludes competitors, and sets prices. It is also illegal for two or more companies to conspire to set prices or to allocate marketing areas, as this reduces free competition.

U.S. antitrust laws have been amended to permit competing companies to form partnerships for joint research in order to meet global competition. Thus, for example, it is legal for General Motors, Ford, and Chrysler to do joint research on materials, oil and reformulated fuel, batteries, and electronic systems for control of vehicles.

Bankruptcy

Bankruptcy of a corporation does not in itself cause dissolution. However, some bankruptcy proceedings leave the corporation without assets with which to do business. In addition, some state statutes provide that when a corporation is insolvent, its creditors may force dissolution.

Court Order

Occasionally a corporation's assets are seriously threatened with irreparable harm because the board of directors or the shareholders cannot resolve an internal dispute. In some states a court can order dissolution if interested parties petition for dissolution. This rarely happens.

The Internet has had a major impact on investing in corporations. In the past, stock transactions could only be made through hiring the services of a stock broker. Now, those same transactions can be made from your home computer through an Internet brokerage. The advantages? With online trading you can make stock trades at any time of the day. Even better, commissions on online trades are much lower. (For example, if you order 500 shares of stock at $25 per share from a full-service brokerage, your commission could be as much as $250, or 2 percent of the total. You could make the same trade online for about $30—a mere 0.24 percent.) The number of accounts with online brokerages is expected to exceed 14 million by the end of 2002.

Investors also can find a wealth of online information about corporations to help make wise investment decisions. Or, they can plug into sites that scroll stock market symbols with the day's current stock prices. Bottom line: if you invest in stocks, using the Internet could help your money grow faster.

Answer the following questions about legal concepts.

1. Generally, __?__ shareholders do not vote in corporate elections.

2. Samson Corporation combines with Goliath Corporation to from a new corporation called Barney's Inc. Is this a merger. **True or False?**

3. Which of the following may result in a corporate dissolution? **(a) corporate bankruptcy (b) irresolvable internal corporate dispute (c) state-ordered forfeiture of the corporate charter (d) all of the above**

4. No-par stock is originally sold at a price set by the market. **True or False?**

5. Directors have the ultimate control of corporate affairs. **True or False?**

6. If a cumulative preferred stock dividend is not paid in a particular period, it remains due and payable in full before the common shareholders receive any additional dividends. **True or False?**

7. Which rule protects corporate officers from being held personally liable (criminally or civilly) to parties outside the corporation for honest errors of judgment made in carrying out the corporate business? **(a) immunity rule (b) corporate officer shield (c) business judgment rule (d) none of the above**

Study the following situations, answer the questions, then prepare arguments to support your answers.

8. All directors of the ABC Avionics Corporation were also officers of the corporation. As directors, all were involved in the unanimous decision to follow the advice of De Moreal, the dynamic president. He had presented engineering and marketing studies in support of a proposal to build a small helicopter that could also be used as an automobile on public highways. After further study, the directors, as officers, proceeded with the plan to design, produce, and market the vehicle. Many problems caused abandonment of the project after the corporation had spent more than $25 million developing it. Several stockholders sued the directors/officers for the full amount. Are they liable?

9. Fleener was employed as a director and vice president of Mt. Everest Productions, a manufacturer of outdoor sports equipment. Without informing the other directors of the corporation, she bought control of a small company that manufactured specialty nylon and composite fabrics. It sold large quantities of its products to Mt. Everest at a profit. Its prices were fair and competitive, and the quality superior. Was Fleener's conduct legal? Was it ethical?

10. The CEO of the Consolidated Hands of Help, a nonprofit New York Corporation, was shown to be using corporate funds to maintain several limos and various houses for himself around the country. He responded that he needed these to enable him to better to recruit donors. The board of directors agreed with his position. A shareholder brought suit claiming that more than 12,000 homeless could be helped for what was being paid for the luxury items. The suit sought to recover the expenditures from the CEO and the board members. Will it be successful? Why or why not?

11. Bridges Inc., a large construction company dealing in federal highway construction contracts, showed earnings of $2 million for its latest fiscal year. The Board of Directors voted to pay out the $2 million in dividends. There are 2,000,000 preferred shares outstanding. Each preferred share has a stated dividend of $0.50. There are 2,000,000 common shares outstanding. How much will be paid out in dividends to all the common shareholders?

12. In exercise 11, if the preferred shares were participating on a one-to-one ratio with the common shares, how much would the common shareholders receive? How much would the preferred shareholders receive in total? If the preferred shares also were cumulative and had not been paid last year, how much would they receive in total this year? How much would the common shareholders receive this year as a consequence?

POWERS OF THE CORPORATION

WHAT'S YOUR VERDICT?

Ruiz organized a corporation in which he owned all the stock. His wife and two daughters were directors with him. Mrs. Ruiz served as vice president and their daughters served as treasurer, and secretary, respectively. Mr. Ruiz served as president.

If Ruiz died, could the business continue indefinitely because it is a corporation?

In general, a corporation can be formed for any lawful purpose. The corporation is then allowed to exercise all powers that are necessary, convenient, and lawful in achieving that purpose.

Powers vary among corporations, but some are inherent in almost every corporation. These powers include the following.

Perpetual Succession

In most jurisdictions, the corporation is the only form of business organization that may be granted the power of perpetual succession. This means that regardless of changes in the shareholders (owners), the corporation may continue indefinitely or for whatever period originally requested by the incorporators. During this time, the death or withdrawal of a director, manager, or shareholder has no legal effect on the corporation's continuity. In *What's Your Verdict?* Ruiz's business could continue. But even a corporate business may end when a majority of its owners decides to end it or upon the death or retirement of an officer whose services were essential.

Corporate Name

A corporation can select any name to identify itself unless that name is identical or deceptively similar to the name of another business already operating in that geographical area. Most states require that the name selected indicate that the business is a corporation, to alert the public of the owners' limited liability. Corporations do this by including a descriptive word in the name, such as Company, Corporation or Incorporated (or Co., Corp., or Inc.).

Any business organization has the legal power to use a fictitious name. However most states require that fictitious names be registered in a designated government office, along with information about the owners.

Bylaws

A corporation can make its own reasonable rules and regulations for the internal management of its affairs. Called bylaws, these rules specify times for meetings of shareholders and directors, for example, and define duties of officers.

Power to Conduct Business

In achieving its purpose(s), a corporation may use any legal means to conduct authorized business. Thus, the corporation has the power, in its own name, to

a. make contracts

b. borrow money and incur other liabilities

c. lend money and acquire assets, including all forms of real and personal property

d. make, indorse, and accept commercial paper (orders or promises to pay money)

e. issue various types of stock and bonds. **Bonds** are long-term notes issued in return for money borrowed and usually secured by a mortgage or deposit of collateral. Unsecured bonds are **debentures**.

f. mortgage, pledge, lease, sell, or assign property

g. buy back from owners its own stock, unless this would make it impossible for the corporation to pay its debts or to pay off any superior class of stock. Such purchases are sometimes made to boost the market price of the stock, to eliminate dissident shareholders, to acquire shares for employee purchase and bonus plans, or to reduce the size of the corporation

h. acquire and hold stock in other corporations provided this does not violate antitrust laws

i. make reasonable donations or gifts for civic or charitable purposes to promote goodwill in accord with corporate social responsibility

j. hire and fire agents, independent contractors, and ordinary employees

k. establish pension, profit sharing, and other incentive plans for employees

l. sue and be sued

Other Implied Powers

A corporation may do any legal act that is necessary or convenient for the execution of its express powers. This would extend to such matters as doing pure and applied research and development (R & D) work, leasing space and equipment, advertising, and buying life and health and liability insurance for officers and other employees.

RIGHTS OF SHAREHOLDERS

WHAT'S YOUR VERDICT?

Berling owns 400 shares of stock in a corporation that has 1,000 voting shares. Niles and Piper, who together own the remaining 600 shares, decide to keep Berling from electing any one of the three directors.

Can they do so?

Status as a shareholder does not give one the right to possess any corporate property or to participate directly in management. However, shareholder status does confer the following important rights.

Right to a Stock Certificate

If a corporation issues stock certificates, a shareholder has the right to receive a certificate as evidence of ownership of shares in the corporation. One certificate may represent one or more shares. Many large corporations have an independent trust company serve as registrar and transfer agent for the corporation's securities. Often shareholders give such trust companies, or the corporation, the right to retain possession of the shares for safekeeping.

In most states, corporations may issue *uncertified stock*. These shares are not represented by a piece of paper, but their ownership and transfers are registered on books kept by or for the issuing corporation.

Right to Transfer Shares

A shareholder generally has the right to sell or to give away any shares owned. This right is sometimes restricted in closely held corporations, where the owners may want to limit ownership to employees or to members of a given family. Accordingly, the corporation's articles of incorporation may provide that an owner who wants to sell shares must first offer them to the corporation or to the other stockholders.

Right to Attend Shareholder Meetings and to Vote

A shareholder may attend shareholder meetings and vote shares owned in any class of stock that has the right to vote. Regular meetings are usually held annually at the place and time designated in the articles or bylaws. Notice of the regular meetings usually is not required. Reasonable notice is required for special meetings.

In a corporate election, a shareholder usually is entitled to the number of votes that equals the number of shares of voting stock held. Having a *minority position* means owning less than 50 percent of the voting shares. To safeguard the interests of such shareholders, many states provide for *cumulative voting* in the election of directors. Under this plan, each shareholder has the right to cast as many votes as the number of shares of stock held, multiplied by the number of directors to be elected. The shareholder may cast all available votes for one candidate or distribute them among two or more candidates.

In *What's Your Verdict?* if three directors are to be elected by cumulative voting, Berling could concentrate his 1,200 votes on one candidate (400 shares × three positions). Niles and Piper have a combined voting power of 1,800 votes (600 × three positions). They can elect two directors by dividing their votes and casting 900 for each. If this were not in effect, Niles and Piper could keep Berling from electing anyone to the board because, with only 400 votes for each position, he could be outvoted each time.

A shareholder that does not wish to attend meetings and to vote in person ordinarily has the right to vote by **proxy** (see the illustration below). Most of the millions of people who individually own comparatively few shares of stock in various corporations cast their votes in this manner. The management, or anyone seeking control of the corporation, mails the necessary proxy forms to all shareholders and solicits their votes. The shareholders may then sign and return the forms. Shareholders who are satisfied with the corporation's performance typically give their proxies to incumbent directors, giving them authority to cast the votes. Federal law requires that the proxy form give the shareholder an opportunity to specify by ballot approval or rejection of particular proposals.

Proxy voting, especially when there is no right of cumulative voting, usually enables present directors and officers of large corporations to remain in control indefinitely and then to name their successors. The power of proxy should be exercised with a sense of social responsibility, recognizing the rights not only of owners, but also of employees, customers, and others.

Right to Increase Capital Stock

Shareholders alone have the right to increase the *capital stock* (total shares of stock) of the corporation. This is usually done by majority vote, on the recommendation of the board of directors. In some corporations, when the capital stock is increased, each shareholder may have a right to purchase additional shares to maintain the percentage of interest in the corporation owned before the increase. This is called the **preemptive right**. It enables shareholders to protect their proportionate interest possessed in past and future profits, and proportionate voting power.

Practically, if there is no preemptive power, little usually is lost. Most individual shareholders in large corporations own too few shares to be concerned about their voting power.

The sale of new shares to outsiders brings in new capital that should increase the total profits, thus benefiting all shareholders. Sometimes large blocks of unissued shares are needed by the directors to purchase whole companies; the preemptive right could prevent such action.

THE BACK-PACK CORPORATION
Proxy

The undersigned hereby appoints GEORGE KINNARD and MARY ANN CONNERLY and each of them, proxies, and with power of substitution (i.e., power to name replacements), to attend the Annual Meeting of shareholders of The Back-Pack Corporation, at the company's main office in Green Bay, Wisconsin, on April 15, 20--, commencing at 10 a.m. and any adjournment thereof, and there to vote all the shares of the undersigned for election of Directors, and on any other business that may properly come before the meeting.

Dated: *March 20, 20--*   *Roberta J. Hogan*   (L. S.)
                                           Signature

Proxy # 125413   Roberta J. Hogan
                        37 Winona Lane
Account # 0590363   Des Moines, Iowa

Right to Share the Profits

Each shareholder is entitled to a proportionate share of the profits that are distributed on the class of stock owned. These dividends usually are paid in money, but they may be shares of stock. Occasionally products of the corporation are distributed as dividends. Even when profits are earned, the board of directors may decide to retain them in the business for future needs of the firm. In effect, the stockholders are thus forced to make an additional investment in the business. Ideally, this should cause the price of stock to go up, and the stockholders can sell out if they so choose. Under unusual circumstances, courts will intervene to compel distribution of dividends at the request of shareholders who claim that there is an unreasonably large surplus of retained and unused or underutilized earnings.

Right to Share in a Distribution of the Capital

If a corporation is dissolved, its creditors have first claim upon the assets of the business. After their claims have been satisfied, any remaining assets or proceeds from the sale of assets are distributed to the shareholders. Preferred stockholders generally have priority over common stockholders in such distribution.

Right to Inspect Corporate Books of Account

A shareholder has the right to inspect and to make appropriate records of the accounting books of the corporation. However, this inspection right may be denied if it is not made at a reasonable time and place, in good faith, and with proper motive. Yet this restriction is understandable in light of the many thousands of people who own shares in large corporations. If the books were open without restriction, competitors could buy a few shares simply to gain an unfair advantage by such inspection.

A Question of ETHICS

Mammoth Corporation was one of the success stories of the 1960s. Mammoth was a conglomerate consisting of many unrelated companies in fields from high-tech agriculture to manufacturing children's clothing. Now its stock was at an all time low. Bill Predator, president of Shark Inc., did some simple math. He figured that if he bought all the shares of Mammoth at their market value today, he would spend little more than $5 billion. Then he could break the company up and sell it in pieces to waiting buyers. The pieces would sell for more than $10 billion. However, this would leave the majority of Mammoth's 30,000 employees without jobs. Are Predator's plans legal? Are they ethical? Should the government allow him to go through with the plans?

THINK ABOUT LEGAL CONCEPTS

Answer the following questions about legal concepts.

1. Shareholders will always be paid dividends as long as the corporation makes a profit. **True or False?**

2. A rule adopted by a corporation's board of directors that calls for a stockholder meeting every six months is termed a(n) **(a) article of incorporation (b) bylaw (c) corporate amendment, (d) none of the above.**

3. Unsecured bonds issued by a corporation are termed __?__ .

4. All common stockholders must vote their shares in every corporate election. **True or False?**

5. Unless a shareholder possesses a stock certificate, there is no ownership interest in the corporation. **True or False?**

Study the following situations, answer the questions, then prepare arguments to support your answers.

6. Lomax and Widener were among some 5,000 common shareholders of the Commonwealth Commodities Corporation. They owned 15 percent of the stock and were dissatisfied with the performance of the directors and managers because the company had shown a loss on operations for three successive years. Therefore they decided to solicit proxies from the other shareholders in order to elect a new "management team." The incumbent managers refused to let the two inspect the books to get the current list of shareholders. The managers called Lomax and Widener "troublemakers" and said that "losses were caused by world overproduction of grains and the strong U.S. dollar which priced us out of the export market." This was true, according to most experts. Can Lomax and Widener get a court order to compel disclosure of the names?

7. Plush Play Products, Ltd., produced toy animals and dolls. A new doll called "Tootsie Twins" proved to be so popular that the factory could not meet the demand. The dolls were commanding premium prices in toy stores. Shortly before Christmas, the board of directors of Plush Play Products voted a dividend that was to include one pair of the "Twins," valued at the low $10 cost of production, for each stockholder. All shareholders with more than one share would receive the balance of their dividends in cash. Lane, a stockholder, sued the directors to prohibit the doll distribution. He claimed that the corporation could earn more by selling the dolls. Should the injunction be issued?

8. Ben invested $1 million in a company making computerized maps. The company was owned by its CEO who had a majority owned more than 50 percent of the stock. Each year Ben waited for dividends to be paid on the shares he owned. However, the CEO increased her pay each year to levels that cancelled out any possible earnings and, therefore, payment of dividends. Are the CEO's actions legal? Why or why not?

With the corporate form of business organization . . .

1. Directors should take their work seriously, even if they are outsiders. They should obey all laws, study the corporate records, and use independent judgment on policy decisions. To "rubber stamp" management proposals is to invite lawsuits by disgruntled shareholders if losses occur.

2. Corporate officers should be selected with great care because they make most of the day-to-day management decisions. Directors tend to rely on the advice of the officers.

3. Shareholders should not casually sign proxies that give directors continued control.

PREVENT LEGAL DIFFICULTIES

Shareholders should try to exercise their voting rights after studying the annual reports and comparing the corporation's progress with that of similar corporations.

4. Shareholders with a minority position have a better chance to be represented on the board if the company uses cumulative voting.

5. It is usually risky to buy stock in new or small, closely held corporations because they are more likely to fail. The majority of shareholders may favor themselves with high salaries as officers and pay low or no dividends, and it may be difficult to sell the shares to others.

6. The buyer of preferred stock who desires greater assurance of receiving dividends should seek cumulative and participating shares.

CHAPTER IN REVIEW

CONCEPTS IN BRIEF

1. A corporation can be created only by government grant available routinely under incorporation statutes in all states or by special legislative acts of the U.S. Congress.

2. In some states, corporate existence begins when properly prepared articles of incorporation are filed with the office of the Secretary of State. In some states, charters or certificates of incorporation are issued.

3. Corporations are a favored form of business organization because of advantages of potential perpetual life, limited liability of shareholders, easy transferability of shares, better access to capital, and professional management. A major disadvantage is double taxation. Small corporations may eliminate double federal taxation by electing to be taxed like partnerships, under subchapter S of the Internal Revenue Service code.

4. Shareholders generally have a right to receive a properly executed stock certificate; freely transfer their shares of stock, attend shareholder meetings and vote if they hold voting stock; maintain their ownership percentage by buying an appropriate portion of new stock issues, if there is a preemptive right; receive a proportionate share of the profits when dividends are declared; share proportionally in distributions of capital; inspect the corporate books, subject to reasonable restrictions.

5. Certain classes of shares may be nonvoting. If preferred, they have priority in the distribution of dividends. They also may have priority in the distribution of capital upon termination.

YOUR LEGAL VOCABULARY

Match each statement with the term that it best defines. Some terms may not be used.

1. Signers of the articles of incorporation
2. Non-voting stock conveying the right to receive a stipulated dividend before any common shareholders receive their dividends
3. Application to a state for a corporate charter
4. Units of ownership in a corporation
5. Power to vote shares for shareholders
6. Distributions of corporate earnings
7. Rules for the internal organization and management of a corporation
8. Combination of two companies into one new one
9. Basic stock in a corporation conveying the right to vote and to receive dividends to its owner
10. Rule that protects management from being personally held criminally or civilly liable for a business decision made within the scope of power and authority granted by the corporate charter and applicable laws
11. Individuals elected by the shareholders to be responsible for the overall direction of the corporation

articles of incorporation
bond
business judgment rule
bylaws
common stock
consolidation
debentures
directors
dividends
incorporators
liquidation
merger
preemptive rights
preferred stock
promoters
proxy
shareholder
shares of stock

12. Must dividends be paid to common shareholders every time there is a profit? Why or why not?

13. Must dividends be paid to preferred shareholders regardless of whether or not the corporation has made a profit? Why or why not?

14. Are preemptive rights more important in a small corporation or a large publicly held corporation? Why?

15. Why should preferred shareholders have priority over common shareholders in a corporate liquidation?

WRITE ABOUT LEGAL CONCEPTS

16. Devise a better way than cumulative voting of insuring minority opinions are represented on a corporate board. Write an outline that sums up your plan.

17. Write an essay stating your opinion about whether it is ever appropriate for the courts to violate the business judgment rule and punish individual officers for their criminal actions on behalf of the corporation.

18. **HOT DEBATE** Write a persuasive opening statement that emphasizes the legal and ethical points in favor of trying the executives as an exception to the business judgment rule. Or, write a persuasive opening statement that emphasizes the points in favor of dismissing the charges.

THINK CRITICALLY ABOUT EVIDENCE

19. Hull organized a corporation to manufacture antibiotics for cattle. She owned most of the capital stock. All went well until a faulty batch of the drugs caused the serious illness or death of more than 3,000 cows. After a series of lawsuits, the corporation was forced into bankruptcy with some $200,000 in debts unpaid. Could Hull be held personally liable for these debts?

20. In its press release, Able Products, a Virginia corporation, announced that it was forming a joint venture with Hyallah, Inc., a toy making corporation chartered in South Korea. In the release, Hyallah was referred to as a public, foreign corporation. Lin, the CEO of Hyallah, pointed out the terms "public and foreign" were legally incorrect. Is he correct and why or why not?

21. Charlene Bertram owned 98 percent of the stock of Traces of Beauty, Inc. The company had been founded in the 1920s by her maternal grandmother. The company had been run by profes-

sional managers after the grandmother died and left Charlene her stock. Traces imported cosmetics from France, England, and Sweden. The products were then sold directly to consumer by mail, 1-800 numbers, and on the Internet. While on trip to Italy, Charlene found a new line of cosmetics that dazzled her. Without consulting any of the company officers, Charlene negotiated an exclusive distributorship for Traces with the Italian cosmetic maker. Upon her return to the states, Charlene met with the company president and told her about the deal. The president was shocked and noted that carrying the Italian line would breach an existing contract with the French cosmetic firm. This contract made Traces millions of dollars over the last 10 years. The president then consulted the corporate legal staff to see if there was any way out of the contract with the Italian firm. Assume you are the company attorney. How would you answer the question posed by the president? Explain your answer.

22. Pillsbury believed that the U.S. involvement in the Vietnam War was wrong. When he learned that Honeywell, Inc., had a large governmental contract to produce antipersonnel fragmentation bombs, he became determined to stop such production. Pillsbury learned that a trust set up by his grandmother for his benefit owned 242 shares of the stock, but these shares were voted by the trustee. Therefore Pillsbury bought just one share in his own name. As a shareholder, he petitioned the court to order Honeywell to produce its shareholder ledgers and all records dealing with weapons manufacture. He wanted to communicate with other shareholders to change the board of directors and then to have the corporation stop making munitions. Should the court grant his request? (*Pillsbury v. Honeywell, Inc.*, 291 Minn. 322, 191 N.W.2d 406)

23. A group of shareholders of the Manganese Corporation of America sued the corporation and four officers who were also directors. The group of shareholders sought to recover damages for the corporation and all its shareholders. Evidence indicated that the officers and directors had negligently caused the corporation's assets to drop from $400,000 to $30,000 in less than two years by being wasteful, careless, and unwise. Are the officers and directors liable for the losses? (*Selheimer v. Manganese Corporation of America*, 423 Pa. 563, 224 A.2d 634)

24. General Telephone Company of Florida owned more than 1 percent of the stock of Florida Telephone Corporation. General sought to examine the latter's stock records in order to make a list of the names, addresses, and holdings of all shareholders. Florida refused, claiming that General intended to gain this information in order to buy more shares and thus get control of the corporation. Can General get a court order to compel the disclosure? (*Florida Telephone Corporation v. State ex ref. Peninsular Telephone Company*, 111 So. 2d 677, Fla.)

25. This is a suit, brought on behalf of all the shareholders of the corporation. Schlensky, a minority stockholder in the Chicago National League Ball Club (Inc.), owner of the Chicago Cubs, sued the corporation and its board of directors, including Philip K. Wrigley. Wrigley also was president and owned about 80 percent of the voting stock. Schlensky alleged negligence and mismanagement for failure to install floodlights to permit night games. He claimed that funds for the installation could be obtained and would be far more than recaptured by increased ticket sales. Allegedly Wrigley thought that baseball was a daytime sport and that night games would have a deteriorating effect on the neighborhood surrounding the ball park, and the other directors acquiesced. The trial court dismissed the complaint, and Schlensky appealed. How should the appellate court rule? (*Schlensky v. Wrigley*, 237 N.E.2d 776, Ill.)

26. The two young attorney-shareholders in Ched Realty sought to buy out the shares of the two other shareholders in the company after the untimely death of the latter two. The attorneys cited a clause in a shareholder agreement that allowed them to buy the shares at "book value or $200 per share, whichever was greater." At the time, the book value of the shares was negative, as the assets of the long-standing corporation had been depreciated to nothing. However, the market value of the shares was well over $40,000 per share. The estates of the two deceased shareholders sued to block the sale for $200 per share claiming that the deceased shareholders were not fully aware of what they were signing because they were older and had not completed high school. The lower court disallowed the shareholder agreement. The two attorneys appealed. Should the appeals court overturn the lower court's ruling? Why or why not? (*Rosiny v. Schmidt*, 587 N.Y.S.2d 929)

27. After decades of operating as a partnership, the Bay Minette Flower Shop was incorporated in the early 1970s. Prior to its incorporation it had opened an account with a wholesaler, M & M Wholesaler Florist, Inc. M & M continued to supply Bay Minette and was never told of the incorporation. Finally, in the early 1990s, M & M sued the Bay Minette Flower Shop and its owners personally for an overdue debt. Should the court allow the piercing of the corporate veil to attach liability to the stockholders of Bay Minette because they did not inform M & M of the change in status? Why or why not? (*M & M Wholesale Florist, Inc. v. Emmons*, 600 So.2d 998)

BACKGROUND Creditors brought suit to "pierce the corporate veil" of On Top Roofing, Inc., and thereby go beyond corporate limited liability to affix full personal liability on its owners. The court with original jurisdiction denied the creditors' request, and they appealed.

EVIDENCE On Top Roofing, Inc., was incorporated in 1977 as Russell Nugent Roofing, Inc., but changed its name to On Top Roofing Inc., in 1985. Russell and Carol Nugent were the sole shareholders, officers, and directors of the corporation. On Top ceased doing business in 1987 when RNR Inc., was incorporated with Russell and Carol Nugent as the sole shareholders, officers, and directors of the corporation.

RNR went out of business in 1988 and RLN Construction, Inc. was incorporated in its stead with Russell and Carol Nugent again the sole shareholders, officers, and directors of the corporation. RLN Construction went out of business in 1989 and Mr. Nugent then formed Russell Nugent Inc.

All the companies were located at the same address, 614 Main in Grandview, Missouri, which was owned by the Nugents and used the same business telephone number. Although three directors were required, only Carol and Russell Nugent had been directors for several years.

Mr. Nugent's corporations did not produce records of any annual meetings in 1988 or 1989. In 1987, K. C. Roofing Center (the plaintiff) advanced about $45,000 in roofing supplies to

On Top, which went unpaid, and fostered this suit.

Mr. Nugent testified that he stopped buying materials from suppliers when they refused to advance any more materials on credit.

Finally, it was shown that Carol and Russell Nugent received rent for 614 Main in amounts varying with the success of the corporations they owned and in 1986 included a $99,290 rent payment in addition to their $100,000 salaries for that term.

PRACTICE JUDGING

1. **Have the Nugents used the corporate form for its proper purposes? Why or why not?**

2. **Should the corporate protection of limited liability be pierced here to make the Nugents fully personally liable for the debts of On Top Roofing?**

3. **Should the suppliers of On Top and the other Nugent corporations have any blame allocated to them for their being in their current position?**

FORMS OF ORGANIZATION FOR SMALL BUSINESS

CHAPTER 33

LESSONS

33-1 TRADITIONAL SMALL BUSINESS FORMS

33-2 NEW AND EVOLVING SMALL BUSINESS FORMS

HOT DEBATE

Once the IRS relaxed its standards on limited liability corporations (LLCs), many regular corporations and other business entities have moved to the LLC form. As a consequence, there has been a significant drop in state tax revenue from corporations. Therefore, the attorneys general from more than 30 states have brought suit against the IRS for its action. Assume you are the attorney general for the state of New York, which fought against the LLC trend for years. You have just followed the lead of the other states and filed suit against the IRS.

Where Do You Stand?

1. **List and discuss the legal reasons in support of your suit.**

2. **List and discuss the legal reasons in favor of the IRS's actions.**

> ## GOALS
>
> ● **Discuss the advantages and disadvantages of the limited partnership and subchapter S corporation**
>
> ● **Identify the type of information required from members of a limited partnership**
>
> ● **Compare and contrast forming a limited partnership with forming a subchapter S corporation**

LIMITED PARTNERSHIP

WHAT'S YOUR VERDICT?

Dr. Melbourne decided to invest as a limited partner in a business that manufactured a new form of collapsible luggage. The business did well. One day, when he was in the business's main office, the general partner mentioned that she was going to move the business into another field of manufacture. Dr. Melbourne, who had invested 80 percent of the capital to start it, blurted out, "Oh, no, you're not, not with my money." The general partner, in front of all the front office personnel, immediately retracted her decision. Later, one of the front office secretaries, Jim, won his suit against the partnership for sexual harassment. He could only collect $500,000 of the $1,000,000 damage award from the business. Therefore, he went after Dr. Melbourne's private fortune. Jim cited the incident in the front office as proof that Dr. Melbourne was a general partner and, as a consequence, fully personally liable.

Will Jim be able to recover the remaining damages from Dr. Melbourne's private fortune?

partnership agreement are not set out by the partners themselves, the law will impose its own terms. However, the government intrudes further into the domain of the partners in a limited partnership than it does in a general partnership. In the eyes of government, this additional intrusive behavior is warranted due to the limited liability provisions afforded the limited partners.

Forming a Limited Partnership

Unlike a general partnership, a limited partnership can only be created by following the procedures set forth in the state statute. Some states have adopted the Uniform Limited Partnership Act (ULPA), and others have adopted the Revised Uniform Limited Partnership Act (RULPA). Under the Uniform Limited Partnership Act (ULPA) and unlike the general partnership, a limited partnership can be created only by proper execution, recording, and publication of a certificate that identifies the partners and states basic facts about their agreement.

As indicated in the sample limited partnership certificate on this page, the limited partnership is legally formed at the time of the filing as

I n a *limited partnership,* there must be at least one general partner with unlimited liability. However, one or more partners may be limited partners. Limited partners are liable only to the extent of their investment in the business.

The general partners in a limited partnership have a great deal of freedom in setting up their business as they see fit. They are the ultimate decision-maker about such factors as who gets what share of the profits and losses, and who has what responsibilities in making the business a success. Like a general partnership, if the terms of the

---

CERTIFICATE OF LIMITED PARTNERSHIP

1. **Name** (must contain without abbreviation the words "Limited Partnership")— BURNIN' HOT CHARCOAL, A LIMITED PARTNERSHIP
2. **Address of Office** (need not be a place of business but must be location in this state where records required by RULPA are kept)—350 BARBQ LANE, WESTOWN, NM
3. **Agent for Service of Process** (must be either a natural resident, domestic corporation, or foreign corporation authorized to do business in New Mexico)— HOWARD FERNANDEZ, 1339 SAVORY STREET, LIBERTY, NM
4. **Name and Address of Each General Partner**—MARGARET WHITTAKER, 1313 HIDEAWAY HAVEN, BLUFFTON, NM
5. **Latest Date Upon Which the Limited Partnership is to Dissolve**—MARCH 13, 2013
6. **Any Other Matters the General Partners Determine to Include Therein**—N/A

FILED WITH THE SECRETARY OF STATE, MARCH 13, 2000, AND EFFECTIVE AS OF THAT DATE.

long as there has been "substantial" compliance with the RULPA filing requirements. If the filing requirements are not met, all business participants are treated as general partners.

Record Keeping for a Limited Partnership

In addition to the information contained in the Certificate of Limited Partnership filed in the appropriate office (usually with the Secretary of State), the RULPA requires certain records to be kept at the office specified in paragraph 2 of the certificate. These records include:

1. a list of the last known addresses of the general and limited partners with each properly identified as general or limited

2. copies of the certificate of limited partnership and all amendments thereto

3. copies of the limited partnership's local, state, and federal income tax returns for the three most recent years

4. copies of any currently effective partnership agreement and any financial statements issued for the three most recent years

5. unless contained in the partnership agreement—the amount of cash and property contributed or pledged by any partner, times of any future contributions by any partner, events that might lead to the limited partnership's dissolution and winding up

Any of these records are obtainable by subpoena and are subject to inspection and copying by the reasonable request of any partner during ordinary business hours.

Under the ULPA, limited partners who participate in any managerial decisions lose their status and

become liable without limit as general partners. This rule has been relaxed and redefined by the Revised Uniform Limited Partnership Act (RULPA), which has been adopted by a majority of the states. Under the provisions of the RULPA, a limited partner does not participate in the managerial control of the business solely by doing such things as consulting with the general partner(s), acting as an agent or employee for the partnership, attending meetings of the general partners, or by participating in the restructuring of the partnership.

Finally, with few exceptions, if a limited partner knowingly allows her or his name to be used in the name of the limited partnership that limited partner is liable to creditors who extend credit without actual knowl-

edge that she or he is a limited partner.

In *What's Your Verdict?* the answer would depend on the state that had jurisdiction over the case. In a state that has not adopted the RULPA, Jim would be able to recover the remaining $500,000 against the private fortune of Dr. Melbourne. If the RULPA were in place, however, Dr. Melbourne would probably be able to keep his private fortune intact.

This is because the RULPA does allow limited partners to participate in decisions that pertain to the structuring of the partnership. Consequently, if the lawyer for Dr. Melbourne could show how the move into another field of manufacture would necessitate such restructuring, his private fortune would be safe.

SUBCHAPTER S CORPORATION

Mike worked on an assembly line in an automobile plant outside Detroit. In his off-hours he also owned and operated a small propane distributorship, Warm-up, Inc. Regretfully last winter was the mildest on record in Michigan, and Mike's business barely broke even. Next winter is projected to be even warmer. Sure that he's going to lose money, Mike expresses his regrets to you that he still isn't a sole proprietorship because then he could take his losses against his other income for tax purposes.

Would the S corporation form help him?

Almost two decades ago, Congress authorized a new corporate form. It was intended to give small business owners an alternative to the traditional corporate form governed by subchapter C of the Internal Revenue Code. Subchapter C corporations are subject to **double taxation** —the corporation is taxed on corporate income and corporate shareholders are taxed on dividends. The alternative form is the **S corporation**, governed by subchapter S of the Internal Revenue Code.

Under the subchapter S form, an eligible corporation elects to be taxed as an S corporation. The earnings are treated the same as a gain (or loss) from a partnership and only taxed at the individual owner's level. This elimination of double taxation has resulted in many businesses adopting this form. Even though additional alternatives are now available (see next lesson on Limited Liability Corporations and Partnerships, for example), businesses still choose the subchapter S form.

Mike in *What's Your Verdict?* should choose the subchapter S corporation form for Warm-up, Inc. Electing to be taxed as an S corporation will allow him to take his business losses against his work income next year and avoid double taxation of income in the good years. In addition, the best elements of the corpo-rate form, such as limited liability, perpetual life, and free transferability of ownership interests will be maintained.

Eligibility Requirements for an S Corporation

In order to qualify as an S corporation under the IRS code, the business must satisfy several requirements.

1. Timely filing—A corporation wanting to be taxed as an S corporation must file the appropriate form indicating such an election with the IRS before March 15 of the tax year in which the election is to be effective. The election must reflect the unanimous choice of the stockholders. Any election of an S-qualified company to resume being taxed as a C corporation must also be the unanimous decision of shareholders.

2. Domestic Corporation—The S corporation status is reserved for businesses incorporated in the United States.

3. Identity of Shareholders—Only natural persons, estates, or certain types of trusts can be shareholders in an S corporation. Other corporations, partnerships, and non-qualifying trusts cannot. In addition, non-resident aliens cannot be shareholders.

4. Number of Shareholders—The corporation must have 75 or fewer stockholders.

5. Classes of Stock—The corporation can have only one class of stock. The shareholders in that class do not have to have the same voting rights.

Formation of an S Corporation

Note that the S corporation is not so much a corporate form as it is a tax status. To form such an entity, one needs to form a corporation in the normal fashion and then make a qualified filing with the IRS.

A Question of ETHICS ?

Paul Seaman met with his lawyer, Raoul Chavez, to discuss changing his regular corporation to a subchapter S. It was obvious to Chavez that Seaman was in a hurry to make this change. It also was obvious that he had no idea that the change did not involve incorporating a new company. Rather, as Chavez knew, it only required filing a single one-page form with the IRS. The whole process could be done in five minutes by a paralegal. Chavez paid his paralegals $48 per hour, so it would cost him only about $4 to get the job done. However, Chavez's normal charge for an incorporation was $540. What should Chavez charge Seaman for changing Seaman's corporation to a subchapter S?

THE UNABOMBER

Beginning in 1978, for nearly 18 years certain university professors, airline executives, and other innocent victims were targets of bombs placed at or sent to their businesses or homes. In all, three people were killed and 23 were wounded.

The perpetrator of the bombings sent taunting letters critical of law enforcement to the media, but the letters provided few clues. In 1987 a witness to one of the bombings in Salt Lake City provided the FBI with a description of a man in sunglasses and a hood. Because his early targets had been university professors and airline executives, the FBI dubbed him the "Unabomber."

The big break in the case occurred when the Unabomber sent a 56-page, 35,000-word long manuscript entitled "Industrial Society and Its Future" to the *New York Times*, the *Washington Post*, and other individuals and publications. A letter to the *Times* and the *Post* with the manuscript said the bombings would stop if "a legitimate media outlet" would print the manifesto and three follow-up documents. After consultation with the FBI, which wanted as many people as possible to have the chance to read the manifesto, both papers decided to meet the Unabomber's demands. The two papers pooled their resources, and the manifesto was printed in its entirety in the *Washington Post*.

Publication of the manifesto led authorities to the Unabomber, Theodore Kaczynski. His brother David recognized that the anti-technology ideas in the manifesto were similar to Theodore's, and, after much anguished soul-searching, he turned him in. Theodore Kaczynski, the man who had eluded the law for more than 20 years, was found in a ramshackle cabin deep in the woods and arrested.

Kaczynski pled guilty prior to trial, admitting that he had been the perpetrator in each of the 16 bombings. Kaczynski was sentenced to life in prison.

Questions to Consider

1 Do you think the *New York Times* and the *Washington Post* were right to publish the Unabomber's manifesto? What were the pros and cons they had to weigh in making their decision?

2 Kaczynski's lawyers wanted him to be declared a paranoid schizophrenic, but he resisted. What effect, if any, might his mental state have had on his situation?

Answer the following questions about legal concepts.

1. There have to be at least two general partners in a limited partnership. **True or False?**

2. RULPA stands for the ___?___ Uniform Limited Partnership Act.

3. A limited partner might be held personally liable to the firm's creditors by letting her/his name be used in the limited partnership's name. **True or False?**

4. Which of the following records do not have to be kept in the limited partnership's designated office within the certifying state? **(a) tax records for the last five years (b) names and addresses of all the general partners (c) names and addresses of all the limited partners (d) all of the above**

5. A subchapter S corporation can include as a stockholder a venture capitalist living in Kyoto, Japan. **True or False?**

6. What is the maximum number of stockholders in a subchapter S corporation? **(a) 15 (b) 50 (c) 75 (d) unlimited**

7. All a corporation's shareholders must assent before the subchapter S status can be assumed. **True or False?**

Study the following situations, answer the questions, then prepare arguments to support your answers.

8. Judith's brother, a famous actor, left her a fortune. She wanted to invest part of it in a start-up business venture. At a party, Judith met Hector, an electrical engineer with an invention that he wanted to market. Judith liked the idea and wanted to capitalize the venture with $150,000. However, she wanted to be able to maintain control over who had an ownership interest in the business and all the business losses for tax purposes, and keep her liability limited to what she had invested in the concern. Hector had no money to invest but did have the rights to the invention and some managerial skills. What business form would you recommend? Why?

9. In a state in which only the ULPA is in effect, Dee was a limited partner in a small manufacturing business. One day she insisted that the general partner hire her sister as his administrative assistant. Did her action make her as liable as a general partner for the debts of the business?

10. In exercise 9, if RULPA is in effect, would Dee be liable as a general partner for the business debts?

11. In their certificate of limited partnership, the partners of a limited partnership accountancy firm neglected to include the address of their agent. It was a good faith mistake. Did their filing create a limited partnership nonetheless?

12. Eriq wanted to start a tennis court repair business. To get the supplies and capital equipment needed, he decided to form a corporation and issue stock. Some 83 investors, including a closely held corporation owned by his dad, bought stock. Later, Eriq wanted to elect the subchapter S form of corporation. Can he do so? Why or why not?

13. Tracy wanted to start a company to make Christmas ornaments. Her mother agreed to help fund the company by buying stock in it. Tracy's attorney suggested that she utilize the subchapter S form for the business. Tracy knew that the subchapter S form only had one class of stock. She worried that if she and her mother both had the same level of ownership, her mother might try to manage the company. Tracy thought it might be a better idea to form a regular corporation and sell her mother preferred stock with no voting rights. The lawyer shook her head. "That means you'll likely have to pay thousands more in taxes. Instead, let me tell you some good news about the subchapter S stock." What was that good news?

14. Tracy (in exercise 13) mentioned to her lawyer that she wanted to be sure that, if her company were successful, she could pass its ownership on to either or both of her two daughters. She mentioned that she was worried that, like a partnership, the subchapter S corporation would end when she died. Is this correct? Why or why not?

G O A L S

● **Explain how limited liability companies and partnerships are organized**

● **List the relative advantages of the LLC and LLP**

● **Identify the disadvantages in an LLC and LLP**

CULTURAL DIVERSITY IN LAW

Wyoming

LLC Pioneers

LIMITED LIABILITY CORPORATION (LLC)

WHAT'S YOUR
VERDICT?

Tim wanted a business form that had the limited liability protection of the corporation for all its owners and that was not subject to double taxation.

What form would you recommend?

For years, the best forms of business organization for small businesses were the limited partnership and the subchapter S corporation. These forms, however, had flaws and limitations that needed to be improved upon. These improvements began to appear in the American West in 1977. The Cultural Diversity in Law feature on this page explains the introduction of the **limited liability corporation (LLC)** form of business organization in the United States.

Formation of an LLC

Similar to a corporation or limited partnership, a limited liability corporation (LLC) must be formed and operated in accordance with the law in the state in which it was organized. In most states, an LLC is formed by filing **articles of organization** in an appropriate state

In 1977 legislators in Wyoming took a bold step toward providing the ultimate in business organization alternatives to Americans. They based their actions on forms of business organizations that existed in Europe and South America. The Wyoming state legislature passed a statute that authorized creation of a limited liability corporation (LLC) in their state. In essence, the LLC offered limited liability protection and taxation as a partnership, but lacked the limitations of the subchapter S or limited partnership alternatives.

For more than a decade, however, the LLC itself remained an alternative only in Wyoming and Florida (Florida imitated Wyoming's creative action by passing a similar statute in 1982). Interest in LLCs mushroomed in 1988, when the Internal Revenue Service ruled that LLCs would be taxed as partnerships at the federal level. By late 1997, every state in the union had an LLC-empowering statute.

State of _____
ARTICLES OF ORGANIZATION

1. **Name***—The Moot Point LLC
2. **Nature of Business**—Retailer of the finest in accessories for the successful attorney
3. **Office address**—1339 W. Synchronicity Blvd., Coincidence, Colorado
4. **Agent for Service of Process**—Ben Acausal, 1339 W. Synchronicity Blvd., Coincidence, Colorado
5. **Name and address of organizer(s)**—Ben Acausal , 1339 W. Synchronicity Blvd., Coincidence, Colorado
6. **Names of initial LLC members**—Ben and Susan Acausal, 1339 W. Synchronicity Blvd., Coincidence, Colorado.

*Note that the business's name must include the LLC designation or the full Limited Liability Company title.

office (usually the Secretary of State's office). A typical "articles of organization" submission is shown on this page.

The owners of an LLC are known as **members**, Their liability is limited to the amount that they have invested in the business, and the earnings of the LLC are taxed as a partnership. However, some states allow certain members to declare themselves as fully personally liable at the time of organization. This is often a plus with potential creditors.

Advantages of LLCs

The significant advantages that make LLCs more attractive than traditional forms are

1. No limitation on the number of members (the S corporation currently limits the number of stockholders to 75).

2. No limitations as to whom or what can be a stockholder in an LLC. Therefore, foreign nationals, corporations, and other business entities can all be shareholders.

3. Members are allowed to participate completely in managing the business. There are no worries of losing the limited liability status for those who do manage, as might be the case even under RULPA.

Disadvantages of the LLC

Prior to 1997, LLCs were subject to an IRS test. This test determined if the LLC could avoid being taxed at up to the federal maximum corporate rate of 34 percent on earnings and then again at the personal rate of the owners (up to 39.6 percent). It required that an LLC not possess more than two of the following four characteristics:

1. centralized management (this would be unlike the partnership form that allows each general partner to manage and allows the pass through of earnings without taxation)

2. perpetuity of life (this ability to continue on indefinitely is very corporate and therefore unlike a partnership)

3. limited liability (again this is indicative of a corporation—a status that must bear double taxation

4. free transferability of ownership—This is also indicative of a corporation and not of the partnership form the LLC must imitate to get away from double taxation

Just as the IRS arbitrarily determined the rule that prevented the LLC from enjoying all the advantages of the form, the IRS later just as arbitrarily revoked the rule. With the revocation the main disadvantages of being in the LLC form were eliminated. The only significant problem in LLC formation today is usually the tax problems associated with transferring assets from a partnership or corporation to the LLC.

Today, unless the business entity is either a corporation formed under a state incorporation statute (not an LLC statute), a publicly traded corporation, or particular types of foreign-owned corporations, it will be presumed by the IRS to be desirous of being taxed as a partnership. If the business entity wants to be taxed as a corporation, it can achieve this end by simply checking the appropriate box on the IRS form.

Most of the states which previously required the filer of the articles of organization to choose two or fewer of the four attributes mentioned above are in the process of amending their LLC statutes to reflect the change in the IRS policy. With this removal of the last barriers to LLC use for smaller corporations, it would be difficult to imagine recommending any other form to Tim in *What's Your Verdict?*

LIMITED LIABILITY PARTNERSHIP

WHAT'S YOUR VERDICT?

Drs. Bryant, Rico and Ferrar wanted to form a partnership. Dr. Rico, however, was concerned about the possibility of being held personally liable for malpractice claims of her partners.

Is there a business form that could protect Dr. Rico from such claims?

With all the advantages of the LLC, it is hard to imagine a need for any other small business form. However, as mentioned above, already-existing business entities might find it difficult to convert to an LLC form. Especially for partnerships constructed for professionals, the difficulty is not limited to taxation problems but extends to the complexity of ending the partnership, valuing the interests, and then fairly reestablishing the concern as an LLC.

As a consequence, in 1991, Texas created the **limited liability partnership (LLP)**. This form offered ease of conversion from an existing partnership, avoidance of double taxation, and partial limited liability protection. In six years almost all the states had enacted LLP statutes, mostly by simply amending already-existing partnership statutes.

Under the majority of the LLP statutes, the limited liability protection extends only to shield against the consequences of the tortious acts of others involved in the partnership. The Texas statute, for example, protects innocent partners from the consequences of errors, omissions, negligence, incompetence, or malfeasance stemming from partnership operations. Therefore, if a partner commits professional malpractice and the recovery from it exceeds the amount of liability insurance coverage the partnership or that individual carries, the other partners will not have their personal fortunes endangered. In *What's Your Verdict?* Dr. Rico would be protected from personal liability for malpractice claims against Drs. Bryant and Ferrer if they formed an LLP. The partners remain responsible for other debts such as wages, or loans.

Medical malpractice is a form of professional malpractice, in which a professional breaches his or her duty of ordinary care. An example of medical malpractice would be a surgeon amputating the wrong limb of a patient. Medical malpractice may also apply to misdiagnosing patients' medical problems.

In the United States, about 80,000 die each year due in part to medical malpractice. Only 2 percent of the patients who are victims of medical malpractice seek compensation through filing a lawsuit.

Doctors are not required to purchase medical malpractice insurance. If the doctor is not insured, a patient has little hope of collecting damages.

Answer the following questions about legal concepts.

1. LLCs are modeled on a type of business form that has existed for many years in Europe and South America. **True or False?**

2. The first state to allow LLCs was __?__ .

3. An LLC can have no more than 75 members. **True or False?**

4. Which of the following could not be an LLC member? **(a) corporation, (b) partnership, (c) foreign, nonresident, national, (d) all of the above can be members**

5. LLCs are still subject to double taxation. **True or False?**

6. For professional partnerships, the main advantage of an LLP over an LLC is the ease of transferring to the LLP form. **True or False?**

Study the following situations, answer the questions, then prepare arguments to support your answers.

7. Phil Rosato and his three brothers formed a business to manufacture baseball mitts. A minor league baseball club, the Carolina Copperheads, wanted to invest in the club so as to have specialty gloves made for it by the Rosatos. Also, due to the depreciation of their newly purchased equipment, the Rosatos were sure to have losses for the first two years. Thereafter, the profits should be substantial. As far as the Copperheads are concerned, why would the LLC form be better for the Rosatos than the S corporation?

8. All four Rosato brothers plan to continue working at their current jobs for the first year or so after the business starts up. How will the LLC form help them tax-wise? Once the Rosatos' business starts to show a profit in the third year, how will the LLC form help them even more?

9. If the Rosatos' business grows, the likelihood of marketing their gloves in Japan seems great. The Rosatos feel that, should they decide to penetrate the Japanese market, they would want to bring in as a member their long-time friend, Mickie Hosaido. Mickie is a Japanese national living in Tokyo. How would the LLC form facilitate bringing Mickie into the business better than the S corporation form?

10. To facilitate going international, the Rosatos will probably have to "go public" and list their stock on a major stock exchange. How will this affect their choice of business form?

11. One of the Rosato brothers is a doctor. Having heard about the LLC form, he went to his attorney and asked about forming an LLC in place of his current limited partnership. The attorney suggested that Dr. Rosato and his partners use the LLC form instead. Why might the lawyer have made such a suggestion?

1. Be sure to carefully evaluate the advantages and disadvantages of each of the small business forms mentioned in this chapter before choosing among them.

2. Remember that the death, disability, or withdrawal of a partner may place the partnership business in serious jeopardy due to the necessity of dissolution.

3. Realize the limitations inherent

PREVENT LEGAL DIFFICULTIES

in the subchapter S form of business organization.

4. Compare the various LLC statutes in order to select the best state in which to organize.

5. Consider the tax consequences of moving from your current form of business organization to an new one.

6. Remember the limited liability inherent in the LLP is typically a protection against financial loss stemming from tortious conduct, not other potential sources of liability.

CHAPTER IN REVIEW

CONCEPTS IN BRIEF

1. The optimal form of business organization for a small business is one offering limited liability, no limits on ownership, and freedom from double taxation.

2. Several forms of business organization are available for the small business that offer a reasonable approximation of the optimal form. These include the limited partnership, subchapter S corporation, and the limited liability corporation.

3. The limited partnership must still have one general partner who is fully exposed to potential liability.

4. Even under RULPA a limited partner must be very careful about the extent of her or his involvement with a partnership. If the limited partner oversteps his limits, she or he may be fully personally responsible for the business liabilities.

5. The subchapter S corporation is a convenient alternative to double taxation as long as the business qualifies for the election.

6. The subchapter S corporation does have limits on its usage such as no more than 75 stockholders, the stockholders cannot be other corporations or non-resident aliens, and there can only be one class of stock.

7. The LLC form does away with almost all the disadvantages of the subchapter S corporate form while still keeping limited liability and freedom from double taxation.

8. The LLP form is a reasonable alternative to the full partnership form of business organization and can be assumed with little or no tax consequences by existing partnerships.

9. Typically, the LLP form extends only to shield against the consequences of the tortious acts of others involved in the partnership. It does not prevent recovery against individual members of the partnership for contractual problems, for example.

YOUR LEGAL VOCABULARY

Match each statement with the term that it best defines.

1. Owners of an LLC
members

2. Form of business organization that offers limited liability only to tortious conduct *LLC*

3. Form of business organization in which earnings are treated the same as a gain (or loss) from a partnership and only taxed at the individual owner's level
S Corporation

4. Document filed with the state to organize an LLC
articles of organization

5. Taxation of a corporation as an entity based on its earnings and then of the shareholders on corporate dividends *double taxation*

6. Form of business organization easily converted to a partnership that avoids double taxation and affords partial limited liability protection
LLP

articles of organization
double taxation
limited liability
    corporation (LLC)
limited liability
    partnership (LLP)
members
S corporation

7. What records must a limited partnership keep as specified in paragraph 2 of the Certificate of Limited Partnership?

8. What is the financial effect for a business of organizing as an LLC?

9. What was the rationale behind the four-factor IRS test for LLCs?

10. Why is there a prohibition against ownership of a subchapter S corporation by another corporation?

WRITE ABOUT LEGAL CONCEPTS

11. Fill out an articles of organization form for an imaginary business or one that you are familiar with.

12. Suppose you and a friend decide to start a business writing and selling computer programs.

Make a list of the pros and cons of each form of business organization you are considering.

13. **HOT DEBATE** Write a persuasive opening statement that emphasizes the legal, ethical and economic points in favor of New York's petition.

THINK CRITICALLY ABOUT EVIDENCE

14. West Virginia Tank and Tower Inc. bought and sold used water towers. One of its 75 stockholders was a Canadian living in Chicago; the remainder were United States citizens. When the company filed its corporate tax return on April 15 of 1996, they elected to be taxed as an S corporation for the tax year their return covered (1995). Will the IRS allow their election? Why or why not?

15. Della Octaves, a well-known opera singer, was a limited partner in "Octaves and Clark, a limited partnership." The Florida real estate development concern's only project was the construction and management of Octaves Area, a residential retirement complex for senior citizens. When the partnership approached a group of local banks for an expansion loan, it did not mention that Octaves was just a limited partner. The loan was for $1.5 million and is now in default. Can the banks collect what is due from Octaves' personal fortune?

16. Three doctors were in a limited liability partnership with Dr. S. Kay Bell. The practice's offices were in Dallas, Texas. During a minor plastic surgery, one of Dr. Bell's partners severed an

artery of a patient and the patient died. The family brought suit and recovered more than $4 million dollars. The negligent surgeon is financially exhausted after paying nearly $1.5 million dollars of the recovery. The partnership's liability policy has covered all but $1 million of the rest. Now the other doctors want to take out a loan in the partnership's name to cover the remaining million. Dr. Bell has come to you for advice as to whether or not she should go along with the idea. How would you advise her? Why?

17. Quiet Running, a closely held LLC, produces electric cars. It recently secured the rights to a patent that will allow it to produce such cars with a cruising range of nearly 500 miles. In order to meet the anticipated demand, it needs a large amount of capital to set up a new factory. You are the corporate counsel and are attending a board meeting when one of the company's financial advisors suggests that the company "go public" with their stock. What advice would you give as to the potential impact of doing so on the company's organizational form?

18. A limited partnership was formed to promote a boxing match between professional football player Lyle Alzado and an ex-boxing heavyweight champion, Muhummad Ali. The limited partner in the deal was to be the firm of Blinder, Robinson and Co. with Alzado and others joined together in an organization known as Combat Associates to be the general partner. Alzado personally guaranteed that if the proceeds of the match were to be less than $250,000 he would make up the difference. In preparation for the match, Blinder, Robinson and Co.'s president participated in interviews and a promotional rally. In addition, the company allowed one of its offices to be used as a ticket office and also held parties. When the proceeds came to less than $250,000, Blinder sued Alzado for the shortfall. Alzado counterclaimed contending that Blinder, Robinson and Co. had acted in such a way that it had become a general partner. How should the court rule on the general partner issue? Why? (*Blinder, Robinson, and Co. v. Alzado,* 713 P. 2d 1314)

19. Ward Parkway was a wholly owned subsidiary of Kroh Brothers Development Company. Ward Parkway was also the general partner in West Tech, a limited partnership. Boatmen's Bank made a $1.3 million loan to West Tech but deposited it in the Kroh Brothers Development Company accounts. Section 620.60(2) of the ULPA states that an act of a partner that is not apparently for the carrying on of the business of the partnership in the usual way does not bind the partnership unless authorized by the other partners. No such authority was forthcoming from any partnership when Jacob D. Mondahein, executed the note for the loan as vice president of West Parkway. Mondahein also directed Boatmen's to put the money in the Kroh Brothers account. Should Boatmen's be able to collect its money from West Tech? Why or why not? (*West Tech, Ltd. v. Boatmen's First National Bank of Kansas City,* 882 F. 2d 323)

20. Harry Weltman brought suit against various owners of the Spirits of St. Louis professional basketball team. Weltman alleged that as a limited partner in the team he should receive a share of payments due under a business settlement agreement. The decision in the case rested partly on which state's laws should be used in the case. The limited partnership was formed in Delaware, but the case was being heard in the federal court of the Eastern District of Missouri. Which state's laws should be used? Why?

(*Weltman v. Silna,* 739 F. Supp. 477)

21. Allright Missouri, Inc. (Allright), a Missouri corporation, was a limited partner in Downtown Development Associates, Ltd. (Downtown). The limited partnership was formed to develop two city blocks located in an area known as Lacledes Landing in downtown St. Louis, Missouri. When questions arose as to the transfer of some of Downtown's land to another limited partnership, Allright and many other limited partners sought to sue Downtown. Should limited partners be allowed to sue the partnership they are a part of? Why or why not? (*Allright Missouri, Inc. v. Billeter,* 829 F. 2d 635)

22. When American National Insurance Co. had a foreclosure sale on a limited partnership's property to recover an amount owed. The proceeds fell short by almost $1.5 million. To recover the shortfall, American National sought to recover against individuals who became partners after the obligation was undertaken by the limited partnership. Can it do so? Why or why not? (*American National Insurance Co. v. Gilroy, Sims and Associates,* 874 F. Supp. 973)

23. Ramsey Homebuilders was a limited partnership that constructed residential properties in the state of Alabama. Ramsey was the general partner in the firm while two others were limited partners. Ramsey had a bad credit history. So, when funds were needed to increase the partnership business, his signature alone often was not enough. Flanagan Lumber Company at first denied credit to the partnership. Pitman was one of the two limited partners and the possessor of a longstanding credit account with Flanagan. Pitman contacted Flanagan's credit manager and was able to get an account opened in Ramsey Homebuilders' name. When the partnership failed to pay off its account, Flanagan sued Pitman, alleging that his vouching for the partnership's credit made him responsible for the partnership's debt. The trial court found that Pitman had exercised control of the business by securing credit for it. Therefore, Pitman was held personally liable for the Flanagan debt. Pitman appealed to the Supreme Court of Alabama. Control is defined as "the power or authority to manage, direct, supintend, regulate, govern, administer, or oversee" according to Black's Law Dictionary. Did Pitman exercise control and therefore become liable for the debt? Why or why not? (*Pitman v. Flanagan Lumber Co.,* 567 So.2d 1335)

CASE FOR LEGAL THINKING

United States v. Dormilee Morton
U.S. District Court for the Eastern District of Missouri, 682 F. Supp. 999

BACKGROUND Until his death, Cody Morton, deceased husband of the defendant, operated a construction business out of the family home. Upon Cody's death, Dormilee Morton succeeded to her husband's ownership interest in the business.

In the years before the construction company finally ceased doing business, it became liable for at least 16 unpaid quarters of withholding taxes for its laborers. The Internal Revenue Service then brought this suit.

Dormilee Morton contends that she should not be held liable for the overdue taxes because she was not a general partner in the business but, at most, a limited partner.

FACTS The evidence showed that from time to time Mrs. Morton would sign bank notes and supporting documents granting security interests in the business equipment. The signatures would be in the form of "Dormilee Morton and Steven Morton (son) d/b/a Morton Construction Company. Mrs. Morton also provided funds for the business, kept the telephone listing for the business in her home, and received the business's mail.

Partnership tax returns signed by Steven Morton listed Dormilee as a partner and she received her share of the profits and losses on the Partner's tax form each year.

Mrs. Morton contributed all the capital assets to the Morton Construction Company. She granted the Bank of Salem, as lender of money, a security interest in the machinery and equipment of the business. She paid the assessed penalty for failure to file a partnership return for the period ending the year 1980. She also acknowledged that she owed the taxes assessed for the business in 1981 and 1982. Mrs. Morton also took advantage of the 50 percent distribution share of the 1984 business loss on her 1984 individual return.

In her defense, Dormilee notes Steven Morton's indication on the appropriate tax forms that the Morton Construction Company was a limited partnership and that Steven was the general partner. Dormilee was referred to only as a "silent" partner on one of the forms.

LOWER COURT After a failure to make the required deposits of federal withholding and FICA taxes or to otherwise pay the amounts of these taxes over to the United States, a delegate of the Secretary of the Treasury properly and timely made assessments against Dormilee Morton and Steven D. Morton, partners, Morton Construction Company. The amount determined to be due and payable for said delinquent taxes, penalties and interest was $44,460.52. Notices of federal tax liens under the Internal Revenue Code for the assessments were promptly filed with the recorder of deeds of Dent County, Missouri.

ISSUE Were Mrs. Morton's actions indicative of a general partner or was she merely a limited partner and therefore not liable for the back taxes, interest, and penalties sought by the Internal Revenue Service.

PRACTICE JUDGING

1. Should Dormilee be held liable for the back taxes as a general partner?

2. What facts were most persuasive in causing you to reach your judgment in deciding the issue in question 1?

3. What rule of law was most significant in reaching your decision on that issue?

LESSONS

34-1 CONSTITUTIONAL AND HISTORICAL BASIS FOR REGULATION

34-2 AREAS OF REGULATION

HOT DEBATE

A new federal agency regulation calls for parents to report directly to the agency every time their child misses school and the reason for his or her absence. The data will be used to double-check school district attendance reports in order to insure proper distribution of federal funds. School districts from all over the United States join in a class action suit in federal court against the agency and its new regulation.

Where Do You Stand?

1. List the legal reasons supporting the school districts' suit.

2. List the reasons for the federal agency's regulation.

GOALS

● **Discuss the historical background that led to the formation of administrative agencies**

● **List the advantages of agency regulation**

● **Explain how a person can appeal decisions made by administrative agencies**

WHY ARE ADMINISTRATIVE AGENCIES NEEDED?

WHAT'S YOUR VERDICT?

Charles W. Bean was exposed to a nerve gas attack during combat in the Persian Gulf. When he sought compensation for the resulting disability, the Veteran's Administration (VA) held a hearing on his claim and denied it. He appealed to a regional VA board that upheld the result of the hearing. He then appealed to a national review board of the VA with the same result.

To what court must Bean take any subsequent appeal? What will be the basis for review at that level?

As the pace and complexity of life in this country increased, the ability of the federal government or state governments to make timely and proper laws regulating commerce declined markedly. This was especially true for the federal government, which in Article 1, Section 8, of the U. S. Constitution had been given the responsibility for regulating **interstate commerce** (trade and other commercial intercourse between or among the states).

For example, it took more than 40 years for the federal government to recognize the problems posed by the "trusts" and then to pass and apply corrective legislation. These trusts were nearly complete monopolies of such areas of commerce as oil, sugar, whiskey, and even plumbing fixtures. By the time Congress acted, an irreversible and very detrimental consolidation of vast economic power had occurred. Many experts have identified this consolidation as one of the main factors in causing the Great Depression of the 1930s. In turn, the Great Depression, for at least its first four years, proved to be beyond the corrective reach of that same governmental system that failed to control the trusts.

Reaction to the Depression

In reaction to the Great Depression, a new responsiveness on the part of government to business problems was believed to be needed. The first step to generating that responsiveness was taken by a new Congress elected in the fourth year of the Depression along with a new President, Franklin D. Roosevelt. That first step, in particular, was the creation of a large number of administrative agencies to regulate the commercial environment. In statute after statute, Congress created new agencies. They delegated a portion of congressional

power in a specific area of commerce to each agency. The staff of each agency consisted of people with considerable expertise in the area they were empowered to regulate. This expertise was expected to allow agencies to respond to developing problems with effectiveness and speed. This response almost always came in the form of rules and regulations.

These new regulators and the web of regulations they created were not met with open arms. Up to the time of the Depression, the U.S. Supreme Court had placed a very restrictive definition upon "interstate commerce." In particular, the Court repeatedly defined such commerce as that which actually flowed over state lines (for example, a shipment of tires by train or truck from an Illinois plant to a Michigan car manufacturer).

All other domestic commerce was considered **intrastate commerce** (commerce conducted wholly within one state). The Constitution left the regulation of intrastate commerce exclusively to the individual states. Unfortunately, when trying to confront a national problem like a depression, the division of labor between the federal and state governments brought on by these definitions produced uneven and often ineffective regulation.

The degree of regulation that the new federal agencies felt necessary to counter the country's economic problems caused them to interfere in what had been previously defined as intrastate commerce. This in turn resulted in the U.S. Supreme Court's invalidation of many of the agencies and their activities as unconstitutional. Finally, in 1937, the Supreme Court changed its mind. In cases involving social security and minimum wages for women and children, it yielded to pressure. The Court allowed interstate commerce to be redefined to include not just goods actually transported over state lines

LAW and the INTERNET

The Internet makes the world just a mouse-click away. For the world of business, that mouse-click means more consumers for your product. But when a company or individual does business over the Internet, the "intrastate vs. interstate" distinction becomes blurred. For instance, if a dispute arises, which court has jurisdiction? In *CompuServe v. Patterson* the court dealt with this very question.

Patterson was a CompuServe subscriber who conducted a small, part-time business only through the Internet. He interacted with CompuServe (headquartered in Ohio) via modem. Although Patterson was an individual (not a large business) from Texas, and had never been to Ohio except via the Internet, the courts found Ohio had jurisdiction in the suit against him brought by CompuServe. Because Patterson was a software developer who used the CompuServe's shareware service, consumers downloaded his software from CompuServe's server in Ohio. The Court of Appeals found that although it was burdensome for Patterson to defend his suit in Ohio, he knew he was making an Ohio connection when he entered into his agreement with CompuServe.

but any activity within the states that might affect such commerce.

This redefinition greatly enlarged the job of the federal government. It had the long-term effect of creating and empowering even more agencies at the federal level. The Supreme Court has since held that the rules and regulations passed by an agency acting with the powers Congress delegated to it have the force and effect of federal law. The regulation of our economy by agencies has probably worked a greater change in the way we live than did the Declaration of Independence or the Constitution.

The Interstate Commerce Commission, the Food and Drug Administration, the Federal Trade Commission, the Securities and Exchange Commission, the National Labor Relations Board, the Federal Communications Commission, the Environmental Protection Agency, the Consumer Product Safety Commission, the Equal Employment Opportunity Commission, and many other agencies are the result. Many of the

state governments have followed the federal government's example by setting up their own extensive system of agencies.

Agency Powers and the Checks and Balances of Our Constitution

The founders of our country were fearful of the consolidation of too much power in the hands of any one person, government, or part thereof. As a consequence, they took the powers of government and split them among the legislative, executive, and judicial branches of our federal government. The founders also built into the Constitution a system of checks and balances that allowed one branch to check the others' use of power.

These principles (separation of powers and checks and balances) were thrown aside in order to create a workable, responsive, and effective set of agencies. If the EPA, OSHA, or the NLRB or any other such agency prosecutes you for a rule violation,

Appeals. This is what Charles Bean must do in *What's Your Verdict?* The review power of the federal courts is severely limited where agencies are involved.

Court Review of Agency Decisions

Court reviews of agency decisions are generally limited to three areas. The limits exist because of the expertise possessed by agency personnel and because of the heavy caseloads of the courts of appeal.

the judge in the hearing will be an agency employee. The prosecutor will be from the agency. The people who made the rule that you are charged with violating will be employees of the agency. In most instances, this produces a rather predictable result. The agency wins. In fairness to the agencies, they are staffed with people who have great expertise in their particular area of regulation. However, expertise does not always guarantee responsibility, objectivity, or restraint.

Once a course of action is set, an agency has an array of powers to carry it out. These include the abilities to investigate and prosecute for rule violations, conduct searches, subpoena evidence, and issue cease-and-desist orders.

An initial agency determination may be appealed, but the appeal will go before agency-staffed appellate bodies. After exhausting your administrative remedies, you may take your appeal to the federal Circuit Courts of

DUE PROCESS First, the reviewing court of appeals checks to be sure that due process has been given to the parties involved. **Due process** involves notifying parties of the charges and of the upcoming hearing or trial. Due process also includes providing parties with an opportunity to appear at the proceeding to present evidence, confront witnesses, and otherwise defend themselves.

ACTIONS WITHIN POWERS GRANTED TO THE AGENCY Second, the reviewing court checks to make sure that the action

CULTURAL DIVERSITY IN LAW

International

Environmental Laws

Protecting our environment is a global issue. Nations all over the world enact legislation and enter treaties concerning this issue. In general, poor countries are less likely to place environmentally friendly regulations on businesses than are wealthy nations. This is due in part because the poor nations do not have the manufacturing technology needed for nonpolluting production processes.

The differences in environmental laws between poor and wealthy nations is sometimes considered by foreign investors when deciding where to locate new production facilities. For example, investors in a steel factory may be more likely to locate the facility in a poor nation, which does not require extensive pollution-control equipment. Locating in a less strict regulatory environment would result in the investors' saving millions of dollars. But the ethics of such decisions are definitely in question.

Many international treaties include provisions to protect the environment. For example the General Agreement on Tariffs and Trade (GATT), places restrictions on importing and exporting products that have been produced using an environmentally harmful production process.

Regional treaties also spotlight environmental concern. The North American Free Trade Agreement (NAFTA) has caused Mexico to have more concern for protecting the environment in order to participate in the benefits of the treaty. The European Union (EU) has passed the Single European Act, making the environment an official responsibility. It also has issued a "Green Paper" to achieve a uniform system of civil liability in cases of environmental damage.

causing the appeal is within the powers granted to the agency by Congress. However, most of the empowering legislation from Congress for agencies contains very broad language when it comes to designating areas of responsibility. The next lesson discusses some of these areas and the agencies with the regulatory responsibility for them.

DECISIONS NOT ARBITRARY AND CAPRICIOUS

Finally, the court reviews the record of the agency proceedings to ensure that the agency has not acted in an arbitrary or capricious fashion. In other words, the court checks to be sure there is a reliable basis in the record for the agency action. If the agency action passes the three tests (due process, within the agency's powers, and not arbitrary or capricious) then the agency's action stands. This is the review to which Charles Bean's case in *What's Your Verdict?* will be subjected.

A Question of ETHICS

As drafted, the Interstate Commerce Clause of the U.S. Constitution restricted federal regulation of the economy to commerce that physically crosses state lines. Now, to combat an economic depression in the nation, lawyers are urging that the clause be reinterpreted to include any commerce that affects interstate commerce. The federal government could then regulate almost any commerce within the states. If the interpretation is not changed, the depression may be greatly prolonged. You are a Justice of the U.S. Supreme Court. You know in your heart the drafters of the Constitution did not intend for the clause to be interpreted in this way. How do you cast your vote and why?

THINK ABOUT LEGAL CONCEPTS

Answer the following questions about legal concepts.

1. Under the interpretation given it before the Depression, the term interstate commerce meant commerce that actually crossed state lines. **True or False?**

2. Congress' responses to problems in the economy have often been too slow. **True or False?**

3. The consolidation of legislative, executive and judicial powers in an agency violates the principle of separation of powers. **True or False?**

4. Which of the following is looked upon as being necessary for due process? **(a) notice of a hearing concerning one's interests (b) the opportunity to present evidence (c) the opportunity to confront witnesses (d) all of the above**

5. Which of the following is not a focus of review of agency decisions by the federal appellate courts? **(a) was the decision based on a reliable basis in the record? (b) was due process afforded? (c) does a state agency have the same job? (d) all of the above are considered on review**

THINK CRITICALLY ABOUT EVIDENCE

Study the following situations, answer the questions, then prepare arguments to support your answers.

6. Bill Freiheit owned a small manufacturing business that shipped goods to various customers around the country. Could his company's shipments be regulated by a federal agency with appropriate powers?

7. Bill's company (in exercise 6), which was in the center of the state, gave off some pollutants through its smokestacks. A federal agency told the company that it had to clean up the discharges even though they did not reach other states. How did the agency have the power to do so?

8. Bill's workforce did not wear protective glasses during its use of power equipment in the manufacturing plant. Another federal agency came in and told Bill to provide the glasses and insure that the employees wore them when necessary. How did the agency have the power to do so?

9. Finally, Bill's workforce was surveyed by another federal agency. Bill's company was ordered to promote more minority workers to achieve a racial balance in the workforce similar to the surrounding community. How did the agency have the power to do so?

10. Bill appealed each of these decisions. What appellate route does each appeal have to take to reach the U.S. Supreme Court?

GOALS

● **Describe the areas of responsibility for the major agencies**

● **Discuss limitations on governmental regulation of business**

MAJOR AGENCIES AND THEIR AREAS OF REGULATION

WHAT'S YOUR VERDICT?

Candace Merriwhether decided to take her company public. To do so she will have to issue several million dollars of stock to the general public.

What agency would be most involved in regulating the transaction?

The major federal agencies involved in the regulation of business are as follows:

INTERSTATE COMMERCE COMMISSION The oldest federal agency, the Interstate Commerce Commission (ICC) created in 1887, regulates the various modes of interstate and land transportation. It was originally created to deal with abuses, such as unfair rates, in the railroad industry.

FEDERAL RESERVE SYSTEM'S BOARD OF GOVERNORS This Board determines crucial economic policies involving the money supply, credit availability, and interest rates.

FEDERAL TRADE COMMISSION In 1914 the Federal Trade Commission (FTC) was created to help the antitrust division of the Justice Department enforce laws against anti-competitive business activities. It now is involved in protecting consumer rights, preventing monopolistic behavior, and eliminating unfair and deceptive trade practices.

SECURITIES AND EXCHANGE COMMISSION Created in 1934, the Securities and Exchange Commission (SEC) regulates the enforcement of laws regulating the disclosure of information perti-nent to the buying and selling of stocks and bonds. It also regulates the stock exchanges themselves. It is this agency that would be most involved in Ms. Merriwhether's stock sale in *What's Your Verdict?*

NATIONAL LABOR RELATIONS BOARD Charged with preserving employees' rights to join labor unions and to participate in collective bargaining, the National Labor Relations Board (NLRB) has been in operation since 1935. As the years progressed, it was also charged with eliminating employer, employee, and union unfair labor practices.

FEDERAL COMMUNICATIONS COMMISSION Also created in 1934, the Federal Communications Commission (FCC) controls all interstate channels of communication and channels of communication between the United States and foreign nations. This includes satellite, telegraph, telephone, radio, and television forms of communication.

EQUAL EMPLOYMENT OPPORTUNITY COMMISSION A result of the campaign for civil rights, the Equal Employment Opportunity Commission (EEOC) came on line in 1964 charged with the elimination of workplace discrimination based on race, religion, sex, color, or national origin. Later legislation added elimination of discrimination based on age or disability to the EEOC's responsibilities.

OCCUPATIONAL SAFETY AND HEALTH ADMINISTRATION Enabled by legislation passed by Congress in 1970, the Occupational Safety and Health Administration (OSHA) has developed and issued rules to govern the health and safety.

CONSUMER PRODUCT SAFETY COMMISSION Sharing the burden of consumer protection primarily with the FTC, the Consumer Product Safety Commission (CPSC) was given its mission in 1972. It researches the safety of various consumer products including toys. It also collects data on mishaps with products and has banned various products including toys, baby cribs, and fireworks.

FOOD AND DRUG ADMINISTRATION Charged with enforcing a number of pure food and drug acts, the Food and Drug Administration (FDA) has a complex scheme of testing and review that any new drug must pass before it can be marketed to the American public. The drugs must be shown to be both effective and safe. The FDA also conducts food product inspections and regulates the availability and use of medical devices such as prosthetics and pacemakers.

ENVIRONMENTAL PROTECTION AGENCY Motivated by our nation's concern for environmental safety, the Environmental Protection Agency (EPA) was created by a government reorganization in 1970. The reorganization placed the enforcement of already existing anti-pollution acts (the Clean Air and Clean Water Acts, for example) in the hands of this newly formed agency. The EPA also regulates the creation, marketing, and use of various hazardous chemicals, as well as handling cleanups of toxic dumpsites around the country.

NUCLEAR REGULATORY COMMISSION The Nuclear Regulatory Commission (NRC), created by Congress in 1975, is charged with insuring the safety of our nuclear power plants. It regularly conducts training sessions and inspections to fulfill its role.

LIMITATIONS ON AGENCY POWERS

WHAT'S YOUR VERDICT?

A state environmental protection agency held an unannounced meeting to discuss possible new regulations governing air quality. Had they been aware of the meeting, manufacturers in the state would have been interested in having representatives attend the meeting and provide input. However, the agency did not want anyone other than the agency members to know about the meeting.

Did the agency violate any statutes by having the secret meeting?

State and federal agencies have limitations on their powers. Statute and the Constitution create some of these limitations.

Limitations on State Regulation

States may regulate business, but they may not impose an unreasonable burden on interstate commerce or deprive anyone of a constitutional right. Likewise, states may not enact laws or regulations that conflict with federal laws or regulations covering the same subject matter. The federal government's laws and agency regulations have supremacy over state laws and regulations.

The Public's Right to Know

To protect the public from secret governmental action, statutes have been enacted to create public accountability for agency activities.

FREEDOM OF INFORMATION ACT The Freedom of Information Act requires that information in federal agency records be made available if properly requested. If an agency refuses to provide information for a legitimate request, the action can be challenged in court.

SUNSHINE ACTS The federal government (by the Sunshine Act of 1976) and many states (by similar state sunshine laws) require most meetings of major administrative agencies to be open to the public. These laws typically require that advance notice be given of meetings, along with the expected topics of discussion. In *What's Your Verdict?* the state environmental protection agency likely violated a state sunshine law in not giving advance notice of its meeting.

ADMINISTRATIVE PROCEDURE ACT To keep the public informed, the Administrative Procedure Act (APA) requires that each federal agency publish proposed and final versions of regulations in the *Federal Register*, a governmental publication containing agency regulations and presidential proclamations and orders.

Answer the following questions about legal concepts.

1. The first federal agency was created in response to the Great Depression of the 1930s. **True or False?**

2. Toxic chemical wastes are the area of responsibility of the ___?___ Protection Agency.

3. The ___?___ was created to help the Department of Justice enforce the country's antitrust laws.

4. Safety in the workplace is the area of responsibility of the **(a) FTC (b) FCC (c) EEOC (d) none of the above**

5. The government regulates the New York and American Stock Exchanges. **True or False?**

6. Which of the following is not a statute enacted to create public accountability for agency activities? **(a) Administrative Procedure Act (b) Sunshine Acts (c) Interstate Commerce Act**

Study the following situations, answer the questions, then prepare arguments to support your answers.

7. Marc Azado's plant ships its manufactured goods to various other plants in other states by truck, railroad, and plane. What agency regulates these shipments?

8. Azado's truck drivers communicate with headquarters and with one another by phone, fax, and radio. What agency regulates these communications?

9. Azado's employees are considering being represented by a union. What agency regulates the employees' right to choose a collective bargaining agent?

10. Azado's manufacturing processes produce some toxic chemicals as by-products. What agency regulates the transportation and disposal of such waste?

11. Azado's plant produces a part of a children's toy bobsled. What agency supervises the safety of such a product?

12. Azado's goods are competitively priced with goods produced offshore. Nonetheless, his shipping costs are abnormally high from his plant to the west coast states. To what federal agency would he address his concerns about high shipping rates?

13. Azado pursues the issue of high shipping rates to the appropriate agency. He discovers that the rates were raised at a hearing held in Seattle several months ago. He wants to try and get the rates lowered once again but needs information on why they were raised in the first place. To find out he must access the appropriate agency records. Under what act will he be able to obtain these records?

14. Azado obtains and reads the records. He then starts a campaign to have the new rates changed back to their previous level. Finally the agency decides to hold a hearing on the matter. What act will make certain that adequate notice of the hearing is available to Azado so he may have his views presented?

1. Know the likely areas of regulation to which your business will be subjected.

2. Collect and index supporting documentation in the areas of regulation.

3. Understand the procedure and structure of any agency you are dealing with.

PREVENT LEGAL DIFFICULTIES

4. Handle regulatory issues quickly and in the necessary detail. Regulators and regulations do not go away. Minor inquiries become serious ones if not treated expeditiously.

5. Join trade associations and other lobbying groups to have a unified voice with others similarly situated.

CHAPTER IN REVIEW

CONCEPTS IN BRIEF

1. Agency regulation was prompted by the failure of Congress to be able to effectively control various crucial business areas.

2. The span and depth of agency regulation was increased many fold by a reinterpretation of the Constitution's interstate commerce clause.

3. The first agencies were created during the Great Depression. Each agency was delegated a portion of congressional power in a specific area. Agencies were staffed with people who were experts in specific areas. This allowed them to respond to problems fast and efficiently.

4. To allow for greater responsiveness and effectiveness in agency regulation, the doctrines of separation of powers and checks and balances were abandoned. Consequently, the legislative, executive, and judicial powers were consolidated in agency hands.

5. In 1937 the Supreme Court redefined "Interstate commerce" to include goods as well as any activity within the states that might affect commerce. This redefinition enlarged the federal government's job because it created and empowered more federal agencies.

6. The review powers of the federal courts over agency decisions only extend to whether due process was afforded, whether an agency decision was arbitrary or capricious and, finally, whether the agency acted within the powers granted to it by Congress.

7. Limits exist from statutes and the Constitution on governmental regulation of business. Protection against secret governmental action is provided through the right to know what agency records contain, through the requirement of open agency meetings, and through the requirement that agency regulations be published in the *Federal Register.*

YOUR LEGAL VOCABULARY

Match each statement with the term that it best defines. Some terms may not be used.

1. Agency regulating television broadcasting

2. Agency regulating collective bargaining

3. Agency regulating safety of drugs

4. Agency regulating the disposal of toxic waste

5. Agency regulating toy safety

6. Agency regulating interest rates

7. Agency regulating unfair trade practices

8. Agency regulating the national stock exchanges

9. Commerce conducted wholly within one state

10. Government publication containing agency regulations

11. Notice of charges or potential rulemaking coupled with opportunity to appear, present evidence, and confront witnesses if warranted

CPSC
due process
EEOC
EPA
FCC
FDA
Federal Register
Federal Reserve System's
   Board of Governors
FTC
ICC
interstate commerce
intrastate commerce
NLRB
NRC
OSHA
SEC

12. What factors prevent Congress from acting effectively in regulating commerce?

13. In the Constitution, why did the founders of our country separate the executive, legislative, and judicial powers of government?

14. Historically, what role did the Great Depression play in the development of agencies?

15. Why do many people believe that a greater revolution took place when the Supreme Court changed the definition of Interstate Commerce than during the American Revolution?

16. How extensive is the review power of the federal courts over agency decisions?

WRITE ABOUT LEGAL CONCEPTS

17. On balance, do you believe empowering the agencies with executive, legislative, and executive authority has produced a better regulatory result than would have existed with a separation of powers?

18. How would you change the review power over agency decisions of the federal courts?

19. **HOT DEBATE** Write a persuasive opening statement that emphasizes the legal, ethical, and economic points in favor of the school districts' petition. Or, write a persuasive opening statement for the Attorney General of the United States that emphasizes the legal, ethical, and economic points in favor of sustaining the regulation.

THINK CRITICALLY ABOUT EVIDENCE

20. Joan owned a small factory in West Virginia. After investigation, OSHA ruled that her workers needed safety goggles different from those she had been providing. The new goggles had lenses two hundredths thicker than the ones that had been in use. They cost almost $20 more per pair ($25 vs. $5). For health purposes, each employee is required to change goggles after every eight hours of wear. Consequently, the increased cost might put Joan out of business, as her competition in northern Mexico does not have to provide any goggles to their employees. At a hearing she requested, Joan presented evidence that the old goggles would stop any flying object just as well as the new ones. OSHA had adopted its goggle standard after extensive hearings and evidentiary submissions. An OSHA hearing examiner therefore ruled in the agency's favor and ordered Joan to buy the approved goggles. Can Joan appeal the decision? If so, to whom?

21. Under what circumstances could Joan, in exercise 20, appeal the agency's decisions to a federal court? Which court?

22. Review the facts of Joan's case as though you were the federal court with appropriate jurisdiction. Do you uphold the hearing examiner?

23. Suppose the U.S. Supreme Court refuses to hear Joan's appeal. Does she have any other reasonable alternative?

24. Considering the nature of Joan's experience and contrasting it with the reasons why regulation of the United States economy was placed in the hands of the administrative agencies, evaluate how well the system is functioning in achieving its objectives. Are there procedures you would change? Would you expand or restrict the reach of the agencies? In what way(s)?

ANALYZE
REAL CASES

25. When the Department of Commerce required that all baby crib mattresses should pass a test involving possible ignition by a burning cigarette, the manufacturers of the mattresses appealed the decision claiming it was arbitrary and capricious to apply such a test to baby cribs. Decide. (*Bunny Bear v. Peterson*, 473 F.2d 1002)

26. When an inspection revealed a dangerous accumulation of coal dust in a mine, the inspector issued a citation for a violation of the Mine Safety and Health Act. After a hearing, the owner was fined $2,000. The owner appealed to the federal courts on the basis that the hearing judge who imposed the fine had made his determination based almost exclusively on the testimony of the inspector who issued the citation. Is that sufficient evidence on the record to avoid the decision being deemed arbitrary and capricious? (*Buck Creek Coal, Inc. v. Federal Mine Safety and Health Administration*, 52 F. 2d 133)

27. Concerned with the possible spread to employees of AIDS and other diseases, OSHA reviewed the protective practices of dentists and their assistants. It then set forth an extensive and, according to the American Dental Association, costly set of rules involving use of protective gloves, masks, etc., by dentists and their assistants. OSHA did so in responding to its charge by Congress to determine whether potential safety rules could significantly reduce a health risk without threatening the existence of an industry. Did OSHA make an error by failing to consider the effect of the increased cost on consumers? Why or why not? (*American Dental Association v. Martin*, 984 F.2d 823)

28. When a bank failed in Livingston, New Jersey, the Federal Deposit Insurance Corporation (FDIC) paid up to $100,000 per account to depositors and then sought to recover the lost money. In performing this latter act, the FDIC issued a subpoena for the personal financial records of two of the directors of the failed bank. The directors refused saying that this intruded on their right of privacy. The FDIC responded that knowledge gained from the subpoenas might indicate whether the directors had violated their fiduciary duties. Should the records be surrendered? Why or why not? (*FDIC v. Wentz*, 55 F.2d 905)

29. After carefully complying with the rules of due process, the Atomic Energy Commission (AEC) was about to issue new rules for nuclear reactor safety when the Natural Resources Defense Council (NRDC) brought suit to stop it. The NRDC argued that, due to the hazards of the nuclear industry, more than just mere compliance with due process was necessary. Although doing so was in compliance with the Administrative Procedure Act, the AEC had shortened a proceeding that might have produced a more extensive record from which arguments could have been made against issuing a license to a new nuclear power plant. The case ultimately came before the U.S. Supreme Court. Should the rulemaking process start again after new and more complex requirements of due process are fulfilled? (*Vermont Yankee Nuclear Power Corp. v. NRDC*, 435 U. S. 519)

30. The Federal Savings and Loan Insurance Corporation (FSLIC) insured savings and other accounts in savings and loan institutions across the nation. Its controlling agency, the Federal Home Loan Bank Board (FHLBB) examined the savings and loans that were insured by the FSLIC to determine whether or not they were being run correctly. When the FHLBB was examining a Texas based Savings and Loan, the Vision Banc S & L, it became suspicious of a very large loan made by Vision to Sandsend Financial Consultants, Ltd. The FHLBB then subpoenaed the financial records of Sandsend from a bank, the West Belt. Sandsend then successfully sued to void the subpoena. The FHLBB appealed. The appellate court noted that the FHLBB's subpoena power was not limited to parties directly associated with an investigation and that the court's review power over an agency's action in issuing a subpoena was limited to two questions: (1) whether the investigation has a proper statutory purpose, and (2) whether the documents sought are relevant to the investigation. Should the appellate court go along with the District Court and uphold the voiding of the subpoena or should it reverse the District Court and order the subpoena enforced? Why? (*Sandsend Financial Consultants, Ltd. v. Federal Home Loan Bank Board*, 878 F.2d 875)

FACTS Coach Tarkanian took over a mediocre basketball program at the University of Nevada at Las Vegas. Within four years his team was in the "Final Four" of the NCAA Tourney. Then after a lengthy investigatory process, the NCAA detailed 38 violations of its rules by UNLV personnel, mainly concerning player recruitment. Ten of the violations involved Coach Tarkanian. The NCAA placed UNLV on probation for two years. UNLV removed Tarkanian from the program for the two-year period. Faced with a drastic cut in salary, Coach Tarkanian brought suit. He alleged that his disciplining was an action of the state government and that his right to due process guaranteed under the Fourteenth Amendment of the U.S. Constitution had been denied him because the university administration had accepted the NCAA determination without giving him notice and a hearing. The university and the NCAA responded that no such due process was required, as the NCAA was a private body and therefore not subject to the requirements of the Fourtenth Amendment.

LOWER COURT DECISION The Nevada Supreme Court rejected the NCAA and university positions. Due process had been denied Coach Tarkanian. The case was then appealed to the U.S. Supreme Court.

U.S. SUPREME COURT DECISION In a 5 to 4 decision, the Supreme Court concluded as follows: Embedded in our Fourteenth Amendment jurisprudence is a dichotomy between state action, which is subject to scrutiny under the Amendment's due process clause, and private conduct, against which the Amendment affords no shield, no matter how unfair that conduct may be. . . . As a general matter, the protections of the Fourteenth Amendment do not extend to private conduct abridging individual rights. Careful adherence to the state action requirement preserves an area of individual freedom by limiting the reach of federal law and avoids the imposition of responsibility on a state for conduct it could not control. In this case Tarkanian argues that the NCAA was a state actor because it misused power that it possessed by virtue of state law. He claims specifically that UNLV delegated its own functions to the NCAA, clothing the Association with authority both to adopt rules governing UNLV's athletic programs and to enforce those rules on its behalf.

These contentions fundamentally misconstrue the facts of this case . . . the NCAA's several hundred other public and private member institutions each similarly affected those policies. . . . They did not act under color of Nevada law. It necessarily follows that the source of the legislation adopted by the NCAA is not Nevada but the collective membership. UNLV retained the authority to withdraw from the NCAA and establish its own standards. The University alternatively could have stayed in the Association and worked through the Association's legislative process to amend rules or standards it deemed harsh, unfair, or unwieldy.

The Supreme Court then concluded that the NCAA actions were not state actions and, therefore, Tarkanian could not sue the NCAA for violation of his Fourteeneth Amendment rights. The Court, however, did concede that UNLV's decision to suspend the coach was a state action.

ENTREPRENEURS AND THE LAW

PROJECT 6 FORMS OF BUSINESS ORGANIZATIONS

BUSINESS BOOMS

Ben Windows watched as the crane lowered the new Reelshield sign onto the top of the steel pedestal in front of his factory. The last 18 months had been amazing. Orders from the trade journal ads were coming in steadily. Even the $2,000 unit price hadn't deterred buyers. The independent salespeople also were producing. Sales were at an all-time high, even though the economy was in a recession. Patricia Johns had created an efficient front office. And the production line had yet to miss a deadline. Of the five production technicians working for Ben, three were ex-cons, and their performance record was flawless.

BUSINESS ORGANIZATION

On a personal level, Kristen and he were still in love. Wedding plans had been finalized for the coming June. Her family was coming around. Her mother had been helping Kristen prepare for the wedding. Her dad had toured the plant and inspected the books. Kristen's dad only made one comment with a negative ring. He felt Ben's business should not be in the sole proprietorship form. "Even with insurance," he commented, "one bad mistake or defective Reelshield and you are in serious trouble." Ben had only nodded when the comment was made. He had just settled such a suit for less than $1,000. Nevertheless, Ben decided to take the matter up with his attorney. It was time for a meeting with her anyway. Ben called her and explained that he wanted to look into alternative forms of organizing his business.

GOVERNMENT AGENCIES

Ben also asked his attorney if there were any other potential problems that he could avoid by adequate legal review and preparation. He replied, "Yes, there are. I realize you are somewhat familiar with dealing with the government because of the OSHA requirement for protective shields. There are more government agencies out there just waiting to make your life more complex. I'll draw up a list and detail what they will be looking for. I'll also brief you on what you should do when they appear." "Great," said Ben.

ACTIVITIES

Divide into teams and perform one or more of the following activities, as directed by your teacher.

BRAINSTORM

Make a list of all the different forms of businesses Ben should consider. Then record the advantages and disadvantages of each form. As a group, decide which form of organization Ben should choose. Present your decision to the class, explaining the reasons you chose the particular form of organization.

PREPARE LEGAL DOCUMENTS

Assume that Ben has chosen the subchapter S form of business organization. Prepare the articles in incorporation for the business. (Each team member should prepare a different section of the articles. Then assemble the document and submit it to your teacher.)

RESEARCH AND PRESENT

Each team member should prepare a report about a different government agency that Ben will need to deal with. The report should detail the types of regulations that the agency imposes on businesses. Members should then present their reports to the team. (Agencies to report on include the Interstate Commerce Commission, Federal Trade Commission, Securities and Exchange Commission, Federal Communications Commission, National Labor Relations Board, Equal Employment Opportunity Commission, Occupational Safety and Health Administration, and the Environmental Protection Agency.)

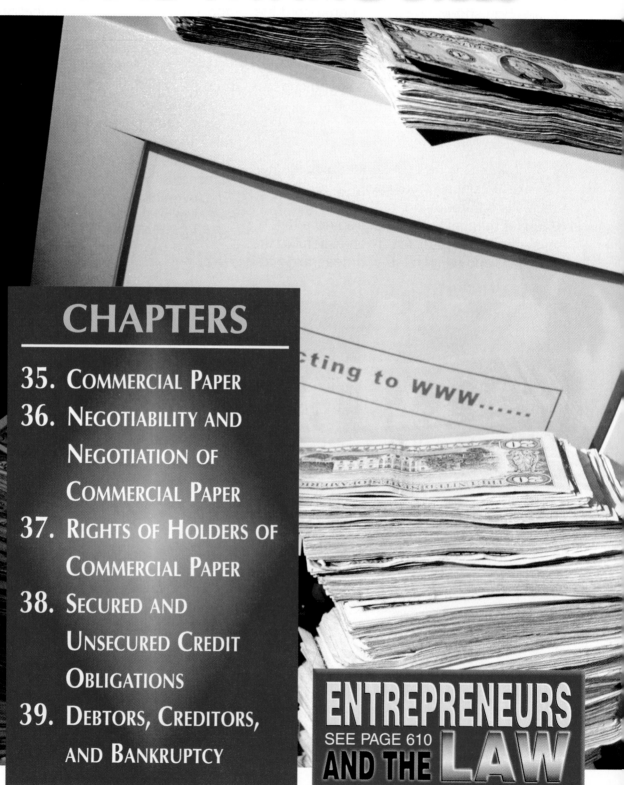

UNIT SEVEN

BORROWING MONEY AND PAYING BILLS

ENTREPRENEURS
AND THE LAW
SEE PAGE 610

Melissa Kugler began working in the banking industry in 1994, directly after high school. Her only prior work experience had been as a receptionist in the radiology department of a nearby hospital. Ironically, that receptionist job led to her current career in banking. "One bit of advice I would offer is that you neither know where life may lead nor what opportunities a job may provide—networking can be invaluable and may open doors to realizing your ultimate career goal."

While working at the hospital, a part-time co-worker noticed Melissa's excellent people skills. She suggested Melissa apply for a teller opening at the bank where she is now employed. Melissa knew that she wanted to work in business and accounting. She also wanted to continue working with people.

Melissa's skills and interests proved to be of tremendous value to her career once she began working at the bank. In 1995, Melissa was promoted to Assistant Head Teller. One year later, she received a promotion to Head Teller.

Melissa is currently studying for a degree in General Banking through night courses at a local community college. She is also taking advantage of American Institution of Banking classes offered through her employer. "On-the-job training was an important component of my training as a bank teller and also during my transition into a supervisory role."

Melissa has found that strong interpersonal skills are essential to her career field. Most of her responsibilities involve interacting with others, including tellers, bank staff, and bank customers. "I have to review staff performance, conduct monthly staff meetings, train staff on new policies and procedures, and coordinate the training of new tellers. I often listen to customer needs and address their concerns. These varied aspects of my job demand that I be able to draw the best from others."

Organizational skills are also very important for banking positions such as Melissa's. Melissa must routinely balance a variety of tasks that require great attention to detail. She supervises the workflow of the tellers, handling any problems that might arise. She and other staff members compile and sort information for a variety of reports and prove ATM and night deposits bags every day. "Some of my responsibilities are fairly routine: processing customer transactions, approving over-limit transactions, opening or processing new customer accounts, and operating the drive-in window when necessary."

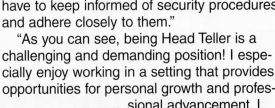

Considering the amount of money that tellers handle, legal issues concern Melissa on a daily basis. "Because I have to account for all monies that enter and leave this branch of the bank, I have to prove the vault cash daily. In addition, I order cash for our branch weekly and verify shipments when they arrive. I supply tellers with cash, and maintain and balance the daily cash flow. I have to keep informed of security procedures and adhere closely to them."

"As you can see, being Head Teller is a challenging and demanding position! I especially enjoy working in a setting that provides opportunities for personal growth and professional advancement. I would say if a person is good at math, willing to learn and to apply what they've learned, and has a professional attitude, banking is definitely a career to consider."

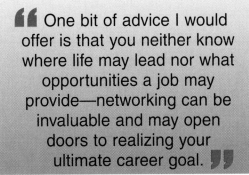

> **❝** One bit of advice I would offer is that you neither know where life may lead nor what opportunities a job may provide—networking can be invaluable and may open doors to realizing your ultimate career goal. **❞**

LESSONS

35-1 BASIC TYPES OF COMMERCIAL PAPER

35-2 SPECIALIZED FORMS OF COMMERCIAL PAPER

HOT DEBATE

One day at the mall you accidentally leave your car unlocked. When you return, your console has been broken into and some things stolen. Two weeks later you receive your bank statement and cancelled checks. You discover that someone has written a bad check on your account. Then you recall that one of your checkbooks was in the console and, obviously, has been taken. You call the bank insisting that, because they have paid a check that you did not issue, they should re-credit your account the amount you have lost. The bank refuses, even though you point out it is in their contract with you only to pay over your signature and that the signature on the bad check doesn't even look like yours. Finally, you bring suit against the bank on the issue.

Where Do You Stand?

1. **List the legal reasons supporting your suit.**

2. **List the reasons supporting the bank's decision not to re-credit your account for the bad check.**

GOALS

● **Explain the importance of commercial paper**

● **Describe the basic types of commercial paper and their uses**

WHAT IS COMMERCIAL PAPER?

WHAT'S YOUR VERDICT?

Marsha shocked her friend Benito by claiming that the bank she had her checking account with was really her debtor and that she could collect whenever she wanted. Benito stared at her, then laughed. "Who are you trying to kid?" he asked. "When did a bank ever take a loan from a depositor?" Marsha smiled back and said, "It happens every day."

Is she correct?

Unconditional written orders or promises to pay money are collectively defined as **commercial paper**. Most of the laws governing the legitimacy and use of commercial paper are in the Uniform Commercial Code (UCC). However, other laws are important to commercial paper as well. For example, commercial paper is not valid if used in illegal transac-tions, such as gambling or drug trafficking as defined in criminal codes.

The check is the most common form of commercial paper. Like other forms of commercial paper, it was developed centuries ago to serve as a relatively safe substitute for money. When traveling and dealing with dis-tant sellers, merchants would leave their valuable gold or silver with their bankers. Then, when the merchants wanted to pay a seller for purchases, they simply wrote an order addressed to their bank. The order directed the bank to deliver a specified amount of the gold or silver to whomever the seller designated.

The bank could tell if the order was authentic by comparing the sig-nature on the order with the mer-chant's signature that it had on file. The bank then complied with the order because, once the merchant had deposited the gold or silver, the bank was the merchant's debtor. Consequently, if the merchant appeared and demanded the gold or silver, the bank had to give it back.

This is still true today. Banks are the debtors of the depositors, as Marsha correctly stated in *What's Your Verdict?* They compete with one another to borrow funds from their depositors and then lend what they have borrowed to others. Checks are called demand instruments because they enable depositors to withdraw their money or have it paid in accor-dance with their order. Marsha can "collect" what is owed to her by writ-ing a check at any time.

TYPES OF COMMERCIAL PAPER

WHAT'S YOUR VERDICT?

Nightwing purchased a personal computer for her new business. After comparing software, she selected an integrated accounting and inven-tory program. The program cost more than $700, and she had to borrow the money from her friend Fyffe. In exchange, Nightwing gave Fyffe an IOU for that amount. The IOU was signed and dated.

Was it commercial paper?

Today, commercial paper can be grouped into two categories. The first consists of unconditional orders to pay money. The second category is composed of unconditional promises to pay money.

"Unconditional," as used to define commercial paper, means that the legal effectiveness of the order or promise does not depend on any other event. Accordingly, an instrument that reads in part "Pay to the order of Sam after he delivers the bike to me" would not be commercial paper because its enforceability is conditional upon delivery of the bike.

Unlike unconditional orders or promises to pay a sum of money, an IOU (such as the one Nightwing gave to Fyffe in *What's Your Verdict?*) only acknowledges the debt. The law holds that such an acknowledgment is far short of a promise or order to repay. Therefore, an IOU is not enforceable as commercial paper.

Of the four main types of commercial paper, two—the draft and the check—are unconditional orders to pay money. The other two—the promissory note and the certificate of deposit—are unconditional promises to pay money. These four main types are discussed below.

Drafts

A **draft** or **bill of exchange** is an unconditional written order by one person that directs another person to pay money to a third. The person directed to pay may be a natural person or an artificial "legal" person, such as a corporation.

If it is not necessary to specify that a particular person receive the money, the order may be made payable to "cash" or to "bearer." Then the person in legal possession of the order may collect on it. However, the order must be either

Sanford bought a used amplifier for her electric guitar from Minton for $600. She paid Minton $100 down and promised to pay the remaining $500 by her next payday. A few days after the sale, Minton bought a state-of-the-art, low-distortion speaker system for $750 at a clearance sale at Downtown Audio. As partial payment to Downtown Audio, Minton drew a draft (see the illustration below) on the $500 Sanford owed him. To be sure Sanford had enough time to get the money, Minton made the draft payable to the order of Downtown Audio thirty days after sight. Upon receiving the draft, Downtown immediately presented it to Sanford who indicated her willingness to pay in thirty days by writing the date and her signature on the front of the paper along with the word "accepted."

effective upon demand or at a definite date, such as the "thirty days after sight" as shown in the illustration below.

The person who executes or draws the draft and orders payment to be made is the **drawer**. The **drawee** is

the party ordered to pay the draft. The **payee** is the party to whom commercial paper is made payable. The drawee is usually the debtor of the drawer. Minton in *In This Case* is the drawer, Sanford is the drawee, and Downtown Audio is the payee.

Drafts are sometimes classified in terms of the time of payment. A draft may be payable "at sight" (also termed being payable "on demand"). This is called a **sight draft**, which is presented to the drawee by the one holding the draft. The drawee on a sight draft is expected to pay immediately.

If a draft is payable on a set date, at the end of a specified period after sight, or at the end of a specified period after the date of the draft, it is a **time draft**. Minton's draft in the illustration is a time draft. When a time draft is payable a number of days or months after sight, it must be presented to the drawee for acceptance in order to start the running of the specified time.

Acceptance is the drawee's promise to pay the draft when due. Such a promise is usually evidenced by the signature of the acceptor on the face of the instrument along with words indicating the acceptance. When a draft states it is payable a number of days or months "after date," the time starts running immediately from the date of the draft.

Checks

A **check** is a type of draft by which a bank depositor orders the bank to pay money, usually to a third party (see the illustration at the top of the next page). Checks are usually written on special forms that are magnetically encoded to simplify check processing for the banking system. However, checks may be written on blank paper, on forms provided by the depositor, on rawhide, or on other materials and still be legally effective. The drawee, though, must always be a bank for the instrument to qualify as a check.

$ *500.00*   Nashville, Tennessee *January 20* 20 __

Thirty days after sight

Payee — Pay to the Order of *Downtown Audio*

Five hundred and 100/no ————— Dollars

For Classroom Use Only

Drawee — *Accepted January 21, 20-- Margaret H. Hanford* } *Jay A. Minton*

Drawer

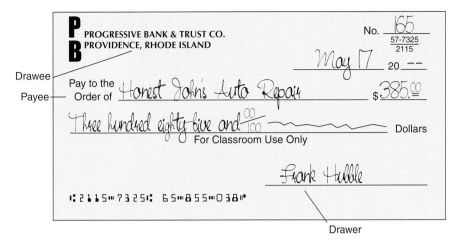

Progressive Bank & Trust Co.
PROVIDENCE, RHODE ISLAND

No. 165
57-7325
2115

May 17 20 __

Drawee

Payee — Pay to the
Order of Honest John's Auto Repair $385.00

Three hundred eighty-five and 00/100 ———— Dollars

For Classroom Use Only

Frank Hubble

⑆2115⑈7325⑆ 65⑈855⑈038⑈

Drawer

HONOR AND DISHONOR The bank, according to the contract between it and the depositor, agrees to **honor** (pay when due) each check as long as sufficient funds remain in the depositor's account. The bank owes that duty as a debtor of the depositor in return for being able to use the depositor's funds until the depositor demands their return. This means that the bank must retain a sizable percentage of the deposited funds so that it can pay properly drawn checks when presented. The remainder of the deposited funds is loaned at interest to pay for the bank's operations and to return a profit to the bank's owners.

A person who deliberately issues a check knowing that there are insufficient funds in the account to pay the check when it is presented at the drawee bank is guilty of a crime. The bank will **dishonor** (refuse to pay when due) the instrument and the payee or current owner of the check will not get money for it from that source. In addition, if a check is issued to pay a debt, the payoff is not effective until the check is presented to and honored by the drawee bank.

STOP-PAYMENT ORDERS When a check has been lost or stolen, the drawer should direct the bank not to pay it. Such an instruction is called a **stop-payment order**. If the drawee bank still pays the check, the bank must re-credit the account. The bank, not the depositor, must bear any loss. Oral stop-payment orders are good

for only two weeks unless they are confirmed in writing. Written stop-payment orders are good for six months, but lapse at the end of that time unless renewed.

PRECAUTIONS AND CARE Care must be taken to prevent checks from being altered. When writing a check, do not leave space for someone to insert figures and words that would change the amount of the instrument. Certainly, never sign a blank check. Do not give anything of value in return for a check that appears to have been altered in any manner. In addition, be wary of a check that may have been issued in connection with illegal activities, for example, gambling. Courts usually consider such instruments void.

Promissory Notes

A **promissory note** is an unconditional written promise by a person or persons to pay money according to

the payee's order or to pay money to the bearer of the instrument. The payment may have to be made on demand or at a definite time according to the stated terms on the face of the note (see the illustration below). The person who executes a promissory note is the **maker**. (If two or more persons execute the note, they are termed "co-makers" and are equally liable for payment.)

Many financial institutions will not lend money unless some personal or

$ 3,000.00   Las Vegas, Nevada December 20 20 __

Payee —   Sixty days _____ after date I promise to pay to

the order of First National Bank

Three thousand and no/100 ———— Dollars

For Classroom Use Only

Payable at First National Bank Building, Las Vegas, Nevada

with interest at 9 % a year.

No. 6 Due February 20, 20-- _____ Eric Gordon

Maker

real property is offered as security by the would-be borrower. The security ensures that the loan will be paid when due. If the debtor fails to pay, the creditor can force the sale of the property and then take the proceeds of that sale to cover the amount the debtor owes. When personal property is offered as security and so indicated on the face of the note, the paper is a **collateral note**. When real property is the security for payment, the paper is a **mortgage note**.

Certificates of Deposit

A **certificate of deposit** is an instrument bearing a bank's written acknowledgment of the receipt of money, together with an unconditional promise to repay it at a definite future time (see the illustration on the right). A certificate of deposit is often called a CD.

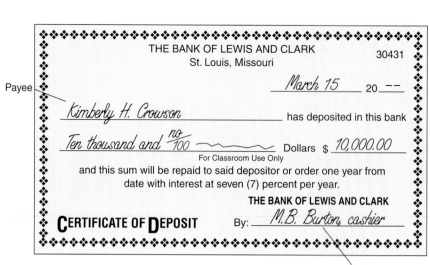

Payee

THE BANK OF LEWIS AND CLARK
St. Louis, Missouri   30431

March 15 20 __

Kimberly H. Crowson _____ has deposited in this bank

Ten thousand and $\frac{no}{100}$ ~~~~~ Dollars $ _10,000.00_

For Classroom Use Only

and this sum will be repaid to said depositor or order one year from date with interest at seven (7) percent per year.

THE BANK OF LEWIS AND CLARK

CERTIFICATE OF **D**EPOSIT   By: _M.B. Burton, cashier_

Maker

Federal law prohibits banks from paying out CDs and other long-term deposits before maturity without a penalty to the depositor. Usually the penalty is a sharp reduction in the amount of interest payable on the funds. This inhibits depositors from withdrawing funds before maturity and permits the banks to lend the funds to others on a long-term basis. Consequently, interest rates on CDs are usually significantly higher than the rates on savings or checking accounts (from which the depositor is far more likely to withdraw funds).

THINK ABOUT LEGAL CONCEPTS

Answer the following questions about legal concepts.

1. Commercial paper is an invention of the twentieth century. **True or False?**

2. The Uniform Commercial Code controls the use of most commercial paper. **True or False?**

3. With checking accounts, banks are the creditors of their depositors? **True or False?**

4. A note secured by land is a mortgage note. **True or False?**

5. A depositor's instruction to his or her bank not to pay a particular check is referred to as a(n) __?__ .

THINK CRITICALLY ABOUT EVIDENCE

Study the following situations, answer the questions, then prepare arguments to support your answers.

6. Hubble paid Honest John's Auto Repair $385 by check for the repair of his car's transmission. When the job proved defective, Hubble telephoned his bank and ordered it to stop payment on the check. Three weeks later, however, the bank honored the check and paid Honest John's the $385 out of Hubble's account. Did the bank make a mistake?

7. Burger was the owner and president of a small surfboard manufacturing company. She also owned the land and buildings the company occupied. When she needed to raise cash to finance a major expansion, her financial advisers told her that the best way to do so was by using the building and land as a source of funds. How could Burger do this?

8. Carl's boy, Jared, wanted a new sports car. He convinced Carl to sign a promissory note in favor of the car dealership for the $47,000 purchase price. Jared also signed the note. Four months later, Jared stopped making payments and drove the car to Mexico and sold it. Jared has taken up permanent residence in Juarez, Mexico. Is Carl nonetheless obligated to pay off the balance of the note?

G O A L S

● Identify the various specialized forms

● Explain the purpose of the specialized forms

● Describe how and when to properly use them

SPECIALIZED FORMS OF COMMERCIAL PAPER

WHAT'S YOUR VERDICT?

Dr. Pugh, of Santa Ana, California, needed expensive drugs to treat a patient with a rare nerve disease. Drugtek, the supplier of the drug, was a New York corporation. It would not ship COD, extend credit, or accept personal checks from customers outside the state.

What other means of payment could Dr. Pugh use to satisfy Drugtek?

The four types of commercial paper described in the previous lesson are the most frequently used. However, certain forms of commercial paper are available to meet specialized needs. Typically, these forms provide for an extremely safe, non-cash means of transfer of monetary value. Specialized forms that meet this need include those described in the following sections.

Certified Checks

A person offered a personal check as payment may fear the bank will not honor the check because of insufficient funds in the drawer's account. But if the bank has already agreed to pay the check, only if the bank fails will the payee or current owner of the check not receive the money due.

A personal check that has been accepted by a bank before payment is a **certified check**. At the time of certification, the bank draws funds from the depositor's account and sets them aside in a special account in order to pay the check when it is presented. In addition, the bank marks

the front of the check with either the word "accepted" or "certified," along with the date and an authorized signature of the bank. In *What's Your Verdict?* Dr. Pugh could use a certified check if Drugtek will accept it.

Cashier's Check

A check that a bank draws on itself is a **cashier's check** (see the illustration below). Banks use such checks to pay their own obligations. Persons who wish to pay others but who do not have checking accounts or find it

impractical to use their personal checks also may purchase them from a bank. Because it is relatively risk-free (only the bank may stop payment on the check), a payee is usually willing to take such a check. This could be the most appropriate type of check for Dr. Pugh.

Drawee

Payee

First State Security Bank
Santa Ana, CA 92703

1203
81-13
820

December 15 20 --

Pay to the Order of _Drugtek_ $ 1,375.50

The sum of $1,375 and 50cts   Dollars

For Classroom Use Only

CASHIER'S CHECK
⑆08 20⑈00 ⑈3⑆   _Martha C. Todd_
as ASSISTANT MANAGER of First State Security Bank

Drawer

Letters of credit are specialized types of commercial paper used in international transactions. The letter of credit is issued by a bank on behalf of an account holder. It represents the bank's promise to pay, accept, or negotiate the beneficiary's draft up to a certain amount of money, in the stated currency, and within a prescribed time limit.

The two types of letters of credit are *documentary* letters of credit and *standby* letters of credit. Documentary letters of credit are used in transactions involving the sales of goods. Standby letters of credit are used to guarantee that a party will fulfill monetary obligations involving construction, service, or sales contracts.

Other documents may be required in a letter of credit transaction. These include a commercial invoice describing the goods, a marine insurance policy, a country of origin certificate, a certificate of analysis or inspections, customs declarations, and packing slips.

Teller's Check

A draft drawn by a bank on funds that it has on deposit at another bank is a **teller's check**. Such a document is a draft drawn by one bank on a second bank. Individuals and busi-

ness firms may also use these instruments when a substantial sum is involved. The purchase of such a draft is another possibility open to Dr. Pugh.

Money Orders

Persons who do not have checking accounts often use money orders. A **money order** is a draft issued by a post office, bank, express company, or telegraph company for use in paying or transferring funds for the purchaser. For example, a money order purchased at one post office orders the post office in the hometown of the payee to make payment. Dr. Pugh also could use a money order.

Traveler's Checks

Travelers are rightfully wary of carrying a lot of cash. Retailers and hotelkeepers worldwide are under-

standably reluctant to take checks from people from other regions and even other countries. The traveler's check was devised to overcome these problems and meet the needs of both groups. A **traveler's check** is a draft drawn by a well-known financial institution on itself or its agent.

The buyer signs the traveler's checks when purchased. Later, when used to pay for a purchase, the traveler writes in the name of the payee and then signs again, in the presence of the payee. The payee then deposits and collects the traveler's check in the same manner as other checks. The payee's ability to compare the two signatures, coupled with the reputation of the financial institution that issued the instrument, usually reduces the risk to the point where businesses worldwide accept traveler's checks.

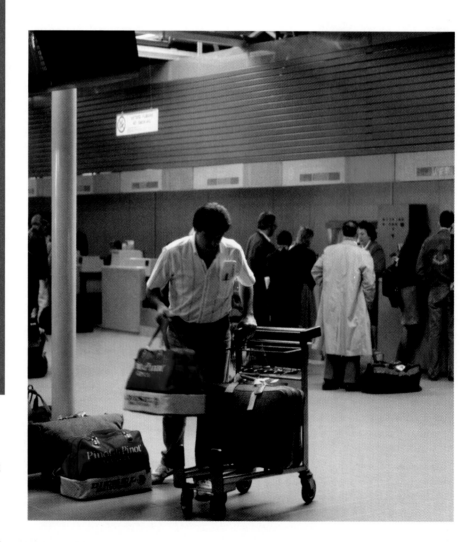

Answer the following questions about legal concepts.

1. Only the drafting bank can stop payment on a cashier's check. **True or False?**

2. When a bank accepts liability on a personal check before it is presented for payment the check is said to be certified. **True or False?**

3. A __?__ draft is a draft drawn by a bank on favorable monetary balances it has in other banks.

4. A personal check that has been accepted by a bank before payment is a
(a) **cashier's check**
(b) **certified check**
(c) **traveler's check**
(d) **teller's check**

5. Individuals that do not have checking accounts often use money orders. **True or False?**

Study the following situations, answer the questions, then prepare arguments to support your answers.

6. Horace ordered a new pair of running shoes from a discount 1-800 number. He paid by cashier's check. When he finds out that his new shoes are defective, he calls the bank to stop payment on the check. Can he stop payment? Who is liable on the instrument?

7. Horace's sister Henrietta has just moved to New York City. She doesn't have a bank account as yet and does not want to carry around much cash. She does have a check made payable to her by a car dealership to which she sold her car upon arriving in New York. What could she do with the check to make sure it will be honored when she cashes it?

8. Several months pass. Henrietta has become adjusted to the big city and wants to return home to Wisconsin to visit. She does not want to carry cash with her. What kind of commercial paper would you recommend that she use to carry her funds with her? It must be usable to pay many small amounts and be trusted by merchants in Wisconsin.

9. The Downhome State Bank of East Orange, N. J., has just completed building a new branch office building. It wants to pay the various contractors. The Bank has more than $800,000 in credits owed to it by the William Penn Bank in nearby Pennsylvania. What instrument might the Downhome Bank use to pay the contractors out of the amount owed it by the William Penn?

1. Prepare commercial paper accurately and handle it with care knowing it has significant value.

2. Be sure you do not leave enough blank space for someone to insert figures and words that would change the face amount of an instrument.

3. If you lend money, get a promissory note made out in your favor in return. If practical, ask for security for the loan and clearly identify the

PREVENT LEGAL DIFFICULTIES

collateral on the face of the instrument.

4. Use traveler's checks and credit cards on long trips. Do not carry a lot of cash.

5. Never sign a blank piece of commercial paper. Take care not to let your blank checks be stolen. Your negligence may render you liable for any forgeries that consequently occur.

6. Remember that an oral stop-payment order is good for only 14 days unless confirmed in writing. A written stop-payment order is good for six months and can be renewed.

CHAPTER IN REVIEW

CONCEPTS IN BRIEF

1. Commercial paper was developed hundreds of years ago to serve as a safer, more convenient substitute for precious metals and currency.

2. There are four important types of commercial paper including drafts, checks (a special type of draft), promissory notes, and certificates of deposit (CDs).

3. Drafts, including checks, are unconditional *orders* by one party to another party to pay money on demand or at a specified future time to a third party. Initially, three parties are involved: the drawer, who gives the order to pay; the drawee, who is so ordered; and the payee, to whom pay-

ment is to be made.

4. A check is a special type of draft in that
   - the drawee of a check is always a bank
   - a check is drawn against funds the drawer has on deposit in the bank
   - a check is always payable on demand

5. Promissory notes and certificates of deposit are unconditional *promises* to pay money on demand or at a definite time in the future. Initially, two parties are involved in notes and CDs: the maker, who promises to pay; and the payee, to whom payment is promised.

YOUR LEGAL VOCABULARY

Match each statement with the term that it best defines. Some terms may not be used.

1. Unconditional written promise or order to pay money

2. Person to whom commercial paper is made payable

3. Drawee's promise to pay draft when due

4. Draft written on bank by depositor

5. Bank's agreement to pay check when due

6. Person who executes a promissory note

7. Check drawn by bank on itself

8. Draft drawn by a bank on its balance with another bank

9. Unconditional written order to pay money to a third person on demand or when presented for payment

10. Written instrument acknowledging a bank's receipt of money and promising to repay it at a definite future time

11. Unconditional written order from one person directing another to pay money to a third person

12. Draft issued by a post office, bank, or express company for use in transferring funds for the draft's purchaser

acceptance
bank draft
cashier's check
certificate of deposit
certified check
check
collateral note
commercial paper
dishonor
draft
drawee
drawer
honor
maker
money order
mortgage note
payee
promissory note
sight draft
stop payment order
teller's check
time draft
traveler's check

13. Why was commercial paper created?

14. Could you write a check on an ordinary piece of paper?

15. What is the difference between a check and a draft?

16. Why is it not advisable to write a check, draft, or other piece of commercial paper with a pencil?

17. What is the purpose of having the purchaser sign the traveler's checks when buying them?

WRITE ABOUT LEGAL CONCEPTS

18. If a good customer comes into a bank and wants to stop payment on a cashier's check she had purchased and had the bank issue, how could the bank protect itself in doing so?

19. How does a certificate of deposit vary from a promissory note?

20. **HOT DEBATE** Write a persuasive opening statement that emphasizes the legal, ethical, and economic points in favor of your petition. Or, write a persuasive opening statement for the bank that encompasses the economic and legal reasons why the loss should fall on the depositor in this situation.

THINK CRITICALLY ABOUT EVIDENCE

21. Joseph McReynolds gave the following signed instrument to Helen Harrison after borrowing $5,000 from her: "This acknowledges my legal duty to pay Helen Harrison $5,000." It was dated and signed by McReynolds. Is the instrument commercial paper?

22. Chen wanted to order skis that she had seen advertised in a national magazine. The advertisement expressly said, "Do not send cash or personal checks. No COD orders accepted." How could Chen pay?

23. Thruster owns Discovery Electronic Works, a small company that manufactures portable computers. The company is doing well but needs to expand and update its product line. Thruster plans to use credit to do both. What specific types of commercial paper will be used if:
    a. Discovery Electronic Works borrows $15,000 out of the $20,000 needed to pay for a ship-

ment of integrated circuit chips and uses the chips as security for payment?
    b. Discovery Electronic Works borrows $65,000 out of the $100,000 needed to buy a building for a new assembly line and uses the real property as security for payment?

24. You are working as a checkout clerk at Surprise Discount, Inc., a local department store. Sarah Johnson, an elderly lady, comes through your line with what she describes as "the perfect gift for my great-grandson." She says that she never expected to find it for under $200 much less the $110 that it is marked at. She writes out a check for the purchase. After she has left the store, you realize that she has written the check for $15.50 rather than the $115.50 purchase price plus tax. However, there is plenty of room to alter the amount to the correct figure. Should you do so?

ANALYZE
REAL CASES

25. While in Shreveport, Louisiana, Claypool wanted to play poker for money stakes at the Crystal Bar. He persuaded Parker to stand good (pay) for any losses he might have. Before the night was over, Claypool's losses amounted to $6,000. Afterwards, Claypool gave Parker a promissory note for $10,473.14 to cover the $6,000 in gambling losses and a legitimate previous loan. When the note came due, Claypool refused to pay. Parker sued, and Claypool defended on the grounds that the note was illegal and void, because it originated in a gambling debt. Will Parker recover? (*Parker v. Claypool,* 78 So. 2d 124)

26. Purchasers of land developed by Holiday Interval, Inc., signed writings in which they promised to pay a certain sum of money at a definite time in the future. However, according to the signed instruments, the payments were due only if specified structures were built in the complex within two years of the signings. Some of these instruments were labeled "promissory note." Were any of the writings commercial paper? (*In re Holiday Interval, Inc.,* 94 Bankr. 594)

27. Gunn contracted to sell Tak, a broker from Hong Kong, 60,000 metric tons of UREA, a fertilizer, at $400 a ton. In connection with this $24 million sale, Gunn entered another contract agreeing to pay Tak a commission for all Tak's sales of the fertilizer. After 10,000 tons of UREA had been sold, paid for, and delivered, Gunn bought and delivered to Tak a cashier's check from the Empire Bank of Springfield for $150,000 payable to Tak's order. Shortly after, Gunn learned that the balance of the order for the remaining 50,000 tons of UREA had been canceled by Tak. Consequently, Gunn went to court and obtained an injunction from the court to the bank to stop payment on the cashier's check. Shortly after the court acted, the cashier's check was transferred by Tak to Lai, who now claims the right to collect the face amount. Should the court order the bank to honor the stop payment order, or must the bank pay Lai the face amount of the check? (*Lai v. Powell, Judge,* 536 S.W.2d 14)

28. In a Missouri circuit court, Kleen was convicted of issuing an insufficient funds check. He appealed, pointing out that he had merely signed a blank check form in Missouri and then given the form to his truck driver. The truck driver carried the signed blank check form to Memphis, Tennessee, where someone at the Herring Sales Company filled in the company name as the payee and also filled in the amount. Herring kept the check in return for a truckload of meal that was transported by Kleen's truck and driver back to Kleen's business in Nevada, Missouri. Kleen therefore contended that even though the check was drawn on the Citizen's Bank of Nevada, the alleged criminal act occurred in Tennessee, where the signed blank form was made a check and was issued. Consequently, Missouri had no jurisdiction, and his conviction should be overturned. You decide. (*State v. Kleen,* 491 S.W.2d 2)

29. Henry Thomas purchased a new car on October 22 and gave Frazier Buick Company a check for the full amount. The company then signed over the certificate of title to Thomas. Unfortunately, Thomas died the next day, and Frazier Buick immediately repossessed the car without cashing the check. The administrator of Thomas' estate then sued the company on behalf of the estate for $500 actual damages, since she "had [the car] sold" for $500 above the price Thomas had paid for it at Frazier Buick. She also asked for $2,500 in punitive damages for the company's abrupt and insensitive action in repossessing the car. Will the estate recover? (*Hickerson v. Con Frazier Buick Company,* 264 S.W.2d 29)

30. General Motors Acceptance Corporation (GMAC) financed the purchase of a Jeep by Azevedo. It then held the positon of lienholder on the vehicle and was noted as such on the vehicle's title and car insurance policy. The policy was taken out by Azevedo but listed GMAC as the beneficiary. Therefore, if the vehicle was involved in an accident and damaged, the insurance company, Abington Casualty, was to pay GMAC the value of the loss. Later, after the Jeep was damaged in an accident, Azevedo submitted a claim on the policy. After suitable appraisals of the loss, Abington issued a check with joint payees, Azevedo and GMAC. Abington then delivered the check to Azevedo who deposited it in his bank with his indorsement but without GMAC's. The bank paid on the check in full to Azevedo even without the indorsement. GMAC never received the benefit of the funds. Now it has brought suit against Abington to recover for its loss. Is GMAC entitled to the insurance money? (*General Motors Acceptance Corporation v. Abington Casualty Insurance Co.,* 602 N.E.2d 1085)

Means v. Clardy
Western District Missouri Court of Appeals, 735 S.W. 2d 6

BACKGROUND Rick Means and Fred Barry owned an apartment building which they wished to sell. On July 18, 1980, they entered into a contract for deed with respondents, Joan and Gary Doerhoff. The agreement provided that the Doerhoffs would receive the apartment in exchange for 6.81 acres of land in Maries County, Missouri, and a note purportedly executed by Nancy Clardy, respondent Bruce Clardy's mother. At that time, several of the monthly installments were in arrears.

FACTS Means and his brother, Fred Barry, brought this lawsuit. They were seeking to collect on a promissory note in the amount of $31,000 purportedly signed by a Nancy Clardy. Clardy had supposedly signed the note as partial payment for a cabinetmaking business that she allegedly purchased.

Two weeks after the note was issued, a partial payment of some $5,000 was to be made thereon. Afterwards the remainder of the principal and interest was "to be paid in cabinets figured at the prevailing builder's price for Jefferson City" and in a final lump sum payment.

When the note was not paid, Means and Barry brought this suit for the nearly $22,000 still due.

LOWER COURT DECISION During the trial, Nancy Clardy testified that she did not sign either the note or a bill of sale buying the business. She alleged that her son, Bruce, had done so and had drawn $5,000 from a "remodeling" fund to make the initial payment on the note. Bruce took the Fifth Amendment (protection

against self-incrimination) when asked about this at the trial. However, a witness to the signing of the promissory note and the bill of sale testified that Bruce Clardy placed the signatures of Bruce and Nancy Clardy on the note.

(Nancy Clardy's signature on the Bill of Sale for Doerhoffs' cabinet business was notarized by John Gross. Gross later testified that Nancy Clardy had not signed any documents in his presence but that as a favor to Bruce he notarized the Bill of Sale after Bruce told him that Nancy Clardy had signed it.)

The trial court held that Bruce Clardy had indeed signed the note for both parties. As a consequence, Nancy Clardy was not liable. Means and Barry then brought this appeal.

APPEALS Means and Barry bring an appeal from the decision of the court below disallowing their recovery partially on the basis of the instrument in question not being commercial papaer.

ISSUE Is the instrument a negotiable promissory note or a mere contract?

PRACTICE JUDGING

1. Is the instrument commercial paper? Why or why not?

2. If it is not commercial paper, Means and Barry are merely assignees. In such case, it will be much more difficult to collect the amount due. The law favors people trying to collect on commercial paper over those trying to collect merely on contractual rights. Why is this?

3. Do you think Means and Barry deserve to collect? Do you think they will?

LESSONS

36-1 REQUIREMENTS OF NEGOTIABILITY

36-2 PROPER INDORSEMENT AND NEGOTIATION

HOT DEBATE

You are president of your own company. Earlier this morning your secretary, Elizabeth, placed a stack of checks to pay the monthly bills on your desk for your signature. As you glanced through them you spotted a $5,000 check for electronic items to your old friend Bill Hutton's company. Later that week, you run into Bill and he mentions that he hasn't sold you anything in ages. You investigate and find that, over the last year and a half, Elizabeth has had you sign over $125,000 in checks made out to your suppliers for goods they didn't provide. She then took the checks, forged the payee's signature to indorse them in blank, and deposited them in her account to be used to cover gambling debts. Your attorney sues her and the bank that took the checks over her forgeries to recover the money. It is discovered that Elizabeth has few assets. She just sold her home and gambled away those proceeds as well.

Where Do You Stand?

1. List the legal reasons supporting your suit.

2. List the legal reasons why the loss should fall on you.

GOALS

- Explain the importance of proper negotiation
- List the requirements of negotiability
- Identify when an instrument is negotiable

WHAT IS NEGOTIATION AND WHY IS IT IMPORTANT?

WHAT'S YOUR VERDICT?

Montez was preparing to open her new business, a hobby store. However, in talking with her accountant, Montez indicated that she wanted to do business on a cash-only basis because taking checks or promissory notes is too risky.

Is this advisable?

If commercial paper is to be accepted instead of cash, the person or business firm receiving it must be assured that there is a very great chance the instrument will be paid. Today, the Uniform Commercial Code (UCC) provides that assurance. To do this, the UCC empowers a qualified owner of commercial paper to overcome many of the legal defenses the person who is obligated to pay the instrument might raise to keep from paying.

To enable the owner to overcome most common defenses and collect on commercial paper, the promise or order to pay money must be negotiable. **Negotiable** means that it must be in writing, contain an unconditional promise or order payable in a sum certain, be payable on demand or at a definite time, and be payable to the bearer or to someone's order. (These requirements are prescribed by statute and are discussed in the following section.) An instrument must be negotiable in order to be classified as commercial paper. In fact, another term meaning commercial paper is **negotiable instruments**.

The party trying to collect on it must acquire the instrument with the promise or order to pay money in the correct manner. **Negotiation** means the proper transfer of negotiable instruments so that the person receiving the instrument has the power to collect on it by overcoming certain defenses of the person who must pay it off. If an instrument is not negotiated, it is considered to have been only assigned. The parties' rights are governed by contract law rather than the law of negotiable instruments.

Unless a valid defense prevents it, an assignee may still collect in full on the instrument that is only transferred by assignment. However more defenses are available with assigned than with negotiated instruments. Therefore, a person would prefer to hold a negotiable instrument than an assigned instrument because the chances of collection are greater.

In *What's Your Verdict?* the accountant would probably advise Montez that significant protection would be afforded her by the UCC if she were to take properly transferred negotiable instruments. Such protection would drastically reduce the risk of not being able to collect. Refusing to accept commercial paper would probably mean losing customers. If they were denied the safety and convenience of using checks and notes in her store, they might not shop there at all.

REQUIREMENTS TO MAKE AN INSTRUMENT NEGOTIABLE

WHAT'S YOUR VERDICT?

Because he had to sign more than 3,000 company documents each week, Bill Capeci, the company president, had a rubber stamp made that read "Downtown Furniture Factory, by Bill Capeci, President." He even used this stamp to sign the company's payroll checks.

Is such a practice legal?

According to the UCC, whether or not an instrument is negotiable is determined by what appears on its face at the time it is issued. In particular, the instrument must

1. be in writing and be signed by the maker or drawer
2. contain an unconditional promise or order

3. be payable in a sum certain in money
4. be payable on demand or at a definite time
5. be payable to the bearer or to someone's order

Negotiability does not require that the instrument state that something of value has been given for the paper. But identifying such value given is often a good idea and will not defeat negotiability. Likewise, the ability to negotiate (but not the ability to collect on) an instrument is not affected by the fact that it is **antedated** (dated earlier than the date of issuance), **postdated** (dated later than the date of issuance), or even undated. If a date is not present, any owner who has possession and who knows the date on which the paper was issued may enter it.

Writing Signed by the Maker or Drawer

To be negotiable, commercial paper must be in writing and signed by the maker or drawer with the intent that it create a legal obligation. Because of the writing, commercial paper is subject to the parol evidence rule when its terms are challenged at law. (Under the parol evidence rule, oral testimony cannot be used to contradict terms in a complete, final, written contract.) However, oral evidence *may* be used to show failure of consideration or breach of contract.

The writing may consist of a printed form with the terms typed or written in. Or, the paper may be totally handwritten. The law is very flexible in this regard. An ink pen, a typewriter, even a pencil may be used, although a pencil is not recommended because it invites alteration. Any medium is satisfactory as a writing surface as long as the result is recognizable as a writing.

If there are conflicting terms within the writing, those written in by hand prevail over both typewritten and printed form terms. Similarly, typewritten terms prevail over printed form terms. In addition, an amount expressed in words prevails over an amount expressed in figures.

As far as the signature is concerned, the form it takes does not alter its legal effectiveness as long as the writer placed it there with the intent to authenticate the instrument. For example, a legally effective signature may be made with a rubber stamp, as in *What's Your Verdict?*

A trade or assumed name may be used in signing if it is intended as one's signature. Also, one person may legitimately sign another person's name if authorized to do so as an agent. A manager may sign commercial paper as an agent for a corporation. Any individual who is unable to write her or his name because of illiteracy or a physical handicap may sign with a mark, typically an "X." However it is an advisable practice to have another person then insert the name of the signer next to the mark and sign as a witness.

The location of the signature is generally immaterial as long as it appears on the face of the instrument. Thus, the signature may appear anywhere in the body of the instrument as long as the signer's status as maker or drawer is clear.

Unconditional Promise or Order

To be negotiable, a promissory note or a certificate of deposit must contain an unconditional promise to pay money. Similarly, a check or a draft must contain an unconditional order to pay money. Simply acknowledging a debt as in "I owe you $100" is not enough. There is nothing in such a statement to indicate that the money will ever be repaid. The use of the word "unconditional" means that the promise or order to pay money must be absolute, that is, free of any limits or restrictions. "I promise to pay Ann Kiersten $1,000 if my mare foals in the next year" would be conditional

upon an event that might not occur. Therefore, the instrument that included the statement would not be negotiable.

Likewise, to promise payment out of a certain fund or account "only" would make the obligation conditional on enough money being in the account. Making payment subject to another agreement would make the obligation conditional on the agreement being properly performed. Such conditions would restrict the free flow of commercial paper. Conditions would require a prospective purchaser of the paper to deal with the uncertainty that the condition might not have been satisfied. This would mean that collection might not be legally possible.

On the other hand, a phrase entitling the holder to reasonable attorney's fees upon default or enhancing the possibility of collection, such as "secured by a mortgage," would improve the potential for negotiation by reducing the uncertainty of collection.

Courteous or considerate language, such as "please pay to the order of" or listing the obligor's bank account number (without the word "only" following) for the convenience of others, does not affect negotiability. However, contrary to rules for privately issued instruments, checks of the government that are restricted to payment from one account (such as "pay out of social security account only") are still negotiable. Finally, instruments that merely acknowledge the source of the obligation, as in "pay to the order of Merrick Miller as per contract," also are negotiable.

Payable in a Sum Certain in Money

To be negotiable, commercial paper must call for the payment of a sum certain in money. **Money,** for this purpose, is any official currency or coin acceptable as a medium of exchange either in the United States or in any foreign country at the time the commercial paper is written. Thus, commercial paper that is collectible in the United States but that has the amount expressed in an acceptable foreign currency is negotiable.

Often, the foreign currency is simply changed into U.S. dollars on the day the paper is payable. However, if the paper requires that the foreign currency be used as the medium of payment, the commercial paper is payable in that currency.

Payment must be solely in money and not money plus a good or ser-

vice. On the other hand, paper that gives the obligee (creditor) a choice of money or something else, for example, "I promise to pay to the order of Vera Spielman $10,000 or thirty-five ounces of gold at the obligee's option" would be negotiable, since the obligee could choose money as payment. If the choice to pay in money or a good or service was the obligor's (debtor's), the instrument is not negotiable. In such a case the obligor could choose to make payment in something other than money.

An instrument is still negotiable if it requires that the amount be paid

- with interest or a discount. (The interest rate may vary. For example, if the instrument reads "interest to be set at 2% plus prime bank rate," the instrument would still be negotiable.)
- by installment, perhaps with an **acceleration clause** that makes the entire balance due and payable upon the happening of a certain event (for example, the obligor's default by missing an installment payment)
- with bank charges for exchanging one national currency into another
- with costs of collection and reasonable attorney's fees in case the paper is not paid

In fact, most of these provisions usually tend to make the commercial paper more attractive to prospective owners.

Payable on Demand or at a Definite Time

Negotiability also requires that an instrument be payable on demand or at a definite time. **Payable on demand** means that the commercial paper is written so as to be payable immediately upon presentment (demand for payment) or at sight. If no time of payment is specified, an instrument is interpreted as being payable on demand.

Payable at a definite time means that the commercial paper is written payable on or before an identified calendar date. It is also acceptable for an instrument to be payable within a set period after an identified calendar date or a fixed period, such as 90 days after sight. An instrument is not negotiable if it is payable at or after an event that is sure to occur but whose date cannot be determined beforehand. For example, a note payable "30 days after the death of Sam Larue" would not be negotiable. Such a promise might be honored by the person making it or it might be legally enforceable as part of a contract. However, that has nothing to do with whether the instrument is commercial paper and can therefore be negotiated.

Payable to Bearer or to Someone's Order

The final requirement is that the paper contain the words of negotiability by being made payable to

CULTURAL DIVERSITY IN LAW

International

Hard vs. Soft Currency

Hard currencies are those that are freely traded on world markets. Currencies considered "hard" are those of the United States, Europe, and Japan. The value of hard currency is set on the open market—that is, by what buyers and sellers will pay for it at any given time. Values of hard currency also may be affected by government intervention, interest rates, or other market factors.

Soft currencies, on the other hand, have fixed exchange rates. Examples are the Russian ruble, the Indian rupee, or the Chinese renminbi. These currencies are purchased at the rates the countries' governments establish for them.

bearer or to a specified person's order. When commercial paper is legally collectible by the party in possession of it, it is referred to as **bearer paper**. The party in possession of bearer paper is called the bearer. To qualify as bearer paper, the face of a piece of commercial paper can read "pay to the order of bearer," "pay to bearer," "pay to (a named party) or bearer," "pay to cash," or any other way that does not identify a specific payee.

In contrast, when commercial paper is made payable to the order of a specified payee, it is called **order paper**. Such phrasing shows the intent of the maker or drawer to have the paper payable to the named payee or to anyone to whom the paper is subsequently negotiated by order of that payee. Order paper may read "pay to the order of Charles Blevins" or whatever specific party the maker or drawer intends. It may also read "pay to Charles Blevins or order." However, if it only reads "pay to Charles Blevins," it is not negotiable. An exception under the 1990 version of the UCC is a check. A check may be negotiable without being payable to order or bearer. Check forms ordinarily contain the preprinted words "Pay to the order of," however.

Order paper may be made payable to the order of more than one party. These parties can be named either jointly ("pay to the order of Jeannette Edwards and Anthony Edwards") or individually ("pay to the order of Emilio Morales or Daniel Elliott"). In the former example, both parties have to sign the instrument to negotiate it further. In the latter example, either Emilio or Daniel acting alone can sign and cash it.

THINK ABOUT LEGAL CONCEPTS

Answer the following questions about legal concepts.

1. Although it is not advisable, a check can be written in pencil. **True or False?**

2. If there is a conflict between the amount of a check written in numerals and a different amount written out in words, the amount written in numbers will prevail, as numbers are clearer. **True or False?**

3. A promissory note is physically issued on June 6 of this year. Which of the following dates placed on the face of the instrument would make it antedated? **(a) June 5 (b) June 7 (c) The instrument cannot be antedated**

4. A signature can be written anywhere on the face of an instrument. **True or False?**

5. Commercial Paper cannot be signed with an "X." **True or False?**

THINK CRITICALLY ABOUT EVIDENCE

Study the following situations, answer the questions, then prepare arguments to support your answers.

6. C.W. Bean wrote a check payable to Christopher John for the full purchase price of Christopher's used pickup. Bean put "$7,500" in numerals on the payee line for the amount of the check but wrote out "seven thousand eight hundred dollars" below it. If no other evidence were presented as to the sale price, what would a court hold as to the amount of the check?

7. On April Fool's Day, a friend gives you a $25 check that she has deliberately antedated to April 1 of the previous year. If she has adequate funds in her account when you present the check, can you still collect on it?

8. On August 7, you sell your car to pay for your college tuition. The buyer asks that you not cash the payoff check until his payday on the first of September, since he needs the money in his account for family expenses. You promise not to cash it, but when you go to register for classes you find that the tuition amount must be paid immediately or else you cannot enroll. Your only source of funds is the check, and you did tell the buyer that the money was to go for your tuition. You know that according to the law, a check is a demand instrument. Can you cash it? Should you cash it?

9. Campbell wrote the following by hand: "I, Gary Campbell, promise to pay to the order of Allison J. Nagy $2,500." Campbell then delivered it to Nagy. In a dispute that arose later, it was argued that because the instrument lacked Campbell's signature, was not dated, and was without a time of payment, it was not negotiable. Do you agree?

GOALS

● Explain the ramifications of improperly transferring commercial paper

● Identify the various types of indorsements

● Use the proper indorsement(s) to achieve a chosen purpose

HOW IS COMMERCIAL PAPER TRANSFERRED?

WHAT'S YOUR VERDICT?

Rainquest awakened one morning with a severe toothache. The pain was worse by noon, so she made an afternoon appointment with her dentist. When Rainquest arrived at the dentist's office, the receptionist informed her that she still owed $175 for previous treatment. By coincidence, Rainquest had with her a check made out to her order in that amount. Rainquest gave it to the receptionist as payment. The receptionist examined it, then returned it to Rainquest and asked her to sign the back.

Is Rainquest's signature necessary to transfer the check to the dentist?

As mentioned previously, commercial paper is usually transferred by negotiation. Negotiation may give the transferee greater rights than if the paper is merely assigned. This is true because, in an assignment, the transferee receives only the rights of the transferor. In negotiation, the transferee, if qualified, may receive additional rights granted under the UCC.

In particular, negotiation for value may be to a party who has no knowledge of defects in the original transaction in which the paper was created. This could give that innocent transferee the power to overcome many defenses against payment that the party obligated to pay might have otherwise used. These defenses include breach of contract and failure of consideration, which are explained in the next chapter.

If the transfer of commercial paper does not qualify as a negotiation, it is legally considered as having been assigned. As such, it is subject to contract law. To enable a transferee to receive rights available under the UCC, it is critical to know the proper way to transfer commercial paper. The proper method of transfer in a specific instance depends on whether the instrument is order or bearer paper.

If the instrument is order paper (payable to the order of a named person), the named person or her or his agent must sign the paper on its reverse side. In *What's Your Verdict?* the receptionist properly requested that Rainquest sign the back of the check. Then the paper must be delivered to make the negotiation complete and proper.

A signature on the back of an instrument to transfer the paper is termed an **indorsement**. (*Indorsement* is the spelling used by the UCC and in the law of negotiable instruments, and so will be used in this text. The popular spelling of this word is *endorsement*.) An owner of commercial paper who signs on its reverse indorses the paper and is an **indorser**. The party to whom the paper is indorsed is the **indorsee**. A party who has physical possession of commercial paper that is payable to his or her order or who is in possession of bearer paper is a **holder**. Therefore, a bearer is a holder, as is a person in possession of paper payable to his or her order.

If the paper is bearer paper, it may be negotiated by delivery alone. The bearer may simply hand the paper to the transferee. Many transferees, however, will require the bearer to indorse the paper. This generally allows the future holders to pursue the transferor for payment of the paper's value if there are problems collecting it from the maker or drawee.

WHAT'S YOUR VERDICT?

Gordon Marshall paid his ex-wife, Gloria Marshall, her monthly alimony by indorsing a weekly paycheck with his name only and handing it to her. While shopping, Gloria had her purse stolen. The thief found the check and promptly bought goods with it at the Penny-Ante Quick Shoppe, which accepted it in good faith. Penny-Ante can legally collect on the check.

What other kind of indorsement might have protected Gloria from this loss?

Indorsements are classified by whether any words, other than the indorser's signature, have been added and, if so, what words.

Blank Indorsements

A blank indorsement consists of just the indorser's signature (see the illustration below). Because it is quickly written, the blank indorsement is the most common. It does not specify a particular person to whom the paper is being transferred. Therefore, it transforms order paper into bearer paper. Even a finder or a thief may negotiate an instrument with a blank indorsement. A blank indorsement is satisfactory and safe for the indorser if

1. value is immediately received for it, or
2. the paper is deposited in a bank at the time of indorsement

Special Indorsements

A **special indorsement** makes the paper payable to the order of a designated party. Recall that, unless the instrument is a check, the words "Pay to the order of" must be used on the face of the instrument to achieve the same result. In an indorsement, the more concise wording "Pay to Gloria Marshall" is as effective as "Pay to the order of Gloria Marshall." The paper will be order paper as a result of either wording.

To be properly negotiated, order paper requires the signature of the party named in the indorsement. A forged signature used as an indorsement cannot pass title. Therefore, unlike the situation with paper having a blank indorsement, a thief or a finder of the paper could not legally cash it.

Transferees who receive commercial paper with blank indorsements may protect themselves by writing that the paper is payable to them above the indorser's signature. This is perfectly legal and restores the order character of the instrument. For example, as shown in the illustration to the right, Gloria Marshall could have taken the blank indorsement of Gordon Marshall and written above it "Pay to the order of Gloria Marshall" or "Pay to Gloria Marshall." Then the thief would have had to forge her signature to pass the instrument. The

law states that the loss generally falls on the person who takes from the forger. Therefore, if Penny-Ante had accepted the check with a special indorsement, it would have been unable to collect.

It is important to note that there are exceptions to the above rule. Innocent holders may be allowed to collect despite the forgery. These exceptions require negligence on the part of the maker or drawer. For example, suppose that a dishonest employee fraudulently gets an employer to sign a check made payable to a frequent supplier of the business but for a nonexistent shipment. The employee then takes the check, forges the supplier's indorsement, and cashes it. The employer must pay it, because it was the employer's negligence that placed the employee in a position to commit the forgery. The employer can then try to recoup the loss from that dishonest employee.

Another exception occurs when an impostor tricks the maker or drawer of commercial paper into giving the impostor an instrument that is made payable to the person who is being impersonated. The impostor then forges the indorsement of the party being impersonated and cashes the check. The instrument is effective against the maker or drawer, who was negligent in not properly

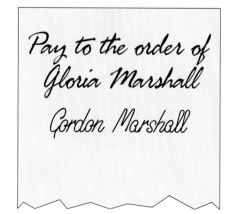

identifying the party to whom the paper was given.

Qualified Indorsements

If the maker or drawee of an instrument fails to pay it, the indorsers may be required to pay it. Adding "without recourse" or equivalent words such as "not liable for payment" over a blank or special indorsement can eliminate this potential secondary liability based on signature. The result is a **qualified indorsement**. A qualified indorsement eliminates the indorser's secondary liability because of his or her signature's appearing on the instrument. If the maker or the drawee does not add such wording, the result is an **unqualified indorsement**, and the indorser may be liable to subsequent holders.

Even though secondary liability is avoided by qualifying the indorsement, certain warranties still may bind a transferor. These warranties are implied by law against all transferors and may still require the indorser to pay if the instrument cannot be collected. The warranties guarantee that

1. the transferor is entitled to enforce the paper
2. all signatures are genuine
3. the instrument has not been altered
4. the transferor has no knowledge of a bankruptcy proceeding against the maker, drawer of an unaccepted draft, or an acceptor, and
5. there are no defenses of any type good against the transferor

The warranty liability of a qualified indorser is the same as the warranty liability of an unqualified indorser. The warranties are very broad in coverage.

The transferor of bearer paper who does not indorse it (and therefore does not acquire secondary liability

on her or his signature as an indorser) still is accountable for these warranties. However, warranty liability runs only to the immediate transferee. If the transferor does indorse the bearer paper, the implied warranties are extended to protect the transferees beyond just the immediate transferee.

To be totally without potential liability on a piece of commercial paper, a qualified indorser might add "without warranties" and thus eliminate all warranty liability. However, it will be extremely difficult to find a transferee that will give significant value for the instrument to a potential transferor under such circumstances.

Restrictive Indorsements

A **restrictive indorsement** directs the use of the proceeds from the instrument or imposes a condition upon payment of the instrument by the indorser. For example, "Pay to Chase Larue to be held in trust for his oldest son, Tommy," would be a restrictive indorsement, since it directs what is to be done with the proceeds of the paper. "For deposit only" and "for collection" also are restrictive indorsements.

In addition, a restrictive indorsement might impose conditions on payment such as "Pay to Kiersten Alexis upon her delivery of her 1965 Mustang to me." Such a condition, if on the face of the instrument, would destroy negotiability, but this is not true if included in an indorsement. However, a future holder is bound by the condition and cannot collect the instrument against the restrictive indorser until the condition is satisfied.

FYI

Frank Abignale was a master embezzler and thief. He was wanted in many states for various schemes that were ingenious in their simplicity. Abnigale was caught when an Eastern Airlines pilot offered him the courtesy of taking the controls of a plane. Abnigale was flying free, wearing an Eastern Airlines pilot's uniform. Regrettably, he had no idea how to fly.

His identity revealed, Abnigale made a deal with the authorities. He would write and talk about the schemes he knew so well to alert financial institution personnel to their vulnerability. His schemes included electronically encoding his own checks to route them to banks in faraway parts of the country. He would also encode his own account number on blank deposit slips and then leave them in the lobbies of financial institutions where he held accounts. Patrons would come in without their own slips, fill in their account numbers on the bogus slips, and the funds would be deposited in Abnigale's account.

What are the elements that make schemes like Abnigale's work? Can you think of any potential areas where precautions against such schemes need to be taken?

WHAT IS AN ACCOMMODATION PARTY?

Sometimes a person who desires to borrow money or to cash a check is not well known in the community or has not established credit. To make her or his commercial paper acceptable, the person might arrange for, someone who is known and has a good credit rating to join in signing the paper (as in *What's Your Verdict?*). Such a cosigner is an **accommodation party**. Under such circumstances, a person who signs as a maker (as did Burk's mother), or as drawer, indorser, or acceptor, becomes primarily liable in that role. It is as though they received the value from the transfer of the instrument. The obligee of the instrument does not have to try to collect from the accommodated party (Burk) before proceeding against the accommodation party (his mother).

However, if the accommodation party is collected against, he or she has the right to seek compensation from the accommodated party. In *What's Your Verdict?* if Burk's mother had to pay the note, she could try to recover from him. However, if the party accommodated is collected against, he or she has no legal right to any contribution from the accommodation party simply because the latter was a cosigner.

Answer the following questions about legal concepts.

1. Bearer paper does not have to be indorsed in order to be negotiated. **True or False?**

2. All indorsements are either blank or special. **True or False?**

3. Commercial paper payable immediately upon presentment is __?__ .

4. "Without recourse" is a __?__ indorsement.
   (a) **blank indorsement**
   (b) **special indorsement**
   (c) **qualified indorsement**
   (d) **none of the above**

5. The type of indorsement that directs the use of the proceeds from the instrument is called a(n) __?__ indorsement.

Study the following situations, answer the questions, then prepare arguments to support your answers.

6. An impostor representing himself as the campaign chairman for Senator Walton Knudson's reelection approached Jean. Jean supported Knudson, so she made out a check to the "Walton Knudson Campaign Fund" for $500. The impostor forged the fund's indorsement and cashed the check as partial payment for a new car. Can the car dealership enforce the instrument against Jean's checking account?

7. Lisa received a promissory note for $1,000 payable to bearer. She indorsed it "to Vince Leonard" and delivered it to him. Later Vince simply delivered the note to the Renaissance Record Shop for a laser disc player and a collection of greatest hits of the Sixties, Seventies, and Eighties. Was Vince's action a proper negotiation?

8. In return for repairing their car, you take a check from a couple in an old station wagon. The car is packed with what looks like all their worldly goods. You have a feeling that either the account is closed or that the check will not be paid or, most likely, both. What indorsement can you use to limit your liability to subsequent holders of the instrument?

9. If you also wrote in "without warrantees" above your indorsement in exercise 8 would that help limit your liability?

10. Your friend wants to buy a car but his credit rating is poor. He asks you to cosign the note with him so that the transaction will go through. If you do so, could you later be required to pay the full amount of the note?

1. Remember that even if an instrument is not negotiable commercial paper, it may still be a valuable contract or creditor's claim and be freely transferable by assignment.

2. If you issue commercial paper that is payable on demand, be ready to pay at any time. Keep funds available to meet such a demand. Civil and even criminal penalties may result from your failure to do so.

3. Only issue bearer paper or create it by indorsement if you

PREVENT LEGAL DIFFICULTIES

immediately transfer it and receive value in exchange or immediately deposit it.

Otherwise unauthorized persons may misuse the bearer paper with the loss falling to you.

4. Where it is a practical option, if you are the payee of commercial paper, include a clause for the payment of reasonable attorney's fees and collection costs by the issuer in case of default.

5. Do not sign as an accommodation party unless you are prepared to pay the full amount of the instrument.

CHAPTER IN REVIEW

CONCEPTS IN BRIEF

1. To be negotiable, an instrument must
   - be in writing and signed by the maker or drawer
   - contain an unconditional order (if it is a draft or a check) or promise (if it is a note or a CD)
   - call for payment of a sum certain in money
   - be payable on demand or at a definite time
   - be payable to the bearer or to the order of a specified person.

2. In conflicts between terms written by various means, the handwritten version prevails over the typewritten version, and the typewritten version prevails over the printed version. Amounts expressed in words prevail over amounts expressed in figures.

3. Although the order or promise given in commercial paper must be unconditional, certain terms may be added to an instrument without destroying negotiability. An example is a provision for the recovery of collection costs or reasonable attorney's fees in case of default.

4. Commercial paper payable to order may be negotiated only by the proper indorsement and delivery. Commercial paper payable to the bearer may be negotiated by delivery alone.

5. Indorsement may be blank or special. By the use of appropriate phrases, indorsements may also be qualified and/or restrictive.

6. Qualified indorsers have some potential liability on an instrument unless less they add the words "without warranties" above their signatures, along with "without recourse."

7. An accommodation party is liable to all subsequent holders of the paper who give value for it, but an accommodation party is not liable to the party accommodated.

YOUR LEGAL VOCABULARY

Match each statement with the term that it best defines. Some terms may not be used.

1. Paper that is to be paid on presentment or at sight

2. Dated later than the date of issuance

3. Indorsement that eliminates the indorser's secondary liability to pay if the primarily liable party does not

4. Indorsement consisting only of the signature of the indorser

5. Person who signs as maker, drawer, acceptor, or indorser to lend name and credit to another person

6. Indorsement that directs the use of the proceeds from an instrument or imposes a condition on payment

7. Indorsement that makes a paper payable to a particular party or to his or her order

8. Dated prior to the date of issuance

9. Official medium of exchange in the United States or a foreign country at the time a piece of commercial paper is issued

10. Negotiable instrument payable to the order of a specified payee

11. Commercial paper legally collectable by the party in posession

acceleration clause
accommodation party
antedated
bearer
bearer paper
blank endorsement
holder
indorse
indorsement
indorser
money
negotiable
negotiation
order paper
payable at a definite time
payable on demand
postdated
qualified indorsement
restrictive indorsement
special indorsement
unqualified indorsement

12. In today's world, which is more important, cash or alternative mediums of exchange such as commercial paper or credit cards? Why?

13. Why do we want to reduce the risk of taking commercial paper?

14. How is the risk of taking commercial paper reduced for the average holder?

15. In interpreting the face of a piece of commercial paper, why does handwriting prevail over typing and typing over printing?

16. Why do we allow "reasonable attorney's fees" to be acceptable as part of a "sum certain?" Surely nothing can be less certain.

17. Why is it so important that the face of commercial paper bear the words "payable to order" or "payable to bearer?"

18. Why do we allow holders to eliminate their signature-based liability to future holders by using a qualified indorsement?

19. Why are warranties extended to all subsequent holders by a holder who indorses the paper?

20. **HOT DEBATE** Write your attorney's opening statement persuading the court that the loss incurred due to Elizabeth's forgery should not fall on you. Or, write the bank's attorney's opening statement persuading that the loss should not fall on the bank.

21. Parnell was the maker of a promissory note payable to LaSalle. The note was complete and legally correct in all respects but contained the following additional terms. Do any of the added terms destroy the negotiability of the note?
    - "This note is prepared as a result of a service contract between the parties dated 3/13/—"
    - "This note is secured by a mortgage on the maker's residence at 67 Park Central West, Pierre, South Dakota."
    - "This note is payable in Canadian dollars, with exchange."

22. Smith paid Coleman $500 for possession of a bearer note made out in the amount of $750. The note is payable upon the death of Coleman's uncle. Is the note negotiable?

23. Anton drew a check for $750 payable to bearer. Anton gave the check to Brewster. Brewster negotiated it by delivery to Charlois. Charlois negotiated it by delivery to Deltoid. Deltoid tried to collect but found that Anton's bank account lacked the necessary funds for payment. May Deltoid collect from either or both of the prior holders, and if so, under what circumstances?

24. Krosby was starting a new business and needed cash. He convinced the Finance Bank to lend him $10,000 against his new equipment. However, the bank insisted that his prominent friend, Hopper, or someone of equal financial means indorse the note as well. What would be the extent of Hopper's potential liability from such an act?

25. Fell sold his collection of baseball memorabilia to his friend Ryun. Ryun gave him a promissory note in partial payment. The note read that it would be paid "as soon as the authenticity of the collection can be established." Is the note negotiable?

ANALYZE REAL CASES

26. Associates Discount Corporation sought court enforcement of a note it held. The note stated that Fitzwater owed a large sum of money for a tractor that had been delivered to him. Fitzwater, the signer and obligor on the note, wanted to testify to the effect that the tractor was never delivered. May he do so? (*Associates Discount Corporation of Iowa v. Fitzwater,* 518 S.W.2d 474)

27. On May 8, 1957, Brookshire was convicted of issuing a check with intent to defraud. On January 1, 1957, Brookshire had given a check dated December 31, 1957, to pay his taxes for 1956. On January 7 or 8, 1957, Brookshire's bank dishonored the check due to insufficient funds. Under these circumstances, should an intent to defraud be inferred from Brookshire's issuing a postdated check? If not, should the conviction be overturned? (*State v. Brookshire,* 329 S.W.2d 252)

28. In May 1963, Ferri executed a note promising to pay $3,000 to Sylvia's order "within ten years after date." Two years later, Sylvia demanded payment. When refused, Sylvia sued Ferri. Is the note due at a definite time? If so, when? If not, why not? (*Ferri v. Sylvia,* 214 A.2d 470)

29. A $10,000 certificate of deposit (CD) "payable to the Registered Depositor hereof" was issued to John D. Cox by Commercial Bank of Liberty. Cox then used the CD as security for a loan made by the Kaw Valley Bank. When Cox defaulted on the loan, Kaw Valley sought to collect on the CD but Liberty refused to pay. Kaw Valley brought suit but could only collect if the CD was negotiable. Was it? (*Kaw Valley Bank Etc. v. Commercial Bank of Liberty,* 567 S.W.2d 710)

30. A manager of Impact Marketing empowered to issue checks issued six post-dated checks on the company's account. Each check was made out to Bell in return for the legal work he was to perform for Impact. Bell sold the checks to Financial Associates. Financial Associates then proceeded to collect on four of the six instruments. However, Impact Marketing stopped payment on the last two when the services that Bell was to provide were terminated. In seeking to collect on the last two instruments, Financial maintained that it was a holder in due course. It therefore had the right to overcome Impact's defenses. These defenses centered on the fact that the checks were postdated and issued for a promise that was fulfilled. Decide. (*Financial Associates v. Impact Marketing,* 394 N.Y.S. 2d 814)

31. Statham issued a check. The payee then indorsed the instrument over to Kemp Motor Sales. When Statham discovered a failure of consideration in the contract with the payee, Statham stopped payment. In attempting to collect on the instrument, Kemp maintained that it was a holder in due course. Statham defended by claiming that Kemp could not collect because Statham discovered the failure before Kemp initiated collection attempts on the check. Decide. (*Kemp Motor Sales v. Statham,* 171 S.E.2d 389)

32. Haas, a trusted employee of a firm by the name of Trail Leasing, Inc., used her access to her employer's blank checks to defraud Trail Leasing of almost $40,000. She did this by making checks payable to the firm's bank, Drovers First American. She then had the checks signed by an authorized officer of the firm when she obtained cash for them. Once it discovered the fraud, Trail Leasing sued the Bank to recover its losses. The decision depended on whether or not the bank was a holder in due course of the checks that Haas cashed on the Trail Leasing account. Certainly the Bank had taken the instruments in good faith without notice of defect or dishonor. However it was an open question if Drovers had given value as the funds had come directly out of the Trail Leasing account. Decide. (*Trail Leasing, Inc. v. Drovers First American Bank,* 447 N.W.2d 190)

33. When an employee of Epicycle cashed a payroll check at Money Mart Check Cashing Center, Inc., the instrument was deposited with others into Money Mart's bank account. Regrettably the check was subsequently returned marked, "payment stopped." When Money Mart attempted to collect on the check at a later date, it maintained that it was a holder in due course. Epicycle defended against the collection efforts by maintaining that Money Mart could not be a holder in due course as it failed to even inquire about the validity of the check before taking it. Decide. (*Money Mart Check Cashing Center, Inc. v. Epicycle Corp.,* 667 P. 1372)

Federal Deposit Insurance Corp. v. Culver
United States District Court, Kansas, 640 F. Supp. 725

BACKGROUND When Texan Nasib Ed Kalliel entered into a business deal with the Rexford State Bank of Rexford, Kansas, the bank was in excellent financial shape. Kalliel suggested that he had a plan to rescue several farmers from the financial disaster that many in the farming industry at that time were experiencing. He suggested that if the bank would loan its money to farmers in trouble, he would guarantee the loan repayment through one of his companies. Unfortunately, the bank did not have enough capital to make adequate loans to all the farmers who needed them. Consequently, the bank agreed to take deposits from a New Jersey firm in the form of high-yield large certificates of deposits. Most of the new deposits went directly to farm loans. However, about 20 percent were "farmed out" to Kalliel himself and his companies.

FACTS Kalliel and a Missouri farmer, Gary Culver, agreed to a working relationship in which Kalliel would manage the business end and Culver the production end of the Culver farm. When Culver told Kalliel that he must have $30,000 to prevent foreclosure, the Rexford Bank provided the money. Shortly thereafter a Bank representative approached Culver and induced him to sign a blank promissory note form. The Bank's representative maintained to Culver that the note was nothing more than a receipt for the money. Later the amount, interest rate, and due date on the note were filled in. However $50,000 was entered as the amount instead of $30,000. When the Rexford Bank later became insolvent, the FDIC bought the note as it did the remaining outstanding Rexford Bank notes. The FDIC then sought to collect on the note as it was mature and no collection efforts had ever been started on it.

ISSUE The FDIC moved for summary judgment. Culver defended that the circumstances surrounding the issuance of the note provided him with the defense of fraud in the execution which would be good even against the holder in due course position of the FDIC. The FDIC maintained its right to collect, as under the UCC the defense of fraud in the execution is available only as long as there has not been "reasonable opportunity to obtain knowledge of its character or its essential terms" provided to the maker of the note. The FDIC maintained that Culver's failure to take notice of the nature of the form of the instrument that he was presented as a "receipt" was negligence and that, therefore, it could collect to the full value of the face of the note.

PRACTICE JUDGING

1. Should the FDIC's request for summary judgement against Culver be granted? Why or why not?

2. If Culver had just signed a blank piece of paper after being told that the bank would make a receipt out of it by printing the appropriate words around his signature, would he be able to avail himself of the defense of fraud in the execution? Why or why not?

3. If the Bank had made the note payable for an unreasonable amount, such as $1,000,000 could the FDIC have been a holder in due course?

LESSONS

37-1 COLLECTION AND DISCHARGE OF COMMERCIAL PAPER

37-2 DEFENSES TO COLLECTION OF COMMERCIAL PAPER AND ELECTRONIC FUND TRANSFERS

HOT DEBATE

Buanna Myers sat at her desk at the Commerce Bank of Statusville. She was deciding whether or not to buy a promissory note from Alyssia Thomas, the proprietor of Alyssia's Autos. The maker of the note was Televangelist Robert Shore, as president of Mercyland, a not-for-profit corporation that managed low-cost rental properties. Buanna knew that many of the transactions originating with Alyssia's Autos had resulted in lawsuits, mainly because the vehicles Alyssia sold were substandard. The note from Mercyland was for $78,000 for a bus just purchased. Buanna knew that her higher ups at the bank would insist on collecting, even from Mercyland. She also knew that if she didn't buy the note, someone else would.

Where Do You Stand?

1. Assume Buanna buys the note and the bus is defective. Should the bank be able to collect? Why or why not?

2. As the attorney for Mercyland, what arguments can you make to allow the cost for repairs to be offset from the amount due on the note?

GOALS

- Explain the importance of being a holder in due course
- Tell how to qualify as a holder in due course
- Discuss the ways commercial paper is discharged

HOLDER IN DUE COURSE

WHAT'S YOUR VERDICT?

Donna paid Alanna $500 for a promissory note with a face value of $10,000. The note was bearer paper, and Alanna refused to indorse it, saying that she had to leave town and therefore her indorsement would not do any good. Donna knew Alanna had recently been indicted for participation in a blackmail scheme. When Donna tried to collect on the note, the maker refused to pay claiming he had signed it only because Alanna had threatened to reveal certain incriminating facts to the Internal Revenue Service.

Is Donna a holder in due course and thereby able to overcome the obligor's defense and collect?

A holder is a person who has physical possession of bearer or order paper payable to the order of that person as a payee or indorsee. All holders have the right to assign, negotiate, enforce payment, or discharge the paper, with or without payment in return. However, when trying to collect on an instrument, a party who qualifies as either a holder in due course or a holder through a holder in due course is legally placed in a much better position than a mere holder or an assignee.

To be a **holder in due course (HDC)**, a person must qualify as a holder and, in addition, take the commercial paper in good faith, give value for it, and not have knowledge of any defense, adverse claim to, or dishonor of the instrument.

Sometimes, for example if the instrument is overdue and the acquirer knew or should have known of its status, a person cannot be an HDC. Such a person could still qualify as a **holder through a holder in due course (HHDC)**. An HHDC is a holder who takes commercial paper anytime after an HDC. An HHDC normally has the same rights as an HDC. Note, however, that according to the Uniform Commercial Code (UCC), persons cannot improve their position on commercial paper through reacquisition.

If an individual had been a mere holder the first time she had an instrument and she then sold it to a person who qualified as an HDC, reacquiring the instrument from that HDC would still leave her with only her original rights as a mere holder, not those of an HHDC. In collecting, either an HDC or an HHDC can overcome more of the defenses that the obligor on an instrument might raise against payment than a mere holder can overcome.

Limited and Universal Defenses

Defenses that are good against everyone except an HDC or an HHDC are termed **limited defenses**. (These were labeled *personal defenses* under pre-UCC law, but this term may still be used in some jurisdictions.) Defenses that are good against all plaintiffs suing on a negotiable instrument are called **universal defenses**. (These are also known as *real defenses* under pre-UCC law, but this term may still be used in some jurisdictions.) These defenses are discussed in Lesson 37-2.

Qualifications of an HDC

For a holder to be considered an HDC and thereby able to overcome limited defenses, the holder must take the paper in good faith and give value without notice of defense or dishonor.

TAKE IN GOOD FAITH AND GIVE VALUE Taking paper in good faith requires that the holder act honestly, not just in the immediate transaction, but in relation to the complete set of circumstances surrounding the paper. In addition, although the courts generally do not consider the adequacy of the value given for commercial paper, the amount given may attract the court's judgment as to the good faith of the parties involved. For example, if the value given is small in relation to the face value of the instrument, fraud or some other unconscionable act that would prevent the holder from being considered an HDC may be implied by the court.

In *What's Your Verdict?* Donna's knowledge of Alanna's alleged criminal activities and the small value given will probably disqualify her from being an HDC. There was an implied lack of good faith in the situation.

Besides giving value in good faith, an HDC must not know the paper is overdue. For example, a time instrument is overdue the day after the maturity date, or, if payments are to be made in installments, the paper is overdue if even a single installment is late. If an instrument is due on demand, it is overdue a reasonable time after it is issued. However, the UCC specifies that a check is overdue 30 days after issue. Also every holder is charged with knowledge of what is on the instrument, so failing to notice the date is no excuse. Similarly, if the date has been altered, as from May 5 to May 15, and if the alteration is not recognizable by a reasonable person, an innocent holder is accountable only for the date as altered (May 15).

Finally, to qualify as an HDC a holder must not know of any defenses against enforcement of the paper, any claims of ownership from third parties, or any previous dishonors of the paper. Any such knowledge attributable to the holder when he or she acquired the paper would prevent that holder from being considered an HDC. As a consequence, that holder might be legally unable to overcome an obligor's limited defenses against payment of the paper.

These considerations come into play only in a very small minority of cases involving commercial paper. In the vast majority, the instruments are discharged without problems, as discussed in the following section.

HOW IS COMMERCIAL PAPER DISCHARGED?

WHAT'S YOUR
VERDICT?

Hofstra owed $7,700 on a note held by Duvall. On the due date Hofstra offered Duvall a prize quarterhorse worth more than $7,700 as payment instead of cash.

Must Duvall accept the quarterhorse as payment, or can he demand cash?

The obligation to pay on commercial paper may be discharged in the following ways.

By Payment

As mentioned, the vast majority of commercial paper is paid and discharged according to its terms. The maker usually pays a note or a certificate of deposit. A check is usually paid upon demand by the bank on which it is drawn. Other types of drafts are usually paid by the drawees who have accepted the drafts. Regardless of the type of instrument or who is paying, by law the commercial paper terms must dictate that payment be made in money. At maturity or on demand, however, the holder (obligee/creditor) may agree to some form of substitution.

For instance, the holder may agree to take different kinds of property, such as other commercial paper or even a quarterhorse, as in *What's*

Your Verdict? in place of a monetary payment. Absent such agreement though, the holder, Duvall, has the right to demand payment in money or to consider the obligor, Hofstra, in default. However, if Duvall agreed to the substitution, the note would be discharged.

When an obligor pays a holder the amount due on commercial paper, the obligor should obtain possession of the paper. Otherwise, a dishonest holder who retains the paper might falsely claim that it had not been paid and demand a second payment. Such a dishonest holder could also negotiate it wrongfully to an innocent third party, who then might also be entitled to payment. Even if the amount due on paper is paid only in part, this fact should be shown by appropriate notation on the paper itself. Mistakenly marking a note paid and returning it to the maker does not discharge the obligation by itself.

A Question of
ETHICS ?

You are the President of the Commerce Bank of Statusville. In your hands is a promissory note for $78,000 signed by Robert Shore as president of Mercyville, the charity mentioned in the Hot Debate. Although the bus is still in good shape, the note is in default due to a steep decline in contributions. Mercyville is on its last legs and cannot pay its creditors. However, none of the creditors have as yet enforced the various outstanding notes. They do not want to cause the charity to close and put hundreds of homeless people back on the street. Unlike the other creditors, the Commerce Bank is owned by parties from out of state. As a consequence, you are being told to file suit for payment, regardless of the consequences. Your job may be in danger if you do not act according to their wishes. What do you do?

However, it is very difficult evidence for the obligee to overcome in order to be still allowed to collect.

By Cancellation

The obligation to pay commercial paper may also be discharged by cancellation. **Cancellation** in this context consists of any act by the current holder that indicates an intent to end the obligation of payment. Knowingly tearing up the paper, burning it, or just drawing a line through the name of a potential obligor, like an indorser, would be excellent evidence of an intent to discharge one or all obligations arising from the instrument. If the cancellation was the result of fraud, an accident, or a mistake, the cancellation does not discharge the instrument.

By Alteration

A fraudulent change to or completion of commercial paper by a party to the instrument will discharge the obligation of the other party. For example, suppose that it is shown to the satisfaction of a court that the holder of a note fraudulently changed the rate of interest due from 7 to 17 percent. In such a case, the maker would not be obligated to pay it. However, the original parties to the paper would still be bound to make payment in accordance with the original terms if the paper later came into the hands of an HDC or an HHDC.

By Impairment of Collateral

If a holder extends the time of payment, releases the principal debtor, or impairs collateral provided as security for payment of the negotiable instruments, any party whose rights are affected and who did not consent is discharged.

As a Contract

A negotiable instrument may be discharged in the same ways as an ordinary contract for the payment of money. For example, a discharge could occur by novation, by accord and satisfaction, or by operation of law, such as in bankruptcy or because of the running of the statute of limitations.

THINK ABOUT LEGAL CONCEPTS

Answer the following questions about legal concepts.

1. A mere holder can discharge the commercial paper she holds even without being paid for it. **True or False?**

2. A mere holder of a note can sell it to a party who qualifies as an HDC, and then reacquire it and have the rights of an HDC. **True or False?**

3. Which of the following would not discharge an instrument? **(a) payment (b) alteration (c) transfer to a previous owner (d) all of the above would discharge the instrument**

THINK CRITICALLY ABOUT EVIDENCE

Study the following situations, answer the questions, then prepare arguments to support your answers.

4. On October 1, Sven Bollinger took a third party check from Tim Wallace in partial payment for a used stereo Sven sold Tim. The check was made out on August 31 payable to Tim. He indorsed it in blank upon transfer. Can Sven be a holder in due course on the instrument?

5. Ficklin was an unqualified indorser on a note for $10,000. Dixon, the holder of the note, mistakenly believed that Ficklin was in financial ruin. Thinking that she could not collect on the note, Dixon struck out Ficklin's indorsement. Is Ficklin still potentially liable on the instrument?

6. A promissory note payable to James O'Brien was indorsed in blank by him and given to Karen Shaw as a gift. She indorsed the note in blank and negotiated it to Tim Leary for value and in good faith, without knowledge of any defenses or dishonor. Tim Leary indorsed the note, "Pay to Francisco Perez, Tim Leary," and delivered it to Perez. Perez knew that Marcum Bros. had a claim against the note. Perez negotiated the note to Karen Shaw. If she now tries to collect on the note from the maker, can the maker effectively raise a limited defense? If Perez had tried to collect from the maker, could the maker have effectively raised a limited defense against payment?

GOALS

- Explain the importance of the difference between limited and universal defenses
- Identify the various types of limited and universal defenses to the collection of commercial paper
- Discuss the rights and duties involved in electronic fund transfers

WHAT ARE THE LIMITED DEFENSES TO COLLECTION?

WHAT'S YOUR VERDICT?

Santana owned "Hello, Cleveland!" a business that provided touring rock groups with transportation from one concert to another. He bought a large used recreational vehicle (RV) to convert for such a purpose from Trail's Used Car and RV Center. Trail assured Santana that the odometer reading of 25,275 on the RV was correct. Santana paid for the vehicle with $15,000 in cash and by issuing a $45,000 promissory note payable to Trail's order. Santana later learned from state authorities that the true odometer reading was 125,275 miles. Santana wanted to avoid the contract because of the fraud. In the meantime, Trail had negotiated the note to the Continental Bank, an HDC, for $41,000.

Must Santana pay Continental the $45,000 as promised?

Even though the emphasis in this and the next section is on defenses, it is once again important to realize that most commercial paper is enforceable according to its terms and is promptly paid. Only in the exceptional case do defenses to collection come into play. In such instances, however, the holder's risk of not being able to collect is greatly reduced if he or she is an HDC and thereby is able to overcome the limited defenses that might be raised against such collection.

Limited defenses are good against all holders except an HDC or an HHDC. Against ordinary holders they are just as effective in barring collection as the universal defenses discussed later in this chapter. The following are the limited defenses.

Breach of Contract or Failure of Consideration

Often commercial paper is issued as a result of a contractual agreement, as in *What's Your Verdict?* Ordinary or mere holders are subject to defenses that arise when the terms of such a contract are not fulfilled or the consideration (or partial consideration) is not given as bargained for by the person who issued the instrument. In *What's Your Verdict?* for example, if Trail had failed to deliver the RV on time, it would have been a breach of contract or, if the RV were defective, a failure of consideration. In either instance only an HDC or an HHDC could have collected on the note. An ordinary holder, like Trail, could not have overcome the defenses.

Fraud in the Inducement

If a person uses fraud to induce another to issue commercial paper (as Trail did to Santana in *What's Your Verdict?*), the party defrauded has a limited defense to use against holders who try to collect. However, in *What's Your Verdict?* Continental Bank is an HDC, and therefore Santana must pay the note. Santana can then seek to recover from Trail.

Fraud in the inducement occurs when the issuer is aware that an obligation based on commercial paper is being created and knows the essential terms. However, the person is persuaded to issue the paper because of fraudulent statements. This should not be confused with *fraud in the execution,* where the issuer is unaware that an obligation based on commercial paper is being created or is unaware of the nature or essential terms of the commercial paper. Fraud in the execution is a universal defense covered later in this chapter.

Temporary Incapacity to Contract—Excluding Minority

Contractual obligations made when a person is experiencing a temporary loss of capacity, such as through insanity or intoxication, are voidable. The law establishes a limited defense against commercial paper issued during such periods of temporary loss of capacity.

Ordinary Duress

Duress can be either a limited or a universal defense depending on its severity. Ordinary duress, typically from severe economic threat or a legitimate threat of criminal prosecution, does not strip away a person's capacity to contract. It does improperly force the person to enter into a contract. As a consequence, ordinary duress provides a limited defense against collection of any commercial paper that originates in such a contractual setting.

Prior Payment or Cancellation

If the obligee pays the amount due on a piece of commercial paper but does not obtain the instrument or at least have it marked "paid," the instrument could continue circulating. If it does, and ends up in the hands of an HDC, that party could then enforce it against the obligor a second time because prior payment or cancellation only produces a limited defense.

Conditional Delivery or Nondelivery

Assume that a check or a note is delivered under a separate agreement that the instrument is to be negotiated only upon the happening of a certain event. Before the condition is satisfied, the paper is negotiated regardless. The resulting defense of conditional delivery is good only against ordinary holders.

For example, concert promoters give a $10,000 earnest money check to the agent of a famous rock group. The agent agrees to cash the check only if the group appears for the promoters' performance. If the group does not appear, yet the agent indorses the check to an HDC in exchange for some new sound equipment, the promoters will have to pay it and try to collect their loss from the agent or the rock group.

Nondelivery is also merely a limited defense. In such a case, an instrument is properly prepared or indorsed but only circulated as a

result of theft or negligence. If the instrument is in bearer form, a later HDC could enforce it, but a mere holder could not.

Unauthorized Completion

A maker or drawer who signs a negotiable instrument but leaves the amount blank runs a great risk. In such an instance, someone else typically is authorized to complete the paper when, for example, a final price is negotiated. If the amount actually entered is not within authorized limits and the instrument is transferred to a holder in due course, the amount would have to be paid to the HDC because unauthorized completion is only a limited defense.

Theft

A mere holder cannot collect on the instrument if the holder or a person through whom she or he obtained the instrument acquired it by theft. An HDC can require payment in such circumstances, however.

WHAT ARE THE UNIVERSAL DEFENSES TO COLLECTION?

WHAT'S YOUR VERDICT?

Tomassen threatened Bisque that if Bisque did not issue a promissory note for $5,000 in Tomassen's favor, Bisque's wife would be seriously harmed. Bisque signed and delivered the note to Tomassen, who then sold it to an HDC for $4,500.

Can the HDC collect on the note against Bisque?

Defenses that are good against all kinds of holders, including HDCs and HHDCs, are universal defenses. They include the following.

Permanent Incapacity to Contract and Minority

If a person is declared permanently insane or a habitual drunkard by judicial proceeding, the person is not responsible for any obligation

incurred thereafter on commercial paper. Either status poses a universal defense to the making, drawing, accepting, indorsing, or accommodating of another party on an instrument.

Just as a minor may avoid contractual responsibilities, her or his refusal to pay on a piece of commercial paper is a universal defense. This is true whether the minor signs as

maker, drawer, acceptor, indorser, or in any other capacity.

Illegality

Commercial paper issued in connection with illegal conduct, such as illegal gambling or prostitution in most states, is unenforceable even by an HDC or an HHDC.

Forgery or Lack of Authority

When one person signs the name of another with the intent to defraud, a forgery has been committed. Such an act is a crime. Forgery on commercial paper produces a universal defense for the person whose signature has been forged. If the intent to defraud is lacking, but a person signs another's signature without authorization, the signer does not commit forgery.

However, the effect on an HDC would be the same unless the person whose name was signed later ratified (approved) the signing. Both the forger and the unauthorized signer would be liable for the instrument regardless.

Alteration

An **alteration** is a party's unauthorized change to or completion of a negotiable instrument intended to change the obligation of a party. If the alteration was made fraudulently, the person whose obligation is affected no longer has liability on the instrument. Other alterations do not discharge a party, and the instrument may be enforced according to its original terms.

Even if the alteration was fraudulent a payor bank, a drawee, or a person taking the instrument for value, in good faith and without notice of the alteration can enforce the instrument according to its original terms. These parties also can enforce the terms as filled in on an incomplete instrument altered by unauthorized completion. If the $15 amount payable on a check is altered to read $150, an HDC or HHDC could collect on the instrument, but only $15. If, by negligence, the person sued on the check substantially contributed to making the alteration possible, that person cannot use the defense of alteration.

Fraud in the Execution of the Paper or as to the Essential Terms

Sometimes trickery is used in such a way that even a careful person who signs does not know and has no reasonable opportunity to learn of the nature or essential terms of the document. Such a person has a defense of fraud against even an HDC or an HHDC. For example, a celebrity signs an autograph on a blank sheet of paper. The "fan" then prints or writes a promissory note around the signature. Or suppose the signer of the paper is not able to read because

he or she is illiterate in English or has broken glasses, and the person planning to defraud gives a false explanation of the essential terms or substitutes one paper for another before the signing. Not even an HDC or an HHDC can collect in these cases.

Duress Depriving Control

While ordinary duress is a limited defense, duress that deprives control is a universal one. For example, a person who signs a note or draft because another person is threatening to shoot him with a gun has a defense good against even an HDC or an HHDC. In *What's Your Verdict?* the threat of physical harm against an immediate family member (or the home) would result in a universal defense being available to Bisque against collection of the paper.

Claims and Defenses Stemming From a Consumer Transaction

Although not defined as a universal defense by the UCC, by Federal Trade Commission (FTC) rule any defense a

consumer could raise against the seller of a good or service can be raised against commercial paper originating in the same transaction. Defenses such as breach of contract, failure of consideration, and fraud in the inducement are thereby made good even against an HDC or HHDC in the proper circumstances. A **consumer transaction** is one in which a party buys goods or services for personal or household use. A notice stating that a piece of commercial paper originated in a consumer transaction and that the debtor's defenses are good against holders must be given in bold print on the instrument.

Prior to the "consumer revolt" of the 1960s, the holder in due course doctrine allowed collection in both consumer transactions and business transactions. For example, if you pruchased a defective car whose transmission fell out on the way out of the used car lot, you would still have to pay off in full any promissory note that you signed to buy the car. You could seek compensation only from the used car dealer.

WHAT'S YOUR
VERDICT?

Snyder left her purse in her unlocked car while visiting a friend. When she returned to the car, the purse had been stolen. Her automatic teller card was in the purse. Snyder immediately notified the police of the theft but did not notify her financial institution for three days. During that time the thief took out $2,100 in cash advances using the card.

Who is liable for the $2,100 loss?

A transfer of funds that requires a financial institution to debit or credit an account and that is initiated by the use of an electronic terminal, computer, telephone, or magnetic tape is an **electronic fund transfer (EFT)**.

EFTs are basically conducted without such paper instruments as checks or drafts. Automated teller machines, point-of-sale terminals in stores, pay-by-phone systems that eliminate check writing, and automated clearinghouse networks that credit payroll checks directly to accounts are examples of devices that facilitate EFTs.

Electronic Fund Transfers Act

Commercial paper law, due to its emphasis on the need for a writing, was generally inapplicable to EFTs. Therefore, the federal government enacted the Electronic Fund Transfers Act (EFTA) to protect consumers making such transfers. The EFTA emphasizes that the use of such transfers is to be purely voluntary. When an EFT is used, the consumer must immediately receive a written receipt and later must receive a statement of all transfers during a particular period. If the consumer detects an error of overbilling, it must be reported within 60 days of the date the statement was

CULTURAL DIVERSITY IN LAW

International

Electronic Data Interchange

A form of electronic fund transfer used widely in international transactions is *electronic data interchange (EDI)*. With EDI, transport documents such as bills of lading, and others, such as import-export papers and invoices, are sent via computer to their destinations. Use of EDI helps to speed up international transactions for multinational corporations and other companies who do business internationally

Rules governing the EDI transfer of bills of lading and other transport documents have been adopted by an international trade organization, the Comite Maritime International (CMI). The rules govern the problem of negotiating the transport documents. The party who has the right to control and transfer the goods is designated as the "holder" in the computer records. According to CMI, EDI can be used for transport documents only upon agreement of all parties involved in the transaction.

sent. The error is reported to the institution responsible for the EFT. The institution then has 10 business days to investigate and to report the results in writing. If the institution needs more time, it can use up to 45 days, but during this time the funds must be made available to the consumer.

In the case of unauthorized transfers, Congress rejected the idea present in commercial paper law requiring full liability on the part of a depositor who negligently allows such a transfer (by losing a check, for example). Instead, Congress chose to divide the risk of unauthorized transfers between the consumer and the financial institution, even if the depositor is negligent. As a consequence, as long as notification is given to the financial institution within two business days of learning of the loss or theft of the card, the consumer is responsible only for the lesser of $50 or the value obtained in unauthorized transfers prior to the notification. However, if more than two days have elapsed before notification, the consumer may be responsible for up to a maximum of $500.

In *What's Your Verdict?* because three days went by before Snyder gave notification of her loss, she will probably have to pay $500 and the financial institution will have to absorb the other $1,600.

UCC Article 4A

While consumer electronic fund transfers are governed by the EFTA, electronic fund transfers by businesses are governed by Article 4A of the UCC. These transfers generally involve large sums of money between highly sophisticated parties. Speed in making the transfer is often very important.

Study the following situations, answer the questions, then prepare arguments to support your answers.

8. A 17-year-old student contracts to pay $3,000 for a 12-month modeling course. She pays $500 down and gives a note for the balance, payable in 23 monthly installments. Advertisements for the course promise "exciting, high-paying jobs." However, it becomes clear that the only jobs offered are to model clothes at local schools. The student decides to avoid the contract but is told that the note has been transferred to a bank that is a holder in due course. Must she pay as promised?

9. You contract for aluminum siding to be installed on the building of your skateboard manufacturing business. You sign a promissory note for $10,000 payable to the order of the siding company. Later, although the siding company has gone out of business without doing the job, a bank demands payment of the note. The bank purchased the instrument from the siding company for $9,500 and is a holder in due course.

Are you legally required to pay the note?

10. While Freed was on vacation and unreachable, the real estate she had been interested in buying came on the market. Although not authorized to do so, Freed's secretary called the seller, negotiated a price for the property, and drew a check on Freed's account by copying Freed's signature from another document. Could an HDC to whom the seller negotiated the check collect against Freed if she did not ratify the instrument?

11. When Torres leased an apartment from Leon, they used a printed form provided by Leon, the landlord. One sentence stated: "No advance deposits shall be required other than for one month's rent." However, Leon had typed in: "Tenant shall pay a $400 refundable cleaning and repair deposit upon taking possession. No charge shall be made for ordinary wear and tear." Torres drew a line through the $400 and wrote in $200. Both parties signed and each received a copy of the lease. Which provision governs the refundable deposit—the printed ($0), the typewritten ($400), or the handwritten ($200)?

For your protection . . .

1. When you acquire commercial paper, try to do so in a manner that qualifies you for the rights of a holder in due course. Do this by giving value in good faith for it and by taking only paper that is not overdue or subject to any defense, claim, or dishonor of which you have knowledge. If that is impossible, become an HHDC by acquiring the paper from an HDC.

2. When you are acquiring commercial paper, require the transferor to give an unqualified indorsement in your presence. Verify the transferor's identity carefully. If the signature is a forgery, the loss would

PREVENT LEGAL

DIFFICULTIES

generally fall on the party who took from the forger.

3. When you receive commercial paper, work to minimize defenses that can be used against you if you try to collect.

4. If you pay your obligation on commercial paper in full, have the paper so marked and signed by the holder, then obtain possession of it immediately. Have partial payments noted on the paper as well.

5. When using EFT, retain your receipts and use them to verify your statements. Immediately report any lost or stolen EFT cards or any other breach of security surrounding your use of EFT to the financial institution that issued your card. This will minimize your potential losses.

CHAPTER IN REVIEW

CONCEPTS IN BRIEF

1. A holder in due course can overcome limited defenses offered against payment of the paper. An ordinary holder's right to collect is subject to such defenses.

2. Ordinary holders, holders in due course, and holders through holders in due course are all subject to universal defenses.

3. Limited defenses include breach of contract or failure of consideration, fraud in the inducement, temporary incapacity to contract (excluding minority), ordinary duress, prior payment or cancellation, conditional delivery or nondelivery, unauthorized completion, and theft.

4. Universal defenses include permanent incapacity to contract and minority, illegality, forgery or lack of authority, alteration, fraud in the execution of the paper or as to its essential terms, and duress depriving control, among others.

5. Obligations on commercial paper may be discharged by payment, cancellation, alteration, impairment of collateral, or in an ordinary contract for payment of money could be discharged.

6. The Electronic Fund Transfers Act (EFTA) protects consumers making electronic transfers. The use of such transfers by consumers is to be purely voluntary.

7. If a consumer reports the loss or theft of an EFT card within two business days after learning of it, the consumer's liability on an unauthorized EFT is limited to $50. Otherwise, the consumer's loss is limited to $500.

8. Electronic fund transfers by businesses are protected by Article 4A of the UCC. Such transfers usually involve large sums of money and high speed transfers.

YOUR LEGAL VOCABULARY

Match each statement with the term that it best defines. Some terms may not be used.

1. One who takes commercial paper after an HDC and thereby acquires the same rights

2. Holder who takes commercial paper in good faith without knowledge of any defect or overdue status and who gives value for it

3. Defenses good against all obligees

4. Defenses good against all obligees except HDCs and HHDCs

5. An act, such as drawing a line through an indorser's signature, done with the intent to discharge that person's obligation on a negotiable instrument

6. A debit or credit to an account that is initiated by the use of a terminal, computer, telephone, or magnetic tape

7. A party's unauthorized change to or completion of a negotiable instrument intended to change the obligation of a party

alteration
cancellation
consumer transaction
electronic fund transfer
  (EFT)
holder in due course
  (HDC)
holder through a holder
  in due course (HHDC)
limited defenses
universal defenses

8. Why does an HHDC have the same rights as an HDC?

9. Even though the amount of value is immaterial, how might the amount paid to the face value affect a person's chances to be an HDC?

10. In what ways can electronic transfers benefit (a) consumers and (b) the banking industry? Do you see any disadvantages to using electronic transfers rather than commercial paper?

WRITE ABOUT LEGAL CONCEPTS

11. Explain the importance of the status of holder in due course.

12. In what ways can commercial paper be discharged?

13. What was the purpose of the Electronic Fund

Transfers Act and how does it accomplish that purpose?

14. HOT DEBATE Write a persuasive letter from the Reverend Robert Shore to the president of the Commerce Bank of Statusville asking for more time to pay the note.

THINK CRITICALLY ABOUT EVIDENCE

15. Abbiatti operated her own computer repair business. To work on the newer models, she purchased a set of advanced instruments for $2,300 from CompRepare, Inc. She paid $300 down and signed a 180-day negotiable note payable to CompRepare for the balance. After using the tools, she realized they were not of the precision required or promised. She refused to pay. In the meantime, the note had been sold to the People's Commercial Bank, an HDC, for $1,850. Can the bank overcome Abbiatti's defense and collect?

16. When Rebel T. Clef, a rock star, landed at the local airport, a young woman persuaded him to sign his autograph on a blank sheet of paper. The woman was a skilled typesetter. She went home and printed all the essential language of a promissory note around the signature. After filling in the amount of $15,000 and inserting her name as payee, she sold the note to an HDC. Is Rebel legally obligated to pay the $15,000?

17. Eaton owed Fobair $1,500 for supplies he purchased the year before for his business. Fobair met Eaton in a restaurant one day and loudly demanded either cash or a signature on an inter-

est-bearing note or he would "haul you into court and sue you for all you've got." Eaton signed, and Fobair promptly sold the note to Livingston, an HDC. Now Eaton refuses to pay the note, claiming it was signed under duress. Will this be a valid defense to payment?

18. Tilly needed another freezer for her ice cream store. She purchased a used one from Worth and paid with a check for $1,275. Worth had assured her that the freezer was in good working order. However, when the unit was installed in Tilly's business, it did not work. Upon removing the back panel, Tilly found that the motor was defective and had not been in working order for several years. What is her defense against collection of the check by Worth? Would Tilly's defense be good against an HDC?

19. By mistake, the Downtown Bank returned a $1,000 note to its maker, Hall. Hall knows that the note had not been paid and that it is highly unlikely that the bank discharged his obligation as a gift. Should he contact the bank and inform it of the mistake?

ANALYZE REAL CASES

20. On May 2, as part of the $96,500 purchase price of some real estate, Collins issued a 30-day note for $66,500. Just before the due date, Collins ordered his attorney, Sanders, to have money available from Collins' account to pay the note. The attorney had the money and did pay the note, but directed the payees to indorse the instrument in blank rather than mark the note paid. Sanders then, without Collins' knowledge, took the note and, on June 3, pledged it as security to the Oswego Bank for a loan the bank had made to the attorney. When Sanders defaulted on the loan, the bank tried to collect against Collins. Was the Oswego Bank an HDC and therefore able to overcome Collins' defense of prior payment? (*Collins v. First National Bank of Oswego, Kansas,* 746 S.W.2d 424)

21. The Pierces purchased siding for their home from the Globe Remodeling Company, Inc. They gave a promissory note for $3,044.40 in payment. In exchange, they were to receive sufficient siding for the job, properly installed, together with $1,200 in cash. Globe indorsed the note to the Gramatan Company, Inc. Gramatan then sold it without indorsement to its affiliate, the plaintiff, Gramatan National Bank, for $2,250. The bank had previously placed Globe on its "precautionary list" because it knew that in other sales, Globe had not performed as promised. The bank also knew that similar Globe notes were being litigated and that federal law enforcement officials had been investigating Globe's activities. In this case, only about $400 had been paid to the Pierces. In addition, only about one-half the siding had been delivered, and none had been installed. The Pierces refused to pay the note, and the bank sued. Is the bank a holder in due course? (*Gramatan National Bank and Trust Co. v. Pierce,* 159 A.2d 781)

22. A vacuum cleaner sales representative approached The Charltons and offered them a deal called the "club plan." Under its terms, the Charltons were to make appointments in their area for sales representatives to demonstrate the cleaners. For each appointment leading to a sale, the Charltons were to receive $25. After some discussion, the couple read and signed the club plan. Then the sales representa-tive mentioned that because they were to be agents for the company, he wanted to leave a vacuum cleaner with them. He then had them sign a "receipt" for the cleaner. Taking his word for the nature of the document (although they could have read the instrument), the Charltons then signed the receipt. Only later, when approached by the Local Finance Company for payment, did the Charltons find out that the receipt was actually a promissory note. Can they successfully defend against payment by claiming fraud in the execution? (*Local Finance Co. v. Charlton,* 289 S.W.2d 157)

23. Cameo State Bank mistakenly believed that a credit life insurance policy had paid an $8,000 note it held. Consequently, it marked it "paid" and returned it to the heirs of the maker. Having discovered the mistake, the bank now asks the court to void the release and enforce the note against the estate. Has the note been discharged? (*Cameron State Bank v. Sloan,* 559 S.W.2d 564)

24. Ognibene withdrew $20 at an automated teller machine (ATM) through the use of his Citibank card and the entry of his confidential personal identifica-tion number. As he did so, he was evidently observed by an individual who was using a tele-phone between Ognibene's ATM and an adjacent ATM. The individual was seemingly reporting to the bank that the adjacent ATM was not working. The person, speaking into the telephone said, "I'll see if his card works in my machine." He then borrowed Ognibene's card and inserted it in the other ATM several times, finally stating, "Yes, it seems to be working." Then he returned Ognibene's card. Later, Ognibene discovered $400 had been withdrawn from his account by the person. Ognibene then sued the bank to have the $400 recredited to his account claiming it was an unauthorized transaction under the EFTA. The bank refused, stating that by giving the other person the card, Ognibene had "authorized" the transaction and was fully liable even though Ognibene had obviously not benefited from the transaction at all. Do you agree with the bank or with Ognibene? (*Ognibene v. Citibank N.A.,* 446 N.Y.S. 2d 845)

FACTS The Kraemers needed money. They owned certain pieces of real estate in Jefferson County, Missouri, and decided to use it as collateral for a loan. To accomplish this, they went to the office of George Pickles, a real estate dealer in the area. There they executed a negotiable promissory note in the principal sum of $50,000, payable five years after date. The note bore the interest rate of 8 percent. They then executed a deed of trust on their real estate as security for the loan.

The promissory note and the deed of trust were in favor of Grace A. Wheeler, the daughter of George Pickles. Ms. Wheeler was merely acting as a "straw party" for her father. As a consequence, she claimed no interest in the notes and indorsed them without recourse to her father, George Pickles. The note provided that payments thereon were to be made at the office of George Pickles. The deed of trust also allowed that the debtors could make payments in multiples of $1,000 at any time on the note.

During the next three years, plaintiffs made more than $12,000 in payments on the notes. Whenever these payments were made, Mr. Pickles would hand to the plaintiffs a printed form of receipt showing the date of payment, the amount paid on the principal, and the amount of the principal remaining to be paid. No indorsement of payment on the note itself was ever made.

Ultimately, Mrs. J. C. Leber purchased the note for $45,000. At that time no notice was given to her of the payments rendered by the Kraemers. Later Mr. Pickles received two other payments on the note but did not remit them to Mrs. Leber.

When Mr. Pickles died before the note matured, Mrs. Leber contacted the Kraemers and for the first time advised them that the note had been purchased by her and that she had been advised by Mr. Pickles' business associate that now "she could do her own collecting."

When the Kraemers and Mrs. Leber could not agree on the amount due on the note, she began foreclosure proceedings. Ultimately, the property was sold and the proceeds deposited in the office of the circuit clerk for disposition by the court.

LOWER COURT DECISION The lower court refused to give the Kraemers full credit for their payments. They appealed.

COURT OF APPEALS OPINION The note was a negotiable instrument of such a character that plaintiffs were bound to have known that it could and probably would be negotiated and passed into the hands of a third party. As a consequence plaintiffs in making payments on this note should have ascertained that the person to whom payment was made either owned the note or had possession thereof for the purpose of collection.

PRACTICE JUDGING

1. Should the Kraemers have to pay the full amount to Mrs. Leber? Why or why not?

2. What other alternatives do the Kraemers have in this situation?

3. Who could the Kraemers sue for their losses in this matter if they must pay the full amount on the note to Mrs. Leber? What legal barriers might they have to overcome to successfully recover their funds in each instance?

LESSONS

38-1 ESTABLISHING A SECURITY INTEREST

38-2 CREATION AND PERFECTION OF SECURITY INTERESTS

HOT DEBATE

The People's Bank of Charlottesville, Rhode Island, decided to increase the charge for issuing a bad check to $30. Notice of this change was provided by mail to each depositor. The next month, Bill Jones' paycheck did not clear because his employer declared bankruptcy. All the checks Bill issued to pay his bills bounced. The bank then charged his account $270 ($30 for each of nine insufficient fund checks). After negotiations failed, Bill sued the bank to get them to recredit the $270.

Where Do You Stand?

1. As Bill's attorney, list the legal reasons supporting your suit.

2. As the bank's attorney, list the reasons the loss should be Bill's not the bank's.

GOALS

- **Distinguish between debtors and creditors**
- **Discuss the importance of protecting both creditors and debtors**
- **Describe a secured transaction**

WHO ARE DEBTORS AND CREDITORS?

WHAT'S YOUR
VERDICT?

Chang, a college student majoring in physics, won a $2,500 prize in a science project competition. She deposited the money in her checking account at the Ranchers and Merchants State Bank.

Is the bank a debtor or a creditor of Chang?

A **debtor** is a person or a business that owes money, goods, or services to another. Whatever is owed is generally called the **debt**. The **creditor** is the one to whom the debt is owed.

At first, the debtor-creditor relationship may seem to be heavily weighted in favor of the creditor. In fact, the creditor generally faces a higher risk of loss. However, both parties benefit. The debtor gets needed or wanted goods or services that might not otherwise be obtainable. The creditor puts available capital to work and is paid for this. Each needs the other. If either fails to perform the contract as promised, both are likely to suffer some loss. Understandably, default is more likely to be by the debtor who fails to pay when due. But usually creditors can and do screen would-be debtors for creditworthiness, and thus limit defaults to a tolerable level.

A legally enforceable debt normally arises out of a contract where something of value has been exchanged for a promise to provide money, goods, or services. In *What's Your Verdict?* Chang transferred her money to the bank in exchange for the bank's promise to either keep it safe and return it upon demand by Chang or pay it to someone else as she may order in writing. Therefore, the bank is the debtor and Chang is the creditor.

During the Middle Ages, charging any interest on loans was illegal.

Today it is legal and very common. Prudent borrowing of money is recognized as beneficial to all parties involved. Extension of credit, whereby a buyer gets goods today and pays later, facilitates economic growth. This economic growth provides more jobs for producers and more goods for consumers. Accordingly, the debtor-creditor relationship is encouraged and protected by law. This protection makes creditors more secure when lending money or selling on credit. At the same time, the law protects debtors by forbidding unfair credit and collection practices.

F Y I

A *bad check* is a check written when the amount of money in a checking account is not enough to cover it. Writing a bad check is a crime in all states. Under typical bad check statutes, it is a crime to write a check with intent to defraud, knowing that the funds are not sufficient to cover the check when presented for payment.

A Question of ETHICS ?

In the Middle Ages it was unethical for anyone to loan money at interest. The practice was forbidden by the Church and punished in the Church's courts. Why do you think charging interest was considered unethical? Do you agree? Why is charging too much interest (as with usury or loan sharking) considered illegal today? Do you think these practices should be illegal? Why or why not?

WHAT'S YOUR VERDICT?

Andrus loaned a friend, O'Shea, $300 cash for a down payment on a new type of videodisc player that would also play compact audio discs. O'Shea financed the remaining $900 of the purchase price through the seller, giving the seller a security interest in the goods. Later, O'Shea stopped making payments while she still owed Andrus the $300 and the retailer $500. The retailer repossessed the player and resold it for $480.

Would Andrus get a share of the $480 to help pay back the $300

All purchases are made either with cash or credit. No debt is involved in a cash transaction. In a credit purchase, however, payment is delayed and a debt, owed by the buyer to the seller or finance company, is created.

In a sale on credit, the seller is understandably concerned about getting paid in full and on time, as promised by the buyer. One legal device that encourages such performance by buyers and is used fre-quently by sellers on credit is called a **secured transaction**. This device gives sellers a reassuring sense of security or freedom from anxiety and fear of loss on the sale.

A secured transaction is a business deal that creates a security interest in personal property or fixtures. As dis-cussed in the chapters on property, fixtures are items of personal property that have become permanently attached to realty. **Security interest** is the interest in or claim against the

CULTURAL DIVERSITY IN LAW

Colombia

Debt Collection

Rather than operating through the courts, credi-tors who try to collect bills in Colombia go through collection agencies. These agencies, known as *chepitos*, basically harass creditors into paying their bills. On behalf of a creditor, chepitos go to the debtor's home or business and carry a sign advertising that a debtor lives or works there. The *chepitos* remain at the site until the bill is paid. Colombian lawyers do not approve of this practice and would like to see it banned.

debtor's property, created for the pur-pose of assuring payment of the debt. **Collateral** is the property that is sub-ject to the security interest of the creditor.

In a secured transaction, if the debtor-buyer defaults by failing to pay as promised, the creditor-seller, or lender, may exercise the legal **right of repossession**. This means the seller on credit (or the finance company that has provided money for the pur-chase) takes the goods back, resells them, and uses the net proceeds (after expenses of the repossession and resale) to pay the balance due. If there is any excess, it is returned to the original debtor-buyer. If there is still a remaining balance due, the seller can sue the original debtor-

Every year we hear of new scams designed to get our money illegally. One new threat is from businesses posing as banks on the Internet. These businesses are not banks. State and federal governments have not legally chartered them, and therefore their deposits are not feder-ally insured.

At least ten such bogus banks have popped up on the Internet so far. The FBI is investigating some of these bogus banks and have put them on an "alert list." The investigation is for possible fraud, tax eva-sion, money laundering, and other potential criminal activity. These cyberschemers typically advertise sky-high interest rates on customers' deposits. To combat this, Internet banking safeguards are being formed to protect con-sumers. A proposal that Internet banks post certification to show they are chartered is one of the proposed safeguards. Consumers can contact the Federal Deposit Insurance Corporation (FDIC) to confirm the legiti-macy of any bank doing business on the Internet. Check before you become the next scammed cyberbanking consumer.

LAW and the INTERNET

buyer to collect. Creditors, be they sellers on credit, or lenders of money, are more likely to be paid if they are secured parties. A **secured party** is a person who has a security interest in collateral owned by the debtor-buyer.

In contrast, a creditor holding a defaulted unsecured claim must first sue, get a court judgment, and then execute (enforce) that judgment against the debtor's property. Other creditors of the debtor may have equal rights in that property. If the debtor's financial obligations are discharged in bankruptcy, the unsecured creditor may receive nothing or only a few cents for each dollar of the unpaid debt rightly claimed.

In *What's Your Verdict?* the retailer could keep the full $480 because of its security interest in the player. It could also sue O'Shea for the remaining $20 of the $500 owed. It would have the right of an unsecured creditor such as Andrus, for this $20 balance.

Answer the following questions about legal concepts.

1. In reference to the bank account of a depositor, the bank is the depositor's creditor. **True or False?**

2. During the Middle Ages it was illegal to charge interest on a loan. **True or False?**

3. The __?__ holds the security interest. **(a) debtor (b) creditor (c) collateral**

4. Repossession is a right that may have to be exercised by the debtor. **True or False?**

5. A secured party is in a superior position to an unsecured party when it comes to collecting a debt. **True or False?**

THINK CRITICALLY ABOUT EVIDENCE

Study the following situations, answer the questions, then prepare arguments to support your answers.

6. When Dodrill started her own copying and duplicating business, she entered into several contractual arrangements. First, she bought $900 worth of paper from Springfield Business Supply, promising to pay the money within 30 days. Then, using her bank credit card, she purchased spreadsheet and word processing software. In addition, she bought several desktop-copying units from the manufacturer on a 24-month installment purchase plan. The plan permitted the seller to repossess the machines if Dodrill defaulted on payments. Finally, Dodrill borrowed $2,000 from the Ozark Region National Bank to meet current expenses, giving a U.S. Treasury bond as security for repayment. Which of the transactions entered into by Dodrill involved a debtor-creditor relationship? Which relationships were secured? Which were unsecured?

7. Fanno pondered the pros and cons of buying versus leasing a costly computer system for his business. "There are so many improvements coming along," he said, "that I could be stuck with an obsolete white elephant if I buy. On the other hand, leasing eventually costs more because the lessor earns a profit too." Finally he bought the needed machine under a five-year secured transaction. He told a friend, "If something better comes along while we're still making payments, I'll simply default and let the seller repossess the obsolete equipment. Could Fanno legally default as planned? Would it be ethical if this shifted the loss on the obsolete gear to the seller? How would the seller "have the last laugh" in this situation?

HOW ARE SECURITY INTERESTS CREATED?

WHAT'S YOUR VERDICT?

Sonia had to pay a dental bill. She borrowed the needed money from her brother and gave him a paper on which she had written "IOU $575. Sonia Aponte, March 8, 20—."

Was this document a pledge, making the loan a secured transaction?

Before the Uniform Commercial Code (UCC) was enacted, many types of legal transactions gave creditors special rights in the property of debtors. Each type had distinct rules for its creation, maintenance, and execution. These rules varied from state to state. Their number and technical nature created a situation that enabled unscrupulous individuals to take advantage of the unsuspecting or the uninformed.

The UCC, however, solved many of the problems by making secured transactions the only legal means of giving a creditor a security interest in another's property. The creditor in such a transaction is the secured party, and the personal property subject to the security interest is the collateral. These UCC provisions apply only to personal property. Contracts involving real property as security, such as mortgages and deeds of trust, are still governed by a variety of other state laws.

A security interest under the UCC can be created only with the consent of the debtor. Such consent is usually given if suitable collateral is avail-able, because otherwise the creditor simply refuses to deal. The agreement may be expressed orally or in writing, depending on which of two basic types of secured transactions is used.

A security interest is created when three things take place. First, there must be an agreement between the debtor and creditor that the creditor will have a security interest. Second, the creditor must give value. Third, the debtor must have rights (either ownership or possession) in the collateral. These three things can occur in any order. When the last of the three occurs, the security interest becomes enforceable against the debtor.

When the Creditor Has Possession of the Collateral

In the first type of secured transaction, the creditor obtains possession of the collateral. This transaction, which may be based on an oral or written agreement, is called a **pledge**. The debtor may be buying the property, or the debtor may already own or have possession of the property, but it is now given as security for a

loan of money. Sonia created no pledge in *What's Your Verdict?* Her IOU is merely a written acknowledgment of the debt. It is not a formal promissory note, and there was no agreement to create a security interest. She gave no collateral as security for payment. The IOU is not a pledge or other type of secured transaction.

In a pledge, upon default by the debtor, the creditor has a legal right to sell the property and apply the proceeds of the sale to the debt. Any surplus is returned to the debtor. Any deficit remains an obligation of the debtor and is collectible as an unsecured claim through a lawsuit.

When the Debtor Retains Possession of the Collateral

In the second type of secured transaction, the debtor retains possession of the collateral under written contract with the secured party. This contract, which creates or provides for the security interest, is a **security agreement**. The security agreement must contain sufficient information to clearly identify the collateral, and the debtor must sign it.

It is this second type of secured transaction that enables a consumer to buy an automobile, major kitchen appliance, or other costly item on credit. The debtor gets immediate possession and use of the goods. But the seller (or the bank or finance company) that lends money needed for the credit sale has the right to take the goods back if a payment is missed or if the contract is breached.

In a similar manner, a retail merchant can buy a shipment of goods on credit from a wholesaler or manufacturer. The retailer then routinely sells the goods to customers who get clear title. When the goods are sold to such consumers, the merchant gets paid and in turn pays the supplier. The supplier continues to be protected by the security interest that

remains in all of the goods in the shipment that are still unsold.

This second type of secured transaction also is used in lending money, because a lender often demands the security of collateral. Suppose you want to borrow $1,000 from a bank.

By giving the bank a security interest in your car or other valuable personal property, such as your personal computer, your promise to repay the loan is strengthened. This is true because the bank has the legal right to repossess the collateral in case of default

and then to sell it and apply the proceeds of the sale to repay the loan. If the bank approves the loan, which it is very likely to do with this added security, you obtain the desired money and still have the use of your property.

When the borrower retains possession of the collateral, the secured party may have problems repossessing the goods in case of default. Repossession must be accomplished without committing a breach of the peace (that is, without violence, actions likely to produce violence, or other violation of the law). Also the secured party may find that the collateral has been improperly maintained, subjected to the claims of other creditors, or even sold. Even so, the UCC gives the secured party maximum protection against most such occurrences, provided the security interest has not only been properly created but has also been "perfected."

HOW DOES A CREDITOR PERFECT A SECURITY INTEREST?

WHAT'S YOUR
VERDICT?

The Old Salt Fishing Supply House sold on credit to Abernathy an expensive sonar device for locating large schools of fish. Abernathy had the sonar installed on his 80-foot commercial fishing boat. Old Salt retained a security interest in the sonar and filed a financing statement. Before the sonar was paid for, Abernathy took out a loan from Hoa Tien and used the sonar as collateral

When Abernathy defaulted on the loans, could Old Salt enforce its security interest in the sonar?

It is possible for a debtor to agree to give many different creditors, each unaware of the others, a security interest in the same goods. The UCC therefore specifies that the first creditor to perfect a security interest has priority over all other creditors.

A **perfected security interest** exists when the security interest is superior

to all other claims in the collateral. If there is only one creditor, there is no need to perfect the security interest. A security interest is valid against a debtor whether or not it has been perfected. Upon default, the creditor with priority may repossess and resell the goods. For example, Old Salt in *What's Your Verdict?* could repossess

and resell the sonar. Such priority creditor takes as much of the proceeds from the sale of the collateral as is necessary to satisfy his or her claim against the debtor. Then any other creditors share in the remaining proceeds.

Notice Through Possession
A perfected security interest results when the creditor gives proper notice of the existence of the security interest to all other potential creditors. Such notice may be given in a number of ways. For example, a creditor in possession of the collateral, as in a pledge, needs to take no additional steps for protection. Possession alone is notice to any possible subsequent buyer or creditor of the debtor that a security interest may exist. The creditor who has possession, thereby, has a perfected security interest. If a cred-

This **FINANCING STATEMENT** is presented to a filing officer for filing pursuant to the Uniform Commercial Code. **3 Maturity date (if any):**

1 Debtor(s) (Last Name First) and address(es)	2 Secured Party(ies) and address(es)	For Filing Officer (Date, Time, Number, and Filing Office)
Daley, John C. and Ava G. **116 Seashore Drive** **Biloxi, MS 39534**	**Adam Cranston** **485 Magnolia Street** **Gulfport, MS 39501**	

4 This financing statement covers the following types (or items) of property:

"Smooth Sailin" Houseboat

Check ⊠ if covered: ☐ Proceeds of Collateral are also covered ☐ Products of Collateral are also covered No. of additional sheets presented:

Filed with _____

By: ___*John C. Daley*___ ___*Ava G. Daley*___ By: ___*Adam Cranston*___
Signature(s) of Debtor(s) Signature(s) of Secured Party(ies)

Filing Officer Copy—Alphabetical

This form of financing statement is approved by the Secretary of State.

STANDARD FORM—UNIFORM COMMERCIAL CODE—UCC-1

itor is able to repossess collateral upon default, the act of retaking possession also perfects the security interest even though the interest had not been perfected previously.

Notice Through Filing a Financing Statement

When the debtor has the goods, it may be necessary for the creditor to file a financing statement to perfect the creditor's interest. A **financing statement** is a brief, written notice of the existence of a security interest in the identified property. (See the example in the illustration above.) It must include the following:

1. the names and addresses of both the debtor and the creditor
2. the signature of the debtor (although the creditor may also sign and commonly does)
3. a statement describing the items of collateral

If crops or things attached to buildings or land are involved, the land where such property is located must also be described. If the security agreement extends to products to be derived from the original collateral, such as the calves of cows, or proceeds from the resale of such collateral, these facts must be stated. The security agreement itself may be filed instead of the financing statement if it meets the necessary requirements.

On the financing statement, any description that identifies the property reasonably well suffices even though it might be necessary to ask questions to determine exactly what property was intended. Of course, a debtor who possesses two automobiles, a motorcycle, a racing bicycle, and a mountain bicycle should not list an unspecified one of these vehicles as "my favorite wheels."

Filing a financing statement gives **constructive notice** that a security interest in specific property exists. This means that the law presumes everyone has knowledge of the facts on file. Anyone sufficiently concerned may get actual notice by checking the public records. The place of filing is specified by the state's version of the UCC and also depends on the nature of the collateral. Filing may be required centrally in the office of the secretary of state, or locally in the office of the clerk in the county where the grounds are located, or both.

As explained in the following paragraphs, there are special provisions for perfecting the security interest that depend on whether the property in question is tangible or intangible.

Tangible Property

When tangible property is used as collateral, the procedure for perfecting the creditor's security interest depends on whether the goods are

- consumer goods—used primarily for personal, family, or household purposes
- farm products—crops, livestock, unmanufactured products of the farm, and farm supplies

- inventory—business goods that are intended for sale or lease, or if they are raw materials, work in process or materials used or consumed in a business
- equipment—goods used by a business in performing its function, such as telephone equipment or computers

Goods can be in only one of these four classes at a given time. Their classification may change, however, if their use changes. For example, a television is classified as inventory if held by a dealer for resale. If used as a closed-circuit system in the store for security, it is equipment. If installed in the buyer's home for entertainment, it is a consumer good.

CONSUMER GOODS Filing is not required to protect the seller's security interest in consumer goods against other creditors of the buyer. This rule relieves retail merchants, who sell many thousands of articles on installment plans, of what would be a heavy burden in paperwork and in payment of filing fees. In case of default in payment, the creditor may repossess the goods from the original buyer. Although not legally obligated, most creditors tolerate late payment for perhaps ten or more days. They typically impose a penalty charge for use of this privilege.

Filing would be required for consumer goods if the consumer already owned the goods and was simply borrowing against them as security. Filing also is necessary, even in initial purchases, if the seller wants protection against a third person who might innocently buy the good for personal, family, or household use from a dishonest debtor. Such a buyer of consumer goods, who gives value and does not know of the security interest, acquires clear title if there has been no filing.

On the other hand, if a filing is in the public records, the third party is bound by the filed security interest even if unaware of its existence. Therefore, the television set that was installed in the buyer's home for entertainment and then sold to a good-faith purchaser for value must nevertheless be returned to the unpaid creditor who had filed a financing statement.

Because there are so many motor vehicles on the roads, most states provide that instead of filing as described above, a special office and procedure are utilized. Thus, the security interest in motor vehicles is often perfected by noting its existence on the certificate of title to the vehicle that is registered in the proper state office.

An exception to the filing requirement is also made when fixtures are sold on credit. Fixtures are items of personal property that are permanently attached to real property in a manner that makes the law treat them like real property. A filing to protect a security interest in fixtures must include in the financing statement a description of the real property involved.

IN THIS CASE

Tokuda bought a household refrigerator for $795 from the Super-Circuit Sales Company in a secured transaction. Super-Circuit did not file a financing statement. When $500 was still owed, Tokuda sold the refrigerator to Goto, a neighbor, who paid $600, honestly assuming that Tokuda had paid for it in full and could therefore transfer it with a clear title. If Tokuda thereafter fails to make any payment as required, Super-Circuit cannot take the refrigerator away from Goto. Instead, it must pursue Tokuda. Goto obtained clear title because Super-Circuit had not filed a financing statement.

FARM PRODUCTS A security interest in farm products is perfected by filing or by taking possession of the products upon default. This applies to farm products bought on credit and to those used as security for loans. Most states require filing a financing statement for farm products with the clerk at the courthouse of the county where the products are stored.

INVENTORY A security interest in inventory is perfected by filing or by taking possession of the inventory upon default. This is true whether the inventory is bought on credit or is put up as security for a loan. However, because inventory generally is purchased by business firms for the very purpose of reselling, a person buying from such a debtor in the ordinary course of business gets clear title to the goods even if aware of the security interest. For example, if you buy a stove at an appliance store, you get title to it free of the security interest held by the unpaid manufacturer or wholesaler who originally sold it to the store on credit.

EQUIPMENT A security interest in equipment is perfected by filing or by taking possession of the equipment upon default. This applies whether the equipment is bought on credit or is put up as security for a loan. If the equipment is a motor vehicle, a notation on the certificate of title may substitute for filing in perfecting the interest. As with inventory, perfection of a security interest in equipment requires filing with the state government, usually in the office of the secretary of state.

Intangible Property

The second major classification of collateral—intangible property—represents value in rights to money, goods, or promises to perform specified contracts. Legal documents or other writings are generally evidence of intangible property. Intangible property includes the accounts receivable of a business, the rights to performance under a contract, bills of lading or airbills, warehouse receipts, commercial paper, and bonds or stocks.

The procedure used in perfecting a security interest in intangible property depends on the classification of that property. A security interest in accounts receivable or contractual rights that cannot be possessed in a physical sense must be perfected by filing unless the transaction does not cover a significant part of the debtor's accounts receivable or other contractual rights.

For documents used in bailments, such as bills of lading, airbills, and warehouse receipts, the creditor may either file a financing statement or take possession of the goods upon default. To perfect a security interest in commercial paper (promissory notes, stock certificates, or bonds), possession by the creditor, upon default of the debtor, is essential.

HOW ARE SECURED TRANSACTIONS TERMINATED?

WHAT'S YOUR
VERDICT?

The Nosmans bought a new flat-screen wall television for their recreation room for $2,000 including the credit carrying charge. They paid $400 down and agreed to pay the balance in eight monthly installments of $200 each. The seller, Silitech, Inc., retained a security interest in the television. After making six payments, the Nosmans defaulted. Silitech repossessed the television.

What must Silitech do to be able to legally keep the set in settlement of the unpaid $400 balance?

Most secured transactions are routinely terminated when the debtor pays the debt in full and the creditor releases the security interest in the collateral. If the creditor has filed a financing statement, this release is made when the creditor files an acknowledgment of the full payment, called a **termination statement**, with the governmental office that has the financing statement. Filing the termination statement informs potential buyers and creditors that the property is no longer collateral. For consumer goods, the termination statement must be filed within 30 days of the payoff or within ten days of a written request by the debtor. Otherwise the creditor must pay $100 plus damages to the debtor.

If the debtor defaults by failing to pay as promised, the secured creditor who does not have possession of the collateral may take possession of it. This may be done without legal proceedings, provided it does not involve a breach of the peace. The creditor may then sell, lease, or otherwise dispose of the collateral. This right of sale also applies after default for the benefit of the secured creditor who has retained possession of the property. The proceeds at disposition are applied to the reasonable expenses of retaking, holding, preparing for resale, and reselling. They also are applied to payment of reasonable attorney's fees and other legal expenses incurred. What remains of the proceeds then goes to pay off the secured debt. In some cases, other creditors may have subordinate or secondary security interests in the collateral, and these are now paid off if proper claims have been made. Finally, if any surplus remains, it goes to the debtor. If there is any deficiency, the debtor is obligated to pay it unless otherwise agreed.

Even when in default as to payment or other performance of the security agreement, the debtor does not forfeit all rights. For example, the debtor may pay the balance due and the expenses of the creditor and **redeem** the collateral any time before the creditor has disposed of it or contracted for its disposal.

As an alternative to resale, the secured creditor may retain the collateral in full settlement of the debt. Written notice of the creditor's intention to keep the collateral must be given to the debtor. If the debtor (or any other person entitled to receive notice) objects in writing within 21 days, the creditor must dispose of the collateral in a commercially reasonable manner by a public or private sale.

Additional protection is given to consumers who have paid 60 percent or more of the debt. In these situations, the creditor may not keep the collateral in satisfaction of the debt unless the consumer agrees in writing. In the absence of such a written agreement, the creditor must sell the collateral within 90 days after the repossession. This law seeks to protect consumers in situations where the value of the goods exceeds the amount of the debt.

In *What's Your Verdict?* the Nosmans paid $400 down and $1,200 in monthly installments. The total ($1,600) was more than 60 percent ($1,200). Therefore, Silitech must obtain the Nosmans' written consent before Silitech can keep the television. Without that consent, the television must be resold in a commercially reasonable manner.

Answer the following questions about legal concepts.

1. Secured transactions must be conducted in accordance with the Uniform Commercial Code in order to be legally effective. **True or False?**

2. A security interest can be created solely with the consent of the creditor. **True or False?**

3. When the creditor keeps the collateral in a secured transaction, the transaction is known legally as a ___?___ .

4. The contract that creates or provides for a security interest is called a(an)
   (a) **starter agreement**
   (b) **financing statement**
   (c) **security agreement**

Study the following situations, answer the questions, then prepare arguments to support your answers.

5. Taft borrowed $50 from a friend, agreeing to repay $5 each week. Although the agreement was informal and oral, Taft gave the friend her high school class ring to hold until the debt was paid in full. Did the friend have a perfected security interest in the ring?

6. The Bartons were "strapped for cash" but needed to have their child's teeth straightened. The corrective work would cost more and take longer if they waited until a later date. Therefore, they pledged their electric range, refrigerator, microwave oven, television, sofa, two armchairs, and complete dining room set as security for a loan of $1,500 from the Happy Home Finance Company. All of the listed property was in excellent condition, having been purchased recently with $10,000 the Bartons had won in a lottery. Did Happy Home Finance Company obtain a perfected security interest in these consumer goods as soon as it gave the money to the Bartons? Did Happy Home act ethically in demanding the listed security from the Bartons?

7. Cuisine International sold kitchen equipment on credit to the Shoreline Resort. In the security agreement and in the financing statement, the collateral was identified as "food service equipment delivered to the Shoreline Resort." When Shoreline was unable to pay its creditors, including Cuisine, some creditors claimed that the collateral description was too vague to create a valid security interest. Were they correct?

Suggestions for buyer or borrower in a secured transaction . . .

1. Be sure you understand the entire security agreement before you sign it. If you have any doubts, have the seller, or preferably your lawyer, banker, accountant, or other trustworthy counsel, examine the form and explain it to you.

2. Never sign any security agreement that has blank spaces to be filled in later. Draw lines in any blank spaces not used.

3. Know what any charges are for, especially service charges.

PREVENT LEGAL DIFFICULTIES

Ask for a detailed listing if it is not offered.

4. Find out if there are any penalties for late payment of installments or if there are any discounts for making payments before they are due.

5. Include express warranties or other promises of the seller in the written contract to avoid later difficulty of proof under the parol evidence rule.

6. Always get a copy of the agreement, signed by the other party.

7. After payment in full, check to be sure that a termination statement has been properly filed.

CHAPTER IN REVIEW

CONCEPTS IN BRIEF

1. Secured transactions are of two types: those in which the creditor has possession of the collateral, called pledges, and those in which the debtor has possession.

2. Property used as collateral is classified as either tangible property (goods) or intangible property. Goods are further classified as consumer goods, farm products, inventory, or equipment. In perfecting a security interest, proper classification of the property must be known. Intangible property includes such things as accounts receivable, bills of lading, airbills, warehouse receipts, notes, bonds, and other contractual rights.

3. A security interest may be perfected by the creditor having or taking possession of the collateral or by the filing of a financing statement. An exception may apply in the case of a motor vehicle: Most states provide that a notation on the certificate of title perfects such a security interest.

4. The financing statement is used to give notice that a security interest in specific property exists. The statement identifies the parties and the collateral. Usually the financing statement and the security agreement are separate writings. However, the security agreement may be filed in place of the financing statement if it meets the legal requirements.

5. After default in a secured transaction, the debtor has the following rights:
   - To pay all that is owed and to redeem the collateral held or repossessed by the creditor at any time before the creditor arranges to dispose, or actually does dispose, of it.
   - Under certain specified circumstances, to demand that the collateral be sold and the proceeds applied to the payment of the debt.

6. Upon the debtor's default, the secured creditor has the following rights:
   - To sell or otherwise dispose of the property. If the creditor does not have the property, he or she may repossess it.
   - Under certain specified circumstances, to retain the property in settlement of the debt.

7. When the debtor has fully paid the obligation in accordance with the security agreement, the secured party has the responsibility for clearing the official records by filing a termination statement.

YOUR LEGAL VOCABULARY

Match each statement with the term that it best defines. Some terms may not be used.

1. Contract that creates or provides for a security interest

2. A person or business that owes money, goods, or services to another

3. An interest in or claim against specified property of the debtor, such interest being created in favor of the creditor to assure payment of the debt

4. Secured party's right to take back collateral to use in satisfying a debt

5. The property that is subject to the security interest of the creditor

6. A filing by a creditor releasing a security interest in collateral

7. To pay the balance due and the expenses of the creditor in exchange for receiving the collateral

8. Legal method or device creating a security interest in personal property or fixtures in order to protect creditors

collateral
constructive notice
creditor
debt
debtor
financing statement
pledge
redeem
repossession
secured party
secured transaction
security agreement
security interest
termination statement

9. Is the debtor-creditor relationship heavily weighted in favor of the creditor?

10. Why should the law protect the debtor-creditor relationship?

11. Is an I.O.U. a promise to repay a debt? Why or why not?

12. What are examples of intangible property in which a security interest may be taken?

WRITE ABOUT LEGAL CONCEPTS

13. When a creditor is selling collateral upon default, in what circumstances does the creditor not have to give reasonable notice to the debtor?

14. Why is it important to have a termination statement filed promptly?

15. **HOT DEBATE** Write a persuasive opening statement that emphasizes the legal, ethical, and economic points in favor of Bill's petition. Write a persuasive opening statement for the bank that encompasses the economic and legal reasons why the loss should fall on Bill.

THINK CRITICALLY ABOUT EVIDENCE

16. D'Artole, an accountant, bought for her personal use a new portable computer with a hard disk for $7,500. She paid $1,000 down and then paid $150 per month for several months under a security agreement she had signed with the seller, the Computer Clinic. Finally, she paid off the remaining balance with her Christmas bonus. The next May she needed a $5,000 loan to take advantage of a business opportunity. She offered the computer as collateral, but the lender refused, saying there was still a security interest in favor of the Computer Clinic on file. D'Artole did not get the loan as a result. What are her rights in this situation?

17. At the county fair, Gull used cash to buy two cows and a bull, all purebred Holsteins. The seller was Spade, a newcomer in the area. Soon after, Gull was surprised and chagrined when the local banker told him that Spade had defaulted on a related loan given to Spade in a secured transaction. The bank had a perfected security interest in the animals. When it repossessed them, Gull protested: "How was I supposed to know that? I never had any notice of the bank's interest.

Where's the proof?" Did Gull actually have legal notice of the bank's interest in, and prior claim to, the animals? Did Spade act ethically in their deal? What can Gull do now?

18. You buy a new read-only memory unit for your personal computer under a contract that permits the seller to repossess it if you miss a payment. The seller has officially recorded these facts. If you sell the memory unit to a friend before you have paid in full for the unit, does your friend get clear title?

19. Burney loaned Sampson $4,000 to buy a car. Sampson issued a promissory note in favor of Burney for that amount. Also, when he registered the new car, Sampson had Burney's name entered on the title as lienholder. Later Sampson took out a loan from the First National Bank of Pennsboro. After a few months, he defaulted on both the bank loan and the promissory note. The bank filed suit and obtained a judgment against Sampson that it sought to execute against the car. Burney maintained his security interest in the car took precedence over the Bank's claim. Who won?

ANALYZE
REAL CASES

20. Shelton purchased an automobile on credit from Erwin. Both Shelton and Erwin clearly intended to create a security interest in the car in favor of Erwin. As a consequence, they signed a bill of sale that set out the terms of payment of the balance due and that also required that Shelton insure the auto until paid for in full. Shelton later obtained a title certificate from the state that clearly showed Erwin as the holder of a first lien on the car. Did these actions and documents give Erwin a security interest in the car? (*Shelton v. Erwin,* 472 F.2d 1118)

21. Speigle fell behind in his car payments to Chrysler Credit Corporation. He had made 14 monthly payments on a 36-month contract, and Chrysler had accepted several late payments. Then he was out of work and money, and he was almost a month in default on a current payment. Speigle visited the Chrysler office to negotiate a solution to his problem. While in the office, one employee of Chrysler parked a car behind Speigle's car, blocking it so it could not be moved. Another employee told him it was repossessed. Speigle sued, claiming that Chrysler's conduct was inequitable and in breach of the peace. Do you agree? (*Speigle v. Chrysler Credit Corporation,* 56 Ala. App. 469, 323 So. 2d 360)

22. The Uniform Commercial Code excludes "money" from its definition of goods. As a consequence, a perfected security interest cannot be obtained in money merely by the creditor's taking possession of it. Midas Coin Company transferred possession of some rare U.S. coins to the St. John's Community Bank as security for a loan. Did the bank have a perfected security interest? (*In re Midas Coin Co.,* 264 F. Supp. 193)

23. The Franklin State Bank repossessed the Parkers' automobile because of the Parkers' delinquency in payments. At the time, Mr. Parker and his son were giving the engine of the car a tune-up in their garage. The vehicle was not mechanically operational because the spark plugs, points, condenser, and air filter had been removed. Franklin did not try to determine why the car was not mechanically operational. Instead, after a three-day notice to the Parkers, the bank sold the car at a private sale to an auto parts dealer for $50. The bank then sued the Parkers to recover the substantial balance of the purchase price remaining and unpaid. Which party should win the suit? Why? (*Franklin State Bank v. Parker,* 136 N.J. Super. 476, 346 A.2d 632)

24. When Ziluck submitted the application for his Radio Shack credit card, he signed an application that had the following statement about the signature line: "I have read the Radio Shack Credit Account and Security Agreement, including the notice provision in the last paragraph thereof. . . . And I agree to the terms of the Agreement and acknowledge receipt of a copy of the agreement." The Security Agreement referred to was on the back of the application and read in part: "We retain a security interest under the Uniform Commercial Code in all merchandise charged to your Account. If you do not make payments on your Account as agreed, the security interest allows us to repossess only the merchandise that has not been paid in full." Ziluck later filed for bankruptcy. The bankruptcy court had to determine whether or not this was a valid security agreement. It decided that it was not because (1) the signature was on the opposite side of the form from the "Agreement," and (2) any collateral subject to the agreement would be improperly described. Radio Shack appealed the decision of the bankruptcy court. Does Radio Shack have a case? Why or why not? (*In re Ziluck,* 139 Bankruptcy Reporter 44)

25. Calcote bought a car using a loan from Citizens & Southern National Bank. The bank obtained a security interest in the car. Calcote later defaulted on the loan and the bank repossessed the car. The bank then sent notice of the repossession, the bank's plans to sell the repossessed car at a private auction, and Calcote's right to demand a public sale to her at the last known address that the bank had. Calcote did not get the certified letter, yet the car was thereafter sold at a private sale with more than 150 dealers invited to participate. Calcote then brought suit against the bank due to its failure to properly notify her and dispose of the vehicle in a commercially reasonable fashion. Do you think the bank acted improperly? Why or why not? (*Calcote v. Southern National Bank,* 345 S.E.2d 616)

26. The Fishes bought some very expensive jewelry from Odom's Jewelers. They were to pay monthly installments on the purchase price until it was fully paid. When they fell behind in their payments, they orally agreed to return the jewelry to Odom's to hold until the purchase price was paid. While Odom's held the jewelry, the Fishes filed for bankruptcy. Did Odom's have a security interest in the jewelry? (*In re Fish,* 128 Bankruptcy Reporter 468)

CASE FOR LEGAL THINKING

FACTS Holiday Intervals sold "time share" deeds for the Holiday Shores resort it was developing at the Lake of the Ozarks, Missouri. These deeds entitled buyers to spend one week per year at one of Holiday's units. Many of the buyers agreed to pay the purchase price through installment contracts. Some of these installment contracts contained a separate promissory note section that repeated the buyer's installment obligations in the form of a promissory note, while other contracts contained no promissory note section. Holiday obtained financing for construction of the units by assigning its copies of the installment contracts and promissory notes to the banks. The banks did not seek to perfect their security interests in these installment contracts and promissory notes. Instead they assumed that they had perfected their security interests by possession of the buyers' installment contracts and promissory notes.

After Holiday ran into financial difficulties, Holiday Owners (one of Holiday's creditors) and various other creditors filed an involuntary bankruptcy petition against Holiday. Holiday Owners has operated the resort since Holiday's failure.

When a bankruptcy petition is filed, claims against the debtor's estate are automatically stayed. In order to obtain the installment contract proceeds, the creditors separately moved for relief from the automatic stay on the ground that they obtained perfected security interests in the

installment contracts through possession of the contracts. In the alternative, the creditors claimed that even if they had not perfected their security interests as to all installment contracts, they had at least done so to those installment contracts containing promissory notes. The bankruptcy court rejected both arguments and denied the banks' motion for relief from the automatic stay.

DISTRICT COURT DECISION The district court affirmed the bankruptcy court's decision in part and reversed in part, holding that the banks had perfected their security interests in those installment contracts which contained promissory notes, but not in the other installment contracts which did not. All parties then appealed.

PRACTICE JUDGING

1. In reaching its decision, the federal appeals court noted the rule that the seller's interest in a land sale contract is a general intangible. If this is so, how is perfection to be achieved?

2. Given your answer to the above question, have the creditors perfected or are their interests to be treated the same as any other unsecured creditor and, therefore, subject to the stay?

DEBTORS, CREDITORS, AND BANKRUPTCY

CHAPTER 39

LESSONS

HOT DEBATE

Norm was a foreign correspondent for a large national television network. One afternoon he took his expensive watch to a jewelry shop to be repaired. The jeweler recognized Norm and told him he watched his network. The jeweler said the watch would be ready the next day. Norm left the store. He then received a call telling him to pack and head for Eastern Russia. When he went to get his watch, almost four months later, the jeweler told him he had sold it after sending Norm ten reminders. Norm responded that there was no mail service where he had been. The jeweler shrugged and said he was just following the state's artisan's lien laws. Norm's attorney ultimately brought suit against the jewelry store for damages.

Where Do You Stand?

1. **What are the jewelry store's reasons for selling the watch?**

2. **What are the legal reasons supporting Norm's suit?**

╔══════════════════════════════════════╗

G O A L S

● **Discuss four types of laws that protect creditors**

● **Explain how liens are created**

● **Explain how liens can protect creditor's rights**

╚══════════════════════════════════════╝

LAWS PROTECTING CREDITORS

WHAT'S YOUR
VERDICT?

Spang borrowed $7,500 from Wagner. Spang promised to repay the money in 24 months with interest at 9 percent per year. Spang gave Wagner shares of American Telephone common stock, which had a market value of $8,000, to hold as security for the payment. The stock was to be returned when the debt was paid.

What was Wagner's legal status?

The primary concern of a typical creditor is that the loan be promptly paid when due. If it is not paid, and especially if costly efforts to collect it prove fruitless, the creditor usually suffers a financial loss. When feasible, such bad debt losses are shifted to other borrowers through higher fees and charges. Thus, it is in the interest of all society that fair and honest loans be collectible with minimum difficulty and expense. Legislation to protect creditors will be discussed in the following sections.

Laws Allowing Secured Debts

Most helpful for creditors are laws that permit them to acquire a legal interest in (a right in or a claim to) specific property of the debtor. The Uniform Commercial Code governs the secured transactions created under its Article 9. This security interest is enforceable in court if the debtor defaults by failing to pay in accordance with the loan agreement or credit extension.

Regardless of how it is created, a creditor who holds a security interest

(as Wagner did in *What's Your Verdict?*) is a secured creditor. A creditor with a security interest in specific property has a lien against that property. A **lien** gives the creditor the right, in case of default on a payment that is due, to sell the property and to use the proceeds from the sale to pay the debt. Usually, the debtor keeps possession of the liened property as long as the debt is not in default. Mortgages on homes are common examples of this type of secured debt. However, a default occurs if a scheduled payment is missed. The creditor may then exercise the right to obtain a court order for sale of the property. If the secured property is personal and movable, such as a car or television, the creditor may peacefully repossess (seize control or possession of) it.

PLEDGES Some secured debt arrangements permit the creditor to have possession of the property until the debt is paid. In the pledge, for example, personal property is given to a creditor as security for the payment of

a debt or for the performance of an obligation. The property may be either goods or documents representing property rights (for example, corporate stock). The **pledgor** (debtor) voluntarily gives up possession of the property. The **pledgee** (creditor) gets possession. Normally, the debt is paid when due or the legal obligation is performed. Then the property is returned to the pledgor.

While the pledge lasts, the pledgee must treat the property with reasonable care. The property may, however, be repledged to a third party on terms that do not prevent the pledgor from getting the property back when the debt is paid.

A **pawn** is a pledge of tangible personal property, usually of small size and comparatively high value. This type of pledge includes such durable and readily resalable items as jewelry, cameras, and musical instruments. It excludes intangible property rights, stocks and bonds, as well as other valuable documents. A pawnbroker lends money at interest and takes possession of tangible personal property from the borrower as security for repayment. The borrower who pawns goods gets a receipt known as a pawn ticket. When the borrower repays the debt together with interest due and turns in the pawn ticket, the pawnbroker returns the goods.

Because thieves sometimes use pawnbroking to convert stolen goods into cash, special statutes regulate the business. These laws require that the pawnbroker be licensed, post a bond, and keep accurate records open to police inspection. If stolen goods are found in the pawnshop, they may be seized without compensation to the pawnbroker. Also, maximum limits are imposed on the rate of interest pawnbrokers may charge.

Goods that are pawned must be held by the pawnbroker for a time prescribed by law (four months is typical) before they can be sold. In most states, the rights of the parties to the proceeds of the sale are the same as for ordinary pledges. In some states, the pawnbroker automatically gets title to pawned and unclaimed goods at the end of a specified time.

INVOLUNTARY LIENS Although most liens are created with the consent of the debtor-owner, statutes in many states create liens in favor of the creditor without such consent. These involuntary liens include the mechanic's lien and the artisan's lien.

The **mechanic's lien** allows a person who has not been paid for labor or materials furnished to build a home, building, or other real property improvement to file a legal claim against the property. If the debt is not paid, the realty may be sold. The holder of the mechanic's lien gets the amount owed from the proceeds. Thus, such a lienholder is entitled to the amount owed from the sale proceeds even before other claimants, such as a bank with a mortgage on the property, gets any money.

The **artisan's lien** allows persons

who have not been paid for services, such as repairing a car or providing a hotel room, to retain possession of the car or the luggage that has been brought onto the premises until they are paid. If payment is not made, these retained goods may be sold to pay the debts that are due. A lien-holder who gives up possession of the property before the debtor pays for the services loses the artisan's lien.

Laws Involving Third Parties

In addition to liens, other means of protection are available to creditors. For example, a creditor who wishes assurance beyond the debtor's promise to pay may demand that a creditworthy third party assume the liability. This is **suretyship**, a contractual relation in which a third party agrees to be primarily liable for the debt or obligation if payment or performance becomes overdue. Three parties are involved. The **principal debtor** owes the debt or obligation. The creditor is the one to whom the obligation is owed. The **surety** is the third party who promises to be liable in case of default by the principal debtor. The surety may be bound by an oral contract, because a suretyship is a primary obligation. Nevertheless, such agreements are usually put in writing.

Suretyship contracts are discharged in much the same way as other contracts. If the debtor pays, the surety is discharged. The surety also is discharged if the creditor releases the debtor or alters the obligation, as by extending the time of performance, without the surety's consent. But a surety who is required to pay the creditor has a legal right to collect from the principal debtor.

If there are cosureties, any cosurety who pays the full debt may get a judgment against the other cosureties for their proportionate share of the debt. This is called the **right of contribution**.

Like suretyship, the guaranty relationship protects the creditor. In it,

the third party, the **guarantor**, agrees to pay if the principal debtor fails to do so. But unlike a surety, the guarantor is only secondarily liable. In effect, the guarantor merely promises that the debtor will pay when the debt comes due. However, this means that the creditor must first sue the defaulting debtor and get a judgment that proves to be uncollectible. In contrast, in a suretyship, such a suit is not necessary. The surety in effect insures that the debt will be paid when due. The surety has primary liability equal to that of the debtor. The contract creating the guaranty relationship must be in writing and signed by the guarantor to be enforceable under the statute of frauds.

Laws Concerning Unsecured Debts

When the debt is small or the credit standing of the borrower is very good, the creditor may be willing to take an **unsecured debt**. This is a debt based only on the oral or written promise of the debtor.

Upon default, an unsecured creditor is in a much weaker position than a secured creditor because, in order to collect, the unsecured creditor must sue the debtor for breach of contract. Then, upon obtaining judgment, the creditor must take legally prescribed steps to collect. This is costly and time-consuming. Moreover, some debtors may prove to be dishonest and may move without leaving a forwarding address. Or they may have no assets that the creditor can take.

In other instances, debtors may even avoid some of their obligations by going into bankruptcy. It is certainly better for the creditor to have a security interest in some asset of the debtor. For example, in *What's Your Verdict?* the common stock could be converted into cash by the secured creditor (Wagner) if the debtor (Spang) defaults.

Laws Allowing Garnishment of Wages

One other method for creditor protection is the **garnishment** of wages. Once a creditor's claim is shown to be legally valid and fair in a court hearing, the creditor may receive a portion of the debtor's wages directly from the debtor's employer. The amount that can be garnished by all creditors, however, is generally limited by the Consumer Credit Protection Act to 25 percent of the debtor's take-home pay.

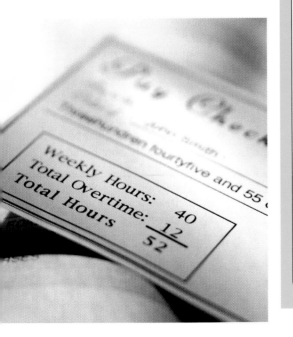

THINK ABOUT LEGAL CONCEPTS

Answer the following questions about legal concepts.

1. The creditor's primary concern is that the loan be paid when due. **True or False?**

2. A __?__ gives a creditor the right upon default to repossess and sell the subject property. **(a) lean (b) debt (c) lien (d) none of the above**

3. In a pledge the debtor keeps possession of the property. **True or False?**

4. An artisan loses his or her artisan's lien by giving up possession of the repaired property. **True or False?**

5. In a suretyship, the surety is secondarily liable. **True or False?**

THINK CRITICALLY ABOUT EVIDENCE

Study the following situations, answer the questions, and then prepare arguments to support your answers.

6. After graduating from high school, Jack Tern decided to become a truck driver. The A-OK Truck Driving Academy offered a two-week, intensive, one-on-one (instructor-student) course with training on two- and three-axle tractors and on 45-foot single and double trucks, for $4,000 cash. Since Jack had no money, A-OK agreed to take his written promise to pay the tuition fee in monthly installments of $130 for four years provided he could get a surety or guarantor to promise to pay if he defaulted. Jack's Uncle Joe signed a guaranty agreement, and Jack enrolled and completed the course. After six months, however, he lost his job as a truck driver and could not continue making the monthly payments. Can A-OK immediately demand payment from Jack's Uncle Joe?

7. Gary Meter took his very expensive watch in for repair to Mike's service center. The bill for the repair came to over $375. When Gary heard how much it was, he told Mike that he could pay him at the first of the month. Gary also informed Mike that the watch had been given to him by his grandmother who was celebrating her hundredth birthday in two days. Gary then asked if he could take the watch with him without paying, so that he could wear it to his grandmother's birthday party. Mike sympathized with Gary and let him do so. When the first of the month came around, Gary did not pay. Mike waited until the end of the month. Then he decided to try and collect by legal means. Does Mike still have an aritsan's lien he can enforce against Gary? Why or why not? What are his other alternatives? Are they as effective as the lien?

GOALS

- Discuss six types of laws that protect debtors
- Discuss the advantages and disadvantages of using credit cards

LAWS PROTECTING DEBTORS

WHAT'S YOUR VERDICT?

The Santaros decided to rent an unfurnished apartment. Reliable Finance Company was among the sources they used for funds to buy the furniture they needed. Reliable gave them a copy of the loan contract showing only the amount to be paid per installment and the number of payments.

Could they demand further information?

There are six important types of laws designed to protect debtors. They do this by

1. setting maximum interest rates

2. requiring clear and complete advance disclosure of loan terms

3. changing the terms of unconscionable contracts

4. correcting specific abuses of the credit system

5. requiring the creditor to record a public notice when certain debts have been paid

6. canceling most debts and giving the debtor's financial life a fresh start

Laws Setting Maximum Interest Rates

Usury laws that set maximum interest rates were discussed in the chapters on contracts. Usually such laws apply only to loans of money. They do not govern carrying charges imposed on credit purchases of goods and services "on time." A few states do regu-late such charges as interest. They do this on the theory that the store, in effect, borrows money and re-lends it to the customer-debtor to finance the purchase on credit.

Laws Requiring Disclosure of Terms

A consumer loan arises when a person borrows money primarily for personal, family, household, or agricultural purposes. It is often called a personal loan to distinguish it from a business or commercial loan.

The federal Truth in Lending Act (part of the Consumer Credit Protection Act) was designed to protect consumers when they become debtors. This law requires complete and clear disclosure of loan terms. In particular, it requires creditors to furnish debtors with certain information. The law does not limit the percentage amounts that may be charged. However, it requires creditors make a full disclosure of interest and finance charges whenever the consumer loan is repayable in four or more installments or carries a finance charge.

The **finance charge** is the total added cost when one pays in installments for goods or services. The creditor must also declare the true equivalent annual interest rate or annual percentage rate (APR). Thus, 1 1/2 percent a month must be stated as 18 percent a year. Under the law, a credit sales contract must also state such details as the cash price of the item; the down payment or trade-in allowance, if any; an itemized list of finance charges; and the total amount to be financed. In *What's Your Verdict?* Reliable Finance is obligated to tell the Santaros the total cost of their loan expressed in dollars and cents and to show the actual APR.

The Truth in Lending Act does not apply to first mortgage loans on homes. Fortunately, interest rates on home loans are usually comparatively low. No doubt this is true because the security behind such loans, namely the houses, tends to be high and can be protected by insurance.

Any creditor who willfully and knowingly violates the Truth in Lending Act may be fined, imprisoned, or both. The violator must also pay the debtor twice the finance charge (but no less than $100 nor more than $1,000) plus court costs and attorney's fees.

An increasing number of consumers lease automobiles and other equipment instead of buying the items. A big advantage of leasing for some persons is that it requires no down payment. However, in the end, the total price paid in leasing usually is higher than a cash or credit purchase would be. This is especially true for those who maintain their automobiles properly and keep them for perhaps five or more years.

The federal Consumer Leasing Act extends the protection of the Consumer Credit Protection Act to consumer lessees. Before the contract is signed, the lessor must comply with full disclosure requirements.

Laws Challenging Unconscionable Contracts

The UCC provides that a court may find that a contract or a clause of a contract is unconscionable, that is, grossly unfair and oppressive. An unconscionable contract or clause offends an honest person's conscience and sense of justice. The terms need not be criminal nor violate a statute. They may simply be unethical. Contracts of adhesion are more likely to be unconscionable because one of the parties dictates all the important terms and the weaker party either must take it as offered or not contract. An example is a contract for emergency repairs in which an unscrupulous mechanic may take unfair advantage and grossly overcharge a motorist who is unfamiliar with automobiles and their maintenance and repair. If the contract is challenged in court, a judge who decides that a clause of the contract is unconscionable may

- refuse to enforce the contract
- enforce the contract without the unconscionable clause, or
- limit the clause's application so that the contract is no longer unfair

The law is not designed to relieve a person of a bad bargain. One may still be legally bound by the purchase of overpriced, poor quality, or unneeded goods.

Laws Prohibiting Abuses in the Credit System

Laws have been enacted to correct such specific problems as the relative inability of women to get credit, unfair debt-collection practices, and inaccurate credit reports.

Federal Equal Credit Opportunity Act

This act makes it unlawful for any creditor to discriminate against an applicant because of sex or marital

status. In the past, women had difficulty obtaining credit. This was true even for women who had jobs. It was especially true for married women who worked as homemakers. The act was created to make such discriminations illegal. Major provisions of the act are the following:

1. A creditor may not refuse, on the basis of sex or marital status, to grant a separate account to a creditworthy applicant.

2. A creditor may not ask the applicant's marital status if the applicant applies for an unsecured separate account.

3. A creditor may not prohibit a married female applicant from opening or maintaining an account in her maiden name.

4. A creditor shall not request information about birth control practices or childbearing intentions or capability.

5. Married persons who have joint accounts have the right to have credit information reported in both their names in order to provide a credit history for both. In the past, upon divorce or upon death of the husband, the wife would often be denied credit because the joint account had been listed in the husband's name only.

Federal Fair Debt Collection Practices Act

This act makes abusive and deceptive debt-collection practices illegal. The act applies to professional bill collectors or agencies that regularly try to collect consumer debts for clients. Prohibited practices include the following:

1. harassment of debtors (as with a series of letters that contain menacing or threatening language, or with repeated telephone calls, especially at night)

2. abusive and profane language

3. threats of violence

4. contact with third parties (relatives, neighbors, friends, and employers)

5. communication with the debtor at work

The act is aimed at aggressively insensitive and irresponsible professional collection agencies. It does not apply to individual creditors who personally try to collect money due them. Nor does it apply to "in-house" debt collection efforts of the creditor or of employees of the creditor. However, a seriously abused debtor may sometimes succeed in a civil action against any debt collector for damages. The legal basis could be the tort of defamation, assault, invasion of privacy, or intentional infliction of mental suffering.

Federal Fair Credit Billing Act

This act provides the following protections to credit card holders:

1. Creditors must mail bills at least 14 days before the due date, must acknowledge billing inquiries within 30 days, and must settle any complaints within 90 days.
2. Creditors may not send repeated, insistent letters demanding payment until disputes over the billing are settled.
3. Credit card holders may withhold payment for items that prove defective without being held liable for the entire amount owed. This applies only in case of purchases of more than $50 made in the buyer's state or within 100 miles of the buyer's home.

The Fair Credit Billing Act also permits merchants to offer discounts to customers who pay cash instead of using credit cards. Thus, gasoline service stations often charge a few cents less per gallon to customers who pay cash. This is fair because extending credit is costly for sellers even though it may increase sales volume.

Federal Fair Credit Reporting Act

This act regulates credit rating service companies that review personal financial records of credit applicants. Aided by computers, these companies or agencies maintain voluminous files covering pertinent information about millions of individuals and business firms that buy goods and services on credit. Retailers, wholesalers, and manufacturers routinely supply such credit rating agencies with data about their experience with customers. In turn, credit rating agencies relay relevant information to cooperating member firms that request it when someone asks them for a credit purchase.

The Retailers Credit Association, composed of retail merchants who sell on credit, is an example of a credit rating agency. It determines the prospective buyer's credit rating. A **credit rating** reflects the evaluation of one's ability to pay debts. Under the law, if credit is denied because of information in a credit report, the company denying credit must tell the applicant. The applicant may then demand that the reporting agency disclose the general nature of the contents of its file (except medical information) and the names of parties who were given this information. However, names of those who provided the information need not be disclosed.

If there is any demonstrated error in the report, the credit-reporting agency must correct it. Upon request, it must notify the inquirers who had been misinformed. The agency must make the disclosures and reports without charge if the applicant acted within 30 days of getting notice of a denial of credit. Similar rules apply when an individual is denied an insurance policy or employment contract because of an unfavorable credit report.

Credit Repair Organizations Act

The Credit Repair Organizations Act, passed in April 1997, governs companies that help consumers "repair" their credit histories. By law, these organizations must notify you of your rights (by providing a copy of the government document entitled

You get an e-mail message stating that for an up-front fee of $200, your bankruptcy entry—or any other negative information on your credit report—can be cleared as if it never occurred. The problem is, if that negative information is accurate (if that bankruptcy really did happen), the information cannot legally be removed for ten years. Negative information other than bankruptcy cannot be removed for seven years.

If the negative information is not accurate, you can correct it yourself for free. "Operation Eraser" was the first combined effort of federal and state officials since the Credit Repair Organizations Act took effect. The operation targets credit repair fraud, much of which is conducted via the Internet. If consumers follow the advice of these operations, they would be committing a felony under federal law. The federal credit repair statute has very specific regulations that for-profit credit repair organizations must follow.

The Federal Trade Commission offers free educational materials over its website, should you have questions about your credit report.

"Consumer Credit File Rights Under State and Federal Law") before you sign a contract with them. The law states that a credit repair company cannot

- make false claims about its services
- charge you until they complete the promised services
- perform any services until you have signed a written contract and completed a three-day waiting period.

Any contract you make with a credit repair service must specify

- the payment terms for services, including the total cost of these services

- a detailed description of the services they will perform
- how long it will take them to achieve the results
- guarantees they offer
- repair company's name and business address

Laws Requiring Notice of Debt Payment to be Recorded

As a practical matter, debtors should always request receipts, especially when paying in cash. In some states, a debtor is not required to pay a debt unless such a receipt is given. Most financial institutions return paid and canceled checks to the drawers (writers) of the checks. Such canceled checks serve as receipts. It is often

helpful for this purpose to indicate on the face of each check the purpose for the payment. Even without such notation, it can serve as evidence of payment. When a secured debt is paid in full, the law generally permits the debtor to require the creditor to record that fact in the public records.

Laws Allowing Debtors to Cancel Debts and Start Over

Bankruptcy laws have been enacted to help debtors who have become overburdened with debts. These laws are described in detail in the next lesson.

SPECIAL LAWS FOR CREDIT CARDS

WHAT'S YOUR
VERDICT?

Tomlinson applied for and received a gasoline credit card. After using it several times, Tomlinson sold the automobile, bought a bicycle, and laid the card aside. Several weeks later, she received a bill for $79 from the oil company for purchases made by someone else. Tomlinson realized that the card had been lost or stolen and so notified the company.

Must she pay the $79?

Instead of carrying large amounts of cash (which could be lost or stolen), or writing checks (which are not accepted by many restaurants and retail stores), millions of consumers buy goods and services by using credit cards. A credit card identifies the holder as a person entitled to obtain goods or services on credit. The issuer of the card specifies the limit of available credit, and before a large sale is made, the seller can contact the issuer to determine if this limit has been exceeded.

Usually a credit card is made of plastic, is embossed with the holder's name and identification number, and has a place on the back for the

holder's signature. Annually, billions of dollars of credit purchases are made with this "plastic money." Some credit cards are intended for specialized purchases such as gasoline or oil. Some are limited to use in specific retail outlets, such as department stores or gas stations. Some are all-purpose cards, usually issued by banks, and intended for purchases from any cooperating seller. Examples are MasterCard, Visa, and Discover cards.

A credit card usually is issued in response to a consumer's written application. The consumer who signs the card is bound in a contractual relation with the issuer and is liable

for all purchases made with the card by the holder or by others with the holder's permission.

Under federal law, the cardholder is also liable for unauthorized use of the credit card by any other person, such as a thief or a dishonest finder.

This liability is limited to $50 and is imposed only if the

1. cardholder had asked for and received the credit card or had signed or used it

2. card issuer had given adequate notice of the possible liability for unauthorized use

3. card issuer had provided the cardholder with a description of how to notify the card issuer if the card is lost or stolen

4. card issuer had provided positive means for identification on the card, such as space for the holder's signature or photograph

5. unauthorized use happened before cardholder notified issuer that card was lost or stolen

Thus, the loss or theft of a credit card should be reported immediately to the issuer. In *What's Your Verdict?* Tomlinson would probably be liable for only $50 of the charges. The thief would be criminally liable for forgery and larceny.

Most credit card agreements require the cardholder to pay the amount charged on the card within a specified number of days after the closing date shown on the billing statement. If the cardholder fails to do so, he or she is contractually obligated to pay interest or finance charges on the unpaid balance. Some states set limits on the rates that can be charged credit card holders. These limits are relatively high (usually about 18 percent a year) and should be avoided whenever possible by paying the full amount due within the grace period. Fifteen days is common but it may be more or fewer. Customers seldom earn 18 percent on their money when they lend or invest it. As you can see, credit may be easily obtained—but it is not cheap.

Credit cards offer convenience and protection from loss for the consumer. But they can cause a significant increase in the cost of goods and services purchased. This is true even when balances due are paid before carrying charges are added.

Realistically, the seller must pay the credit card company for its service in bookkeeping and in prompt payment for purchases made. Commonly, this cost to the seller is a charge of between 3 percent and 6 percent of the sales prices. Such amounts paid to the credit card company are passed on to customers, both cash and credit, through higher prices for goods sold.

In addition, credit cards have a great potential for abuse through overuse by owners and misuse by thieves or finders of lost cards. Some

A Question of ETHICS

Patricia Blakemore's husband often abused her after coming home drunk late at night. Finally, she reported him to the police. For a while, with the help of intensive counseling, he had not attempted to harm her. But she could tell he was returning to his old ways. Sooner or later, she knew he would beat her again. She needed to get away. However, he kept the checkbook and money under his control and signature. If she could just take one of the credit cards, she could get enough cash advances to live on until she could get a job. The problem was that she was not a cosigner on the cards. Nonetheless, she knew the personal identification numbers for each card and had used them before at his direction. Of course, this time she would be using the money solely for her own use. Patricia paused. Should she go ahead with what she was contemplating?

consumers fail to plan and save for their purchases. Instead, they often use their credit cards impulsively to purchase goods and services not really needed. Sometimes, the payments for these purchases, when added to other living expenses, total more than the debtor's income. Debtors who find themselves in this situation may consult debt-counseling services that now operate in many cities. These services assist debtors in budgeting their income and expenses in a disciplined plan to pay off creditors and to avoid being forced into bankruptcy.

Answer the following questions about legal concepts.

1. Laws protecting debtors by setting maximum interest rates are ___?___ laws.

2. The Truth in Lending Act, as part of the Consumer Credit Protection Act, limits the percentage rate of interest or finance charges that can be added to installment sales. **True or False?**

3. The UCC provides that a court may find a contract or contractual clause ___?___ if it is grossly unfair. As a result, the contract or clause may not be enforced.

4. Which of the following is not a part of the Equal Credit Opportunity Act? **(a) creditor may not ask applicant's marital status if the application is for an unsecured separate account (b) credit may not be refused on the basis of race (c) creditor may not prohibit a married female applicant from opening an account in her maiden name (d) creditor shall not request information about the applicant's birth control practices**

5. A consumer who applies for, receives, and signs a credit card is bound in a contractual relation with the issuer. **True or False?**

THINK CRITICALLY ABOUT EVIDENCE

Study the following situations, answer the questions, then prepare arguments to support your answers.

6. During the warranty period, the Arnaudos returned their home computer for repair to the seller, Computerville Inc. Later, after the express warranty period had expired, the Arnaudos stopped making their regular monthly $100 payments for the computer because the problem continued. Computerville then gave its claim for the $1,900 balance to Bulldog Services, a collection agency. Bulldog had a clerk telephone the Arnaudos at least once a day and once a night, usually after 1 AM. Every Sunday, a uniformed Bulldog agent would park the company truck in front of the Arnaudos' house. The truck had these words in large type on both side panels: "Bulldog Services. We Chase Deadbeats." The agent would then try to talk about the claim with any person entering or leaving the house. Was Bulldog Services acting legally? Was Bulldog Services acting ethically?

7. Shortly after graduation from college, Matilda Smith applied for credit at a local department store. The store denied her application, citing the unfavorable credit report it had received from the Alpha-Omega Credit Bureau. Matilda assumed that the negative report stemmed from a prolonged dispute with a major retail chain over goods she had not ordered. Recently, the retail store acknowledged its error. What can Matilda do to clear her name?

WHAT IS BANKRUPTCY?

WHAT'S YOUR VERDICT?

Bill Cooper, owner of Cooper's Petstores, decided he had to face the fact that he was overextended. The new store in the Blakerstown Mall had such an expensive monthly payment on its five-year lease that it was about to cause Bill to close down the whole chain. This would mean the loss of jobs for his 35 employees as well as his own financial ruin. In fact, he had been unable to make his monthly payments on the business's truck and to his suppliers for the last three months. Several suppliers had stopped deliveries to him. He had discussed the situation with his attorney and they were to meet later today to consider filing bankruptcy.

If bankruptcy is Cooper's only alternative, what form of bankruptcy would you recommend?

Under the U.S. Constitution Congress has exclusive power to establish uniform laws on bankruptcies. **Bankruptcy law** has a dual purpose. It protects debtors by giving them a new economic start, free from most creditors' claims. Bankruptcy law also protects creditors by setting up a framework to give them a fair treatment in their competition for the debtor's assets. The federal Bankruptcy Code provides the following forms of possible relief for debtors.

Chapter 7 Liquidation, or "Straight Bankruptcy"

Chapter 7 involves the sale for cash of the nonexempt property of the debtor and the distribution of the proceeds to creditors. Nonexempt prop-

erty includes such assets as bank accounts, stocks, and bonds. Liquidation results in the discharge of most of the debtor's financial obligations.

Chapter 11 Reorganization

This relief is designed to keep the corporation, partnership, or sole proprietorship in active business with no liquidation. The debtor or a committee of creditors files a plan for reorganization. The bankruptcy court must approve this plan. The court will approve the plan if it is reasonable and if it was created in good faith. Chapter 11 reorganization would probably be ideal for Cooper's Petstores in *What's Your Verdict?*

Under Chapter 11, claims of both secured and unsecured creditors, as well as the interests of the owners of

the business, may be "impaired," meaning reduced. The plan to reorganize must be in the best interests of the creditors, and each class of creditors that is adversely affected must accept it. A class of creditors accepts the plan when a majority that represents two-thirds of the amount of that group's total claim votes to approve the plan. Even when only one class (for example, the bondholders) accepts the plan the Bankruptcy Court may approve it under a so-called "cramdown provision." This requires that the creditors or the owners who object are either unaffected by the plan, or are paid in full before any junior (or lower) class of claimant is paid.

Chapter 13 Extended Time Payment Plan

Chapter 13 relief is available only to individuals who have regular income. This plan also avoids liquidation of assets. The debtor must have regular income, unsecured debts of less than $250,000, and/or secured debts of less than $750,000. The debtor must submit a plan for the installment payment of debts within three years with a possible extension to five years.

During this time, the creditors may not file suit for payment of any debts. Both secured and unsecured debts (other than a claim, such as a promissory note and mortgage, secured by the debtor's principal residence) may

be reduced in amount or extended in time for payment. The plan must be "in the best interests of the creditors," who might otherwise receive even less in a Chapter 7 liquidation.

A major advantage of the Chapter 13 proceeding is that upon completion of payments called for under the plan, the court grants a discharge for almost all debts. The only exceptions are for certain long-term debts, such

as payments for a house and payments of alimony and child support.

Chapter 12 Plan

Congress added Chapter 12 relief to the Bankruptcy Code in 1986 for family farm owners. The eligibility requirements are set to exclude large agricultural operators. This plan is similar in operation to the Chapter 13 proceeding for other debtors.

PROCEDURE FOR CHAPTER 7 BANKRUPTCY

WHAT'S YOUR
VERDICT?

Jack Gilbert was talking to his fellow law school student, Chase Adamson, about finances and said, ". . . after I graduate, I'm going to declare bankruptcy and get rid of all these student loans." Chase looked at Jack and said, "Whoa, buddy. I just finished the course on bankruptcy and there's something about the law you should know that might change your plan."

What does Chase know about bankruptcy that Jack does not?

Liquidation under Chapter 7 of the Bankruptcy Act may be voluntary or involuntary.

Voluntary Bankruptcy

With a few exceptions, any person, business, or other association may request voluntary bankruptcy. A person does not have to be insolvent (unable to pay debts when they are due) to file. Husbands and wives may file jointly.

Involuntary Bankruptcy

Any person or business, except farmers and charitable institutions, owing

$10,000 or more to a single petitioning unsecured creditor and unable to pay debts when they come due may be forced into involuntary bankruptcy. However, if a person has more than 12 creditors with unsecured claims totaling at least $10,000, at least three must sign the involuntary bankruptcy petition.

In either voluntary or involuntary bankruptcy proceedings, the debtor, under oath, must file the following information with the court:

- a list of all creditors and amounts owed to each

- a list of all property owned, including property claimed to be exempt from seizure

- a statement explaining the debtor's financial affairs
- a list of current income and expenses

To conceal or fraudulently transfer assets or to provide false information knowingly is a crime under the bankruptcy laws.

After the petition is filed, a trustee is then selected. The trustee's duties are to find and to protect the assets of the debtor, liquidate them, and pay the claims against the debtor's estate with the proceeds. Such claims would include court costs, back wages owed to the debtor's employees, taxes, and claims of the general creditors. Secured creditors would seek payment of the secured debts directly against the collateral. Secured debts would be enforced ahead of any other claims.

There are certain types of claims that cannot be discharged by bankruptcy. These include the following:

- certain taxes
- alimony and child support
- claims against the debtor for property obtained by fraud, embezzlement, or larceny
- judgments against the debtor for willful and malicious injury to the person or property of another (but claims for injuries caused by negligence are discharged)
- student loans owed to the government or to a nonprofit school of higher learning, unless the loan became due more than seven years before the bankruptcy, or an undue hardship would be imposed on the debtor or on his or her dependents. (In *What's Your Verdict?* this is the information Chase thought Jack should have.)
- judgments against the debtor resulting from driving while intoxicated
- claims not listed by debtor

Exempt Property

Certain assets of the debtor are exempt from seizure to satisfy creditor's claims. These exemptions are specified in the federal bankruptcy laws which are revised every three years. Individual states have been empowered to disallow the use of these exemptions and substitute their own. The states can also create their own list and let the petitioner choose between state and federal exemptions. Under the federal law exempt property currently includes the following:

- up to $15,000 in equity in the debtor's home
- up to $2,400 interest in one motor vehicle
- up to $1,500 interest in the debtor's tools of trade
- alimony and support payments, social security payments, and welfare and pension benefits
- up to $400 per item of household goods and furnishings, wearing apparel, books, animals, crops, and musical instruments (the total value of exempted items cannot exceed $8,000)
- up to $1,000 in jewelry
- up to $15,000 in personal injury and other awards

Liquidation and Distribution of Proceeds

Once the assets of the debtor are brought under the trustee's control, they are liquidated. The proceeds of the liquidation are then used to pay the creditors. The law provides an order of priority for payout as follows:

1. secured creditors
2. administrative expenses such as court costs, trustee's and attorney's fees
3. unpaid wages, salaries, and commissions earned within 90 days of the filing of the petition, limited to $4,000 per claimant

4. unsecured claims from contributions to be made to employee benefit plans for services provided within 180 days of the filing of the petition and limited to $4,000 per employee
5. claims by farmers and fishers up to $4,000, against debtor operators of grain storage or fish storage or processing facilities
6. consumer deposits up to $1,800 per claimant given in connection with the rental, purchase, or lease of property or services not actually provided
7. paternity, alimony, maintenance and support debts
8. certain unpaid taxes such as property and income
9. claims of all general creditors and those with residual unsatisfied claims from the above categories

If any amount is left after all the above classes of claimants have been satisfied, it is turned over to the debtor. After the procedure is concluded, all eligible debts of the debtor are considered discharged. The debtor cannot file a petition in bankruptcy again until 6 years have elapsed. Bankruptcy stays on a credit report for 10 years.

Answer the following questions about legal concepts.

1. Under the U.S. Constitution, Congress has exclusive power to establish uniform laws on bankruptcies. **True or False?**

2. Chapter ___?___ relief is available only to individuals. **(a) 7 (b) 10 (c) 13 (d) none of the above**

3. Chapter 12 was added to the Bankruptcy Code in 1986 for family farm owners. **True or False?**

4. Which of the following is not a required filing by a voluntary debtor in bankruptcy? **(a) list of all creditors and amounts owed to each (b) list of all property owned, including property claimed to be exempt from seizure (c) statement explaining the debtor's financial affairs (d) all of the above must be filed**

Study the following situations, answer the questions, and then prepare arguments to support your answers.

5. Mark is greatly upset and wonders if he should report what appears to him to be a flagrant abuse of the bankruptcy law. The individual debtor in question has been living for years in a house that is worth at least $100,000 and maybe much more. Recently, the debtor went through a bankruptcy, yet he and his family still live in the house. Is such a result possible without violating the bankruptcy laws? What chapter of the laws might make it possible?

6. Under the state exemptions to the bankruptcy act allowable under the law of a large southwestern state, there is a one-acre exemption for the debtor's home. Two brothers, Robert and Lyle Quest, are forced into involuntary bankruptcy due to some precious metal speculations. Robert lives in a penthouse atop a $62 million office building he owns. Lyle's penthouse is atop a $71 million building that he owns. Each claims the one acre due under the state law. The creditors claim that they should be able to reach all the value in the one acre except for the $15,000 exemption allowed by the federal law. Who wins?

7. Robert, in exercise 6, separated his rare china collection into 1,217 individual pieces, each worth less than $400, and claimed them as exempt property. The state law's exemption is the same as the federal one for personal property. May Robert exempt his whole collection? Why or why not?

8. One month before being forced into bankruptcy, Lyle retired from his position as president of the brothers' company. He then began drawing an amount equal to his old salary ($4 million per year) as his pension. He claimed that the pension was exempt from his creditors' claims as the state exemption mirrored the federal exemption in the area. Is he correct?

Using credit wisely . . .

1. In applying for credit, always be accurate and honest. Lies about one's credit history are often exposed.

2. If you give property as security for a debt, be sure it is returned or properly released when the debt is paid.

3. Protect your rights by learning about them and exercising them when appropriate. The Fair Credit Reporting Act, Fair Credit Billing Act, Equal Credit Opportunity Act, Fair

PREVENT LEGAL DIFFICULTIES

Debt Collection Practices Act, and related statutes are of limited value without consumer

demand for their enforcement.

4. Be cautious about entering into a credit agreement as a surety or a guarantor.

5. A person who repairs your television, watch, car, or other personal property can exercise an artisan's lien on the property, retaining possession until paid, or eventually selling the goods. Before work is begun get a detailed written estimate of anticipated cost.

CHAPTER IN REVIEW

CONCEPTS IN BRIEF

1. When one owes money to another, the relationship is that of debtor and creditor.

2. A debt may be secured or unsecured. If secured, the debtor gives the creditor possession of the security, or a nonpossessory lien against specified property until the debt is paid. If unsecured, the creditor does not get a lien against specific property. However, the creditor may successfully sue the debtor, and then have the sheriff seize cash deposits or other available assets of the debtor to satisfy the court judgment. To the extent necessary, the sheriff sells the assets (real and personal property) at a public sale.

3. A lien gives the creditor the right to sell specified property of the debtor to pay the debt. Any excess money received goes to the debtor. If there is a shortage, the creditor normally may sue for the balance due.

4. Goods or documents representing property rights may be delivered to the creditor as security for a loan. This creates a pledge and gives the creditor the right to sell the goods or the documents in case of default. Upon performance of the obligation, the pledgor (debtor) has a right to have pledged property returned.

5. Creditors may proceed against the general assets of the debtor in the following two cases:
   - when secured debts are in default and are not paid in full by proceeds from sale of the property pledged, and
   - when unsecured debts are not paid.

6. In answering for the debt of another upon default, the surety assumes a primary liability. The guarantor is liable secondarily after the creditor has exhausted all remedies against the debtor, including judgment of a court and attempted execution.

YOUR LEGAL VOCABULARY

Match each statement with the term that it best defines. Some terms may not be used.

1. Car repairer's right to retain possession of the car until paid or if not paid, to sell the car to pay the repair bill

2. An interest in property allowing its sale by creditor upon default by debtor

3. A debt in which the creditor lacks a secured interest in collateral

4. A loan for personal, household, or agricultural purposes

5. A court-ordered procedure by which a portion of a delinquent debtor's wages are paid to satisfy the debt

6. The total added cost when one pays in installments for goods or services

7. Procedure based on federal law that protects creditors and debtors in cases in which the latter are unable or unwilling to pay their debts

8. The evaluation of a party's ability to pay debts

9. Party who agrees to be primarily liable for debt created in favor of the principal debtor

10. A party who agrees to be secondarily liable to the principal debtor

artisan's lien
bankruptcy law
consumer loan
credit rating
finance charge
garnishment
guarantor
lien
mechanic's lien
pawn
pledgee
pledgor
principal debtor
surety
suretyship
unsecured debt

11. What class of people do the mechanic's and artisan's liens serve? Why?

12. Why would the state be interested in allowing creditors the use of the lien?

13. What standards are required for the sale of pledged material when the pledgor has not redeemed them?

14. What is the legal difference in a surety and a guarantor?

15. In choosing between sureties and guarantors, which ones should creditors prefer? Why?

16. What does a signature on a credit card indicate? If the card is lost or stolen, generally what is the card holder's liability?

WRITE ABOUT LEGAL CONCEPTS

17. Draft a list of bankruptcy exemptions for your state. Explain why you have chosen the ones you did.

18. Why is there a separate Chapter 13 bankruptcy for wage earners?

19. **HOT DEBATE** Write a persuasive opening statement that emphasizes the legal, ethical and economic points in Norm's favor. Or, write a persuasive opening statement for the jeweler that encompasses the economic and legal reasons why the loss should fall on Norm.

THINK CRITICALLY ABOUT EVIDENCE

20. You are thinking of buying an automobile and plan to borrow money to help you pay cash for the purchase. Is there a limit on how much interest a lender can charge you? Suppose you decide to rely on dealer financing, paying the dealer or finance company a series of monthly installments. Is there any limit on the annual percentage rate (APR) of the financing charge the seller may add to the price of the car?

21. An acquaintance brags that she will finance her college education with government-insured student loans and then go bankrupt after graduation to avoid paying them. Is this possible? Is this ethical?

22. All five of your credit cards are stolen from your motel room while you are skiing. Fortunately you discover the loss within a few hours and immediately notify the credit card companies by telephone. On the following day, you also notify them by mail. However, within a week, the thief uses your credit cards to charge $1,875 in purchases. Eventually, each credit card company bills you for $50 of the purchases made with its card. By what authority did they do this? Must you pay these bills?

23. Alex gets paid at the end of the month. A week before payday, Alex ran out of cash. His classmate Roger agreed to lend him $10, "for 20 when you get paid." Translated, this means that Roger lends Alex $10 now in exchange for $20 to be paid after seven days. Is this, contract legal? Is it ethical?

24. When Lola came home from college for spring break, her mother gave her a credit card. "You can sign my name, but don't spend more than $100," she told Lola. Lola went on a buying spree with her friend Joyce and together they bought $575 worth of clothing using the credit card. Now her mother refuses to pay more than $150, stating, "$100 I authorized, and $50 is the legal maximum for unauthorized purchases." The credit card company sues for $575. Who wins?

ANALYZE
REAL CASES

25. Medias and other pawnbrokers objected to an Indianapolis city ordinance that regulated their business. The ordinance required an applicant for a pawnbroker's license to establish good character by the certificate of three landowners. The ordinance also provided that the licensee keep specified records and supply information to the chief of police. Finally, the ordinance specified that the licensee hold all pledged articles for 96 hours, and it required that the licensee take the thumbprints of all persons from whom he or she bought or received goods. Are these regulations arbitrary and unreasonable? (*Medias v. City of Indianapolis,* 216 Ind. 155, 23 N.E.2d 590)

26. Sniadach owed the Family Finance Corporation (FFC) $420 under a written promise to pay. When this debt became overdue, the creditor obtained a court order that summarily garnished her wages. Her employer had $63 in wages earned by her but not yet paid, and it agreed to hold one-half of them subject to the court order. Sniadach sued the FFC and asked the court to reverse the garnishment order, claiming that it violated her right to due process under the Fourteenth Amendment. She had received the summons and complaint on the same day that her employer was notified and froze her wages. Thus, she had no opportunity to be heard and to present her side of the case before the garnishment took effect. The trial court denied her motion, and the Wisconsin Supreme Court affirmed. She now appeals to the U.S. Supreme Court. How should it rule? (*Sniadach v. Family Finance Corporation,* 395 U.S. 337)

27. Todd was one of seven cosureties. When the principal debtor defaulted, Todd paid the debt and sued the other cosureties. Is Todd entitled to a judgment for one-seventh of the debt against each of the cosureties or to a judgment for six-sevenths of the debt against each? (*Todd v. Windsor,* 118 Ga. App. 805, 165 S.E.2d 438)

28. In his divorce decree, Elliot was ordered to pay $102 of his weekly wages of $467.47 from his job at a General Motors plant for child support. Months later, U.S. Life Credit Corporation (USLC) recovered a judgment against Elliot in municipal court. With court approval, USLC then garnished 25 percent of Elliot's $467.47 per week to pay off the judgment amount. The U.S. Secretary of Labor then filed a lawsuit against the municipal court and USLC contending that the payments to USLC and for child support, taken together, violated the 25 percent of disposable income restriction on garnishments imposed by the act. You decide. (*Donovan v. Hamilton County Municipal Court,* 580 F. Supp. 554)

29. When Hardison filed for bankruptcy, one of his main creditors was General Finance Corporation (GFC) to which he owed $2,800. After the GFC debt and others were discharged as a result of the bankruptcy procedure, he received a letter from GFC informing him that his credit was still good with it. By telephone, Hardison then arranged for a $1,200 loan from GFC. However, when he appeared to pick up the money, GFC informed him that it was going to make the loan only if he agreed to pay back not only the $1,200, but also an additional $1,200 from the first loan. Hardison then signed a consumer credit contract agreeing to those terms. Later, Hardison filed a lawsuit claiming that GFC should have included the amount from the previously discharged debt in the "total finance charge" in the truth-in-lending statement shown him at the time of the transaction, rather than as a part of the "total amount financed." Hardison wanted damages available under the Truth in Lending Act. Should he receive them? (*Hardison v. General Finance Corporation,* 738 F.2d 893)

30. When the Richmonds filed for Chapter 7 liquidation under the Bankruptcy Code, their unsecured debts totaled a little more than $19,000. All but $225 of the unsecured debts was owed on credit cards. The trustee in bankruptcy noted that the Richmond's monthly expenses included voluntary payments in support of their grandchildren. The trustee also pointed out to the court that, if these payments were stopped, the Richmonds would have an additional $300 per month with which to pay off the credit cards. In fact, under a three year Chapter 13 plan, the Richmonds could pay off more than 90 percent of the credit card debt in 36 months. As a consequence, the trustee filed a motion to dismiss the Richmond's case, contending that to grant relief to them would be an abuse of Chapter 7. The court noted that in making such a decision, it must decide whether the debtors are seeking an advantage or are truly needy in the sense that their financial situation warrants dismissal of the debts. How should the judge decide this case, and why? (*In Re Richmond,* 144 Bankruptcy Reporter 539)

BACKGROUND Prior to 1976, a student could attend school on student loans guaranteed by the government and then discharge them immediately upon graduation, before starting employment, under the terms of the Bankruptcy Act. Congress ultimately closed the loophole except for those for whom paying back the loans posed an "undue hardship."

Mary Lou Baker filed for bankruptcy protection under the "undue hardship" provisions to relieve her of the burden of repaying educational loans totally some $6,635. The loans were from three institutions of higher learning: The University of Tennessee at Chattanooga, Cleveland State Community College, and the Baroness Erlanger School of Nursing.

FACTS Mary Lou Baker was a mother of three with a monthly take-home pay of less than $650. Her monthly expenses for herself and the children (her husband had left town) were nearly $1,000. She did not receive any public aid and had no other income according to the record. However, just prior to filing this action, her church had paid her January heating bill to prevent her from being without heat in her home.

Of her three children, one had difficulty reading and another required special and expensive shoes. Baker herself had not been well and her medical bills had gone unpaid prior to the bankruptcy filing.

In the bankruptcy petition she filed, Mrs. Baker seeks a discharge of her educational loans based on the hardship provision.

COURT DECISION Ralph Kelley, Bankruptcy Judge, rendered the court's decision:

In 1976 the Congress passed the Educational Amendments which restricted a discharge in bankruptcy (of student loans). The restriction was designed to remedy an abuse by students who, immediately upon graduation, would file bankruptcy to secure a discharge of educational loans. These students often had no other indebtedness and could easily repay their debts from future wages. . .

This court concludes that under the circumstances of this case, requiring the debtor to repay the debts owed to the three defendants of $6,635.00 plus interest would impose upon her and her dependents an undue hardship.

In passing the Educational Amendments of 1976 and including these amendments in the Bankruptcy Reform Act of 1978, Congress intended to correct an abuse. It did not intend to deprive those who have truly fallen on hard times of the "fresh start" policy of the new Bankruptcy Code.

PRACTICE JUDGING

1. What sort of standard does the court identify here for future debtors when it says petitioner Baker had "truly fallen on hard times?" What sort of standard would you propose?

2. Presume Mrs. Baker did her best at each institution but still ended up either without the sought-after degree or without a job commensurate with the money expended to qualify for it. Does the government, as guarantor of such educational loans, find itself being forced into evaluating how successful each applicant may be before issuing them the money?

ENTREPRENEURS AND THE LAW

PROJECT 7 BORROWING MONEY AND PAYING BILLS

FINANCIAL SETBACK

Ben was upset. His plan to finance a major expansion of his current plant by personally borrowing money from his bank and in-laws hadn't worked. Too many delays and unseen expenses had driven him to the brink of bankruptcy. The business was still going strong, but his personal "fortune" was exposed. He finally told Kristen about the problem. She immediately suggested that he talk it over with a bankruptcy attorney. She also called another attorney who specialized in corporate financing. As usual Ben went ahead with her suggestion for the meeting.

FINANCIAL SOLUTION

Ben looked down in total dismay as he listened to the attorney's report. Not only would he go down in flames, but he probably would take his in-laws with him. Finally, he realized that the bankruptcy attorney had stopped speaking. "That's it then, isn't it." Ben said. "Not quite, sir," said the attorney. "This is our expert on corporate finance, Mr. Whorton. I think he may have some good news for you." Ben looked up. "Haven't had any of that since the twins were born." Ben pointed to a picture on his desk of his beautiful daughters. "Well, Mr. Windows, I think you could have saved yourself a lot of grief if you had just come to us in the first place. You have a lot of unencumbered capital equipment and grounds around here. We could go to your current creditors and offer them secured positions in return for their backing off on trying to collect according to their current schedule. However, the best idea would be to set up a financing package that will let you complete your current expansion and even give you capital to buy whatever supplies and equipment you need to make even more money. I've taken the liberty of preparing a plan with several options, including secured and unsecured instruments, equity capitalization and some combinations of the two."

Ben started to relax. If he understood correctly, not only would he be able to save the company but his hopes and plans for the expansion as well. When the attorneys left, Ben emerged from his office with a big smile on his face. For the first time in more than six months, he was going home early to his wife and children.

Divide into teams and perform one or more of the following activities, as directed by your teacher.

PRESENT

Assume your team is the bankruptcy attorney who explained the bankruptcy issues to Ben. Each team member should consider one of the following issues and prepare a short presentation on it: (1) Which form of bankruptcy might be most helpful to Ben? (2) What will be the effect of bankruptcy on the business? (3) What should be Ben's plan to pay off his in-laws? (4) What could be salvaged for Ben if he does declare bankruptcy. After each member presents to the team, the team should prepare a presentation covering all the issues for the class.

BRAINSTORM

As a team, brainstorm a list of financing options for the business.

DEBATE

After your list from the brainstorming activity is compiled, debate the pros and cons of each alternative, given Reelshield's current position. Make a recommendation about which financing option seems best for the company.

CONSTITUTION OF THE UNITED STATES

We the People Of the United States, in Order to form a more perfect Union, establish Justice, insure domestic Tranquility, provide for the common defence, promote the general Welfare, and secure the Blessings of Liberty to ourselves and our Posterity, do ordain and establish this Constitution for the United States of America.

ARTICLE I

Section 1. All legislative Powers herein granted shall be vested in a Congress of the United States, which shall consist of a Senate and House of Representatives.

Section 2. The House of Representatives shall be composed of Members chosen every second Year by the People of the several States, and the Electors in each State shall have the Qualifications requisite for Electors of the most numerous Branch of the State Legislature.

No Person shall be a Representative who shall not have attained to the Age of twenty five Years, and been seven Years a Citizen of the United States, and who shall not, when elected, be an inhabitant of that State in which he shall be chosen.

*Representatives and direct Taxes shall be apportioned among the several States which may be included within this Union, according to their respective. Numbers, which shall be determined by adding to the whole Number of free Persons, including those bound to Service for a Term of Years, and excluding Indians not taxed, three fifths of all other Persons. The actual Enumeration shall be made within three Years after the first Meeting of the Congress of the United States, and within every subsequent Term of ten Years, in such Manner as they shall by Law direct. The number of Representatives shall not exceed one for every thirty Thousand, but each State shall have at Least one Representative; and until such enumeration shall be made, the State of New Hampshire shall be entitled to chuse three, Massachusetts eight, Rhode Island and Providence Plantations one, Connecticut five, New-York six, New Jersey four, Pennsylvania eight, Delaware one, Maryland six, Virginia ten, North Carolina five, South Carolina five, and Georgia three.

When vacancies happen in the Representation from any State, the Executive Authority thereof shall issue Writs of Election to fill such Vacancies.

The House of Representatives shall chuse their Speaker and other Officers; and shall have the sole Power of Impeachment.

Section 3. The Senate of the United States shall be composed of two Senators from each State, chosen by the Legislature thereof, for six Years; and each Senator shall have one Vote.

Immediately after they shall be assembled in Consequence of the first Election, they shall be divided as equally as may be into three Classes. The Seats of the Senators of the first Class shall be vacated at the Expiration of the second Year,

*Sections of the Constitution which are crossed out in this text have been amended and are no longer in effect.

of the second Class at the Expiration of the fourth Year, and of the third Class at the Expiration of the sixth Year, so that one third may be chosen every second Year; ~~and if Vacancies happen by Resignation, or otherwise, during the Recess of the Legislature of any State, the Executive thereof may make temporary Appointments until the next Meeting of the Legislature, which shall then fill such Vacancies.~~

No Person shall be a Senator who shall not have attained to the Age of thirty Years, and been nine Years a Citizen of the United States, and who shall not, when elected, be an Inhabitant of that State for which he shall be chosen.

The Vice-President of the United States shall be President of the Senate, but shall have no Vote, unless they be equally divided.

The Senate shall chuse their other Officers, and also a President pro tempore, in the Absence of the Vice-President, or when he shall exercise the Office of President of the United States.

The Senate shall have the sole Power to try all Impeachments. When sitting for that Purpose, they shall be on Oath or Affirmation. When the President of the United States is tried, the Chief Justice shall preside: And no Person shall be convicted without the Concurrence of two thirds of the Members present.

Judgment in Cases of Impeachment shall not extend further than to removal from Office, and disqualification to hold and enjoy any Office of honor, Trust or Profit under the United States: but the Party convicted shall nevertheless be liable and subject to Indictment, Trial, Judgment and Punishment, according to Law.

Section 4. The Times, Places and Manner of holding Elections for Senators and Representatives, shall be prescribed in each State by the Legislature thereof; but the Congress may at any time by Law make or alter such Regulations, except as to the Places of chusing Senators.

The Congress shall assemble at least once in every Year, ~~and such Meeting shall be on the first Monday in December,~~ unless they shall by Law appoint a different Day.

Section 5. Each House shall be the Judge of the Elections, Returns and Qualifications of its own Members, and a Majority of each shall constitute a Quorum to do Business; but a smaller Number may adjourn from day to day, and may be authorized to compel the Attendance of absent Members, in such Manner, and under such Penalties as each House may provide.

Each House may determine the Rules of its Proceedings, punish its Members for disorderly Behaviour, and, with the Concurrence of two thirds, expel a Member.

Each House shall keep a Journal of its Proceedings, and from time to time publish the same, excepting such Parts as may in their Judgment require Secrecy; and the Yeas and Nays of the Members of either House on any question shall, at the Desire of one fifth of those Present, be entered on the Journal.

Neither House, during the Session of Congress, shall, without the Consent of the other, adjourn for more than three days, nor to any other Place than that in which the two Houses shall be sitting.

Section 6. The Senators and Representatives shall receive a Compensation for their Services, to be ascertained by Law, and paid out of the Treasury of the United States. They shall in all Cases, except Treason, Felony and Breach of the Peace, be privileged from Arrest during their Attendance at the Session off their respective Houses, and in going to and returning from the same; and for any Speech or Debate in either House, they shall not be questioned in any other Place.

No Senator or Representative shall, during the Time for which he was elected, be appointed to any civil Office under the Authority of the United States, which shall have been created, or the Emoluments whereof shall have been encreased during such time; and no Person holding any Office under the United States, shall be a Member of either House during his Continuance in Office.

Section 7. All Bills for raising Revenue shall originate in the House of Representatives; but the Senate may propose or concur with Amendments as on other Bills.

Every Bill which shall have passed the House of Representatives and the Senate, shall, before it becomes a Law, be presented to the President of the United States; If he approve he shall sign it, but if not he shall return it, with his Objections to that House in which it shall have originated, who shall enter the Objections at large on their Journal, and proceed to reconsider it.

If after such Reconsideration two thirds of that House shall agree to pass the Bill, it shall be sent, together with the Objections, to the other House, by which it shall likewise be reconsidered, and if approved by two thirds of that House, it shall become a Law. But in all such Cases the Votes of both Houses shall be determined by yeas and Nays, and the Names of the Persons voting for and against the Bill shall be entered on the Journal of each House respectively. If any Bill shall not be returned by the President within ten Days (Sundays excepted) after it shall have been presented to him, the Same shall be a Law, in like Manner as if he had signed it, unless the Congress by their Adjournment prevent its Return, in which Case it shall not be a Law.

Every Order, Resolution, or Vote to which the Concurrence of the Senate and House of Representatives may be necessary (except on a question of Adjournment) shall be presented to the President of the United States; and before the Same shall take Effect, shall be approved by him, or being disapproved by him, shall be repassed by two thirds of the Senate and House of Representatives, according to the Rules and Limitations prescribed in the Case of a Bill.

Section 8. The Congress shall have Power To lay and collect Taxes, Duties, Imposts and Excises, to pay the Debts and provide for the common Defence and general Welfare of the United States; but all Duties, Imposts and Excises shall be uniform throughout the United States;

To borrow Money on the credit of the United States;

To regulate Commerce with foreign Nations, and among the several States, and with the Indian Tribes;

To establish an uniform Rule of Naturalization, and uniform Laws on the subject of Bankruptcies throughout the United States;

To coin Money, regulate the Value thereof, and of foreign Coin, and fix the Standard of Weights and Measures;

To provide for the Punishment of counterfeiting the Securities and current Coin of the United States;

To establish Post Offices and post Roads;

To promote the Progress of Science and useful Arts, by securing for limited Times to Authors and Inventors the exclusive Right to their respective Writings and Discoveries;

To constitute Tribunals inferior to the supreme Court;

To define and punish Piracies and Felonies committed on the high Seas, and Offenses against the Law of Nations;

To declare War, grant Letters of Marque and Reprisal, and make Rules concerning Captures on Land and Water;

To raise and support Armies, but no Appropriation of Money to that Use shall be for a longer Term than two Years;

To provide and maintain a Navy;

To make Rules for the Government and Regulation of the land and naval Forces;

To provide for calling forth the Militia to execute the Laws of the Union, suppress Insurrections and repel Invasions;

To provide for organizing, arming, and disciplining, the Militia, and for governing such Part of them as may be employed in the Service of the United States, reserving to the States respectively, the Appointment of the Officers, and the Authority of training the Militia according to the discipline prescribed by Congress;

To exercise exclusive Legislation in all Cases whatsoever, over such District (not exceeding ten Miles square) as may, by Cession of particular States, and the Acceptance of Congress, become the Seat of the Government of the United States, and to exercise like Authority over all Places purchased by the Consent of the Legislature of the State in which the Same shall be, for the Erection of Forts, Magazines, Arsenals, dock-Yards and other needful Buildings; And

To make all Laws which shall be necessary and proper for carrying into Execution the foregoing Powers, and all other Powers vested by this Constitution in the Government of the United States, or in any Department or Officer thereof.

Section 9. The Migration or Importation of such Persons as any of the States now existing shall think proper to admit, shall not be prohibited by the Congress prior to the Year one thousand eight hundred and eight, but a Tax or duty may be imposed on such Importation, not exceeding ten dollars for each Person.

The Privilege of the Writ of Habeas Corpus shall not be suspended, unless when in Cases of Rebellion or Invasion the public Safety may require it.

No Bill of Attainder or ex post facto Law shall be passed.

No Capitation, or other direct, Tax shall be laid, unless in Proportion to the Census or Enumeration herein before directed to be taken.

No Tax or Duty shall be laid on Articles exported from any State.

No Preference shall be given by any Regulation of Commerce or Revenue to the Ports of one State over those of another: nor shall Vessels bound to, or from, one State, be obliged to enter, clear, or pay Duties in another.

No Money shall be drawn from the Treasury, but in Consequence of Appropriations made by Law; and a regular Statement and Account of the Receipts and Expenditures of all public Money shall be published from time to time.

No Title of Nobility shall be granted by the United States: And no Person holding any Office of Profit or Trust under them, shall, without the Consent of the Congress, accept of any present, Emolument, Office, or Title, of any kind whatever, from any King, Prince, or foreign State.

Section 10. No State shall enter into any Treaty, Alliance, or Confederation; grant Letters of Marque and Reprisal; coin Money; emit Bills of Credit; make any Thing but gold and silver Coin a Tender in Payment of Debts; pass any Bill of Attainder, ex post facto Law, or Law impairing the Obligation of Contracts, or grant any Title of Nobility.

No State shall, without the Consent of the Congress, lay any Imposts or Duties on Imports or Exports, except what may be absolutely necessary for executing its inspection Laws: and the net Produce of all Duties and Imposts, laid by any State on Imports or Exports, shall be for the Use of the Treasury of the United States; and all such Laws shall be subject to the Revision and Controul of the Congress.

No State shall, without the Consent of Congress, lay any Duty of Tonnage, keep Troops, or Ships of War in time of Peace, enter into any Agreement or Compact with another State, or with a foreign Power, or engage in War, unless actually invaded, or in such imminent Danger as will not admit of delay.

ARTICLE II

Section 1. The executive Power shall be vested in a President of the United States of America. He shall hold his Office during the Term of four Years, and, together with the Vice-President, chosen for the same Term, be elected, as follows

Each State shall appoint, in such Manner as the Legislature thereof may direct, a Number of Electors, equal to the whole Number of Senators and Representatives to which the State may be entitled in the Congress: but no Senator or Representative, or Person holding an Office of Trust or Profit under the United States, shall be appointed an Elector.

The Electors shall meet in their respective States, and vote by Ballot for two Persons, of whom one at least shall not be an Inhabitant of the same State with themselves. And they shall make a List of all the Persons voted for, and of the Number of Votes for each; which List they shall sign and certify, and transmit sealed to the Seat of the Government of the United States, directed to the President of the Senate. The President of the Senate shall, in the Presence of the Senate and House of Representatives, open all the Certificates, and the Votes shall then be

~~counted. The Person having the greatest Number of Votes shall be the President, if such Number be a Majority, of the whole Number of Electors appointed; and if there be more than one who have such Majority and have an equal Number of Votes, then the House of Representatives shall immediately chuse by Ballot one of them for President, and if no Person have a Majority, then from the five highest on the List the said House shall in like Manner chuse the President. But in chusing the President, the Votes shall be taken by States, the Representation from each State having one Vote; A quorum for this Purpose shall consist of a Member or Members from two thirds of the States, and a Majority of all the States shall be necessary to a Choice. In every Case, after the Choice of the President, the Person having the greatest Number of Votes of the Electors shall be the Vice-President. But if there should remain two or more who have equal Votes, the Senate shall chuse from them by Ballot the Vice President.~~

The Congress may determine the Time of chusing the Electors, and the Day on which they shall give their Votes; which Day shall be the same throughout the United States.

No Person except a natural born Citizen, or a Citizen of the United States, at the time of the Adoption of this Constitution, shall be eligible to the Office of the President; neither shall any person be eligible to that Office who shall not have attained to the Age of thirty five Years, and been fourteen Years a Resident within the United States.

~~In Case of the Removal of the President from Office, or of his Death, Resignation, or Inability to discharge the Powers and Duties of the said Office, the Same shall devolve on the Vice-President, and the Congress may by Law provide for the Case of Removal, Death, Resignation or Inability, both of the President and Vice-President, declaring what Officer shall then act as President, and such Officer shall act accordingly, until the Disability be removed, or a President shall be elected.~~

The President shall, at stated Times, receive for his Services, a Compensation, which shall neither be increased nor diminished during the Period for which he shall have been elected and he shall not receive within that Period any other Emolument from the United States, or any of them.

Before he enter on the Execution of his Office, he shall take the following Oath or Affirmation: "I do solemnly swear (or affirm) that I will faithfully execute the Office of President of the United States, and will to the best of my Ability, preserve, protect and defend the Constitution of the United States."

Section 2. The President shall be Commander in Chief of the Army and Navy of the United States, and of the Militia of the several States, when called into the actual Service of the United States; he may require the Opinion, in writing, of the principal Officer in each of the executive Departments, upon any Subject relating to the Duties of their respective Offices, and he shall have Power to grant Reprieves and Pardons for Offenses against the United States, except in Cases of Impeachment.

He shall have Power, by and with the Advice and Consent of the Senate, to make Treaties, provided two thirds of the Senators present concur; and he shall nominate, and by and with the Advice and Consent of the Senate, shall appoint Ambassadors, other public Ministers and Consuls, judges of the supreme Court, and all other Officers of the United States, whose Appointments are not herein otherwise provided for, and which shall be established by Law: but the Congress may by Law vest the Appointment of such inferior Officers, as they think proper, in the President alone, in the Courts of Law, or in the Heads of Departments. The President shall have Power to fill up all Vacancies that may happen during the Recess of the Senate, by granting Commissions which shall expire at the End of their next Session.

Section 3. He shall from time to time give to the Congress Information of the State of the Union, and recommend to their Consideration such measures as he shall judge necessary and expedient; he may, on extraordinary Occasions, convene both Houses, or either of them, and in Case of Disagreement between them, with

Respect to the Time of Adjournment, he may adjourn them to such Time as he shall think proper; he shall receive Ambassadors and other public Ministers; he shall take Care that the Laws be faithfully executed, and shall Commission all the Officers of the United States.

Section 4. The President, Vice-President and all civil Officers of the United States, shall be removed from Office on Impeachment for, and Conviction of, Treason, Bribery, or other high Crimes and Misdemeanors.

ARTICLE III
Section 1. The judicial Power of the United States, shall he vested in one supreme Court, and in such inferior Courts as the Congress may from time to time ordain and establish. The Judges, both of the supreme and inferior Courts, shall hold their Offices during good Behaviour, and shall, at stated Times, receive for their Services, a Compensation, which shall not be diminished during their Continuance in Office

Section 2. The judicial Power shall extend to all Cases, in Law and Equity, arising, under this Constitution, the Laws of the United States, and Treaties made, or which shall be made, under their Authority; to all Cases affecting Ambassadors, other public Ministers and Consuls; to all Cases of admiralty and maritime Jurisdiction; to Controversies to which the United States shall be a Party; to Controversies between two or more States; between a State and Citizens of another State; between Citizens of different States between Citizens of the same State claiming Lands under Grants of different States, and between a State, or the Citizens thereof; and foreign States, Citizens or Subjects.

In all Cases affecting Ambassadors, other public Ministers and Consuls, and those in which a State shall be Party, the supreme Court shall have original Jurisdiction. In all the other Cases before mentioned, the supreme Court shall have appellate Jurisdiction, both as to Law and Fact, with such Exceptions, and under such Regulations as the Congress shall make.

The Trial of all Crimes, except in Cases of Impeachment, shall be by Jury; and such Trial shall be held in the State where the said Crimes shall have been committed; but when not committed within any State, the Trial shall be at such Place or Places as the Congress may by Law have directed.

Section 3. Treason against the United States, shall consist only in levying War against them, or in adhering to their Enemies, giving them Aid and Comfort. No Person shall be convicted of Treason unless on the Testimony of two Witnesses to the same overt Act, or on Confession in open Court.

The Congress shall have Power to declare the Punishment of Treason, but no Attainder of Treason shall work Corruption of Blood, or Forfeiture except during the Life of the Person attained.

ARTICLE IV
Section 1. Full Faith and Credit shall be given in each State to the public Acts, Records, and judicial Proceedings of every other State; And the Congress may by general Laws prescribe the Manner in which such Acts, Records and Proceedings shall be proved, and the Effect thereof.

Section 2. The Citizens of each State shall be entitled to all Privileges and Immunities of Citizens in the several States.

A Person charged in any State with Treason, Felony, or other Crime, who shall flee from Justice, and be found in another State, shall on Demand of the executive Authority of the State from which he fled, be delivered up, to be removed to the State having Jurisdiction of the Crime.

~~No Person held to Service or Labour in one State, under the Laws thereof, escaping into another, shall, in Consequence of any Law or Regulation therein, be discharged from such Service or Labour, but shall be delivered up on Claim of the Party to whom such Service or Labour may be due.~~

Section 3. New States may be admitted by the Congress into this Union; but no new State shall be formed or erected within the Jurisdiction of any other State; nor any State be formed by the Junction of two or more States, or Parts of States, without the Consent of the Legislatures of the States concerned as well as of the Congress.

The Congress shall have Power to dispose of and make all needful Rules and Regulations respecting the Territory or other Property belonging to the United States; and nothing in this Constitution shall be so construed as to Prejudice any Claims of the United States, or of any particular State.

Section 4. The United States shall guarantee to every state in this Union a Republican Form of Government, and shall protect each of them against Invasion; and on Application of the Legislature, or of the Executive (when the Legislature cannot be convened) against domestic Violence.

ARTICLE V

The Congress, whenever two thirds of both Houses shall deem it necessary, shall propose Amendments to this Constitution, or, on the Application of the Legislatures of two thirds of the several States, shall call a Convention for proposing Amendments, which, in either Case, shall be valid to all Intents and Purposes, as Part of this Constitution, when ratified by the Legislatures of three fourths of the several States, or by Conventions in three fourths thereof, as the one or the other Mode of Ratification may be proposed by the Congress; Provided that no Amendment which may be made prior to the Year One thousand eight hundred and eight shall in any Manner affect the first and fourth Clauses in the Ninth Section of the first Article; and that no State, without its Consent, shall be deprived of its equal Suffrage in the Senate.

ARTICLE VI

All Debts contracted and Engagements entered into, before the Adoption of this Constitution, shall be as valid against the United States under this Constitution, as under the Confederation.

This Constitution, and the Laws of the United States which shall be made in Pursuance thereof; and all Treaties made, or which shall be made, under the Authority of the United States, shall be the supreme Law of the Land; and the Judges in every State shall be bound thereby, any Thing in the Constitution or Laws of any State to the Contrary notwithstanding.

The Senators and Representatives before mentioned, and the Members of the several State Legislatures, and all executive and judicial Officers, both of the United States and of the several States, shall be bound by Oath or Affirmation, to support this Constitution; but no religious Test shall ever be required as a Qualification to any Office or public Trust under the United States.

ARTICLE VII

The Ratification of the Conventions of nine States, shall be sufficient for the Establishment of this Constitution between the States so ratifying the Same.

Done in Convention by the Unanimous Consent of the States present the Seventeenth Day of September in the Year of our Lord one thousand seven hundred and Eighty seven and of the Independence of the United States of America the Twelfth In Witness whereof We have hereunto subscribed our Names,

G.o Washington Presid.
and deputy from Virginia

AMENDMENT I

Congress shall make no law respecting an establishment of religion, or prohibiting the free exercise thereof; or abridging the freedom of speech, or of the press, or the right of the people peaceably to assemble, and to petition the Government for a redress of grievances.

AMENDMENT II

A well regulated Militia, being necessary to the security of a free State, the right of the people to keep and bear Arms, shall not be infringed.

AMENDMENT III

No Soldier shall, in time of peace be quartered in any house, without the consent of the Owner, nor in time of war, but in a manner to be prescribed by law.

AMENDMENT IV

The right of the people to be secure in their persons, houses, papers, and effects, against unreasonable searches and seizures, shall not be violated, and no Warrants shall issue, but upon probable cause, supported by Oath or affirmation, and particularly describing the place to be searched, and the persons or things to be seized.

AMENDMENT V

No person shall be held to answer for a capital, or otherwise infamous crime, unless on a presentment or indictment of a Grand Jury, except in cases arising in the land or naval forces, or in the Militia, when in actual service in time of War or public danger; nor shall any person be subject for the same offence to be twice put in jeopardy of life or limb, nor shall be compelled in any criminal case to be a witness against himself, nor be deprived of life, liberty, or property, without due process of law; nor shall private property be taken for public use without just compensation.

AMENDMENT VI

In all criminal prosecutions, the accused shall enjoy the right to a speedy and public trial, by an impartial jury of the State and district wherein the crime shall have been committed; which district shall have been previously ascertained by law, and to be informed of the nature and cause of the accusation; to be confronted with the witnesses against him; to have compulsory process for obtaining witnesses In his favor, and to have the assistance of counsel for his defence.

AMENDMENT VII

In Suits at common law, where the value in controversy shall exceed twenty dollars, the right of trial by jury shall be preserved, and no fact tried by a jury shall be otherwise re-examined in any Court of the United States, than according to the rules of the common law.

AMENDMENT VIII

Excessive bail shall not be required, nor excessive fines imposed, nor cruel and unusual punishments inflicted.

AMENDMENT IX

The enumeration in the Constitution of certain rights shall not be construed to deny or disparage others retained by the people.

AMENDMENT X

The powers not delegated to the United States by the Constitution, nor prohibited by it to the States, are reserved to the States respectively, or to the people.

AMENDMENT XI

The Judicial power of the United States shall not be construed to extend to any suit in law or equity, commenced or prosecuted against one of the United States by Citizens of another State, or by Citizens or Subjects of any Foreign State.

AMENDMENT XII

The Electors shall meet in their respective states, and vote by ballot for President and Vice-President, one of whom, at least, shall not be an inhabitant of the same state with themselves; they shall name in their ballots the person voted for as President, and in distinct ballots the person voted for as Vice-President, and they shall make distinct lists of all persons voted for as President, and of all persons voted for as Vice-President, and of the number of votes for each, which lists they shall sign and certify, and transmit sealed to the seat of the government of the United States, directed to the President of the Senate; The President of the Senate shall, in the presence of the Senate and House of Representatives, open all the certificates and the votes shall then be counted; The person having the greatest number of votes for President shall be the President, if such number be a majority of the whole number of Electors appointed; and if no person have such majority, then from the persons having the highest numbers not exceeding three on the list of those voted for as President, the House of Representatives shall choose immediately, by ballot, the President. But in choosing the President, the votes shall be taken by states, the representation from each state having one vote; a quorum for this purpose shall consist of a member or members from two-thirds of the states, and a majority of all the states shall be necessary to a choice. And if the House of Representatives shall not choose a President whenever the right of choice shall devolve upon

~~them, before the fourth day of March next following, then the Vice-President shall act as President, as in the case of the death or other constitutional disability of the President~~ The person having the greatest number of votes as Vice-President, shall be the Vice-President, if such number be a majority of the whole number of Electors appointed, and if no person have a majority, then from the two highest numbers on the list, the Senate shall choose the Vice-President; a quorum for the purpose shall consist of two-thirds of the whole number of Senators, and a majority of the whole number shall be necessary to a choice. But no person constitutionally ineligible to the office of President shall be eligible to that of Vice-President of the United States.

AMENDMENT XIII

Section 1. Neither slavery nor involuntary servitude, except as a punishment for a crime whereof the party shall have been duly convicted, shall exist within the United States, or any place subject to their jurisdiction.

Section 2. Congress shall have power to enforce this article by appropriate legislation.

AMENDMENT XIV

Section 1. All persons born or naturalized in the United States and subject to the jurisdiction thereof, are citizens of the United States and of the State wherein they reside. No State shall make or enforce any law which shall abridge the privileges or immunities of citizens of the United States; nor shall any State deprive any person of life, liberty, or property, without due process of law; nor deny to any person within its jurisdiction the equal protection of the laws.

Section 2. Representatives shall be apportioned among the several States according to their respective numbers, counting the whole number of persons in each State, excluding Indians not taxed. But when the right to vote at any election for the choice of electors for President and Vice-President of the United States, Representatives in Congress, the Executive and Judicial officers of a State, or the members of the Legislature thereof, is denied to any of the male inhabitants of such State, being twenty-one years of age, and citizens of the United States, or in any way abridged, except for participation in rebellion, or other crime, the basis of representation therein shall be reduced in the proportion which the number of such male citizens shall bear to the whole number of male citizens twenty-one years of age in such State.

Section 3. No person shall be a Senator or Representative in Congress, or elector of President and Vice-President, or hold any office, civil or military, under the United States, or under any State, who, having previously taken an oath, as a member of Congress, or as an officer of the United States, or as a member of any State legislature, or as an executive or judicial officer of any State, to support the Constitution of the United States, shall have engaged in insurrection or rebellion against the same, or given aid or comfort to the enemies thereof. But Congress may by a vote of two-thirds of each House, remove such disability.

Section 4. The validity of the public debt of the United States, authorized by law, including debts incurred for payment of pensions and bounties for services in suppressing insurrection or rebellion, shall not be questioned. But neither the United States nor any State shall assume or pay any debt or obligation incurred in aid of insurrection or rebellion against the United States, or any claim for the loss or emancipation of any slave; but all such debts, obligations and claims shall be held illegal and void.

Section 5. The Congress shall have power to enforce, by appropriate legislation, the provisions of this article.

AMENDMENT XV

Section 1. The right of citizens of the United States to vote shall not be denied or abridged by the United States or by any State on account of race, color, or previous condition of servitude.

Section 2. The Congress shall have power to enforce this article by appropriate legislation.

AMENDMENT XVI

The Congress shall have power to lay and collect taxes on incomes, from whatever source derived, without apportionment among the several States, and without regard to any census or enumeration.

AMENDMENT XVII

The Senate of the United States shall be composed of two Senators from each State, elected by the people thereof, for six years; and each Senator shall have one vote. The electors in each State shall have the qualifications requisite for electors of the most numerous branch of the State legislatures.

When vacancies happen in the representation of any State in the Senate, the executive authority of such State shall issue writs of election to fill such vacancies; Provided, That the legislature of any State may empower the executive thereof to make temporary appointments until the people fill the vacancies by election as the legislature may direct.

This amendment shall not be so construed as to affect the election or term of any Senator chosen before it becomes valid as part of the Constitution.

AMENDMENT XVIII

~~**Section 1.** After one year from the ratification of this article the manufacture, sale, or transportation of intoxicating liquors within, the importation thereof into, or the exportation thereof from the United States and all territory subject to the jurisdiction thereof for beverage purposes is hereby prohibited.~~

~~**Section 2.** The Congress and the several States shall have concurrent power to enforce this article by appropriate legislation.~~

~~**Section 3.** This article shall be inoperative unless it shall have been ratified as an amendment to the Constitution by the legislatures of the several States, as provided in the Constitution, within seven years from the date of the submission hereof to the States by the Congress.~~

AMENDMENT XIX

The right of citizens of the United States to vote shall not be denied or abridged by the United States or by any State on account of sex. Congress shall have power to enforce this article by appropriate legislation.

AMENDMENT XX

Section 1. The terms of the President and Vice-President shall end at noon on the 20th day of January, and the terms of Senators and Representatives at noon on the 3rd day of January, of the years in which such terms would have ended if this article had not been ratified; and the terms of their successors shall then begin.

Section 2. The Congress shall assemble at least once a year, and such meeting shall begin at noon on the 3rd day of January, unless they shall by law appoint a different day.

Section 3. If, at the time fixed for the beginning of the term of the President, the President elect shall have died, the Vice-President elect shall become President. If a President shall not have been chosen before the time fixed for the beginning of his term, or if the President elect shall have failed to qualify, then the Vice-President elect shall act as President until a President shall have qualified; and the Congress may by law provide for the case wherein neither a President elect nor a Vice-President elect shall have qualified, declaring who shall then act as President, or the manner in which one who is to act shall be elected, and such person shall act accordingly until a President or Vice-President shall have qualified.

Section 4. The Congress may by law provide for the case of the death of any of the persons from whom the House of Representatives may choose a President whenever the right of choice shall have devolved upon them, and for the case of the death of any of the persons from whom the Senate may choose a Vice-President whenever the right of choice shall have devolved upon them.

Section 5. Sections 1 and 2 shall take effect on the 15th day of October following the ratification of this article.

Section 6. This article shall be inoperative unless it shall have been ratified as an amendment to the Constitution by the legislatures of three-fourths of the several States within seven years from the date of its submission.

AMENDMENT XXI

Section 1. The eighteenth article of amendment to the Constitution of the United States is hereby repealed.

Section 2. The transportation or importation into any State, Territory, or possession of the United States for delivery or use therein of intoxicating liquors, in violation of the laws thereof, is hereby prohibited.

Section 3. This article shall be inoperative unless it shall have been ratified as an amendment to the Constitution by conventions in the several States, as Provided in the Constitution, within seven years from the date of the submission hereof to the States by the Congress.

AMENDMENT XXII

Section 1. No person shall be elected to the office of the President more than twice, and no person who has held the office of President, or acted as President, for more than two years of a term to which some other person was elected President shall be elected to the office of the President more than once. But this Article shall not apply to any person holding the office of President when this Article was proposed by the Congress, and shall not prevent any person who may be holding the office of President, or acting as President, during the term within which this Article becomes operative from holding the office of President or acting as President during the remainder of such term.

Section 2. This article shall be inoperative unless it shall have been ratified as an amend-

ment to the Constitution by the legislatures of three-fourths of the several States within seven years from the date of its submission to the States by the Congress.

AMENDMENT XXIII

Section 1. The District constituting the seat of Government of the United States shall appoint in such manner as the Congress may direct:

A number of electors of President and Vice-President equal to the whole number of Senators and Representatives in Congress to which the District would be entitled if it were a State, but in no event more than the least populous State; they shall be in addition to those appointed by the States, but they shall be considered, for the purposes of the election of President and Vice-President, to be electors appointed by a State; and they shall meet in the District and perform such duties as provided by the twelfth article of amendment.

Section 2. The Congress shall have power to enforce this article by appropriate legislation.

AMENDMENT XXIV

Section 1. The right of citizens of the United States to vote in any primary or other election for President or Vice-President, for electors for President or Vice-President, or for Senator or Representative in Congress, shall not be denied or abridged by the United States or any State by reason of failure to pay any poll tax or other tax.

Section 2. The Congress shall have power to enforce this article by appropriate legislation.

AMENDMENT XXV

Section 1. In case of the removal of the President from office or of his death or resignation, the Vice-President shall become President.

Section 2. Whenever there is a vacancy in the office of the Vice-President, the President shall nominate a Vice-President who shall take office upon confirmation by a majority vote of both Houses of Congress.

Section 3. Whenever the President transmits to the President pro tempore of the Senate and the Speaker of the House of Representatives his written declaration that he is unable to discharge the powers and duties of his office, and until he transmits to them a written declaration to the contrary, such powers and duties shall be discharged by the Vice-President as Acting President.

Section 4. Whenever the Vice-President and a majority of either the principal officers of the executive departments or of such other body as Congress may by law provide, transmit to the President pro tempore of the Senate and the Speaker of the House of Representatives their written declaration that the President is unable to discharge the powers and duties of his office, the Vice-President shall immediately assume the powers and duties of the office as Acting President.

Thereafter, when the President transmits to the President pro tempore of the Senate and the Speaker of the House of Representatives his written declaration that no inability exists, he shall resume the powers and duties of his office unless the Vice-President and a majority of either the principal officers of the executive department or of such other body as Congress may by law provide, transmit within four days

to the President pro tempore of the Senate and the Speaker of the House of Representatives their written declaration that the President is unable to discharge the powers and duties of his office. Thereupon Congress shall decide the issue, assembling within forty-eight hours for that purpose if not in session. If the Congress, within twenty-one days after receipt of the latter written declaration, or, if Congress is not in session, within twenty-one days after Congress is required to assemble, determines by two-thirds vote of both Houses that the President is unable to discharge the powers and duties of his office, the Vice-President shall continue to discharge the same as Acting President; otherwise, the President shall resume the powers and duties of his office.

AMENDMENT XXVI

Section 1. The right of citizens of the United States, who are eighteen years of age or older, to vote shall not be denied or abridged by the United States or by any State on account of age.

Section 2. The Congress shall have power to enforce this article by appropriate legislation.

AMENDMENT XXVII

No law, varying the compensation for the services of the Senators and Representatives, shall take effect, until an election of Representatives shall have intervened.

THE DECLARATION OF INDEPENDENCE

IN CONGRESS, JULY 4, 1776. A DEC-LARATION BY THE REPRESENTATIVES OF THE UNITED STATES OF AMERICA, IN GENERAL CONGRESS ASSEMBLED.

WHEN in the Course of human Events, it becomes necessary for one People to dissolve the Political Bands which have connected them with another, and to assume among the Powers of the Earth, the separate and equal Station to which the Laws of Nature and of Nature's God entitle them, a decent Respect to the Opinions of Mankind requires that they should declare the causes which impel them to the Separation.

WE hold these Truths to be self-evident, that all Men are created equal, that they are endowed by their Creator with certain unalienable Rights, that among these are Life, Liberty, and the Pursuit of Happiness That to secure these Rights, Governments are instituted among Men, deriving their just Powers from the Consent of the Governed, that whenever any Form of Government becomes destructive of these Ends, it is the Right of the People to alter or to abolish it, and to institute new Government, laying its Foundation on such Principles, and organiz-ing its Powers in such Form, as to them shall seem most likely to effect their Safety and Happiness. Prudence, indeed, will dictate that Governments long established should not be changed for light and transient Causes; and accordingly all Experience hath shewn, that Mankind are more disposed to suffer, while Evils are sufferable, than to right themselves by abolishing the Forms to which they are accustomed. But when a long Train of Abuses and Usurpations, pursuing invariably the same Object, evinces a Design to reduce them under absolute Despotism, it is their Right, it is their Duty, to throw off such Government, and to provide new

Guards for their future Security. Such has been the patient Sufferance of these Colonies; and such is now the Necessity which constrains them to alter their former Systems of Government. The History of the present King of Great-Britain is a History of repeated Injuries and Usurpations, all having in direct Object the Establishment of an absolute Tyranny over these States. To prove this, let Facts be submitted to a candid World.

HE has refused his Assent to Laws, the most wholesome and necessary for the public Good.

HE has forbidden his Governors to pass Laws of immediate and pressing Importance, unless suspended in their Operation till his Assent should be obtained; and when so suspended, he has utterly neglected to attend to them.

HE has refused to pass other Laws for the Accommodation of large Districts of People, unless those People would relinquish the Right of Representation in the Legislature, a Right inestimable to them, and formidable to Tyrants only.

HE has called together Legislative Bodies at Places unusual, uncomfortable, and distant from the Depository of their public Records, for the sole Purpose of fatiguing them into Compliance with his Measures.

HE has dissolved Representative Houses repeatedly, for opposing with manly Firmness his Invasions on the Rights of the People.

HE has refused for a long Time, after such Dissolutions, to cause others to be elected; whereby the Legislative Powers, incapable of Annihilation, have returned to the People at large for their exercise; the State remaining in the mean time exposed to all the Dangers of Invasion from without, and Convulsions within.

HE has endeavoured to prevent the Population of these States; for that Purpose obstructing the Laws for Naturalization of Foreigners; refusing to pass others to encourage their Migrations hither, and raising the Conditions of new Appropriations of Lands.

HE has obstructed the Administration of Justice, by refusing his Assent to Laws for establishing Judiciary Powers.

HE has made Judges dependent on his Will alone, for the Tenure of their Offices, and the Amount and Payment of their Salaries.

HE has erected a Multitude of new Offices, and sent hither Swarms of Officers to harrass our People, and eat out their Substance.

HE has kept among us, in Times of Peace, Standing Armies, without the consent of our Legislatures.

HE has affected to render the Military independent of and superior to the Civil Power.

HE has combined with others to subject us to a Jurisdiction foreign to our Constitution, and unacknowledged by our Laws; giving his Assent to their Acts of pretended Legislation:

FOR quartering large Bodies of Armed Troops among us:

FOR protecting them, by a mock Trial, from Punishment for any Murders which they should commit on the Inhabitants of these States:

FOR cutting off our Trade with all Parts of the World:

FOR imposing Taxes on us without our Consent:

FOR depriving us, in many Cases, of the Benefits of Trial by Jury:

FOR transporting us beyond Seas to be tried for pretended Offences:

FOR abolishing the free System of English Laws in a neighbouring Province, establishing therein an arbitrary Government, and enlarging its Boundaries, so as to render it at once an Example and fit Instrument for introducing the same absolute Rule into these Colonies:

FOR taking away our Charters, abolishing our most valuable Laws, and altering fundamentally the Forms of our Governments

FOR suspending our own Legislatures, and declaring themselves invested with Power to legislate for us in all Cases whatsoever.

HE has abdicated Government here, by declaring us out of his Protection and waging War against us.

HE has plundered our Seas, ravaged our Coasts, burnt our Towns, and destroyed the Lives of our People.

HE is, at this Time, transporting large Armies of foreign Mercenaries to compleat the Works of Death, Desolation, and Tyranny, already begun with circumstances of Cruelty and Perfidy, scarcely paralleled in the most barbarous Ages, and totally unworthy the Head of a civilized Nation.

HE has constrained our fellow Citizens taken Captive on the high Seas to bear Arms against their Country, to become the Executioners of their Friends and Brethren, or to fall themselves by their Hands.

HE has excited domestic Insurrections amongst us, and has endeavoured to bring on the Inhabitants of our Frontiers, the merciless Indian Savages, whose known Rule of Warfare, is an undistinguished Destruction, of all Ages, Sexes and Conditions.

IN every stage of these Oppressions we have Petitioned for Redress in the most humble Terms. Our repeated Petitions have been answered only by repeated Injury. A Prince, whose Character is thus marked by every act which may define a Tyrant, is unfit to be the Ruler of a free People.

NOR have we been wanting in Attentions to our British Brethren. We have warned them from Time to Time of Attempts by their Legislature to extend an unwarrantable Jurisdiction over us. We have reminded them of the Circumstances of our Emigration and Settlement here. We have appealed to their native Justice and Magnanimity, and we have conjured them by the Ties of our common Kindred to disavow these Usurpations, which, would inevitably interrupt our Connections and Correspondence. They too have been deaf to the Voice of Justice and of Consanguinity. We must, therefore, acquiesce in the Necessity, which denounces our Separation, and hold them, as we hold the rest of mankind, Enemies in War, in Peace, Friends.

WE, therefore, the Representatives of the UNITED STATES OF AMERICA, in GENERAL CONGRESS, Assembled, appealing to the Supreme Judge of the World for the Rectitude of our Intentions, do, in the Name, and by Authority of the good People of these Colonies, solemnly Publish and Declare, That these United Colonies are, and of Right ought to be, FREE AND INDEPENDENT STATES; that they are absolved from all Allegiance to the British Crown, and that all political Connection between them and the State of Great-Britain, is and ought to be totally dissolved; and that as FREE AND INDEPENDENT STATES, they have full Power to levy War, conclude Peace, contract Alliances, establish Commerce, and to do all other Acts and Things which INDEPENDENT STATES may of right do. And for the support of this Declaration, with a firm Reliance on the Protection of divine Providence, we mutually pledge to each other our Lives, our Fortunes, and our sacred Honor.

Signed by ORDER and in BEHALF of the CONGRESS,
JOHN HANCOCK, President.

ATTEST.
CHARLES THOMSON, SECRETARY.

PHILADELPHIA: PRINTED BY JOHN DUNLAP.

GLOSSARY OF LEGAL TERMS

A

Acceleration clause clause making the entire balance of a debt due and payable upon a certain event (typically default)

Acceptance in contracts, occurs when a party to whom an offer has been made agrees to the proposal; in commercial paper, drawee's promise to pay the draft when due

Accession right of an owner of property to an increase in that property

Accommodation party party lending his or her credit standing to insure the payment of an instrument

Accord agreement between the parties to a contract to change the obligation required

Accord and satisfaction parties' agreement to change the obligation required by their original contract and the performance of the new obligation

Actual bailment bailee's receipt and acceptance of the goods themselves

Administrative agency governmental body formed to carry out particular laws

Administrator/administratrix court-appointed representative for a decedent (male/female)

Adoption legal process that creates a parent-child relationship

Adulterated product does not meet minimum standards for purity and quality

Adverse possession occurs when someone adversely and exclusively possesses, in an open and notorious way, the land of another private person; possession is continuous and for the statutory period

Affirmative action plan court-ordered plan to remedy past discrimination by bringing the percentages of minorities and women in the workforce up to their corresponding percentages in the pool of qualified applicants

Age of majority age at which a person can be legally bound to contracts

Agency legal relationship in which one person is authorized to alter another's legal relationships

Agency shop establishment in which nonunion members are not required to join the union but must pay union dues

Agent one who is authorized to alter the legal relations of another

Alien corporation corporation chartered in another nation

Alimony economic maintenance paid by wage earner to his/her spouse/ex-spouse

Allocation of markets competitors' agreement to split market areas between themselves

Alteration in contracts, material change in the terms of a contract made intentionally by one party without consent of the other; in commercial paper, party's unauthorized change to or completion of a negotiable instrument intended to change the obligation of a party

Amendment change or alteration

Americans with Disabilities Act of 1990 (ADA) prevents employers from engaging in unjustified discrimination against people based on their disabilities

Annulment court order that cancels a marriage because of a problem that existed from the beginning of the marriage

Antedated dated earlier than the date of issuance

Anticipatory breach notification, before the scheduled time of performance, of refusal to perform contractual terms as agreed

Antitrust laws laws that prohibit competing companies from price fixing or dividing up sales regions

Apparent authority agency authority created when a principal leads the third party to believe that someone has particular agency authority

Appellate briefs written arguments on the issues of law submitted by opposing attorneys

Appellate court reviews decisions of lower courts to determine if a significant error of law was made during trial

Applicant pool people qualified for a particular job

Arbitrator independent third party who develops a binding and enforceable resolution to a dispute

Arson willful and illegal burning of a building

Articles of Confederation loose form of charter for common government adopted by the 13 colonies prior to adoption of the Constitution

Articles of incorporation application to a state for a corporate charter

Articles of organization document filed with the state to organize an LLC

Artisan's lien lien for unpaid services assessed against personal property that has been improved

Assault intentional threat to physically or offensively injure another

Assignee party to whom a transfer of contractual rights is made

Assignment transaction by which a party transfers contractual rights to another

Assignment of a lease tenant transfers to a third party his or her interest in a lease

Assignor one who transfers contractual rights

Associate circuit court court that hears minor criminal cases, state traffic offenses, and lawsuits involving amounts of no more than $25,000

Assumption of risk person is aware of a danger on the job but agrees to do it anyway

Attractive nuisance something that attracts children to trespass

Auction public sale to the highest bidder

Authorization card signature on card indicates that a worker wants to be represented by a particular union

Automobile insurance insurance providing liability and other coverages for the operation of a motor vehicle

B

Bailee person having temporary possession and control of another person's goods, holding them in trust for a specified purpose

Bailee's lien right of a bailee to retain possession of the bailed property until payment is made

Bailment transfer of possession of personal property without transfer of ownership

Bailor party who gives up possession of the property

Bait and switch improper business practice involving luring buyers with an understocked, low-priced good only to sell them a more profitable one

Bankruptcy legal proceedings discharging debts and distributing assets

Bankruptcy law federal law-based procedure for the benefit and relief of creditors and their debtors in cases in which debtors are unable or unwilling to pay their debts

Bargaining unit any group of employees whose employment contract is negotiated together

Barter exchange of goods for goods

Battery harmful or offensive touching

Bearer party in possession of bearer paper

Bearer paper commercial paper legally collectible by the party in possession

Beneficiary party for whose benefit a trust is managed; also, recipient of the amount to be paid under an insurance policy

Bid rigging competitors' agreement that one bidder will have the lowest bid for a particular job

Bigamist someone who knowingly marries while still married to another

Bilateral contract offeree can accept offer by giving a promise to the offeror instead of performing the contracted-for act

Bill of exchange (also called **draft**) unconditional written order from one person directing another to pay money to a third person

Bill of Rights first ten amendments to the U.S. Constitution

Bill of sale receipt that serves as written evidence of the transfer of ownership of goods

Blacklist employers compile a list of employees identified as pro-union and send it to other employers to make it difficult for the employees to find work

Blank indorsement indorsement consisting only of the indorser's signature

Blue-sky laws laws prohibiting the sale of worthless stocks and bonds

Bona fide occupational qualification (BFOQ) job requirement that compels discrimination against a protected class

Bona fide seniority system system that rewards employees for length of employment rather than merit

Bonds long-term notes a corporation issues

Boycott refusal to buy or use an employer's goods or services

Breach of contract failure to provide complete performance of contractual obligations

Bribery offering or giving something of value to improperly effect performance of another party

Bulk transfer transfer, generally by sale, of all or a major part of the goods of a business in one unit at one time

Burglary entering a building without permission when intending to commit a crime

Business ethics ethical principles used in making business decisions

Business judgment rule rule that protects management and other parties involved in a corporation from being held personally liable (criminally or civilly) for honest errors in judgment made in the course of business

Business law group of laws that governs business situations and transactions

Business necessity defense to disparate treatment employment discrimination case showing that an employer's actions were meant to advance the business rather than to create unjustified discrimination

Bylaws rules and regulations for the internal management of corporate affairs

C

Cancellation ending a contract for sale of goods because of breach, while retaining other remedies; also, any act that shows an intent to end the obligation of payment of commercial paper

Capacity ability to understand

Carrier's lien carrier's right to retain possession of the goods until the charges for transportation and incidental services are paid

Case law made when an appellate court endorses a rule to be used in deciding court cases

Cashier's check check drawn by a bank on itself

Casual seller seller who does not meet the definition of a merchant

Casualty insurance insurance that covers for losses due to accident, chance, or negligence

Casual workers persons who do not work regularly for a certain employer

Causation linking a job requirement with underrepresentation of a protected class in the workforce

Caveat emptor let the buyer beware

Caveat venditor let the seller beware

Cease-and-desist order governmental order requiring that certain improper conduct be stopped

Certificate of deposit bank's written acknowledgement of the receipt of money with an unconditional promise to repay it at a definite future time

Certification selecting a bargaining representative by a majority secret vote of the workers in the bargaining unit; NLRB then recognizes that union as the exclusive negotiator for all the employees in the bargaining unit

Certified check check upon which liability has been accepted by the drawee bank

Charitable trust created for the fulfillment of an altruistic purpose

Check draft written on a bank by a depositor

Child custody care and control of a minor

Child support money paid by a parent to provide child with economic maintenance

CIF "cost, insurance, freight" price

Civil disobedience open, peaceful violation of a law to protest its alleged injustice

Civil law group of laws used to provide remedy for wrongs against individuals

Civil rights personal, human rights recognized and guaranteed by the U.S. Constitution

Class action court procedure allowing a party to bring suit on his or her behalf and for those similarly situated

Close (or **closely held**) **corporation** private corporation whose stock is held by only one or a small number of shareholders

Closed shop employer agrees that workers must belong to the recognized union before they can be hired

COD collect on delivery

Code laws grouped into an organized form

Codicil formal, written, and witnessed amendment to a will

Coinsurance clause in a fire policy that requires the insured to maintain coverage equal to a certain percentage of the total current value of the insured property

Collateral property subject to the security interest of the creditor

Collateral note note on which personal property is offered for collateral

Collateral promise promise to pay a debt or default of another

Collective bargaining process by which the union and employer negotiate a contract of employment that binds both sides

Collision insurance automobile insurance that protects against upset and direct and accidental damage due to colliding with another object

Commercial paper unconditional written promise or order to pay a sum of money

Commingling mixing the money of the agent and the principal together

Common carrier one who agrees, for a fee, to transport goods that are lawful and fit for shipment for anyone who applies

Common law law based on current standards or customs of the people

Common-law defenses defenses in a negligence suit that include the employee's assumption of risk, the employer's contributory negligence, and co-worker negligence

Common-law marriage marital relationship legalized by the couple holding themselves out as husband and wife and sharing home and property for an extended period

Common stock basic stock in a corporation conveying to its owner the right to vote and to receive dividends

Community property property owned equally by spouses

Compensatory damages amount of money awarded to compensate for a plaintiff's loss

Competency license state requirement for people in certain occupations and businesses to pass exams and receive a license

Complete performance doing all the things promised in a contract

Composition of creditors agreement by all creditors to accept something less than the total amount of their claims as full payment

Compounding a crime accepting something of value for a promise not to inform on or prosecute a suspected criminal

Comprehensive insurance insurance that covers against all damage to the insured's car except that caused by collision or upset

Condemnation forcing a property owner to transfer property to a government in exchange for just reasonable compensation

Conditional estate estate where continued ownership is dependent upon some act or event

Consent order voluntary, court-enforceable agreement between the government and an offender requiring the termination of an illegal or questionable practice

Consequence-based reasoning form of ethical reasoning that evaluates the results of an action

Consequential damages money awarded to a party for foreseeable injuries caused by the other party's breach

Consideration that which is given or received in a contract

Consignment bailment in which ownership remains with the manufacturer or wholesaler until the goods are sold

Consolidation two or more corporations combine to form a new one

Conspiracy agreement between two or more persons to commit a crime

Constitutional law law made when the fundamental, supreme law of the land is adopted, amended, or interpreted

Constructive bailment occurs when the bailee receives and accepts a symbol of the personal property rather than the property itself

Constructive eviction tenant moves out of leased premises because the landlord caused the premises to become unfit for its intended use

Constructive notice legal presumption that everyone has knowledge of facts on public file

Constructive trust created to require a person holding property to transfer it to another because retention would be a wrongful and unjust enrichment of the holder

Consumer individual who acquires goods primarily for personal, family, or household use

Consumer loan loan for personal, household, or agricultural purposes

Consumer Products Safety Commission (CPSC) agency regulating the safety of various products including toys

Consumer transaction transaction in which a party buys goods or services for personal or household use

Contempt of court action that hinders the administration of justice in court

Contract agreement that courts will enforce

Contract of adhesion contract in which the more powerful party dictates all the important terms

Contract to sell transaction in which transfer of ownership is to take place in the future

Contractual capacity ability to understand that a contract is being made and its general meaning

Contractual duties legal obligations created by a contract

Contractual rights something a party will receive under a contract

Contributory negligence in personal injury law, plaintiff's own negligence is a partial cause of an injury; in employment law, employee does something carelessly to contribute to her or his injury or death

Conversion using property in a manner inconsistent with the owner's rights

Conveyance transfer of an estate from a grantor to a grantee by a deed

Cooling-off period stopping a labor dispute by federal court order for a period of 80 days

when a national emergency strike is threatened

Co-ownership ownership existing when two or more persons have the same ownership rights in the same property

Copyright protects the expression of a creative work, such as the work of an artist, author, or composer

Corporation legal entity created by the authority of federal or state law

Corrective advertising advertising to correct improper and false impressions

Counteroffer offeree's response to an offer which modifies it

Court governmental forum that administers justice under the law

Court of record accurate, detailed report of what went on at trial

Covenants not to compete agreements involving price fixing, market allocations, and terminated employees for the purpose of protecting a company's interests

Co-worker negligence one worker causes the injury of another

Creditor party to whom a debt is owed

Credit rating evaluation of a party's ability to pay debts

Credit sale sale that, by agreement of the parties, calls for payment for the goods at a later date

Crime punishable offense against society

Criminal act specific conduct that violates a criminal statute

Criminal insanity defense based on the accused's inability to know right from wrong

Criminal intent intent to commit an evil act in violation of a statute

Criminal law group of laws that defines and sets punishments for offenses against society

Cumulative preferred stock preferred stock whose dividends remain due and payable beyond one corporate fiscal year

Custody care and present control of another's personal property under the owner's direction

D

Damages monetary award to compensate for the loss caused by a tort

Deadlock collective bargaining situation in which the union and employer cannot agree on important issues

Debentures unsecured bonds

Debt that which is owed to a debtor

Debtor person or business that owes money, goods, or services to another

Decedent person who dies

Decertification election process by which employees can reject union representation or select a different union

Declaration of Independence document drafted by representatives of the 13 original colonies that asserts the rights desired by the colonists

Decree for specific performance court order for a defendant to do exactly what he or she promised to do in the contract

Dedication transferring real property by donating it to the government, such as to a city for use as a park or roadway

Deed legal document used to transfer ownership of real property

Defamation false statement that injures one's reputation

Default failure to perform a legal duty or failure to perform an agreement

Defense at criminal law, a legal position that allows the defendant to escape criminal liability

Delegation of duties turning over to another party one's duties under a contract

Delivery shift of physical possession of the property to the new owner

Democracy governmental system in which citizens vote directly to decide issues

Demurrage fee for delay by party shipping goods in loading or by party receiving goods in unloading

Directors individuals elected by the shareholders to be responsible for the overall direction of a corporation

Disability physical or mental condition that substantially limits a major life activity

Disaffirmance both parties to a contract return the consideration

Discharge of contract termination of contractual duties that ordinarily occurs when the parties perform as promised

Discharged for cause employee is discharged because of violating an employment obligation

Discharged without cause employee's discharge is not due to his or her conduct

Disclaimer sign, label, or warning reducing a bailee's duty of care; also, notice of exclusion in a warranty

Dishonor bank's refusal to pay a check when due

Disparate impact employer treats members of a protected class less favorably than other employees; has the effect of eliminating members of a protected class

Dissolution change in partnership relationship due to a partner ceasing his association with its ongoing purpose; also, term for divorce or the ending of a marriage in some states

Dividends distributions of corporate earnings

Divisible contracts contracts for which separate consideration is given for the legal and illegal parts

Divorce court action terminating a marriage

Doctrine of capture grants ownership of fluid minerals to the party who extracts them

Domestic corporation corporation doing business in the state in which it is chartered

Donee person receiving a gift

Donor person giving a gift

Dormant partner partner neither known to the public nor active in management

Double taxation taxation of a corporation as an entity based on its earnings and then of the shareholders on corporate dividends

Draft (also called **bill of exchange**) unconditional written order from one person directing another to pay money to a third person

Drawee party ordered to pay a draft

Drawer party that executes a draft and orders payment to be made

Due process in administrative agency decision-making, notice of charges or potential rulemaking coupled with opportunity to appear, present evidence, and confront witnesses if warranted

Due process of law constitutional requirement for fundamental fairness in our legal and court system

Duress occurs when one party uses an improper threat or act to obtain an expression of agreement

Duty of accounting requires agent to account to the principal for all money and property of the principal that comes into the agent's possession

Duty of confidentiality requires agent to treat information about the principal very carefully

Duty of loyalty and honesty requires

employee to look out for the best interests of the employer

Duty of loyalty and obedience requires agent to place the interests of the principal above the interests of all others

Duty of obedience requires employee to follow the reasonable orders and rules of the employer

Duty of reasonable care and skill requires agent to exercise the degree of care and skill any reasonably prudent person would use in a similar situation

Duty of reasonable performance requires employee to perform assigned duties at the prescribed time and in the prescribed manner

Duty of reasonable skill requires employee to perform job tasks with competence

E

Easement irrevocable right to the limited use of another's land

Easement appurtenant easement which benefits nearby land

Easement by prescription making systematic use of another's property for a long period of time, typically 15 to 21 years, resulting in the law's acknowledging an easement arising from the use

Easement in gross easement that is personal and that does not benefit neighboring land

Economic strike work stoppage in which the dispute is over wages, hours, or conditions of employment

Electronic fund transfer (EFT) debit or credit to an account initiated by the use of a terminal, computer, telephone, or magnetic tape

Emancipation severing the child-parent relationship

Embezzlement taking of another's property

or money by a person to whom it has been entrusted

Eminent domain power of the government to take private property for public use in exchange for the fair market price

Employee party who works under the supervision of another for pay

Employer party who engages another to work for pay

Employment contractual relationship in which one party engages another to work for pay under the supervision of the party paying

Employment at will employment relationship whereby employee may be discharged at any time because no agreement was made about length of employment; alternately, employee may quit the job at any time without liability for breach of contract

Employment discrimination treating individuals differently on the basis of race, color, gender, national origin, or religion

Encumbrances claims of third parties against the goods

Endorsements (also called **riders**) modifications made to the standard fire policy to satisfy an insured's needs

Environmental Protection Agency (EPA) agency regulating the creation, marketing, and use of hazardous chemicals, as well as the disposal of toxic waste

Equal Employment Opportunity Commission (EEOC) agency charged with eliminating workplace discrimination based on race, religion, sex, color, national origin, age, or disability

Equal rights of possession attribute of co-ownership which means that no co-owner can exclude any other co-owner from any physical portion of the property

Equity basic fairness

Escheat reversion of property to the state

Estate bundle of ownership rights in, and powers over, realty; also, property of the deceased

Ethics deciding what is right or wrong action in a reasoned, impartial manner

Eviction legal action taken to remove a tenant from possession of all the landlord's real property

Evidence materials presented to prove or disprove alleged facts

Ex parte injunction injunction issued by a judge after hearing only one side of an argument

Exclusions exceptions to insurance coverage

Executed contract contract that has been fully performed

Executor/executrix intestate's personal representative appointed to settle the estate (male/female)

Executory contract contract that has not been fully performed

Existing goods physically existing goods owned by the seller

Express authority agency authority directly communicated by the principal to the agent

Express trust trust in which the terms are explicitly stated by the settler

Express warranty assurance of quality or performance explicitly made by the seller

Extortion improperly obtaining money or other things of value by use of force, fear, or the power of office

Extraordinary bailment bailment that requires an unusually high standard of care

Extraordinary care duty arising from an extraordinary bailment in which the bailee is liable for all damage, loss, or injury

F

Face value stated maximum amount that could be paid under a policy

Fair use limited use of copyrighted works by critics, researchers, news reporters, and educators

False imprisonment depriving a person of freedom of movement without consent and without privilege

False or misleading advertising advertising that improperly deceives or conceals material facts

False pretenses obtaining property by lying about a past or existing fact

Featherbedding forcing an employer to pay for services not performed

Federal Communications Commission (FCC) agency regulating all interstate and international channels of communication

Federal Register government publication containing agency regulations

Federal Reserve System's Board of Governors agency regulating interest rates

Federal Trade Commission (FTC) agency regulating unfair trade practices

Fee simple absolute greatest possible bundle of ownership rights in, and powers over, an estate

Felony crime punishable by more than one year in jail, a fine of more than $1,000, or both

Fidelity bond insurance policy that pays the employer money in the case of employees' theft

Fidelity insurance provides coverage against financial loss caused by dishonesty

Fiduciary duties legal requirement that the agent serve the best interests of the principal; specific fiduciary duties are loyalty and obedience, reasonable care and skill, confidentiality, and accounting

Finance charge total added cost when one pays in installments for goods or services

Financing statement brief, written notice of the existence of a security interest in the identified property

Fire insurance property insurance that covers for loss or damage due to fire (and usually smoke as well)

Firm offer binding offer stating in writing how long it is to be held open

Fixture item of personal property that has become permanently attached to realty and is thus transformed from personalty into realty

FOB shipping term meaning "free on board"

Food and Drug Administration (FDA) agency regulating safety of food and drugs on the market

Forbearance refraining from doing what one has a right to do

Foreclosure legal process where a party with a lien on realty can, after default, cause the property to be sold to pay the debt

Foreign corporation corporation doing business in a state other than the one in which it was chartered

Forgery falsely making or materially altering a writing to defraud another

Fraud intentional misrepresentation of an existing, important fact

Fraudulent misrepresentation party to a contract knows that a statement he or she made is untrue

Full warranty express warranty that obligates the seller to repair or replace a defective product without cost to the buyer within a reasonable time

Fundamental ethical rules form of ethical reasoning that evaluates the act but not its consequences

Fungible goods goods of an essentially identical nature

Future goods goods that are not both existing and identified

Future interest nonpossessory estate made up of ownership power retained by the grantor of a conditional estate

G

Gambling activity involving an agreement with the following: payment to participate, chance to win based on luck rather than skill, and a prize for one or more winners

Garnishment court-ordered procedure by which a portion of a delinquent debtor's wages are paid to satisfy the debt

General duty clause type of law OSHA enforces that requires employers to provide a work environment free from hazards likely to cause serious physical harm or death

General jurisdiction court that can hear almost any kind of case

General partnership all partners assume full liability for debts of the firm

Genuine agreement agreement to enter into a contract that is evidenced by words or conduct between the parties

Gift voluntary transfer of ownership without consideration

Good faith purchaser innocent third party to a fraudulent transfer of goods who gives value to the goods and acquires rights in them

Goods items of tangible, movable, personal property

Grant transferring ownership of realty with a deed

Grantee person receiving ownership with a deed

Grantor person giving up ownership with a deed

Gratuitous agency agency relationship where the agent receives no consideration

Gratuitous bailment arises when only one of the parties benefits from the bailment

Guarantor party agreeing to be secondarily liable in case of default by the principal debtor

H

Heirs persons who, by statute, are entitled to property not disposed of by a decedent's will

Holder party in possession of commercial paper payable to his or her order or to bearer

Holder in due course (HDC) party that takes commercial paper in good faith without knowledge of any defect or overdue status and gives value for it

Holder through a holder in due course (HHDC) party that takes commercial paper after an HDC and thereby acquires the same rights

Holographic will will written and signed entirely by the hand of the maker

Honor bank agrees to pay a check when due

Hostile environment interference with an employee's ability to work through unwelcome comments, gestures, or touching of a sexual nature

I

Identified goods designated subject matter of a particular sales contract

Immunity freedom from prosecution for a crime

Impartiality idea that the same ethical standards apply to everyone

Impeachment case trying a government official for misconduct in office

Implied authority agency authority that is implied from the grant of express authority or because of an emergency

Implied warranty warranty obligation implicitly imposed by law on all sellers

Incorporators signers of the articles of incorporation

Indemnify to make good a loss

Independent contractor one who contracts to do something for another but is free of the latter's direction and control

Indivisible contracts contracts for which legal and illegal parts cannot be broken out as separate items

Indorsee party to whom commercial paper is indorsed

Indorsement signature on the reverse side of commercial paper

Indorser owner of commercial paper who signs it on the reverse

Infraction minor misdemeanor

Infringement unauthorized copying, sale, display, or performance of a copyrighted work

Inland marine insurance insurance that covers against loss or damage to personal property where the property is located or while it is being transported by any means other than by sea

Innocent misrepresentation party to a contract does not know that a statement he or she made is untrue

Insurable interest potential to sustain loss if the insured property is damaged or destroyed or if the insured person is injured or dies

Insurance agreement under which one party will pay to offset a loss to another

Insured party protected or covered if the loss occurred

Insurer party who will indemnify if loss occurs

Integration clause contract clause stating that both parties agree that the terms written in the contract constitute the entire and final agreement

Integrity doing what is right even under pressure to act otherwise

Intellectual property purely intangible personal property that one cannot touch or move

Intentional tort tort in which the defendant means to commit the injurious act

Inter vivos trust trust created during the lifetime of the settlor

Interference with contractual relations enticing or encouraging a person to break a contract

Interstate commerce trade and other commercial intercourse between or among businesses in different states

Interstate Commerce Commission (ICC) regulates the various modes of interstate and land transportation

Intestate to die without a will

Intoxication mental impairment caused by voluntary use of alcohol, drugs, or inhalants

Intrastate commerce commerce conducted wholly within one state

Invasion of privacy unwelcome and unlawful intrusion into one's private life so as to cause outrage, mental suffering, or humiliation

Involuntary bailment arises without consent of the bailee; raises issue of whether the goods are lost or misplaced

J

Joint tenancy co-ownership of property with equal interests and the right of survivorship

Joint venture partnership formed by two or more persons or firms combining resources and skills for one complex project

Judgment final result of a trial

Jurisdiction power of a court to decide a case

Jury panel of citizens sworn by a court to decide issues of fact in court cases

Justice title of a judge on the state supreme court or federal Supreme Court

Juveniles individuals over 13 and under 18 years of age who have special status under the criminal law

L

Land basic physical element of realty

Landlord (also called **lessor**) one who, through a lease, transfers to another exclusive possession and control of real property

Larceny wrongful taking of another's property with the intent to deny them possession

Laws enforceable rules of conduct in a society

Lease agreement in which one party receives temporary possession of another's real property in exchange for rent

Leasehold estate tenants' ownership interest in real estate

Legal duties obligations or standards of conduct toward other persons that are enforceable by law

Legal rate of interest rate specified by statute when interest is called for but no percentage is stated in the contract

Legal rights benefits to which a person is justly entitled by law

Legal tender currency or coins

Legal value change in the legal position of a party as a result of a contract

Lessor (also called **landlord**) one who, through a lease, transfers to another exclusive possession and control of real property

Liability insurance insurance that covers personal injury or property damage claims for which the insured is legally responsible

License in real property, a temporary, revocable right to some limited use of another's land

Licensee person whom the possessor of land has permitted to be on that land

Lien legal right in another's property as security for the performance of an obligation such as the repayment of a loan

Life estate estate that lasts only for the grantee's life

Life insurance insurance that pays to a named beneficiary or the deceased's estate upon the death of the insured

Limited defenses defenses good against all obligees except HDCs and HHDCs

Limited liability corporation (LLC) form of business organization offering limited liability, taxation as a partnership, and few of the restrictions for use encountered in the S corporation or limited partnership

Limited liability partnership (LLP) form of business organization easily converted to a partnership that avoids double taxation and affords partial limited liability protection

Limited partner partner with limited liability in a limited partnership

Limited partnership partnership form authorized by state statute requiring at least one general partner but allowing limited liability for the rest

Limited warranty warranty providing a level of protection less than a full warranty

Liquidated damages damages agreed upon before a possible breach of contract

Liquidated debt debt for which the parties agree that the debt exists and on the amount of the debt

Liquidation process by which a corporation's life is ended

Litigate to resolve disputes in court

Lockout employer shutdown of operations to force a union to agree to the employer's position

Lost property property that the owner unknowingly leaves somewhere or accidentally drops

Lottery game involving the three elements of prize, chance, and consideration

M

Main purpose rule exception to a statute of frauds provision making a third party liable for an oral promise to pay another's debt if the main purpose of the promise serves the promisor's own interest

Major breach breach that discharges the other party's duty to perform

Majority rule elected representatives vote for laws acceptable to the majority of people they represent

Maker person who executes a promissory note

Marine insurance insurance that covers for loss of or damage to vessels, cargo, and other property exposed to the perils of the sea

Marital consortium mutual obligations of wife and husband undertaken to fulfill the purposes of their union

Marriage legal union of a man and woman as husband and wife

Material facts important facts that influence both parties' decisions about a contract

Maximum rate of interest rate of interest at which, by statute, lenders may not exceed

Mechanic's lien lien against realty available to one who has supplied labor or materials to improve it

Mediation attempt by a neutral third party to achieve a compromise between two parties in a dispute

Mediator independent third party who tries to develop a non-binding solution acceptable to both sides of a dispute

Members owners of an LLC

Mental incapacity condition in which a party to a contract is unable to understand the consequences of the contractual act

Merchant seller who deals regularly in a particular type of goods or who claims special knowledge in a certain type of sales transaction

Merger combination of corporations in which one absorbs another

Mineral right ownership of the minerals on and beneath a parcel of realty

Minimal care duty arising from a bailment in which the bailee must not ignore, waste, or destroy the property

Minor individual under the age of majority (18 in most states)

Minor breach breach that does not discharge the other party's duty to perform

Minority minor part of a person's life (typically under the age of 18)

Mirror image rule requires that the terms in the acceptance must exactly match the terms contained in the offer

Misdemeanor crime punishable by up to one year in jail, a fine of less than $1,000, or both

Mislaid property property that is intentionally placed somewhere but then forgotten

Mitigate damages to act to minimize one's injury

Money official medium of exchange in the United States or any foreign country

Money order draft issued by a post office,

bank, express company for use in transferring funds for the draft's purchaser

Moral rights legitimate claims on other people which flow from each person's status as a human being

Mortgage note note on which real property is used as security for payment

Multinational corporation (MNC) corporation that has a significant investment of assets in foreign countries

Municipal court city courts, usually divided into traffic and criminal divisions

Mutual mistake both parties to a contract have an incorrect belief about an important fact

Mutual-benefit bailment consideration is given and received by both bailor and bailee

N

National emergency strike work stoppage that involves national defense or major industries or that would imperil national health or safety

National Labor Relations Board (NLRB) agency regulating collective bargaining

Necessaries things needed to maintain life and lifestyle

Negligence most common tort based on carelessness

Negligence suit suit brought by an employee against an employer that claims the employer's carelessness caused the employee's injury

Negotiable written unconditional promise or order for a sum certain payable on demand or at a definite time

Negotiable instruments another term for commercial paper

Negotiation proper transfer of a negotiable instrument so that the person receiving the

instrument has the power to collect on it by overcoming defenses of the person who must pay it off

Neutral on its face label for a workplace policy that does not seem on the surface to discriminate against any protected class

No-fault divorce divorce proceeding in which the requesting spouse does not have to show cause

No-fault insurance insurance that requires that the parties to an automobile accident be covered by their own insurance company, regardless of who is at fault

Nominal consideration token amount identified in a written contract when parties either cannot or do not wish to state the amount precisely

Nominal damages token amount awarded when rights have been violated but there is no actual injury

Nominal partner person who is not a partner but who is held out as such

Nonfreehold estate (also called **tenancy**) estate that involves ownership for a limited period of time

Non-necessaries things that are relative luxuries

Nonprofit corporation business organization for a social, charitable, or educational purpose

Non-trading partnership partnership that provides professional and noncommercial assistance or advice

Novation contractual party's release of the other party from the duty of performance and the acceptance of a substitute party

Nuclear Regulatory Commission (NRC) agency charged with insuring safety of nuclear power plants

Nuncupative will orally made will

O

Obligor one who owes a duty under a contract

Occupancy acquisition of title by taking possession of personal property that belongs to no one else

Occupational Safety and Health Act (OSHA) law enacted in 1970 that created the Occupational Safety and Health Administration

Occupational Safety and Health Administration (OSHA) federal agency that administers the Occupational Safety and Health Act by enacting safety regulations and inspecting workplaces

Offer proposal by an offeror to do something, provided the offeree does something in return

Offeree party to whom an offer is made

Offeror party who makes an offer to form a contract

Offset deducting the cost of completing or fixing a minor breach from payment of the contract price to the breaching party

Open shop establishment in which nonunion members are not required to join the union or to pay union dues

Option separate contract arising when the offeree gives the offeror something of value in return for a promise to leave an offer open

Option contract underlying contract to keep an option open

Order paper commercial paper made payable to the order of a specified payee

Ordinance legislation enacted by a town, city, or county board or commission

Ordinary care duty created by mutual-benefit bailment in which bailee is liable only if negligent in some fashion

Original jurisdiction power to hear the case in full for the first time

Output contract agreement to purchase all of a particular producer's production

Ownership in severalty ownership of all property rights by oneself

P

Parol evidence (also called **parol statements**) spoken words inadmissible in court

Parol evidence rule rule under which oral testimony cannot be used to contradict terms in a complete, final, written contract

Participating preferred stock preferred stock whose holder, after the preferred dividends are paid, shares in remaining dividends as a common shareholder

Parties' principal objective method of contract interpretation focused on the main goals of the parties to the contract

Partnership association of two or more persons, as co-owners, to carry on a business for profit

Partnership agreement explicit statement, orally or in writing, of the terms and conditions agreed to by the partners for running the partnership

Partnership at will partnership in which a partner may withdraw at any time without liability to other partners

Past consideration act that has already been performed cannot be consideration for a promise in the present

Patent government grant of exclusive right to make, use, and sell a product or process which is novel, non-obvious, and useful

Pawn pledge of tangible personal property

Payable at a definite time commercial paper payable on or before an identified calendar date

Payable on demand commercial paper payable on sight or when presented

Payee party to whom commercial paper is made payable

Payment delivery of the agreed-upon price and the concurrent acceptance of it by the seller

Payroll deductions money deducted from an employee's paycheck

Perfected security interest exists when the security interest is superior to all other claims in the collateral

Performance fulfillment of contractual promises as agreed

Periodic tenancy arises when the leasehold is for a renewable period of time with rent due at stated intervals

Perjury crime of lying under oath

Personal property (also called **personalty**) tangible, movable property and intangible property

Personalty another name for personal property

Picket to walk with signs at employer's business to publicize dispute or influence opinion

Plea bargaining agreement with prosecutor allowing defendant to plead guilty to a lesser crime than the more serious one he or she would likely be charged with

Pledge secured transaction in which the creditor has possession of the collateral

Pledgee creditor in a pledge who takes possession of property given up by pledgor

Pledgor debtor in a pledge who voluntarily gives up possession of the property

Policy written contract of insurance

Political party private organization of citizens who select and promote candidates for public office

Positive law law based on the dictates of a central political authority

Postdated dated later than the date of issuance

Power of attorney any writing that appoints someone as an agent

Power to terminate both agent and principal may terminate the relationship at any time

Preemptive rights enables shareholders to protect their proportionate voting power and interest in past and future profits

Preferred stock non-voting stock conveying the right to receive a stipulated dividend before any common shareholders receive their dividends

Premium consideration for insurance contract

Prenuptial agreement legal contract resolving property and other claims that might result from a marriage

Price fixing competitors agree to charge the same amount for a product or service

Price consideration for a contract to sell or sale of goods

Primary boycott employees' refusal to buy their employer's products or services

Primary promise promise to pay another's debt that is not conditioned upon the other person's failure to pay

Principal one who authorizes another to alter his or her legal relations

Principal debtor person who owes the debt or obligation

Prior appropriation rights water ownership system that grants the first party to use the water priority over other potential users in subsequent years

Private corporation corporation established for a private purpose

Private trust trust created for private reasons

Privity of contract relationship or connection between parties to a legally binding agreement

Privity of estate chain of ownership connections between the original promisee and the current owner of an estate

Probate court administers wills and estates

Procedural defense defense based on problems with the way evidence is obtained or the way the accused person is arrested, questioned, tried, or punished

Procedural law group of laws that define the methods for enforcing legal rights and duties

Procedural unconscionability element of unconscionability shown by how the contract is created

Profit-making corporation private corporation organized to produce a profit for its owners

Promisee person to whom the promise or action is given in exchange for the other person's promise or action

Promisor person who gives the promise or action in exchange for the promise or action of another

Promissory estoppel promise is enforced even though no consideration is given for it

Promissory note unconditional written promise to pay money to order or to bearer

Promoters those who sell a business idea and the corporate form for it

Property tangible and intangible things and their corresponding legal rights and interests

Property insurance insurance that covers for losses resulting from perils such as fire, theft, or windstorm

Protected classes groups that employment law protects

Proximate cause legally recognizable cause of harm

Proxy power to vote shares for shareholder

Public corporation corporation established for a governmental purpose

Public service corporation private company that furnishes an essential public service

Puffing greatly exaggerated sales talk

Punishment penalty provided by law and imposed by a court

Punitive damages money a court requires a defendant to pay in order to punish and make an example of the defendant

Q

Qualified indorsement indorsement limiting or eliminating signature-based liability for the indorser

Quasi-contract obligation that is enforced as if it were a contract in order to prevent unjust enrichment of one party

Quid pro quo one thing exchanged for another; type of sexual harassment case in which a supervisor seeks sexual favors from a subordinate in exchange for continued employment or a favorable term or condition of employment

Quitclaim deed transfers any interest the grantor may have in the real property, but doesn't guarantee that the grantor owns anything or that the grantee receives anything

R

Ratification acting toward the contract as though one intends to be bound by it; principal's assent to unauthorized acts of an agent

Real property (also called **realty**) land, water, and minerals in the earth; airspace above the land; and things permanently attached to the land

Realty another name for real property

Receiving stolen property receiving or buying property known to be stolen from another so as to deny the rightful owner of possession

Redeem to pay the balance due and the expenses of the creditor in exchange for receiving the collateral

Release party settles a claim at the time the tort occurs, and the liability is unliquidated because the extent of damages is uncertain

Remedy action or procedure followed to enforce a right or to compensate for an injury

Rent consideration given by a tenant in return for temporary possession of a property

Representation election conducted by a union if workers wish to be represented by a union but management will not voluntary recognize it

Republic governmental system in which citizens elect representatives to decide issues

Requirements contract seller agrees to supply all of the needs of a particular buyer

Resale price maintenance manufacturer attempts to influence the retail price of its product

Rescission backing out of the transaction by asking for the return of what you gave and offering to give back what you received

Restitution restoring or making good a loss; repayment of money illegally obtained

Restrictive covenant promise as a part of a contract or deed limiting the owner's use of the realty

Resulting trust implied trust formed to hold property for its original owner

Revenue license required license imposed by governments on certain occupations for the sole purpose of raising money

Revocation withdrawing an offer before it is accepted

Riders (also called **endorsements**) modifications made to the standard fire policy to satisfy an insured's needs

Right of contribution cosurety who pays the full debt is entitled to judgment against the other cosureties for their proportionate share of the debt

Right of partition attribute of co-ownership which allows any co-owner to require the division, usually financial, of the property among the co-owners

Right of repossession right of a secured party to take back collateral to use in satisfaction of the debt

Right of survivorship right of one joint tenant to ownership of property when the other joint tenant dies

Right to air space power of the owner of a parcel of realty to use the air space above the surface

Right-to-work laws state laws which ban the union shop, the closed shop, and the agency shop

Riparian rights water ownership system in which those abutting the water own the right to use it

Risk potential loss that is insured against

Robbery wrongful taking of another's property from their person or presence by threat of force of violence

S

Sale contract in which ownership of goods transfers from the seller to a buyer for a price

Sale of an undivided interest sale involving a person who sells a fractional interest in a single good or in a number of goods that are to remain together

Sale on approval goods are delivered to the buyer in an "on trial" or "on satisfaction" basis

Sale or return completed sale in which the buyer has the option of returning the goods

Satisfaction performance of the new contractual obligation parties have agreed to substitute for their original obligation

Scofflaw person who does not respect the law

Scope of authority in employment law, range of acts an organization has authorized an employee to do; in agency, range of acts authorized by the principal

S corporation form of business organization governed by subchapter S of the Internal Revenue Code, under which earnings are treated the same as a gain (or loss) from a partnership and only taxed at the individual owner's level

Secondary boycott striking employees try to encourage customers to stop buying products or services of a third party

Secret partner partner not known to the public but active as a manager

Secured party person who has a security interest in collateral owned by the debtor-buyer

Secured transaction legal method or device creating a security interest in personal property or fixtures in order to protect creditors

Securities and Exchange Commission (SEC) agency regulating the disclosure of information pertinent to buying and selling stocks as well as the national stock exchanges themselves

Security agreement contract that creates or provides for a security interest

Security interest interest in or claim against specified property of the debtor created for the purpose of assuring payment of the debt

Self-defense use of force that appears reasonably necessary for self-protection of an intended victim

Separate property property owned by either spouse at the time of marriage or received as a gift or inheritance

Separation stage in the divorce process in which the spouses maintain their marital rights and obligations but do not live together

Servicemark word, mark, or symbol that identifies a service as opposed to a product

Settlor creator of a trust

Shareholder (also called **stockholder**) person owning share of stock in a corporation

Shares of stock units of ownership in a corporation

Sight draft draft on which payment is due immediately when presented to the drawee

Silent partner partner known to the public but who takes no active managerial role

Small loan rate of interest higher interest rates that loan companies and pawnbrokers may charge on loans up to $2,000

Social insurance government-sponsored insurance protecting against financial problems related to retirement, survivorship, disability, and declining health

Sole proprietorship form of business owned by one person who has total unlimited liability

Sovereignty freedom from external control

Special indorsement indorsement making the paper payable to the order of a designated party

Special partnership partnership formed for a single transaction

Specialized jurisdiction court that hears only one specific type of case

Spendthrift trust trust created to protect the beneficiary's interest in a property from the beneficiary's creditors

Spot zoning treatment of a single property in a manner inconsistent with the treatment of similar properties in the area

Standard Fire Policy fire insurance contract that covers for losses resulting from fire, lightning strike, or removal from premises endangered by fire

Stare decisis doctrine that requires lower courts to follow existing case law in deciding similar cases

Statute of frauds law stating that certain agreements are not enforceable in court unless they are evidenced by a signed writing

Statute of limitations state laws setting time limit for bringing a lawsuit

Statutes laws enacted by state or federal legislatures

Stockholder (also called **shareholder**) person owning share of stock in a corporation

Stop-payment order instruction by the depositor to a financial institution not to pay a particular instrument drawn on it

Strict liability holding a defendant liable without a showing of negligence

Strike collective work stoppage by employees to pressure the employer to give in to union demands

Subletting tenant transfers to a third party all the property for a period less than the remaining time of the lease or part of the property for part or all of the remaining term of the lease

Subpoena written court order compelling a person to appear and testify

Substantial performance performance of all but a minor contractual duty

Substantive defense defenses that disprove, justify, or otherwise excuse the alleged crime

Substantive law group of laws that defines rights and duties

Substantive unconscionability element of unconscionability established by the terms of the agreement

Substitution parties' replacement of their original contract with a new contract

Surety third party agreeing to being primarily liable for debt in case of default by the principal debtor

Suretyship being primarily liable for a debt created in favor of the principal debtor

Surface right ownership of the surface of a parcel of realty

System of checks and balances division and allocation of the powers of government between its various branches

T

Teller's check draft drawn by a bank on its balance with another bank

Tenancy at sufferance tenant remains in possession after a lease has expired

Tenancy at will results if a party possesses land with the owner's permission but without an agreement as to the term of the lease or the amount of the rent

Tenancy by the entireties usual form of co-ownership between husband and wife, carrying equal interest and the right of survivorship

Tenancy for years leasehold that is for a definite period of time, such as six months, one year, or ninety-nine years

Tenancy from month to month periodic tenancy in which the rent is paid by the month

Tenancy in common form of co-ownership in which the shares may be unequal and there is no right of survivorship

Tenancy in partnership form of co-ownership by which the partners hold partnership property

Tenant (also called **lessor**) one who, through a lease, is given possession of real property

Tender offer to perform an obligation

Tender of delivery to place the goods at the buyer's disposal or to give notice to the buyer that delivery can be received

Termination conclusion of the legal existence of the partnership

Termination statement filing by a creditor releasing a security interest in collateral

Test of the reasonable person objective legal test used by jurors or judges to determine whether the offeror has shown an intent to contract

Testamentary capacity testator must know the kind and extent of property involved, persons who stand to benefit, and that he or she is making an arrangement to dispose of his or her property after death

Testamentary intent clear intention to make a will

Testamentary trust trust created after the death of a settlor in accordance with directions in the person's will

Testate to die with a valid will

Testator/testatrix maker of a will (male/female)

Testimony statements by witnesses under oath

The Good standard for judging right and wrong

Third party one who deals with an agent who represents the principal

Time draft draft payable on a date set on the instrument or one that is payable after the running of a specified period after the draft's date

Tort private or civil wrong for which the law grants a remedy

Trade fixture personalty attached to leased realty by a business tenant; usually treated as personal property even if permanently attached

Trade secret unpatented formula or process not known to others and which is valuable in business

Trademark unique word, mark, symbol, or device that identifies a product of a particular manufacturer or merchant

Trading partnership partnership that buys and sells goods and services commercially

Traveler's check draft drawn by a financial institution on itself and signed by purchaser who must sign again in presence of payee for validation

Trespass (also called **trespass to land**) to be on the land of another without right or permission of the owner

Trial court first court to hear a dispute

Trust legal vehicle used to transfer the immediate control of property to another party

Trust account checking account which assists an agent in avoiding the commingling of funds

Trustee legal entity having title to the property named in a trust

U

Unconscionable term or contract that, under the UCC, is grossly unfair and oppressive

Unconscionable contract grossly unfair contract for the sale of goods

Unconstitutional law that conflicts with a constitution and is therefore invalid

Underinsured motorists coverage compensates the insured when the negligent driver does not have sufficient insurance to cover damages

Undisclosed principal principal whose identity is kept secret from the third party by the agent

Undue influence occurs when one party to a contract is in a position of trust and wrongfully dominates the other party

Unemployment compensation government payments to those who recently lost their jobs through no fault of their own

Unequal treatment (also called **disparate treatment**) employer treats members of a protected class less favorably than other employees

Unfair labor practice strike work stoppage in which the dispute is over unfair labor practices

Unfair labor practices union or employer actions which violate the rights of employees with respect to union activity

Unfair trade practice dishonest, fraudulent or anticompetitive business method

Unilateral contract offeror promises something in return for the offeree's performance and indicates that this performance is the way acceptance must be made

Unilateral mistake occurs when one party holds an incorrect belief about the facts related to a contract

Uninsured motorists protection allows the insured to collect damages from his or her own insurance company when they are not collectible from the person who caused the harm

Union shop establishment in which all workers must join the union within a stated period

Universal defenses defenses good against all obligees

Universalizing mental test to identify illogical actions

Unqualified indorsement indorsement without wording limiting or eliminating liability for the indorser

Unsecured debt debt in which the creditor lacks a secured interest in collateral

U.S. Constitution document that consists of seven articles that provide a workable framework for our federal government

Usury lending money at a rate higher than the state's maximum allowable rate

V

Variance granted by a city or county to allow a landowner to make some use of his or her land that is inconsistent with the general zoning ordinance

Vendee buyer in sales of goods and contracts to sell

Vendor seller in sales of goods and contracts to sell

Verdict jury's decision in a case

Vicarious criminal liability substituted criminal liability

Vicarious liability legal doctrine by which one party is held liable for the torts of another

Vocational rehabilitation retraining an injured worker for a different job

Voidable contract contract in which the injured party can withdraw, thus cancelling the contract

Voidable marriage valid marriage that can be terminated by one or both parties due to improper grounds

Void marriage marriage considered invalid from the beginning

W

Wager bet on the uncertain outcome of an event

Waiver contractual party's intentional and explicit giving up of a contractual right

Warranty statement about the product's qualities or performance that the seller assures the buyer is true

Warranty deed transfers grantor's interest in the property and protects the grantee by providing several enforceable grantor's warranties

Warranty of habitability requires a landlord to provide residential property in a condition fit for human living

Warranty of merchantability warranty requiring that the goods fit the ordinary purposes for which goods are used

Warranty of the principal's capacity assumption of the law that the agent promises the third party that the principal has capacity

Water right ownership of water running over or under a parcel of realty

White-collar crime crime typically committed in the workplace that does not involve violence or force nor does it cause injury to people or physical damage to property

Will legal expression by which a person directs how his or her property is to be distributed after death

Winding-up period period following dissolution in which the ongoing business of the partnership is concluded, its obligations are satisfied, and each partner's share is distributed

Within the statute of frauds contracts required to be in writing to be enforceable in court

Without the statute of frauds contracts which are not governed by the statute of frauds, thus not required to be in writing

Witness individual with personal knowledge of important facts

Work permit document obtained from the state allowing a person under 18 years old to work

Workers' compensation payment employer makes to an insurance fund that compensates employees for injuries that occur on the job

Workers' compensation statutes laws that require most employers to buy insurance to pay benefits to injured employees

Workforce pool persons actually in the workforce

Writ of certiorari order to a lower court to produce the record of a case for the Supreme Court to review

Wrongful discharge firing an employee in retaliation for reporting violations of law by the company

Y

Yellow-dog contracts employment contracts in which new employees promise not to join a union

Z

Zoning ordinance law adopted by a city or county to regulate the location of residential, business, and industrial districts

CASE INDEX

A

ABC News v. Food Lion, 600
ABC Trans., etc. v. Aeronautics
    Forwarders, Inc., 388
Advent Systems, Ltd. v. Unisys
    Corporation, 229
Agricultural Insurance Co. v.
    Constantine, 310
Aircraft Sales and Serv. v. Gannt, 310
Allen v. Houserman, 310
Allen v. Whitehead, 92
Allright Missouri, Inc. v. Billeter, 520
Ambassador Insurance Co. v. Kenneth I.
    Tobey, Inc., 400
American Dental Association v. Martin,
    532
American National Insurance Co. v.
    Gilroy, Sims and Associates, 520
American Trading and Production Corp
    v. Shell International Marine, Ltd.,
    194
Antrell v. Pearl Assurance Company,
    358
Armored Car Service Inc. v. First
    National Bank of Miami, 310
Associates Discount Corporation of
    Iowa v. Fitzwater, 562

B

Bailey v. Utah State Industrial
    Commission, 462
Baldwin v. Peters, Writer & Christensen,
    112
Baxter International, Inc. v. Morris, 164
Blevins v. Cushman Motors, 261
Blinder, Robinson, and Co. v. Alzado,
    520
Board of Trustees of the University of
    Alabama v. Calhoun, 372
Bowen v. Roy, 32
Boyar v. Wallenberg, 340
Brammer v. Taylor, 372
Brown v. Board of Education, 13
Buck Creek Coal, Inc. v. Federal Mine

Safety and Health Administration,
    532
Bunny Bear v. Peterson, 532
Burchett v. Marcum, 401
Burger Man, Inc. v. Jordan Paper
    Products, Inc., 228
Burkhardt v. Smith, 326
Burks v. Poppy Construction Company,
    32
Burne v. Franklin Life Ins. Co., 164

C

Calcote v. Southern National Bank, 590
California v. Cabazon, 156
Cameron State Bank v. Sloan, 576
Cameron v. Terrell Garrett, Inc., 400
Campbell Soup Co. v. Wentz, 209
Cargill, Inc. v. Wilson, 228
Carma v. Marathon, 141
Carpenter v. Koehring Company, 92
Carter v. Reichlin Furriers, 310
Cast v. Petsinger, 486
Cherberg v. Peoples National Bank of
    Washington, 341
Chicago Title Insurance Co. v.
    Renaissance Homes, Ltd., 164
City of Chicago v. Commonwealth
    Edison Company, 32
Clackamas County v. Holmes, 326
Clement v. Clement, 486
Clover Park School District v.
    Consolidated Dairy Products
    Company-Darigold Farms, 126
Collins v. First National Bank of
    Oswego, Kansas, 576
Colorado Carpet Installation, Inc. v.
    Palermo, 228
Colorado-Kansas Grain co. v.
    Reifschneider, 228
Commission v. A Juvenile, 64
Commonwealth v. Feinberg, 76
CompuServe v. Patterson, 524
Connecticut National Bank v.
    Chadwick, 372
Cooper v. Isaacs, 486

Cousineau v. Walker, 126
Crist v. Nesbit, 276
Curless v. Curless, 276

D

Danbury Hatters, 419
David v. Lose, 310
David v. Serges, 388
Davison v. Wilson, 358
Davis v. McDougall, 326
Desfossess v. Notis, 388
Dixon v. Mercury Finance Company of
    Wisconsin, 164
Dolitsky v. Dollar Savings Bank, 296
Donnelly v. Yellow Freight System, Inc.,
    64
Donovan v. Hamilton Country
    Municipal Court, 608
DuPont v. Christopher, 296

E

Eckis v. Sea World Corporation, 462
Edgewater Motels, Inc. v. Gatzke, 410
Edward L. Mangan v. Joseph J. Mangan,
    Jr., 372
Eldredge v. Jensen, 340
Elektra Records Company v. Gem
    Electronic Distributors, Inc., 296
Employers' Casualty Company v. Bratch,
    453
Engel v. Vernon, 486
Epson v. CBC Corporation, 112
Estate of Witlin v. Rio Hondo
    Associates, 486

F

Faith v. Singleton, 372
Falls Industries, Inc. v. Consolidated
    Chemical Industries, Inc.,
    242
FDIC v. Wentz, 532

INDEX

J

Japan, product liability in, 251
Jews, murder during World War II, 41
Job safety, 449–450
John (King of England), 36
Joint custody, 271
Joint tenancy, 291
Joint venture, 475
Joseph, Franz, 46
Judgment, 88
    confess, 480
Judicial branch of government, 10,
    44–45
Jurisdiction
    defined, 6
    general, 55
    original, 54
    specialized, 55, 59–60
Jury
    civil, 88
    defined, 54
    evolution of, 6–7
    Japanese court system and, 251
    right to trial by, 37, 71
Justice (supreme court judge), 59
Juvenile courts, 59–60

K

Kaczynski, Theodore, 512
Kansas
    common-law marriage in, 265
    juveniles tried as adults in, 60
    marriage laws in, 266
Kentucky
    juveniles tried as adults in, 60
    marriage laws in, 266
    Uniform Marriage and Divorce Act
      adopted by, 264
Kidnapping, Lindbergh case, 116
King, Dr. Martin Luther, Jr., 28
King's Bench, 6–7
Korean War, 50
Kugler, Melissa, 537

L

Labels, warning, 248
Labor laws, history of, 419
Labor Management Relations Act,
    422
Labor-Management Reporting and
    Disclosure Act, 425

Lamm, Sharon, 377
Land
    defined, 313
    duties owed to those entering your,
      322
    others' rights in your, 320–321
    trespass to, 83, 322
Landlord, 329
    duties of, 335–336
    liability for injuries on property, 333
    rights of, 335
Landrum-Griffin Act, 425
Lanham Act, 285
Larceny, 69
    bankruptcy and property obtained
      by, 604
    insurance against, 344
Law
    case, 10
    civil, 11
    Constitution as supreme, 45
    consumer protection by, 245
    criminal, 11
    culture and, 19
    death and the, 361–363
    employment terms imposed by, 404
    evolution of, 5
    as institution, 20
    justification for violating, 28–29
    mistake of, 120
    procedural, 12
    stages in growth of, 5
    substantive, 12
    what is? 5
    See also Laws
Law of capacity, 142–153
Law-equity courts, 8
Law and the Internet
    bogus banks, 580
    copyright law and websites, 284
    credit repair fraud, 598
    cybercontracts, 129
    divorce information, 270
    e-mail ownership, 288
    e-mail threats, 26
    freedom on speech, 56
    intrastate vs. interstate commerce,
      524
    "Living Trust Makers," 368
    online fraud, 199
    online stock trades, 497
    real estate schemes, 336
    right to privacy, 40
    Social Security Administration
      online, 354
    spamming, 248

Law in the Media
    Food Lion case, 600
    Kevorkian mercy killing, 364
    Lindbergh kidnapping case, 116
    Menendez brothers murder, 269
    Tucker execution, 12
    Unabomber, 512
    women and crime, 442
Laws
    administrative, 10
    allowing secured debts, 593–594
    antitrust, 69, 495
    blue-sky, 159
    child-labor, 408–409
    conflicting, 10–11
    consumer protection
      adulteration, 250–251
      lemon laws, 250–251
      licensing, 250
      safety, 251
      sanitation, 250–251
      See also Laws, product liability
    criminal, 66–77
    defined, 5
    divorce, 270–271
    ethics and, 25–29
    labor, history of, 419
    personal injury, 78–80
    product liability, 85–86. *See also*
      Laws, consumer protection
    protecting creditors, 593–595
    right-to-work, 422
    sources of our, 9–10
    statutes as, 9
    types of, 9–13
    See also Law
Lawyer
    contingency fee, 87
    as professional agent, 392
    right for representation by, 71
Lease(s)
    breach of, 336
    defined, 329
    tenant's right to assign, 332–333
    types of, 329–331
Leasehold estate, 329–330
Legal duties, 40
Legality of contracts, 99, 154–165
Legal problems. *See* Prevent Legal
    Difficulties
Legal rate of interest, 156
Legal rights, 40
Legal system, origin of our, 6–8
Legal tender, 190
Legal value
    as consideration requirement, 129

PHOTO CREDITS

3 Courtesy of Barbara Cicognani; 34 CORBIS/Robert Holmes; 40 top Asman Custom Photo; 93 UPI/Corbis-Bettmann; 97 Courtesy of Gail Hallock; 98 Roger Ressmeyer/© CORBIS; 119 CORBIS/ Adam Woolfitt; 136 CORBIS/Philip Gould; 182 CORBIS/Vittoriano Rastelli; 213 Courtesy of Kathryn Redwine; 281 Courtesy of Warren Zaretsky; 317 CORBIS/Joseph Sohm; ChromoSohm Inc.; 377 Courtesy of Sharon Lamm; 467 Courtesy of Richard Nella; 491 CORBIS/ Raymond Gehman; 499 CORBIS/Wolfgang Kaehler; 502 CORBIS/Alison Wright; 507 CORBIS/Paul A. Souders; 541 CORBIS/Steve Raymer; 544 CORBIS/Todd Gipstein; 537 Courtesy of Melissa Kugler; 570 CORBIS/Neal Preston; 604 CORBIS/Caroline Penn; 624 CORBIS/Museum of the City of New York; 7, 35 North Wind Picture Archives; 37 right, 51 CORBIS/Bettmann; 42, 423 CORBIS/Leif Skoogfors; 114, 418, 488 CORBIS/Michael S. Yamashita; iv, v, vi, vii, viii, ix, x, xi, 2, 4, 11, 13, 17, 18, 20, 22, 23, 26, 29, 37, 40 bottom, 46, 47, 52, 53, 56, 60, 61, 65, 66, 69, 73, 78, 80, 85, 86, 89, 95 top right, 95 bottom right, 95 center, 95 top left, 95 bottom left, 96, 99, 101, 103, 108, 109, 116, 117, 123, 128, 129, 130, 132, 137 top, 137 bottom, 142, 145, 148, 149, 154, 157, 161, 166, 167, 169, 172, 173, 174, 176, 177, 183, 184, 188, 189, 190, 191, 195, 196, 199 top, 199 bottom, 201, 202, 203, 204, 205, 211 top right, 211 bottom right, 211 center, 211 top left, 211 bottom left, 212, 214, 215, 216, 218, 223, 225 top, 225 bottom, 230, 232, 235, 239, 243, 244, 246, 248, 251, 252, 256, 257, 261, 262, 264, 265, 270 top, 270 bottom, 272, 273, 279 top right, 279 bottom right, 279 center, 279 top left, 279 bottom left, 280, 282, 284, 288 top, 288 bottom, 292, 293, 298, 301, 306, 307, 312, 314, 318, 320, 323, 328, 330, 335, 336 top, 336 bottom, 337, 342, 344, 348, 349, 350, 354 top, 354 bottom, 355, , 375 top right, 375 bottom right, 375 center, 375 top left, 375 bottom left, 380, 376, 378, 381, 382, 385, 389, 360, 366, 368, 369, 390, 391, 394, 396, 397, 402, 403, 404, 405, 408, 411, 412, 413, 422, 424, 427, 432, 433, 437, 439, 442, 443, 448, 450, 454, 457, 459, 465 top right, 465 bottom right, 465 center, 465 top left, 465 bottom left, 466, 468, 470, 471, 476, 477, 480, 482, 483, 487, 494, 496, 497, 500, 502, 508, 510, 512, 515, 516, 517, 522, 523, 524, 525, 527, 529, 535 top right, 535 bottom right, 535 center, 535 top left, 535 bottom left, 536, 538, 545, 549, 550, 553, 555, 558, 559, 564, 571, 572, 573, 578, 579, 580, 581, 583, 587, 591, 592, 594, 595, 597, 598 top, 598 bottom, 599, 600, 603, 604, 605, 611 top right, 611 bottom right, 611 center, 611 top left, 611 bottom left, PhotoDisc